DB2 for OS/390 Development for Performance

AF789939

List of Chapters

Acknowledgments

This book has over 14,000 contributors since 1984 from attendees of seminars and courses upon which it is based.

Special gratitude goes to the leading professionals in the world of DB2 who graciously reviewed and significantly contributed to some or all chapters of the book.

- **Lou Agosta, Ph.D.,** Independent Consultant, North Sheridan Rd 8C, Chicago, IL 60660, phone: 773-784-7978, email: lagosta@ibm.net
- **Peter Backlund,** DB2 Consultant, Sweden, email: pbacklu@ibm.net
- **Marilyn Bohl,** VP Engineering, Work Process Systems, Inc., email: bohl@wpsi.com
- **Richard Bolesta,** PLATINUM technology, inc., bolesta@platinum.com
- **Willie Favero,** BMC Software, Inc., wfavero@ibm.net
- **Michael Hannan,** DB2 Applications Design, SQL & Performance Tuning Specialist, Melbourne, Australia, phone: + 66 419 356 145, email: mhannan@C031.aone.net.au
- **Frank J. Ingrassia,** I M S I, 4720 Little John Trail, Sarasota, FL, 34232 USA, phone: 941-371-1930, email: FrankJIngrassia@prodigy.net
- **Robert W. Lyle**
- **Blaine Lucyk,** DB2 Specialist, 43 Compton Road, Regina, SK, Canada S4S 2Y2, phone: 306-761-0164, email: blucyk@stones.com

The review process requires a great deal of work. The reviewers took their valuable time from their busy schedule to provide outstanding comments that have been incorporated in the book. The book is greatly improved as a result of the excellent input of these reviewers. It is the reader that benefits the most from their dedication to DB2 and contributing their knowledge to the book.

This book is dedicated to Fleurette Ann Wiorkowski, the greatest achievement of my life, and to John J. Wiorkowski and Iva Ann Johnson who made me what I am.

ISBN 0-9668460-1-X

Gabrielle & Associates
9922 Lincolnshire Court
Rockwall, TX 75087
USA

Web site: http://www.GabrielleDB2.com
Email: Gabrielle@GabrielleDB2.com
Telephone: 972-412-8866
FAX: 972-412-8867

Table of Contents

Concepts and Components

Creating STOGROUPs, Databases, and Buffer Pools

Creating Tablespaces

Creating Tables and Views

Index Usage for Performance

Index Design for Performance

The Basics of SQL Data Manipulation

Concurrency Control

Program Development

Batch Processing

Triggering Actions in DB2

Stored Procedures

User Defined Functions

Program Preparation and Execution

Join Performance

Subselects and Table Expressions

Parallel Processing

Programming for Performance

The Optimizer

Explaining the Access Path Chosen by the Optimizer

Load and Check Data Utilities

Runstats and Reorganization

Copy, Quiesce, Report, Recover, & Rebuild

INDEX

Concepts and Components

CO.1 INTRODUCTION

DB2 is based on the relational model which was invented and first published by Dr. E. F. Codd in 1970. Prior to Dr. Codd's invention at IBM, database management systems (DBMS) had no theoretical foundation. Rather, they were developed heuristically as needed. For example, hierarchical DBMS are based on bill of material processing to meet the requirements of the space program for building spacecraft. Network DBMS are based on a model for communications networks.

The invention of the relational model started a great deal of research into DBMS, both in the academic world and in industry. Thousands of articles were published on the relational model and how it can be used in industry during the 1970s, 1980s, and 1990s. Chris Date gives comprehensive coverage of the relational model, System R, and DB2 in several of his many books. System R was the first major prototype developed during 1974 to 1979. Portions of the prototype were used in the DB2 and SQL/DS products. IBM researchers turned their attention to R* research during 1980 to 1982 which grew into distributed capability among multiple DB2 subsystems on mainframes. The next step was Starburst research dealt with distributed capability for DBMS on mainframes, work stations and personal computers (PCs). Research into extensions for DB2 continues at the IBM Database Technology Institute.

DB2 was first announced as a product by IBM in June of 1983. There have been a number of versions and releases since the original announcement as summarized below. More are expected in the future.

- V1.1 June 1983
- V1.2 Feb. 1986
- V1.3 May 1987
- V2.1 April 1988
- V2.2 October 1988
- V2.3 September 1990
- V3.1 March 1993
- V4.1 September 1994
- V5.1 April 1996
- V6.1 May 1998
- V7.1 April 2000

The DB2 for OS/390 home page on the World Wide Web (WWW) provides for the latest information, useful software that can be downloaded at no cost, and access to the DB2 manuals. The address is http://www.software.ibm.com/data/db2/os390/.

CO.2 DB2 USAGE ARCHITECTURE

All usage of data in DB2 is through the structured query language (SQL). SQL consists of data definition, data manipulation, and data control components as shown in Figure CO.1. We will briefly describe each of these components in this section and indicate where details on the components can be found in the book.

Figure CO.1. DB2 usage architecture

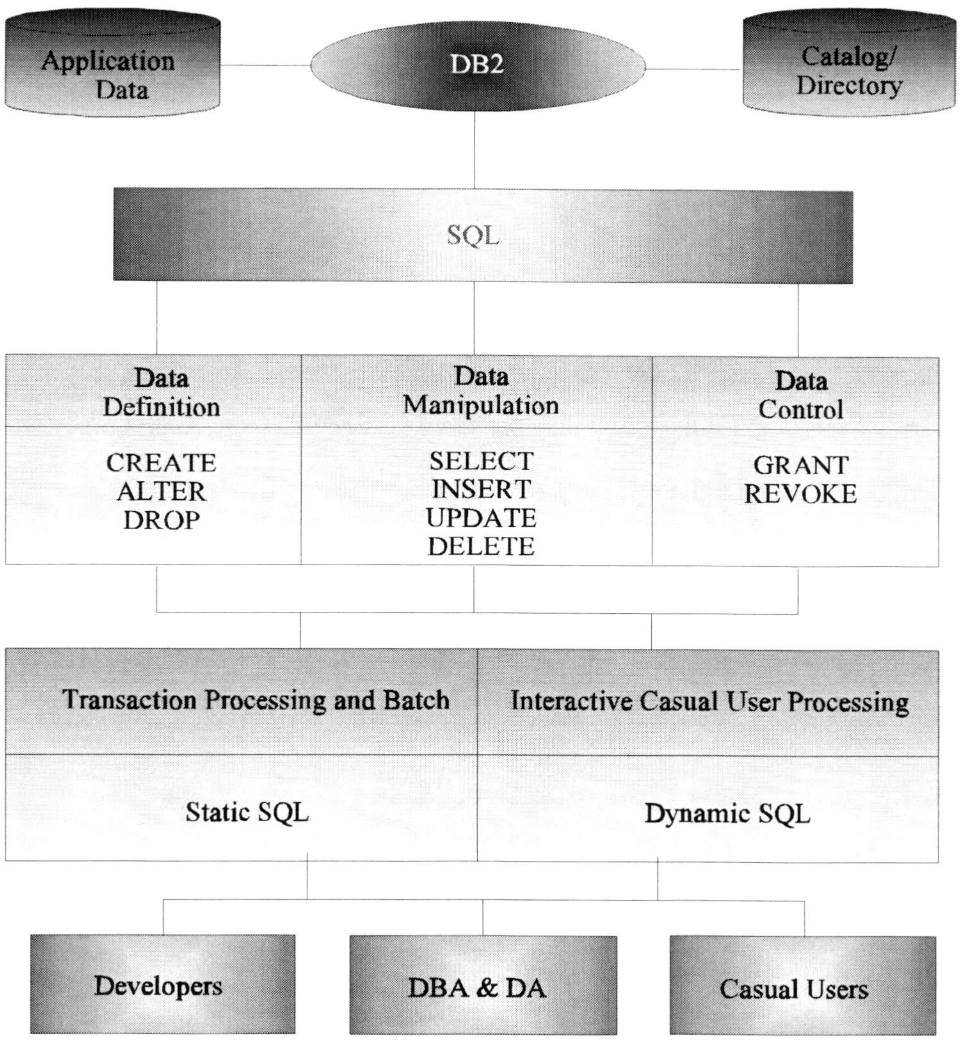

SQL Data Definition

The data definition language (DDL) component of SQL provides for creating, altering, and dropping objects including storage groups, databases, tablespaces, tables, indexes, views, aliases, and synonyms as discussed in Chapters CD, TS, CT, and ID. DB2 automatically records information about objects that you create and alter in one or more catalog tables. When objects are dropped, DB2 deletes the rows describing the objects. The three basic data definition statements are CREATE, ALTER, and DROP.

A storage group consisting of one or more DASD devices to house tables and indexes is one of the first objects to be created. If a storage group is not created before creating a table, a tablespace is automatically created in the default SYSDEFLT storage group in the default DSNDB04 database. You will want to create a storage group, database, and tablespace before creating a table rather than taking the defaults in most cases.

Most parameters that are specified to control the creation of objects can be changed with the ALTER statements. The DROP statement provides for deleting objects that have been created and removing their definitions from the catalog tables.

SQL Data Manipulation

The data manipulation language (DML) component of SQL provides for selecting, inserting, updating, and deleting rows of a table. Typically when a person uses the term *SQL* they are referring to the DML portion of the language.

The four basic data manipulation statements are SELECT, INSERT, UPDATE, and DELETE. The SELECT statement provides for retrieving one or more rows from one or more tables. The INSERT statement provides for inserting one row into one table. An INSERT with a subselect allows for INSERTING many rows into a table as selected from another table. An UPDATE statement provides for changing one or more columns in one or more rows of a table. The DELETE statement provides for deleting one or more rows from a table. The use of these statements is described in Chapters SL and PD. Developing and tuning SQL statements for performance are discussed in Chapters JP, ST, PP and throughout the book.

DML, DDL, and DCL statements can be executed interactively or embedded in programs written in REXX, PL/1, C, Java, FORTRAN, and Assembler. Typically, DDL and DCL statements are executed interactively. DML statements are executed interactively and embedded in host programs.

Binding SQL DML into a Plan or Package

All static SQL DML statements are bound into a plan or package. The bind process takes one or more SQL DML statements and compiles them into a usable control structure for execution. The result of the bind is an application plan or package. Static SQL means the SQL DML statements in a host program are bound into a plan or package and stored in the directory. The plan or package does not have to be bound again when executed if you are using the default bind parameters. Dynamic SQL means that bind processing is required for each SQL statement each time it is executed if you are using the default bind parameters. This is a major distinction between static and dynamic SQL DML. However, this distinction is blurred for static SQL when using reoptimization as discussed in Chapter OP and for dynamic SQL when using the dynamic cache and the KEEPDYNAMIC YES bind parameter as discussed in Chapters PD and PE. Plans, packages, and the bind process are described in Chapter PE.

SQL statements executed using SQL processing using file input (SPUFI) or an interactive product such as IBM's query management facility (QMF) are executed dynamically. Most CASE tools and fourth generation languages provide the option to execute the SQL statements statically or dynamically. REXX is an interpretative language. Therefore, SQL is executed dynamically from a REXX program. The use of Open Database Connectivity (ODBC) results in the use of dynamic SQL.

Some application systems products that can be purchased from software companies and application programs developed in-house at user companies use dynamic SQL in their host programs.

If objects that a plan or package depends on are dropped (an index, table, view, etc.), a primary or foreign key is added, or privileges are revoked, the plan or package is marked as invalid. An automatic rebind occurs when the plan or package is next executed. It will be successful if required objects and privileges exist. Otherwise, an error will be issued.

The Optimizer

Part of the bind process is optimization. The optimizer determines a good access path for each data manipulation statement based on statistics in the catalog tables describing the data and indexes. This avoids developers and business professionals having to know how the data is stored and navigate through the database as is required with older non-relational DBMS. Chapter OP covers the optimization process in detail. You can determine the access path chosen by the optimizer using EXPLAIN. EXPLAIN causes rows to be inserted into PLAN_TABLE describing the access path chosen to locate data as described in Chapter EX.

SQL Data Control

The data control language (DCL) component of SQL provides for granting privileges to technical and business professional that allow them to perform various operations including the definition and manipulation of objects. Privileges given using the GRANT statement and can be removed using the REVOKE statement. The DB2 SQL Reference and DB2 Command Reference provides details on the privileges required for each operation.

Authorization IDs: A person is identified to DB2 using an authorization identifier (AUTHID). The primary AUTHID is required and usually is an individual's TSO user identifier (ID), CICS ID, or IMS ID. Optionally, each person can also have up to and including 245 secondary AUTHIDs that are assigned through connection or signon exits. This is usually done in conjunction with security software products like RACF, ACF2, or TOP SECRET.

Project team members can be assigned a secondary AUTHID of say POSYSTEM. Privileges can be granted to POSYSTEM rather than to each team member's primary AUTHID which eases the management of security. Composite privileges are all primary and secondary AUTHID privileges. The current SQLID is any of the composite IDs as set by the connection and signon exits or the SET statement executed interactively or from a host program. A person can set their current SQLID to POSYSTEM by executing:

```
SET CURRENT SQLID = 'POSYSTEM'
```

Authority to perform actions: No one can take any action on any DB2 object or resources until the person is granted privileges. An exception is the person who installs the DB2 subsystem. That person has install system administration (SYSADM) privileges.

Explicit and implicit privileges: Explicit privileges are granted using the DCL GRANT statement. Implicit privileges are received automatically by virtue of the person taking some action. For example, a person can explicitly be granted privileges to create a table. The person has implicit privileges to execute SQL DML, load data into the table, and explicitly grant privileges on the table to others.

Single and grouped capabilities: An individual privilege can be granted to an AUTHID to create a table or select from an existing table, for example. A grouped privilege can be granted to an AUTHID. For example, the database administration (DBADM) privilege allows a person to create tablespaces, tables, views, indexes and manipulate these objects using DML statements and control the usage of the objects by granting and revoking privileges to AUTHIDs using DCL statements. Figure CO.2 shows the individual privileges that can be granted as well as the privileges within boxes can be granted as a group.

Figure CO.2. Single and grouped privileges

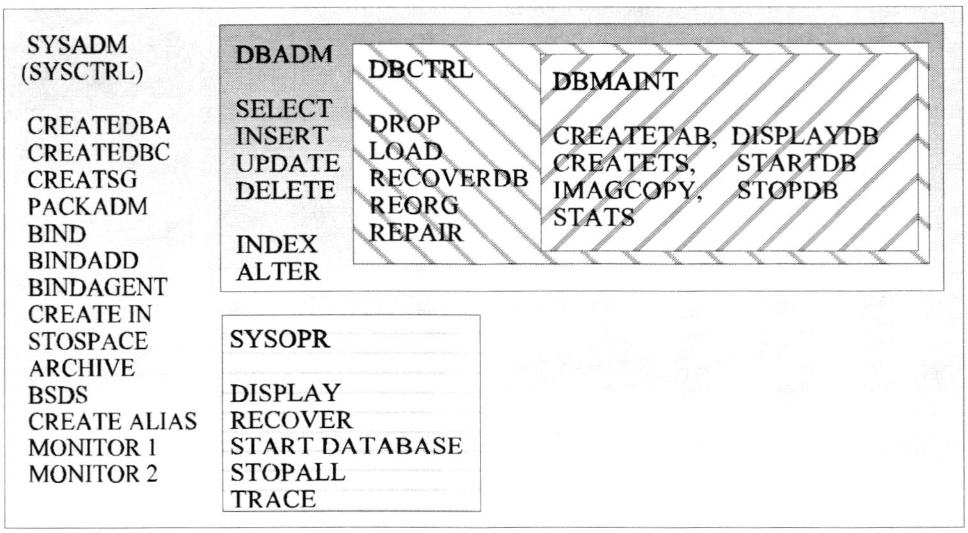

SQLCODE and SQLSTATE

The SQLCODE and SQLSTATE provide information on the status of executing an SQL statement. These codes are reported after the execution of every SQL statement for both static and dynamic SQL. The codes are returned after the execution of SQL interactively and are returned in the SQL communications area (SQLCA) when the SQL statements are embedded in a host program as discussed in Chapter PD.

An SQLCODE of 0 means that the statement executed successfully. If the code has a value of +100, no rows qualified for the SQL statement or no more rows qualify when selecting a number of rows. A three-digit positive integer is an informative or warning message. A three-digit negative integer indicates an error condition. A brief message accompanies the SQLCODE and SQLSTATE when executing SQL interactively and some information is provided in the SQLCA for embedded SQL. More detail is available from the *Messages and Codes* manual and by calling a sample program as discussed in Chapter PD.

The SQLSTATE reports similar information as the SQLCODE. The SQLSTATE conforms to the American National Standards Institute (ANSI) standard. The same value is reported for all relational DBMS that comply with the standard. This means that programs receive the same status as to the result of executing a statement on different relational DBMS. The SQLSTATE is a five-digit character standard code with a range of '00000' to '65535'. The first two digits indicate the error class. The last three digits indicate the specific error. For example, a values of '00000' means successful execution and '02000' means that no rows qualify or no more rows qualify.

SQL99 Standard

The SQL99 standard consists of the following five volumes. They are available from the web site http://webstore.ansi.org/ at a cost of $20.00 per volume.

- ANSI/ISO/IEC 9075-1-1999 Information Technology - Database Language - SQL Part 1: Framework (SQL/Framework)
- ANSI/ISO/IEC 9075-2-1999 Information Technology - Database languages - SQL - Part 2: Foundation (SQL/Foundation)
- ANSI/ISO/IEC 9075-3-1999 Information Technology - Database Languages - SQL - Part 3: Call-level Interface (SQL/CLI)
- ANSI/ISO/IEC 9075-4-1999 Information Technology - Database languages - SQL - Part 4: Persistent Stored Modules (SQL/PSM)
- ANSI/ISO/IEC 9075-5-1999 Information Technology - Database Languages - SQL - Part 5: Host Language Bindings (SQL/Bindings)

Utilities

A number of utilities are provided with DB2 for the management and maintenance of databases, tablespaces, tables, and indexes. The utilities are summarized below and covered in detail in Chapters LC, RR, and CR.

- **The LOAD** utility reads records from a sequential file and loads rows into one or more tables.

- **RUNSTATS** collects statistics describing tablespaces, tables, and indexes. It optionally updates the catalog tables with the statistics.

- **REORG** restores storage efficiencies of tablespace and indexes.

- **COPY** makes a full or incremental copy of only the pages in a tablespace changed since the last copy.

- **MERGECOPY** combines the copies.

- **REPORT** produces reports on all the tables and tablespaces in a referential integrity structure and the data sets needed for a recovery. A referential integrity structure is a group of related tables that must conform to certain rules as discussed in Chapter CT.

- **CHECK DATA** checks for violations of referential integrity (optionally deletes rows) and checks the consistency of a table and its indexes.

- **QUIESCE** establishes a point of consistency for a list of tablespaces to provide for recovering related tablespaces to currency or to a point-in-time.

- **RECOVER** restores data from copies made with the COPY utility and applies updates as recorded in the log data sets. This applies only to tablespaces prior to V6. It also applies to indexes in V6.

- **REBUILD INDEX** causes a tablespace scan to extract the indexed values, sort of the indexed values, and build of the indexes serially prior to V6. REBUILD INDEX and RECOVER INDEX are aliases in V4 and V5.

- **REPAIR** is used to correct erroneous data and turn off pending states.

- **STOSPACE** determines the space allocation of tablespaces and indexes, and updates the catalog tables with the information.

- **MODIFY** can be used to delete old copies and logs that are no longer needed for a recovery.

The Catalog Tables

DB2 inserts rows into the catalog tables describing all objects created, including storage groups, databases, tablespaces, tables, indexes, views, aliases and synonyms. It changes the rows when the objects are altered and deletes the rows when the objects are dropped. DB2 records information about all privileges that are granted. It records information about all plans and packages that are bound. Statistics determined by the RUNSTATS and STOSPACE utilities are recorded in the catalog tables. Indeed, the execution of most of the utilities updates the catalog tables, particularly the SYSIBM.SYSCOPY table. We will see in Chapter CT how the COMMENT ON and LABEL ON statements can be used to describe tables and columns.

You can insert, update, and delete data used by the optimizer as discussed in Chapter RR and OP. The most common direct manipulation of the catalog tables is to report on information placed there by DB2. We will see a number of examples of doing this throughout the book. All catalog tables have a qualifier of SYSIBM. For example, the full name of a local catalog table is SYSIBM.SYSCOPY. Typically, the SYSIBM qualifier is not used in discussion of the catalog tables. However, it must be used when selecting from them as will be seen in the following example.

If you are given an assignment to work on the POSYSTEM and tables in the application system are created with the authorization ID of POSYSTEM, you can determine the table layout of the tables in the application system with the statement:

```
SELECT NAME, COLTYPE, LENGTH, SCALE,
       NULLS, FOREIGNKEY, COLNO
FROM   SYSIBM.SYSCOLUMNS
WHERE  TBCREATOR = 'POSYSTEM'
ORDER BY TBNAME, COLNO;
```

You may want to determine information on indexes created on the S table. This can be accomplished with the statement:

```
SELECT I.TBCREATOR, I.TBNAME, I.CREATOR,
       I.NAME, I.UNIQUERULE, I.CLUSTERING,
       K.ORDERING, K.COLNAME, K.COLSEQ,
       K.COLNO
FROM   SYSIBM.SYSKEYS K,
       SYSIBM.SYSINDEXES I
WHERE  I.TBCREATOR = 'POSYSTEM'
AND    I.TBNAME    = 'S'
AND    I.CREATOR   = K.IXCREATOR
AND    I.NAME      = K.IXNAME
ORDER BY I.NAME, K.COLSEQ;
```

Control Center

The Control Center provides a graphical user interface for the management of DB2 for OS/390 objects from a PC/workstation. One of the many options available is to get information from the catalog table as indicated by the arrow in Figure CO.3. The Control Center itself runs on DB2 for non-OS/390 platforms which includes DB2 Connect for the PC/workstation. There are several prerequisites that must be installed to allow for the use of the Control center including the enablement of stored procedures using Work Load Manager (WLM) in goal or compatibility mode.

Figure CO.3. Control center panel

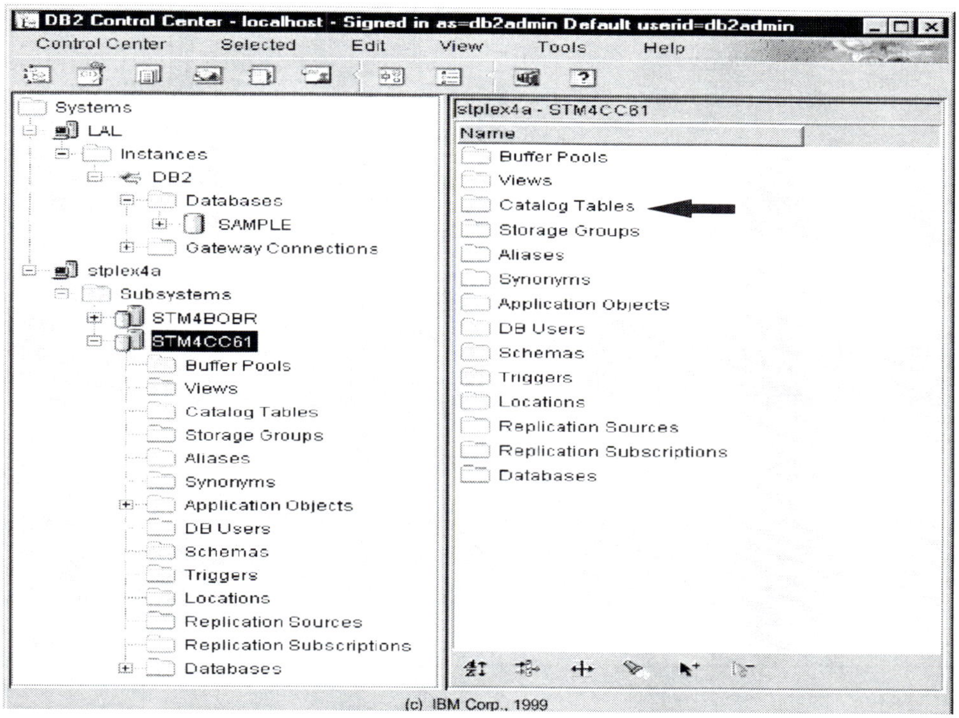

There are several prerequisites that must be installed to allow for the use of the Control center including the enablement of stored procedures using WLM in goal or compatibility mode.

The Directory

The directory tables like the catalog tables are maintained by DB2 when you take certain actions.

However, you cannot select directly from the directory tables like the catalog tables. There are methods for getting information on most of the five tables and tablespaces in the directory database DSNDB01.

1) The database descriptors (DBD) describing objects in a database are maintained in the DBD01 tablespace and accessed by DB2 using a hashing algorithm. You can get information on objects in a database using the DISPLAY DATABASE command like:

```
-DISPLAY DATABASE(DASPJDB)
```

2) DB2 maintains the start and stop relative byte addresses of log records in the SYSLGRNX table in the SYSLGRNX tablespace. (An overview of logging is in Section CO.4 and the details are in Chapter CR.) This information is used by DB2 to locate updates in the log to apply to a copy during a recovery. The information is accessed by DB2 using the DSNLLX01 and DSNLLX02 indexes. You can get information from SYSLGRNX using the REPORT utility.

3) DB2 tracks the progress and status of utilities that have been submitted but not successfully completed in the SYSUTILX tablespace. It accesses the information using the DSNLUX01 and DSNLUX02 indexes. You can get information about the progress and status of a utility by naming it in the DISPLAY UTILITY command like:

```
-DISPLAY UTILITY(RUNSPJ)
```

4) Application plans that result from a bind are stored by DB2 in the SCTR table in the SCT02 tablespace. The DSNSCT02 index is used by DB2 to locate the required plan when it is executed. Similarly, application packages that result from a bind are stored in the SPTR table in the SPT01 tablespace. The DSNSPT02 index is used to locate the required package when it is executed.

How Many Bytes?

The number of bytes of central, expanded, and DASD storage used in a computer complex has been growing by leaps and bounds since mainframes first became widely used in the 1960s. The abbreviations and the number of bytes they represent are summarized in Figure CO.4.

Figure CO.4. Number of byte units

Abbre.	Desc.	Number of Bytes Base 2	Number of Bytes Base 10
KB	Kilobytes	1,024	1,000
MB	Megabytes	1,048,576	1,000,000
GB	Gigabytes	1,073,741,824	1,000,000,000
TB	Terabytes	1,099,511,627,776	1,000,000,000,000
PT	Petabytes	1,125,899,906,842,624	1,000,000,000,000,000

CO.3 DB2 INTERACTIVE

DB2 interactive (DB2I) is a menu-driven tool for executing dynamic SQL using SPUFI, generating data structures from the catalog tables for inclusion in host programs, program preparation and execution of DB2 commands and utilities. These options are shown in Figure CO.5.

Figure CO.5. DB2I primary option menu

```
DSNEPRI                    DB2I PRIMARY OPTION MENU           SSID: DSN
COMMAND ===> _

Select one of the following DB2 functions and press ENTER.

 1  SPUFI                  (Process SQL statements)
 2  DCLGEN                 (Generate SQL and source language declarations)
 3  PROGRAM PREPARATION (Prepare a DB2 application program to run)
 4  PRECOMPILE             (Invoke DB2 precompiler)
 5  BIND/REBIND/FREE       (BIND, REBIND, or FREE plans or packages)
 6  RUN                    (RUN a SQL program)
 7  DB2 COMMANDS           (Issue DB2 commands)
 8  UTILITIES              (Invoke DB2 utilities)
 D  DB2I DEFAULTS          (Set global parameters)
 X  EXIT                   (Leave  DB2I)

PRESS:  END to exit                            HELP for more information
```

SQL Processing Using File Input (SPUFI)

SPUFI is useful for executing multiple SQL statements as keyed into a member of a partitioned data set (PDS) or sequential file that you have created before using SPUFI. Do replace 'AUTHID.SPUFI.IN(MEMBER)' in option 1 of the SPUFI Panel as shown in Figure CO.6 with the name of a PDS that already exists and specify a member name to identify SQL statements that you want to retain. A PDS member is used to key and edit SQL statements. 'AUTHID.SPUFI.OUT' in option 4 should be replaced with the name of a sequential data set into which you want the results of the execution to be written. DB2 creates this data set automatically and reuses it for each execution of SQL from a member of the 'AUTHID.SPUFI.IN' PDS in the example. Options 5 through 9 are described well on the SPUFI panel. You will probably want to use the indicated defaults except for option 5 after the first execution. You can place an 'N' for option 5 after you have changed the defaults that are reviewed in the next paragraph to avoid having the CURRENT SPUFI DEFAULTS panel displayed each time that you use SPUFI.

Figure CO.6. SPUFI panel

```
DSNESP01                        SPUFI                        SSID: DSN
===>
Enter the input data set name: (Can be sequential or partitioned)
 1 DATA SET NAME..... ===> 'AUTHID.SPUFI.IN(MEMBER)'
 2 VOLUME SERIAL..... ===>        (Enter if not cataloged)
 3 DATA SET PASSWORD. ===>        (Enter if password protected)

Enter the output data set name:   (Must be a sequential data set)
 4 DATA SET NAME..... ===> 'AUTHID.SPUFI.OUT'

Specify processing options:
 5 CHANGE DEFAULTS... ===> Y (Y/N - Display SPUFI defaults panel?)
 6 EDIT INPUT........ ===> Y (Y/N - Enter SQL statements?)
 7 EXECUTE........... ===> Y (Y/N - Execute SQL statements?)
 8 AUTOCOMMIT........ ===> Y (Y/N - Commit after successful run?)
 9 BROWSE OUTPUT..... ===> Y (Y/N - Browse output data set?)

For remote SQL processing:
10 CONNECT LOCATION   ===>

PRESS: ENTER to process     END to exit     HELP for more info.
```

Most of the default values on the SPUFI defaults panel in Figure CO.7 are good. You will want to change option 1 from RR to CS to minimize lock contention as discussed in Chapter CC. Do be cautious with option 2 which allows you to specify the maximum number of lines that are returned in the output file regardless of the number that qualifies. The default value of 250 is a reasonable starting point. However, if you need to review or search the results of more than 250 lines, do increase this value.

Figure CO.7. SPUFI defaults

```
DSNESP02                CURRENT SPUFI DEFAULTS                SSID: DSN
===>
Enter the following to control your SPUFI session:
 1 SQL TERMINATOR .. ===> ;  (SQL Statement Terminator)
 2 ISOLATION LEVEL . ===> RR (RR=Repeatable Read, CS=Cursor Stability)
 3 MAX SELECT LINES  ===> 250(Maximum number of lines to be
                              returned from a SELECT)
Output data set characteristics:
 4 RECORD LENGTH ... ===> 4092 (LRECL= logical record length)
 5 BLOCKSIZE ....... ===> 4096 (Size of one block)
 6 RECORD FORMAT.... ===> VB (RECFM= F, FB, FBA, V, VB, or VB)
 7 DEVICE TYPE...... ===> SYSDA (Must be a DASD unit name)

Output format characteristics:
 8 MAX NUMERIC FIELD ===> 33 (Maximum width for numeric field)
 9 MAX CHAR FIELD .. ===> 80 (Maximum width for character field)
10 COLUMN HEADING .. ===> NAMES (NAMES, LABELS, ANY, or BOTH)

PRESS: ENTER to process    END to exit    HELP for more info.
```

A brief war story will demonstrate why the value specified for option 3 can be very important. A person was testing a batch update program and wanted to verify that the rows were being changed correctly. The person selected the rows from the table updated by the batch program and found that changed rows did not appear in the SPUFI output. The person spent a good deal of time trying to debug the batch program thinking that it was in error. After a good deal of time and frustration debugging a program that was working correctly, it was discovered that the real problems was that the changed rows appeared correctly beyond the first 250 rows displayed by SPUFI.

After you have made any changes to the defaults, press the ENTER key before pressing F3 to exit to ensure the changes take effect.

You are presented with an interactive system productivity facility (ISPF) panel for keying and editing SQL statements that you want to execute as indicated in Figure CO.8. If there is more than one SQL statement in the input file, each statement must be terminated with a semicolon (";"). The use of the semicolon for terminating SQL statements when using the QMF product is optional.

Figure CO.8. ISPF panel for keying and editing SQL statements

```
EDIT ----------'AUTHID.SPUFI.IN(MEMBER)'------------- COLUMNS 001 072
COMMAND INPUT ===> ;;;                                SCROLL ===> PAGE
************************** TOP OF DATA ****************************
000100 SELECT SN, PN, JN, QTY
000200 FROM   SPJ
000300 WHERE  SN = 'S4';
000400
000500 -- 2 hyphens can be used followed by comments
000600
000700 SELECT JN, JNAME, CITY
000800 FROM   J
000900 WHERE  JN = 'J2';
*********************** BOTTOM OF DATA ****************************
```

When you are ready to execute the SQL statements, key three semicolons (";;;") on the command input line, then press F3 like:

```
COMMAND INPUT ===> ;;;
```

The three semicolon are not required. However, they do save having to pass through several panels and pressing F3 to go past the panels to get into ISPF browse mode to review the results of executing the SQL statements. You do need to press F3 with or without the three semicolons.

The SQL statements that you keyed and their results are displayed in ISPF browse mode as shown in Figure CO.9. You can return to the ISPF editor by keying three semicolons (";;;") on the command line and pressing F3. Again the three semicolons avoid going thru intermediate panels. If you prefer to return to the SPUFI panel, simply press F3 without entering the three semicolons.

Figure CO.9. Results in browse mode

```
  Menu  Utilities  Compilers  Help
 ------------------------------------------------------------------------------
 BROWSE    RDAGXW.SPUFI.OUT                              Line 00000000 Col 001 080
********************************* Top of Data **********************************
---------+---------+---------+---------+---------+---------+---------+---------+

 SELECT SN, PN, JN, QTY
 FROM   SPJ
 WHERE  SN = 'S4';
---------+---------+---------+---------+---------+---------+---------+---------+
SN       PN       JN              QTY
---------+---------+---------+---------+---------+---------+---------+---------+
S4       P6       J3              300
S4       P6       J7              300
DSNE610I NUMBER OF ROWS DISPLAYED IS 2
DSNE616I STATEMENT EXECUTION WAS SUCCESSFUL, SQLCODE IS 100
---------+---------+---------+---------+---------+---------+---------+---------+

 -- 2 hyphens can be used followed by comments
 Command ===>                                                  Scroll ===> PAGE
  F1=Help    F3=Exit    F5=Rfind  F12=Cancel
  Menu  Utilities  Compilers  Help
 ------------------------------------------------------------------------------
 BROWSE    RDAGXW.SPUFI.OUT                              Line 00000019 Col 001 080

 SELECT JN, JNAME, CITY
 FROM   J
 WHERE  JN = 'J2';
---------+---------+---------+---------+---------+---------+---------+---------+
JN       JNAME                CITY
---------+---------+---------+---------+---------+---------+---------+---------+
J2       Punch                Rome
DSNE610I NUMBER OF ROWS DISPLAYED IS 1
DSNE616I STATEMENT EXECUTION WAS SUCCESSFUL, SQLCODE IS 100
---------+---------+---------+---------+---------+---------+---------+---------+
---------+---------+---------+---------+---------+---------+---------+---------+
DSNE617I COMMIT PERFORMED, SQLCODE IS 0
DSNE616I STATEMENT EXECUTION WAS SUCCESSFUL, SQLCODE IS 0
---------+---------+---------+---------+---------+---------+---------+---------+
DSNE601I SQL STATEMENTS ASSUMED TO BE BETWEEN COLUMNS 1 AND 72
DSNE620I NUMBER OF SQL STATEMENTS PROCESSED IS 2
DSNE621I NUMBER OF INPUT RECORDS READ IS 13
DSNE622I NUMBER OF OUTPUT RECORDS WRITTEN IS 37
******************************** Bottom of Data ********************************
 Command ===>                                                  Scroll ===> PAGE
  F1=Help    F3=Exit    F5=Rfind  F12=Cancel
```

Schema Definition in Batch

Often DB2 objects discussed in Chapters CD, TS, and CT are created using SPUFI. Optionally, objects can be created with a schema processor executed in batch (cannot be executed interactively nor within a host program). Schema definitions are provided for conformance to ISO/ANSI standards. A schema name is an option to a qualifier name for objects that require a qualifier including tables, indexes, aliases, and views as discussed in Chapters CT and ID. A schema can also include a collection of distinct types, functions, stored procedures, and triggers as discussed in Chapters CT, TR, UD, and SP. These objects can use the schema name as the qualifier or the user SQLID of the creator of the objects.

Here is an example of what can placed in a file and used as input to the schema processor. The schema processor is executed using the batch program DSNHSP with JCL from prefix.SDSNSAMP(DSNTEJ1S). The input is read from SYSIN data set and the output written to SYSPRINT. The schema processor sets the current SQLID to the value of the specified schema AUTHID (POSYS in the example) before executing any of the statements in the schema definition.

```
CREATE SCHEMA AUTHORIZATION POSYS;

CREATE TABLE S
 (SN     CHAR(6)  NOT NULL PRIMARY KEY,
  SNAME  CHAR(20) NOT NULL WITH DEFAULT,
  STATUS SMALLINT NOT NULL WITH DEFAULT,
  CITY   CHAR(15) NOT NULL WITH DEFAULT);

GRANT SELECT ON S TO PUBLIC;

CREATE VIEW AMSTERDAM S AS
  SELECT SN, SNAME, STATUS, CITY
  FROM   S
  WHERE  CITY = 'Amsterdam';
```

There are some differences in processing statement using the schema processor and SPUFI. All statements are executed even if one or more statements results in a negative SQL code unlike SPUFI which terminates when the first error is encountered. All statements executed by the schema processor are rolled back and must be resubmitted for successful execution as with SPUFI. The schema processor allows for performing actions on an object that does not yet exist when statements are executed in sequence. For example, you can grant privileges on a table that is created later in the schema definition as in the previous example. This is not true for SPUFI. The creation of a table with a column defined as a PRIMARY KEY or UNIQUE results in automatic creation of a unique index (does not apply when using SPUFI).

Only one schema definition is accepted by the schema processor in a single job.

CO.4 DB2 SUBSYSTEM ARCHITECTURE

The DB2 subsystem consists of three required address spaces and two or more optional address spaces as shown in Figure CO.10. The three required address spaces are the Systems Services, Database Services, and Internal Resource Lock Manager address spaces. The fourth Distributed Data Facility address space is optional but highly advisable if distributed processing is required. The fifth Stored Procedure address space is optional and also highly advisable in a distributed environment. Indeed, there can be multiple stored procedure address spaces managed dynamically by the OS/390 and OS/390 operating system.

Figure CO.10. DB2 subsystem architecture

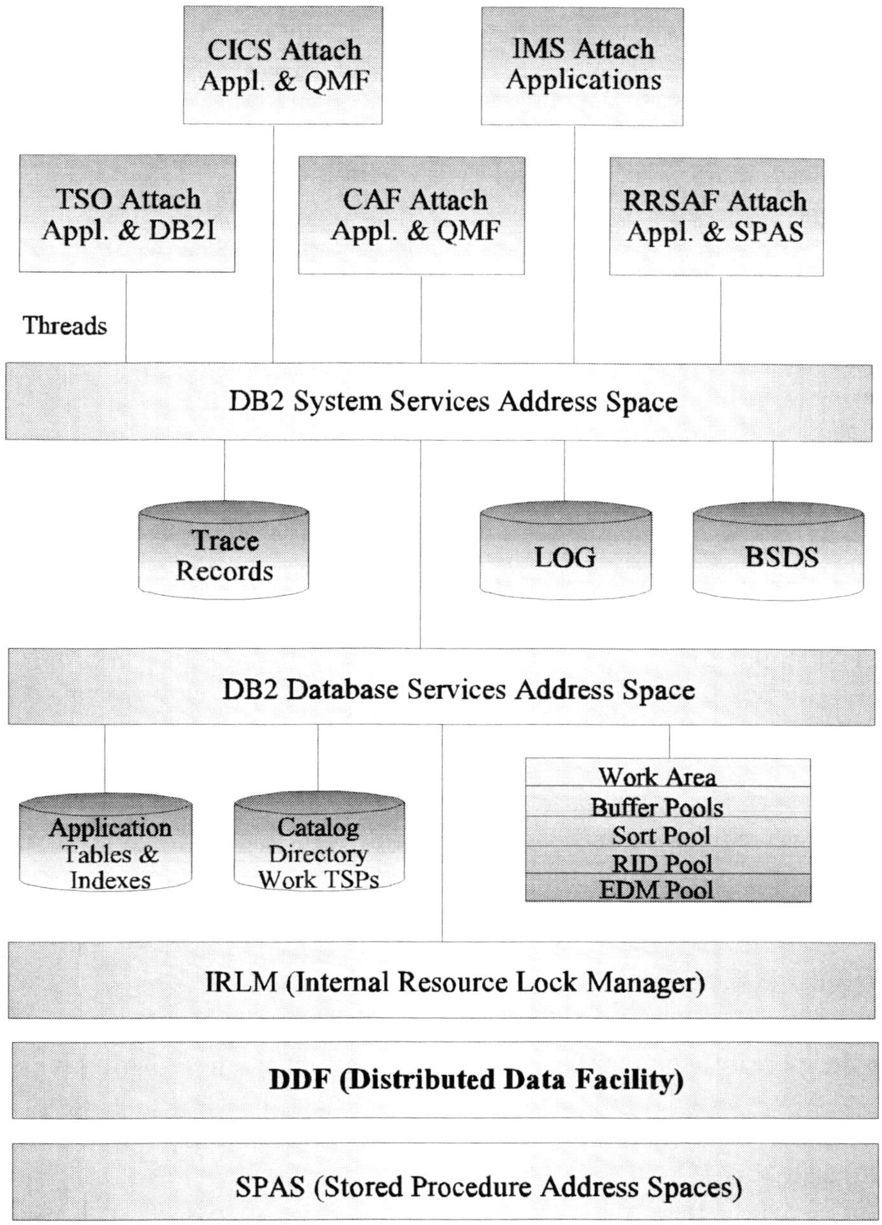

Attaches and Threads

Access to the DB2 subsystem is through the Customer Information Control System (CICS), Information Management System (IMS), Time Sharing Option (TSO), Call Attachment Facility (CAF), Recoverable Resource Manager Services Attachment Facility(RRSAF), or the DSNU attachment facility for utilities.

The System Services address space uses one of the attachment facilities to establish a thread of communication with the DB2 subsystem when the first SQL statement is executed in a plan or package. A thread is a task control block (TCB) that is used to describe an application's connection existence, trace its progress, and provides the ability to perform processing in DB2. A thread is deallocated upon completion of processing or can be canceled with the cancel thread command like:

```
-CANCEL THREAD (414)
```

The value of 414 in the example is a token used to identify the thread. It can be determined using the DISPLAY THREAD command. -CANCEL THREAD (414) NOBACKOUT (V7) avoids rollback which can be length. However, it is necessary to recover effected objects for data integrity.

Thread reuse is available when using CICS, and IMS wait for input (WFI) and IMS Fast Path (IFP). Thread reuse means that a thread can be reused by a defined transaction rather than allocating and deallocating the thread each time that a transaction is executed. This has performance advantages if the transaction is executed one or more times every 30 to 45 seconds. A savings of 5 to 20 percent of CPU time for transactions with 10 or fewer SQL statements can be realized. The work avoided with the use of and the activities performed when a thread is created, used and deallocated are described in Section CO.10.

System Services Address Space

The System Services Address Space is also known as DSN1MSTR. This address space is responsible for a number of activities in DB2. It is responsible for starting and stopping the DB2 subsystem when the START and STOP commands are executed. Indeed, it is responsible for all command processing including starting and stopping traces, starting and stopping a database, and displaying information about threads and databases.

System Services collects statistics, accounting, performance, audit, global, and monitor trace records when the appropriate trace is started. This information is available from performance monitor products which use the instrumentation facility interface to access the trace records.

Logging and Recovery Management

System Services is responsible for logging and recovery management. It writes a before and after image of all updated rows to the log buffer in central storage as shown in Figure CO.11. Each log record is assigned a relative byte address (RBA) when it is written to the log. An RBA is an offset from beginning of the log where log records can be found. It can be thought of a log record sequence number. The RBA is 6 bytes (48 bits) in length with a maximum value of 2^{48}. It is used to locate log records to be applied to an image copy during a recovery.

Figure CO.11. Logging and recovery

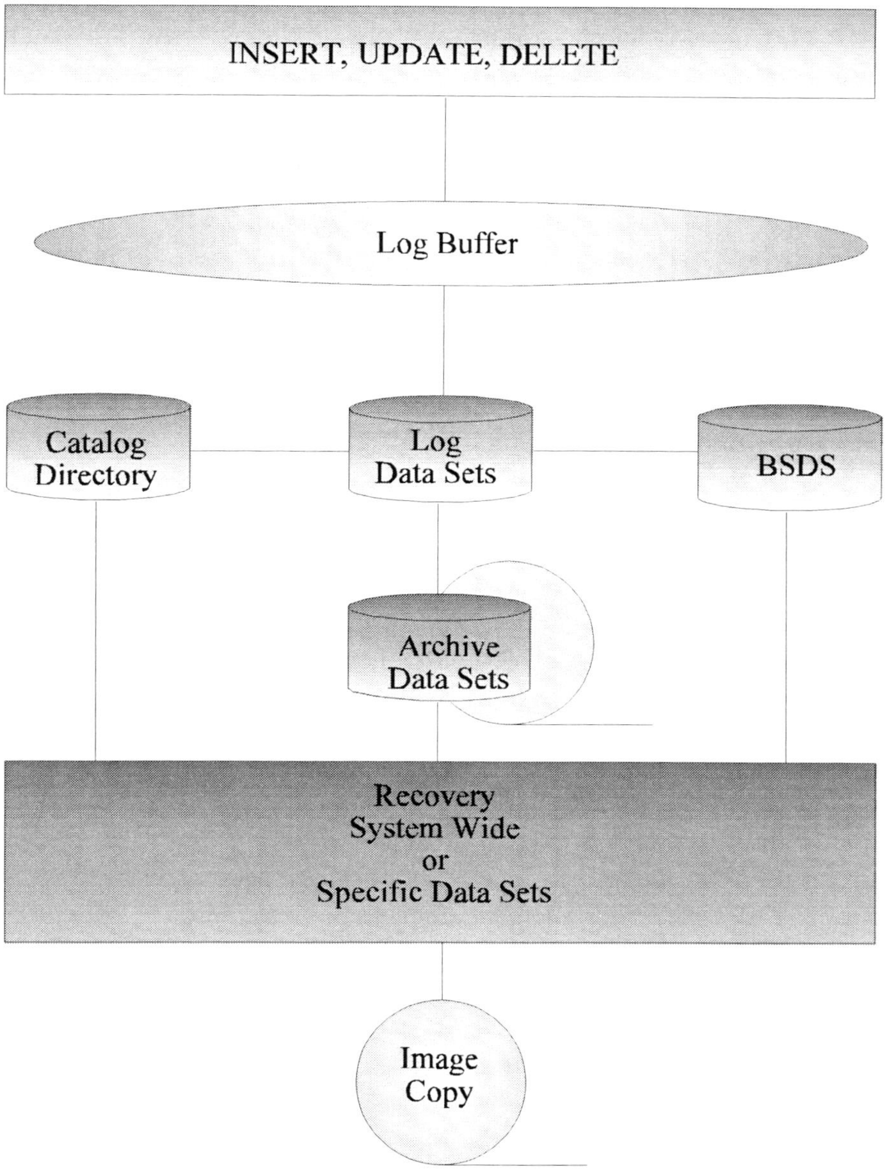

The OUTPUT BUFFER in central storage is used to log before and after images of updated data. The buffer is 4000 KB by default (can be 40 to 400,000 KB in V6). The goal is to size the output buffer to minimize a force write of the buffer to active log. The size can be specified in DSNZPARM DSN6LOGP OUTBUFF or the DSNTIPB installation panel. You can change a copy of DSNZPARM macros in prefix.SDSNSAMP(DSNTIJUZ) and executing it. The "prefix" portion of the PDS name is specified by the person who installs DB2 on the DSNTIPA1 installation panel. The value DSN610 is the default for Version 6. The 6 portion of the name indicates the version and the 10 portion indicates the release of DB2.

The WRITE THRESHOLD is the number of contiguous 4 KB output buffer pages that are allowed to fill before data is written to the active log data set. It can be 1 to 256 with a default of 20. A value within the range of 32 to 128 is reasonable. A high value is good for SQL statements that update and delete a large number of rows. The value can be specified in DSNZPARM DSN6LOGP WRTHRSH or on the DSNTIPB installation panel. Regardless of the value specified the log buffer is written to the active log on DASD when a commit is issued by any program to ensure that no committed data is lost. Commit processing is discussed in Chapter CC.

The NUMBER OF LOGS is the number of data sets per active log copy. You can have from 2 to 31 active log data sets with a default of 3. The default is a good starting point. If you need more active log data sets, the number can be specified on the DSNTIPB installation panel.

The ARCHIVE LOG FREQ is the interval in hours at which the active log is offloaded to the archive log. You can specify a value of 1 to 200 with a default of 24 hours. The default is a good starting point and can be changed on the DSNTIPB installation panel. An image copy of critical tablespaces taken every 24 hours is a good choice to decrease the likelihood that the archive log will be required for a recovery. Recovery from the active log improves recovery time significantly over having to use the archive log.

The UPDATE RATE is an estimate of the number of inserts, updates, and deletes expected per hour. The DSNTINST CLIST assumes that 400 bytes of data are logged for each insert, update, and delete when it calculates this value. For example, 10 GB of data can be logged per hour for processing millions of updates and inserts. The value can be specified on the DSNTIPB installation panel.

The ARCHIVE LOG FREQ and UPDATE RATE can be used to determine the size of the active logs.

LOGLOAD determines when checkpoints are taken for DB2 subsystem restart. DB2 takes periodic checkpoints to ensure that all committed units of recovery are written to the tablespaces and all uncommitted units of recovery are rolled back to reduce recovery time. The information written during a checkpoint is used for recovery of one or more tablespaces when the RECOVER utility is executed and when DB2 is started after an abend due to a power failure for example. If LOGLOAD is too large, restart of DB2 time is increased A checkpoint is taken when 50,000 log records have been written by default (can specify 0 or 200 to 16000000).

LOGLOAD can be dynamically changed until DB2 is restarted with a command like (V6):

```
SET LOG LOGLOAD(150000)
```

The new value takes affect following the next system checkpoint. Indeed, you can initiate a system checkpoint like:

```
SET LOG LOGLOAD(0)
```

If LOGLOAD is to be changed permanently, it can be changed using the LOGLOAD parameter in DSNZPARM or by using the field CHECKPOINT FREQ on installation panel DSNTIPN. A good goal is to take a checkpoint every 15 to 20 minutes. The LOGLOAD values can be calculated based on a formula invented by Joel Goldstein: Take the DB2PM "Write-NoWait" value and divide it by the statistics interval which is typically 15 or 30 minutes and multiply by 20 minutes. A checkpoint is also taken when switching from one active log data set to another, at the end of a successful restart, and at normal termination of DB2. The active log should be sized to contain data for about 10 checkpoints.

The LOAD parameter value in DSNZPARM can be determined like:

Tracking Recovery Information

BSDS: System Services manages the boot strap data set (BSDS) which contains the beginning and ending RBA of the active and archive log data sets. This is a wrap around inventory of checkpoints. Dual active and archive logs, and the BSDS are managed by Systems Services by default. The log data set pairs can be written to DASD. It is important to spread data sets across multiple DASD devices, channels, and control units to minimize I/O contention. Data Facility Storage Management Subsystem data facility product (DFSMSdfp, frequently referred to simply as SMS) can be used to write archive logs to tape units. Optionally, one set of logs can be written to DASD and one to tape units.

Recovery Information in the Catalog and Directory: The catalog table SYSCOPY contains a record of all copies. The most recent copy is written to the tablespace by the recovery utility for a recovery. The directory table SYSLGRNX contains the start and stop RBA for each tablespace and index to locate updates in the log to apply to a copy during a recovery.

INPUT BUFFER is used for reading the active and archive log data sets. It is 60 KB with no option to change the size (V6). Each RECOVER utility job has an input buffer.

Fast Log Apply (V6)

The log can be read with up to and including 100 parallel prefetch tasks. Log records are sorted with a single pass of the log. This enables multiple log records to be applied to a page or series of pages with fast log apply. Multiple log apply tasks are used to apply log records in parallel. This avoids having to repeatedly read a single page for each log record that applies to the page. Fast log apply is not the default. It must be enabled with the LOG APPLY STORAGE field on the DSNTIPL installation panel.

Monitor Statistics for Resizing Log

The log buffer and active log data set should be sized so that a recovery can be done without access to the archive log to minimize unavailability of the data during a recovery. If the archive log must be accessed, the log buffer and/or active log data set sizes should be increased in size. Figure CO.12 contains partial log statistics from the DB2 PM Statistics Report. If READS SATISFIED FROM ARCHIVE LOG A is high, consider increasing the size of the active log.

Figure CO.12. Partial log statistics from the DB2 PM Statistics Report

LOG ACTIVITY		QUANTITY
READS SATISFIED-OUTPUT BUFF		269.00
READS SATISFIED-OUTP.BUF(%)		98.18
READS SATISFIED-ACTIVE LOG		5.00
READS SATISFIED-ACTV.LOG(%)		1.82
READS SATISFIED-ARCHIVE LOG	A	0.00
READS SATISFIED-ARCH.LOG(%)		0.00
TAPE VOLUME CONTENTION WAIT		0.00
WRITE-NOWAIT		298.9K
WRITE OUTPUT LOG BUFFERS		19200.00
BSDS ACCESS REQUESTS		377.00
UNAVAILABLE OUTPUT LOG BUFF	B	0.00
CONTR.INTERV.CREATED-ACTIVE		6980.00
ARCHIVE LOG READ ALLOCATION		0.00
ARCHIVE LOG WRITE ALLOCAT.		0.00
CONTR.INTERV.OFFLOADED-ARCH		0.00
READ DELAYED-UNAVAIL.RESOUR		0.00
READ DELAYED-ARCH.ALLOC.LIM		N/A
LOOK-AHEAD MOUNT ATTEMPTED		0.00
LOOK-AHEAD MOUNT SUCCESSFUL		0.00

It should be possible to write the log buffer to the active log without a wait. If write request to the active log must wait, do increase the output buffer size. An alternative is to adjust the write threshold if you believe that the size of the write threshold might be too close to the size of the output buffer. A high value for UNAVAILABLE OUTPUT LOG BUFF B in Figure CO.12 indicates that adjustments are needed.

Chapter CR contains a detailed description of logging, making copies, and recovery.

Instrumentation Facility Interface

The Instrumentation Facility Interface (IFI) in the System Services Address Space writes records describing the work done by all of the DB2 subsystem address spaces depending on the trace that has been started. Records can be written by AUTHID, plan, class, and instrumentation facility component ID (IFCID) to GTF, SMF, etc. data sets. The IFCID is an identifier of records written as described in the sample library prefix.SDSNSAMP(DSNWMSGS).

The accounting trace can be started like:

```
-START TRACE(ACCTG) PLAN(SUPDATE) AUTHID(FLEUR)
  CLASS(1,2,3,7,8) IFCID(...) DEST(GTF)
```

One or more plan names and AUTHIDs can be specified using the PLAN and AUTHID parameters. The CLASS parameter provides for specifying groups of IFCID records to be collected. The IFCID parameter provides for specifying that only specific records are to be collected. The accounting trace records are also identified as storage management facility (SMF) record ID of 101.

The requested accounting trace records are written each time an application thread is created and used, and when a distributed data facility thread changes from an active to inactive state. Accounting records include:

- CPU and elapsed time
- Number of synchronous I/Os
- Number of latches, locks taken/released, timeouts, deadlocks, and lock avoidance
- Number of SQL statements executed by type
- Text of SQL

Following is an estimate of the additional CPU cost by class when the trace is turned on:

Class	Increase in CPU Costs
1	< 5 %
2	1-10 %, higher value if fetch intensive environment because fetch costs are low relative to the cost of writing the trace records
3	< 1 %
7 & 8	< 1 %

The statistics trace can be started like:

```
-START TRACE(STAT) PLAN(SUPDATE) AUTHID(FLEUR)
  CLASS(1,2,3) DEST(GTF)
```

The records are written when DB2 is started and stopped, at specified intervals, when there is a switch to another active log data set, and when a distributed data facility thread changes from an active to inactive state. The statistics trace collects information on overall DB2 subsystem usage including:

- Total threads created, commits, and commands issued
- Log manager statistics
- Total number of SQL statements executed by type
- Total number of binds
- Number of locks taken/released, timeouts, and deadlocks
- Buffer pool usage
- Record ID pool usage
- Environmental Descriptor Manager pool usage
- Distributed data facility statistics

The activation of the statistics trace is low cost. It simply enables the use of the statistics. These statistics are always collected regardless of whether the trace as been turned on.

The statistics trace records are also identified as SMF record ID of 100.

The performance trace can be started like:

```
-START TRACE(PERFM) PLAN(SUPDATE) AUTHID(FLEUR)
  CLASS(4) IFCID(6) DEST(GTF)
```

The performance trace can collect information for all or specific DB2 operations depending on the trace classes started. It can trace operations done for one or more of resource managers, including storage management, data manager, and relational database services. The performance trace is resource intensive. If only the default classes of 1, 2, and 3 are turned on, the increase in CPU costs can be 5 to 30 percent. The performance trace is best used only when necessary and the records collected should be limited as much as possible using the PLAN, AUTHID, CLASS, and IFCID parameters particularly when more than the default classes are activated.

The performance trace records are also identified as SMF record ID of 102.

The global trace is used for servicing DB2. The increase in CPU costs can be 10 to 150 percent while the trace is turned on.

The audit trace records information if auditing is specified when a table is created and security related classes can be turned on.

The monitor trace records information for online monitoring and user-written programs.

Monitoring products are usually used to analyze the trace records in real time and through batch reports. Some monitors insert data into tables for analysis with SQL. DB2 performance monitor (DB2PM) is the monitoring product sold by IBM.

Recommendation: Do execute the DISPLAY TRACE command periodically to determine if unnecessary traces are turned on. Traces could have been turned on or an analysis and not turned off after the analysis. Also beware of the use of DSNTRACE DD DUMMY.

Database Services Address Space

The Database Services address space is also known as DSN1DBM1. This address space is responsible for managing most application work when SQL statements and utilities are executed as well as the catalog and directory tables. It consists of two major components, data manager and the relational data system.

Data manager (DM) interfaces with buffer manager for getpage and release page (relpage) of data and index pages, and sets write pending indicating that a page must be written to the tablespace. It also interfaces with buffer manager for latch processing and with the Internal Resource Lock Manager for locks. DM interfaces with log manager for writing log records. It services utilities with data access and manipulation. It manages the directory tables. DM does all referential integrity and table constraint checking. It performs Enterprise System Architecture (ESA) compression and decompression of data. DM is best known for applying stage 1 predicates on pages in the buffer. (A predicate is a condition specified in the WHERE clause of SQL statements that must be met for the row to qualify for processing.) The use of stage 1 predicates reduces CPU costs as discussed in Chapter PP and throughout the book. DM passes qualifying rows one column at a time to the relational data system for further processing.

Relational Data System (RDS) applies stage 2 predicates on columns passed from DM. It does join processing and a good deal of subselect processing. It does internal sorts of rows as required by SQL statements and sorts record IDs if list prefetch is chosen as part of the access path by the optimizer. RDS interfaces with the environmental data manager for access to plans, packages, and DBDs. It manages the catalog tables, VSAM control blocks, and working storage.

CO.5 BUFFER POOLS

DB2 manages a number of shared pools in the Database Services address space including the buffer pools, sort pool, record ID pool, environmental descriptor pool, and working storage. These pools can be used by all SQL statements as they are executed. The pools are in central storage and can be paged to expanded storage by OS/390.

The primary goal of the buffer pools is to reduce I/O wait time. Indeed, this is true for all of the pools. If we assume a "typical" online transaction with 0.5 second response time, about 68 percent of the time is spent waiting for pages to be read from DASD as shown in Figure CO.13.

Figure CO.13. Resources required by a "Typical" transaction.

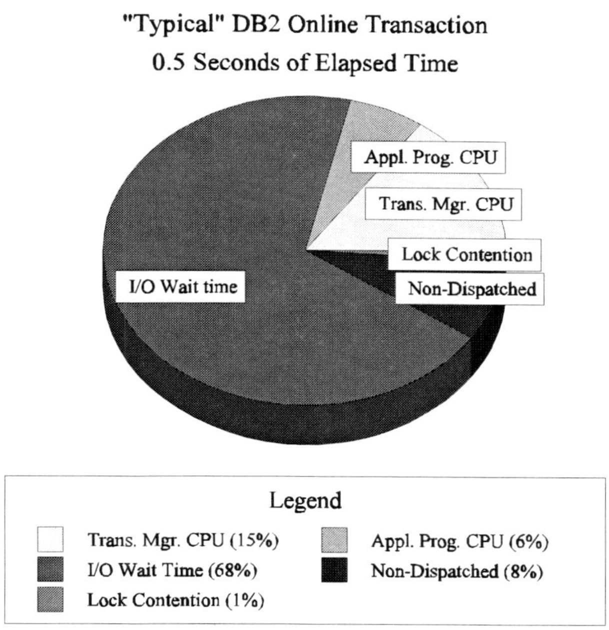

Buffer manager keeps frequently referenced tablespace and index pages in the buffer pools to minimize I/O to DASD. DM issues getpages for the pages that it needs to do its work. Buffer manager searches the buffer pool to determine if the page is already in the pool as a result of having read the page for another user. If the page is present, DM can work on the page without a physical I/O to DASD. If the page is not present in the buffer pool, buffer manager passes a read request to Data Facility Product (DFP) manager. It is the DFP media manager that issues the physical I/O. A read of a single page at random with a single I/O is called a *synchronous* I/O. It is performed under the user Task Control Block (TCB) priority. The CPU time for issuing the I/O appears in the accounting trace records and can be used to bill users for their usage of the resources. Sequential I/O is used to read up to and including 32 pages with a single I/O. This is referred to as *asynchronous* I/O. It is performed under the DB2 Service Request Block (SRB). This means that the CPU time used to issue the I/O does not appear in accounting records for bill back, monitoring, and tuning. The number of I/O issued is collected for all types I/O.

Buffer manager is responsible for a number of activities in addition to keeping frequently processed pages in up to 50 4 KB pages, 10 8 KB, 10 16 KB, and 10 32 KB page buffer pools as indicated in Figure CO.14. How these 80 buffer pools can be managed is discussed in Chapter CD.

Figure CO.14. Buffer manager responsibilities

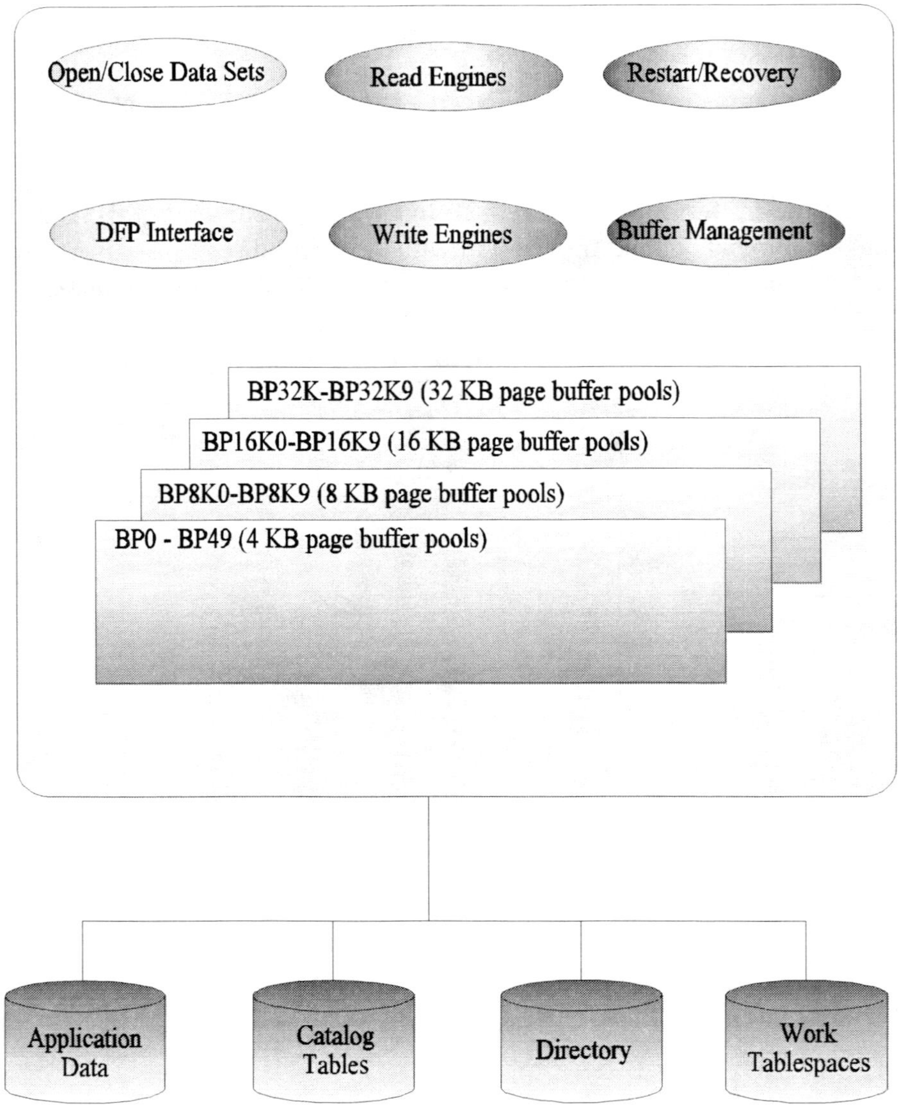

When Data Sets are Opened

Before I/O can be issued, the underlying data sets for the tablespaces and indexes must be opened by buffer manager if they are not already open as a result of earlier processing. The acquire and release parameters specified when SQL statements are bound determines when the data sets are opened and closed. (These parameters are best known for determining when table and tablespace locks are acquired and released and are discussed in Chapters CC and PE.) If acquire of use is specified, the data sets are opened when an SQL statement is executed that requires the tablespace or index is executed. If acquire of allocate is specified, all data sets used by the thread are opened when the thread is allocated. Buffer manager maintains a counter for each open data set. The counter is incremented by one for each user of the data set. The counter is decremented by one when a commit is issued if the plan or package was bound with release of commit. If release of deallocate was specified, the counter is decremented when the thread is deallocated.

Read Engines

The component of buffer manager responsible for reading multiple pages with a single I/O is called the *read engines*. Buffer manager can allocate a number of read engines, each of which can read pages from a data set. The read engines perform read ahead processing with asynchronous I/O. This means that buffer manager attempts to have the required pages in the buffer pool when DM issues a getpage. One of three types of prefetch is used to read up to and including 32 4 KB pages with a single I/O assuming that the buffer pool being used contains 1000 or more pages. (BP0 has 2000 pages by default.)

1) Asynchronous sequential prefetch always reads 32 data or index pages with a single I/O. The optimizer determines whether sequential prefetch should be used. It is frequently used for tablespace and index space scans. The details of the use of sequential prefetch are given in Chapters BP and OP.

2) Asynchronous dynamic prefetch is similar to sequential prefetch. The difference is that if the optimizer does not choose to use sequential prefetch but prefetch appears to be beneficial during the process of reading pages, dynamic prefetch is activated based on a sequential detection algorithm covered in Chapter BP.

3) Asynchronous list prefetch can read up to and including 32 data pages as identified from the index pages. The optimizer determines whether list prefetch should be used. Index processing is required prior to the use of list prefetch as discussed in Chapter PP.

Prefetch of 32 4 KB pages means reading 128 KB of data. The same principle applies to 8, 16, and 32 KB pages. The prefetch quantity is 128 KB of data (16 8 KB pages, 8 16 KB pages, and 4 32 KB pages.

Write Engines

Write engines perform write behind processing. Write engines are basically the opposite of read engines in that they are used to write up to and including 32 pages rather than read them. SQL statements need not wait while updated pages are being written to DASD in the great majority of cases. Up to 10 percent of updated pages for a single data set are written using asynchronous deferred write in 1 to 32 page groups by default. The page IDs are sorted and the pages are written in sequence as they appear on DASD to minimize seek time. Pages can be read and updated by many users without physical reads and writes as discussed in Chapter CD.

Asynchronous deferred writes are triggered by thresholds and specific activities. If more than 10 percent of the pool or 64 pages (whichever is larger) are occupied by updated pages for a single data set, deferred write is initiated. The 64 page limit is used to determine when pages updated by the load, reorganization, and recover utility are written. If less than or equal to 50 percent (default) of the pool is stealable, the updated pages are written to DASD. If there is a shortage of space in the buffer pool and a page slot must be reused, updated pages at the beginning of the least recently used chain are written to DASD. A DB2 checkpoint causes all updated pages to be written to DASD. If you execute the QUIESCE utility with write of yes, stop the database, tablespace, or index space, or stop the DB2 subsystem, updated pages are written to DASD. A switch to read-only processing or a close of a data set causes the updated pages to be written to DASD.

Once deferred write is started, write processing continues until 60 percent (default) of the pages are available for use in a buffer pool.

CO.6 SORT POOLS

There are three types of sorts used with DB2: the utilities use an external sort (DFSORT for example), sort of record IDs, and sort of rows as required by SQL statements. This section describes how DB2 sorts rows as required by SQL statements.

DM issues getpages for the required pages and buffer manager locates the pages in the buffer pool or initiates physical I/O to read the pages from DASD as shown in Figure CO.15. DM applies the stage 1 predicates and passes only the qualifying rows one column at a time to RDS. RDS applies the stage 2 predicates to further minimize the number of rows that must be processed further. This processing in the database services address space occurs with or without a sort.

Figure CO.15. Sort processing

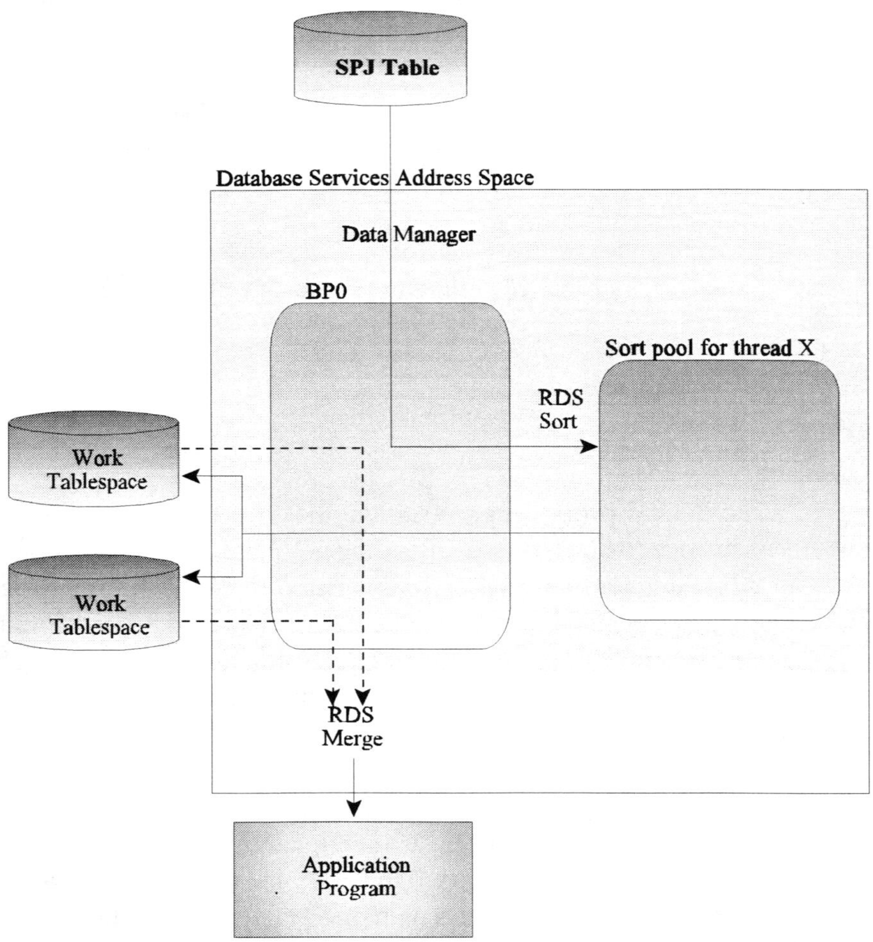

If a sort is required, RDS sorts the rows in a sort pool using a tournament sort. The default size of a sort pool is 1,000 KB. The size can be changed in the SORT POOL SIZE field of the installation panel DSNTIPC or DSNZPARM DSN6SRPM SRTPOOL.

A sort pool is allocated in working storage for each thread that requires a sort. A SELECT statement can require multiple sorts if it has a UNION and ORDER BY clause, for example. The maximum number of nodes in a tournament sort tree is 16,000. The optimal sort pool size for a single sort can be calculated as:

```
16,000 (maximum nodes in a sort tree) *
(16 bytes of control information + sort key length + sort data
length) * the number of sorts
```

For example, assume a statement selects four 10 byte columns--SN, PN, JN, QTY--and the statement does a UNION *and* an ORDER BY on one of the 10 byte columns. The multiplier of 2 in the following example of estimating the space to sort the data is for the two sorts, one sort for the UNION and one sort for the ORDER BY.

```
16,000 * (16 + 10 + 40) * 2 = 2,112,000 bytes
```

Notice that the more columns selected and sorted the more space is required. This suggests that only the columns that are required be selected and sorted for the best performance. If columns in the ORDER BY clause are not in the SELECT clause, they need to be included in the sort data length. If the sort cannot be done in the sort pool, as many rows as possible are sorted and written to a logical work file on work tablespaces in the DSNDB07 database. Each batch of sorted rows is considered a run. Each run is written to a work tablespace via the buffer pool assigned to DSNDB07, read from work tablespaces via buffer pool assigned to DSNDB07, sorted runs must be merged before rows can be returned to the user.

The number of logical work files containing sorted rows can be minimized with a sort pool of 2 MB in the example and for similar statements that require sorts. Minimizing the number of work files written to DASD and merging them reduces the costs of a sort significantly. It is a challenge to estimate the sort pool size for the many SQL statements that require a sort. Do identify a few SELECT statements that require a sort and for which you want to maximize performance. Use the formula to calculate the sort pool size in central storage so that the sort can be done with minimal use of the work files. Of course, you must work within the constraints that you have on the use of central storage. However, you can probably justify more central storage to save CPU and elapsed time required for sorts.

The buffer pool (BP0 by default) assigned to DSNDB07 is used for writing the runs to DASD and merging them. Buffer manager places limits on the amount of a buffer pool that can used. If 20 percent of the buffer pool assigned to DSNDB07 is stealable, up to 10 percent of the sum of the four buffer pools used to determine the default sort pool can be used for I/O to the work tablespaces and merging. Do have sufficient space in the buffer pool for this processing to avoid degrading performance of the sorts.

Create and Size Work File Tablespaces for the Workload: The system administrator must be sure there are enough work file tablespaces and that the work file tablespaces are large enough to support sorts required by many SQL statements and other processing. This means creating perhaps five to seven work file tablespaces in most cases rather than using the two provided by default at installation time. Less than or equal 16,000 node runs are written to logical work files in DSNDB07 work tablespaces via BP0 (default). Logical work files (LWF) are allocated in physical work tablespaces (PWT). If 2 PWT are allocated, LWFs are allocated like:

- LWF1 placed on PWT1
- LWF2 placed on PWT2
- LWF3 placed on PWT1
- LWF4 placed on PWT2
- LWF5 placed on PWT1

Space is freed with a commit (not using CURSOR WITH HOLD) or rollback.

The number and size of work file tablespaces is highly dependent on the size and frequency of sorts on the DB2 subsystem. One possible approach is to create each of five to seven work file tablespaces with 500-1000 cylinders of primary quantity (PRIQTY) each and 25-50 cylinders of secondary quantity (SECQTY). Then monitor the space usage. A good indication of whether there is insufficient work space is to determine if the work tablespaces have gone into secondary extents. An important indicator of too small of a work tablespace is an extent failure. This indicates the work tablespace is too small for the workload. This does not occur for other tablespaces unless the maximum number of extents have been taken. It is necessary to stop DSNDB07 to add, delete, and change work tablespaces and start it for further use. The work tablespaces should be spread across multiple DASD devices, channels, and control units. This minimizes seek time and I/O contention. It allows for parallel I/O for merging the logical work files.

Chuck Hoover did extensive research to determine the breakeven point between DB2 V5 sort and DFSORT. He found it to be 2.2 million 225 byte rows which were sorted in about 3.4 minutes. DB2 sort costs increase rapidly beyond this point. DFSORT sort costs increase much more slowly. This suggests the use of DFSORT when sorting more data.

DSNDB07 is used for trigger processing, data for global temporary tables, materialization of table expression and views, correlated and non-correlated subselect processing, star join processing, and more in addition to sort processing.

A tag sort is used if the row of qualifying columns plus overhead is greater than 4 KB. This means that the required columns are sorted and a tag (pointer) is used to locate columns in the row that are not sorted. This increases sort costs significantly which is one of many reasons for selecting only the required columns especially when a sort is required.

CO.7 RID POOL

Four byte record IDs (RIDs) follow indexed values in leaf pages and reference rows on data pages. RIDs are discussed in detail in Chapters IU and PP. If the optimizer chooses list prefetch as part of the access path, DM retrieves the qualifying RIDs from the index leaf pages and places them in the RID pool. In most cases, the RIDs are sorted and duplicate page identifiers are eliminated before list prefetch I/Os are issued. This allows for retrieving the pages in the sequence in which they appear on DASD, thus minimizing seek time. The elimination of duplicate page identifiers avoids DM having to issue multiple getpages for multiple rows on a page. DM can get the page once and process all of the qualifying rows on the page.

A primary distinction between list prefetch, and sequential and dynamic prefetch, is that list prefetch requires access to the index pages to get the RIDs, process them in the RID pool, and issue one I/O to retrieve between 2 and 32 data pages. In contrast, sequential and dynamic prefetch does not require prior access to one or more indexes and can be used on the index pages as well as the data pages.

List prefetch is always used with a hybrid join and multiple index processing. It is also used with single index processing as discussed in Chapter PP.

The RID pool can be specified as 16 KB to 1 GB with the default being 4,000 KB. The RID pool size can be specified as RID POOL SIZE on installation panel DSNTIPC or DSNZPARM DSN6SPRM MAXRBLK.

CO.8 EDM POOL

Environmental Descriptor Manager (EDM) pool contains plans, packages, and DBDs required for execution of SQL. Buffer manager reads these objects from the directory into the EDM pool via BP0. The EDM pool is analogous to a buffer pool in that the goal is to keep frequently used objects in the pool and minimize I/O to DASD.

Skeleton cursor table (SKCT) and skeleton package table (SKPT) are basically master copies of a plan and package. SKCT and SKPT sections are loaded as SQL statements are executed. Each section contains code structures for one or more SQL statements and is 4 KB in size. A complex SQL statement can span multiple sections. Only those sections required as the program runs must be in the EDM pool for execution. The sections for a SKCT or SKPT are chained in non-contiguous space in the EDM pool. SKCT and SKPT allocation occurs when the first SQL statement is executed in a program at thread allocation time. The Cursor Table (CT) and Package Table (PT) are copies of the SKCT and SKPT sections. Each active user has an individual copy. Each section is allocated as needed during execution. The EDM manager attempts to keep a copy of the SKCT and SKPT in the pool in order to make a copy for a new user who executes the plan or package to avoid I/O to the directory for each user execution. When a BIND REPLACE, REBIND, FREE, or DROP is issued, the SKCT and SKPT are read from the directory.

Figure CO.16. EDM Pool

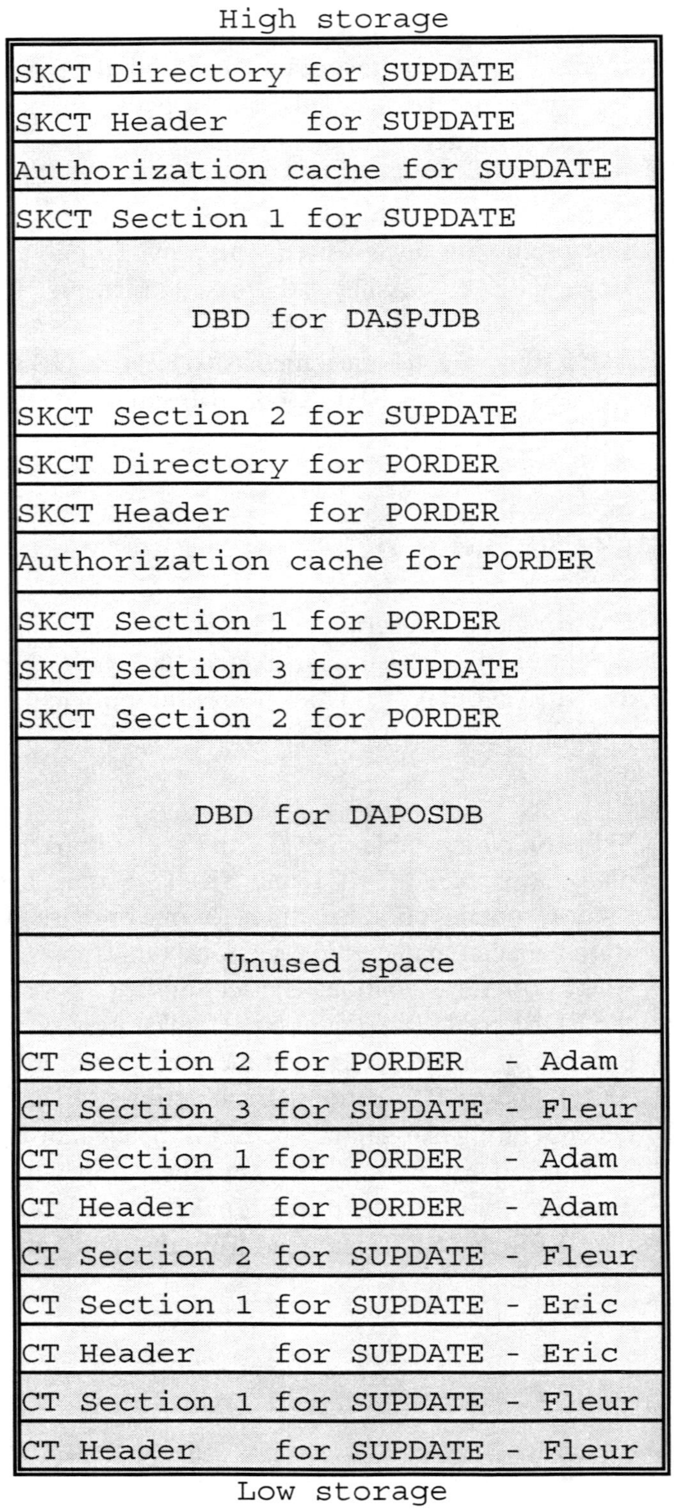

An example of how the EDM pool is used will be given with reference to Figure CO.16. Assume that Fleur is the first person that executes the SUPDATE plan. The SKCT directory, header, and section 1 for the plan are read from the SCTR table in tablespace SCT02 and a copy is made and allocated in low storage as a CT. The SKCT directory, header, authorization cache, and section 1 are placed in high storage for use by additional users who execute the plan. Next Eric executes the same SUPDATE program, the EDM manager makes a copy of the SKCT information that was already read from the directory for Fleur. We will assume that Fleur continues executing statements in the program and requires another section, section 2. It is read from the directory, a copy is made in low storage and the SKCT for the section is placed in high storage. When Eric executes an SQL statement in section 2, a copy is made for him in low storage based on the SKCT and header in high storage read and processed for Fleur. This processing continues as Fleur and others execute the plan.

Next, assume that Adam executes the PORDER plan. The SKCT directory, header, and first required section are read from the directory. The CT copy is made and placed in low storage where it is executed. The SKCT objects are placed in high storage for use as a master copy for others to execute the PORDER plan. As Adams executes more SQL statements in the PORDER plan, more sections are processed as described.

If a plan or package is bound or deleted, the EDM manager must read the new SKCT or SKPT from the directory or issue an error message if the plan has been deleted.

The DBD for the database being processed, DASPJDB in the example, would have been read from the directory tablespace DBD01 and placed in the EDM pool prior to plan allocation.

The cursor table database block (CTDB) is a portion of the header with information on objects manipulated. There is one CTDB for each DBD used by the plan and package. The cursor block (CUB) is a linked child of the CTDB for each cursor. The CUB contains control information on the position in a table and on a leaf page if an index is used, information needed for CURSOR WITH HOLD, index lookaside, and sequential detection. (These topics are discussed in Chapters PD, IU, and BP.)

If acquire of allocate is specified, a static CUB is built in the header at bind time which improves performance but requires more space in the EDM pool. The PLSIZE column in the catalog table SYSPLAN has the header size. If acquire of use is specified, a dynamic CUB is built in working storage at execution time.

The release parameter specified with a bind also effects the use of the EDM pool and deallocation of resources. Release of deallocate has performance advantages over release of commit as can be seen in the comparison of processing required using the two options in Figure CO.17.

Figure CO.17. Release parameter effect on the EDM pool

Release of Commit	Release of Deallocate
CUB counters are reset with a commit work. Index lookaside and sequential detection must be re-initialized.	CUB counters are not reset with a commit work which increases the benefits of index lookaside and sequential detection and reduces costs.
CT and PT space is reusable after a commit work.	CT and PT space is not reusable until thread deallocation which avoids having to recreate the CT/PT.
RDS portion of the header counters decremented by 1 at commit (unless CURSOR WITH HOLD is used). Space for the DM portion is held.	RDS portion of the header counters are not decremented by 1 until thread deallocation. Sections, DM, and RDS portions of the header are held until thread deallocation which minimizes the resources required.
If header counter is 0, SKCT and SKPT section space is reusable.	If header counter is 0, SKCT and SKPT section space is not reusable until thread deallocation which decreases the chances of rereading the directory.
DBD counter of users decremented by 1 for DBDs at commit (unless CURSOR WITH HOLD is used).	DBD counter of users is not decremented by 1 until thread deallocation which decreases the chances of having to reread the DBD.
Data set counter of users decremented by 1 at commit.	Data set counter of users is not decremented by 1 until thread deallocation.

Release of Commit	Release of Deallocate
Global temporary table logical work file space is released with a commit.	Many uses of the same temporary table do not cause repeated allocation and deallocation of the logical work files. Beware of holding onto space for a long period of time if you do not plan to use it.

Recommendation: Acquire of allocate and release of deallocate has performance advantages. The use of these parameters does require more space in the EDM pool. Usually, the use of more storage is a positive trade-off to decrease I/O and CPU usage, and improve performance. The exception is when more than 2 GB of space is required in DSN1DBM1 using 32 bit addressing (64 bit addressing is expected in the future which can allow 9 exabytes of addressable space). The parameters are particularly important to maximize the benefits of thread reuse. Indeed, thread reuse has minimal benefits without the use of the parameters. About the only disadvantage is that a plan or package cannot be rebound until it is deallocated. This can be a long time if the plan or package is frequently executed. It is necessary to find a time in a production environment where the plan or package can be deallocated for a rebind.

Acquire of allocate and release of deallocate do not increase the likelihood of lock contention in most cases as discussed in Chapter CC.

Authorization and the EDM Pool

An authorization cache in the EDM pool can be used to minimize I/O to determine if the user AUTHID has authority to execute a plan. The authority of an AUTHID is checked once in the SYSPLANAUTH and SYSPACKAUTH catalog tables and stored in the plan or package cache if the user is authorized for execution. This avoids checking the AUTHID each time it is used. Use of the cache requires that a plan be bound with a cache size of 256 to 4,096 bytes. The default of 1024 bytes allows for storing 124 AUTHIDs with a base portion of 32 bytes. If more than 124 AUTHIDs attempt to execute a plan, the space is reused and it is necessary to verify privileges the next time that the reused AUTHID slot attempts to execute the plan. This suggests that the cache size be made larger or that privileges be granted to the public as will be discussed in a moment.

The package cache is 32 KB which allows for about 400 AUTHIDs by default. (The size can be changed in DSNZPARM or PACKAGE AUTH CACHE field of DSNTIPP installation panel.) The package cache is a global cache for all packages. It is necessary to GRANT EXECUTE ON collid.* TO AUTHIDS for use of the package cache. There is a plan cache for each plan by default.

A good alternative to using plan and package caches is to grant execution privileges to the public. This causes a bit to be turned on in the SKCT or SKPT to avoid further authorization checks as long as it remains in the EDM pool. A security software product can be used to control who can execute which plans and packages. If you choose this option, do specify CACHESIZE of 0 for each applicable plan and use 0 as the global package cache to avoid wasting space in the EDM pool. The default of 1024 for a plan cache can be changed to 0 on the installation panel DSNTIPP to avoid having to specify CACHESIZE of 0 each time a plan is bound.

DBDs in the EDM Pool

The DBD contains descriptor blocks for each object in a database including each tablespace, table, index, etc. as discussed in Chapter CD. Figure CO.18 summarizes the space required for each object in a DBD.

Figure CO.18. Space for each object in a DBD

Bytes	Each Object in a DBD
160	Tablespace
104	Tablespace partition
64	Table in segmented tablespace
90	Table in nonsegmented tablespace
10	Column in each table
158	Index
100	Index partition
10	Index column in each index
24	Referential integrity relationship

DBDs are shared resources. One copy is used for all SQL referencing objects in the database. DBD can be broken into 32 KB chunks to avoid having to allocate contiguous space in EDM pool (V6) as shown in Figure CO.16. This minimizes EDM pool fragmentation where sufficient space is available but it is not contiguous. However, it is advisable to avoid creating too many objects in a database resulting in a large DBD because it is necessary to log the entire DBD when objects in the DBD are created, dropped, or altered.

If space fragmentation is a problem and the pool cannot be increased in size, consider executing the DISPLAY DATABASE command and name frequently used databases after starting the DB2 subsystem like:

```
-DISPLAY DATABASE (DASPJDB, DAEMPDB)
```

This results in loading DBDs in contiguous space. It also avoids transactions having to wait for initial loading of DBDs as objects in the database are referenced.

If there is insufficient space to load a DBD, a -904 SQLCODE is issued indicating resource unavailable. No SQL statement referencing objects in the database can be executed until space is available to load the DBD from the directory.

EDM Pool Size

The EDM pool should be sized to retain frequently used plans, packages, and DBDs. If DYNAMIC SQL YES is specified on installation panel DSNTIP4, more space is required for skeletons of dynamic SQL. Data spaces can be used for the EDM pool as discussed in Chapter PD when using the dynamic cache. The default size is 14,812 KB. Sizing the EDM pool for the workload is second only in importance to sizing the buffer pools for the workload to achieve good performance of application systems. Both the EDM and buffer pools can be sized based on a hit ratio. That is, the required pages should be found in central storage 80 to 90 percent of the time. The hit ratio for the EDM pool can be calculated as:

```
1 - (number of loads from directory / number of requests)
```

For example, if the number of loads from the directory is 20 and the number of requests is 100, the hit ratio is 0.80. That is, the required SKCT or SKPT sections are found in the EDM pool 80 percent of the time based on:

```
0.80 = 1 - (20 / 100)
```

A good hit ratio not only reduces I/O to the directory but also reduces the costs of allocation and deallocation of CTs, PTs, SKCTs, SKPTs, and DBDs. In addition, it reduces the costs of re-initializing counters and control information if release of deallocate is used.

The least recently used (LRU) algorithm is used to reuse space in the EDM pool when it is full. The CTs and PTs space is reused before SKCT and SKPT space. If there is insufficient space in EDM pool, a -904 SQLCODE is received with reason code 00C90089 indicating that resources are not available to allocate a plan, package, or DBD.

Locating Plans and Packages

The precompiler reads the host program with embedded SQL, comments out the SQL statements, and writes a copy of the statements to the database request modules (DBRM) library. The DBRM name, section number, and consistency token are written to the modified host program by the precompiler. This processing is detailed in Chapter PE.

DB2 uses an index on the plan name and section to locate the plan in the directory based on the information placed in the modified host program by the precompiler. It uses an index on the location.collection.name.contoken.rds#.seq# to locate the package in the directory. Information about the location and collection can be determined from the plan depending on a number of factors to be discussed. This information must be determined to allow for a matching index scan to locate the required package. (There is also an index on version.location.collection.name.contoken to guarantee uniqueness.)

Locating package information: The package name is in the modified host program similar to the plan name. However, in order for DB2 to do a matching index scan to locate a specific package, it must determine the location and collection since they are the two leading columns of the composite index. The location is in the current server special register if SET CURRENT SERVER has been used to set it. If the current server special register is blank, the local server is assumed. The collection ID is in the current package set special register if SET CURRENT PACKAGE SET has been used to set it. If the current package set special register is blank, DB2 uses the first collection entry in the plan header for a matching index scan on the location.collection.name.contoken.rds#.seq# composite index. If the package is not found in the first collection, the second, third, etc., collection entry is used in a matching index scan. If the package is not found in the last collection, a -805 SQLCODE is received or -812 SQLCODE if last entry is "*" at execution time.

Recommendation: The search algorithm suggests that the most frequently used collection should be named first in the PKLIST when the plan is bound. The PKLIST and relationship between plans and packages are discussed in Chapter PE.

Space for Plans and Packages

If many DBRMs are bound to a plan, the plan header and directory portions are large which can result in EDM pool fragmentation and unavailable space at execution time. This is because the plan header and directory must be in contiguous space. If there is insufficient contiguous space in the EDM pool to load a large header and directory, a -904 SQLCODE is received with the reason code of 00C90089.

The EDM manager attempts to minimize fragmentation of space by tracking the number of sections previously allocated for plans and packages. Based on this information, the EDM manager attempts to allocate a block of space to contain the number of frequently used sections when next executed.

One of many advantages of packages over binding many DBRMs into a plan as discussed in Chapter PE is that packages reduce the size of the plan header and directory compared to a plan with many DBRMs. The plan does not have a listing of SQL sections in its packages. Packages also avoid redundant SKCT sections in the EDM pool for a DBRM bound into multiple plans.

One of the few disadvantages of packages, and a rather minor one assuming that you do not have an extreme shortage of EDM space, compared to binding many DBRMs into a plan, is that a package like a plan must be on a 4 KB boundary, and has a header and directory. This means that 10 packages may use 40 KB compared to 10 DBRMs bound to a plan that may use only 20 KB, for example.

Compiled Assignment Procedures

Compiled column assignment procedures are used to move columns to host variable output areas to reduce CPU time. There are three procedures IPROC, UPROC, and SPROC for inserts, updates, and selects. These procedures increase the plan/package size in the EDM pool and directory. This space is minimized by setting a limit of the procedure size at bind time. If the procedure exceeds 4 KB, it is not stored in the directory with the plan/package. Rather the procedures are compiled at run time if more than three rows are processed. The systems administrator can disable or modify the 4 KB and greater than three row threshold with the hidden DSNZPARM parameter SPRMSPS.

If the compiled assignment procedures are generated at run time after processing three rows, the procedures are lost with a commit if the release of commit is specified with a bind. It is best to use release of deallocate so that the procedures are retained across commits. This is one of many advantages of using release of deallocate as discussed in Chapter CC.

CO.9 WORKING STORAGE

Working storage is a general central storage work area that can be paged to DASD by OS/390. It is

5,960 KB in size by default. DB2 has a variety of uses for this work area. The bind and rebind process uses some space in working storage. There is 24 KB used per thread that uses static SQL in addition to the plan and package in the EDM pool. There is 76 KB of working storage used per thread that uses dynamic SQL in addition to a miniplan and space for SKCT if the dynamic cache is used in the EDM pool. A compression directory for each compressed tablespace is kept in working storage when the tablespace is processed. Control blocks for open data sets are kept in working storage. Space is used for in-memory tables, in-memory indexes, etc., to improve performance of SQL statements as discussed in Chapter ST.

CO.10 THREAD CREATION, USE, AND TERMINATION

A thread is created when the first SQL statement in a program is executed which requires about 50,000 instructions. This thread allocation, execution of SQL, commit processing, and termination of the thread requires a number of activities as summarized in Figure CO.19 along with a brief summary of how to minimize the resources required for the activities. More detail on the activities are discussed throughout the book. The activities marked with an asterisk (*) are those that are not required for a transaction that is using thread reuse. That is, the transaction is using a protected thread and the thread is reused by the transaction every 30 to 45 seconds in most cases. Clearly thread reuse has significant performance advantages for frequently executed transactions.

Figure CO.19. Activities required for thread creation, use, and termination

Activity	Minimize Resources Required
Create thread	
Sign on	Verify authority to connect
*Write account record	One record for all trans. with thread reuse
Load SKCT header	Minimize number of DBRMs bound to a plan
Create CT header	Minimize number of DBRMs bound to a plan
*Check exec authority	Use authorization cache or grant to public
Acquire all TSP locks	Use acquire allocate if most SQL executed
Increment claim count	Use acquire allocate if most SQL executed
Load all DBDs	Use acquire allocate if most SQL executed
Log.open all datasets	If acquire allocate
Each SQL executed	
*Load SKCT section	Size EDM pool to hold frequently used SKCT
*Create CT copy	Release deallocate avoids space reuse
*Load SKPT hdr/dir/sec	If package, load SKPT now (not with plan)
*Create PT copy	Release deallocate avoids space reuse
*Acquire TSP locks	Use acquire allocate if most SQL executed
*Load DBDs	Use acquire allocate if most SQL executed
*Log. open data sets	Use acquire allocate if most SQL executed
Process SQL	Use efficient SQL & programming techniques
Commit processing	
Write log records	Commit every 10 updates for transactions
Release page locks	Above & use lock table for batch
*Release TSP locks	Use release deallocate
*Free CT/PT sections	Release deallocate avoids space reuse
Decrement claim count	Use release deallocate
Log. close data sets	Use release deallocate
Terminate thread	(Not done if thread reused)
*Write account record	One record for all trans. with thread reuse

Activity	Minimize Resources Required
*Release TSP locks	Not released if thread reuse
*Free CT/PT space	Not freed if thread reuse
*Free working storage	Not freed if thread reuse
*Log. close data sets	If release deallocate

*Thread reuse minimizes or eliminates resources required.
SK represents SKCT and SKPT sections.

The cost of commit processing is reduced with thread reuse since table or tablespace intent locks need not be released and CT sections are not freed. Notice that many of the items marked with an asterisk indicating that the work need not be repeated with thread reuse are influenced by the acquire and release parameters specified at bind time. Indeed, thread reuse saves few resources without specifying ACQUIRE(ALLOCATE) and RELEASE(DEALLOCATE) at bind time. The ACQUIRE and RELEASE parameters are discussed in Chapter CC.

CO.11 IRLM ADDRESS SPACE

The Internal Resource Lock Manager (IRLM) address space is used to take and releases locks when data is selected or updated. It is also known as the IRLMPROC. Its size is 335,000 KB by default. It is advisable to retain the default PC value of N so that the extended common service area (ECSA) is used and about 5 percent savings in CPU time can be realized. If PC of Y is specified, cross memory services is used for lock requests.

The primary goal of the IRLM is to avoid one person's updates being written over by another person's updates. It basically serializes updates. The IRLM also provides for synchronizing several updates in conjunction with a unit of recovery.

Chapter CC is devoted to the work done by the IRLM.

CO.12 DISTRIBUTED DATA FACILITY

Distributed Data Facility (DDF) is an optional fourth address space that manages a distributed environment. It is also known as DSN1DIST.

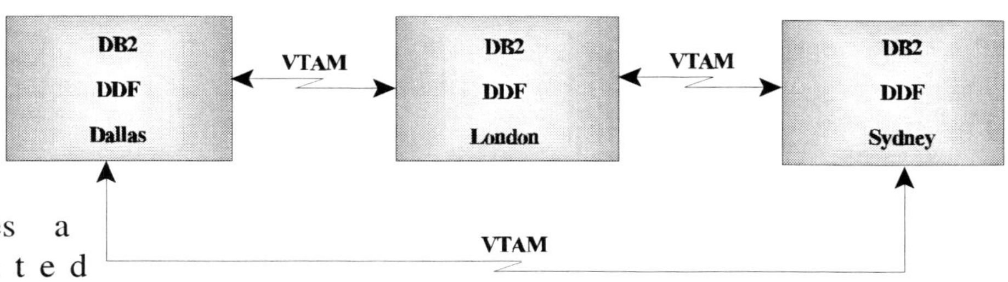

DDF is responsible for establishing and managing a connection with one or more remote DBMSs. The BSDS contains the DB2 location name and password. Virtual telecommunications access method (VTAM) is used for remote site communications as shown in Figure CO.20.

Figure CO.20. Distributed data facility

Multi–Site Update

DDF provides for updating data on multiple remote DBMSs within a remote unit of recovery when using the CICS, IMS, IMS batch, TSO, CAF, and RRSAF attaches. Coordinated recovery is supported among all relational DBMSs that conform to distributed relational database architecture (DRDA), support multi-site updates, and do two-phase commit processing. DB2 Universal Database (UDB) has this support on a number of platforms including OS/390, Windows 2000, NT, 98, 95, Unix, AIX, Linux, HP-UX, Solaris, UNMA-Q, OS/2, and OS/400.

Most DBMS software companies support or plan to support DRDA.

DB2 for OS/390 supports DRDA application directed distributed facilities and system directed distributed facilities, which is an earlier implementation.

Application directed distributed facilities provide for selecting, inserting, updating, and deleting rows from multiple sites using multiple DBMSs. The remote site must be designated with the CONNECT statement or the entire three part name of the table including the location must be used before executing static or dynamic SQL at a remote site at present. Three part names of objects are discussed in Chapter CT. Location independence is available thru the use of three part names without the use of a CONNECT statement in V6.

System directed distributed facilities uses the DB2 private protocol (not DRDA). This means that only DB2 for OS/390 can be used as a client or server (not other DBMSs). This is an older distributed facility for which support is expected to be discontinued in the future. It has only one primary advantage over application directed distributed facilities prior to V6. It has location independence which means that a developer need not be concerned with the location of the data. Rather, the database administrator (DBA) creates aliases for tables that indicate their locations and defines the distributed environment in the communications database. Developers name the aliases without specifying the locations in their SQL statements. DB2 determines the location based on information in the catalog table SYSTABLES placed there as a result of creating the alias. This can be done in with DRDA in V6.

There are a number of disadvantages to the older system directed distributed facilities. Even though SQL statements are embedded in the host program as static SQL, the text of the statements is transmitted to the remote site and executed dynamically. There is a good deal of overhead when transmitting data. Five bytes of overhead are required per column value transmitted. In contrast, DRDA does not have column overhead. Plans and packages that use the private protocol can be identified from the catalog tables SYSSTMT and SYSPACKSTMT with an 'A' in the STATUS column.

Distributed Request in DataJoiner

DataJoiner provides for a distributed request. This means that one SQL statement can reference tables in multiple DBMSs at multiple sites. Two phase commit processing is supported as with application and system directed distributed facilities. A global catalog provides for location transparency.

DataJoiner includes global optimization which determines where most of the processing should be done based on the size of the answer set at each site, the MIPS (million of instructions per second) rating of computers at each site, and the communications links and their speed between the sites.

Classic Connect is a separate order able component of DataJoiner. It provides for read-only access to IMS and VSAM data including joins with relational tables.

Detailed information about DataJoiner and related products is available on the world wide web using the address http://www.software.ibm.com/data/datajoiner/aboutdj.html.

CO.13 STORED PROCEDURE ADDRESS SPACES

Stored procedures are subroutines or main programs that are callable from a remote or local site. A primary goal of stored procedures is to reduce the interchange of messages in a client/server environment. The calling program can call multiple stored procedures at multiple sites with two phase commit processing.

The stored procedure address spaces are allied address spaces. DB2 manages the DSN1SPAS address space. It can start, stop, and display information about the address space. Multiple address spaces can be managed by the WLM component of OS/390 using compatibility or goal mode based on the work load and assigned priorities. There are several advantages to multiple address spaces. You can dedicate high priority threads to an address space. A single stored procedure or group of procedures can be dedicated to an address space. You can isolate stored procedures so that one does not abend and cause another to abend.

The many advantages of stored procedures in general as well as how to use them are discussed in Chapter SP which is dedicated to the subject.

CO.14 SUMMARY

The same language, namely SQL, is used by DBAs, developers, and business professionals to create, manipulate, and control information in DB2. This offers a good deal of flexibility and facilitates communication on the usage of DB2. The catalog tables provide accurate and up to the second information on all objects in DB2.

The systems services address space is used to manage the overall DB2 subsystem. The database services address space is used to manage application data and indexes as well as the catalog tables and the directory tables.

The buffer pools, EDM pool, sort pool, RID pool, and working storage are used to achieve and maintain good performance. The buffer pool and EDM pool are particularly important in minimizing I/O.

The use of DDF and stored procedures positions DB2 for OS/390 as the super server in a distributed environment.

EXERCISES

1. Is static or dynamic SQL used when using SPUFI and QMF? Is static or dynamic SQL usually used when embedding SQL in a host program?

2. A plan or package is produced and stored in the DB2 directory as a result of binding static or dynamic SQL?

3. What is the purpose of SQLCODEs and SQLSTATEs?

4. What is the purpose of the optimizer?

5. How are you known to DB2?

6. How are the catalog tables used by DB2? How can you use the catalog tables?

7. How can you access information in the directory?

8. When is a thread allocated for a COBOL program?

9. Trace statistics are collected by which address space on which address spaces?

10. How do you read and analyze trace statistics in most cases?

11. DM and RDS are executed from which address space?

12. The buffer pools, EDM pool, sort pools, RID pool, and general working storage are part of which address space?

13. Which of the pools are not shared among multiple programs executing concurrently?

14. The tuning of which two components affects performance more than any other tuning of the DB2 subsystem?

15. Why is it important to size the EDM pool to achieve an 80 percent hit ratio or better?

16. What is the purpose of read engines?

17. What is the purpose of write engines?

18. What are the SKCT and SKPT and where are they kept during execution?

ANSWERS

1. Dynamic SQL is used when using SPUFI and QMF. Static SQL is usually used when embedding SQL in a host program.

2. A plan or package is produced and stored in the DB2 directory as a result of binding static SQL.

Dynamic SQL is bound at run time and is not stored in the directory.

3. SQLCODEs and SQLSTATEs give a description of whether an SQL statement is executed successfully, the statement was executed but resulted in a warning, or the statement was not successfully executed because of an error condition.

4. The purpose of the optimizer is to choose a good access path for retrieving or changing data without the person writing the SQL having to know how the data is stored other than the table and column names.

5. You are known to DB2 through your authorization ID. This can be your TSO user ID, CICS ID, IMS ID, or a secondary authorization ID.

6. DB2 records information on all objects created, plans and packages that are bound, privileges granted, and utilities execution in the catalog tables. You can select from the catalog tables to get information on objects that have been created, plans and packages that have been bound, privileges granted, and the status of objects after executing utilities if you have authority to select from the catalog tables.

7. You can access most information in the directory but not with SELECT statements. The DISPLAY DATABASE command can be used to get information on databases. The REPORT utility can be used to get information on the resources required for a recovery. The DISPLAY UTILITY command can be used to get information on utilities that have been submitted and have not completed successful execution. Information on the plans and packages in the directory cannot be accessed. Information is available from several catalog tables on plans and packages.

8. A thread is allocated for a host program (including one written in COBOL) when the first SQL statement is executed in the program. A thread is not allocated when the program initially executes COBOL statements before it executes SQL.

9. Trace statistics are collected by the systems services address space on all of the address spaces including systems services, database services, IRLM, DDF, and stored procedures address spaces.

10. Typically trace statistics are read and analyzed using a performance monitor product.

11. DM and RDS are executed from the database services address space.

12. The buffer pools, EDM pool, sort pools, RID pool, and general working storage are part of the database services address space.

13. The sort pool is not shared among multiple programs executing concurrently. A sort pool is allocated and used for a single program.

14. The tuning of the buffer pools and EDM pool affects performance more than any other tuning of the DB2 subsystem.

15. Is it important to size the EDM pool to achieve an 80 percent hit ratio or better to minimize I/O and resources to read and allocate the plan, package, and DBD each time a program is executed.

16. Read engines are used by buffer manager to read up to and including 32 pages with a single I/O

for sequential prefetch, dynamic prefetch, and list prefetch.

17. Write engines are used by buffer manager to write up to and including 32 pages with a single I/O for deferred write.

18. The SKCT and SKPT are basically master copies of the plans and packages kept in the EDM pool during execution.

FIGURES

Creating STOGROUPs, Databases, and Buffer Pools

CD.1 INTRODUCTION

A database is a collection of tablespaces, tables, and indexes in DB2. These are physical objects that occupy space on DASD. Before physical objects are created it is necessary to provide space on DASD using storage groups or user defined data sets. Figure CD.1 shows the use of a storage group with two volumes of DASD. A database is created referencing the storage group. Tablespaces and indexes are created referencing the database and optionally referencing other storage groups as discussed in Chapter TS. A tablespace can contain one or multiple tables, and one or multiple indexes can be created on a table. A view unlike physical objects does not occupy space on DASD. A view is a way of looking at some or all columns and rows in one or more tables as discussed in Chapter CT.

Figure CD.1. DB2 objects

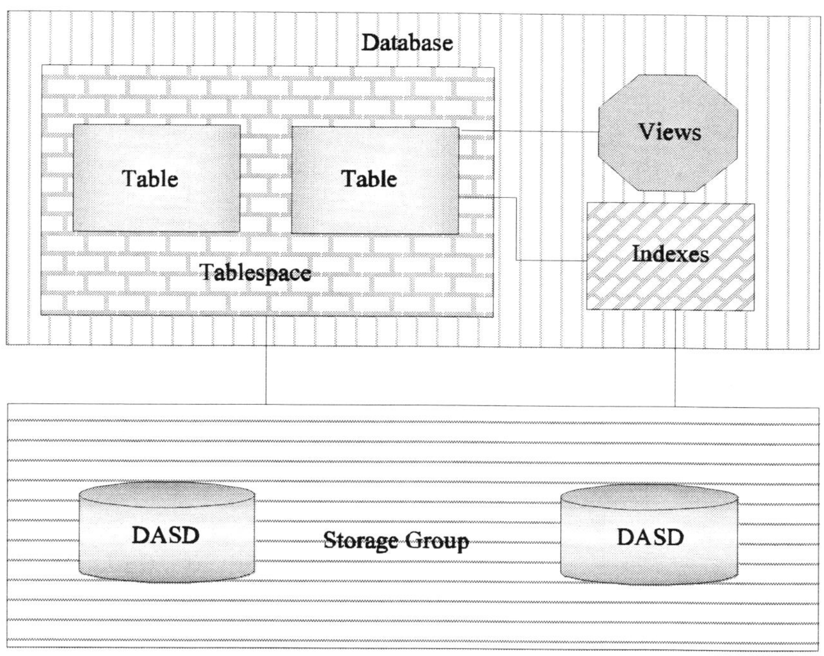

The creation of databases is straightforward but there are a number of guidelines that should be considered in sizing the database. The data must be brought into central storage for processing. We will discuss the many options that you have available on designing buffer pools to contain the data depending on how it is processed.

CD.2 SPACE FOR TABLESPACES AND INDEX SPACES

Tablespaces and indexes reside in virtual storage access method (VSAM) data sets. DB2 creates a VSAM linear data set (LDS) when you create a tablespace or index if you are using storage groups. If more than one data set is required to house a large tablespace, DB2 creates them. Multiple data sets used for a tablespace or index are referred to as a page set. Optionally, you can create a LDS or entry sequence data set (ESDS). We will first look at how to create storage groups and user defined data sets, and then at the pros and cons of these alternatives as well as data set placement on DASD.

Create a Storage Group

Here is an example of creating the storage group DASPJSTG consisting of two volumes.

```
CREATE STOGROUP DASPJSTG
   VOLUMES (VOL1, VOL4)
   VCAT VCATID;
```

The VOLUMES parameter is used to give the volume serial identifiers of DASD for the storage group. Volumes are used by DB2 in the order in which they are listed in the VOLUMES parameter. Once the first volume is filled, DB2 uses the volume listed second, third, etc. Optionally, you can use VOLUMES ('*') to have Data Facility Storage Management Subsystem data facility product (DFSMSdfp) control placement of tablespaces and indexes across volumes. The DFSMSdfp product is often referred to simply as SMS as is done in this book. The VCAT parameter is used to specify the integrated catalog facility (ICF) high level qualifier of the catalog name (or alias if the name is more than 8 bytes), VCATID is used in the example.

If there is more than one DB2 subsystem on a processor and you are not using sysplex data sharing, do create a separate ICF catalog for each DB2 subsystem. Otherwise, more than one tablespace can be created with the same VSAM data set name and the tablespaces will use the same VSAM data set. Obviously, this can result in data integrity problems.

A volume assigned to a storage group is not dedicated to it. Non-DB2 data sets can be allocated on the volume and a volume can be assigned to more than one storage group. The maximum number of volumes in a storage group is 133. The volumes must be of the same device type.

Typically, the systems administrator creates storage groups. Indeed, the person who creates storage groups must have SYSADM, SYSCTRL, or CREATESG privileges.

Alter a Storage Group

Volumes can be added and removed from a storage group like:

```
ALTER STOGROUP DASPJSTG
  ADD    VOLUMES(VOL6)
  REMOVE VOLUMES(VOL4);
```

There is no loss of data when removing a volume. Once a volume is removed, no more objects will be placed on the volume. The execution of the reorganization, load replace, or recover utilities result in the object being placed on another volume in the storage group. If all volumes are removed from a storage group, objects must be altered to place them in another storage group. Otherwise, the utilities will have no space to place the data.

The DROP STOGROUP DASPJSTG statement can be used to remove a storage group. If any page sets refers to the storage group, a -616 SQLCODE is issued and the storage group is not dropped. It is necessary to first alter tablespaces and indexes to reside in another storage group after stopping the objects.

User Defined Data Sets

An alternative to using storage groups is to create VSAM data sets using the IDCAMS program to execute access method services (AMS) commands to create, alter, and delete data sets. Some VSAM parameters can be tailored, other must have specific values, and some are ignored by DB2.

Some parameters can be tailored to specific requirements, for example, LDS or ESDS, STAGE and NODESTAGEWAIT for 3850 MSS and TO or FOR can be used to prevent deletion for a specified period of time.

Some parameters must have specific values when using ESDS data sets, for example, NONINDEXED, RECORDSIZE of 4089, CONTROLINTERVALSIZE of 4096, and SHAREOPTIONS (3,3) or SHAREOPTIONS (1,3) for shared databases.

Some parameters will not be used by DB2, for example, SPANNED, EXCEPTIONEXIT, SPEED, BUFFERSPACE, and WRITECHECK.

A strict naming convention must be used when creating the VSAM data sets for use by DB2. The naming convention follows the form c.s.d.p.i.t, for example:

Tablespaces are named like:

```
ICFNAME.DSNDBD.DASPJDB.PTSP.I0001.A001
```

Indexes are named like:

```
ICFNAME.DSNDBD.DASPJDB.PTSPX.I0001.A001
```

Here is a brief description of each node of the data set name:

```
c = ICFNAME (ICF catalog name or alias) to be specified in USING
VCAT clause on the CREATE TABLESPACE statement

s = DSNDBD for VSAM data
    DSNDBC for VSAM cluster

d = Database name into which the tablespace or index is to be
created

p = Tablespace name to be used in the CREATE TABLESPACE statement
or index name to be used in CREATE INDEX statement

I = The literal I0001

t = The literal "A" followed by a 3-digit data set number (001, for
example)
```

Naming convention used with reorganization: If you are using shadow copies with the reorganization utility as discussed in Chapter RR, the naming convention is extended. You must explicitly create the shadows using a naming convention like:

```
ICFNAME.DSNDBD.DASPJDB.PTSP.S0001.A001 for the tablespace
ICFNAME.DSNDBD.DASPJDB.PTSPX.S0001.A001 for the index name
```

Notice that the "I" node is a literal S0001 rather than I0001. No data set should have a name with an "I" node of "T0001". This name is used as an intermediate name during the renaming of data sets. Each partition must have a "t" node of A0nnn where *nan* is equal to the partition number to be reorganized. The data sets must be LDS with SHAREOPTIONS (3,3) or SHAREOPTIONS (1,3) if ROSHARE OWNER. The original data and shadows must have the same master catalog and component passwords.

Comparison of Storage Groups and User Defined Data Sets

DB2 professionals responsible for creating tablespaces and indexes need not be knowledgeable in creating and maintaining VSAM data sets when using storage groups. DB2 creates, alters, and deletes the necessary VSAM data sets for tablespaces and index spaces. Even if the developer is knowledgeable of VSAM, it is certainly a time consuming task to create 450 data sets for 150 tables each of which has two indexes on average, for example.

If a tablespace exceeds the maximum number of bytes allowed for a VSAM data set, DB2 will automatically create additional data sets as needed to allow for up to 64 GB of data for a tablespace or 16 TB (V6) of data for large partitioned tablespaces when using storage groups. If user defined data sets are used, you must know when the additional data sets are required and create and maintain then. It is necessary to delete the underlying data sets after dropping a tablespace or index for the space to be reusable when using user defined data. In contrast, DB2 automatically deletes the data sets when objects are dropped when using storage groups.

The ALTER statement can be used to change the space allocation for tablespaces and indexes when using storage groups. In contrast, when using user defined data sets, you must make the changes using IDCAMS commands typically after unloading the data and before reloading the data as discussed in Chapter RR. In addition, the selects from the catalog tables described in Chapter RR cannot be used for space management because the space allocations for user defined data sets are not in the catalog tables. One technique used by some developers is to alter to use storage groups, execute the STOSPACE utility, and alter back to use VCAT.

User defined data sets are used by some developers to control the placement of data sets on DASD and to comply with storage management policies of the organization.

Data Set Placement on DASD

Small to medium (a few cylinders, for example) tablespaces and indexes can be placed on contiguous DASD space. This is advisable because minimal seek time will be required to access the indexes followed by the tablespace.

It is important to spread large tablespaces and indexes across multiple volumes, channels, and control units. This will spread I/O activity across the devices and also provides for efficient DB2 parallelism. Figure CD.2 shows the separation of tablespaces from their associated indexes on DASD. This is a good strategy. It avoids having to seek to the tablespace after having located reference to rows using indexes. Work can be done on the tablespace and indexes in parallel with minimal seek time.

Figure CD.2. Separation of tablespaces and indexes

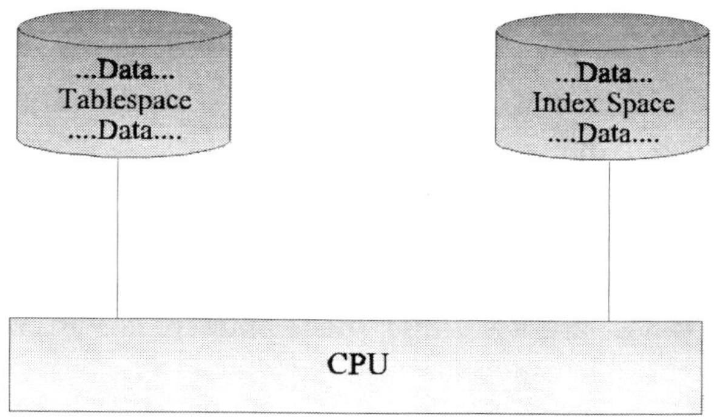

You do have direct control over placement of data sets on DASD when using user defined data sets. However, this is a manual and time consuming process. Some DASD placement control can be achieved when using storage groups by creating a storage group for tablespaces and a separate storage group for indexes. If you need to favor some frequently processed tablespaces or indexes, they can be placed in a storage group along with infrequently processed data to minimize seek time. You need to create and manage storage groups for data set placement. A technique used by some developers is to assign only one or a few DASD volumes to a storage group and create or alter tablespaces and indexes to achieve the required volume separation. You can create a storage group for specific tablespaces and another one for specific indexes.

SMS is a good product for managing DASD. However, special considerations are required for data set placement. You can assign data sets to specific storage classes based on an established naming convention to achieve separation. For example, if the index names begin with X, VCAT.*.*.X* can be used for the assignment of indexes. The guarantee space option of SMS can be used to specify the volume ID where the data sets are to be placed. Of course, for the named data set, the advantages of using SMS for space management is lost. Other alternatives are to use separate SMS storage groups or an exit can be used to determine placement of data sets.

Dr. Lou Agosta clarifies the use of GUARANTEED SPACE = YES in that it tells SMS three things. First, do not execute the Automated Class Selection (ACS) routines to determine volume placement of the data set based on its name, storage class, performance characteristics, or other data set attributes. Second, place the data set on the user-specified device. Third, space is not guaranteed in that if there is no space available where the data set is supposed to be placed, no space is allocated. Lou cautions that "GUARANTEED SPACE" does not really guarantee anything, much less space. Rather the DBA (or responsible person) has to guarantee space is available on the specified volume. Space is "guaranteed" by the DBA, not by SMS or DB2.

Recommendation: Consider using a naming convention to control placement of data sets.

CD.3 CREATING A DATABASE

The CREATE DATABASE statement causes the initial creation of a Database Descriptor (DBD). Descriptive information about objects and object IDs are placed in the DBD by DB2 as the objects are created. Object IDs are two-byte small integers assigned by DB2 to objects when they are created. They are used internally by DB2 to manage objects. DBDs reside in the environmental descriptor manager (EDM) pool along with plans and packages in central storage when SQL data manipulation statements are executed that reference objects in the database. The DBD is divided into 32 KB chunks to minimize fragmentation of space in the EDM pool. The maximum number of databases that can be created on a DB2 subsystem is 65,279. Here is an example of creating the DASPJDB database.

```
CREATE DATABASE DASPJDB
  STOGROUP DASPJSTG
  CCSID EBCDIC
  BUFFERPOOL BP1
  INDEXBP BP2;
```

The maximum length of a database, storage group, or tablespace name is eight alphanumeric characters. The STOGROUP, BUFFERPOOL, and INDEXBP (V6) parameters establish a default storage group, buffer pool for tablespaces, and buffer pool for indexes for objects created in the database. The defaults can be overridden when creating tablespaces and indexes in the database. If the buffer pools for tablespace and indexes are not specified, the installation default of BP0 is used. The installation default can be changed from BP0 to another buffer pool for application tablespaces and yet another buffer pool for application indexes on installation panel DSNTIP1 or DSNZPARM DSN6SYSP TBSBPOOL and IDXBPOOL (V6). The STOGROUP, BUFFERPOOL, and INDEXBP parameters can be altered as shown in the following statement. We will discuss the CCSID parameter later in this section.

```
ALTER DATABASE DASPJDB
  STOGROUP DANEWSTG
  BUFFERPOOL BP3
  INDEXBP BP4;
```

Factors that Affect Placement of Objects in a Database

Creating a database is very straightforward. There are a number of considerations in designing a database. In general, one database is created for an application system. However, this depends to a very large extent on the number of objects that need to be created and managed within an application system or a subject area.

Concurrency and the DBD: An exclusive lock is taken on a DBD when objects are created, altered, or deleted. The bind of static and dynamic SQL requires a share lock on the DBD. Such operations must wait for commit processing to release the exclusive lock required by a data definition statement. Locks are held during the bind and execution of dynamic SQL until commit processing. The utilities take locks on the DBD. These factors suggest that placing too many objects in a database can result in lock contention.

Logging: When objects are created, altered, and dropped, and when segmented tablespaces are reorganized, the entire DBD is replaced and logged. A large DBD increases the resources required for logging and the required size of the logs considerably.

Administration and privileges can be at the database level: Database administration (DBADM) privileges can be granted at the database level. This allows a person with DBADM privileges to create, alter, and delete objects in the database, use utilities on the objects, execute commands on the \objects including START and STOP, and execute DISPLAY database commands. This suggests that objects to be managed by an AUTHID be placed in a database and the AUTHID be given DBADM authority.

Databases for business professionals: If business professionals are given the privilege to create their own personal tables or save data using an interactive tool such as Query Management Facility (QMF), exercise caution as to the number of users that use a given database to avoid lock contention and ease management of the objects in the database. You might consider a database for each department of about 10 users as a rule of thumb.

Location of Objects in Databases: You need not be concerned with the location of objects in various databases when issuing SQL data manipulation statements. DB2 will make this determination at bind time based on information in the catalog and directory tables.

Database Size

The maximum number of objects allowed by DB2 in a database is 10,000. (The theoretical maximum size of a DBD is 2 GB.) However, you do not want too many objects in a database nor do you want it to be too large for the reasons discussed in the previous subsection, this subsection, and in Chapter CO.

DB2 limits the DBD size to < 25 percent of the EDM pool. A -904 SQLCODE (00C9008F reason code) is received (resource unavailable). This limit is imposed by DB2 at run time and can result in an unpleasant surprise. Do be cautious regarding too large of a DBD for the EDM pool and workload. Tablespaces and indexes cannot be altered to use another database. It is necessary to unload the data, drop the tablespace, create the tablespace, table, and indexes, load the data, grant privileges, execute RUNSTATS, and rebind plans and packages (or accept an automatic rebind).

DBD Increases in Size: If tables are created and dropped in a segmented tablespace, the DBD increases in size. This can occur in a test environment, and in a decision support system where users create and drop their own objects, drop and recreate data entry type tables, etc. In order to make the space reusable it is necessary to perform several steps:

- Reorganize the tablespace which places a Relative Byte Address (RBA) in SYSCOPY beyond the dropped table.

- Delete old image copies of the tablespace with the MODIFY utility as discussed in Chapter CR. For example, the -MODIFY RECOVERY TABLESPACE DASPJDB.DASPJTSP DELETE DATE(*) command will delete all image copies for the DASPJTSP tablespace in the DASPJDB.

- Take 1 to 4 image copies for local and recovery sites with one tablespace scan as described in Chapter CR.

Control information in the DBD is no longer required for recovery, and the object IDs can be reused for future recoverability after the procedure is performed. In one case a 2.5 MB DBD was reduced to 113 KB by following the procedure.

An alternative is to rebuild the DBD from the catalog tables using the REPAIR utility like:

```
REPAIR DBD REBUILD DATABASE DASPJDB
```

EBCDIC and ASCII Encoding Schemes

IBM stores data using the Extended Binary Coded Decimal Interchange Code (EBCDIC) encoding scheme on mainframes data sets in most cases. Tables will contain data in EBCDIC format by default. The default is Coded Character Set Identifier (CCSID) of EBCDIC as shown in the earlier CREATE DATABASE statement. Optionally, the data can be stored using American Standard Code for Information Interchange (ASCII) encoding scheme by specifying CCSID ASCII when creating a database, tablespace, table, global temporary table, and on the installation panel DSNTIPF.

The CCSID of EBCDIC or ASCII can be specified when creating a database or tablespace in which case all tables created in the database or tablespace use the specified encoding scheme. Optionally, the CCSID can be specified for specific tables and global temporary tables as they are created and the format need not match the format of other tables in the database and tablespace. However, all tables referenced in an SQL statement must be defined with the same encoding scheme. Data to be loaded into a table using the LOAD utility can be in EBCDIC or ASCII format with the default being EBCDIC format.

Most personal computers (PC) and work stations store data using the ASCII encoding scheme. If a table is going to be processed mostly by a client on a PC or work station, storing the data using the ASCII encoding scheme has advantages. It avoids the costs of translating from the EBCDIC to the ASCII encoding scheme before the data is transmitted to a client and translation from ASCII to EBCDIC when data is returned to the mainframe. When a table is accessed from an EBCDIC application (3270 terminal users, batch applications, etc.), DB2 translates from ASCII to EBCDIC automatically. However, a sort results in ASCII sequence.

You can ALTER CCSID identifier to include/exclude the Euro symbol for newly created objects. Existing tablespaces can be altered as discussed in Chapter TS.

CD.4 BUFFER POOLS

One or more buffer pools must exist to hold data and index pages in the central storage while they are being processed. A buffer pool consists of a virtual pool which resides in central storage and optionally a data space in central storage and a hiperpool (Hiper is derived from the first two characters of *high* and the first three characters of *performance*.) which resides in expanded storage. How virtual pools, data spaces, and hiperpools are used and managed is discussed throughout the remainder of this section.

Advantages of Virtual Pools

The primary purpose of buffer pools is to hold frequently referenced data and index pages in storage to minimize the number of I/O to DASD, the I/O transfer time, the CPU time to issue the physical I/O, and I/O contention. Buffer manager uses look-aside buffering to minimize these costs. For example, a user can cause one or more pages to be read into a virtual pool by executing SQL statements. The user can select and update the data while it resides in a virtual pool or data space. Other users can select and update the same pages without incurring I/O to DASD. A user must commit any inserts, updates, and deletes before subsequent users can process the same data. The updated page need not be written to the database immediately after it is committed and before the next user reads or updates the same page. However, the changed data is logged to DASD to avoid any loss of data in case of a power failure, for example. Chapter CC contains a detailed description of the serialization of update activity to ensure data integrity.

Disadvantages of Small Virtual Pools

If a virtual pool is too small for the workload, it is considered a small virtual pool. The hit ratio is the percentage of times that a page is found in the pool and a physical I/O is not required. It is used to determine if the virtual pool is too small for the workload as discussed later in this section.

There are a number of thresholds used for controlling how the buffer pool is used as discussed in Section CD.7. Frequently exceeding these thresholds can adversely affect performance. For example, the optimizer may have requested sequential prefetch, list prefetch, dynamic prefetch, or parallelism at bind time. These efficient techniques cannot be used at run time or are discontinued during execution if there is insufficient space in the virtual pool. In addition, deferred write can be disabled which detracts from the performance of writing updated pages to DASD.

If the virtual pool is too small for the workload, two critical thresholds can be reached. If 95 percent of the pages are marked in-use (data management threshold), an I/O is issued for each row rather than the usual process of reading a page and processing all qualifying rows on the page. If 97.5 percent of pages are marked in-use (immediate write threshold), writes are synchronous to the log and data. This means that the I/O to write an updated page is not issued until after the completion of the I/O to the log. Normally, I/O to the data pages is issued immediately after issuing I/O to the log.

Example of hitting the 95 percent threshold: A batch job at a particular company normally completed using about one minute of CPU time. One evening the operator noticed that the job was still running after using about 30 minutes of CPU time. The operator canceled the job, knowing that there must be a problem. The next day an investigation was done into the cause of the problem. It was discovered that the 95 percent threshold had been reached and over 6 million getpages had been issued compared to the more typical 430,000 getpages for the job. The problem was that a getpage was issued for each row rather than for each page in most cases.

An IBM test was done on a 3090-200 computer was done to get an idea of the effect of buffer pool size on the transaction rate. The transaction rate went from 32 transactions per second with 2000 pages in the buffer to 42 transactions per second with 8000 pages in the buffer while maintaining 0.4 second response time.

Sizing the buffer pool for the workload is the single most important tuning of a DB2 subsystem to achieve good application system performance. It impacts the number of I/O that must be issued, the I/O time, the number of getpages, and CPU time to issue the I/O and getpages.

Page Size Depends on Buffer Pool Assignment

The data page size is determined by your choice of a buffer pool when creating a database, tablespace, or index space. BP0, BP1, BP2, through BP49 house 4 KB pages, BP8K0 thru BP8K9 house 8 KB pages (V6), BP16K0 thru BP16K9 house 16 KB pages (V6), and BP32K, BP32K1, BP32K2, through BP32K9 house 32 KB pages. Do be cautious with the use of BP32. It contained 32 KB pages in earlier versions of DB2. BP32 contains 4 KB pages and BP32K contains 32 KB pages.

BP0 is used by the utilities and when reading and writing the work tablespaces in DSNDB07 by default. This can be changed as will be discussed. BP0 is used when DB2 processes the catalog tables and directory tables. This cannot be changed at present.

4 KB page buffers should be used for most tablespaces and is used for all indexes.

8, 16, and 32 KB page buffers are useful for long rows with a length greater than 2037 (½ of 4 KB less overhead). This is because only one row fits on a 4 KB page and the remainder of the page cannot be used. if the tablespace has rows longer than 4 KB including the page overhead, it is necessary to use 8, 16, or 32 KB size pages. The goal is to minimize the amount of unusable space on a page.

Large page sizes reduce resources required for serialization, which is particularly important in a sysplex data sharing environment. One-fourth the resources for page registration and serialization are required when using 16 KB pages compared to 4 KB pages assuming page level locking. However, larger page sizes open the door for increased serialization contention.

If mostly batch processing where most rows are processed on a page, the number of getpage and relpage are reduced which reduces CPU time.

Larger page sizes require more I/O time and virtual storage usage for most row lengths. A 32 KB page must be brought into the virtual pool to process 1 row of say 100 bytes, for example. Contiguous virtual storage is required for each of the 8, 16, or 32 KB page. This can result in fragmented space where there is space for a number of 4 KB pages but insufficient contiguous space for the larger page sizes, particularly 32 KB pages. The I/O transfer time for 32 KB pages is 8 times that of using 4 KB buffers (8 * 4 KB page = 32 KB page) which is clearly not desirable for average row lengths.

Even if you have no 32 KB page tablespaces, a 32 KB page buffer pool is required in case a select from multiple tables gives a result row of over 4 KB. In this case DB2 automatically uses the 32 KB page buffer pool.

Buffer Management

An overview of the work done by buffer manager was covered in Chapter CO. In this section, we will look at the details of how buffer management locates a required page to satisfy an SQL statement. The buffer manager is a very important component of DB2. It was invented, developed, and remains under the management of Dr. Jim Teng. Indeed, IBM hold several patents on the buffer manager as a result of his work.

A virtual pool (VP) is created using a GETMAIN instruction when the first data set is opened that references the VP. The VP is deleted when all data sets using a buffer pool are closed to avoid wasting space.

Buffer pages are located using a hash table of anchor points and buffer headers as indicated in Figure CD.3. The page set ID and relative page number within the page set are input to the hashing algorithm. The result is a pointer to an entry in an anchor point table which points to a buffer header.

The number of anchor points in the table is MAX(624, 0.2 * number of buffers in the pool). (The anchor point table is dynamically reconfigured when the pool size is changed.)

Figure CD.3. Locating a page in the buffer

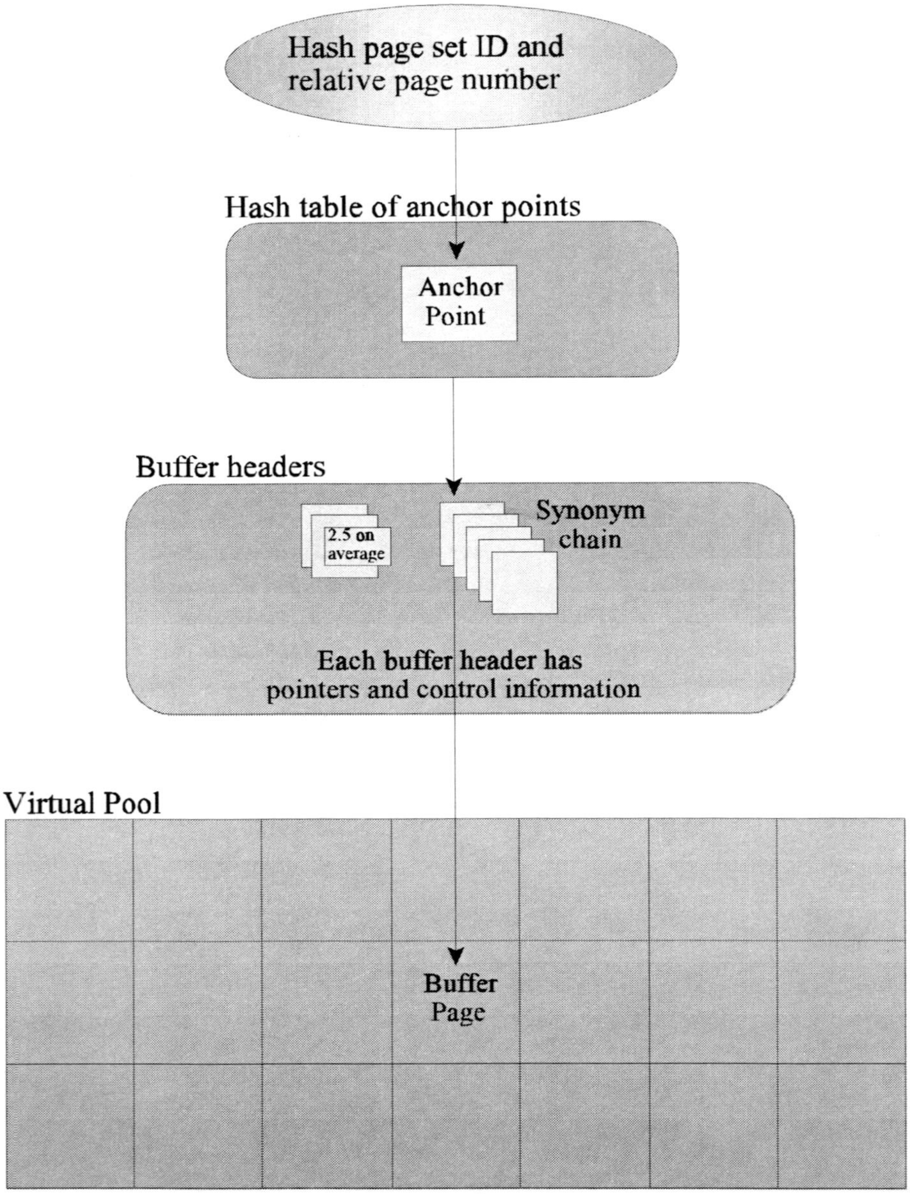

A hashing algorithm always results in producing duplicate values. These duplicate values of synonym pointers are managed in the buffer header. There are a maximum of 5 synonym pointers with an average search of 2.5 based on a Poisson distribution. In addition, the buffer header contains a pointer to a buffer page or a value of 0 indicates that the page is not in buffer. It contains chains of page addresses for reuse of pages, deferred write, etc. There is also control information, counters, flags, etc. in the buffer header. A good deal of information on the operations of buffer manager is from Chuck Hoover's mini books (as he calls them) published by his employer Compuware, Inc.

If the page is not in the virtual pool and a hiperpool exists, similar structures and processing are used to determine if the page is in the hiperpool.

Reuse of Buffer Pages

A buffer pool will be filled with pages read and updated for various processing. The buffer pages are reused based on how they are read, processed, and placed on reuse chains in the buffer headers. The pages are reused in the following order.

1) Most Recently Used (MRU) pages are reused first. Pages read for parallel processing (pages from a large table can be placed on the MRU chain and pages from a small table can be placed on the LRU chain) are placed on the MRU chain of pages in the buffer header. Also placed on the chain are pages read for merging of sorted rows and pages read for some utilities. Basically MRU pages are those that are very unlikely to be rereferenced by others.

2) Sequential Least Recently Used (SLRU) pages are reused after all the page slots on the MRU chain have been reused. SLRU pages are those that are read with sequential, dynamic, and list prefetch. If a SLRU page is referenced at random, it is placed on the LRU chain to allow others to reference the page for as long as possible. No more than 80 percent of the buffer is used for sequentially read pages by default.

3) Least Recently Used (LRU) pages are those that are read at random using a matching index scan, for example. Twenty percent of the buffer is reserved for random reads by default. Randomly read pages can also use the 80 percent of pages used for sequential read pages if the space is not already in use.

There are SLRU and LRU chains for the reuse of hiperpool pages.

4) A first-in-first-out (FIFO) algorithm can be used for the reuse of pages. It is a lower cost method for reuse of pages than LRU as will be discussed.

You can specify LRU or FIFO by buffer pool.

Status of Buffer Pool Pages

Each page in a virtual pool has a status indicating how the page can be used.

A buffer page cannot be used to receive a page from DASD if it is marked as in-use or considered an updated page. An in-use page is one where data manager (DM) has issued a getpage and has not issued a set write pending or released the page (relpage). An updated page is one where DM has set write pending on for the page and buffer manager has placed the page on a deferred write queue for the data set.

A buffer page can be used to receive a page from DASD if the page is available, stealable or empty. An available page is one that has not been used since the virtual pool was first allocated. A stealable page is one where DM has issued a getpage and relpage, and write pending is not active. A page slot is not stealable if the page or row has a S, U, or X lock in most cases. An empty page is one that has been moved to the hiperpool.

All hiperpool pages are stealable.

CD.5 BUFFER POOL HIT RATIOS

As discussed at the beginning of Section CD.4, sizing the buffer pool for the workload is critical to the performance of application systems. A good measure of whether the buffer pool has been sized for the workload and whether more or less space is required is the hit ratio. The hit ratio is the percentage of time that a page is found in the buffer pool when requested by DM and a physical I/O is not required. A good goal is to locate a required page in the buffer pool 80 to 90 percent of the time, assuming that the pages are referenced by one or more users.

The buffer pool hit ratio can be calculated using the formula:

```
(getpages - synchronous reads - asynchronous reads) / getpages
```

If your hit ratio is low, do increase the buffer pool size. Take measurements and calculate the hit ratio again. If the hit ratio is still too low, increase the buffer pool size again and calculate the hit ratio. Repeat this process until the hit ratio flattens out as shown in Figure CD.4.

Figure CD.4. Buffer hit ratios

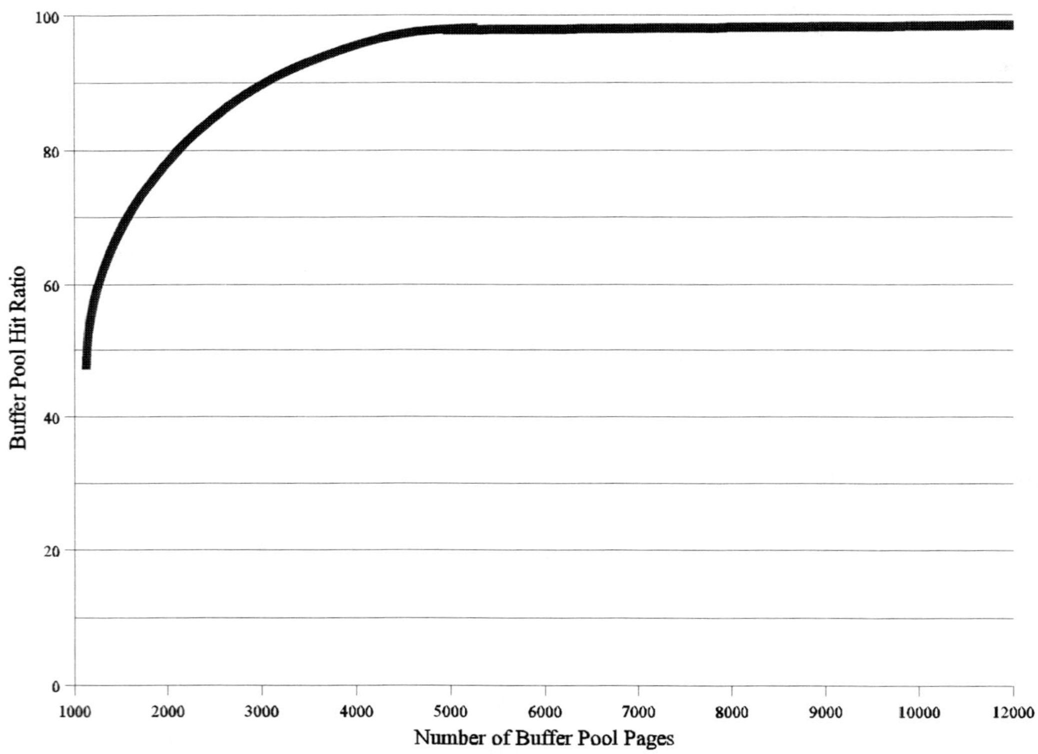

Notice that the hit ratio is less than 50 percent in the example when using a 1000 page buffer pool. As the number of pages assigned to the buffer pool increases so does the hit ratio until about 5000 pages have been assigned to the buffer pool. At this point the hit ratio is approaching 98 percent. Adding pages to the buffer pool increases the hit ratio very little. The goal of increasing the hit ratio until it flatten out has been accomplished at about 5000 pages. If you run out of central storage space to assign to the virtual pool before the required hit ratio is reached, consider using hiperpools.

Initial sizing of a buffer pool can be accomplished using two techniques. Set the number of virtual pool pages equal to number of getpages per second. This yielded a 60 percent hit ratio in one case. An alternative is to size the pool to contain 10 to 20 percent of the tablespaces and indexes pages assigned to a pool. In one case when the virtual pool was sized to contain 10 percent of the data and index pages, a 90 percent hit ratio was achieved.

CD.6 Data Spaces and Hiperpools

Additional storage for buffer pools can be made available though the use of data spaces and hiperpools. This section describes data spaces and hiperpools in terms of what they are, how they can be used, and the advantages and disadvantages of the spaces

Managing within Limits

A word of 4 bytes and 32 bits where 1 bit is used as a parity bit is used for addressability on most computers including mainframes and PCs. This gives an architectural limit of addressable storage of 2 GB, calculated as 2^{31}. Therefore, an address space is limited to 2 GB. Database services resides in an address space in central storage with 0.4 GB of DB2 code, working storage, EDM pool, RID pool, sort pool, and virtual pools. This limits the size of the pools, in particular the virtual pool. A data space (V6) provides for addressing 8 million pages. If you are using 4 KB pages that means 32 GB of space calculated as 32 GB = 8 million * 4 KB page. A hiperpool (high performance pool) provides for addressing 8 GB calculated as 2 GB per hiperpool times 4 which is the maximum number of hiperpools that an be used with a buffer pool. Hiperpools reside in expanded storage only (ESO) (also known as cache) type hiperspace. SCROLL type hiperspace cannot be accessed in a cross memory environment. Therefore, it cannot be used for hiperpools.

Virtual Pool, Data Spaces, and Hiperpools Comparison

Data spaces and hiperpools both provide relief from the 1.6 GB (2 GB is the current limit per address space less other central storage required by DB2) virtual pool limit if this is an issue at your company. They both reside outside of the database services address space (DBM1). Virtual pools and data spaces reside in central storage as contrasted to hiperpools which reside in expanded storage. The primary benefit of data spaces is their size of 32 GB if 1.6 GB is a constraining factor (not part of 2 GB limit per address space). They are expected to provide additional benefits in the future with OS/390 processor enhancements that will provide for larger real memory.

Virtual pools are byte addressable in contrast to data spaces and hiperpools which are page addressable as used by DB2. This means that a data space and hiperpool page must be moved to central storage for comparisons and extraction of columns and rows. Programs like buffer manager and data manager can manipulate data directly in a virtual pool (unlike a data space and hiperpool). Only the virtual pool can contain common areas, system data, and programs. Buffer management of buffers must be done in the virtual pool. Data spaces pages are copied (MVCL) into a lookaside buffer in DBM1 (1 buffer for each page size of 4, 8, 16 and 32 KB pages) for comparisons and extraction of columns and rows when getpages are issued by data manager. Changed pages are copied to virtual pool when a relpage is issued. The lookaside buffer is sized and managed by DB2 based on the number of active threads (10 to 40 MB, for example, with an initial size of 1 MB). Architecturally, data spaces are byte addressable. However, they are managed by DB2 at the page level through the use of the lookaside buffer. A data space page requires 128 bytes in the virtual pool. More space is required to manage hiperpools in comparison. The use of data spaces can increase CPU time by from 1 to 10 percent.

All three types of spaces can contain data and index pages. However, updated pages must reside in the virtual pool or data space. Updated pages must be written to DASD before they can be moved to a hiperpool. Pages reside in a virtual pool or hiperpool, not both. An updated page (also known as a *dirty page*) must be written to DASD before being cached in a hiperpool. Pages in a hiperpool are read-only.

OS/390 can page out virtual pool and data space pages to expanded storage or DASD. Pages can be read directly into virtual pool and data space. In contrast, pages must goes through virtual pool to be placed in hiperpool. Hiperpool requires a move page (MVPG) hardware instruction and asynchronous data mover facility (ADMF) microcode unlike other 2 types of spaces.

Figure CD.5 summarizes the comparison of virtual pool, data spaces, and hiperpools.

Figure CD.5. Virtual pool, data spaces, and hiperpools comparison

Feature	Virtual Pool	Data Space	Hiper-pool
Type of storage	Central	Central	Expanded
Maximum size	1.6 GB	32 GB	8 GB
Outside of the database services address space (DBM1)	No	Yes	Yes
Addressability	Byte	Page	Page
Can contain common areas, system data, & programs	Yes	No	No
Contain updated pages not written to DASD	Yes	Yes	No
Subject to OS/390 paging	Yes	Yes	No
Pages can be read directly into space	Yes	Yes	No
Requires MVPG hardware instruction & ADMF	No	No	Yes

Data Space Specifics

If more than 1.6 GB of central storage is needed for buffers, data spaces are a good choice. A data space can support no more than one virtual pool. However a virtual pool can have one or more data spaces assigned to it. The use of data spaces increases CPU usage by about 1 to 10 percent based on preliminary results. Details on data spaces and hiperspaces are in the *OS/390 MVS Programming: Extended Addressability Guide* manual.

Hiperpool Specifics

If you decide to use a hiperpool, there is a one-to-one correspondence between a hiperpool and virtual pool. A hiperpool is created when its virtual pool is created. Typically the hiperpool is larger than its corresponding virtual pool although this is not a requirement. Buffer manager moves pages from the virtual pool to the hiperpool and from the hiperpool to the virtual pool. The paging is similar to what is done by the OS/390 operating system when it moves pages to and from central storage and DASD. A hiperpool is somewhat like DASD in that it is used to store tablespace and index pages. Also, it is like DASD in that the unit of data transfer is at the 4 KB page level.

Getting a Page from the Hiperpool: Pages are read from DASD into a virtual pool and passed to a hiperpool. The MVPG instruction and ADMF microcode is used for the page movement. For example, a getpage is issued by data manager. This causes buffer manager to look for the page using its hashing algorithm. If the page is in the virtual pool, the getpage is satisfied. If the required page is not in the virtual pool, buffer manager checks the hiperpool using the same hashing algorithm. If the page is found in the hiperpool, the page is moved to the virtual pool and is no longer addressable in the hiperpool. The getpage is satisfied. If the required page is not in the hiperpool, buffer manager initiates a physical I/O to DASD and accepts the page into the virtual pool. The getpage is satisfied. If there is no hiperpool the sequence of events are the same as described except that buffer manager does not look for the page in expanded storage.

A hiperpool is of limited value for sequentially read pages because it is unlikely that the pages will be rereferenced. A hiperpool is most useful for randomly read and processed pages.

Expanded storage for a hiperpool: Do be cautious of defining a hiperpool as being larger than available expanded storage. OS/390 informs buffer manager that the data has been discarded due to an expanded storage shortage when buffer manager attempts to move a page from the hiperpool. Buffer manager reads the data from DASD. A count of the number of times that this occurs is maintained and reported as hiperpool read failures to reflect a shortage of expanded storage. Of course, shortages detract from efficient use of hiperpool.

OS/390 Paging

If OS/390 paging is experienced, reduce the size of the virtual pool, use data spaces, or hiperpools. Hiperpools are favored if expanded storage is less costly than central storage on your computer. They are also well suited to most read-only tablespaces and indexes. This suggests the assignment these objects to a buffer pool with a hiperpool assigned to it.

Do avoid paging of pages in central storage to auxiliary or expanded storage (uses LRU algorithm). It detracts from performance significantly. Page faults result if pages are in auxiliary or expanded storage. The pages must be reread for processing. If PAGE-INS REQUIRED FOR WRITE and PAGE-INS REQUIRED FOR READ statistics are high, insufficient central storage space is available for the buffers. Do seriously consider the use data spaces or hiperpools.

Relative Cost and Speed of Storage Types

The cost of all types of storage has been decreasing in price and increasing in speed since mainframes first became available in the 1960s, and this trend continues. We will use the prices and speeds in Figure CD.5 as relative estimates. You may purchase the storage at lower prices than indicated in the figure. Central and expanded CMOS storage are priced very similarly at present. There is very little cost savings by using hiperpools. However, the relative prices for bipolar computers are similar to those shown. For example, central storage costs about three times that of expanded storage. The speed of central storage is about 1000 times faster than that of expanded storage at the high end of the speed range. That is, both the sequential and random speeds of central storage are about 100 nanoseconds (ns) compared to expanded storage speeds of 10 to 100 microseconds (μs). Central and expanded storage are both integrated circuitry.

Figure CD.6. Relative cost and speed of storage

Storage	Cost/MB	Sequential Speed	Random Speed
Processor Cache	$100 K	10 ns	10 ns
Central Storage	3 K	100 ns	100 ns
Expanded Storage	1.2 K	10-100 μs	10-100 μs
3990 Cache	1 K	2 ms	2 ms
3390 DASD/Array	10	2 ms	20 ms
Optical Library	3	10 ms	10 sec
Tape Library	1	2 ms	2 min

The most economical direct access storage with a good sequential and random speed of 2 and 20 milliseconds (ms) is DASD. This makes DASD a good choice for storing the bulk of the data and indexes. Certainly, most companies do just that. DASD cache compares favorably with expanded storage but has a dramatically slower random speed at the time of writing. DASD cache is expected to compare more favorably with expanded storage in the future. Central and expanded CMOS storage are priced very similarly at present. Therefore, there is very little cost savings by using hiperpools. You may want to consider the use of hiperpools with CMOS processor if you are constrained by the 1.6 GB limit for a virtual pool. (Hiperpool space is not included in the 1.6 GB limit.) Low update tablespaces and indexes are a good choice for a buffer pool with a hiperpool.

DASD cache on 3990s with cylinder prestaging is used for random I/O by DB2. The cache is not used for sequential prefetch by default. It can be enabled by specifying SEQCACH of SEQ in the DSNZPARM macro DSN6SPRM or on the DSNTIPE installation panel. Further control is available through the use of SPRMPF32 in DSNZPARM. If SEQCACH of BYPASS is used, SPRMPF32 in DSNZPARM can be set to a non-zero value (0 is the default). This results in 3 contiguous prefetch requests before bypassing prefetch. Enabling the use of the cache with sequential prefetch is a good choice for tablespace scans and non-matching index scans which makes it useful for batch and utility processing, and for data warehousing applications provided that the pages are rereferenced. If the pages are rarely rereferenced, the cache does not improve performance. Indeed, the cache can degrade performance for random I/O by as much as 100 to 200 percent depending on the cache controller. Record rather than track caching degrades performance less, depending on how it is used.

If it is appropriate in your environment to enable the cache for sequential prefetch, it should be disabled for the DSNDB07 tablespaces. Otherwise, many concurrent accesses to logical work files on the work tablespaces will overload the cache. The cache can be disabled by specifying the volume

IDs that contain work tablespaces. If you are using SMS to manage DB2 data sets, you can disable the cache at the data set level.

CD.7 CUSTOMIZING VIRTUAL POOLS AND HIPERPOOLS

If you are experiencing OS/390 paging of the virtual pool, do use data spaces or hiperpools. A primary objective is to avoid paging.

If insufficient central storage is available for data spaces, consider sizing of hiperpools in expanded storage. A reasonable starting point is to have the hiperpool two to four times the size its virtual pool. If the hiperpool is less than its corresponding virtual pool or the hiperpool does not improve the hit ratio, the additional CPU time required for moving pages to and from the hiperpool is not justified in most cases.

The sizing of the hiperpool (HP) should be analyzed similar to the sizing of the virtual pool as discussed in Section CD.5. The first formula in Figure CD.7 for calculating the hit ratio is the same one suggested in the earlier section on calculating the hit ratio. The result of using the formula is the percentage of pages found in a pool (with and without a hiperpool). It can be used for both the virtual pool and hiperpool. You will also want to look at the hit ratio for only the virtual pool and for only the hiperpool which are the second and third formula in the figure.

Figure CD.7. Formula for calculating hit ratios

Ratio	Formula
Buffer pool hits (VP and HP if any)	(getpages - sync reads - asynch reads) / getpages
Virtual pool hits (subtract HP reads if any)	(getpages - HP reads - synch reads - asynch reads) / getpages
Hiperpool hits	HP reads / getpages

Size and Thresholds of Pools

The default sizes and thresholds of BP0 are shown in Figure CD.8. The use of a hiperpool is not the default. Information about virtual pools and hiperpools is recorded in the boot strap data set (BSDS) and can be changed dynamically without stopping and starting DB2. The ALTER BUFFERPOOL command can be used to change the size and thresholds of the pools. Indeed it is also used to create and delete virtual pools and hiperpools. Following is an example of the command specifying default thresholds for the virtual pool and hiperpool. The virtual pool size is set as the default and the hiperpool is made twice the size as a starting point. The assigned values remain in effect until the next ALTER BUFFERPOOL command is executed.

```
-ALTER BUFFERPOOL(BP0)
     VPSIZE  (2000) HPSIZE (4000)
     VPSEQT  (80)   HPSEQT   (80)
     VPPSEQT (50)   PGSTEAL (LRU)
```

```
VPXPSEQT(50)    VPTYPE   (PRIMARY)
DWQT     (50)   CASTOUT  (YES)
VDWQT    (10)
```

Figure CD.8. Virtual Pool and Hiperpool Thresholds

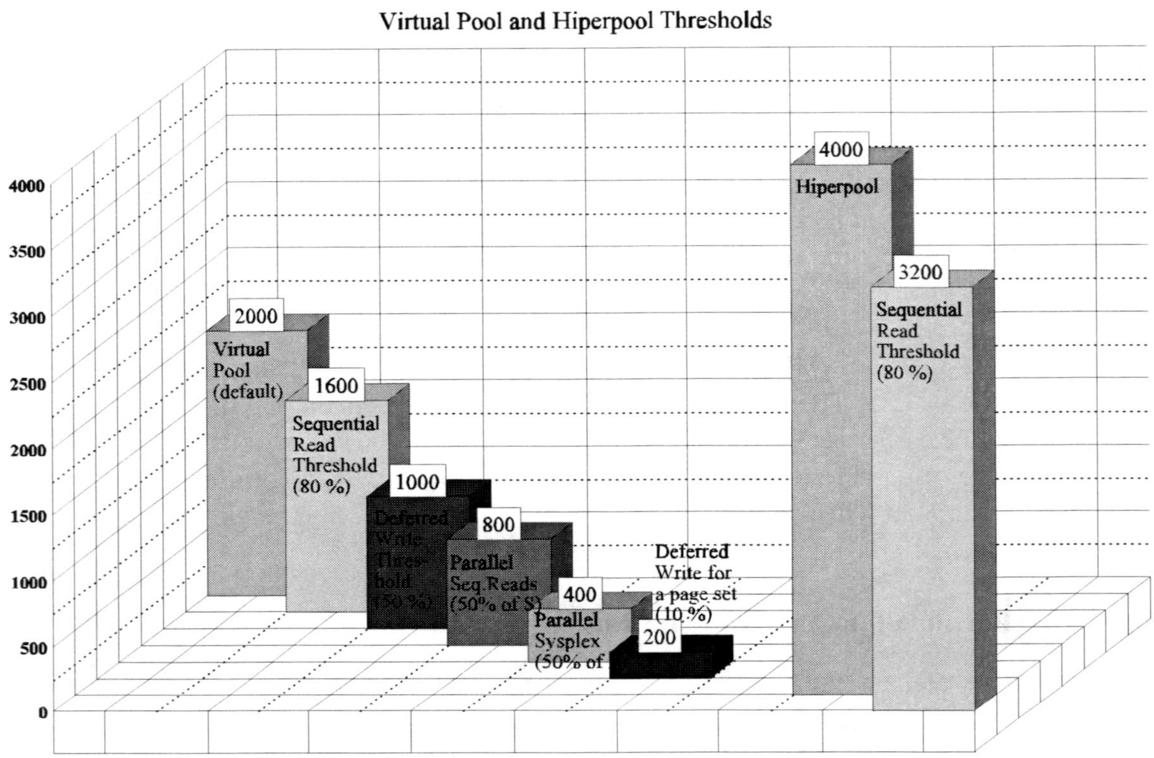

The buffer pool name follows the ALTER BUFFERPOOL command in parentheses. Following is a description of each of the parameters and guidelines on the values that should be considered.

VPSIZE is used to specify the number of page buffers in the virtual pool. There can be 0 to 400,000 4 KB pages in a 4 KB virtual pool. The default of 2000 pages in BP0 should be increased or more virtual pools should be created, assuming medium to heavy usage. This determination can be made based on the hit ratio.

HPSIZE is used to specify the number of buffers in a hiperpool. There can be 0 to 2,097,152 4 KB pages. ADMF uses 128 of these pages for control information used in moving pages to and from the hiperpool.

VPSEQT limits the number of pages that can be used for sequential reads in the virtual pool. The default is 80 percent and the value can be between 0 and 100 percent. Zero turns off prefetch and sequential data is purged after being read. Consider less than 80 percent for virtual pools used primarily for online transactions with matching index scans. Do be cautious of too low a percentage for the few cases where prefetch is beneficial. Do avoid thrashing where pages must be read more than once because the page slots are used by another process before they are used by the process that caused the initial read.

HPSEQT limits the number of pages that can be used for sequential reads in the hiperpool. The default is 80 percent and the value can be between 0 and 100 percent. Pages read with prefetch are not moved to the hiperpool if 0 is specified. This is a good choice if prefetched pages are not reused, for example, tablespace and index spaces used primarily for data warehousing and batch processing. This is the only threshold that applies to a hiperpool.

VPPSEQT limits the number of pages in a virtual pool that can house pages read using I/O and central processor (CP) parallelism as discussed in Chapter PL. VPPSEQT is a percentage of VPSEQT. The default is 50 percent of VPSEQT and can be between 0 and 100 percent. That is parallelism can use 40 percent of pool by default and in the example. The purpose of this threshold is to avoid too many pages being used for I/O and CP parallelism, which can degrade the performance of other processing. Zero turns off all modes of parallelism, which is not advisable in most cases.

VPXPSEQT limits the number of pages that can be used by an assisting DB2 for sysplex parallelism. VPXPSEQT is a percentage of VPPSEQT. The default is 50 percent of VPPSEQT and can be between 0 and 100 percent. That is, an assisting DB2 in sysplex parallelism can use 20 percent of the pool by default and in the example. The purpose of this threshold is to avoid too many pages being used for assisting in sysplex parallelism. Zero disallows a DB2 subsystem from being an assistant for sysplex parallelism and is not advisable in most cases.

DWQT indicates the percentage of in-use pages before deferred write is triggered in the virtual pool. Deferred write continues until in-use pages are 10 percent below the threshold. The default is 50 percent and the value can be between 0 and 90 percent. If 0 is specified, buffer manager uses the MIN(40, 1 percent value) for 4 KB BPs. The write I/O is issued for 32 pages after 40 pages have been updated. This allows for retaining the most recent 8 hot pages including the space map page in the buffer.

VDWQT indicates the percentage of the virtual pool that can contain updated pages from a single page set. Updated pages are written to the table when the threshold is reached. The default is 10 percent and the value can be between 0 and 90 percent. If 0 is specified, buffer manager uses the MIN(40, 1 percent value) for 4 KB BPs with the DWQT condition. VDWQT should be less than DWQT. VDWQT is overridden by most utilities. Optionally, you can specify a number of updated pages before initiating deferred write for a data set. For example, if VDWQT (0, 100) is used, 0 means not to use a percentage and 100 means to write pages for a page set afer 100 pages have been updated.

DWQT and VDWQT thresholds of 90 percent are a good choice for tablespaces and indexes frequently updated. Regardless of these values, all updated pages are written to DASD at checkpoint, stop database, and stop DB2. Do be cautious of specifying too high a value for DWQT and VDWQT. This can result in delays while writing updated pages to DASD when the thresholds are reached, delays during checkpoint processing, a shortage of write engines, and a delay with stop processing. There are 300 write engines available.

PGSTEAL(LRU) (default) causes pages to be reused on a least recently used basis. It requires maintenance of page chains to determine the least recently used pages. It is a good choice in most cases.

PGSTEAL(FIFO) causes page to be reused on a first-in-first out basis (V6). The algorithm is less costly to maintain than use of the LRU algorithm. It reduces latch contention for buffer pool management. It can be useful for a buffer pool that experiences little or no I/O. For example, a buffer pool sized to page fix pages in memory. Another use of FIFO is for a buffer pool used to house very large tables that are referenced at random with little reuse of pages in the buffer.

Recommendation: Consider assigning object to separate buffer pools when FIFO has advantages. FIFO is a good choice for buffer pools designed to page fix pages in buffer

FIFO is used when VDWQT threshold is reached.

VPTYPE(PRIMARY) means virtual pool resides in the primary address space (database services address space, DBM1). This is the default.

VPTYPE(DATASPACE) means virtual pool resides in a data space.

The VGPTYPE parameters can be specified on DSNTIP1, DSNTIP2, DSNTIP6, installation panels. You can alter the VPTYPE like other parameters. However, altering VPTYPE requires reallocation of the buffer pool. You can reallocate a buffer pool without restarting DB2. The following example changes BP8 VPTYPE to a data space.

```
-ALTER BUFFERPOOL(BP8) VPSIZE(0)
-ALTER BUFFERPOOL(BP8) VPSIZE(10000) VPTYPE(DATASPACE)
```

The new parameter values takes effect when buffer pool is next allocated.

VPTYPE for BP0 requires restarting DB2 or the following procedure can be used. Issue the ALTER command like:

```
-ALTER BUFFERPOOL(BP8) VPSIZE(0)
```

Use -STOP DATABASE command to stop all table spaces and indexes that are using BP0. Issue the ALTER command once again like:

```
-ALTER BUFFERPOOL(BP8) VPSIZE(10000) VPTYPE(DATASPACE)
```

Use -START DATABASE command to start all table spaces and indexes that are using BP0.

The procedure to change BP0 can be used to change any buffer pool without waiting for reallocation of the buffer pool.

CASTOUT(YES) allows OS/390 to discard pages in the hiperpool if expanded storage is needed for other processing or usage of pages in the hiperpool is low. This is the default.

If hiperspace is stolen by OS/390, buffer manager move page instructions will fail. Pages thought to be in the hiperpool must be read from DASD. Attempts to move pages from the virtual pool to the hiperpool will fail. Of course, performance can be adversely affected. Stolen hiperspace will be returned by OS/390 when it is no longer required for use by others.

CASTOUT(NO) does not allow OS/390 to steal expanded storage from the hiperpool in most cases. Exceptions are that pages can be stolen if the hiperpool is deleted, hiperspace storage area is explicitly released, OS/390 hiperspace maintenance is required, or the address space owning the hiperspace is swapped out (DB2 is not swappable). CASTOUT NO basically pins (page fixes) pages in expanded storage and favors DB2 application systems over other processing on the computer. This can adversely affect other applications on the computer.

Alter of the CASTOUT parameter does not take effect immediately as is the case for all other ALTER BUFFERPOOL parameters.

Creating, Deleting, and Changing Pools

The ALTER BUFFERPOOL command can be used to create, delete, and change the size of a virtual pool and hiperpool. Here is an example of creating BP1 with 4000 pages, a hiperpool with 8000 pages, and use of default values for thresholds.

```
-ALTER BUFFERPOOL(BP1)
     VPSIZE(4000)
     HPSIZE(8000);
```

A virtual pool or hiperpool can be deleted by setting the VPSIZE or HPSIZE to 0. This causes all processing in the buffer pool to be quiesced. Here is an example of deleting virtual pool BP5.

```
-ALTER BUFFERPOOL (BP5)
     VPSIZE(0);
```

Any attempted access to an object assigned to BP5 receives a resource unavailable message. It is necessary to ALTER all objects assigned to a BP before deleting it. An exclusive lock is taken on the DBD to alter assignment of an object to a buffer pool. Stop tablespace and index space is an alternative to quiesce plans and packages that hold a share lock on the DBD. However, this does result in unavailability of objects during quiesce processing and execution of ALTER statements.

Here is an example of increasing the size of BP0 to 8000 pages, its hiperpool to 32,000 pages, and retaining the current thresholds.

```
-ALTER BUFFERPOOL (BP0)
     VPSIZE (8000)
     HPSIZE(32000);
```

Changing the size of the virtual pool or hiperpool causes buffer manager to dynamically reconfigure the hash table for the pools and sets the sizes in the BSDS. The changes remain in effect until the buffer pool is altered again.

Thresholds that Cannot be Altered: There are only two thresholds that cannot be altered. These are the data management threshold (DMTH) and the immediate write threshold (IWTH) which are permanently set at 95 and 97.5 percent. These thresholds are discussed at the beginning of Section CD.4 as reasons for insuring that the virtual pool is well sized for the workload. These thresholds are necessary to slow activity because there is insufficient space available in the virtual pool. Basically, buffer manager has no space to place newly read pages. Hiperpools have no effect on the thresholds.

CD.8 DETERMINING USAGE OF POOLS

The DISPLAY command can be executed to determine the current status and activity of virtual pools and hiperpools like:

```
-DISPLAY BUFFERPOOL(ACTIVE)
     DETAIL(INTERVAL) LIST(ACTIVE) LSTATS
```

BUFFERPOOL(ACTIVE) requests statistics on all active buffer pools and is the default. Optionally, you can specify the name of specific buffer pools (BP0, BP1, BP32K for example) in place of the ACTIVE parameter value. Another choice is to specify BUFFERPOOL(*) which indicates that you want information on all active and inactive buffer pools.

DETAIL(INTERVAL) requests statistics accumulated since the last incremental display and is the default. DETAIL(*) requests accumulated statistics since the buffer pools first became active.

LIST(ACTIVE) requests statistics on all open and in-use tablespaces and indexes and is the default. LIST(*) requests statistics on all open tablespaces and indexes in-use and not in-use.

LSTATS provides information on I/O delays by database, tablespace, and index. The statistics are incremental since the last display.

DBNAME and SPACENAM parameters can be specified along with the name of a database, tablespace or index space when using the LIST and LSTATS parameters. If LIST is not specified, LIST(ACTIVE) is used. A specific name can be given, a range of names separated by a colon, or the wild card of asterisk can be used to take advantage of a naming convention. For example, the following command provides information on all databases beginning with DADB and all tablespaces that begin with DATSP:

```
-DISPLAY BUFFER POOL(ACTIVE)
     DBNAME(DADB*) SPACENAM(DATSP*)
```

Figure CD.9 is an example of a report on all active buffer pools. Notice that the beginning of the report gives the size and thresholds of BP0 as requested in the DISPLAY command. The hiperspace that houses the hiperpool is @001DB2T. The three-digit number is a sequence number of each hiperspace in the hiperpool with a maximum value of 4. The last four bytes are the DB2 subsystem name. The tablespaces currently using the buffer pool are listed along with a count of the number of users. The statistics on each data set are given, including the number of current and changed pages in the VP as well as the maximum. Similar statistics are given for the HP except that the number of changed pages is not given because changed pages must be written to the tablespaces before they are cached in the HP. The synchronous and asynchronous I/O delays including the average and maximum delays, and the total pages are given in the report.

Figure CD.9. Report of displaying BP0 information

```
-DISPLAY BUFFERPOOL(BP0), LIST(ACTIVE), LSTATS

BUFFER POOL NAME BP0, BUFFER POOL ID 0, USE COUNT 10

VIRTUAL BUFFER POOL SIZE = 2000 BUFFERS
   ALLOCATED             = 2000 TO BE DELETED      = 0
   IN USE/UPDATED        =  400

HIPERPOOL SIZE           = 9000 BUFFERS, CASTOUT  = YES
   ALLOCATED             = 9000 TO BE DELETED      = 0
   BACKED BY ES          = 9000

THRESHOLDS -
   VPSEQENTIAL           = 80   HP SEQUENTIAL      = 80
   DEFERRED WRITE        = 50   VER DEFERRED WR    = 10
   PARALLEL SEQUENTIAL   = 50   ASSISTING PAR SEQT= 50

HIPERSPACE NAMES - @001DB2T

TABLESPACE = DSNDB01.DBD01,     USE COUNT = 2
           = DSNDB06.SYSDBASE,  USE COUNT = 1
           = DSNDB06.DSNDLX01,  USE COUNT = 4

STATISTICS FOR DATASET 1 -

  VP CACHED PAGES -
    CURRENT       =        12   MAX                =   40
    CHANGED       =         8   MAX                =   20

  HP CACHED PAGES -
    CURRENT       =        40   MAX                =   80

  SYNCHRONOUS I/O DELAYS    -
    AVERAGE DELAY =        22   MAXIMUM DELAY      =   35
    TOTAL PAGES   =        23

  ASYNCHRONOUS I/O DELAYS -
    AVERAGE DELAY =         3   MAXIMUM DELAY      =    5
    TOTAL PAGES   =       640
```

More detail can be gotten by adding the parameter DETAIL to the DISPLAY command as indicated in Figure CD.10. Again the report begins with the size and thresholds of BP0. We have more detail including the number of random and sequential getpages, and synchronous I/O. We are happy to see that the 95 percent DMTH threshold has not been reached since the DISPLAY command was last executed. The number of sequential prefetch requests, prefetch I/Os, and pages read are shown in the report. Similar statistics not shown in the example are reported for list and dynamic prefetch. Prefetch has not been disabled because of no buffers and no read engines. The DWQT and VDWQT thresholds have not been hit as indicated by the zeros for the DWT HIT and VERTICAL DWT HIT field on the report. Hiperpool activity is reported for the reads and writes not using ADMF and when using ADMF. The number of I/O issued for parallelism is reported as zero. Of course, since parallelism has not been used since the last time the DISPLAY command was executed, parallelism has not been degraded.

Figure CD.10. Report of displaying BP0 detail information

```
-DISPLAY BUFFERPOOL(BP0), DETAIL

BUFFER POOL NAME BP0, BUFFER POOL ID 0, USE COUNT 10

VIRTUAL BUFFER POOL SIZE = 2000 BUFFERS
   ALLOCATED             = 2000 TO BE DELETED      =    0
   IN USE/UPDATED        =  400

HIPERPOOL SIZE           = 9000 BUFFERS, CASTOUT   = YES
   ALLOCATED             = 9000 TO BE DELETED      =    0
   BACKED BY ES          = 9000

THRESHOLDS -
   VPSEQENTIAL           =   80 HP SEQUENTIAL      =   80
   DEFERRED WRITE        =   50 VER DEFERRED WR    =   10

HIPERSPACE NAMES - @001DB2T
INCREMENTAL STATISTICS SINCE 10:14:30 MAR 12, 1993
RANDOM GETPAGES      =   219614 SYN READ I/O (R)  =  7883
SEQ.   GETPAGES      =  7645409 SYN READ I/O (S)  =   521
DM CRITICAL HIT      =        0

SEQUENTIAL PREFETCH -
  REQUESTS           =    72960 PREFETCH I/Os     = 52838
  PAGES READ         =  1627587

Above 3 lines repeated for list and dynamic prefetch

PREFETCH DISABLED -
  NO BUFFER          =        0 NO READ ENGINE     =      0
SYS PAGE UPDATES     =   102335 SYS PAGE WRITTEN   =  17336
ASYNC WRITE I/O      =     1803 SYNC WRITE I/O     =      0
DWT HIT              =        0 VERTICAL DWT HIT   =      0
NO WRITE ENGINE      =        0
HIPERPOOL ACTIVITY (NOT USING ASYNCH. DATA MOVER FACILITY
  SYNC  HP READS     =    14920 SYNC  HP WRITES    =    225
  ASYNC HP READS     =     7928 ASYNC HP WRITES    =   1121
  READ FAILURES      =        0 WRITE FAILURES     =      0
HIPERPOOL ACTIVITY (USING ASYNCH. DATA MOVER FACILITY)
  SYNC HP READS      =   330372 HP WRITES          = 992577
  READ FAILURES      =        0 WRITE FAILURES     =      0
I/O PARALLEL ACTIVITY -
  PARALLEL REQUESTS  =        0 DEGRADED PARALLEL  =      0
```

The BSDS reports do not show pool sizes even though this information is maintained in the BSDS.

CD.9 GUIDELINES ON THE USE OF MULTIPLE VIRTUAL POOLS

There are a number of guidelines to consider when deciding which tablespaces and indexes to assign to which buffer pools based primarily on the type of data and processing expected. Some of the strategies reviewed below will be good choices for your application system.

A separate virtual pool can be used for data and index pages. This is a particular good choice for very large tables of, say, 10 million rows or more, for example. The tablespace virtual pool can be relatively small if random page processing is expected and it is unlikely that the data pages will be referenced and remain in buffer. The index virtual pool should be large to increase the likelihood that the index pages will remain in the buffer. Basically, this configuration assumes that you are willing to accept a physical I/O for most data pages but want to avoid as many I/O to the index as possible, depending on the size of the index and the buffer pool used for the index. One company found that this strategy reduced response time from 3.7 to 0.7 seconds.

If tablespaces and indexes are frequently scanned, consider pinning them in a hiperpool. The goal is to basically make the pages resident in the hiperpool so that they are rarely read from DASD, which reduces I/O time dramatically. One company pinned a 1,655,000 row table on 138,000 pages in a hiperpool. Before doing this a tablespace to satisfy a COUNT(*) required 316 elapsed and 8 CPU (TCB, task control block) seconds. After creating a hiperpool to contain the tablespace, the elapsed time dropped to 13 seconds and 8 CPU seconds. The amount of hiperpool space required can be reduced by using data compression as discussed in Chapter TS. If a 50 percent compression ratio is achieved, the hiperpool space required can be reduced by half. The CPU time is expected to increase, particularly for decompression during a tablespace scan.

Place frequently used reference tables in a separate virtual pool sized to basically page fix the pages.

Tablespaces and indexes used by frequently executed transactions can be placed in a separate virtual pool to avoid competition for space with less critical transactions.

Consider placing tablespaces and indexes primarily used for batch processing in a separate buffer pool. This avoids batch programs taking space that could be used by online transactions. An alternative, is to lower the VPSEQT and HPSEQT thresholds assuming that batch programs, rather than transactions, are using prefetch.

Frequently updated tablespaces and indexes can be placed in a separate virtual pool with the deferred write thresholds set high (DWQT and VDWQT at 90 percent for example). Do be cautious of hitting the DMTH and IWTH thresholds, delays in writing the pages to DASD when the thresholds are reached, running short of write engines, and delays when the DB2 subsystem is stopped, particularly with a large virtual pool. Consider adjusting the checkpoint frequency to write updated pages to DASD less frequently. Do be cautious because the checkpoint frequency applies to all virtual pools. This strategy allows pages to be repeatedly updated with minimal writes to DASD. However, do be cautious of a significant performance degradation during checkpoint processing while many updated pages are being written to DASD. Very little other work can be accomplished during this processing. There is no reason to use a hiperpool because dirty pages are not placed in the hiperpool.

Tablespaces and indexes that are usually not rereferenced can be placed in a separate small virtual pool. If a large percentage of pages are read with prefetch and the pages are not referenced, a large virtual pool will not increase the hit ratio. However, the virtual pool should be large enough to enable prefetch of 32 pages (1000 pages) assuming prefetch is used. Set the deferred write threshold low (11 percent allows for 3 deferred write I/O of 96 pages). This reduces writes of updated pages to DASD at checkpoint time. There is no reason for using a hiperpool if pages are usually not rereferenced.

If application tablespaces, indexes, and work tablespaces are not assigned to BP0 in a production DB2 subsystem, BP0 can be made relatively small for the directory and catalog I/O (minimum of 56 pages). This strategy assumes that the EDM pool is sized to minimize I/O to the directory through BP0, the sort pool size has been set for the workload, security checking does not require excessive

I/O to the authorization tables, and there is very low usage of reoptimization and dynamic SQL.

Do assign work tablespaces in work database DSNDB07 to a separate virtual pool. This avoids work tablespaces taking buffer pages that would otherwise be used for application data and indexes. It also avoids sort merge pass degradation, work file request rejections, and workfile prefetch being aborted. The VPSEQT threshold can be set at 80 to 90 percent of the virtual pool for sequential reads using this strategy. The use of 100 percent is not advisable because the buffer pool is accessed at random for some work files including for some subselect and join processing, for example. BP7 is a convenient buffer pool to use for the DSNDB07 database.

Objects used for data warehousing applications can be placed in a separate virtual pool. This avoids space being taken from transaction usage.

Consider temporarily assigning tablespaces, indexes, and work tablespaces to various virtual pools for analysis of buffer usage. This is useful in determining the size of virtual pools and assignment of objects to them.

It is important to avoid effect of having pages in buffer pool when testing different formulation of SQL and other testing scenarios. One way of accomplishing this is to alter tablespace and indexes to use a different buffer pool, run tests, alter tablespace and index to use original buffer pool, and repeat processing until testing is complete. An alternative is to stop/start tablespaces and indexes used in the tests. This requires that pages be read into the buffer pool when next accessed.

There are many variations on the use of multiple virtual pools and hiperpools. Do not be afraid to experiment and come up with a strategy that works well for your tablespaces and indexes in your environment.

Configuration of your buffer pools and thresholds is a challenge. The workload changes throughout the day. Time and resources are needed to monitor and tune for the workload. If you do not have the time and resources to meet the challenge, consider one buffer pool, particularly if you require 10,000 pages or less. This minimize the possibility of a shortage of space in one buffer pool with sufficient space in another buffer pool regardless of the configuration.

CD.10 ADJUSTING I/O PRIORITY

It is straightforward to assign CPU priority by address space. However, I/O to tablespaces and indexes are issued using the priority of the database services address space. This means that the same priority is given to online transactions using CICS and IMS as that given to batch jobs, utilities, and data warehousing applications. Usually there is a service agreement with the business professionals that online transaction will execute with an agreed upon response time. This response time is difficult to achieve if there are many types of applications executing on a DB2 subsystem.

Your OS/390 systems programmer can use work load manager (WLM) to set goals which allows WLM to automatically adjust the I/O priority, CPU usage, and central storage to favor online transactions in certain address spaces and batch programs executing in other address spaces. If WLM is not used at your company, an alternative to having all I/O issued under the priority of the database services address space is to manually adjust the I/O priority similar to that shown in Figure CD.11. Your systems programmer should consider giving database services a medium priority and CICS or

IMS the highest I/O priority. TSO and data warehousing applications can be given low to medium priority with batch processing having the lowest I/O priority. Your systems programmer can accomplish this adjustment using SYS1.PARMLIB like:

- SYS1.PARMLIB(IEAIPSxx), IOQ = PRTY (not FIFO)
- SYS1.PARMLIB(IEAIPSxx), PGN = ..., IOP = ...

Figure CD.11. Adjusting I/O priority

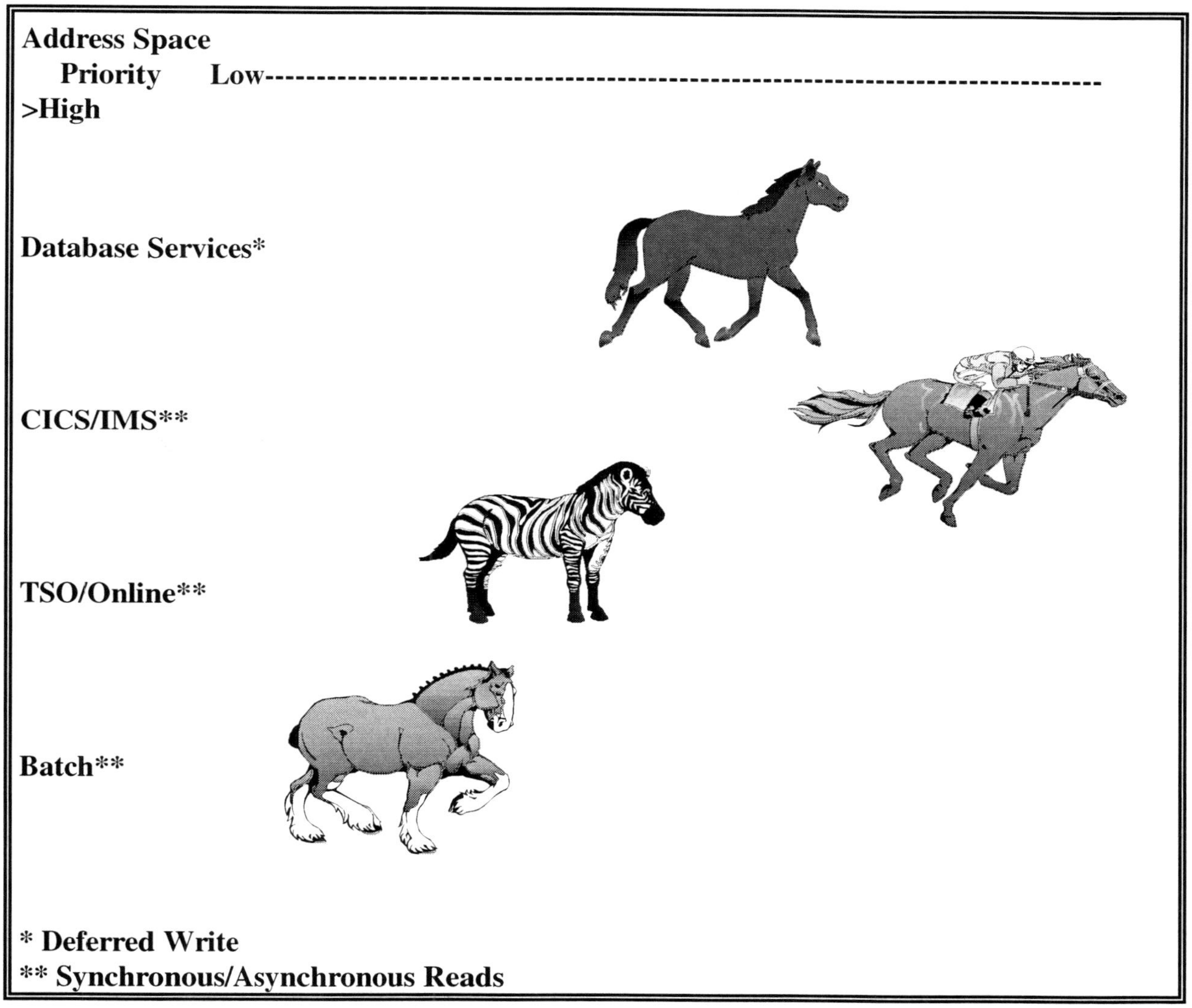

Test Results of Adjusting I/O Priority

IBM tested the results of adjusting the I/O priority similar to that shown in Figure CD.11 using the Relational Transaction Workload (RTW). The tests were done on a 9121-480 computer with 3390-2 DASD behind one 3990 controller. There were 2000 pages in BP0 and the sequential read threshold was set at the default of 80 percent.

Figure CD.12 shows the results of the tests in terms of transactions per second. FIFO means that all

I/O was issued under the priority of the database services address space which is the case if the I/O priority is not adjusted and you are not using WLM. IOPQ means that the I/O priority of transactions was set higher than that of tablespace scan processing. There were two tablespace scans on two DASD volumes running continually during the online transaction processing. The tests were done with three think times. The first pair of bars reflect a slow think time where the user needed to look at the screen for awhile to decide the action to be taken. Notice that the transactions per second did not change when using the I/O priorities rather than the default FIFO priority. The second pair of bars reflect medium think times where the user needed to look at the screen for a shorter period of time. In this case the transactions per second again did not change. The third pair of bars reflect a fast think time where the user needed to look at the screen for a short period of time to make a decision as to what action to take. In this case the transactions per second improved from 18 to 27 transactions per second.

Figure CD.12. Transactions per second with and without adjusting I/O priority

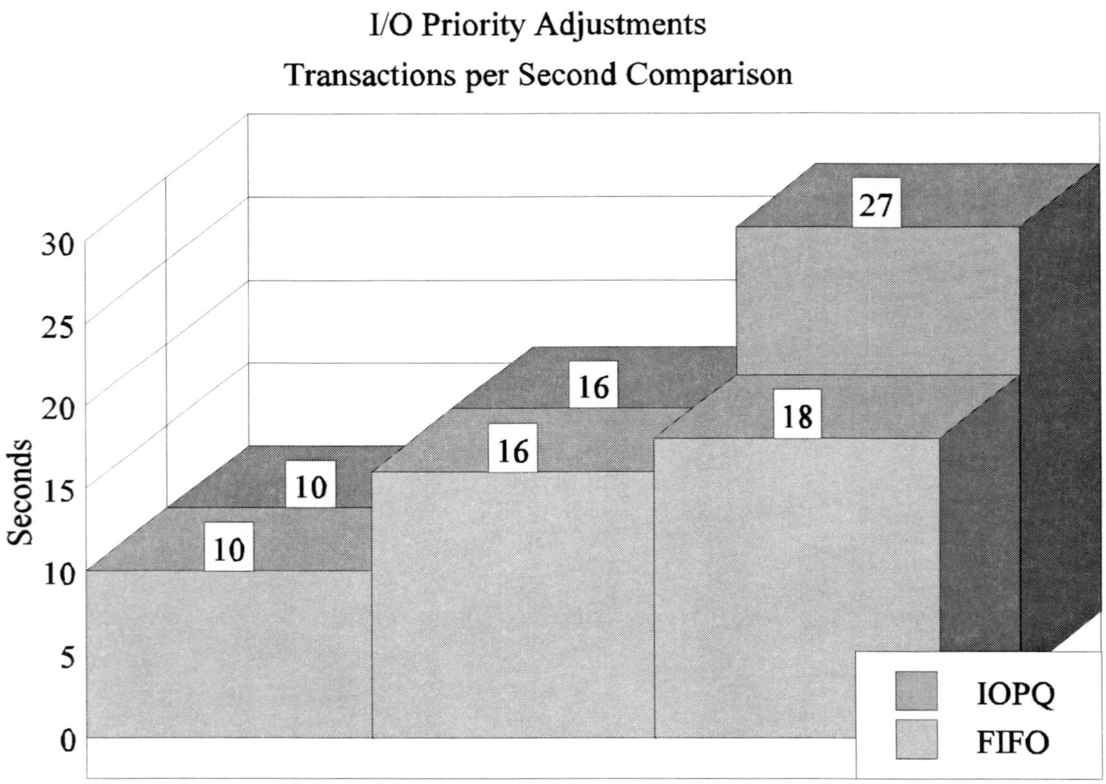

Figure CD.13 shows the results of the tests in terms of response time. The tests were done again with three think times. The first pair of bars for a slow think time shows a little better response time when assigning I/O priorities rather than using the default FIFO priority. The second pair of bars for the medium think time shows the response time improved from 0.67 to 0.42 seconds. The third pair of bars for a fast think time shows the response time improved from 1.5 to 0.85 seconds

Figure CD.13. Response time with and without adjusting I/O priority

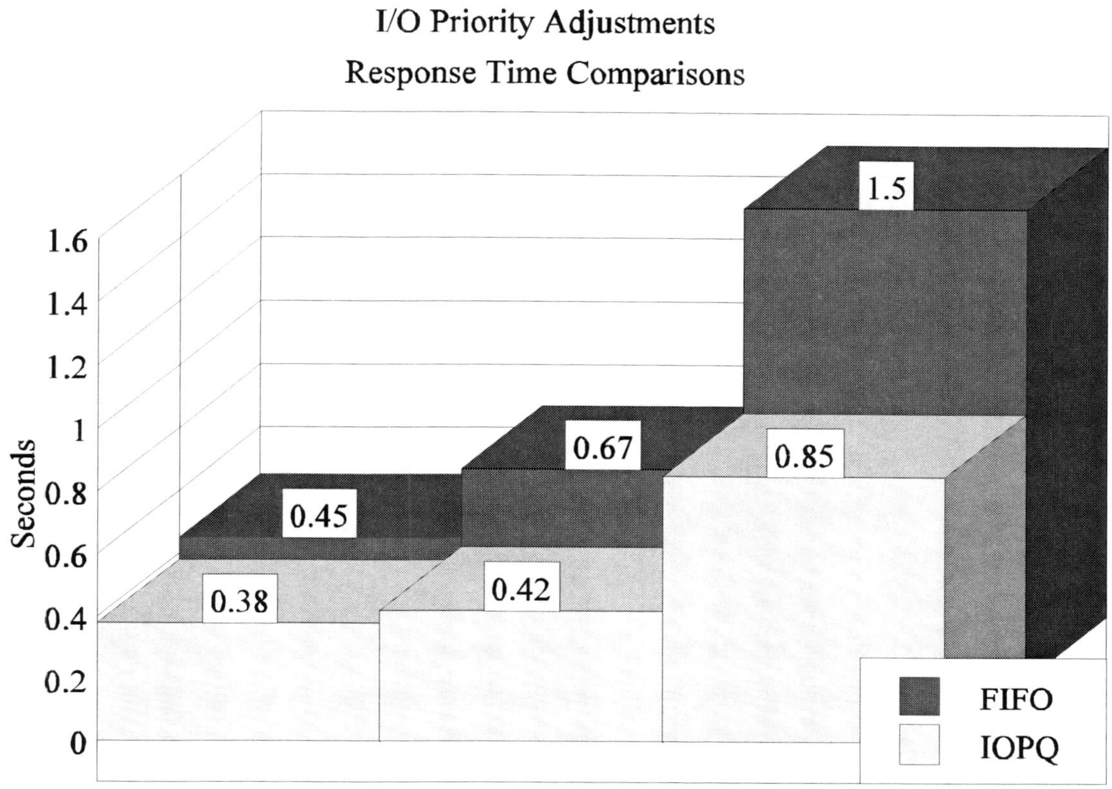

The tests were repeated with the buffer pool increased to 4000 pages. The sequential read threshold was decreased to 25 percent. This means that only 25 percent rather than 80 percent of the buffer pages can be used for tablespace scans. The online transactions can use 75 percent of the buffer pages without them being stolen by the continually running tablespace scans.

The transactions per second did not change for the slow and medium thinkers. It did increase for the fast thinkers -- from 18 and 27 transactions per second to 25 and 30 transactions per second.

The response time improvements with and without adjusting the I/O priority were greater with the larger buffer pool and more of it dedicated to online transactions as shown in Figure CD.14. The response time for the transactions was improved for all three think times, with the fast thinkers experiencing the greatest improvements. The response time without adjusting the I/O priority remained about the same at 1.49 in the first case and 1.5 seconds with the increased buffer space available to the online transactions. However, the response time went down to 0.85 seconds when adjusting the I/O priority to favor the online transactions with the smaller buffer pool and went down further to 0.44 seconds with the increased number of buffer pages available to the online transactions.

Figure CD.14. Response time with and without adjusting I/O priority using a larger BP

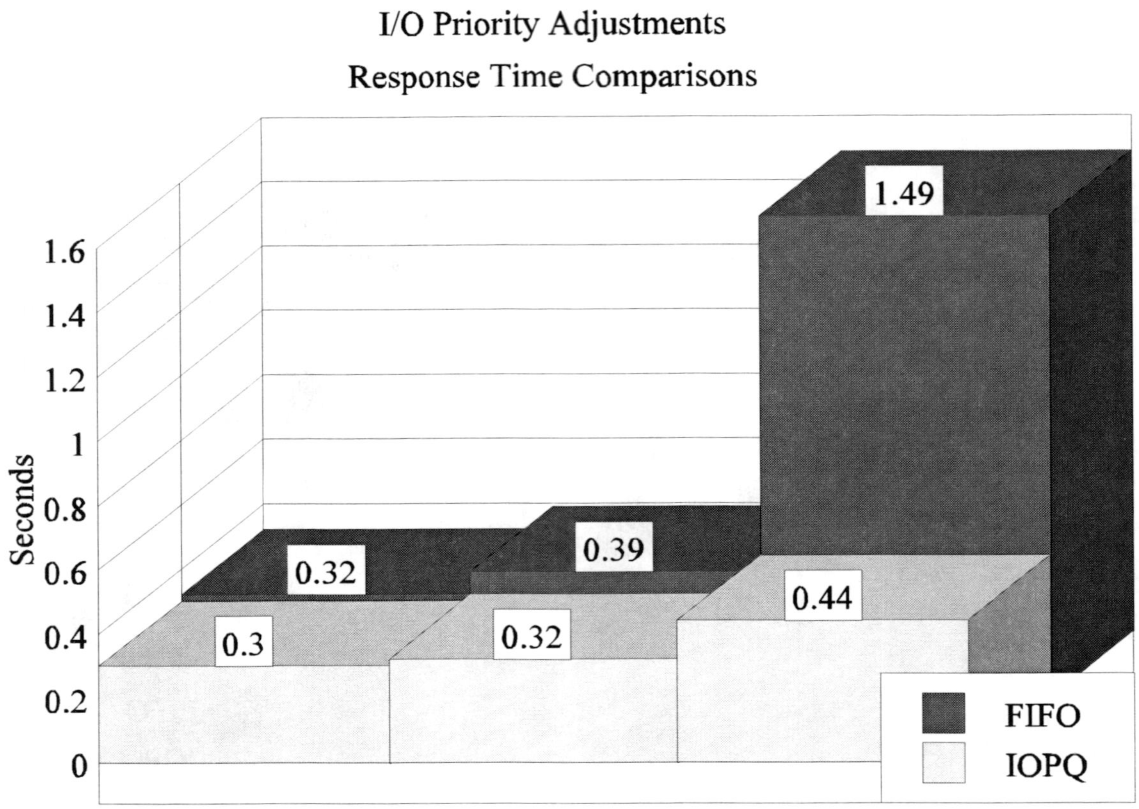

The transactions per second and response time test results give you an idea of whether you should consider running similar tests in your environment and, if justified, adjust the I/O priorities to favor online transactions. An alternative is to use OS/390 workload manager.

CD.11 SUMMARY

The use of storage groups allows DB2 to create, delete, and alter VSAM data sets, thus saving you a good deal of time and effort. Do be cautious about using DBDs that are large for the available space in the EDM pool. Space in the EDM pool is require for the execution of plans and packages.

The buffer pool configuration affects performance more than any other single factor. Do achieve a buffer hit ratio that is suitable for your environment. Consider the use hiperpools and data spaces for a buffer pool if more than 1.6 GB is required. There are more advantages expected in future for data spaces. If there is insufficient central storage available to achieve a good hit ratio or there are addressability constraints, consider the use of expanded storage. Expanded storage is more costly than DASD storage but significantly less costly than central storage when using bipolar processors. Hiperpool random I/O of 100 μs is over 2000 times faster than DASD, which makes it very good for moderately read data.

The ALTER BUFFERPOOL command can be used to dynamically create, delete, and change virtual pool and hiperpool sizes and thresholds based on your analysis of the sizes and thresholds required for your environment. The DISPLAY command gives good information on the current configuration of buffer pools and statistics on their usage.

EXERCISES

1. a) What is a general guideline when sizing a DBD?

b) Why is the guideline important?

c) How should objects be organized in databases?

2. a) The DBD can continue to increase in size after all required objects have been created. What causes this to happen?

b) What are two types of processing that result in the DBD increasing in size?

c) What can be done to allow for reuse of DBD space after tables are dropped?

3. Why is it advisable to stop a database before altering objects in the database?

4. a) There are a number of advantages to using storage groups versus user defined data sets (USING VCAT). What is the disadvantage?

b) How can the disadvantage be minimized? For example, how can you place tablespaces on one volume and indexes on another volume?

c) What is a disadvantage of using SMS for management of DASD and how can it be minimized?

5. What are the disadvantages if a buffer pool is too small for the usage of tablespaces and indexes assigned to it?

6. a) If a page is read and updated by user A, is it necessary to write the changed page to DASD and reread it for user B?

b) How does DB2 avoid losing the updates in central and expanded storage in case of a power failure?

c) How is data integrity maintained?

b) DB2 logs the changed page to DASD in case of a power failure where all data in the buffer pool would be lost.

c) DB2 maintains data integrity using locks and latches to serialize updates so that one user's updates is not overwritten by another users update.

7. a) What is meant by a buffer page being in-use?

b) What is meant by a buffer page being stealable?

8. a) What is a buffer pool hit ratio?

b) What is a good goal for a hit ratio?

9. If you do not have any 32 KB data pages, is it necessary to have a 32 KB buffer pool? Why?

10. What are the benefits of using 8, 16, or 32 KB pages?

11. What type of storage is used by a virtual pools, data spaces, and hiperpools?

12. What are some reasons for using data spaces and hiperpools?

13. What are some advantages of using data spaces compared to hiperpools?

14. a) How are virtual pools, data spaces, and hiperpools created, modified, and deleted?

b) How are their thresholds changed?

15. Which ALTER BUFFERPOOL parameter does not take effect immediately after the ALTER command is executed?

16. How can you determine the number of sequential, dynamic and list prefetch I/O that are used to read pages into BP4?

ANSWERS

1. a) A general guideline when sizing a DBD is that it should not exceed about 5-10 percent of the EDM pool size, or about 250-500 KB, assuming the default EDM size.

b) A DBD that is too large for the EDM pool can result in a resource unavailable message at execution time if there is insufficient space for loading the DBD.

c) The organization of objects in DBDs can be along the lines of subject areas. That is, logical groupings of objects can be placed in a database based on application usage. All objects in a payroll/personnel system can be placed in a database. If this results in a DBD that is too large, the objects relating more to payroll can be placed in one database and the objects relating more to personnel can be placed in another database. Consideration should be given to the administration of database objects so that the appropriate authority can be granted at the database level.

2. a) The DBD increases in size as existing tables are dropped and recreated in a segmented tablespace.

b) 1) A data entry table may have rows inserted for a period of time (for example, daily, weekly, etc.) followed by processing the data, dropping the table, and recreating it. A good alternative is to use the mass delete algorithm. 2) Ad hoc users may create and drop tables for their own personal use in an interactive environment.

c) The DBD space can be made reusable by reorganizing the tablespace, deleting old image copies, and taking an image copy of the tablespace as detailed in Section CD.3.

3. Stopping the database and starting it again after an alter of objects results in the updated DBD being read into the EDM pool. This allows DB2 to recognize the new parameters.

4. a) The disadvantage of using storage groups is that there is less control over placement of tablespaces and index spaces on specific volumes, channels, and control units.

b) If one volume is placed in a storage group for a large tablespace and another volume is assigned to another storage group for indexes, you can achieve separation of the data and indexes by assigning them to the two separate storage groups. This example can be generalized to other types of access and space management. For example a heavily used tablespace and infrequently used data sets can be placed in a storage group with a single volume. In contrast, placing several heavily used tablespaces in a single storage group with one volume will lend to excessive DASD arm movement.

c) SMS does not "know" the difference between tablespaces and index spaces. It is necessary to use separate SMS storage groups and guarantee space on a volume for specific data sets, or an exit can be used to determine placement. A good alternative is to assign data sets to specific storage classes based on an established naming convention to achieve separation. For example, if index names begin with X, VCAT.*.*.X* can be used. However, caution must be exercised as pointed out by Dr. Lou Agosta.

5. If a buffer pool is too small for the usage of tablespaces and indexes assigned to it, the performance of SQL statements that process the tablespaces and indexes is likely to be adversely affected. The number of physical I/O to DASD is likely to be higher than it should be and the I/O wait time will be excessive. This adversely affects the response time of online transactions and the elapsed time of batch and data warehousing applications. It also increases the CPU time because the CPU is used to issue the physical I/O.

6. If a page is read and updated by user A, it is not necessary to write the changed page to DASD and reread it for user B. User B can reread the page as long as user A has committed the update and the buffer pool has sufficient space to hold the page.

b) DB2 logs the changed page to DASD in case of a power failure where all data in the buffer pool would be lost.

c) DB2 maintains data integrity using locks and latches to serialize updates so that one user's updates are not overwritten by another user's updates.

7. a) An in-use buffer page is one where DM has issued a getpage and has not yet issued a relpage or set write pending.

b) A stealable page is one where DM has issued a getpage and relpage, and write pending is not active.

8. a) A buffer pool hit ratio is the percentage of time that the page is found in the buffer pool when DM issues a getpage and buffer manager does not have to issue a physical I/O.

b) A good goal for a hit ratio is 80 to 90 percent or more assuming that pages are referenced. Keep in mind that if you are using a hiperpool, hit ratios can be calculated for the buffer pool, virtual pool, and hiperpool.

9. It is necessary to have a 32 KB buffer pool even if you do not have any 32 KB data pages. The buffer pool is needed to process result rows of over 4 KB selected from multiple 4 KB page tablespaces.

10. The benefits of using 8, 16, or 32 KB pages have to do with space requirements and the costs serialization. If the row length is greater than ½ of a 4 KB page size less overhead, the larger page sizes can be used to save space by choosing a page size that fits a multiple of the row length without wasting space. Serialization cost can be reduced by using larger page sizes assuming that you are locking at the page level. This is particularly important in a sysplex data sharing environment. However, be cautious of serialization contention since data is being locked on the larger page sizes.

11. Virtual pools and data spaces reside in central storage. A hiperpool resides in expanded storage. The term *buffer pool* refers to all three types of spaces.

12. If your need for buffer pool space exceed the 1.6 GB limit. Data spaces and hiperpool are a good choice. If expanded storage costs less than central storage, the use hiperpools is a good choice to achieve cost savings. Data spaces and hiperpool can be used to reduce OS/390 paging and improve performance.

13. Some advantages of using data spaces compared to hiperpools is that data spaces reside in central storage, have a larger maximum size, can contain common areas, system data, and programs, can contain updated pages, and pages are read directly into a data space.

14. a) Virtual pools, and hiperpools are created, modified, and deleted using the ALTER BUFFERPOOL command. DB2 manages data spaces with no controls available to the system administrator.

b) Virtual pools, and hiperpools are changed using the BUFFERPOOL command.

15. The VPTYPE parameter used to designate private or data space usage does not take effect immediately after issuing the ALTER BUFFERPOOL command. The buffer pool must be deallocated and reallocated for the parameter to take effect.

16. The number of sequential, dynamic and list prefetch I/O that are used to read pages into BP4 can be determined by specifying BUFFERPOOL(BP4) and the DETAIL parameter on the DISPLAY command.

FIGURES

Creating Tablespaces

TS.1 INTRODUCTION

We begin this chapter with a description of the three types of tablespaces. Information is provided upon which to base your decision as to which type of tablespace is best for your data. Many parameters are used to instruct DB2 on how to manage the objects. These parameters are analyzed in detail to assist you in deciding the best design of your tablespaces. The many pros and cons of the parameters are discussed along with real world experiences and test results to give you a basis for your design. Do explicitly specify all of the parameters when creating a tablespace. Otherwise, default values which may not be appropriate for your application system will be used. The goal is to design tablespaces that can effectively and efficiently store the data for your application system. The design provides a basis for ease of access and manipulation of the data by online transactions, batch programs, and utilities. The result is high performance with minimal use of I/O, CPU, and elapsed time.

Three Types of Tablespaces

All types of tablespaces resides in a page set of one or more VSAM data sets. The page size can be 4, 8, 16 or 32 KB, depending on your buffer pool choice as discussed in Chapter CD.4. Most often the 4 KB page size is used. The data page format is the same for all types of tablespaces.

A segmented tablespace can house one or more tables (no limit). The tablespace is divided into segments of from 4 to 64 pages, and each segment is dedicated to a table. A table can occupy multiple segments.

A simple tablespace can house one or more tables (no limit) like a segmented tablespaces. Rows from multiple tables can be interleaved on a page under the developer's control and maintenance.

A partitioned tablespace can house one table. The tablespace is divided into parts. Each part is housed in a separate VSAM data set.

The term *nonsegmented* tablespace refers to simple and partitioned tablespaces.

TS.2 SEGMENTED AND SIMPLE TABLESPACES

A segmented tablespace is divided into segments as the name suggests. A segment can consist of 4, 8, 16, 32, or 64 pages. You determine the segment size by specifying one of these values with the parameter SEGSIZE. The segment size applies to all of the tables in a tablespace. Each segment is dedicated to a table. The LOAD and REORG (reorganization) utilities leave segments of a table in contiguous space on DASD.

Segment sizes of 32 and 64 pages have advantages, assuming that most tables in the tablespace require 32 or more pages. The benefits of prefetch are maximized. The prefetch quantity is 32 pages, assuming a buffer pool of 1000 pages or more. A smaller segment size can result in reading pages for another table when there are multiple tables in a tablespace. SEGSIZE of 32 or 64 minimizes the number of space map pages as discussed in Section TS.9. Both values result in about 5,000 data pages following a space map page. SEGSIZE 32 results in 4,800 data pages following each space map page and SEGSIZE 64 has 5,504 data pages following each space map page. The resources required to search for free space are minimized when using a SEGSIZE of 32 or 64. There is an increased likelihood that the space map pages will remain in the buffer pool with the larger SEGSIZE values.

SEGSIZE 32 results in fewer pages being reserved for the 16 page compression and decompression dictionary as discussed in Section TS.8 than does SEGSIZE 64. This fact can serve as the tie breaker for using a SEGSIZE OF 32 rather than 64 when using compression. If you need to avoid wasting 16 pages of a 32 page segment used for the dictionary, consider SEGSIZE 16.

Small tables should be placed in tablespaces with a small segment size. If you plan to place no more than one table in a tablespace, the SEGSIZE should match the table size. If you plan to place multiple small tables in a tablespace, consider using the average table size in pages as the SEGSIZE.

Advantages of Segmented Tablespaces

A primary advantage of a segmented tablespace over a nonsegmented tablespace is that more detailed information is available on the space map page for the location of free space to maintain clustering and variable length rows as detailed in Section TS.9. A tablespace scan of a segmented tablespace scans only the segments of the table being processed. This is in contrast to scanning the entire tablespace of a simple tablespace even if only one of multiple tables in the tablespace needs to be processed. The space map pages are used to identify pages that contain active rows of the table being processed in a segmented tablespace. This also avoids scanning empty segments and segments containing only deleted data.

The optimizer has a better estimate of the number of pages that contain rows for a table. It uses SYSTABLES.NPAGES which has the number of pages that contain active rows of a table. This is in contrast to using what is usually a higher value in SYSTABLES.NACTIVE for simple tablespaces. NACTIVE contains the number of pages in a tablespace up to the high preformatted page. The COPY utility does not copy empty pages due to a dropped table or the use of the mass delete algorithm when making a full image copy. It uses the space map pages to identify pages that contain active rows. The mass delete algorithm is an efficient method for deleting all of the rows in a table, particularly when there are multiple tables in the tablespace. The details on the use of the algorithm are covered in Chapter BP.

Advantages of Multiple Tables in a Tablespace

If you plan to place multiple tables in a tablespace, it should be a segmented tablespace. We will look first at the advantages of multiple tables in a tablespace followed by the pros and cons of using a segmented or simple tablespace to house them.

Related small to medium sized tables can be placed together in a nonpartitioned tablespace. One reason for doing this is that most utilities operate at the tablespace or partition level. Therefore, fewer utilities need to be prepared and executed. This may appear to be a trivial point until you think about the number of tables in your application system and the number of utilities that must be prepared, tested, and executed on a routine basis. An experience at one company will be used to illustrate the point. The developers chose to place one table per tablespace. They had about 300 tables in the application system. They developed and tested 300 RUNSTATS, REORG, COPY, and RECOVER utilities. This is a total of 1200 utility jobs (300 tablespaces * 4 utilities) plus the LOAD utility and a few CHECK DATA, CHECK INDEX, REPAIR, and other utilities. Operations refused to accept the routine scheduling of so many utility jobs. The developers had to go back to the drawing board and combine related tables into fewer tablespaces.

A primary reason for considering multiple tables in a tablespace is to ease the management of referential integrity structures with respect to the utilities. Indeed, one of the reasons for the DB2 developers inventing segmented tablespaces is for the efficient management of multiple tables in a tablespace as detailed in the next section. It is particularly important for synchronizing related tables when copying and recovering them as discussed in Chapter CR. If referential integrity is defined to DB2 and all related tablespaces are not recovered to together, they are placed in a check pending status. Check pending must be turned off before you can select and update the related tables.

Fewer VSAM data sets for fewer tablespaces need to be open at any one time. This is particularly important when there are many tablespaces and indexes in many applications system on a DB2 subsystem. Limits on the number of open data sets are discussed in Section TS.6. Deferred write allows many users to update pages for multiple tables and write the updated pages to the tablespace in 32 page chunks as discussed in Chapter CO.

Placing multiple very small reference tables in a single tablespace is a good choice. This avoids a minimum allocation of two tracks for each table and management of a header and space map page for each table.

Multiple Tables in a Simple Versus Segmented Tablespace

There are a number of reasons why if you decide to have multiple tables in a tablespace, it should be a segmented tablespace. These reasons also point out a number of advantages of segmented tablespaces. As already mentioned, a tablespace scan of a simple tablespace is over all pages in a tablespace regardless of whether a page contains a row from the table being processed. For example, scanning the S table requires scanning tables S, P, J, and SPJ if they are in the same tablespace. In addition, empty pages due to deleted rows are processed in a simple tablespace scan. In contrast, a tablespace scan is over only non-empty pages which contain rows of the accessed table when using a segmented tablespace. It is basically a table scan.

An implicit or explicit LOCK TABLE statement locks all tables in a simple tablespace. In contrast, it locks only the referenced table in a segmented tablespace.

The reorganization utility does not recluster data if there is more than one table in a simple tablespace. In contrast, a reorganization reclusters the data for each table regardless of the number of tables in a segmented tablespace.

Reorganization is required to reuse space occupied by a dropped table in a simple tablespace. In contrast, a reorganization is not required to reuse space occupied by dropped tables in a segmented tablespace. This makes segmented tablespaces a particularly good choice for QMF users who frequently create and drop tables explicitly or implicitly. Deleted row space is immediately reusable for all types of tablespaces without a reorganization.

Recommendation: Clearly, segmented tablespaces have significant advantages over nonsegmented tablespaces for multiple tables.

Disadvantages of Multiple Tables in a Tablespace

Although it is clear that, if you want multiple tables in a tablespace, it should be a segmented tablespace, the next question to be addressed is whether one or multiple tables should be placed in a tablespace. The following issues apply to segmented and simple tablespaces.

As mentioned earlier, most utilities operate at the tablespace or partition level including the REORG, RUNSTATS, COPY and RECOVER utilities. However, you may need different scheduling for each table. In addition, you may need to recover only one table which is not possible with multiple tables in a tablespace.

Reallocation of space is at the tablespace level. However, you may need to reallocate space for a specific table without reorganizing multiple tables.

Different tables may need different tablespace parameter values, PCTFREE, FREEPAGE, SEGSIZE, LOCKSIZE, LOCKMAX, MAXROWS etc. as discussed throughout this chapter.

The compression dictionary for one table may not be the best for another table. The compression dictionary is discussed in Section TS.8.

If a load replace is done of a table, all tables in a tablespace are lost. This is because load replace uses the VSAM REUSE parameter which resets the entire tablespace to empty. An alternative is to use the mass delete algorithm followed by load resume or insertion of rows in a segmented tablespace

Utilities operate at the tablespace or partition level and the pending states apply at these levels, not at the table level. This can result in limited availability if there is more than one table in the tablespace. All tables are unavailable even though only one table needs to be operated on by a utility or caused a pending state to be turned on.

Recommendation: Do not mix frequently and infrequently updated tables in a tablespace. Most of the issues discussed have to do with update activity on a table.

Most companies place one table in one tablespace except for small reference tables. Multiple small reference tables are typically placed in one tablespace.

Simple Tablespaces

There are few advantages of simple tablespaces over segmented tablespace even if you decide to have one table per tablespace. A simple tablespace does have fewer space map pages to be read and updated compared to a segmented tablespace as discussed in Section TS.9. However, there are few space map pages for both types of tablespace. A simple tablespace has a space map page every 10,760 data pages compared to every 4,800 pages using SEGSIZE 32 and to even 5,504 pages using SEGSIZE 64. A simple tablespace does not have segments; therefore, there is no need to be concerned that segments of a table can become dispersed and fragmented. In addition, you can avoid inserting rows in clustering sequence as discussed in Section TS.7.

A potential advantage of a simple tablespace compared to a segmented tablespace is that rows from multiple tables can be interleaved on a page. For example, a parent row describing a job can be followed by multiple dependent rows from the SPJ table. This would result in fewer I/O when information is needed on both jobs and parts used on the job. However, more I/O are required when processing only the parent or dependent rows. The reason that interleaving of rows is little more than a potential advantage is that DB2 does not support the interleaving. For example, inserted rows are not necessarily interleaved. The reorganization utility does not interleave rows.

If you decide to interleave rows from multiple tables on a single page, you must do a good deal of planning and work. For example, it is necessary to interleave rows on a sequential file before loading multiple tables from a single sequential file. This can be done by sorting on the primary key (PK) and foreign key (FK). (The PK and FK are discussed in Chapter CT.) Creation of the clustering index on the PK and FK encourages maintenance of clustering for inserts. Insertion of PK rows followed by the corresponding FK rows encourages maintenance of the interleaved rows but does not guarantee it. When doing a reorganization, it is necessary to pause the utility after the unload, sort on the PK and FK, and restart the utility using the PHASE parameter. A good deal of manual intervention is required for interleaving of rows and is seldom used.

You may find that there are a number of simple tablespaces at your company. This situation frequently exists because the tablespaces were created in the early days of DB2 before segmented tablespaces were supported. There is no option for altering from a simple to segmented tablespace. It is necessary to unload the data, drop the tablespace, create the tablespace, table, and indexes, load the data, grant privileges, execute RUNSTATS, and rebind plans and packages (or accept an automatic rebind). Many companies do not want to take the time and resources to do this unless there are great benefits from doing so. A justification for converting from simple to segmented tablespaces is if reorganizations are more frequent than desired; the frequency can be reduced by using segmented tablespaces where free space is managed more efficiently as discussed in Section TS.9.

TS.3 ANALYSIS OF TABLESPACE PARAMETERS

The parameters that can be specified when creating a tablespace are included in the following example of creating the PTSP tablespace in the DASPJDB database.

```
CREATE TABLESPACE PTSP
  IN DASPJDB
  USING STOGROUP DASPJSTG
    PRIQTY 7200
    SECQTY  720
    ERASE NO
  BUFFERPOOL BP0
  SEGSIZE  32
  PCTFREE  10
  FREEPAGE 31
```

```
LOCKSIZE PAGE
  LOCKMAX 0
MAXROWS 255
CLOSE NO
DEFINE YES
COMPRESS NO
TRACKMOD YES;
```

Creation and usage of storage groups, databases, and buffer pools, and global buffer pools are described in Chapter CD. The database to house the tablespace is named using the IN clause of the CREATE TABLESPACE statement. The USING STOGROUP clause indicates the storage group to be used for space allocation of the tablespace. The name of the storage group to contain the tablespace need not be the same as that specified when creating the database to contain the tablespace. If you prefer to use a user-defined data set to house the tablespace, you must first create the VSAM data set. You then specify the high level qualifier of the data set in the USING VCAT clause rather than using the USING STOGROUP clause. The buffer pool to be used for processing the data pages is specified using the BUFFERPOOL parameter. If this parameter is not specified, the buffer pool specified when the database was created is used. BP0 is used if a buffer pool was not specified when creating the database.

All parameters specified in the CREATE TABLESPACE statement can be changed with the ALTER statement except for placement of the tablespace in a database, the segment size, and the number of partitions. In order to change these parameters it is necessary to unload the data and drop the tablespace, which also drops all dependents of the tablespace as discussed in Chapter CT.8.

Here is an example of altering all parameters that can be changed with the ALTER statement.

```
ALTER TABLESPACE DASPJDB.PTSP
  USING STOGROUP DATOMSTG
    PRIQTY 14400
    SECQTY   720
  ERASE YES
  PCTFREE 15
  FREEPAGE 7
  MAXROWS 255
  LOCKSIZE ROW
    LOCKMAX 10001
  CLOSE YES
  BUFFERPOOL BP1
  COMPRESS NO
  TRACKMOD NO;
```

You can alter from USING VCAT to USING STOGROUP or the opposite. It is necessary to stop the tablespace to ensure no access to the data can occur during this type of alter. Then start the tablespace after the alter has executed successfully.

You can ALTER CCSID identifier to include/exclude the Euro symbol for newly created objects as discussed in Chapter CD. This is also true for existing tablespaces. However, there are a number of steps that must be followed as described in the *SQL Reference* manual.

Primary and Secondary Space Allocation

The primary and secondary quantities are specified using the PRIQTY and SECQTY parameters. The required space is requested 1 K byte units. DB2 automatically converts the space allocation to cylinders or tracks. For example, there are 720 KB on a cylinder and 48 KB bytes on a track of a 3390 DASD volume and 600 KB on a cylinder and 40 KB on a track of a 3380 volume. Both the PRIQTY and SECQTY should be in multiples of cylinders if more than one cylinder is required. If the PRIQTY or SECQTY is less than one cylinder, track allocation is used.

Do use DB2 Estimator to accurately estimate the PRIQTY and allow for growth. Avoid data sets going into secondary allocations because seek time is increased if a data set is spread across DASD in multiple extents. You have heard the saying that on a clear day you can see forever; well, on a cluttered disk you can seek forever. Some DASD devices lessen the importance of multiple extents. However, there is still an overhead in managing multiple extents for most devices.

It is not necessary to stop and start the tablespace and indexes to alter PRIQTY and SECQTY in V5 with APAR PQ04053. The new space allocation can be used immediately because DB2 uses space as reflected in the catalog tables. However, LISTCAT will not show the new allocation until after REORG, LOAD REPLACE, RECOVER, or REBUILD INDEX.

Space Allocation: Data Facility Product (DFP) media manager allocates space for DB2. If insufficient contiguous space is available to satisfy the PRIQTY on a volume, space can be taken on up to and including 5 extents. If more than five extents are required, the data set is not allocated.

Secondary Space Allocation: If available space in the current extent is less than 10 percent of MIN(half of SECQTY, half of PRIQTY), secondary extension is done by media manager. If the SECQTY is not specified, the default is MAX(10 percent of PRIQTY, 3 times the page size).

The maximum number of extents on multiple volumes is 119 (on a single volume in V6). Four of the 123 VSAM extents are reserved by DB2. The maximum number of extents on multiple volumes is 251 with 4 of the 255 VSAM extents reserved by DB2 in V6.

Preformatting space: Two cylinders or tracks are preformatted at a time for tablespaces and indexes when the objects are created (also format header and space map pages), there is no space on candidate page and no space formatted at end of data set for an INSERT statement or UPDATE of a row such that it is too long to fit on the original page. Preformatting consists of writing X'00' on the pages. This can be resource intensive for a program inserting a large number of rows or updating variable length rows such that they no longer fit on the page. It requires more resources when the program inserts or updates a row that requires the preformatting of two cylinders or tracks. This preformatting of space during an application program execution can be minimized by having the LOAD and REORG utilities preformat the space by using the PREFORMAT parameter as discussed in Chapters LC and RR.

LISTCAT shows the preformatted space as the high used RBA and the allocated space as the high allocated RBA. It does not show the altered space until after a reorganization, load replace, or recover. These utilities delete and define the VSAM data sets.

Tablespace Size: The tablespace size is limited by the RID size in the indexes. Four byte RIDs are used for tablespaces less than or equal to 64 GB. The first 3 bytes (24 bits) of a 4 byte RID are used to reference a data page. These 24 bits give the limit of 64 GB for the tablespace, calculated as 2^{24} = 16 MB * 4 KB page for nonpartitioned tablespaces.

A partitioned tablespace can be up to and including 16 terabytes (TB) (V6). Section TS.7 discusses how to define a tablespace greater than 64 GB. All indexes on these very large tablespaces have 5 byte RIDs. The first 4 bytes (32 bits) of the 5 byte RID are used to reference a data page. The limit of 16 TB for is based on 2^{32} = 4 GB * 4 KB page. The limit in V5 is 1 TB.

ERASE Parameter

The ERASE parameter determines the action to take when a tablespace is dropped. The alter of this parameter requires that the tablespace or index be stopped.

ERASE YES provides added security by filling the data set with zeros when the tablespace is dropped.

ERASE NO means that the tables in a tablespace are not accessible using SQL statement after the tablespace is dropped. However, theoretically someone can dump the DASD device and still see the data before another data set is written over the space. ERASE NO has performance advantages when dropping a tablespace. This is the default.

TS.4 FREE SPACE FOR UPDATING AND INSERTING ROWS

Free space should be specified for tablespace and indexes that have random insert, update, and delete activity. Free space in the tablespace is important for maintaining rows in sequence according to the clustering index and to manage variable length rows. Free space in the index pages minimizes page splitting as discussed in Chapter ID. The amount of free space can be specified using the PCTFREE and FREEPAGE parameters.

The PCTFREE parameter provides for specifying the amount of space to be left free at the bottom of each table and index space page by the LOAD, REORG, RECOVER INDEX, and REBUILD INDEX utilities. The defaults of 5 percent for tablespace pages and 10 percent for index space pages are used unless you specify a value based on the row length in your table as discussed this section.

The FREEPAGE parameter provides for specifying how often an empty page should be interspersed in the tablespace and index space. The default is 0 blank pages with a maximum of 255. Empty pages are brought into the buffer pool when pages are read with sequential and dynamic prefetch. Do specify an appropriate number for your tablespace as discussed in this section.

The LOAD, REORG, RECOVER INDEX, and REBUILD INDEX utilities and build of a newly created index leaves the specified free space as indicated in Figure TS.1.

Figure TS.1. Free space within pages and between pages

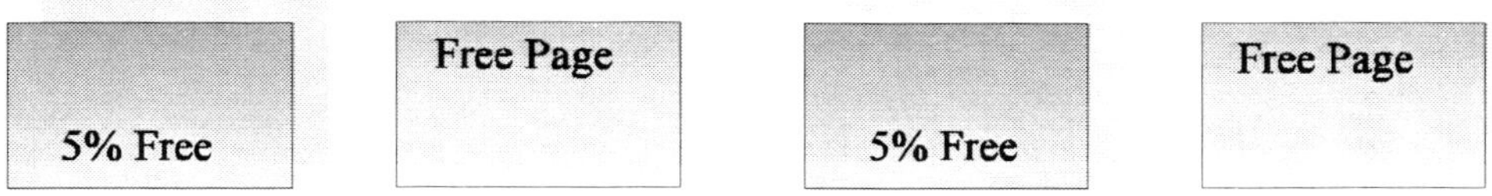

Search for Free Space

It is important to understand how DB2 searches for free space in segmented and non-segmented tablespaces in order to decide the values to specify for the PCTFREE and FREESPACE parameters. DB2 maintains rows in sequence according to the clustering index as discussed in Chapter ID. The target page for the row is the page with rows having a higher and/or lower value. This is the first choice for INSERTING the row. If there is no free space on the target page to insert the row to maintain the rows in sequence, the space map page, as discussed in Section TS.9, is analyzed to determine if there is any free space within the target segment.

SEGSIZE 32 is used in the CREATE TABLESPACE statement at the beginning of Section TS.3. For this tablespace, the second choice is to insert the row within the 32 page segment based on free space information in the space map page control block for the target segment. If the row is inserted within the target segment, it is considered a near page.

The third choice is to insert the row within the range of pages covered by the space map page. Availability of space is determined by analyzing the remaining control blocks in the space map page to determine if there is sufficient free space to insert the row. If the row can be inserted using this search or the following searches, it is considered a far page.

The fourth choice is to scan the space map pages from the current segment to the end of the tablespace for any available space to determine if the row can be inserted with a maximum of 3 pages being accessed with no free space.

The fifth choice is to allocate a new segment at end of tablespace. If no more extents can be allocated, the sixth choice is to scan the space map pages from the beginning of the tablespace in an attempt to reuse space previously occupied by deleted rows at the beginning of the tablespace. If still no free space can be found, a -904 SQLCODE indicating resource unavailable is issued.

The search for free space in a nonsegmented tablespace uses a similar algorithm except the initial search is forward and backward 16 pages within the space map page (less than or equal 3 pages are read). An exception is when using MEMBER CLUSTER parameters as discussed in Section TS.7. Space obtained from the deletion of all rows in a table using the mass delete algorithm and dropping a table is not reusable until after a reorganization.

Free pages used as near pages: FREEPAGE provides for INSERTING a row near the candidate page when the candidate page is full as indicated in Figure TS.2. FREEPAGE 31 provides for a near page within a segment when using a segmented tablespace with a SEGSIZE of 32 pages. FREEPAGE 15 provides for a near page when using a nonsegmented tablespace.

Figure TS.2. Near and far pages

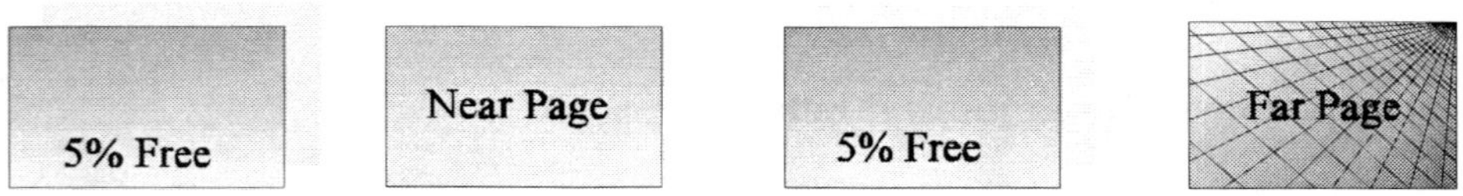

Use of Free Space to Maintain Variable Length Rows

DB2 maintains variable length rows for compressed rows, rows with VARCHAR columns, and when EDITPROC and FIELDPROC are used as discussed in Chapter CT. Also, variable length rows are maintained after a column has been added to a table with the ALTER statement and before a reorganization. Variable length rows can be increased in length with an update. DB2 cannot place a row that is expanded in length in exactly the same position (assuming that there is no free space following the row). LOAD and REORG pack the rows on a page and leave the specified amount of space at the bottom of the page.

If there is insufficient free space on the page to expand a row in length, DB2 will gather all available free space in an attempt to keep the row on its original page. If it cannot get enough free space, it will use its free space search algorithm to locate a near or far page to place the row and leave a pointer in the original location pointing to the new location. If the row is increased in length again in the future with insufficient space on the page, the row is moved again and the first pointer changed to point to the new location. This avoids a chain of pointers that must be followed to locate a moved row. Perhaps of even more significance for improved performance is that the use of a pointer avoids having to update each index referencing the table to point to the new location of the row.

Prefetch I/O time can be adversely affected by moved rows. If there is a pointer to a moved row within the 32 pages prefetched, a synchronous I/O is issued to locate the moved row. The prefetch I/O does not continue until the I/O for the moved row is completed. Although this may sound like a trivial point, one company found that the average time to read a page was 50 ms after many rows had been moved. This is in contrast to an average I/O time of 1.7 ms per page after a reorganization which eliminates pointers to moved rows. Obviously, your results will be different. However, the reason for giving company experiences and test results is to provide an order of magnitude difference for your decision making process. In this case, it is an issue of whether variable length rows should be used when the rows are frequently increased in length and insufficient free space has been specified assuming random update activity.

Estimating Free Space for Variable Length Rows

If you have a good deal of update activity that increases variable length rows in length and the update activity is random throughout the tablespace, 10 percent free space is a reasonable starting point. If the update activity is concentrated in only some areas of the tablespace, the free space is of limited value. The free space is left in every page throughout the tablespace but is not used except in the areas where the update activity occurs.

The initial free space that you specify can be adjusted based on the NEARINDREF and FARINDREF columns in SYSTABLEPART. NEARINDREF is the number of rows that have been moved from their original position due to an increase in row length and insufficient free space on the page. FARINDREF is the number of rows that have been moved to a far off position. The distinction between near and far pages is discussed earlier in this section. The RUNSTATS utility must have been executed recently for these statistics to accurately reflect the current condition of the tablespace. If (NEARINDREF+FARINDREF)*100/CARDF > 5, consider increasing the PCTFREE and reorganizing the tablespace to eliminate the pointers to moved rows and provide more free space for future update activity. Another indication that more free space is needed is if the CLUSTERRATIOF in SYSINDEXES falls below 80 percent too quickly after a reorganization.

When you alter a table and add an additional column, do consider a reorganization, depending on the amount of free space that you have on the pages, the length of the added column, and how many rows will be given new values for the newly added column before the next scheduled reorganization. If you believe that free space must be gathered on many pages and that it will be necessary to search for free space often, it is best to do a reorganization so that DB2 can expand all the rows and space on each row to provide for the newly added column.

If you have a good deal of insert activity and are compressing the rows, determine the average row length using DSN1COMP, REORG, or LOAD. Estimate the free space such that one or more additional compressed rows fit on a page on average and allow more free space for expanding rows with updates. There is a 50 percent chance that updating a compressed row will increase it in length.

An alternative for compressed data with high insert activity is to specify PCTFREE 0 and apply the PN57245 APAR. This APAR causes the LOAD utility to mark the pages as full. Compressed and fixed length rows are then inserted at the end of the tablespace. This avoids getpages, synchronous I/O, and lock requests to search for free space to insert rows.

Free Space to Maintain Clustering

Free space should be a multiple of the record length for fixed length rows or the average length for variable length rows. This is particularly important to maintain the rows in clustering sequence. Here is an example of estimating the required free space to insert one row on a page assuming a 100 byte row.

```
0.03 = ceiling ((100 byte row length + 6 byte row prefix + 2
byte page directory entry) / 4074)
```

Three percent free allows one row to be inserted on a page before DB2 must use its search algorithm to locate free space. If you expect that typically multiple rows will be inserted on a large percentage of the pages at random, multiply the 3 percent by an estimate of the number of rows to be inserted per page between reorganizations.

If the table has been created, the calculation can be done based on statistics in the catalog tables like:

```
SELECT TB.NAME,TB.COLCOUNT, TB.CARDF, TB.NPAGES, TB.RECLENGTH,
  INTEGER((((TB.RECLENGTH+2.0)/4074.0)*100.0)+0.9),
  TSP.FREEPAGE, TSP.PCTFREE
FROM SYSIBM.SYSTABLES TB,
SYSIBM.SYSTABLEPART TSP
WHERE TB.CREATOR = 'Authid'
AND   TB.TYPE    = 'T'
AND   TB.TSNAME  = TSP.TSNAME
ORDER BY TB.NAME;
```

Add a multiplier to the end of the arithmetic expression with the number of rows expected to be inserted on a page.

Recommendation: Consider checking existing tablespaces to determine if they have an appropriate amount of free space specified. If not, ALTER them to have a percent free that will allow one or more rows to be inserted on a page.

Estimate Free Space Needed between Reorganizations

The reorganization frequency has a significant impact on the amount of free space needed. The REORG utility reallocates the free space specified on the CREATE and ALTER statements. You can base the estimate of free space on the expected percentage or number of rows to be inserted less rows to be deleted over some period of time for which reorganizations are being considered, weekly for example, assuming random insert and delete activity throughout the tablespace.

Estimate based on percentages: If 10 percent of the total number of rows are randomly inserted and 5 percent are deleted on a weekly basis and weekly reorganizations are planned, do calculate free space to allow for 5 percent additional rows. The percentage of rows deleted is subtracted from the percentage of rows to be inserted because deleted row space is immediately reusable. Five percent times 40 rows is 2 rows, assuming a row length of 100 bytes with 40 rows per page. We use the earlier example where 3 percent free space is required to insert 1 row on a page. The 3 percent is multiplied by 2 which is the estimated number of rows to be inserted minus the number of rows to be deleted after applying the percentages to the maximum number of rows that fit on a page. This results in PCTFREE 6 needed to allow for the insertion, deletion, and reorganization estimates.

Estimate based on number of rows: You can base the estimate of free space on the number of rows and pages rather than percentages. Estimate the number of rows to be inserted on a weekly basis less the number of rows to be deleted. Also estimate the number of data pages. If representative data has been loaded and RUNSTATS executed, SYSTABLES.NPAGES contains the number of data pages. Divide the estimated number of rows to be inserted after subtracting the number of rows to be deleted (60,000, for example) by the number of pages (30,000, for example). Estimate the average number of rows to be inserted on a page as the number of additional rows to be inserted divided by the number of pages, which gives 2 rows in the example (60,000 rows / 30,000 pages). Multiply the average number of rows to be inserted on a page by the calculated percent free that allows for 1 row. The result is again 6 percent (3 percent free for 1 row * 2 rows).

Avoid Too Much Free Space

Certainly the appropriate use of free space is important. However, there are some tablespaces that do not benefit from free space. Indeed, PCTFREE 0 should be specified on the tablespaces and indexes to avoid using the default free space if the parameter is not specified at all. The use of free space wastes DASD space and more I/O is required to select the same number of rows if a page is only partially filled with rows because of the unnecessary use of free space. This is particularly significant for batch programs that process many rows.

If a tablespace is read-only or has very low insert and update activity, no free space is needed. If rows are always inserted and deleted at the end of the table, only the free space on the last page is used and the free space on all the other pages is wasted. Indeed, this applies to a situation where rows are typically inserted, updated, and deleted in only a few specific areas of the tablespace. Free space is best utilized where the insert, update, and delete activity is close to random.

A skewed distribution of insert/delete activity can result in free space in some pages rarely being used. A work around is to load sections with no insert/delete activity with no percent free. Specify a percent free with alter and load resume sections with high insert/delete activity. Index page splitting is another issue to deal with and is discussed in Chapter ID.

Different partitions frequently have different update activity. If this is true for your partitioned tablespaces, do customize the free space by partition. Of course, partitions that contain historical data should have 0 percent free.

TS.5 PARAMETERS THAT CONTROL LOCKING

The values specified for the LOCKSIZE and LOCKMAX parameters are the first steps in controlling locks taken by DB2. MAXROWS also influences the amount of data that is locked. These parameters are discussed in this section. A detailed description of locks and latches is given in Chapter CC.

Locksize for a Tablespace

The LOCKSIZE parameter is used to indicate the granularity of locking, which can be the row, page, table, or tablespace level.

LOCKSIZE ROW gives the maximum concurrency but can be resource intensive, particularly in a sysplex data sharing environment.

LOCKSIZE PAGE is a good choice in most cases. Escalation to a larger granularity of lock occurs only if repeatable read is used, LOCKMAX 0, and the optimizer chooses a tablespace or non-matching index scan. If these conditions are encountered, a warning is issued at bind time with a +806 SQLCODE, indicating that escalation will occur at run time.

LOCKSIZE ANY usually results in a page lock and is the default. Escalation to a larger granularity of lock occurs if NUMLKTS or LOCKMAX is exceeded as discussed in the next two sections.

LOCKSIZE TABLE can be used for segmented tablespaces.

LOCKSIZE TABLESPACE reduces CPU time (about 5-15 percent over page locks) and virtual storage usage. It is an excellent choice for read-only tables and tables used by only one user in an ad hoc environment, for example. If page or row locking is needed for online transactions but others do not need access to the data during batch processing during the evenings or weekends, a LOCK TABLE statement can be issued in the batch program as discussed in Chapter BP.

Changing the Lock Size: The lock size can be changed with the ALTER statement. Execution of the statement causes a quiesce of the tablespace and an X lock is taken to ensure that no one is processing the data during the change. It is advisable to execute the ALTER statement during low activity on the tablespace to avoid a timeout. The new LOCKSIZE takes effect immediately after the ALTER is successful. It is not necessary to rebind plans and packages to use the new lock size. You may want to do a rebind if you are changing between a page and row lock size. Additional CPU time is estimated for row locking compared to page locking and can result in a different access path being chosen by DB2.

Maximum Number of Locks

The numbers of row and page locks any one thread can hold on one table or tablespace are limited including locks taken for referential integrity enforcement. This limit can be set using the LOCKMAX parameter, the NUMLKTS parameter in DSNZPARM, and on the installation panel DSNTIPJ. If the limit is exceeded, the row and page locks are released and the lock is escalated to a share (S) or exclusive (X) lock based on the intent to share (IS) or intent exclusive (IX) held on the table or tablespace. If LOCKPART YES is specified on the CREATE TABLESPACE statement (not the default), only accessed partitions are locked.

No INSERT, UPDATE, and DELETE statements can be issued on the tablespace if the escalation is to an S lock. SELECT statements are denied if the escalation is to an X lock. Sporadic lock contention is usually the symptom of the problem. The cause of the lock escalation is difficult to determine. Unfortunately, no positive or negative SQLCODE is issued to allow for a commit or rollback to release the locks. The number of lock escalations that occurred can be determined from the statistics trace. It is necessary to use the performance trace to determine the programs that caused the escalation.

Control of Lock Limits and Escalation

If LOCKMAX of SYSTEM is specified when the tablespace is created, the NUMLKTS in DSNZPARM is used, which has a default that a maximum of 1000 locks on the tablespace can be taken before escalation. NUMLKTS can be set to zero to disallow escalations. LOCKMAX can be specified for the lock size of row, page, and any when the tablespace is created along with a value from 0 to 2,147,483,647. Zero means no escalation will occur which is the default when using lock size of page. If LOCKSIZE of ANY is specified and LOCKMAX is not specified, the NUMLKTS value is used. LOCKMAX of SYSTEM is the default when using LOCKSIZE of ANY.

Recommendation: NUMLKTS and LOCKMAX of 0 are a good choice in most cases. These parameter values avoid the difficulty of determining what escalations have occurred because escalation cannot occur.

Lock Limit per Thread

There is a second limit that applies to the maximum number of locks that can be held on any number of objects by one thread. This limit can be specified in NUMLKUS of DSNZPARM. The installation panel DSNTIPJ can be used to specify both the NUMLKTS and NUMLKUS limits.

The NUMLKUS lock limit is 10,000 by default. If the limit is exceeded, a -904 SQLCODE is issued and the cursor is automatically closed. If a fetch or close cursor is attempted, a -501 SQLCODE indicates that the cursor is not open for a fetch or close and -507 indicates the same for an update or delete.

The purpose of NUMLKUS is to avoid taking more locks than can be held by the internal resource lock manager (IRLM) based on the space given to the lock manager.

Recommendation: Do not specify a limit of 0 for NUMLKUS because it means that there is no limit. If the IRLM space is filled and a lock request is issued, the IRLM abends, and can cause DB2 to abend as well.

Maximum Number of Rows on a Page

You can specify a value between 1 and 255 to indicate the maximum number of rows on a data page. The maximum number of rows that can be placed on a page is a function of the fact that the last byte of a RID is used to reference a slot in the page directory. (The page directory is discussed in Section TS.9.) Of course, a byte consists of 8 bits. The maximum of 255 rows per data page is calculated as 2^8-1. If the MAXROWS parameter is not specified, the maximum number of rows on a page is 255 by default. This is a good choice if you have very short rows because rows are simply short or they are short due to the use of compression as discussed in Section TS.8.

MAXROWS 1 (or a small number) is a good choice in some cases. It avoids using free space to control the number of rows on a page when heavy random insert activity is expected and row locking is not advisable. This avoids an older technique where 99 percent free is specified to allow 1 row and 1 index value per data and index page. Dummy rows are loaded to match the number of expected pages that will be used. The dummy rows are hidden with a view that excludes a value written in the dummy rows.

MAXROWS 1 (or a small number) has advantages over row locking in a data sharing environment.

TS.6 LOGICAL AND PHYSICAL CLOSE OF DATA SETS

VSAM data sets for tablespaces, partitions, and indexes are opened when first accessed. It can be resource intensive when the required data sets are not open. In one case it required 14 seconds to open 25 tablespaces and 40 indexes. This can detract from performance during prime time. After starting and stopping DB2 or a database, consider opening data sets during non-prime time if it is a problem in your environment. This can be done by executing a program that inserts a row into a table in each tablespace and each partition that is frequently accessed and then issues a rollback.

CLOSE YES or CLOSE NO can be specified to indicate when the data set is to be closed. Close of yes is the default. The close parameter has very little effect unless DSMAX or the OS/390 limit of open data sets per address space is reached. An exception is that CLOSE YES allows for removal of inter-DB2 R/W interest and data sets are closed before reaching the limits when using sysplex data sharing.

The default maximum number of open data sets per DB2 subsystem is 2000. The limit can be changed in DSNZPARM DSN6SPRM DSMAX. The theoretical maximum number of open data sets is 32,767 with OS/390 V2.6 and V5 APAR PQ18543. The practical limit is determined by the space below the 16 MB line. There can be about 15,000 open data sets if OS/390 scheduler work area is below 16 MB line or about 20,000 open data sets if OS/390 Scheduler Work area is above 16 MB line. If either the DB2 or space below the 16 MB line is exceeded, -904 SQLCODE indicating resource unavailable is issued.

Switch to Read-Only Status

If a tablespace, index, or partition is not updated for 10 minutes or 5 checkpoints or QUIESCE is executed, the data set is switched to read-only processing (also known as a pseudo-close). The specified limits are the default and can be changed in DSNZPARM DSN6SYSP using the PCLOSET and PCLOSEN parameters. The switch to read-only status applies to objects created with CLOSE of YES and NO.

Switch to read-only status consists of a number of actions:

- Changed pages are written to DASD.
- Write RB-RBA (Recovery Based-RBA) to the HPGRBRBA field in the header page. It is used for logonly recovery without an image copy.
- Write RBA of last committed update to SYSLGRNX and close the log range entry. This allows for skipping log records up to the RBA when the data set is next updated to minimize recovery time.
- Information about a read-only data set is not written with a checkpoint. This saves resources at checkpoint time.

Logical Close of Data Sets

A counter is maintained for each data set indicating the number of users actively using the data set. The counter is decremented by one at commit or deallocation time, depending on the release parameter value specified at bind time and discussed in Chapter CC. If a data set no longer has users, that is the counter is zero and no locks are held, the data set is placed at end of a drain queue as indicated in Figure TS.3.

Figure TS.3. Drain queue

Data Set	Drain Queue	FIFO Close
A	Oldest with no active users	1st to close
B	Previous with no active users	2nd to close
C	Most recent with no active users	3rd to close

A logical open occurs when a data set is next referenced. A logical open means that the data set is removed from the logical close drain queue. It is not physically opened by DFP.

Physical Close of Data Sets

Thresholds are used to determine when a data set is physically closed. If 99 percent of DSMAX is reached (includes count of tablespaces created with close of yes and no), there is an asynchronous physical VSAM close of 3 percent of the data sets at the beginning of drain queue on a first-in-first-out (FIFO) basis. If the OS/390 limit is exceeded, the data sets are closed synchronously.

CLOSE YES data sets are closed first followed by CLOSE NO if 3 percent of the data sets have not been closed. CLOSE YES is a good choice for data sets processed infrequently. CLOSE NO is good for data sets processed frequently. It saves about 0.25 to 1.0 seconds of CPU time to open a data set depending on the processor used.

Data sets are physically closed when the database, tablespace, partition, index, or DB2 is stopped. The physical close of data sets is like switching to read-only processing in that changed pages are written to DASD, the RB-RBA is written to the header page, the RBA of last committed update is written to SYSLGRNX, and the log range is closed.

Limit the Number of Open Data Sets

The objective is to limit the number of data sets that are open at any one time to the number of data sets that are used more than a few times a day. There is no reason to keep data sets open if they are used only weekly or only a few times a day, for example. Working storage in database services address space is required for each open data set. About 1.8 KB is required for each open data set (300 bytes below the 16 MB line or 900 bytes above the 16 MB line, depending on the scheduler work area placement.) Although 1.8 KB is not much space, when multiplied by the maximum number of data sets that can be opened for an address space, the space requirement becomes up to 18 MB, which can be significant depending on the availability of central storage.

In addition, resources are required to physically close data sets when stopping databases, tablespaces, and the DB2 subsystem. In one case it required 30 minutes to close 10,000 data sets when the command -STOP DB2 MODE(QUIESCE) was issued. The DB2 developers improved processing so that it is not necessary to close data sets at shutdown, resulting in a 3.3X improvement with 1000 open data sets. However, it is still necessary to write updated pages in the buffer pool to DASD at shutdown. In addition, restart after an abend of DB2 requires that log records be processed for all open data sets.

Do size DSMAX carefully. It controls the number of open data sets and number of data sets to be closed when the 99 percent threshold is reached. Adjust the DSMAX value based on monitoring the number of open data sets at any one time on your DB2 subsystem.

Definition of VSAM Data Sets

The DEFINE YES (default) means that VSAM data sets are defined with an application tablespace or index is created. DEFINE NO means that VSAM data sets are not defined until rows are placed in the tablespace and referenced in indexes by the LOAD utility or INSERT statements. This is useful to avoid defining all data sets for a purchased application system where not all options are chosen and thus not all data sets are required. It can be useful if you are approaching the limit of open VSAM data sets. It applies only to STOGROUP defined data sets. A 100 SQLCODE is received from a SELECT statement if the data set has not been defined.

TS.7 PARTITIONED TABLESPACES AND INDEXES

A partitioned tablespace is divided into parts. Each part is in a separate VSAM data set. There must be a partitioning index to designate which rows go into which partitions. The partitioning index is itself partitioned into the same number of VSAM data sets as used for the tablespace partitions as shown in Figure TS.4.

Figure TS.4. Partitioned tablespace and index

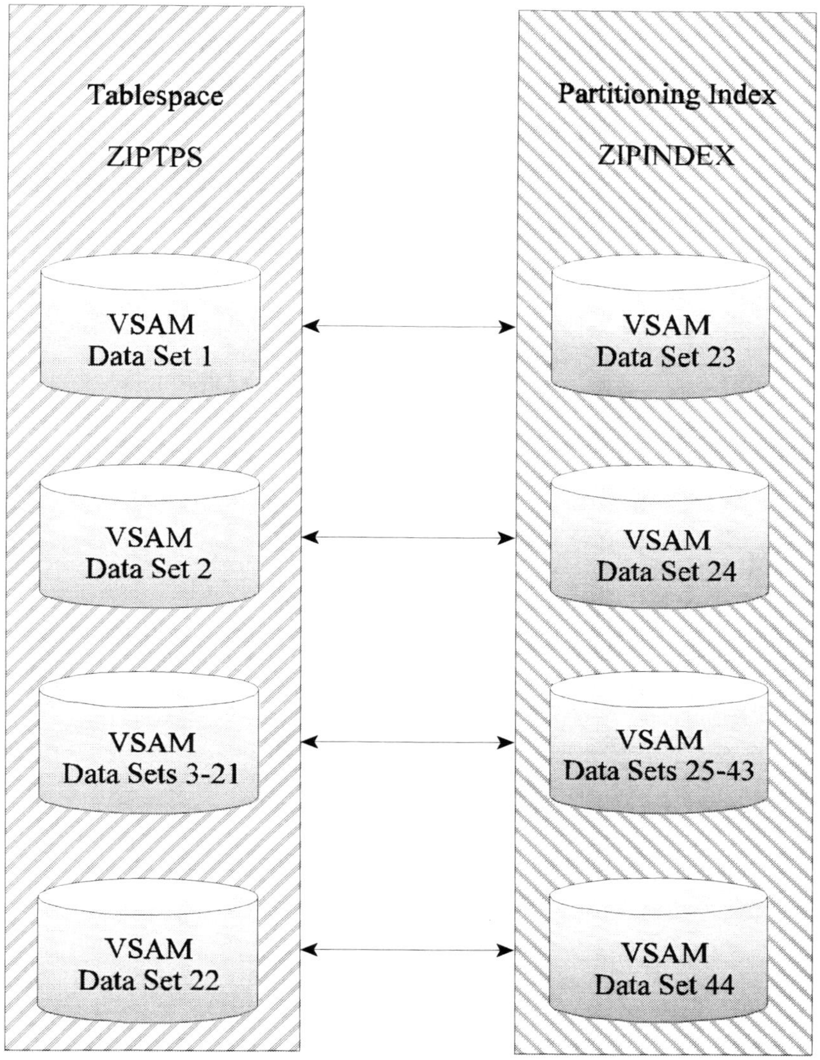

Create a Partitioned Tablespace

All of the tablespace parameters described in this chapter apply to a partitioned tablespace. The parameters describing space requirements, free space, and compression can be specified differently for individual partitions. The NUMPARTS, PART, and LOCKPART parameters apply only to partitioned tablespaces.

The following CREATE TABLESPACE statement creates a partitioned tablespace with 22 partitions as indicated in the NUMPARTS parameter. The storage group and amount of space required for all partitions can be specified. You can name one or more partitions and specify a different storage group and space allocation for each of them. In the following example, the DAZ00STG group and the indicated space allocation will be used for all partitions except those explicitly named in parentheses with the PART parameter. In most cases each actively used partition should be placed on a different DASD device on multiple channels and control units to maximize parallel I/O and DB2 parallelism. In the example, PART 1 uses the DAZ01STG storage group with a different space allocation, free space, and compression. (Data compression is discussed in the next section.) PART 2 uses the

DAZ02STG storage group, the same space allocation as PART 1, different free space, and does not use compression.

```
CREATE TABLESPACE ZIPTSP
   IN DAZIPDB
   USING STOGROUP DAZ00STG
     PRIQTY 7200
     SECQTY    0
     ERASE NO
   PCTFREE   0
   FREEPAGE  0
   NUMPARTS 22
   (PART 1 USING STOGROUP DAZ01STG
             PRIQTY 14400
             SECQTY   720
             ERASE NO
           PCTFREE 20
           FREEPAGE 7
           COMPRESS YES,
    PART 2 USING STOGROUP DAZ02STG
             PRIQTY 14400
             SECQTY   720
             ERASE NO
           PCTFREE 15
           FREEPAGE 7)
   MEMBER CLUSTER
   LOCKSIZE PAGE
     LOCKMAX 0
   LOCKPART YES
   BUFFERPOOL BP0
   CLOSE NO;
```

The LOCKSIZE, LOCKMAX, BUFFERPOOL, and CLOSE parameters apply to all parts of a partitioned tablespace and were discussed in the earlier sections of this chapter. The LOCKPART parameter applies only to partitioned tablespaces.

MEMBER CLUSTER is an optional parameter for partitioned and simple tablespaces (V5 APAR PQ02897). The purpose of this parameter is to minimizes contention (particularly p-locks) and overhead when INSERTING rows in specific areas of a partition or simple tablespace (not a segmented tablespace at present) including at the end. (This is often referred to as hot spot inserts.) MEMBER CLUSTER causes rows not to be inserted in the data pages in sequence according to the explicitly created clustering index nor the implicit clustering index (usually the first index created) as is usually the case (discussed in Chapters IU and ID). Rather rows are inserted to avoid p-lock contention in a sysplex data sharing environment. Each data sharing member gets its own space page and attempts to insert rows within the range of pages covered by the space map page. Each space map page covers 199 data pages. This is in contrast to the usual case where 10,000 data pages are covered by a space map page for nonsegmented tablespaces. Also, insert processing does not wrap to the first space map page after processing the last space map page.

The duration for holding a page p-lock is extended when using MEMBER CLUSTER. This significantly reduces p-lock negotiation in a sysplex data sharing environment. (P-lock negotiation occurs when another data sharing member requests release of a held p-lock by a data sharing member so it can process the data). The p-lock is held until another agent requests the p-lock unconditionally or the buffer page is stolen.

MEMBER CLUSTER is useful for a partitioned and simple tablespace where multiple concurrent data sharing members have hot spot inserts, row locking is used, rows are inserted at end of a partition based on the clustering index, and records are not sorted in clustering sequence before insertion with a batch program. The disadvantage of using the parameter is that it can require more frequent reorganizations to regain clustering.

You can identify tablespaces created with MEMBER CLUSTER like:

```
SELECT CREATOR, NAME, DBNAME, TYPE
FROM   SYSIBM.SYSTABLESPACE
WHERE  TYPE IN ('I', 'K');
```

MEMBER CLUSTER is not needed to avoid transaction lock contention for inserts. If the target page is locked, the row is inserted in a near or far page as if there is no free as discussed in Chapter CC.

LOCKPART YES results in partitions being locked only as they are accessed. This is referred to as selective partition locking. If the default of LOCKPART NO is used, the entire partitioned tablespace is locked. If LOCKSIZE of PAGE, ANY, or ROW is used, the LOCKPART parameter applies to the parent locks of intent to share (IS), intent exclusive (IX), and share with intent exclusive (SIX) discussed in Chapter CC. If lock escalation occurs because the LOCKMAX or NUMLKTS value is exceeded, the escalation is to the partition level (not the tablespace level) as discussed in Section TS.5. The LOCKPART parameter does not apply when using a LOCKSIZE of TABLE and TABLESPACE, if the LOCK TABLE IN EXCLUSIVE MODE statement is executed without the PART parameter, or the plan is bound with ACQUIRE(ALLOCATE).

The maximum size and number of partitions depend on whether the DSSIZE parameter defines partitions as greater than or equal 8 GB, the LARGE parameter is specified, or more than 64 partitions are defined when the tablespace is created. If any of these conditions are not met, the maximum size of a partitioned tablespace is the same as that for a nonpartitioned tablespace, which is 64 GB. If there are from 1 to 16 partitions, each partition can be 4 GB each. If there are from 17 to 32 partitions, each partition can be 2 GB each. If there are from 33 to 64 partitions, each partition can be 1 GB each. The maximum number of partitions is 64.

If the DSSIZE parameter can be used to define partitions as greater than or equal 8 GB, the LARGE parameter is specified, or more than 64 partitions are defined when creating a partitioned tablespace. The maximum number of partitions is 254. Each data partition, index partition, and nonpartitioning index (NPI) can contain 64 GB of data, and a maximum of 16 TB of data in the entire tablespace (V6). It is advisable to use the DSSIZE parameter rather than the LARGE parameter for upward compatibility. There are several prerequisites to having a data set greater than 4 GB. It is necessary to use SMS managed data sets (DFSMS V1.5) with a SMS data class, ACS (Automatic Class Section), and extended addressability (EA) must be enabled to allow data sets larger than 4 GB. The DSSIZE clause can be specified on the CREATE TABLESPACE statement with 8GB or more and up to and including 254 partitions.

```
DSSIZE 8G NUMPARTS 254
```

In order to change the DSSIZE, it is necessary to drop and recreate the tablespace. It is not possible to alter the DSSIZE.

If DSSIZE is not specified and more than 64 partitions are specified, the maximum data set size is 4 GB and the maximum partitioned tablespace size is 1 TB. This is the limit in V5 in any case.

The Partitioning Index

A partitioning index is required on a partitioned tablespace to designate which rows are to be placed in which partition. The partitioning index must be the CLUSTER index as indicated in the following CREATE statement. The partitioning index is divided into parts corresponding to the parts of the tablespace. Each part is a separate and distinct index referencing rows in its corresponding data partition.

```
CREATE INDEX ZIPINDEX
  ON ZIPTB (ZIPCODE)
  CLUSTER
    (PART 1 VALUES(1000000.)
      USING STOGROUP DAX01STG
        PRIQTY 7200
        SECQTY  720
      PCTFREE  20
      FREEPAGE  7,
     PART 2 VALUES(2000000.)
      USING STOGROUP DAX02STG
        PRIQTY 7200
        SECQTY  720
      PCTFREE  15
      FREEPAGE  7,
     PART 3 VALUES(3000000.)
      USING STOGROUP DAX03STG
        PRIQTY 7200
        SECQTY  720,
     PART 4 VALUES(4000000.)
      USING STOGROUP DAX04STG
        PRIQTY 7200
        SECQTY  720,
     PART 5 VALUES(5000000.)
      USING STOGROUP DAX05STG
        PRIQTY 7200
        SECQTY  720,
           .
           .
           .
     PART 22 VALUES(22000000.)
      USING STOGROUP DAX22STG
        PRIQTY 14400
        SECQTY   720)
  PCTFREE   0
```

```
FREEPAGE  0
BUFFERPOOL BP0
CLOSE NO;
```

Most of the parameters used when creating the partitioning index have the same meaning as the corresponding parameter used when creating a tablespace. Index usage and design are discussed in Chapters IU and ID. The storage group, space allocation, and free space can be specified differently for each index partition as when creating a partitioned tablespace.

Each partition number must be named along with the limit key value for the columns in the partitioning index. Each limit key value is the maximum value that can be placed in a partition. Indeed, the limit key values are used to determine which row to insert into which partition. In the example, all rows with zip codes less than or equal to 1,000,000 are placed in partition 1 of the index and data pages. All rows with zip codes greater than 1,000,000 and less than or equal 2,000,000 are placed in partition 2 of the index and data pages. This principle applies to partitions 3 through 21.

The limit key specified for the last partition works differently depending on whether the tablespace can contain more than 64 GB of data. If the tablespace cannot contain more than 64 GB of data, all rows with a zip code less than or equal to as well as those greater than 22,000,000 are placed in the last partition of 22. Basically, the limit key is not enforced on the last partition. If the tablespace can contain more than 64 GB, the upper limit is enforced. Rows with a zip code greater than 22,000,000 are not loaded by the LOAD utility. They are written to the discard data set if one is specified as described in Chapter LC. An INSERT statement receives a negative SQLCODE if it attempts to insert a row with a value greater than 22,000,000 in the partitioning index column.

The first 255 bytes of a partitioning index identify the partition number (V6) and 255 bytes is the maximum length of columns in an index. The example assumes that the column used for the upper range values is declared as an integer. If there are any decimal columns described in the upper range values, the values must be specified with a decimal point (1000000. for example). If descending order is specified, values are the lowest rather than the highest values as used in the example.

The partitioning index must be the clustering index. This presents design challenges. You may want to partition on certain columns and have your clustering index on other columns for the performance benefits of clustering as discussed in Chapters IU and ID.

The columns that participate in the partitioning index can be updated (V5 APAR PQ16946) if the partitioned tablespace is created after application of the APAR. This facility is not intended for heavy update activity where the update causes the row to change partitions. If the update causes a row in partition 5 to be moved to partition 10, parts 5 through 10 of the tablespace, partitioning index, and all NPIs are drained. Other cannot access the parts until a commit is issued. This is necessary to avoid a row disappearing from index access temporarily. An alternative is to select the row, save the columns, delete the row, and insert the row after changing the column in the partitioning index. This process requires the update of all indexes on the table as does the use of the UPDATE statement but minimizes lock contention. Do be cautious if the tablespace is a parent in a referential integrity structure. If the delete cascade or set null rules are in effect, you must manage the dependent tables before deleting rows from the parent partitioned tablespace. Referential integrity is discussed in Chapter CT.

The partitioning index cannot be altered or dropped. It defines the limit key for each partition. That is a row greater than the value specified using the PART and VALUE clause of the create tablespace statement cannot be placed in the specified partition. We will discuss some challenges and alternatives for managing the challenges that result from this rule in the following sections.

Advantages of Partitioning

A partitioning tablespace provides for dividing a large tablespace into smaller more manageable pieces. It improves the availability of data. For example, you can execute a utility or program on one partition and execute another utility or program on other partitions concurrently.

You can spread partitions on multiple DASD devices, channels, and control units. This improves performance by reducing I/O time for online transactions accessing the data at random and batch programs accessing data in different partitions.

Partitioning provides for DB2 parallelism on multiple partitions which is particularly useful in reducing the elapsed time required to process many rows. It also allows for scanning a few partitions rather than the entire tablespace in a limited partition scan. These techniques are discussed in Chapter BP.

Tablespace and index parameters can be specified and altered on individual partitions.

SMS can archive infrequently used partitions and automatically recall them when next accessed to save DASD space.

Partitioning is Not a Panacea

A primary cost of partitioning is maintaining NPIs. An NPI is one index that references rows in all data partitions. All indexes on a table in a partitioned tablespace other than the partitioning index are NPIs. NPI are divided into logical parts which can be processed independently like the physical parts of the partitioning index. This provides for partition independence as discussed in Chapter LC and a sophisticated access path discussed in Chapter IU. PIECESIZE provides for placing NPI in separate data sets and spreading them on different DASD to reduce I/O contention as discussed in Chapter ID.

Reorganization of a single data partition of a tablespace with NPIs can approach but not exceed reorganization of the entire tablespace. The RIDs of NPIs are updated in place only if the RID has changed, to reduce costs. However, load replace of a partition requires that NPI RIDs pointing to replaced rows be deleted and RIDs pointing to new rows be inserted. The load of the second through last partition uses insert mode on the NPIs, which are similar to that when using an INSERT statement.

The load and reorganization of all partitions at once requires fewer resources than processing each partition individually, particularly if there are NPIs. However, processing one or a few partitions leaves all other partitions available for use by others.

Estimating the Number of Partitions

A number of factors must be considered in determining the number of partitions that are best. Business requirements may well determine the number of partitions. For example, it may be necessary to partition by month so that a history of monthly data can be maintained. Processing requirements are a major consideration. It may be necessary to do batch processing in a particular sequence which requires that the clustering index be on the columns that determine the sequence of batch processing as discussed in Chapter BP. Also, the clustering index is valuable in avoiding searches, joins, sorts, and other processing discussed in Chapters IU and ID. The clustering and partitioning index are one and the same.

The number of partitions best for DB2 parallelism depends on whether SQL statements are I/O and/or CPU intensive, and the number of processors, DASD devices, control units, and channels available.

I/O Intensive: If "other read I/O time" (time that DB2 is waiting for pages to be read into a buffer pool) from DB2PM is close to the total elapsed time (accounting trace class 3), the SQL is I/O intensive. You can estimate the number of partitions as the elapsed time divided by the processor time multiplied by the number of processors that can be used. If a representative SQL statement requires 60 elapsed minutes and 30 processor minutes, and there are 10 processors available, 20 partitions is a good goal assuming sufficient I/O paths are available based on:

```
20 = 60 elapsed minutes / 30 processor minutes * 10 processors
```

Processor Intensive: If the processor time is about 70 percent or more of the elapsed time (accounting trace class 2), the SQL is processor intensive. This suggests that the number of partitions should be greater than or equal to the number of processors not dedicated to other higher priority work.

Do avoid one or more partitions that are considerably larger than other partitions. This limits the maximum degree of parallelism as discussed in Chapter PL.

Small tablespaces can be partitioned to encourage join parallelism. The small partitioned tablespace is likely to be the outer table of a join. The number of partitions in the outer table determines the maximum degree of parallelism as discussed in Chapter PL.

Maximum Number of Partitions: The number of partitions and your choice of the partitioning index are very important and cannot be changed with an ALTER statement. It is necessary to unload the data, drop the tablespace, create the tablespace, table, and indexes, load data, grant privileges, execute RUNSTATS, and rebind plans and packages (or accept an automatic rebind). Do consider defining the maximum number of partitions allowed. If the tablespace will not exceed 64 GB, 64 partitions can be defined and four byte RIDs are used for all indexes on the table in the tablespace. If the tablespace is greater than 64 GB and less than 16 TB, 254 partitions can be defined and five byte RIDs are used for all indexes on the table in the tablespace.

Limit Key for Each Partition

Once you have determined the number of partitions required, the next question is what limit key values need to be specified to get about the same number of rows in each partition. The following SELECT statement gives the limit key value for each of four partitions on a million row table assuming a partitioning index on SN, PN, and JN. There can be more rows in one partition than others depending on the cardinality of the column. The limit key value is the value that occurs about every 250,000 rows. This is the reason for the values of 250000, 500000,750000, and 1000000 in each of the outer SELECTS for each UNION ALL block.

```
SELECT 'Part 1 limit key = ',
  MAX(SN CONCAT PN CONCAT JN)
FROM   SPJ AS SPJ1
WHERE 250000 >
  (SELECT COUNT(*)
   FROM   SPJ AS SPJ2
   WHERE  SPJ2.SN < SPJ1.SN
   OR    (SPJ2.SN = SPJ1.SN
   AND    SPJ2.PN < SPJ1.PN)
   OR    (SPJ2.SN = SPJ1.SN
   AND    SPJ2.PN = SPJ1.PN
   AND    SPJ2.JN < SPJ1.JN))
UNION ALL
SELECT 'Part 2 limit key = ',
  MAX(SN CONCAT PN CONCAT JN)
FROM SPJ AS SPJ1
WHERE 500000 >
  (SELECT COUNT(*)
   FROM   SPJ AS SPJ2
   WHERE  SPJ2.SN < SPJ1.SN
   OR    (SPJ2.SN = SPJ1.SN
   AND    SPJ2.PN < SPJ1.PN)
   OR    (SPJ2.SN = SPJ1.SN
   AND    SPJ2.PN = SPJ1.PN
   AND    SPJ2.JN < SPJ1.JN))
UNION ALL
SELECT 'Part 3 limit key = ',
  MAX(SN CONCAT PN CONCAT JN)
FROM   SPJ AS SPJ1
WHERE 750000 >
  (SELECT COUNT(*)
   FROM   SPJ AS SPJ2
   WHERE  SPJ2.SN < SPJ1.SN
   OR    (SPJ2.SN = SPJ1.SN
   AND    SPJ2.PN < SPJ1.PN)
   OR    (SPJ2.SN = SPJ1.SN
   AND    SPJ2.PN = SPJ1.PN
   AND    SPJ2.JN < SPJ1.JN))
UNION ALL
SELECT 'Part 4 limit key = ',
  MAX(SN CONCAT PN CONCAT JN)
FROM   SPJ AS SPJ1
WHERE 1000000 >
  (SELECT COUNT(*)
   FROM   SPJ AS SPJ2
   WHERE  SPJ2.SN < SPJ1.SN
   OR    (SPJ2.SN = SPJ1.SN
   AND    SPJ2.PN < SPJ1.PN)
   OR    (SPJ2.SN = SPJ1.SN
   AND    SPJ2.PN = SPJ1.PN
```

```
   AND     SPJ2.JN < SPJ1.JN))
GROUP BY 1, 2
ORDER BY 1 ASC, 2 DESC;
```

The statement is very resource intensive. It requires a great deal of CPU and I/O time because it is a correlated subselect. Do execute it when the resources are available. Hopefully the statement will have to be executed only once or a few times to provide information on the limit key values needed for partitioning.

An alternative is to sort rows and report on the upper range value every 250,000 rows as determined by host language code using a cursor on:

```
SELECT SN, PN, JN
FROM   SPJ
ORDER BY SN, PN, JN
```

Although this technique may be considered brute force, it is likely to perform better than the correlated subselect.

Partitioning Index Alternatives

We will consider a number of alternatives for designing the partitioning index along with the pros and cons of the alternatives. Hopefully, these alternatives will be useful for the design of your partitioned tablespaces and indexes.

Use of a pseudo random number has some advantages. It provides for spreading insert activity throughout the tablespace and provides for appropriately equal partition sizes. It avoids hot spot insert activity which is useful in a data sharing environment and is an alternative to MEMBER CLUSTER.

The disadvantages of partitioning on a pseudo random number should be considered carefully. A random number is not useful to avoid sorts for ORDER BY, GROUP BY, DISTINCT, and joins in most cases. The usefulness of sorting input in sequence for batch match/merge processing is unlikely (good batch technique discussed in Chapter BP.) Partitioning on a random number does not allow for the clustering partition index on a column with a business meaning for searches, joins, and sort avoidance. It does not allow for partitioning according to business requirements (by month, order ID, invoice ID, etc.). If high insert activity is expected, a large number of random I/O can detract from performance. The use of a partition scan is unlikely. In most cases, it is necessary to create one or more NPI to provide index access to columns with a business meaning. Additional space is required for each row (19 bytes per row if a ROWID column is used) and for an index that is rarely used to satisfy a user request. Typically partitioned tablespaces have a larger number of rows making the additional space required for data and the partitioning index significant.

Techniques for Generating Pseudo Random Number: ROWID data type column containing pseudo random numbers can be created as described in Chapter CT and used as described in Chapters IU and PD.

Restrictions on Use of ROWID Column as Partitioning Index: It is not possible to use the LOAD utility to load at the partition level (must load entire tablespace). Only the first 17 bytes of partitioning index are used as the limit key. It is necessary to specify upper range value in hexadecimal like:

```
CREATE INDEX SPJX ON SPJ(SPJ_ROWID)
  CLUSTER (PART 1 VALUES(X'3FFF'),
  CLUSTER  PART 2 VALUES(X'7FFF'),
  CLUSTER  PART 3 VALUES(X'BFFF'),
  CLUSTER  PART 4 VALUES(X'FFFF'))
```

If the restrictions present problem, an alternative is to determine the maximum required number of partitions, 64 or 254, for example. Define a partitioning index on a partitioning column containing a generated random number between 1 and 64 or 1 and 254.

Partitioning on the PK: The PK is a good choice if you have frequent batch processing in PK sequence and the index can be used for searches, joins, and to avoid sorts. However, there is a disadvantage of this technique if the partitioning tablespace is a parent table with dependent tables defined and the columns constituting the partitioning index are frequently updated. Recall from the topic on defining the partitioning index that the UPDATE statement cannot be used to change the partitioning index values and the complexities involved in managing the dependent tables.

Partitioning on a Sequential Value: Partitioning on a sequential value has advantages. For example the partitioning index can be on an ascending date, order number, or invoice number. The maximum number of partitions in a large tablespace (254) can be defined for sequentially inserted rows. This allows for 21 years and 2 months of monthly data before it is necessary to drop and recreate the tablespace. If you are partitioning by a sequential order or invoice number over a 20 year period, for example, specify a limit key value for each of the 254 partitions to accommodate the orders or invoices. You have a good deal of flexibility in specifying the limit key value for the unused partitions because the limit key can be altered followed by a reorganization as discussed in the following subsection (V6).

Partitioning on a sequential value has additional advantages. You can load or load resume the most current partition while all other partitions are available for other processing. There is no need to reorganize or execute RUNSTATS on earlier partitions once they are populated in sequence or reorganized and RUNSTATS has been executed after the data in a partition has stabilized. You can use 0 PCTFREE and 0 FREEPAGE on all partitions to reduce space requirements.

If you use this technique, do use the ALTER statement to make the unused partitions very small and purge an obsolete partition with load replace of 0 records or use a dummy input file to minimize space requirements.

Partitioning Index Control Table: Each row can be assigned a value of 1, 2, 3, etc. as a partition number in a column defined for this purpose. Rows with a value of 1 are placed in partition 1, rows with a value of 2 are placed in partition 2, etc. The partition number column has advantages when used with a control table. The control table is used to associate a partition number with a time period or range of order numbers, for example. The control table allows for placing the clustering index on a column that will benefit from clustering. It also provides for reuse of partition numbers when rolling months or ranges of order numbers. Only the oldest partition is unavailable while executing a load replace of the partition with new data.

We will use an example to demonstrate the use of a control table, assuming that the requirement is to partition by month and retain a two year history. The control table contains the partition number, the first and last day of a month. The Reuse Begin and Reuse End columns contain the date range that replaces the oldest partitions date ranges as indicated in Figure TS.5.

Figure TS.5. CONTROL table for partitioning by month

PART_NO	MONTH_BEGIN	MONTH_END	Reuse Begin	Reuse End
1	~~1992-01-01~~	~~1992-01-31~~	1994-01-01	1994-01-31
2	~~1992-02-01~~	~~1992-02-29~~	1994-02-01	1994-02-28
3	1992-03-01	1992-03-31		
...	...	...		
24	1993-12-01	1993-12-31		

The control table is used to determine the partition number before selecting from the target HISTORY table. If the user requests information on rows with a date between 1992-03-15 and 1992-03-20, the following SELECT statement can be used to determine the partition number of the partition that contains the rows required.

```
SELECT PART_NO
FROM   CONTROL
WHERE  MONTH_BEGIN <= '1992-03-15' --Dates
AND    MONTH_END   >= '1992-03-20';--requested
```

Assume that the HISTORY table has a composite partitioning index on the partition number (PART_NO) and order date (ORDER_DATE). A matching index scan can be used on the partitioning index based on the PART_NO determined from the CONTROL table and order dates required by the user like:

```
SELECT ACCOUNT_NO, AMOUNT
FROM   HISTORY
WHERE  PART_NO = 3
AND ORDER_DATE BETWEEN '1992-03-15'
                   AND '1992-03-20';
```

If you do not want developers and business professionals who access the data directly to be aware of the CONTROL table, a view can be used to "hide" the CONTROL table. The disadvantage of the technique is that the CONTROL table is an additional reference table to be accessed and must be maintained.

This technique can be used for partitioning by order number, invoice number, or any column values. It is one of the most popular techniques used for managing partitions.

Altering the Limit Key

One or more partition limit keys can be altered (V6). This has a number of advantages. It is useful to accommodate changing business requirements. It may be necessary to alter the limit key of partitions that have grown larger than expected and beyond the limit of a partition size. This allows for moving rows from one partition to another. It allows for activating more partitions in the future than are not required at present. You can activate additional partitions that have been previously defined for new time periods and deactivate old partitions that are no longer required. Partitions can be resized so that each partition is approximately equal in size. This improves parallel processing performance as discussed in Chapter PL. In addition, the size of partitions is important in maximizing the availability of critical data during utility and batch processing.

The altered partitions are placed in REORG pending (REORP) status. Rows cannot be selected, inserted, updated, and deleted from the altered partitions while the partitions are in this pending status. It is necessary to reorganize the altered partitions plus the next partition, the entire tablespace, load replace the tablespace, or drop the tablespace. An exception is that the last partition is not placed in REORG pending if tablespace does not allow for more than 64 GB of data. All plans and packages that reference the partitioned tablespace are marked as invalidate. The first access of a plan or package causes all of them to be rebound. The rebinds are successful if altered partitioned have been reorganized successfully. Otherwise, a -904 SQLCODE is received when there is an attempt to run a plan or package that accesses the tablespace.

Example of Altering Limit Keys: Assume that about one-half a million calls are estimated per month and it has been decided to specify a limit key of the last day of each month in 1999. However, November and December have over 1 million calls per month as shown in Figure TS.6.

Figure TS.6. Number of rows in each of 12 partitions

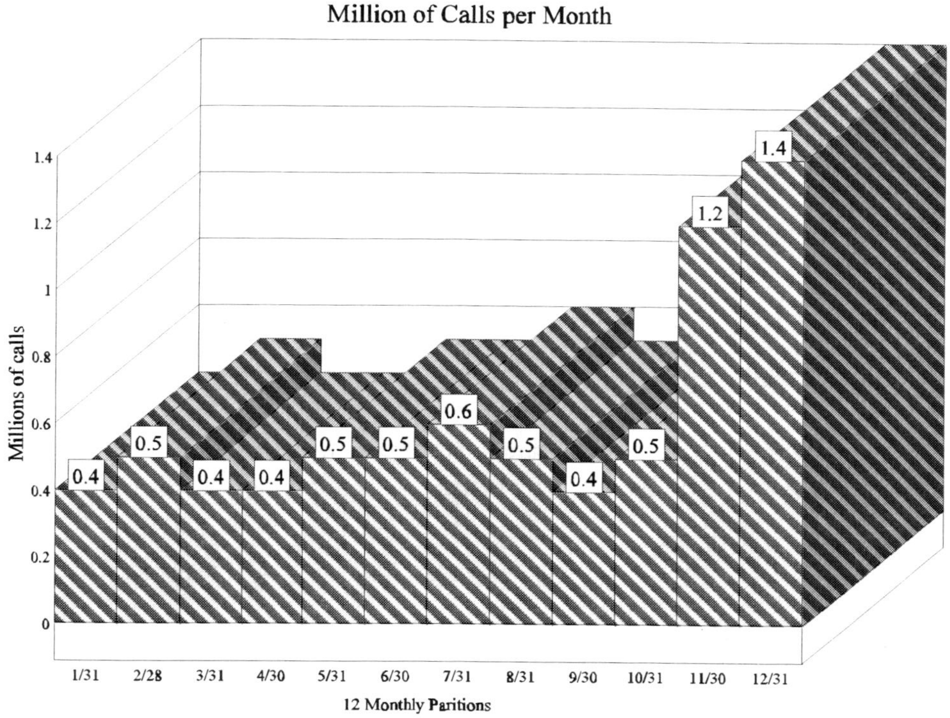

It is decided to alter the two large partitions for November and December to make them more consistent in size with the other partitions at about one-half million rows in each partition. Also the limit key for an unused partition to allow for calls in January of 2000 is specified to activate partition 15.

```
ALTER INDEX MONTH_LIMIT
  PART 11 VALUES ('1999-11-15'),
  PART 12 VALUES ('1999-11-30'),
  PART 13 VALUES ('1999-12-15'),
  PART 14 VALUES ('1999-12-31'),
  PART 15 VALUES ('2000-01-31');
```

Parts 11 through 16 are placed in REORG pending status. It is necessary to reorganize these partitions as discussed in Chapter RR. It is not necessary to reorganize the last partition (16) if tablespace is <= 64 GB. Do consider rebinding plans and packages that reference the tablespace to avoid automatic rebinds when they are next executed.

Current and Historical Data

Current and historical data are often placed in a single tablespace. However, they have many different characteristics. Current data is frequently updated, which requires free space to accommodate updates and page or row locking. It is necessary to periodically execute the reorganization, RUNSTATS, image copy, and other utilities. Rebind of plans and packages are needed periodically as well. The index design for current data frequently differs from that required for historical data.

Historical data is rarely updated. This means that zero free space and a LOCKSIZE of TABLE or TABLESPACE is a good choice. It is not necessary to periodically execute the reorganization,

RUNSTATS, image copy, and other utilities. Rebind of plans and packages are needed infrequently. You can also support more indexes with low update activity. This is particularly important in a data warehousing environment.

You can create a view with UNION ALL of the current and historical data so tables appear as one (V7) provided duplicates do not occur or are acceptable. Do select from the current data, UNION ALL, and select from historical data. This causes the current data to be searched first. If UNION is required and many rows qualify and must be sorted, an alternative is to have application programs and ad hoc users determine when to process current and/or historical tables.

There are some disadvantages of separate current and historical tables. The current data must be placed in the historical table periodically. Also, the current data table begins with 0 rows periodically.

Recommendation: If the disadvantages of separate current and historical tables are manageable, do maintain the data in separate tables. This reduces the costs and complexity of maintaining the tablespace and indexes significantly.

TS.8 DATA COMPRESSION

COMPRESS YES is specified to cause DB2 to compress data in a tablespace. (Compression does not apply to indexes, the catalog and directory.) A dictionary is built containing frequently occurring bytes and a corresponding bit pattern. For example, if John occurs frequently in the tablespace, it is placed in the dictionary along with a bit pattern of say 0110. (12 bits are used rather than the 4 shown in the example.) Each occurrence of John is replaced in the tablespace with the bit pattern, including the occurrence of John in the names Johns, Johnson, Johnsen, Johnston, Johnstone, etc. using enterprise system architecture (ESA) compression. Column boundaries are ignored. This is in contrast to using a compaction algorithm where 40 bytes of blanks are represented by 1 blank preceded by a count of 40, for example.

Data with repetitive patterns is a good candidate for compression. For example, names and codes for cities, states, countries, departments, divisions, string of blanks, etc. Numeric values that occur frequently like 199.99, 100.00, 1998, identifiers where only the last few digits vary, etc. are also good candidates. Graphic and image data do not compress well.

Savings and Costs of Compression

There are many factors to consider in determining the savings and costs of compression.

DASD space: Significant DASD space savings can be achieved with compression. Between 40 to 70 percent less DASD space is required with compression, depending on the characteristics of the data, with a typical savings of 50 to 60 percent. There are additional savings in terms of I/O, depending on the type of processing. If the data is compressed by 50 percent, twice as many rows fit on a page and half the number of I/O need to be issued for sequential processing. Random processing has a greater chance that the required row is in the buffer pool since more rows fit in the buffer. This results in a reduction in the number of I/O, I/O time, and CPU time to issue I/O. It reduces the amount of data sent across I/O channels, elapsed time, virtual pool and hiperpool space requirements, and log space required. Compressed data is logged in compressed form. Log records can be decompressed by calling DSNWLI and passing 0306 in the IFCID area.

CPU costs with and without hardware assist: If your computer has the CMPSC instruction, hardware compression will be used to compress and decompress the data. If the computer does not support ESA compression, software compression is used. CPU time is required to compress and decompress the data. You can expect an overall increase in CPU time of from 1 to 5 percent, more toward the 1 percent for hardware compression and more toward the 5 percent for software compression. In general, software compression requires about 3.5 times more CPU time than hardware compression.

Lock Contention: There is an increased potential for lock contention with more rows on a page when using page locking.

Type of processing influences costs: Decompression of all columns in a row is required even if only a few columns are needed. This is particularly costly for long rows because the cost is per byte. Decompression of all rows is required when doing a tablespace scan. It is necessary to decompress rows before applying predicates to determine if the row qualifies. If an index is used to locate qualifying rows, only the identified rows are decompressed. Some of the decompressed rows may not be needed based on additional predicates that are applied after the row is located using an index.

Utilities that require decompression: Several utilities must decompress all rows in the tablespace including REORG, RUNSTATS, RECOVER INDEX, REBUILD INDEX, and DSN1PRNT.

Dictionary Creation and Maintenance: Computer and people resources are required to create, refine, and maintain the compression and decompression dictionary.

Transmission of Data: The data is decompressed before it is transmitted in a distributed environment. This avoids having to keep the dictionary synchronized at multiple sites. VTAM can optionally compress data for transmission and decompress it at the receiving site.

How to Use Compression

COMPRESS YES is specified on the CREATE TABLESPACE statement to use compression. COMPRESS NO is the default. Compression can be specified at the partition level to allow for compressing some but not all partitions. This offers the opportunity to compress partitions that are infrequently updated and not compress partitions that are frequently updated to reduce the CPU costs of compression.

The ALTER TABLESPACE statement can be used to turn compression on and off. It is not necessary to drop and recreate the tablespace or unload and reload the data. However, you must reorganize or unload and reload the data to gain or eliminate compression.

Some but not all rows in a table can be compressed. Only rows that become shorter are stored in compressed form. The first byte of a 6 byte row prefix contains X'00' for a normal row, X'04' for a compressed row, and X'20' for an overflow row.

The ALTER TABLE statement can be used to add a column to a table when using ESA compression, unlike when using EDITPROC compression.

Impact of Compression on the Optimizer and by Program Type

The optimizer factors in compression when choosing an access path and the resources required to process compressed data differ depending on the type of program.

Impact on Access Path: The optimizer includes additional CPU time in its estimate for decompression based on PCTROWCOMP (percentage of rows compressed) in SYSTABLES for compressed tablespaces and SYSTABSTATS for compressed partitions. The row length is also included in the calculations because the CPU cost is per byte. A high PCTROWCOMP results in a higher CPU cost estimate. This means that a matching index scan is more likely and a lower degree of parallelism is likely. The use of non-compressed indexes to locate the compressed data minimizes the number of rows that need to be decompressed. A tablespace scan requires the decompression of every row before applying predicates to determine if the row qualifies and should be passed to the relational data system (RDS) for further processing. No compression or a low PCTROWCOMP results in a lower CPU estimate per row. This means that a tablespace and non-matching index scan with data reference is more likely and a higher degree of parallelism is likely. Index-only access is not affected by compression because indexes are not compressed.

ESA compression does not use EDITPROC which reduces costs because it is not necessary to do an EDITPROC call and return. Other techniques used for compression use EDITPROC. The optimizer factors in a fixed increase in CPU cost when EDITPROC is used. The estimate is somewhat lower than reality in most cases. The estimate is of limited accuracy because the costs depend on the specific compression and decompression algorithm used with EDITPROC.

Program Types: Among the different program types and processing, batch programs, some utilities, and decision support applications that process many rows will likely experience an increase in CPU time with a decrease in I/O and elapsed time. This is because many rows are typically scanned and decompressed which increases CPU time but decreases I/O and elapsed time because there are more rows per page. Online transactions that process a few rows will probably not have a significant increase in CPU time, I/O usage is unlikely to decrease, and response time is unlikely to increase significantly, typically few rows are processed in online transactions and these rows are usually located using an index which is not compressed.

Capacity Planning Estimates

DB2 Estimator can be used to estimate the changes in CPU, I/O, elapsed time, DASD space when using compression. You can import descriptions of existing tables and SQL statements into DB2 Estimator. Estimate the costs of frequently executed SQL with and without the compression option and compare the estimates.

An alternative is to estimate the CPU costs to compress and decompress the data based on the costs per byte. The CPU time to compress and decompress data is covered in Chapter OP. The CPU and elapsed time for SQL and utility execution tests are reported at the end of this section.

Very Short and Very Long Rows

The length of uncompressed rows impacts the savings and costs of compression.

Very short rows: Very short uncompressed rows will not result in significant saving in most cases. One row is compressed at a time. The 6 byte row prefix and 2 byte page directory entry are not compressed.

Very Long Rows: At least one additional row should fit on a page to realize savings. A very long row may not be compressible such that an additional row will fit on a 4 KB page. If this is the case, consider 8, 16, or 32 KB page which allows for several long compressed or uncompressed rows. This is a good choice if there are frequent sequential scans. Do keep in mind that the I/O time is increased by 8x for a 32 KB page compared to a 4 KB page. This is particularly important if only one or a few rows are frequently processed on a 32 KB page that contains many rows. This can increase elapsed time and require more space in the buffer pool.

Updating and Logging Variable and Fixed Length Rows

Logging of updated rows is affected by whether a row is variable or fixed in length and the sequence of columns in a row.

Updating Variable Length Rows: Compressed rows and rows with VARCHAR columns are variable in length. If a variable length row is updated, made longer, and there is no free space on the page to expand the row, the row must be moved to a near or far page as discussed in Section TS.4. There is an increased probability that the update of any column (not just VARCHAR columns) will cause rows to be moved to a near or far page due to a lack of free space on the page for a longer row. This can require more frequent reorganizations.

Logging of variable length rows: A variable length row is logged from first changed byte to the end of row. Placing frequently updated variable length and fixed length columns in a variable length row at the end of the row reduces logging. If the row length is changed by an update, the length field at the beginning of the row is also logged as shown in Figure TS.7. If the row is variable in length because of VARCHAR columns and the VARCHAR columns are not frequently updated, the frequently updated fixed length columns should be placed at the end of the row to reduce logging. Placement of VARCHAR toward the end of the row and before frequently updated column decreases the CPU cost of calculating the offset of the columns following VARCHAR columns.

Figure TS.7. Logging of variable length rows

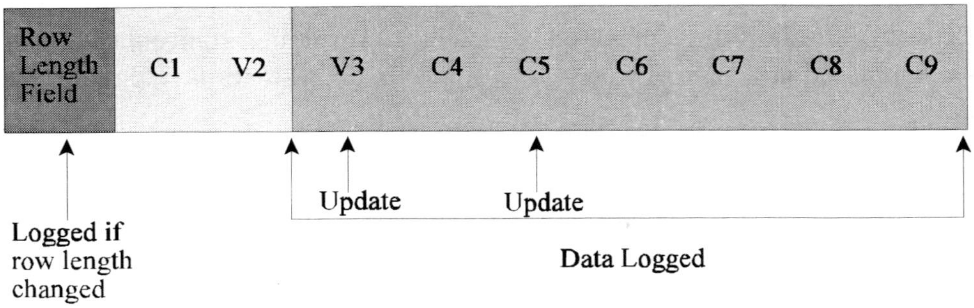

Logging of Fixed Length Rows: Less logging is required for fixed length rows. DB2 logs from the first changed byte to the last changed byte. This suggests that frequently updated columns be placed contiguously to reduce logging. Column C4 in Figure TS.8 should be placed before C3 or after C5 in the example.

Figure TS.8. Logging of fixed length rows

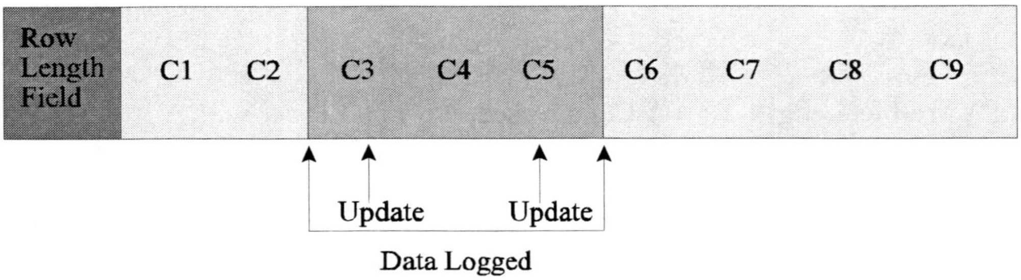

Estimating DASD Savings

DSN1COMP can be used to estimate savings for compression. It can be executed against any data set with a DB2 page format. A good choice of input to DSN1COMP is a full or incremental image copy. You probably have an image copy and it does not interfere with the availability of the tablespace to use it for the estimate of DASD savings. If you do not have an available image copy, you can take a copy of the tablespace being considered for compression using DSN1COPY or the image copy utility and use it as input to DSN1COMP. An alternative is to stop the tablespace or partition in a VSAM LDS and use it as input to DSN1COMP.

Here is an example of the parameters that can be specified on the EXEC statement to execute DSN1COMP.

```
DSN1COMP 4K NUMPARTS(24) SIZE(4096)
FREEPAGE(31) PCTFREE(5) FULLCOPY REORG ROWLIMIT(20000)
```

The first parameter, 4K, is the data set page size used for SYSUT1 and is the default. If the tablespace uses a 8, 16, or 32 KB page size, the appropriate value is specified rather than 4K. NUMPARTS indicates the number of partitions. NUMPARTS(0) is used if the tablespace is not partitioned and is the default. SIZE is the number of entries in the dictionary. You can specify 512, 1024, 2048, or 4096. 4096 is a good choice. If a smaller dictionary size is specified, DSN1COMP requires fewer resources to produce the estimates discussed below. However, the estimates may not be as accurate. The actual compression and decompression dictionary usually has 4,096 nodes of 8 bytes each on 16 pages. The number of bytes is 65,536 calculated as 2 dictionaries * 4,096 nodes * 8 bytes or 16 pages * 4,096 bytes. The default of 16 pages for the dictionary can be changed in DSNZPARM.

The values for FREEPAGE and PCTFREE should be specified as on the CREATE TABLESPACE statement as discussed in Section TS.5. FULLCOPY indicates that the input will be a full image copy of the tablespace. INCRCOPY is an option to indicate that the input will be an incremental copy. REORG means that the estimate should be determined with the sampling algorithm used with REORG. This is in contrast to the method used by LOAD where the dictionary is built based on the first *n* rows as will be discussed in this section. ROWLIMIT(20000) indicates the number of rows that should be evaluated to produce the estimates, 1,000,000 is the maximum. If the number specified is too small, the DSN1941 message is issued indicating that limit should be made larger. The DSSIZE parameter should be specified for tablespaces greater than 64 GB.

Example of DSN1COMP Report

DSN1COMP reports on the number of KB bytes and pages with and without compression along with an estimate of the percentage of bytes that will be saved with compression. It gives the average compressed and uncompressed row length. The report also includes the number of rows scanned to build the dictionary, the number of rows processed to provide the compression estimate, and the number of entries in the dictionary. Figure TS.9 is an example of the report produced by DSN1COMP.

Figure TS.9. Example of DSN1COMP report

```
DSN1940I DSN1COMP COMPRESSION REPORT

      1,289 KB WITHOUT COMPRESSION
        736 KB WITH COMPRESSION
         43 PERCENT OF BYTES WOULD BE SAVED

      2,108 ROWS SCANNED TO BUILD DICTIONARY
     20,000 ROWS SCANNED TO PROVIDE COMPRESSION ESTIMATE
      4,096 DICTIONARY ENTRIES

         81 BYTES FOR AVERAGE UNCOMPRESSED ROW LENGTH
         52 BYTES FOR AVERAGE COMPRESSED ROW LENGTH
         16 DICTIONARY PAGES REQUIRED
        358 PAGES REQUIRED WITHOUT COMPRESSION
        225 PAGES REQUIRED WITH COMPRESSION
         37 PERCENT OF THE DB2 DATA PAGES WOULD BE SAVED

DSN1994I DSN1COMP COMPLETED SUCCESSFULLY, 20,002 PAGES
PROCESSED
```

The data page estimate includes space for the page header, trailer, ID map, and row prefix. However, you do need to add space for the dictionary when estimating the amount of DASD space required for the tablespace or partition.

RUNSTATS Statistics

Statistics collected by RUNSTATS are useful in making decisions regarding data compression. SYSTABLEPART.PAGESAVE is the percentage of pages times 100 saved as a result of compression in a tablespace or partition. For example, assume 30,000 pages without compression, 40 percent savings means that 18,000 pages are required for the compressed data. If PAGESAVE contains a negative number, either the data should not be compressed or the dictionary needs to be rebuilt. For example, -3 means that 30,900 pages are required for the compressed data.

If PAGESAVE decreases over time with update activity, it is likely that the characteristics of the compressed data have changed with insert, update, and delete activity. The dictionary needs to be rebuilt using the reorganization utility to maintain good compression. The average number of bytes per row before and after compression is also useful in determining if the dictionary needs to be rebuilt. These averages are reported by the REORG, LOAD, and DSN1COMP utilities.

RUNSTATS calculates the percentage of rows compressed out of the total number of active rows in the table and places the value in SYSTABLES.PCTROWCOMP. It also places similar percentages for each partition of a partitioned tablespace in SYSTABSTATS.PCTROWCOMP. These statistics are used by the optimizer to estimate the CPU costs of various access paths.

Compression/Decompression Dictionary

Each tablespace and each partition must have a dictionary for compression and decompression. This accounts for the fact that each partition may have different characteristics. A segment in a segmented tablespace is dedicated to the dictionary. For example, SEGSIZE 32 results in 32 pages being dedicated to the dictionary. Of course, savings as a result of compression should be greater than the number of pages required by the dictionary to justify compression. The dictionary is placed after the header and first space map pages and before the data pages. Both the LOAD and REORG utilities can build the dictionary. They validate the dictionary after it has been built and log the build of the dictionary if log of yes is specified.

LOAD build of the dictionary: LOAD builds a tree of 4096 nodes from which it builds the dictionary based on the first *n* rows loaded into a tablespace during the RELOAD phase. It processes the number of rows necessary to build the dictionary. The value for *n* depends on the characteristics of the data. It is usually a small value of a few thousand rows. The first *n* rows are not compressed to avoid processing the rows twice. Typically, the percentage of uncompressed rows is very small.

If the first *n* rows of the tablespace are not representative of most rows in the tablespace the dictionary can be less than optimal, resulting in less of a savings due to compression than required. This can be compensated for by taking a sample of the rows that are representative of the data with respect to compression, load a table with the sample which results in building the dictionary, delete the sample rows, and load all of the rows for the table or multiple tables. You can avoid deleting the rows in the table used to build the dictionary by deleting the records in the file used in the sample before loading the table or multiple tables.

An alternative is to reorganize the data and have the REORG utility build a new dictionary. We will see shortly that REORG uses a sampling algorithm to build the dictionary. You must decide whether the sampling algorithm results in a good dictionary for your data. An example of a case where you may want to sample the data yourself is for a telephone directory where common names like Johnson, Jones, and Smith appear toward the end of the table, assuming that the table is loaded in sequence by last name. Consider randomizing the sequence for the dictionary build if this can result in a problem. For example, sort by telephone number, in this example, assuming little or no relationship between telephone number and name. If there are multiple tables in a tablespace and the first *n* rows of the first table are not representative of all the tables in the tablespace, similar problems are likely to occur.

Another word of caution is that rows inserted by a host program into a tablespace that has never been loaded or reorganized are not compressed until a reorganization.

The KEEPDICTIONARY parameter of LOAD replace and resume avoids the costs of rebuilding the dictionary and replacing a dictionary built and refined by REORG.

REORG build of the dictionary: REORG like LOAD builds the dictionary based on the first *n* rows. REORG uses a sampling algorithm to refine the tree as it unloads the data at intervals:

- ½ of 1 thru 1,000 rows
- 1/4 of 1,001 thru 2,000 rows
- 1/8 of 2,001 thru 3,000 rows
- Etc. up to 1/1000

You can expect 2 to 10 percent additional savings based on this refinement of the dictionary assuming that the first *n* rows are representative of the entire tablespace with one or multiple tables in the tablespace. REORG reclaims any space not used by the dictionary. A patented "pruning" process is used to reduce the dictionary size. This reduces the costs of traversing the dictionary tree for compression and decompression of the rows processed for SQL statements. Of course, the additional savings and the dictionary size depends on the characteristics of the data.

REORG builds the dictionary during the UNLOAD phase. This applies to UNLOAD CONTINUE (default) and UNLOAD PAUSE. UNLOAD ONLY unloads data in decompressed form and does not build a dictionary.

The KEEPDICTIONARY parameter of REORG as with LOAD reduces the costs of executing the utilities. Perhaps even more important is that KEEPDICTIONARY with REORG avoids recompressing the data. The rows are decompressed as they are unloaded with and without the KEEPDICTIONARY parameter. This is necessary to extract the indexed values, sort them, and rebuild the indexes. The unloaded data contains decompressed indexed values and compressed rows which are reloaded to the tablespace. The default for both utilities is to build the dictionary. (It does not compress the rows LOAD used to build dictionary.)

KEEPDICTIONARY is a good choice in most cases, assuming that the characteristics of the data have not changed with respect to compression between reorganizations. Do monitor the average compressed row length and SYSTABLEPART.PAGESAVE. If these values indicate a loss of compression efficiency, do rebuild the dictionary to maximize the benefits of compression. The CPU and elapsed time are reduced significantly based on test results at the end of this section. Do try REORG with and without KEEPDICTIONARY with your data or use DB2 Estimator to get an idea of the differences in costs.

REORG INDEX does not use compression since the indexes are not compressed and the utility rebuilds the indexes based on a scan of the leaf pages. REORG INDEX is a good choice over routine reorganizations of the tablespace and indexes with an occasional REORG TABLESPACE with mostly transaction processing as discussed in Chapter RR.

Use of the Dictionary During Execution of SQL

The dictionary is read into database services address space working storage via a virtual pool when compressed data is first accessed. Data manager (DM) validates the dictionary after it is placed in working storage. The dictionary remains in storage while compressed data is being processed (64 KB per open compressed data set). DM interfaces with hardware and software compression. RDS always receives decompressed data.

Processing an update on a compressed row starts with locating the row to be updated. If the row is compressed, it is decompressed. Any exit routines are executed. The columns are changed according to the SET clause. If there are indexes on the updated columns, they are updated. Any exit routines are executed again. The changed row is compressed. If the compressed row is shorter than the row before compression, the compressed row is written to the tablespace. Otherwise, the decompressed row is written.

Ziv-Lempel-Welch Compression Algorithm

The Ziv-Lempel-Welch algorithm used for hardware and software compression was invented by Ziv and Lempel as published in the article Compression of Individual Sequences via Variable-Rate Coding. Welch explained the algorithm in his article "A Technique for High Performance Data Compression", after which it became popularly used in PKZIP on PCs, Stacker on OS/2, UNIX Compress, and VM and OS/390 Terse.

The dictionary is a tree like structure initialized with all possible values. The tree structure will be explained assuming only three possible values, a, b, and c, assigned the values of 1, 2, and 3 as shown in Figure TS.10.

Figure TS.10. Dictionary tree structure

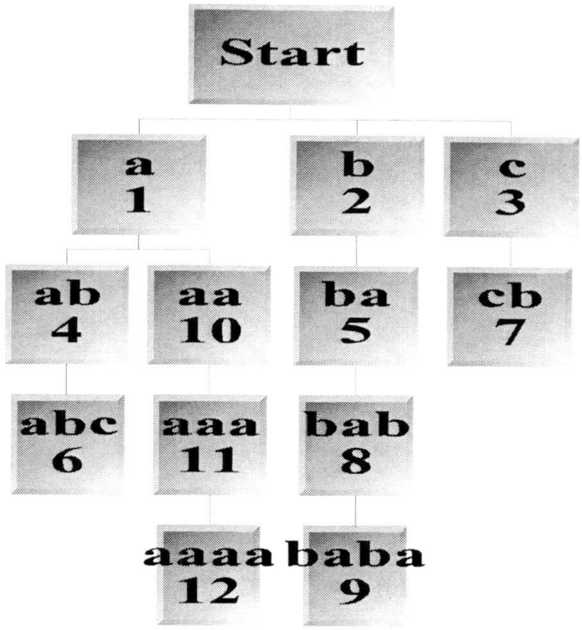

Build of dictionary: We will assume in the example that the dictionary is initially built from an input string of ababcbababaaaaaaa. The dictionary is built in steps as detailed below. The underlined characters are those currently evaluated. The lighter characters represent the node under which a new string is added.

1) ababcbababaaaaaaa
a is present in initialized dictionary
Add next character of b

2) ababcbababaaaaaaa
Assign 4 to ab under node a since a is the prefix of the last character added b.
Add next character of a

3) ababcbababaaaaaaa
Assign 5 to ba under node b since b is the prefix of the last character added of a
Add next character of b

4) ababcbababaaaaaaa
ab is already in dictionary
Add next character of c

5) ababcbababaaaaaaa
Assign 6 to abc under node ab since ab is the prefix of the last character added of c
Add next character of bc

6) ababcbababaaaaaaa
Assign 7 to cb under node c since c is the prefix of the last character added of b
Add next character of a

7) ababcbababaaaaaaa
ba is already in dictionary
Add next character of b

8) ababcbababaaaaaaa
Assign 8 to bab under node ba since ba is the prefix of the last character added of b
Add next character of a

9) ababcbababaaaaaaa
ba is already in dictionary
Add next character of b

10) ababcbababaaaaaaa
bab is already in dictionary
Add next character of a

11) ababcbababaaaaaaa
Assign 9 to baba under node bab since bab is the prefix of the last character added of a
Add next character of a

12) ababcbababaaaaaaa
Assign 10 to aa under node a since a is the prefix of the last character added of a
Add next character of a

13) ababcbababaaaaaaa
aa is already in dictionary
Add next character of a

14) ababcbababaaaaaaa
Assign 11 to aaa under node aa since aa is the prefix of the last character added of a
Add next character of a

16) ababcbababaaaaaaa
aa is already in dictionary
Add next character of a

17) ababcbababaaaaaaa
aaa is already in dictionary
Add next character of a

18) ababcbababaaaaaaa
Assign 12 to aaaa under node aaa since aaa is the prefix of the last character added of a

Compression of the data is accomplished by finding the prefix of a string in the dictionary similar to building the dictionary and outputting the corresponding code. The lighter characters below now represent the string located in the dictionary. The corresponding code in the dictionary is output. The final compressed data contains 1 2 4 3 5 8 1 10 11 1. Here is an example of the steps required to output the compressed data.

```
1)    ababcbababaaaaaaa
```

Add next character of b to produce a prefix of a

2) ababcbababaaaaaaa
Locate a prefix and output code of 1
Add next character of a

3) ababcbababaaaaaaa
Locate b prefix and output code of 2
Add next character of b

4) ababcbababaaaaaaa
a prefix has been processed above
Add next character of c

5) ababcbababaaaaaaa
Locate ab prefix and output code of 4
Add next character of b

6) ababcbababaaaaaaa
Locate c prefix and output code of 3
Add next character of a

7) ababcbababaaaaaaa
b prefix has been processed above
Add next character of b

8) ababcbababaaaaaaa
Locate ba prefix and output code of 5
Add next character of a

9) ababcbababaaaaaaa
b prefix has been processed above
Add next character of b

10) ababcbababaaaaaaa
ba prefix has been processed above
Add next character of a

11) ababcbababaaaaaaa
Locate bab prefix and output code of 8
Add next character of a

12) ababcbababaaaaaaa
Locate a prefix and output code of 1
Add next character of a

13) ababcbababaaaaaaa
a prefix has been processed above
Add next character of a

14) ababcbababaaaaaaa
Locate aa prefix and output code of 10
Add next character of a

16) ababcbababaaaaaaa
a prefix has been processed above
Add next character of a

17) ababcbababaaaaaaa
aa prefix has been processed above
Add next character of a

18) ababcbababaaaaaaa
Locate aaa prefix and output code of 11

```
19)    ababcbababaaaaaaa
       Last character of a, output code of 1
```

Decompression of the data is simple. It is accomplished by finding the code in the dictionary and outputting the corresponding value to produce the original string: ababcbababaaaaaaa.

CPU and I/O Time Test Results

It is always best to estimate the CPU and I/O times for your data in your environment. An alternative is to use DB2 Estimator. IBM reported on the average timings of 12 samples of customer data in the manual *DB2 V3 Performance Topics,* GG24-4284. An ES/9000 9121-742 was used for hardware compression and a 3090-300J was used for software compression. Some of the test results of SQL CPU time (class 2) percent increase are summarized in Figure TS.11.

Figure TS.11. SQL CPU Time Percent Increase and Decrease

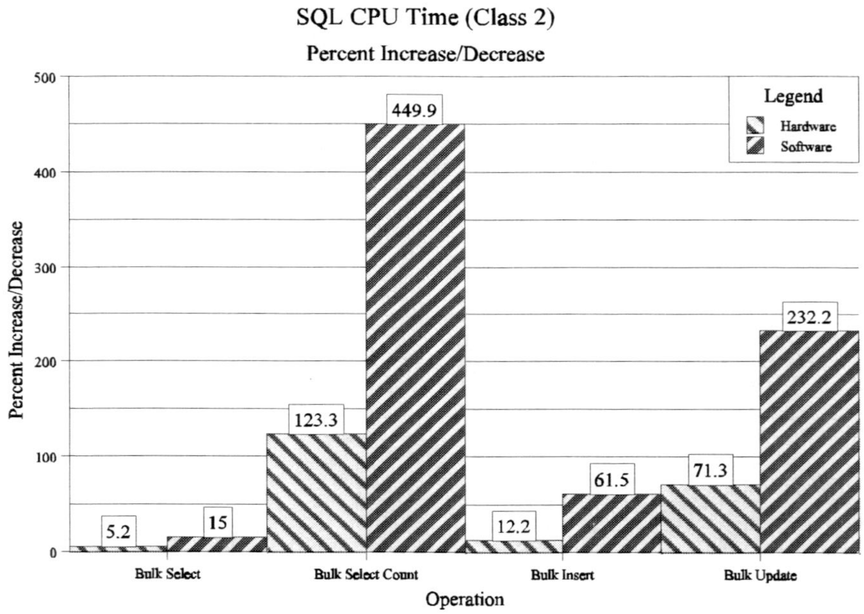

Notice that the hardware compression resulted in significantly less CPU time than software compression. The selection of a large number of rows is the least expensive of the operations. The compression algorithm was optimized for decompression by IBM. The most expensive operation summarized in the figure is a tablespace scan to count the number of rows in the table. Every row must be decompressed before it is processed. The update of a large number of rows is more expensive than INSERTING a large number of rows because the data must be decompressed, updated, and then compressed for updates. This is in comparison to inserts where the rows only need to be compressed. The deletion of rows was not measured because the rows need not be compressed or decompressed in order to be marked as being deleted, assuming that the rows to be deleted are located with an index.

The class 2 elapsed time percent increase and decrease for selecting, counting, INSERTING, and updating the rows are summarized in Figure TS.12.

Figure TS.12. SQL elapsed time percent increase and decrease

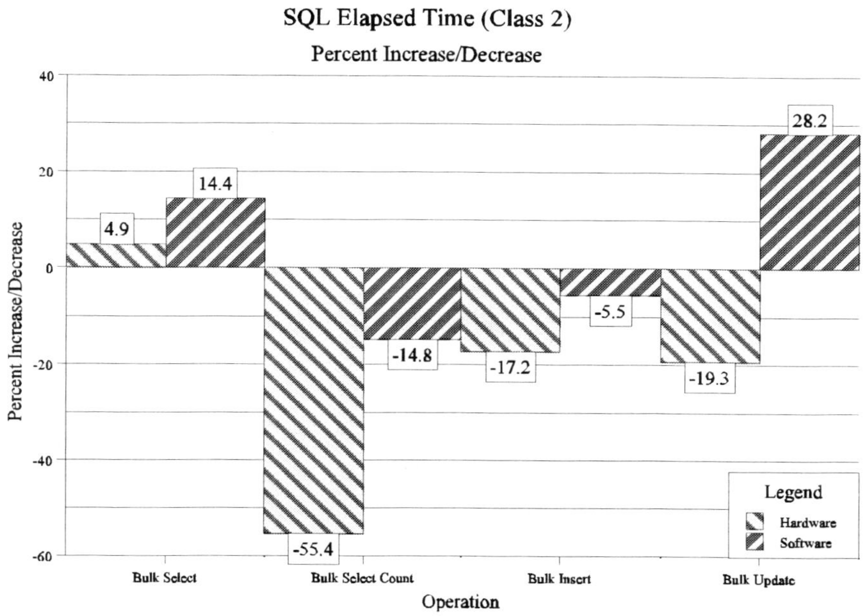

Notice that the elapsed time increase in Figure TS.12 to select a large number of rows is a little less than the CPU time in Figure TS.11. The tablespace scan to count the rows decreased significantly because there are fewer pages of compressed data to be scanned than there would be uncompressed data. The insertion and update of a large number of rows using hardware compression also shows a decrease in the elapsed time for similar reasons. The increase in elapsed time for the updates using software compression is surprising.

The effect of compression on frequently executed utilities was tested. The results of the average CPU time increase and decrease from the tests are summarized in Figure TS.13.

Figure TS.13. Utility CPU time percent increase and decrease

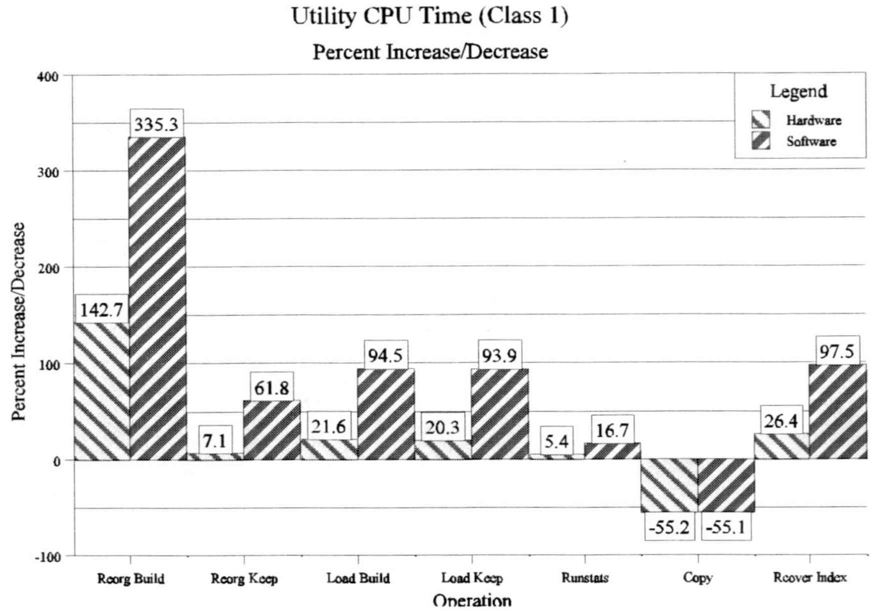

Notice that most of the utilities experienced an increase in CPU time (class 1) using both hardware and software compression. Again we see that the CPU time increased more with software compression, compared to hardware compression. The greatest increase in CPU time was for reorganizations with rebuilding of the dictionary. When using KEEPDICTIONARY, the increase in CPU time was dramatically less. This substantiates the recommendation for using KEEPDICTIONARY if there is not a loss in compression efficiency between reorganizations.

There is a good decrease in CPU time when doing an image copy. Compression and decompression are not required when making a copy. The compressed data is copied. Indeed, there is a decrease in the CPU time because less CPU time is necessary to issue fewer I/O on a smaller number of compressed data pages. Both CPU and elapsed time savings will be about the same as the percentage of pages saved. Similarly, recovery (rebuild in V6) savings will be about the same as the copy savings prior to the log apply.

The average utility elapsed time test results are similar to the CPU time test results for the utilities with some notable exceptions as shown in Figure TS.14.

Figure TS.14. Utility elapsed time percent increase and decrease

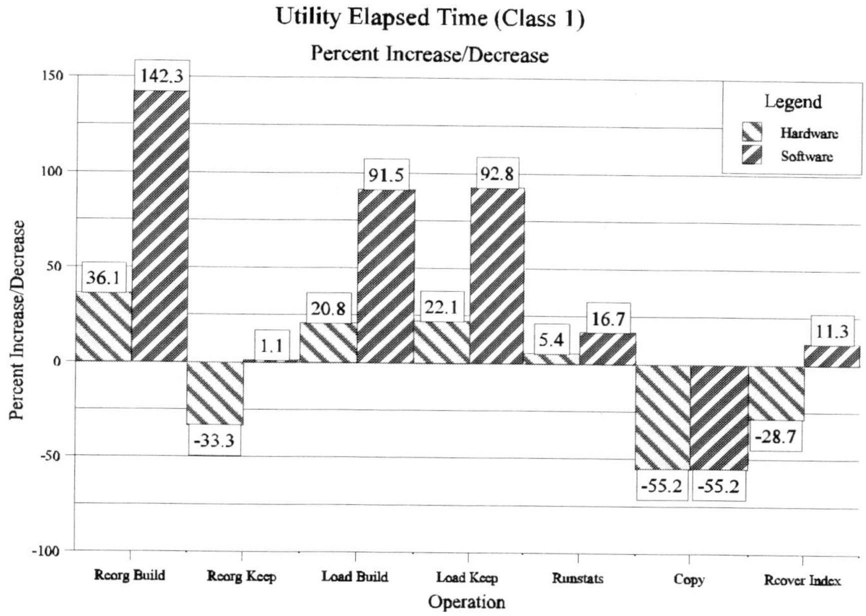

The elapsed time increase was substantially less than the CPU time increase for building the dictionary and compressing the rows with the new dictionary. Again, this is due in large part to the reduced number of I/O required with fewer data pages due to compression. The elapsed time actually decreased with hardware compression and not having to recompress the data because of keeping the dictionary. Again, because fewer data pages are required when using compression, the RECOVER INDEX utility prior to V6 (the REBUILD INDEX in V6) had a reduction in elapsed time when using hardware compression. Overall, compression is a good choice to reduce elapsed time for image copies, recovery, and reorganization with keep dictionary.

TS.9 STRUCTURE OF TABLESPACES

All three types of tablespaces consist of a header page, space map page, compression and decompression dictionary if compression is used, and a number of data pages as shown in Figure TS.15. Space map pages occur throughout the tablespace followed by many data pages. The number of data pages that follow a space map page depends on the type of tablespace and the segment size if segmented tablespaces are used.

Figure TS.15. Header, space map, dictionary and data pages

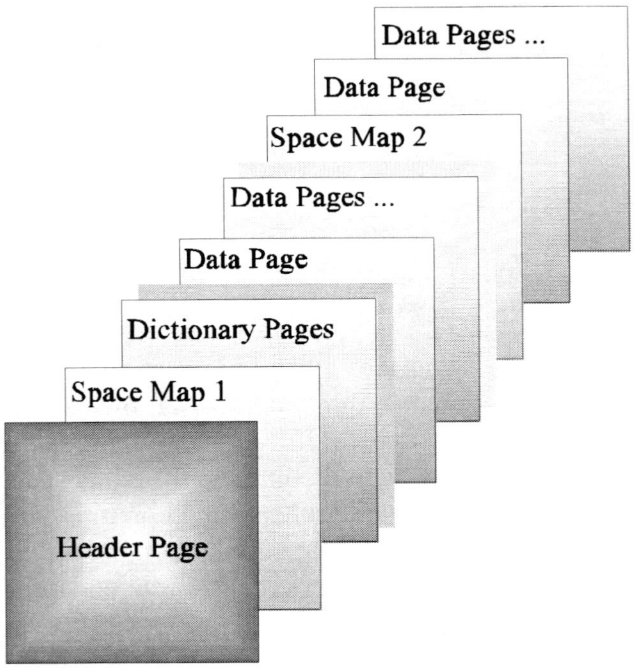

Common Header and Trail Data

All pages begin with a common header consisting of 12 bytes. The first field is a 1 byte flag. The second field is a 6 byte LOGRBA of when the page was last updated and logged. The third field is a 1 byte log ID. The fourth field is a 3 byte page number within the page set. The fifth and last byte contains the page status.

The header page also includes the database ID (DBID), page set ID (PSID), and tablespace ID (OBID). Each of these IDs is 2 bytes in length. Following the IDs is the 6 byte relative byte address (RBA) to which the RECOVER utility has recovered a page set or partition. The HPGRBRBA is the recovery based RBA (RB-RBA) used in logonly recovery. It is updated when the data set is switched to read-only status, the data set is closed, the QUIESCE utility is executed with WRITE YES, the tablespace is stopped, and when DB2 is stopped as discussed in Section TS.6. The level ID follows and is used to detect a down level error as discussed in Chapter CR. The timestamp of when the tablespace was created, the DB2 subsystem name, and additional information are in the header page.

Common trail byte: All pages end with a common trail byte which is used to indicate if the page is broken. The fourth bit must match the fourth bit in the page header.

Space Map Pages

There are three uses of the space map pages. The first use of a space map page is to provide DB2 with information on the location of free space on the data pages that follow. The second use is to indicate pages that have been modified since the last copy by default. This information is used by the COPY utility to determine which pages should be copied when making an incremental copy as discussed in Chapter CR. The third use of a space map page is to identify segments of a segmented tablespace.

A segment header follows the 12 byte common header data on the space map page for a segmented tablespace. The first 2 bytes contains the maximum number of pages covered by the space map page. For example, if the segment size is 4 pages, the number of pages following the space map page is 1,712. If the segment size is 32 pages, the number of pages following the space map page is 4,800. If the segment size is 64 pages, the number of pages following the space map page is 5,504. The second 2 bytes contains the segment size of 4, 8, 16, 32, 64 pages. The third 2 bytes contain the number of free segments. The fourth 2 bytes contain the lowest free segment number. The fifth field of 4 bytes contains the offset of the last formatted page within the scope of space map pages. The sixth and last field of 4 bytes is reserved for future use.

A 7 byte segment block header follows the segment header of a segmented tablespace. The first 4 bytes contain a pointer to the next segment block on the space map page. The second 2 bytes contain the table object ID (OBID). The third field is a 1 byte flag.

The space map pages of a nonsegmented tablespace contain the header data and the number of pages covered by the space map page in a 4 byte field. A space map page covers 10,760 4 KB pages or 87,216 32 KB pages. The next 4 bytes are the last used entry. The last 6 bytes are reserved for future use.

The space map page segment blocks of a segmented tablespace contains a pointer to a page within the pages of a segment that it describes as indicated in Figure TS.16. Following the pointer is information on the availability of free space within a segment. Four bits are used to describe each page. The meaning of the bit values are:

0 - Page is empty and unformatted
1 - Page is emptied with mass delete
2 - Page is empty and formatted
3 - Page has space for longest row
4-10 Values indicate the difference between the minimum and maximum row size in 12.5 percent increments for placing variable length rows
11-14 Values reserved for future use
15 - Page has less than the minimum row space available or is full

Figure TS.16. Segmented space map page and tablespace

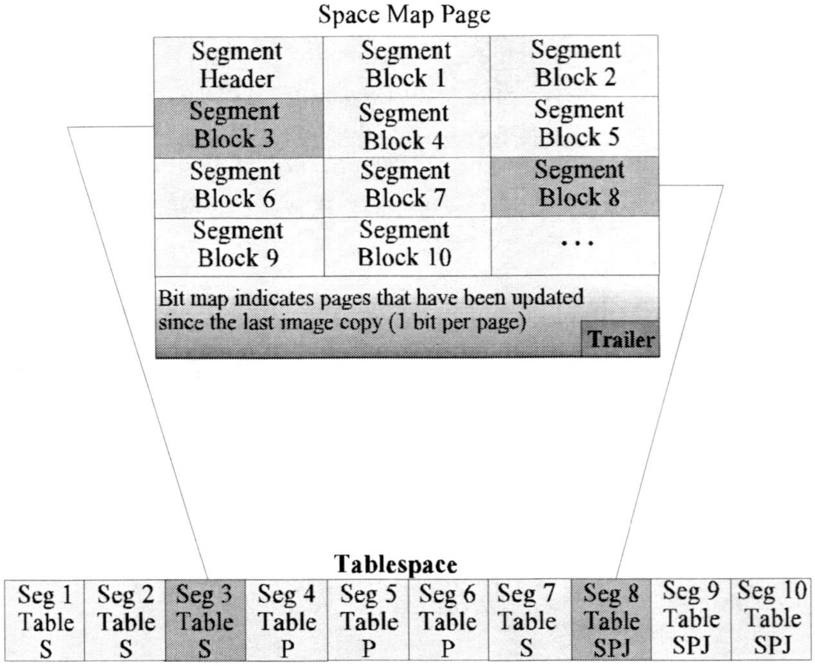

DB2 tests the 4 bits to determine if there is space available on a page to insert a row or update a row and make it longer. This minimizes I/O to the data pages to locate free space.

Only 2 bits are used for nonsegmented tablespaces to indicate that space is available for the largest, average, or smallest row or that the page is full. This limited information on the availability of free space is a primary reason that segmented tablespaces have advantages over nonsegmented tablespaces.

Bit Map Describing Updated Pages

There is a bit map at the bottom of each space map page for segmented and nonsegmented tablespaces. The bit map has a bit corresponding to each page within the range of pages covered by the space map page. A bit is turned on when a row is inserted, updated, or deleted after the last image copy was made by default. For example, if a row is inserted on page 10, the tenth bit is turned on. The image copy utility turns off the bits that correspond to the pages that it copies. The utility uses the bit map to determine if it should make an image copy and whether the copy should be a full copy or an incremental copy of only the pages that have changed since the last copy as described in Chapter CR.

The TRACKMOD parameter can be used to control maintenance of the space map page (V6). The default for this parameter is yes. It results in the processing described in the previous paragraph. Maintenance of the space map page can result in contention due to turning on a bit for each row that is inserted, updated, or deleted. The contention is more likely in a sysplex data sharing environment. If you encounter a problem or anticipate a problem due to heavy insert, update, and delete activity, use TRACKMOD NO.

The trade-off of TRACKMOD NO is that incremental copies execute more slowly because the RBA is used to determine which pages should be copied. It is necessary to compare the currently active RBA for a data set with the RBA on the page to determine if the page should be copied. This is in contrast to using the bit map on the space map pages to identify the pages that must be copied when executing the incremental copy utility as discussed in Chapter CR.

You can determine if modification of pages are being tracked from the column TRACKMOD in SYSTABLESPACE. Blank in the column indicates that changed pages are tracked in the bit map on the space map page. *N* indicates that the default has been changed. Changed pages are not tracked in the space map page.

Page Layout

All data pages in all three types of tablespaces have the same layout. The first 12 bytes on each data page contains the common page header described at the beginning of this section. Following the common page header are 2 bytes indicating the total free space on the page, 2 bytes containing the offset to contiguous free space, 2 bytes containing the offset to 1st chained hole, 1 byte containing the number of ID map entries, and the last byte is reserved for future use.

Although the terms row and record are often used interchangeably, there is a difference in DB2. A row in a table consists of all of the columns in the row. A record is the row plus the row prefix (RP) of 6 bytes as indicated in Figure TS.17. The RP begins with a 1 byte row type. It has a value of X'00' for a normal row, X'04' for a compressed row, and X'20' for an overflow row. Next comes a record length of 2 bytes, a 2 byte OBID of the table, and finally a 1 byte map ID for the directory entry at the bottom of the page.

Figure TS.17. Page layout

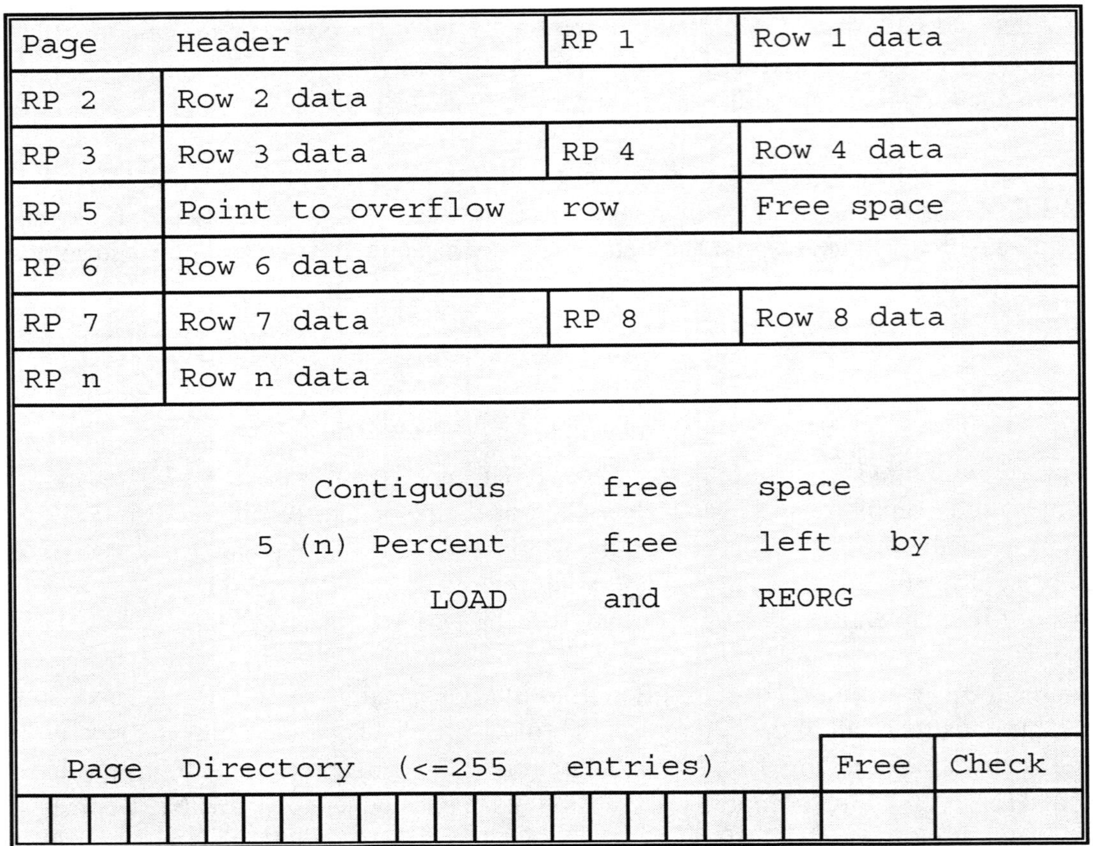

Record = RP (Row Prefix) + Row

The page directory contains up to 255 map IDs, each of which is 2 bytes in length. This maximum number of directory entries corresponds to the maximum number of rows on a page discussed with respect to the MAXROWS parameter in Section TS.5.

The last 2 bytes on the page contain the ID of the first free ID map entry (1 byte) and a common check byte (1 byte).

TS.10 SUMMARY

Segmented tablespaces have significant advantages over simple tablespace for one or multiple tables per tablespace, managing related tables, and the management of free space to maintain clustering and variable length rows. Do be cautious of mixing tables with different update activity in a single simple or segmented tablespace. A SEGSIZE of 32 is a good choice for all but very small tables.

Do choose a percent free to match the update activity and adjust it to match your reorganization requirements. Free space should be a multiple of the record length. Otherwise, there can be unusable space on every page. If there is random insert, update, and delete activity, FREEPAGE of 31 is a good choice for segmented tablespaces, assuming a SEGSIZE of 32, and 15 is a good choice for nonsegmented tablespaces.

LOCKSIZE of PAGE reduces locking costs and avoids unexpected lock escalations that can occur with LOCKSIZE of ANY. MAXROWS can be used to control the number of rows on a page. Do use CLOSE of NO for frequently processed tablespaces.

Do consider partitioning large tablespaces for improved availability and manageability of the parts. Partitioning provides for spreading I/O across multiple DASD devices, channels and control units. It also provides for DB2 parallelism and limited partition scans. Do specify a larger number of partitions than will every be used, perhaps the maximum number of partitions allowed, because it is not possible to alter the number of partitions. It is necessary to drop and recreate the tablespace and all related objects. However, the limit key of each partition can be altered which offers a good deal of flexibility if a sufficient number of partitions have been specified.

DSN1COMP provides good information on whether compression will result in significant savings in DASD space and the number of data pages that need to be processed. These savings may well justify the increased CPU time in many cases. The increase in CPU time is frequently not significant for online transactions that process only a few rows. Hardware compression costs substantially less than software compression.

RUNSTATS statistics on compressed data can be used to monitor compression savings, determine when the dictionary should be rebuilt, and collect statistics for use by the optimizer in access path selection. LOAD and REORG can build and refine the dictionary. KEEPDICTIONARY is a good choice once the dictionary is refined and characteristics of the data with respect to compression do not change.

EXERCISES

1. a) If there is insufficient contiguous space on a volume for the PRIQTY allocation, will a resource unavailable message be issued?

b) Why should the SECQTY be specified in multiples of cylinders rather than tracks if the tablespace is expected to occupy multiple cylinders?

c) Why is it important to estimate the PRIQTY carefully and avoid the use of SECQTY allocations?

2. a) How does DB2 use free space?

b) What are the consequences of having insufficient free space when variable length rows are used?

c) What are the consequence of having insufficient free space with respect to maintaining the rows in sequence.

d) What are some considerations that apply to both variable length rows and sequencing of the data?

3. a) Several formula to estimate the amount of free space for tablespaces were presented. What key point should be kept in mind when estimating the free space for a table?

b) What are some characteristics of tables that should have zero free space?

4. a) When will the blank pages left as a result of the FREEPAGE parameter be used?

b) Why is FREEPAGE 31 a good choice when using SEGSIZE of 32?

c) Why is FREEPAGE 15 a good choice when using nonsegmented tablespaces?

5. a) What are the characteristics of tablespaces that can be created with a lock size of table or tablespace?

b) What are the benefits of using lock size of table or tablespace?

6. a) What conditions suggest the need for row locking?

b) What are the costs of row locking?

c) What are some of the conditions that require a page lock even though lock size of row is specified?

d) What are some alternatives to row locking?

7. What are the advantages of a segmented tablespace over a simple tablespace regarding the space map page?

8. a) What are the advantages of multiple tables per segmented tablespace?

b) What are the disadvantage of multiple tables per segmented tablespace?

c) How does the frequency of updates affect the decision to group tables in a tablespace?

9. What are the advantages of a simple tablespace over segmented tablespace?

10. What are the advantages of a partitioned tablespace?

11. What is a disadvantage of a partitioned tablespace without NPIs?

12. a) What are some advantages of using a control table to determine the range of values in a partition?

b) What are some disadvantages of using a control table to determine the range of values in a partition?

ANSWERS

1. a) No. If there is insufficient contiguous space available to satisfy the PRIQTY on a volume, space will be taken on up to and including 5 extents. If more than 5 extents are required, a resource unavailable message will be issued.

b) If the PRIQTY or SECQTY is less than or equal to one cylinder, then track allocation is used, which detracts from performance.

c) One should avoid data going into secondary allocations because excessive seek time can be experienced. The secondary allocation is usually far away from the primary allocation and arm movement is one of the most time consuming aspects of locating data on DASD.

2. a) DB2 uses free space to maintain variable length rows and to maintain the rows in clustering sequence.

b) If there is insufficient free space, variable length rows have to be moved to a near or far page, which requires additional CPU and I/O. A pointer to the new location of the row is left in the original row space on the page. Two I/O to the data pages are required to locate the moved row for future processing.

c) If there is insufficient free space, it will not be possible to insert a row on a page in clustering sequence. Additional CPU and I/O are required to locate space for the row. Performance of transactions and batch programs that rely on the rows being in sequence will degrade as more and more rows are placed out of sequence.

d) The page is dynamically reorganized to gather free space, which adds to the number of instructions that must be executed, and the page is locked during the process. The data will need to be reorganized more frequently if there is insufficient free space to maintain clustering and variable length rows.

3. a) The free space should be a multiple of the row length. For example, the default of 5 percent free will not allow for a row to be inserted if the row is more than 200 bytes in length. The 200 bytes of free space on the data pages will never be used.

b) Read-only tables, those with very low insert/delete activity, and tables where rows are always inserted/deleted at the end of the table do not benefit from free space being available. There is no need to waste space on each page and cause more pages to be used and processed than necessary.

4. a) If a variable length row cannot be increased in length on a page or a row cannot be inserted on the target page to maintain clustering sequence because of insufficient space on a page, space on the blank page will be used.

b) If space is not available on the desired page, the search algorithm for free space in a segmented tablespace begins with trying to place the row within the target segment. FREEPAGE of 31 leaves a blank page within each segment when using SEGSIZE of 32.

c) The search algorithm for free space in a nonsegmented tablespace begins with looking for space within plus or minus 16 pages as indicated on the space map page. FREEPAGE of 15 leaves a blank page within the 16 page range.

5. a) Read-only tables are very good candidates for lock size of table or tablespace. Consideration can be given to using lock size of table or tablespace for tables with very low insert/delete activity (reference tables that rarely change for example). Private tables created by an ad hoc user and used only by that user benefits from a lock size of table or tablespace.

b) There is no need to lock at the row or page level or execute the instructions for lock avoidance (discussed in Chapter CC) for read-only tables and those that are rarely updated.

6. a) Tablespaces that experience high update activity in frequently executed online transactions. Programs that process only a few rows. Very small tables that are frequently updated. Short rows with many rows on a page (compression frequently results in short rows). Rows usually inserted at the end of a table or updates concentrated in any specific areas of the table.

b) If a program typically processes multiple rows on a page, a lock is required for each of the rows processed (rather than a single lock on the page).

c) If a variable length row is increased in length or space on a page is dynamically reorganized to gather free space, a page lock is necessary.

d) Lock avoidance and the UR isolation level reduces costs for read-only processing without row locking. UR must be used cautiously as discussed in Chapter CC.

7. The space map page of a segmented tablespace offers a number of advantages over a simple tablespace. The space map page is used to locate free space more efficiently and to implement the mass delete algorithm. It is used to locate only the pages with active rows for the table being processed during a tablespace scan and the COPY utility uses the space map page to identify only the pages with active rows. The optimizer has a better estimate of the number of pages that contain rows for a table.

8. a) One advantage of multiple tables in a tablespace is that fewer utilities need to be developed and scheduled in production because most utilities operate at the tablespace level. Recoverability of related tables in a single tablespace is improved. Fewer tablespaces need to be open. Deferred write applies to all tables in the tablespace. These advantages apply to a number of very small reference tables in a single tablespace. In addition, a header and space map page for one or a few pages need not be maintained and a track is not required for each table.

b) The disadvantage of multiple tables in a tablespace is that utilities cannot be scheduled for individual tables as required and all tables are unavailable while a utility is executing in most cases. Pending states apply at the tablespace level. Different tables may need different tablespace parameter values (PCTFREE, SEGSIZE, LOCKSIZE, LOCKMAX, etc.), but only one is definable. If compression is used, the compression dictionary may not be best for all tables in the tablespace.

c) If tables with a different update activity are grouped in a tablespace the above disadvantages are more intense. It is best not to mix frequently and infrequently updated tables in a tablespace.

Most companies place one table in one tablespace except for small reference tables. Multiple small reference tables are typically placed in one tablespace.

9. There are few advantages of a simple tablespace over a segmented tablespace. The fact that there are more space map pages for segmented tablespaces versus simple tablespaces is not considered a significant increase in space in most cases. (A segmented tablespace with a SEGSIZE of 64 has a space map page every 5,504 pages or 4,800 for a SEGSIZE of 32 versus a simple tablespace with a space map page every 10,760 pages.) The advantage of being able to interleave related rows on a page is overshadowed by the fact there are no automatic facilities to maintain the interleaving of rows on a page.

10. The advantage of a partitioned tablespace is that it provides for dividing a large table into multiple

parts for improved availability and ease of management. Utilities can operate on a single partition while other partitions are available for processing by SQL and other utilities in most cases. Elapsed time for reading a large number of rows can be reduced through the use of parallelism on multiple partitions. Multiple batch jobs can operate on multiple partitions in parallel through application design. Parts of the tablespaces can be placed on multiple DASD devices and channels to reduce I/O contention. Large tables usually have parts that are frequently processed and parts that are rarely processed. The rarely processed parts can be archived using SMS and will be automatically recalled when an SQL statement requires data in the partition. The partitions that are rarely updated can be given 0 percent free to avoid wasting space. In addition, the parts that are rarely accessed can be placed on slower less expensive devices.

11. A disadvantage of a partitioned tablespace without NPIs is that the partitioning index cannot be altered for additional ranges of values. This is particularly troublesome for historical data where it is necessary to drop old partitions and add new partitions.

12. a) The advantage of using a control table to determine the range of values in a partition is flexibility of adjusting the upper range values of rows to be placed in a partition. This is particularly important for historical data where it is necessary to remove partitions containing data that is no longer needed and add partitions for a new time period.

b) The disadvantage of using a control table is that it must be maintained through application design and development. It must be accessed each time that rows are accessed in the partitioned tablespace. However, if there is not a well defined partitioning index, other alternatives can result in significant performance problems.

FIGURES

Creating Tables and Views

CT.1 INTRODUCTION

The table is DB2's basic unit for data manipulation. A table is sometimes referred to as a base table to distinguish it from a view, which is a virtual table derived from one or more base tables. In a base table, each column holds values for an entity attribute, identified in the column heading. Each row contains a value for each column, with a few exceptions that will be explained later, with all the values in a given column being of the same data type.

CT.2 CREATING TABLES

The table name can be a three part name consisting of LOCATION.AUTHID.NAME. The LOCATION can be used to direct the execution of SQL statements to another relational DBMS. The default is the location where the SQL DML (data manipulation language) or DDL (data definition language) statements are executed. AUTHID (authorization identification) is the current SQLID (SQL identifier) of the person who creates the table. NAME is the name specified when the table is created. Typically, the LOCATION and AUTHID are not specified when creating tables and views and are not specified when using SQL DML statements. Control of the AUTHID for SQL DML is discussed in Chapter PE.

Creation of global temporary and declare temporary tables are discussed in Chapter SP.

Figure CT.1 shows a typical statement for creating a table--in this case for storing information about suppliers. The developer lists within parentheses after the table name, each column name for the table, followed by the data type and length of the column, and whether null values are allowed in the column. (A null indicates that an actual value is either unknown or inapplicable. Nulls hold practical and performance implications to be discussed in a moment.) The maximum length of a column name is 18 and the maximum number of columns in a table or view is 750 except for a dependent table which has a maximum of 749.

Figure CT.1. CREATE TABLE statement

```
CREATE TABLE S
 (SN      CHAR(6)  NOT NULL,
  SNAME   CHAR(20) NOT NULL WITH DEFAULT,
  STATUS SMALLINT WITH DEFAULT NULL
    CONSTRAINT STATUS_C
      CHECK (STATUS BETWEEN 10 AND 200),
  CITY    CHAR(15) WITH DEFAULT 'London'
    CONSTRAINT CITY_C
      CHECK (CITY IN ('Rome', 'Oslo', 'London'),
  AUTHID_OF_INSERTER CHAR(8) WITH DEFAULT USER,
  DATE_RECORDED DATE NOT NULL WITH DEFAULT,
  PRIMARY KEY (SN))
CCSID EBCDIC
RESTRICT ON DROP
AUDIT NONE
DATA CAPTURE NONE
VALIDPROC CHECKS
IN DASPJDB.STSP;
```

Column order holds performance implications. When an update changes data, DB2 records the change in a log, which is used to recreate the change if the tablespace must be recovered after a failure. Because DB2 logs only that portion of a row from the first to the last changed byte, placing frequently updated columns next to each other minimizes logging, saving on both processing and storage. And, as we shall see, listing variable-length columns last provides the best performance. First, let us look at data types.

Data Types

DB2 offers all the IBM standard data types and some special data types summarized in Figure CT.2. Data type synonyms are available for compatibility with the ANSI (American National Standards Institute) and ISO (International Standards Organization) standards. The synonyms are indicated with an "*" in the figure.

Figure CT.2. Basic data types and lengths

Data Types	N B	COBOL Declaration	PL/1 Declaration	C Declaration
SMALLINT	2	01 V PIC S9(4) COMP-4.	DCL V BIN FIXED(15);	short int id;
INTEGER	4	01 V PIC S9(9) COMP-4.	DCL V BIN FIXED(31);	long int id;
DECIMAL or NUMERIC*	<=16	01 V PIC S9(n)V9(m) COMP-3.	DCL V DEC FIXED(S,P);	decimal (x,y)
REAL or FLOAT(n) n <= 21	4	01 V COMP-1.	DCL V BIN FLOAT(21);	float id;
DOUBLE PRECISION, DOUBLE, or FLOAT(n) 22<=n<=53	8	01 V COMP-2.	DCL V BIN FLOAT(53);	double id;
CHAR	255	01 V PIC X(n)	DCL V CHAR(n);	char id [m];
VARCHAR or CHAR VARYING* or CHARACTER VARYING*	4046	01 V. 49 VL PIC S9(4) COMP. 49 VN PIC X(n).	DCL V CHAR(n) VAR;	struct char var id {len & data};
LONG VARCHAR	32714			
GRAPHIC	254	01 V PIC G(n)	DCL V GRAPHIC(n);	wchar_t var id;
VARGRAPHIC	4046	01 V. 49 VL PIC S9(4) COMP. 49 VN PIC G(n) DIS-1.	DCL V GRAPHIC(n) VAR;	struct var id {len & data};
LONG VARGRAPHIC	32714			
DATE	4	01 V PIC X(10)	DCL V CHAR(10)	char id [>=11];
TIME	3	01 V PIC X(8)	DCL V CHAR(8)	char id [>=9];
TIMESTAMP	10	01 V PIC X(26)	DCL V CHAR(26)	char id [>=27];

*SQL92 standard.

"N B" is the number of bytes required by the data type. Do add one byte if nulls are allowed.

C character declarations use one byte for the NULL-terminated form.

Numeric Data Types

DB2's data types offer developers a number of choices, some of which affect performance. An INTEGER, for example, requires 4 bytes, which can represent a value of up to 2,147,483,648. If the developer knows that the item's value will never exceed 32,767, however, he or she may use SMALLINT, which can represent values up to that amount but needs only 2 bytes. The shorter representation can save storage and speed processing and I/O operations.

A packed decimal column with a maximum value of 99999.99 can be defined with a data type of DECIMAL(7,2). Seven is the precision of the number and 2 is the scale. This means that 7 is the total number of digits in the number and 2 of the digits are to the right of the decimal point. Four bytes are required to store the value. If the column is defined as DECIMAL(6,2), four bytes are still required to store the value, but the maximum value is 9999.99 because 4 bits are required to represent the sign. This suggests that odd precision should be used to avoid wasting space for each column value and allow for the largest number of digits per byte of storage.

DB2 allows for very large packed decimal values with a maximum value of 10^{31} - 1 provided that DEC31 is specified in DSNZPARM using DECARTH=DEC31 or on the installation panel DSNTIP4 (DEC15 is the default). DEC31 allows for a values of 10 nonillion. A nonillion comes in after a million, billion, trillion, quadrillion, quintillion, sextillion, septillion, and octillion to give you an idea of the magnitude of the number. Section SL.4 discusses an alternative for managing these large values in a host program.

Character Data Types

Most character data types including CHAR, VARCHAR, and LONG VARCHAR use a single byte character set (SBCS). That is, each character requires one byte to represent a character. Graphic data types use a double byte character set (DBCS). This data type uses two bytes to represent ideograms in the Asian business language of Katakana. Mixed data strings allow for a mixture of SBCS and DBCS with shift codes used to delimit DBCS characters. Data subtypes of SBCS, MIXED, and FOR BIT DATA can be specified for string data types. FOR BIT DATA indicates that the bits need not be associated with a coded character set identifier (CCSID).

VARCHAR with Care

VARCHAR or LONG VARCHAR is required if the character string is more than 255 bytes because the maximum length of the CHAR data type is 255 bytes as can be seen in Figure CT.2. The VARCHAR data type also offers DASD space savings, but there are trade-offs to be considered. The data type has space allocated according to the actual length of each data item, not including trailing blanks, up to the maximum specified in the CREATE TABLE statement. The CHAR data type, on the other hand, allocates the same amount of space--that specified in the statement--regardless of each item's length. If the value is, in fact, shorter than the allocated amount, the remaining bytes are filled with blanks.

It may seem at first that VARCHAR would always use space more efficiently than CHAR. This is not always true, however, because each VARCHAR entry must carry a 2-byte prefix indicating its length. If the values' lengths do not vary significantly, this 2-byte cost on each item can outweigh the gains of space savings on the shorter items.

Analysis of VARCHAR and CHAR space usage: The following SELECT statement is useful in determining the space used and saved by using a CHAR column compared to a VARCHAR column. You will want to change the name of a table (SYSIBM.SYSCOLUMNS in the example) with a VARCHAR column to the name of the table of interest to you. Also, change NAME to the name of the column defined as VARCHAR and change 18 to the value used to define the VARCHAR column.

```
SELECT 18 * COUNT(*) AS CHAR18,
  SUM(2 + LENGTH(NAME)) AS VARCHAR18,
  18 * COUNT(*) - SUM(2 + LENGTH(NAME)) AS BYTES_SAVED,
  18 AS AVG_CHAR18,
  AVG(2 + LENGTH(NAME)) AS AVG_VARCHAR18,
  18 - AVG(2 + LENGTH(NAME)) AS COL_B
FROM SYSIBM.SYSCOLUMNS;
```

Here is the results of the SELECT statement:

CHAR18	VARCHAR18	BYTES_SAVED	AVG_CHAR18	AVG_VARCHAR18	COL_B
147852	84061	63791	18	10	8

In this case there is a savings of 63,791 bytes if the column is defined as VARCHAR. This suggests that VARCHAR is a good choice. A VARCHAR column is often useful with descriptive text where the user sometimes enters a short description and other times they enter a long description.

However, there are some additional factors that should be considered before making a final decision. The space savings should result in one or more additional rows fitting on a page. Otherwise, there is no real saving in DASD space and I/O. This is because storage and I/O is at the page level. The use of VARCHAR also costs storage space when a VARCHAR column is indexed. The storage space used for each index value does not vary. Instead DB2 inserts blanks to pad each value to its maximum length. In any case, long columns make poor candidates for indexes because they can cause additional levels in the index structure which requires additional I/O to traverse the index structure. The use of a VARCHAR column causes a row to be variable in length as does DB2 data compression. The implications of this for performance and logging are discussed in Chapter CD.

Index only processing of an index on a column declared as VARCHAR is not possible by default. It is necessary to access the data pages to retrieve the length of significant bytes in the column to return to the host program. The length is not stored in the index pages. Index only processing can be enabled by changing RETVLCFK to YES in DSNZPARM DSN6SPRM macro after applying V5 APAR PQ10465. It is necessary to rebind plans and packages that reference VARCHAR columns to take advantage of index only processing. If index only processing is chosen by the optimizer as part of the access path, values returned to host program are fully padded with blanks and the maximum length of the VARCHAR column is returned in the 2 byte length field. This can require changes to programs that expect only leading significant bytes and the length of the significant bytes in the 2 byte length field. If index only processing is not chosen by the optimizer as part of the access path with the current bind or a future bind, only significant bytes (non-trailing blanks) are returned to the host program. The 2 byte length field contains the length of the significant bytes.

Caution: Programs must be designed to handle an access path with or without index only processing of VARCHAR indexes if index only processing is enabled for the DB2 subsystem.

Compression has advantages over the use of VARCHAR columns, particularly if there are several potential VARCHAR columns in a row. There are a couple of advantages of VARCHAR over compression. Trailing blanks are not passed to relational data system (RDS) and to the host program. Instead, a row is decompressed at the data manager (DM) level and trailing blanks are passed to RDS and the host program. Only if a VARCHAR column is made longer is the row moved to a near or far page if there is not sufficient space on the page. In contrast, an update of any column in a compressed row has a fifty percent chance of causing the rows to be increased in length and moved to a near or far page if there is not sufficient space on the page.

The ALTER TABLE statement can be used to change the maximum length of a VARCHAR column (V5 APAR PQ16674), for example:

```
ALTER TABLE S
ALTER COLUMN SNAME SET DATA TYPE VARCHAR(200);
```

It is not always clear what the new length should be. The following SELECT statement is useful in making this determination. It reports on the column lengths and number of times each length occurs for a given table (SYSIBM.SYSCOLUMNS in the example).

```
SELECT COL_LENGTH, COUNT(*)
FROM (SELECT LENGTH(NAME) AS COL_LENGTH
      FROM SYSIBM.SYSCOLUMNS) AS L
GROUP BY COL_LENGTH
ORDER BY COL_LENGTH;
```

The results of execution of the statement are:

COL_ LENGTH	N_ OCCUR
2	52
3	111
4	469
5	874
6	1,182
7	1,191
8	1,128
9	857
10	613
11	457

The column NAME is defined as VARCHAR(18). Based on the data currently in the column, the column can be declared as VARCHAR(11) which is the maximum length of values in the column. Your data is likely to have a much wider difference in the current definition and the desired definition of the column. Of course, you will want to allow space for values that are not currently in the column.

Altering the length of a VARCHAR column invalidates plans, packages, and dynamic cached statements that reference the column.

It is not necessary to rebuild an index on an altered VARCHAR column immediately. The index is maintained with old and new lengths for up to and including 16 alters. However, REBUILD INDEX, REORG INDEX, or REORG TABLESPACE should be used to rebuild the index as soon as possible to maximize performance.

There are restrictions on VARCHAR columns that can be altered. The column cannot be referenced in a referential integrity structure, view, temporary table, stored procedures, EDITPROC, VALIDPROC, and FIELDPROC.

There are restrictions on the operations that can be performed on a column declared as VARCHAR with a length greater than 255 bytes since it is considered a long string like LONG VARCHAR. It is not possible to place an index on the column, it cannot be used with a predicate other than LIKE, a function other than SUBSTR, a subselect, a UNION without ALL, ORDER BY, GROUP BY, or DISTINCT. (These functions are discussed in Chapter SL.)

Numerals as Numeric Types

Developers sometimes are tempted to declare variables consisting of numeric identifiers--such as employee identifications or part numbers--as character types. These numbers will not be used in calculations so the developer feels safe in treating them as character variables. The perceived advantage is that the approach avoids the data exceptions that occur after data entry mistakes--the keying in of a character rather than a numeral for a numeric type. A validation procedure would catch such an error, but the lack of thorough validation does occur. Consequently data exceptions may occur, requiring costly program reruns. If a character type had been declared originally, however, the system would accept the mistake and keep running.

This shortcut can be expensive, however. Putting aside the question of tolerating misinformation, using a character type for numeric data holds tangible disadvantages. One is that it uses unnecessary storage space. SMALLINT, which can handle numbers up to 32,767, requires only 2 bytes. The five characters needed to represent values that high require 1 byte each--a 3-byte cost per data value. One company saved 3500 cylinders of 3390 DASD by converting a numeric identifier from CHAR(5) to SMALLINT. If the column is indexed, the space cost of this approach more than doubles. In addition, when there are fewer pages in a table, fewer I/O are required to perform a tablespace scan.

Another reason to use the appropriate type is that occasional users find it confusing to have to enclose some numerals in quotation marks--those that have been declared as characters--in their database requests. Finally, when DB2 eventually supports enforcement of domains, difficulties will be encountered. The domain of a column with all numeric data is misrepresented when the column is declared as a character data type. The number of possible values in a column declared as a numeric data type differs from that for a character data type. The optimizer has more accurate information on the number of possible values in a column when the declared data type reflects the data to be placed in the column as discussed in Chapter OP. Clearly all of these potential problems argue strongly in favor of declaring numeric identifiers as numeric types.

Date and Time

Three data types allow for the manipulation of dates and times and for the automatic recording of when rows are inserted. This capability is useful for keeping track of when orders are entered, for example. The data types are DATE, TIME, and TIMESTAMP. Figure CT.3 summarizes the format of the available DATE and TIME data types.

Figure CT.3. Date and time data types

Format*	Date	Date Example	Time	Time Ex.
ISO (International Standards Organization)	YYYY-MM-DD	1987-05-23	HH.MM.SS	20.10.30
USA (IBM USA Standard)	MM/DD/YYYY	05/23/1987	HH:MM AM	08:10 PM
EUR (European Standard)	DD.MM.YYYY	23.05.1987	HH.MM.SS	20.10.30
JIS (Japanese Industrial Standard Christian Era)	YYYY-MM-DD	1987-05-23	HH:MM:SS	20:10:30

```
*An exit can be used to define other formats
```

TIMESTAMP, which represents both date and time in the ISO format plus six digits of microseconds, is useful when a large number of sources are entering data into the same table at the same second and the organization wants to differentiate the entries by time. It is almost a million times less likely that two sources will enter data at the same microsecond than at the same second, though it can happen, particularly in a multiprocessor system or across international time zones.

The time and date columns are declared in the CREATE TABLE statement by stating the column name followed by the type name: DATE_RECORDED DATE, for example. As with numeric types, the lengths need not be declared. In fact, DATE requires 4 bytes, TIME 3 bytes, and TIMESTAMP 10 bytes. The internal representation is like a packed decimal representation without the four sign bits. Because the time and date types are very specialized, they do not correspond directly to types provided by host-languages. Host-language variables that receive values from time and date columns must be declared as character types: 10 bytes long for DATE corresponding to the 10 characters in the standard date formats, 8 bytes for TIME, and 26 bytes for TIMESTAMP. When the DATE and TIME variables are used in calculations, a process discussed in Chapter SL, the host-language variable that receives the results must be declared as a decimal type: DECIMAL(8,0) for DATE, DECIMAL(6,0) for TIME, and DECIMAL(14,n) for TIMESTAMP, with n=0 through 6, depending on the format required.

Specifying the Date and Time Format: The ISO format is the installation default and can be changed in DSNZPARM. (Also, an exit can be used to define other formats.) Do be cautious of setting USA as the default. The unload and reload of a table with a column containing time results 0 seconds. This can result in duplicate primary keys that have time as part of the key. Use of the sample program DSNTIAUL to unload data outputs time in the format HH:MM AM or HH:MM PM by default. In addition, dates extracted into a sequential file do not sort chronologically.

Recommendation: The use of the ISO format as the installation default is a good choice. You can specify a different format at precompile time for reporting purposes. For example, specification of USA, EUR, or JIS overrides the installation default. Another alternative is the use of the CHAR scalar function (discussed in Chapter SL) can be used to specify the format like:

```
SELECT CHAR(ORDER_DATE, USA) FROM ...
```

The CHAR function can be used to override the installation and precompile specifications for specific columns.

Identity Column

Unique, sequential, and recoverable values for each row in a table can be automatically generated by DB2 by defining the column as an identity column as shown in the following example (V6 APAR PQ30652). The use of an identity column has significant performance advantages over the use of using a table with the last sequence number as discussed in Chapter PD. IBM compared these two techniques. Their test results show 634 transaction per second using an identity column with CACHE 20 compared to 106 transactions per second using a table with last sequence number.. Details of the tests can be found in the *DB2 UDB Server for OS/390 Version 6 Technical Update* (SG24-6108) manual.

```
CREATE TABLE S_ID
  (SN_ID  INTEGER GENERATED ALWAYS AS IDENTITY
    (START WITH 1, INCREMENT BY 1, CACHE 20),
   SNAME  CHAR(20) NOT NULL WITH DEFAULT,
   STATUS SMALLINT WITH DEFAULT 99,
   CITY   CHAR(15) NOT NULL WITH DEFAULT,
   PRIMARY KEY (SN_ID)) --not required
     IN DASPJDB.STSP;
```

The data type of an identity column can be INTEGER, SMALLINT, or DECIMAL with a scale of 0. The column can be a distinct type based on one of these data types. Distinct types are discussed later in this section in the subsection Creating and Using Distinct Types. An identity column can be designated on a declare temporary table (not on a create temporary table).

Following is a description of each of the clauses that can be used when defining a column as an identity column.

GENERATED ALWAYS (default) means that an explicit value cannot be specified with an INSERT and UPDATE statement. The identity column should not be specified in the field specification of the LOAD utility. LOAD generates the sequential values. DB2 generates values if the identity column is not specified in an INSERT statement with a subselect. DB2 guarantees unique values without having to create a unique index.

GENERATED BY DEFAULT means that an explicit value can be provided. If an explicit value is not provided, DB2 generates a value. This is useful for data propagation where is it necessary to copy the content of a table to another table or unload and reload a table. Caution must be exercised when using GENERATED BY DEFAULT. Insertion of a value within the range of values currently being used by DB2 fails. Uniqueness is not guaranteed except for previously DB2 generated values. You can create a unique index to guarantee unique values. If this is done, developers need to check for -803 SQLCODE indicating an attempt to insert a duplicate value in a column with a unique index.

AS IDENTITY designates the column as an identity column. The column is implicitly NOT NULL. Only one identity column is allowed for a table.

START WITH provides for generating numbers starting with a number other than 1 which is the default. If you need to override the default, the value specified must be a valid number for the chosen data type. It can be a positive or negative number. If it is a positive number, it is an ascending number. If it is a negative number, it is a descending number.

INCREMENTED BY provides for incrementing the number with a value greater than 1 (1 is the default). The value must be valid for the chosen data type.

CACHE 20 means that 20 (default) preallocated values are kept in memory by DB2. This improves performance as discussed in Chapter PD. A value of between 2 and 2,147,483,648 can be specified.

NO CACHE means preallocated numbers are not kept in memory. This is useful if it is necessary to assign numbers in sequence as the rows are inserted in a sysplex data sharing environment.

The integrity of an identity column is maintained in a sysplex data sharing environment where multiple processors can be inserting rows at the same time. Each processor is assigned 20 (default) preallocated numbers if the cache is used. Therefore, numbers are not necessarily assigned in the order of row insertion by various processors.

Recoverability of the counter value is achieved by reconstructing it from the logs if DB2 abends and there is no cache.

Gaps can appear in the generated sequence numbers when using INCREMENT BY 1. Transaction A can be inserting rows at the same time as transaction B. Transaction A may not have its rows with strict sequential numbering within a UR. If a rollback occurs or if DB2 abends before all numbers in the cache (if used) are assigned, numbers are not reused. The preallocated numbers lost from the cache are not used in the future. The highest number allocated is used after a recovery to a point-in-time which can result in gaps in the sequence numbers unless SYSSEQUENCES is recovered to the same point-in-time.

Restrictions: EDITPROC cannot be used on the table nor can FIELDPROC be used on the identity column.

CREATE TABLE ... LIKE ... INCLUDING IDENTITY causes the newly created table to inherit the identity column of the old table. This does not apply to creating a table like a view.

The ALTER table statement can be used to add an identity column. If the table is populated when the ALTER is issued, the table is placed in the REORG pending state. Execution of the reorganization utility (discussed in Chapter RR) assigns the unique sequential values and removes the pending state.

Identity column catalog tables: SYSSEQUENCES has one row for each identity column including the last assigned value and the definition of the column. SYSSEQUENCESDEP has one row for each identity column including the name of table that has the identity column and release dependencies.

SYSCOLUMNS.DEFAULT column has the value of I for AS IDENTITY and GENERATED ALWAYS or J for AS IDENTITY and GENERATED BY DEFAULT.

Inserting rows into a table with an identity column and determining the last sequence number inserted are discussed Chapter PD.

Large Object Data Types and Requirements

The term large objects (LOB) is used to refer to the data types of:

- Character large object (CLOB)
- Binary large object (BLOB)
- Double byte character large objects (DBCLOB)

These LOB columns are designed for large character data (a book, for example), photograph, video or audio data, and large double byte character data (a book, for example). The number of bytes in a LOB column value can be 1 to 2,147,483,647 bytes except a DBCLOB is limited to 1,073,741,823 bytes because each symbol requires two bytes. The default for CLOBs and BLOBs is 1,073,741,823 bytes, and for DBCLOBs the default is 524,288 double-byte characters. LOG YES on the tablespace is used by default if the LOB default sizes or smaller are used. If a value larger than the default is specified, LOG NO is required.

A table created with a LOB column must also include a ROWID column. If the CURRENT RULES special register is set to 'STD', DB2 implicitly creates the LOB table space, auxiliary table, and an index on the auxiliary table for each LOB column in the base table. The naming convention used by DB2 is described in the *SQL Reference* manual. The utility REPORT TABLESPACESET can be used to identify the LOB tablespaces that DB2 implicitly created. If the special register is set to 'DB2' (default), you need to create these objects using the CREATE TABLESPACE, CREATE AUXILIARY TABLE, and CREATE INDEX statements.

The LOB data is actually stored in an auxiliary table in a LOB tablespace. Each LOB column in a table must be stored in a separate auxiliary LOB tablespace. It is necessary to have one LOB tablespace for each partition if the base table is partitioned.

The ROWID column in the base table is used to locate the LOB in the auxiliary table. The LOB column in the base table is an indicator column defined as VARCHAR(4) that can be used to avoid having to move a LOB column of up to 2,147,483,647 bytes into a host program.

Details on creating and using LOBs can be found in the *Administration Guide, Application Programming and SQL Guide*, and *SQL Reference* manuals.

ROWID Data Type

Direct row access provides for locating a row directly without the I/O and CPU time required to locate a row with an index or tablespace scan (V6). It is useful to locate a row a second time after retrieving the row ID value using an index or tablespace scan. A ROWID column uniquely and permanently identifies rows in a table. The following CREATE and ALTER statements are examples of establishing the SPJ_ROWID column as a ROWID data type in the SPJ table.

```
CREATE TABLE SPJ
 (SN   CHAR(6) NOT NULL,
  PN   CHAR(6) NOT NULL,
  JN   CHAR(6) NOT NULL,
  QTY  INTEGER NOT NULL WITH DEFAULT
  SPJ_ROWID ROWID GENERATED ALWAYS NOT NULL);
```

The ALTER TABLE statement can be used to add a column with a data type of ROWID. DB2 immediately generates a unique row ID value for each existing row. However, it is not physically stored in the database until reorganization.

```
ALTER TABLE SPJ
  ADD SPJ_ROWID ROWID GENERATED ALWAYS NOT NULL;
```

The usage of a ROWID column is discussed in the TS, IU, and PD Chapters.

Restrictions on ROWID column: A ROWID column is implicitly defined as NOT NULL. It is advisable to specify NOT NULL in the column definition for clarity. It is not possible to allow for nulls and a default cannot be defined. However, a select of a ROWID column can return null if no rows qualify. Additional restrictions include:

- ROWID column cannot be declared a primary or foreign key.
- Only one column in a table can be defined with a ROWID data type.
- Cannot have a ROWID column on a temporary table.
- FIELDPROC and CHECK CONSTRAINT cannot be defined on column.
- EDITPROC cannot be used on a table with a ROWID column.
- Private protocol does not support a ROWID column.
- Column distribution statistics are not collected (all values are unique).

Internal and External ROWID Length: The internal length (space in buffer pool and on DASD, for example) is 19 bytes. The first 2 bytes are a length field and the remaining 17 bytes contain the row ID. The external length is 40 bytes. A host variable to receive a row ID is declared similar to a VARCHAR declaration like:

```
01   SPJ-ROWID
     49   SPJ-ROWID-LEN PIC 9(4)USAGE COMP.
     49   SPJ-ROWID     PIC X(40).
```

It is also necessary to declare the host variable as a ROWID for processing by precompiler like:

```
EXEC SQL BEGIN DECLARE SECTION END-EXEC.
01   SPJ-ROWID SQL TYPE IS ROWID.
EXEC SQL END DECLARE SECTION END-EXEC.
```

Row ID values are generated by DB2 when a row is inserted into a table. They cannot be changed with an UPDATE statement (-151 SQLCODE). The ROWID column contains a pseudo random number in the first 6 bytes consisting of the low order bytes of the OS/390 store clock in reverse order by bit, other identifying information that is proprietary to IBM, and RID (changes with a reorganization) in the format of bit data. It can be specified in a WHERE clause and displayed like:

```
X'F0DFD230E3C0D80D81C201AA0A2801000000000000203'
```

GENERATED ALWAYS clause of a ROWID column definition means that DB2 always generates row ID values and is the default. This is a good choice in most cases. It disallows the insertion of a value into ROWID column without OVERRIDING USER VALUE clause discussed below.

GENERATED BY DEFAULT means that DB2 generates a row ID value only if one is not provided in the INSERT statement or to the LOAD utility. This declaration is useful for data propagation using an INSERT with a subselect and the LOAD utility. If a value is not found in a row from the subselect or in the input file of LOAD, DB2 assigns a value. GENERATED BY DEFAULT is required if the LOAD utility is to accept row ID values from an input file. LOAD requires that a two byte length field precede the row ID value to describe its length. If LOAD encounters a duplicate row ID value, it abends.

A ROWID column must have a valid value for each row. Recall that NOT NULL is used for a ROWID column. If a valid row ID value does not exist when an insert is attempted, a -407 SQLCODE is received.

Indexing a ROWID Column: An index is not required if the column is defined using the GENERATED ALWAYS clause. A unique single column index is required on the ROWID column when using GENERATED BY DEFAULT. Indeed, it is not possible to insert or load data until the index is created.

If SQLRULES(STD) is used with GENERATED BY DEFAULT, an index is automatically created on the ROWID column. The index name is always 18 characters. The first character is 'I', followed by 10 characters of the column name (if the column name is less than 10 characters, underscore characters are used as padding), and 7 characters of randomly generated characters assigned by DB2. COPY NO is used when the index is created. This means that the index cannot be copied and recovered (it must be rebuilt).

Index only processing can be used to retrieve a row ID value if RETVLCFK is changed to YES in the DSNZPARM DSN6SPRM macro. This allows for index only processing on a variable length column. Be cautious of the implications for the entire DB2 subsystem discussed above in the subsection "VARCHAR with Care".

Inserting Rows with a ROWID Column: The GENERATED clause determines if and how rows can be inserted into a table with a ROWID column. If GENERATED ALWAYS is used, it is not possible to insert a value into a ROWID column without the OVERRIDING USER VALUE clause. The GENERATED BY DEFAULT is useful for data propagation. Indeed, it is required if the LOAD utility is to accept row ID values from an input file. The clause allows the option of specifying a ROWID column in an INSERT statement with a subselect from another table (subselect can include ROWID column).

Inserting Rows with GENERATED ALWAYS: Following is an example of inserting a row into the SPJ table with the SPJ_ROWID declared as GENERATED ALWAYS. A -798 SQLCODE is received if there is an attempt to insert a value into SPJ_ROWID. The negative SQLCODE can be avoided with the use of the keyword DEFAULT in place of specifying a value. An alternative is not to specify the ROWID column and a corresponding value.

```
EXEC SQL
INSERT INTO SPJ (SN, PN, JN, QTY, SPJ_ROWID)
  VALUES ('S10', 'P40', 'J7', 400, DEFAULT) END-EXEC.
```

OVERRIDING USER VALUE clause is needed for an insert with a subselect if the ROWID column is declared as GENERATED ALWAYS. It is used to have DB2 ignore any values for ROWID column. This causes DB2 to generate row ID values. The clause is useful when inserting rows into a table from another table when the GENERATED ALWAYS clause is used. It allows for specifying the ROWID column in the INSERT and subselect. Any value in the SPJ.SPJ_ROWID column in the subselect is ignored. DB2 generates a values for the SPJ_TEST.SPJ_ROWID column in the example:

```
EXEC SQL
INSERT INTO SPJ_TEST (SN, PN, JN, QTY, SPJ_ROWID)
OVERRIDING USER VALUE
  SELECT SN, PN, JN, QTY, SPJ_ROWID
  FROM   SPJ
  WHERE  SN < 'S4' END-EXEC.
```

Inserting Rows with GENERATED BY DEFAULT: Following is an example of inserting a row into the SPJ table with SPJ_ROWID declared as GENERATED BY DEFAULT. The SPJ_ROWID column and a corresponding value should not be specified. DB2 generates a value for the ROWID column.

```
EXEC SQL
INSERT INTO SPJ (SN, PN, JN, QTY, SPJ_ROWID)
  VALUES ('S10', 'P40', 'J7', 400, DEFAULT) END-EXEC.
```

An attempt to insert a invalid (non-generated DB2 value) results in a -399 SQLCODE.

The OVERRIDING USER VALUE is not used if the ROWID column is defined as GENERATED BY DEFAULT. DB2 generates values for SPJ_TEST.SPJ_ROWID. The SPJ.SPJ_ROWID values are ignored.

```
EXEC SQL
INSERT INTO SPJ TEST (SN, PN, JN, QTY, SPJ_ROWID)
OVERRIDING USER VALUE
  SELECT SN, PN, JN, QTY, SPJ_ROWID
  FROM   SPJ
  WHERE  SN < 'S4' END-EXEC.
```

The ROWID columns in the two tables do not reference the same rows. For example, it is not possible to retrieve the corresponding row from SPJ_TEST using a SPJ_ROWID from SPJ. This is true regardless of the GENERATED clause value.

Domains

C. J. Date defines a domain as a pool of values from which one or more columns draw their actual values. E. F. Codd suggests that data types should be used to enforce domains. A date data type is a good example of enforcement of a domain through a DB2 data type. A column defined as a date data type must contain a year value between 1 and 9999, a value between 1 and 12, and a day value between 1 and 31. Table check constraints provide for some validation of data and facilities for domain support. Distinct types, table check constraints, and triggers (discussed in Chapters TR) can be used to enforce domains (V6).

Creating and Using Distinct Types

You certainly do not want to compare or do arithmetic operations on US dollars and Euro. They have different values at different times. Similarly, pounds and kilograms are units of weight but should not be compared or used together in arithmetic operations. The same principle applies to temperatures in centigrade and Fahrenheit, distance in miles and kilometers, and many other data types. Errors can be avoided by declaring the appropriate columns as their particular distinct type. Once you define a column with a distinct type, the column can be used only with another column defined with the same distinct type in comparisons, function invocations, stored procedures calls, and assignments. Distinct types are also known as user-defined data types and are considered strong typing.

Built-in data types refer to the basic data types in DB2, including DECIMAL, INTEGER,

SMALLINT, CHAR, etc.. Distinct types are represented internally as DB2 built-in data types. They can be used with DRDA (Distributed Relational Database Architecture) (not private protocol distributed processing).

The use of distinct types begins with the CREATE DISTINCT TYPE statement to assign it a name and specify the built-in data type used to store the data. The name of a distinct type has a qualifier which optionally can be the current SQLID or a schema name as discussed in Chapter CO. The following two statements create US_DOLLAR and EURO distinct types both of which are stored as DECIMAL(9,2). You will want to create a distinct type for each country's currency where your company does business.

```
CREATE DISTINCT TYPE US_DOLLAR AS DECIMAL(9,2)
  WITH COMPARISONS;

CREATE DISTINCT TYPE EURO      AS DECIMAL(9,2)
  WITH COMPARISONS;
```

The WITH COMPARISONS clause means that only like distinct types can be compared The clause is required for all but large objects (LOB).

Consider the use built-in data types of DECIMAL rather than NUMERIC, and DOUBLE or REAL rather than FLOAT to increase portability across platforms.

The following CREATE TABLE statement uses the US_DOLLAR distinct type for the SALARY column and EURO for the COMM column.

```
CREATE TABLE EMP
 (EMPNO      CHAR(6)          NOT NULL,
  FIRSTNME   VARCHAR(12)      NOT NULL,
  MIDINIT    CHAR(1)          NOT NULL,
  LASTNAME   VARCHAR(15)      NOT NULL,
  WORKDEPT   CHAR(3)                  ,
  PHONENO    CHAR(4)                  ,
  HIREDATE   DATE                     ,
  JOB        CHAR(8)                  ,
  EDLEVEL    SMALLINT                 ,
  SEX        CHAR(1)                  ,
  BIRTHDATE  DATE                     ,
  SALARY     US_DOLLAR                ,
  BONUS      DECIMAL(9,2)             ,
  COMM       EURO                     ,
  PRIMARY KEY (EMPNO));
```

Use of Distinct Types to Avoid Invalid Operations

Let's see how the use of distinct types avoid invalid operations. Here is an incorrect statement to determine employees who have a salary greater than their bonus and their commission.

```
SELECT EMPNO, LASTNAME, SALARY,  BONUS,  COMM
FROM   EMP
```

```
WHERE   SALARY > BONUS
AND     SALARY > COMM;
```

The SALARY distinct type of US_DOLLAR avoids the incorrect operations. It is not valid to compare SALARY in US dollars with BONUS declared as DECIMAL(9,2). Similarly, SALARY cannot be compared to BONUS declared with the distinct type of EURO. The following error message is received.

```
SQLCODE = -401, ERROR: THE OPERANDS OF AN ARITHMETIC OR COMPARISON
OPERATION ARE NOT COMPARABLE
SQLSTATE   = 42818 SQLSTATE RETURN CODE
```

Another invalid statement shows that arithmetic operations cannot be done on unlike distinct types and built-in data types. Here is an attempt to determine the total income for employee '00200'.

```
SELECT EMPNO, LASTNAME, SALARY + BONUS + COMM
FROM   EMP
WHERE  EMPNO = '00200';
```

The statement does not execute successfully because it is not possible to add columns defined as US_DOLLAR, DECIMAL, and EURO in an SQL statement. The following error results from the attempt.

```
DSNT408I SQLCODE = -440, ERROR:  NO FUNCTION BY THE NAME + HAVING
COMPATIBLE ARGUMENTS WAS FOUND IN THE CURRENT PATH
DSNT418I SQLSTATE   = 42884 SQLSTATE RETURN CODE
```

It is necessary to take an overt actions to allow comparison and arithmetic operations between distinct types and built-in data type data types. DB2 automatically creates functions for this purpose. These cast functions are automatically dropped when the distinct type is dropped. Optionally, you can create sourced functions as discussed in Chapter UD. If you need to perform operations with two or more different distinct types, it is necessary to create functions for this purpose.

Cast To and From Distinct Types

DB2 automatically generates cast functions to allow for operations on a distinct type and built-in data type with the same name and qualifier or schema as the distinct type for which they were created. Two cast functions are created automatically when a distinct type is created. One cast function has the name of the built-in data type, DECIMAL in our example. This cast function provides for casting from the built-in data type (DECIMAL) to the distinct type (US_DOLLAR). Cast functions named US_DOLLAR and EURO are also created automatically by DB2. These cast functions provide for casting literals and host variables from the distinct types of US_DOLLAR and EURO to the built-in data type DECIMAL. The use of cast functions are evaluated at stage 1 and can use a matching index scan (discussed in Chapter PP).

It is not possible to compare SALARY declared as US_DOLLAR with a literal or host variable which uses built-in data types. The following statement to determine employees whose salary is greater than 20,000.00 results in a -401 SQLCODE. DB2 has no way of knowing whether 20,000.00 is in US dollars as is the column.

```
SELECT EMPNO, LASTNAME, SALARY, BONUS, COMM
FROM   EMP
WHERE  SALARY > 20000.00;
```

Use of functions to compare a literal or host variable with distinct types: The US_DOLLAR cast function can be used to determine employees whose salary is greater than 20,000.00 like:

```
SELECT EMPNO, LASTNAME, SALARY, BONUS, COMM
FROM   EMP
WHERE  SALARY > US_DOLLAR(20000.00);
```

An alternative is to designate salary as decimal and make the comparison.

```
SELECT EMPNO, LASTNAME, SALARY, BONUS, COMM
FROM   EMP
WHERE  DECIMAL(SALARY) > 20000.00;
```

An attempt to use the EURO(20000.00) fails with a -401 SQLCODE as it should. It is incorrect to compare salary in US dollars with Euros. They have different values depending upon the current exchange rate.

One should not do arithmetic operations and compare US_DOLLAR, DECIMAL, and EURO values. We will review some additional uses of the cast functions if you find it necessary to do the manipulations in some situations on some types of data. The real goal is to review various uses of the functions.

If it is required for some reason in another situation with other types of data, that the DECIMAL function be used to designate each distinct type as decimal to allow arithmetic operations and comparisons. The following statement adds salary in US dollars, bonus in decimal, and commission in Euro as well as identifying employees whose salary in US dollars is greater than their bonus in decimal and their salary is greater than their commission in Euro.

```
SELECT EMPNO, LASTNAME, DECIMAL(SALARY) +
  BONUS + DECIMAL(COMM)
FROM   EMP
WHERE  DECIMAL(SALARY) > BONUS
AND    DECIMAL(SALARY) > DECIMAL(COMM);
```

The CAST function syntax is an alternative to designate each distinct type as decimal to allow the same operations as in the previous statement. However, this formulation is evaluated at stage 2 and cannot use a matching index scan.

```
SELECT EMPNO, LASTNAME, CAST(SALARY AS DECIMAL) +
  BONUS + DECIMAL(COMM)
FROM   EMP
WHERE  CAST(SALARY AS DECIMAL) > BONUS
AND    CAST(SALARY AS DECIMAL) > CAST(COMM AS DECIMAL);
```

These functions do not convert from one unit of measure to another. User-defined functions are required for this purpose as discussed in Chapter UD.

The CAST function can be used to designate COMM (defined as Euro) as decimal in a comparison with a decimal literal or host variable. The developer needs to know that the literal or host variable is in Euro for a valid operation. DB2 has no way to enforce this. Following is a statement to identify employees who have a bonus greater than 100.00. The developer must know that the literal of 100.00 or host variable containing 100.00 is in Euro or is a required comparison in using other data types to achieve accurate results.

```
SELECT EMPNO, LASTNAME, SALARY, BONUS, COMM
FROM   EMP
AND    CAST(COMM AS DECIMAL) > 100.00;
```

There is no way to cast salary defined as US_DOLLAR and bonus defined as DECIMAL to EURO for performance of arithmetic operations and to do comparisons of different distinct types. Indeed, this is a primary goal of distinct types. The following statement

```
SELECT EMPNO, LASTNAME, CAST(SALARY AS EURO) +
  CAST(BONUS AS EURO) + COMM -- COMM is defined as EURO
FROM   EMP
AND    CAST(SALARY AS EURO) < CAST(BONUS AS EURO)
AND    CAST(SALARY AS EURO) < COMM;
```

results in:

```
DSNT408I  SQLCODE  =  -461,  ERROR:   A  VALUE  WITH  DATA  TYPE
MKTGXW.US_DOLLAR CANNOT BE CAST TO TYPE EURO
DSNT418I SQLSTATE   = 42846 SQLSTATE RETURN CODE
```

Conversion of salary in US dollars to Euro and bonus in decimal to Euro can be done with an external user-defined function (UDF) written in a host language to do the required calculations as described in Chapter UD.

Uses of US_DOLLAR Cast Function: Recall that DB2 automatically generates a cast function with the name of the distinct type (US_DOLLAR in the examples) in addition to the cast function with the name of the built-in function (DECIMAL in the examples). Thus far we have concentrated mostly on the DECIMAL cast function. A couple more examples using the US_DOLLAR function will further clarify when the cast functions can and cannot be used.

Comparisons can be done between distinct types and built-in data types by designating a column defined with a decimal built-in data type, literal, or host variable as an US_DOLLAR distinct type. The following example uses the US_DOLLAR case function is designate bonus as US dollars. This provides for identifying employees whose salary in US dollars is greater than their bonus defined with a built-in data type of decimal. Once again, the developer must take care that this is in fact a legitimate comparison.

```
SELECT EMPNO, LASTNAME, SALARY, BONUS, COMM
FROM   EMP
WHERE  SALARY > US_DOLLAR(BONUS);
```

It is not possible to use a function to designate a literal or host variable as a distinct type in an arithmetic operation as in the following example. If you need to add 1000.00 Euro to employee commissions defined with an EURO distinct type, it is necessary to use a sourced UDF to allow the addition or use any arithmetic operation as discussed in Chapter UD. Also, sourced functions are useful in minimizing the need for casting and avoiding -410 SQLCODEs.

```
SELECT EMPNO, LASTNAME, SALARY, BONUS, COMM + EURO(1000.00)
FROM   EMP
AND    SALARY > US_DOLLAR(20000.00);
```

This statement results in:

```
DSNT408I SQLCODE = -440, ERROR:  NO FUNCTION BY THE NAME + HAVING
COMPATIBLE ARGUMENTS WAS FOUND IN THE CURRENT PATH
DSNT418I SQLSTATE   = 42884 SQLSTATE RETURN CODE
```

Additional factors that require your consideration are pointed out with examples of SQL statements using distinct types with host variables in Chapter PD.

Privileges for the creation and usage of distinct types are similar to UDF as discussed in Chapter UD except there is no package involved.. You can grant usage privileges on distinct types and cast functions automatically created by DB2 to others like:

```
GRANT USAGE ON DISTINCT TYPE US_DOLLAR TO PUBLIC;
```

Dropping Distinct Types: You can drop a distinct type using the RESTRICT clause as in the following example. This means that there are no tables defined using the distinct type, and no UDF and stored procedures dependent on the distinct type. If there is difficulty dropping distinct types, select from SYSROUTINES to determine the dependencies and drop them first.

```
DROP DISTINCT TYPE US_DOLLAR RESTRICT;
```

The drop of a distinct type results in DB2 automatically dropping cast functions that it created automatically.

Table Check Constraints

The CHECK clause of the CREATE TABLE statement can be used to define rules for having DB2 validate the data when rows are inserted and updated. This eliminates the need for developers to write, test, and maintain host language code to check constraints in many cases. The table check constraint avoids having to repeatedly code for rules in multiple programs. There is no need to be concerned that a constraint may not be properly coded in all programs because of a misunderstanding or a new person joins the team who is not aware of the constraints that must be enforced. The LOAD and CHECK DATA utilities will validate the data according to the constraints defined in the table check constraints.

There is a single source of information about the constraints as recorded in the catalog tables. The constraints can be dynamically added or dropped if the business constraints change without modification to one or more host programs. In addition, constraints are uniformly enforced across all interfaces to DB2 (QMF, for example). This allows for power users to update the data directly and have the data validated according to the constraints defined to DB2.

Definition of Constraints

Most positive conditions that can be specified in a WHERE clause predicate of a SELECT statement as discussed in Chapter SL can be used in defining a constraint. The conditions can be joined with AND and OR Boolean operators provided that a constraint definition does not exceed 3800 bytes. The defined constraints will be checked when rows are inserted and updated. If a constraint is violated, a -545 SQLCODE is issued and the row is not inserted or updated.

Figure CT.1 has examples of creating a S table with two constraints named STATUS_C and CITY_C. The STATUS_C constraint does not allow a row to be inserted if the value for the STATUS column is outside of the between 10 and 200 range. Also, a status value cannot be updated to be outside of the range. Null does not violate a constraint. A row can be inserted into the S table without specifying a value for status.

The constraint name is the column name or a variation on the column name being checked followed by "_C" in the example. The constraint name can be 18 bytes in length. The constraint name is placed in the SQLERRMC field of the SQL Communication Area (SQLCA) when a constraint is violated. It is useful in describing an error to the user as discussed in Chapter PD.

Rules for Defining Constraints

There are some rules for defining constraints. The first operand must be a column name. The second operand can be a literal or column from the row being checked. If the second operand is a literal, basically the column must have equal or greater precision than the literal. For example, one cannot compare a literal with a value greater than 32,767 to a SMALLINT column and a literal of 140.95 with an INTEGER column. If the second operand is a column, it must have matching data type and length with the first operand. The exception is that compatible character strings can have different lengths.

It is necessary to exercise caution when defining constraints. DB2 does not check the semantics of a constraint definition, any more than it will the WHERE clause of a SELECT statement. For example, the following definition of a constraint on status is allowed but no one can insert any rows with a status value into the table.

```
CONSTRAINT STATUS CHECK (STATUS > 100 AND STATUS < 80)
```

A column cannot be compared to a column function, a special register, host variables, parameter markers, EXISTS and quantified predicates, subselects, and the CHECK clause cannot reference another table.

Referencing Another Table for Validation Purposes

The most restrictive rule is that the CHECK clause *cannot* reference another table. One would prefer to reference a table containing all valid cities rather than having to list them in an IN list as is done for the CITY constraint in Figure CT.1. Another table can be referenced in a trigger definition for validating data. Triggers are available in V6.

You may want to list all valid values in an IN list if the values are static to achieve improved performance over triggers. The values are searched by Data Manager (DM) in central storage which holds significant performance advantage as discussed in Section CT.5. Do list the values that are frequently referenced first in the IN list because the values are searched sequentially. The constraints can be added and dropped with an ALTER statement. For example, a constraint on a STATE column can be defined by listing all of the 50 states in an IN list. The constraint can be dropped and a trigger referencing a STATE table can be created in the future. This may or may not be desirable from a performance point of view. It may be that the table check constraints will have performance advantages over triggers, depending on the implementation of triggers.

Adding Constraints to a Populated Table

The ALTER statement can be used to add constraints to a populated table like:

```
ALTER TABLE S
  ADD CONSTRAINT SN_C
    CHECK (SN BETWEEN 'S1' AND 'S99999');
```

Plans and packages do not require a rebind to take advantage of constraint enforcement. The constraints are checked depending on the CURRENT RULES special register when adding constraints. The CURRENT RULES special register can be set to the SQL standard before executing the ALTER statement like:

```
SET CURRENT RULES = 'STD'
```

The DB2 rule is the default and has advantages. Check pending is turned on and no SQL manipulation statements can be executed until check pending is turned off. After adding a number of constraints, the CHECK DATA utility can be executed to check all of the defined constraints and turn off check pending if there are no violations or you have specified that violating rows should be written to an exception table. The DB2 rule has performance advantages when adding more than one constraint.

ALTER TABLE Statement

Many of the parameters specified when creating a table cannot be altered after the table is created. Figure CT.4 is an example of an ALTER TABLE statement that specifies all parameters that can be altered. Special conditions that apply to altering a specific parameter are discussed along with a description of the parameters.

Figure CT.4. ALTER TABLE statement

```
ALTER TABLE S
  ADD COUNTRY CHAR(20) WITH DEFAULT (USA)
  DROP CONSTRAINT STATUS_C;
  ADD CONSTRAINT SN_C
    CHECK (SN BETWEEN 'S1' AND 'S99999')
  FIELDPROC FSN
  VALIDPROC VALIDSN
  AUDIT ALL
```

```
DATA CAPTURE CHANGES
DROP RESTRICT ON DROP
DROP PRIMARY KEY;
```

The ALTER statement in Figure CT.4 has an example of adding a new COUNTRY column to S table in Figure CT.1. When a column is added to a table, it is recommended that the reorganization utility with an inline copy be executed before many values are placed in the new column. This causes space to be allocated for the newly added column and provides a copy of the table with the newly added column. If the reorganization utility is not executed after adding a new column to a table, there is good chance that most updates to place a value in the new column will cause the row to be moved to a page with free space available for the row that is expanded in length as discussed in Chapter CD.

A table can be renamed with the RENAME statement and authorizations are transferred to the new table name. For example, the S table is renamed to SUPPLIER in the statement:

```
RENAME TABLE S TO SUPPLIER;
```

There are some restrictions on renaming a table. It cannot be renamed if a trigger or view is defined on the table. You can rename a tables acted on by a trigger. However, it is necessary to drop the trigger and recreate it to reference the new table name. RENAME does not apply to synonyms and aliases.

To Null or Not Null

Nulls can be used when actual values are unknown or inapplicable. DEFAULT NULL or no null specification clause is the default and tells DB2 to insert or load a row even though there is no value specified for a column.

It is perhaps easiest to understand the concept of nulls by considering the problem that arises when they are unavailable. What value should be placed in the cost column of a product information table for an item whose cost has not been set? A value of 0 is inaccurate because the product surely has a cost. A null value solves the problem by showing that the item carries a cost but that it is not known.

The ability to make this distinction takes resources. The use of nulls requires 1 byte of storage for every value in a column that allows nulls and another byte for every value in an index created from a column with nulls. The extra byte provides a prefix for each value that indicates whether it is in fact null. The null prefix is HEX '00' if the value is present and HEX 'FF' if it is not. These extra bytes can add up. A 100,000-row table with 10 columns allowing nulls requires 1 million bytes for the capability. If five of those columns are indexed, another ½ million bytes are needed. Index page splitting will occur for inserting sequential values as discussed in Chapter ID. Application programmers that select data from a column with nulls must know that nulls are allowed in columns and remember to code a null indicator and there is the processing time for testing the null indicators.

Null can also present difficulties for occasional database users and programmers. Null values do not compare as equals in joins, for example. Suppose a database includes one table describing projects and another describing employees who might work on them. A user may request a report requiring an inner join of columns from each table--perhaps a list of the salaries being paid to workers assigned to each project. If some projects have no workers assigned to them, that fact might be indicated with nulls in the project table assignment column because an employee identification would not be applicable as an entry. Those projects with null values for the assignment column will not show up in the report, however, because the inner join ignores them. This may be fine if the report's purpose is to show salaries being paid for active projects. If the report was meant to show how much was being paid in salaries, by project, however, it would be misleading since it would not show the projects for which no salaries were being paid. If the problem is recognized, an outer join can be used as discussed in Chapters JP and ST.

The developer can avoid this and similar problems by using a non-meaningful value in place of null as a code that, in this case, would relate to an "unassigned" row in the employee table. For example, an employee ID of zero in the employee table would carry "unassigned" in the name column, and inactive projects would list zeros for employee IDs in the open slots.

An advantage of using nulls is that they allow for accurate averages in columns that include them. The nulls do not enter into the sum of values or contribute to their count. Consider a column of salaries that must use zeros for employees whose salaries are unknown. If the salaries for 10 employees totaled $300,000, the average is $30,000. If information on a new hire whose salary was unknown were added to the table and the salary was listed as zero, the salary column would still total $300,000, but the count of employees would now be 11. The column average would be $27,272.27. If null was used, the average would not change. One way around this problem if the developer does not wish to use nulls is to specify NOT NULL for the salary column, use zero in place of nulls, and compute the average for values where the salary is not equal to zero. This scheme does not work if the column includes volunteers, and the average should reflect that fact. To avoid this additional problem, the developer might use an impossible salary--perhaps -1--as the null replacement and take the average of salaries not equal to -1.

When null is used in an arithmetic calculation, the result is null unless the SQL statement specifies special handling for nulls. For example, if a statement requests the subtraction of employees' insurance payments from their salaries and the insurance payment value is null, the result is null. The same principle applies to addition and multiplication. Division by null is like division by zero and results in a negative SQLCODE indicating an error. Chapter SL discusses the use of the COALESCE and VALUE functions to substitute values for nulls in SQL expressions. Figure CT.5 summarizes how nulls are treated when manipulated by SQL statements.

Figure CT.5. How nulls are treated by SQL statements

- Null is =, >, < no value.
- Null does not participate in an inner join.
- Addition, subtraction, and multiplication involving null results in null.
- Division by null results in a negative SQLCODE.
- Concatenation of a null results in a null
- All column functions exclude nulls except for COUNT(*) which counts the number of rows.
- Outer join produces null for columns in a table with no match on the join columns in the other table as discussed in Chapters JP and ST.
- If no rows qualify in a subselect, the result is null.
- If no rows qualify with a column function calculation, the result is null and requires a null indicator to avoid a negative SQLCODE.
- Existence of a null is tested with WHERE QTY IS (NOT) NULL (not QTY = NULL).

- ORDER BY sorts all nulls as higher than non-nulls and GROUP BY groups nulls together.

Programmers must be aware of which columns allow nulls. Whenever they write a program that SELECTS data from a column with nulls, they must declare a null indicator variable and reference it in each SELECT statement for the column. This coding is not difficult. But if it is not done--the programmer does not know or forgets that nulls apply--a negative SQLCODE results. Chapter PD discusses programming for nulls.

WITH DEFAULT NULL is not widely used on column definitions because of exceptions and complexities in managing nulls.

Not Null

DB2 requires that some value be assigned to every row in every column for which NOT NULL is specified. For certain kinds of columns, the developer will almost never allow nulls. A primary key, by definition, must uniquely identify each row. Therefore a unique value should always be inserted into the primary key column. Any column can be declared unique by creating a unique index on it, meaning that DB2 will not allow duplicate values to be inserted in it. In fact, all primary key columns should have a unique index created to guarantee that no values are repeated. In most cases a column that must contain all unique values should be declared NOT NULL and a unique index created. If a column must contain all unique values and multiple null entries can occur in the column, the column must allow for nulls and an index created with the UNIQUE WHERE NOT NULL clause as discussed in Chapter ID. A foreign key column should not contain nulls if there is an absolute dependency of the foreign key table on the primary key table as discussed in Section TS.3. The primary key column, any column that should have only unique values, and frequently the foreign key column should be declared NOT NULL. If a column is added to a table with the ALTER statement, the column cannot be declared as NOT NULL because there are no values initially in a new column.

Not Null with Default

If the developer specifies NOT NULL WITH DEFAULT for a column in the CREATE TABLE statement, DB2 automatically places zeros in empty numeric columns, blanks in empty character columns, and the current date, time, or timestamp in columns with the corresponding date data type.

If a table includes columns for ORDER_DATE and RECEIVED_DATE, the current date is appropriate for the first but not the second when a row is first inserted. An alternative for RECEIVED_DATE is '0001-01-01' or '9999-12-31' (all zeros is not a valid date). The date of '0001-01-01' is used by the reorganization utility after a date column is added to a table with the ALTER statement.

Primary key columns can be declared NOT NULL or NOT NULL WITH DEFAULT. They cannot be assigned a default value. NOT NULL WITH DEFAULT allows a zero or blank as a primary key value, however, probably not the intended unique identifier. Since NOT NULL WITH DEFAULT makes little sense for a column with a unique index in any case, only one zero or blank is allowed. A possible exception is the use of timestamp as a primary key that would allow for the automatic recording of the timestamp when the row is inserted.

Assignment of a Default Value

A specific value can be specified to be used when an actual value is not available by using the WITH DEFAULT clause on the column definition. For example, if no value is specified for the S.CITY column, the value of London will be used as defined in the WITH DEFAULT 'London' clause in Figure CT.1.

A literal, USER, CURRENT SQLID, and NULL can be specified as the default. USER causes the primary AUTHID of a person who inserts a row to be placed in the column. The column AUTHID_OF_INSERTER will have the primary AUTHID of the person who inserts a row if no value is specified in the Figure CT.1 CREATE TABLE example. CURRENT SQLID causes the current SQLID of a person who inserts a row to be placed in the column. USER and CURRENT SQLID provide some auditing capability. WITH DEFAULT NULL or no parameter value causes the column to be treated as null if no value is provided.

A column specified NOT NULL WITH DEFAULT or WITH DEFAULT and a value can be added to a table with an ALTER statement. The newly added column will contain the default values after a reorganization. NOT NULL cannot be specified for columns added to a table with the ALTER TABLE statement. A newly added column will obviously contain nulls until its values are inserted. If the developer wants to specify NOT NULL for a new column, he or she must drop the table and re-create it.

Coded Character Set Identifier

The CCSID can be specified as EBCDIC or ASCII when creating a table, tablespace, or database as discussed in Chapter CD.

Restrict on Drop

Tables can be dropped by accident. It is very difficult to recover from an accidental drop of an object because the drop results in all information on the object being removed from the catalog tables. The clause WITH RESTRICT ON DROP can be used to minimize the possibility of an accidental drop when a table is created as shown in Figure CT.1. This is not the default. The restriction can be added to an existing tables like:

```
ALTER TABLE P
ADD RESTRICT ON DROP;
```

Once the restriction has been placed on a table, no one can drop the table. In addition, no one (not even SYSADM) can drop the tablespace and database that contains the table. It is necessary to remove the restriction before the table can be dropped. The restriction can be removed like:

```
ALTER TABLE P
DROP RESTRICT ON DROP;
```

Do beware of including the ALTER to remove the restriction in a SPUFI file before the DROP statement. This defeats the purpose of disallowing the drop of an object. Consider placing the

ALTER to remove the restriction in a separate SPUFI file that must be executed before the SPUFI file containing the DROP statement. This minimizes accidents that are very difficult to recover from.

Data Capture

The DATA CAPTURE CHANGES parameter causes log records to be written to the log in expanded format rather than logging only part of an updated row as discussed in Chapter TS. A before and after image of the entire row is logged. This increases costs of logging somewhat and number of log data sets required. If ESA compression is used, the log record will be in compressed form which reduces the space required on the log.

DATA CAPTURE NONE is the default. DATA CAPTURE CHANGES is useful for auditing, replication of data, and disaster recovery. When these functions are required, DATA CAPTURE CHANGES reduces costs compared to application program processing in most cases. The expanded log records can be read by an assembler program using DSNDQJ00 in DSNMACS which contains a mapping macro. There are a number of software products that will read the expanded log records and do processing for auditing, replication of data, and disaster recovery. IBM's program offering for replication of data is DPropD (Data Propagator) and the RRDF (Remote Recovery Data Facility) program offering has a log apply feature for disaster recovery.

The data capture feature can be added to the catalog tables with the ALTER statement (V5 APAR PQ13031). (Utility (DSNUTIL) logged events are not captured by design.) This provides for maintaining shadow catalog tables that can be used by SQL generators and general access to the catalog to reduce lock contention. DPropD (Data Propagator) program offering can be used to propagate changes to the shadow catalog from the catalog at specified intervals of time.

Auditing a Table

DB2 will audit a table's use--keep a record of SQL statements that access it--if the table's creator requests such an audit in the table's CREATE statement and the system administrator specifies that the audit is to occur. With the clause AUDIT CHANGE, the developer requests that records be kept for each insert, update, or delete statement. An AUDIT ALL clause requests records for SELECTS as well. An audit record consists of the SQL statement, the primary AUTHID of the individual issuing the statement, and a timestamp indicating when the statement was issued. AUDIT NONE asks that no auditing be done and is the default.

Before and after images of changed data are not part of the audit record. If a before and after image of the changed data is required, DATA CAPTURE should be considered.

EDITPROC, FIELDPROC, and VALIDPROC

The EDITPROC, FIELDPROC, and VALIDPROC parameters provide for specifying a program that will be executed automatically when a row is processed depending on the specific procedure specified. Figure CT.6 shows how a row is passed through an EDITPROC when the row is inserted, updated, or selected. The same processing is done with a FIELDPROC. A row is passed through a VALIDPROC when it is inserted, updated, or deleted.

Figure CT.6. Processing a row with an EDITPROC

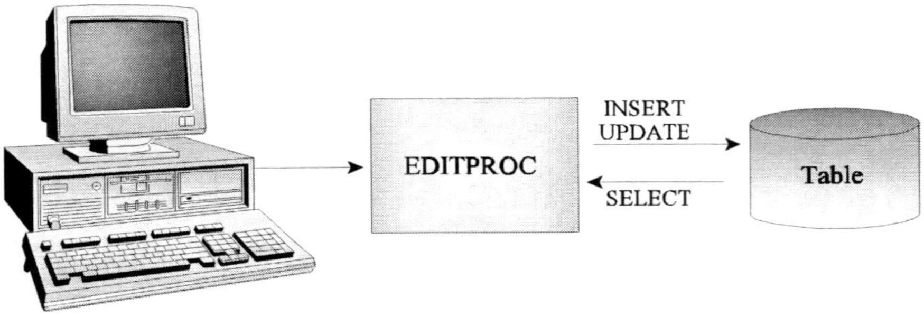

The procedure must be written in assembler, it operates in privileged mode, can issue no I/O, and SQL statements cannot be issued from a procedure. Procedures are exits from DB2. The sample library, SDSNSAMP, contains sample procedures. Once a procedure has been developed, tested, and its name specified following the keyword of EDITPROC, FIELDPROC, or VALIDPROC on the CREATE TABLE statement, its use is transparent to application programs. Figure CT.1 has an example of specifying a VALIDPROC with the procedure name of CHECKS.

EDITPROC and FIELDPROC can be used to compress, encrypt, or manipulate the data for some other purpose. An EDITPROC can operate on an entire rows. FIELDPROC operates on individual columns.

Several software companies offer products for compressing data with the use of EDITPROC. IBM provides a sample procedure DSN8HUFF in the sample library SDSNSAMP. ESA compression is a good alternative for compressing data as discussed in Chapter TS.

FIELDPROC procedures are useful for changing the usual EBCDIC collating sequence. Sorts done on data represented in EBCDIC result in strict alphabetical order, for example, while an organization may want to use exceptions to that order. In an employee list, for example, it may want MacDonald and McDonald next to each other rather than having MacGraw in between. An assembler program invoked using FIELDPROC can account for the special order. Similarly, sorts of EBCDIC represented data do not account for accent marks, sorting words that contain them out of alphabetical order. A FIELDPROC routine can solve the problem of handling accent marks, common in languages other than English.

FIELDPROC can be specified only on a column declared as a character data type (not a numeric data type). It can be used for translating a character code to a name or description when the data is selected. State code is frequently stored in a row rather than the longer state name. The state code of AL can be translated to Alabama automatically for reporting purposes when a row is selected, for example.

FIELDPROC and WITH DEFAULT cannot be used on the same column definition. EDITPROC and FIELDPROC routines affect the way DB2 stores the data. Therefore, they cannot be added to or dropped from a table after it has been created, nor can a column be added to a table that includes an EDITPROC routine. A FIELDPROC routine can be added to a table with a column that is added with an ALTER TABLE statement.

A VALIDPROC routine can be used to check data as they are entered to ensure the values are within permitted ranges. If the routine detects a mistake, it can issue an error message and does not permit the update, insertion, or deletion. It is not invoked when data are retrieved. A VALIDPROC routine provides for centralized validation of data to avoid writing the validation logic into multiple application programs. However, one cannot select from another table from the VALIDPROC routine. This limits the amount of validation that can be done. Check table constraints are a good alternative to the use of a VALIDPROC routine. Check table constraints can be easily defined and altered without having to develop an assembler routine and provide performance advantages in most cases.

Since VALIDPROC does not affect how the data are stored, an ALTER TABLE statement may add or drop a VALIDPROC routine. A column may also be added to a table that employs a VALIDPROC routine. The routine, unless revised, will not, however, operate on the new column.

IN Clause

The IN clause designates the database and tablespace to house the table. If the IN clause is not specified, the default database DSNDB04 is used and DB2 automatically creates the tablespace using the default storage group SYSDEFLT. In this case, very little space is allocated to the tablespace--12 KB of primary and 12 KB of secondary space. The default tablespace name is the same as the table name if the table name is <= 8 alphanumeric characters, first position is not a number, and name is not currently used for another table or index space. Otherwise, the first 4 characters of table name are used followed by a digit and 3 characters for uniqueness. And if left to DB2 to create the tablespace, DB2 creates a simple tablespace. It was seen in Chapter TS that there are significant advantages of a segmented tablespace even for one table per tablespace. These factors suggest that the developers will, in most cases, want to create their own tablespace and database in which to house the table.

Row Length Considerations

To fit as many rows as possible on each page and avoid wasted space, developers should consider several factors related to row length. DB2 permits a maximum of 255 rows per 4KB data page regardless of their length. This limitation is due to a page's directory, which can list only that many rows. All eight bits of the last byte in the record identifier (RID) are used to locate a slot in the page directory. Thus, 2^8-1 = 255 rows per page is the maximum.

The developer should avoid row lengths of slightly more than 2037 bytes including overhead. Rows cannot be split across pages. Only one 2038-byte row can fit on a page, leaving almost half the page empty. This requires twice as many I/O operations to access the same number of rows as would be needed if the length were slightly less than 2037 bytes and two rows could fit on each page.

Similarly a row of more than 4074 bytes including overhead will not fit on a 4 KB page but will need a 32 KB page. Developers should use 32 KB pages only when one or more rows will not fit on a 4 KB page. Contiguous space in an assigned 32 KB page size buffer pools is required for 32 KB pages. The large pages also requires eight times the I/O transfer time as 4 KB pages. However, if long textual data is being stored, it is best to use a 32 KB page rather than artificially splitting the row across multiple 4 KB pages.

Creating LIKE Tables

Frequently developers want to create tables exactly like existing ones on the same DB2 subsystem. For example, they may want to create a test table just like an existing production table. A TEST.SPJ table can be created like an existing PROD.SPJ table with the statement:

```
CREATE TABLE TEST.SPJ LIKE PROD.SPJ IN DATSTDB.DATESTSP;
```

The IN clause is used to designate the database and tablespace that is used for the new table.

COMMENT ON Statements

Developers can use the COMMENT ON statement to enter in the catalog tables, SYSIBM.SYSTABLES and SYSIBM.SYSCOLUMNS, textual descriptions of the tables and columns they have created. These descriptions can be used as part of the documentation for the application system. In effect, the COMMENT ON statement inserts the developer's description in the catalog table REMARKS column in the row describing the table or column the statement specifies. Since the REMARKS column is a 254-character VARCHAR column, the description in the COMMENT ON statement cannot exceed 254 characters.

The COMMENT ON statement for a table identifies the table and, following the keyword IS, gives the description itself within single quotation marks--for example:

```
COMMENT ON TABLE AUTHID.SPJ IS
  'SPJ SHOWS THE RELATIONSHIP BETWEEN
   SN, PN, JN AND HAS THE PN QUANTITY';
```

The COMMENT ON statement for a single column also names the column:

```
COMMENT ON COLUMN AUTHID.SPJ.SN IS
  'SN IS THE SUPPLIER ID';
```

The developer can, however, use a single statement to enter descriptions of several of a table's columns. To do that, he or she names the table in the COMMENT ON statement and, within parentheses, specifies the column names and their associated descriptions--for example:

```
COMMENT ON AUTHID.SPJ
  (SN IS 'SN IS THE SUPPLIER ID',
   PN IS 'PN IS THE PART ID',
   JN IS 'JN IS THE JOB ID');
```

LABEL ON Statements

The LABEL ON statement's purpose is to create labels that substitute for table or column names when interactive reports are generated. For example, a LABEL ON statement may create a label 'SUPPLIER ID' for the SN column in the example SPJ table. Whenever an interactive request generates a report using the column, the values are returned with the label rather than column name as a heading. Labels may be up to 30 characters.

The LABEL ON syntax is similar to that of the COMMENT ON statement. Columns can be labeled individually, or several from the same table can be labeled with a single statement--for example:

```
LABEL ON COLUMN AUTHID.SPJ.SN IS
  'SUPPLIER ID';

LABEL ON AUTHID.SPJ
  (SN IS 'SUPPLIER ID',
   PN IS 'PART ID',
   JN IS 'JOB ID');
```

The COMMENT ON and LABEL ON statements can be used on a table, view, or alias.

CT.3 REFERENTIAL INTEGRITY

Referential integrity means that every foreign key value (not including null) must have a corresponding primary key value to which it refers. (Primary and foreign keys are discussed in Chapter CO.) We will use the supplier/part/job (SPJ) database in Figure CT.7 which consists of four tables to discuss referential integrity (RI). Three of these tables are parent tables--S, P, and J-- with primary keys of SN, PN, and JN. The dependent table is SPJ which has three foreign keys, SN, PN, and JN. These foreign keys reference the parent tables of S, P, and J. The SPJ table has a composite primary key consisting of the SN, PN, and JN columns. These tables will be used in examples to show the purpose of RI, the rules needed to enforce RI, and how to implement RI using DB2 or application logic. Indeed, the tables are used throughout the book in examples.

Figure CT.7. Suppliers, part, job, and suppliers/part/job tables

S (Supplier Table)

SN	SNAME	STATUS	CITY
S1	Smith	20	London
S2	Jones	10	Paris
S3	Blake	30	Paris
S4	Clark	20	London
S5	Adams	30	Athens

P (Part Table)

PN	PNAME	COLOR	WEIGHT	CITY
P1	Nut	Red	12	London
P2	Bolt	Green	17	Paris
P3	Screw	Blue	17	Rome
P4	Screw	Red	14	London
P5	Cam	Blue	12	Paris
P6	Cog	Red	19	London

J (Job Table)

JN	JNAME	CITY
J1	Sorter	Paris
J2	Punch	Rome
J3	Reader	Athens
J4	Console	Athens
J5	Collator	London
J6	Terminal	Oslo
J7	Tape	London

SPJ (Supplier/Part/Job)

SN	PN	JN	QTY
S1	P1	J1	200
S1	P1	J4	700
S2	P3	J1	400
S2	P3	J2	200
S2	P3	J3	200
S2	P3	J4	500
S2	P3	J5	600
S2	P3	J6	400
S2	P3	J7	800
S2	P5	J2	100
S3	P3	J1	200
S3	P4	J2	500
S4	P6	J3	300
S4	P6	J7	300
S5	P2	J2	200
S5	P2	J4	100
S5	P5	J5	500
S5	P5	J7	100
S5	P6	J2	200
S5	P1	J4	100
S5	P3	J4	200
S5	P4	J4	800
S5	P5	J4	400
S5	P6	J4	500

Consider the J and SPJ tables shown in Figure CT.7. If the J2 row is deleted from the J table, the SPJ table as it now stands does not make sense. The rows in SPJ referring to J2 are meaningless since there is no longer such a job. The potential for this kind of anomaly exists whenever any changes are made to foreign key columns and whenever primary key columns are updated or deleted. If a foreign key is defined on JN in the SPJ table referencing the J table with a primary key defined, DB2 will not allow the deletion of J2 rows in the SPJ table.

A table with a foreign key is called a dependent table and a table whose primary key is associated with a foreign key is called a parent table. DB2 allows a parent table to exist without associated dependent tables. Such tables are called independent tables. A dependent table can reference multiple parent tables. And, of course, tables can have both primary and foreign keys. However, a parent table can have only one primary key consisting of one or more columns.

Creating the Primary Key

The first step in setting up a new table's RI is to specify the primary key in the CREATE TABLE statement (Figure CT.1). The syntax is straightforward. After the key words PRIMARY KEY, the column or columns that comprise the key are listed in parentheses. Only one primary key can be defined per table, as the relational model dictates.

The SQL standard states that the primary key should be declared on the column definition with the keywords PRIMARY KEY rather than after the column definitions. If the standard is used, the column must be declared as NOT NULL. Another option to comply with the standard is to specify UNIQUE in the column definition which forces the creation of a unique index. This parameter also requires that the column be declared as NOT NULL. PRIMARY KEY and UNIQUE cannot both be specified in a column definition.

The developer must create a unique index on the column or columns that constitute the primary key or are specified in the UNIQUE clause. A unique index on the primary key provides for an efficient mechanism for DB2 to enforce the requirement that every primary key value be unique—a requirement called entity integrity in relational terms. If there is no unique index on the specified primary key and columns declared as unique, DB2 considers the table definition incomplete. (The STATUS column in SYSIBM.SYSTABLES equals 'I' when a table is incomplete.) DB2 will not allow SQL data manipulation access to an incomplete table and utilities that require access to the table will fail. An incomplete table can be altered, dropped, and an index can be created.

A unique index is created automatically on a column defined as a PRIMARY KEY or UNIQUE when a table is created using the schema processor which complies with the SQL92 standard.

Recommendation: It is advisable to define a primary key even if there are no dependent tables that reference the primary key table. It clearly documents the primary key in the catalog tables and forces the creation of a unique index on the primary key. There are no rules or performance implications to defining a primary key without having dependent tables. Indeed, the rules that apply to a parent table do not apply to a table with a primary key defined if there are no foreign keys defined referencing the table.

Creating Foreign Keys

The foreign key clause in the CREATE TABLE statement first designates a name for the referential constraint following the keywords FOREIGN KEY. The constraint name is SNFK for the SN foreign key in the SPJ table (Figure CT.8). The constraint name is used in error messages to identify a violated constraint as discussed in Chapter PD. It cannot exceed eight characters and must be unique for a given table. The RI constraint name cannot be the same as a table check constraint name.

Figure CT.8. Creating a foreign key table

```
CREATE TABLE SPJ
 (SN      CHAR(6)   NOT NULL,
  PN      CHAR(6)   NOT NULL,
  JN      CHAR(6)   NOT NULL,
  QTY     INTEGER   NOT NULL WITH DEFAULT,
  PRIMARY KEY (SN, PN, JN),
  UNIQUE (SN, PN, JN),     -- Optional
  FOREIGN KEY SNFK (SN) REFERENCES S
    ON DELETE RESTRICT,  -- Default
  FOREIGN KEY PNFK (PN) REFERENCES P
    ON DELETE CASCADE,   -- Not Realistic
  FOREIGN KEY JNFK (JN) REFERENCES J
    ON DELETE SET NULL) -- Not Realistic
IN DASPJDB.SPJTSP;
```

The developer specifies in parentheses following the constraint name the column or columns that serve as the foreign key. A foreign key column must have the same data type and length as the primary key column. If the foreign key is a composite consisting of more than one column, the columns must be specified in the same order as the composite primary key columns. The primary and foreign keys do not need to match in terms of the null attribute, default values, and column names. The foreign key clause next identifies the single table that the key references. Naming the primary key column is optional. There can be only one primary key for a table; therefore the primary key reference is implicit. DB2 does not allow a foreign key to reference more than one parent table. If you wish to conform to the SQL standard, the column declared as the primary key or declared as being unique can be referenced.

ROWID and LOB columns cannot be defined as primary or foreign keys.

RI Rules

The foreign key clause goes on to identify the type of rule to be enforced when rows are deleted from the primary key table. After the keywords ON DELETE, the developer states whether DB2 should RESTRICT the deletion, CASCADE it to the foreign key table, or set the corresponding values in the foreign key to null (SET NULL). If you wish to conform to the SQL standard, NO ACTION can be specified which is like RESTRICT except as to when enforcement occurs with self-referencing tables as will be discussed. The correct rule defined depends on the business rules and the meaning of the data to the business. Each of the rules are described and examples of when and when not to use each rule is given.

The RESTRICT and NO ACTION rule means that a row cannot be deleted from the parent table if there is a matching foreign key value. In Figure CT.8, for example, because DELETE has been specified on the SNFK referential constraint, which references the S table, if an attempt is made to delete S4 from the S table, a negative SQLCODE will be issued and the S4 row will not be deleted. The RESTRICT rule is a good choice in this relationship. One would not want to delete information about a supplier where parts supplied by that supplier are currently being used on jobs. If information about the supplier is lost and a defective part is discovered, it will be necessary to contact the supplier to order a replacement part.

The CASCADE rule means that when a row is deleted from the parent table, all rows with a matching foreign key value will be deleted in all dependent tables that reference the parent table. For example, if P6 is deleted from the P table, all P6s will be deleted from the SPJ table. This is not a good choice in this case. One would not want to delete information about a part that is currently being used on a job. The RESTRICT rule is a good choice in this relationship.

The CASCADE rule is useful if the foreign key rows have no meaning without a primary key row. For example, if an employee leaves the company and the row describing the employee is deleted from the employee table, there is no reason to keep information about the employee's skills. This example assumes that skills are maintained in a SKILLS table that has been defined with a foreign key that references the employee table.

The SET NULL rule means that when a row is deleted in the primary key table, all rows with a matching foreign key will be set to null in all dependent tables that references the parent table. If J7 is deleted from the J table, all J7s will be set to null in the SPJ table. Of course, this means that JN in the J table must allow for nulls. Again, the RESTRICT rule is a good choice for this relationship. The goal has been to show examples of all three rules with the SPJ database.

Explicit and Implicit RI Rules

An explicit RI rule having to do with the deletion of a primary key and its effect on the matching foreign keys are specified with the ON DELETE clause when a foreign key is designated referencing a primary key as discussed. There are also implicit rules that come into play if a foreign key is designated having to do with the update of a primary key, insertion of a foreign key, and update of a foreign key value.

The update of a primary is not allowed if there is a matching foreign key value. For example, the update of S4 to be S10 would lead to potential problems. If a replacement part supplied by S4 is required for P6 that is used for J3, one should not contact S10 because it was S4 that supplied the part assuming that S10 is a new supplier with no relationship with S4. If S10 is a new supplier who is taking responsibility for parts supplied by S4, it is necessary to delete S4 and insert S10. It will be necessary to develop a procedure to deal with the S4 rows in the SPJ table before the deletion depending on the delete rule defined. The SQL for one possible procedure is:

```
INSERT INTO S (SN) VALUES ('S10');
UPDATE SPJ SET SN = 'S10' WHERE SN = 'S4' WITH RR;
DELETE FROM S WHERE SN = 'S4';
```

If the reader is not familiar with basic SQL data manipulation, Chapter SL can be read before reading this chapter.

The insert of a foreign key is allowed only if the value already exists in the parent table. If this implicit rule did not exist, one could insert an orphan row in a dependent table with no matching primary key value.

The update of a foreign key can occur only if the new foreign key value already exists in the parent table. If this implicit rule did not exist, one could update a foreign key such that there would be no matching primary key value. Again this would result in an orphan row in a dependent table.

No Constraint Checking Required

There are two cases where no constraint checking is required.

The insertion of a primary key into a parent table is unrestricted with respect to the dependent tables. For example, one can insert a row describing a new supplier without having already placed an order from the supplier. Of course, a duplicate primary key cannot be inserted into a parent table because of entity integrity.

The deletion of a foreign key from a dependent table is unrestricted. For example, the S4, P6, J3 row can be deleted when J3 is completed with no adverse effect on the parent tables.

Figure CT.9 summarizes the explicit and implicit RI rules.

Figure CT.9. Summary of explicit and implicit RI rules

- **Delete of a primary key** depends on the defined foreign key rule:
  - Restrict or no action causes the primary key delete to be rejected if there is a matching foreign key (default).
  - Cascade results in the primary key value and all foreign key values being deleted.
  - Set null results in the primary key value being deleted and all foreign key values set to null.

- **Update of a primary key** value can occur only if there is no matching foreign key value.

- **Insert of a foreign key** value only if the value exists as a primary key in the parent table.

- **Update of a foreign key** can occur only if the new foreign key value exists in the parent table.

- **Insert of a primary key** into a parent table is unrestricted with respect to dependent table (duplicate primary keys are not allowed).

- **Delete of a foreign key** from a dependent table is unrestricted.

The ALTER statement can be used to add or drop primary and foreign keys provided that the developer has the appropriate privileges. Adding a foreign key, however, turns on check pending and no SQL data manipulation statements can be issued. This is because values that violate RI may already exist in the foreign key column. The CHECK DATA utility can be used to turn check pending off as discussed in Chapter LC.

Altering a table with respect to RI constraints can invalidate plans and packages. SELECTS from the catalog tables can be used to determine the invalidated plans and packages so that they can be explicitly rebound or DB2 will automatically rebind the plans and packages when next executed.

Foreign Keys and Nulls

Foreign and primary key columns need not have the same null attribute. Whether a foreign key column should allow nulls or not depends on the nature of the data. This can be thought of in terms of whether there is an absolute or conditional dependency of the dependent table on the parent table.

Absolute Dependency: If in the foreign key table a row's information has no business meaning or makes no sense without the associated information in the primary key table, the foreign key column should be declared as NOT NULL. For example, imagine a CUSTOMER_ORDER table with information on product orders that includes a foreign key referencing the CUSTOMER table that describes customers who have placed the orders. If there can be no order without a customer, there must always be a relationship between the description of an order in the CUSTOMER_ORDER table and the description of its customer in the CUSTOMER table. Consequently, there must be a foreign key value in the CUSTOMER_ORDER table referencing a primary key value in the CUSTOMER table. This is an example of an absolute dependency where the foreign key in the CUSTOMER_ORDER table should be declared NOT NULL.

Conditional Dependency: There need not always be a foreign key value for every row depending on the business rules. Consider an EMPLOYEE table describing employees and including a foreign key referencing a DEPARTMENT table describing the departments to which they are assigned. If the company allows employees to be unassigned, the EMPLOYEE table's foreign key to the DEPARTMENT table should allow for nulls. This is an example of a conditional dependency. If the company had a rule requiring that every employee be assigned to a department, the relationship between the two tables would be absolute and the foreign key should be declared as NOT NULL.

Developers should pay special attention, however, to the null attributes of composite foreign keys. Improper use of nulls in composite foreign keys can lead to violations of RI. In the case of composite keys, DB2 considers the entire key null if any one of its columns is null. This can result in foreign key values without matching primary key values, a violation of RI. If a null appears anywhere in the SN, PN, or JN columns of SPJ, DB2 will allow an insert. (None of the columns should allow for null because the three columns constitute the primary key of SPJ. Assume for a moment that SN, PN, and JN are not the primary key of the SPJ table.) The following insert will be allowed even though there are no matching primary key values in the P and J tables of P99 and J99 because a SN is not specified and the column allows for nulls.

```
INSERT INTO SPJ
VALUES ('P99', 'J99', 200);
```

The problem can be avoided by not allowing for nulls in any columns of a composite key.

CT.4 RELATIONSHIPS THAT REQUIRE SPECIAL HANDLING

There are some relationships that require special handling. There are restrictions on which delete rule can be used with self-referencing tables, cycles, and delete-connected tables through multiple paths. If an attempt is made to define an invalid delete rule for these types of relationships, a negative SQLCODE will be issued. There are two types of SQL data manipulation restrictions that will result in a negative SQLCODE at bind or run time. Most of these restriction are required due to subtle conditions that are best understood through illustrations. Study of the accompanying examples should clarify the potential problems that are avoided by imposing restrictions.

Self-Referencing Constraint

A self-referencing table is one that has a foreign key that references the primary key in the same table. In the supplier example, for instance, if each supplier were owned by another, higher-level supplier, those ownerships might be recorded in a new column in the S table. Figure CT.10 shows such a modified S table, S_O table, with the S_OWNER column containing the ownership indications. For example, S2 is owned by S1, S3 by S2, and so on. A nullable foreign key is a good choice for a self-referencing table. Without a nullable foreign key, the fact that S1 has no owner cannot be recorded in a straightforward manner.

Figure CT.10. Self-referencing table

Cascade or No Action

SN	SNAME	STATUS	CITY	S_OWNER
S1	Smith	20	London	null
S2	Jones	10	Paris	S1
S3	Blake	30	Paris	S2
S4	Clark	20	London	S3
S5	Adams	30	Athens	S4

A self-referencing table is useful for a table with information for bill-of-material processing, an organization chart, and budgets allocated by the president of an organization to vice presidents, directors, and managers, for example.

By definition, the foreign key in a self-referencing table must specify the delete rule of NO ACTION or CASCADE. The restrict rule would be of little practical value because its enforcement would be limited to barring deletion of any primary key value that had a dependent foreign key value. This would assure that an existing "ownership" relationship could not be removed from the table, but at the cost of greatly limiting changes to the table. In the example, for instance, only S5 could be deleted because it is the only supplier that does not own another.

The DELETE SET NULL rule is not suitable for a self-referencing constraint because it holds the potential for unpredictable results. For example, this statement would call for deletion of any supplier that does not report to another—in other words, any supplier whose S_OWNER value is null:

```
DELETE FROM S_O WHERE S_OWNER IS NULL;
```

If DELETE SET NULL were in effect, when the SN = S1 row was deleted, S1 in S_OWNER would be set to null. If the rows were processed in order, when the SN = S2 row was deleted, S2 in the S_OWNER column would be set to null. Eventually, all the rows in this table would be deleted—if the rows were processed in order. If the rows were not processed in order or if the values in the S_OWNER column were not in sequence, fewer rows would be deleted.

If the CASCADE rule is used, when any primary key value is deleted, all rows with key values below it in the hierarchy of ownerships are also deleted. If S3 is deleted from the S_O table, for example, the deletions cascade to the SN = S4 row, then to the SN = S5 row. This is the desired result assuming that a decision has been made to stop doing business with S3 and its subsidiaries.

Beware of the CASCADE Rule: Do be cautious when using the CASCADE rule. If the president of an organization is deleted, then all of the employees of the organization will be deleted. The NO ACTION rule can be used where such an accident can occur to avoid unintentionally deleting more rows than required.

Cannot Insert Multiple Rows with a Subselect: There must be an existing primary key value for every inserted foreign key value. In the example, an attempt to insert a row with an S_OWNER value of S10 will fail because there is no S10 in the primary key. This problem can surface when a subselect is used to insert values from one table into another, self-referencing table. If DB2 detects such a violation during processing, it issues a negative SQLCODE. The rule is that more than one row cannot be inserted into a self-referencing table with a subselect.

A self-referencing constraint must be created with an ALTER TABLE statement. This is because the parent table with the primary key must exist before the related foreign key can be defined. If either the DELETE SET NULL or DELETE RESTRICT rule is specified as the self-referencing constraint, DB2 issues an error message when execution of the ALTER TABLE statement defining the invalid constraint is attempted.

DB2 supports cursor-controlled updates of the primary key and deletions involving self-referencing constraints in version 4 unlike previous versions of DB2. This complies with the SQL standard.

Cycles

A cycle is a situation in which tables are related to each other through both primary and foreign key relationships. In the simplest case, one table is a primary key table to the other; the second table is a primary key table to the first. For example, consider the tables in Figure CT.11. One is a modified J table, or J_S table, that includes a column, SUPERVISOR, showing each job's supervisor. Supervisors are employees of course. The JN column is the primary key. The other table is an employee table, which includes a column, ASSIGNED_JOB, showing the employee's job assignments. The EMPLOYEE column is the primary key. The SUPERVISOR column in the J_S table is defined as a foreign key to the employee table. ASSIGNED_JOB in the employee table is a foreign key to the J_S table. This is a two-table cycle.
Some cycles consist of more than two tables—foreign keys may connect several tables before the loop closes.

Figure CT.11. Relationship with a Cycle

JN	JNAME	CITY	SUPERVISOR
J1	Sorter	Paris	E700
J2	Punch	Rome	E200
J3	Reader	Athens	E500
J4	Console	Athens	E300
J5	Collator	London	E800
J6	Terminal	Oslo	E100
J7	Tape	London	E400

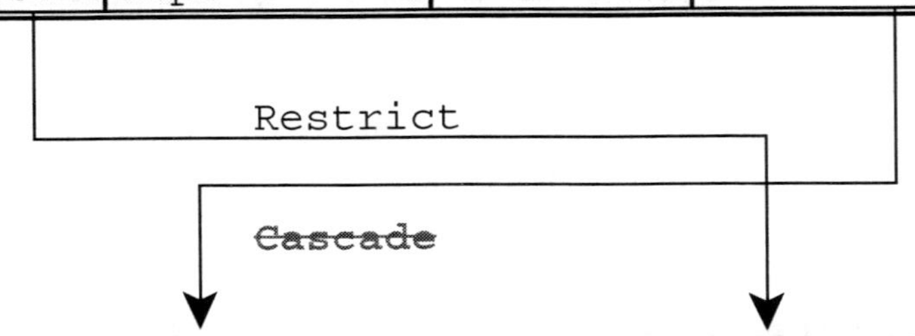

EMPLOYEE	...	ASSIGNED_JOB
E100		J6
E200		J2
E300		J4
E400		J7
E500		J3
E600		null
E700		J1
E800		J5

Restrictions: There are restrictions on the type of delete rules that may be used with either two-table or greater than two-table cycles. The CASCADE DELETE rule may not be used in a two-table cycle. In a cycle with more than two tables, at least one of the foreign keys participating in the cycle must employ the RESTRICT or SET NULL rule. DB2 will issue an error message when a CREATE statement with constraint definitions violating these restrictions attempts to execute.

To understand the kind of problem that might occur in cycles consider what would happen in the example if the foreign key on the SUPERVISOR column were defined with the CASCADE rule and that on the ASSIGNED_JOB column were defined with a RESTRICT rule. In that case, every time the row for an employee who is a supervisor is deleted from the EMPLOYEE table, rows in the J_S table showing that employee as a supervisor would also be deleted. Notice what happens when there is an attempt to delete 'E400' from the Employee table. The deletion would cascade to the J7 row in J_S table. That deletion, however, is barred by the restrict rule constraining deletions of JNs that appear in the ASSIGNED_JOB column.

In some cases, even with a valid cycle, some deletions may be impossible. In the example, even if both foreign keys were defined with the restrict rule—a cycle that DB2 would allow—there would be no way to delete most of the rows in both tables. For example, the 'E400' row could not be deleted from the EMPLOYEE table because of the foreign key restriction on the SUPERVISOR column. Neither could the row with 'E400' be deleted from the J_S table because of the ASSIGNED_JOB foreign key's restriction against deleting J7. This kind of difficulty can be avoided in a cycle by defining at least one of the foreign keys with the DELETE SET NULL rule and allowing nulls in the foreign key column.

Delete-Connected Tables

Tables related with a foreign key are called delete-connected tables because a deletion in the primary key table can affect or be affected by the contents of the foreign key table. If the delete rule connecting the two tables is cascade, then tables that are delete connected with the foreign key table are also delete-connected on its primary key table. In other words, a table can be delete connected with its grandparent. In Figure CT.12, for example, the J and PJ tables are delete connected by a foreign key on the JN column. Because the JN column's foreign key rule is cascade, the SPJ table, which is delete connected with the PJ table, is also delete connected with the J table.

Figure CT.12. Delete connected tables through multiple paths

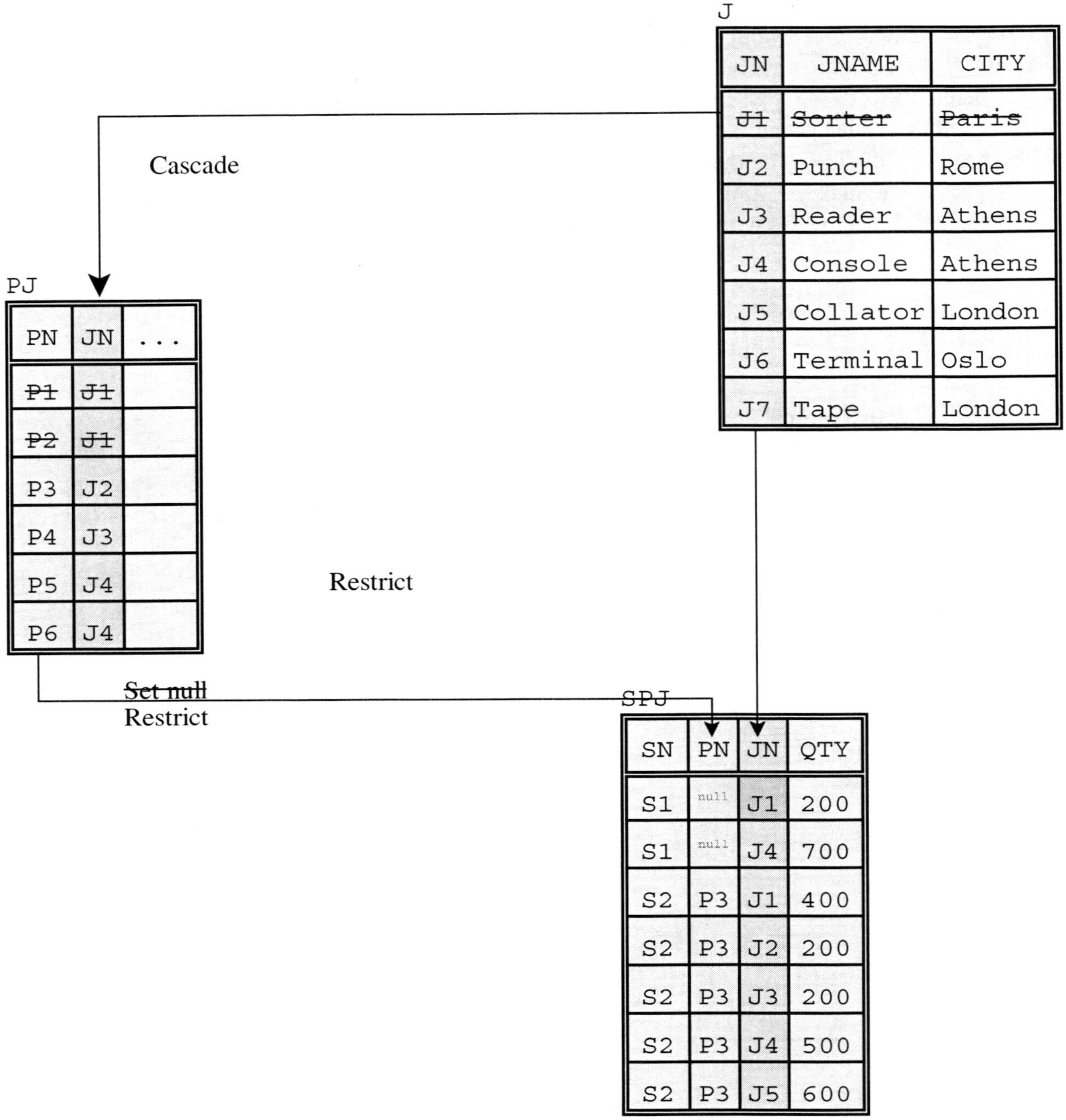

Problems can arise when two tables are delete connected through more than one path. In Figure CT.12, for example, the foreign key relating the J and SPJ tables directly would make those tables delete connected through two paths—the direct connection and the path through the PJ table. Because of the possibility of differing results depending on the order of processing such delete-connected tables through multiple paths, DB2 restricts their definition.

Restrictions: The foreign keys that establish a table's multiple delete connections—in the example, PN and JN in the SPJ table—must all be defined to have the same delete rule, and the rule may not be the SET NULL rule. Both must be defined either by the restrict rule or by the cascade rule. The cascade rule is crossed out in Figure CT.12 to indicate that it is not a valid rule. DB2 will issue an error message whenever a CREATE or ALTER TABLE statement attempts to define keys that violate these restrictions.

Let us look at one of the problems that might occur if DB2 allowed such multiple path delete connections. If the foreign key on PN in the SPJ table to the PJ table is defined by the crossed out cascade rule and the foreign key on JN in the SPJ table to the J table is defined by the restrict rule and a statement attempted to delete 'J1' from the J table, if DB2 first processed a cascade rule to the PJ and SPJ tables, because of the cascade J1 would be deleted from all three tables (crossed out in the figure). If DB2 first checked the constraint between the J and SPJ table, it would find J1 as a foreign key value in the J table and restrict all deletions.

Invalid Delete with Subselect

When a cascade rule is in effect, DB2 will not allow deletions based on a subselect that references the table from which the deletions are being made. This example illustrates the problem: Consider the two tables in Figure CT.13. One is the familiar S table, with SN as a primary key. The other is the JSUP table, which shows which suppliers supply which jobs. Each job has both a primary and secondary supplier. The PRIMARY_S and SECONDARY_S columns are foreign keys referencing the S table, with both the RI rules specified as delete cascade.

Figure CT.13. Invalid subselect delete

SN	SNAME	STATUS	CITY	S_OWNER
S1	Smith	20	London	null
S2	Jones	10	Paris	S1
S3	Blake	30	Paris	S2

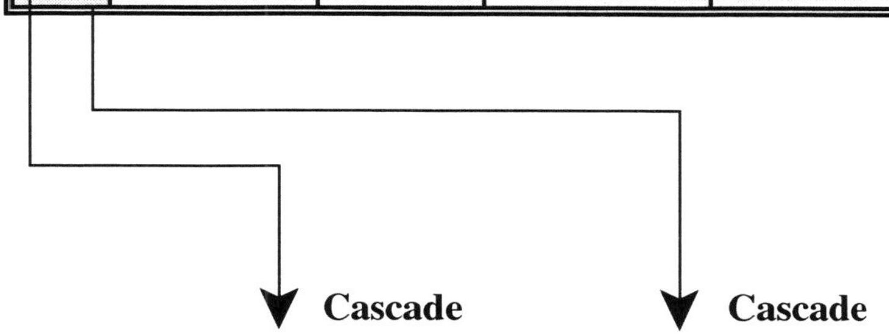

JN	PRIMARY_S	SECONDARY_S
J1	S1	S2
J2	S1	S2
J3	S2	S3

The following subselect might be used to delete from the S table all suppliers who are not used as secondary suppliers on any job.

```
DELETE FROM S SX WHERE SN NOT IN
  (SELECT SECONDARY_S
   FROM   JSUP
   WHERE  JSUP.SECONDARY_S = SX.SN);
```

The results of this statement, however, will be different depending on the order in which the rows are processed. If SN = S1 is evaluated in the subselect first, the NOT IN clause evaluates as true because S1 is not a secondary supplier. Therefore, S1 is deleted from the S table. Since it is a primary key value, and the cascade rule is in effect, the S1 rows in JSUP are also deleted. When SN = S2 is evaluated in the subselect, the NOT IN clause also returns true, since the previous cascade delete had eliminated the two jobs in which S2 had been secondary supplier. S2, therefore, is also deleted and its deletion cascades to eliminate the J3 row. Now, when SN = S3 is evaluated in the subselect, the NOT IN clause returns true and S3 is deleted.

Suppose, however, that S3 is the first value from the S table to be evaluated in the subselect. In that case, the NOT IN clause would return false because, at this point in the processing, the J3 row still exists, with S3 as its secondary supplier, and the S3 row will not be deleted. To avoid this kind of anomaly, at bind time, when DB2 encounters a DELETE statement containing this type of subselect combined with a cascade delete rule, instead of binding the statement it issues an error message.

CT.5 DB2 VERSUS APPLICATION ENFORCED INTEGRITY

The advantages of defining RI to DB2 are similar to those of defining table check constraints to DB2. Developers can be relieved of the time and effort to develop, test, and maintain their programs to enforce the constraints. In addition, the SQL that appears to be best for enforcing the RI constraints in applications can result in errors.

SQL Insert that Can Violate RI

The following SQL statements appear to be a reasonable approach to inserting a row with a SN foreign key value of S11 into the SPJ dependent table if there is a matching primary key in the S table.

```
SELECT SN
FROM   S
WHERE  SN = 'S11';

IF SQLCODE = 0
  INSERT INTO SPJ (SN, PN, JN, QTY)
  VALUES ('S11', 'P1', 'J2', 200);
```

The problems is that S11 can be deleted after the SELECT statement is executed with a 0 SQLCODE and before the INSERT statement is executed resulting in an S11 row in the dependent table without a matching S11 in the parent table. There are techniques that can be used to hold a lock on the S11 row in the parent table until the dependent row has been successfully inserted and committed as discussed in Chapter CC. However, a new developer may not be aware that an apparently simple technique can result in violating RI.

SQL Update that Can Violate RI

Another situation is even more subtle and the possibility of an error cannot be avoided with locking techniques. The goal is to update a foreign key value of S2 to S10 in the SPJ table provided there is a matching primary value of S10 in the parent table. The following UPDATE statement with an EXISTS subselect is a possible approach but can result in violating RI.

```
UPDATE SPJ SET SN = 'S10'
  WHERE SN = 'S2' AND EXISTS
  (SELECT SN FROM S WHERE SN = 'S10');
```

An EXISTS subselect returns a true or false to the UPDATE statement as discussed in Chapters SL and ST and locks are released. If a true is returned, the update of SPJ will be successful. The problem is that someone can delete S10 from the parent table after the true condition is determined from the EXISTS subselect and before the update is complete. This will result in S10 being an orphan in the SPJ dependent table. Again, there is the potential for violating RI when using application enforcement of constraints. Indeed, there are few foolproof techniques for implementing RI in application programs without the possibility of introducing erroneous data as discussed in the IBM manual, *DB2 Referential Integrity Usage Guide* (GG24-3312).

Performance of DB2 Enforced and Application Enforced Constraints

The performance considerations for DB2 enforcing RI constraints and table check constraints are similar. Both types of constraints are recorded in the Database Descriptor (DBD). DM checks the constraints in central storage as recorded in the DBD. (The DBD is held in the environmental descriptor (EDM) pool in central storage.) This avoids having a host program execute SQL statements to enforce RI. In the case of check table constraints that are defined with an IN list, SELECTS from a reference table are also avoided.

No code is added to the plan or package for RI and table check constraints when they are defined to DB2. SQL statements need not be executed in application programs to enforce the constraints. SQL statements require execution of code to go through the Application Program Interface (API), RDS, DM, buffer manager, Internal Resource Lock Manager (IRLM) or lock avoidance and back through the layers of code to return the SQLCODE to the host program. Significantly fewer instruction must be executed by DM to check the constraints found in the DBD.

The trade-off is that the DBD will be larger and may require a larger EDM pool. There is always concern about the DBD size because the DBD must be in contiguous space in the EDM pool as discussed in Chapter CD. On the other hand, there may be a savings of space in the EDM pool. It depends on the number of bytes required to store the constraint definitions in the DBD compared to the number of bytes saved in the plan or package as a result of having fewer SQL statements. It is possible that the decreased size of the plan or package will offset the increased size of the DBD in the EDM pool. If more space is required in the EDM pool for a larger DBD, trading more storage for reduced number of instructions that must be executed and reduced number of I/O is usually a very positive trade-off. Very large DB2 installation do need to be concerned with a shortage of space within the 2 GB current architectural limit. The 2 GB limit is due to the 31 bits used for addressability (2 gigabytes = 2^{31} = 2,147,483,648). The future may bring 63 bit addressability, allowing for 9 exabytes (9 exabytes= 2^{63} = 9,223,372,036,854,779,000).

The performance trade-offs of having DB2 enforce table check conditions with =, <, <=, >, >=, BETWEEN, IN, LIKE, and NULL comparisons versus having the host program check the condition before attempting to insert or update a row may not be positive. If the host program discovers that the row should not be inserted or updated, the INSERT or UPDATE statement will not be executed at all. Certainly, there is a savings if one can avoid executing a statement.

DB2 verifies that data manipulation adheres to all applicable RI rules as the processing occurs. This is called inflight verification. As processing changes a row's values, DB2 checks for RI violations and takes the specified action if it discovers any. If a restrict rule is in effect, for example, processing stops when a violation occurs. This inflight checking provides improved performance compared with checking in advance or with allowing processing to continue to a commit work point and then rolling back the processing if a violation had occurred. The NO ACTION rule causes enforcement to occur at end of statement processing when deleting more than one row in a self-referencing table.

RI processing does require resources, however, which the installation must take into account. For example, if DB2 were enforcing a restrict rule on the JN foreign key, when a user attempted to delete J2, DB2 would have to first search for J2 in the SPJ table, taking the necessary concurrency control locks, performing the I/O operations, and so on. This processing can be very intensive if the number of changes of key values is high.
In most cases, DB2 integrity enforcement will be more efficient than that done by an application. When DB2 enforces the rules, its checking will always use an available index on a primary or foreign key column, whereas for an application's checking, depending on how the checking is coded, the optimizer may not employ an index.

Application-Enforced Integrity

There are some situations in which application-enforced integrity might make sense. For example, DB2's rules may not match an organization's policy for using the data in question. In some cases, the organization might rather have a primary key update cascade to the foreign key rather than having DB2 bar the change with its implicit restrict rule. Such a cascade is permitted by the relational model.

The application design may be such that referential integrity cannot be violated in most cases. It may be that the PK and FK rows are always inserted, updated, and deleted within the same unit of recovery by an application program. Caution should be exercised in making the decision to use application enforced RI. Although it appears that all cases are covered in programs, they may not be. As additional programs are added to the application system or modifications are made to existing programs, the constraints may not be checked correctly.

RI enforcement by DB2 can add to the costs of INSERTING or updating a large number of rows by a batch program. For example, consider a situation in which there is a foreign key on the SN column of the SPJ table that references the SN in the S table. Suppose that the batch program must insert 100,000 rows into the SPJ table, with each new row indicating the receipt of a part from supplier S1. Before allowing insertion of each new row, DB2 would have to check to see that S1 exists in the S table. The person who writes the program knows, however, that the check can be made only once for the entire batch. It is necessary to hold a lock on S1 in the parent table while INSERTING rows into the dependent table to avoid the parent row being deleted during the inserts.

DB2 does not allow exceptions to integrity rules once they have been defined. In the above example, for instance, the developer may want to have DB2 enforce the rule on the SN foreign key at all times except during batch insertions. The LOAD utility, described in Chapter LC, provides a means for shutting off constraint checking during batch insertions. For batch updates, the only way to shut off that enforcement would be to use an ALTER statement to drop the key from the SPJ table. After the batch update, the key could be added again. In both cases, however, check pending is turned on. Techniques for turning off check pending are discussed in Chapter LC. In addition, there are performance advantages to having a program delete rows from a dependent table before deleting the rows from the parent table.

Checking for Constraint Violations

If DB2 is not used to validate data according to defined table check and RI constraints, SQL statements can be developed and executed to do this. This can be resource intensive, particularly for determining if there are any RI violations. All foreign key values in the JN column of the SPJ table that are not in the primary key JN column of the J table can be identified with either of the following statements.

```
SELECT SN, PN, JN, QTY
FROM   SPJ
WHERE  NOT EXISTS
   (SELECT 1
    FROM   J
    WHERE  J.JN = SPJ.JN);
```

Execution of a NOT EXISTS subselect for each of multiple dependent tables can be resource intensive. If RI is defined to DB2, the CHECK DATA utility can be used to validate the data. This utility will optionally delete violating rows and write an image of the rows to an exception table without logging. Using the utility to check for violations of RI and table check constraints has performance advantages.

Even if DB2 is not used to enforce RI, costs can be reduced compared to executing multiple NOT EXISTS subselects by adding RI constraints with the ALTER statement and executing the CHECK DATA utility. After executing the utility, the ALTER statement can be used to remove the constraints when using application enforced RI.

LOAD with ENFORCE CONSTRAINTS applies to RI and table check constraints. If a row violates a constraint, it will be written to a discard data set by default. This provides for some validation of the data by LOAD and minimizes the need to insert rows with a batch host program if the target tablespace or partition can be made unavailable during a load or load resume.

Another advantage of having DB2 enforce constraints is that the constraints are well documented in the catalog tables. Although application enforced constraints may be well documented initially, additional programs that are written over the years and modifications to existing programs are not always documented. Chapter PD contains SELECT statements from the catalog tables to obtain information about RI and table check constraints defined to DB2 and how the information can be used for error management.

CT.6 VIEWS

The name *view* well describes its object's function: to provide particular views of base tables. Views are virtual tables, made up of columns and rows from base tables and other views, but their data are not stored separately. Instead the developer defines a view in terms of a SELECT statement. DB2 records the defining statement in catalog tables SYSIBM.SYSVTREE and SYSIBM.SYSVLTREE and resolves it into base table references when an SQL statement using the view is bound. The process is transparent to users, who perceive and deal with views as if they were base tables in most cases.

Views are useful in providing access and update security. Rather than allowing users access to all rows and columns in a base table, developers can grant the use of views that show only columns and rows approved for the users. Views provide for ease of use and have performance advantages without increasing the costs of executing SQL statements significantly.

Security and Views

It is common practice at a company that managers are allowed to see information about employees in their department and no others. Here is an example of how views can be used to enforce such a policy. A MGR_PRIVILEGES table can be created containing the manager's AUTHID in the column USER_ID and the manager's employee number in the column MGRNO like:

```
CREATE TABLE MGR_PRIVILEGES
   (USER_ID CHAR(8) NOT NULL,
    MGRNO   CHAR(8) NOT NULL,
PRIMARY KEY (USER_ID));
```

Some examples use the EMP (employee) and DEPT (department) tables to make the examples more intuitive. These tables are described in the *Application Programming and SQL Guide* manual. The following MGR_EMP view definition allows managers to see only employees in their departments.

```
CREATE VIEW MGR_EMP AS
   SELECT EMPNO, FIRSTNME, MIDINIT
     WORKDEPT, PHONENO, HIREDATE, JOB,
     EDLEVEL, SEX, BIRTHDATE, SALARY,
     BONUS, COMM
   FROM  EMP, DEPT, MGR_PRIVILEGES
   WHERE MGR_PRIVILEGES.USER_ID= USER   -- special register
   AND   MGR_PRIVILEGES.MGRNO   = DEPT.MGRNO
   AND   EMP.WORKDEPT           = DEPT.DEPTNO;
```

Access to the view can be granted to the public while allowing a manager to see only employees in his or her department. USER is a special register that contains the AUTHID of the person using the view. DB2 locates the AUTHID in the MGR_PRIVILEGES table and determines the MGRNO. The MGRNO in turn is used to locate the employees who have a manager with the value in the DEPT table by setting the column MGR_PRIVILEGES.MGRNO equal to DEPT.MGRNO in a join. This join processing disallows updates of the view as will be seen shortly. If managers need to update employee rows, a separate view must be created for each manager and privileges granted to each manager to update the view.

Ease of Use and Performance

Views are useful for providing casual users and programmers easy and efficient access to data from several base tables. Managers need not be aware that three tables are accessed to provide the required information about employees in their departments. They simply select from the MGR_EMP view. The manager may need to look at the net salary of employees frequently but does not want to be bothered with keying the calculation of gross salary minus the various deductions. This can also be error prone. A person may forget to subtract some of the deductions on occasion which will give incorrect gross salaries. The term *derived* column is sometimes used to describe the gross salary as calculated in a view definition.

Naming standards frequently result in table and column names that are difficult to remember and are not what the business professional uses when referencing an object. A view can be created that uses the terms that are used by the business professionals.

Users are concerned with business processes and cannot be expected to know how to write complex SQL statements and formulate statements that perform well. Developers can create a view of complex operations that do perform well for users.

Resolution of Views

The results of a select from a view are not written to a work area in most cases. Rather the optimizer transforms the select from the view to a select from the underlying base tables and determines a good access path for the transformed statement. A manager may want to review the record of all employees in his/her department that were hired before January 1, 1983, and keys the statement:

```
SELECT EMPNO, FIRSTNME, MIDINIT
  WORKDEPT, PHONENO, HIREDATE, JOB,
  EDLEVEL, SEX, BIRTHDATE, SALARY,
  BONUS, COMM
FROM  MGR_EMP
WHERE HIREDATE < '1983-01-01';
```

The transformed statement will look like:

```
SELECT EMPNO, FIRSTNME, MIDINIT
  WORKDEPT, PHONENO, HIREDATE, JOB,
  EDLEVEL, SEX, BIRTHDATE, SALARY,
  BONUS, COMM
FROM  EMP, DEPT, MGR_PRIVILEGES
WHERE MGR_PRIVILEGES.USER_ID= USER
AND   MGR_PRIVILEGES.MGRNO   = DEPT.MGRNO
AND   EMP.WORKDEPT           = DEPT.DEPTNO
AND   HIREDATE < '1983-01-01';
```

Notice that the transformed SELECT statement is the same as the SELECT statement used to define the view with the additional predicate of HIREDATE < '1983-01-01' specified by the manager. Basically the SELECT statement that defines the view is merged with the SELECT from the view.

Cost of Views

In most cases, views cost only a few milliseconds of CPU time when DB2 binds the SQL, a one-time cost for static SQL. For dynamic SQL, using QMF for example, that CPU cost is paid each time a view is used. There are some cases where the use of views can detract from performance.

View Materialization: There are some cases where the rows that qualify according to the SELECT statement that defines the view must be written to a work file. For example, if the SELECT statement has a GROUP BY with a column function, the result of the GROUP BY and column function is written to a work file before the processing is done for the select from the view. This is an example of view materialization that is discussed in Chapter ST.

Retrieving Columns from One Table in a View Join: If a view definition involves a join, you should not select from only one of the tables. Consider the following view involving a join:

```
CREATE VIEW S_SPJ AS
 (SELECT SN, SNAME, STATUS, CITY, QTY
  FROM   S, SPJ
  WHERE  S.SN = SPJ.SN);
```

Here is a select of columns from the S table which is one of the two tables referenced in the view:

```
SELECT SNAME, STATUS, CITY
FROM   S_SPJ;
```

Join processing is done even though only columns from the S table are selected. This is necessary to return the correct results according to the view definition because the view qualifies only suppliers which have parts in the SPJ table. However, the person who SELECTS from the view may not realize that he or she is not seeing all of the suppliers in the S table. In addition, performance will be adversely affected by having to do join processing when only columns from one table are required. It is important to understand the view definition before selecting from a view.

An alternative to minimize the possibility of someone selecting from only one table based on a view of multiple tables is to use a view naming convention with the number of tables referenced in the view as part of the view name. For example, the view name S_SPJ_2 indicates that two tables are referenced in the view definition.

View Restrictions

The developer may use almost any SELECT statement in a view definition. However, DB2 does not allow creation of views with statements including UNION ALL, UNION, or ORDER BY operations, perhaps because the second and third operators can entail costly sorts. And it does not create a view from a statement including a FOR UPDATE OF clause, a clause used in embedded SQL that indicates the selected data is to be updated.

You can define a view with UNION and UNION ALL in V7. Do use UNION if no duplicate rows qualify or are acceptable. Do select from table that most frequently contains qualifying rows, UNION

ALL, select from table that is less likely to have qualifying rows. DB2 searches the first table first. It may not be necessary to access the second table at all depending on the number of rows fetched.

Updateability of Views: DB2 also does not update certain other views. For example, it makes no sense to update views that include column functions (AVG, SUM, COUNT, MIN, and MAX) because DB2 has no way of knowing what values to assign to the base tables. For example, if the average QTY is increased by 100, should DB2 increase each value by 100? Trying to update views that contain column functions would entail ambiguities and logical inconsistencies between the views and base tables. A view with a scalar function (such as date/time and string functions) in the SELECT clause cannot be updated. DB2 issues an error message when a program or user tries to update a view containing any of the column and scalar functions.

A view definition that contains a GROUP BY or DISTINCT cannot be updated because it can require a sort. If the rows are sorted into a work file, the rows in the base table can change after a copy of the sorted rows are written to the work file. Similarly, a view with a table expression in the FROM clause cannot be updated because the table expression results may be written to a work file. In addition, a view definition of a calculated value or constant cannot be updated although a row can be inserted into such a view.

Nor does DB2 update views created with joins. In other words, DB2 does not update a view when it finds more than one table listed in the CREATE VIEW statement's FROM clause. But developers may use subselects to create undatable views from multiple tables. In some cases, DB2 will update a view drawn from multiple tables with a subselect when it will not update the equivalent view created with a join. In recasting a join statement as a subselect, the developer should take care that the statements are, in fact, equivalent and care should be taken that the reformulated statement will perform well.

WITH CHECK OPTION Parameter

The WITH CHECK OPTION parameter is required to avoid an insert or update of a row using a view such that the row is not visible when a select is issued using the view. For example, this view definition allows a user to see only suppliers in London:

```
CREATE VIEW LONDON_S AS
  SELECT SN, SNAME, STATUS, CITY
  FROM   S
  WHERE  CITY = 'London';
```

A user can insert a row using the view for a supplier in Athens with the statement:

```
INSERT INTO LONDON_S VALUES
  ('S20','Thomas',50,'Athens');
```

A user can also update a row that he or she can see through the view even though he or she will not be able to see the row after it is updated like:

```
UPDATE LONDON_S
  SET   CITY = 'Athens'
  WHERE CITY = 'London';
```

The WITH CHECK OPTION parameter must be added to the end of a CREATE VIEW statement to avoid a user being able to insert or update a row such that the row is not visible when selecting from the view. In any case, a user cannot delete and select a row that does not qualify according to the view.

Views created on views including a check option are also checked according to the specified criteria by default. The default parameter is CASCADE. The default can be over-ridden by specifying the LOCAL parameter which means that the WITH CHECK OPTION applies only to the view created with the option and does not apply to views referencing the view created using the WITH CHECK OPTION.

There is a performance concern regarding the WITH CHECK OPTION. An index on columns specified in predicates will not be used to locate a row to be updated unless list prefetch is chosen to access the data pages.

The WITH CHECK OPTION has been used to provide some data validation in releases of DB2 prior to the availability of table check constraints discussed in Section CT.2 of this chapter. The table check constraints and triggers are better suited for validating the data.

Privileges to Create a View

A person needs no special privilege to create a view. The creator of the view will have the same privileges on the view as on the underlying base tables and can grant privileges to others.

Database administration (DBADM) authority allows the person holding the privilege to perform most operations on most objects in a database for which the authority is held. Views are an exception. DBADM of a database which contains tables referenced by a view created by someone else does not have privileges on the view. This avoids a person with DBADM privileges having access to a table in another database owned by another person. For example, if this restriction did not apply, a person could create a view referencing two tables from two different databases. If the person with DBADM privileges on one database could select from the view, he or she would be able to see information from a table in another database that is not covered by the DBADM authority.

System administration (SYSADM) authority is required to create a view for an AUTHID that is not one of DBADMs composite privileges.

Levels of Views

Developers can create views on other views and on combinations of views to any number of levels as long as the view references no more than 225 base tables directly or indirectly. As shown in Figure CT.14, for example, VIEW I can be created over some columns and rows in TABLE A; VIEW II can be created on TABLE A and TABLE B; VIEW III can be created on VIEW I and VIEW II; and so on. While this offers a great deal of flexibility, it can also create a great deal of confusion if levels are too deep. The higher-level views depend on those at the lower levels. If a lower-level view or table is dropped, higher-level views depending on it will also be dropped automatically and without a warning. In Figure CT.14, for example, if VIEW I is dropped, VIEW III and VIEW IV are dropped. If TABLE A is dropped, all of the views are dropped.

Figure CT.14. Levels of views

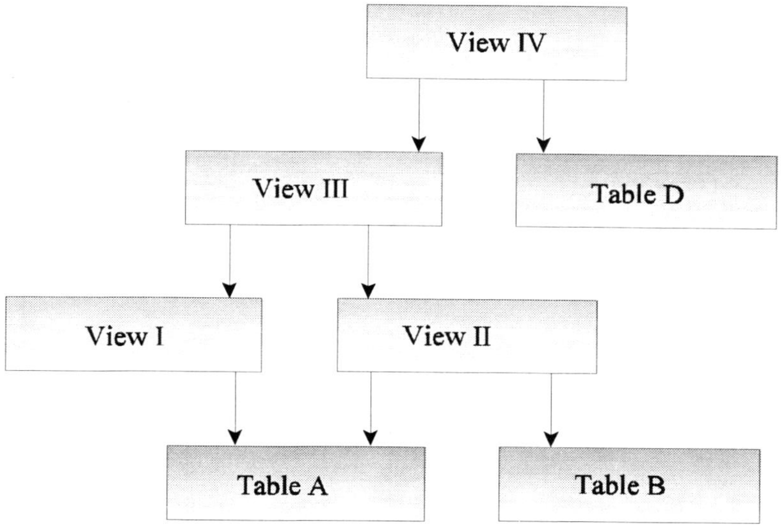

Table Restructuring

Views provide for a layer of data independence when tables must be restructured. Assume that a number of programs have been developed referencing the P table in Figure CT.6. It has been decided to build new automated warehouses and it is necessary to add a new column to the P table containing the size of each part in cubic feet so that robots can move the parts from one bin to another. It is also necessary to create a warehouse table to account for several warehouses in different cities. The CITY column will be removed from the P table and placed in the WAREHOUSE table along with the PN. The P table can be unloaded, dropped, and recreated with the name of P_NEW without the CITY column. A view with the name of the original P table can be created that also references the new WAREHOUSE and P_NEW tables like:

```
CREATE VIEW P AS
  SELECT PN, PNAME, COLOR, WEIGHT, CITY
  FROM   P_NEW, WAREHOUSE
  WHERE  P_NEW.PN = WAREHOUSE.PN;
```

Programs that select from the original P table will not need to be revised. This is because the view identifies the same information as the original P table. SQL statements will be automatically rebound when they are next executed after the drop of the original P table or can be explicitly rebound during non-prime time. Notice, however, that the FROM clause includes two tables. DB2 will not update the view, so applications performing updates on the original view will not work with this one.

Views Not Theoretically Undatable

Not all views are undatable in theory. C. J. Date provides an example of a view that utilizes the tables in Figure CT.6 that is not theoretically undatable in his book *An Introduction to Database Systems.*

Consider the view created by this statement:

```
CREATE VIEW CITY_PAIRS (S_CITY, P_CITY) AS
  SELECT S.CITY, P.CITY
  FROM   P, S, SPJ
  WHERE  P.PN   = SPJ.PN
  AND    SPJ.SN = S.SN;
```

This view contains city pairings, each showing a city where a part supplier is located, taken from table S, and a city where the user organization stores the part, taken from table P. P1, for example, is kept in London. It is supplied by S1, also located in London. The row in the CITY_PAIRS table is London-London. P1 is also supplied by S5 in Athens, creating an Athens-London pair. Here is the complete view:

S_CITY	P_CITY
London	London
Paris	Rome
Paris	Paris
Paris	London
London	Paris
Athens	Paris
Athens	London
Athens	Rome

The view is not undatable because the view definition requires a join of the S, P, and SPJ tables. Indeed, this view is not theoretically undatable because it cannot be determined which rows in the underlying base tables should be updated. Some examples will demonstrate the point. Consider this UPDATE statement:

```
UPDATE CITY_PAIRS
  SET    S_CITY = 'Dallas',
         P_CITY = 'New York'
  WHERE  S_CITY = 'Paris'
  AND    P_CITY = 'London';
```

Which city should be updated in the S table? Which in the P table? The obvious ambiguity makes the attempted update meaningless. A similar problem occurs with this DELETE statement:

```
DELETE FROM CITY_PAIRS
  WHERE S_CITY = 'London'
  AND   P_CITY = 'Rome';
```

Are all London suppliers and Rome parts to be deleted from the base tables S and P? And consider this INSERT:

```
INSERT INTO CITY_PAIRS
  VALUES ('Dallas','New York');
```

Are NULLS to be inserted in all columns except CITY in the base tables? The INSERT, if allowed, would not provide for a primary key value in the S and P tables.

Whether a view involving a join is undatable is not always obvious. Indeed the question of theoretically undatable views is a fertile one for researchers. Some views of joins that DB2 does not currently update, however, are theoretically undatable, particularly those joined on the primary and foreign keys. DB2 may provide the ability to update those views in a future release. E. F. Codd discusses view updateability in-depth in his book *The Relational Model for Database Management Version 2*.

CT.7 SYNONYMS, ALIASES, AND QUALIFIERS

Synonyms and aliases are useful for creating a more meaningful name for use by a person using a table or view. They are sometimes used by developers to manage the leading qualifier of a table or view. Test and production tables frequently have the same table name with a different qualifier for each set of tables. Developers need to test their programs using the test tables and have a straightforward method for referencing the production tables after their programs are tested successfully. For example, a developer needs to select and update from the TEST.SPJ table in a program that is being developed in a test environment. It is known that when the program is migrated to the production environment, the table will have a different qualifier, say PROD.SPJ. Developers do not want to reference TEST.SPJ in all FROM clauses because it would be necessary to change the program to reference PROD.SPJ when the program is moved to production.

Use of Synonyms

Synonyms were one of the few methods available for managing references to test and production tables in early releases of DB2. The developer can create a synonym like:

```
CREATE SYNONYM SPJ FOR TEST.SPJ;
```

This allows the developer to simply reference SPJ in all FROM clauses. Then after the move of the program to a production DB2 subsystem, a synonym is created to point to the production table:

```
CREATE SYNONYM SPJ FOR PROD.SPJ;
```

This seems like a straightforward procedure but there are some complicating factors that revolve around the fact that a synonym is specific to the AUTHID that created it. The consequences are that when a table or view is dropped directly or indirectly by dropping a tablespace or database, the synonym is also dropped. It is not uncommon in a development environment to drop and recreate objects. After this has occurred, a program that was working fine will no longer execute until the referenced synonym is recreated. Typically a number of developers are writing programs that reference a table. Each developer or a person with the appropriate authority must set his or her current SQLID to that of the developer and recreate the synonym for that developer. This has proved to be quite cumbersome at a number of companies.

Use of an Alias

An alternative to the use of a synonym is to use an alias which is not specific to an AUTHID like synonyms. Aliases are designed for a client/server environment using DRDA (V6) and the private protocol to avoid having to reference the location qualifier of a table or view. They can be used in a local environment as well with or without specifying the location like:

```
CREATE ALIAS SPJ FOR DALLAS.TEST.SPJ
```

The advantage is that the alias is not dropped when the table is dropped and in fact the table does not need to exist when the alias is created.

The procedures using synonyms and alias cannot be used in a sysplex data sharing environment because the catalog tables are shared across multiple DB2 subsystem. The procedures require creating two synonyms or aliases with the same name. Creation of the second synonym or alias will fail as being a duplicate of the first in a data sharing environment.

Use of a Qualifier

Another alternative for referencing test tables in test and production tables in production from the same program, perhaps the best of the three, is the use of a qualifier and secondary AUTHIDs. Each person can be assigned up to 245 secondary AUTHIDs and each person on a project team can be assigned the same secondary AUTHID. For example, each person working on the TEST.SPJ table can be assigned the secondary AUTHID of TEST. This allows the developer to set his or her ID to TEST and issue any SQL statement interactively without having to specify the qualifier of TEST. Also when the developer binds that SQL statements into a plan or package, the qualifier parameter can be specified as QUALIFIER(TEST) which causes all unqualified table names to be qualified with TEST. Then the migration to production requires only that the bind statement specify QUALIFIER(PROD). Indeed the value specified as the qualifier does not have to be a secondary AUTHID. However, secondary AUTHIDs do provide for avoiding qualifying interactive SQL and allows for granting of privileges to a single ID shared by a number of developers.

Synonym, alias, and secondary AUTHID are <u>not</u> part of SQL. This means that another technique will be required if the programs are used on a DBMS that does not support these features. The use of an alias is supported by IBM family of relational DBMSs including DB2/2 and DB2/6000 V2.

CT.8 DROPPING OBJECTS

We have discussed creating objects in the order that they must be created in Chapters CD and TS. A database must be created before a tablespace, a tablespace must be created before a table, a table must be created before creating synonyms, views, and indexes as shown in Figure CT.15.

Figure CT.15. Sequence of creating objects

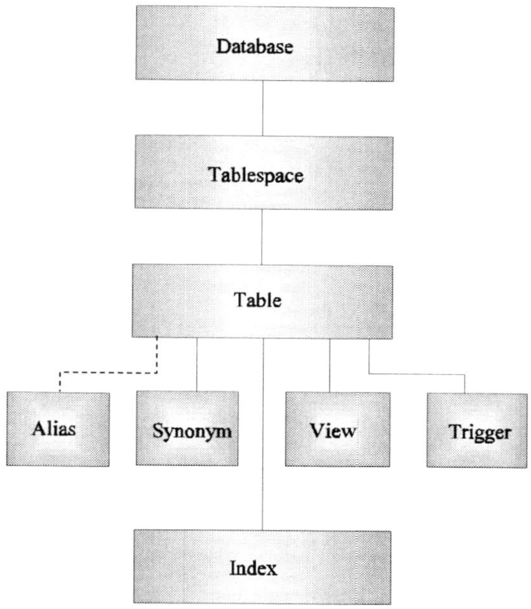

Each object can be dropped with the DROP statement by specifying the type of object and the object name, for example:

```
DROP DATABASE    Name_of_Database;
DROP TABLESPACE  Name_of_Tsp;
DROP TABLE       Name_of_Table;
DROP SYNONYM     Name_of_Synonym;
DROP ALIAS       Name_of_Alias;
DROP VIEW        Name_of_View;
DROP INDEX       Name_of_Index;
```

Dependent Objects

Dropping an object causes all dependent objects to be dropped. For example, if you drop a database all objects in the database are dropped and all privileges on the objects are revoked. If you drop an object further down in the hierarchy of objects, the lower objects are dropped. For example, if you drop a table, the synonyms, aliases, views, indexes, and triggers (Chapter TR) of table are dropped and privileges revoked. If the data is to be retained, do unload the data before performing a drop that will drop the table.

Recommendation: If the objects are to be recreated, save the CREATE statements in a file, develop CREATE statements based on SELECTS from catalog tables before dropping objects, or use a software product to generate CREATE statements from the catalog tables before dropping the objects.

CT.9 SUMMARY

DB2 offers developers considerable flexibility in designing tables and using views. A number of data types are available to choose from including data types for date and time periods. Also, the ROWID data type can be used to locate a row without index usage or a tablespace scan. This can prove useful in locating a row a second time efficiently after retrieving the row ID value using an index or tablespace scan.

There are a number of options for dealing with unknown or inapplicable values for a row. Not null with default or defining default values avoids complexities of managing nulls. There are advantages in saving development time and costs by defining business rules with the check table constraints and RI constraints. Constraints can be changed as required without modifying programs and the constraints are enforced uniformly regardless of the method used to change rows. There are performance trade-off that must be considered in defining constraints and the design of tables in general.

RI requires that every foreign key value, other than null, have a corresponding primary key value. If changes to the data were allowed to violate that rule, the tables would likely contain errors after inserting, updating, and deleting rows. Several rules governing data changes will protect against RI violations. Developers define the rules to DB2 when tables are created and can subsequently change the rules with the alter statement. DB2 then enforces the rule whenever changes that will affect the key are attempted. Developers should know how to implement all integrity rules and how to use DB2's RI facilities. They should also be aware of limitations on certain data manipulations imposed by DB2's implementation of integrity rules that ensure predictable and repeatable results.

EXERCISES

1. Develop a CREATE statement for an employee table named EMP in the database DAYOURDB and tablespace EMPTSP with the following column names. Specify NOT NULL for the EMPNO, have blank as the default for MIDINIT, and NOT NULL WITH DEFAULT for all of the other columns.

Column name	Data type and length
EMPNO	6 bytes of character data
FIRSTNME	1 to 12 bytes of character data
MIDINIT	1 byte of character data
LASTNAME	1 to 15 bytes of character data
WORKDEPT	3 bytes of character data
PHONENO	4 bytes of character data
HIREDATE	Date data type
JOB	8 bytes of character data
EDLEVEL	Numeric values < 32 K
SEX	1 byte of character data
BIRTHDATE	Date data type
SALARY	Packed decimal 9 with 2 decimal places
BONUS	Packed decimal 9 with 2 decimal places
COMM	Packed decimal 9 with 2 decimal places

2. What is the fully qualified name of the table created in the first exercise?

3. Where should FIRSTNME and LASTNAME be placed in the CREATE TABLE statement developed for the first exercise, and why?

4. Is VARCHAR(12) for FIRSTNME and VARCHAR(15) for LASTNAME a good choice? Why?

5. The SQL statement SELECT AVG(SALARY) FROM EMP yields incorrect results. What could be the problem and how can the problem to avoided?

6. a) Write a column definition clause to be included in a CREATE TABLE EMP statement such that when the user does not specify a WORKDEPT for an employee, the value of 'UNK' will be placed in the column.

b) Write a column definition clause such that when a row is inserted into the EMP table, the HIREDATE will be recorded automatically.

c) Write a column definition clause such that a row cannot be inserted into a table unless the EDLEVEL is greater than 12.

7. Create a distinct type of fahrenheit and one for centigrade. Use the built in data type of integer.

8. Will the following statement execute successfully? Why?

Assume that the WEATHER table has a TEMP_F column defined with the distinct type of fahrenheit and a TEMP_C column with a distinct type of centigrade.

```
SELECT TEMP_F, TEMP_C
FROM   WEATHER
WHERE  TEMP_F > TEMP_C
AND    DATE_W = '2000-01-17';
```

9. **Will the following statement execute successfully?**

```
SELECT TEMP_F, TEMP_C
FROM   WEATHER
WHERE  INTEGER(TEMP_F) > 70
AND    DATE_W = '2000-01-17';
```

10. **Will the following statement execute successfully? Why?**

```
SELECT CAST(TEMP_F AS CENTIGRADE) + TEMP_C
FROM   WEATHER
WHERE  CAST(TEMP_F AS CENTIGRADE) > TEMP_C
AND    DATE_W = '2000-01-17';
```

11. If the following DROP statement fails, what might you consider investigating?

```
DROP DISTINCT TYPE FAHRENHEIT RESTRICT;
```

12. Write an ALTER statement to avoid someone accidentally dropping the EMP table.

13. Write an ALTER statement to avoid someone accidentally dropping the EMP table.

14. Will AUDIT and/or DATA CAPTURE write information so that a report of the before and after image of inserted, updated, and deleted rows can be generated?

15. Write a statement to create a BOARD_MEMBER table in the DABMDB database and DABMTSP tablespace with the same definition as the EMP table.

16. What is the primary goal of RI?

17. a) Why is it advisable to define a primary key even if there are no foreign keys in a dependent table referencing the parent table?

b) What are the costs associated with doing this?

18. A table, ORDERS, storing information on orders placed by customers, has the CUSTNO column as a foreign key to the CUSTOMER table. What delete constraint is appropriate.

19. A table, DEPENDENTS, storing information on employees' dependents, has the EMPNO column

as a foreign key to the EMPLOYEE table. What delete constraint is appropriate for handling cases when employees leave the company?

20. A table, SUPERVISORS, containing information on which employees are assigned to supervise which jobs, has a foreign key to the employee table. What delete constraint is appropriate for handling cases when employees assigned as supervisors leave the company?

21. Are there any restrictions on the insertion of a foreign key row?

22. Are there any restrictions on the update of a foreign key value?

23. Are there any restrictions on the insertion of a primary key row?

24. Are there any restrictions on the deletion of a foreign key row?

25. What are some advantages of defining RI constraints to DB2?

26. What are some advantages of enforcing RI constraints in application programs?

27. Create a view named WORKDEPT such that the manager of the DBA (department) can see only the employees in the DBA department. Assume that the manager can update information about the employees in the DBA WORKDEPT. Are there any special considerations that apply to the view definition?

28. What are some uses of views?

29. Should the WITH CHECK OPTION be used in the definition of a view where users only select data and do not insert rows and update rows?

30. What functions cannot be specified in the SELECT statement that defines a view?

31. If users are to insert, update, and delete rows, what functions cannot be specified in the view definition?

32. What are the advantages of using the QUALIFIER parameter to specify the qualifier of tables and views when doing a bind and rebind of plans and packages compared to using synonyms and aliases?

ANSWERS

1. Here is a CREATE TABLE statement for the EMP table.

```
CREATE TABLE EMP
 (EMPNO      CHAR(6)       NOT NULL,
  FIRSTNME   VARCHAR(12)   NOT NULL WITH DEFAULT,
  MIDINIT    CHAR(1)       WITH DEFAULT ' ',
  LASTNAME   VARCHAR(15)   NOT NULL WITH DEFAULT,
  WORKDEPT   CHAR(3)       NOT NULL WITH DEFAULT,
  PHONENO    CHAR(4)       NOT NULL WITH DEFAULT,
  HIREDATE   DATE          NOT NULL WITH DEFAULT,
```

```
  JOB         CHAR(8)      NOT NULL WITH DEFAULT,
  EDLEVEL     SMALLINT     NOT NULL WITH DEFAULT,
  SEX         CHAR(1)      NOT NULL WITH DEFAULT,
  BIRTHDATE   DATE         NOT NULL WITH DEFAULT,
  SALARY      DECIMAL(9,2) NOT NULL WITH DEFAULT,
  BONUS       DECIMAL(9,2) NOT NULL WITH DEFAULT,
  COMM        DECIMAL(9,2) NOT NULL WITH DEFAULT)
IN DAYOURDB.EMPTSP;
```

2. The fully qualified name of the table created in the first exercise is LOCATION.AUTHID.EMP where LOCATION is the current location of the person who enters the statement and AUTHID is the current SQLID of the person who enters the statement.

3. Placement of the VARCHAR columns FIRSTNME and LASTNAME as the last columns in the row minimizes the number of bytes that must be logged when rows are updated which improves performance.

4. It is doubtful that the number of letters in a person's first and last name will vary greatly within the maximum allowed characters of 12 and 15. An additional 2 bytes are required for the length field for each first and last name resulting in little DASD space savings if any. If an index is created on one or both of the columns, the shorter values will be padded with blanks resulting in no savings in the index pages. Index only processing is not possible. It is always necessary to get the length value from the data pages for SELECT statements. In addition, program development time and costs are increased with the added work for managing VARCHAR columns as discussed in Chapter PD.

5. The salary column has been specified NOT NULL WITH DEFAULT, and some rows contain zeros for unknown salaries. The problem can be avoided by excluding 0 salaries from the average calculation like:

```
SELECT AVG(SALARY)
FROM   EMP
WHERE  SALARY ¬= 0;
```

An alternative is to have DB2 substitute null for a 0 salary.

```
SELECT AVG(NULLIF(SALARY, 0))
FROM   EMP;
```

If you want to avoid developers having to exclude 0 from the average, the SALARY column can be defined as allowing for nulls. The SELECT statement will then ignore null values in taking the average.

6. a) The column definition clause to cause 'UNK' to be placed in a column when the user does not specify a department for an employee is "WORKDEPT CHAR(3) WITH DEFAULT 'UNK'".

b) The column definition clause to cause the HIREDATE to be recorded automatically when a row is inserted into the EMP table, is "HIREDATE DATE NOT NULL WITH DEFAULT".

c) The column definition clause such that a row cannot be inserted into a table unless the EDLEVEL is greater than 12 is "EDLEVEL SMALLINT NOT NULL CONSTRAINT EDLEVEL_C CHECK (EDLEVEL > 12)"

7. Here are the CREATE statements for two distinct type, one for fahrenheit and one for centigrade using the built-in data type of integer.

```
CREATE DISTINCT TYPE FAHRENHEIT AS INTEGER WITH COMPARISONS;

CREATE DISTINCT TYPE CENTIGRADE AS INTEGER WITH COMPARISONS;
```

8. The following statement will not execute successfully because a comparison cannot be made between a column defined with a distinct type of FAHRENHEIT and a column TEMP_C column defined with a distinct type of CENTIGRADE. An SQLCODE of -401 is returned.

```
SELECT TEMP_F, TEMP_C
FROM   WEATHER
WHERE  TEMP_F > TEMP_C
AND    DATE_W = '2000-01-17';
```

9. The following statement will execute successfully and the correct results received assuming that the value 70 is in fahrenheit (not centigrade). The statement results in a -401 SQLCODE without the use of the INTEGER cast function. The developer is taking an overt action to by using the INTEGER function to make the comparisons. The same principle applies if a host variable is used in place of 70. Host variables are always defined with built in data types. Host languages do not support the definition of a field as a distinct types.

```
SELECT TEMP_F, TEMP_C
FROM   WEATHER
WHERE  INTEGER(TEMP_F) > 70
AND    DATE_W = '2000-01-17';
```

10. The following statement will not execute successfully (-461 SQLCODE). It is not possible to cast a distinct type TEMP_F (distinct type of FAHRENHEIT) to a different distinct type (CENTIGRADE). One of the primary goals of distinct types is to avoid arithmetic operations and comparison of unlike distinct types. An UDF needs to be developed in a host language with the correct formula to convert fahrenheit to centigrade.

```
SELECT CAST(TEMP_F AS CENTIGRADE) + TEMP_C
FROM   WEATHER
WHERE  CAST(TEMP_F AS CENTIGRADE) > TEMP_C
AND    DATE_W = '2000-01-17';
```

11. If the following DROP statement fails, consider determining if there are any UDF and stored procedures dependent on the distinct type by selecting from SYSROUTINES.

```
DROP DISTINCT TYPE FAHRENHEIT RESTRICT;
```

Once the drop is successful, all automatically created cast functions created by DB2 when the distinct type is created are dropped automatically.

12. Here is an ALTER statement to avoid someone accidentally dropping the EMP table.

```
ALTER TABLE EMP
```

```
ADD RESTRICT ON DROP;
```

13. DATA CAPTURE (not AUDIT) causes information to be recorded in the log so that a report of the before and after image of inserted, updated, and deleted rows can be generated.

14. A statement to create a BOARD_MEMBER table with the same definition as the EMP table in the DABMDB database and DABMTSP tablespace is:

```
CREATE TABLE BOARD_MEMBER LIKE EMP IN DABMDB.DABMTSP;
```

15. The primary goal of RI is to insure that every non-null foreign key value in a dependent table has a corresponding primary key value in the parent table. For example, you would not want to have an unpaid bill of $100,000 and not have information on the customer for billing purposes.

16. a) The definition of a primary key, even if there are no foreign keys referencing the parent table, clearly documents the primary key in the catalog tables and requires the creation of a unique index on the primary key columns.

b) There are no costs associated with defining a primary key if there are no foreign keys referencing the parent table. No special processing is required in this case.

17. The restrict delete rule should be defined such that information about a customer cannot be deleted if there is an outstanding order placed by the customer.

18. A cascade delete is a good choice in this case because there is no reason to maintain active information on an individual's dependents when that individual is no longer employed. However, there may be a requirement to archive data on the former employee before deleting information.

19. A SET NULL constraint is a good choice because, although the employee has left the company, the job still exists and the supervisory position needs to be filled.

20. A foreign key row cannot be inserted unless there is a primary key value matching the foreign key value in the row to be inserted. This is an implicit rule.

21. A foreign key value can be updated to only a value that appears in the primary key column of the parent table. This is an implicit rule.

22. The only restriction on the insertion of a primary key row is that the primary key value cannot already exist in the table. There are no other restrictions regardless of whether or not there are foreign keys referencing the parent table.

23. There are no restrictions on the deletion of a foreign key row.

24. There are a number of advantages to defining RI constraints to DB2. You can be sure that RI is enforced uniformly regardless of how the data is updated. It is not necessary to develop SQL and procedural code to maintain RI integrity and be concerned that the constraints may not be understood and enforced in all cases. It is likely that DB2 enforced integrity will perform better than application enforced integrity because the RI enforcement is done at a lower level and FK indexes are always used to enforce the constraints, assuming that they have been created. There is more flexibility in

enforcing constraints. For example, if business rules are changed, the constraints can be changed by dropping existing constraints and adding new constraints without changing any application programs. One can always determine what constraints are enforced by selecting from the catalog tables. The DB2 utilities can be used to enforce the constraints.

25. An advantage of enforcing RI constraints in application programs is if it is believed that RI cannot be violated in some cases and it is not necessary to check the constraints in those cases. One should be very careful with this belief. There may be cases where RI can be violated. Business rules may dictate that constraints should be enforced differently than what is allowed by DB2. Application design may allow checking the existence of a PK and holding a lock so that the PK cannot be updated or deleted while inserting or updating a number of matching FK rows.

26. The following CREATE VIEW statement will allow the manager of the DBA department to see only employees in this department.

```
CREATE VIEW MGR_WORKDEPT AS
  SELECT EMPNO, FIRSTNME, MIDINIT, LASTNAME, WORKDEPT,
  PHONENO, HIREDATE, JOB, EDLEVEL, SEX, BIRTHDATE,
  SALARY, BONUS, COMM
  FROM   EMP
  WHERE  WORKDEPT = 'DBA';
```

The SELECT defining the view cannot reference more than one table in the FROM clause when the user plans to update data using a view.

27. Views can be used to enforce column and row level security, provide for automatic calculation of values without the user having to know the correct expression, ease the use of SQL, help ensure good performance of SQL statements, and provide independence in applications from the structure of base tables.

28. There is no need to use the WITH CHECK OPTION in a view definition if users can only select data and cannot insert rows and update rows. The option is useful in not allowing users to insert rows they cannot see, or update rows they can see to be rows they cannot see.

29. ORDER BY, UNION, UNION ALL, and FOR UPDATE OF cannot be specified in a view definition.

30. If users are to insert, update, and delete rows, the SELECT statement that defines the view should not include a column or scalar function, derived columns, DISTINCT, GROUP BY, and HAVING clauses, and more than one table in the FROM clause of a view definition.

31. Use of the QUALIFIER parameter avoids having to be concerned with duplicate synonym and alias names on the same DB2 subsystem and when using sysplex data sharing. The QUALIFIER parameter avoids having to recreate synonyms when objects are dropped and recreated.

FIGURES

Index Usage for Performance

IU.1 INTRODUCTION

DB2 can use indexes in a variety of ways to locate required rows efficiently. In the same way that an index in a book is used to quickly locate a particular item of interest, DB2 can use an index to locate a page containing a requested row to avoid scanning the entire tablespace. An index in a book contains keywords that the authors believe are useful to you in locating information. DB2, on the other hand, must be prepared to locate *any* value in the indexed column. Therefore, all unique values that appear in the indexed column are placed in the index.

In this chapter, we describe the basic index structure and how indexes are used to locate data. This is similar to both type 1 and 2 indexes. Type 2 indexes were introduced in V4. Type 1 indexes were removed from DB2 in V6. Index design issues and how the index manager process pages when rows are inserted, updated, and deleted are described in Chapter ID.

Index Structure

Figure IU.1 is a conceptual representation of a fragment of the index structure used by the index managers to reference data pages containing information on jobs and their names. The last row of boxes represents data pages. If the job table has a million 100-byte rows, there are about 30,000 data pages. Clearly, it is too costly to scan all data pages when only a few rows are required.

Figure IU.1. Index structure

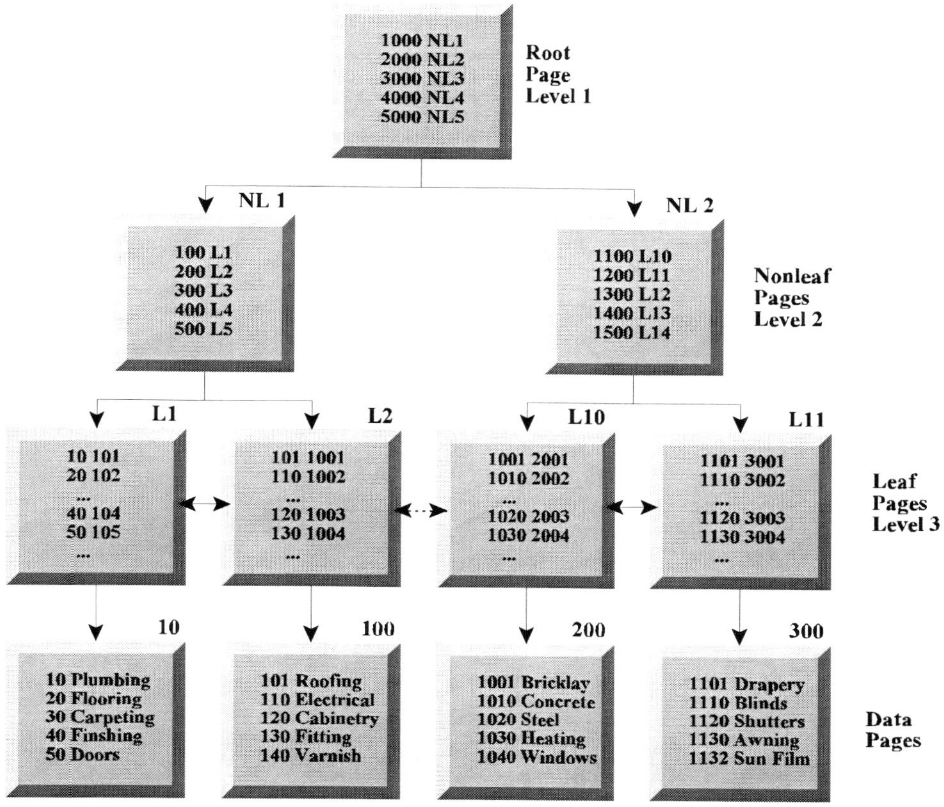

You are likely to need indexes on columns that are frequently searched or joined. In our example, it is the job number (JN) column. At the bottom of the index are the leaf pages represented by the boxes just above the data pages in Figure IU.1. Each leaf page contains indexed values followed by one or more *record identifiers* (RIDs). If the index is on a column with all unique values, the primary key for example, each value has one RID following it. If the index is on a column that contains duplicate values, a CITY column for example, each city in the in the index has one or more RIDs following it. If there are 200 jobs in Dallas, a leaf page entry has the value of Dallas followed by 200 RIDs.

A RID is four bytes in length (except for tablespaces greater than 64 GB (gigabyte) as discussed in Chapter TS. The first three bytes of the RID reference a data page. The fourth byte of the RID points to a slot in the page directory that contains the offset of the row on the page. If the tablespace is greater than 64 GB, the RIDs of indexes on tables in the tablespace are five bytes in length with the first four bytes referencing a data page and the fifth byte points to a slot in the page directory.

If there is an index on a 10-byte column, there will be about 4,000 leaf pages. Certainly, it is better to scan 4,000 leaf pages than to scan 30,000 data pages. However, we do not want to 4,000 leaf pages just to locate a few rows.

Figure IU.1 shows that an index has nonleaf pages above the leaf pages. The nonleaf pages contain the upper range value of each of the leaf pages along with a pointer to each leaf page. For example, the nonleaf page NL1 has the upper range value of 100 with a pointer of L1 referencing the first leaf page, an upper range value of 200 with a pointer of L2 referencing the second leaf page, and so on. Leaf pages between L3 and L9 are not shown, and the leaf pages with a pointer greater than L11 are not shown in the figure. Because of space limitations, only the two of the 16 nonleaf pages are shown in the figure.

The *root page* is at the top of the index. It contains the upper range value for each of the nonleaf pages along with pointers to the nonleaf page. The root page in the example has an upper range value of 1000 with a pointer of NL1 to the nonleaf page with the values less than 1000. The root page also contains an upper range value of 2000 with a pointer of NL2 to the nonleaf page with values less than 2000 and so on for each nonleaf page in the index.

Clustering Indexes

The clustering index determines how rows are physically ordered in a table. Data manager uses the clustering index to determine where to insert a row. For example, the clustering index on JN causes rows to be maintained in sequence on JN. An insert of JN 105 causes the row to be inserted on the same page as JN 101 and 110, assuming there is free space on the page. Rows are maintained in logical sequence on the column designated as the clustering index. A table can have at most one clustering index.

Cluster Ratio: The *cluster ratio* is the percentage of rows in sequence on the data pages. It is a value computed by the RUNSTATS utility, described in Chapter RR. You can designate only one index as the clustering index on a table. However, several indexes may have a good cluster ratio.

Consider an example of how you can have a high cluster ratio on two columns. Assume that the clustering index is on an employee number and that employee numbers are assigned sequentially as new employees are hired. There is also an index on a timestamp column of when the employee was hired. Both of these indexes will have a very high cluster ratio after they are reorganized using the REORG utility. There are many situation where this can occur that are not so obvious. By selecting the CLUSTERRATIOF column in the SYSINDEXES catalog table, you might be surprised to see a number of your indexes with a good cluster ratio. (CLUSTERRATIOF rather than CLUSTERRATIO is used by the optimizer once it is populated in V6 as discussed in Chapter RR.) The optimizer considers the cluster ratio for any index with a cluster ratio greater than five percent when determining if and how an index should be used as discussed in Chapter OP.

The terms clustering and non-clustering suggest different index structures. This is not true. Clustering and non-clustering indexes have the same index structure. Clustering refers to how rows are sequenced on the data pages. The cluster ratio is 100 percent in Figure IU.1 because all rows on the data pages are in sequence on job number.

Well-Clustered Indexes Can Help Avoid Sorts: An index can be used to avoid a sort of data rows. The values on the index leaf pages are maintained in logical sequence. The index manager can follow forward pointers to scan the leaf pages in sequence. The optimizer may choose to scan the leaf pages and follow the RIDs to the rows and retrieve them in sequence. The optimizer is likely to do this if the cluster ratio is 80 percent or more.

The use of an index to avoid a sort of rows is useful for retrieving rows in sequence to satisfy an ORDER BY, GROUP BY, DISTINCT, and to avoid sorts for joins.

If the cluster ratio is low, the use of the index to avoid the sort is too costly. This is because excessive seek time can be required to the data pages to retrieve the rows in sequence. For example:

- Atlanta RID references a row on cylinder 100
- Chicago RID references a row on cylinder 1
- Dallas RID references a row on cylinder 50
- Houston RID references a row on cylinder 2
- New York RID references a row on cylinder 75
- San Jose RID references a row on cylinder 3, etc.

IU.2 BASIC INDEX USAGE

Now that we have described the index structure, let's look at some ways DB2 uses an index. In this section, we describe matching index scans (with and without referencing the data pages), non-matching index scans, and index screening.

Matching Index Scan

DB2 can find a specific row with only a few I/O operations by following a path down through the index structure. For example, a matching index scan can be used to find job 110:

1. The index manager compares the value 110 to the upper range values in the root page and determines that it is less than 1000, which indicates that the nonleaf page NL1 should be accessed next.

2. Job 110 is compared to the upper range values in NL1. Job 110 is greater than 100 but less than 200 indicating that leaf page L2 contains job 110.

3. Leaf page L2 has the RID 1002 that points to the page 100 containing the row for job 110.

Using a matching index scan with data reference, the job is located with three I/Os to the index pages and one I/O to the data pages. If it is not necessary to access the data pages to satisfy a SELECT statement, the processing is referred to as a matching index scan *without* data reference.

If the index is being used frequently, there is a good chance that the root page, some nonleaf pages, and perhaps some leaf and data pages will be found in the buffer pool from previous searches. This can further reduce the number of I/Os.

Non-matching Index Scan

All of the leaf pages are scanned in a non-matching index scan. Data pages are accessed for each value that qualifies in a leaf page. It is not necessary to start at the top of the index structure to locate each row that is required. There are times when it is not possible or it is not efficient to perform a matching index scan. In these cases a non-matching index is best. A non-matching index scan without data reference is used if it is not necessary to access the data pages to get additional columns that are not in the leaf page to satisfy a SELECT statement.

A matching index scan followed by a scan of the leaf pages can be done to satisfy a range predicate (some form of greater than, less than, BETWEEN, or LIKE). For example, a SELECT statement that requests jobs between 101 and 1030 (WHERE JN BETWEEN 101 AND 1030) is likely to result in a matching index scan to locate job 101 followed by a scan of the leaf pages until all of job 1030 have been processed.

IU.3 INDEX LOOKASIDE AND ONE-FETCH ACCESS

Index Lookaside

Index lookaside is a refinement of a matching index scan. Index lookaside begins with a matching index scan. For a leaf page and the next higher nonleaf page, DB2 saves the lowest and highest values, log relative byte address (RBA), and page identifiers. Before doing a second matching index scan, DB2 goes through the following process:

1. It checks to see if the next required value is within the range of saved values for the leaf page. If the value is within the range of values on the leaf page, the value is located on the leaf page.

2. If the value is not within the range of values for the leaf page, DB2 checks to see if the value is within the range of saved values for the next higher nonleaf page. If the value is within the range of values for the nonleaf page, a getpage is issued on the nonleaf page.

3. If the value is not present, a matching index scan is performed. In the context of index lookaside, this is referred to as absolute positioning.

Advantages of Index Lookaside: There are a number of advantages to index lookaside processing. In many cases, a matching index scan is avoided for each value required. Data Manager (DM) issues a release and getpage on a leaf page only after processing all qualifying values on the page.

This is in contrast to issuing a release and getpage for each of 213 values on a leaf page. (The number of indexed values on a leaf is 213 using the example of a 10-byte indexed column and the default of 10 percent free space).

Index lookaside avoids a matching index scan for each required value--all qualifying values are processed before the page is released, and sequential or dynamic prefetch can be used on the leaf pages. These factors result in a significant reduction in the number of getpages, physical I/O, lock requests, and CPU time. This technique is particularly useful for the inner table of nested loop and hybrid joins, correlated subselects, repeated execution of any SQL statement that processes multiple rows, and a singleton select in a programming loop. Index lookaside is not an option of the optimizer. It is a technique coded into DB2 processing. Therefore, the only indication of its use is a reduction in resource consumption as seen in the accounting trace records.

A word of caution is in order. The saved identifiers are reset each time that a commit work is issued when the plan or package is bound with RELEASE(COMMIT). We recommend RELEASE(DEALLOCATE) to maximize the benefits of index lookaside and to gain other performance benefits.

One-Fetch Index Access

The column functions of MIN and MAX can be satisfied by a one-fetch index access. To do this, the MIN function requires an ascending index, and MAX requires a descending index. The one-fetch index access applies to an index on a single column and a composite index on multiple columns. If the minimum or maximum value is requested on the non-leading column of a composite index, it is necessary to specify equal predicates on the leading columns of the index.

The minimum value is stored as the first value in the first leaf page of an ascending index of a single column index. The maximum value is on the last leaf page and can be located with a non-matching index scan.

It is sometimes puzzling as to how the index manager can use one fetch to locate the maximum value with a descending index but cannot do that with an ascending index. The reason has to do with the fact that a descending index is stored and processed like an ascending index after one's complement is done on the indexed values. This basically flips the bits (the bit pattern 0001 becomes 1110 for example) so that now the maximum value is the first value on the first leaf page of a descending index.

Restrictions: A one-fetch index access cannot be used if there is more than one table, more than one column function, and if GROUP BY is used in the select. Also, the leading columns of a composite index must have equal predicates.

Use of one-fetch index access: There are many uses of a one-fetch index access that result in excellent performance. We will use an example to determine the employee who has the highest seniority with the company in each department. There are many similar uses including determining the oldest order placed by a customer, oldest deposit in an account, oldest insurance policy, etc. In this example assume a composite index and SELECT statement like:

```
CREATE INDEX WKDEPTX ON EMP (WORKDEPT, HIREDATE ASC);

SELECT EMPNO, WORKDEPT, HIREDATE
FROM   EMP AS E1
WHERE  HIREDATE =
  (SELECT MIN(HIREDATE)
   FROM   EMP AS E2
   WHERE  E1.WORKDEPT = E2.WORKDEPT);
```

The optimizer is likely to choose a matching index scan on WORKDEPT and an one-fetch index access on HIREDATE.

Similarly, you can use the MAX column function with an descending index on date to determine the most recently hired employee, the most recent order placed by a customer, the most recent deposit in an account, the most recent insurance policy, etc.

IU.4 LIST PREFETCH AND MULTIPLE INDEX USAGE

List prefetch is a prerequisite of multiple index usage. List prefetch has significant advantages in its own right. We will first look at list prefetch followed by multiple index usage.

List Prefetch

List prefetch is a method for using a single I/O to retrieve up to and including 32 data pages that contain qualifying rows according to one or more predicates. It is necessary to get the RIDs from one or more indexes and place them in the RID pool. The RIDs are sorted, and duplicate page identifiers (first three bytes of the RID) are eliminated using an in-memory sort without work files.

Advantages of List Prefetch: With list prefetch, the seek time to locate pages is minimized by reading pages sequentially as they appear on DASD. There are fewer I/Os to the data pages because the RIDs are sorted and reduced before accessing the data pages. All qualifying rows on a page are processed with list prefetch. This is in contrast to a having to do a matching index scan for each of several rows that might qualify on a page.

Skip-sequential processing is used with list prefetch. That is, unreferenced data pages are skipped. For example, if pages 5, 7, 10, 15, 20, 23, 27, and so on, are required and pages 5, 10, 15, 20, 25 are in the buffer pool, only 7, 23, 27 must be read from DASD. (Buffer manager also avoids rereading pages that are already in the buffer pool for sequential and dynamic prefetch.)

Assuming a buffer pool of 1000 or more pages, one I/O can be issued to read up to and including 32 pages as identified by RIDs from the leaf pages. This is in contrast with sequential and dynamic prefetch where one I/O is issued to access the next 32 pages in most cases. Sequential and dynamic prefetch have the advantage that they can be used on the index *and* data pages. They do not require prior access to an index as does list prefetch. Sequential and dynamic prefetch are discussed in more detail in Chapter BP and list prefetch is discussed further in Chapter PP.

Multiple Index Processing

DB2 can use multiple indexes on a table to satisfy multiple predicates joined by AND and OR. The qualifying RIDs are obtained from the indexes for each of the predicates, sorted, and duplicate page identifiers are eliminated--a union process for OR; and an intersection process for AND. Then from the resulting list, DB2 uses list prefetch to retrieve the data from the data pages in sequence as they appear on DASD.

Consider a separate index on SN and PN with the following SELECT statement:

```
SELECT SN, PN, JN, QTY
FROM   SPJ
WHERE  SN = 'S5'
AND    PN = 'P5';
```

A matching index scan can be used to locate S5 in a leaf page. S5 might supply P5 to many jobs and have a number of RIDs following the value of S5. As an example, assume that RIDs 1002, 3003, and 4005 follow S5 as shown in Figure IU.2. These RIDs are written to a temporary work area, which we call work area A in the RID pool. A matching index scan can be used to locate P5 in a leaf page with RIDs 1002 and 2004 following the part number. These RIDs are written to a temporary work area B in the RID pool.

Figure IU.2. Use of multiple indexes

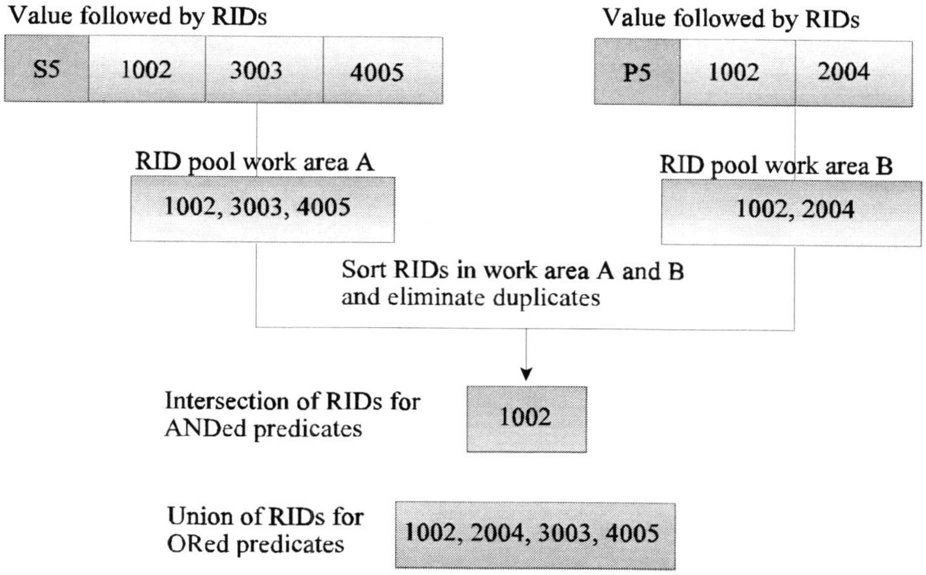

The SELECT statement requires those rows with both S5 *and* P5. To identify the RIDs that have both values, DB2 intersects the RIDs in temporary work areas A and B. RID 1002 is the only RID that appears in both lists of RIDs for S5 and P5. Rather than having to read five pages identified by RIDs 1002, 3003, 4005, 1002 (for the second row on the page referenced by RID 1002), and 2004, only one I/O to the one data page identified by RID 1002 is read with a list prefetch I/O.

Multiple index processing can also be used for ORed predicates like:

```
SELECT SN, PN, JN, QTY
FROM   SPJ
WHERE  SN = 'S5'
OR     PN = 'P5';
```

As for the ANDed predicates, RIDs are located for S5 and P5 and written to temporary work areas in the RID pool. A union of the RIDs is done for the OR condition with the result shown at the bottom of Figure IU.2. That is, the unique RIDs from both lists are required because the OR condition is satisfied if the row has either S5 or P5. I/O is reduced for an ORed condition because duplicate page identifiers are eliminated. In the example, the original list of five RIDs is reduced to four RIDs by eliminating the duplicate 1002 page ID.

Both the intersection and union of the RIDs start by sorting the RIDs and eliminating duplicates on the page identifiers. This is all that is necessary for the union. For the intersection, it is necessary to identify the RIDs that appear in both lists. The sort results in the RIDs being in the same sequence as the pages are on DASD, which minimizes the seek time. List prefetch is used to read up to 32 pages with a single I/O. Multiple-index processing is discussed in more detail in the Chapter PP.

Logical Partitioning Index Usage

A nonpartitioned index contains RIDs referencing all partitions of a partitioned tablespace. The first few bits of a RID are used to determine which partition the RID is referencing. The number of bits used depends on the number of partitions. This allows for *logical* partitioning as shown in Figure IU.3. For example, RID R4 indicates that it is referencing a row in partition 2, RID R3 indicates it is referencing a row in partition 1.

Figure IU.3. Logical partitioning of a nonpartitioned index

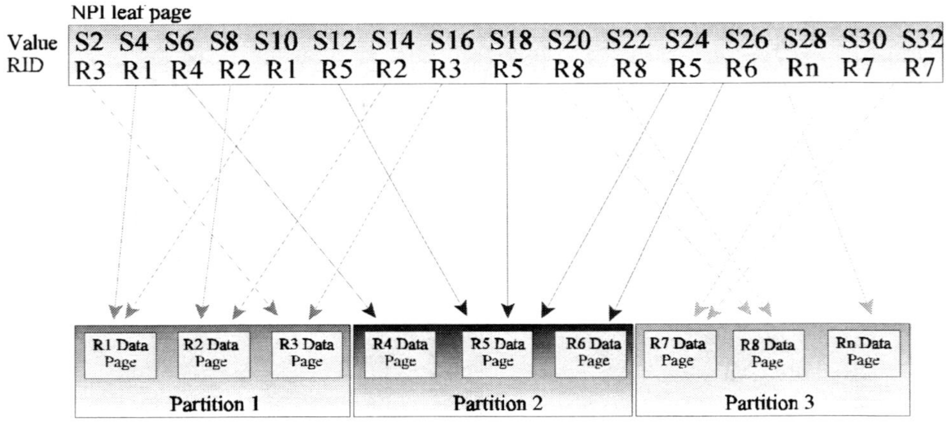

Logical partitioning allows for narrowing the search using a single index. This has performance advantages over using multiple index processing. For example, assume that there is a nonpartitioning index on CITY and a partitioning index on DATE_RECEIVED with 12 monthly partitions and a WHERE clause of:

```
WHERE CITY          = 'Rockwall'
AND   DATE_RECEIVED = '1993-09-16'
```

A matching index scan on CITY can be used to locate the RIDs for rows with Rockwall. The first few bits of the RIDs following Rockwall are used to determine those RIDs that point to rows in partition 9 with September 16, 1993 data. List prefetch is then used to access the rows identified by the RIDs. This has significant performance advantage over using multiple index processing with the CITY and DATE_RECEIVED indexes, particularly if there are few rows for Rockwall and many rows for 1993-09-16.

The same principle applies to ranges of values and noncontiguous partitions in V6. For example, only parts 2, 3, 9, and 10 are scanned for:

```
WHERE   CITY          = 'Rockwall'
AND    (DATE_RECEIVED BETWEEN '1994-02-15' AND '1994-03-15
OR      DATE_RECEIVED BETWEEN '1994-09-27' AND '1994-10-15)
```

IU.5 COMPARING METHODS FOR LOCATING DATA

This chapter has described a number of methods for using indexes to locate data efficiently. Let's compare some of these methods using a 10,000-row table with 200 pages. The following SELECT statement is used:

```
SELECT PN, PNAME
```

```
FROM    P
WHERE   CITY = 'Dallas';
```

Tablespace Scan: One approach is to do a tablespace scan to locate all of the parts in Dallas. Initially, one might think that 200 I/Os will be required for each of the 200 pages in the tablespace. The use of sequential prefetch reduces the number of I/O substantially to only 7 (200/32). However, most of your tablespaces contain more than 10,000 rows on 200 pages. Dividing by 32 is not sufficient to give good performance for large tables. You may decide to create an index on the CITY column.

Matching Index Scan: The optimizer computes a *filter factor* to determine if an index is appropriate to locate the rows for Dallas. The filter factor is an estimate of the percentage of rows that will qualify based on a predicate. It is necessary to know the cardinality of a column to compute the filter factor. The *cardinality* of a column is the number of distinct values in the column. If we assume that there are 20 distinct cities in the CITY column, the filter factor formula for an equal predicate is very simple. You want one value with an equal predicate, Dallas in the example. You want 1 out of the 20 distinct value in the column. That is, 1 divided by 20 or 5 percent of the rows. (The filter factor formulas for other predicates are in Chapter OP.)

The filter factor can be multiplied by the number of rows to give an estimate of the number of I/Os required. In the example, this is 5 percent of 10,000 rows, or 500 I/Os to the data pages plus I/Os to the index. It is rather surprising that the number of I/Os estimated to the data pages using an index is higher than the number of I/Os using a tablespace scan. This is because the index has few distinct values, and we are assuming a zero cluster ratio. The low cardinality of 20 means that typically there will be about 2.5 qualifying rows on each page. That is, a matching index scan without list prefetch must be done for each page 2.5 times. Notice that 2.5 times the number of pages in the tablespace is 500 (2.5 * 200), which is the I/O estimate assuming a zero cluster ratio. Figure IU.4 represents the multiple accesses to the same data page.

Figure IU.4. Use of low cardinality non-clustered index

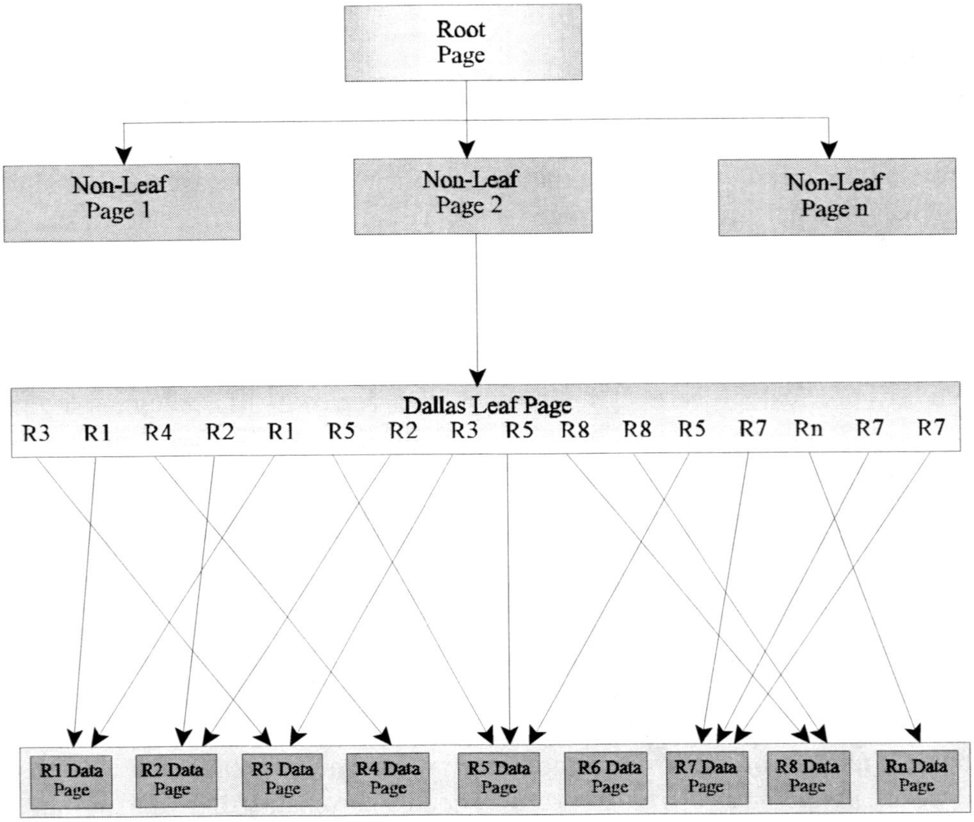

The optimizer recognizes a low cardinality index on the CITY column and considers list prefetch. If list prefetch is chosen, the I/O estimate to the data pages is 7 (200 / 32), which is the same as the tablespace scan. Actually, the number of I/Os is higher than the tablespace scan, because I/O is required to the index pages to get the RIDs to use in the list prefetch operation. Also adding to the costs is the fact that the RIDs are placed in the RID pool and sorted before issuing the list prefetch I/O.

Matching Index Scan with a Clustering Index: If you have a large table and believe that it is important to avoid a tablespace scan to locate rows for a particular city, consider making the low cardinality index on CITY a clustering index. The I/O estimate using a clustering index is much lower because if the cluster ratio is 100 percent, the optimizer can multiply the filter factor times the number of pages. That gives an I/O estimate of 10 (0.05 * 200 pages). The I/O can be reduced further. If eight or more pages are estimated to contain qualifying rows, prefetch can be used to get the up to and including 32 pages with a single I/O. (This is a simplified example. Actually, the optimizer can factor in the cluster ratio as discussed in Chapter OP.)

A high cluster ratio index on a column with a low cardinality means that the rows for a given value are grouped together on the data pages, as shown in Figure IU.5. Most of the rows for Dallas are grouped together on the data pages.

Figure IU.5. Use of low cardinality clustering index

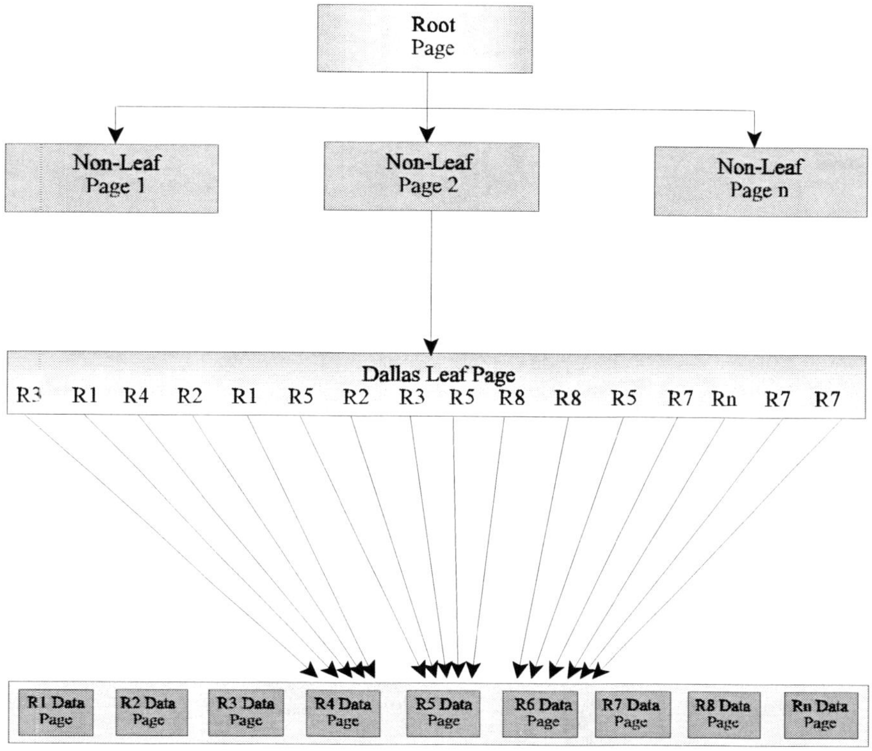

IU.6 USING COMPOSITE INDEXES

A composite index is an index consisting of more than one column. The primary key on the SPJ table consists of the columns SN, PN, and JN and should have a unique composite index on the columns to guarantee unique values. A matching index scan can be done on all columns of a composite index if equal predicates are used as in the WHERE clause:

```
WHERE SN = 'S1'
AND   PN = 'P1'
AND   JN = 'J4'
```

In order to use a matching index scan with a composite index, it is necessary to specify at least the leading column (first column) of the composite index in the WHERE clause. Without specifying the leading column, it is like trying to find a name in a telephone book without knowing the first few characters of the name. If you wanted to find a name ending in "son", it would be necessary to scan the entire telephone book. The index manager is faced with a similar problem. It must scan the tablespace or all index leaf pages if the leading column of a composite index is not specified in the WHERE clause.

Recall that the root and nonleaf pages have the upper range values that are used to navigate through the index structure to locate the required value on a leaf page and finally the data page. If the leading column of a composite index is not specified, it is not possible to compare the required value with upper range values in the nonleaf pages.

A matching index scan with a composite index on SN, PN, and JN cannot be used to satisfy the following WHERE conditions because there is not a predicate on SN.

```
WHERE PN = 'P1'

WHERE PN > 'P1'
AND   JN = 'J4'

WHERE JN > 'J4'
```

The optimizer may choose to do a non-matching index scan rather than a tablespace scan because there are usually fewer leaf pages than data pages.

A matching index scan can be done if the first column of the composite index is specified in the WHERE clause. This applies to equal and range predicates as indicated in the examples with comments:

```
WHERE SN = 'S1'-- Match on S1 and process all S1s

WHERE SN > 'S1' -- Match on S1 and scan past S1s
```

The index manager will be able to match on columns, SN and PN, when the following WHERE clause is used:

```
WHERE SN = 'S1' -- Match on S1 and P1, scan past P1s
AND   PN > 'P1'
```

However, a range predicate specified on a column of a composite index breaks the number of columns that can be used in a matching index scan. For example, a range predicate is specified on the second column of the composite index, PN, in the following example. Therefore, the index manager can only do a matching index scan on SN and PN even though there is an equal predicate on JN.

```
WHERE SN = 'S5' -- Match on S5 and P4, scan for J3s
AND   PN >='P4'
AND   JN = 'J3'
```

It is a bit like finding a name in a telephone book that begins with "John" and ends with *n*. If you don't know the characters in between, you can turn to the page with "John", but you will have to scan all of the names beginning with "John" to find those ending with *n* (Johnson, Johnsen, and Johnston, for example).

The index manager is actually doing a bounded search as you would in looking for the names. You won't scan past the names that begin with "John". Here is an example of a WHERE clause that can use a bounded search on the SN, PN, and JN composite index:

```
WHERE SN = 'S5' -- Match on S5 and P4, scan for J3s
AND   PN BETWEEN 'P4' AND 'P8'
AND   JN = 'J3'
```

The index manager can do a matching index scan to locate S5 and P4. It scans the leaf pages looking for J3 until it completes the scan including the P8s. This is a form of index screening.

Index Screening

Index screening means that a matching index scan is done on the leading columns of a composite index followed by applying additional predicates on the composite index leaf pages. An example will demonstrate the process assuming a composite index on SN, PN, and JN. A matching index scan can be used to locate S5 followed by a scan of the leaf pages to locate only S5s that supply parts for JN > 'J4' for the statement:

```
SELECT SN, PN, JN, QTY
FROM   SPJ
WHERE  SN = 'S5'
AND    JN > 'J4';
```

The goal is to reduce the number of data pages that must be processed by applying predicates on the index pages. List prefetch processing can be used on the RIDs identified with index screening. This also applies to a non-matching index scan.

Non-matching index scan versus a tablespace scan: If a tablespace scan is chosen by the optimizer because a value for the leading column of a composite index is not provided by the user, consider encouraging a non-matching index scan with index screening. This guideline assumes that there are fewer leaf pages than data pages and the cost of the leaf page access in addition to data page access is justified.

We will consider two examples of encouraging a non-matching index scan assuming that a value for SN is not provided by the user. The technique requires that the lowest possible value in the column is moved to :SN. A literal will probably result in the optimizer recognizing that a low value does not narrow search, particularly with a range predicate.

```
SELECT SN, PN, JN, QTY
FROM   SPJ
WHERE  SN > :SN
AND    JN = :JN
AND    PN = :PN;
```

If SN has a low cardinality which still results in a tablespace scan, consider:

```
SELECT SN, PN, JN, QTY
FROM   SPJ
WHERE  JN = :JN
AND    PN = :PN;
AND    SN IN
   (SELECT SN
    FROM   ALLSN);
```

If a non-matching index scan is still not chosen, consider adding OPTIMIZE FOR 1 ROW before the ";" for both statements as discussed in Chapter PD, IN subselect can be transformed to an IN list as discussed in Chapter ST, and can match on three columns as discussed in Chapter PP.

Index and Column Cardinalities

The index and column cardinalities used by the optimizer depend on whether the index is a composite or single-column index. For a composite index, it also depends on the type of predicate that is specified on the columns in the WHERE clause. Following are the cardinalities used by the optimizer based on the type of index and the predicates used.

FIRSTKEYCARDF column in SYSINDEXES contains the number of distinct values of the first column in an index. It is the value used by the optimizer in calculating the filter factor for a predicate on a single-column index.

FULLKEYCARDF column in SYSINDEXES contains the number of distinct values of all bytes in a composite index. It is the value used by the optimizer in calculating the filter factor if an equal predicate is coded on each column in the composite index.

COLCARDF column in SYSCOLUMNS contains the same value as FIRSTKEYCARDF for the first column of a composite index. The value is used by the optimizer in calculating the filter factor if an equal predicate is not coded on each column in the composite index.

COLCARDF contains a statistical estimate of the number of distinct values in the non-leading columns of a composite index or a non-indexed column. You can get this information into the catalog by running the RUNSTATS utility using the TABLE and optionally the COLUMN parameters as discussed in Chapter RR. If a matching index scan cannot be used on all columns in a composite index, COLCARDF is used by the optimizer in calculating the filter factor. COLCARDF is also used in calculating the filter factor for predicates on non-indexed columns as discussed in Chapter JP.

If the index is partitioned, FIRSTKEYCARDF and FULLKEYCARDF in SYSINDEXSTATS and COLCARDF in SYSCOLSTATS are used by the optimizer in calculating the filter factor for predicates on the partitioning index of a partitioned tablespace.

Using Index Cardinalities with Composite Indexes

Here are some examples to illustrate how the index cardinalities can be used for a composite index on SN, PN, and JN where equal predicates are not specified on all columns in the index. Assume the following cardinalities and filter factors for equal predicates:

- SN cardinality of 10 and filter factor of 0.10
- PN cardinality of 2,000 and filter factor of 0.0005
- JN cardinality of 500 and filter factor of 0.002

If the 'middle' columns in a composite index are not specified in the WHERE clause, the use of FIRSTKEYCARDF and FULLKEYCARDF do not give a good estimate of the percentage of rows that qualify. The FIRSTKEYCARDF is 10 with a filter factor is 0.10 for an equal predicate on the first column of the composite index, and FULLKEYCARDF is 5000 with a filter factor of 0.0002 if there are equal predicates specified on all columns in the composite index.

Consider the following SELECT statement on a 10,000-row table with 200 pages:

```
SELECT SN, PN, JN, QTY
FROM   SPJ
WHERE  SN = 'S4'
AND    JN = 'J7';
```

Based on the FIRSTKEYCARDF of 10 for SN, the optimizer can estimate that 1000 (0.10 * 10,000) rows qualify by multiplying the filter factor times the number of rows in the table. This suggests that J7 uses about 1000 parts from S4. Based on the cardinality of all three columns in the composite index (FULLKEYCARDF), the optimizer can estimate that 2 (0.0002 * 10,000) rows qualify. This suggests that J7 uses 2 parts from S4. It is not clear whether 1000 or 2 rows will qualify based on the FIRSTKEYCARDF or FULLKEYCARDF, because not all columns in the composite index are specified with equal predicates.

The optimizer can calculate a better estimate if COLCARDF has been updated for the missing 'middle' column (PN). Otherwise, the optimizer interpolates values between the FIRSTKEYCARDF and FULLKEYCARDF filter factors, similar to fitting a line between the two known points and estimating the middle point as the filter factor.

If the leading column but not the trailing columns of the composite index is specified in the WHERE clause, another method must be used to estimate the I/O required and whether the index should be used to efficiently locate the required rows. For example, the trailing JN column is not specified in:

```
SELECT SN, PN, JN, QTY
FROM   SPJ
WHERE  SN = 'S4'
AND    PN = 'P5';
```

If the correlation statistics for columns in a composite index are requested of RUNSTATS as discussed in Chapter RR, the optimizer will use the statistics as discussed in Chapter OP. Another optional statistic collected by RUNSTATS available for use by the optimizer is COLCARDF.

The filter factor can be calculated as the filter factor for the predicate on SN based on FIRSTKEYCARDF or COLCARDF times the filter factor for the predicate on PN based on COLCARDF. Multiplication of the filter factors results in a smaller estimate in the percentage of rows that qualify. One would expect a smaller percentage of the rows to qualify if each row must satisfy the two ANDed predicates. The filter factor for the example is 0.00005 (0.10 * 0.0005). It is estimated that use of the index is a good choice even though the last column of the index is not specified in the WHERE clause. If COLCARDF has not been updated, the default filter factor of 0.04 is used, which makes it rather likely that the index will be chosen by the optimizer for a matching index scan.

Use of an Index with Update

All columns in a composite index must be specified with equal predicates to use an index to locate a row to be updated where the indexed columns are changed unless the optimizer chooses to use list prefetch. A matching index scan on a composite index composed of SN, PN, JN cannot be used to locate the row to be updated for the following statement because PN is not in the WHERE clause.

```
UPDATE SPJ
```

```
SET     PN = 'P1'
WHERE   SN = 'S1'
AND     JN = 'J1';
```

There is an exception. If list prefetch is used to access the data pages after index processing, the index can be used to locate the required rows. This is because DB2 must verify that the values have not changed since the RIDs were located, placed in the RID pool, and list prefetch issued. You can encourage the use of list prefetch by specifying a column that is not in the index if it is not chosen as part of the access path. You might add a predicate on a column that is not in the composite that does not disqualify rows like:

```
AND QTY >= 0
```

A matching index scan on all three column in the composite index can be used for

```
UPDATE  SPJ
SET     PN = 'P1'
WHERE   SN = 'S1'
AND     PN = 'P4'
AND     JN = 'J1';
```

because equal predicates are specified on all columns in the index.

Of course, a matching index scan can be used on a single column index with an equal predicate to locate a row to be updated like:

```
UPDATE  S
SET     SN = 'S9'
WHERE   SN = 'S8';
```

If an indexed column is to be updated, there are a number of cases where the index cannot be used to locate a row to be updated:

- A range predicate is used on the indexed column to be updated except when list prefetch is used.
- An arithmetic expression is used on an indexed column in the WHERE or SET clause.
- The indexed column is specified in the FOR UPDATE OF clause.
- The indexed column is specified in a view definition WHERE clause using the WITH CHECK OPTION (described in Chapter CT).

These restrictions on index usage are necessary to avoid missing rows or going into a looping condition. For example, if an index on STATUS is chosen as the access path, rows will be retrieved in sequence on status for:

```
UPDATE  S
SET     STATUS = :STATUS
WHERE   STATUS > :OLD-STATUS;
```

An update of status from 10 to 50 would cause the cursor position to jump to status 50, skipping the statuses in between.

If an index were used on SN, a looping condition could be caused by:

```
UPDATE S
SET    SN = SN + 1
WHERE  SN BETWEEN 5 AND 15;
```

SN would be changed from 5 to 6, 6 qualifies for the BETWEEN and would be updated again to a value of 7, 7 qualifies for the BETWEEN and would be updated again to a value of 8, and so on. This is probably not the desired result and would use a considerable amount of CPU time. Therefore, an index is not used to locate the rows to be updated with a range predicate.

In some cases an arithmetic expression can be removed from a SET clause or predicate and placed in the host language code. However, a range predicate cannot be replaced with an equal predicate to achieve the same results.

An index *can* be used to locate rows to be deleted with no restriction. The clustering index *is* always used to determine where to insert a row.

Index-Only Processing

Most DB2 professionals know intuitively that index-only processing is a good thing. An example supports that intuition. A million-row table with 100-byte rows occupies about 28,572 pages (ceiling(1,000,000 / floor(3870/(100 byte row + 8 bytes))). An index on a 10-byte column occupies about 4695 (ceiling(1,000,000 / floor (3634 / (10 byte column + 4 byte RID + 3 bytes)) leaf pages. Obviously, processing all leaf pages is more efficient than processing all data pages. Even if only a few values are required, avoiding I/O to the data pages results in savings.

Consider including frequently-retrieved columns in the index if index-only processing can be achieved. When index-only processing is used, it makes a non-clustered index as efficient as a clustered index because the values are always processed in sequence on the leaf pages.

Following are a few examples of the types of SELECT statements that can be satisfied with index-only processing. Comments are used to indicate how the processing can be accomplished. Assume that all columns referenced are indexed. Assume also that there is a composite index on SN, PN, JN in the SPJ table and a composite index on CITY and SN in the S table. The SN, PN, and JN columns are the primary key (PK) of the SPJ table. The SN column is the PK of the S table. The SN column in the SPJ table is a foreign key (FK) referencing the S table.

```
SELECT MIN(QTY) -- One-fetch index access
FROM   SPJ;      -- with an ascending index

SELECT AVG(QTY) -- Scan leaf pages
FROM   SPJ;

SELECT COUNT(*) -- Index with smallest number of pages
```

```
FROM    S;

SELECT SN           -- Match on CITY, then scan
FROM   S            -- leaf pages for ORDER BY
WHERE  CITY = 'Paris'
ORDER BY SN;

SELECT S.SN, PN, JN -- Search and join using
FROM   S, SPJ        -- PK & FK indexes only
WHERE  S.SN = SPJ.SN
AND    S.SN > 'S2';

SELECT SNAME
FROM   S SX
WHERE  EXISTS        -- True/False returned
  (SELECT SN, PN, JN -- using PK index only
   FROM   SPJ
   WHERE  SN = SX.SN
   AND    PN = 'P5'
   AND    JN = 'J7');
```

Index only processing of an index on a column declared as VARCHAR is not possible by default. The default can be changed as discussed in Chapter CT along with some words of caution regarding possible program changes to allow for index only processing of VARCHAR columns.

IU.7 DIRECT ROW ACCESS WITHOUT INDEX USAGE OVERVIEW

A column with a data type of ROWID provides for locating a row a second time using direct row access. It is necessary to locate the row with an index or tablespace scan the first time to get the row ID. The second access requires the specification of the ROWID column in the WHERE clause to locate the row directly. The column PLAN_TABLE.PRIMARY_ACCESSTYPE = 'D' (PLAN_TABLE is discussed in Chapter EX) shows the optimizer choice of using a ROWID column for direct row access without index usage or a tablespace scan.

Large Objects (LOBs) require the use of a single ROWID column to identify the location of a large object. A ROWID column is required for a table with a LOB column. It provides for locating the LOB data in an auxiliary tables using an index on the auxiliary table.

A ROWID column can be used to locate a row efficiently the second time to verify that row has not changed since it was displayed and before it is updated as discussed in Chapter PD.

A ROWID can be used as a partitioning key to spread insert activity throughout the tablespace as discussed in Chapter TS. Caution should be exercised in using this technique. It is not possible to have the clustering index on a column that can be used to efficiently process data for online transactions and batch programs (the partitioning index is the clustering index). In addition, if high insert activity is expected, a large number of random I/O can detract from performance.

IU.8 SUMMARY

In this chapter, we described the various ways that indexes can be used to efficiently locate data. These include matching and non-matching index scans with and without data reference, multiple index processing, index lookaside, list prefetch, one-fetch index access for MIN with an ascending index and MAX with a descending index, use of composite indexes, and index screening.

EXERCISES

1. a) Under what conditions would you like to see the optimizer choose a matching index scan?

b) Under what conditions is it best not to use a matching index scan?

2. a) If a matching index scan is used, under what conditions will only one leaf page and one data page be processed?

b) Under what conditions will more than one leaf and data page be processed when using a matching index scan?

3. a) What is the meaning of a cluster ratio of 80 percent?

b) Is there a difference between the structure and basic access paths for clustering and non-clustering indexes?

c) What is the difference between clustering and non-clustering indexes?

4. a) Would you like to use an index to retrieve rows in sequence to avoid a sort? Why?

b) Under what conditions would you not want to use an index to retrieve rows in sequence to avoid a sort? Why?

5. a) What are the advantages of list prefetch?

b) How is list prefetch different from sequential and dynamic prefetch?

6. a) What is the filter factor?

b) What is the filter factor formula for an equal predicate?

c) How is the number of I/O estimated?

7. a) What is the purpose of index lookaside?

b) What are the benefits of index lookaside?

8. What is the advantage of multiple index usage?

9. Assume a composite index on SN, PN, and JN.

Which of the following WHERE clauses can use a matching index scan? Which columns will DB2 be able to match on?

```
WHERE SN  = 'S5'
AND   PN >='P4'
AND   JN  = 'J3'

WHERE PN  > 'P4'
AND   JN  = 'J6'

WHERE SN  > 'S2'

WHERE SN  = 'S2'
AND   PN  > 'P4'

WHERE SN  = 'S2'
AND   PN  = 'P4'
AND   JN  = 'J6'
```

10. Assume a composite index on SN, PN, and JN.
Please note on each of the following WHERE clauses whether the optimizer will use FIRSTKEYCARDF, FULLKEYCARDF, or COLCARDF (assuming that COLCARDF has been updated by RUNSTATS).

```
WHERE SN  = 'S2'
AND   PN  = 'P4'

WHERE SN  = 'S5'
AND   JN  = 'J6'

WHERE SN  = 'S5'
AND   PN >='P4'
AND   JN  = 'J3'

WHERE SN  = 'S2'
AND   PN  = 'P4'
AND   JN  = 'J6'
```

11. Assume a composite index on SN, PN, and JN.

a) Can a matching index scan be used for the following WHERE clause on a SELECT statement?

```
WHERE   SN = 'S2'
AND     JN = 'J6'
```

b) Can a matching index scan be used for the following WHERE clause on an UPDATE statement assuming that columns in the composite index are updated?

```
WHERE   SN = 'S2'
AND     JN = 'J6'
```

12. Assume an index on all columns in the WHERE and FOR UPDATE OF clauses. Which of the

following statements can or cannot use a matching index scan assuming list prefetch is not chosen as part of the access path? Give the reasons that the statement can or cannot use a matching index scan.

a)
```
UPDATE SPJ SET QTY = :QTY * 1.1
  WHERE QTY > 50;
```

b)
```
QTY = QTY + 10

UPDATE SPJ SET QTY = :QTY
  WHERE QTY = 100;
```

c)
```
EXEC SQL DECLARE SCURSOR CURSOR FOR
         SELECT SN, SNAME, STATUS
         FROM   S
         WHERE  STATUS > :NEW-STATUS
         FOR UPDATE OF STATUS, CITY
END-EXEC.
```

d)
```
CREATE VIEW EUROPE AS
  SELECT SN, SNAME, STATUS, CITY
  FROM   S
  WHERE  CITY IN ('London', 'Paris', 'Rome')
WITH CHECK OPTION;

UPDATE EUROPE
  SET CITY = :CITY
  WHERE CITY = 'Paris';
```

13. a) Are there any special conditions for using a matching index scan to locate a row to be deleted?

b) Are there any special conditions for using an index to insert a row?

14. Why might you want to use a matching index scan on a column with a cardinality of 20?

15. Can a one-fetch index scan with index only processing be done for the following statement. Assume a descending composite index on CITY and STATUS.

```
SELECT CITY, MAX(STATUS)
FROM   S
WHERE  CITY = 'Copenhagen';
```

16. How can direct row access be used? What are the major prerequisites to using direct row access?

ANSWERS

1. a) A matching index scan is the best choice for an online transaction that displays a few rows to the user.

b) A matching index scan is not a good choice if many rows are to be processed (more than 10-15 percent, for example) in a batch program.

2. a) A matching index scan using a unique index with an equal predicate requires that only one leaf page and one data page be processed.

b) If you are using a range predicate on a unique or nonunique index, it is likely that more than one leaf page and one data page will be processed. Indeed, if you are using an equal or range predicate on an index with a low cardinality, it is likely that more than one leaf page and one data page will be processed.

3. a) A cluster ratio of 80 percent means that 80 percent of the rows are in sequence on the data pages according to the indexed columns.

b) There is no difference between the structure and basic access paths for clustering and non-clustering indexes. A matching index scan, non-matching index scan, list prefetch, index lookaside, one-fetch index access, use of multiple indexes, use of composite indexes, and index-only processing can be used with clustering and non-clustering indexes.

c) The clustering index is used to determine where rows should be inserted to maintain the rows in sequence of the columns in the clustering index.

4. a) The use of an index to avoid a sort has significant advantages if there is a good cluster ratio. It avoids retrieving all qualifying rows and sorting them before the first row can be returned to the program.

b) It is best not to use an index to avoid a sort if many rows will be retrieved and the cluster ratio is low. This is because the seek time to DASD can result in more elapsed time than would be required to retrieve the rows out of sequence and sort them.

5. a) List prefetch results in reading only data pages with qualifying rows based on the predicates evaluated using one or more indexes. The pages are read in sequence as they appear on DASD, which reduces seek time. All qualifying rows on a page can be processed without a getpage and I/O to the same page for each qualifying row on the page. This is in contrast to, say, three matching index scan for three rows on a page.

b) List prefetch requires prior access to one or more indexes to get the RIDs. It reads only the data pages identified by the RIDs in one or more indexes. List prefetch is not be used on index pages. Sequential and dynamic prefetch can be used on index and data pages. Sequential and dynamic prefetch reads the next 32 pages with one I/O even if all of the pages do not have qualifying rows. List prefetch reads only pages with qualifying rows. It can issue one I/O for less than or equal to 32 pages based on the qualifying RIDs.

6. a) The filter factor is an estimate of the percentage of rows that will qualify according to the coded predicate.

b) The filter factor formula for an equal predicate is one divided by the cardinality of the indexed column.

c) The I/O estimate is based on the filter factor multiplied by the number of rows and pages in the tablespace. If the cluster ratio is high, the number of pages is the stronger factor. If the cluster ratio is low, the number of rows is the stronger factor. How the cluster ratio is factored into the I/O estimate is discussed in Chapter OP.

7. a) The purpose of index lookaside is to minimize the number of matching index scans.

b) The benefits of index lookaside are a reduction in the number of getpages, I/O, and CPU time.

8. Qualifying RIDs from multiple indexes are sorted and duplicates on the page identifier are eliminated to reduce the number of I/Os to the data pages. Taking the intersection of identified RIDs for ANDed predicates can significantly reduce the number of I/Os to the data pages. The intersection of RIDs from two indexes means that only pages referenced by RIDs that qualify from both indexes need to be processed. Taking the union of identified RIDs means that DB2 can access a data page once and retrieve all the qualifying rows. If you have ORed two predicates on two columns, both indexes on the two columns must be used in multiple index processing. Otherwise, a matching index scan is not possible to achieve the correct results with two indexes on the two columns or one composite index on the two columns. List prefetch is used on the manipulated RIDs to achieve the advantages discussed for list prefetch.

9. The columns that DB2 will use in a matching index scan are noted.

```
WHERE SN  = 'S5'  -- Match on S5 and P4, scan for J3s
AND   PN >='P4'
AND   JN  = 'J3'

WHERE PN  > 'P4'  -- Cannot do a matching index scan
AND   JN  = 'J6'  -- Must specify the leading column

WHERE SN  > 'S2'  -- Match on S2 and scan past

WHERE SN  = 'S2'  -- Match on S2 and P4, scan past P4s
AND   PN  > 'P4'

WHERE SN  = 'S2'  -- Match on S2, P4, J6
AND   PN  = 'P4'
AND   JN  = 'J6'
```

10. The use of FIRSTKEYCARDF, FULLKEYCARDF, or COLCARDF cardinalities are noted.

```
WHERE SN  = 'S2'  -- FIRSTKEYCARDF
AND   PN  = 'P4'  -- COLCARDF on PN

WHERE SN  = 'S5'  -- FIRSTKEYCARDF
AND   JN  = 'J6'  -- COLCARDF on JN

WHERE SN  = 'S5'  -- FIRSTKEYCARDF
AND   PN >='P4'   -- COLCARDF on PN
AND   JN  = 'J3'

WHERE SN  = 'S2'  -- FULLKEYCARDF
AND   PN  = 'P4'
AND   JN  = 'J6'
```

11. a) A matching index scan on one column can be used for the WHERE clause on the SELECT statement.

b) A matching index scan cannot be used for the WHERE clause on an UPDATE statement unless list prefetch is chosen by the optimizer. The middle column of the composite index is not specified.

12. a) A matching index scan cannot be used because of the arithmetic expression in the SET clause in the following statement. An arithmetic expression in the WHERE clause will also disallow the use of an index. The range predicate in the WHERE clause also disallows the use of a matching index scan. The reason is that a value can re-occur and cause a loop if an index were used on QTY.

```
UPDATE SPJ SET QTY = :QTY * 1.1
  WHERE QTY > 50;
```

b) A matching index scan can be used with an <u>equal</u> predicate and no arithmetic expression in the WHERE and SET clause for the following statement.

```
QTY = QTY + 10

UPDATE SPJ SET QTY = :QTY
  WHERE QTY = 100;
```

c) A matching index scan cannot be used on STATUS and CITY. If an index were used on a column in a FOR UPDATE OF clause, it could result in missing rows or going into a looping condition.

```
EXEC SQL DECLARE SCURSOR CURSOR FOR
         SELECT SN, SNAME, STATUS
         FROM   S
         WHERE  STATUS > :NEW-STATUS
         FOR UPDATE OF STATUS, CITY
END-EXEC.
```

d) A matching index scan cannot be used on CITY because the column is specified in the CREATE VIEW WHERE clause with the WITH CHECK OPTION.

```
CREATE VIEW EUROPE_S AS
  SELECT SN, SNAME, STATUS, CITY
  FROM   S
  WHERE  CITY IN ('London', 'Paris', 'Rome')
    WITH CHECK OPTION;

UPDATE S SET CITY = :CITY
  WHERE CITY = 'Paris';
```

13. a) A matching index scan can be used to locate a row to be deleted like locating a row for a SELECT statement. There are no special conditions regarding DELETE statements.

b) The clustering index is always used to determine where a row should be inserted if the index has been designated with the CLUSTER keyword when the index is created.

14. If there is a skewed distribution of values where some of the 20 distinct values appear very

infrequently and others appear very frequently on most pages in the tablespace, you may want to use the index to efficiently locate the infrequently occurring values. This is described in more detail with some alternatives for dealing with the situation in Chapter OP.

15. An one-fetch index scan with index only processing can be used with an descending composite index on CITY and STATUS. This is because there is a matching index scan on the leading column of the composite index.

```
SELECT CITY, MAX(STATUS)
FROM   S
WHERE  CITY = 'Copenhagen';
```

16. Direct row access can be used to locate a row directly without the use of a tablespace scan or index. The major prerequisites to direct row access are that the table must have a column defined as a ROWID data type, the row ID must be determined before it can be used in a WHERE clause, and a reorganization has not occurred between the time that the row ID was determined and when it is used.

FIGURES

Index Design for Performance

ID.1 INTRODUCTION

It is important for both DBAs and programmer/analysts to understand how to use indexes. DBAs are usually concerned with physical design and maintenance, and programmer/analysts must understand how to write SQL statements that make the best use of indexes. Chapter IU describes the methods used by the index manager to efficiently locate rows.

This chapter describes issues related to designing indexes. It identifies the characteristics of columns that should and should not be indexed, and it describes the characteristics of columns that benefit the most from having a clustering index. Information about designing composite indexes are addressed.

ID.2 INDEX DESIGN GUIDELINES

Indexes can be used in a variety of ways and have a number of advantages. The primary advantage of indexes is the ability to process a small percentage of the rows efficiently with minimal I/O and CPU usage. We would like to see index usage when selecting, updating, deleting, and joining a small percentage (less than 5 to 10 percent) of rows in medium to large tables. A clustering index improves performance for processing a larger percentage of rows (less than 30 to 50 percent), particularly when the rows must be processed in sequence. Indexes can also be used to avoid access to data pages with index only processing. There are many reasons for having many indexes. However, there are costs associated with maintaining indexes that requires minimizing the number of indexes on a table.

Each time a row is inserted or deleted, the corresponding operation must be performed on each index. Each time an indexed column is updated, the record identifier (RID) must be deleted and inserted for the new value. The costs of changing indexes is often more than the costs of changing the data. In addition, there is increased exposure to contention (latches and P-locks when using row locking and sysplex data sharing).

Whenever DB2 loads or reorganizes a table, it must build or rebuild each index to it. Whenever it recovers a tablespace, it must also recover or rebuild the indexes. The index itself may need to be reorganized (rebuilt) more frequently than the tablespace as a result of index page splitting as discussed in Section ID.5. Finally, indexes require DASD space. Using indexes efficiently is a matter of selecting those whose performance benefits outweigh these costs. The benefits depend on the way the data are to be used and the table size.

Columns that Should Be Indexed

Primary keys and foreign keys are often searched or joined over a small percentage of rows and are good candidates for indexes. Indeed, the primary key must have a unique index to guarantee unique values in the column. If there is no index on the foreign key, an update of a primary key value requires a tablespace scan of each dependent table. This scan is done to verify that the old value does not exist in a dependent table. Similarly, when a row is deleted from a parent table and no index exists on the foreign key, it is necessary to do a tablespace scan on each dependent table to enforce the delete rule, described in Chapter CT. Both DB2 enforced and application enforced referential integrity benefit from having an index on the foreign key.

Joins are often performed on the primary key and foreign key columns; therefore, an index on these columns makes the join much more efficient in most cases.

Figure ID.1 Summarizes the characteristics of columns that benefit from an index.

Figure ID.1. Characteristics of columns that benefit from an index

- Primary key and foreign key columns
- Columns which must have unique values to satisfy a business requirement
- Columns that have column functions computed frequently (COUNT, SUM, AVG, MIN, and MAX for example)
- Columns used to test for the existence of a value (if the value does not exist, no data pages will be accessed)
- Columns which are searched or joined over less than 5 to 10 percent of the rows when considering a non-clustering index
- Columns which are searched or joined over less than 30 to 50 percent of the rows when considering a clustering index
- Columns frequently used together in a WHERE clause can benefit from a composite index to avoid maintaining multiple indexes
- Columns frequently used in an ORDER BY, GROUP BY, or DISTINCT clause to avoid sorts

Columns that Benefit from Clustering

The choice of the column or columns to be included in the clustering index determines where DB2 inserts rows. The keyword CLUSTER, specified when the index is created, instructs DB2 to maintain the rows on the data pages in sequence according to the indexed column as described in Chapter IU.

The optimizer is likely to use the clustering index to avoid a sort for ORDER BY, GROUP BY, DISTINCT, and join processing. A column where these operations are often performed is a good candidate for the clustering index.

Columns frequently searched or joined over a range of values using the operators BETWEEN, >, <, or LIKE are good candidates for clustering. A clustering index means that values are maintained in sequence on the data pages. A matching index scan can be used followed by a non-matching index scan to satisfy the range predicate. DB2 can use sequential prefetch to scan the data pages and the leaf pages.

A column with few distinct values (a *low cardinality*) is a good candidate for clustering if an index is required on the column at all. Generally it is not a good idea to create an index on a column with a low cardinality because the index does not narrow the search. However, if an index is required, a clustering index on such a column is a good choice because all of the like values are grouped (clustered) together on the data pages.

In earlier releases of DB2, the primary key was often chosen as the clustering index to allow for cursor repositioning operations. The use of the OPTIMIZE FOR *n* ROWS clause makes it unnecessary to use the clustering index for cursor repositioning, as described in Chapter PD. However, if there is batch processing requirements in which the input is in primary key sequence, the primary key is a good choice for the clustering index, as described in Chapter BP.

The foreign key is a good candidate for frequent one-to-many joins (where many is large such as greater than 1000, for example). If all of the foreign key rows are grouped together on the data pages, the join processing is more efficient. An index on the foreign key is also useful for cascading deletes and set nulls of foreign key rows with RI constraint processing. If all of the J7s are grouped together on the data pages of a dependent table, a cascade delete of J7s can efficiently locate and delete all J7s that are grouped together.

Figure ID.2 summarizes the characteristics of columns that benefit from a clustering index. No one column has all of the characteristics listed here. Consider the trade-offs when deciding which column or columns should have the clustering index.

Figure ID.2. Characteristics of columns that benefit from a clustering index

- Column frequently processed in sequence using the operators ORDER BY, GROUP BY, or DISTINCT
- Column frequently searched or joined over a range of values using predicates such as BETWEEN, >, <, or LIKE
- Column with a low index cardinality or skewed distribution (if an index is required)
- Primary key column is a good candidate for batch processing
- Foreign key column is a good candidate for frequent one-to-many joins and enforcement of referential integrity (the many foreign values will be clustered together)

When using a partitioned tablespace, the clustering index must be the partitioning index.

Recommendation: It is very important to specify a clustering index based on your analysis of how the data is processed. If you do not create an index using the parameter CLUSTER, then by default the first index created (or more precisely the first index on the chain of indexes in the database descriptor (DBD) is used to determine where to insert rows.

One problem with allowing DB2 to default to a clustering index is that when indexes are dropped and recreated, the first index on the chain may not be created first. DB2 starts using the new first index on the chain of indexes in the DBD to determine where to insert rows; what you thought was the clustering index is no longer used as such.

The REORG utility does not resequence rows if a clustering index is not explicitly declared. Further, the parameter SORTDATA on the REORG utility statement is ignored if there is no clustering index declared on a table. This can severely detract from performance. SORTDATA required 74 percent less elapsed time when reorganizing data with a cluster ratio of 80 percent in one case. Another deterrent to good reorganization performance is when SHRLEVEL CHANGE and NOSYSREC is used without an explicitly defined clustering index. With a clustering index defined, the rows are not written to SYSREC during unload and need not be sorted. However, without an explicitly defined cluster index this processing is necessary. The REORG OFFPOSLIMIT threshold applies only to explicitly defined clustering indexes as discussed in Chapter RR.

Consider using the following SELECT statements to verify that all tables created over the years do in fact have a clustering index.

```
SELECT I.TBCREATOR, I.TBNAME, I.CREATOR,
       I.NAME, I.CLUSTERING
FROM   SYSIBM.SYSINDEXES I
WHERE NOT EXISTS
   (SELECT 1
    FROM   SYSIBM.SYSINDEXES X
    WHERE  X.CLUSTERING = 'Y'
    AND    X.CREATOR    = I.CREATOR
    AND    X.NAME       = I.NAME)
ORDER BY I.TBCREATOR, I.TBNAME;
```

Recommendation: The rows that are returned from the SELECT statement do not have a clustering index defined. It is recommended that all tables have an explicitly declared clustering index.

Exception: If MEMBER CLUSTER is specified when creating a partitioned or simple tablespace as discussed in Chapter TS, rows are not clustered.

When Clustering Is Not Useful: Depending on the type of predicates used on the columns, some columns do not benefit from having a clustering index. If equal predicates are used on a column with a unique index, clustering has no advantage. One matching index scan can be used to locate the one row. With the exception of batch processing, there is generally no advantage to having a clustering index on a primary key with a unique index if equal predicates are used. If few rows are processed (less than 20, for example), the cost of using a non-clustering index can be acceptable. In addition, if the processing is mostly index-only processing, there is no need to access the data pages and the order of rows on the data pages does not matter.

Analyze How Data is Used

To understand the cost vs. benefits of using indexes, you must analyze how the data is used to determine which columns should be indexed. Identify columns that are frequently searched or joined, and estimate the percentage of rows processed by frequently executed SQL statements. Consider creating the clustering index on the column most frequently searched or joined in sequence. Consider non-clustering indexes on searched or joined columns in which less than 5 to 10 percent of the rows are to be selected, updated, deleted, and joined.

Refine this analysis with an estimate of the percentage of the rows that are inserted, updated, and deleted over a given period of time. Minimize the number of indexes when inserting, updating, and deleting more than about 10 percent of the rows on a weekly basis. If heavy update activity is concentrated on a weekly, monthly, quarterly, or annual basis, consider the techniques for avoiding index maintenance described in Chapter BP.

Composite indexes are useful when columns are frequently referenced together. They reduce the number of indexes that must be maintained and increase the chance of index-only retrieval.

These are only general guidelines. The physical design of the tables and indexes requires an analysis of how the data is to be processed. A process analysis matrix sometimes called a CRUD (Create, Retrieve, Update, and Delete) matrix is useful in summarizing how the data will be processed. Figure

ID.3 is an example of such a matrix.

Figure ID.3. Process matrix

	Transaction/Program*							
Table Card/ Column Card	SPJUP	PJASG	SPJST	PUONJ	ORDP	RECP	FIND	JUSP
S 500K	I1/D1							
SN 500K	P	J1	J1		J1		S1	
SNAME 300K		S1	S1		S10		S1	
STATUS 10	U1	S1			S10		>P	
CITY 20	U1	S1			S10		P	
P 1000K	I1/D1							
PN 1000K	P	J1	J1	J1-P	J1		S1	J1
PNAME 900K		S1	S1	S1	S1		S1	S60
COLOR 30K		S1					S1	S60
WEIGHT 15K		S1					S1	S60
CITY 20	U1	S1			P		P	
J 2000K	I9/D7							
JN 2000K		J1	J1	J1-P			S1	J1-P
JNAME 900K		S1	S1	S1			S1	S1
CITY 20	U1	S1		S1			P	
SPJ 10000K		I1				I10K		
SN 1000K		J1	J1		J1-S9			
PN 2000K		J1	J1	J1-S1	J1-P			J1
JN 3000K		J1	J1	J1-S9				J1
QTY 90K		U1	S1	S9				
Frequency+	10W	3000D	8000D	500D	2000D	2W	1000D	90000D

*Note P (Equal predicate, >P range), Sn (Select column, number of rows), In (Insert), Dn (Delete), Jm (Join, m=x for one of many joins) in each cell

+Frequency of execution: D (Daily), W (Weekly), M (Monthly), A (Annual)

Tables and columns are listed as rows of the matrix. Beside each table is noted the table cardinality (the number of rows in the table) and beside each column is noted the column cardinality (the number of distinct values in the column). Each column of the matrix has the name of a transaction or batch program.

For each cell in the matrix, note S*n* (Select column), I*n* (Insert), and D*n* (Delete) in each cell where *n* represents the number of rows processed. Joins are noted with J*m* where *m* represents one of many joins. If a predicate is specified on the column to narrow the search, note a P for an equal predicate, >P for a greater-than predicate, and so on. The last row in the matrix is for the frequency of execution; D (Daily), W (Weekly), M (Monthly), and A (Annual) are convenient notations. The form of the matrix is not critical. The important thing is to perform a detailed analysis of how the data will be processed and summarize the processing requirements to provide a basis for design of the indexes. The process matrix will also prove useful in tuning the design of the tables.

To make process analysis more manageable, identify the top 10 programs or top 10 percent of the programs for which performance is most critical. The indexes identified will likely be beneficial to most of the programs. You can do more tuning of the index design when the transaction and batch programs are tested.

ID.3 DESIGNING COMPOSITE INDEXES

A composite index (a single index composed of more than one column) can be used for the following:

- To uniquely identify a row for a primary key.
- To reduce the total number of indexes and provide for index-only processing.
- To narrow a search with ANDed predicates efficiently, as in the following example:

```
SELECT SN, PN, JN, QTY
FROM   SPJ
WHERE  SN = 'S1'
AND    PN = 'P1'
AND    JN = 'J1';
```

Separate indexes on SN, PN, and JN would require processing RIDs from each of three separate indexes before accessing the data pages. If a large number of RIDs qualify, this can mean unacceptable delays for online transactions.

The three separate indexes can be best, however, if frequent OR conditions are specified in a WHERE clause. A matching composite index scan cannot be used with ORed predicates because rows can be missed (although a non-matching index scan can be used). The following SELECT statement and the SPJ table in Figure ID.4 demonstrate the point.

```
SELECT SN, PN, JN, QTY
FROM   SPJ
WHERE  SN = 'S4'
OR     PN = 'P1'
OR     JN = 'J1';
```

Figure ID.4. Missed rows with ORed predicates on a composite index

SN	PN	JN	QTY
S1	P1	J1	200
S1	P1	J4	700
S2	P3	J1	400
S2	P3	J2	200
S2	P3	J3	200
S2	P3	J4	500
S2	P3	J5	600
S2	P3	J6	400
S2	P3	J7	800
S2	P5	J2	100
S3	P3	J1	200
S3	P4	J2	500
S4	P6	J3	300
S4	P6	J7	300
S5	P2	J2	200
S5	P2	J4	100
S5	P5	J5	500
S5	P5	J7	100
S5	P6	J2	200
S5	P1	J4	100
S5	P6	J4	500

If a matching index scan is used to locate the S4 row in the table followed by a scan of the remaining leaf pages, P1s and J1s above S4 will be missed as indicated by the shading in Figure ID.4.

Three separate indexes on the three columns can be used to identify all rows. In addition, multiple indexes have advantages if the WHERE clause does not specify the leading columns of the composite index.

It is possible to use a matching index scan with ORed predicates on the same column. A good way of thing about it is if the ORed predicates can be transformed to an IN (list), multiple matching index scan can be used. For example two matching index scans can be used on a composite index on SN, PN, and JN or a single index SN.

```
SELECT SN, PN, JN, QTY
FROM   SPJ
WHERE  SN = 'S1'
OR     SN = 'P4':
```

ORed predicates are on the same column are equivalent to:

```
SELECT SN, PN, JN, QTY
FROM   SPJ
WHERE  SN IN ('S1', 'P4');
```

Sequence of Columns in Composite Index Design

Composite index design, like the design of indexes in general, depends on how the data is to be processed. The sequence of columns in a composite index can significantly effect performance.

Design to maximize the number of matching columns: The first column of a composite index must be specified in the WHERE clause to perform a matching index scan. When a range predicate is used on a column, DB2 cannot match on any following columns in the composite index. Columns where equal predicates are usually specified in the WHERE clause should be placed first in the composite index.

Design to avoid sorts: Indexes can be used to avoid sorting rows. This is particularly important if many rows qualify and only a few rows will be fetched, as described in Chapter PD. Consider ordering columns in a composite index to allow for use of the index to avoid sorts for ORDER BY, GROUP BY, DISTINCT, and joins.

Design for index only processing: Index-only processing avoids I/O to the data pages. If only one or two additional columns are required in addition to the columns in a composite index, those columns should be considered for inclusion in the composite index. You will want to avoid adding a column to a primary key index because it can make the composite index non-unique and the column must be carried in dependent tables.

Minimize the number of leaf pages that must be scanned: Avoid placing a low cardinality column first in a composite index. Otherwise, you may find that many leaf pages are scanned even though a matching index scan is the chosen access path. For example, suppose that many online transactions allow the users to scroll forward in the data using a common cursor repositioning technique with a WHERE clause of:

```
   SN >= 'S2'   AND
 ((SN  = 'S2'   AND
   PN  = 'P3'   AND
   JN  > 'J3')  OR
  (SN  = 'S2'   AND
   PN  > 'P3')  OR
  (SN  > 'S2'))
```

A matching index scan can be used only for the first column in the composite index because of the range predicate on SN. Suppose SN has a cardinality of 20 with a uniform distribution of values, the column is 10 bytes in length, and there are one million rows in the table. That means that there are about 50,000 S2s (one million rows divided by a cardinality of 20) with various PNs and JNs following the S2s that must be scanned and tested for the predicates coded. If the PN or JN columns are placed first in the index, the number of values that must be scanned and tested is reduced significantly, assuming that the PN or JN columns have many distinct column values.

Exception: It might be necessary to have a low cardinality column first to avoid frequent sorts. Having a low-cardinality column first is not a problem if most of the SQL statements can specify an equal predicate on the first column and if the second column has a good cardinality and can be specified in the WHERE clause. If the low cardinality column must be placed first, do collect COLCARDF and consider collecting frequency and correlation statistics.

Analyzing Existing Indexes

If there are three or more columns in a composite index and the columns are correlated, it is important to have RUNSTATS collect correlation statistics by specifying the KEYCARD parameter as described in Chapter RR. Otherwise, the optimizer can choose a less than optimal access path. Chapter OP describes correlated columns, how to determine if the columns are correlated, and how the optimizer chooses an access path with and without correlation statistics.

Consider investigating composite indexes where non-matching index scans are used. You can easily determine these indexes by selecting from the plan table and the SYSINDEXES catalog table using the following SELECT statement. The PLAN_TABLE is described in Chapter EX.

```
SELECT DISTINCT I.NAME, I.CLUSTERING, I.UNIQUERULE,
         I.COLCOUNT, P.MATCHCOLS
FROM    SYSIBM.SYSINDEXES I, AUTHID.PLAN_TABLE P
WHERE   P.ACCESSCREATOR = I.CREATOR
AND     P.ACCESSNAME    = I.NAME
AND     I.CREATOR       = 'Authid'
AND     I.NAME LIKE 'ABC%' -- Use naming convention
AND     P.MATCHCOLS = 0
AND     I.COLCOUNT  > 1;
```

The P.MATCHCOLS will contain 0 for SQL statements that use a non-matching index scan. If you find composite indexes that are frequently used with non-matching index scans, you may want to investigate reordering columns in the composite index to allow for matching index scans on one or more columns.

You might be able to reorder the columns so that a number of statements that were not using a matching index scan can do so. Don't forget to consider SQL that was doing a matching index scan on the old column order that cannot with the new column order. Request an explain of the access paths with the new ordering of the columns and again execute the select from the PLAN_TABLE and SYSINDEXES to determine if the new order is best overall compared to the old order.

During your analysis, consider using DEFER YES when you create an alternative composite index to avoid building the index until you have evidence that the new order is best. (DEFER YES is described in Section ID.7.) Indeed, you might want to create several composite indexes with various column orderings using DEFER YES and request explain of the access paths chosen by the optimizer for SQL statements that access the table. Based on your analysis, use the column order that maximizes the number of matching columns and minimizes sorts for most SQL statements or those that have critical performance requirements.

No match on all columns: The following SELECT statement identifies SQL statements that do not have a match on all columns in composite indexes:

```
SELECT DISTINCT I.NAME, I.CLUSTERING, I.UNIQUERULE,
         I.COLCOUNT, P.MATCHCOLS
FROM    SYSIBM.SYSINDEXES I, AUTHID.PLAN_TABLE P
WHERE   P.ACCESSCREATOR = I.CREATOR
AND     P.ACCESSNAME     = I.NAME
AND     ICREATOR     = 'Authid'
AND     I.NAME LIKE 'ABC%'   -- Use naming convention
AND     P.MATCHCOLS =
       (SELECT MAX(MATCHCOLS)
        FROM    AUTHID.PLAN_TABLE P
        WHERE   P.ACCESSCREATOR = I.CREATOR
        AND     P.ACCESSNAME     = I.NAME)
AND     I.COLCOUNT  >
       (SELECT MAX(MATCHCOLS)
        FROM    AUTHID.PLAN_TABLE P
        WHERE   P.ACCESSCREATOR = I.CREATOR
        AND     P.ACCESSNAME     = I.NAME)
ORDER BY I.NAME;
```

Index not used by static SQL: The following SELECT statement identifies indexes that are not used in any static SQL statements:

```
SELECT I.TBNAME, I.NAME, I.CLUSTERING, I.UNIQUERULE
FROM   SYSIBM.SYSINDEXES I
WHERE  I.CREATOR = 'Authid'
AND    I.NAME LIKE 'ABC%' -- Use naming convention
AND    I.NAME NOT IN
      (SELECT PL.BNAME
       FROM   SYSIBM.SYSPLANDEP PL
       WHERE  PL.BCREATOR = 'Authid'
```

```
          AND     PL.BNAME LIKE 'ABC%'
          AND     PL.BTYPE     = 'I')
AND       I.NAME NOT IN
         (SELECT PK.BNAME
          FROM    SYSIBM.SYSPACKDEP PK
          WHERE   PK.BQUALIFIER = 'Authid'
          AND     PK.BNAME LIKE 'ABC%'
          AND     PK.BTYPE        = 'I')
ORDER BY I.TBNAME, I.NAME;
```

If it is doubtful that dynamic SQL and future static SQL will use the indexes, drop them to avoid the overhead of index maintenance. There are a couple of cases where you may still need the index. The index may be necessary to guarantee unique values in a column and for enforcing referential integrity constraints.

ID.4 DATA-ONLY LOCKING

Transaction locks are not taken on index pages. *Data-only locking* is done on a row, page, table, or tablespace. It is not necessary to access a data page; DB2 builds a lock name based on object identifiers (object ID, page set ID, RID, etc.).

Index-only processing requires data-only locking for each qualifying value. Predicate evaluation is done before determining if the entry is committed when using a matching or non-matching index scan (not for tablespace scan). This applies to leaf page access to obtain RIDs for list prefetch. A data-only lock must be taken for each qualifying RID if lock avoidance is not successful. The techniques used on data pages for lock avoidance are used on the index pages to avoid data-only locks. (Lock avoidance is discussed in Chapter CC.)

If there is an attempt to access a row identified by a RID found in a leaf page that references a data page that has an X lock, for example, a -911 SQLCODE is issued.

Locks Taken with RR

When using SQL with repeatable read (RR), DB2 ensures that a row is not inserted into a range of values that are locked for RR. It also has to handle the case of insertions after the last value in the index. Srr (rr is an attribute of an IRLM share lock) locks are taken on value/RID pairs for SQL bound with RR. An EOF (End of File) lock is used on the index to manage insertions following the last value in the index. This avoids SQL with RR seeing a new row that it had not seen previously if it rereads the data. RR is discussed in Chapter CC.

Let's consider examples of the use of Srr and EOF locks. If the indexed values of 110 and 120 with RIDs 1002 and 1003 in Chapter IU, Figure IU.1, have an Srr data lock, for example, an insert of 115 waits until the other program issues a commit and releases the Srr locks. An insert takes an X data-only lock on the data referenced by RID 1003 for the indexed value of 120. An insert of 1135 encounters an Srr lock on 1130 and requests an X EOF lock.

Latch Processing

Latches are used on index and data pages when the tablespace is created with a ROW, PAGE, or ANY lock size. They are used to maintain integrity of the index pages similar to data pages as discussed in Chapter CC. They are used to avoid attempts to process data on a page that is being reorganized to reclaim free space and to avoid processing data that is being updated. One would not want to read a partially updated data page or composite index on SN, PN, and JN as a result of the UPDATE statement:

```
UPDATE SPJ
    SET SN = 'S4' -- Update applied
        PN = 'P4' -- Update not applied
        JN = 'J4' -- Update not applied
WHERE   SN = 'S3'
        PN = 'P3'
        JN = 'J3';
```

Latches prevent someone seeing 'S4', 'P3', and 'J3' on the composite index or data page while the values are being changed from 'S3', 'P3', and 'J3' to 'S4', 'P4', and 'J4'. Latch processing is required for each qualifying row with and without index-only processing. Latches are discussed in Chapter CC.

ID.5 INDEX STRUCTURE MODIFICATION

Index structure modification (SMOD) operations are required when index pages are removed from the index structure as a result of all values being deleted from an index page or when an inserted row needs to be referenced on an index page that is full. The index manager maintains a balanced index structure. That is, the number of I/Os to traverse an index structure is always the same regardless of the path taken through the index.

Consider what would happen if the index manager did not maintain a balanced index structure. High insert activity down a particular path of the index structure would cause additional nonleaf page levels to be created. Look at Figure IU.1 in Chapter IU. If two additional index levels were to be added down the job 111 path, the number of index I/Os to locate the job would increase from 3 to 5, resulting in an unbalanced index structure. Users tend to access newly inserted rows frequently. If an unbalanced index structure were used, these users would have additional I/Os down the longer path.

Index Page Splitting

The index manager maintains a balanced index structure by using free space in the index when index entries are inserted or updated. If the free space on an index leaf page is used up, the next insert or update causes the page to split, with half the values remaining on the original page, and half of the values placed on a new page. The nonleaf page above the split page must be updated to point to the new lower-level leaf page. This process can continue up to the root page. If there is no free space in the root page to account for a new nonleaf page, the root page is split, and a new root page is created, resulting in an extra level being added to the index structure. When an additional level is added to the index, an additional getpage and I/O are required for every matching index scan. (An I/O is not required if buffer manager locates the page in the buffer pool.)

Recommendation: Reorganize indexes when additional levels have been added to the index, or if there are many half full pages as a result of page splitting. Chapter RR provides SELECT statements from the catalog tables that can be used to identify these conditions.

Access During Structure Modification

Processing must be serialized during a page split and update of the next higher level page in the index. This is done by turning on the structure modification bit (SM_bit). The SM_bit is used to avoid others having to do latch processing. In addition, a tree lotch is taken. A lotch is a cross between a latch and a lock. It is taken by the index manager (not using the IRLM). SQL statements can traverse the index while the X lotch is held. However, if an SQL statement encounters a page with the SM_bit turned on, it will have to request an S lotch and wait for the X lotch to be released. Again, a lock is not taken for commit duration. These factors mean that the index page will be unavailable for a short period of time.

SQL statements can access any index pages other than the one being split, its parent and dependent pages. For example, assume that an insert of 115 into the index represented in Chapter IU Figure IU.1 results in a page split. Others cannot use the leaf page containing 101 through 130, and they cannot use the next higher page until structure modification (SMOD) processing completes. Others can use all other leaf and nonleaf pages. They can see values 1001 through 6000, for example. If an SQL statement attempts to look at values on the affected pages, they will see that the SM_bit is on and will request an S lotch. The S lotch request must wait for the X lotch to be released. It is not necessary to serialize others until the program causing the SMOD operation issues a commit work. The index manager allows a non-matching index scan, index lookaside, and index screening that is in progress to continue, provided it does not encounter the page being split.

Insertion of Sequential Values

Often rows are inserted such that they must be referenced in the last leaf page of an index. For example, if there is an index on a timestamp, sequentially assigned IDs for orders, job IDs, employee IDs, etc. reference to the newly inserted row must be placed in the last leaf page. This applies to clustering and non-clustering indexes.

The index manager adds a newly allocated page when the last leaf page becomes full rather than splitting it. This reduces CPU, I/O, serialization contention, and latch wait time. However, if the first column of the index allows for nulls, the index manager cannot do this special processing. A column that allows for nulls has a null indicator of X'FF' as the first byte of the column. This results in nulls always being inserted on the last leaf page rather than the next sequential value.

This special processing applies only to the last leaf page, not the ones at the beginning or middle of the index. It is necessary to reference the new leaf pages in the next higher nonleaf page using the SMOD technique discussed in this section. If there are areas in the index where there is a great deal of insert activity without a corresponding deletion of indexed values in the same pages, consider using 0 percent free in the index pages as discussed in the section on creating indexes. Any requested free space is left by the utilities LOAD, REORG, and REBUILD INDEX in every leaf page and is rarely used on all but the last leaf page.

ID.6 COLUMNS THAT SHOULD NOT BE INDEXED

Columns with a low cardinality, a skewed distribution, or many unknown values make poor candidates for indexing. The use of an index on these types of columns often does not reduce the number of data pages that must be processed, and it costs more to maintain the index.

Low Cardinality Indexes

A non-clustering index on a column with a low cardinality is of limited or no value in satisfying search conditions. This is because it is likely that one or more rows will qualify on each data page. If most pages in a table must be processed it is best to use a tablespace scan and take advantage of sequential or dynamic prefetch.

You can estimate the average number of occurrences of a value on each data page by multiplying the filter factor times the number of rows and divide by the number of data pages. For example, assume a cardinality of 20 on a city column in a million row table on 30,000 data pages. The filter factor for an equal predicate is one divided by 20--five percent of the rows are required with an equal predicate. Five percent of one million rows (50,000) divided by 30,000 data pages gives an estimate of 1.7 rows on each data page for a given city, assuming a uniform distribution of values on the data pages. If you require all rows for Dallas, it is best to do a tablespace scan because there is typically one or more qualifying rows on each data page with a uniform distribution of values. A screen can be filled with 12 rows using one sequential prefetch I/O to return 54.4 rows for Dallas in the buffer pool or 7 random reads to the data pages returns 11.9 rows to fill a screen. The use of a non-clustering index on city increases the number of I/O (I/O are required to the index pages) and offers no benefit. A general rule of thumb is to avoid creating an index on any column for which, on average, each distinct value appears one or more times on each data page.

In addition, an index on a column with a low cardinality means that many RIDs follow the index value. This chain of RIDs is called a *synonym chain*. In the example, there are typically 50,000 RIDs following a value in the leaf pages.

Look at your existing indexes to see if they can be used to reduce the number of I/Os to data pages. The following SELECT from the catalog tables calculates the number of times a given value appears on a data page on average, assuming a uniform distribution of values. The AVG_PER_PAGE_S is the average occurrences for a single column index and the AVG_PER_PAGE_C is the average for a composite index.

```
SELECT I.CREATOR, I.TBNAME, I.NAME,
       I.FIRSTKEYCARDF, I.FULLKEYCARDF,
       C.NAME, C.COLCARDF, T.CARDF, T.NPAGES,
       (T.CARDF*1.0)/T.NPAGES/I.FIRSTKEYCARDF
          AS AVG_PER_PAGE_S,
       (T.CARDF*1.0)/T.NPAGES/I.FULLKEYCARDF
          AS AVG_PER_PAGE_C
FROM   SYSIBM.SYSINDEXES I,
       SYSIBM.SYSTABLES  T,
       SYSIBM.SYSCOLUMNS C,
       SYSIBM.SYSKEYS    K
WHERE  I.FIRSTKEYCARDF > 0
```

```
AND     I.FULLKEYCARDF  > 0
AND     T.CARDF         > 0
AND     T.NPAGES        > 0
AND     I.UNIQUERULE= 'D'
AND     T.TYPE       = 'T'
AND     I.CREATOR    = 'PAT'
AND     K.IXCREATOR  = I.CREATOR
AND     C.TBCREATOR  = I.CREATOR
AND     T.CREATOR    = I.CREATOR
AND     T.NAME       = C.TBNAME
AND     T.NAME       = I.TBNAME
AND     C.NAME       = K.COLNAME
AND     K.IXNAME     = I.NAME;
```

If you are considering creating a non-clustering index and are concerned that the index might not minimize the number of data pages to be processed, evaluate the cardinality before creating the index. Do this by counting the number of distinct occurrences of a value in a column. For example, if you are considering an index on SPJ.SN, the following statement gives the cardinality of the column.

```
SELECT COUNT (DISTINCT SN)
FROM   SPJ;
```

If there are very few distinct values (less than 20 or less than 5 percent of the total number of rows, for example), a non-clustering index is of little value in minimizing I/O to the data pages. It is best to use a tablespace scan with sequential prefetch because most data pages will have qualifying rows. Even for an online transaction, there is a good chance that a single prefetch I/O of 32 pages using a tablespace scan will retrieve the required rows to display to the user, assuming that rows with like values are spread throughout the tablespace. There are exceptions. The index may be needed to locate infrequently occurring values in a skewed distribution of values or to avoid sorts.

Skewed Distribution of Values

We have been assuming a uniform distribution of values (also referred to as a flat distribution of values). A uniform distribution of values means that each city occurs the same number of times as every other city in a table. Indeed, this is the assumption made by the optimizer for static SQL using host variables. A column with a skewed distribution of values--some values occur much more frequently that others--has similar problems as one with a low cardinality, at least for the frequently occurring values. Figure ID.5 is an example of a skewed and uniform distribution of values.

Figure ID.5. Skewed and uniform distribution of values

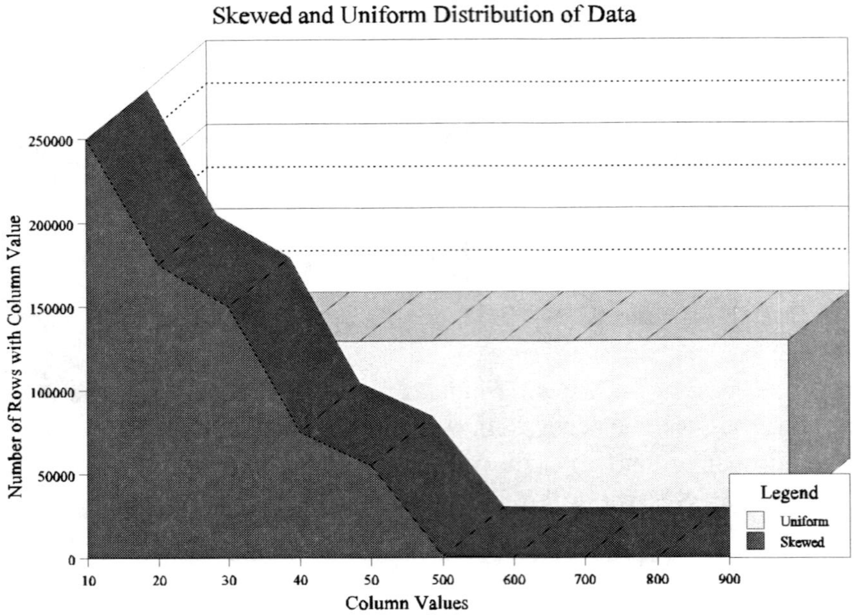

If you are considering indexing a column on STATUS, for example, and suspect that the distribution might be skewed, the following SELECT statement provides information on whether the distribution is skewed.

```
SELECT STATUS, COUNT(*)
FROM   S
GROUP BY STATUS
ORDER BY 2;
```

Figure ID.6 shows an example of the result of the SELECT statement. Using an index to locate the rows with a status of 900 in a million row table is desirable because only 50 rows qualify. It is probably worthwhile to use an index to locate rows with a status of 500 to 900 to avoid a tablespace scan. However, a tablespace scan is best to locate the rows with a status between 10 and 50 because of their frequent occurrences. We certainly do not want to use an index to locate 250,000 rows with a status of 10. A tablespace scan is best for processing one-fourth of the rows.

Figure ID.6. Identifying a skewed distribution of values

```
          Number of
Status    Occurrences
______    ___________

900            50<———————Good use of index
800           150
700           300
600           480
500           875

etc.          etc.

 50         55000<———————Poor use of index
 40         75000        Tablespace scan is best &
 30        150000        long synonym chain of RIDs
 20        175000
 10        250000
```

There are several long synonym chains. For example, 250,000 RIDs follow the value of 10, 175,000 RIDs follow the value of 20, 150,000 RIDs follow the value of 30, and so on. Ideally, we would not create an index at all on a column with a skewed distribution of values because of the long synonym chains and the problems of using the index to locate infrequently occurring values and not using the index to locate frequently occurring values.

The RUNSTATS utility determines the ten (default) most frequently occurring values in a tablespace and records them in the COLVALUE column of SYSCOLDIST along with the frequency of occurrence in the column FREQUENCYF. The FREQUENCYF is the percentage of rows time 100 that contains the value in the column COLVALUE. Similar statistics are collected by partition for a partitioned tablespace and are recorded in SYSCOLDISTSTATS. You can review existing indexes to determine if there is a skewed distribution of values in the indexes with:

```
SELECT COLVALUE, FREQUENCY
FROM   SYSIBM.SYSCOLDIST
WHERE  TBCREATOR = 'POSYSTEM'
UNION ALL
SELECT COLVALUE, FREQUENCY
FROM   SYSIBM.SYSCOLDISTSTATS
WHERE  TBCREATOR = 'POSYSTEM';
```

Developers should avoid indexing columns having a skewed distribution of data. Nevertheless, there are times when it is necessary to retrieve infrequently occurring values in such a column with an index rather than a tablespace scan to provide good response time. Techniques for dealing with a skewed distribution are discussed in Chapters PP and OP.

Sparse Index by Application Design: A sparse index references only specific values rather than all values in a column. DB2 does *not* support sparse indexes. However, you can design for a pseudo sparse index. Consider creating a sparse index table, INFREQ_STATUS, containing the primary key and the infrequently occurring values as shown in Figure ID.7.

Figure ID.7. INFREQ_STATUS sparse index table

SN	CITY
S40	Caplen
S53	Rockwall
S54	Rockwall
S67	Childress
S85	Hollis
Etc.	Etc.

The host language programs can join the target S table with the sparse index table. Optionally, a view can be created containing the join so that developers need not be concerned with coding the join. If a view is used, the only programs that must be concerned with the sparse index table are those that maintain it.

If the user requests an infrequently occurring status, the following statement will return the required results from the target S table.

```
SELECT SN, SNAME, STATUS, CITY
FROM   INFREQ_STATUS, S
WHERE  INFREQ_STATUS.STATUS  = :STATUS
AND    INFREQ_STATUS.SN      = S.SN;
```

If the user requests a status that occurs frequently, a 100 SQLCODE will be received for the statement. It is necessary to execute a statement that will do a tablespace scan to get the frequently occurring status.

Advantages of a sparse index table: The advantages are that it is not necessary to maintain a large index on a skewed distribution of values with a long synonym chain of RIDs and the few infrequently occurring values can be processed efficiently.

Disadvantages of a sparse index table: It is necessary to access the INFREQ_STATUS table in addition to the S table in most cases. The INFREQ_STATUS table must be maintained with infrequently occurring values and the corresponding primary key. Programs that change the S table must maintain the sparse index table in addition to the target table. A trigger can be developed to maintain the sparse index table as discussed in Chapter TR. DB2-enforced referential integrity can provide some assistance as well. If you define INFREQ_STATUS.SN as a foreign key referencing the S table using the cascade rule, any time that you delete an SN from the S table, DB2 automatically deletes the corresponding SN from the INFREQ_STATUS table.

Many Unknown Values

A column with many unknown values results in a long synonym chain of RIDs. Consider a customer account table where the customer is asked for their social security number, but it is not required. Many customers do not know their social security numbers when they apply for accounts. The column may be declared as allowing nulls, not null with default, or having a default value assigned automatically when a row is inserted into the table with an unknown social security number. Regardless of the choice for dealing with unknown social security numbers, there will be a long synonym chain of RIDs following the null or unknown value. A column with many unknown values is not a good candidate for an index. However, it may be needed to process the known values.

Management of a Synonym Chain

An indexed column which contains a skewed distribution of values or many unknown values is like a low cardinality index in that columns with this type of data result in long synonym chains of RIDs that are costly to maintain.

Recommendation: Avoid indexing columns with a low cardinality, a skewed distribution of values, or many unknown values. All three of these conditions result in long synonym chains of RIDs.

The index manager stores the highest RID on a leaf page in the next higher nonleaf page as shown in Figure ID.8. This allows for locating the page containing the required RID directly without scanning a large number of leaf pages. Once the required page is located, a binary search of the RIDs on the page speeds the process further.

Figure ID.8. Synonym chain management

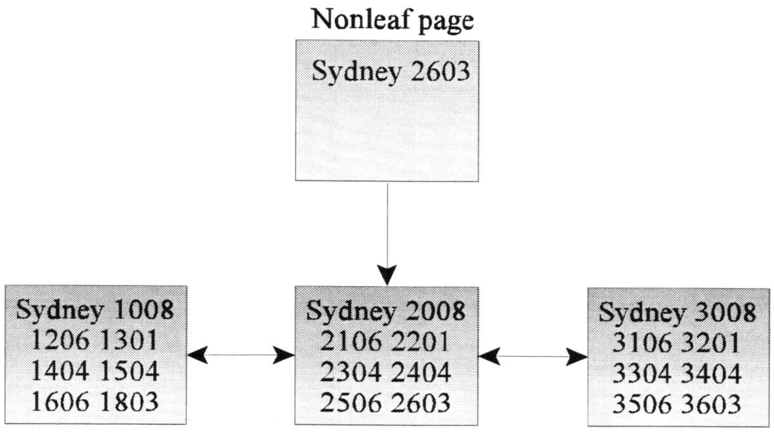

RIDs Maintained in Sequence: The index manager maintains RIDs in sequence. This allows for a binary search to locate the required RID for an update or delete, and to make a slot for an insert with a nonunique index. When a new RID is inserted following an indexed value, it must be inserted in sequence. If the new RID is not the highest RID for the value on the target leaf page, the existing RIDs must be shifted right within a single leaf page to maintain the sequence. If there is not enough space to insert the RID on the target leaf page, the leaf page is split.

Each indexed value in a unique index leaf page is followed by one RID. A nonunique index can have many RIDs following a value on a leaf page. The value occurs only once on a leaf page followed by as many RIDs as fit on the page. The value is repeated on as many leaf pages as necessary to contain all of the RIDs required to reference each row that contains the value.

Additional Columns That Should Not Be Indexed

Figure ID.9 summarizes the cases where you should be careful about indexing columns. The first three items dealing with a column with a low cardinality index, skewed distribution of values, and many unknown values have been described in this chapter.

Figure ID.9. Beware of Indexing Some Types of Columns

- Avoid indexes on columns with a low cardinality.
- Avoid indexes on columns with a skewed distribution.

- Avoid indexes on columns that frequently have unknown values.
- Minimize indexing columns that are frequently updated, because delete and insert processing is required on the index.
- Minimize indexing wide columns (more than 30-50 percent of the row length, for example) because the number of index pages will approach the number of data pages. However, the index will be of value for matching index scans where only a few leaf pages need to be scanned.
- VARCHAR column are padded to their full length in an index.
- Minimize indexes on tables in a tablespace that occupy less than eight pages because the optimizer assumes that less than 8 pages will fit in a buffer pool.

The remaining items in Figure ID.9 are additional guidelines to consider in designing your indexes. The last guideline has significant exceptions. You should always have an index on the primary key, regardless of the number of pages. The optimizer is likely to use the index for the inner table of joins. An index is used for RI constraint checking and to ensure uniqueness for the primary key. List prefetch is considered if two or more pages are estimated to contain qualifying rows. Finally, index only processing can be used.

There is a method for encouraging index usage over a tablespace scan for small tables, small tables that grow rapidly in size, and those where RUNSTATS has not been executed in a test environment, for example (V6 APAR PQ33429). NPGTHRSH installation panel can be set to any value (default is 0). For example, 10 means that all tables with NPAGES < 10 or NPAGES = -1 favor index usage. Do be cautious of using this option. A tablespace is better than index usage in some cases, many of which are discussed in Chapter BP. The parameter effects all SQL. If it is necessary to encourage index usage consider using OPTIMIZE FOR 1 ROW (discussed in several chapters) or optimization hints at the statement level (discussed in Chapter EX) because these techniques are at the statement level.

Of course, a column should not be indexed unless it can be used to narrow the search significantly for frequently executed programs where a tablespace scan would be too costly.

Logically Sequenced Indexed Values

Indexed values are maintained in logical sequence to avoid shifting values down into free space at the bottom of a leaf page. When the LOAD, REORG, or REBUILD INDEX utilities builds the index pages with the values in sequence, it leaves the specified free space at the bottom of a page. For example, assume that the values of 10, 20, 30, and 40 have been loaded into a table. The insertion of the value 25 goes into the free space at the bottom of the page to avoid shifting of the values 30 and 40 into free space as shown in the first box in Figure ID.10.

Figure ID.10. Comparison of insertion of values in index and data pages

```
Index
Leaf Page

    10   1001
    20   1002
    30   1003
    40   1004
--->25   1005
```

```
Data Page
   100

    PN 10 row
    PN 20 row
    PN 30 row
    PN 40 row
--->PN 25 row
```

The index manager uses a key map area in leaf and nonleaf pages to retrieve the values in physical sequence to avoid a sort, for example. A two-byte key map entry contains the offset of each value on the page. A new value can be inserted into any available free space on the page without shifting values. It is necessary to shift the key map entries to maintain logically sequenced values. Shifting key map entries into adjacent free space left by utilities requires less processing than shifting values so that the page is unavailable for a shorter period of time. The latch can be released when the processing is complete. Recall that a latch is not held for commit duration.

The key map is conceptually like the page directory at the bottom of a data page. The row for PN 25 is inserted at the bottom of the page in the free space left by a utility without having to shift rows down to insert 25 in between 20 and 30, assuming that the clustering index is on PN. The page directory is used to locate a row without having to maintain the rows in physical sequence according to the column with the clustering index as indicated in the second box of Figure ID.10.

The key map does not limit the number of values on a page like the page directory limits the number of rows on a page. The index manager attempts to insert a key map entry and value until the page is full.

Reuse of Space From Deleted Values

RIDs are marked as deleted by turning on a bit in a byte preceding each RID. It is not necessary to shift RIDs immediately to fill space from a deleted RID. The space is reusable after a commit. This is important for updates as well because the update of an indexed value uses delete processing followed by insert processing.

When a threshold of pseudo deleted and committed RIDs is reached (thought to be 10 percent), a DELETE statement causes pseudo deleted RIDs to be physically deleted. Physical deletion results in shifting RIDs to fill in the gap of pseudo deleted RIDs while holding a latch. In addition, three or fewer index pages that have all pseudo deleted RIDs within the range of pages addressed by the space map page are deleted. The limit of deleting three index pages at a time is to avoid sporadic poor performance of the SQL statement that causes the deletions. The space map page is used to track pages with only committed pseudo deleted RIDs. This provides for deleting index pages where all RIDs are marked as deleted but the pages are never accessed again for inserts, for example.

SQL using RR results in physical deletions when the percentage threshold is reached within a page. RIDs are physically deleted when the table or tablespace has an X lock. Of course, when an index is rebuilt by a utility, pseudo deleted RIDs are physically removed.

Inserting a RID reuses space from a pseudo deleted RID and the associated value if all RIDs for the indexed value are deleted. For example, Figure ID.11 shows how the RID of 7002 can replace the pseudo deleted RID of 8004 following the indexed value of Sydney. However, if a RID 4003 must be inserted between 3006 and 5001, free space from pseudo deleted RIDs and deleted values must be gathered. An X latch is held on the page during the process.

Figure ID.11. Deletions and reuse of space

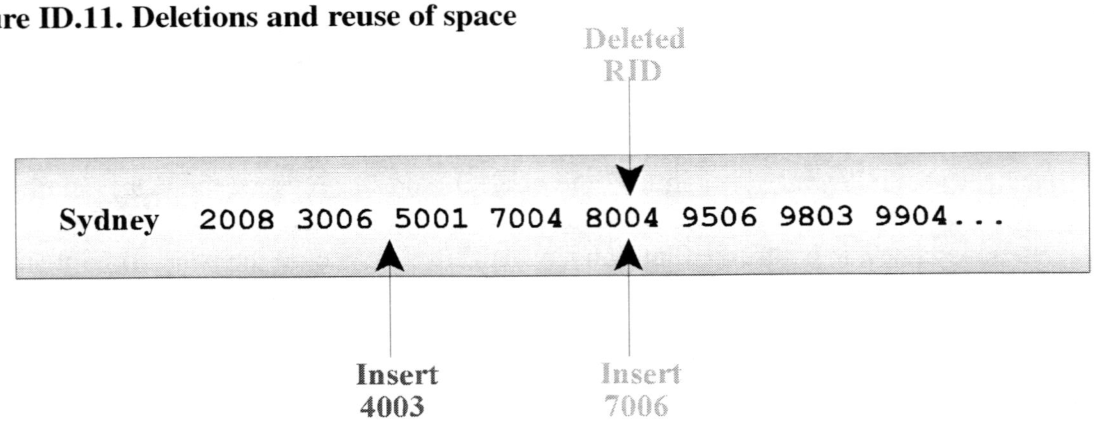

Suffix Truncation in Nonleaf Pages

It is not necessary to store the entire upper range column value in nonleaf pages in order to determine which lower level nonleaf or leaf page to access. Only the leading portion of a value needs to be stored. For example, Gim is sufficient to reference a leaf page containing Giles, Gilford, Gilkey, Gill, and so on. Halc is sufficient to reference a leaf page containing Halbach, Halbert, Halbrook, and so on. These truncated variable length values are sufficient to traverse the index tree. (Gim rather than Gil and Halc rather than Halb is used because the value in the nonleaf page must be strictly greater than the value in the leaf page.) This is called *suffix truncation,* and it is used in the root and nonleaf pages. Suffix truncation reduces the number of trailing blanks that are stored in the nonleaf pages of an index on a VARCHAR column.

Truncated values means that more upper range values and pointers to lower levels in the index tree will fit on a nonleaf page resulting in increased *fanout*. That is, fewer nonleaf pages are required with suffix truncation. Fewer levels result in fewer getpages and I/O to do a matching index scan. Also, less DASD space is required in many cases.

There are no single-level indexes. If all the required indexed values and RIDs fit on a single leaf page, there is a root page with a last page pointer.

ID.7 CREATING AND ALTERING INDEXES

Following is an example of creating a unique ascending index on the PN column in the P table to provide a basis for analyzing the parameter for the CREATE statement.

```
CREATE UNIQUE INDEX PNX
  ON P (PN)
  USING STOGROUP DASPJSTG
    PRIQTY 7200
```

```
    SECQTY  720
    ERASE NO
  PCTFREE  10
  FREEPAGE 63
  CLUSTER
  DEFER NO
  PIECESIZE 4 M
  BUFFERPOOL BP0
  CLOSE NO;
```

PCTFREE and FREEPAGE: PCTFREE is the percentage of free space left at the bottoms of index pages by utilities that build indexes including LOAD, REORG, and REBUILD INDEX. The default is 10 percent. The PCTFREE value should allow for the insertion of multiples of the indexed value, flag, RID, and key map entry for unique indexes. Less free space is required for nonunique indexes because the indexed value is not repeated for each occurrence of a value. No more than 10 percent free space is left in the nonleaf pages to minimize the number of levels in an index.

If page splitting has resulted in an additional index level or many half-full pages, reorganize the index. For highly volatile data, it might be necessary to increase the free space value with the ALTER statement to reduce the frequency of reorganizations required in the future.

A FREEPAGE value of 63 as shown in the previous example means that a blank page will be left within every 64 pages. The index manager first analyzes the space map page to determine if there is an available page within plus or minus 64 pages of the page that must be split. If space is found, it is considered a near page. Otherwise a scan of the space map pages is done to locate a free page to accommodate a page split. Use a FREEPAGE of 31 or less if page splits are frequent and occur throughout the leaf pages.

PCTFREE and FREEPAGE of 0 is a good choice if there is low insert and update activity or insert and update activity is concentrated in specific areas of the index, sometimes called "hot spots". This is because the free space is distributed evenly throughout the index and will be quickly used in the hot spots but wasted in most areas of the index. There is no reason to allow for free space in an index on a column where values are always inserted in sequence at the end of the index. This also applies to a tablespace where the clustering index is on a sequential value.

UNIQUE: This parameter designates a unique index. A negative SQLCODE will be issued if there is an attempt to insert or update a column such that it would result in a duplicate value in the columns designated as a unique index. One null entry is allowed.

UNIQUE WHERE NOT NULL: This parameter is like the UNIQUE parameter except that it allows any number of null entries in the column. As an example of its use, assume there is a business rule where only one employee can be assigned to a job but there can be jobs with no employees assigned. The following table shows that J3 and J4 exist but no employees are currently assigned to the jobs.

J (Job Table)

JN	JNAME	CITY	EMPNO
J1	Sorter	Paris	900
J2	Punch	Rome	400

J3	Reader	Athens	(null)
J4	Console	Athens	(null)
J5	Collator	London	100
J6	Terminal	Oslo	300
J7	Tape	London	200

Be careful about allowing multiple null entries in a unique composite index. If any part of a composite index contains null, duplicates are allowed. For example, two entries of "S4 null J6" are allowed in a composite unique index. This is in conformance with the SQL standard.

CLUSTER: This parameter designates the clustering index. The importance of the clustering index and the characteristics of columns that benefit from clustering are discussed in Section ID.2 and Chapter IU.

ASC or DESC: An ascending (ASC) index is the default. If a descending index is required, DESC must be specified.

PIECESIZE: PIECESIZE provides for separating pieces of a nonpartitioning index on separate DASD devices to achieve multiple I/O paths. The piece size can be between 254 KB and 64 GB in with a maximum of 254 pieces (data sets) (V6). The partitioned tablespace must be defined as allowing for more than 64 GB by specifying the DSSIZE parameter with a value of 4 GB or larger or you can specify the LARGE parameter as discussed in Chapter TS. The prerequisites to exceeding 4 GB data sets are also discussed in Chapter TS. The PIECESIZE is filled completely by LOAD and REORG. The primary plus secondary quantities should be divisible evenly into PIECESIZE for the best space utilization.

Space allocation, CLOSE, and BUFFERPOOL: The guidelines for index space allocation, CLOSE and BUFFERPOOL are similar to the corresponding parameters specified when creating a tablespace as discussed in Chapter CD.

Index rules: The maximum number of columns in an index is 64 and the maximum number of bytes in the indexed columns is 255. No column can appear more than once in an index. The same column can appear in multiple indexes.

When to Create and Build Indexes

In most cases, indexes should be created after a table is created and before the LOAD utility is used to populate the table. The LOAD utility builds the indexes after extracting the indexed values while inserting rows into the table. The extracted indexed values are sorted and the indexes are built efficiently one at a time.

If a table already has rows when an index is created, a tablespace scan is performed to extract the indexed values. The indexed values are sorted and built similar to LOAD processing.

There are some significant processing differences between creating an index before or after the table is loaded. When building an index on a populated table, the internal DB2 sort is used to sort the indexed values. It uses logical work files in the work tablespaces in the database DSNDB07. The index build abends if there is not enough space in the work database, which is a real possibility. The work tablespaces are usually sized by the system administrator to accommodate sorts for SQL statements, not the build of indexes on large tables. LOAD, on the other hand, uses an external sort (such as DFSORT), which has performance advantages when sorting a large number of rows.

In addition, a lock is held on the DBD while the index is being built, preventing the execution of all data definition statements and binds of SQL referencing objects in the database. If multiple indexes are created on a populated table, the processing is repeated serially for each index created.

Defer Building of Indexes

When creating indexes on a populated table, consider using DEFER YES on the CREATE INDEX statement. This results in minimal processing. The underlying VSAM data set to receive the index is created, rows are inserted into the catalog tables describing the index, the DBD is updated with information on the new index, recover pending is set for the index, and a +610 SQLCODE is issued to indicate that the index is not usable.

The REBUILD INDEX or REORG TABLESPACE utilities can be used to build the indexes at a time that is good for other activity in the system. The build uses processing similar to the LOAD utility. This has significant performance advantages. In one case there was a 37 percent savings in elapsed time and a 23 percent savings in CPU time using DEFER YES followed by building an index on a 394,785 row table. It required 572 elapsed and 59 CPU seconds with DEFER NO compared to 359 elapsed and 45 CPU seconds with DEFER YES and building the index.

Caution must be exercised in the timing of creating the indexes and building them. The optimizer can choose to use the index before it is built. Even if no plans and packages are bound between the time that the index is created and the time that it is built, a -904 SQLCODE indicating that a resource is unavailable can be received. This is because insert and delete statements must update all indexes. DB2 will see the newly created but unbuilt index in the DBD and attempt to insert a reference to a new row or delete a reference to a row when a delete is attempted.

Recommendation on when to use DEFER YES: Perhaps the most important case when you will want to use DEFER YES is when you believe it is necessary to use INSERT statements to populate a new table rather than the LOAD utility as suggested in Chapter BP. INSERT statements issued in a host language program results in excessive index page splitting and the same leaf page is updated repeatedly. These inefficiencies can be avoided by inserting rows that have been sorted in clustering sequence into a new table before creating indexes. Consider using the sort utility to check for duplicates on a column that will have a unique index to avoid errors when the index is built. After inserting the rows, create the indexes with DEFER YES, and then use REBUILD INDEX, or REORG TABLESPACE.

DEFER YES is useful for testing the usefulness of additional indexes without the cost of building the indexes. It is best to update the index statistics in the catalog tables with an estimate of the statistics that will be collected when RUNSTATS is executed after the index is built. If this is not possible, the optimizer will use default statistics to determine an access path. SQL that may benefit from the additional indexes can be explained to determine if the resources required to build and maintain the indexes are worthwhile.

If it is necessary to drop indexes before executing a batch job to avoid the costs of index maintenance as discussed in Chapter BP, DEFER YES is a good choice when re-creating the indexes.

Altering Indexes

Most index parameters can be altered. The CLUSTER, UNIQUE, UNIQUE WHERE NOT NULL, and DEFER parameters cannot. An alter of parameters that affects how the index is stored on DASD requires the index to be rebuilt before the new parameter value can be utilized for the index. These parameters are PCTFREE, FREEPAGE, and PIECESIZE. Here is an example of altering an index.

```
ALTER INDEX PNX
  USING STOGROUP DATOMSTG
    PRIQTY 14400
    SECQTY   720
    ERASE NO
  PCTFREE  25
  FREEPAGE 15
  PIECESIZE 8 M
  BUFFERPOOL BP1
  CLOSE YES;
```

ID.10 Creating Additional Indexes on the Catalog Tables

If you frequently select from the catalog tables with predicates on the indicated columns in Figure ID.12, creation of indexes on the columns avoids a tablespace scan in most cases. Based on your usage of the catalog tables you may not require all of the indexes and perhaps there are additional indexes that can be created for your frequent accesses to the catalog tables.

Figure ID.12. ID. Create additional indexes on the catalog tables

Catalog Table	Columns	Used to Determine
SYSCOLUMNS	NAME, TBNAME, TBCREATOR	Table layout without TBNAME and TBCREATOR (there is an index on TBCREATOR, TBNAME, NAME)
SYSDBRM	NAME	Information about program from which DBRM was created
SYSDBRM	PLNAME	Name of the application plan of which this DBRM is a part
SYSFOREIGNKEYS	CREATOR, TBNAME, RENAME, COLSEQ	Referential integrity relationships
SYSPACKDEP	DNAME	Objects dependent on a package
SYSPLANDEP	DNAME	Objects dependent on a plan

SYSRELS	CREATOR, TBNAME, RELNAME	Referential integrity relationships
SYSSYNONYMS	TBCREATOR, TBNAME	Synonyms on a table
SYSSTMT	PLCREATOR, PLNAME, NAME, STMTNO	SQL statements used by a plan. Can be a very large index.
SYSVIEWDEP	DCREATOR, DNAME	Tables and views that have a view defined on them
SYSVOLUMES	SGCREATOR, SGNAME	Volume ID of volumes in a given storage group if not managed by SMS

ID.8 SUMMARY

Index design and usage affects application performance more than any other single factor in the design and development of application systems. DB2 provides a multitude of indexing options. It is difficult to predict how tables will be accessed. However, it is essential to carefully analyze how SQL will be used in online transactions, batch programs, and data warehousing applications to determine which columns should be indexed. A process matrix is a good tool for doing this.

The choice of which column should have the clustering index is very important. The characteristics of columns that benefit most from having a clustering index are where the index can be used to retrieve data in sequence without a sort, to facilitate efficient join processing, to satisfy range and string searches, and for batch processing. For columns with a low cardinality or skewed distribution a clustering index is best if an index is required at all. No single column will have all of these characteristics, and you must consider the many trade-offs when deciding which column should have the clustering index.

EXERCISES

1. a) Why should you limit the number of indexes on a table?

b) Are there types of tables that can have more indexes than others?

2. In general, how should you determine which columns should be indexed?

3. a) How does the index created with the CLUSTER parameter affect the data and index?

b) Does the clustering index structure and maintenance differ from a non-clustering index structure and maintenance?

4. a) If an index is not created with the keyword CLUSTER, how does DB2 determine where to insert a row in a table?

b) How is a reorganization affected by the lack of an index created with the keyword CLUSTER?

5. a) Why is the clustering index or any index with a good cluster ratio important?

b) What are some of the various ways that an index with a good cluster ratio can be used?

6. a) What are the advantages of having the clustering index on the PK?

b) What type of processing results in little benefit to having the clustering index on the PK?

7. a) What are the advantages of having the clustering index on the FK?

b) What are the characteristics of a FK that results in less benefit from having a clustering index?

8. a) Is the clustering index a good choice on a column with a low cardinality, skewed distribution of values, or many unknown values, if an index is required? Why?

b) What are the disadvantages of having an index on a column with a low cardinality, skewed distribution or many unknown values?

9. What are some guidelines for composite index design?

10. a) Can index only processing be done with data only locking?

b) Is it necessary to access a data page to take a data-only lock for index processing?

11. a) Is lock avoidance used on indexes?

b) How can one get a -911 SQLCODE when accessing an index page?

ANSWERS

1. a) It is more costly to insert/update/delete index pages than data pages. Even if there is only one index on a table, the costs are higher because of the possibility of page splitting for inserts and maintenance of RIDs when rows are deleted. The update of a row results in changing the row on a page (a variable length row that has been increased in length may need to be moved if there is insufficient space). The update of an index requires that the indexed value and/or RID be removed from an index page and inserted in another index page in most cases. The more indexes that are on a table the higher the cost of maintenance. It costs about 3 times as much to maintain 3 indexes. There is also the additional costs for each index when executing the load, reorg, and recover utilities.

b) More indexes can be created on tables that have very low insert/update/delete activity. Be cautious about too many indexes on tables that contain extracted data. Even though the data is not updated in the table, the extracted data must be refreshed periodically -- frequently with a load replace.

2. It is necessary to do a process analysis to determine which columns should be indexed. You should identify columns which are frequently searched or joined and estimate the percentage of rows that will be processed. If the percentage is small and the table is large, consider indexes on those columns.

Certainly an index is required on the PK, and indexes should be seriously considered on FKs.

3. a) DB2 attempts to maintain the rows in sequence on the column with the clustering index as long as there is free space. There is no affect on the index itself.

b) No, the clustering index has exactly the same structure and is maintained like non-clustering indexes through page splitting. Issues specific to the clustering index will be discussed in subsequent exercises.

4. a) DB2 uses the first index on the DBD index chain to determine where a row should be inserted. If indexes are dropped and recreated, the first index created may be different when the indexes are recreated.

b) Data is not reclustered by the reorganization utility. The SORTDATA parameter on the REORG statement is ignored. SORTDATA significantly improves reorganization performance in the majority of cases. For example, the reorganization of a tablespace with an 80 percent cluster ratio required 74 percent less elapsed time when SORTDATA was used in one case. An exception is when the cluster ratio is 100 percent, in which case the elapsed time was increased by 4 percent. In addition, it is not possible to avoid writing data to SYSREC when using REORG with SHRLEVEL CHANGE during the unload and sort which detracts from performance.

5. a) An index with a good cluster ratio provides an efficient access path for selecting, updating, and deleting rows.

b) An index with a good cluster ratio is useful in retrieving rows in sequence without the delay, I/O, and CPU time that is required to retrieve all qualifying rows and sort them before the first row can be returned to the user. All 3 join methods have performance advantage when a clustering index can be used.

6. a) If there is a good deal of batch processing in sequence on the PK, the clustering index offers significant advantages. The clustering index is also important for cursor repositioning in a batch program for restart and when a -911 or -913 is received.

b) Cursor repositioning in an online transaction that requires the processing of only a few rows to be displayed to the user does not require a clustering index when OPTIMIZE FOR *n* ROWS (where *n* is small) is used in most cases. (This clause is discussed in Chapter PD.) An index with almost any cluster ratio can be used to retrieve a few rows in sequence. In addition, many online transactions use equal predicates on the PK in which case clustering of the data has little or no benefit.

7. a) A one-to-many join (1 PK and many FK values) where the many matching FKs are clustered on the data pages can result in enhanced join performance. In addition, DM can enforce the cascade or set null constraint efficiently with the FK values clustered on the data pages. For example, the deletion of S4 from the S table requires that all S4s be located and deleted from the SPJ table when the cascade delete constraint is defined. A matching index scan can be used to locate S4 in the FK index. The S4 value has all RIDs pointing to the S4 FK rows following the value of S4 in the leaf pages. Also, most of the pages identified by the RIDs are in sequence on DASD, making the deletion of all S4 rows quite efficient.

b) If the FK column has a high cardinality, there will be few duplicate FK values in most cases and the benefits of a) will not apply. For example, a one-to-one relationship between the PK and FK would result in little or no benefit in having the clustering index on the FK.

8. a) Yes, the duplicate values are grouped together on the data pages so that a single matching index scan can be done followed by scanning the leaf pages and dipping down to retrieve the rows that are grouped together on the data pages.

b) The index is of very little value in processing a large percentage of rows which frequently qualify when there is a low cardinality, skewed distribution of values, or many unknown values. Indeed, I/O to the index adds to the processing costs. A tablespace scan with asynchronous prefetch is the best access path when processing a large percentage of the rows. If the cardinality is <= 3, it is very doubtful that the optimizer will choose to use a matching index scan. There is a good probability that the required values to display to the user will be on the first 32 pages prefetched with 1 I/O for a tablespace scan when there is a low cardinality. An index with a low cardinality, skewed distribution, or many unknown values results in a long synonym chain of RIDs that are costly to maintain when deleting, updating, and inserting rows.

9. It is best to place columns used with equal predicates first in a composite index. Try to order columns to minimize sorts. Consider adding columns to the index to allow for index only access. (Avoid adding a column to a PK index if the column must be carried in the dependent tables.) Avoid placing a low cardinality column first in a composite index unless it is necessary to avoid frequent sorts <u>or</u> the first column can be specified with an equal predicate <u>and</u> the second column with a good cardinality can be specified in most WHERE clauses.

10. a) The index manager can do index only processing without access to data pages.

b) It is not necessary to access a data page to take a data-only lock. The lock name is based on data page identifiers including the object ID, page set ID, RID, etc.

11. a) Yes, if the RBA of when the index page was last updated and logged is < RBA for the index space, no data-only lock is required. The techniques used on data pages for lock avoidance are used on index pages to avoid data-only locks.

b) The index manager attempts to get a data-only lock when an index page is accessed if lock avoidance is not successful. If the data page is already locked, a -911 SQLCODE will be received. The lock name for the data-only lock is the same as the lock name for the data page lock. This is necessary to ensure data integrity.

FIGURES

The Basics of SQL Data Manipulation

SL.1 INTRODUCTION

The label *structured query language* is a misnomer in that the language it refers to provides much more than query capabilities. It also provides data definition and data control facilities and, as this chapter describes, rich data-manipulation capabilities. The name is misleading in another sense. Although the language serves well for interactive queries and updates, it can also be embedded within host-language programs for database access. With only a few minor additions to the syntax, embedded SQL works exactly the same as interactive SQL.

The primary data-manipulation functions provided by SQL are SELECT, UPDATE, INSERT, and DELETE. The SELECT capabilities provide a powerful, flexible collection of methods for finding desired data within a database. UPDATE, INSERT, and DELETE allow for the changing, addition, and removal of rows, respectively. We will examine all of these capabilities in detail by looking at examples of statements that employ them. The examples refer to the tables presented in Figure CT.6. By working through the example statements manually—referring to the tables and identifying selected rows, for example—one can easily grasp each statement's meaning.

SL.2 SELECT STATEMENTS

All SELECT statements take this basic form:

```
SELECT SNAME, CITY
FROM   S
WHERE  SN = 'S4';
```

In general, the SELECT clause indicates the column or columns that are to provide the information; the FROM clause indicates the table or tables that contain those columns; the WHERE clause, contains the conditions by which the information is to be selected. Each condition is referred to as a predicate. A SELECT list may contain up to 750 columns and a FROM clause up to 15 tables.

The WHERE clause contains one or more conditions that must be met before a row is included in the returned set. A condition may be that a row's value must relate to some other value in a particular way. SQL allows the standard comparison operators: the “equal to” (=), “not equal to” (!=, ¬=, or <>), “greater than” (>), “greater than or equal to” (>=), “less than” (<), and “less than or equal to” (<=) operators. The > and < operators can be preceded by ! or ¬ to represent negation. The comparators are referred to as simple operators and apply to alphanumeric as well as numeric values.

In the statement above, for example, the WHERE clause stipulates a search for information related to a supplier with a supplier number (SN) equal to S4. The WHERE clause can stipulate multiple search criteria through the use of the AND and OR Boolean operators. In addition, another kind of SELECT statement, called a subselect, may serve as a search criterion. Section SL.10 introduces this facility and the performance implications are discussed in Chapter ST.

SELECT *

An asterisk (*) after SELECT indicates that all columns in the selected rows are to be returned. The asterisk avoids the need to specify all the column names or even to know what they are. SELECT * should not be used in host-language programs, however. Such use would detract from data independence in this way: When an SQL statement SELECTS data for use by a program, the program must have a host variable to receive a value from each column selected. If a column were added to the table, the embedded SELECT * would automatically pass its value to the program. If there is no host variable, DB2 has no place to store the returned value for access by the program. Similarly, if a column were deleted, SELECT * would not return the correct values to the program. If the columns to be selected had been listed, however, the added columns would not have affected the program and the deleted column would affect only the programs referencing the column. In addition, SELECT * detracts from good performance as discussed in Chapter PP.

This example illustrates the use of SELECT * and the operation of a simple WHERE clause. The problem is to determine from the example tables the jobs that use part number P6 supplied by supplier S5 and the number of parts (QTY) assigned to each of those jobs. The Supplier/Part/Job (SPJ) table in Figure CT.6 contains all of that information. This statement SELECTS it:

```
SELECT *
FROM   SPJ
WHERE  SN = 'S5'
AND    PN = 'P6';
```

The SELECT * clause indicates that all column values from the appropriate rows are to be returned. The FROM clause indicates the rows are to be found in the SPJ table. And the WHERE clause stipulates that only rows in which SN equals S5 and PN equals P6 are to be returned. Single quotation marks in the statement identify character string values. Before reading the report returned by this SELECT statement, presented below, try locating in the SPJ table the rows that satisfy the WHERE criteria. Here is the report with the needed information:

SN	PN	JN	QTY
S5	P6	J2	200
S5	P6	J4	500

Notice that SELECT * returns the columns in the order in which they were defined in the CREATE TABLE statement, and the column names are returned as headings.

Naming a Result with AS

A SELECT statement produces a report when executed interactively using QMF or SPUFI, for example. The column headings of the report are the same as the column names in a table as was seen in the previous examples. You may want the report headings to be different than the column names. This can be accomplished with the AS clause. Here we want the QTY column to have a report heading of NUMBER_OF_PARTS:

```
SELECT SN, PN, JN, QTY AS NUMBER_OF_PARTS
FROM   SPJ
WHERE  SN = 'S5'
AND    PN = 'P6';
```

The report produced with the AS clause looks like:

SN	PN	JN	NUMBER_OF_PARTS
S5	P6	J2	200
S5	P6	J4	500

The AS clause is particularly useful in naming a calculated expression as we will see in this section.

Selecting Nulls

SQL statements that test for the presence of nulls hold the potential for a programming difficulty. It may seem natural for programmers to test for nulls in the same way they test for any other value. A typical SQL statement to locate suppliers with a status of 30 would be:

```
SELECT SN, SNAME, STATUS
FROM   S
WHERE  STATUS = 30;
```

The equals sign would not be correct syntax, however, for a statement that seeks null salaries. As DB2 sees it, a null does not equal—or compare in any way with—anything. SQL therefore provides a special predicate using the verb IS to test for nulls. In this case, the proper statement would be: WHERE STATUS IS NULL.

SELECT Using OR or IN

A user or programmer can limit a search to rows containing any one of a number of values by using a series of OR operators in the WHERE clause or by using the IN operator. Consider a request for information about suppliers S1, S3, and S4. We would like to know the parts supplied by each, how many of each part is supplied, and the jobs in which they are used. All of that information is contained in the SPJ table. Using the OR operator, this statement returns the necessary rows:

```
SELECT SN, PN, JN, QTY
FROM   SPJ
WHERE  SN = 'S1'
OR     SN = 'S3'
OR     SN = 'S4';
```

The SELECT returns all columns from the SPJ table for rows having a supplier number of S1, S3, or S4. The equivalent statement using the IN operator is:

```
SELECT SN, PN, JN, QTY
FROM   SPJ
WHERE  SN IN ('S1', 'S3', 'S4');
```

The statement might be read as "Return all column values from the SPJ table for rows with supplier numbers included in the set of numbers consisting of S1, S3, and S4." The responses to the statements are the same:

SN	PN	JN	QTY
S1	P1	J1	200
S1	P1	J4	700
S3	P3	J1	200
S3	P4	J2	500
S4	P6	J3	300
S4	P6	J7	300

If the user requires the selection of a varying list of values, consider the use of an IN subselect from a temporary table as discussed in Chapters ST and SP.

Range SELECTS

SQL also allows users to retrieve rows associated with ranges of search values—for example, all rows from the Part (P) table containing weight values greater than or equal to 12 and less than or equal to 14. The language provides two equivalent ways of formulating these requests. One way uses the symbolic relationship operators. Those operators would be used to report on parts with weights included within the range just stated in the following way:

```
SELECT PN, WEIGHT
FROM   P
WHERE  WEIGHT >= 12
AND    WEIGHT <= 14;
```

The alternative uses the BETWEEN operator:

```
SELECT PN, WEIGHT
FROM   P
WHERE  WEIGHT BETWEEN 12 AND 14;
```

Besides being easier to type and perhaps a bit easier to grasp, this second statement holds performance benefits—explained in Chapter PP—over the one using the symbolic operators. One must remember, however, that the BETWEEN operator includes within its range the numbers used in the statement. A way to remember is to understand that the range defined by the BETWEEN operator is equivalent to that created by the *less than or equal to* and *greater than or equal to* operators. (NOT BETWEEN does not include the end points.)

The report returned by either statement is:

	WEIGHT
P1	12
P4	14
P5	12

String Searches

The LIKE operator specifies searches for values that contain any character or string of characters. The operator allows the user to specify the location of the target character or string within a longer string by using underscores and the percent (%) sign. Each underscore represents a character position of any value. The % sign is a wild card standing for any number of alphanumeric values. Examples will illuminate the points.

The following statement requests a search for the name of any supplier in the Supplier (S) table whose name includes a K:

```
SELECT SN, SNAME
FROM   S
WHERE  SNAME LIKE '%K%';
```

The % signs indicate that any combination of characters can precede or follow the K or only the value of K exists in the SNAME. A scan of the S Table's SNAME column reveals that two values fit the criteria: Blake and Clark.

If a string search is being done within a host-language program, the host-language variable used to provide the value to be found must match the length of the column being searched. If that variable is short, it must be padded with underscores or the % sign. In the example above if the column being searched is CHAR(5), the host variable must contain %K%%%. The additional % signs, not needed with interactive SQL, pad the variable to the required five character length. Such padding is not necessary for a column declared as VARCHAR. Chapter PD discusses host-language variables more fully.

A request for suppliers with a K in the fourth position of their names demonstrates the use of the underscore with the LIKE operator:

```
SELECT SN, SNAME
FROM   S
WHERE  SNAME LIKE '_ _ _K%';
```

The one value satisfying this request is Blake.

Negating a Predicate

The NOT operator in the WHERE clause allows the SELECT to search for rows that do not meet the stated criteria. The word NOT preceding another operator causes this negation. The symbol ¬=

placed before a comparison operator negates it. For example, these statements return suppliers not located in London or Athens:

```
SELECT SN, SNAME, CITY
FROM   S
WHERE  CITY NOT IN ('London', 'Athens');
```

or

```
SELECT SN, SNAME, CITY
FROM   S
WHERE  CITY ¬= 'London'
AND    CITY ¬= 'Athens';
```

SL.3 COLUMN FUNCTIONS AND ARITHMETIC CALCULATIONS

SQL offers a number of built-in mathematical functions called column functions for use in the SELECT clause that allow users to request data on the basis of simple mathematical operations or according to several numeric properties. It returns, for example, the sum or average of the values that meet the search criteria, and it identifies the minimum or maximum value found. In addition, SQL allows users to request computations—addition, subtraction, multiplication, division, and combinations of those operations—on the selected data. The operators are AVG, SUM, MIN, MAX, COUNT, and DISTINCT and the familiar arithmetic symbols +, -, *, and /. The built-in functions, except for COUNT, ignore nulls in their calculations. Examples best explain the functions' use.

MIN, MAX, and AVG

The SPJ table (Figure CT.6) contains the quantity of each part each supplier supplies for each job. To find the minimum, maximum, and average number of parts supplied by supplier S2, the SELECT statement must identify the quantities in rows where supplier number is S2 and apply the MIN, MAX, and AVG operators to those amounts:

```
SELECT MIN(QTY), AVG(QTY), MAX(QTY)
FROM   SPJ
WHERE  SN = 'S2';
```

Eight rows satisfy the WHERE clause. In those rows, the minimum QTY value is 100, and the maximum is 800. The average QTY for those rows is 400. The statement returns:

MIN(QTY)	AVG(QTY)	MAX(QTY)
100	400	800

Headings above the resulting values may or may not be returned depending on the interactive tool that is being used and whether the AS clause is used. The AS clause can be used to assign a name to the result of a column function or to a calculated expression. The AS name appears as the column heading when using QMF or SPUFI as will be seen in the following example.

Math in the SELECT Clause

Suppose we want to know the difference between the maximum quantity and the average for parts supplied by S2. A simple adjustment of the SELECT clause, inclusion of a minus sign, provides the answer:

```
SELECT MAX(QTY) - AVG(QTY) AS DIFFERENCE
FROM   SPJ
WHERE  SN = 'S2';
```

DIFFERENCE
400

The SELECT clause can handle more complex calculations. When functions are used in combination in SELECT equations, SQL follows the standard order of operations. It first computes expressions within parentheses, beginning with the innermost set if parentheses are nested. Then it performs multiplication and division before addition and subtraction. For example, to calculate the difference between the maximum quantity and average quantity that we have just found as a percentage of the average, we must divide the difference by the average and multiply by 100. Here is that computation in the SELECT clause:

```
SELECT (MAX(QTY) - AVG(QTY)) / AVG(QTY) * 100
```

The parentheses enclosing the subtraction are necessary to ensure the operation is performed first, as the computation demands. The answer in this case is 100. Suppose the parentheses were forgotten. The clause would be:

```
SELECT MAX(QTY) - AVG(QTY) / AVG(QTY) * 100
```

SQL would perform the division and multiplication first (400/400*100 = 100) and then the subtraction (800 - 100 = 700), not the intended computation.

COUNT Column Function

The COUNT column function can be used to count the number of rows in a table or the number of rows that meet a specified condition. When COUNT is followed by an asterisk in parentheses and there is no WHERE clause, the number of rows in the table is returned.

```
SELECT COUNT(*) AS NROWS
FROM   SPJ;
```

NROWS
24

If a WHERE clause is specified, the COUNT function counts all rows that satisfy the condition.

```
SELECT COUNT(*) AS NROWSP3
FROM   SPJ
WHERE  PN = 'P3';
```

NROWSP3
9

DISTINCT Function

Although the DISTINCT function is not a column function per se, it can be used with column functions. It filters out all redundant column values in the rows satisfying the WHERE clause or, if no WHERE clause is used, of the entire table. For example, the following statement would be used to find the unique supplier number and part number pairs that appear in the SPJ table. Notice that DISTINCT applies to all the columns in the SELECT clause even though commas separate the columns.

```
SELECT DISTINCT SN, PN
FROM   SPJ;
```

SN	PN
S1	P1
S2	P3
S2	P5
S3	P3
S3	P4
S4	P6
S5	P1
S5	P2
S5	P3
S5	P4
S5	P5
S5	P6

DISTINCT can work with column functions, removing the repeated values before performing the specified function. For that use, DISTINCT is specified within parentheses, along with the name of the column being acted upon. Here we want to determine the number of unique PNs in the SPJ table:

```
SELECT COUNT (DISTINCT PN) AS UNIQUEPN
FROM   SPJ;
```

UNIQUEPN
6

SL.4 DATA-TYPE CONVERSIONS

DB2 offers a number of scalar functions that can be used in the SELECT or WHERE clause for converting the data types of values from columns, host-language variables, and calculations. Scalar functions act on a single value in contrast to a column function which usually acts on multiple values in a column. We will discuss many of the basic scalar function in this chapter. There are many user defined function and you can develop more as discussed with Chapter UD. The performance implications of scalar and column functions are discussed in Chapter PP.

The scalar function DIGITS converts a numeric value to a character string with leading zeros and without a sign or decimal point. If the value is a SMALLINT type, the result is a 5-byte string; if it is an INTEGER type, the result is a 10-byte string; and if it is a DECIMAL, the result has the same number of digits as the original value.

The function CHAR can be used to convert a decimal data type to a character string. This can be useful for converting very large numbers to a character representation for reporting purposes. Most host languages support a decimal value no greater than the equivalent of DECIMAL(15). DB2 supports numbers up to and including DECIMAL(31) if DEC31 is specified in DSNZPARM. The following statement converts a very large DEBT column value to a character string for reporting with a sign and decimal point assuming that :DEBT is declared as PIC X(33) in a COBOL program. EXEC SQL and END-EXEC are discussed in Chapter PD.

```
EXEC SQL SELECT CHAR(DEBT)
     INTO   :DEBT
     FROM   BUDGET
     WHERE  ID = :ID
END-EXEC.
```

If you need to override the DEC15 default for the DB2 subsystem when using dynamic SQL (discussed in Chapter PD), the CURRENT PRECISION special register can be set like:

SET CURRENT PRECISION = ' DEC31'

You can determine the current precision like:

SET :HVDEC = CURRENT PRECISION

The function DECIMAL can be used to convert a numeric value in a character data type to a decimal data type. For example, assume NUMERICID = '123456 ', DECIMAL (NUMERICID, 6,0) results in a decimal value of 123456. Notice that the trailing blanks are truncated.

The function DECIMAL can also be used to convert any numeric data type into a packed decimal data type. If the numeric value to be converted is called BALANCE, the command DECIMAL (BALANCE, 6,2) changes it to a packed decimal with a precision of six and two decimal places. A typical conversion of a calculation would be DECIMAL (AVG(BALANCE, 6,2)), which computes the average of BALANCE and returns it with a precision of six and two decimal places. FLOAT(BALANCE) converts a numeric BALANCE to a double precision floating point number.

The INTEGER function works in a similar fashion to convert any numeric type to an integer. It is particularly useful for rounding off numerals. For example, INTEGER (AMOUNT + 0.5) rounds up and truncates to an integer any numeric AMOUNT with a fractional part of 0.5 or more and rounds down to an integer any decimal amount with a fractional part less than 0.5. The result is a 4-byte binary number. The ROUND user-defined function discussed in Chapter UD is a good alternative and offers a good deal of flexibility. When INTEGER is used with a mathematical function such as SUM, the order of the functions in a statement is important. For example, the clause INTEGER (SUM (AMOUNT + 0.5)) sums the AMOUNT values and round off the result. The command SUM (INTEGER (AMOUNT + 0.5)) rounds off the AMOUNT values before summing.

The HEX function converts any data type other than LONG VARCHAR to hexadecimal representation. The results are presented as a VARCHAR type with twice as many bytes as the original value. The HEX function is useful for converting values in the START_RBA column of the catalog table SYSIBM.SYSCOPY. This column presents the relative byte address (RBA) to which the RECOVER utility should recover in a log. The utility requires that the RBA be presented in hexadecimal representation.

Finally the VARGRAPHIC function converts a character string of 254 bytes or fewer to a double-byte DBCS representation, which is used for Asian Katakana ideograms.

SL.5 STRING MANIPULATION FUNCTIONS

DB2 provides several scalar functions for manipulating character strings.

Substring Function

The substring function (SUBSTR) extracts a portion of a character string, with numbers presented with the string value's name indicating which alphanumeric value begins the extract and the number of characters to be included. For example, SUBSTR (SNAME, 1,3) instructs DB2 to begin with the first character in the SNAME value and include three bytes. If the SNAME value were JACKSON, the function's result would be JAC. If there are not enough characters to fill the receiving host variable or column, the result is padded with trailing blanks.

One interesting use for SUBSTR in conjunction with DIGITS is to break apart intelligent identification numbers (those including codes). For example, the seventh digit of a part identification number of INTEGER type might indicate the city in which it is stored. An SQL statement like this might be used to select according to that digit:

```
SELECT  CITY, QTY
FROM    INVENTORY
WHERE   SUBSTR (DIGITS (PARTID), 7,1) = '4';
```

In the WHERE clause, DIGITS converts PARTID to a character string, and SUBSTR extracts the seventh character. If that character is '4', the search criterion is satisfied.

Concatenation Function

The concatenation function is in a way the reverse of the substring function. Rather than taking strings apart, as SUBSTR does, concatenation puts them together. The function can be used to combine any combination of character variables and literals. Concatenation is used in the SELECT clause to format results or in a WHERE clause to put data in the desired format for processing and is invoked with the CONCAT operator. In the statement's results, the character string coming before CONCAT is joined with that after the CONCAT operator. Literals are enclosed in single quotes.

For example, the following statement finds the names and colors of parts stored in London, and returns them, separated by a comma and a space:

```
SELECT  PNAME CONCAT ',' CONCAT COLOR
FROM    P
WHERE   CITY = 'London';
```

Nut   , RED
Screw , RED
Cog   , RED

Notice that these results assume that PNAME has been declared as CHAR(5). For CHAR columns, the concatenation takes place after the trailing blanks that pad a value to the column's length. For VARCHAR columns, concatenation takes place immediately after each value's final character.

If PNAME is declared VARCHAR, the results is:

Nut, RED
Screw, RED
Cog, RED

Another string manipulation function, LENGTH, counts the number of bytes, or characters, in a CHAR or VARCHAR value, excluding bytes used as null and VARCHAR indicators. LENGTH includes a count of trailing blanks for CHAR columns. VARCHAR columns have no trailing blanks. The result is an integer.

STRIP Function

The STRIP function can be used to remove a specified character (blank is the default) from leading, trailing, or both the leading and trailing (default) positions of a character data type column or field. If the CITY column has the value of ' Copenhagen ', the function STRIP(CITY, BOTH, ' ') results in 'Copenhagen'. Actually all that is needed in this case is STRIP(CITY) to give the result of 'Copenhagen'. This is because the second operand of BOTH is the default and the default for the third operand is blank (' ').

You can indicate that only the leading or trailing specified characters are to be removed. For example, if the AMOUNT host variable contains '0014.950' and the function STRIP(AMOUNT, LEADING, '0') is applied the result is 14.950 with the leading zeros stripped off. Similarly, the function STRIP(AMOUNT, TRAILING, '0') results in 0014.95 with the trailing zeros stripped off.

COALESCE and VALUE Functions

COALESCE and VALUE are synonyms. COALESCE conforms to the SQL standard. These scalar functions provide flexibility for handling nulls and zeros in computations. Without the use of one of these functions, for example, division by null or zero would result in a negative SQLCODE, which indicates an error. If the COALESCE function is applied to the division by zero or null, the result is a null. The calculation COALESCE (AMOUNT/PERCENT) returns null whenever PERCENT is zero or null.

COALESCE can also be used to substitute a numeric value for any nulls used in computations. That function is used by identifying the value to be substituted for nulls after the name of the data item used in the computation. For example, in the calculation NET_SALARY - COALESCE (INSURANCE, 0), zero is subtracted from NET_SALARY whenever INSURANCE is a null. Otherwise if the null was subtracted, the result would also be null. Similarly, adding a null or multiplying by null results in null.

NULLIF Function

The NULLIF function is useful for dealing with a value used to represent that no valid value exists. Chapter CT discusses alternatives for representing unknown values. One alternative is to define a column such that a specified value will be placed in the column when a row is inserted into the table without giving a value for the column. For example, the WEIGHT column can be defined as WEIGHT INTEGER WITH DEFAULT -1. This results in a -1 being placed in the WEIGHT column if the user does not know the weight of a part when information about a new part is inserted into the table.

If the user requests the total weight of parts in London for shipment to Edinburgh, the -1 value should not be included in the sum. This can be accomplished like:

```
SELECT SUM(NULLIF(WEIGHT, -1))
FROM   P
WHERE  CITY = 'London';
```

The NULLIF function avoids including any -1 values in the summation. If the first and second operands are equal, a null is returned and, as we saw in Section SL.5, null is not included in the calculation of a column function. In the example, if WEIGHT = -1, a null is returned and is not included in the summation. If the first and second operands are not equal, the first operand value is returned and in this case included in the summation which is the desired result. Although, the user should be notified if the total weight does not include some parts to be shipped to Edinburgh, particularly if the user is estimating the costs to ship the parts and the costs are based on the weight.

SL.6 DATE AND TIME FUNCTIONS AND CALCULATIONS

DB2 offers a number of functions for working with its three date and time data types—DATE, TIME, and TIMESTAMP—and a number of calculations that may be used with the data types. The flexibility of the DATE and TIME data types begins with the formats of the dates and times they represent, which include international, U.S., European, and Japanese standards. Examples of the formats are given in Figure CT.3. The International Standard Organization's (ISO) formats are the defaults, but the system's installer can change these defaults. The default values are used unless the SQL statement using DATE or TIME specifies otherwise. The format can also be chosen for an application program at precompile time.

The CHAR function is used in SQL statements to specify a format for a DATE or TIME value other than the default. For example, if the default is the ISO standard but the programmer wants to use the USA standard, the CHAR function used with the column name makes the conversion. The syntax is CHAR(DATE_COL, USA), where DATE_COL is the column name and USA is the desired format. The conversion returns the date as a character string with USA punctuation, 06/23/1987, for example. If the punctuation is not desired, the HEX function can be used like: HEX(DATE_COL). The CHAR function can also be used to convert the results of date or time calculations to character strings rather than the decimal representation that would otherwise result. For example, CHAR(DATE_COL - 60 DAYS) would subtract 60 days from the value in the DATE_COL column and return the result as a character string. CHAR includes the delimiters—the dashes or slashes—that are part of the DATE representation.

DB2 offers a number of scalar functions for extracting only part of a DATE, TIME, or TIMESTAMP. For example, MONTH(DATE_COL) returns only the month. If DATE_COL held 12/15/1989, 12 would be returned. The DAY and YEAR functions work similarly for the day or year portion of a DATE value. And the HOUR, MINUTE, and SECOND functions return those portions of TIME values. The MICROSECOND function returns the microsecond portion of a TIMESTAMP column.

DATE and TIME values may participate in several types of calculations. One type involves the addition or subtraction of labeled durations. For example, any number of years, months, or days may be added to or subtracted from a DATE value. The syntax simply identifies the date column, followed by a plus or minus sign, followed by the number of units and the unit's name—YEARS, MONTHS, or DAYS. But the result of the addition or subtraction is not so straightforward.

YEAR and MONTH Calculations

In most cases, the YEARS or MONTHS calculation results in the same date as the original DATE value, plus or minus the number of units indicated, regardless of the number of days in the interval covered by the addition or subtraction. Consider the calculation DATE_COL + 1 MONTHS, for example, when the DATE value is '09/30/1989'. Although the following month, October, has 31 days, DB2 does not add that many days. Instead it returns '10/30/1989', the same date plus one month.

Remember, that is in most cases. Some dates, however, exist in some months or years, but not others. For example, the calculation '08/31/1989' + 1 MONTH could not result in '09/31/1989', since September has only 30 days. In these cases, DB2 returns the last day of the appropriate month; in the example, '9/30/1989'. The same principle applies to a labeled duration calculation that would result in February 29 of a non-leap year.

Use of the DAYS units provides more precise results, with the result date being exactly the number of days added or removed from the original date as the number indicated in the calculation—for example, '09/30/1989' + 31 days = '10/31/1989'.

Last Day of Month Calculations

Often a program may have to know the last day of the current month—so that bills can be sent out on that date, for example. But the last date of a month might be the twenty-eighth, twenty-ninth, thirtieth, or thirty-first. The following clause using a combination of DATE and string functions can determine the current month's last date, no matter the month or year.
Imagine a PARTS_ORDERED table that includes a column, SCHED_DATE, showing the scheduled delivery date for all ordered parts. For accounting purposes, we want to know which parts are scheduled to be delivered after the last day of the current month. This statement finds that information:

```
SELECT PN
FROM   PARTS_ORDERED
WHERE  SCHED_DATE
       DATE(SUBSTR(CHAR(CURRENT DATE, ISO), 1,8)
       CONCAT '01')
       + 1 MONTH - 1 DAY;
```

The clause beginning "DATE" determines the current month's last date. Assuming a current date of February 15, 1989, the following list presents the results of each element in the clause, beginning with the innermost parentheses:

```
1. CHAR(CURRENT DATE, ISO)  = 1989-02-15
2. SUBSTR(..., 1,8)         = 1989-02-
3. (...CONCAT '01')         = 1989-02-01
4. (...) + 1 MONTH          = 1989-03-01
5. (...) - 1 DAY            = 1989-02-28
```

In the first step, the CHAR function puts the current date into a character string in the ISO format. The second step uses the substring function to truncate that date to just the year and month. Step three's concatenation sets the date to the first of the month. Step four's addition of a month sets the date at the first day of the next month. The final step subtracts a day, resulting in the final day of the current month. DATE at the beginning converts the date to the DATE data type for DB2's use in the comparison.

TIME Calculations

Addition or subtraction of time units to a TIME value is similar to date calculations but without some of the complications. The labeled units are HOURS, MINUTES, and SECONDS. The time calculations take into account the 24-hour representation for the ISO, European, and Japanese formats and the 12-hour representation for the USA format. For example, if 12 hours were added to a non-USA format TIME value of '16.30.00', the result would be '04.30.00'. If 12 hours were added to a USA format TIME value of '04:30 AM', the result would be '04:30 PM'. All of the labeled durations available for TIME and DATE values may also be used in TIMESTAMP calculations. In addition, MICROSECOND can be used in TIMESTAMP calculations.

Subtracting DATE and TIME Values

DATE values may be subtracted from one another but not added, and TIME values may be subtracted from one another but not added. In addition, DATE or TIME values may be subtracted, respectively, from special registers called CURRENT DATE and CURRENT TIME, which represent exactly what their names say. DB2 also provides CURRENT TIMESTAMP and CURRENT TIMEZONE, the latter of which provides the time duration of the local time zone from GMT (Greenwich Mean Time). (GMT is now known as the universal time coordinate). When subtraction of these values occurs, the results take the special form YYYYMMDD, which is a packed decimal type representing the number of years, months, and days that the subtraction yields. For example, if the CURRENT DATE is '06/20/1989', subtracting a DATE value of '03/30/1987' yields 00020221, for 2 years, 2 months, and 21 days.

DB2 performs subtractions on dates with differing formats. For instance, using the PARTS_ORDERED table from the above example and assuming SCHED_DATE is in ISO format, DB2 can handle this statement to determine which parts are due to arrive at least two years after December 31, 1989:

```
SELECT PN
FROM   PARTS_ORDERED
WHERE  YEAR(SCHED_DATE - '12/31/1989') > 2;
```

Notice that SCHED_DATE is in the ISO format but '12/31/1989' is in USA date format. Notice also that '12/31/1989' is not even identified as a date. It is merely a character string. DB2 recognizes the string's format as a date and treats it as such.

The DAYS Function

The DAYS function provides a way to calculate the number of days between two DATE values. DAYS determines the number of days between a given date and 12/31/0000. That number by itself is rarely useful; however, by determining the DAYS values for two dates and subtracting one from the other, DB2 finds the number of days separating the two dates. For example, for a DATE_COL1 value of '02/28/1989' and a DATE_COL2 value of '01/31/1989', the calculation DAYS(DATE_COL1) — DAYS(DATE_COL2) returns 28.

Day of the Week: The DAYS function is useful in determining the day of the week of a given date in a column or host variable of DATEREC prior to V6, for example.

```
SELECT DAYS(DATEREC)  -  (DAYS(DATEREC) -1) / 7 * 7
FROM   PARTS_ORDERED;
```

The values returned are 1, 2, 3, 4, 5, 6, or 7 representing Monday, Tuesday, Wednesday, Thursday, Friday, Saturday, or Sunday.

DAYOFWEEK user-defined function can be used to retrieve the day of the week (1 represents Sunday) as discussed in the UD Chapter in V6.

A similar calculation can be used to determine the Monday on or before DATEREC:

```
SELECT DATE((DAYS(DATEREC)  - 1) / 7 * 7 + 1)
FROM   PARTS_ORDERED;
```

If the Monday after DATEREC is required, the following calculation provides the date:

```
SELECT DATE((DAYS(DATEREC)  - 1) / 7 * 7 + 1 + 7)
FROM   PARTS_ORDERED;
```

If Tuesday is required, -2, +2 rather than -1, +1 should be used in the calculation. If Wednesday is required, -3, +3 rather than -1, +1 should be used. For Thursday and the remaining days of the week increment by -1 or +1 for each of days.

Converting to the DATE Data Type

If dates are stored as character or numeric types in a format DB2 does not accept, the DATE function and string manipulations in an SQL statement can convert them to the proper type and format. Suppose ORDER_DATE is stored as a CHAR(6) type in the form YYMMDD. This statement converts ORDER_DATE values to a DATE type in the ISO format:

```
SELECT DATE ('19'
       CONCAT SUBSTR(ORDER_DATE,1,2,) CONCAT '-'
       CONCAT SUBSTR(ORDER_DATE,3,2)  CONCAT '-'
       CONCAT SUBSTR(ORDER_DATE,5,2))
FROM   PARTS_ORDERED
WHERE  SN = 'S4';
```

Looking at an example date helps one understand how the statement works. Suppose ORDER_DATE has the value of 880131. The statement in the parentheses begins with '19'. Concatenated with that is the substring of ORDER_DATE, beginning with the first position and including two characters—'88'. That yields '1988'. The next concatenation adds the hyphen, '1988', and the next adds a two-character substring from ORDER_DATE beginning at position 3—'01'. So far, we have '1988-01'. The next concatenation adds another hyphen and the final one adds the final two characters from the string—'1988-01-31'. The DATE function then converts that character string to the DATE data type.

If ORDER_DATE were stored as a DECIMAL or INTEGER, the conversion statement would be only slightly different, having to account first for the conversion from the numeric to character type before the substring function can be used. The following statement handles the conversion of either DECIMAL or INTEGER types:

```
SELECT DATE('19'
       CONCAT SUBSTR(DIGITS(ORDER_DATE),1,2) CONCAT '-'
       CONCAT SUBSTR(DIGITS(ORDER_DATE),3,2) CONCAT '-'
       CONCAT SUBSTR(DIGITS(ORDER_DATE),5,2))
FROM   PARTS_ORDERED
WHERE  SN = 'S4';
```

The DATE function is also useful in counting the number of orders placed since the first of last month including this month regardless of today's date.

```
SELECT COUNT(*)
FROM   PARTS_ORDERED
WHERE  ORDER_DATE >
       DATE(SUBSTR(CHAR(CURRENT DATE, ISO),1,8)
       CONCAT '01') - 1 MONTH;
```

Use of Scalar Functions without Selecting from a One Row Table

Most host languages do not support all of the scalar function available in DB2. The SET or VALUE statement provide for the use of the scalar functions within a host program. For example, you can determine the month portion of ORDER_DATE like:

```
EXEC SQL SET :MO = MONTH(ORDER_DATE) END-EXEC.
```

<u>or</u>

```
EXEC SQL VALUES(MONTH(ORDER_DATE)
         INTO   :MO END-EXEC.
```

Use of functions interactively require selecting from a one row table as in the following example. The catalog table SYSIBM.SYSDUMMY1 is designed for this purpose.

```
SELECT MONTH(ORDER_DATE)
FROM   SYSIBM.SYSDUMMY1;
```

Recommendation: The SET and VALUES statements have performance advantage over selecting from a one row table. Therefore, do consider the use of these statements in a host language program.

SL.7 SELECTING BY GROUPS

The GROUP BY clause may be used in SELECT statements for searches designed to return a single value—a sum or minimum, for example. But rather than performing the search and returning the value for an entire column, GROUP BY separates the rows into groups according to duplicate values in the named column and then operates on each group. In other words, the GROUP BY operator creates a separate group for each distinct value in the named column. Then it performs the column function on each group and returns a single row for each group. Grouped by CITY, for example, the Supplier table has three groups: for London, Paris, and Athens. This statement, then, finds the maximum supplier status in each city:

```
SELECT CITY, MAX(STATUS)
FROM   S
GROUP  BY CITY;
```

CITY	MAX(STATUS)
London	20
Paris	30
Athens	30

A HAVING clause works like a WHERE clause to qualify a search, but the HAVING clause criteria applies to each groups created with a GROUP BY clause rather than to individual rows, for example:

```
SELECT CITY, MAX(STATUS)
FROM   S
GROUP  BY CITY
HAVING COUNT(*) > 1;
```

CITY	MAX(STATUS)
London	20
Paris	30

SQL applies the HAVING clause criteria to each group. In this case, it counts the values in each group, eliminates any group having fewer than two, and returns the maximum value for those remaining. Basically it eliminates unwanted groups. A way of thinking about the HAVING clause is to pretend that the GROUP BY results are written to a work file (this is true only if a sort is required) like:

CITY	COUNT(*)
London	2
Paris	2
Athens	1

The conditions specified in the HAVING clause (HAVING COUNT(*) > 1 in the example) is applied to the pretend work file. Athens is not included in the result as indicated by the being crossed out in the table. This is because there is only one supplier in the city. The unwanted group is eliminated.

GROUP BY can establish groups according to the values in more than one column, creating a separate group for each unique combination of values in the columns specified. A select from the SPJ table might group according to supplier number and part number (GROUP BY SN, PN). In that case, the S1-P1 combination represents a group, consisting of two rows, the S2-P3 combination forms a group with seven rows, and so on. The number of columns that may be used in a GROUP BY clause is limited by the total number of bytes in their columns. Theoretically DB2 allows columns totaling 4000 bytes to make up a GROUP BY clause, which should allow enough columns to satisfy almost any request.

Notice that any column included in the SELECT clause of a statement that contains a GROUP BY clause must either have an associated column function or appear in the GROUP BY clause. The function returns a single value based on the information in the indicated column for the grouped rows. But which of the group's values would the select return if no function was specified? For example, suppose that in the above statement, the SELECT clause had included the SNAME column. Which supplier name would SQL return with the London row?

SL.8 SEQUENCING THE QUALIFYING ROWS

JN	PN	QTY
J1	P3	400
J2	P4	500
J4	P1	700
J4	P3	500
J4	P4	800
J4	P5	400
J4	P6	500
J5	P3	600
J5	P5	500
J6	P3	400
J7	P3	800

An ORDER BY clause, placed at the end of a select, tells SQL the sequence in which to present the results. The user can specify sequencing by one or more of the columns. It is not necessary to select columns specified in ORDER BY clause (V5 APAR PQ23778). SQL sequences first according to the first column indicated. Then within each group created by the first sequence, it sequences according to the second column indicated, and so on—for example:

```
SELECT JN, PN, QTY
FROM   SPJ
WHERE  QTY >= 400
ORDER BY JN, PN;
```

The rows are sequenced by job numbers—J1, J2, J4, J5, J6, J7. Then within groups of rows having duplicate job numbers, the rows are sequenced by part number—J4-P1, J4-P3, J4-P4, and so on. As with the GROUP BY statement, the maximum number of columns that may be used with an ORDER BY depends on the total length of the column values, with 4000 bytes being the limit.

The ORDER BY clause need not identify the returned column or columns to be used in the sequence by name. Instead it can identify them by their position in the SELECT clause. An equivalent ORDER BY clause for the above statement would be ORDER BY 1, 2. This facility is useful for substituting for long column names.

The position must be specified if the ORDER BY is on a calculated expression or an AS name can be assigned. For example, it is necessary to ORDER BY 4 or the AS name of INCREASE in the statement:

```
SELECT JN, PN, QTY, QTY * 1.10 AS INCREASE
FROM   SPJ
ORDER  BY INCREASE;
```

DB2 sequences null values as being higher than any other value. It will sequence in ascending or descending order. Ascending is the default. A user specifies descending order by placing the word DESC after the column in the ORDER BY clause—for example, ORDER BY PN DESC.

SL.9 CASE EXPRESSIONS

CASE expressions can reduce the number of SQL statements that must be developed, tested, and maintained. They offer performance benefits, particularly when multiple tablespace scans for each of several SELECT statements can be avoided with the use of a CASE expression.

A CASE expression yields a constant or computed value based on finding which of several conditions are true. CASE can be used in a SELECT statement in SET, or the WHERE clause of an UPDATE statement. The expression in a CASE clause is similar to SELECT and WHERE clause expressions.

One use of a CASE expression is to report on text rather than a code that appears in a column of a table. A column name tested for equality can be in the CASE or WHEN clause. Here is an example of testing the SEX column for a value of 'M' and 'F' and returning the value of 'Male' and 'Female' for the corresponding code.

```
SELECT EMPNO, LASTNAME,
CASE SEX
     WHEN 'M' THEN 'Male'
     WHEN 'F' THEN 'Female'
     ELSE 'UNKNOWN'
END AS GENDER
FROM   EMP
WHERE  WORKDEPT = 'D4';
```

If the ELSE clause is not used, null is the result for a row that does not match the WHEN condition. The AS name following the END delimiter is optional. In the example, GENDER is the column heading for a report generated using an interactive tool.

A good way to read a CASE expression is to say in case an 'M' is found in the SEX column, then return 'Male'. In case an 'F' is found in the SEX column, then return 'Female'. If neither value tested in the WHEN clauses is found, then return 'UNKNOWN'.

Additional details on CASE expressions is in Chapter PP.

SL.10 SUBSELECTS

Subselects are SELECTS that work in conjunction with other SELECTS, providing values that determine part of the search criteria. In simple as opposed to correlated subselects, DB2 usually first performs the subselect, or inner select, presented within parentheses below the primary, or outer, select. The value or values returned for the subselect provide values for the search criteria for the primary select.

In correlated subselects, the subselect's search criteria depend on values from the table identified in the outer select. SQL evaluates the outer select first and passes a value to the subselect, which returns values one at a time to be used in completion of the outer select. Both types of subselects can best be explained through examples.

To understand a simple subselect, consider a search for parts that exceed the average weight of all the parts kept in London. A subselect can determine the average weight and pass that value to a primary select that locates the heavier parts:

```
SELECT PNAME, WEIGHT
FROM   P
WHERE  WEIGHT >
  (SELECT AVG(WEIGHT)
   FROM   P
   WHERE  CITY = 'London');
```

PNAME	WEIGHT
Screw	17
Bolt	17
Cog	19

Subselect Returning Multiple Values

Subselects can also pass multiple values to the primary select, most frequently done by using the IN operator in the primary select to address a set of values returned by the subselect. To determine the part number and name of parts supplied by supplier S2, for example, a subselect can locate S2's part numbers in the SPJ table and pass that set to a select that finds those parts' names in the P table. The statement for this select is:

```
SELECT PN, PNAME
FROM   P
WHERE  PN IN
   (SELECT PN
    FROM   SPJ
    WHERE  SN = 'S2');
```

PN	PNAME
P3	Screw
P5	Cam

The primary select can also use three other operators—ALL, ANY, and SOME—to address sets of values returned by the subselect. Used in the select's WHERE clause, ALL, ANY, or SOME instructs the select to find rows based on their comparison to the values in the returned set. For ALL, each returned row satisfies the comparison against all values in the set. For ANY and SOME, which are equivalent, each satisfies the comparison against at least one value in the set. For example, the following statement determines all parts that weigh more than each and every part stored in Paris:

```
SELECT PNAME, WEIGHT, CITY
FROM   P
WHERE  WEIGHT > ALL
   (SELECT WEIGHT
    FROM   P
    WHERE  CITY = 'Paris');
```

The words ANY and ALL are somewhat ambiguous and do not naturally carry to some users the operators' precise meanings. Moreover, SQL's handling of unknown values with respect to these operators can be misleading. Since searches provided by the ANY, ALL, and SOME operators can be performed with equivalent statements using more straightforward terminology, users may be wise to avoid these operators entirely rather than having to deal with their somewhat confusing distinctions. For example, selecting parts that weigh more than each and every part stored in Paris is the same as selecting parts that weigh more than the heaviest part stored in Paris. The MAX operator can identify those rows.

```
SELECT PNAME, WEIGHT, CITY
FROM   P
WHERE  WEIGHT >
   (SELECT MAX(WEIGHT)
    FROM   P
    WHERE  CITY = 'Paris');
```

If COALESCE(MAX(WEIGHT), 0) is used, all parts > 0 are returned.

The MIN operator can perform the function of ANY or SOME. To say that a given value is greater than any or some of the values in a set is the same as saying that it is greater than the least value in the set and that the different formulation returns the same results.

Care must be exercised if there is a possibility that no rows will qualify for the subselect when using ALL and MAX interchangeably since the result can differ. If there are no parts in Paris, all weights are greater than an empty set, but no weights are greater than a null from MAX. If there are parts in Paris, MAX returns the same results as does ALL. MIN and ANY or SOME return the same results regardless of whether rows qualify in the subselect. No weights are greater than an empty set, and no weights are greater than a null MIN.

Nulls are also troublesome if they appear in rows in a table processed in a subselect. Assume for a moment that the PN column contains a null in the SPJ table and that there is a P99 in the P table. It is necessary to determine information on parts in P that are not used on jobs in SPJ, and the statement used is:

```
SELECT PN, PNAME, COLOR, WEIGHT, CITY
FROM   P
WHERE  PN NOT IN
  (SELECT PN
   FROM   SPJ);
```

The P99 in the P table is not identified. The rational is that the unknown value in the SPJ might be P99. Either of the following two formulations of the request identifies the P99 that is not currently being used on any job.

```
SELECT PN, PNAME, COLOR, WEIGHT, CITY
FROM   P
WHERE  PN NOT IN
  (SELECT PN
   FROM   SPJ
   WHERE  SPJ.PN IS NOT NULL);
```

The subselect excludes any nulls with the predicate WHERE SPJ.PN IS NOT NULL. These are just a few of the potential problems when dealing with nulls and the reason that most developers do not allow for nulls in most columns.

Nested Subselects

A subselect can pass an intermediate answer set to a subselect that uses it in defining the search criteria that allow it to pass an intermediate answer to another subselect, and so on for up to 15 subselects in a single SQL statement. Each subselect can reference up to 15 tables in the FROM clause. A single SQL statement including its subselects cannot exceed 32,767 bytes.

In most cases, SQL executes the innermost subselect first and works its way up. This is a non-correlated subselect (correlated subselects are discussed in the Correlated Subselects subsection that follows). For example, a search to locate the part number and name for parts supplied by supplier Jones would be similar to the search presented above in which we found the part numbers and names for parts supplied by S2. In this case, however, an additional subselect is needed to find Jones's supplier number. The necessary statement is:

```
SELECT PN, PNAME
FROM   P
WHERE  PN IN
  (SELECT PN
   FROM   SPJ
   WHERE  SN =
     (SELECT SN
      FROM   S
      WHERE  SNAME = 'Jones'));
```

PN	PNAME
P3	Screw
P5	Cam

Correlated Subselects

In a correlated subselect, the outer select identifies a table from which SQL draws values for use in the subselect. The outer select passes one value from a row at a time from the identified table to the subselect, which uses the column specified in the subselect to perform the subselect. For example, to determine the names of parts used on job 1, the search can check each part listed in the P table against all the parts listed in the SPJ table. When the part number (PN) from P matches the PN from SPJ, and the job number equals J1, the select returns that part's name. The correlation name of PX as specified with the AS clause in the outer select (first select) is used in the inner select (second select) to refer back to the outer select. An alternative to specifying the AS name in the FROM clause is to separate the table name form the correlation name with a space (FROM P PX, for example). This statement satisfies the search:

```
SELECT PNAME
FROM   P AS PX
WHERE  'J1' IN
  (SELECT JN
   FROM   SPJ
   WHERE  SPJ.SN = PX.PN);
```

To perform this search, SQL first passes the first part number from the P table to the subselect. The subselect uses the part number, P1 for example, from that row in its search. This search finds P1 used in two jobs—J1 and J4—which make up the set returned to the outer select for evaluation with the IN operator. Since J1 is the first value returned, the outer select returns PNAME from the P1 row in the P table—Nut. SQL continues the process by passing to the subselect each subsequent part number from the P table in turn. Try continuing the search using the remaining values from the P table.

Chapter ST discusses the performance implications of subselects.

SL.11 INTERSECTION AND DIFFERENCE

In set operations, *intersection* represents the values common to both original sets. *Difference* represents the values of one set that do not also belong to the second set. EXISTS and NOT EXISTS subselects can be used to determine the intersection and difference. The subselect (second select in parentheses) returns a true or false to the outer select (first select) depending on the subselect evaluation. For EXISTS, if there is a value satisfying the subselect, the operator returns true. For NOT EXISTS, if there is no value satisfying the subselect, the operator returns true. The outer select includes a row whenever the subselect returns a true evaluation.

Intersection: A select to determine the cities that have both suppliers and part stocks represents the intersection of the two sets of city values from S and P tables.

This statement can be used to determine that intersection (SELECT CITY rather than SELECT 1 in the subselect can be specified as discussed in Chapter ST):

```
SELECT DISTINCT CITY
FROM   S AS SX
WHERE  EXISTS
  (SELECT 1
   FROM   P
   WHERE  P.CITY = SX.CITY);
```

CITY
London
Paris

DB2 performs the search by passing the first city from S to the subselect, which finds a match for London and therefore returns a true evaluation. The outer select therefore includes the row, returning London. Then it continues the process for each subsequent row. The shaded area in Figure SL.1 represents the intersection. Notice that the only cities that appear in both S and P are London and Paris.

Figure SL.1. Intersection

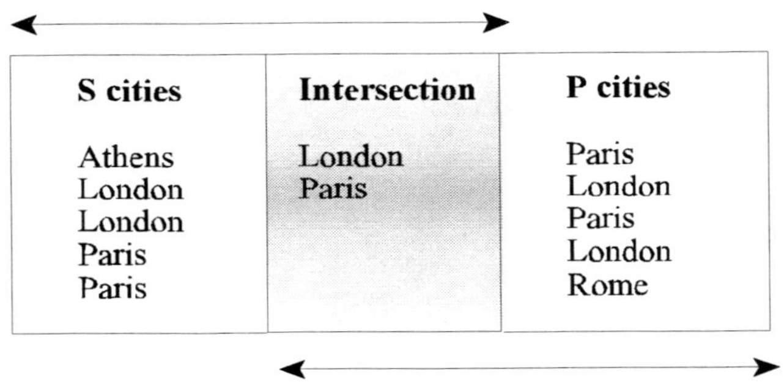

Difference: Similarly a search to determine whether there are any cities with parts but no suppliers, found by subtracting the cities in S from those in P, would represent a difference. The statement to determine this difference is:

```
SELECT DISTINCT CITY
FROM   P AS PX
WHERE  NOT EXISTS
  (SELECT 1
   FROM   S
   WHERE  CITY = PX.CITY);
```

CITY
Rome

If the CITY value from a row in P does not match any CITY value in S, the subselect returns a true value for the NOT EXISTS operator, causing the outer select to return that CITY. In this case, the difference between PART cities and SUPPLIER cities is Rome. The shaded area in Figure SL.2 represents the difference. Notice that Rome is the only remaining P city after subtracting the S cities.

Figure SL.2. Difference

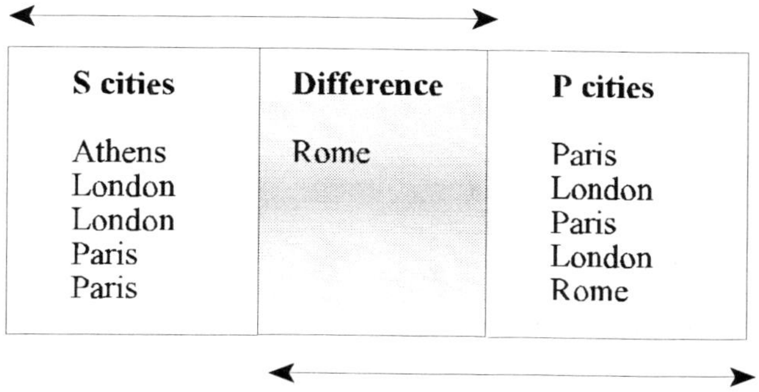

SL.12 NESTED TABLE EXPRESSIONS

A nested table expression looks a bit like a subselect in that it is a SELECT statement enclosed in parentheses. However, a table expression appears in the FROM clause and a subselect appears in the WHERE clause. Here is an example of using a table expression to determine the suppliers who supply > 1000 parts to jobs.

```
SELECT SN, TOTAL_PARTS
      FROM   (SELECT SN, SUM(QTY) AS TOTAL_PARTS
              FROM   SPJ
              GROUP BY SN) AS SUMQTYBYSN
      WHERE   TOTAL_PARTS > 1000;
```

SN	TOTAL_ PARTS
S1	900
S2	3200
S3	700
S4	600
S5	3100

The result of the table expression is given a name. In the example, the name is SUMQTYBYSN. The result of column functions can also be given a name, the sum of QTYs in the SPJ table is named TOTAL_PARTS. This name can be referenced in the outer select. The following table shows the results of only the table expression in parentheses. Typically, the results of a table expression with GROUP BY, DISTINCT, and column function are written to a work file. There are many types of table expressions that are not written to a work file as described in Chapter ST.

The results of the table expression can be tested in the outer select. That is, the SN qualifies in the outer select if the TOTAL_PARTS calculated in the table expression are greater than 1000. Here is the result of the SELECT statement with the table expression:

SN	TOTAL_ PARTS
S2	3200
S5	3100

SL.13 JOINS

In general, joins combine information from two or more tables by comparing all the values that meet the search criteria in the designated column or columns of one table with all the values in corresponding columns of the other table or tables. When the values meet the comparison criteria, the rows containing them are joined and used for the select. This kind of join is called an *inner join. Outer joins*, discussed in Chapter JP, do not require a match in both columns to be joined.

A simple example illustrates the join concept. To find all suppliers of part P4, their names, cities, and amounts they supply, columns must be drawn from tables S and SPJ. The first step can be to find the P4 suppliers, identified by supplier number, in the SPJ table. Those rows, shaded in Figure SL.3, provide the quantities supplied.

Figure SL.3. A join

SPJ

SN	PN	JN	QTY
S1	P1	J1	200
S1	P1	J4	700
S2	P3	J1	400
S2	P3	J2	200
S2	P3	J3	200
S2	P3	J4	500
S2	P3	J5	600
S2	P3	J6	400
S2	P3	J7	800
S2	P5	J2	100
S3	P3	J1	200
S3	P4	J2	500
S4	P6	J3	300
S4	P6	J7	300
S5	P2	J2	200
S5	P2	J4	100
S5	P5	J5	500
S5	P5	J7	100
S5	P6	J2	200
S5	P1	J4	100
S5	P3	J4	200
S5	P4	J4	800
S5	P5	J4	400
S5	P6	J4	500

S (Supplier Table)

SN	SNAME	STATUS	CITY
S1	Smith	20	London
S2	Jones	10	Paris
S3	Blake	30	Paris
S4	Clark	20	London
S5	Adams	30	Athens

Result of Join

SNAME	CITY
Blake	Paris
Adams	Athens

The next step is to find the suppliers' names and cities by matching the SN values associated with P4 in the SPJ table with the SN values in the S table—that is, by comparing the values for equality. When a match is found, the combined row provides the information for the select.

The FROM clause of the SELECT statement for the join must include the tables that participate. The WHERE clause identifies the columns to be compared and the type of comparison. Although most joins involve a match of values—called a *natural join* or *equi-join*—any of the comparison operators may be used. The statement needed for this join is:

```
SELECT SNAME, CITY, QTY
```

```
FROM    S, SPJ
WHERE   S.SN = SPJ.SN
AND     PN   = 'P4';
```

Although not a requirement, in most cases, the columns on which the tables are joined have the same name, data type, and length. When they have the same name, it must be qualified by the table name—SPJ.SN, for example.

Three-way Joins

A SELECT statement may join up to 15 tables, but joins of many tables are not common. The additional joins are simply added to the WHERE clause. Suppose, for example, that we wish to find the name of P4 along with the other information requested in the above search. Part names are included in the P table, so including that table in the join is one way to expand the search. In this case, we join the P and SPJ tables on the PN column. The necessary statement is:

```
SELECT SNAME, S.CITY, PNAME,
  QTY
FROM    S, SPJ, P
WHERE   S.SN    = SPJ.SN
AND     SPJ.PN = P.PN
AND     P.PN    = 'P4';
```

SNAME	CITY	PNAME	QTY
Blake	Paris	Screw	500
Adams	Athens	Screw	800

Notice that the CITY column in the SELECT clause is modified by the S table name to distinguish it from the CITY column in the P table, also part of the joined tables.

Joins Using Comparisons Other Than Equality

Any of SQL's comparison operators may be used as the basis on which tables are joined. The following example search, while perhaps of limited utility except to a port authority, demonstrates such a join. In the example, we want DB2 to compare the ship length in the ship table to the dock length in the dock table to determine which docks are long enough to accommodate a ship pulling into port. The SELECT returns the dock ID that can be communicated to the ship. The necessary statement is:

```
SELECT SHIP_LENGTH, DOCK_ID
FROM    SHIP, DOCKS
WHERE   SHIP_LENGTH < DOCK_LENGTH;
```

Joining a Table with Itself

SQL can join a table with itself, treating the table as if it were two identical copies of itself. A request to find the combined quantity of parts P2 and P6 for each supplier that supplies both parts for the same job demonstrates a join of a table with itself. To grasp how this join works, imagine that there are actually two SPJ tables, as shown in Figure SL.4. The statement is:

```
SELECT I.SN, I.JN, I.PN, I.QTY, II.QTY, I.QTY + II.QTY
FROM    SPJ I, SPJ II
```

```
WHERE   I.SN   = II.SN
AND     I.PN   = 'P2'
AND     II.PN  = 'P6'
ORDER BY 7;
```

I.SN	I.JN	I.PN	I.QTY	II.PN	II.QTY	I.QTY+II.QTY
S5	J2	P2	200	P6	200	400
S5	J4	P2	100	P6	500	600

To evaluate the statement, consider that each row of SPJ I is compared against each row of SPJ II. I.SN must equal II.SN because the request deals with the activity of individual suppliers. I.JN must equal II.JN because the activity relates to one job. Joining rows that meet those criteria and include parts P2 and P6 provides the answer. Those rows are shaded in Figure SL.4. In practice the search would probably be narrowed to P2 and P6 before the join.

Figure SL.4. Joining a table to itself

SPJ I

SN	PN	JN	QTY
S1	P1	J1	200
S1	P1	J4	700
S2	P3	J1	400
S2	P3	J2	200
S2	P3	J3	200
S2	P3	J4	500
S2	P3	J5	600
S2	P3	J6	400
S2	P3	J7	800
S2	P5	J2	100
S3	P3	J1	200
S3	P4	J2	500
S4	P6	J3	300
S4	P6	J7	300
S5	P2	J2	200
S5	P2	J4	100
S5	P5	J5	500
S5	P5	J7	100
S5	P6	J2	200
S5	P1	J4	100
S5	P3	J4	200
S5	P4	J4	800
S5	P5	J4	400
S5	P6	J4	500

SPJ II

SN	PN	JN	QTY
S1	P1	J1	200
S1	P1	J4	700
S2	P3	J1	400
S2	P3	J2	200
S2	P3	J3	200
S2	P3	J4	500
S2	P3	J5	600
S2	P3	J6	400
S2	P3	J7	800
S2	P5	J2	100
S3	P3	J1	200
S3	P4	J2	500
S4	P6	J3	300
S4	P6	J7	300
S5	P2	J2	200
S5	P2	J4	100
S5	P5	J5	500
S5	P5	J7	100
S5	P6	J2	200
S5	P1	J4	100
S5	P3	J4	200
S5	P4	J4	800
S5	P5	J4	400
S5	P6	J4	500

Chapter JP discusses the three types of join processing used by DB2 and the performance implications of joins.

SL.14 UNION

In set operations, a union includes values that appear in either or both of the original sets, with duplicate values excluded from the results. Columns participating in a union must be of compatible data type—broadly defined, a numeric type can be unioned with another numeric type and a character type can be unioned with another character type.

In general, a union consists of multiple SELECT statements combined with UNION operators. Each SELECT identifies the column or columns on which the union is to be performed. The participating SELECTS must specify the same number of columns or literals, and literals can be specified instead of columns. The SELECT statements also identify the columns to be included from each table in the union operation. For example, this statement determines the suppliers included in either or both the S and SPJ tables:

```
SELECT SN
FROM   S
UNION
SELECT SN
FROM   SPJ;
```

SN
S1
S2
S3
S4
S5

In many cases, rows, or column values, will be selected from each table in a union for different reasons. In those cases, literals printed out with each returned value allow users to keep track of why it was selected. A SELECT clause's literals, which are enclosed in single quotation marks, print out along with the values returned by the select.

Consider, for example, a search for parts that weigh more than 16 pounds and parts that are supplied by S2. The first set of parts can be found in the P table and the second set in the SPJ table. A union of the two sets returns all the parts requested. Literals used with each SELECT identifies in the report the reason each part is included. Since each SELECT associates a different literal with each returned value, duplicate part numbers selected from the two tables may be included. The necessary statement is:

```
SELECT PN, 'WEIGHT > 16' AS CRITERIA
FROM   P
WHERE  WEIGHT > 16
UNION
SELECT PN, 'SUPPLIED BY S2' AS CRITERIA
FROM   SPJ
WHERE  SN = 'S2'
ORDER BY CRITERIA, PN;
```

PN	CRITERIA
P3	SUPPLIED BY S2
P5	SUPPLIED BY S2
P2	WEIGHT > 16
P3	WEIGHT > 16
P6	WEIGHT > 16

If the output is to be sorted, the ORDER BY clause must appear after the final SELECT and must specify the columns to be sorted by the AS name. An alternative to the AS name is to specify the numeric position of the column and literal in the statement like: ORDER BY 2,1 . UNION automatically eliminates duplicate rows returned by the participating SELECT statements. The UNION ALL instructs DB2 to leave duplicates in the union's results.

Performance implications of UNION and UNION ALL are discussed in Chapter PP.

SL.15 INSERTING, UPDATING, AND DELETING DATA

SQL allows users to change the values of stored data. The statements required for inserts, updates, and deletes are straightforward.

Inserts

All INSERT statements begin with the words "INSERT INTO" followed by the name of the table to receive the inserts and, in parentheses, the columns to receive the data. The data to be inserted can be specified within parentheses in a VALUES clause, or they can be selected from another table. If all of a table's columns are to receive data, their names need not be specified in the INSERT INTO clause. The following statement, for example, inserts the specified values into all the columns in the S table:

```
INSERT INTO S
  VALUES ('S10', 'JOHNSON', 50, 'DALLAS');
```

If the column names are not specified in the INSERT INTO clause, the values must be listed in the order that the columns were specified in the CREATE TABLE statement. Each inserted value must have a compatible data type and length specified for the column that receives it.

When SQL is embedded in a program, even if all of a table's columns are to be included in an insert, it is good practice to specify them anyway; that way, if a new column is added to the table, the insert program will not have to be changed to account for it. If the columns are named in the INSERT statement, the values to be inserted must be in the order of the named columns. If the user does not specify a column name and a value for a column, a third column named STATUS in the following example, DB2 inserts the row provided that the missing column is declared as NOT NULL WITH DEFAULT, WITH DEFAULT value, or WITH DEFAULT NULL. If the column is defined as NOT NULL, the row is not inserted and a negative SQLCODE is received.

```
INSERT INTO S (SN, SNAME, CITY)
  VALUES ('S10', 'JOHNSON', 'DALLAS');
```

Flexibility of VALUES clause: You can include expressions discussed throughout the book like special-registers, labeled durations, case expressions, cast specifications, arithmetic expressions, scalar functions, constants, host variables, and non-table user-defined functions in the VALUES clause (V6). Following is an example of using the scalar function CONCAT to insert 'Smith John' in the SNAME column. The statement also shows how to use the DEFAULT key word to indicate that the value specified as the default when the table is created should be inserted into the STATUS column. You can also use NULL to indicate that null is to be inserted into the column. These keywords allow for specifying the column name and indicating that the default or null is to be inserted into a column.

```
INSERT INTO S (SN,   SNAME,   STATUS, CITY)
   VALUES ('S99', 'Smith ' CONCAT 'John',  DEFAULT,
           'Dallas');
```

When a SELECT statement is used with an INSERT, the select copies the data it retrieves into the specified table rather than returning it to the user or program. Developers find the method useful for building a small test table from a subset of a production table, as demonstrated by this example:

```
INSERT INTO S_TEST
  SELECT SN, SNAME, STATUS, CITY
  FROM   S
  WHERE  SN  < 'S4';
```

You can insert into a table with a subselect from the same table (V6). Do be cautious of a -803 SQLCODE indicating duplicate primary key values.

If a medium to large number of rows are to be inserted into a table, the LOAD utility has significant performance advantage as discussed in Chapter LC.

If table reference in the subselect is empty (S table in example), a +100 SQLCODE and '02000' SQLSTATE is returned. If the receiving table is self-referencing (referential integrity discussed in RI section), the subselect must not return more than one row unless NO ACTION is used when defining the FK.

Updates

An update, which changes values already stored, includes an UPDATE clause, which indicates the table containing the information to be changed, and a SET clause, which indicates the columns to be changed and their new values. It also uses a WHERE clause to identify specific rows to be changed. Suppose supplier S1 has moved to Dallas and increased its status by 10. Its new name is not known. The necessary update of the S table would require this statement:

```
UPDATE S
SET CITY    = 'DALLAS',
    STATUS = STATUS + 10,
    SNAME   = NULL
WHERE SN    = 'S1';
```

Notice that DB2 updates numeric columns based on arithmetic calculations as in the STATUS column. Notice also that an equal sign is used to assign a null to a column, in contrast to the test for a null with a SELECT statement, which requires the special IS operator.

An update can also use a subselect. For example, Supplier Blake has sent an additional 10 of each parts it supplies to jobs recorded in the SPJ table, but the person wanting to update QTY does not know Blake's supplier number. This UPDATE statement with a subselect handles the change:

```
UPDATE SPJ
SET QTY = QTY + 10
WHERE SN IN
   (SELECT SN
    FROM   S
    WHERE  SNAME = 'Blake');
```

Update Based on Results of Subselect

You can set a column equal to the result of a subselect that returns only one value. If more than one row qualifies in the subselect a -811 SQLCODE is returned (V6 APAR PQ30383). Following is an example of updating the SPJ table based on bolts having been assigned a new PN in the P table for SN of S4.

```
UPDATE SPJ
```

```
SET PN =
 (SELECT PN
  FROM   P
  WHERE  PNAME = 'Bolt')
WHERE SN = 'S4';
```

The following statement is an extension of the previous statement to show that multiple columns in a table can be set to multiple columns resulting from a subselect and that an expression can be used in the subselect.

```
UPDATE SPJ
SET (PN, QTY) =
 (SELECT PN, :QTY * 1.1
  FROM   P
  WHERE  PNAME = 'Bolt');
```

A GROUP BY in a statement usually results in more than one row qualifying. Therefore, it is not allowed when updating columns according to the result of a subselect, rather a -815 SQLCODE is returned. The SET clause can include an expression, NULL provided that the column being updated allows for nulls, or the keyword DEFAULT (meaning the default established when creating a table as discussed in Chapter CT).

If no rows qualify in the subselect, null is returned. The column is assigned null if it allows for null based on the creation of the table. If the column does not allow for null, an error of -407 SQLCODE is received.

You can use a correlated subselect as a condition. For example, the STATUS column can be set to the number of times a supplier is used on a job

```
UPDATE S AS S1
SET STATUS =
 (SELECT COUNT(*)
  FROM   SPJ AS SPJ1
  WHERE  S1.SN = SPJ1.SN);
```

It is not possible to update a table referenced in the subselect.

Deletes

DELETE statements identify the table from which rows are to be removed and, through a WHERE clause, the specific rows. For example, this statement to delete from the J table jobs performed in Rome removes the only row that satisfies the WHERE criterion—that for job J2:

```
DELETE FROM J
  WHERE CITY = 'Rome';
```

Subselects can also identify rows to be deleted.

SL.16 SUMMARY

SQL provides rich data access and manipulation capabilities. This chapter provides a grounding in those capabilities including information on SQL syntax and on how to employ the SQL operators. Mastering this information is only the first step in learning to use SQL with DB2, however. One must also understand how to use it within programs and understand DB2's implementation of SQL to be able to formulate the most efficient statements. Chapters PD through EX discuss how to develop programs for DB2 and efficient use of SQL.

EXERCISES

Most of the exercises are based on the tables found in Figure CT.6. Please refer to the figure when writing the needed SQL statements and to verify the results of the statements.

1. There is frequently more than one way to write a statement to obtain results. Write two SELECT statements to determine the PN, PNAME, and WEIGHT of parts that weight 15 pounds or more and 20 pounds or less.

2. Write a SELECT statement to determine the suppliers in Athens assuming that most people have keyed the first three letters of the city correctly but may have misspelled the remaining portion. Give the results of the statements including the SN, SNAME, and CITY.

3. Write a statement to determine the minimum weight of parts in London. Give the results of the statement including the PN and PNAME.

4. Write a statement to compute the average status for suppliers by city from the S table and have the rows sequenced by CITY. Use AVGSTATUS as the heading of the report column for the averages. Give the results of the statement.

5. Use the GROUP BY operator to find how many P5s are available, on average, from each supplier that supplies it. The SELECT should provide each SN that supplies P5 on a job in the SPJ table and the average. Further, report on only the SN that provide P5 with an average quantity greater than 300. Have the column heading of AVGQTY appear in the report for the averages and show the results.

6. Write a statement to identify the SNs in the SPJ table that have 3 in the second position of the SN column and show the results.

7. Write the SELECT clause to determine the microsecond portion of a column ORDER_TIMESTAMP that has been declared as a timestamp data type.

8. Write a SELECT clause to add one month to the date 8/31/1987 and give the result.

9. Write a SELECT clause to add 30 days to a column DATEREC containing '01/31/1987' and give the result (1987 is not a leap year).

10. Write a SELECT clause to subtract 1/31/1987 from 3/31/2001 and give the results.

11. Write a statement to determine the jobs using parts from supplier Blake and give the results. Include the SN, SNAME, PN, JN, and QTY.

12. Write a statement to determine the names of all jobs using part numbers P1 or P6 and the quantities used. Sequence the results by JNAME and QTY; include the PN with each returned row. Give the results.

13. The requirement is to determine the PN, PNAME, COLOR, WEIGHT, and CITY from the P and SPJ tables. The following statement satisfies the requirement but returns duplicate rows. Modify the statement to eliminate the duplicate rows.

```
SELECT P.PN, PNAME, COLOR, WEIGHT, CITY
FROM   P, SPJ
WHERE  P.PN = SPJ.PN
AND    QTY  = 200;
```

14. Write a SELECT statement to report SN, SNAME, STATUS, and a description of each suppliers status. The description is poor, average, or excellent based on a status of 10, 20, or 30, respectively.

15. Write a statement to report PN, PNAME, WEIGHT, and whether the part is considered heavy or light. A part is considered heavy if it weighs greater than or equal 15 and light if it weighs less than 15. Give the results.

16. Develop a SELECT statement with a CASE expression to calculate the total sales by month during the first 3 months of the year for DIVISION = 'CENTRAL'. Assume that the SALES table has one row per month. Each row has 1 for January, 2 for February, and 3 for March in a MONTH column. The sales amount is in the SALES_AMOUNT column.

17. Reformulate the following statement without using a table expression.

```
SELECT S.SN, SNAME, CITY, TOTAL_PARTS
FROM   S,
    (SELECT SN, SUM(QTY) AS TOTAL_PARTS
     FROM   SPJ
     GROUP BY SN) AS SUMQTYBYSN
WHERE S.SN = SUMQTYBYSN.SN;
```

SN	SNAME	CITY	TOTAL_ PARTS
S1	Smith	London	900
S2	Jones	Paris	3200
S3	Blake	Paris	700
S4	Clark	London	600
S5	Adams	Athens	3100

18. Write two formulations of a statement to determine PNs in the SPJ table that are not in the P table.

19. Write two formulations of a statement that identifies all of the suppliers in Dallas or that have a status of 30 and give the results including the SN, SNAME, CITY, and STATUS. Assume that there are no duplicate rows or that duplicate rows are acceptable.

20. Write a statement to insert a row into the S table with a SN of S6, SNAME of Flora, STATUS of 40, and CITY of Rome.

21. A new packing requirement increases the weight of parts by 10 percent. Write an update statement to increase the weight of all parts by 10 percent.

22. The warehouse in Paris has been closed. Delete all of the rows from the P table for Paris.

ANSWERS

1. The parts that weigh between 15 and 20 pounds can be determined with the BETWEEN predicate or the >= and <= predicates like:

```
SELECT PN, PNAME, WEIGHT
FROM   P
WHERE  WEIGHT BETWEEN 15 and 20;

SELECT PN, PNAME, WEIGHT
FROM   P
WHERE  WEIGHT >= 15
AND    WEIGHT <= 20;
```

PN	PNAME	WEIGHT
P2	Bolt	17
P3	Screw	17
P6	Cog	19

2. All of the suppliers in a city beginning with ATH are identified with:

```
SELECT SN, SNAME, CITY
FROM   S
WHERE  CITY LIKE 'ATH%';
```

SN	SNAME	CITY
S5	Adams	Athens

3. The following statement determines the minimum weight of parts in London and the results follow.

```
SELECT PN, PNAME, MIN(WEIGHT)
FROM   P
WHERE  CITY = 'London'
GROUP BY PN, PNAME;
```

PN	PNAME	
P1	Nut	12
P4	Screw	14
P6	Cog	19

Notice that the minimum weight does not have a column heading in the report because the AS clause is not used.

4. The following statement computes the average status for all suppliers in each city of the S table and sequences the results by CITY. The averages have the column heading of AVGSTATUS.

```
SELECT CITY, AVG(STATUS) AS AVGSTATUS
FROM   S
GROUP BY CITY
ORDER BY CITY;
```

CITY	AVGSTATUS
Athens	30
London	20
Paris	20

ORDER BY in addition to GROUP BY is required to insure that the rows are returned in sequence.

5. The following statement gets each of the SNs from SPJ into a group and computes the average quantity for those SNs that supply P5 to a job and have an average quantity greater than 300. The averages have a column heading of AVGQTY.

SN	AVGQTY
S5	333

```
SELECT SN, AVG(QTY) AS AVGQTY
FROM   SPJ
WHERE  PN = 'P5'
```

```
GROUP BY SN
HAVING AVGQTY > 300;
```

6. The substring scalar function can be used to identify the SNs with 3 in the second position of the identifier.

```
SELECT SN
FROM   SPJ
WHERE  SUBSTR(SN,2,1) = '3';
```

SN
S3
S3

7. The SELECT clause to determine the microsecond portion of the column ORDER_TIMESTAMP is:

```
SELECT MICROSECOND(ORDER_TIMESTAMP)
```

8. The SELECT clause to add one month to the date 8/31/1987 is:

```
SELECT '08/31/1987' + 1 MONTH
```

The result is '09/30/1987' because there are 30 days in September.

9. The SELECT clause to add 30 days to a column DATEREC is:

```
SELECT DATEREC + 30 days
```

The result is '03/02/1987'.

10. The SELECT clause to subtract 1/31/1987 from 3/31/2001 is:

```
SELECT '03/31/2001' - '01/31/1987'
```

The result is 00140200 which means 14 years and 2 months are between the two dates.

11. The following join gets information about the supplier Blake from the S table and the PN, JN, and QTY of parts from the SPJ table.

```
SELECT SPJ.SN, SNAME, PN, JN, QTY
FROM   SPJ, S
WHERE  SPJ.SN = S.SN
AND    SNAME  = 'Blake';
```

SN	SNAME	PN	JN	QTY
S3	Blake	P3	J1	200
S3	Blake	P4	J2	500

12. It is necessary to select from the SPJ and J table to get all of the jobs using PNs P1 or P6 with the quantity of parts used on the jobs. The ORDER BY clause results in the required sequence.

```
SELECT JNAME, QTY, PN
FROM   SPJ, J
WHERE  SPJ.JN = J.JN
AND    PN IN ('P1', 'P6')
ORDER BY JNAME, QTY;
```

JNAME	QTY	PN
Console	100	P1
Console	500	P6
Console	700	P1
Punch	200	P6
Reader	300	P6
Sorter	200	P1
Tape	300	P6

13. The DISTINCT function can be used to eliminate the duplicate rows like:

```
SELECT DISTINCT P.PN, PNAME, COLOR, WEIGHT, CITY
FROM   P, SPJ
WHERE  P.PN = SPJ.PN
AND    QTY = 200;
```

14. The following SELECT statement reports on poor, average, and excellent suppliers with only one tablespace scan. The results follow the statement.

```
SELECT SN, SNAME, STATUS,
CASE STATUS
     WHEN 10 THEN 'Poor'
     WHEN 20 THEN 'Average'
     WHEN 30 THEN 'Excellent'
     ELSE 'Invalid'
END AS STATUS_DESC
FROM   S;
```

SN	SNAME	STATUS	STATUS_DESC
S1	Smith	20	Average
S2	Jones	10	Poor
S3	Blake	30	Excellent
S4	Clark	20	Average
S5	Adams	30	Excellent

15. The following statement reports on PN, PNAME, WEIGHT, and whether the part is considered heavy or light. Notice that the column WEIGHT must be in the WHEN clauses because a comparison other than equal is done.

```
SELECT PN, PNAME, WEIGHT,
CASE
WHEN WEIGHT <  15 THEN 'Light'
WHEN WEIGHT >= 15 THEN 'Heavy'
     ELSE 'No weight'
END AS WEIGHT_DESC
FROM   P;
```

PN	PNAME	WEIGHT	WEIGHT_DESC
P1	Nut	12	Light
P2	Bolt	17	Heavy
P3	Screw	17	Heavy
P4	Screw	14	Light
P5	Cam	12	Light
P6	Cog	19	Heavy

16. Here is a SELECT statement with a CASE expression to calculate the total sales by month for the central division during the first 3 months of the year.

```
SELECT SUM(CASE WHEN MONTH = 1
           THEN SALES_AMOUNT ELSE NULL
           END) AS JAN_SUM,
```

```
          SUM(CASE WHEN MONTH = 2
              THEN SALES_AMOUNT ELSE NULL
              END) AS FEB_SUM,
          SUM(CASE WHEN MONTH = 3
              THEN SALES_AMOUNT ELSE NULL
              END) AS MAR_SUM
FROM      SALES
WHERE     DIVISION = 'CENTRAL';
```

17. The table expression

```
SELECT S.SN, SNAME, CITY, TOTAL_PARTS
FROM   S,
      (SELECT SN, SUM(QTY) AS TOTAL_PARTS
       FROM   SPJ
       GROUP BY SN) AS SUMQTYBYSN
WHERE S.SN = SUMQTYBYSN.SN;
```

can be reformulated as a join:

```
SELECT S.SN, SNAME, CITY, SUM(QTY) AS TOTAL_PARTS
FROM   S, SPJ
WHERE  S.SN = SPJ.SN
GROUP  BY S.SN, SNAME, CITY;
```

Both give the same results:

SN	SNAME	CITY	TOTAL_ PARTS
S1	Smith	London	900
S2	Jones	Paris	3,200
S3	Blake	Paris	700
S4	Clark	London	600
S5	Adams	Athens	3100

The table expression has performance advantages. In the table expression, each unique SN with the sum of QTYs is written to a work file and only those unique SN must be joined with the S table. In contrast, the join requires joining each SN, including duplicates, in SPJ with each SN in the S table, then sorting the rows for the GROUP BY and calculating the sum of the QTYs. Performance implications of CASE expressions are discussed in Chapter PP.

18. The PNs in SPJ but not in the P table can be identified using a NOT EXISTS or NOT IN subselect like:

```
SELECT PN
FROM   SPJ AS SPJX
WHERE  NOT EXISTS
  (SELECT 1
   FROM   P
   WHERE  PN = SPJX.PN);

SELECT PN
FROM   SPJ
WHERE  PN NOT IN
  (SELECT PN
   FROM   P);
```

No rows qualify from the statements. There is no PN in the dependent SPJ table that is not in the parent P table.

19. Two predicates on CITY and STATUS can be ORed or a UNION ALL can be used to identify any suppliers in Dallas or that have a STATUS of 30 because we are assuming that no duplicate rows qualify or duplicate rows are acceptable.

```
SELECT SN, SNAME, CITY, STATUS
FROM   S
WHERE  CITY = 'Dallas'
OR     STATUS = 30;

SELECT SN, SNAME, CITY, STATUS
FROM   S
WHERE  CITY = 'Dallas'
UNION ALL
SELECT SN, SNAME, CITY, STATUS
FROM   S
WHERE  STATUS = 30;
```

SN	SNAME	CITY	STATUS
S3	Blake	Paris	30
S5	Adams	Athens	30

There are no suppliers in Dallas.

20. Here is a statement to insert the row into the S table:

```
INSERT INTO S (SN, SNAME, STATUS, CITY)
  VALUES ('S6', 'Flora', 40, 'Rome');
```

21. The following statement increases the weight of all parts by 10 percent. Do be cautious when you do not specify a WHERE clause for UPDATE and DELETE statements. Keep in mind that all rows in the table are affected.

```
UPDATE P
SET WEIGHT = WEIGHT * 1.10;
```

22. The following statement deletes all of the rows from the part table for Paris.

```
DELETE FROM P
WHERE  CITY = 'Paris';
```

FIGURES

Concurrency Control

CC.1 INTRODUCTION

Concurrency is the process of allowing multiple users or applications to use the same data. However, we also want to ensure that one user or program does not change data while another is in the process of using or changing that data, a situation that can lead to errors or inconsistencies in the data. DB2 manages concurrency with several types of locks that restrict access to data while the data are being used. Generally, DB2 SELECTS the appropriate lock type based on concurrency requirements inherent in the transaction. These are called *implicit locks*. However, it is also possible for programmers to use *explicit locks* in their programs to lock a table for specific periods. The IRLM (Internal Resource Lock Manager) controls all locks. A hashing algorithm based on the data set identifier and page number is used to locate a hash table entry point to a chain of hashing synonyms to determine if the required lock is available. About 250 bytes per lock are required in most cases.

If locks are not available to control concurrency, serious errors can occur. Assume the Johnsons have a $1,000 checking account balance. Mrs. Johnson withdraws $200 at 10:01:01.001 A.M. At precisely that instant plus a millisecond, before her transaction completes and the new $800 balance is entered, Mr. Johnson withdraws $300. His deduction is taken from the still-intact $1,000, and a new balance of $700 is written to the account, overwriting Mrs. Johnson's work. Mrs. Johnson received her $200, but the transaction was lost. Since the final balance should have been $500, the bank also lost. A lock on the account during Mrs. Johnson's transaction would have held Mr. Johnson's transaction at bay. A number of other errors are possible when more than one transaction accesses the same data at the same time.

The specific points in a transaction when DB2 acquires or releases locks and the amount of data covered by any particular lock depends on decisions the designer makes during tablespace creation and when issuing a bind command. Locks involve important performance tradeoffs. Locking large units of data can result in poor response times because users and programs must wait their turns at the data. Locking smaller units of data can allow better access to the data (better concurrency) but can require considerable CPU time and virtual storage for managing the locks. To use locks most efficiently and to insure data integrity, you must understand the options for controlling locks, how DB2 reacts to your choices, and the application traffic. Figure CC.1 summarizes the lock size and type determinants.

Figure CC.1. Lock size and type determinants

- The lock sizes and lock limits declared on the tablespaces in the SQL CREATE statements defining them.
- The installation limits for number of locks per tablespace (NUMLKTS) and number of locks per user (NUMLKUS).
- The isolation level, current data, and acquire/release options you choose.
- Type of SQL statements--whether SELECT or UPDATE, for example--within a commit scope.
- Clauses that can be specified on SELECT statements.
- The access path chosen by the optimizer.
- The presence of explicit LOCK TABLE statements.

Protecting the Transaction's Work

Locks protect data while DB2 performs the logical units of recovery necessary to complete a database transaction, such as the withdrawal of funds from a savings account or the addition of a part to an inventory. Typically, such transactions require a series of updates, insertions, and deletions and internal operations such as fetching and summing data. The total of these steps represents the transaction's unit of recovery (UR). (A UR is also known as a unit of work (abbreviated as UOW)). For the savings withdrawal, for example, the transaction must make an entry in the account, adjust and enter the new balance, and adjust and enter the bank's new cash position. To maintain consistency, for a transaction to be successfully completed and recorded, all of its steps must be completed. Otherwise none of the work should be recorded.

Generally DB2 begins acquiring locks on a transaction's affected data when the first SQL statement in a program is executed and holds them until the UR is complete or the program terminates. When the work is complete, DB2 commits it, records it in an active log data set, and can write the changed data to the tablespace at the commit point or later along with other changed pages to make the process more efficient. Although these logical units of recovery are obviously of importance to the logic of the program, there are also recovery and concurrency considerations tied to the UR.

Of relevance to concurrency, once the change is safely recorded in the log, any locks on the data can be released and the pages can be used by others without requiring additional physical I/O. Use the COMMIT or COMMIT WORK statement within TSO and CAF programs to indicate the end of a UR. The statements and processes used to commit a UR with CICS and IMS are discussed in Chapter PD. You can also COMMIT to establish shorter units of recovery within a larger application logical unit of recovery if this is permitted by business rules. This provides for releasing locks so that others can get at the data. In addition, it creates smaller units of recovery and can reduce the time it takes to restart a program in the event that it fails in the middle of UR. This may or may not be acceptable to the business process. In some cases, all of the changes must be made to the data or none of the changes are to be made to the data.

In the event of a failure, DB2 uses the information in the log to roll back values changed by the failing transaction since the last commit point. If no commit was issued, then all database changes since the transaction started will be rolled back. After the rollback, DB2 releases the locks and issues an error message. Locks themselves can in certain circumstances prevent transactions from completing as a result of a deadlock or timeout.

Latches: Latches are similar to locks in that they are used to maintain the integrity of data. However, internal latches require about one-tenth the number of instructions as locks. Latch processing is at the page level and is required for each qualifying row to avoid processing data that is in the process of being updated. This is particularly important when using lock avoidance and uncommited read as will be discussed in Sections CC.5 and CC.6. For example, you would not want to see the new supplier name of Jones before the new status of 50 is applied as a result of the statement:

```
UPDATE S
   SET SNAME   = 'Jones',  -- Update applied
   STATUS      = 50         -- Update not applied
WHERE  SN      = 'S4';
```

Latches are maintained by DB2, not by IRLM. Latches have advantages over locks. Deadlocks cannot occur with latches, not between each other or with other locks. DB2 avoids deadlocks (or deadlatches, if you prefer) involving latches by requesting only conditional locks while holding a latch, or by requesting latches in a specific order. Latches are not held until a commit is issued as are locks. Rather they are released once the work involving the latched page has been completed.

Although IBM considers detailed information on latches as proprietary, you can monitor their activity using accounting or monitor class 3, IFCIDs 0226 and 0227.

CC.2 DEADLOCKS AND TIMEOUTS

Certain transactions executing at the same time can lock each other out of data that they need to complete their logical units of recovery. Since neither can complete its work and commit, neither can release its locks. Nevertheless, each waits for the other in a situation called a deadlock or, by some, a deadly embrace.

We refer to the Johnsons again for a simple example to illustrate deadlocks. Assume that their checking account balance is again $1,000 and that they also have a $2,000 savings account balance. Assume also that the system is programmed to consider that a transfer from one account to the other is a single transaction, made up of a withdrawal and deposit. Mrs. Johnson attempts to withdraw $200 from the savings account and deposit it in the checking account. At the same time, Mr. Johnson tries to transfer $300 from checking to savings. Mrs. Johnson's transaction begins by locking the savings account so the deduction can be made without threat of a concurrent change. Mr. Johnson's work begins with a lock on the checking account for the same reason. Mrs. Johnson's transaction tries to continue with an update of the checking account but cannot gain access because of Mr. Johnson's lock. His transaction cannot complete because it encounters his wife's lock on the savings account. Neither transaction can release its lock until it completes and its work is committed. Neither transaction can complete. Mr. and Mrs. Johnson, or at least their transactions, are in deadly embrace (Figure CC.2).

Figure CC.2. Deadlock

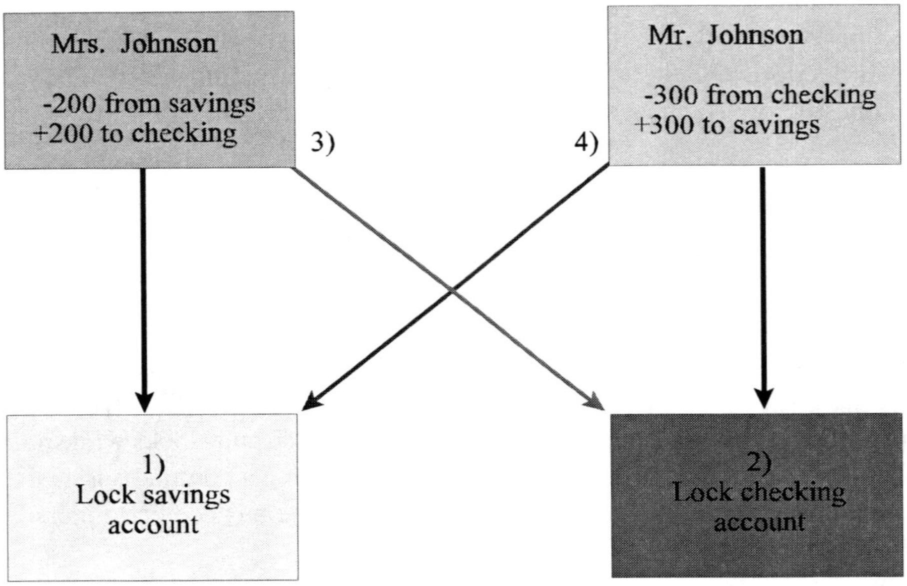

DB2 resolves a deadlock by rolling back any action already taken by the transaction in the deadlock that has the fewest log records or most current lock if IMS is the transaction manager. This rollback releases that transaction's locks and allows the other transaction to continue. In this example, DB2 releases Mr. Johnson's lock on the checking account, which allows Mrs. Johnson to complete her business. Then Mr. Johnson's transaction can try again.

Detecting Deadlocks: The IRLM checks for deadlocks every 5 seconds unless the system administrator has changed this default value on the DSNTIPJ installation panel. When a deadlock occurs, a -911 or -913 SQLCODE is returned to the application program and console message DSNT376I or DSNT375I is written for a timeout and deadlock.

In most cases you will see a -911, which means that a rollback of all changes during a current unit of recovery has occurred. If you are using CICS and ROLBE=YES is specified in the RCT (Resource Control Table), the transaction can be restarted by specifying the task in the PCT (Program Control Table). If you are using CICS and ROLBE=NO, a -913 is received, the locks for the SQL statement which caused the -913 are released, and the other locks are held until the program rolls back or commits the unit of recovery. Open cursors are closed. A -913 can occur in a non-CICS environment. CICS provides a transaction restart facility for handling deadlocks that works with DB2 transactions.

Deadlock and timeout using IMS/DC are managed depending on the type of region used.

- IMS message driven BMP, MPP, IFP deadlock and timeout results in rollback, abend code of 0777, and IMS reschedules the transaction. No SQLCODE is returned to program.

- IMS non-message driven region results in rollback with -911 SQLCODE if rollback is successful. If the rollback is not successful, IMS issues a code of 0777 and program abends. No SQLCODE is returned to program.

- DL/1 batch results in abend with a completion code of 04E and reason code of 00D44033.

- Deadlock between DB2 and DL/1 results in a timeout. The last lock requestor is rolled back. The other unit of work continues processing.

Programming Recommendation: Typically a program should call a subroutine or module to process SQLCODEs. Depending on the error code and the error routine, the program might automatically reissue Mr. Johnson's transaction or send him a message asking him to reenter the request. Chapter PD discusses error handling in more detail.

To avoid deadlocks, it is best that all concurrently executing programs access the tables in the same order. For example, processing tables in alphabetic order of table names can prevent deadlocks on data pages. Any predetermined order followed by all programs will accomplish the same goal. However, the user doesn't control the order of table access within a statement.

Timeouts

The IRLM services requests for locks on a first-in, first-out basis. If a lock required by a program is unavailable because it is being used by another program, that program is suspended until the lock becomes available. If the locked resource is not available within an installation-specified time, a timeout occurs. By default, IRLM tries for 60 seconds to get the lock.

Specifying the Timeout Interval: Installation panel DSNTIPI has a RESOURCE TIMEOUT field that allows the systems administrator to specify the minimum number of seconds before a timeout can occur. DB2 uses the timeout period and a multiplier to determine if a timeout has occurred. Different types of programs use different multipliers. Most transactions use a multiplier of 1. However, IMS DL/I batch and IMS Fast Path non-message processing use a multiplier of 6, the BIND command uses 3, and IMS batch message programs use 4. Utilities use a multiplier of 6. The STOP DATABASE command tries 15 times before a timeout.

If IRLM cannot get a lock within the time limit, a -911 or -913 is issued, similar to a deadlock. The reason code indicates whether the negative SQLCODE is a result of a deadlock or timeout and console message DSNT376I or DSNT375I is written.

Changing the Timeout Factor: The system administrator can change certain timeout multipliers, as shown here:

Type of Process	How to Change Timeout Multiplier
Utilities	UTILITY TIMEOUT field of DSNTIPI
IMS BMP	BMPTOUT subsystem parameter
DL/I Batch	DLITOUT subsystem parameter

Deadlocks and Timeouts in a Distributed Environment

If two processes are running on separate DB2 subsystems at different locations, a deadlock is reported as a timeout. DB2 provides the option at the subsystem level to timeout a distributed thread (user) which is inactive, holding a lock, and has not committed. The condition is checked every three minutes. Once the condition is detected, a rollback occurs and all resources are released. The requester thread is canceled if timed out. DB2 effectively issues a -CANCEL DDF THREAD command. This avoids using resources to derive results that cannot be transmitted to the requester. If a thread is to be canceled, the systems administrator must specify the timeout period in seconds on IDLE THREAD TIMEOUT of DSNTIPR installation panel or the IDTHTOIN of DSNZPARM (not the default). The timeout does not apply to an inactive thread that is not holding a lock and to indoubt threads.

CC.3 LOCK SIZES AND TYPES

DB2 determines its locking strategy for each transaction during the bind process in most cases. DB2 locks data in units of differing sizes: row or page, table, tablespace. DB2 does not take transaction locks on indexes at all, but uses data-only locking. A variety of lock types can be used with these locks, offering different concurrency levels.

Determining the Lock Size

When creating or altering the tablespace, you can specify a lock size (ROW, PAGE, TABLESPACE, or TABLE) or choose ANY, indicating that DB2 should choose the lock size whenever the table is accessed. In that case, DB2 usually chooses a lock size of PAGE.

Decisions about lock sizes depend on how the particular table and indexes will be used, with the general tradeoff between response times and CPU and virtual storage usage in effect. Smaller lock sizes, such as row locks, can offer greater concurrency, but because they are usually more numerous than page, table or tablespace locks, they can require considerable CPU resources.

Advantages and Costs of Row Locking

Even with row locking, it is necessary to serialize processing at the page level to gather free space for such things as expanding a variable-length row. A page latch is taken to serialize processing while gathering free space on a page, but the latch is not held until commit.

There are some situations that might benefit from row locking:

- A high transaction rate is required with high update activity. Row locking allows multiple programs to update different rows on the same page at the same time (although not at the same instant because of page latching for each qualifying row).

- If a program processes only a few rows and there are lock contention problems, row locking can help by locking only those few rows rather than locking all the rows on a page, which might be locking out another program that is trying to process different rows on that page.

- There are small tables that are frequently updated. Row locking can allow more access to needed rows on a page.

- There are short rows with many rows on a page. If you are using data compression, this is often the case. With page locking, more data is unavailable to other applications. Row locking means that only the needed rows are locked.

- Updates and deletes concentrated in specific areas of a table are considered "hot spots". Lock contention in these hot spots is minimized with row locking.

Row locking is *not* required to reduce lock contention when INSERTING rows at the end of a table or in any concentrated area of the table. If the page is locked when an insert of a row is attempted, the row is inserted in a near or far page as if there is no free space on the page. The tradeoff is that clustering is lost more quickly. There is also the additional I/O required to search for a page to insert the row in many cases. In balance, however, it is usually worth these tradeoffs to avoid lock contention.

Costs: There are costs associated with locking at the row level versus the page level. More locks means more lock overhead. For example, if a transaction processes two rows on a page, you've doubled the costs to take locks. However, the cost to release locks is not doubled because only one call is required to release the locks. If your batch process processes most rows on the page, you could increase locking cost many times. A worst case scenario is if the batch program processes all rows on each page. If there are 40 rows on a page, row locking can require up to 40 times the number of locks as that required for page locking.

IBM tested updating 23,826 rows with a single dynamic UPDATE statement using V4 on a 50 MIPS processor as reported in the manual *Locking in DB2 for MVS/ESA Environment,* SG24-4725. The elapsed time when using a page locksize was almost half that required when using a row locksize as shown in Figure CC.4. The CPU time was increased about 50 percent when using row locking. Using these test results, we can estimate the CPU time required to take a lock at about 51 microseconds ((3.27 - 2.08) / (23,983 - 660). The number of lock requests was dramatically higher with row locking at 23,983 compared to 660 for page locking.

Figure CC.3. Comparison of elapsed and CPU class 2 time using page and row locking

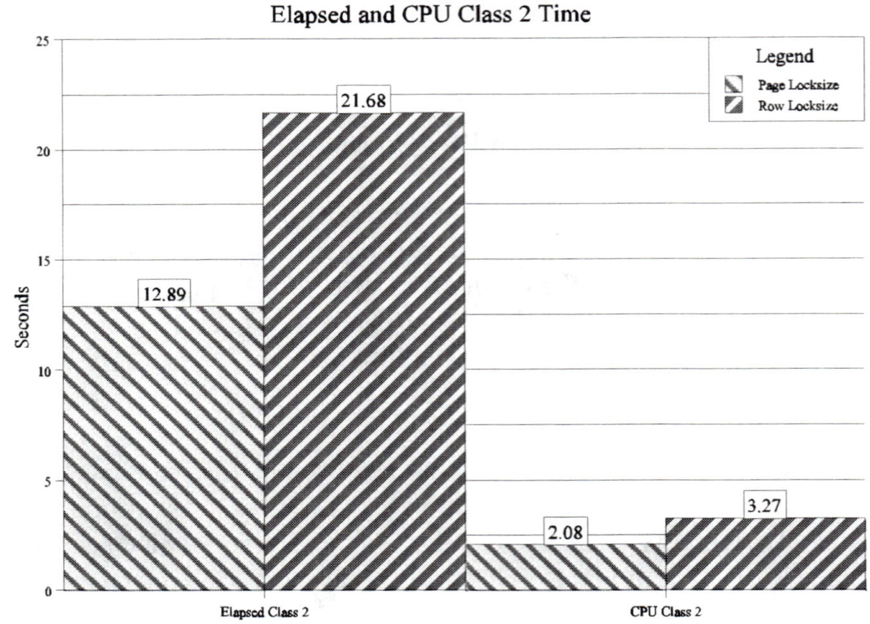

Recommendation: If lock contention is not a problem now, do not use row locks.

Use of page locks provides the best performance in most cases (assuming that the table or tablespace locksize is not appropriate for the processing). If lock contention continues to be a problem, consider altering to a row lock size. Use a monitor to determine if lock contention has been reduced with a row lock size and if the cost increase is acceptable.

If row locking is necessary for online transactions during the day, but the table undergoes batch processing at night, consider altering the table to a lock size of page before executing the batch program. Alter it back to row locking after it executes. Plans and packages do not require a rebind when the locksize is altered. The use of LOCK TABLE statement as an alternative is discussed in Section CC.10.

Share, Update, and Exclusive Locks

Locks can be taken in share (S), exclusive (X), or update (U) mode. *Share* locks allow two or more programs to read simultaneously but not change the locked unit, with each taking a share lock. DB2 uses share locks when it responds to SELECT statements. An *exclusive* lock bars all other users from the locked unit while an update takes place. After a program has taken an exclusive lock, no other transaction can read the data or take any kind of lock against it. (Uncommitted read is an exception to be discussed.) It is necessary for DB2 to read a row before it can be updated or deleted, and during this read a less restrictive *update* lock can be taken.

Before changing a value, DB2 can take an S or U lock against the page or row and then *promote* that to an X to make the change. It could take an X lock initially, but that would limit concurrency unnecessarily, since there would be many cases in which a program can read data in anticipation of changing it but then not make the change at all. By using lock promotion, concurrent users can read the data until the last possible moment before the change--if the change is made at all.

However, this approach also increases the possibility for deadlocks. Between the time the update transaction takes the S lock and promotes it to an X lock, a second update transaction is also entitled to take an S lock against the same page. Each share lock would hold, waiting for the other to be released so it could take an exclusive lock and make its change. Neither will be released, of course, because each is preventing the other from taking the X lock it needs to complete.

The U lock avoids these deadlocks in certain cases while still affording a high level of concurrency. A U lock is compatible with S locks but not with other U locks or X locks. Chapter PD discusses how to select rows and declare an intent to update or delete the rows. This processing results in a U lock being taken while looking for a page to change. Before the change is actually made, the lock is promoted to an X lock after existing S locks held by other programs are released. (The matrix in Figure CC.5 shows compatibility among the different modes of page- or row-level locks.)

Figure CC.4. Page and row lock compatibility

Program A has lock

Program B can take lock

Lk	X	U	S
X	-	-	-
U	-	-	Y
S	-	Y	Y

If and when the program wants to make the change, it waits for preceding S locks to be released and promotes the U to an X lock. The S locks are likely to be released because none of them represents an update transaction vainly waiting its turn for an X lock. If one of the concurrent transactions were for an update, it would have had a U lock, barring the second update transaction and avoiding a deadlock. Between the time a transaction acquires a U lock and promotes it, other transactions can acquire share locks, enabling them to read the data. The update transaction must wait for all previous S locks taken by other transactions to be released before promoting to an X lock for the change if the change is needed. If a change is not made, the U lock is released depending on the isolation level used and always when a commit work is issued.

Update locks are available at the page level and are used when searching for a row to be updated or deleted. They are usually used when a cursor is used to fetch the data and the user has specified an isolation level of cursor stability. The DECLARE {name} CURSOR statement with the FOR UPDATE OF clause invokes the use of U locks. (Cursors and the FOR UPDATE OF clause are discussed in PD.) DB2 also uses U locks while searching for data to be updated without a cursor, particularly for updates that affect multiple rows.

CC.4 LOCK LIMITS AND ESCALATIONS

DB2 provides administrators with the ability to limit the number of locks that can be taken by any one program or interactive user for a particular tablespace and within the entire DB2 subsystem.

Control at the Tablespace Level

Use the LOCKMAX clause of the CREATE TABLESPACE to limit the number of locks that an application can take on that tablespace. You can specify an integer from 1 to 2,147,483,647. A zero (0) means that lock escalation is disabled. The value SYSTEM means that the value specified in the NUMLKTS subsystem parameter is used. The system administrator can change the default maximum value of 1000 on the DSNTIPJ installation panel or by specifying NUMLKTS in DSNZPARM. If you do not specify LOCKMAX when creating a tablespace with a lock size of ANY, the system value is used. If you do not specify LOCKMAX when creating a tablespace with a lock size of ROW or PAGE, the default of zero is used.

The value specified for LOCKMAX applies to tablespaces defined with LOCKSIZE ANY, PAGE, or ROW. DB2 counts all page and row locks against this value. The count includes locks required for triggered SQL statements that are invoked and those taken for the enforcement of referential integrity when it is defined to DB2. Although the tables may not be explicitly referenced in SQL statements, a count of the locks are included and checked against the NUMLKTS and NUMLKUS limits. This can result in exceeding the limits, even though an analysis of the SQL statements might not lead to that conclusion.

When a program reaches the NUMLKTS limit, the intent lock of the tablespace is escalated to an S or X lock. If the tablespace is segmented, then escalation occurs for the table lock. If LOCKPART of YES is specified when the tablespace is created, only the accessed partitions are locked. The individual page or row locks are released after the escalation.

Recommendation: No positive or negative SQLCODE is issued when locks are escalated as a result of meeting the lock limit for the tablespace. In most cases, it is best to disable lock escalation. Do this by specifying 0 for LOCKMAX and NUMLKTS. Use lock controls on the thread level to control the total number of locks taken by a single transaction or batch program.

This recommendation is less critical in V6. This is because message DSNI031I is written to the operator along with database and tablespace name, partition number, lock state (escalated to S or X lock), plan or package name, statement number, etc.

Control on the Thread Level

The NUMLKUS parameter in DSNZPARM and the DSNTIPJ installation panel is the maximum number of page or row locks that a single thread can hold at any one time. This value applies for objects created with a lock size of ROW, PAGE, or ANY. The default value is 10,000.

If a user or program exceeds the value in NUMLKUS, a -904 SQLCODE is returned to the program. The cursor is automatically closed. The program's error module can then choose to commit or roll back to release the locks. If a fetch or close cursor is attempted, a -501 indicates that cursor is not open for a fetch or close and a -507 indicates the curser is not open for an update or delete.

Recommendation: Do not choose zero for NUMLKUS. A zero means that the thread can hold an unlimited number of locks; unlimited, that is, until IRLM runs out of storage.

If a program attempts to get a lock and the IRLM has no space available, the program abends. The IRLM does not abend, rather it writes a message to console when it does not have enough space to take additional locks (V5 APAR PQ07327).

```
DXR175E irlmnm IRLM IS UNABLE TO OBTAIN STORAGE - storage_type
```

The IRLM address space needs to be increased in size or programs that accumulate a large number of locks need be identified and revised to commit more frequently.

Avoiding Lock Limits

To avoid exceeding lock limits, commit work frequently, which causes the locks to be released. (Commit frequency is discussed in Chapter PD.) Use of the cursor stability or uncommited read isolation levels for fetching data, discussed in Section CC.6, further reduces the chances that a program will exceed the lock limits.

If you can tolerate the possible loss of concurrency, issuing a LOCK TABLE statement in the program can also help reduce the number of locks taken. The explicit lock means that data and index page locks are not taken against the tablespace, and any previous locks are released.

CC.5 LOCK AVOIDANCE

Lock avoidance is a technique used by DB2 to reduce the number of locks that must be taken during read-only SELECT processing. If lock avoidance is successful, a qualifying row is returned to the program without taking a lock. (Lock avoidance also applies to checking dependents for a primary key update or for delete with a restrict constraint.)

If no rows qualify on a page, it is not necessary to lock a page or row when lock avoidance is successful. This applies to read-only SELECT statements as well as to UPDATE and DELETE statements bound with the isolation level of cursor stability or read stability. Isolation levels are discussed in Section CC.6.

Lock avoidance applies to read-only SELECT statements and ambiguous SELECTS bound with CURRENTDATA(NO) (YES is the default). No lock is taken for a singleton select with CURRENTDATA(NO) unless the isolation level of RR or RS is used in which case a lock is taken.

The clause FOR FETCH ONLY explicitly declares a SELECT statement as read-only. (FOR READ ONLY syntax complies with the SQL standard and has the same meaning as FOR FETCH ONLY.) If a row will not be updated and can change after it is fetched, use FOR FETCH ONLY in the cursor declaration like:

```
EXEC SQL DECLARE SCURSOR CURSOR FOR
         SELECT SN, SNAME, STATUS
         FROM S
         WHERE STATUS > :NEW-STATUS
         FOR FETCH ONLY
END-EXEC.
```

It is advisable to add the FOR FETCH ONLY clause to all new SELECT statements to clearly indicate that the SELECT statements are used to only read rows and the rows will not be updated or deleted after they are read. You should also consider adding the clause to SELECT statements in programs that are being revised. The FOR FETCH ONLY clause clearly designates the statement as read-only. It is clear to the developer, to someone revising the program, and to DB2.

An ambiguous cursor means that DB2 cannot determine if the cursor is read only because it does not have a FOR FETCH ONLY, FOR READ ONLY, or FOR UPDATE OF clause. If the cursor is not the target of WHERE CURRENT OF clause on an UPDATE or DELETE statement, it is considered ambiguous. In addition, if the cursor is in a plan or package that contains a PREPARE or EXECUTE IMMEDIATE statement, it is considered ambiguous because a fetched row could be modified by a dynamic SQL statement. You can allow lock avoidance for ambiguous cursors by specifying CURRENTDATA(NO) at bind time.

Why Read-Only Data?

Why is lock avoidance used only for read-only data? Data can change after it is read because no locks are taken. An obvious consequence \can be illustrated using the Johnson's bank account once again. Assume that Mr. and Mrs. Johnson have a balance of 1000 dollars in their checking account. If Mrs. Johnson withdraws 1000 dollars and, before the balance of 0 is committed, Mr. Johnson withdraws the same amount. A bank will not stay in business very long if this is allowed to happen.

A more subtle example shows how a read-only SELECT statement can result in erroneous processing. Assume the program reads a row and an SQLCODE of 0 is returned. An UPDATE or DELETE statement is executed but the program does not check the SQLCODE again. The developer assumes that the update or delete was executed successfully because the required row was read successfully. Processing continues as if the row was successfully updated or deleted. However, it is possible that the row was not updated or deleted because it was changed after it was read and before the update or delete was issued. To avoid this problem, use the FOR UPDATE OF clause on the SELECT statement if a returned row might be updated or deleted. Do be cautious with the use of the FOR UPDATE OF clause. It disallows some efficient techniques for processing the data as discussed in Chapter PD.

How DB2 Lock Avoidance Works

To avoid locks, DB2 must first determine if the data has been committed. If it has, it does not need to take a lock on it. It compares the log relative byte address (RBA) of the oldest active UR for a particular tablespace or partition against the RBA in the page header that indicates when the page was last updated. Typically, many URs are active at any one time as represented in Figure CC.6. The arrows indicate the beginning and end of a UR. Notice that URs F and H have not ended their URs. DB2 tracks the oldest active UR for each page set--this is called the *commit log sequence number* (CLSN). The CLSN is 10 in the example. This means that all data on a page with an RBA less than 10 has been committed.

Figure CC.5. CLSN used in lock avoidance

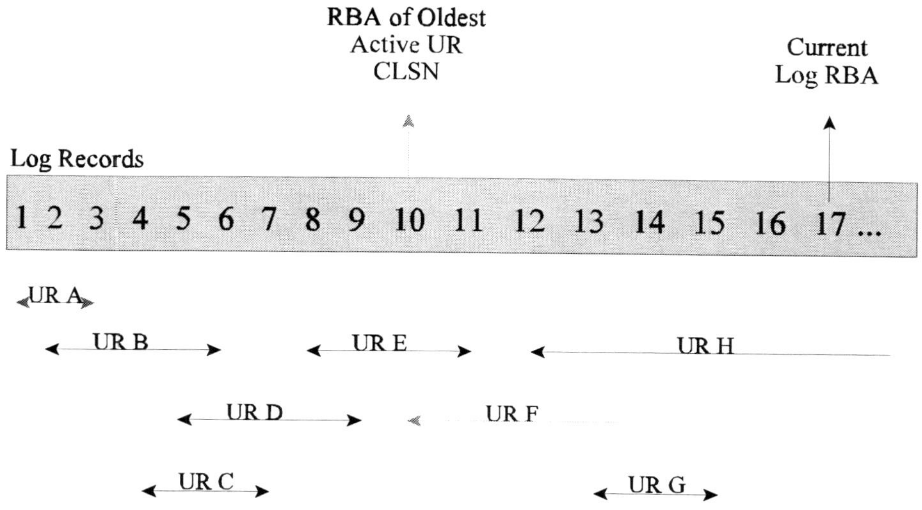

Assume that someone SELECTS a row from a page that was last updated with an RBA of 3 as recorded in the page header (Figure CC.7). Because 3 is earlier than the CLSN of 10, it is safe to assume that everything on the page has been committed. DB2 can avoid taking a lock on that page. A latch is taken at the time the page is read.

Figure CC.6. Lock avoidance implementation

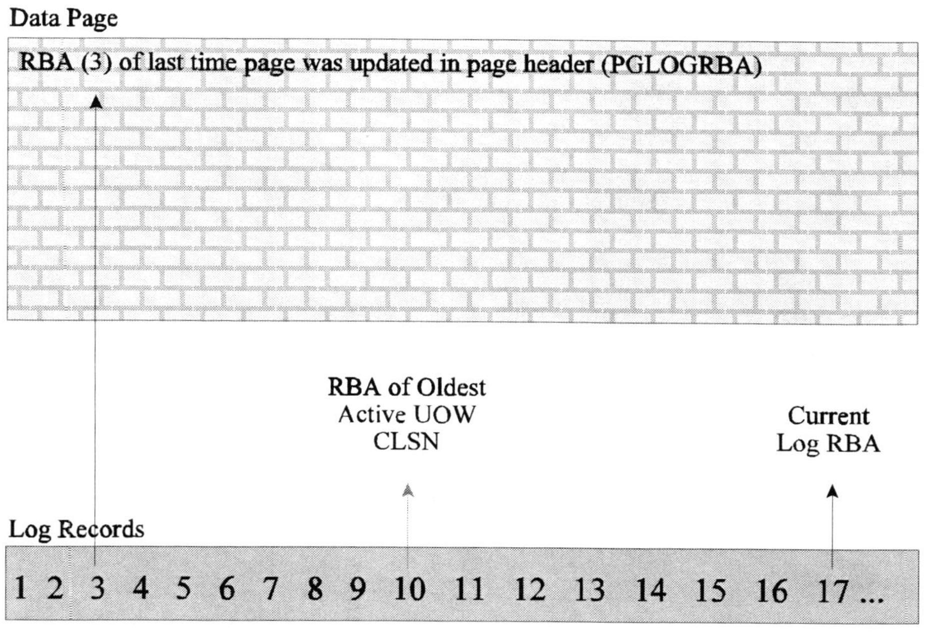

If the page RBA is 12, however, it is still possible that data on that particular page has been committed, because the CLSN is for the entire tablespace or partition, not the particular page or row DB2 is looking at. To determine whether this particular page has uncommited data on it, DB2 checks the possibly uncommited (PUNC) bit that is maintained for each row in the row prefix. The PUNC bit is turned on by insert and update activity on a row and when a page is being reorganized. The bit is turned off when the page or row is locked or CLSN processing is successful and > 25 percent of the bits are on.

If the PUNC bit is on, a lock is attempted. However, if the PUNC bit is off, the page or row lock is avoided, the row is returned to the program, and the row can be selected or updated by others. For example, if Program A has a U or X lock on a page and is processing row 10 on that page, Program B can read row 15 on that same page.

Recommendations: Use lock avoidance whenever possible by fulfilling the prerequisites in Figure CC.8. The use of lock avoidance improves concurrency and performance.

Figure CC.7. Prerequisites for using lock avoidance

- The LOCKSIZE must be ROW, PAGE, or ANY
- Cursor stability must be specified at bind time
- Applies to read-only SELECT statements and ambiguous SELECTS bound with CURRENTDATA(NO) (YES is the default)
- Applies to pages with no qualifying rows for SELECT, UPDATE, and DELETE statements bound with cursor stability and read stability and with CURRENTDATA of YES and NO

Monitoring Lock Avoidance: Performance class 7, IFCID 0223, and performance class 6 or accounting class 1, IFCID 0218, contain information on lock avoidance.

CC.6 ISOLATION LEVELS

If an SQL statement embedded in a host-language program might return multiple rows, you must declare in the program a cursor that presents them to the host program one at a time, usually within a repeatedly executed block. DB2 can handle locking for these cursor reads in different ways. The choices, called *isolation levels*, are uncommited read (UR), cursor stability (CS), read stability (RS), and repeatable read (RR). RR is the default. The levels apply to data covered by ROW, PAGE, and ANY lock sizes.

How to Specify Isolation Level: Specify the isolation level at bind time for all statements in a plan or package, or on individual statements using the WITH clause of the SELECT statement. The isolation level specified on a WITH clause, as shown below, overrides the bind isolation level. This capability can give you more flexibility in designing your applications for concurrency.

```
SELECT SN, SNAME, STATUS, CITY
FROM   S
WHERE CITY = 'Vancouver'
WITH UR;
```

If the WITH clause is not specified, the package bind isolation level is used if specified. If the package isolation level is not specified, the plan isolation level is used.

Uncommitted Read (UR)

UR means that a program can read data that has not yet been committed by another program. No locks are taken except for the special S mass delete lock used to serialize UR readers and mass deleters, which requires an X mass delete lock. In addition, an IX lock on any tablespace in the work file database (DSNDB07, usually) is taken to avoid a drop for the tablespace that is being processed. UR, like all of the isolation levels, cause SQL to be serialized with most utilities, depending on the phase of processing, by using claim and drain processing as discussed in Chapter LC.

If using UR, your program can be reading data that is in the process of being changed. It provides a high level of concurrency, but do not use UR if seeing uncommited data could affect a business decision.

When Not to Use UR

There are many cases where errors can result from reading uncommited data. You do not want to read data with a read-only SELECT statement and then update the row just fetched--the row could have changed after it was fetched. Do not use UR when balancing financial accounts or when balancing the number of parts received and sold.

Here is a more subtle example. One should not schedule the manufacture of an item if all of the materials are not available. This can result in idle time in a plant. It can also result in defective merchandise in an automated manufacturing environment. For example, chemicals may be added automatically at a point in the manufacturing process. There may not be enough chemicals in a container because a previously manufactured item used the last of the chemical. A program may not see the shortage because it read a row while there was an X lock to subtract the amount used by the last item.

A dramatic example is the possibility of scheduling train usage of railroad tracks where two trains are on a collision course. While reserving a room at a hotel for a person when a room is not available is not catastrophic, it can result in a person not having a place to sleep for the night and is likely to result in the permanent loss of a guest for the hotel.

Restrictions: UR can only be specified for read-only SELECT statements for similar reasons as given for the use of lock avoidance.

If the WITH UR clause is not specified and UR is used as the bind isolation level, UR will be used for read-only SELECTS and cursor stability will be used for non-read-only SELECTS.

When to Consider Using UR

If business professionals are willing to see the data even if it is currently being updated, UR may be considered. Consider a case where a newly inserted row is displayed to the user but is subsequently rolled back. Did the data exist? Yes, it did exist for a moment in time. It is reminiscent of the philosophical questions regarding existence addressed in the early 1600s. Descartes is credited with ending the debate with his statement: "I think, therefore I am."

Your users may not have a philosophical bend. It is best to ask them some questions in terms of their application system. Formulate some worse case scenario and ask them if UR is acceptable. Figure CC.9 contains some questions to stimulate thinking. The important point is for you and your business professionals to decide when it is appropriate to use UR. Even after users understand and accept the consequences of using UR, consider including a timestamp on screens and reports to indicate the time to six digits of microseconds when the data existed as presented.

Figure CC.8. Questions for considering the use of UR

Ask users the following types of questions, modified for the particular application under discussion:

- Is it acceptable to see a row that was inserted or updated but for which a rollback occurred rather than a commit?
- Is it acceptable for a passenger to reserve an airline seat even though the last seat is being sold to someone else? Some airlines do allow tickets to be over-sold.
- Is it acceptable for a customer to order an item even though the last item is being sold to someone else? This is a policy used by some catalog companies. The customer is notified that the item is on back order with a follow-up letter.
- Is it acceptable to see the total number of Fords in Perth while the last car is being purchased for scheduling the manufacture of Fords in Australia, scheduling shipments of Fords to Perth, or a potential buyer in Perth?
- Is it acceptable to see the total number of Fords sold at 10:30.20 on September 27, 1994 since the beginning of the month while a car is being sold at 10:30.19 and committed at 10:30.21?

Tables that are always updated in a single-threaded batch program without other programs executing are good candidates for UR. It is appropriate to use UR when accessing data extracted for a data warehousing application and for historical data that is never updated. It may be appropriate to use UR when computing a column function where the results do not have to be exact. For example, the average price of an item since the beginning of the year may be acceptable even though the price of the item is being updated but has not been committed or rolled back. There are probably some reference tables that are rarely updated (a state code table, for example) where UR is justified. The use of UR when selecting from the catalog tables is a good choice in most cases. You can read locked pages and avoid locking others out. A SPUFI plan bound with UR is not provided with DB2. If it is acceptable to use UR with SPUFI in a test environment, consider rebinding the RR SPUFI plan with UR, assuming that the RR SPUFI plan is not used. An alternative is to add the clause WITH UR to your read-only SELECT statements.

Determining Where UR Is Being Used

If there is a possibility that someone might use UR without realizing the full consequences of reading uncommited data, the SELECT statements in Figure CC.10 will prove useful. The SELECTS from the catalog tables can be used to identify plans and packages that were bound with UR or that have WITH UR on a SELECT statement. In addition, IFCIDs 0060, 0061, 0065, 0108, 0112, 0113, 0177, and 0124 from performance trace classes 3, 10, and 11, or monitor trace class 1 shows the isolation level used at execution time, which is useful for programs using dynamic SQL.

Figure CC.9. SELECT statements to identify the use of UR

```
SELECT DISTINCT Y.PLNAME
FROM   SYSIBM.SYSPLAN X,
       SYSIBM.SYSSTMT Y
```

```
WHERE (X.NAME = Y.PLNAME
AND     X.ISOLATION = 'U')
    OR Y.ISOLATION = 'U'
ORDER BY Y.PLNAME;

SELECT DISTINCT Y.COLLID, Y.NAME,
       Y.VERSION
FROM   SYSIBM.SYSPACKAGE  X,
       SYSIBM.SYSPACKSTMT Y
WHERE (X.LOCATION  = Y.LOCATION
AND    X.LOCATION  = ' '
AND    X.COLLID    = Y.COLLID
AND    X.NAME      = Y.NAME
AND    X.VERSION   = Y.VERSION
AND    X.ISOLATION = 'U')
    OR Y.ISOLATION = 'U'
ORDER BY Y.COLLID, Y.NAME, Y.VERSION;
```

Cursor Stability (CS)

Under CS, if a lock is taken at all on a particular page or row, that lock is released after the cursor moves to another page or row. However, if a row is inserted, updated, or deleted with or without the FOR UPDATE OF clause, locks continue to be accumulated for pages and rows that are changed. In most cases, the lock on the last page or row accessed is released when COMMIT is issued, when an SQLCODE of +100 is issued, and when the cursor is closed. The lock is also released if a row or page is returned to an intermediate work file. To prevent holding a lock on the last row or page, close the cursor when it is no longer needed.

Caution: Compared to RR and RS, CS provides more concurrency; however, because it allows other users to access the pages or rows a given program has already read in the midst of a process, this isolation level may allow the data to be changed by another program without the knowledge of the original program. For example, consider a program that reads through a table of plumbing parts to be sure all those needed for a particular job are in stock before submitting an order for any of them. If CS is used, another program might scoop up the last number 5 elbow pipe between the time the original program saw it was available and the time when the order including it was placed.

CS also opens the possibility--though usually only a slight one--that rows can be mistakenly processed twice or not at all. Consider an application, SREPORT, that SELECTS suppliers from the Supplier table in Supplier Number order. At the same time, an update program, SCHANGE, is changing supplier numbers. If SCHANGE increases the Supplier Number of a row that SREPORT has processed into a range that it is yet to process, SREPORT might very well select that row twice. In Figure CC.11, for example, SREPORT has processed rows S1, S2, and S3. While it is processing rows S4 and S5, SCHANGE changes S3 to S6. SREPORT will almost surely process the row again if the search has been using an index. The update will have added a pointer from the index for value S6 to the row. Even if the search is using a tablespace scan that does not return to the page that held the changed value, it might still encounter the row again if the update had caused it to be moved. The reverse problem occurs--SREPORT misses a row--when SCHANGE lowers the row's SN into a range SREPORT has already processed.

Figure CC.10. Double processing under CS

```
UPDATE S
 SET    SN = 'S6'
 WHERE  SN = 'S3';
```

SN	SNAME	STATUS	CITY
S1	Smith	20	London
S2	Jones	10	Paris
S3	Blake	30	Paris
S4	Clark	20	London
S5	Adams	30	Athens
S6	Blake	30	Paris

An isolation level of RR or RS, under which SREPORT holds locks on pages or rows until all processing is complete, would avoid most of these problems. (LOCK TABLE may be required in some cases.) But whether RR or RS should be used depends on the application and the processing schedule. Running batch update and reporting programs in sequence rather than concurrently avoids these double or missed processing problems. Also, the seriousness of these problems varies. If the only difficulty that arises from rare processing anomalies is that a plumbing parts inventory might say there are 1,020 $0.02 bolts available when there are only 1,000, the inconsistency may be tolerable. (The data in the table is correct. It is a matter of what the program saw while it was processing the data.) If, on the other hand, the application might say a banking customer has $2 million rather than $1 million, there is considerable risk.

CURRENTDATA Option

We introduced the CURRENTDATA option in the discussion on lock avoidance. It is important to understand, though, that the CURRENTDATA option can affect results in those cases where a cursor is not accessing data through a work file. CURRENTDATA(YES) tells DB2 that the data on which your cursor is positioned must remain "current" with the data in the base table. In most cases, use CURRENTDATA(NO) to take advantage of lock avoidance. CURRENTDATA(YES) is the default in Version 4. (CURRENTDATA(NO) was the default prior to Version 4.) You must explicitly specify CURRENTDATA(NO) to take advantage of lock avoidance in Version 4.

Read Stability (RS)

Under RS, DB2 takes a lock on the page or row the cursor is accessing and holds the lock only for rows that satisfy predicates. Locks on qualifying rows or pages are held until the program issues a COMMIT. If no rows qualify on a page, a lock is not taken unlike when using RR. Lock avoidance can be used for stage 1 processing but is not used if the row passes stage 1 processing and is rejected at stage 2. (Stage 1 and 2 predicates are discussed in Chapter PP.)

No other program can update or delete a row that is part of the answer set returned to the application. However, it is possible that additional rows can be inserted (or a non-qualifying row updated) that can satisfy the predicate the second time around.

RS and NC (No Commit) conforms to the SQL standard. DB2 does not accept NC as an isolation level. If the SQL is bound with NC on a server that supports NC and the SQL is executed on DB2, it is treated as UR.

Repeatable Read (RR)

Under RR, all page and row locks are held as the cursor moves through the rows. Locks are held even for non-qualifying rows, and are not released until the next commit point. This effectively locks out all other application processes from accessing those pages or rows.

If RR is specified and at bind time the optimizer does not find a usable index for a matching index scan, the optimizer chooses a table or tablespace lock and issues a message, DSNX103I, alerting you that a table or tablespace lock will be used to avoid accumulating a lock on every page or row for a tablespace scan or non-matching index scan.

S or U Locks with RR or RS: By default, DB2 takes S locks on rows or pages when using RS or RR. This has performance advantages if FOR UPDATE OF is used and updates are infrequent. You can use the RRULOCK DSNZPARM value YES to have DB2 take U locks directly rather than initially taking S locks and then changing them to a U when a row is located for update or delete. This can provide some performance advantage if you use RR or RS isolation with frequent updates.

KEEP UPDATE LOCKS: The KEEP UPDATE LOCKS clause causes X locks to be taken immediately rather than taking S and U locks initially on rows or pages that have qualifying rows. The clause applies when using FOR UPDATE OF and WITH RS or WITH RR. If WITH RS is specified, locks are held even though the row does not qualify at stage 2 and is not returned to the program. If WITH RR is specified, locks are taken on all rows or pages including rows that fall within the range of the selection expression (predicates and CASE expressions, for example). The locks are released with a commit. The KEEP UPDATE LOCKS clause avoids some types of deadlocks. The clause is specified like:

```
EXEC SQL DECLARE SCURSOR CURSOR FOR
         SELECT SN, SNAME, STATUS
         FROM   S
         WHERE  STATUS > :NEW-STATUS
         FOR UPDATE OF SNAME
         WITH RS KEEP UPDATE LOCKS
END-EXEC.
```

Recommendations for Isolation Levels

If a program can tolerate reading "dirty data", UR offers the best concurrency and performance. However, most programs do require some sort of concurrency control. CS with CURRENTDATA(NO) is a good choice to take advantage of lock avoidance in most cases.

If a program requires greater control than that offered by CS, consider RS. It offers greater control over the data but does not lock non-qualifying rows and pages as does RR. In most cases, it holds fewer locks than RR. Both RS and RR have the additional risk of having the page or row locks promoted to a table or tablespace lock if the maximum number of locks per tablespace is exceeded. If a cursor's SQL statement requires DB2 to create and process an intermediate work file--as it would for sorts and for processing several types of subselects, for example--RR or RS holds its locks during the processing, which could be a long time. It also risks an error code if the NUMLKUS limit is exceeded.

CC.7 INTENT LOCKS

When an SQL statement in a transaction first accesses a tablespace with a page or row level lock, DB2 first takes a particular type of lock, called an intent lock, at the table and tablespace level for a segmented tablespace or tablespace level for a nonsegmented tablespace. It later takes an S, U, or X lock against the page or row on which the data reside as SQL is executed. In a sense, the intent locks act as traffic signals that regulate the use of page and row level locks, and signal to concurrent transactions the type of access the pages or rows are undergoing.

Intent locking reduces the processing needed to manage the locks, while allowing a high degree of compatibility among concurrent locks. For example, if a given transaction needs the data it is about to read to remain unchanged, DB2 can take a share lock against the table or tablespace, which allows subsequent transactions to read but not change the data. The transaction must also be sure, however, that no changes are underway before it takes the S lock. That is where the intent lock comes in. For any X lock on a page or row in the tablespace, which would indicate an imminent change, DB2 will have taken an intent lock on the table or tablespace.

Instead of having to search all page or row locks to find those applying to a specific page, DB2 can look for the one tablespace intent lock, in this case a share with intent exclusive (SIX) lock. If it finds it, the transaction knows it must wait for the current changes to be completed before it proceeds with an update.

Types of Intent Locks

There are three types of intent locks: Intent share (IS), intent exclusive (IX), and share with intent exclusive (SIX).

Intent share: The transaction intends to read but not update data pages and, therefore, takes S locks on them; it tolerates concurrent transactions taking S, IS, SIX, IX, or U locks.

Intent exclusive: The transaction intends to read or change data and therefore take an X lock against the data pages; it tolerates concurrent transactions taking IX or IS locks.

Shared with intent exclusive: The transaction intends to read or change data; it tolerates other transactions taking an IS lock on the tablespace, which allows them to read data by taking S page locks. They cannot change the data.

A primary purpose of intent locks is cause a program to wait for a required S, U, or X lock at the table and tablespace level until the necessary locks have been released from the rows and pages and there is a compatible intent lock.

Allowable Combinations of Table and Tablespace Locks

The matrix in Figure CC.12 shows the allowable combinations of table and tablespace lock. Locks are at the partition level when using a partition scan as discussed in Chapter PL. The last two rows in the matrix indicate when row or page locks can be taken depending on the current tablespace lock. The matrix shows the type of activity each lock will allow in the data pages or rows beneath it. Note, for example, that if transaction A holds an IX lock, it allows subsequent transactions to take IX or IS locks, permitting those transactions eventually to take exclusive or share locks, which allow them to change or read a page or row. IS and IX intent locks are the most common when using a lock size of row and page.

Figure CC.11. Table and tablespace lock compatibility

Program A has lock

Program B can take lock

Lock	X	U	SIX	IX	S	IS
X	-	-	-	-	-	-
U	-	-	-	-	Y	Y
SIX	-	-	-	-	-	Y
IX	-	-		Y	-	Y
S	-	Y	-	-	Y	Y
IS	-	Y	Y	Y	Y	Y
ROW	-	-	S	S/X	-	S/X
PAGE	-	-	S	S/X	-	S/X

CC.8 ACQUIRING AND RELEASING LOCKS

Page or row locks are always taken when required during a program's execution and they are always released when the program executes a COMMIT or ROLLBACK statement. To a certain extent, however, you can control at which points DB2 acquires or releases locks against table and tablespaces, including intent locks. Use the BIND parameters ACQUIRE and RELEASE to indicate this.

Acquiring Locks

There are two options for acquiring table and tablespace locks: USE and ALLOCATE.

ACQUIRE(USE) causes DB2 to obtain a table or tablespace lock only when it executes an SQL statement that references a table in the tablespace. DB2 uses ACQUIRE(USE) when checking referential integrity constraints, regardless of the ACQUIRE parameter you specify at bind time. ACQUIRE(USE) is the default for plans and is effectively used for packages which do not allow for an ACQUIRE parameter.

ACQUIRE(ALLOCATE) gets locks on all tables and tablespaces referenced directly and indirectly by a program when it allocates the program's thread--just before it executes the first SQL statement in the program. If a SELECT statement appears in the same program as an INSERT, UPDATE, or DELETE statement, a more restrictive IX lock is taken, even if those particular statements are never executed. This has certain advantages in that it is not necessary to first take an IS lock on a tablespace and then change it to an IX lock for an INSERT, UPDATE, or DELETE statement executed on same tablespace.

A program for which ALLOCATE is specified must wait for all referenced tables and tablespaces to be available for the required locks before it can execute. This may delay that program's execution, but it minimizes the chance for deadlocks that exists when a number of programs execute concurrently against the same tables and tablespaces. However, this is not usually a problem anyway because the tablespace IS and IX locks are compatible. A program can have an IX lock at the table or tablespace level when executing an INSERT, UPDATE, or DELETE statement. Another program can be holding an IX or IS lock and be updating data or selecting data on another page.

Benefit of ACQUIRE(USE): ACQUIRE(USE) provides greater concurrency because the tablespace locks are not taken until they are actually needed. It allows for selective partition locking which is discussed in Chapter CD.

Releasing Locks

There are two options for releasing table and tablespace locks: COMMIT and DEALLOCATE. RELEASE(COMMIT) releases table and tablespace locks at commit or rollback points. RELEASE(DEALLOCATE) holds these locks until the thread is deallocated and the program terminates. DB2 follows a plan or package's RELEASE parameter for referential integrity checking.

RELEASE(DEALLOCATE) only serializes access to pages and rows when using S, U, and X locks at the table or tablespace level as a result of one of the following conditions: a LOCKSIZE of table or tablespace is used, the LOCK TABLE statement is executed, or lock escalation has occurred.

Benefits of RELEASE(DEALLOCATE): RELEASE(DEALLOCATE) has performance benefits. Counter and control information is not reset for sequential detection, index lookaside, and dynamically-generated compiled assignment procedures. It is not necessary to re-initialize processing including (IPROC, UPROC, and SPROC) after each commit as discussed in Chapter CO. RELEASE(DEALLOCATE) avoids taking and releasing the same locks repeatedly when using thread reuse in CICS and WFI (Wait for Input) in IMS, and in a data sharing environment. Figure CC.13 summarizes when lock sizes are acquired and released.

Figure CC.12. When locks are acquired and released

- Page and row locks are taken when required during execution of the program.
- Page and row locks are released depending on the use CS, RR, and RS but always with a commit or rollback
- Table and tablespace locks are acquired and released depending on the acquire and release parameter specified at bind time.
- IS and IX are usually taken at the table and tablespace levels when using page and row locking. This can be verified with EXPLAIN as discussed in Chapter EX.
- S, U, and X locks can be taken on individual rows and pages when IS and IX locks are in effect at the table and tablespace levels.

All combinations of ACQUIRE and RELEASE parameter values are valid except for ACQUIRE(ALLOCATE) with RELEASE(COMMIT) (Figure CC.14). The ACQUIRE option is not available for packages because DB2 always uses ACQUIRE(USE). These choices affect the amount of processing required for managing the locks and whether and when users and programs can access the data.

Figure CC.13. ACQUIRE and RELEASE sequences for tablespace locks

```
        unlock             lock table/tablespace                  unlock
PLAN A ——— ACQUIRE(USE) ———————————————— RELEASE(COMMIT) ——

        unlock             lock table/tablespace                  unlock
PLAN B ——— ACQUIRE(USE) ————————————— RELEASE(DEALLOCATE) ——

                           lock table/tablespace                  unlock
PLAN C ACQUIRE(ALLOCATE) ————————————— RELEASE(DEALLOCATE) ——
```

Recommendation: ACQUIRE(USE) and RELEASE(DEALLOCATE) provide good concurrency when using page or row locking and maximize performance.

To hold exclusive locks as short a time as possible, it is advisable to group INSERT, UPDATE, and DELETE statements together in a host language program followed by a COMMIT. If these SQL statements are interspersed with host language code, the locks are held while executing the host language code.

CC.9 EXPLICIT LOCK TABLE STATEMENT

The LOCK TABLE statement within a program overrides and releases all lock sizes and types that otherwise would be in effect for the accessed tables except for an intent lock held at the tablespace level. The explicit table lock allows use of the table lock size for specific programs that update heavily even though a LOCKSIZE of row, page, or any was specified when the tablespace was created. Use the LOCK TABLE statement to avoid having a program take a large number of row or page locks.

It is a good alternative to RR and RS when a large percentage of a table's rows or pages are to be updated.

The statement takes the form LOCK TABLE {name} IN SHARE MODE or LOCK TABLE {name} IN EXCLUSIVE MODE. While the statement requires the table's name, in nonsegmented tablespaces, DB2 takes the lock against the tablespace containing the referenced table. The LOCK TABLE statement locks only the specified table if it is in a segmented tablespace with an intent lock at the tablespace level. A PART parameter can be used to specify a specified partition that is be locked along with the name of a table in a partitioned tablespace, for example LOCK TABLE {name} PART 5 IN EXCLUSIVE MODE. The lock does not take effect until the statement executes, even if ACQUIRE(ALLOCATE) had been specified at bind time. If an IX lock is already held, an SIX is acquired. If SIX, U, or X lock is already held, locking the table in share mode has no effect. The explicit lock releases according to the RELEASE parameter specified at bind time.

Do issue LOCK TABLE after each commit if RELEASE(COMMIT) is used. The table lock is released with a commit. Page or row locking is used if LOCK TABLE is not issued again.

The LOCK TABLE statement does not operate on views or on tables located on another DBMS, including another DB2 subsystem. If a LOCK TABLE statement is used on a view, DB2 returns a negative SQLCODE (-156). An error may be issued at bind time depending on the precompiler being used to avoid the execution time error condition. To use the LOCK TABLE statement for a view, you must specify the underlying base table. Installations can use this feature to control use of LOCK TABLE statements. When developers are authorized to use only views, access to base tables is barred, thus enforcing the prohibition against LOCK TABLE statements except in special cases.

If you can afford to lock out all access to a table, locking the table has performance advantages. Figure CC.15 summarizes the elapsed and CPU minutes used by one program with and without LOCK TABLE. Notice that there is a saving of about 30% in elapsed and CPU time by using LOCK TABLE in this one case. An alternative is to start the tablespace in read-only mode in which case no locks are taken.

Figure CC.14. Effect of LOCK TABLE on performance

	Elapsed Minutes	CPU Minutes
No Lock Table	110	28
Lock Table Exclusive	78	20

An alternative to using the LOCK TABLE statement is to start the tablespace in read-only mode in which case no locks are taken. This avoids modifying the program and going through program preparation. It also allows for placing the tablespace in read-only mode when a batch read-only window is available and allowing for updates by other programs when the window is not available. The DASPJTSP can be started in read-only mode like:

```
-START DATABASE(DASPJDB) SPACENAM(DASPJTSP)
   ACCESS(RO)
```

CC.10 MONITORING LOCKS

There are a number of tools within DB2 that can be used to monitor locks. If lock contention becomes a problem, these tools can be quite useful in determining the lock size and type of locks so that corrective action can be taken. The EXPLAIN statement gives the lock mode in the PLAN_TABLE column TSLOCKMODE. (The use of EXPLAIN is discussed in Chapter EX.) If you see a value other than IS, IX, or N, investigate to see if your program is locking out other programs from reading or updating data when it executes.

Chapter PD discusses the SQLCA data structure used to communicate information between DB2 and a program. The field SQLERRMC contains a message indicating the database, tablespace or index space, page number, and index subpage involved in the lock contention. The message is positional, beginning with the DB2 error code and describing the object involved in the lock contention as indicated in Figure CC.16.

Figure CC.15. Lock contention message

```
----|----1----|----2----|----3----|----4----|----5----

00C9008E 00000301 PROTO    .ICLOSE2 .X'0003B6'.X'01'

    Position 01-08  =  DB2 error code
    Position 10-17  =  Resource type
    Position 19-26  =  Database name
    Position 28-35  =  Tablespace or index space
    Position 37-45  =  Page number (hex)
    Position 47-51  =  Index sub-page number (hex)
```

Typically the system or database administrator has authority to issue the -DISPLAY DATABASE command. This command gives current table and tablespace locks held and lists resources that are waiting for locks when the LOCKS parameter is specified.

If an UR is active across up to and including 255 checkpoints (default is 0, no limit), the message DSNR035I is written to the operator along with AUTHID, plan name, and etc. The UR continues. You can specify the number of checkpoints as UR CHECK FREQ on DSNTIPN installation panel or DSNZPARM URCHKTH.

Recommendation: Do modify the program to commit more frequently if the number of checkpoints within a UR is high.

Any of three traces can be turned on for general monitoring and accounting. The *statistics* trace records gives the total number of times a condition occurred for all SQL executed in the DB2 subsystem (class 1 and 3). The conditions specifically related to locking are suspensions, deadlocks, timeouts, and lock escalations. The *accounting* trace records give similar information but can be for specific authorization IDs, plans, and packages (class 1, 3, and 8). These records also give the maximum number of page locks held by a plan, which is useful for tuning lock limits and to determine if the program needs to issue a COMMIT more often to stay within those limits. The *performance* trace records show the progression of locks in detail but are very costly to have turned on for all plans and packages. Up to three times the usual number of DB2 instructions are executed while the full trace is turned on. Also, the result of the performance trace is very lengthy and difficult to read. It is a last resort in problem determination.

You will want to use a performance monitor to analyze the results of the trace data. IBM's DB2PM product provides good information on locking through the locking, accounting, and statistics reports. A number of software companies sell performance monitors for analysis of the statistics collected by DB2.

CC.11 LOCKS ON THE CATALOG TABLES AND DIRECTORY

Pages in the catalog tables and the directory are locked whenever an object is created or dropped. A lock against catalog table pages or the directory from a given developer, user, or program may bar others from creating objects, binding SQL, or even executing SQL. It is advisable to issue a COMMIT after each CREATE, ALTER, or DROP statement to avoid holding locks any longer than necessary. All access to the catalog table pages by an internal plan for data definition language (DDL) statements and binds use RS regardless of the isolation level of the program executing the statements (including SPUFI). Drain processing is used for DDL to avoid X tablespace locks. An exception is the creation of an index on a table in a segmented tablespace. This is because of no claim/drain processing is done at the table level when using segmented tablespaces. Catalog tables are subject to lock escalation just as are application tables when using a locksize of ANY after accumulating more than 1000 locks (default). These factors suggest frequent commits when using DDL. Locks are taken on the database descriptor (DBD) in the directory for a number of operations (including an X lock during object creation, alteration, and deletion, during index build, and an S lock during plan or package bind).

Locks are acquired at bind time on the catalog tables, and directory. An IX lock is taken on most catalog tablespaces, X lock on the SKCT and SKPT in directory (also locked for DROP and REVOKE statements), and S lock on the DBD. At execution time an IS lock is taken on the SYSPLANAUTH and SYSPACKAUTH catalog tables to check execution authority, S lock on SKCT and SKPT in the directory, and no locks are required on the DBD except for dynamic SQL, in which case an S lock is taken. The operations and locks are summarized in Figure CC.17 from the *IBM Locking in DB2 for MVS/ESA Environment* manual

Figure CC.16. Locks taken on the catalog and directory

Object of Locking	Static SQL	Dynamic SQL	Bind	Create Table	Alter Table	Drop Table Space	Grant	Revoke
Catalog Table Space	IS (a)	IS (b)	IX	IX	IX	IX	IX	IX
SKCT or SKPT	S	S	X	-	X ©	X (d)	-	X
DBD	- (e)	S (f)	S	X	X	X	-	-

(a) IS locks on the catalog table spaces are held only for a short time to check execute authority if the plan or package is not public or the authorization list is not cached in the EDM pool.
(b) Except when checking EXECUTE authority (see Note a), IS locks on the catalog table spaces are held until the COMMIT point.
(c) SKCT or SKPT is marked invalid if a referential constraint (such as a new primary key or foreign key) is added or changed, or the AUTHID attribute is changed in the table.
(d) SKCT or SKPT is marked invalid as a result of a drop table space operation.
(e) If the DBD is not in the EDM pool, S-locks are acquired on the DBD table space, which efficiently locks the DBD.
(f) Share lock is not taken on the DBD if the package or plan is cached (APAR PQ24634)

Several DB2 subsystem plans are used in bind operations, to validate user's authority, to perform service tasks, and for utilities as summarized in Figure CC.18. These locks can cause processing to be serialized.

Figure CC.17. DB2 subsystem plans that are locked

Plan	Description
DSNBIND	Used for all binds. Is a major contributor to the length of time required to complete a bind.
ACT	Used to validate a user's authority to access a specified plan. Is executed each time a thread is created with a lock of short duration.
BCT	Used to perform service tasks and handle requests from DB2 resource managers with lock usually of short duration.
DSNUTIL	Used by utility control program DSNUTILB. The lock duration varies with specific utility function.

CC.12 SUMMARY

It is difficult to point to typical transactions as guides for concurrency control decisions. Two extreme cases, however, summarize the tradeoffs available between resource usage and concurrency levels.

To allow many concurrent programs to change data at the cost of CPU time and virtual storage usage, consider:

- Use a page locksize. Use row locking only if your performance monitor indicates that lock contention is occurring on data pages.
- Have DB2 hold locks for as short a time as possible by employing ACQUIRE(USE) and RELEASE(DEALLOCATE) and by setting isolation level at CS with CURRENTDATA(NO) to take advantage of lock avoidance for ambiguous SELECT statements in most cases. Consider using UR when appropriate.
- Use FOR FETCH ONLY (or FOR READ ONLY) when writing new SELECT statements and when revising old ones.
- In programs, issue frequent commits, hold off updates to as near a commit point as possible, and commit before waiting for terminal input.

To accommodate mostly read-only programs and batch programs that can afford to limit other program access while using a minimum amount of resources:

- Use a lock size of table or tablespace. The isolation level has no effect when using a lock size of table or tablespace.
- Use ACQUIRE(ALLOCATE) and RELEASE(DEALLOCATE).
- Commit work infrequently.

These guidelines minimize the demand for resources, but there can be no concurrent updates by multiple programs.

These are the extremes. Each application has a unique mix of transactions with differing performance characteristics and needs that determine your concurrency control choices.

If acceptable, use CURRENTDATA(NO) to allow lock avoidance for ambiguous SELECT statements and UR to eliminate locking.

EXERCISES

1. What LOCKSIZE is best if there will be no concurrent update activity?

2. What LOCKSIZE should be used when concurrent update activity is expected?

3. Assume a LOCKSIZE of page. A very small sample of data (2-3 pages) has been loaded into tables for testing of programs under development. Developers are frequently experiencing lock contention. What is the problem and possible solution to the problem?

4. Is a lock size of row required to minimize lock contention when there is heavy insert activity at the end of the table or in any concentrated area of the table? If this type of heavy insert activity is expected, what value should be specified for PCTFREE and FREEPAGE?

5. How can you avoid lock escalation when using a lock size of row, page, or any? How can the lock escalation be isolated to a particular program or SQL statement?

6. If your program holds an S, U, or X lock on a page and it is using an isolation level of cursor stability (CS), repeatable read (RR), or read stability (RS), which SQL statements can another program execute successfully that act on the page? If the other programs are using the UR isolation level, which SQL statements can they execute successfully?

7. How do CS, RS, and RR differ with respect to how long page locks are held? How long are locks held with CS on a SELECT statement with the FOR UPDATE OF clause?

8. What are the primary requirements to take advantage of lock avoidance?

9. If no rows qualify on a page for a SELECT, UPDATE, or DELETE statement, will a lock be taken on the page or row if the CS or RS isolation level is used with the CURRENTDATA parameter of YES or NO.

10. Besides lock avoidance, what are the other benefits of read-only SELECT statements?

11. Assume that you select a row and display it to a user with a CICS pseudo-conversational or an IMS online transaction. Page locking is used, the plan is bound with CURRENTDATA(YES), and an isolation level of CS, RR, or RS is used. You issue an UPDATE statement based on information keyed by the user. Can you be certain that no one has changed the row after the row was displayed to the user and before the UPDATE statement was executed? What is an alternative for dealing with the situation?

12. What effect do the BIND and REBIND parameters ACQUIRE and RELEASE have on when row and page locks are acquired and released?

13. Under what conditions can RELEASE(DEALLOCATE) reduce concurrency, assuming the use of row or page locking and the CS isolation level?

14. What are the advantages of RELEASE(DEALLOCATE)?

15.
Bonnie Baker, an outstanding consultant and speaker, encountered the following locking procedure during an assignment. You will find her resolution in the answer. What are the problems with the procedure?

1. Use "LOCK TABLE tablename IN EXCLUSIVE MODE" to lock the table that will be updated and to override the page-level locking normally used for the table. (Bypass the LOCK TABLE statement if a parameter so indicates.)

2. Read two million records from a transaction file.

3. As each transaction record is read, perform an update to a DB2 table.

4. Commit after every five updates (commit frequency chosen for restartability, because of the fear of long-running rollbacks, and in anticipation of the eventual need to run concurrently with online programs).

5. Bind with RELEASE COMMIT.

ANSWERS

1. A LOCKSIZE value of table or tablespace is best if no concurrent update activity will take place.

2. In most cases, a LOCKSIZE of page is best when concurrent update activity is expected.

3. Locks are taken at the page level. One-half to one-third of the rows in the very small tables of 2-3 pages are being locked each time a change is made to the tables. Consider using row locking, a larger PCTFREE value, or cause each row to occupy a separate page by adding dummy columns to the table. If the table is large in production, consider using page locking.

4. Row locking is *not* required to reduce lock contention when INSERTING rows at the end of a table or in any concentrated area of the table. If the page is locked when an insert of a row is attempted, the row is inserted in a near or far page as if there is no free space on the page. PCTFREE and FREEPAGE should be zero when heavy insert activity is expected in concentrated areas of the table. There is no reason to waste space on each page by specifying a value for PCTFREE and it is not useful to leave a blank page every 63 pages or less. The free space and blank pages are used in the concentrated areas but wasted in most areas of the tablespace. Indeed, PCTFREE and FREEPAGE of 0 is the best choice, particularly for inserts at the end of the table. This causes DB2 to simply add additional pages for the new rows, rather than using its search algorithm to find free space somewhere in the tablespace.

5. Use LOCKMAX of 0, which is the default when using LOCKSIZE of ROW or PAGE, to avoid lock escalation. When using LOCKSIZE ANY, specify a LOCKMAX of 0, or set the NUMLKTS to 0 in DSNZPARM. To determine which program or SQL statement is causing lock escalation, it is necessary to turn on a performance trace.

6. If your program is using an isolation level of CS, RR, or RS and holds an S or U lock on a page, other programs can read the page but not insert, update, or delete rows on the page. If your program holds an X lock on a page, other programs cannot select, insert, update, or delete rows on the page. If other programs are using UR, they can select rows on the page that has an S or X lock while your program is executing select, insert, update, or delete statements that act on the page.

7. With CS isolation, a page lock is released when you fetch a row on another page. With RS isolation, locks are held on pages processed with qualifying rows. With RR isolation, locks are held on pages processed with qualifying and non-qualifying rows. A commit or rollback causes all page locks to be released with all three isolation levels. When using a SELECT statement with the FOR UPDATE OF clause and CS, locks on updated pages are held until a commit or rollback occurs.

8. Lock avoidance applies to read-only SELECT statements and ambiguous SELECTS bound with CS or RS and CURRENTDATA(NO), and when row or page locking is used. These options must be specified explicitly, because RR and CURRENTDATA(YES) are the defaults.

9. If no rows qualify on a page for a SELECT, UPDATE, or DELETE statement, the page or row is not locked if CS or RS and CURRENTDATA of YES or NO.

10. Read-only SELECT statements allow for the use of the UR isolation level and the blocking of data for transmission. It also increases the likelihood that parallel processing can be used for the SQL statement.

11. The row can change after it is displayed to the user and before the UPDATE statement is executed because locks are released when a screen is displayed. One of the several alternatives presented to deal with the situation is to save the primary key and all columns displayed before displaying the screen. Use a fully qualified UPDATE statement on all of the saved columns. The UPDATE statement is successful only if the row has not changed since it was displayed to the user. If the row has changed, the program receives an SQLCODE of +100 indicating that the row was not found to be updated. This means that the row has changed or was deleted after it was displayed and before the UPDATE statement was executed.

12. The ACQUIRE and RELEASE parameters do not affect when row and page locks are acquired and released.

13. RELEASE(DEALLOCATE) can reduce concurrency when using row and page locking if lock escalation has occurred to an S or X lock at the table or tablespace level or if a program issues the LOCK TABLE statement. Once an S table or tablespace lock is in effect, no other program can execute an INSERT, UPDATE or DELETE statement on the table. Once an X table or tablespace lock is in effect, no other program can execute a SELECT, INSERT, UPDATE or DELETE statement on the table.

14. RELEASE(DEALLOCATE) has performance advantages. This is because counter and control information is not reset for sequential detection, index lookaside, and dynamically-generated compiled assignment procedures. It is not necessary to re-initialize processing after each commit. Thread reuse in CICS and WFI (Wait for Input) in IMS benefit when RELEASE(DEALLOCATE) is used.

15. Bonnie Baker gives the following analysis.

First, the initial LOCK TABLE statement did indeed eliminate page-level locking -- but only for one unit of work. At the first commit, the X table lock and IX tablespace lock were released (because that's what RELEASE COMMIT does). When the second unit of work began, the locks acquired by the LOCK TABLE statement had been released. So the table resumed its normal page-level locking -- an IX lock on the tablespace, an IX lock on the table, and X locks on every single page updated. Each commit then released any page locks. (Page locks are always released at commit, regardless of the RELEASE parameter.) But each and every commit also released the table and tablespace intent locks. At the beginning of each new unit of work the intent locks on the tablespace and table had to be reacquired. Not good. Especially for a program that intended to acquire no page locks, just two big locks, one on the tablespace and one on the table, and keep them for the duration of the program run.

Second, because the commits were done after every five updates, the UPROC (discussed in Chapter CO) was barely built when it was destroyed by the commit (because that's what RELEASE COMMIT does). This job paid for the building of 400,000 UPROCs without enjoying the benefit of a single one. The premature demise of the UPROC was very expensive. Again, not good.

FIGURES

Program Development

PD.1 INTRODUCTION

Programs written in a number of host languages--COBOL, PL/1, C, FORTRAN, Assembler, APL2, BASIC, Ada, Prolog, REXX, and Java--can contain SQL statements that access DB2 data. That is, SQL statements embedded in a host language can update a DB2 database or return selected values from the database to a program. When you develop a program to use DB2 data, you must develop the host-language source code and the embedded SQL. The maximum number of table that can be referenced in a SELECT, INSERT, UPDATE, DELETE, and CREATE VIEW statement is 225.

Static and Dynamic SQL

SQL works within host-language programs in two ways--statically and dynamically. With static SQL, you know the SQL statement to be used and can therefore code it in the program. This allows the statements to be bound before executing the program, and that bound SQL remains static during execution. (All of the host languages that support SQL can use static SQL except for BASIC and APL2, which, because they are interpretive languages, bind SQL statements each time they are executed.) Static SQL, although less flexible than dynamic SQL, usually offers the best performance for online transactions with a high transaction rate.

With dynamic SQL, the program can formulate statements based on choices made and entered by the user as the program runs. In this case, the program must have code that allows the program to construct the statement, submit it to the bind process, execute it, and deal with its results. An alternative is to dynamically execute an SQL statement so that the optimizer can use the content of host variables in its access path selection process. (We will discuss dynamic SQL in more detail in Section PD.11.)

With a few additions, embedded SQL uses the same syntax that interactive SQL uses. You must indicate where an SQL statement begins and ends in order to set it apart from the host language code. The beginning delimiter is always EXEC SQL, which immediately precedes the statement. In COBOL, END-EXEC. signifies the statement conclusion; in PL/1, a semicolon performs that function. FORTRAN recognizes the end of a line as the statement end. Each SQL statement must have a beginning and ending delimiter.

Figure PD.1 is a fragment of a COBOL program showing the four data manipulation statements. It contains minimal COBOL code to show the SQL and does not show complete COBOL logic. For example, logically it is impossible to reach the DELETE statement.

Figure PD.1. Embedded SQL in a COBOL fragment

```
EXEC SQL SELECT SN, SNAME, STATUS, CITY
         INTO   :SN,:SNAME,:STATUS,:CITY
         FROM   S
         WHERE  SN = :SN-IN
END-EXEC.

IF SQLCODE = 0
   MOVE 'YES' TO SN-PRESENT.

IF SN-PRESENT = 'NO '
   EXEC SQL INSERT INTO S( SN, SNAME, STATUS, CITY)
                   VALUES(:SN,:SNAME,:STATUS,:CITY)
   END-EXEC.

IF SN-PRESENT = 'YES'
   EXEC SQL UPDATE S SET STATUS = :STATUS
            WHERE  SN = :SN-IN
   END-EXEC.

GO TO ACCEPT-NEXT-S.

EXEC SQL DELETE FROM S
         WHERE SN = :SN-IN
END-EXEC.
```

IBM-Provided Sample Programs

DB2 provides a number of sample programs that include code that might be useful for building your own programs. Most developers keep model or skeleton programs in their source libraries to use in developing new programs. DB2's library of sample programs can provide starting points for these skeletons. They are in the SDSNSAMP library, and the load modules are in the SDSNLOAD library. There are sample programs for batch, CICS, IMS, and ISPF. Here are a few member names of the SDSNSAMP library of sample programs that you may find useful:

- DSN8BC3 contains a sample COBOL program
- DSN8BP3 contains a sample PL/1 program
- DSN8BD3 contains a sample C program
- DSN8BF3 contains a sample FORTRAN program

The sample programs are described in the *Application Programming and SQL Guide* manual.

PD.2 USING HOST LANGUAGE VARIABLES

When a SELECT statement returns values to a program rather than to a user's terminal, the program must have host-language variables to receive them, and the SELECT statement must include information indicating those variables. Host variables in embedded SQL are identified by a colon preceding the variable names. If a host variable name is split for readability, in COBOL a hyphen must join the two parts (:SN-IN, for example); in PL/1 an underscore joins the two (:SN_IN). DB2 column names must be split with an underscore. These seemingly trivial points are the source of frustration at precompile time for COBOL developers. It is easy to remember the distinction but difficult to key the hyphen or underscore, depending on whether it is a host variable or column name.

An INTO clause in an embedded SELECT statement identifies the host variables that are to receive the selected values. Here is a typical SELECT statement embedded in COBOL:

```
EXEC SQL SELECT SN, S_NAME, S_ADDRESS
  INTO :SN, :S-NAME, :S-ADDRESS
  FROM  S_DETAIL
  WHERE SN = :SN-IN
END-EXEC.
```

Values from the columns SN, S_NAME, and S_ADDRESS are received by the host variables :SN, :S-NAME, and :S-ADDRESS, respectively.

A single host language data structure cited once in an SQL SELECT ... INTO statement can receive values from multiple columns. Consider the following definition of a COBOL data structure S-DETAIL:

```
01   S-DETAIL.
     05   SN          PIC X(2).
     05   S-NAME      PIC X(30).
     05   S-ADDRESS PIC X(60).
```

S-DETAIL can receive values from three columns. The values are assigned to the lower-level variables in the order in which the columns are listed in the SELECT statement. In this example:

```
EXEC SQL SELECT SN, S_NAME, S_ADDRESS
  INTO :S-DETAIL
  FROM  S_DETAIL
  WHERE SN = :SN-IN
END-EXEC.
```

SN, S_NAME, and S_ADDRESS are received by the variables SN, S-NAME, and S-ADDRESS, respectively.

Programming Recommendation: As the above examples demonstrate, there can be equivalent SELECT ... INTO statements using several individual host variables or a single multilevel variable. It is usually better, however, to avoid using multilevel variables. For one thing, if lower-level variables are added or deleted from the multilevel variable, the SQL statement referencing it will no longer work--the columns cited will no longer match the lower-level variables. For another, in order for column values to match the lower-level variables, the statement may have to select more columns than are actually needed for the application, a waste of processing resources, as discussed in Chapter PP.

Varying-length Variables

The COBOL language deals with variable length character data through the use of 49-level variables. Here is an example of defining the 49-level host variables to receive a VARCHAR column value.

```
01   SNAME.
     49   SNAME-LENGTH PIC S9(4) COMP.
     49   SNAME-TEXT   PIC X(30).
```

:SNAME-LENGTH contains the number of bytes in :SNAME-TEXT when selecting SNAME. SNAME-TEXT should be the same length as defined for the column (VARCHAR(30)). It is advisable to move space to SNAME-TEXT before selecting a column value into the host variable. Otherwise, unexpected characters can appear after the column value. For example, if the SNAME column contains Blake, the SNAME-LENGTH field will contains 5, the first five bytes of SNAME-TEXT will contain Blake, and the remaining 25 bytes will contain whatever was there before the move of data from the column to the host variable.

For UPDATE and INSERT statements, the program must calculate SNAME-LENGTH if it is unknown. Otherwise, trailing blanks are stored in the VARCHAR column. There are three alternatives for determining the number of characters before trailing blanks.

1) Assign each character of the value to an array, count the number of trailing blanks, and subtract the value from the total length of the string.

2) Use the following COBOL statement:

```
UNSTRING SNAME-TEXT DELIMITED BY '  ' COUNT IN SNAME-LENGTH.
```

3) POSSTR scalar function can be used determined the position in a string of another string:

```
EXEC SQL SET :SNAME-LENGTH =
  POSSTR('ERIC CLARK        ', '  ') - 1 END-EXEC.
```

:SNAME-LENGTH contains 10 (there are 10 bytes in ERIC CLARK before training two blanks) with the use of UNSTRING and POSSTR. Be careful of the use of these two techniques. It assumes that two blanks are not embedded in a character string. For example, if the string is 'EricbbClark', 'Clark' will be lost.

Qualifying a Variable by Table Name

When the same column name appears in more than one table, a host-language variable for each column's values must indicate to which table it refers. In a COBOL program, outside of SQL statements, the usual syntax for qualifying a variable applies. Inside SQL statements, however, DB2 requires a different format. For example, if the S_NAME column is included in both the Supplier table and the S_DETAIL table, each reference to an S-NAME host-language variable must identify the appropriate table. Outside of SQL statements, the COBOL references might be S-NAME OF S-DETAIL or S-NAME IN S-DETAIL. Inside SQL statements, however, the qualification format joins the table name and column name with a period. For example, S-DETAIL.S-NAME indicates that the variable refers to the S_NAME COBOL 05 level in the S_DETAIL 01 level. Used in an SQL statement, that format looks like this:

```
EXEC SQL SELECT S_NAME
  INTO: S-DETAIL.S-NAME
  FROM  S_DETAIL
  WHERE SN = :SN-IN
END-EXEC.
```

Programming for Nulls

If a host program is to receive a value from a column that allows nulls, the program requires variables for both the value and its associated null indicator. A null indicator variable is declared in the program as any other variable. For simplicity, programmers usually name the null indicator variable with a variation on the name of its associated variable. For example, a variable to receive values from the SNAME column, which allows nulls, might be called :SNAME. The associated null indicator variable might be called :SNAME-INDNULL. You can use the DCLGEN option of DB2I to generate an array of null indicator variables as discussed in Chapter PE.

The null indicator variable must be included in the SELECT ... INTO statement, as shown in this example:

```
EXEC SQL SELECT SNAME
  INTO :SNAME:SNAME-INDNULL
  FROM  S
  WHERE SN = :SN-IN
END-EXEC.
```

Notice that no comma or space separates the variable and associated null indicator variable in the statement.

If SNAME has a value, SNAME-INDNULL contains a value of 0. If SNAME is null, SNAME-INDNULL contains a -2 and a +305 SQLCODE is returned.

If a column contains nulls and you don't include a null indicator, the program receives a -305 SQLCODE.

Even if no columns allow for nulls, it may be necessary to use a null indicator to avoid a -305 SQLCODE. For example, if the average salary of employees in department X is computed and there are no employees in the department, the result is null and a null indicator must be coded on the SQL statement to avoid a negative SQLCODE.

Recommendation: If a null indicator is needed, you should test the null indicator for a positive SQLCODE as well as testing for negative SQLCODEs.

For example, if an SQL statement moves a null from a nullable integer column into a small integer host variable, it sets the null indicator at -2 and issues a +304 SQLCODE. The host variable will have the same value as before the SQL statement was executed.

INSERTING Nulls: INSERTING a null also requires special handling. Outside of the SQL INSERT statement, the program must move a negative number to the null indicator for the column receiving the null value. For example, if the user does not provide a value for STATUS, a -1 can be moved to the null indicator associated with the STATUS column like:

```
MOVE -1 TO STATUS-INDNULL.

EXEC SQL INSERT INTO S
   (SN, SNAME, STATUS, CITY ) VALUE
  (:SN,:SNAME,:STATUS:STATUS-INDNULL, :CITY)
END-EXEC.
```

Data Type Compatibility

Although host variable names need not match the names of the columns that provide their values, the data types must be compatible, and the lengths should match. When DB2 generates the data structures, it creates host-language structures that match the columns' definitions in the catalog tables. Mismatch errors generally occur in working storage variables defined by programmers. Mismatches can also occur when a SELECT clause's calculation produces a value too large for its variable or when a user enters a value with the wrong type or length.

Some mismatches are not allowed. DB2 issues a negative SQLCODE when a mismatch occurs. For example, a statement is not allowed to execute if it attempts to move a number into a numeric data type with insufficient precision to handle it--a value over 32,767 into a small integer, for example. And if a SELECT clause's calculation results in a value too large for its host variable or is an impossible value, a number divided by zero, DB2 simply leaves the variable set at its previous value and issues a negative SQLCODE.

However, DB2 automatically corrects for some mismatches, allowing processing to continue. For example, it removes the fractional part of a column's decimal or float value when moving it into an integer or small integer host variable. For example, 430.90 is truncated to 430. DB2 also truncates the trailing characters of a character column's value when moving it to a host variable that is not long enough to hold it.

These corrections can lead to incorrect or unanticipated results if the program does not account for them. To describe the data corrections it has made, DB2 uses SQLCODEs and null indicator values. For example, if a statement moves a value from a nullable integer column into a small integer host variable, it sets the null indicator at -2 and issues a +304 SQLCODE.

Recommendation: To determine if any of these data conversion situations have occurred, test for the null indicator's value in host-language code following the SQL statement. It is always best to avoid the problem by ensuring that column and host variable data types match. Not only does that avoid anomalous results, but also it saves on the processing DB2 must otherwise perform to correct mismatches.

Data Type Conversion Functions

DB2 has many functions, called scalar functions, that can be used to convert from one data type to another. This can be handy when data has to be moved into a host variable of another type. For example, assume you have a DEBT column defined as DECIMAL(31). This means that the column can contain 31 digits. However, most host languages only support the equivalent of DECIMAL(15). The CHAR scalar function can be used to convert the column DEBT to a character string, which can then be moved to a host variable defined as CHAR(33) or PIC X(33) as shown here:

```
EXEC SQL SELECT CHAR(DEBT)
  INTO :DEBT
  FROM BUDGET
END-EXEC.
```

A number of additional functions are discussed in Chapter SL.

Affect on Access Path: In most cases, when you use a scalar function on a column in a WHERE clause, a matching index scan cannot be used.

Use of Distinct Types

Distinct types provide for ensuring that designated columns can only be compared and arithmetic operation performed on columns defined with the same distinct type. For example, it should not be possible to compare a column containing distance measured in miles and another column containing distance in kilometers. Nor should it be possible to perform arithmetic on the two column. One should not add miles and kilometers, for example, the result is not accurate. Chapter CT describes how to create distinct types for each of the two columns and how DB2 automatically generates cast functions to designate miles as a built-in data type and the opposite. Additional operations can be done on distinct types with user-defined functions as described in Chapter UD.

Use of Host Variables and Literals with Distinct Types: Host variables defined with built-in data types and literals can be used to receive and assign distinct type values in SELECT, INSERT, UPDATE, and DELETE statements. DCLGEN generates fields with the built-in data types for the distinct types of US_DOLLAR for SALARY, EURO for COMM, and DECIMAL built-in data type for COMM. Indeed, all three columns are stored using the built-in data types specified when the distinct types are created as discussed in Chapter CT.

```
10 SALARY                    PIC S9(7)V9(2) USAGE COMP-3.
10 BONUS                     PIC S9(7)V9(2) USAGE COMP-3.
10 COMM                      PIC S9(7)V9(2) USAGE COMP-3.
```

Host variables cannot be defined as distinct types. This is the reason that cast functions are automatically generated when distinct types are created. Cast functions provide for comparisons in a WHERE clause and arithmetic operations on distinct types as discussed in Chapter CT. However, assignment of the distinct type column values to host variables do not require cast functions. Here is an example of the use of the DECIMAL cast function to all for the comparison of a column salary with a distinct type of US dollars with a host variable defined with a built-in in data type of decimal.

```
EXEC SQL
SELECT EMPNO, LASTNAME, SALARY, BONUS, COMM
 INTO :EMPNO,:LASTNAME,:SALARY,:BONUS,:COMM
FROM   EMP
WHERE  EMPNO             = :EMPNO
```

```
AND     DECIMAL(SALARY) > :SALARY END-EXEC.
```

A cast function is not required to assign literals to distinct type columns as shown in the following INSERT statement. The last line of the statement assigns 50000.00, 2000.00, and 20000.00 to the columns SALARY, BONUS, and COMM which are defined with the distinct types of US_DOLLAR, DECIMAL (is a built in data type), and EURO.

```
EXEC SQL
INSERT INTO EMP
(EMPNO, FIRSTNME, MIDINIT, LASTNAME,
 WORKDEPT, PHONENO, HIREDATE,
 JOB, EDLEVEL, SEX, BIRTHDATE,
 SALARY, BONUS, COMM)
VALUES
('00201','FLEUR','A' ,'JOHNSON',
 'D11','4501', '1974-03-03',
 'DESIGNER', 16, 'M', '1941-05-29',
  50000.00,  2000.00, 20000.00) END-EXEC.
```

Similarly, host variables defined as built-in data types can be used to assign values to distinct type columns with the SET clause of a UPDATE statement. The data types of each column in the SET clause are preceded with '--'.

```
EXEC SQL
UPDATE EMP
  SET SALARY   = :SALARY, --US_DOLLAR
      BONUS    = :BONUS,  --DECIMAL
      COMM     = :COMM    --EURO
  WHERE EMPNO = :EMPNO END-EXEC.
```

A DELETE statement is like a SELECT statement in that the cast function of DECIMAL is used to designate a column defined with a distinct type of US_DOLLAR to allow the comparison with a host variable defined with a built in data type of decimal in the WHERE clause.

```
EXEC SQL
DELETE FROM EMP
  WHERE DECIMAL(SALARY) > :SALARY END-EXEC.
```

PD.3 COMMIT AND ROLLBACK WORK

To ensure that updates will be applied to the database, the program must make sure the changes are committed. A commit turns responsibility over to DB2 to make sure that all changes are applied to the database. The changes are seen by subsequent SQL statements on that data, even though the data is not usually written immediately to the table. DB2 tries to keep pages in the buffer pool so that others can select and update them without having to do a read or write from DASD. There are a number of thresholds and operations that cause buffer manager to write pages to the table which are discussed in Chapter CD.

Commit and rollback processing closes all the cursors and releases locks. For more information about how commit processing affects the concurrency of an application, see Chapter CC.

Changes can also be rolled back, ensuring that those changes will not be reflected in the database.

When Is Work Committed or Rolled Back?

Work is committed when a program ends normally. Work is rolled back when a program abends. It is best to explicitly request a commit or rollback. How this is done depends on the transaction manager that is used.

TSO and CAF (Call Attached Facility) commit and rollback points are:

- ♦ EXEC COMMIT or EXEC COMMIT WORK
- ♦ EXEC ROLLBACK

CICS commit and rollback points are:

- ♦ EXEC CICS SYNCPOINT
- ♦ EXEC CICS RETURN (to CICS)
- ♦ TERMINATE (DL/1)
- ♦ EXEC CICS ROLLBACK

IMS commit and rollback points are:

- ♦ GU call to I/O PCB (MODE=SNGL)
- ♦ CHKP or XRST calls
- ♦ ROLL or ROLB

When using CICS and IMS online transactions, most programs display a screen and issue a statement that results in a commit. The commit processing applies to DB2 and DL/1 data.

How Often to Commit Work

The recommendation is often given, and rightly so, that to achieve the best concurrency, and to shorten restart times, programs should commit frequently. Because commit processing has costs of its own, particularly with respect to logging, it can be a challenge to decide how often to commit.

IBM tested this effect on DB2 V4 with a 50 MIPS processor as reported in the manual *Locking in DB2 for MVS/ESA Environment*, SG24-4725. The test consisted of updating 8,664 rows in a 90,972 row table on 2,178 pages using a matching index scan. Figure PD.6 summarizes the test results.

Figure PD.2. Commit frequency

Commit Freq.	Elapsed Seconds Class 2	CPU Seconds Class 2	Commits	Updates per Commit	Get-pages	Max. Locks Held	STS
8664	3.13	1.46	1	8664	242	242	1
1000	5.19	1.86	9	963	247	28	2

Commit Freq.	Elapsed Seconds Class 2	CPU Seconds Class 2	Commits	Updates per Commit	Get-pages	Max. Locks Held	STS
500	8.82	1.91	18	482	254	15	6
100	17.79	1.98	86	101	321	4	13
50	31.58	2	170	51	406	3	28
10	90.21	2.37	867	10	998	2	81
1	686.2	6.92	8664	1	8678	1	670

Notes:

Commit Frequency	Commit every *n* updates
Elapsed Class 2	Elapsed time executing DB2 calls
CPU Class 2	CPU time executing DB2 calls
Commits	Number of commits (close to number of rows updated, 8664, divided by commit frequency)
Updates per Commit	Number of rows updated, 8664, divided by commits
Getpages	Number of getpage requests
Maximum Locks Held	High-water-mark for the number of locks held by the program
STS	Service task switch suspensions (in this example, corresponds to synchronous log writes).

*Logs on 3380 DASD, 3390 DASD with fast write will reduce elapsed time

Consider these tests results as relative numbers. That is, a commit every 10 updates compared to commit after each update required about one-seventh of the elapsed time. The elapsed time goes down further with a commit every 100 and 1000 updates and still further if a LOCK TABLE is issued. As always, your results will vary depending on your specific CPU model, DASD hardware, workload, and other variables in your environment. It is always best to test the effect of a commit frequency in your environment and base your decision on your results.

Recommendation: The results in Figure PD.6 suggest that, for best performance, avoid committing after every update. If business requirements permit, a good commit frequency for an online transaction is about every 10 updates to minimize CPU time and I/O. A good target for batch processing is to commit every 1000 updates. (Batch processing is discussed in Chapter BP.) Use a LOCK TABLE statement to reduce resource consumption further.

PD.4 MAINTAINING DATA INTEGRITY AFTER DISPLAYING A SCREEN

DB2 automatically issues the equivalent of a commit work when a program displays a screen using CICS pseudo-conversational or IMS, depending on the mode of operation. (To be precise, locks are released when control is returned to CICS when using pseudo-conversational. Displaying a screen is one of the operations that causes control to be returned to CICS.) A commit (or its equivalent depending on the transaction manager used as discussed in Section PD.3 of this chapter) should be issued before a program asks for terminal input when using CICS conversational, TSO, and CAF where a commit is not issued automatically to release locks. If locks are not released until after the input is provided, the person entering the information ends up determining how long those locks will be in effect. If he or she leaves for a coffee break or answers the telephone before remembering to provide the required input, those locks can block others from the data for a considerable amount of time.

Consider a potential data integrity problem. Assume that Eric requests information about P4, the information is displayed to the screen, and commit processing occurs. Eric is interrupted by a telephone call or goes on a break. Meanwhile Fleur requests information on P4 as well. She updates information about the part and it is committed. Eric returns to his screen, updates the now old data and his update is written over Fleur's update. Fleur's update is lost. Certainly, this is not acceptable. There are several alternatives and variations on the alternatives to avoid having one persons update written on top of another persons update.

The information on P4 can be saved before displaying the screen like:

```
PN-OLD      = 'P4'
PNAME-OLD   = 'Screw'
COLOR-OLD   = 'Red'
WEIGHT-OLD = 14
CITY-OLD    = 'London'
```

Eric can change any of the values and the transaction issues:

```
UPDATE P
   SET PN     =   :PN
       PNAME  =   :PNAME
       COLOR  =   :COLOR
       WEIGHT =   :WEIGHT
       CITY   =   :CITY
 WHERE PN     =   :PN-OLD
 AND   PNAME  =   :PNAME-OLD
 AND   COLOR  =   :COLOR-OLD
 AND   WEIGHT =   :WEIGHT-OLD
 AND   CITY   =   :CITY-OLD;
```

If no one has made a change to P4 since the row was displayed, the update is successful and returns an SQLCODE of 0. If DB2 returns SQLCODE = 100, it indicates that the row no longer exists as it did when originally displayed, or it indicates that the row was deleted since it was displayed and the user should be informed.

The technique performs well because DB2 changes only the required information. If an indexed value has not been changed, DB2 does not update the index. If the user did not change any value, the data page is not written to DASD, and it is not logged. Lock and latch processing is done in all cases.

If there is a timestamp column in the row, an alternative that can minimize the number of columns that must be saved and used in the WHERE clause is to save only the primary key and timestamp when the row was displayed. Update the row with the new data and new timestamp when the row is changed. If there is not already a timestamp column on the row and you do not want to add 10 bytes to the row length, include a two- or four-byte counter. Have all programs that update the column update the counter column and use it in the WHERE clause to qualify the update.

Another technique for handling this kind of problem is to have the program reread the row with the FOR UPDATE OF clause after the user enters the new data. Compare it with the values saved before the screen was displayed. The update is issued if the data has not changed between the time that the row was displayed and the changed data was read by the program. The disadvantage of this technique is that the row must be reread before it is updated. There are some additional concerns with the FOR

UPDATE OF clause that are discussed in the Section PD.7 of this chapter. This requires more programming effort, and the additional read of the data detracts from performance.

If the table has a column declared as a ROWID data type (P_ROWID column in the example), it can be used to provide for direct row access without the use of an index or tablespace scan. A ROWID column does add 19 bytes to the row length. (Declaration of a ROWID column is discussed in Chapter CT, its basic usage in Chapter BIU, and more on its usage in the next section including the reason for specifying the primary key in the WHERE clause as a fallback access path.) The UPDATE statement can be issued as:

```
UPDATE P
   SET PN       =   :PN
       PNAME    =   :PNAME
       COLOR    =   :COLOR
       WEIGHT   =   :WEIGHT
       CITY     =   :CITY
 WHERE PN       =   :PN-OLD
 AND   P_ROWID  =   :P-ROWID
 AND   PNAME    =   :PNAME-OLD
 AND   COLOR    =   :COLOR-OLD
 AND   WEIGHT   =   :WEIGHT-OLD
 AND   CITY     =   :CITY-OLD;
```

Can verify that row has not changed with any techniques discussed

PD.5 USAGE OF DIRECT ROW ACCESS

Direct row access provides for locating a row directly without the I/O and CPU time required to locate a row with an index or tablespace scan (V6). It is necessary to retrieve the ROWID value through the use of an index or tablespace scan before it can be used in an SQL statement for direct row access.

A ROWID column can be used in a SELECT clause, WHERE clause of SELECT, UPDATE, and DELETE, an INSERT statement, accepted as input to the LOAD utility if GENERATED BY DEFAULT (discussed in Chapter CT) is used, and can constitute all or part of an index.

Direct Row Access Requirements

Direct row access applies only to stage 1 predicates. Simple Boolean term predicates qualify for direct row access, for example:

```
WHERE C1 = :HV
```

The C1 column must be declared with a ROWID data type. The :HV host variable represents a non-column defined as described in Chapter CT.

An index must exist on C1 to allow:

```
WHERE C1 IN (:HV1, :HV2, :HV3)
```

This is equivalent to:

```
WHERE C1 = :HV1
OR    C1 = :HV2
OR    C1 = :HV3
```

Direct row access cannot be used for ORed predicates on different columns, for example:

```
WHERE C1 = :HV1
OR    C2 = :HV2
```

Direct row access can be used on ANDed predicates where one predicate is on a ROWID column, for example:

```
WHERE C1 = :HV1
AND   C2 = :HV2
```

If there are multiple predicates and a ROWID column in the WHERE clause, the optimizer is likely to ch0ose direct row access on the ROWID column if the above criteria are met.

Parallelism and list prefetch are not used with direct row access either as a primary or fallback access path. If an SQL statement qualifies for both direct row access and parallelism or list prefetch (multiple index processing and hybrid join require list prefetch), direct row access is chosen.

Changing from Direct Row Access to ACCESSTYPE at Run Time

A second access path is chosen when direct row access is chosen by the optimizer. The PLAN_TABLE.PRIMARY_ACCESSTYPE = 'D' indicates director row access. The PLAN_TABLE.ACCESSTYPE indicates index usage or a tablespace scan. The second access path allows for an alternative access path if direct row access cannot be used at run time.

A saved row ID value before a reorganization cannot be used to locate a row after a reorganization. This is because a row ID value gives the location of a row and the location of a row changes with a reorganization. Therefore, do not save a row ID column value before a reorganization and expect to locate the same row after a reorganization. A subtle situation must be avoided. Reorganization (including online reorganization) can be executed while a program is executing after the program commits and before it completes processing. If a reorganization after a commit can be performed, retrieve the row ID again after the commit. Do not save row IDs in a table or file and use them after a commit. If an index exists on the row ID column, the beginning portion of the row ID is used to locate row. If the RID in the index does not match the RID in row ID column, the fallback access path is used.

Do take the necessary steps to avoid a tablespace scan when direct row access is expected. Certainly, the I/O and CPU time will be much more costly with a tablespace scan compared to direct row access in the great majority of cases. Users quickly become accustom to very good response time with direct row access and will even more quickly complain when a tablespace scan occurs. The same principle applies to a batch program that performs well most of the time but poorly when DB2 cannot use direct row access at run time.

Do provide for a good fallback access paths: A good choice is to specify the primary key in the WHERE clause assuming an index on the primary key. An alternative is to specify a predicate on a column with a usable index. Another alternative is to use an index on the column defined with a ROWID data type.

PD.6 USING CURSORS

When executing a SELECT statement interactively, all qualifying rows are returned as the user pages through the results. A host language program must declare and manage a cursor to receive more than one row from a SELECT statement. A cursor allows the SELECT to qualify a set of rows and return them one at a time. Imagine the set of rows being returned to a screen display. A screen cursor can point to one row at a time. A host language program must use a DB2 cursor to process one row at a time.

Declaring and Opening Cursors

A declarative SELECT statement is used to establish a cursor. (Because it is a declarative rather than executable statement, it can be placed in the data or procedure division of a COBOL program but must physically come before the OPEN.) The declaration takes the form DECLARE {name} CURSOR FOR, in which the cursor's name follows the word DECLARE. Here is a complete example declaration:

```
EXEC SQL DECLARE SCURSOR CURSOR FOR
  SELECT SN, SNAME, STATUS, CITY
  FROM   S
  WHERE  STATUS > :OLD-STATUS
  AND    SN     > :OLD-SN
  FOR FETCH ONLY
END-EXEC.
```

The FOR FETCH ONLY clause is optional but highly advisable if you are not going to update or delete a row that is fetched. It informs DB2 that the SELECT statement is read-only. There are a number of processes in DB2 that require read-only SELECT statements or an ambiguous SELECT bound with CURRENTDATA(NO) including lock avoidance, some forms of parallel processing, and blocking of data for transmission (SELECT with DISTINCT, ORDER BY, or GROUP BY clause is an additional criteria for qualifying as read-only in this case). Most of these processes significantly improve performance and concurrency. An alternative form of the clause is FOR READ ONLY, which complies with the SQL standard.

The program calls on the cursor for processing through two statements: one for opening the cursor and the other for fetching its rows. The OPEN statement readies the SELECT for execution. DB2 attempts to process one qualifying row at a time to pass to the program--unless all rows are required by a sort, for example. The OPEN statement simply uses the key word OPEN followed by the cursor's name:

```
EXEC SQL OPEN SCURSOR END-EXEC.
```

Fetching from the Cursor

The FETCH statement identifies the cursor to be used and employs an INTO clause to indicate the host variables that are to receive the values from each row:

```
EXEC SQL
  FETCH FROM SCURSOR INTO :SN, :SNAME, :STATUS, :CITY
END-EXEC.
```

As with the SELECT ... INTO statement used when a single row is returned, the variables used in a FETCH ... INTO statement must be of compatible data type with the columns that supply their values. The FROM clause of the FETCH statement is optional according to DB2 and is required by the SQL standard. A number of cursors can be opened at one time, on a single table or on multiple tables.

Typically a FETCH statement is coded within a program loop, which returns after processing a row to receive the next row. DB2 does not have to return all rows requested by a cursor's statement when the cursor is opened or at the first fetch unless one of the following is true:

- The statement requires a sort or an intermediate work file for a subselect, in which case all rows must be processed. Use of an index, which allows rows to be retrieved in order, avoids sorts.

- If materialization is required, rows identified by a view definition or table expression are written to a work area not including rows disqualified by predicates. (Materialization is discussed in Chapter ST).

- If list prefetch is used, all RIDs must be retrieved and sorted, in most cases before the first row can be returned to the program. (List prefetch is discussed in Chapter PP.)

A FETCH causes the cursor to advance to the next row. Because the program usually has to process all selected rows, a test for the existence of rows usually controls the loop. DB2 communicates with programs about the processing status through SQLCODEs (Section PD.8). The +100 SQLCODE indicates that the fetch found no rows or no more rows. The program can test for a +100 SQLCODE and move out of the loop when it is encountered. The 0 SQLCODE means one or more rows were found.

Singleton Select Versus a Cursor

A cursor is *not* needed when you retrieve a single row with an equal condition on a primary key for example. Indeed, a singleton select outperforms a cursor select if only one row is required because it requires only one trip between the host program and DB2. DB2 does manage an internal cursor used to fetch the one row. A second internal fetch is executed to return a 0 SQLCODE if a qualifying row is found or a -811 SQLCODE if more than one row qualifies. However, do avoid executing a singleton select many times to retrieve many rows.

A cursor select requires three trips between the host program and DB2 - first for the open cursor, second for a fetch (can have multiple fetches), and third for the close cursor. A combination of a singleton select and a cursor is a good choice if more than 40 to 50 percent of the time, zero or one row qualifies. In this case issue a singleton select and if -811 SQLCODE is received, open a cursor and fetch the required rows. The *DB2 for OS/390 Application Design Guidelines for High Performance,* SG24-2233, manual offers test results that suggests this guideline.

Exception: A cursor may be needed to influence the access path with OPTIMIZE FOR *n* ROWS as will be discussed.

Closing and Reopening Cursors

A CLOSE statement--EXEC SQL CLOSE SCURSOR END-EXEC.--closes the cursor. A Commit statement also closes all open cursors except those declared using the WITH HOLD clause discussed later in this section. After a cursor has been closed, it can be reopened without having to be declared again.

Conceptually, when a cursor is reopened, its SELECT statement is executed again. If the values that set the SELECT's criteria have not changed, the SELECT returns the same set of rows depending on the locking choices made as discussed in Chapter CC. This becomes a problem if a program closes a cursor in the midst of processing the set and then reopens the cursor to resume processing. If the program does not change the value that determines the search criteria to reflect the fact that some rows have been processed, the reopened cursor returns the original set (exceptions are discussed in Chapter CC). The program then begins processing rows that have already been processed rather than resuming at the next row after where the cursor was closed. One way to solve this problem is to track the cursor's position.

Tracking the Cursor's Position

To track the cursor's position as it works through the set of rows, use the last row processed to reset the search criteria. This technique works only if the search returns unique column values in an order that the program can follow. This is the case if the search criteria include a primary key column, which by definition includes only unique values, and the results are ordered by that column. DB2 can use an index to return the ordered rows, or it will get the qualifying rows and sort them. To allow for this cursor tracking technique, you should include a primary key in the predicate of a cursor declaration, and order the results by that column even when the search does not require it.

For example, the SCURSOR declared above might be used in an application to credit bonuses to suppliers with greater than a certain status. That status can be determined by the application's user, entered in response to a prompt and read into variable :OLD-STATUS. That variable is all that is needed to set the original search criteria to identify the suppliers to be credited. However, you may want to be able to commit in the midst of this processing or display a screen and resume processing at the proper row when the cursor is reopened. Because SN is a primary key, if the SELECT returned the rows in order by SN, the program can track the cursor's movement precisely through the set. Set the original :OLD-SN value at "blank." If the user enters 10 for :OLD-STATUS, SCURSOR's SELECT statement returns:

SN	SNAME	STATUS	CITY
S1	Smith	20	London
S3	Blake	30	Paris
S4	Clark	20	London
S5	Adams	30	Athens

The cursor initially points to the first row. Then as the rows process according to the FETCH-INTO statement, the program saves the current SN in :OLD-SN. If the cursor closes after the program completes its second loop through the statement, :OLD-SN will equal S3. When the cursor reopens, its SELECT statement using that value returns:

SN	SNAME	STATUS	CITY
S4	Clark	20	London
S5	Adams	30	Athens

Processing can complete in order.

If the rows are not returned in supplier number order, which is likely in a tablespace scan without an ORDER BY clause, this technique would skip rows for processing. Consider the effect, for example, if the cursor's SELECT statement returns rows in this order:

SN	SNAME	STATUS	CITY
S1	Smith	20	London
S3	Blake	30	Paris
S2	Jones	10	Paris
S4	CLARK	20	London
S5	Adams	30	Athens

After the second fetch loop :OLD-SN equals S3. When the cursor is closed and reopened after this fetch, the cursor's SELECT statement does not return the S2 row.

Recommendation: Do not assume that rows will always be returned in the correct sequence, even if they are now. The access path can change in the future as a result of a new index added to the table, changes made to the optimizer, or any number of changes that can occur in the future. The only way to ensure that the rows are returned in the required sequence is to use the ORDER BY clause.

Optimizing for a limited number of rows: If the number of qualifying rows is large, performing a sort to satisfy the ORDER BY every time the cursor is opened is likely to be prohibitively expensive. Frequently, only 15 rows or the number that will fit on a screen to be displayed to a user is all that is required for online transactions. The OPTIMIZE FOR *n* ROWS ($n = 15$ in this example) clause informs the optimizer that only a small number of rows is required, and it is likely that it will choose to use an ascending index to locate the rows in sequence and avoid a sort. (Chapter PP discusses how DB2 can use indexes to avoid a sort.)

```
SELECT SN, SNAME, STATUS, CITY
FROM   S
WHERE  SN > :OLD-SN
ORDER BY SN
FOR FETCH ONLY
OPTIMIZE FOR 15 ROWS
```

Care should be exercised in using OPTIMIZE FOR *n* ROWS. You can fetch beyond the number that you specify for *n* for any number of qualifying rows. However, a good access path for *n* rows is probably not a good access path for 10,000 rows. It is best to give your best estimate of the number of rows to be fetched. Avoid using OPTIMIZE FOR 1 ROW if you plan to fetch more than one row. This is a special case that the optimizer recognizes, and it will not use sequential prefetch, list prefetch, and multiple index processing for a select from a single table.

Cursor Repositioning with a Composite Primary Key

When a cursor is controlled by a composite primary key, reopening in sequence can be complex. Consider a composite primary key on the SN, PN, and JN columns of the SPJ table (Figure PD.2). Assume that the last row fetched contains the values of S2, P3, J3, and 200 before a screen is displayed, a commit is issued, or the cursor is closed.

Figure PD.3. Reopening a cursor with a composite primary key

```
SN >= 'S2' AND
((SN  = 'S2' AND
  PN  = 'P3' AND
  JN  > 'J3') OR

 (SN  = 'S2' AND
  PN  > 'P3') OR

 (SN  > 'S2'))
ORDER BY SN, PN, JN
OPTIMIZE FOR 12 ROWS
```

SN	PN	JN	QTY
S1	P1	J1	200
S1	P1	J4	700
S2	P3	J1	400
S2	P3	J2	200
S2	P3	J3	200
S2	P3	J4	500
S2	P3	J5	600
S2	P3	J6	400
S2	P3	J7	800
S2	P5	J2	100
S3	P3	J1	200
S3	P4	J2	500
S4	P6	J3	300
S4	P6	J7	300
S5	P2	J2	200
S5	P2	J4	100
S5	P5	J5	500
S5	P5	J7	100
S5	P6	J2	200
S5	P1	J4	100
S5	P3	J4	200
S5	P4	J4	800
S5	P5	J4	400
S5	P6	J4	500

```
NOT (SN  = 'S2'  AND
     PN  = 'P3'  AND
     JN <= 'J3') AND

NOT (SN  = 'S2'  AND
     PN  < 'P3') AND

    (SN >= 'S2')
ORDER BY SN, PN, JN
OPTIMIZE FOR 12 ROWS
```

Alternative 1: The basic approach to finding the next row using a composite primary key is the same as that described above for when a single-column primary key is used. The last key values processed are saved in host language variables, in this case, :OLD-SN, :OLD-PN, and :OLD-JN. Then this series of selection criteria in the cursor's SELECT statement will reopen it at the next row:

```
WHERE (SN = :OLD-SN AND
       PN = :OLD-PN AND
       JN > :OLD-JN) OR
      (SN = :OLD-SN AND
       PN > :OLD-PN) OR
      (SN > :OLD-SN)
ORDER BY SN, PN, JN
OPTIMIZE FOR 12 ROWS
```

In this case, OLD-SN = 'S2', OLD-PN = 'P3', and OLD-JN = 'J3'. The first portion of the criteria returns the next row, which holds the values 'S2', 'P3', and 'J4' as shown in Figure PD.2. The predicates on the left and right side of the figure show the rows that qualify for each group of predicates. Notice that no matter what values the host variables hold, the results always include the next row, and the ORDER BY clause assures it will be the next one processed. As explained in Chapter IU, however, DB2 does not use a matching index scan when satisfying an SQL statement that uses the 'OR' operator on multiple columns of a composite index. A non-matching index scan or multiple index processing on the one composite index can be used, but this can result in poor performance if the table is medium to large in size with many leaf pages to scan.

Alternative 2: All of the predicates in the previous example are surrounded by parentheses and an additional ANDed predicate is added to allow for a matching index scan on the first column of the composite index like:

```
WHERE   SN >= :OLD-SN AND
       ((SN  =  :OLD-SN AND
         PN  =  :OLD-PN AND
         JN  >  :OLD-JN) OR
        (SN  =  :OLD-SN AND
         PN  >  :OLD-PN) OR
        (SN  >  :OLD-SN))
ORDER BY SN, PN, JN
OPTIMIZE FOR 12 ROWS
```

This formulation does have the advantage that it allows for a matching index scan on the first column. If the first column has a low cardinality (a small number of distinct values), this can require the scan of many leaf pages which can negatively affect performance.

Alternative 3: A third alternative, similar to the first alternative uses negative logic to eliminate the ORed conditions like:

```
WHERE NOT (SN  =  :OLD-SN  AND
           PN  =  :OLD-PN  AND
           JN <=  :OLD-JN) AND
      NOT (SN  =  :OLD-SN  AND
           PN <   :OLD-PN) AND
          (SN >=  :OLD-SN)
ORDER BY SN, PN, JN
```

This alternative can use a matching index scan on the first column of the composite index. However, the negative logic makes the formulation confusing. A good way to ease the understanding of the formulation is to think "but not" where you see "AND NOT".

Alternative 4: Compare a concatenation of the three columns in the composite index with a concatenation of the three host variables containing the last values processed. This is very similar to coding the repositioning statement for a single column primary key.

```
SELECT SN, JN, PN
FROM   SPJ
WHERE  SN BETWEEN 'S2' AND :HIGH-VALUES
AND    SN CONCAT PN CONCAT JN >
```

```
      :OLD-SN CONCAT :OLD-PN CONCAT :OLD-JN
ORDER  BY SN, PN, JN
OPTIMIZE FOR 12 ROWS
```

Unfortunately, this straightforward concatenation technique cannot use an index because the concatenation is evaluated at stage 2. In order to use a matching index scan the predicate must be evaluated at stage 1. (Stage 1 and 2 processing is discussed in Chapter PP) The BETWEEN predicate allows for a matching index scan on the first column of the composite index and a scan on the remaining leaf pages. However, each occurrence of SN, PN, JN beyond S2 and including S2 must be passed to stage 2 for concatenation and evaluation, which increases the costs substantially.

Alternative 5: An easy alternative is not to commit or close the cursor until the leading column changes. In the example, process all S2 and then reposition on S3. This can be a usable technique for batch processing where the cardinality of the first column is suitable for commit processing.

Alternative 6: If the table being accessed is small, processing resources are plentiful, and run time is unimportant either of the above five approaches work fine. A sixth approach maximizes the number of columns that can be used in a matching index scan. This technique requires several cursors and more programming logic, as indicated in the following pseudo code. The number of cursors that must be coded and managed can be minimized by using separate cursors only for the leading columns with a low cardinality followed by alternative 2.

```
SELECT SN, PN, JN, QTY
FROM   SPJ
WHERE  SN = :OLD-SN
AND    PN = :OLD-PN
AND    JN > :OLD-JN
ORDER BY SN, PN, JN
OPTIMIZE FOR 12 ROWS

IF SQLCODE = 100
   More rows needed to fill screen,
   process cursor for next SELECT

SELECT SN, PN, JN, QTY
FROM   SPJ
WHERE  SN = :OLD-SN
AND    PN > :OLD-PN
ORDER BY SN, PN, JN
OPTIMIZE FOR 12 ROWS

IF SQLCODE = 100
   More rows needed to fill screen,
   process cursor for next SELECT

SELECT SN, PN, JN, QTY
FROM   SPJ
WHERE  SN > :OLD-SN
ORDER BY SN, PN, JN
OPTIMIZE FOR 12 ROWS

IF SQLCODE = 100
   All qualifying rows have been fetched
```

The first SELECT statement can use a matching index scan on all three columns of the composite index and will probably return enough rows to be displayed to the user. If not, the second SELECT can use a matching index scan on two of the columns in the composite index and will probably return enough rows to be displayed to the user. If not, the third SELECT can use a matching index scan on one of the columns in the composite index. If not enough rows are fetched to fill a screen before receiving a 100 SQLCODE, there are not enough qualifying rows to be displayed.

Using CURSOR WITH HOLD

The CURSOR WITH HOLD clause in a cursor declaration statement avoids closing the cursor and repositioning to the last row processed when the cursor is reopened. CURSOR WITH HOLD is useful for batch processing and can be used with TSO, CAF, DL/1 batch, a background CICS task, and IMS BMP. CURSOR WITH HOLD can be coded but will be ignored when used with CICS pseudo-conversational or IMS interactive processing because DB2 repositions by saving the last primary key value in a way much like what was discussed above. The saved values are maintained with the thread. When a screen is displayed using CICS pseudo- conversational and IMS, a commit is effectively issued, all cursors are closed, the thread is deallocated, and the last primary key value is lost. Indeed, it is not desirable to hold resources while a user is looking at the data or answering a telephone call.

The declaration looks like this:

```
EXEC SQL DECLARE SCURSOR CURSOR WITH HOLD FOR
  SELECT SN, SNAME, STATUS, CITY
  INTO :SN,:SNAME,:STATUS,:CITY
  FROM   S
  WHERE  STATUS > :NEW-STATUS
  FOR FETCH ONLY
END-EXEC.
```

A FETCH must be the first statement after a commit is issued when using CURSOR WITH HOLD. Locks are released on with a commit assuming RELEASE LOCKS of YES (default) on installation panel DSNTIP4 or in DSNZPARM DSN6SPRM RELCURHL (V6).

Dynamically prepared SQL is kept in the Environmental Descriptor Manager (EDM) pool past a commit point without using the dynamic cache as discussed in Section PD.11.

CURSOR WITH HOLD has the advantage that cursor repositioning logic need not be executed after each commit. This has performance advantages for batch programs. However, cursor repositioning logic is still required in a batch program. Recall from Chapter CC that locks can be released as a result of a -911 or -913 SQLCODE from a deadlock or timeout. The cursor position is released when the locks are released. (The LOCK TABLE statements can be issued at the beginning of the program to avoid deadlocks and timeouts.) You will also need to develop cursor repositioning logic for application program restart processing. If a program abends, obviously CURSOR WITH HOLD cannot hold position.

Restrictions: CURSOR WITH HOLD disallows parallelism and is ignored in stored procedures when using the DB2 established stored procedure address space.

Scrolling Backward

Users sometimes want to take second looks at rows that were previously displayed. They would like to be able to press a key that redisplays those rows.

A technique for scrolling backward is to save the first primary key of each displayed panel as far back as the user is permitted to scroll, and refetch the data. The user may agree that they do not plan to scroll backward more than ten pages, for example. Assume that the first row on the first panel has a primary key of S1, P1, and J1 which is hidden on the panel or saved in a work area. The first row of the second panel has a primary key of S2, P3, and J4. The first row of the third panel has a primary key of S3, P3, and J1. Figure PD.3 shows an example of a technique for scrolling backward three panels.

Figure PD.4. Example of technique for scrolling backward

	SN	PN	JN	QTY	
Display panel 1	S1	P1	J1	200	If user scrolls back
Save S1, P1, J1	S1	P1	J4	700	3 panels,
	S2	P3	J1	400	Display message that
	S2	P3	J2	200	cannot scroll back
	S2	P3	J3	200	further
Display panel 2	S2	P3	J4	500	If user scrolls back
Save S2, P3, J4	S2	P3	J5	600	2 panels,
	S2	P3	J6	400	Reposition using
	S2	P3	J7	800	S1, P1, J1
	S2	P5	J2	100	Display panel 1
Display panel 3	S3	P3	J1	200	If user scrolls back
Save S3, P3, J1	S3	P4	J2	500	1 panel,
	S4	P6	J3	300	Reposition using
	S4	P6	J7	300	S2, P3, J4
	S5	P2	J2	200	Display panel 2

If the user scrolls back one panel after displaying three panels, use the primary key of S3, P3, and J1 as hidden on the panel or saved in a work area to refetch the rows that were displayed using the forward repositioning technique discussed in Section PD.3. If the user scrolls back two panels, use the primary key of S2, P3, and J4 to refetch the rows required to fill the displayed panel and if the user scrolls back three panels, use the primary key of S1, P1, and J1 to reposition and refetch the rows required to fill the displayed panel.

Use of ROWID to Allow for Scrolling Forward and Backward with One Index: You can select required rows in ascending sequence using an ascending index to avoid a sort (opposite is true for a descending index) or DB2 can sort the rows. Save the row ID values in an array or work area as the rows are fetched. Select the rows a second time with the ROWID column in WHERE clause and process the row IDs in reverse sequence from an array or work area. This avoids creating an ascending and descending index on the same column.

The technique may not perform well if many rows are fetched because all row ID values must be fetched, saved, and the rows retrieved a second time in reverse sequence. In addition, seek time can be high depending on the location of the rows. If few rows qualify and must be sorted, consider sorting the rows in the required sequence if an index cannot be used to avoid the sort. However, the technique can be useful for a medium number of rows as an interim solution. The technique may not be necessary in a future release (V7+1 for example) where a bidirectional index can provide for using an ascending index to avoid a descending sort and the opposite. It is unlikely that an ascending index can be used to determine the MAX value with 1-fetch index access (and the opposite) in the near future.

A drawback to the previous two techniques is that other processing may change the data between when the original rows were displayed and the cursor is opened a second time. If rows are inserted, the second series of fetches will return rows that were not seen the first time. If rows were deleted, some rows seen the first time will not be seen the second time the screen is displayed. Actually this can be considered an advantage in that the user sees the data as it currently exists. However, some user prefer to see exactly what they saw the first time even though that it not what exists on the table at the moment.

The problems of more or less rows displayed the second time can be avoided by saving the rows returned by the cursor in a temporary table or some other temporary storage available to the program. Depending on the transaction manager being used, the data can be saved in an array in the program, ISPF internal table, CICS temporary storage, or IMS/DC SPA. An alternative is to use CICS BMS paging or IMS MFS logical paging.

The disadvantage of saving the data to be displayed a second time is that although the user requires the ability to scroll backward through the data, they in fact seldom do scroll backward. Yet, the data is always saved which increases the cost of the transaction substantially. In addition, depending on the locking used, the data may have changed since the data was placed in the temporary area. This is an advantage in that the user sees the same data when scrolling backward. However, complications are introduced when the user also requires the ability to update the data, which may have changed since it was saved. The update transaction must avoid updating a row that has been deleted or writing an update over an updated row that the user did not see. Techniques for accomplishing this are discussed in Chapter CC.

PD.7 EMBEDDED UPDATES AND DELETES

Embedded SQL allows you to update and delete rows with or without a cursor.

Without a Cursor

An embedded UPDATE or DELETE statement can act on all of the rows meeting its WHERE clause criteria in response to a single execution of the statement. Multiple rows therefore may be updated or deleted in a program with the same statement an interactive user would employ for that action. For example, if all parts above a given weight in a particular city were to be reassigned to another city, an application for managing the change might prompt the user to enter the cutoff weight, the city where the parts are to be found, and the city to which they are to be reassigned. If those values were read into variables :WEIGHT-LIMIT, :OLD-CITY, and :NEW-CITY, this embedded statement would update all qualifying parts:

```
EXEC SQL UPDATE P SET CITY = :NEW-CITY,
         WHERE WEIGHT > :WEIGHT-LIMIT
         AND   CITY   = :OLD-CITY
END-EXEC.
```

Notice that it is not necessary to first select the rows and then delete them. This improves performance and saves development time.

With a Cursor

In some cases, however, the updates or deletions are done in conjunction with other processing that requires a cursor. If the rows returned with a cursor are to be updated or deleted, the cursor definition must indicate that fact. A FOR UPDATE OF clause alerts DB2 that the update is coming so that the fetched rows will not be changed before they are updated or deleted. DB2 keeps the rows stable by holding locks. Locks are accumulated on each page or row that is updated after being fetched until a commit or rollback point with or without the FOR UPDATE OF clause. Locks are accumulated on each page or row accessed even if no rows qualify with RR.

If the program to reassign parts over a certain weight from one city to another employed a cursor, its declaration would look something like this:

```
EXEC SQL DECLARE PCURSOR CURSOR FOR
  SELECT PN, WEIGHT
  FROM   P
  WHERE  WEIGHT > :WEIGHT-LIMIT
  FOR UPDATE OF CITY
END-EXEC.
```

Notice that the column being updated need not appear in the SELECT clause, although it usually does.

When a cursor is used for updates, the UPDATE statement must use a WHERE CURRENT OF CURSOR clause to indicate the row to be processed--for example:

```
EXEC SQL
  UPDATE P
  SET CITY = :NEW-CITY
  WHERE CURRENT OF PCURSOR
END-EXEC.
```

The WHERE CURRENT OF clause causes the row at which the cursor points to be updated. The update does not advance the cursor, however. A FETCH ... INTO statement is necessary for that.

Restrictions on Update: Certain SELECT statements return values that are not updatable. For example, what values in a column should be changed to "update" the column's average? Because DB2 has no way of answering that question, it disallows use of the FOR UPDATE OF clause in cursor declarations that include the AVG function, the SUM, COUNT, MIN, MAX, and DISTINCT functions, or the GROUP BY operator. The FOR UPDATE OF clause does not work with an ORDER BY, thus it cannot be used with cursor repositioning logic. Finally, unions, joins, and most subselects create temporary work files, as do a number of the other operations, that cannot be updated since the underlying base tables may be changed independently, creating inconsistencies in the data. Basically, FOR UPDATE OF cannot be used on a read-only cursor. Read-only SELECT statements are discussed in Chapter CC.

FOR UPDATE OF disallows the use of some efficient processing that requires read-only SELECT statements including lock avoidance, and uncommited read as discussed in Chapter CC and block fetch as discussed in Section PD.9.

DB2 does not use index access on columns specified in the FOR UPDATE OF clause unless list prefetch is used. If it were to use an index on a column being updated, some updates would not be applied after the initial update since the index itself would be changed by the update. For example, if an index on the STATUS column were used to retrieve rows, those rows would be returned in STATUS order. An update of STATUS from 10 to 50 would cause the cursor position to skip to a STATUS of 50, missing 20, 30, and 40. If equal predicates are used on the updated column and all preceding columns, an index can be used to locate the row to be updated. An index cannot be used on a column with an arithmetic expression in the WHERE or SET clause. The restriction also applies to columns in predicates when the WITH CHECK OPTION is used in defining a view.

Recommendation: Updating with a cursor, with its need for a cursor declaration, FETCH ... INTO statement, and UPDATE ... WHERE ... CURRENT statement, requires considerably more coding than the simple embedded update statement. A primary purpose of the FOR UPDATE OF clause is to hold locks on all pages or rows updated to avoid others updating the data. But displaying a screen using CICS pseudo-conversational and IMS results in a commit, which releases all locks. Since the cursor update also precludes the use of indexes on columns specified in the FOR UPDATE OF clause, it also carries a performance deficit. For these reasons, and because in most cases an update without a cursor can carry out the same updates as an update with a cursor, it makes sense to avoid cursor updates except for some batch processing.

PD.8 TESTING FOR EXISTENCE

A frequent requirement is to determine whether a particular value exists one or more times in a table. Further processing is based on the results of the existence test. We will review several alternatives for existence tests with an analysis of the performance implications of the alternatives. The reason for reviewing unsatisfactory alternatives is to avoid someone thinking of one of the alternatives and testing it only to determine that it performs poorly.

Alternative 1: Unfortunately, a popular technique for testing for the existence of the occurrence of a value is to count all occurrences of the value. Here is an example of determining the number of occurrences of S4 in the SPJ table.

```
SELECT COUNT(SN)
FROM   SPJ
WHERE  SN = 'S4';
```

This alternative is perhaps the worse technique if you only need to know if the value exists one or more times because it is necessary for DB2 to locate all occurrences of S4 and count them. It performs particularly poorly when there are many occurrences of the value in the predicate. However, the alternative is necessary if you must determine the number of occurrence of a value. It is not necessary if you need to only determine if the value exists one or more times.

Alternative 2: It is not necessary to actually select a column value to determine if a value exists in a table. Indeed, you can select a literal (1, 2, 'ABC', etc.) and based on the SQLCODE returned determine if the value exists, for example:

```
SELECT 1
FROM   SPJ
WHERE  SN = 'S4';
```

Two cases need to be tested if a cursor on the SELECT statement is defined.

a) If the SQLCODE is 0, S4 does exist.

b) If the SQLCODE is 100, S4 does not exist in the table.

If a singleton SELECT statement is used, a third case need to be tested.

c) If the SQLCODE is -811, more than one occurrence of S4 exists in the table and a cursor has not been defined. It is not advisable to depend on the values returned in host variables when a negative SQLCODE is received. Even if you receive values from the first row found today, you may not receive comparable results in the future with a change to DB2. For example, if a subselect is used and no rows qualify in the subselect, the outer table is not tested at all because a -811 is seen by DB2 indicating that no rows quality in the subselect. There are some cases where you will not receive any values at all as shown in the following example.

```
SELECT SN, PN, JN, QTY
FROM   SPJ
WHERE  SN =
   (SELECT SN
    FROM   S
    WHERE  CITY = 'Stockholm';
```

If there are multiple suppliers in Stockholm, the subselect returns a -811 SQLCODE. DB2 does not access the SPJ table at all and therefore no values are returned from the SPJ table. An alternative is to use an IN subselect as discussed in Chapter ST.

Alternative 3: Here is a similar technique to alternative 1 with an effort to cause DB2 to stop processing when the first specified SN is located.

```
SELECT COUNT(DISTINCT SN)
FROM   SPJ
WHERE  SN = 'S95';
```

Unfortunately, at present DB2 does not stop processing when it finds the first S95. Rather it processes all occurrences of the value which detracts from performance if there are more than a few occurrences of the value as the following test results indicate. DB2 may stop processing when it finds the first S95 in the future.

Here is another technique which like the COUNT(DISTINCT SN) formulation attempts to get DB2 to stop processing when it finds the first S95 value.

```
SELECT 1
FROM   SYSIBM.SYSDUMMY1
WHERE  EXISTS
  (SELECT 1
   FROM   S
   WHERE  SN = 'S95');
```

Unfortunately this technique suffers from the same problem as the COUNT(DISTINCT SN) formulation. DB2 does not stop processing when it locates the first occurrence of S95 at present.

The EXISTS statement can be changed to a correlated subselect like:

```
SELECT 1
FROM   SYSIBM.SYSDUMMY1 AS D
WHERE  EXISTS
  (SELECT 1
   FROM   S
   WHERE  SN = 'S95'
   AND    D.IBMREQD = D.IBMREQD);
```

In this case, DB2 stops processing when it finds the first occurrence of S95. A correlated EXISTS subselect has performance advantages over a non-correlated EXISTS subselect. This is because DB2 stops processing when it finds the first occurrence of the value being tested when using a correlated subselect. In contrast, a non-correlated subselect results in DB2 having to process all rows that have the value. Even though the correlated EXISTS subselect has performance advantages, it is not a straightforward test for existence and can be confusing to the person who needs to maintain the program.

Analysis of alternatives 2 and 3: Peter G. Backlund, a Swedish consultant working with DB2 since 1981, did a number of tests to evaluate the performance in terms of CPU time of various alternatives for testing for existence. He wrote a program to execute static SQL statements a number of times in a loop so that any overhead including thread creation can be disregarded. The CPU time measurements are based on a sufficient number of execution of the statements in a loop. The CPU time reported in the next two figures is for one execution. For example, in one case the CPU time for 10 executions is about 8 seconds and for 100 executions about 80 seconds. The CPU time is reported for one execution as 0.8 seconds.

We will use the SPJ table with the columns SN, PN, JN, and QTY that is used throughout the book which is very similar in structure to the table used by Peter G. Backlund . The table used in the tests has 3,522,640 rows and a composite index on the first three columns of the table. The analysis assumes a composite index on SN, PN, and JN. The equivalent of following "SELECT 1" statement with and without a cursor was used to test for existence as well as the "SELECT COUNT(DISTINCT SN)" statement. Figure PD.4 shows the test results.

```
SELECT 1
INTO   :X
FROM   SPJ
WHERE  SN = 'S95'

SELECT COUNT(DISTINCT SN)
INTO   :X
FROM   SPJ
WHERE  SN = 'S95'
```

Figure PD.5. Comparison of test for existence with values in an index

WHERE clause	Number of occurrences of value in WHERE clause	CPU sec. SELECT 1 with no cursor	CPU sec. SELECT 1 with cursor and 1 fetch	CPU sec. SELECT COUNT (DISTINCT SN) with no cursor
SN = 'S95'	0	0	0.0002	0
SN = 'S94'	62519	0	0.0002	0

The test results suggest that the SELECT 1 and SELECT COUNT (DISTINCT SN) with no cursor is a good choice if you expect no rows to qualify in most cases assuming that the columns you are testing are in an index. This suggestion is based on the tests using the predicate SN = 'S95' that use 0.0001 CPU seconds. If more than one row qualifies in a few percentage of the cases (less than 10-20 percent, for example) and you need to know that, consider following the first test with another test using a SELECT 1 statement defined with a cursor. This avoids executing the higher cost (0.0002 CPU seconds) cursor statement 80-90 percent of the time. The idea of first executing a singleton select followed by the possible execution of a cursor select is discussed in Section PD.3 with the guidelines at 40-50 percent. The SELECT COUNT (DISTINCT SN) formulation requires significantly more CPU time (0.2 seconds) if multiple rows exists with the required values as indicated by the test case with a predicate of SN = 'S94'.

If you need the actual count of the number of rows with the value specified in the predicate and most of the time no rows qualify, use the SELECT 1 or SELECT COUNT (DISTINCT SN) with no cursor to maximize your performance. For the few percentage of cases where multiple rows qualify, follow the first SELECT statement with SELECT COUNT(SN) described as alternative 1. You will incur the higher costs for only the few percentage of cases.

Peter G. Backlund also tested cases to determine the existence of values where all values are not in the index. The QTY column is not part of the composite index on SN, PN, and JN in our example. The WHERE clause was varied as shown in Figure PD.5.

Figure PD.6. Comparison of test for existence without all values in an index

WHERE clause	Number of occurrences of value in WHERE clause	CPU sec. SELECT 1 with no cursor	CPU sec. SELECT 1 with cursor and 1 fetch	CPU sec. SELECT COUNT (DISTINCT SN)
SN = 'S93' AND QTY = 900*	0	0.8	0.8	1
SN = 'S92' AND QTY = 800*	260	0.0024	0.0011	1

*QTY column is not part of the composite index.

The required CPU time does not differ for the three formulations of the SELECT statement based on the test results if no rows qualify. However, if a number of rows exists with values that satisfy the SN = 'S92' AND QTY = 800 WHERE clause, the SELECT 1 formulation defined with a cursor has performance advantages with a CPU usage of 0.0011 seconds. The SELECT COUNT (DISTINCT SN) should not be used when a column not in the index is tested for existence. It uses significantly more CPU time (0.8 seconds) than the SELECT 1 formulations with and without a cursor.

Notice that the singleton select in Figure PD.4 requires less CPU time than does the cursor select in Figure PD.5. The processing required for a singleton select compared to a cursor select is discussed in Section PD.3. The second internal fetch to determine if a -811 SQLCODE should be returned can be costly if a good deal of processing is required to determine that there is more than one qualifying row. In contrast, there is no additional costs for a cursor select if a second row is not fetched. In addition, a cursor select can have advantages if OPTIMIZE FOR 1 ROW is needed to influence the access path. We see that a comparison of a singleton select and a cursor select depends on a number of factors.

Alternative 4: A correlated subselect can be used to retrieve rows based on the existence of a value using one SELECT statement. The previous alternatives need an additional SELECT statement to retrieve rows if the required value exists. The following EXISTS subselect returns a true or false to the outer SELECT. If the values tested in the inner select exists, the rows form the S table are returned. This statement returns information on suppliers who supply part P5 where the part is being used on J7:

```
SELECT SN, SNAME, STATUS, CITY
FROM   S AS SX
WHERE EXISTS
  (SELECT 1
   FROM   SPJ
   WHERE  SN = SX.SN
   AND    PN = 'P5'
   AND    JN = 'J7');
```

This formulation has performance advantages and disadvantages. It has performance advantages in that one rather than two SELECT statements need to be executed which reduces the path length (the number of instructions that must be executed). It allows for a matching index scan on the SN, PN, and JN composite index for each row in the S table which initially appears to be a good thing. However, if there are many rows in the S table which require many matching index scans into the SPJ table and the I/O to the SPJ table are pretty much at random, we have a performance disadvantage.

The requirement described in the example can be met by reformatting the statement as a join. The advantage and disadvantages of EXISTs and join formulations are discussed in Chapter ST. If your requirement does not allow for reformulation of a statement to a join, the EXISTs formulation is worth consideration. Even though EXISTs and NOT EXISTs subselects are usually correlated subselects, they can have performance advantages in some cases, particularly if the use of the in-memory table is beneficial for the particular processing required (also discussed in Chapter ST). The best formulation also depends on the number of rows that must be scanned in the outer S table and processed in the SPJ inner table example.

Many factors need to be analyzed to determine which formulation of a request will give the best performance, thus the saying that "it depends". The goal in this book is to give you information on what it depends upon.

PD.9 GENERATING SEQUENCE NUMBERS

It is sometimes necessary to generate sequence numbers for orders, invoices, or perhaps employee identification numbers. Four alternatives are presented for generating sequence numbers along with the associated pros and cons. The first alternative has performance advantages over using an application table to track the last used sequence number.

Alternative 1: An identity column can be defined to DB2 as described in Chapter CT (V6 APAR PQ30652). The definition causes DB2 to generate sequence numbers according to the parameters specified when the column is defined. The SN_ID column of the S_ID table is defined as the identity column. You can insert a row into S_ID table with or without specifying the identity column as in the following examples.

```
INSERT INTO S_ID
(SN_ID, SNAME, STATUS, CITY)
  VALUES
(DEFAULT, 'Johnson',  20, 'Childress');
```

or

```
INSERT INTO S_ID
(SNAME, STATUS, CITY)
  VALUES
('Johnson',  20, 'Childress');
```

It is not possible to insert a value into an identity column defined as GENERATED ALWAYS except if the OVERRIDING USER VALUE clause is used. This use of this clause is not recommended because if it is changed to GENERATED BY DEFAULT, the insert will fail.

```
INSERT INTO S_ID
(SN_ID, SNAME, STATUS, CITY)
  VALUES
(4000, 'Johnson',  20, 'Childress');
```

If a value is specified for an identity column defined as GENERATED BY DEFAULT, the value is inserted into the table. This can result in a duplicate value without a unique index defined on the column. If the GENERATED BY DEFAULT clause is used when the table is created for data propagation, do consider creating a unique index on the identity column.

The guidelines given for insertion of a single row applies to inserting into a table with a subselect from another table.

Determine value inserted: You can determine the last sequence number inserted into a table with the SET statement like:

```
EXEC SQL SET :CURSEQNO = IDENTITY_VAL_LOCAL() END-EXEC.
```

The :CURSEQNO host variable contains the most recently inserted value after a successful insert (V6 APAR PQ36328). This applies to sequence numbers generated by DB2 or assigned by program if GENERATED BY DEFAULT is used. The value can be useful in determining the generated primary key to be used to insert a corresponding foreign key rows. If a value has not been generated since a commit (not savepoint), null is returned. Only the SET statement is supported (SELECT, VALUE, etc statements give unpredictable results particularly if a parallel access path is used). The host variable to receive the sequence number can be defined as DECIMAL(31,0) regardless of the definition of the column. If you need to override the DEC15 default for the DB2 subsystem, the CURRENT PRECISION special register can be set or determined like:

```
SET CURRENT PRECISION = ' DEC31'
SET :HVDEC = CURRENT PRECISION
```

Beware of using IDENTITY_VAL_LOCAL in triggers: A BEFORE trigger returns unpredictable results or null. An AFTER trigger returns the most recent value from a single row insert within the body of the trigger. If VALUES is used, a null is returned. It is not possible to use a function to determine the value assigned in the insert that caused the trigger to be activated nor at any of the 1 to 16 levels of triggers as discussed in Chapter TR.

In the following alternatives we will use the variable SEQNO to represent the required sequence number to be inserted into the target table. The next two alternatives assume that the next sequence number (NEXTSEQNO) is stored in a one row table.

Alternative 2: The NEXTSEQNO is selected with a cursor including the clauses of FOR UPDATE OF, WITH RS (or RR), or KEEP UPDATE LOCKS. These clauses are used to hold an X lock on the one row table containing NEXTSEQNO until a commit is issued. This avoids someone else getting the sequence number and producing a duplicate. An UPDATE statement with the WHERE CURRENT OF clause is used to increment the NEXTSEQNO. The SEQNO is set to the NEXTSEQNO plus one using host language code. A row is then inserted into the target table with the generated SEQNO.

Alternative 3: In this alternative the NEXTSEQNO is incremented immediately in the one row table with an UPDATE statement. This causes an X lock to be held until a commit is issued so that no one else can get the same sequence number. The NEXTSEQNO is decremented by one in a SELECT statement that puts the result in the host variable SEQNO. The row is then inserted into the target table as in alternative 2.

Alternative 4: The maximum sequence number is selected from the target table with the MAX(SEQNO) function. The SEQNO is incremented by one and inserted into the target table. If a -803 SQLCODE is returned, someone else has gotten the same MAX(SEQNO) incremented it by one and successful inserted it into the target table. A unique index on the SEQNO column is required to avoid duplicate sequence numbers being inserted into the target table. It should be a descending index to maximize performance by allowing for one-fetch index access. If the -803 SQLCODE is received, the program must select another MAX(SEQNO) and attempt its insert again repeatedly until a 0 SQLCODE is received indicating a successful insert.

Pros and cons of alternatives: Alternatives 1 (assuming the use of GENERATED ALWAYS), 2, and 3 do not require a unique index on the sequence number column in the target table to avoid duplicates nor is it necessary to manage the -803 SQLCODE. This avoids index maintenance if an index is not required on the column for other purposes. Alternative 2 requires three SQL statements one of which requires a declare cursor, open, and fetch. Alternative 4 requires two SQL statements in most cases and has performance advantages if a unique descending index is maintained. This alternative does not require a one row control table to track NEXTSEQNO with potential lock contention on the control table.

It is likely that there will be lock contention on the control table 10 percent of the time if one transaction per second is executed and the transaction requires 0.1 seconds to execute.

The average wait time for a lock can be calculated with the formula

```
AVG wait time = (P(PL) / (1 - P(PL)) * AVG lock duration
```

where P(PL) is the probability of the page being locked. The following sample calculation assumes that the page will be locked 10 percent of the time and the average lock duration is 0.1 seconds.

```
0.11 seconds  = (0.10  / (1 - 0.10)) * 1 second
```

It is estimated that the average wait time for a lock is about 0.11 seconds. The formula is covered in detail in the manual *Locking in DB2 for MVS/ESA Environment*, SG24-4725.

PD.10 ERROR HANDLING

It is possible to handle error conditions in a variety of ways. Although you can handle error conditions by writing code immediately after the statement that causes the error, most organizations find it more efficient to place all of the error handling within a separate section of the program or in a separate common module that can be used by all programs. Using a common module can avoid redundancy in coding and ease maintenance.

The SQL Communications Area

The SQL Communications Area (SQLCA) is a data structure that must be included in any host-language program using SQL. The SQLCA provides a way for DB2 to pass feedback about its operations to the program. As a program runs, after each SQL statement executes, DB2 returns, via the SQLCA, codes indicating that the execution was successful or identifying errors or special conditions. The program can then test for these codes and handle them appropriately.

The SQLCA will be included in a COBOL program by the precompiler as a result of the statement:

```
EXEC SQL INCLUDE SQLCA END-EXEC
```

Each host language has somewhat different syntax for including the SQLCA in the program. The include syntax and the details on the fields in the SQLCA is described in the *Application Programming and SQL Guide* manual. We describe some of the key fields in the SQLCA.

The SQLCODE field in the SQLCA should be checked after each SQL statement that is executed. If the value is 0, the statement executed successfully. If the value is 100, no rows or no more rows qualify for the statement. If the SQLCODE is any other positive number, it is a warning or informative message. If the SQLCODE is a negative number, there is an error condition.

The SQLSTATE is for compliance with the SQL standard. Its error descriptions are more general in nature than the SQLCODE descriptions. This is because the description must be applicable to any DBMS that complies with the standard. If there is a possibility that your program may execute on a relational DBMS other than DB2 for OS/390, it is a good idea to process the SQLSTATE as well as the SQLCODE to minimize the changes needed to a program when it is executed on another DBMS, such as DB2 Universal Database (UDB) on Windows 2000, NT, 98, 95, Unix, AIX, Linux, HP-UX, Solaris, UNMA-Q, OS/2, OS/400, and other platforms in the future. Many of the SQLCODEs used by these DBMSs are not the same as those used by DB2 UDB for OS/390.

The SQLCODE has more precise description of a condition. The SQLSTATE is more general for multiple DBMSs. It is advisable to check the SQLCODE and/or SQLSTATE after each statement or command is executed.

The SQLSTATE is 5 bytes of character data with a class and subclass. The first 2 bytes are the class and the last 3 bytes are the subclass.

You can define an SQLSTATE with triggers and user-defined functions as discussed in Chapters TR and UD. Do avoid conflicts with SQL92 SQLSTATE values by using the first character of the letters between I and Z or the digits 7, 8, or 9. Details on the SQL92 SQLSTATE rules for defining values can be found in the SQL Reference manual.

The third element in the SQLERRD array is an integer containing the number of rows inserted, updated, or deleted. It is best to use this field to determined the number of rows changed, particularly with an SQL statement that processes more than one row. The alternative of counting the number of rows is more costly. Do keep in mind that the field does not include a count of foreign key rows deleted as a result of the use of a cascade delete constraint or updated due to the use of the set null rule. In addition, it does not include the number of rows deleted using the mass delete algorithm (discussed in Chapter BP.)

Error Message Text

The SQLERRMC field in the SQLCA contains up to 70 bytes of descriptive information about the error or special condition identified by the SQLCODE. A program can display this text during program testing and use the information to write a friendly message to the user describing the error.

Example: Here is an example of using information in the SQLERRMC to inform users about referential constraint violations. If an update statement violates a referential integrity constraint, it is necessary to know the constraint name that was violated. Recall from Chapter CT that a constraint name was given when defining the foreign key. This name can be found in SQLERRMC when a negative SQLCODE is received, usually beginning with a -53. For example, if a -530 is received indicating that an insert or update would have resulted in an orphan dependent row, the SQLERRMC can be moved to a host language structure like:

```
IF SQLCODE = -530
   MOVE SQLERRMC TO CONSTRAINTS.
```

CONSTRAINTS can be defined in working storage like:

```
01   CONSTRAINTS.
     03   PARM-LENGTH       PIC S9(4) COMP.
     03   REF-CONSTRAINT    PIC X(08).
     03   FILLER            PIC X(62).
```

The host variable REF-CONSTRAINT contains the constraint name given when the foreign key was defined.

The violation of a table check constraint is managed similar to referential integrity constraints. (Table check constraints are discussed in Chapter CT.) If you receive a -545, the constraint name is found in the SQLERRMC field.

After you have the constraint name, more information is needed to notify the user. You can extract information about the constraints from the catalog tables, and place the information in an application table for retrieval and analysis in a production environment. The referential integrity constraint name is in the column SYSIBM.SYSFOREIGNKEYS.RELNAME, and the table check constraint name is in the column SYSIBM.SYSCHECKS.CHECKNAME. The following SELECT statements identify the information needed to notify the user about the constraint that was violated for objects created with the authorization ID of POSYSTEM.

```
SELECT F.RELNAME, F.COLNAME,
       F.CREATOR, F.TBNAME,
       R.REFTBCREATOR, R.REFTBNAME,
       C.NAME, C.KEYSEQ, C.COLTYPE, C.LENGTH,C.SCALE
FROM   SYSIBM.SYSFOREIGNKEYS F,
       SYSIBM.SYSRELS        R,
       SYSIBM.SYSCOLUMNS     C
WHERE  F.CREATOR      = 'POSYSTEM'
AND    F.CREATOR      = R.CREATOR
AND    F.TBNAME       = R.TBNAME
AND    F.RELNAME      = R.RELNAME
AND    R.REFTBCREATOR = C.TBCREATOR
AND    R.REFTBNAME    = C.TBNAME
AND    F.COLSEQ       = C.KEYSEQ
```

```
ORDER BY F.RELNAME, F.COLNAME,
         F.CREATOR, F.TBNAME,
         C.NAME, C.KEYSEQ

SELECT C.CHECKNAME, CDEP.COLNAME,
       C.CREATOR, C.TBNAME,
       C.CHECKCONDITION
FROM   SYSIBM.SYSCHECKS   C,
       SYSIBM.SYSCHECKDEP CDEP
WHERE  C.CREATOR        = 'POSYSTEM'
AND    C.TBOWNER        = CDEP.TBOWNER
AND    C.TBNAME         = CDEP.TBNAME
AND    C.CHECKNAME      = CDEP.CHECKNAME
ORDER BY C.CHECKNAME, CDEP.COLNAME,
         C.CREATOR, C.TBNAME;
```

By using an application table that contains SQLCODEs, constraint information, and descriptive text, a program that receives an SQLCODE can select from the table and retrieve the text to display to the user.

Wherever possible, suggest how the user should proceed to resolve the problem. For example, if the user attempts to insert a row into a dependent table that does not have a corresponding parent row, the user needs to be informed and told how to proceed to resolve the problem. Simply displaying the SQLCODE of -530 will be of little value to the user. If the SQLCODE of -551 is received, the user needs to be notified that they do not have the required privilege and who they should contact to get the privilege. If the SQLCODE of -911 is received because of a timeout or deadlock, the user needs to be informed that someone else is currently processing the data. Consider developing retry logic for these situations. Perhaps the program can try to get the data three times and each time inform the user that the data is locked by someone else before giving a message that the user must re-execute the transaction later. A rollback of all insert, update, and delete statements within a UR occurs with an SQLCODE of -911 and must be executed again. In addition, cursor repositioning logic is required.

Detailed Error Descriptions: Some error conditions require a technical person to resolve the problem. If the SQLCODE of -818, -805, or -812 is received, an administrator must investigate and resolve the fact that DB2 cannot find a valid plan or package to execute. Similarly, an SQLCODE of -904 indicating that a resource is unavailable requires that someone find out why that resource is unavailable. Some companies also write a log of error messages to identify error patterns for resolution and to provide information for further analysis. These logs and the person resolving the problem require a detailed description of the error.

Detailed message information can be retrieved using a sample program provided in SDSNSAMP. The assembler program DSNTIAR can be called, passing it the SQLCA ,and it can return up to 960 bytes of text describing the error. It is necessary to define a data structure to receive the message text like:

```
01  ERROR-MESSAGE.
    02  ERROR-L        PIC S9(4) COMP VALUE +960.
    02  ERROR-TEXT     PIC X(120) OCCURS 8 TIMES
                        INDEXED BY ERROR-INDEX.
77  ERROR-TEXT-L     PIC S9(9) COMP VALUE +120.
```

Here is an example of calling DSNTIAR from a program:

```
CALL 'DSNTIAR' USING SQLCA
      ERROR-MESSAGE, ERROR-TEXT-L.
```

DSNTIAR issues OS/390 GETMAINs to allocate storage. If you are using CICS, it is best to call DSNTIAC which issues CICS GETMAINs. This will reduce the amount of CPU time required.

PD.11 CONNECTING TO REMOTE SITES

You can connect to multiple remote sites and update data at various sites within a unit of recovery. When you issue a commit, DB2 takes responsibility for insuring that all updates issued at all sites will be completed or none of the updates will take place with its two-phase commit protocol.

Type 2 Connection

The type 2 CONNECT statement applies to application directed distributed facilities. You can connect to multiple DBMS that conform to Distributed Relational Data Access (DRDA) architecture. A host variable or literal can be specified in the CONNECT statement to indicate the location where the following SQL statements are to be executed. The first CONNECT statement in Figure PD.7 establishes a connection to the content of the host variable :ROME. A row is inserted into the SPJ table in Rome. (The host variable has the same name as the content of the host variable in the example.)

Figure PD.7. Connecting to multiple sites

```
     EXEC SQL CONNECT TO :ROME END-EXEC.
     EXEC SQL INSERT INTO SPJ (SN, PN, JN, QTY)
                VALUES ('S10', 'P40', 'J7', 400) END-EXEC.

     EXEC SQL CONNECT TO :SYDNEY END-EXEC.
     EXEC SQL UPDATE P SET CITY = 'Perth'
              WHERE PN = 'P4' END-EXEC.

--   If DELETE is to occur in :Rome,
--      CONNECT TO     :ROME if SQLRULE(DB2) (default)
--      SET CONNECTION :ROME if SQLRULE(STD)

     EXEC SQL DELETE FROM J
              WHERE  JNAME = 'Electrical'
              AND    CITY  = 'Sydney' END-EXEC.

     EXEC SQL RELEASE :SYDNEY END-EXEC.
--   Next SELECT will execute in :SYDNEY

     EXEC SQL SELECT SN, SNAME, STATUS, CITY
              FROM   S
              WHERE  SN = 'S4'
              FOR FETCH ONLY END-EXEC.

     EXEC SQL COMMIT END-EXEC.
```

```
--    Connection to :ROME still exists (default)

      EXEC SQL CONNECT RESET END-EXEC. -- Return to local site
```

The second CONNECT statement in Figure PD.7 establishes a connection to Sydney. Now two connections exists but only one is active at any one time. That is, all SQL statement after the CONNECT statement will be executed at the location specified in that statement. If further processing is to be done in Rome it is necessary to re-activate the connection to Rome. This is done with either a CONNECT TO :ROME or SET CONNECT TO :ROME if you wish to comply with the SQL standard. The statements preceded by "--" are comments in the example. The DELETE statement is executed in Sydney.

When all processing is complete at a site, it is advisable to release the connection to minimize the resources required by the program and allow others to use the resources. This can be done with the RELEASE statement followed by a COMMIT statement. The connection is not physically broken until the COMMIT statement is executed. The SELECT statement will be executed in Sydney even though the connection has been released. You will want to release connections immediately before a commit to avoid confusion unlike the example with a comment to emphasize the fact that the connection is not physically broken until the commit. It is necessary to hold connections until a commit to ensure a two-phase commit where all updates within the unit of recovery are made at all locations. The connection to Rome still exists after the commit because it was not released prior to the commit. You can return to the program's location with the CONNECT RESET statement. Any SQL statements executed after the reset will be against tables at the program's location. The currently active site can be determined with the following statement.

```
SET :CURRENT = CURRENT SERVER
```

The location of the program is in the host variable :CURRENT. The SQLERRP field in the SQLCA data structure contains a server ID indicating the IBM DB2 product, version, release, and modification level.

Methods for Specifying the Location

Use of the CONNECT TO statement detracts from location independence because the location must be known to move into the :ROME host variable for successful execution of:

```
EXEC SQL CONNECT TO :ROME END-EXEC.
EXEC SQL INSERT INTO SPJ (SN, PN, JN, QTY)
           VALUES ('S10', 'P40', 'J7', 400) END-EXEC.
```

A good alternative is to use an alias when using DRDA (V6) and the private protocol.

```
CREATE ALIAS SPJ FOR ROME.POSYS.SPJ;--prior to executing SQL

EXEC SQL INSERT INTO SPJ (SN, PN, JN, QTY)
           VALUES ('S10', 'P40', 'J7', 400) END-EXEC.
```

The alias (SPJ in the above example) can be specified in SQL statements. This requires the use of the DBPROTOCOL(DRDA) bind parameter which is the default unless changed on DSNTIP5 installation panel or DSNZPARM DSN6SYSP DBPROTCL. The DBPROTOCOL(PRIVATE) parameter is not advisable as will be seen in the next section,

An alternative that detracts from location independence is to use fully qualified table or view names like:

```
EXEC SQL INSERT INTO ROME.POSYS.SPJ (SN, PN, JN, QTY)
            VALUES ('S10', 'P40', 'J7', 400) END-EXEC.
```

Type 1 and 2 Connections

A type 1 connection can be specified to override the default of a type 2 connection with the precompiler parameter of CONNECT(1). Also a type 1 connection is used if the CURRENTSERVER bind parameter is used to designate the initial connection. Type 1 connection results in using the private protocol (also known as system directed distributed facilities). There are several disadvantages of this older protocol. It is possible to connect only to another DB2 subsystem using the DB2 private protocol. It is necessary to commit and break the current connection before establishing another connection. Significantly more bytes must be transmitted compared to the use of the DRDA protocol. Finally, the private protocol is expected to be eliminated in the future.

Type 2 connections use the more current DRDA (also known as application directed distributed facilities) protocol. These connections allow for connection to multiple DBMS that conform to DRDA architecture. The CONNECT(2) parameter is the default for the precompiler.

You must make a decision to use type a 1 or type 2 connection in all packages executed by a transaction. Otherwise, a -808 SQLCODE is received if PROGA has a type 1 connection and PROGB attempts a type 2 connection.

Recommendation: Type 2 connections with the use of the DRDA protocol are recommended rather than type 1 connection which means the use of the private protocol. The advantages of DRDA over the private protocol are discussed in Chapter CO.

Releasing a Connection

The description of the RELEASE statement in Figure PD.7 assumes the default of EXPLICIT. The action to take when a commit is executed is determined by the bind parameter DISCONNECT. DISCONNECT(EXPLICIT) means that all released connections are destroyed. DISCONNECT(AUTOMATIC) means that all remote connections will be destroyed even if they have not been explicitly released. DISCONNECT(CONDITIONAL) means that all remote connections will be destroyed except those with CURSOR WITH HOLD when a commit is executed.

Blocking of Data for Transmission

If a SELECT statement is read only, 32 KB of data and control information is blocked and transmitted in one message. This has significant performance advantages over formatting and transmitting one row at a time. If OPTIMIZE FOR *n* ROWS clause effects the number of rows blocked and transmitted.

- If OPTIMIZE FOR 1 ROW is used, DB2 blocks and transmits MIN(16 rows, 32 KB of data).
- If OPTIMIZE FOR *n* ROWS is used where *n* results in <= 32 KB of data and control information, DB2 blocks and transmits *n* rows at a time with a maximum of 32 KB.
- If OPTIMIZE FOR *n* ROWS is used where *n* results in >= 32 KB of data and control information, DB2 blocks and transmits up to and including 100 32 KB blocks by default. Blocks are transmitted as they are built (it does not wait until 100 blocks have been built). The default can be changed with the parameters EXTRA BLOCKS REQ = 100 and EXTRA BLOCKS SRV = 100 on installation panel DSNTIP5 (can be 0-100).

PD.12 ORGANIZATION CHART PROCESSING (OR BILL OF MATERIALS)

Organization chart structures are not uncommon in application system design. Most companies have an organization chart similar to the one in Figure PD.8. Information is frequently stored according to the reporting structure of employees and cost center allocation of budgets and expenses. This type of structure occurs in manufacturing, commonly called bill-of-material processing, where it is necessary to know the components needed to build a product and the subcomponents of each component. For example, a bill-of-material for an airplane would have at the top level the end product airplane analogous to the president's level shown in the organization chart. At the next level down would be the wings of the airplane rather than the vice presidents, the next level might be the engines rather than the assistant vice presidents, the next level might be the fan of the engine rather than the director, etc. until all components necessary to build the airplane are accounted for.

Figure PD.8. Organization Chart

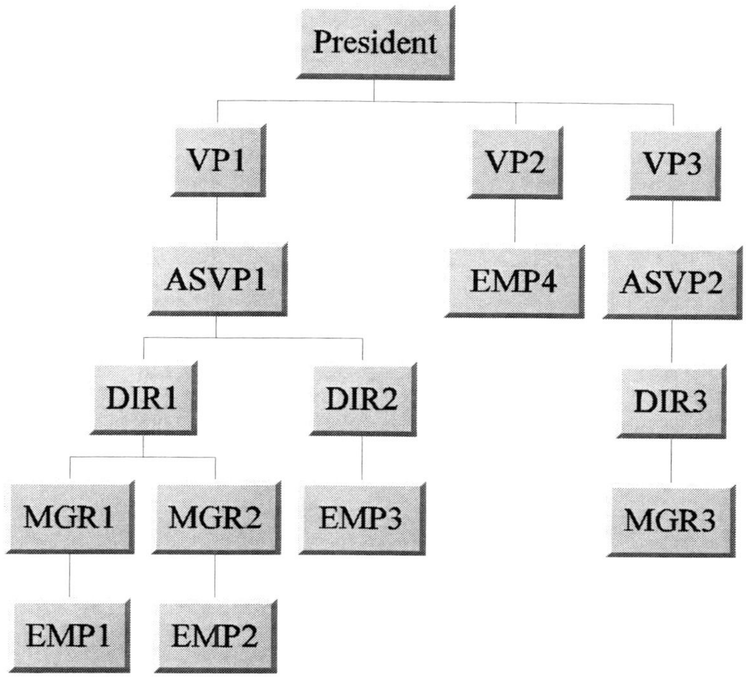

An organizational chart or bill-of-materials can be "flattened" into a table as shown in Figure PD.9. The top level, the president, appears as the parent and each position that reports to the president is listed as a dependent, in the example vice presidents VP1, VP2, and VP3. Each vice president is also listed in the parent column, with the associated reporting employees listed as dependents. Each dependent appears as a parent if he or she has a reporting employee. EMP1, EMP2, EMP3, and EMP4 do not appear in the parent column since they have no one reporting to them. The PL column is a numeric indicator of the level of reporting for the parent and the DL column indicates the level of reporting for the dependent. The PL and DL columns are optional but can be useful for reporting purposes.

Figure PD.9. Organization chart table

PARENT	DEPENDENT	PL	DL
President	VP1	1	2
President	VP2	1	2
President	VP3	1	2
VP1	ASVP1	2	3
VP2	EMP4	2	6
VP3	ASVP2	2	3
ASVP1	DIR2	3	4
ASVP1	DIR1	3	4

PARENT	DEPENDENT	PL	DL
ASVP2	DIR3	3	4
DIR1	MGR1	4	5
DIR1	MGR2	4	5
DIR2	EMP3	4	6
DIR3	MGR3	4	5
MGR1	EMP1	5	6
MGR2	EMP2	5	6

The SQL code to perform an explosion to determine all employees who report directly or indirectly to VP1 is shown along with comments as to the result of each statement:

```
SELECT DEPENDENT    -- ASVP1 is returned
FROM   ORG_CHART
WHERE  PARENT  = &VP1;

SELECT DEPENDENT    -- DIR1, DIR2 is returned
FROM   ORG_CHART    --  one at a time when fetched
WHERE  PARENT  = &ASVP1;

SELECT DEPENDENT    -- MGR1, MGR2, EMP3 is returned
FROM   ORG_CHART    --  one at a time when fetched
WHERE  PARENT  =&DIR1;--  using DIR1, DIR2

SELECT DEPENDENT    -- EMP1, EMP2 is returned
FROM   ORG_CHART    --  one at a time when fetched
WHERE  PARENT  =&MGR1;--  using MGR1, MGR2, EMP3
```

The positions are indicated with QMF parameters for ease of understanding. Each parameter would be replaced by a host variable in a program. The first SELECT determines that ASVP1 reports directly to VP1. The second select determines those employees who report directly to ASVP1, DIR1 and DIR2. The third select determines that MRG1, MGR2, and EMP3 report directly to DIR1. The last select shown determines that EMP1 and EMP2 report to MRG1. Using this approach, a select is needed for each level in the organization chart, and a cursor is necessary for each of the SELECTS. Also needed is logic to save the intermediate values used to determine the next level of reporting, and logic coded in the host language to determine which statement to execute until all reporting levels have been located.

Using Subselects to Reduce Host Language Code

The amount of host language code that needs to be developed can be reduced significantly by having DB2 save the intermediate results using subselects:

```
SELECT PARENT,DEPENDENT,PL,DL
FROM   ORG_CHART
WHERE  PARENT = &VP1 OR PARENT IN
(SELECT DEPENDENT FROM ORG_CHART WHERE PARENT = &VP1 OR PARENT IN
(SELECT DEPENDENT FROM ORG_CHART WHERE PARENT = &VP1 OR PARENT IN
(SELECT DEPENDENT FROM ORG_CHART WHERE PARENT = &VP1 OR PARENT IN
(SELECT DEPENDENT FROM ORG_CHART WHERE PARENT = &VP1 OR PARENT IN
(SELECT DEPENDENT FROM ORG_CHART WHERE PARENT = &VP1 OR PARENT IN
(SELECT DEPENDENT FROM ORG_CHART WHERE PARENT = &VP1 OR PARENT IN
(SELECT DEPENDENT FROM ORG_CHART WHERE PARENT = &VP1 OR PARENT IN
(SELECT DEPENDENT FROM ORG_CHART WHERE PARENT = &VP1 OR PARENT IN
(SELECT DEPENDENT FROM ORG_CHART WHERE PARENT = &VP1 OR PARENT IN
(SELECT DEPENDENT FROM ORG_CHART WHERE PARENT = &VP1 OR PARENT IN
  -- EMP1, EMP2
(SELECT DEPENDENT FROM ORG_CHART WHERE PARENT = &VP1 OR PARENT IN
  -- MGR1, MGR2, EMP3
(SELECT DEPENDENT FROM ORG_CHART WHERE PARENT = &VP1 OR PARENT IN
  -- DIR2, DIR1
(SELECT DEPENDENT FROM ORG_CHART WHERE PARENT = &VP1 OR PARENT IN
  -- ASVP1
(SELECT DEPENDENT FROM ORG_CHART WHERE PARENT = &VP1))))))))))))))
ORDER BY 3,1,4,2;
```

There is a limit of 15 levels using the subselect technique because a maximum of 15 tables can be referenced in an SQL statement. This limit applies even if it is the same table name referenced 15 times as is the case for the table ORG_CHART. Also it will be seen in Chapter ST that an IN subselect results in a tablespace scan which will significantly detract from performance with the 14 subselects in the statement.

Either of the techniques described above for explosions can be used for implosions. For example, an implosion would be used to determine who employee EMP1 reports to directly or indirectly. Each occurrence of the DEPENDENT column would be replaced by the PARENT column and each occurrence of the PARENT column would be replaced by the DEPENDENT column.

Designing Indexes for Performance: Good index design enhances performance for both techniques. A composite index on the parent and dependent columns in that order allows index-only processing to accomplish an explosion. If implosions are frequently required, the composite index would be on the dependent and parent columns in that order.

Simple SQL with Increased Table Costs: The SQL can be simplified significantly by storing the explosion in the table. Figure PD.10 shows a table design where the parent is repeated for each direct and indirect reporting level in the dependent column. The president is not included in the table since only a SELECT * is needed to determine all those that report directly and indirectly to the president.

Figure PD.10. Expanded organization chart table

PARENT	DEPENDENT	PL	DL
VP1	ASVP1	1	2

PARENT	DEPENDENT	PL	DL
VP1	DIR1	1	3
VP1	MGR1	1	4
VP1	EMP1	1	5
VP1	MGR2	1	4
VP1	EMP2	1	5
VP1	DIR2	1	3
VP1	EMP3	1	5
ASVP1	DIR1	2	3
ASVP1	MGR1	2	4
ASVP1	EMP1	2	5
ASVP1	MGR2	2	4
ASVP1	EMP2	2	5
ASVP1	DIR2	2	3
ASVP1	EMP3	2	5
Etc.			

All employees who report directly or indirectly to VP1 can be determined very simply:

```
SELECT DEPENDENT
FROM   EXP_ORG_CHART
WHERE  PARENT = &VP1
FOR FETCH ONLY;
```

The expanded organization chart may be acceptable for a small number of rows (say 10,000) and where business professionals need direct ad hoc access. The expanded version would be unacceptable for a large organizational or bill-of-material structure because of the amount of DASD space that would be required and the complexity of updating the data.

PD.13 EMBEDDED DYNAMIC SQL

Embedded, dynamic SQL is a powerful but costly feature. In many cases, it is too costly for use in high transaction rate applications. Dynamically generated SQL statements are prepared--that is, optimized and bound--just as static SQL--except the plan is not stored in the directory. There are SQL statements that must be used within the host-language program to accomplish that preparation. In addition, if the dynamic statement is a SELECT, the program must be able to determine the data structures needed to receive the selected values and be able to generate those structures, just as the programmer includes the necessary data structures in a host-language program for static SQL as generated by DCLGEN as discussed in Chapter PE. With dynamic SQL, however, a program must dynamically allocate memory to receive the values for them.

Dynamic Statements Other than Select

The host program must first include a variable to receive the SQL statement, which should be a varying-length character variable for COBOL and Assembler, or a varying or fixed-length string variable in PL/1. Make the variable long enough to accommodate the longest statement a user is likely to require. We will call that variable SQLSTATEMENT. It is declared as any other host variable would be. Set the variable equal to an SQL statement in this way:

```
MOVE 'UPDATE SPJ SET QTY = QTY + 10
      WHERE SN = 'S3'
      AND   PN = 'P3'' TO SQLSTATEMENT
```

If the dynamic SQL statement, as here, uses constants instead of host-language variables, DB2 binds and executes it at once in response to a single statement, the EXECUTE IMMEDIATE statement, which looks like this:

```
EXEC SQL EXECUTE IMMEDIATE :SQLSTATEMENT END-EXEC.
```

If a dynamic statement is to be executed again, however, the EXECUTE IMMEDIATE command is an inefficient way of doing it because it requires that the statement be rebound for each execution. The more efficient approach, and the one needed if the statement uses host-language variables or is a SELECT statement, binds the statement once in response to a PREPARE statement and executes it any number of times in response to EXECUTE statements. (In either case, the optimizer returns its relative cost estimate for a dynamic bind from a host-language program as SQLERRD(4) in the SQLCA.)

For a dynamic SQL statement to be executed repeatedly, a host-language variable is needed to reference the bound SQL statement. We will call the variable SQLBOUND. The embedded SQL statement that orders preparation of the code structure is PREPARE, followed by the name of the variable to reference it, followed by the keyword FROM, followed by the name of the source code variable that provides the statement. The PREPARE statement for the example is:

```
EXEC SQL
     PREPARE SQLBOUND FROM :SQLSTATEMENT
END-EXEC.
```

Because the bind process locks the DBD of all databases containing tables being referenced by the SQL statement, be sure to test the SQLCODE for an unsuccessful PREPARE. If a prepare is unsuccessful, branch to a rollback to release the locks.

The statement is now ready for execution, which is invoked by an embedded EXECUTE statement like:

```
EXEC SQL EXECUTE SQLBOUND END-EXEC.
```

Arguments and Parameters

A dynamic SQL statement cannot include a host variable. It can, however, use question marks to indicate variables to which values are assigned and passed to the EXECUTE statement. These question marks are called parameter markers. For example:

```
SQLSTATEMENT = 'UPDATE SPJ SET QTY = QTY + 10
                WHERE SN = ?
                AND   PN = ?'
```

A USING clause in the EXECUTE statement indicates the variables that are to take the places of the question marks. After the statement has been prepared as above, its EXECUTE statement would look like this:

```
EXEC SQL EXECUTE SQLBOUND USING :SN, :PN END-EXEC.
```

The USING clause assigns its variables to the parameters in the order listed. The dynamic statement can execute any number of times with differing values for SN and PN without rebinding.

Dynamic SELECTS

There are two types of dynamic SELECT statements: fixed list and variable list. The first is used when you know when the program is written the number, types, and lengths of variables that are needed to receive returned values. This somewhat limits the usefulness of dynamic SQL. In that case, a COBOL programmer can declare INTO variables in the data division. Most of the other SQL statements, such as INSERT, UPDATE, and DELETE, which return only SQLCA feedback, not data, work quite well dynamically within COBOL or FORTRAN because there is no uncertainty about the data type and length of returned columns. SQL data definition and data control statements also work well within COBOL and other host languages.

If the information about the variables will be developed only as the program executes, a variable-list SELECT is needed. In this case, the program must be able to allocate storage for those variables dynamically. This is possible only with PL/1, Assembler C, and with COBOL programs calling subroutines in these languages. COBOL pointer and set constructs can be used. The IBM sample COBOL program DSN8BCU1 is a good example of how to allocate storage and DSN8BCU2 is the called program that does pointer manipulation. These programs are documented in the *Application Programming and SQL Guide* manual.

The SQL Descriptor Area

For the variable-list SELECT, DB2 provides the program the information it needs to allocate storage through the SQL descriptor area (SQLDA), a data structure similar to the SQLCA in that both communicate information between DB2 and host-language programs. The SQLDA receives a description of the value to be returned from the SELECT statement in the program. DB2 interrogates the catalog tables for the information describing the columns returned by the SELECT and passes that information back to the program. A number of commands are needed to carry out those functions.

The variables for the dynamic SELECT statement are declared just as they would be for non-SELECT statements. The PREPARE statement that invokes the bind process is the same. (The statement to be prepared is restricted, however, in that even if a single value might be returned, the select must use a cursor rather than a SELECT ... INTO clause. Consequently the PREPARE command does not work with a dynamic SELECT statement that includes INTO.)

An INCLUDE statement, INCLUDE SQLDA, which is similar in syntax to INCLUDE SQLCA, is required to bring the SQLDA structure into the program. The DESCRIBE statement, is needed to bring the descriptions of the variables the SELECT will return into the SQLDA. A PL/1 DESCRIBE statement looks like this:

```
EXEC SQL DESCRIBE SQLBOUND INTO SQLDA;
```

DESCRIBE INPUT provides for having a DB2 server to describe the input parameter data into an SQLDA (V5 APAR PQ24584). This improves performance for DRDA and Open Database Connectivity (ODBC) applications by avoiding the expense of additional catalog queries and network messages.

Declaring the Cursor

The dynamic SELECT statement also requires a cursor. Instead of including the actual SELECT statement in the cursor declaration as would be done with static SQL, the declaration here refers to the variable referencing the statement's plan--for example:

```
EXEC SQL DECLARE SCURSOR FOR SQLBOUND;
```

It also requires OPEN and FETCH statements. The OPEN statement is the same as in static SQL, but the FETCH statement is slightly different. Instead of using an INTO clause to fetch values into specified host-language variables, FETCH here employs a USING DESCRIPTOR clause, which indicates the values are to be returned to variables identified in the SQLDA--for example:

```
EXEC SQL OPEN SCURSOR;
     DO WHILE ...
        EXEC SQL FETCH SCURSOR USING DESCRIPTOR SQLDA;
     END;
EXEC SQL CLOSE SCURSOR;
```

Costs of Dynamic SQL

Dynamic SQL is a sophisticated feature of DB2 and can be valuable when required. When performance is an issue, however, use dynamic SQL with care. EXECUTE IMMEDIATE requires that DB2 bind a plan each time it executes a statement dynamically. A prepared statement can be executed repeatedly with only one PREPARE. Indeed, we will see how a prepared statement can be cached to avoid repeated prepares. However, if a dynamic SQL is prepared frequently, I/O to the catalog and CPU costs for access path selection are increased. These costs can be significant and are not likely to be acceptable if a high transaction rate is required. A method for reducing I/O to the catalog tables is discussed in Chapter OP regarding reoptimization which like dynamic SQL requires that the access path be chosen at run time.

Caching of Dynamic SQL

The frequency of PREPARE executions can be reduced by caching the dynamic statements in the EDM pool. Statements cached in the EDM pool can be shared among different threads, plans, and packages. The plans and packages are retained past a commit point. They are not shared with other members of a data sharing group because each member has its own EDM pool.

The caching of dynamic SQL is a good choice if the exact same dynamic statement is executed repeatedly. This is particularly useful for client/server applications and tools that use dynamic SQL. It applies to DRDA, not the private protocol.

If an SQL statement is executed repeatedly, a prepare need not be executed for each execution of the statement. A statement can be prepared, executed, a commit work can be issued, and the statement can be executed again repeatedly without doing another prepare if the statement is found in the cache. The second execution of a dynamic statement costs only about 1.2 percent more in CPU time compared to static SQL. The details of the tests results are in *DB2 for OS/390 Version 5 Performance Topics,* SG24-2213.

The prepared statement and the statement string are saved. If a statement with literals is prepared again, it must be identical to the initially prepared statement to take advantage of the cache. An exception is that leading and trailing blanks are ignored. The following two SELECT statements are not identical. Notice that the second statement has two blanks after "SELECT SN," rather than one blank as in the first statement.

```
'SELECT SN, SNAME FROM S WHERE STATUS = 30';

'SELECT SN,  SNAME FROM S WHERE STATUS = 40';
```

Caching of prepared statements is of no values when using QMF, SPUFI, DSNTEP2, or any interactive tool where users do not execute exactly the same statement with the same literals repeatedly.

The sharing of cached statements requires the same bind authority, bind parameter values for DYNAMICRULES, CURRENTDATA, ISOLATION, SQLRULES, QUALIFIER, and special register values for CURRENT DEGREE and CURRENT RULES.

The execution of the RUNSTATS utility (with all UPDATE options including NONE) causes all cached statements referencing tables and indexes for which statistics were collected to be reprepared when next executed (V5 APAR PQ17905). This allows for access path selection based on new statistics and newly created indexes when the statement is next executed.

Caching of dynamic SQL requires that it be enabled on the DSNTIP4 installation panel by specifying CACHE DYNAMIC SQL of YES. This is not the default. You must make a choice between caching dynamic SQL and reoptimization. The default of NOREOPT(VARS) is required when caching dynamic SQL. This is because the value of parameter markers and special registers used in the WHERE clause are not available when the PREPARE is executed. Therefore, reoptimization and the use of the cache are mutually exclusive. The purpose of the cache is to avoid bind processing including access path selection. The purpose of reoptimization is to determine a good access path for values requested by users.

If you want to reoptimize dynamic SQL that uses parameter markers and special registers at run time and not use the cache, it is necessary to specify the bind parameters REOPT(VARS) and DEFER(PREPARE). REOPT(VARS) does not increase the costs of binding dynamic SQL. DEFER(PREPARE) means that prepare processing is postponed until OPEN, EXECUTE, or DESCRIBE. This allows the optimizer to see the content of parameter markers and special registers for access path selection. Do check the SQLCODE after an OPEN as would be checked after a PREPARE. DEFER(PREPARE) also has the advantage that it reduces network traffic in a client/server environment.

KEEPDYNAMIC(YES): The use of the bind and rebind parameter KEEPDYNAMIC(YES) (not the default) means that a PREPARE need not be issued after a commit, reduces network traffic, and avoids the possibility that a dynamic statement might have to be reprepared because its space was reused by others in the EDM pool when using the cache. Figure PD.11 summarizes the processing with and without use of the cache. Notice that without the cache DB2 must issue an implicit prepare after a commit and with the cache DB2 uses the prepared statement in memory.

Figure PD.11. Processing with and without the cache

Processing	Without Cache	With Cache
PREPARE S1 FROM ... EXECUTE S1 COMMIT	Statement prepared and put in memory	Same
EXECUTE S1 COMMIT	No PREPARE issued. DB2 issues an implicit prepare. Do check SQLCODE for an unsuccessful prepare.	No PREPARE issued. DB2 uses the prepared statement in memory
EXECUTE S1 COMMIT	No PREPARE needed	Same

If a PREPARE is issued, the statement is prepared with and without the use of the cache. This means that you should not code more than one PREPARE for the same SQL statement. Indeed, it is necessary to remove multiple PREPARE statements from existing programs to avoid multiple prepares. If CURSOR WITH HOLD is used, the prepared statement is retained past a commit with and without use of the cache and KEEPDYNAMIC(YES).

KEEPDYNAMIC(YES) results in local and global copies of statements with and without the use of the cache.

Local copies of the prepared statement and statement string are retained in DBSA address space working storage with and without the cache. A global copy of a prepared statement is retained in the EDM pool when using the cache.

If the cache is used, local copies and the global copy are retained after a commit (local copy of prepared statement is made as in use). An OPEN, EXECUTE, or DESCRIBE causes the local copy of the prepared statement to be used after validity checking. DROP, ALTER, or REVOKE statements executed on a dependent object make the local statement invalid. PREPARE causes the local prepared statement to be replaced. The local copy of a prepared statement is discarded when a PREPARE is issued for the same statement, application process ends, rollback, or a statement is marked invalid. The space is reused on a LRU basis.

If the cache is not used, the prepared statement is discarded after a commit, rollback, or PREPARE of an identical statement. OPEN, EXECUTE, DESCRIBE or PREPARE causes a prepare of the saved statement string which is referred to as an implicit prepare.

Cost of Using the Cache

Costs are increased somewhat when using the cache. It is necessary to locate the statement in the cache and, if it is not present because the space has been reused by another plan or package, prepare processing is required. Additional space is required in the EDM pool for the cache. One skeleton copy of a prepared statement is retained in EDM pool. It is advisable to size the EDM pool to avoid having to reread static plans and packages from the directory and to avoid having to repeatedly prepare dynamic statements. Data spaces can be used for the EDM pool similar to the use of data spaces for buffer pools discussed in Chapter CD when using the dynamic cache

A hit ratio for cached dynamic SQL can be calculated similar to calculating a hit ratio for buffer pools. The required fields are in the IFCID (Instrumentation Facility Component ID) records 0002, 0003, and 0148 when using the statistics trace. The field QISEDSC contains the number of pages used for the cache, QISEDSG contains the number of cache search requests, and QISEDSI contains the number of times that a statement was placed in the cache because it was not found there. The hit ratio is calculated like:

```
Hit ratio = (QISEDSG - QISEDSI) / QISEDSG
```

If the hit ratio is low and identical dynamic statements are executed repeatedly, do increase EDM size to avoid rereading static statements from the directory and repreparing dynamic statements. If you are using KEEPDYNAMIC(YES), do increase the MAX KEPT DYN STMTS of 5000 (default if cache used) on the DSNTIPE panel. This results in a 9 MB cache (5000 * 1.8 KB (average prepared statement size)). If space for a cached statement is reused, a dependent object no longer exists, or privileges are revoked, an implicit PREPARE occurs.

User Privileges Required for Dynamic SQL

You will want to use the bind parameter DYNAMICRULES(BIND) (not the default) if the user is allowed to select and update data only through specific programs rather than through any interactive tool. If this parameter is used, the plan or package owner AUTHID privileges are used for all objects referenced in SQL as with static SQL. Also like static SQL, the QUALIFIER value is used for unqualified object names. You cannot use SET CURRENT SQLID and you cannot use dynamic GRANT, REVOKE, ALTER, CREATE, or DROP in a plan/package bound with DYNAMICRULES(BIND).

The default is DYNAMICRULES(RUN) which requires that you grant select privileges on tables to users who will execute the dynamic SQL. INSERT, UPDATE, and DELETE privileges must also be granted if the user is allowed to perform these operations on the data. If the privileges are granted, the users can perform the operations on data directly from tables using QMF, for example, which may violate your security policies. Unqualified object names are qualified by the value in the special register CURRENT SQLID.

Use of Dynamic SQL for Generalized Reporting

Dynamic SQL can be quite useful when used in the proper circumstances. For example, consider using dynamic SQL for generalized reporting programs. If users cannot narrow down the search conditions they use, there can be an excessive number of static SQL statements to code. For example, if there are 20 search conditions, the use of static SQL would require that over a million SELECT statements be developed! (The million estimate is calculated as 1,048,576 = 2^{20} possibilities.)

Some organizations take the "no dynamic SQL" rule as hard and fast. These organizations have fulfilled the generalized reporting tool requirement in many cases by using the BETWEEN predicate for the various search conditions as shown here:

```
SELECT SN, SNAME, STATUS, CITY
FROM   S
WHERE  SN     BETWEEN :SN-LOW      AND :SN-HIGH
AND    SNAME  BETWEEN :SNAME-LOW   AND :SNAME-HIGH
AND    STATUS BETWEEN :STATUS-LOW  AND :STATUS-HIGH
AND    CITY   BETWEEN :CITY-LOW    AND :CITY-HIGH
FOR FETCH ONLY;
```

All variables are initialized with the lowest or highest values for the column. You should consider using 'AAA' and 'ZZZ' or the lowest and highest possible values for the column when using literals. Do avoid initializing the low and high values with X'00' and X'FF' when using reoptimization. The values will be treated as if they are the same value by the optimizer because they are outside the range of A-Z, 0-9, and blank considered in filter factor calculations. This makes the use of indexes likely even though the use of indexes may not give the best access path.

The user is asked which values are required. If a user requests all suppliers in Dallas with a status >= 20, then 20 is moved to :STATUS-LOW and 32,767 is moved to STATUS-HIGH. Dallas is moved to both :CITY-LOW and :CITY-HIGH.

Disadvantage of the Approach: With a statically bound plan, the optimizer might choose multiples index access for the four BETWEENs or some other access path that is less than optimal. Indexes on SN and SNAME should not be used because all values qualify with the host variables initialized to low and high values. We do not want 25 percent of the SN and SNAME RIDs to be placed in the RID pool only to be discarded as discussed in Chapter PP.

If dynamic SQL is used, the developer can build a statement with only the needed predicates on columns specified by the user using the literals requested like:

```
SELECT SN, SNAME, STATUS, CITY
FROM   S
WHERE  STATUS >= 20
AND    CITY    = 'Dallas'
FOR FETCH ONLY;
```

The PREPARE of a simple dynamic SELECT requires about the same CPU time as applying one unnecessary predicate 10,000 times or two unnecessary predicates 5,000 times. In our example, if the S table contains 5,000 rows and the predicates on SN and SNAME are not specified, we can justify the CPU cost of dynamic SQL.

Programming Recommendation: Use static SQL for the few search conditions that are frequently required, such as those needed to fulfill weekly or daily report requests. Embedded dynamic SQL can be used to handle those conditions that are required infrequently. An alternative is the use of reoptimization.

Use of Reoptimization for Generalized Reporting

Reoptimization is an alternative for having the optimizer choose the access path at run as discussed in Chapter OP. It applies to static SQL as well as embedded dynamic SQL with parameter markers.

In one case, a company found that the following SELECT statement required 20 minute with multiple index processing. A much better access path was chosen when the bind parameter REOPT(VARS) was used resulting in only 10 seconds required to achieve the required results.

```
SELECT    A.DOCUMENT_NO,A.PROCESS_DATE,B.DOCUMENT_SEQ_NO,
B.RECORD_TYPE,A.BILL_TO_CD, A.SHIP_TO_CD, A.SORG_CD, A.PAYEE_NAME,
B.PROGRAM_NO,B.PAY_AMT
FROM   TDNFDBA.SLDL_TPC_HEADER_T2 A, TDNFDBA.SLDL_TPC_DETAIL_T3 B
WHERE A.DOCUMENT_NO = B.DOCUMENT_NO
AND A.RECORD_TYPE    = B.RECORD_TYPE
AND A.PROCESS_DATE   = B.PROCESS_DATE
AND A.DOCUMENT_NO   BETWEEN :WS-DOC-NO-MIN AND :WS-DOC-NO-MAX
AND B.RECORD_TYPE   BETWEEN :WS-PMT-TYPE-MIN AND :WS-PMT-TYPE-MAX
AND A.SORG_CD       BETWEEN :WS-SORG-MIN AND :WS-SORG-MAX
AND A.BILL_TO_CD    BETWEEN :WS-BILL-TO-MIN AND :WS-BILL-TO-MAX
AND A.SHIP_TO_CD    BETWEEN :WS-SHIP-TO-MIN AND :WS-SHIP-TO-MAX
AND A.PAYEE_NAME    BETWEEN :WS-NAME-MIN AND :WS-NAME-MAX
AND A.SLS_REGION    BETWEEN :WS-REG-MIN AND :WS-REG-MAX
AND A.SLS_DISTRICT BETWEEN :WS-DIS-MIN AND :WS-DIS-MAX
AND A.SLS_TERRITORY BETWEEN :WS-TER-MIN AND :WS-TER-MAX
AND B.PROGRAM_NO    BETWEEN :WS-PROG-MIN AND :WS-PROG-MAX
AND B.GRP_CD        BETWEEN :WS-GRP-MIN AND :WS-GRP-MAX
AND B.SUBGRP_CD     BETWEEN :WS-SUB-MIN AND :WS-SUB-MAX
AND A.PROCESS_DATE BETWEEN :WS-PROC-DT1-MIN AND :WS-PROC-DT1-MAX
AND A.REFERENCE_NO BETWEEN :WS-REF-NO-MIN AND :WS-REF-NO-MAX
AND B.INVOICE_NO    BETWEEN :WS-INV-NO-MIN AND :WS-INV-NO-MAX
AND B.SHIP_DATE     BETWEEN :WS-SHIP-DT1-MIN AND :WS-SHIP-DT1-MAX
AND A.SLSREP_CD     BETWEEN :WS-SREP-MIN AND :WS-SREP-MAX
AND A.PAY_AMT       BETWEEN :WS-PMT-AMT-MIN AND :WS-PMT-AMT-MAX
ORDER    BY    A.DOCUMENT_NO,A.PROCESS_DATE,B.RECORD_TYPE,
B.DOCUMENT_SEQ_NO;
```

PD.14 SUMMARY

DB2 provides for a number of ways to use SQL with a number of programming languages. The syntax for embedded SQL is virtually the same as the standard interactive SQL with the exception of CURSOR manipulation. Cursor repositioning can be a challenge particularly with a composite primary key. Several techniques for cursor management were discussed.

EXERCISES

1. Assume that TEMP_F (temperature in fahrenheit), TEMP_C (temperature in centigrade) are declared as distinct types. Will the following INSERT statement execute successfully? Why?

```
EXEC SQL
INSERT INTO WEATHER
(DATE_W, TEMP_F, TEMP_C)
VALUES
(:DATE-W, :TEMP-F, :TEMP-C) END-EXEC.
```

2. Under what conditions are all rows processed by DB2 when a cursor is opened or when the first row is fetched?

3. What guidelines should be used to determine the value for *n* in OPTIMIZE FOR *n* ROWS? Why?

4. What value should be used for *n* to inform the optimizer not to use list prefetch and sequential prefetch? What other types of processing are discouraged as well?

5. A program for reviewing the number of parts assigned to a given job periodically repeats rows the user has already seen. What is the problem? Provide a possible solution.

6. If *n* is specified as the number of rows in a table, will it encourage a tablespace scan?

7. What are the disadvantages of the each of the following techniques for cursor repositioning when using a composite index?

```
a) SELECT SN, PN, JN
   FROM   SPJ
   WHERE  SN >= 'S2' AND
          PN >= 'P3' AND
          JN >  'J3'
   ORDER BY SN,PN,JN
   OPTIMIZE FOR 12 ROWS;
```

```
b) SELECT SN, PN, JN
   FROM   SPJ
   WHERE (SN  = 'S2' AND
          PN  = 'P3' AND
          JN  > 'J3') OR
         (SN  = 'S2' AND
          PN  > 'P3') OR
         (SN  > 'S2')
   ORDER BY SN,PN,JN
   OPTIMIZE FOR 12 ROWS;
```

```
c) SELECT SN, PN, JN
   FROM   SPJ
   WHERE NOT (SN  = 'S2'  AND
              PN  = 'P3'  AND
              JN <= 'J3') AND
         NOT (SN  = 'S2'  AND
              PN  < 'P3') AND
             (SN >= 'S2')
   ORDER BY SN,PN,JN
   OPTIMIZE FOR 12 ROWS;
```

```
d) SELECT SN, PN, JN, QTY
   FROM   SPJ
   WHERE  SN = :OLD-SN
   AND    PN = :OLD-PN
   AND    JN > :OLD-JN
   ORDER BY SN, PN, JN
   OPTIMIZE FOR 12 ROWS;
```

IF SQLCODE = 100, more rows needed to fill screen,
process cursor for next SELECT statement

```
SELECT SN, PN, JN, QTY
FROM   SPJ
WHERE  SN = :OLD-SN
AND    PN > :OLD-PN
ORDER BY SN, PN, JN
OPTIMIZE FOR 12 ROWS;
```

IF SQLCODE = 100, more rows needed to fill screen,
process cursor for next SELECT statement

```
SELECT SN, PN, JN, QTY
FROM   SPJ
WHERE  SN > :OLD-SN
ORDER BY SN, PN, JN
OPTIMIZE FOR 12 ROWS;
```

IF SQLCODE = 100,
all qualifying rows have been fetched

```
e) SELECT SN, PN, JN
   FROM   SPJ
   WHERE  SN BETWEEN 'S2' AND :HIGH-VALUES
   AND    SN CONCAT PN CONCAT JN >
          :OLD-SN CONCAT :OLD-PN CONCAT :OLD-JN
   ORDER  BY SN, PN, JN
   OPTIMIZE FOR 12 ROWS;
```

8. Which of the cursor repositioning techniques in the previous question performs the best? Modify one of the statements so that it has the best performance and is easy to understand assuming a high cardinality on the first column of a composite index.

9. Why does the FOR UPDATE OF clause increase the likelihood of lock contention?

10. How can the columns specified in the FOR UPDATE OF clause affect performance?

11. a) A CICS pseudo conversational transaction is to be written to add parts to jobs as requested by the user. The program has been written to display a screen requesting the information required including the SN, PN, JN, and the additional QTY of parts required. Is it advisable to use the following partial SQL?

b) Is the SQL useful for a batch program?

```
EXEC SQL DECLARE SPJCUR CURSOR FOR
         SELECT SN, PN, JN, QTY
         FROM   SPJ
         WHERE  SN = :SN
         AND    PN = :PN
         AND    JN = :JN
         FOR UPDATE OF QTY;
END-EXEC.

EXEC SQL UPDATE SPJ
         SET  QTY = :QTY
         WHERE CURRENT OF SPJCUR
END-EXEC.
```

12. What are the disadvantages of selecting all columns defined into a 01 group level generated by DCLGEN, like:

```
EXEC SQL SELECT SN, S_SNAME, S_ADDRESS
         INTO  :S-DETAIL
         FROM   S_DETAIL
         WHERE  SN = :SN-IN
END-EXEC.
```

13. Under what conditions is an index <u>not</u> used to locate a row to be updated or deleted?

14. Users require the ability to scroll backwards through returned data. a) What questions should you ask users to clarify the requirement?

b) How do answers to those questions affect your decision about how to accomplish the task?

15. a) What is a user requirement that suggests the use of embedded dynamic SQL? b) What are two reasons for using embedded dynamic SQL to satisfy the user requirement? c) How can the costs of using embedded dynamic SQL be reduced? d) Will the use of the dynamic cache be useful in reducing the costs to satisfy this user requirement?

ANSWERS

1. The following INSERT statement will execute successfully. The assignment of a host variables to distinct type columns with and INSERT and UPDATE statement does not require the use of a cast function.

```
EXEC SQL
INSERT INTO WEATHER
(DATE_W, TEMP_F, TEMP_C)
VALUES
(:DATE-W, :TEMP-F, :TEMP-C) END-EXEC.
```

2. If a sort is required, all rows must be processed and sorted when the cursor is opened. (An index can be used to avoid processing and sorting all rows when the cursor is opened.) All qualifying rows for an inner select (second or later SELECT) of a subselect must be retrieved before the outer select (first SELECT) can be processed. Materialization may be required for some views and table expressions when the first FETCH statement is executed. Materialization is discussed in the ST Chapter.

3. It is best to estimate the number of rows to be fetched and use the value for *n* in OPTIMIZE FOR *n* ROWS. For an online transaction, this is usually the number of rows necessary to fill a screen. The optimizer has been enhanced in every release of DB2 and will probably be enhanced in subsequent releases of DB2. If *n* is specified as your best estimate of the number of rows to be fetched, the optimizer is able to estimate the best access path in the current release and in future releases of DB2.

4. OPTIMIZE FOR 1 ROW informs the optimizer not to use list prefetch and sequential prefetch when selecting from a single table. This also discourages prefetch with multiple table access, multiple index access, merge and hybrid join, and parallel processing. OPTIMIZE FOR 1 ROW should be used only if the required performance is not achieved by estimating the actual number of rows to be fetched.

5. The application is using a cursor to present the rows. When a COMMIT executes, the cursor is closed. When it reopens, it SELECTS the original set of rows and resumes processing at the beginning. The program can track the cursor's progress through the set and adjust the cursor statement to accommodate it when the cursor is reopened.

6. If *n* is specified as the number of rows in a table, it will <u>not</u> encourage a tablespace scan. The optimizer estimates the number of rows that will qualify. If *n* is greater than the number estimated by the optimizer, the value is ignored.

7. a) Rows that should be processed can be missed. For example, a row with J1 or P1 will be missed further down in the table.

b) The technique cannot use a matching index scan because of the OR predicates on multiple columns in a composite index. Rows can be missed if a matching index scan is used.

c) If there is a low cardinality on the first column of the composite index, many index pages will be scanned. The technique can use a matching index scan on only the first column.

d) This technique requires that more host language code be developed and tested.

e) A matching index scan cannot be used since concatenation is evaluated at stage 2. The BETWEEN predicate allows for a matching index scan on 1 column. However, like technique c) if there is a low cardinality on the first column of the composite index, many index pages will be scanned. In addition, each value must be passed to RDS (Relational Data System) for stage 2 processing.

8. The technique that performs the best is d), in which there are the same number of SELECT statements as there are columns in the composite index. (You need only develop a SELECT statement for each of the leading columns in the composite index that have a low cardinality.) It provides for a matching index scan on the maximum number of columns possible.

Statement b) can be modified so that a matching index scan can be done on the first column of the composite index like the following statement. It is easier to understand than the NOT formulation which can also use a matching index scan on the first column.

```
SELECT SN, PN, JN
   FROM    SPJ
   WHERE   SN >= 'S2' AND
        ((SN   =  'S2' AND
           PN   =  'P3' AND
           JN   >  'J3') OR
          (SN   =  'S2' AND
           PN   >  'P3') OR
          (SN   >  'S2'))
```

9. Locks are held on each row or page updated until the cursor is closed. This holds true even if the package or plan is bound with cursor stability.

10. An index on columns specified in the FOR UPDATE OF clause that is specified in the SET clause of the UPDATE statement is not used to locate rows depending on the predicate and if list prefetch is used. This is because rows can be missed or a looping condition can occur.

11. a) It is not necessary to select the row before an update is issued. In addition, locks taken for the FOR UPDATE OF clause are not held after the screen is displayed.

b) The FOR UPDATE OF clause on the SELECT statement and WHERE CURRENT OF avoids a separate getpage or physical I/O for the SELECT and UPDATE statement for a batch program.

12. Often, all columns are not required. More CPU time is required for selecting more columns than are required. The likelihood of having to modify a program is increased if a column data type or length needs to be changed, a column is added, or a column is deleted. Performance and data independence are improved by selecting only the columns required by the program. Performance is improved by reducing the number of columns to be passed from DM to RDS and to the host program by selecting only the required columns. This reduces CPU time since the path length is reduced. A sort requires more resources to sort a longer row than necessary.

13. An index cannot be used to locate a row to be updated if there is a range predicate specified on the column to be updated and list prefetch is not chosen as part of the access path. An index cannot be used on a column in a predicate specified in a view that includes a WITH CHECK OPTION clause. An index cannot be used on a column with an arithmetic expression in the WHERE or SET

clause of an UPDATE statement. An index can be used to locate a row to be deleted without any restrictions. The clustering index is used to determine where to insert a row.

14. a) Consider asking the user how many screens they will look back at, how often they tend to scroll backward, and whether they plan to update the rows when they scroll backward.

b) The number of screens that the user will look at a second time will determine the number of Primary keys (one for each screen) that must be saved for reposition processing. If you decide to use a temporary work area, it will allow you to determine the number of rows that will be placed in the temporary work area and to calculate the amount of space required. If they seldom plan to scroll backward, it is very costly to fetch and save all rows for all screens compared to saving only one Primary key for each screen. If the user plans to update rows on the screen when they scroll backward, it will be necessary to use one of the alternatives discussed to insure that a row has not changed since it was displayed and before the update is issued.

15. a) A user requirement that suggests the use of embedded dynamic SQL is where the user needs to request information based on a large number of conditions.

b) One reason is that it is impractical to develop static SQL for each combination of conditions. The second reason is that the multiple BETWEEN conditions required to use static SQL are likely to result in a poor access path.

c) The costs of using embedded dynamic SQL can be reduced by developing static SQL for the frequent combination of conditions requested by most users and use dynamic SQL for the infrequently requested combination of conditions.

d) The dynamic cache is not useful in reducing costs to satisfy this user requirement. This is because it is unlikely that the user will request exactly the same combination of conditions with the same value frequently enough for the dynamic statement to be reused in the cache.

FIGURES

Batch Processing

BP.1 INTRODUCTION

The task of applying hundreds of thousands of updates, inserts, and deletes to a multimillion row table represents a challenging, though not uncommon, programming problem. Seductively easy, and apparently reasonable, approaches can be extremely expensive. We will use a real-world case, altered to use the SPJ example tables, to explore some mass update techniques and their implications.

BP.2 ALTERNATIVES FOR BATCH PROCESSING

The production table, SPJ_PROD, has six million rows. Periodically it receives about 500,000 updates from the identically structured SPJ_UPDATE table. If there is a match on the two tables' primary key columns, the SN, PN, and JN composite, QTY in the SPJ_PROD table's row is updated with the QTY value from the SPJ_UPDATE row. If there is no match, the SPJ_UPDATE row is inserted into SPJ_PROD.

Alternative 1: Matching Index Scan

One approach is to use a cursor statement without a predicate to select the entire SPJ_UPDATE table. Using a programming loop, each primary key value fetched from that cursor is then used in a SELECT statement to search for a match in the SPJ_PROD table.

- If a match is found, a separate statement updates the row.

- If there is no match--which is indicated when the select from SPJ_PROD returns an SQLCODE of 100--another statement inserts the row into the SPJ_PROD table.

This approach seems reasonable, but when it was tried, processing lasted more than *24 hours* before the developer gave up and canceled the job.

This approach can be improved upon slightly by using a cursor and a FOR UPDATE OF clause with the SELECT statement searching the SPJ_PROD table. That would avoid having to find each row being updated twice--once to look for the match and once for the update. But, in light of the more than 24-hour processing for the initial approach, saving one search, even if it cut the work in half, would not be savings enough. Another approach is needed.

Alternative 2: Matching Index Scan Variation

This is similar to the first alternative in that it fetches each row from SPJ_UPDATE with a tablespace scan as was done in the previous example. However, it eliminates the initial SELECT from the SPJ_PROD and the use of the UPDATE with cursor. Instead this approach goes directly to an

UPDATE statement on SPJ_PROD without a cursor. In this UPDATE statement, the search criteria specifies equalities on the primary key columns and the values from SPJ_UPDATE are presented by a cursor and programming loop:

```
EXEC SQL UPDATE SPJ_PROD
         SET QTY = :SPJ_UPDATE.QTY
         WHERE SPJ_PROD.SN = :SPJ-UPDATE.SN
         AND   SPJ_PROD.PN = :SPJ-UPDATE.PN
         AND   SPJ_PROD.JN = :SPJ-UPDATE.JN
END-EXEC.
```

If the statement returns an SQLCODE of +100, indicating no row with that primary key was found, the program inserts the row in SPJ_PROD. If inserts are in the majority, attempt the insert first rather than the update. If the program receives a -803 SQLCODE indicating a duplicate on the primary key, then issue the UPDATE.

DB2 can use an index on the primary key in SPJ_PROD to look for the update matches. But, even so, searches of the 6 million row table, with perhaps as many as 500,000 searches of a 3-level index, plus I/O to the data pages, could require considerable processing. This alternative might be appropriate if a small percent of rows would be updated.

Alternative 3: Dropping and Recreating Indexes

This approach deletes rows from the SPJ_PROD table that have primary key values matching those in SPJ_UPDATE. Then, all rows from the SPJ_UPDATE table are inserted into SPJ_PROD.

To make this process efficient, you must first drop the unique and clustering indexes on SPJ_PROD. This forces a tablespace scan and avoids having to delete and insert values into the index. Then, create a unique index on the primary key in SPJ_UPDATE. By doing this, index-only access can be used to satisfy the delete subselect. The SQL statements are:

```
DELETE FROM SPJ_PROD
WHERE  SN CONCAT PN CONCAT JN IN
  (SELECT SN CONCAT PN CONCAT JN
   FROM   SPJ_UPDATE);
```

and

```
INSERT INTO SPJ_PROD
  SELECT SN, PN, JN, QTY
  FROM   SPJ_UPDATE;
```

One drawback to this approach is that it is not possible to commit work periodically. If there is a failure, the processing must be started again at the beginning.

Because there was no index on the production table, rows were not inserted in clustering sequence. You must recreate the indexes and then reorganize the table, or another way is to do the following steps:

- Unload the table
- Sort the data set in clustering sequence
- Recreate the indexes
- Reload the table

Whichever approach you use, the plans and packages that were invalidated when the indexes were dropped must be rebound.

This approach to batch processing allowed the installation to process the mass update in 3 hours, as opposed to the more than 24 hours required using the initial method. It is possible to come up with even better solutions if the clustering index can be placed on the primary key. (The application developers believed that the clustering index had to be on another column.)

Alternative 4: Match-Merge Processing

The idea behind match-merge processing is to use two cursor SELECT statements: one selecting from the table providing the update values, the other from the production table. The host language program compares the selected values and uses the matching values in an UPDATE statement. Because the rows can be returned by the two SELECTS in order, each table need be read only once.

In the example, the cursors' two SELECT statements are:

```
SELECT SN, PN, JN, QTY
FROM   SPJ_PROD
ORDER BY SN, PN, JN;
```

and

```
SELECT SN, PN, JN, QTY
FROM   SPJ_UPDATE
ORDER BY SN, PN, JN;
```

The returned values are fetched into host language variables. Each set of values from the production table is compared against corresponding values from the update file. (The original case study had the input to the batch program in a table. Most often the input will be in a sequential file.) The first row from the production table is compared with the first record from the update file. If there is no match, the program inserts the row. If there is a match, it updates the row. The program continues processing each compared set of rows and records in this fashion. This approach is illustrated in Figure BP.1.

Figure BP.1. Match-merge processing

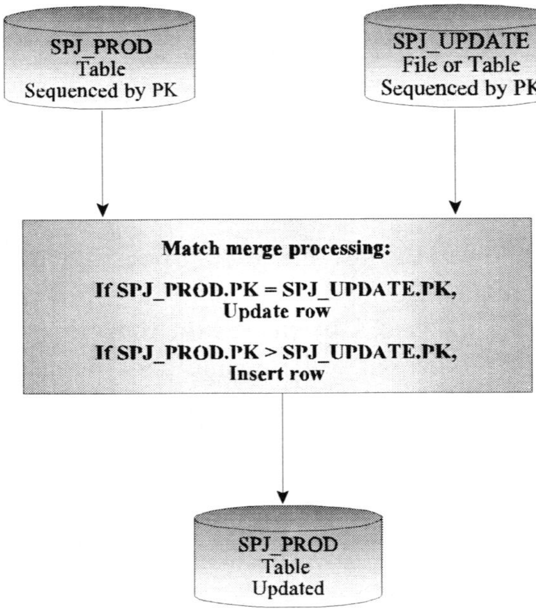

This approach does allow for periodic commit work statements, which can help avoid lengthy restart processing should the program fail.

Designing for Performance: Although this approach does require that all rows in the production be processed, it can be very efficient if more than 10-20 percent of the rows are to be processed. (We will see in Section BP.5 that the percentage may be even lower based on some I/O time estimates.) The key to obtaining the best performance from match-merge processing is to make it so that DB2 will be able to fetch pages in a sequential fashion. This allows DB2 to present the rows without having to do a costly sort, and it also means that it is likely to use *sequential prefetch* for I/O, in which case it can bring 32 pages at a time into the buffer, rather than one page at a time. (One I/O is used to read 32 pages, assuming a buffer pool of 1000 or more pages.)

To accomplish this goal, put a clustering index on the primary key in the production table and sort the update file in sequence on the primary key. Then, be sure to specify the primary key columns in the predicate. The ORDER BY clause in the SELECT statement insures that the rows are returned in order and increases the likelihood that the optimizer will choose to use the index to avoid a sort, assuming that there is a good cluster ratio on the primary key index.

To avoid processing a long series of rows in the production table that do not have a match in the update file, consider counting the number of rows with no match. If the count is greater than some number, 10,000 perhaps, close the cursor and reopen it when the primary key in the production table is greater than or equal to the primary key in the update file.

Alternative 5: Match-Merge Variation using LOAD

The match-merge processing described above is efficient, but it does require maintenance of the indexes on the table. Insert, update, and delete processing of indexes is almost always more costly than doing the same processing on the data. Figure BP.2 illustrates a process in which this index maintenance can be avoided.

Figure BP.2. Match-merge processing with updates and deletes

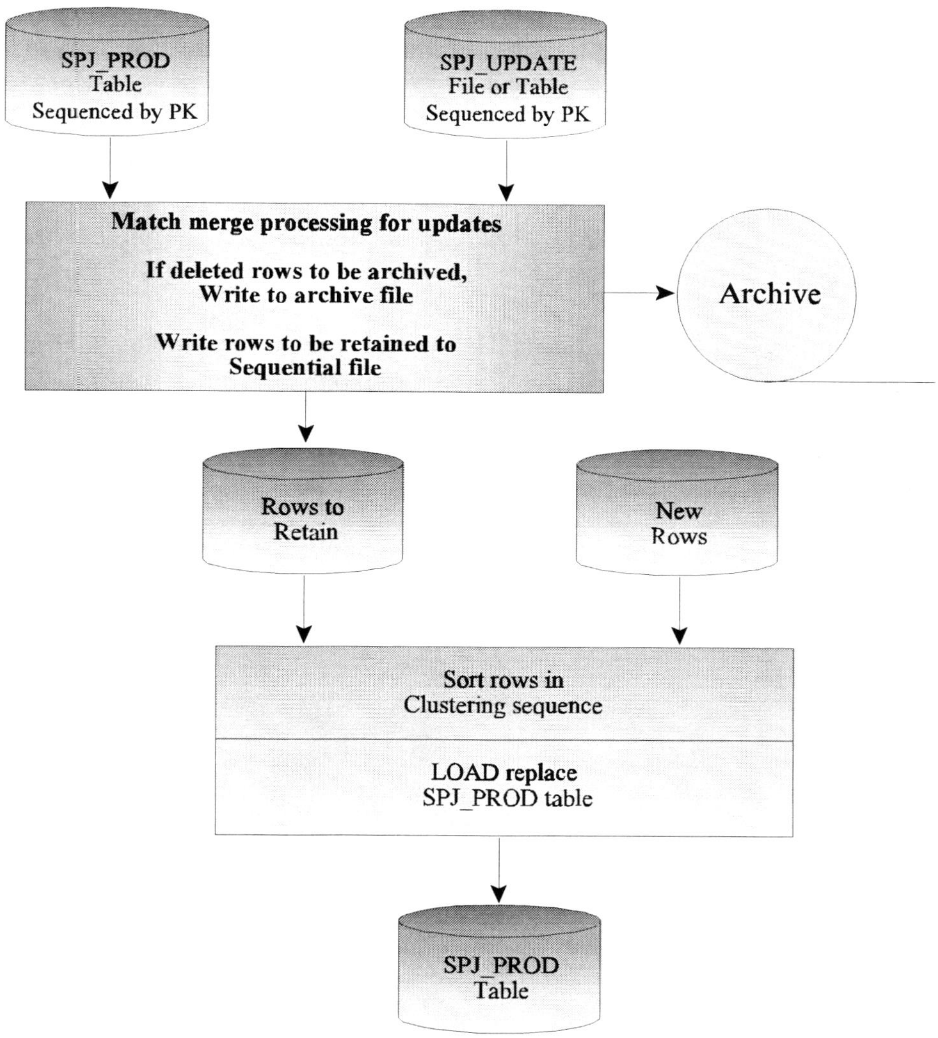

Here is an explanation of the processing in Figure BP.2.

1. Have the production table and the update file sequenced by primary key, the same as described already for match-merge processing.

2. Do match-merge processing similar to that described above, except use host-language code to update the required rows (not an SQL UPDATE statement) and write the updated rows, rows to be retained, and rows to be inserted from the SPJ_UPDATE file into a sequential file (shown as "Rows to Retain" in Figure BP.2). If you are deleting rows and want to keep archives, either use SQL to write deleted rows to an archive table, or use host-language code

to write to an archive sequential file. Do not insert, update, and delete the rows on the production table using SQL INSERT, UPDATE, and DELETE statements. This avoids index maintenance without having to drop the indexes and invalidate plans and packages that use the indexes.

3. If the rows in "Rows to Retain" are not in sequence from the extract and update processing or the new rows to be inserted arrive in a separate file ("New Rows" in Figure BP.2), sort the rows in preparation for the load process.

4. Use the LOAD utility to load and replace the data in the production table. If the production table is in a multi-table segmented tablespace you can use the mass delete algorithm to delete all rows from the production table and use LOAD RESUME. (The mass delete algorithm is discussed in Section BP.7.)

5. Do not log the data as you load it. Instead, create a recovery point by making an image copy of the tablespace after it is loaded. If you are replacing the data, an inline copy can be made as the data is replaced in the tablespace.

Data is unavailable to other applications during the LOAD processing. However, if the table is in a partitioned tablespace, only the partition currently being loaded is unavailable.

BP.3 BENEFITS OF SEQUENTIAL PREFETCH

A tablespace scan is best at times due primarily to the efficiencies of sequential prefetch. Prefetch means that up to 32 pages can be read with a single I/O instruction. The average I/O time for each page read is 1.7 ms (milliseconds) compared to reading each page individually, which requires about 16 ms on a 3390 DASD device.

Sequential prefetch can be used for a tablespace scan and for a non-matching index scan when processing eight or more data or leaf pages. It can be used on the data and index pages after finding a starting position with a matching index scan if the cluster ratio is greater than 80 percent. Prefetch can be used for an update and delete when a cursor is not used. DB2 uses prefetch for its work tablespaces and the utilities use prefetch of up to 64 pages with a single I/O.

Sequential Detection

The benefits of sequential prefetch are so significant that it may be initiated during execution even if not requested by the optimizer. Sequential detection is used to initiate sequential prefetch at execution time if a number of data or index pages are being accessed in sequence. The thresholds for when prefetch can be activated and deactivated can change from one release to another. Currently, if 5 pages of the last 8 pages contain required values, prefetch is activated. If 5 pages of the last 8 pages do not contain required values, prefetch is deactivated. Dynamic prefetch can be repeatedly activated and deactivated for any cursor or non-cursor SQL statement. It can be of significant benefit in processing the inner table in joins and tests for existence.

There are a few cases where sequential detection will not be used. It is not used for referential integrity processing of tables and indexes not explicitly named in the SQL statement. This suggests having an index on the foreign key that can be used in a matching index scan. Sequential detection is not used for update and delete processing if index only processing is not shown in the plan table.

EXPLAIN provides information on the access path chosen by the optimizer by causing rows to be inserted into the PLAN_TABLE as discussed in Chapter EX. EXPLAIN does not show the use of prefetch as a result of sequential detection since it occurs at execution time. The developer can encourage the use of prefetch at bind time, which is shown when using EXPLAIN. The simplest technique for encouraging the use of prefetch is to not use a predicate. Obviously if a predicate is not coded, a tablespace scan is required and the optimizer will almost certainly specify the use of sequential prefetch. However, it is always best to narrow the search with predicates to minimize the number of rows that must be returned to the program. You can code a predicate and inform the optimizer not to use an index to satisfy the predicate by using "OR 0 = 1" in parenthesis with the predicate. For example, if you do not want to use an index on S.SN, code: (WHERE S.SN > 'S4' OR 0 = 1).

The use of ORDER BY on a column with a high cluster ratio index will encourage the use of sequential prefetch on the data and leaf pages as will the use of range predicates like BETWEEN, less than, and greater than. It is best to avoid repeated execution of a singleton select; rather use a cursor when retrieving more than one row in a program. Issue global update and delete statements without first selecting the rows. As was seen in the batch case study, it is best to process the rows in sequence, which means that the updates to be applied to a table should be sorted in the sequence of retrieval of the table.

Deferred Write

Deferred write is like sequential prefetch in that 32 pages are processed with a single I/O. As the name indicates, deferred write is used to write 32 changed pages to a tablespace or index with a single I/O. In addition, the page addresses are sorted so that pages can be written serially across DASD which minimizes seek time to write the page. It is necessary to have sufficient space in the buffer pool and not exceed certain thresholds to take advantage of this efficient processing as discussed in Chapter CD. If you believe that deferred write is not being used because a batch job varies in elapsed time depending on the DB2 workload when the job is executed, for example, check with the system administrator or use a performance monitor to determine if your program is taking advantage of deferred write.

BP.4 I/O TIME ESTIMATES FOR INDEX USAGE VERSUS PREFETCH

To illustrate the possibly great reduction in elapsed time when using sequential prefetch over a matching index scan, we can use a formula to estimate how much I/O time is used in each case. Assume the following:

- 100,000 rows must be located at random in a one million row table with a three-level B-tree index
- 30,000 data pages with row lengths of 100 bytes
- 4,000 leaf pages for a 10-byte indexed column
- 16 ms per page for random read on 3390 DASD
- 1.7 ms per page for sequential prefetch on 3390 DASD

I/O Estimate for Matching Index Scan: We can assume 400,000 I/O operations (100,000 rows x (3-level B-tree +1 for data page)).
The time can vary depending on whether any index pages remain in the buffer. Let's take the worst case first, and assume that no pages remain in the buffer pool. The I/O time is 1.78 hours, calculated as:

400,000 I/O x 16 ms / 1000 for seconds / 60 for minutes / 60 for hours = 1.78 hours of I/O time.

If the root and nonleaf pages remain in the buffer, we can cut the number of I/O operations in half and come up with an estimate of 0.89 hours of I/O time. Index lookaside on leaf pages and sequential detection on index and data pages can reduce I/O time further, depending on the success of these techniques at run time.

Sequential Prefetch I/O Time Estimate: The estimates for this depend greatly on how well the data is clustered. Let's take two extreme cases:

Case 1: Assume that the data is clustered and processed in sequence. The 100,000 required rows are on 3,000 data pages and are referenced on 400 leaf pages. In other words, a fairly limited range of index leaf pages must be referenced. Perhaps only a range of supplier numbers between 20,000 and 80,000 must be updated. In this case, a matching index scan is used to position in the leaf and data pages. Then, sequential prefetch is used to scan across the required pages. In this scenario, we come up with an estimate of 0.10 *minutes* of I/O time (3,400 I/O x 1.7 ms / 1000 for seconds / 60 for minutes).

Case 2: Assume that the data is not well-clustered; the rows to be processed are scattered on most data pages. In this case, DB2 must scan all leaf and data pages. In this scenario, we come up with an estimate of 0.96 minutes of I/O time (34,000 I/O x 1.7 ms / 1000 for seconds / 60 for minutes).

Figure BP.3 is a handy table that uses the above formula to calculate I/O time for the matching index scans, guided tablespace scan (scan of required leaf and data pages), and a tablespace scan based on the percentage of rows read.

Figure BP.3. I/O time estimates for matching index scan vs. prefetch

Percent of Rows Read	**Hours** for MIS* Root & Non leaf Pages Remain in Buffer	**Minutes** for Sequential Prefetch	Minutes for Scan of All Leaf & Data Pages with Prefetch
0.01	0.0888888889	0.00963333333333	0.96333333333
0.05	0.44444444444	0.0481666666667	0.96333333333
0.10	0.88888888889	0.0963333333333	0.96333333333
0.15	1.33333333333	0.1445	0.96333333333
0.20	1.77777777778	0.192666666667	0.96333333333
0.25	2.22222222222	0.240833333333	0.96333333333
0.30	2.66666666667	0.289	0.96333333333
0.35	3.11111111111	0.337166666667	0.96333333333
0.40	3.55555555556	0.385333333333	0.96333333333
0.45	4	0.4335	0.96333333333
0.5	4.44444444444	0.48166666667	0.96333333333

*MIS = Matching Index Scan

The graphic representation of the I/O time estimate in Figure BP.4 shows the dramatic differences using the three methods. Indeed, the difference is even more dramatic than illustrated because the matching index scan processing is in hours while the two lines showing the prefetch I/O time are in minutes. The line representing the matching index scan goes up very quickly with the percentage of data processed. The line representing the prefetch I/O time for the various percentages of data and index pages processed goes up very slowly. The line representing the prefetch I/O time for processing all of the data is flat. It shows that a tablespace scan requires less I/O time than processing less than 10 percent of the data with a matching index scan and scanning a higher percentage of the data and index pages.

Figure BP.4. Graphic of I/O time estimates

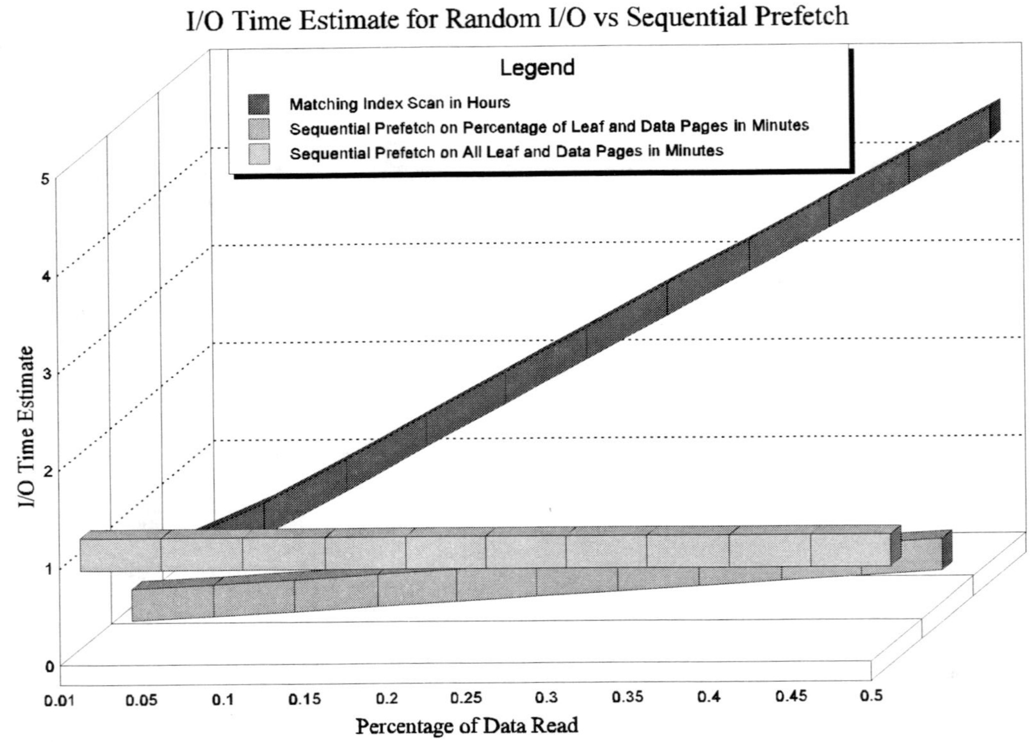

BP.5 LOAD UTILITY VERSUS INSERT STATEMENTS

When large amounts of data must be inserted, the LOAD utility has advantages over application program INSERT statements. In one situation it saved 35 percent in CPU time and ran nine times faster. LOAD has significant advantage for improved performance and in other areas as well.

Logging: All INSERTS are written to the log. With the LOAD utility, you should specify LOG NO and follow the load with a full image copy. Or, better yet, have LOAD make an inline copy as discussed in Chapter LC.

Preformatting: For insert processing, DB2 has to preformat ahead by writing out hex zeroes either 2 cylinders or tracks ahead. LOAD does not have to do this preformatting; it formats the free space at the bottom of the page as part of its deferred write processing.

Free Space for Future INSERTS: LOAD leaves the specified percent free for data and index pages, leaving room for future updates. INSERT does not.

Path length: The LOAD communicates directly with the data manager component of DB2. Insert processing must go through the application program interface and the relational data system before going to data manager. Also, LOAD does not have to check for broken pages as do INSERT and DELETE.

Compression: If you use data compression, LOAD builds the compression dictionary and compresses the data. Rows inserted into a newly created table that has never had rows is not compressed until a reorganization. This is because there is no dictionary. The LOAD and REORG utilities can create and refine the compression/decompression dictionary.

Index Builds: Perhaps the biggest contributor to application program elapsed time for INSERTS are index values being inserted at random in most cases. As we recommended earlier, the data should be sorted in clustering index order before processing. (LOAD does not sort the data.) The data cannot also be sorted in sequence according to the non-clustering indexes. This means that non-clustering index leaf pages will be updated somewhat at random and the same leaf pages will have to be updated repeatedly to point to the rows.

Figure BP.5 is an example of how leaf pages for a non-clustering index must be processed repeatedly and somewhat at random. For example, assume we have an index on supplier city, which is not the clustering index. Record 1 is a row for Dallas and must be referenced on leaf page L3, record 2 is a row for Abilene and must be referenced on leaf page L1, record 3 is a row for Houston and must be referenced on leaf page L4, record 4 is a row for Chicago and must be referenced on leaf page L2, record 5 is a rows for Atlanta and must be referenced on leaf page L1, etc. Notice that the leaf pages are not referenced in sequence. This can result in excessive DASD seek time. In addition, a leaf page must be processed multiple times.

Figure BP.5. Updates to leaf pages of a non-cluster index

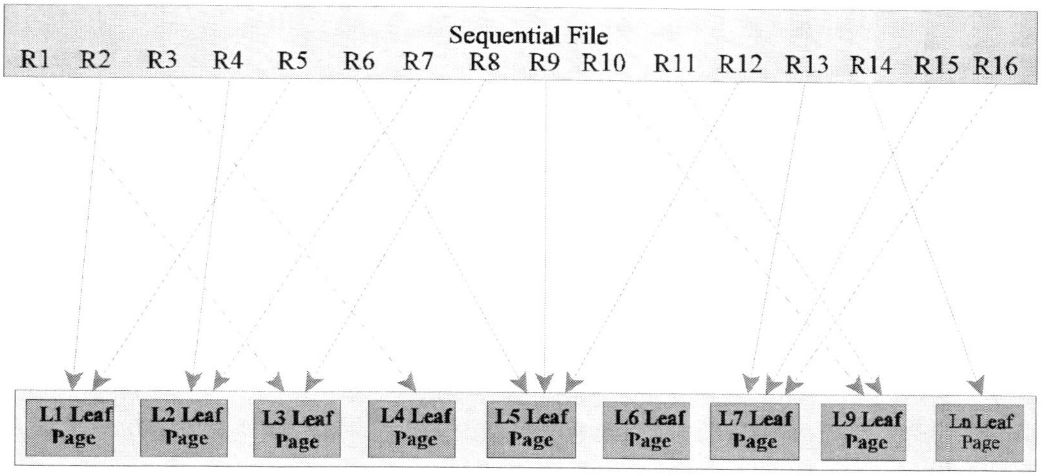

LOAD extracts the index values into a work file as it loads the data. It can then use an external sort facility such as DFSORT to sort non-clustering indexed values. By doing this, it can avoid skipping around the leaf pages, thus significantly reducing seek time. In addition, LOAD does not need to traverse the clustering index to determine where to insert each row.

If you were asked to write a program to insert about 2,000 rows into a quarter of a million row table, you would probably do so without concern for performance. Let's consider a test where one percent of 262,000 rows were added to a table with 2 indexes. LOAD RESUME required 43 elapsed seconds. INSERTS required almost twice as long at 78 elapsed seconds. The test was repeated for adding five percent of 262,000 rows to the table. When adding about 13,000 rows, the difference is even greater with LOAD RESUME requiring 91 elapsed seconds and INSERTS required 377 elapsed seconds. LOAD RESUME was over four times faster in this case. You will find that the larger the percentage of rows to be added to a table, the greater the savings with LOAD RESUME.

Consider using DB2 Estimator to estimate the costs of loading a large number of rows compared to INSERTING the same rows. Figure BP.6 summarizes estimates calculated by DB2 Estimator for DB2 V5. The first is an estimate for loading one million rows into a table with two indexes using an inline copy and the SORTKEYS parameter (discussed in Chapter LC). INSERTING the million rows using a subselect requires 10 times more CPU time than loading the rows and even more I/O and elapsed time. The last estimate is based on the costs of INSERTING one row multiplied by one million which is even more costly than using the subselect.

Figure BP.6. Comparison of LOAD and INSERTING rows using DB2 Estimator V5

Description	CPU Min:Sec	I/O Min:Sec	Elapsed Min:Sec
LOAD with inline copy and SORTKEYS	2:26.06	1:25.77	2:26.06
INSERT with subselect of 1 million rows	22:46.40	44:32.24	57:35.74
1 INSERT * 1 million rows	33:33.00	133:33.00	133:33.00

Why INSERTS Are Used Rather Than LOAD

Considering all the advantages of the LOAD utility, why consider using INSERT statements at all? One simple reality is that not everyone has the authority to use LOAD. Another reason is data availability. During LOAD processing, data is unavailable to other application programs. However, if a tablespace is partitioned, it is possible to load only one partition at a time, thereby reducing the scope of the outage at any given time. When using INSERT, only the pages where rows are inserted are unavailable due to locks taken by DB2 until commit processing, assuming page level locking.

Another reason some people balk at using the LOAD utility is because the data must be validated. For example, perhaps only certain ranges or types of data can be loaded into the table. Consider validating the data and doing any updates or deletes that are required. Write the validated data into a separate file, sort it in clustering sequence and then use LOAD. Another option is to define table check constraints on the table. Those constraints can be enforced by the LOAD utility. Chapter CT has detailed information about check constraints. If triggers reference the table, a major disadvantage of using LOAD rather than INSERT is that triggers are not activated by the LOAD utility.

If table has an identity column, there are plans to use load replace, and original sequential values are to be retained, consider defining the column with the GENERATED BY DEFAULT clause. If the table is defined with an identity column using GENERATED ALWAYS and existing values are to be retained, it is necessary to unload the data, drop the table, recreate the table with GENERATED BY DEFAULT (cannot change back to GENERATED ALWAYS), recreate indexes (consider a unique index on the identity column to guarantee unique values), and load the table.

If it is necessary to insert a large number of rows on a routine basis, use the PREFORMAT parameter when reorganizing the tablespace and loading the table initially. The PREFORMAT parameter causes the two utilities to write X'00' on the tablespace and index pages for the full primary quantity and the last secondary quantity. The high used RBA equals the high allocated RBA after using

PREFORMAT. This will increases the time for executing the utilities but avoids the time during inserts with some inserts requiring more time than others.

Managing Repeated Access to Reference Tables

Many batch programs must access small reference tables to determine such things as whether a valid state has been keyed by a user or to determine if a city is serviced by a particular division. It can be quite costly to use SELECT statements to access these tables repeatedly. A SELECT statement must go through several layers of software through DB2 and back to the program with a cost of from about 20,000 to 40,000 instructions, depending on the specific statement executed.

One way to avoid this cost is to read each reference table into an array in the program. The program can search the array to validate data for each row processed. If you are using COBOL, a SEARCH ALL statement does a binary search of the array, or a SEARCH can be used for a sequential search. Although this technique requires development time and effort, it is well worth the savings that will result when the batch program is repeatedly executed.

BP.6 DELETING A LARGE NUMBER OF ROWS

The deletion of a large number of rows, whether it is a large percentage of the rows in a table or all rows in table, is a costly process. The primary cost is in the deletion of values from the indexes, particularly if there are several indexes on the table. Some alternatives for reducing the cost of index maintenance are discussed.

Deletion of a Large Percentage of Rows in a Table

The reorganization utility can be used to efficiently delete rows that meet specified conditions during the reorganization process (V5 APAR PQ19897). This is done by specifying the DISCARD parameter, the table from which to delete the rows, and conditions under which to delete the rows. Optionally, discarded rows can be written to a discard data set in an external format that can be read by an application program or loaded into an archival table, for example, if SHRLEVEL NONE OR REFERENCE (not CHANGE) is used. Details on this processing is in Chapter RR.

Advantages: REORG ... DISCARD has significant performance advantages over DELETEing rows followed by a reorganization. It avoids having to delete reference to the discarded rows from one or more indexes. There is little or no increase in the cost of a reorganization when using the DISCARD parameter, particularly if the discarded rows are not written to a discard data set. Indeed, the costs of the reorganization may be reduced because fewer rows must be reorganized and referenced in one or more indexes that are rebuilt with a reorganization of a tablespace. Delete processing can be done with a scheduled reorganization. If reorganizations need to be scheduled more frequently to accommodate the delete processing, most SQL processing benefits from more frequent reorganizations.

The costs of logging the deleted rows is saved in comparison with using DELETE statements. This assumes that log of no is used with an inline copy or followed by an image copy with the reorganization. Also X and most S locks if using lock avoidance and latch processing are avoided when using the REORG utility.

Disadvantage: The use of REORG means that others cannot update data in the tablespace or partition during most of the reorganization processing which detracts from 24 hour availability of the data

If it is necessary to delete rows from only some partitions of a partitioned tablespace, then only those partitions are unavailable. Application programs can be designed for a limited partition scan or use of DB2 parallelism discussed in Chapter PL to allow processing of other partitions that are not being loaded.

Delete Many Rows without REORG ... DISCARD: If REORG ... DISCARD is not appropriate for the application an alterative is available to reduce costs. The cost of index maintenance can be avoided when deleting a large percent of the rows in a table by selecting all the rows using a tablespace scan and writing the rows to be retained to a sequential file (not including the rows to be deleted). If the deleted rows need to be archived, they can be written to a separate file. Sort the rows to be retained in clustering sequence and use the LOAD utility with an inline copy to replace the data if there is one table in the tablespace. If there is more than one table in the tablespace, use the mass delete algorithm followed by a LOAD RESUME.

There are a number of advantages to the procedure. It avoids index maintenance, logging of deleted rows, X locks on pages, most S locks if lock avoidance is used, and latch processing. In one case the technique reduced a 26 hour job to 15 minutes of CPU time when index maintenance on seven indexes was eliminated. It is not necessary to follow the procedure with a reorganization because the data is well organized after the processing described. This is an added cost savings because a batch update program frequently needs to be followed by a reorganization. The disadvantage of the procedure is that no one can update the data during most of the processing, which detracts from 24 hour availability of the data. If it is necessary to delete rows from only some partitions of a partitioned tablespace, then only those partitions are unavailable. Application programs can be designed for a limited partition scan or use of DB2 parallelism discussed in Chapter PL to allow processing of other partitions that are not being loaded.

Deletion of All Rows in a Table

Mass Delete Algorithm: The mass delete algorithm is very efficient in deleting all of the rows in a table. It accesses, updates, and logs only the space map pages of the data and indexes. It does not read and write the data and index pages to mark the rows and indexed values as being deleted as is necessary without using the mass delete algorithm. There are restrictions on when the mass delete algorithm can be used:

- The tablespace must be segmented.
- The table cannot be a parent table with dependent tables defined.
- The table cannot be created with a VALIDPROC and DATA CAPTURE CHANGES.
- The DELETE statement cannot reference a cursor and cannot have a WHERE clause.

If these restrictions are met, the following DELETE statement uses the mass delete algorithm to effectively and efficiently delete all of the rows and index entries in the SPJ table.

```
DELETE FROM SPJ;
```

There are a couple of disadvantages of the mass delete algorithm. If there are multiple tables in a tablespace, the space is not reusable for tables other than the one from which all the rows were deleted. The DROP TABLE statement is necessary to free space for use by other tables. The number of rows deleted is not recorded in the SQL communications area (SQLCA) discussed in Chapter PD. This means that the number of rows deleted cannot be reported by SPUFI, QMF, and other interactive tools.

If LOAD RESUME is used to place rows in the table after deleting the existing rows, there is a performance benefit. The LOAD utility does not have to format the existing pages.

Load Replace: An alternative is to LOAD REPLACE the table with a dummy or empty input file. It is particularly useful for a nonsegmented tablespaces and a parent table for which the mass delete algorithm does not work. However, it does place the parent table in check pending state if there are any dependent tables defined. Do be cautious about using LOAD REPLACE if there is more than one table in a tablespace. It will result in losing all tables in the tablespace since LOAD REPLACE deletes and defines the underlying VSAM data sets.

Optionally, the REUSE parameter can be added to the LOAD statement. It causes a logical reset of the data sets (V5 APAR PQ19077) which keeps the data sets at the same location on DASD. This eases the maintenance of data set placement on DASD and improves performance over deleting and redefining the data sets.

BP.7 RUNNING BATCH AND ONLINE CONCURRENTLY

When running batch programs concurrently with online transactions, it is important to take steps to ensure that online transaction performance does not suffer from the batch processing.

Adjusting Priorities

An obvious way to keep batch programs from taking resources from online transactions is to give the batch programs a lower priority. One caveat is to be careful to avoid lock contention; a low-priority batch program can hold onto its locks for a long time, locking out higher-priority transactions.

With OS/390, it is possible to assign priority relative to a set of goals. A set of goals is a particular service class. Workload manager dynamically dispatches work relative to the service class of a particular application type, a particular application, or several other specifications.

If you do not have workload manager, or if you are not using goal mode yet, realize that the I/O of all programs has the dispatching priority of the database services address space. However, it is possible to adjust I/O priority separately for synchronous reads and writes and prefetch reads. Consider speaking to your system programmer about using OS/390 I/O priority scheduling to set the I/O priority of the application's address space. For example, you can set the I/O priority of the CICS address space higher than that of batch. Chapter CD has an example of setting the I/O priority of the database services address space.

Commit Frequency

To avoid having a long-running batch job hold locks on data for long periods of time, the batch program must issue COMMIT WORK statements periodically. Adjust the commit frequency to meet the required response time goals and to minimize lock contention. To determine how often to commit, you must know the maximum amount of time that is acceptable for an online transaction to wait for a lock to be released. We will use the test results discussed in Chapter CC and summarized in Figure BP.7 to analyze the number of pages locked and for what period of time depending on the commit frequency. If the commit frequency is every 10 updates, two pages are locked for about 0.10 seconds (90 seconds of elapsed time executing DB2 calls / 867 commits while updating 8,664 rows). The user will have to wait more than 0.10 seconds to access the two pages if other programs are attempting to process the locked pages and are queued to get locks, a long running SQL statement is executing, or the programs are doing other work while locks are held. If the user can wait more than 0.10 seconds plus the other factors for access to the data being processed by the batch program, consider a commit every 100 or 1000 updates. If the user can wait 0.58 seconds plus the other factors, the batch program can commit every 1000 updates and complete updating 8,664 rows in 5.19 seconds compared to committing after every update and requiring 686.20 seconds (Figure BP.7). Committing based on a specified time has the advantage that you know that the locks taken by the program are held no longer than the specified time. In general, consider committing every 0.5 to 5 seconds. Committing every 0.5 to 1 second gave good test results. These are only general guidelines based on one test. As always it is best to test a scenario that you are considering in your environment.

Figure BP.7. User wait time and commit frequency

Time User Can Wait for Locked Pages*	Number of Pages Locked	Commit Frequency	Time to Update 8664 rows*
0.08+	1	1	686.20
0.10+	2-10	10	90.21
0.22+	4-100	100	17.79
0.58+	28-1000	1000	5.19

*Elapsed time in seconds executing DB2 calls

A DB2 professional attending a course covering this material had a long running batch job that typically required 5.5 hours. He modified the program to commit every 20 seconds rather than after each unit of recovery before going home for the day. The next morning he reported to the class that the job ran for only 57 minutes. (He did not know how many update statements were in a unit of recovery.)

You would like to commit frequently to release locks and you would like to reduce the costs of executing batch programs. During heavy transaction usage, you will need to commit more frequently and during low activity you can commit less frequently to gain the performance benefits. Figure BP.8 is an example of an application table that can be used to specify time periods with heavy and low transaction usage and an appropriate commit frequency.

Figure BP.8. Commit frequency based on time of day

COMMIT_FREQUENCY

Start_Time	End_Time	Frequency
08.00.00	09.00.00	100
09.00.01	11.00.00	10
11.00.01	13.00.00	100
13.00.01	17.00.00	10
17.00.01	07.59.59	1000

Application programs can use the SET statement to determine the time that their batch program is executing by setting a host variable equal to the special register CURRENT_TIMESTAMP and optional do calculations (V6) as in the following example.

```
SET :CURRENT_TIMESTAMP = CURRENT_TIMESTAMP + 30 DAYS END-EXEC.
```

The SET statement can also be used to execute functions as in the following statement. The use of the VALUE ... INTO statement is an alternative for executing functions as discussed in Chapter UD.

Transaction rates are usually low on weekends. If this is the case in your environment and you want to lower the costs of your batch program execution, consider determining whether your program is executing on a weekend like (V6):

```
EXEC SQL SET :DAY-WEEK = DAYOFWEEK(CURRENT DATE) END-EXEC.
```

DAYOFWEEK returns an integer in the range of 1 to 7, where the values of 1, 2, 3, 4, 5, 6, 7 represent Sunday, Monday, Tuesday, Wednesday, Thursday, Friday, Saturday.

It is necessary to use DAYOFWEEK in a SELECT statement from a one row table interactively as in the following example without the use of the formula.

A formula is needed prior to V6 for a host program as well as interactively.

```
SELECT DAYS(CURRENT DATE) - (DAYS(CURRENT DATE) -1) / 7 * 7
FROM   SYSIBM.SYSDUMMY1;
```

If the result is 1, it is Monday, if 2 it is Tuesday, if 3 it is Wednesday, and so forth. On weekends, consider committing after 1,000 updates.

You may also want to consider committing less often on holidays when your transaction rate is low. Figure BP.9 is an example holiday table that can be read to determine the commit frequency.

Figure BP.9. Commit frequency for holidays

COMMIT_FREQ_HOLIDAYS

Date	Holiday	Frequency
1992-01-01	New Years	1000
1992-04-19	Easter	1000
1992-12-25	Christmas	1000
Etc.		

Partition Processing to Fit in a Batch Window

If you have a small batch window where some of the data can be unavailable to transactions for a short period of time, consider partitioning the tablespace such that the batch processing can be done on a partition within the available time period. For example, if a batch job requires one hour and there is a five minute batch window available, consider twenty partitions such that each partition can be processed in three minutes. The additional two minutes that are available allow for overall variation in the workload of the computer. The time also allows for submitting multiple batch jobs, each of which operates on one partition and for the contention expected when multiple batch jobs executing concurrently. The batch program must be designed to process one partition. You may be able to take advantage of a limited partition scan and DB2 parallelism discussed in Chapter PL. Optionally, several jobs, each of which is designed to operate on one partition, can be submitted and executed in parallel.

Partitioning allows for executing most utilities on a single partition with other partitions available for SELECT, INSERT, UPDATE, and DELETE processing. Partition independence is discussed in Chapter LC.

BP.8 DESIGNING RESTARTABLE BATCH PROGRAMS

Restarting a long-running batch update program presents challenges. A simple approach is to issue no commits during processing. All updates are rolled back automatically if a failure occurs. However, this approach is generally not recommended. Even for a 15-minute run, it can take 15 minutes to apply the updates, 30 minutes to roll back, and another 15 minutes to apply the updates a second time. Even worse, during most of this time some, perhaps many, of the pages would have exclusive locks, excluding all other access. Consequently, to avoid the possibility of lengthy rollbacks and holding locks, the batch program should commit work periodically.

We will describe three techniques to allow for commits, one in which restart logic is coded in the program and two in which data is simply copied before processing begins. Note that if a program relies on copies of the data, it must issue a LOCK TABLE statement before it can begin processing. This locks out other updaters, whose updates would be lost if the image copies were restored.

Alternative 1: Restart Logic

When commit works are issued, the program must be able to determine where to resume processing after a failure. The technique for coding this logic is similar to that for reopening a cursor described in Chapter CC. The primary key value of the last row processed before the commit is saved and is used to reestablish position when processing resumes. It is not enough for that key value to be saved in the program, because it will be lost in the failure when the program abends. However, if that key value is saved in another table, a control table, with the update of that table committed along with the processing on the primary data tables, the value is always available to the program when it restarts. This control table contains the last primary key value, control information, intermediate results, and perhaps the commit frequency for future modification if commits need to be more or less frequent.

The restarted program must read the control table to reestablish position and continue processing. (CURSOR WITH HOLD does not hold position after a program has abended.) Recall that ORDER BY is required to avoid missing rows, and an index can be used to avoid a sort. If the input to the update program is on a GSAM file and IMS extended restart is available, it can be used on the input and output files but cannot be used on the DB2 table to re-establish position when the program is restarted.

The development of a generalized application restart program is non-trivial. There are several software companies that sell restart packages. Consider estimating the time it would take to develop a generalized restart program and compare that to the cost of buying one.

Alternative 2: Image Copy

A technique used to avoid developing complex restart logic in a program and to allow for periodic commits is to take an image copy of the tablespaces before submitting the batch job. If the job fails, recover the tablespaces to the image copies and re-run the batch job.

Disadvantage: When using referential integrity, dependent tablespaces will have check pending set on. This can be avoided by quiescing all the related tables to an RBA (relative byte address) point and recovering to the RBA as will be discussed in Chapter CR. Both techniques require that all indexes on all tables must be rebuilt.

Alternative 3: DSN1COPY

Use DSN1COPY, a standalone utility discussed in Chapter CR, to copy all the tablespaces to be updated along with all indexes to sequential files. Then, if a failure occurs, use DSN1COPY again to copy the sequential files back to the tablespaces and indexes and rerun the batch job. This alternative avoids having to rebuild the indexes.

BP.9 EXECUTING BATCH PROGRAMS

Three alternatives are described here: the DSNTEP2 sample program shipped with DB2, TSO TMP, and the call attachment facility.

DSNTEP2 Sample Program

DSNTEP2 is a sample PL/1 program that reads SQL statements and executes them dynamically. It is provided in source form only prior to V6, so you need a PL/1 compiler and run-time library or Language Environment to use it. It is provided in object form in member DSNTEP2L with a DBRM member of DSN@EP21 (V6). DSNTIAD is similar to DSNTEP2, except it is written in Assembler and cannot execute SELECT statements.

DSNTEP2 allows up to 10 errors (MAXERRORS) after which it terminates with a return code of 8. It does not issue a rollback; unlike SPUFI which issues a rollback to the last commit point in such a situation.

Figure BP.10 contains example JCL for executing DSNTEP2. It contains the SQL embedded in the JCL. Usually you will want the SYSIN DD statement to reference a file or PDS member that contains the SQL. It is often referred to as batch SPUFI because people frequently test interactively with SPUFI and use DSNTEP2 to execute the SQL in batch.

Figure BP.10. JCL to execute DSNTEP2

```
//SUPDATE    JOB ... USER=AUTHID
//TERM       EXEC PGM=IKJEFT1B,DYNAMNBR=30
//SYSIN      DD
SELECT * FROM S;
SELECT * FROM P;
/*
//SYSTSIN    DD    *
TIME
DSN SYSTEM(DSN)
RUN PROGRAM(DSNTEP2) PLAN(DSNTEP2)  -
    LIBRARY('PROJ.AUTHID.LOAD')     -
   END
TIME
/*
//
```

Functional comments can be provided in SYSIN (V6 APAR PQ24360). You can specify the maximum number of rows to return for each subsequent SELECT statement (-1 indicates that all rows are fetched).

--#SET ROWS_FETCH 250

You can specify the maximum number of rows to output for each subsequent SELECT statement (-1 indicates that all rows are output).

--#SET ROWS_OUT 250

You can change to/from different terminator characters. This is particularly useful when creating complex triggers.

--#SET TERMINATOR '#'

TSO Terminal Monitor Program

The TSO terminal monitor program (TMP) executes statements as if they were keyed from TSO. It is frequently used to execute batch programs. Figure BP.11 contains sample JCL to execute the TMP which has the name IKJEFT01. The TMP executes statements as if they were keyed interactively using TSO. The DSN610.SDSNLOAD library is the default and is frequently changed to, for example, SYS1.DSN610.SDSNLOAD when the DB2 subsystem is installed. You will need to determine the name given at your installation. All commands like RUN can be executed from the DSN processor. Do change DSN SYSTEM(DSN) to the name given to the DB2 subsystem when it is installed, for example, DSN SYSTEM(DB2T) or DSN SYSTEM(DB2P).

Figure BP.11. JCL to execute a batch program using TSO TMP

```
//SUPDATE    JOB ... USER=AUTHID
//*
//STEP1      EXEC PGM=IKJEFT01,DYNAMNBR=30
//STEPLIB    DD   DSN=DSN610.SDSNLOAD,DISP=SHR
//SYSPRINT   DD   SYSOUT=A
//SYSTSPRT   DD   SYSOUT=A
//SYSUDUMP   DD   SYSOUT=A
//SYSOUT     DD   SYSOUT=A
//REPORT     DD   SYSOUT=A
//PARMIN     DD   DSN=PARMIN.FILE
//*
//SYSTSIN    DD   *
TIME
DSN SYSTEM(DSN)
RUN PROGRAM(SUPDATE) PLAN(SUPDATE) -
    LIBRARY('PROJ.AUTHID.LOAD')    -
    PARMS ('/VALUE1 VALUE2 VALUE3')
END
TIME
/*
```

The TSO TIME command is executed before and after the SUPDATE program in the example. The purpose is to get a rough estimate of the CPU and elapsed times required by the batch program by subtracting the time values.

Alternate TSO Entry Points: TSO provides two alternate entry points, IKJEFT1A and IKJEFT1B, which have some advantages over IKJEFT01. When using either of these entry points, TSO does not intercept errors from a program abend. They also allow the JCL return codes (CODE= parameter) to be passed to the next job step. They act more like a standard OS/390 batch program in the disposition of data sets after a program abend and in the content of a dump after a system or application-initiated abend.

Disposition of Data Sets: You specify the disposition of a data set after a program has abended by coding the DISP parameter on a DD statement. If the disposition parameter is coded as DISP=(NEW,CATLG,DELETE), the data set is deleted if the program abended in a standard OS/390 batch. However, if IKJEFT01 is used to execute a batch program, the data set is cataloged--the middle parameter is used. If IKJEFT1A is used, the data set is cataloged if there is an application abend--a COBOL call to ILBOABN0, a PL/I call to PLIDUMP with the S option, or an assembler ABEND macro is executed. The use of the IKJEFT1B entry point results in the same disposition of the data set as standard OS/390 (Figure BP.12). If there is a system abend as a result, of say, a data exception (0C7), the data set will be deleted as indicated in the third parameter. The dump content and abend code passed to the next step in the job vary, depending upon the entry point used as summarized in Figure BP.13. Again IKJEFT1B more closely resembles standard OS/390 batch. In addition, parameters cannot be passed on a JOB or STEP statement to a program using TMP. It is necessary to pass them through the use of a CLIST. For these reasons, CAF is some times used to execute batch programs. A sample CAF assembler program is in outprefix.SDSNSAMP(DSN8CA).

Figure BP.12. Data set disposition, depending upon the environment

Assume DISP=(NEW,CATLG,DELETE) on DD statement

Program abend	OS/390	IKJEFT1B	IKJEFT1A	IKJEFT01
System abend	DELETE	DELETE	DELETE	CATLG
Application abend	DELETE	DELETE	CATLG	CATLG

Figure BP.13. Dump content and abend code, depending upon the environment

Program abend	OS/390	IKJEFT1B	IKJEFT1A	IKJEFT01
System abend	Appl.	Appl.	Appl.	TSO
Abend code	As is	04C	04C	Not pass
Application abend	Appl.	Appl.	TSO	TSO
Abend code	As is	As is	Not pass	Not pass

Passing Parameters Using TSO TMP: Job step PARM values cannot be passed using DSN. You can use a CLIST to do this, however. Figure BP.14 is an example of a CLIST, AUTHID.TSO.CLIST(EXPARM).

Figure BP.14. CLIST used to pass parameters

```
PROC 0 SUBSYS(DB2P) PARM(DEFAULT)
DSN SYSTEM(&SUBSYS)
RUN PROGRAM(UPDATE) PLAN(SUPDATE) PARM('&PARM') -
    LIBRARY('PROJ.AUTHID.LOAD')
SET &SAVECC = &LASTCC
DATA
END
ENDDATA
/*
```

When you execute the batch program, use JCL like that shown in Figure BP.15. It shows the batch program passing a parameter value and a new subsystem identifier to the CLIST. The alternative to this approach is to pass parameters on the RUN statement, which might not conform to batch standards.

Figure BP.15. JCL using CLIST to pass parameters

```
//STEP2      EXEC PGM=IKJEFT1B,
//                PARM='%EXPARM SUBSYS(DB2T) PARM(value)'
//SYSTSPRT  DD    SYSOUT=*
//SYSPROC   DD    DISP=SHARE,DSN=AUTHID.TSO.CLIST
//SYSTSIN   DD    *
additional TSO commands as needed
/*
```

Call Attachment Facility (CAF)

If you are looking for an attachment that acts more like a standard OS/390 batch program, consider the call attachment facility. Although it has no performance advantage over TSO TMP once the batch program starts executing in its own address space, the return codes, parameter values, and disposition handling are as with any batch job.

CAF provides for direct control over connections to DB2 without the other standard attachments, and it can be used to issue instrumentation facility interface (IFI) calls. It can be used in the following environments:

- OS/390 batch and OS/390 started task
- IMS batch
- TSO background and foreground

The *Application Programming and SQL Guide* manual contains information on how to use the CAF.

BP.10 SUMMARY

The design techniques used for batch programs and online transactions are quite different. Batch techniques should be used for batch processing. Matching index scans, while a good choice for online transactions, are usually not a good choice for batch programs when processing more than 10 to 20 percent of the rows.

It is important to minimize index maintenance for batch update programs. We saw several techniques for doing this, including using LOAD RESUME rather than INSERTING a large number of rows with a host language program.

EXERCISES

1. Why is a tablespace scan often best for batch processing?

2. If a matching index scan is chosen for the predicate WHERE JN > 'J3', what can you do to disallow the use of the index and encourage a tablespace scan?

3. - Assume that you need to write a batch program to update 10 to 20 percent of the rows in a large production table and the input to the program is in a sequential file. Is it important to have the production table and sequential file in sequence on the primary key? Why?

4. What strategy would you suggest for a batch program to process about 50,000 rows to be updated in a million row table named SPJ? The information to be used to update the rows is in a sequential file named UPDATES. About 150,000 rows are to be deleted and archived as indicated by a date range that is input to the program. About 200,000 rows are to be inserted into the table and are currently in a sequential file called INSERTS.

5. What is a major disadvantage to the strategy suggested in the above exercise?

6. How can you minimize the time that the data is unavailable during the batch process?

7. If you have a batch window when all of the data can be made unavailable but the table is too large to be processed within the time frame, what is an approach to consider?

8 What is an advantage of using the mass delete algorithm followed by LOAD RESUME compared to LOAD REPLACE?

9. What are the performance benefits of CURSOR WITH HOLD for a batch program?

10. Should a batch program provide for cursor repositioning logic when CURSOR WITH HOLD is used? Why?

11. Is it advisable to use OPTIMIZE FOR 12 ROWS when repositioning a cursor in a batch program?

12. If prefetch is not chosen as part of the access path by the optimizer, is it possible that prefetch may be used at execution time?

13. Under what condition might the optimizer not choose sequential prefetch for a batch program?

14. Usually a batch job executes in a couple of minutes of elapsed time. Assume that the problem is within DB2, not due to the workload of other software on the computer.

a) Occasionally, the batch job takes several minutes of elapsed time. Why?

b) Occasionally, the batch job takes over 30 minutes of elapsed time. Why?

c) What action can you take?

ANSWERS

1. Sequential prefetch is usually chosen by the optimizer for a tablespace scan. Sequential prefetch results in reading 32 pages with a single I/O, assuming a buffer pool of 1000 pages or more. The average I/O time for a prefetched page is 1.7 ms using 3390 DASD. This is compared to the I/O time for a page read at random, which is 16 ms. In addition, a page read at random means the use of an index, which requires processing a three level index in most cases.

2. Add "OR 0 = 1" to the predicate to disallow the use of a matching index scan. For example, WHERE (JN > 'J3' OR 0 = 1) disallows the use of a matching index scan on JN and encourages a tablespace scan.

3. Yes, it is important to have the production table and sequential file in sequence on the primary key. This allows for match-merge processing with sequential prefetch used on the leaf and data pages with no sort.

4. It is advisable to have the sequence of the table to be updated and the sequence of the UPDATES file match. If the clustering index is on the primary key, a sort can be avoided for an ORDER BY clause. The UPDATES file can be sorted in sequence on the primary key.

A good strategy is to design for a guided tablespace scan with sequential prefetch on the million row tablespace and clustering index. Read the table and UPDATES file until there is a match using match-merge logic in the program. Modify the row and write it to a sequential file named EXTRACTS, for example. The row is not updated in the table to avoid updating indexes. While doing the match-merge processing, test if the row has a date within the range of dates to be deleted. If the row is to be deleted, write it to an archive file and not to the EXTRACTS file if the deleted rows need to be archived.

Sort the EXTRACTS and INSERTS files into a file named COMPLETE. The files can simply be concatenated and a sort is not necessary if the rows are to be added to the end of the table and are in sequence. As one of the last statements in the batch program, use the mass delete algorithm to delete all rows in the table if it is not a parent table and it is in a segmented tablespace. For example, DELETE FROM SPJ with no predicate. Use LOAD RESUME to repopulate the SPJ table with the records in the COMPLETE file and rebuild the indexes. If the table is in a tablespace with no other tables, LOAD REPLACE can be used.

5. A major disadvantage to the technique is that the table is unavailable during the batch processing.

6. Consider using a partitioned tablespace. Design the batch process to update data in one partition at a time. All other partitions are available for reading and updating while the batch program is processing a partition. If one partition can be unavailable for three minutes, for example, size the partitions such that the batch program can process the data in one partition in three minutes.

7. Consider partitioning the tablespace such that a separate batch job can be submitted for each partition (or set of partitions) and can be executed in parallel. For example, assume that the batch job usually requires one hour of elapsed time but you have only 15 minutes available for the job in your batch window. Consider, dividing the tablespace into 10 parts where each part can be processed in about 6 to 10 minutes. Submit 10 batch jobs to process data in each of the 10 parts that will be executed in parallel. Notice that some additional time is allowed in the example. Ideally, the longest running batch job working on one partition will require 10 minutes and we assumed a 15 minute batch window.

8. The mass delete algorithm does not delete/define the data sets as does LOAD REPLACE. This means that LOAD RESUME does not have to reformat existing data and index pages as is necessary when using LOAD REPLACE.

9. CURSOR WITH HOLD avoids the cost of repositioning the cursor after each COMMIT. Another performance benefit is that any temporary work areas are held after a COMMIT and need not be regenerated.

10. A batch program should provide for cursor repositioning when CURSOR WITH HOLD is used. If a rollback occurs because of a deadlock, it is necessary to reposition and redo the processing that was rolled back. In addition, cursor repositioning is necessary for application program restart processing.

11. No, it is not advisable to use OPTIMIZE FOR 12 ROWS, as discussed in Chapter PP, when repositioning a cursor in a batch program if a large number of rows are to be processed before a commit. (CURSOR WITH HOLD is a good choice to avoid the need to execute cursor repositioning logic in most cases.) When it is necessary to reposition after rollback or program restart, it is likely that a large number of rows will be processed. OPTIMIZE FOR 12 ROWS encourages a good access path for processing 12 rows which is probably not a good access path for processing thousands or tens of thousands of rows.

12. Sequential detection may result in dynamic prefetch being used at execution time even though the optimizer did not choose to use prefetch.

13. A singleton SELECT statement that returns one row may be performed in a paragraph repeatedly. The optimizer will choose a good access path to process one row which does not include prefetch. However, at execution time dynamic prefetch may be activated if rows are being retrieved on consecutive pages.

14. a) It may be that DB2 is not able to take advantage of deferred write a good deal of the time because < 50 % of the pages are stealable. DB2 must frequently write updated pages one at a time rather than using the more efficient deferred write and write 32 pages with a single I/O.

b) It may be that > 95 percent of the pages in the buffer pool are marked as in use and DB2 is writing a page for every row that is updated. A one minute batch job required over 30 minutes of elapsed time before it was canceled at a company when the 95 % threshold was exceeded.

c) It is advisable to check with the system administrator to determine if the buffer pool is sized correctly for the workload.

FIGURES

Triggering Actions in DB2

TR.1 INTRODUCTION

Triggers give you the opportunity to turn responsibility for some actions over to DB2. You can define and implement business rules and actions using triggers. Complex validation of data can be done through the use of triggers. Values can be automatically generated each time an INSERT statement is executed. Exception conditions can be checked and the appropriate action taken as defined in a trigger. These actions can be based on a comparison of values before and after an update. You can execute additional INSERT, UPDATE, and DELETE statements after an event based on a trigger definition. Triggers can be used to update summary information after an event, and maintain audit or mirror data.

Order processing tables are used to demonstrate how triggers are created and used. One of the primary tables used in examples is the ORDER table created like:

```
CREATE TABLE ORDER
  (ORDERNO     INTEGER       NOT NULL WITH DEFAULT,
   CUSTNO      INTEGER       NOT NULL WITH DEFAULT,
   ITEMNO      INTEGER       NOT NULL WITH DEFAULT,
   UNIT_PRICE  DECIMAL(9,2)  NOT NULL WITH DEFAULT,
   QTY         INTEGER       NOT NULL WITH DEFAULT,
   WEIGHT      INTEGER       NOT NULL WITH DEFAULT,
   COUNTRY     CHAR(6)       NOT NULL WITH DEFAULT,
   SHIP_COSTS  DECIMAL(9,2)  NOT NULL WITH DEFAULT,
   TAXES       DECIMAL(9,2)  NOT NULL WITH DEFAULT,
   DUTY        DECIMAL(9,2)  NOT NULL WITH DEFAULT,
   ORDER_DATE  DATE          NOT NULL WITH DEFAULT,
   SHIP_DATE   DATE          WITH DEFAULT '9999-12-31',
   PRIMARY KEY (ORDERNO));
```

TR.2 COMPONENTS OF TRIGGERS

Triggers provide for defining actions to DB2 that are to be taken before or after an event on a table.

Before triggers are activated before any action is taken on a table by DB2. These triggers do not activate other triggers. After triggers are activated after actions are taken on a table by DB2. These triggers can result in the activation of other triggers. An event can be an INSERT, UPDATE, or DELETE statement on one table. Triggers do not apply to utilities.

An action can be to execute one or more SQL statements on local tables depending on the conditions defined and type of trigger. An action can occur for each row processed or statement executed. Triggers cannot be used to take an action outside of DB2. However, user-defined functions (UDF) and stored procedures can be invoked from within a trigger definition that takes an action outside of DB2. A program that causes the trigger to be activated cannot access the result of a stored procedure. UDF and stored procedures are discussed in Chapters UD and SP.

The maximum size of a trigger is 3,460 bytes.

BEFORE Trigger to Validate Data

A BEFORE trigger is useful to validate data. For example, a row should not be inserted into a CUSTOMER table if the customer is not in a city where the company does business. Assume that the VALID_CITY table contains all cities where the company does business. The following BEFORE INSERT on the CUSTOMER table trigger ensures that a row can never be inserted unless the company does business in the city.

```
CREATE TRIGGER BCUS10
  NO CASCADE BEFORE INSERT ON CUSTOMER
  REFERENCING NEW AS N
  FOR EACH ROW MODE DB2SQL
  WHEN (N.CITY <>
     (SELECT CITY
      FROM   VALID_CITIES
      WHERE  CITY = N.CITY))
  BEGIN ATOMIC
      SIGNAL SQLSTATE 'IBC10'  ('Not a valid city');
  END#
```

Each component of the CREATE TRIGGER statement is described in this chapter.

Triggers cannot be created on a view, temporary table, auxiliary table, alias, synonym, or catalog table. However, triggers defined on a table referenced in a view are activated when manipulating the view.

Multiple SQL Statements Can be Executed in a Trigger Body

If there is more than one SQL statement in the trigger body, the statements must be preceded by BEGIN ATOMIC and ended with an END statement. These constructs are optional if there is only one SQL statement in the trigger body. If there are more than one statement in a trigger body, each statement must be terminated by a ";".

SPUFI and DSNTEP2 use ";" as a terminator for a complete SQL statement by default. This can result in DB2 seeing only part of the trigger definition. It is necessary to use a different statement terminator when more than one SQL statement appears in a trigger body.

The SPUFI SQL terminator can be changed using the CURRENT SPUFI DEFAULTS panel. The first entry on the panel is SQL TERMINATOR with a default of ";". Key over the ";" terminator with "#" if this is your desired terminator character. The default ";" can be replaced with another character but it cannot be blank (" "), comma (","), underscore (_), double quote ("), single quote ('), left parenthesis "(", and right parenthesis ")". The "#" terminator is used in example CREATE TRIGGER statements in this chapter where there are one or more statements in a SPUFI input file. If ";" must be used to terminate multiple SQL statements in the trigger body, "#" or the designated terminator must be used for all other statements in the file.

The DSNTEP2 terminator can be set with a functional comment embedded in the input file containing the SQL to be executed as read from SYSIN provided the V6 APAR PQ24360 has been installed. If you wish to change the terminator character to "#", the following statement must proceed the use of the terminator.

```
--#SET TERMINATOR '#'
```

The terminator can be changed again within the file so that subsequent SQL statements use the newly defined terminator.

Activation Time

The activation time of a trigger can be BEFORE or AFTER an event as indicated by these keywords in the CREATE TRIGGER statement. The previous CREATE TRIGGER statement applies to the insertion of rows as indicated by "BEFORE INSERT" in the statement. If you also want to ensure that a city value cannot be updated to a city where the company does not do business, a BEFORE UPDATE trigger is required like:

```
CREATE TRIGGER BCUS20
  NO CASCADE BEFORE UPDATE OF CITY ON CUSTOMER
  REFERENCING NEW AS N
  FOR EACH ROW MODE DB2SQL
  WHEN (N.CITY <>
     (SELECT CITY
      FROM   VALID_CITIES
      WHERE  CITY = N.CITY))
        SIGNAL SQLSTATE 'IBC20' ('Not a valid city');
```

NO CASCADE is required for all BEFORE triggers. This is because a BEFORE trigger cannot activate another trigger.

Triggering Event

The event that causes the trigger to be activated can be an INSERT, UPDATE, or DELETE statement executed on the named table in the ON clause. The trigger applies only to the specified statement type. You can name one or more columns in an UPDATE trigger which is advisable. Otherwise, the trigger applies to the update of any columns in the row. It detracts from performance to execute a trigger if it does not apply to the column updated.

Referential Integrity: An action taken as a result of enforcement of referential integrity (RI) can invoke a trigger. For example, if a primary key (PK) row is deleted with dependent tables defined to DB2 with the constraints of DELETE CASCADE or DELETE SET NULL, all corresponding foreign key (FK) rows are deleted or the FK is updated to be null. This results in invoking triggers defined on the affected FK tables. This part of the cascading effect is discussed in Section TR.6.

Granularity

The trigger can apply to each row processed in the table or each statement executed. This is known as the granularity of the statement and is specified with the FOR EACH ROW or FOR EACH STATEMENT clause.

FOR EACH ROW results in the trigger being activated for each row processed in the table. Multiple rows can be processed by an SQL statement as a result of the set oriented nature of SQL. Costs increase as the number of rows processed increases. The trigger does not apply if no rows qualify. It is referred to as a row trigger.

FOR EACH STATEMENT results in the trigger being activated for each UPDATE or DELETE statement executed on the named table. The trigger is activated once even if no rows qualify as a result of the triggering statement. FOR EACH STATEMENT applies to AFTER triggers (not BEFORE triggers). It is referred to as a statement trigger.

Mode

DB2SQL mode is currently implemented in DB2. Additional modes may be available in the future. The SQL92 standard has immediate and deferred modes defined. The clause MODE DB2SQL results in processing like the immediate mode.

TR.3 TRANSITION VARIABLES

Transition variables provide for referencing a row or table before (OLD) and after (NEW) a triggering event. The REFERENCING clause is used to assign transition variables. A correlation name is assigned using an AS clause. Figure TR.1 summarizes the types of transition variables available, gives a brief description, and indicates the type of trigger where the variables can be used. Of course, you can choose your own correlation names rather than those used in the examples.

Figure TR.1. Transition variables

Transition Variables	Description
REFERENCING OLD AS O	O can be used to reference columns <u>before</u> modification. Applies to update and delete triggers.
REFERENCING NEW AS N	N can be used to reference columns <u>after</u> modification. Applies to update and insert triggers.
REFERENCING OLD_TABLE AS OT	OT can be used in a FROM clause and as a correlation name to reference a table <u>before</u> modification. Can count the number of rows in Oslo before a triggering event, for example. Applies to update and delete triggers.

Transition Variables	Description
REFERENCING NEW_TABLE AS NT	NT can be used in a FROM clause and as a correlation name to reference a table after modification. Can count the number of rows in Oslo after a triggering event, for example. Applies to update and insert triggers.

The REFERENCING keyword appears only once for multiple transition variables, for example:

```
REFERENCING OLD AS O NEW AS N OLD_TABLE AS OT NEW_TABLE AS NT
```

The following formulation results in an error:

```
REFERENCING OLD AS O
REFERENCING NEW AS N
```

The use of OLD_TABLE and NEW_TABLE correlation names in the FROM clause, can be used to evaluate a column function (MIN, MAX, AVG, SUM, COUNT) for more than one row in a table before or after a triggering event. You might want to think of the OLD_TABLE and NEW_TABLE as being before and after read-only images of the table. Indeed, the referenced tables cannot be modified.

When Transition Variables Can Be Used

Use of transition variables depends on the activation time, triggering event, and granularity as summarized in Figure TR.2. None of the transition variables are required in a CREATE TRIGGER statement. If used, old row and old table refers to the data before the triggering action. New row and new table refers to data after the triggering action.

Figure TR.2. Rules for the use of transition variables

Activation Time and Triggering Event	FOR EACH ROW Granularity	FOR EACH STATEMENT Granularity
BEFORE INSERT	New row	Not applicable
BEFORE UPDATE	Old row, new row	Not applicable
BEFORE DELETE	Old row	Not applicable
AFTER INSERT	New row, new table	New table
AFTER UPDATE	Old row, new row Old table, new table	Old table, new table
AFTER DELETE	Old row, old table	Old table

The rules for use of transition variable are logical. For example, it is not possible to reference an old row when executing a BEFORE and AFTER INSERT trigger because one does not exist. In addition, there is no new row when executing a BEFORE and AFTER DELETE trigger. All combinations of old and new rows and tables can be referenced only for AFTER UPDATE triggers.

Transition Variables and Performance

Values for AFTER trigger transition variables and transition tables are saved in a DSNDB07 work tablespace until a commit is issued. This can require more space in the work tablespaces. The transition variables are stored in a format similar to the base table. That is the entire row is stored (not just the columns referenced). VARCHAR columns are padded with blanks to their full length.

A work file contains the full set of updated or inserted rows for row and statement triggers. The entire work file is scanned (no index is created) for each row processed for a row trigger and once for a statement trigger when processing transition variables. This detract from performance for large transition tables.

There are costs of work file processing including:

- 24 pages are allocated for each work file initially (more space is allocated as required)
- Creation, use, and deletion of work files
- I/O and/or GETPAGE requests to work files
- Potential contention with work files used for other processing (sorts, data for global temporary tables, materialization of table expression and views, some joins, most subselects, etc.)

If NEW and OLD transition variables are used, two work files are created. There is some savings in using work files in that no logging is done.

Use transition variables only when required to avoid work file processing and maximize performance. Also consider the use BEFORE triggers where possible (work files are not used).

Additional performance considerations: The initialization cost of executing a trigger is about the same as a fetch except when work files are required. If trigger is not executed (update of a column that does not have trigger defined on it but there is a trigger defined on another column of the table, for example), the cost is negligible. The is no overhead for an SQL statement that does not activate a trigger. If an INSERT trigger is defined on a table, there is no overhead for UPDATE and DELETE statements, for example.

An index can be used on column in "subselect" of WHEN condition. An index can be used on VALID_CITIES.CITY in the BCUS10 trigger introduced in Section TR.2.

The Database Descriptor (DBD) is increased in size. The object descriptor (OBD) of a trigger is associated with the table description. This can require more space in the EDM (Environmental Descriptor Manager) pool.

TR.4 TRIGGER BODY AND WHEN CONDITIONS

The trigger body contains actions to be taken based on the results of the WHEN condition (optional). A BEFORE and AFTER trigger body can contain only certain statements.

A BEFORE trigger body can have the following types of statements:

- SELECT
- SIGNAL SQLSTATE
- VALUES
- CALL a stored procedure and invoke a UDF that does not contain an INSERT, UPDATE, or DELETE statement that modifies the triggering table.
- SET transition variable

You can perform most of the functions of a BEFORE trigger in an AFTER triggers. In addition, can modify a table with INSERT, UPDATE, and DELETE statements as summarized:

- SELECT
- SIGNAL SQLSTATE
- VALUES
- CALL of a stored procedure and invoke a UDF
- INSERT
- UPDATE (without cursor to locate row to be updated)
- DELETE (without cursor to locate row to be deleted)

The SELECT, INSERT, UPDATE, and DELETE statements are discussed throughout the book with an introduction in Chapter SL. Calling a stored procedure is discussed in Chapter SP. The use of UDF is discussed in Chapter UD. The remaining statements -- SIGNAL SQLSTATE, VALUES, and SET are discussed in this chapter.

Host variables and parameter markers cannot be used in a trigger body. It is not possible to reference tables and views at a client site nor use dynamic SQL in a trigger. However, you can CALL a stored procedure, and use a function that references objects at a client site, and use dynamic SQL. CALL parameters can be literals, transition variables, table locators, or expressions (not host variables).

WHEN condition controls when the trigger body is executed. If there is no WHEN condition, the trigger body is executed when the trigger is activated. A WHEN condition is similar to a simple WHERE condition. It can include transition variables and subselects. If a row trigger is used, the condition is evaluated once for each modified row. If a statement trigger is used, the condition is evaluated once for each execution of the triggering statement. AND and OR can be used to join multiple conditions within a WHEN condition. All conditions for WHEN clause must be in parenthesis. The result of a WHEN condition can be true, false, or unknown. The trigger body is executed only if the WHEN condition is true.

Recommendation: Use good programming practices when writing the logic of WHEN conditions for good performance.

SIGNAL SQLSTATE

The SIGNAL SQLSTATE statement provides for disallowing successful execution of the triggering statement, statements that would have been invoked by the trigger, and any RI enforcement. For example, an order cannot be deleted before the item is shipped. Assume that the SHIP_DATE column is defined WITH DEFAULT '9999-12-31' for the following CREATE TRIGGER statement.

```
CREATE TRIGGER BORDER40
  NO CASCADE BEFORE DELETE ON ORDER
  REFERENCING OLD AS O
  FOR EACH ROW MODE DB2SQL
  WHEN (O.SHIP_DATE >= CURRENT DATE)
  BEGIN ATOMIC
    SIGNAL SQLSTATE 'IBR40' ('Item has not been shipped');
  END#
```

The error code 'IBR40', in the example, is returned in the SQLSTATE field of the SQLCA (discussed in Chapter PD). The error code must be defined in the program as a 5 character literal consisting of upper case letters and digits. You can avoid conflicts with SQL92 SQLSTATE values by using a first character of the letters between I and Z or the digits 7, 8, or 9.

The error message ('Item has not been shipped'), in the example is returned in the SQLERRMC field of the SQLCA. It must be less than or equal to 70 characters.

All actions under the control of DB2 and Resource Recovery Services (RRS) are rolled back and a -438 SQLCODE is returned to the program. The rollback does not include sending an email message, for example. The error code, message, and -438 SQLCODE are also displayed when an error occurs interactively.

Figure TR.3 summarizes several SQLCODEs issued by DB2 as a result of a severe error encountered in the trigger that results in a rollback. The rollback affects the trigger statement (not the other SQL statements in the program). It applies to the SQL statement that activated the trigger, all triggers, and cascading actions involved (a trigger can be activated by another trigger). The rollback also applies to cascading RI relationships including DELETE CASCADE and DELETE SET NULL.

Figure TR.3. Errors resulting from execution of a trigger

SQLCODE	Description from *Messages and Codes* Manual
-901	Unsuccessful execution caused by a system error that does not preclude the successful execution of subsequent SQL statements.
-906	The SQL statement cannot be executed because this function is disabled due to a prior error.
-911	The current unit of recovery has been rolled back due to deadlock or timeout. REASON reason-code, TYPE OF RESOURCE resource-type, and RESOURCE NAME resource-name.
-913	Unsuccessful execution caused by a deadlock or timeout. REASON CODE reason-code, TYPE OF RESOURCE resource-type, and RESOURCE NAME resource-name.

A -723 SQLCODE ('09000' SQLSTATE) indicates that a statement within the trigger body abended. All statements within the trigger body (not within program) are rolled back. Information is placed in the SQLCA. Warnings are not returned to the program.

TR.5 SET, VALUE, AND CASE IN BEFORE TRIGGERS

The SET, VALUE, and CASE clauses are explained through the use of a number of create trigger examples. The CREATE TRIGGER statements are analyzed to show how to use these clauses as well as the clauses described in previous sections of this chapter.

Use of the SET Statement to Modify a Row

BEFORE triggers can be used to modify data before inserting, updating, or deleting a row. For example, shipping costs are 10 percent higher in cities outside of the USA when the item weight is greater than 25. The following statement is used to increase the shipping costs by 10 percent if the country is not the USA and the weight is greater than 25 before the order is inserted into the ORDER table. Also, the trigger sets the SHIP_DATE to the current date because international orders are shipped on the date of the order.

```
CREATE TRIGGER BORDER10
  NO CASCADE BEFORE INSERT ON ORDER
  REFERENCING NEW AS N
  FOR EACH ROW MODE DB2SQL
  WHEN (N.COUNTRY <> 'USA'
    AND N.WEIGHT    > 25)
      SET N.SHIP_COSTS = N.SHIP_COSTS * 1.1,
          N.SHIP_DATE  = CURRENT DATE;
```

The REFERENCING NEW clause is required for BEFORE INSERT triggers. Other referencing clauses do not apply to the BEFORE INSERT trigger. However, the column qualification is optional for BEFORE INSERT triggers. For example, COUNTRY or N.COUNTRY can be used in the WHEN clause. Similarly SHIP_COSTS or N.SHIP_COSTS can be used in the SET statement.

The WHEN clause is used to test the required conditions. Notice that the two conditions joined by AND are enclosed in parenthesis.

SET Explanation

The SET statement is used to assign values to columns when using BEFORE triggers, in particular INSERT and UPDATE triggers. One or more columns can be set to:

- Expressions (arithmetic operators, DB2 or UDFs, special registers, etc.)
- Default (default value specified for the column when the table was created)
- Null
- Result of a SELECT statement that returns only one row and is enclosed in parenthesis

A SET statement begins with the keyword SET followed by setting one or more columns to a value, each of which is separated by a comma. In the previous example, the use of the SET statement can be seen with reference to the N.SHIP_COSTS and N.SHIP_DATE.

Overriding the Triggering Statement

Here is an example of overriding the triggering statement. Assume that there is a business rule that does not allow the increase in unit price to be greater than 50 percent. This is specified in the WHEN clause. The business rule requires setting the increase to 50 percent of the old unit price as specified in the SET statement.

```
CREATE TRIGGER BINV10
  NO CASCADE BEFORE UPDATE OF UNIT_PRICE ON INVENTORY
  REFERENCING OLD AS O
              NEW AS N
  FOR EACH ROW MODE DB2SQL
  WHEN (N.UNIT_PRICE > 1.5 * O.UNIT_PRICE)
  SET   N.UNIT_PRICE = 1.5 * O.UNIT_PRICE;
```

OLD and NEW transition variables can be defined with UPDATE triggers. Columns on both sides of the SET equal must be qualified with the correlation name. Columns on the left side of the equal must be qualified with the NEW row correlation name (N in the example).

VALUES Statement

The VALUES statement can be used to execute a UDF or stored procedure unconditionally -- once for each row in a row trigger or once for each statement trigger. The previous example is expanded to invoke a UDF.

The ADJINC UDF logs attempts to adjust unit price by more than 50 percent.

```
CREATE TRIGGER BINV10
  NO CASCADE BEFORE UPDATE OF UNIT_PRICE ON INVENTORY
  REFERENCING OLD AS O
              NEW AS N
  FOR EACH ROW MODE DB2SQL
  WHEN (N.UNIT_PRICE > 1.5 * O.UNIT_PRICE)
   BEGIN ATOMIC
     SET     N.UNIT_PRICE = 1.5 * O.UNIT_PRICE;
     VALUES (ADJINC(O.ITEMNO, N.UNIT_PRICE, O.UNIT_PRICE));
   END#
```

ADJINC can be a stored procedure and invoked like:

```
BEGIN ATOMIC
  SET   N.UNIT_PRICE = 1.5 * O.UNIT_PRICE;
  CALL  ADJINC(O.ITEMNO, N.UNIT_PRICE, O.UNIT_PRICE);
END#
```

Invoking a UDF Conditionally

A UDF can be invoked conditionally using a SELECT statement. Assume that the previous business rule has a specification that the price is doubled if the price is less than 2.00 based on the logic in the ADJINC UDF.

```
CREATE TRIGGER BINV10
  NO CASCADE BEFORE UPDATE OF UNIT_PRICE ON INVENTORY
  REFERENCING OLD AS O
              NEW AS N
  FOR EACH ROW MODE DB2SQL
  WHEN (N.UNIT_PRICE > 1.5 * O.UNIT_PRICE)
     BEGIN ATOMIC
       SELECT ADJINC(O.ITEMNO, N.UNIT_PRICE, O.UNIT_PRICE)
       FROM   INVENTORY AS I
       WHERE  O.UNIT_PRICE < 2.00
       AND    I.ITEMNO = O.ITEMNO;
     END#
```

VALUES and CASE

VALUES and CASE can be used to test multiple WHEN conditions. For example, if an item is shipped more than 7 or 14 days after the order is placed, DISCOUNT UDF is executed for discount processing.

```
CREATE TRIGGER BSHIP10
  NO CASCADE BEFORE INSERT ON SHIPMENT
  REFERENCING NEW AS N
  FOR EACH ROW MODE DB2SQL
 BEGIN ATOMIC
    VALUES CASE
      WHEN DAYS(N.SHIP_DATE) - DAYS(CURRENT DATE)
                BETWEEN 8 AND 14
        THEN DISCOUNT ('USH10', 'Between  8 & 14 days')
      WHEN DAYS(N.SHIP_DATE) - DAYS(CURRENT DATE)
                > 14
        THEN DISCOUNT ('USH20', '> 14 DAYS')
          ELSE ' '
   END;
  END#
```

TR.6 AFTER TRIGGERS

An AFTER trigger is executed after its triggering SQL statement and all of its constraints are successful. They can insert, update, and delete rows from tables and views not associated with the trigger. AFTER triggers see the results of BEFORE triggers executed before them.

Cascading Triggers

An AFTER trigger can activate other triggers as a result of its action. This is referred to as cascading triggers. The limit to cascading is 16 levels of nesting including triggers, UDF, and stored procedures. If there is an attempt to execute a 17th trigger, a rollback occurs with -724 SQLCODE and '54038' SQLSTATE. If trigger A is activated after trigger B and completes after trigger B completes, it is not considered a cascading trigger, for example:

```
Trigger B activated
Trigger A activated
Trigger B completes
Trigger A completes
```

Restrictions: It is not possible to modify a table that has been modified at a higher level of nesting (-746 SQLCODE). A trigger cannot reference a remote table in the trigger definition. However, the trigger can invoke a UDF and stored procedure that acts on local and remote data.

Referential Integrity: If a parent row is deleted by an AFTER trigger and it has dependents with DB2 enforced RI, constraints are enforced. For example, cascade delete causes all foreign key rows matching the primary key to be deleted. This results in delete triggers defined on the dependent table being activated. The set null RI constraint causes all foreign keys matching the primary key to be set to null. This results in activation of update triggers defined on the dependent tables.

Beware of too complex of cascading actions. It can be difficult to manage and debug. There is no significant performance difference between invoking a single trigger compare dot invoking the trigger within other nested operations.

AFTER UPDATE of Columns Trigger

It is advisable to name columns for which the trigger is to be executed. This avoids updating a column added with the ALTER statement which invokes the trigger. This is probably not the intent.

Consider an example of inserting a before and after image of information into CUSTOMER_MOD table when the customer name or credit limit of a customer is changed for a customer.

```
CREATE TRIGGER ACUS10
  AFTER UPDATE OF CNAME, CREDIT_LIMIT ON CUSTOMER
  REFERENCING OLD AS O
              NEW AS N
  FOR EACH ROW MODE DB2SQL
    WHEN (O.CNAME        <> N.CNAME
      OR  O.CREDIT_LIMIT <> N.CREDIT_LIMIT)
  BEGIN ATOMIC
    INSERT INTO CUSTOMER_MOD
           (  CUSTNO,  CNAME,   CREDIT_LIMIT)
      VALUES (O.CUSTNO,O.CNAME,O.CREDIT_LIMIT);
    INSERT INTO CUSTOMER_MOD
           (  CUSTNO,  CNAME,   CREDIT_LIMIT)
      VALUES (N.CUSTNO,N.CNAME,N.CREDIT_LIMIT);
```

```
END#
```

Explanation of AFTER UPDATE of columns trigger: Notice that one or more columns can be referenced in the AFTER UPDATE OF clause. You can reference old and new rows in an AFTER trigger. The WHEN clause can contain multiple conditions using OR and AND. One or more SQL statements can be executed in the trigger body. Each statement is terminated with ';'. These statements must be preceded with BEGIN ATOMIC and terminated with END followed by the defined terminator character, "#" in the example.

Additional effects of inserting rows into the CUSTOMER_MOD table: Columns not named in the INSERT statement can be changed automatically. Assume that the CUSTOMER_MOD table has an UPDATER column defined with WITH DEFAULT USER and a CHANGE_TIMESTAMP column defined as NOT NULL WITH DEFAULT. After the trigger executes successfully, the UPDATER column contains the primary AUTHID of the person who executed the program and the CHANGE_TIMESTAMP contains the current timestamp of when the change was made.

Cascade Update with a Trigger

Cascade update means that if a PK value is updated, the corresponding FK value in all dependent tables should be updated automatically. DB2 RI does not support cascade update. However, it can be implemented with a trigger like:

```
CREATE TRIGGER ACUS20
  AFTER UPDATE OF CUSTNO ON CUSTOMER
  REFERENCING OLD AS O
              NEW AS N
  FOR EACH ROW MODE DB2SQL
  BEGIN ATOMIC
    UPDATE  ORDER
      SET   CUSTNO = N.CUSTNO
      WHERE CUSTNO = O.CUSTNO;
    UPDATE  SHIPMENT
      SET   CUSTNO = N.CUSTNO
      WHERE CUSTNO = O.CUSTNO;
 END#
```

The trigger definition results in updating the FK CUSTNO in the dependent ORDER and SHIPMENT table when an UPDATE statement is issued on the CUSTNO in the CUSTOMER table. If the FK appears in multiple dependent tables and cascade update is to occur on each table, it is your responsibility to update each dependent table.

Creation of a trigger of enforce any form of RI or other constraints does not check for any existing violation of constraints in the table. In contrast, creation of RI or table check constraints causes check pending to be turned on. The CHECK DATA utility should then be executed to deal with the violations as discussed in Chapter LC.

Pass Trigger Transition Table to Stored Procedure or UDF

You can pass trigger transition tables to a stored procedures or UDF. For example, after the ORDER table is updated, the results are to be passed to the PROCORD stored procedure.

```
CREATE TRIGGER AORDER20
  AFTER UPDATE ON ORDER
  REFERENCING NEW_TABLE AS NT
  FOR EACH STATEMENT MODE DB2SQL
  BEGIN ATOMIC
    CALL (PROCORD(TABLE NT));
  END#
```

The REFERENCING NEW_TABLE AS NT clause identifies the updated rows. The CALL statement references the NT correlation name as a parameter when calling the stored procedure.

The stored procedure must declare table locator field PROCORD-LOCATOR in working-storage like:

```
01 PROCORD-LOCATOR SQL TYPE IS TABLE LIKE ORDER AS LOCATOR.
01 ORDERNO PIC S9(9) COMP-4.
```

It is necessary to declare a cursor, open, fetch and close the cursor for the transition table in the stored procedure like the following fragment of code:

```
EXEC SQL DECLARE CORDER CURSOR FOR
SELECT ORDERNO
FROM   TABLE(:PROCORD-LOCATOR LIKE ORDER)
WHERE  UNIT_PRICE > 10000 END-EXEC.

EXEC SQL OPEN  CORDER END-EXEC.
EXEC SQL FETCH CORDER INTO :ORDERNO END-EXEC.

EXEC SQL CLOSE CORDER END-EXEC.
```

Example of NEW_TABLE and Column Function

NEW_TABLE and OLD_TABLE with correlation names are useful for evaluating column functions (MIN, MAX, AVG, SUM, COUNT) on one or more rows before or after executing an AFTER trigger. For example, after inserting a row for an ordered item, the user needs to be notified if the total cost (sum of unit price * quantity) of an item (not including shipping costs) exceeds a 10,000 limit.

```
CREATE TRIGGER AORDER10
  AFTER INSERT ON ORDER
  REFERENCING NEW_TABLE AS NT
  FOR EACH ROW MODE DB2SQL
  WHEN (10000.00 >
       (SELECT SUM(NT.UNIT_PRICE * NT.QTY)
        FROM   NT
        WHERE  CUSTNO  = NT.CUSTNO
        AND    ORDERNO = NT.ORDERNO))
  BEGIN ATOMIC
```

```
    SIGNAL SQLSTATE 'IAR10' ('10,000 limit exceeded');
  END#
```

If the limit is exceeded, the error code 'IAR10' is returned in the SQLSTATE field and the error message ('10,000 limit exceeded') is returned in the SQLERRMC field of the SQLCA and a rollback occurs.

The use of REFERENCING NEW_TABLE AS NT provides for the results of the SET statement to be seen when referencing NT in a FROM clause.

Caution: In this particular case, it is doubtful that a customer will order more than their credit limit very often. However, a word of caution is in order particularly where a long rollback can occur often. A rollback is costly as discussed in Chapter BP. Indeed, it can cost twice as much as doing the work initially. Do be cautious of developing triggers that can result in costly rollbacks. If this is a possibility, consider doing the work through program design. For example, sum the cost of line items as they are placed in an array in the program, compare subtotals to the credit limit, and notify the customer when the credit limit is exceeded. If the credit limit is not exceed at the end of the order, insert the rows from the array into the ORDER table.

AFTER DELETE Trigger

Assume that there is a business rule that if a customer is deleted from the CUSTOMER table that all rows for the customer are to be deleted from the ORDER table. The following trigger can be used to implement the business rule.

```
CREATE TRIGGER ACUS20
  AFTER DELETE ON CUSTOMER
  REFERENCING OLD AS O
  FOR EACH ROW MODE DB2SQL
  DELETE FROM ORDER
    WHERE CUSTNO = O.CUSTNO;
```

An alternative is to use DB2 enforced RI as discussed in Chapter RI. A cascade delete can be defined on the dependent ORDER table such that if a row is deleted from the parent CUSTOMER table, DB2 will automatically delete the matching FK rows in the ORDER table. We will see in Section TR.10 that DB2 enforced RI can have performance advantages over implementing RI through triggers.

TR.7 ORDER OF PROCESSING TRIGGERS AND CONSTRAINTS

The order of processing a trigger can affect the results and performance. Figure TR.4 summarizes this order. It can be seen that the order of processing is quite involved. Do consider a naming convention to indicate whether it is a BEFORE or AFTER trigger, the table associated with the trigger, and a sequence number to indicate the order of creation and execution. A naming convention is helpful but not sufficient. The catalog tables are required for an analysis of the processing order of triggers and constraints as discussed in Section TR.9.

Figure TR.4. Order of processing triggers and constraints

- OLD transition variables are bound.
- BEFORE triggers are executed in the order created for each qualifying row based on the timestamp in SYSTRIGGERS.CREATEDTS.
- NEW transition variables are applied for BEFORE triggers.
- RI constraints with DELETE CASCADE or DELETE SET NULL rules are applied before delete triggers or before update triggers on dependent tables.
- Actual insertion, deletion, or update is applied to the table.
- Unique index, RI, and table check constraints are checked. A rollback occurs when first row violates any constraint checked.
- Insertion of a row into the PLAN_TABLE, DSN_STATEMNT_TABLE, and DSN_FUNCTION_TABLE by DB2 does not activate an INSERT trigger on those tables. A trigger defined on these tables is activated when SQL is executed on the tables.
- NEW transition variables are bound before AFTER triggers are executed.
- AFTER triggers are executed after BEFORE triggers based on timestamp of creation. The BEFORE trigger rules above are applied.
- AFTER triggers are executed in the order created for each row modified by the triggering statement and enforcement of RI based on the timestamp in SYSTRIGGERS.CREATEDTS. An AFTER trigger is executed once even if no rows qualify when using the FOR EACH STATEMENT clause.
- SQL statements within the AFTER trigger body are executed in the order written. An executed statement can activate another trigger (or the same trigger) which follows the execution order described.
- An AFTER trigger sees the effect of previously executed AFTER triggers.

Triggers and Special Registers

Special registers are saved before a trigger is activated and restored after the trigger completes. During the execution of a trigger, special registers inherit their value from the triggering SQL operation (insert, update, delete) including:

- CURRENT DATE
- CURRENT TIME
- CURRENT TIMESTAMP
- CURRENT DEGREE
- CURRENT LOCALE LC_CTYPE
- CURRENT OPTIMIZATION HINT
- CURRENT PATH
- CURRENT PRECISION
- CURRENT RULES
- CURRENT SERVER
- CURRENT SQLID
- USER

The CURRENT PACKAGESET special register is set to the qualifier or schema name of the trigger (schema are discussed in Chapter CO. The CURRENT TIMEZONE is set to the OS/390 TIMEZONE parameter.

TR.8 TRIGGER MANAGEMENT

Triggers like most objects in DB2 have a qualifier and an owner as well as privileges to create a trigger. The creation of a trigger results in DB2 automatically creating a package for the trigger. These issues are discussed in this section.

Trigger Naming Convention and Ownership

A trigger name has a qualifier (similar to the qualifier of a table name). The name must be unique for triggers assigned to a table and within a schema. It cannot exceed eight bytes. You can use a qualifier rather than a schema. If a qualifier is not explicitly specified when creating a trigger, the current SQLID of the creator of the trigger is the qualifier when it is created dynamically. If the trigger is created from a host program, the AUTHID used in the REBIND QUALIFIER parameter is the qualifier of the trigger. If a QUALIFIER is not specified when binding a package or plan, the owner of the package or plan is the trigger qualifier.

A schema can be used to logically group triggers, UDF, distinct types (also known as user-defined data types), stored procedures, and other objects (somewhat like a database is a grouping of physical objects). If a schema is used, the qualifier of objects created within a schema is the schema name. Schema creation is done using a batch program (not SPUFI) according to the SQL92 standard as discussed in Chapter CO. The PATH parameter of bind and rebind provides for specifying the schema name for static SQL. The CURRENT PATH special register provides the schema name for dynamic SQL.

The owner of the trigger is the qualifier or schema name. SYSTRIGGERS.SCHEMA contains the qualifier or schema name in the SCHEMA column.

Authority Required for Triggers

SYSADM or SYSCTRL can create and drop triggers. If schemas are used, the CREATEIN privilege can be granted on the schema. One or more of the following privileges are required without SYSADM, SYSCTRL, or CREATEIN:

- TRIGGER privilege on the table upon which the trigger is defined, for example

  ```
  GRANT TRIGGER ON AUTHID.ORDER TO FLEUR; -- or PUBLIC
  ```

- DBADM on the database that contains the table

- ALTER privilege on the table to which the trigger is attached

If transition variables are used, SELECT privileges are required on the table to which the trigger is attached. SELECT privileges are also required on all tables and views referenced in the WHEN condition. Privileges are required on the objects manipulated by SQL in the trigger body as with a host program. If the trigger invokes a UDF or stored procedures, EXECUTE privilege is required on the object. DYNAMICRULES(RUN) is required to execute CREATE TRIGGER as an embedded dynamic SQL statement. The owner of the package or plan must have the required privileges to create a trigger.

The trigger body is executed under the authority of the creator (not the executor). This is similar to static and dynamic SQL with the bind parameter DYNAMICRULES(BIND) for plans and packages.

Trigger Package

A package is created automatically when a trigger is created and has the same name as the trigger. The collection name is the name of the qualifier or schema. The version ID is an empty string which means that multiple versions of a trigger cannot exist. It is not necessary to grant privileges on a trigger package to executors. Triggers are not specified in a package list for the plan containing SQL that invokes trigger.

It is not possible to drop a trigger package. It is dropped automatically when the trigger or triggering table (table named in ON clause) is dropped. You can rebind a trigger package. This is useful if the trigger package has been marked invalid or inoperative due to dropping a referenced table, alias (not synonym), index, adding a column to the trigger table, or revoking a privilege that the trigger package depends upon. Rebind of a trigger package provides for choosing an improved access path based on new indexes or statistics. There is an example of rebinding a trigger package:.

```
REBIND TRIGGER PACKAGE (DACUSID.ACUS20);
```

Figure TR.5 lists the bind parameters used when creating a trigger and thus a trigger package. Only the parameter marked with "*" can be changed with a rebind.

Figure TR.5. Trigger Package Bind Parameters

```
ACTION(ADD)
CURRENTDATA(YES)*
ISOLATION(CS)*
RELEASE(COMMIT)*
EXPLAIN(NO)*
FLAG(I)*
IMMEDWRITE(NO)*
OWNER(AUTHID)
QUALIFIER(AUTHID)
PATH(PATH)
QUERYOPT(1)
DBPROTOCOL(DRDA)
DEGREE(1)
DYNAMICRULES(BIND)
ENABLE(*)
NOREOPT(VARS)
NODEFER(PREPARE)
SQLERROR(NOPACKAGE)
VALIDATE(BIND)
```

*Parameter that can be changed with a rebind of the trigger package

A package cannot be created based on the trigger package with the BIND COPY command. Optionally, you can specify the location as part of trigger package name. However, it must be the current server location where the package resides. It is not possible to do a remote rebind.

Recommendation: Do a REBIND with EXPLAIN(YES) to determine the access path chosen for the trigger. Do consider the use of overriding the default and using RELEASE(DEALLOCATE) as discussed in Chapter CC.

Dropped and Invalid Triggers

The DROP statement can be used to delete a trigger like:

```
DROP TRIGGER BCUS10 RESTRICT;
```

Dropping a trigger automatically drops the trigger package. It is not possible to drop or free a trigger package directly. Drop of a trigger does not cascade and drop other objects. If a triggering table is dropped, the associated trigger and trigger package are also dropped.

Trigger packages like all packages are marked as invalid when an object (referenced table, index, view, etc.) that it depends on is dropped or required privileges are revoked. DB2 attempts an automatic rebind with the next attempt to invoke the trigger. Do consider executing an explicit rebind after re-establishing the dependencies. This avoids automatic rebind during prime time. It also avoids the user getting an error message if the trigger package is marked as inoperative which means that it must be explicitly bound. Fortunately, a trigger package is unlikely to be marked inoperative because if a table is dropped, the trigger is dropped. If an index is dropped, there is always an alternative access path. Invalid and inoperative trigger packages can be identified like:

```
SELECT COLLID, NAME
FROM   SYSIBM.SYSPACKAGE
WHERE  TYPE = 'T'
AND   (VALID = 'N' OR OPERATIVE = 'N');
```

TR.9 TRIGGERS IN THE CATALOG TABLES

You may well want to know the triggering actions that are taken when you manipulate a table. This can be determined by selecting from the catalog tables. Here is a statement to determine information on all triggers created on the CUSTOMER table with a specified owner.

```
SELECT DISTINCT SCHEMA, NAME, TRIGTIME, TRIGEVENT,
  GRANULARITY, CREATEDTS
FROM  SYSIBM.SYSTRIGGERS
WHERE TBNAME  = 'CUSTOMER'
AND   TBOWNER = 'AUTHID';
```

The SCHEMA column contains the name of the schema or qualifier for the trigger.

The NAME column contains the name of the trigger.

The TRIGTIME indicates when the trigger is activated. "B" means that it is activated before an event. "A" means that it is activated after an event.

The TRIGEVENT indicates the event that causes the trigger to be activated. "I" means that the trigger is activated for an insert, "D" for a delete, and "U" for an update.

The GRANULARITY indicates that the trigger is executed once for each statement with a "S" in the column or for each row with a "R" in the column.

The CREATEDTS column contains the timestamp of when the trigger was created. The timestamp is used to determine the order of execution of multiple triggers.

The text (<=3460 bytes) of a trigger with the schema or qualifier of DACUSJDB and name of ACUS20 can be determined like:

```
SELECT TEXT, SEQNO
FROM   SYSIBM.SYSTRIGGERS
WHERE  SCHEMA = 'DACUSJDB'
AND    NAME   = 'ACUS20'
ORDER BY SEQNO;
```

The COMMENT ON statement can be used to describe the trigger in SYSTRIGGERS.REMARKS like:

```
COMMENT ON TRIGGER ACUS20 IS
 'Delete all rows from ORDER table when
  a customer row is deleted';
```

TR.10 TRIGGERS AND CONSTRAINTS

Triggers have a number of valuable usages. However, there are alternatives for some types of triggers and some of these alternatives have performance advantages as discussed in this section.

Trigger and Constraint Similarities

Both triggers and constraints provide for having DB2 enforce rules and actions. Constraints can be RI and table check constraints. They both provide for global enforcement of rules and actions which are uniformly enforced across all interfaces including QMF, for example. They reduce program development time and costs by avoiding having to repeatedly code actions in multiple programs. Further, there are reductions in program maintenance time and costs. Certainly, dropping and recreating triggers and constraints requires less time than modifying programs. Triggers and constraints are automatically recorded in the catalog without concern for maintaining documentation on the actions implemented application programs. These advantages are discussed in more detail in Chapters CT and RI.

Constraints Contrasted with Triggers

RI and table check constraints have performance advantages over triggers in that they are enforced by Data Manager which reduces the path length. Triggers are implemented by the Relational Data Systems through the use of packages which results in more instructions being executed.

Constraints can only test simple predicates without subselects compared to the complex processing that can be defined in triggers. Constraints are good for declarative comparisons. They can be enforced when created. In contrast, the creation of a trigger does not check existing rows nor turn check pending on. Constraints can be enforced with the LOAD and CHECK DATA utilities. There is no utility support for triggers. Unfortunately, validation triggers are not activated when loading data despite the many performance advantages of using the LOAD utility to populate a table for the first time or add rows to a table compared to INSERT statements as discussed in Chapter BP. Constraints apply to INSERT, UPDATE, and DELETE statements. In contrast, a trigger must be created for each required operation.

A major advantage of triggers is that they provide for complex processing and validation of data.

Alternatives to Triggers

Do use the following techniques rather than triggers if they accomplish the goal due to their performance advantages.

- RI constraints when creating tables
- Table check constraints when creating a table
- User defined defaults when creating a table
- Distinct types
- If complex logic is required, consider placing most of the processing in a stored procedure and call the stored procedure from the trigger

- Data replication or propagation to maintain a copy of the data

TR.11 SUMMARY

Triggers provide for having DB2 enforce rules and actions. They can be activated before or after an event.

BEFORE triggers are useful for validation of data before inserting, updating, and deleting data. They can reference other tables in the WHEN clause. Triggers can be used to automatically generate values for newly inserted rows. They can modify row values for which the trigger was activated. However, they cannot modify other rows in the same or other tables.

AFTER triggers can be used to insert, update, delete, and select from a table. It is necessary to define a separate trigger for each operation if the action is to occur for more than one operations. You can compare values before and after an update as well as test a condition and execute one or more statements if the condition is true.

BEFORE triggers are executed followed by AFTER triggers in the order created.

Do be cautious of too complex of cascading triggers, UDFs, and stored procedures.

EXERCISES

The exercises that require the creation of triggers are on the sample EMP and DEPT tables to allow you to test your answers on DB2 for OS/390 without having to create tables.

1. a) What is a logical reason that REFERENCING OLD AS O does not apply to insert triggers?

b) What is a logical reason that REFERENCING NEW AS N does not apply to delete triggers?

2. a) Is it necessary to proceed more than one statement (SQL or trigger statement) in the body of a trigger with BEGIN ATOMIC and end it with END?

b) What terminator must be used following each statement between BEGIN ATOMIC and END?

c) What terminator must be used following the END of BEGIN ATOMIC section?

3. Develop a trigger to validate that an employee to be inserted into the EMP table was born more than 18 years ago. Return an SQLSTATE of 'IBE10' and a message of 'Employee is less than 18 years' in the SQLCA. Rollback the INSERT statement that activated the trigger.

4. Attempt to execute the following statement and review the results.

```
INSERT INTO EMP
(EMPNO,FIRSTNME,MIDINIT,LASTNAME ,WORKDEPT,PHONENO,HIREDATE,
 JOB,EDLEVEL,SEX,BIRTHDATE,SALARY,BONUS,COMM)
VALUES
```

```
('000099','MICHAEL',' ','HANNAN','A00','3978','2000-01-01',
 'PRES',18,'M','1999-07-04',52750.00,1000.00,4220.00);
```

5. Develop a trigger such that MGRNO in the DEPT table cannot be updated to a value not in the EMPNO column of the EMP table.

6. Why can ";" be used as the terminator for the previously created BDEP10 trigger?

7. Attempt to execute the following statement. Why does the update fail.

```
UPDATE DEPT
 SET MGRNO     = '12345'
 WHERE DEPTNO = 'D12';
```

8. Develop a trigger to disallow the deletion of employees whose COMM is greater than their SALARY without further investigation.

9. What program logic can be developed to allow deletion of an employee whose COMM > SALARY despite implementation of the previous trigger?

10. Develop a trigger so that insertion of a new employee into WORKDEPT 'A00' is not allowed if it causes the sum of the salaries for the department to exceed 10,000.00.

11. Assume that updating the MGRNO column in the DEPT table means that a new manager has been assigned to a department and the person is given a 10 percent increase in salary. Develop an AFTER trigger to accomplish this.

12. After a department is deleted, send an email with information on the deleted department to the director. Assume that an EMAILD UDF has been created for this purpose. The function requires input parameters of DEPTNO, DEPTNAME, and MGRNO.

13. Is it possible to alter a trigger?

14. How is a trigger package created?

15. How can you determine the access path chosen for a trigger package.

ANSWERS

1. a) REFERENCING OLD AS O refers to the state of a row before the trigger processing. There is no row prior to inserting a row.

b) REFERENCING NEW AS N refers to the state of a row after trigger processing. There is no row after deleting a row.

2. a) It is necessary to proceed more than one statement (SQL or trigger statement) in the body of a trigger with BEGIN ATOMIC and end it with END.

b) The ";" terminator must be used following each statement between BEGIN ATOMIC and END.

c) You must define the terminator that follows the END of the BEGIN ATOMIC section according to the rules discussed in this chapter. The terminator "#" has been used in examples.

3. Here is a trigger to validate that an employee to be inserted into the EMP table was born more than 18 years ago. The SIGNAL statement is used to return an SQLSTATE of 'IBE10' and a message of 'Employee is less than 18 years old' in the SQLCA. A rollback of the INSERT statement that activated the trigger occurs if the SIGNAL statement is activated.

```
CREATE TRIGGER BEMP10
NO CASCADE BEFORE INSERT ON EMP
REFERENCING NEW AS N
FOR EACH ROW MODE DB2SQL
WHEN (CURRENT DATE - 18 YEARS < N.BIRTHDATE)
BEGIN ATOMIC
  SIGNAL SQLSTATE 'IBE10'
   ('Employee is less than 18 years');
END#
```

4. The result of executing:

```
INSERT INTO EMP
(EMPNO,FIRSTNME,MIDINIT,LASTNAME ,WORKDEPT,PHONENO,HIREDATE,
JOB,EDLEVEL,SEX,BIRTHDATE,SALARY,BONUS,COMM)
VALUES
('000099','MICHAEL',' ','HANNAN','A00','3978','2000-01-01',
'PRES',18,'M','1999-07-04',52750.00,1000.00,4220.00);
```

is:

```
DSNT408I SQLCODE = -438, ERROR:  APPLICATION RAISED ERROR WITH DIAGNOSTIC TEXT:
         Employee is less than 18 years
DSNT418I SQLSTATE    = IBE10 SQLSTATE RETURN CODE
DSNT415I SQLERRP     = DSNXRTYP SQL PROCEDURE DETECTING ERROR
DSNT416I SQLERRD     = 1  0  0  -1  0  0 SQL DIAGNOSTIC INFORMATION
DSNT416I SQLERRD     = X'00000001'  X'00000000'  X'00000000'  X'FFFFFFFF'

         X'00000000'  X'00000000' SQL DIAGNOSTIC INFORMATION
---------+---------+---------+---------+---------+---------+---------+---------+
DSNE618I ROLLBACK PERFORMED, SQLCODE IS 0
DSNE616I STATEMENT EXECUTION WAS SUCCESSFUL, SQLCODE IS 0
```

Notice that -438 SQLCODE was received along with a rollback and the specified SQLSTATE and message. Do be cautious of the terminator used. The question and answer used a terminator of ";". If you executed the CREATE TRIGGER and INSERT statement in the same file, it is necessary to use "#" as the terminator for the INSERT statement assuming that you used "#" as the terminator for the CREATE TRIGGER statement.

5. Here is a trigger such that a MGRNO in the DEPT table cannot be updated to a value not in the EMPNO column of the EMP table.

```
CREATE TRIGGER BDEP10
  NO CASCADE BEFORE UPDATE OF MGRNO ON DEPT
  REFERENCING NEW AS N
```

```
    FOR EACH ROW MODE DB2SQL
    WHEN (N.MGRNO NOT IN
      (SELECT EMPNO
       FROM   EMP))
         SIGNAL SQLSTATE 'IBD10'
            ('Manager is not in the EMP table');
```

6. The ";" can be used as the terminator for the previously created BDEP10 trigger because there is only one statement to be executed and there is no BEGIN ATOMIC and END clause.

7. The update failed because EMPNO '12345' is not in the EMP table which is required by the BDEP10 trigger.

8. The following trigger disallows the deletion of employees whose COMM is greater than their SALARY without further investigation.

```
CREATE TRIGGER BEMP20
NO CASCADE BEFORE DELETE ON EMP
REFERENCING OLD AS O
FOR EACH ROW MODE DB2SQL
WHEN (O.COMM > O.SALARY)
BEGIN ATOMIC
  SIGNAL SQLSTATE 'IBD10'
    ('Good sales person');
END#
```

9. One possibility is to set the COMM for the employee to zero before deleting the employee row.

10. Following is a trigger that does not allow the insertion of a new employee into WORKDEPT 'A00' if it causes the sum of the salaries for the department to exceed 10,000.00.

```
CREATE TRIGGER AEMP10
AFTER INSERT ON EMP
REFERENCING NEW_TABLE AS NT NEW AS N
FOR EACH ROW MODE DB2SQL
WHEN (10000.00 >
 (SELECT SUM(SALARY)
  FROM   NT
  WHERE  WORKDEPT = 'A00'))
    BEGIN ATOMIC
      SIGNAL SQLSTATE 'IAR10'
                         ('A00 salary budget exceeded');
END#
```

The trigger can be tested with the following INSERT statement.

```
INSERT INTO EMP
(EMPNO,FIRSTNME,MIDINIT,LASTNAME ,WORKDEPT,PHONENO,HIREDATE,
JOB,EDLEVEL,SEX,BIRTHDATE,SALARY,BONUS,COMM)
VALUES
('000333','Michael',' ','Hannan','A00','3978','1965-01-01',
'PRES',18,'F','1933-08-14',6000.00,1000.00,8000.00)#
```

11. The following trigger will increase the salary of the EMPNO by 10 percent in the EMP table after updating the corresponding MGRNO column in the DEPT table.

```
CREATE TRIGGER ADEP20
AFTER UPDATE OF MGRNO ON DEPT
REFERENCING OLD AS O
            NEW AS N
FOR EACH ROW MODE DB2SQL
BEGIN ATOMIC
  UPDATE EMP
  SET SALARY  = SALARY * 1.1
  WHERE EMPNO = N.MGRNO;
END#
```

12. Send an email to the director when a department has been deleted using the EMAILD UDF.

```
CREATE TRIGGER ADEP30
  AFTER DELETE ON DEPT
  REFERENCING OLD AS O
  FOR EACH ROW MODE DB2SQL
  BEGIN ATOMIC
    VALUES (EMAILD (O.DEPTNO, O.DEPTNAME, 0.MGRNO));
  END#
```

13. It is not possible to alter a trigger. It is necessary to drop the trigger and recreate it to make any changes.

14. A trigger package is created automatically when the trigger is created.

15. Rebind the trigger package with the parameter EXPLAIN(YES)

FIGURES

Stored Procedures

SP.1 INTRODUCTION

Stored procedures can be subroutines, modules, or main programs. They are developed and executed much like any subroutine except that they are called using SQL CALL rather than CALL. Stored procedures are managed by DB2 after the developer executes the CREATE PROCEDURE statement which updates the SYSROUTINES and SYSPARMS (V6) catalog tables. The calling program can call multiple stored procedures at the local site and multiple remote sites with two phase commit processing.

Stored procedures can be written in COBOL, PL/1, C, assembler, REXX (V6 APAR PQ30219, V5 APAR PQ29706), Java and the SQL procedure language. The SQL procedure language consists of BASIC like procedural code (from SQL99 and ISO standards, also known as Persistent Stored Module (PSM)) and SQL. Stored procedures can contain multiple static and dynamic SQL statements. They can be called from any programming language that allows for an SQL CALL statement including Microsoft Visual Basic and Studio, IBM VisualAge for Java, PowerBuilder, etc. The stored procedure and calling program need not be written in the same language nor run on the same platform. A stored procedure can be written in COBOL, and be called from a C program on the client, for example. It is necessary to use the Language Environment (LE) regardless of the programming language. LE establishes a common run-time environment, provides storage management and condition handling to host programs. LE run-time library and any language specific libraries are specified in the link edit step. Details can be found in the *OS/390 Language Environment for OS/390 & VM Programming Reference* manual. The platform for developing and calling procedures can be DB2 Universal Database (UDB) for OS/390, Windows 2000, NT, 98, 95, Unix, AIX, Linux, HP-UX, Solaris, UNMA-Q, OS/2, OS/400, and other platforms in the future.

A stored procedure can call a procedure (V6). The limit is 16 levels of nesting including procedures, triggers, and UDF at local and remote sites.

Stored procedures are undergoing a good deal of development and expansion at the time of writing.

Advantages of Stored Procedures

A primary advantage of stored procedures is to reduce the costs of formatting and transmitting messages in a client/server environment. These significant costs are reduced by formatting and transmitting a message to execute a stored procedure which can contain any number of SQL and procedural statements. These statements are executed at the remote site and the results transmitted to the caller. Also, lock contention is reduced because most locks are not held while messages are sent and received. In one test, IBM found that the use of stored procedures resulted in 85 percent more transactions per second. Using the client/server workload, the transaction rate was 30.3

transactions per second without the use of stored procedures compared to 56.7 transactions per second with the use of stored procedures.

Stored procedures can be used to manage client processes centrally. Their use avoids having to modify many client programs if the data or processing changes. You can modify stored procedures without affecting the calling program if call parameters are not changed. Stored procedures provide for encapsulating portions of an application program so that the caller need not have knowledge of sensitive data and processing. Procedures can be developed on one platform and deploy on another platform.

External Stored Procedures and SQL Procedures

DB2 offers two types of stored procedures both of which are invoked with EXEC SQL CALL. The costs of executing SQL is the same with and without the use of stored procedures. The term *procedure* is used to refers to both external stored procedure and SQL procedure when the description applies to both. Any differences are noted. This subsection introduces the two types of procedures with subsequent detailed coverage throughout the chapter.

An External stored procedure can be written in a host language as a subroutine or main program. They must be defined to DB2 using the CREATE PROCEDURE statement.

An SQL procedure is developed using the CREATE PROCEDURE statement. The statement also defines the procedure to DB2 as with external stored procedure. The difference is that the SQL procedure is developed within the CREATE PROCEDURE statement using SQL statements and SQL stored procedure language. The language provides for ease of use but limited functionality compared to a full function host language.

The DB2 Stored Procedure Builder (SPB) with a Graphical User Interface (GUI) front end can be used to build SQL procedures. You can be prompted to build a procedure resulting in SQL procedure language and SQL statements. You can build, modify, run, and manage procedures. You can use the SQL procedure language, Java, or REXX. The SPB generates a C program and package which can run on the OS/390, Windows 2000, NT, 98, 95, Unix, AIX, Linux, HP-UX, Solaris, UNMA-Q, OS/2, OS/400, and other platforms in the future. A debugger option is available.

SP.2 CALLING A PROCEDURE

EXEC SQL CALL is required to call a procedure. The procedure name is a three part name consisting of the location, server name, and procedure name; each part has a maximum of 18 bytes. The location portion of the name is the name of the DBMS where the procedure is stored. If it is not specified in the SQL CALL, the content of the current server special register is used. This special register can be set using the CONNECT statement. Location independence is supported using DRDA (V6), therefore the CONNECT statement is not required. The second part of the name, server name, should be SYSPROC when using DB2 for OS/390 as the server. The third component of the name is the procedure name. The three part name can be called using a literal or host variable preceded by a ":" as in the following statement.

```
EXEC SQL CALL :INORUP (:SN-IN, :SN, :SNAME,
```

```
:STATUS, :CITY, :OPERATION, :SCODE) END-EXEC.
```

Each parameter of the SQL CALL can be a host variable (not a data structure) or literal as defined as in the CREATE PROCEDURE statement.

The call parameters can be defined in the linkage section and using clause of the procedure division of the procedure. An example of this in COBOL for the above SQL CALL is in Figure SP.1.

Figure SP.1. Defining a parameter list in COBOL

```
IDENTIFICATION DIVISION.
. . .
DATA DIVISION.
. . .
LINKAGE SECTION.
01   SN-IN       PIC X(2).
01   SN          PIC X(2).
01   SNAME       PIC X(20).
01   STATUS      PIC S9(4) USAGE COMP.
01   CITY        PIC X(15).
01   OPERATION   PIC X(6).
01   SCODE       PIC S9(4) COMP.
```

The fragment of code in Figure SP.2 requires the transmission of a message for each SQL statement and for each test of the SQLCODE. If the code is part of an external stored procedure, it is necessary only to format and transmit the call statement:

```
EXEC SQL CALL :INORUP (:SN-IN, :SN, :SNAME,
     :STATUS, :CITY, :OPERATION, :SCODE) END-EXEC.
```

Figure SP.2. Fragment of code for an external stored procedure

```
EXEC SQL SELECT SN, SNAME, STATUS, CITY
         INTO   :SN,:SNAME,:STATUS,:CITY
         FROM   S
         WHERE  SN = :SN-IN
END-EXEC.

IF SQLCODE = 0
   EXEC SQL UPDATE S SET STATUS = :STATUS
            WHERE  SN = :SN-IN
   END-EXEC.
   MOVE 'UPDATE' TO OPERATION.
   MOVE SQLCODE TO SCODE.
   Return to client

IF SQLCODE = 100
   EXEC SQL INSERT INTO S(SN, SNAME, STATUS, CITY)
                  VALUES(:SN,:SNAME,:STATUS,:CITY)
   END-EXEC.
   MOVE 'INSERT' TO OPERATION.
   MOVE SQLCODE TO SCODE.
   Return to client
```

There are two red manual on stored procedures at the time of writing that you will find quite useful.

- *Developing Cross-Platform DB2 Stored Procedures: SQL Procedures and the DB2 Stored Procedure Builder* (SG24-5485)
- *Getting Started with DB2 Stored Procedures: Give Them a Call through the Network* (SG24-4693) contains a diskette with many sample client and server programs in most languages.

SP.3 RETURNING DATA TO THE CALLING PROGRAM

A result set can be returned to the calling program. The calling program can fetch from the cursors declared and opened in the procedure as if the cursor had been established in the calling program. An alternative is to have the procedure return a single message to the calling program. We will first look at returning a result set.

Return a Result Set to the Caller

The WITH RETURN clause on the cursor declaration and a declare locator host variables provide for the calling program to fetch rows from a cursor declared in a procedure. The WITH HOLD clause is needed if COMMIT ON RETURN of yes is specified in the CREATE PROCEDURE statement as discussed in Section SP.4. The cursor must be declared and opened in the procedure like:

```
EXEC SQL DECLARE SCURSOR CURSOR WITH HOLD WITH RETURN FOR
         SELECT SN, SNAME, STATUS, CITY
         FROM   S
         WHERE  STATUS > :NEW-STATUS
END-EXEC.

EXEC SQL OPEN SCURSOR END-EXEC.
```

The calling program must declare, associate, and allocate a locator host variable as shown in a fragment of a program written in COBOL (Figure SP.3). L1 is declared as a RESULT-SET-LOCATOR in a 01 level data structure and must be variable in length. The L1 result set locator is associated with the procedure :INORUP in an EXEC SQL ASSOCIATE RESULT SET LOCATOR statement after calling the :INORUP procedure. It is also necessary to allocate the cursor name as specified in the procedure DECLARE CURSOR statement with the :L1 locator variable using the EXEC SQL ALLOCATE statement. ALLOCATE does not open the cursor; it must be opened in the procedure. The calling program can then fetch from the SCURSOR cursor declared in the procedure as if it had declared and opened the cursor. The calling program or procedure can close the cursor. The cursor is not closed in the procedure when it ends unless it is explicitly closed.

Figure SP.3. Declare, associate, and allocate a locator host variable

```
EXEC SQL BEGIN DECLARE SECTION END-EXEC.
01  L1 SQL TYPE IS RESULT-SET-LOCATOR VARYING.
EXEC SQL END DECLARE SECTION END-EXEC.
...
EXEC SQL CALL :INORUP (:SN-IN, :SN, :SNAME,
    :STATUS, :CITY, :OPERATION, :SCODE) END-EXEC.
```

```
EXEC SQL ASSOCIATE RESULT SET LOCATOR (:L1)
     WITH PROCEDURE :INORUP END-EXEC.

EXEC SQL ALLOCATE SCURSOR CURSOR FOR RESULT SET :L1
      END-EXEC.

EXEC SQL FETCH SCURSOR INTO :SN-IN, :SN, :SNAME,
    :STATUS, :CITY, :OPERATION, :SCODE END-EXEC.
```

Multiple locator variables can be declared, associated, and allocated for each of multiple cursors. The calling client program can fetch from the cursors in any order independent of the order returned from the procedure provided that DRDA level 3 is supported.

The members of DSN8ED1 and DSN8ED2 in the SDSNSAMP library are sample programs calling procedures.

ODBC and CLI: When using Open Database Connectivity (ODBC) and Call Level Interface (CLI), the calling program must fetch from the result sets in the order returned by the server to comply with the ODBC rules. A procedure can be called from ODBC and CLI calls can be issued from within a procedure. ODBC and X/OPEN CLI can be used by OS/390 application programs which is useful when porting work station server applications to OS/390.

Returning a Single Message

An output parameter can be defined for each row fetched or each column in each row to be returned to the client. This can be cumbersome if the procedure must return a number of columns and rows to be displayed on a screen at the client site.

An alternative is to have the procedure build a character string of 1920 bytes to fill a 24x80 screen based on multiple rows processed and transmitted it to the caller. It is necessary for the client and server programs to establish conventions for the exchange of data. Another possibility is to define an output parameter for each row fetched or each column to return to the client. The second alternative can result in a very long parameter list.

There are generous limit on the number of bytes that can be returned in a single parameter and for the entire procedure. The maximum number of bytes that can be passed in a single parameter of an SQL CALL statement is 32,765. The maximum number of bytes that can be passed to or from a procedure is 5.4 MB.

SP.4 CREATE PROCEDURE STATEMENT

The CREATE PROCEDURE statement is used to describe a procedure to DB2 (V6). This determines how the procedure is to be executed. The statement populates two catalog tables. SYSROUTINES contains a row for every routine including a procedure, user-defined function, and cast function. SYSPARMS table contains a row for each parameter of a routine or multiple rows for table parameters (one for each column of the table). The first example contains only the basic parameters.

```
CREATE PROCEDURE INORUP(IN SN_IN CHAR(2), OUT SN CHAR(2),
  OUT SNAME CHAR(20), OUT STATUS SMALLINT,
  OUT CITY CHAR(15), INOUT OPERATION CHAR(6),
  OUT SCODE SMALLINT)
RESULT SETS 4
EXTERNAL  NAME 'INORUP'
LANGUAGE  COBOL
PARAMETER STYLE DB2SQL
RUN OPTIONS
 'HEAP(,,ANY),BELOW(4K,,),ALL31(ON),STACK(,,ANY,)';
```

INORUP is the name used to call the procedure. The parameters following INORUP in parenthesis must begin with IN, OUT, or INOUT (input, output, or input and output parameter), optionally the name of field can be specified, the last description of the input/output field must designate the data type and length of field.

RESULT SETS 4 indicate that rows can be fetched from 4 cursors, for example.

EXTERNAL NAME is the name of the load module (need not be the same name as the procedure).

LANGUAGE COBOL means that the procedure is written in COBOL. It can be PLI, C, ASSEMBLE, REXX, COMPJAVA, or SQL for SQL procedures.

Create Parameters in Detail

A few of the basic parameters have been discussed in this chapter. The parameters used in the following statement are similar to those used when creating a user-defined function (UDF) in the next Chapter UD. There are some additional parameters that apply only to UDF which are described in that chapter. Please see Chapter UD Section 9 for a summary of the similarities and differences between procedures and UDF.

```
CREATE PROCEDURE INORUP(IN SN_IN CHAR(2), OUT SN CHAR(2),
  OUT SNAME CHAR(20), OUT STATUS SMALLINT,
  OUT CITY CHAR(15), INOUT OPERATION CHAR(6),
  OUT SCODE SMALLINT)
RESULT SETS 4
EXTERNAL  NAME 'INORUP'
LANGUAGE  COBOL
PARAMETER STYLE DB2SQL
COMMIT ON RETURN YES
WLM ENVIRONMENT WLMENVCU
PROGRAM TYPE SUB
STAY RESIDENT NO
CALLED ON NULL INPUT
READS SQL DATA
NO DBINFO
DETERMINISTIC
FENCED
ASUTIME LIMIT 80000
NO COLLID
SECURITY DB2
```

```
RUN OPTIONS 'HEAP(,,ANY),BELOW(4K,,), ALL31(ON),
  STACK(,,ANY,)';
```

EXTERNAL NAME identifies the name of the load module resulting from program preparation of a stored procedure or UDF. 'INORUP' is the external name of the INORUP function. This is the name used in the SQL CALL statement for procedures or in an SQL statement for invocation of a UDF. 'TOTALAMT' is the external name of the TOTAL_AMOUNT UDF in Chapter UD.

LANGUAGE COBOL gives the name of the host program language used to develop the procedure or UDF. It can be COBOL, PLI, C, REXX, Java, or ASSEMBLE for external stored procedures. An SQL procedure requires LANGUAGE SQL.

PARAMETER STYLE DB2SQL indicates the linkage convention that the function program uses to receive input parameters from and return values to the invoking SQL statement. There are no optional parameter values at present. This parameter has the same meaning as when used with triggers (discussed in Chapter TR).

COMMIT ON RETURN NO (default) means that the UR is not to be committed upon successful return (non-negative SQLCODE) from the procedure or invocation of UDF.

COMMIT ON RETURN YES means that the UR is to be committed upon successful return (non-negative SQLCODE) from the procedure or UDF. Reduces message traffic and ensures that locks are released in a timely fashion.

WLM ENVIRONMENT without a name following the parameter means that the procedure or UDF runs in the work load manager (WLM) established stored procedure address space that is specified at installation time. If the parameter is followed by a name, this means that the procedure or UDF runs in the named WLM environment.

WLM ENVIRONMENT followed by (name,*) means that when an SQL application program directly invokes a procedures or UDF, the WLM environment in which the procedure or UDF runs is used. If a procedure or UDF invokes another procedure or UDF, it runs in the same environment that the invoking routine uses.

NO WLM ENVIRONMENT means that the procedure is to run in the DB2-established stored procedure address space (does not apply to UDF). This parameter cannot be used with PROGRAM TYPE SUB, SECURITY USER, SECURITY DEFINER, and parameters with a LOB data type or distinct type based on a LOB data type.

The users of a procedure or UDF must have the appropriate authorization to execute functions in the specified WLM environment. RACF can be used to provide the required authority.

PROGRAM TYPE SUB (default) means that the procedure or UDF is written and executed as a subroutine. Reduces CPU cost for call processing and cleanup (30 K instructions) compared to a MAIN program. However, some languages have restrictions (no I/O for Pl/1, for example). The program must be dynamically loadable (fetchable). It is the developers responsibility to free resources (storage and files, for example).

PROGRAM TYPE MAIN means that the UDF is written and executed as a main program. This option gives you full language capabilities and guaranteed resources are freed (storage, for example).

STAY RESIDENT NO (default) means that the load module of the procedure or UDF does not remain resident in memory. The load module is deleted from memory at end of its processing. This is a good choice for non-reentrant procedures and UDF.

STAY RESIDENT YES means that load module remains resident in memory at the end of its processing. This is a good choice for reentrant load modules that are used frequently.

RETURNS NULL ON NULL INPUT means that UDF is not invoked if any of the input arguments are null. The result returned to the invoking program is null. NOT NULL CALL is a synonym for RETURNS NULL ON NULL INPUT.

CALLED ON NULL INPUT means that the procedure or UDF is invoked regardless of whether the input argument is null or non-null. The result can be null or a non-null value. The procedure or UDF should check for null to determine the required processing. NULL CALL is a synonym for CALLED ON NULL INPUT

READS SQL DATA (default) means that you cannot execute SQL statements that modifies data in a procedure or UDF. It is possible to use statements to read data including SELECT and cursor management statements. Also some statements including DECLARE and related statements, statements for preparation and execution of dynamic SQL, most SET statements, and etc. can be processed.

MODIFIES SQL DATA means that you can execute most SQL DML, DDL, and DCL statements. Except COMMIT, ROLLBACK, SET CONNECTION, and RELEASE cannot be executed. DISALLOW PARALLEL is a good choice to avoid unexpected results if different results can occur when a parallel path is or is not chosen. This is the default when MODIFIES SQL DATA is used.

CONTAINS SQL means that no SQL statements that read or modify data can be executed. It is possible to invoke some statements including DECLARE and related statements, statements for preparation and execution of dynamic SQL, most SET statements, and etc.

NO SQL means that no SQL statements can be executed in the procedure or UDF. However, most DECLARE statements can be used in procedures.

Details on each statement allowed and disallowed in a procedure and UDF based on the chosen parameter is given in the *SQL Reference* manual.

NO DBINFO (default) means that no additional information is passed to the procedure or UDF when it is invoked.

DBINFO means that additional arguments can be passed when the procedure or UDF is invoked, for example the run-time AUTHID, schema name, name of the table or column that the object might be inserting into or updating, and the database server ID that invoked the procedure or UDF. The *Application Programming and SQL Guide* manual contains additional details.

NOT DETERMINISTIC (default) means that the procedure or UDF might not return the same result for identical input arguments. A random number returned from a procedure or UDF that generates values based on the range of input parameters is not the same in most cases, for example. If a parallel path is chosen, different results can be returned. This can be avoided by specifying DISALLOW PARALLEL which is the default when using this parameter. VARIANT is a synonym for NOT DETERMINISTIC.

DETERMINISTIC means that a procedure or UDF always returns the same result for identical input arguments. DAYOFWEEK always returns an integer in the range of 1 to 7, where 1 represents Sunday, for example. NOT VARIANT is a synonym for DETERMINISTIC.

FENCED (default) means that the procedure or UDF runs in an external address space to prevent the function from corrupting DB2 storage.

ASUTIME NO LIMIT (default) means that there is no processor time limit for the procedure or UDF.

ASUTIME with a value provides for specifying the total amount of processor time, in CPU service units, that a single invocation of a procedure or UDF can use. ASU is the amount of CPU time in service units depending on the computer model used. The value can be between 1 and 2 GB. The *OS/390 MVS Initialization and Tuning Guide* manual gives the details. The procedure or UDF is cancelled when the limit is exceeded. The value specified here is not related to the ASUTIME column of the resource limit specification table.

NO COLLID (default) means that the package collection for the procedure or UDF is the same as the package collection of the object that invokes the procedure or UDF. If a trigger invokes the procedure or UDF, the collection of the trigger package is used. If the invoking program does not use a package, the package collection is the value of the CURRENT PACKAGESET special register.

COLLID followed by the name of a collection is the package collection that is used when the procedure or UDF is executed.

SECURITY DB2 (default) means that the AUTHID that is associated with the WLM-established stored procedure address space is used if the object accesses resources that an external security product protects. Procedures and UDFs do not require an external security environment.

SECURITY USER means that the primary AUTHID of the process that invoked the object is used to determine if the function can access resources protected by an external security product. An external security environment should be established for the procedure or UDF if this parameter value is chosen.

SECURITY DEFINER means that the AUTHID of the invoked object owner is used to determine if the procedure or UDF can access resources protected by an external security product. In this case an external security environment should be established for the object as with SECURITY USER.

RUN OPTIONS provides for passing 254 or fewer bytes of options to the LE to be used for the procedure or UDF. If the parameter is not specified, an empty string is passed and the installation defaults are used. The parameters H(,,ANY),STAC(,,ANY,),STO(,,,4K),

BE(4K,,),LIBS(4K,,),ALL31(ON) limits storage that is required by LE. The *OS/390 Language Environment for OS/390 & VM Programming Reference* manual contains details.

ALTER and DROP Procedures

The ALTER PROCEDURE statement can be used to change most parameters. Except the input and output parameters, CALLED ON NULL INPUT, and FENCED parameters cannot be altered.

A procedure can be dropped like:

```
DROP PROCEDURE INORUP RESTRICT;
```

The parameter RESTRICT is required. It avoids dropping a procedure used by a trigger.

SP.5 SAVEPOINT MANAGEMENT

The SAVEPOINT statement provides for establishing a point to which you can rollback or you can release the savepoint (V6 APAR PQ30439). A savepoint with the name of REDO can be established like:

```
EXEC SQL SAVEPOINT REDO UNIQUE ON ROLLBACK RETAIN CURSORS
  END-EXEC.
```

You can rollback work to the named savepoint like:

```
EXEC SQL ROLLBACK TO REDO END-EXEC.
```

Optionally, you can release a savepoint like:

```
EXEC SQL RELEASE SAVEPOINT REDO END-EXEC.
```

A savepoint applies to the DBMS where it is set (not other DBMSs). It is possible to connect to another location within the scope of a savepoint when using the DRDA CONNECT statement. This does not apply when using the private protocol. For example, a savepoint set in Los Angeles is unknown to SQL statements executed in San Francisco and vice versa. It is not possible to use an alias or three-part name to access a remote DBMS with the scope of a savepoint using DRDA and private protocol. This is because developers need not be aware of remote sites involved.

Savepoints can be used in a host program including stored procedures and external user-defined functions defined with MODIFIES SQLDATA. They cannot be used in triggers nested within user-defined functions. Savepoints can be executed statically or dynamically. If they are executed dynamically, it is necessary to bind with DYNAMICRULES of RUN.

Establishing a SAVEPOINT

A savepoint must be given a name of 128 bytes or less. REDO is the name given to the savepoint established in previous and following examples. The are three additional clauses that can be used when defining a SAVEPOINT, two of which are shown in the statement:

```
EXEC SQL SAVEPOINT REDO UNIQUE ON ROLLBACK RETAIN CURSORS
  END-EXEC.
```

UNIQUE means that the savepoint name must be unique within a Unit of Recovery (UR). If you do not use UNIQUE and establish a savepoint with a duplicate name, the first savepoint is destroyed and a new savepoint is established (release rules discussed later in this section do not apply). It is advisable to avoid using the same name for multiple savepoints. Indeed, UNIQUE cannot be used when manipulating savepoints within a loop.

ON ROLLBACK RETAIN CURSORS means not to close cursors opened after establishing a savepoint with a rollback. Cursors are not tracked. However, the cursor may not be useable. For example, if an inserted row is rolled back, an error results from an attempt to update or delete the row.

ON ROLLBACK RETAIN LOCKS means that any locks acquired after establishing the savepoint are not released upon a rollback to a savepoint. Locks are not tracked.

The cost of establishing a savepoint is about the same as fetching a row.

Rollback to a Savepoint

Rollback work to where the REDO savepoint was established can be accomplished with or without the keyword 'WORK'.

```
EXEC SQL ROLLBACK      TO REDO END-EXEC. or
EXEC SQL ROLLBACK WORK TO REDO END-EXEC.
```

If the savepoint name is not specified, a rollback of all savepoints set within a UR occurs.

```
EXEC SQL ROLLBACK END-EXEC.
```

If there is not an active savepoint when the rollback is issued, an error is received.

Savepoints set after the one rolled back are also rolled back. For example, assume that REDO1, REDO2, and REDO3 savepoints are established in the order specified. The rollback to REDO2 rolls back REDO2 and REDO3.

A rollback applies to changes made to the data, schema, and declared temporary tables. Some work is not rolled back including:

- Results of SQL issued on a created temporary table (warning is issued)
- Open or close of cursors
- Changes to cursor positioning
- Acquisition and release of locks
- Caching of rolled back dynamic statements

Release Savepoint

It is not possible to rollback to a savepoint or savepoints established after the named saved point once it is released. A savepoint can be released with either of the statements:

```
EXEC SQL RELEASE    REDO END-EXEC. or
EXEC SQL RELEASE TO REDO END-EXEC.
```

This applies to savepoints established in a main program and subroutines called by the main program. For example, assume that a main program establishes REDO1 savepoint, subroutine A establishes REDO2 savepoint, and subroutine B establishes REDO3 savepoint. If the main program releases REDO1 after it executes and the two subroutines are executed, savepoints REDO1, REDO2, and REDO3 are released.

COMMIT releases all savepoints within the current UR.

SP.6 FUNCTIONS NOT SUPPORTED IN A PROCEDURE

Most functions performed in a DB2 application program can be performed in a procedure with some exceptions.

COMMIT and ROLLBACK

The calling program has control of a unit of recovery (UR) to ensure that all work is committed or rolled back in the calling program and multiple procedures (referred to as two phase commit processing). This is enforced by not allowing the successful execution of COMMIT and ROLLBACK statements in the procedure. These statements must be issued from the calling program to be successful.

There is a work-around to allow the procedure to force the calling program to rollback. If a ROLLBACK is issued from a procedure, the procedure and caller are placed in a must rollback state with both receiving -751 SQLCODE. The caller must issue an explicit rollback or terminate execution, which results in an implicit rollback in the procedure.

Calling a procedure from a procedure (V5): The additional statements that result in a -751 SQLCODE which forces the calling program to issue a rollback are:

- SQL CALL to another procedure
- CONNECT
- RELEASE
- SET CONNECTION
- SET CURRENT SQLID

These restrictions are a result of the inability to call a procedure from another procedure (V5).

Use of CAF: If the call attach facility (CAF) is used by DB2 to manage procedures, it cannot be used by the procedure.

DRDA and the private protocol: A program cannot mix the Distributed Relational Database Architecture (DRDA) with private protocol within a UR. The protocols are also known as application directed (DRDA) and system directed (private protocol) processing.

Access to Non-DB2 Resources

DL/1 databases, message queue series (MQSeries), VSAM, and flat files can be accessed from a procedure in addition to tables. It is necessary to define DD statements for the files in JCL for a procedure address space.

A procedure can change DB2 tables, DL/1 databases, recoverable VSAM files, and MQSeries messages. A COMMIT or ROLLBACK applies to all of these resources. That is, all updates within a UR are committed or rolled back. OS/390 WLM-established procedure address spaces must be used for this two phase commit processing. Procedure address spaces are discussed in Section SP.10.

DB2 notifies OS/390 RRS (Resource Recovery Services) about commit and rollback decisions and RRS passes the decision to other resources. The path length is increased when updating non-DB2 data. It is necessary to use the recoverable resource manager services attachment facility (RRSAF). This is done by specifying the ATTACH(RRSAF) parameter to the precompiler. DSNRLI must be linkedited with the procedure and AMODE(31) is needed to run above the 16 MB line. Any program can use RRSAF rather than CAF or TSO TMP (Terminal Monitor Program). Thread reuse can be used with RRSAF. This is particularly useful for any program that requires that a UOW span multiple data sources.

A procedures can access the external CICS interface (EXCI) for synchronous execution of CICS transactions. The CICS MQI (Message Queue Interface) product can be used for asynchronous execution of CICS transactions.

IMS DL/1 calls cannot be executed from a procedure. However, IMS transactions can be invoked asynchronously using MQI. The CICS EXCI can be used from a procedure synchronously to run a CICS transaction that has DL/1 calls.

SP.7 TEMPORARY TABLES

There are two types of temporary tables that can be created and manipulated much like base tables in any host program including procedures and triggers with some exceptions. There are a number of uses for temporary tables. Rows can be inserted into a temporary table as read from tables, DL/1 databases, VSAM, flat files, and other resources. The rows from the various sources can then be manipulated with SELECT statements. If it is necessary to select the same rows from a table more than once, consider placing the rows in a temporary table to avoid having to select the rows a second time. This is particularly important if the SELECT statement is costly to execute. If you need a varying number of values in an IN (list), consider placing values in temporary table and use a IN subselect referencing the temporary table.

Manipulation of temporary tables: You can use the INSERT and SELECT statements on temporary tables just like on base tables including joining temporary and base tables. WITH RETURN can be used when selecting from temporary tables. How UPDATE and DELETE statements can be used depends on the type of temporary table.

We will describe and analyze the differences between the two types of temporary tables to determine which best suites your requirements:

- CREATE GLOBAL TEMPORARY table
- DECLARE GLOBAL TEMPORARY table

Creation of Global Temporary Tables

A global temporary table can be created like (V5):

```
CREATE GLOBAL TEMPORARY
  TABLE MIAMI_S
    (SN     CHAR(6),
     SNAME  CHAR(20),
     STATUS SMALLINT,
     CITY   CHAR(15));
```

A global temporary table can also be created using the LIKE parameter:

```
CREATE GLOBAL TEMPORARY TABLE MIAMI_S LIKE DALLAS_S;
```

Declaration of Global Temporary Tables

A declare temporary table can be created like (V6 APAR PQ32670):

```
DECLARE GLOBAL TEMPORARY
  TABLE SESSION.NEWYORK_S
    (SN     CHAR(6),
     SNAME  CHAR(20),
     STATUS SMALLINT,
     CITY   CHAR(15))
      ON COMMIT PRESERVE ROWS;
```

A declare temporary table can also be created using the LIKE parameter:

```
DECLARE GLOBAL TEMPORARY TABLE SESSION.MIAMI_S LIKE DALLAS_S;
```

Comparison of Declare and Create Global Temporary Tables

The syntax of declare and create temporary tables are similar. However, there are some major differences in the implementation of the objects that will influence your decision as to which is appropriate for your requirements as summarized in Figure SP.4. Do pay special attention to the notes indicated in parenthesis following the Y and N.

Figure SP.4. Comparison of declare and create global temporary tables

Description	DECLARE GLOBAL TEMPORARY	CREATE GLOBAL TEMPORARY
Create database and segmented tablespace	Y (1)	N
Storage of rows	User created tablespace	DSNDB07 work tablespaces
Same table name can be used in multiple programs	N	Y (2)
Table qualifier	SESSION (3)	Like a base table
Authorization required	N (4)	Y (5)
Recorded in catalog tables	N	Y (6)
When instance of table created	Execution of DECLARE GLOBAL TEMPORARY	Open, insert, select into, or delete is issued
Create index on table	Y	N
Incremental bind at run time	Y	N
Searched DELETE and UPDATE	Y	N (7)
Retain rows in table across commit point	Y if PRESERVE N if DELETE	N (8)
Can rollback changes to last commit or savepoint (UNDO log records used)	Y (except for INSERT statements)	N

Here is a explanation of the notes on the comparison of declare and create global temporary tables:

(1) It is necessary to CREATE DATABASE ... AS TEMP and a segmented tablespace within the database before executing the DECLARE GLOBAL TEMPORARY statement. The size is limited by PRIQTY and SECQTY specified when the tablespace is created. Only one TEMP database can exist on a DB2 subsystem. Each member of a sysplex data sharing group must have a TEMP database if DECLARE GLOBAL TEMPORARY is used on that member. It is recommended that the FOR MEMBER clause be used to designate the member. Otherwise, the member that executes the statement is the designated member and only that member can accept DECLARE statements for the database.

(2) Each program has an instance of the table as defined in the catalog tables as indicated in note 6. Various programs and executions of the same program do not have access to the same rows for both types of temporary tables.

(3) SESSION can be specified on DECLARE statement as the qualifier. If no qualifier is specified, SESSION is used. It is recommended that you reference SESSION.table_name in your SQL statements. Optionally, you can bind with QUALIFIER(SESSION). However, the qualifier applies to all tables in the package or plan. It is likely to result in errors because most base tables do not have a qualifier of SESSION. Incremental bind processing is done for SQL referencing a declare temporary table at run time. Processing is like using dynamic SQL except that the dynamic cache cannot be used. This is because the table does not exist at bind time.

(4) No, except must have select privileges on table referenced in LIKE clause if used.

(5) Yes, privileges required are similar to a base table or you can GRANT CREATETMTAB TO AUTHID.

(6) A row is inserted into SYSTABLES with TYPE = 'G' as a result of the CREATE TEMPORARY TABLE statement. However, each of many programs can have an instance of the table. The rows are deleted when the temporary table is dropped. You can manually update catalog statistics, otherwise default statistics are used. Statistics are useful to the optimizer in determining the table join sequence, for example. Do be cautious of the fact that the statistics apply to all instances of global temporary tables some of which can be large and others small. Regardless of whether you choose to update the statistics, the number of rows and pages are accumulated and kept in memory for use with dynamic SQL without use of the cache.

(7) There are data manipulation restrictions for global temporary tables. It is not possible to UPDATE specific rows in a global temporary table. However, you can reference the temporary table in the WHERE clause of UPDATE of a base table. It is not possible to DELETE from a global temporary table with a WHERE clause or WHERE CURRENT OF. However, you can DELETE FROM table with no WHERE clause. That is delete all rows in the global temporary table.

(8) Global temporary table rows are deleted and space freed with COMMIT (except when using CURSOR WITH HOLD), ROLLBACK, thread deallocation, and DROP TABLE. Declare temporary tables are dropped when the thread that created the table is deallocated.

Items that apply to both types of temporary tables: Rows in a temporary table cannot be shared across multiple programs or multiple executions of the same program. There is no locking, logging, and recovery of temporary tables. Except share locks are taken on the tablespace and database used for DECLARED TEMPORARY TABLES. An exception regarding logging is that UNDO (not REDO) log records are used for DECLARE TEMPORARY TABLE. There are restrictions on temporary tables in addition to those noted in Figure SP.4:

- ♦ Cannot define referential integrity
- ♦ Cannot specify a default for a column
- ♦ Cannot create a column declared as a ROWID or LOB (V6)
- ♦ Cannot create a table LIKE a declare temporary table
- ♦ Cannot issue a LOCK TABLE statement on a temporary table
- ♦ DB2 parallelism cannot be used (true for any data in a work tablespace
- ♦ DBPROTOCOL(PRIVATE) cannot be specified when binding SQL referencing temporary tables

SP.8 PREPARATION OF EXTERNAL PROCEDURES

A external stored procedure is prepared very much like any host program with a precompile, compile, linkedit into an OS/390 load library, and bind. It is necessary to linkedit with the DSNALI (for a static link) or DSNHLI2 (for a dynamic link) language interface module for CAF connection to ssnmSPAS when using a DB2-established procedure address space or RRSAF when using a WLM-established procedure address space. A package (not a plan) must be used for the SQL in a procedure. A client in Dallas can develop a procedure and bind the associated DBRM into a package at the server in Rome, for example:

```
BIND PACKAGE (ROME.SPCOLLID) MEMBER (INORUP)
```

The collection (SPCOLLID in the example) can be specified in the CREATE PROCEDURE statement.. The collection of the caller is used if the column contains blank. A procedure does not require a plan when called from a client. The DDF (Distributed Data Facility) thread of a caller is used to call a procedure. The SQL CALL can be issued from a plan or package. The caller of the procedure needs to be granted privileges to execute the procedure package like:

```
GRANT EXECUTE ON PACKAGE SPCOLLID.INORUP TO FLEUR;
```

Optionally, the privilege can be granted to the public.

Calling a Non-procedure: A module or subroutine (not a procedure) that has a package can be called from a procedure using a CALL statement (not SQL CALL). The procedure and module or subroutine packages can be in the same collection. An alternative is to use the SET CURRENT PACKAGESET to reference a collection that contains the module or subroutine before calling it. If SQL is executed from the calling procedure after calling the module or subroutine, the SET CURRENT PACKAGESET statement must be used to set the collection back to the procedure collection. If a local plan or package calls a local procedure, the PKLIST of the local plan must include the procedure package.

SP.9 SQL PROCEDURES

LANGUAGE SQL designates an SQL procedure as contrasted with an SQL external procedure developed in a host language (LANGUAGE COBOL, for example). Procedural logic can be specified within CREATE PROCEDURE statement using Basic like statements (examples will be given). SQL procedures avoid developers having to know a host language, how to embed SQL in the program, and program preparation provided SPB is used. There are two alternatives for developing an SQL procedure. The CREATE PROCEDURE statement can be developed with SQL and some procedural code. The SPB tool on Windows 2000, NT, 98, or 95 and Unix can be used to develop the procedure on platforms other than the one used for execution of the procedure. The SQL procedure language is complied into a C procedure.

Availability of SQL Procedure Software

At the time of writing SQL procedures can be used with V5 after applying APARs PQ29866, PQ24199, PQ24199, and PQ29706 depending on how you plan to use procedures. The SQL procedure code for V5 is shipped as a zip file sqlproc.zip. It is available from:

http://www.software.ibm.com/data/db2/os390/spb
http://www.software.ibm.com/data/db2/os390/, click on download option

It is necessary to unzip sqlproc.zip into PC files and install into DB2 libraries on OS/390. The use of the SPB requires PC installation of:

- DB2 UDB V6.1
- DB2 Connect V6
- Download OS/390 component of Procedure Builder, upload to OS/390, and install it

A remote Debugger can be installed on your PC and the Debug Tool on OS/390 starting with:

http://www.software.ibm.com/ad/c390/cmvsbeta.htm

Installation details are in the *DB2 for OS/390Version 5 Preview of SQL Procedures* manual available from:

http://www.ibm.com/software/db2/os390/sqlproc

The *OS/390 REXX* manual is available from:

ftp://ftp.software.ibm.com/software/os390/db2server/books/REXXV5.PDF

REXX is required for preparation of SQL procedure.

SQL Procedure Example

Following is an example of an SQL procedure that performs functions similar to the external stored procedure in Section SP.4.

```
CREATE PROCEDURE INORUP
 (IN     SN_IN      CHAR(2),
  OUT    SN         CHAR(2),
  OUT    SNAME      CHAR(20),
  OUT    STATUS     SMALLINT,
  OUT    CITY       CHAR(15),
  INOUT  OPERATION  CHAR(6),
  OUT    SQLCODEOUT INTEGER)
LANGUAGE SQL
PINORUP: BEGIN
  DECLARE SN_IN_SP   CHAR(2);
  DECLARE SN_SP      CHAR(2);
  DECLARE SNAME_SP   CHAR(20);
  DECLARE STATUS_SP  SMALLINT;
  DECLARE CITY_SP    CHAR(15);
  DECLARE SQLCODE    INTEGER;
```

```
  DECLARE SQLSTATE  CHAR(5);

DECLARE SCURSOR CURSOR FOR
  SELECT SN, SNAME, STATUS, CITY
  FROM   S
  WHERE  SN = SN_IN;
OPEN SCURSOR;

S_LOOP: LOOP
  FETCH SCURSOR INTO SN_SP, SNAME_SP,
                     STATUS_SP, CITY_SP;
  IF SQLCODE = 0 THEN
    UPDATE S SET STATUS = STATUS_SP
    WHERE  SN = SN_IN;
    SET OPERATION  = 'UPDATE';
    SET STATUS     = STATUS_SP;
    SET SQLCODEOUT = SQLCODE;
    LEAVE S_LOOP;
  END IF;

  IF SQLCODE = 100 THEN
    INSERT INTO S(SN, SNAME, STATUS, CITY)
           VALUES(SN, SNAME, STATUS, CITY);
    SET OPERATION  = 'INSERT';
    SET SNAME      = SNAME_SP;
    SET STATUS     = STATUS_SP;
    SET CITY       = CITY_SP;
    SET SQLCODEOUT = SQLCODE;
    LEAVE S_LOOP;
  END IF;

END LOOP;
CLOSE SCURSOR;
END PINORUP
```

The first section in parenthesis define input and output variables for the SQL procedure. The DECLARE statements following PINORUP: BEGIN declares SQL variables for use within the SQL procedure. This accomplishes the same goal as defining input and output variables for external stored procedures discussed in Section SP.7. Notice that the receiving variables (host variables) in the SQL are not preceded by a colon as in a host program.

Compound Statement

A compound statement consists of one or more SQL and procedure statements between BEGIN and END. The statements must follow the order:

1. SQL variable and condition declarations
2. Cursor declarations
3. Handler declarations
4. Assignment statements, control-flow statements such as CASE, IF, LOOP, ITERATE, REPEAT, WHILE, GOTO, and SQL statements such as SELECT, INSERT, UPDATE, DELETE, CALL, CREATE TABLE, etc.

BEGIN NOT ATOMIC or BEGIN does not require that all statements before the END statement must execute successfully or all are rolled back

BEGIN ATOMIC means that all statements before the END must execute successfully or all are rolled back. This option is not supported on DB2 for OS/390 at present.

Terminating character: The procedure body has no terminating character. If a statement is nested within other statements in the procedure body, the statement must end with a semicolon (;). If the statement is the only statement in the procedure body, the statement does not have a terminating character.

Procedural Statements for Use in SQL Procedures

Figure SP.5 summarizes procedural statements for use in SQL procedures, most of which were used in the previous example of an SQL procedure. The remaining statements will be used later in this section.

Figure SP.5. Summary of procedural statements for use in SQL procedures

Statement	Description
SET	Assigns a value to an output parameter or to an SQL variable, which is a variable that is defined and used only within a procedure body. The right side of an assignment statement can include SQL built-in functions.
IF	Selects an execution path based on the evaluation of a condition.
CASE	Selects an execution path based on the evaluation of one or more conditions. Similar to usual CASE statement.
LOOP	Executes a statement or group of statements multiple times.
ITERATE	Repeat a labeled set of statements while a specified condition is true.
REPEAT	Executes a statement or group of statements until a search condition is true.
WHILE	Repeats the execution of a statement or group of statements while a specified condition is true.
LEAVE	Transfers program control out of a loop or a block of code including a LOOP, ITERATE, REPEAT, and WHILE which determine where to continue processing.
GOTO	Transfers program control to a labelled statement.

UPDATE with CASE Expression

A CASE expression can be used in an SQL procedure. It is particularly useful with updates to avoid having to select rows, sest conditions in a host program, and execute multiple UPDATE statements for multiple conditions. Following is an example of increasing a given EMPNO (IN EMPNOIN parameter) salary. If the employee is in D1, the salary is increased by 10 percent and they are in D2, the increase is 20 percent provided their bonus plus commission is greater than their salary.

```
CREATE PROCEDURE INCSALARY
 (IN EMPNOIN    CHAR(6))
  LANGUAGE SQL
  MODIFIES SQL DATA
  CASE WORKDEPT
    WHEN 'D1' THEN
         UPDATE EMP
         SET    SALARY = SALARY * 1.1
         WHERE  EMPNO  = EMPNOIN
         AND    BONUS + COMM > SALARY;
    WHEN 'D2' THEN
         UPDATE EMP
         SET    SALARY = SALARY * 1.2
         WHERE  EMPNO  = EMPNOIN
         AND    BONUS + COMM > SALARY;
    ELSE
         UPDATE EMP
         SET    SALARY = SALARY
         WHERE  EMPNO  = EMPNOIN;
  END CASE
END INCSALARY
```

There are some statements that are not supported in DB2 for OS/390 at present. The FOR statements provides another method for executing a group of statement repeatedly in addition to the ones shown in Figure SP.5. The SIGNAL statement provides a method for invoking a handler (discussed in the next subsection DECLARE Handler) or returning an SQLSTATE to invoker of the procedure. RESIGNAL provides a method for repeating a signal with the same or different condition.

Figure SP.6 summarizes statements supported in the body of SQL procedures.

Figure SP.6. Statements that can be used in an SQL procedure

```
DECLARE CURSOR              CALL
OPEN                        ALLOCATE*
FETCH                       ASSOCIATE*
CLOSE                       RELEASE
SELECT INTO
INSERT                      CREATE
UPDATE                      DROP
DELETE                      RENAME
VALUES INTO*                DECLARE GLOBAL TEMPORARY TABLE
                            COMMENT ON
EXECUTE                     LABEL ON
EXECUTE IMMEDIATE
PREPARE FROM                GRANT
                            REVOKE
ROLLBACK*
SAVEPOINT
RELEASE SAVEPOINT
ROLLBACK TO SAVEPOINT
LOCK TABLE

*Not supported in DB2 for OS/390 at present
```

DECLARE Handlers

DECLARE handlers indicate the action to take if a condition is met. They are useful in managing SQLSTATEs and SQLCODEs. It is advisable to test the SQLSTATE in addition to the SQLCODE other than 0 and 100 for compatibility across platforms. The handles are designed to manage SQLSTATEs with a class code of '00', ' 01', or ' 02' in the first two bytes of the SQLSTATE.

Here is an example using the not_found condition handler with a fragment of previous SQL procedure definition as highlighted in bold.

```
DECLARE not_found CONDITION FOR '02000';
DECLARE SQLCODE   INTEGER;
DECLARE SQLSTATE  CHAR(5);
DECLARE SCURSOR CURSOR FOR
  SELECT SN, SNAME, STATUS, CITY
  FROM   S
  WHERE  SN = SN_IN;
DECLARE CONTINUE HANDLER FOR not_found SET NOROWS = 1;
OPEN SCURSOR;
  FETCH SCURSOR INTO SN_SP, SNAME_SP, STATUS_SP, CITY_SP;
CLOSE SCURSOR;
```

All variable names are folded to upper case (not_found becomes NOT_FOUND for example). That is names, variables, labels, etc. are not case sensitive. If you refer to an SQL procedure parameter in the procedure body, do not declare an SQL variable with a name that is the same as that parameter name.

EXIT handler can be used to end a compound statement as in the following example. Assume that RETURN_MESSAGE has been declared as an output parameter.

```
DECLARE SQLCODE    INTEGER;
DECLARE SQLSTATE   CHAR(5);
DECLARE RESOURCE_UNAVAILABLE CONDITION FOR '57011';
DECLARE EXIT HANDLER FOR RESOURCE_UNAVAILABLE
  SET RETURN_MESSAGE = 'Resource unavailable';
DECLARE SCURSOR CURSOR FOR
  SELECT SN, SNAME, STATUS, CITY
  FROM   S
  WHERE  SN = SN_IN;
OPEN SCURSOR;
  FETCH SCURSOR INTO SN_SP, SNAME_SP, STATUS_SP, CITY_SP;
CLOSE SCURSOR;
```

SQLEXCEPTION handler receives control if any SQL statement in the procedure body receives a negative SQLCODE and the execution of the procedure ends. Assume that SQLSTATEOUT has been declared as an output parameter.

```
DECLARE SQLCODE    INTEGER;
DECLARE SQLSTATE   CHAR(5);
DECLARE EXIT HANDLER FOR SQLEXCEPTION
  SET SQLSTATEOUT = SQLSTATE;
DECLARE SCURSOR CURSOR FOR
  SELECT SN, SNAME, STATUS, CITY
  FROM   S
  WHERE  SN = SN_IN;
OPEN SCURSOR;
  FETCH SCURSOR INTO SN_SP, SNAME_SP, STATUS_SP, CITY_SP;
CLOSE SCURSOR;
```

DECLARE CONTINUE HANDLER FOR SQLEXCEPTION can be used to continue processing and does not end the procedure. This can be appropriate for character truncation that returns an SQLSTATE = ' 22001' and SQLCODE = -302 or numeric truncation that returns an SQLSTATE = ' 22003' and SQLCODE = -304.

DECLARE ... FOR SQLWARNING is similar to SQLEXCEPTION except it applies only to the '01' class in the first two bytes of the SQLSTATEs. If an error occurs without a defined handler, execution of compound statement is terminated. If NOT ATOMIC (not the default) is specified within a compound statement, rollback does not occur for an error within the compound statement.

WHILE Statement Used with Handler: This example shows the use of the WHILE statement in addition to a handler.

```
DECLARE at_end INT DEFAULT 0;
DECLARE SQLCODE    INTEGER;
DECLARE SQLSTATE   CHAR(5);
DECLARE SCURSOR CURSOR FOR
  SELECT SN, SNAME, STATUS, CITY
  FROM   S
  WHERE  SN = SN_IN;
```

```
OPEN SCURSOR;
WHILE at_end = 0 DO
  FETCH SCURSOR INTO SN_SP, SNAME_SP, STATUS_SP, CITY_SP;
  IF SQLCODE = 100 THEN SET at_end = 1;
    END IF;
END WHILE
```

WHILE causes one or more statements to be executed until a specified condition is true. The example uses WHILE statement to fetch rows until no rows or no more rows are found in which case at_end = 1 and END WHILE is executed.

The ITERATE statement provides for performing statements within a labeled group of statements. Here is an example using a fragment of a CREATE PROCEDURE statement.

```
DECLARE fcount INTEGER DEFAULT 0;
fetch_12_rows: while (fcount <= 12) do
  FETCH SCURSOR INTO SN_SP, SNAME_SP, STATUS_SP, CITY_SP;
SET fcount = fcount + 1;
ITERATE fetch_12_rows;
```

Each component of the example is described. Fetch 12 rows based on a counter established and initialized to 0 with:

DECLARE fcount INTEGER DEFAULT 0;

Label group of statements and test counter:

fetch_12_rows: while (fcount <= 12) do

Execute required statement (can have multiple statements):

FETCH SCURSOR INTO SN_SP, SNAME_SP, STATUS_SP, CITY_SP;

Increment counter by 1:

SET fcount = fcount + 1;

Iterate named group of statements:

ITERATE fetch_12_rows;

The REPEAT statement is the last SQL procedural statement for which an example has not been shown.

```
fetch_s_loop:
REPEAT
  FETCH SCURSOR INTO SN_SP, SNAME_SP, STATUS_SP, CITY_SP;
UNTIL
  SQLCODE <> 0
END REPEAT fetch_s_loop
```

REPEAT can be used to execute one or more statements until a search condition is true. Condition (SQLCODE <> 0, in the example, is tested after execution of each SQL statement (FETCH SCURSOR INTO in the example). If the condition is true, the SQL procedure statement is not executed again.

The GET DIAGNOSTICS statement determines the number of rows effected by the previous INSERT, UPDATE, DELETE statement. (It is retrieved from the third element of the field SQLERRD in the SQLCA.)

Increase the quantity of parts being used on 'J4' by 20 % as an example of the statement:

```
BEGIN
DECLARE nrows INTEGER;
UPDATE SPJ
SET QTY = QTY * 1.2
WHERE JN = 'J4';
GET DIAGNOSTICS nrows = ROW_COUNT;
END
```

The variable "nrows" contains the number of rows updated.

Preparation of SQL Procedures

There are two basic tasks in the preparation of SQL procedures. You must create a load module and package. This is done by preprocessing the CREATE PROCEDURE statement which generates a C language source program. The CREATE PROCEDURE cannot be executed dynamically using SPUFI or QMF, for example. This applies to SQL procedures (not external procedures). JCL or the SPB is required. The C program is precompiled which generates the DBRM member with the coded SQL and the modified C program (discussed in Chapter PE). The DBRM member must be bound into a package.

The second task is to the define the procedure to DB2 done through the execution of the CREATE PROCEDURE statement in V6. If you are using the SPB, the statement is generated and executed automatically for you. In V5, it is necessary to insert a row into the SYSPROCEDURES catalog describing the procedure as described in Section SP.9.

JCL for Preparation of SQL Procedures without the SPB is in the SDSNSAMP library. The member DSNHPSM preprocesses the CREATE PROCEDURE statement. It reads only one statement from a partitioned data set member. It procedures the C language source program The name of the program is the first 8 bytes of SQL procedure name by default. The name of program, DBRM, and C load module must be the same. Do exercise caution if you override the defaults. The JCL produces an INSERT statement for defining the procedure in SYSPROCEDURES when using V5.

The SDSNSAMP library contains a number of useful members:

DSNHSQL contains JCL which preprocesses, precompiles, compiles, prelink-edits, and link-edits an SQL procedure.

DSNTEJ63 contains JCL to invoke JCL procedure DSNHSQL to prepare SQL procedure DSN8ES1 for execution.

DSN8ES1 contains an SQL procedure that accepts a department number as input and returns a result set that contains salary information for each employee in that department.

DSNTEJ64 contains JCL which prepare the client program DSN8ED3 for execution.

DSN8ED3 contains a C program that calls SQL procedure DSN8ES1. It precompiles the C program generated by DSNHPSM which produces the DBRM containing SQL and the modified C language program. It is then necessary to compile and link-edit the modified C program which produces an executable C language program. The DBRM must be bound into a package (not a plan).

The INSERT INTO SYSPROCEDURES statement produced by DSNHPSM must be executed (V5). But before you execute the statement, do modify the statement if required. For example change the LOADMOD name if it was changed from the default.

Stored Procedure Builder

The SPB is useful in creating and managing procedures using the SQL procedure language, Java, or REXX. The GUI interface provides for being prompted to build procedures as well as viewing and edit generated procedure code. A sample SPB screen is shown in Figure SP.7. You can copy and paste stored procedures across connections. Procedures can be run from the SPB with or without customizing settings to enable remote debugging of installed stored procedures. It generates a C program and package through program preparation managed by the SPB. It can run on Windows 2000, NT, 98, 95, AIX, Solaris, OS/2, AS/400, and other platforms in the future.

Figure SP.7. Sample SPB screen

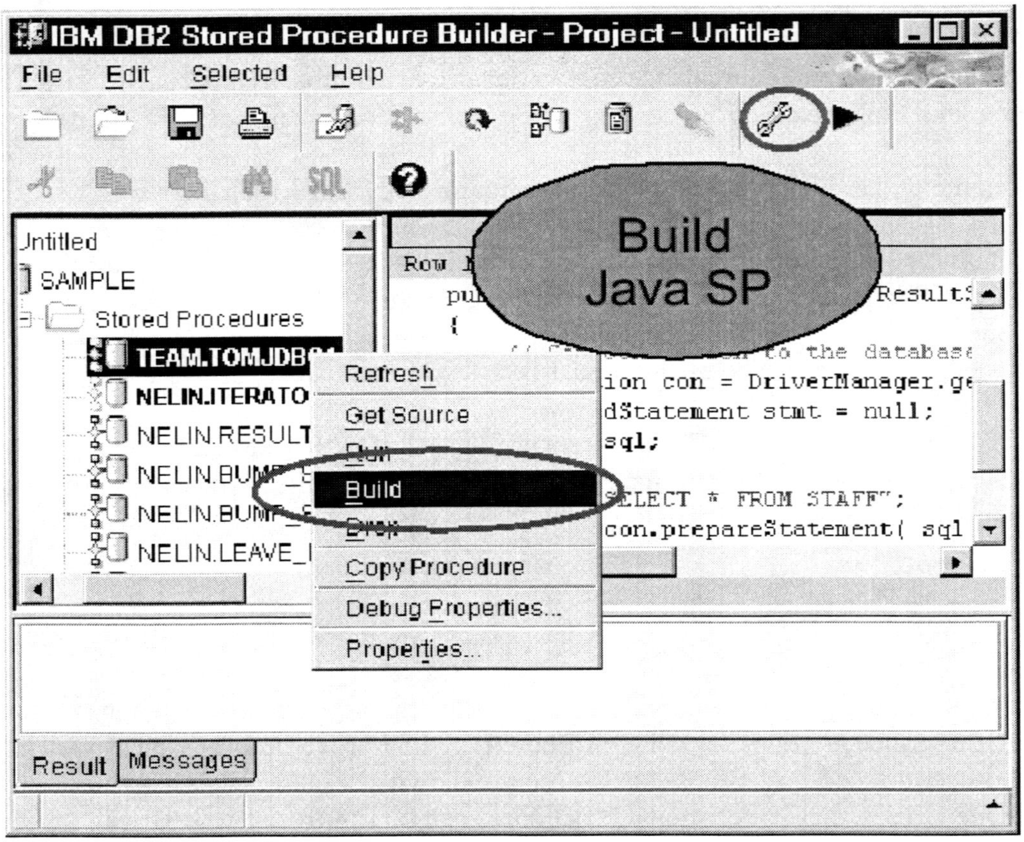

The SPB invokes DSNTPSMP (REXX procedure) using the TSO attach which performs similar steps as described in the previous subsection. DSNTPSMP requires a dedicated WLM-established procedure address space. Do not attempt to run multiple copies of DSNTPSMP concurrently. Optionally, you can use RRSAF (V6 APAR PQ24199). Figure SP.7 is a sample screen used by the SPB.

Optionally, you can use call the DSNTPSMP procedure directly from a program after setting up the environment as described in the V6 APAR PQ30492.

Executing Utilities from a Procedure

Utilities can be executed from an application program by calling the PL/1 DSNUTILS procedure (V5 APAR PQ15684). (The control center uses the procedure to execute utilities.) DSNUTILS must run in a procedure address space managed by WLM. Developers must set call parameters to indicate which utility to execute and provide the required parameters. The utilities are discussed in Chapters LC, RR, and CR. The calling program need not develop JCL for executing utility. DSNUTILS creates the utility statement based on the call parameters which are read from SYSIN by the utility program DSNUTILB. Data set are dynamically allocated.

Example of Setting Parameters and Calling DSNUTILS: Figure SP.8 is an example of a calling program setting parameter values for a reorganization of the DASPJDB.DASPJTSP tablespace. Other parameters not required by the reorganization utility are initialized to ' '.

Figure SP.8. Example of setting DSNUTILS parameters

```
Uid='REORGSPJ',Restart='',Utility='REORG TABLESPACE',
CopyDSN1='SYSADM.COPYDDN.DASPJDB.DASPJTSP',
CopyDEVT1='SYSDA',CopySpace1=10,
Utstmt=
'REORG TABLESPACE DASPJDB.DASPJTSP
 SORTDEVT SYSDA SORTNUM 2
 SHRLEVEL CHANGE
 DEADLINE CURRENT DATE + 1 DAY + 2 HOURS + 30 MINUTES
 MAPPINGTABLE DASPJTSP.MAP_TBL
 MAXRO 240 LONGLOG DRAIN DELAY 900'
```

Figure SP.9 is an example of calling the DSNUTILS procedure.

Figure SP.9. Example of calling DSNUTILS

```
EXEC SQL CALL DSNUTILS(:UID, :RESTART, :UTSTMT, :RETCODE,
:UTILITY, :RECDSN, :RECDEVT, :RECSPACE, :DISCDSN, :DISCDEVT,
:DISCSPACE, :PNCHDSN, :PNCHDEVT, :PNCHSPACE, :COPYDSN1,
:COPYDEVT1, :COPYSPACE1, :COPYDSN2, :COPYDEVT2, :COPYSPACE2,
:RCPYDSN1, :RCPYDEVT1, :RCPYSPACE1, :RCPYDSN2, :RCPYDEVT2,
:RCPYSPACE2, :WORKDSN1, :WORKDEVT1, :WORKSPACE1, :WORKDSN2,
:WORKDEVT2, :WORKSPACE2, :MAPDSN, :MAPDEVT, :MAPSPACE,
:ERRDSN, :ERRDEVT, :ERRSPACE) END-EXEC.
```

The *Utility Guide and Reference* manual has details on the parameters and how to setup the environment to call the DSNUTILS procedure. DSN8EPU in SDSNSAMP contains a sample PL/1 program that calls DSNUTILS. DSNTEJ6U in SDSNSAMP contains sample JCL to prepare and execute DSN8EPU.

Returning Results to Calling Program: The report generated by a utility is written to the SYSIBM.SYSPRINT global temporary table and rows can be fetched from the table by the calling program. The DSNUTILS procedure deletes rows currently in a SYSIBM.SYSPRINT global temporary table instance. It writes the utility output stream (SYSPRINT) to SYSIBM.SYSPRINT global temporary table. Finally, it declares a cursor, opens it, and returns to the calling program like:

```
EXEC SQL DECLARE SYSPRINT CURSOR WITH RETURN FOR
  SELECT * FROM SYSIBM.SYSPRINT
  ORDER BY SEQNO;

EXEC SQL OPEN SYSPRINT;
```

The calling program can now fetch the output from the utility using the SYSPRINT cursor.

SP.10 UPDATING SYSPROCEDURES (V5)

Rows must be inserted into SYSPROCEDURES describing each procedure to be called prior to V6. DB2 only reads this catalog table, it does not maintain it in any way. You can use the INSERT, UPDATE, DELETE statements on the table or LOAD rows as with an application table. Figure SP.10 is a sample INSERT statement to describe the INORUP procedure.

Figure SP.10. Describe a procedure in SYSPROCEDURES

```
INSERT INTO SYSIBM.SYSPROCEDURES
  (PROCEDURE, AUTHID, LUNAME, LOADMOD, LINKAGE,
   COLLID, LANGUAGE, ASUTIME, STAYRESIDENT, IBMREQD,
   RUNOPTS, PARMLIST) VALUES
  ('INORUP', ' ', ' ', 'INORUP', ' ',
   'SPCOLLID', 'COBOL', 0, ' ', 'N', ' ',
   'SN-IN CHAR(2)  IN,  SN CHAR(2) OUT,
    SNAME CHAR(20) OUT, STATUS SMALLINT OUT,
    CITY  CHAR(15) OUT, OPERATION CHAR(6) INOUT,
    SCODE SMALLINT OUT');
```

The columns of SYSPROCEDURES are descriptive of their meaning. The first column, PROCEDURE, must contain the name of the procedure. The AUTHID column can contain the authorization identifier of the caller of the procedure. The example in Figure SP.10 shows the insertion of a blank in the column which indicates that any AUTHID can call the procedure. The LUNAME column is also blank in the example, indicating that the procedure can be called from any location. Multiple rows can be inserted describing a procedure, one for each of many AUTHIDs and LUNAMEs that can call a procedure. The columns PROCEDURE, AUTHID, and LUNAME uniquely identify the rows and make up the primary key of SYSPROCEDURES.

LOADMOD must contain the name of the load module for the procedure. The column can be updated to reflect the version to be used when the procedure is called. LINKAGE of blank means that output parameters can be null but input parameters cannot be null. COLLID contains the name of the collection (SPCOLLID in the example) where the procedure package can be found on the server. LANGUAGE indicates that the procedure is written in COBOL.

The ASUTIME is useful in controlling the amount of CPU time that can be used by host language code plus that used by static SQL and dynamic SQL. The maximum resources that can be used before the procedure is cancelled are given in service units like those specified in the resource limit table (Chapter PP).

STAYRESIDENT of yes is a good choice if the procedure will be executed frequently rather than the default of blank shown in the example. You will probably want the procedure to run above the 16 MB line and can specify this by using the RUNOPTS of HEAP(,,ANY), STACK(,,ANY,),STORAGE(,,,4K),BELOWHEAP(4K,,),LIBSTACK(4K,,),ALL31(ON), linkedit with AMODE(31), RMODE(ANY), and compile a COBOL procedure with RES and DATA(31).

The last column in SP.10, PARMLIST, provides for specifying the names, data types, and lengths of parameters, and whether they are input, output, or both input and output to the procedure as:

- IN (input only to the procedure)
- OUT (output only from the procedure)
- INOUT (input and output to the procedure)

Most data types and lengths can be specified similar to when creating a table (Chapter CT) with some exceptions. DATE, TIME, and TIMESTAMP are *not* valid data type declarations prior to V6. These data types must be declared as CHAR data similar to the data type used for host variables that receive columns from a table. The date and time must have a valid format if the parameter is to be used in an

SQL statement. For example, a valid International Standards Organization (ISO) date format is '1999-04-02'.

More columns can be specified than are shown in the Figure SP.10 example. The RESULT_SETS column allows for specifying the maximum number of result sets that can be returned from the procedure. Procedures are run in a DB2-established procedures address space by default. The WLM_ENV column provides for naming the application environment to be used by the WLM to manage the procedure in one of multiple address spaces. PGM_TYPE provides for specifying that the procedure consists of a subroutine rather the a main program. Development of a procedure as a subroutine or module has performance advantages over developing it as a main program.

EXTERNAL_SECURITY of yes means that a RACF environment will be automatically created by DB2 each time the procedure is invoked so that RACF can manage access to non-SQL resources. The default of no has performance advantages and is a good choice if access to non-SQL resources is not required.

COMMIT_ON_RETURN of yes means that the unit of recovery is automatically committed when control is returned successfully to the calling program. This has performance advantages in that it reduces message traffic and ensures that locks are released in a timely fashion. It reduced the transaction rate from 76.7 to 64.7 transactions per second in one case.

A summary of the column definitions in SYSPROCEDURES is in Figures SP.11 through SP.13.

Figure SP.11. Definition of columns in SYSIBM.SYSPROCEDURES - 1

Column/Data Type	Description
PROCEDURE* CHAR(18) NOT NULL	Name of procedure used in SQL CALL statement.
AUTHID* CHAR(8) NOT NULL WITH DEFAULT	AUTHID of user running the program issuing the SQL CALL. AUTHID after any outbound or inbound translation. blank = Row applies to all AUTHIDs.
LUNAME* CHAR(8) NOT NULL WITH DEFAULT	blank = Row applies to all callers of the procedure (default). Can specify LUNAME of remote or local LUNAME for which this row applies.
LOADMOD** CHAR(8) NOT NULL	Member name of procedure load module.
LINKAGE CHAR(1) NOT NULL WITH DEFAULT	blank = SIMPLE linkage convention is used where input parameters cannot be null. Output parameter can be null. N = SIMPLE WITH NULL, caller can supply null values for any of the parameters defined in PARMLIST (required by SQL procedures).

* PROCEDURE, AUTHID, and LUNAME uniquely identify the row. Multiple rows can be inserted, allowing multiple AUTHIDs and LUNAMEs to call the procedure.

** Procedure version is associated with the load module name. SYSPROCEDURES.LOADMOD can be updated to reflect the version to be used when the procedure is called.

Figure SP.12. Definition of columns in SYSIBM.SYSPROCEDURES - 2

Column/Data Type	Description
COLLID CHAR(18) NOT NULL	Name of package collection containing SQL for the procedure. blank = Uses the same collection name as the calling package or SET CURRENT PACKAGESET collection is used.
LANGUAGE CHAR(8) NOT NULL	'COBOL', 'PLI', 'C', or 'ASSEMBLE' describes the host language used in the procedure.
ASUTIME INTEGER NOT NULL WITH DEFAULT	Maximum number of service units that can be used before the procedure is canceled. Includes CPU time used for host language code, static, and dynamic SQL. 0 = No limit.
STAYRESIDENT CHAR(1) NOT NULL WITH DEFAULT	blank = Load module is deleted from memory after the procedure ends if LE Release 3 is available. 'Y' = Load module remains resident in memory after the procedure ends. Should be reentrant.
IBMREQD CHAR(1) NOT NULL	'Y' = Row came from basic machine readable material (MRM) tape. 'N' = Did not come from MRM.
RUNOPTS*** VARCHAR(254) NOT NULL	blank = Default LE runtime options. 'MSGFILE(OUTFILE), RPTSTG(ON), RPTOPTS(ON)' is an example of LE runtime options.
PARMLIST VARCHAR(3000) NOT NULL	Parameter list expected by the procedure.

*** If program can run above the 16 MB line, use RUNOPTS:

- HEAP(,,ANY),STACK(,,ANY,),STORAGE(,,,4K), BELOWHEAP(4K,,),LIBSTACK(4K,,),ALL31(ON)
- Linkedit with AMODE(31), RMODE(ANY)
- Compile COBOL with RES and DATA(31)

Figure SP.13. Definition of columns in SYSIBM.SYSPROCEDURES - 3

Column/Data Type	Description
RESULT_SETS SMALLINT NOT NULL WITH DEFAULT	Maximum number of result sets that can be returned by this procedure. Default is 0, no results sets will be returned (DB2 and WLM owns).
WLM_ENV CHAR(18) NOT NULL WITH DEFAULT	Blank = Procedure is run in the DB2-established procedures address space (default). Can name application environment with associated JCL to be used for procedure (WLM owns).
PGM_TYPE CHAR(1) WITH DEFAULT 'M'	M = Procedure is a main program (default) and is required for DB2-established address space. S = Procedure is a subroutine and can be used with WLM-established address space (WLM owns).
EXTERNAL_SECURITY CHAR(1) NOT NULL WITH DEFAULT 'N'	N (default) - RACF access to non-SQL resources is not required. Good choice if procedure only accesses SQL objects. Y - RACF environment should be automatically created by DB2 each time the procedure is invoked so that RACF can manage access to non-SQL resources (WLM owns).
COMMIT_ON_RETURN CHAR(1) WITH DEFAULT 'N'	N = UR is not to be committed upon successful return (non-negative SQLCODE) from the procedure (default). Y = UR is to be committed upon successful return (non-negative SQLCODE) from the procedure. Reduces message traffic and ensures that locks are released in a timely fashion (DB2 and WLM owns).

SP.11 PROCEDURE ADDRESS SPACES

In this section we will look at how procedures can run in a single address space established by DB2 or multiple address spaces managed by OS/390 WLM, and how priorities can be assigned. We will also look at the interaction of the caller of a procedure, the DB2 subsystem, and a procedure address space.

DB2-Established Address Space

The DB2-established procedure address space is an allied address space with the name of ssnmSPAS where "ssn" is the DB2 subsystem name, "m" is a subsystem identifier, and "SPAS" represents procedure address space. In this environment, procedures are executed in a FIFO (First-In-First-Out) sequence as they are called under the priority assigned to the ssnmSPAS address space. The systems administrator can start/stop the address space without restarting DB2. If the address space is not explicitly started, DB2 issues an OS/390 START command to activate ssnmSPAS when the first procedure is executed. DB2 START, STOP, and DISPLAY commands can be used to manage procedures and the ssnmSPAS address space. JCL generated during installation can be customized, to include other program libraries, additional DD statements required by procedures, and the region size can be increased from the default of 2048 KB, for example.

Multiple procedures can be run concurrently in the ssnmSPAS address space. If a procedure is to be called from multiple programs, it should be reentrant. (The RENT linkage editor option should be used.) If a procedure is *not* reentrant and STAYRESIDENT = ' ', the load module is loaded for each SQL CALL. This can require an excessive amount of space in the address space.

Eight concurrent task control blocks (TCB) can run procedures by default and a maximum of 1000 can be specified on the installation panel DSNTIPB. You probably want less than 50 procedures running in the address space. Each procedure requires 100 KB of storage below the 16 MB line for each concurrently executing TCB when using LE V3.

Address Spaces Managed by Work Load Manager

Multiple procedure address spaces established and managed by OS/390 WLM have advantages. Multiple address spaces provide for dedicating high priority procedures to an address space with a high priority. A single procedure or group of procedures can be assigned to specific address spaces with the appropriate priority. The assigned priority applies to the execution of host language and SQL code. Procedures can also be isolated so that one procedure does not abend and cause another to abend.

Priority of Procedure Threads

An OS/390 enclave provides for assigning individual dispatching priorities to a single thread or group of threads used by procedures and DDF. (An enclave is a special kind of OS/390 service request block (SRB) that behaves like a TCB.) WLM can be used to assign priorities using goal or compatibility mode. Goal mode provides for defining priorities in terms of the required response time for a given percentage of the time. For example, PROGA should execute in less than two seconds 80 percent of the time. WLM can be used to generate and shut down procedure address spaces based on assigned priorities, the work load, and service classes. When using compatibility mode, the priority is defined in SYS1.PARMLIB using a service class (SRVCLASS) and the systems administrator must manage the address spaces with OS/390 commands. A locally called procedure inherits the priority of the caller (CICS, TSO, etc. for example).

Threads can be classified into different service classes by plan, package, AUTHID and LUNAME, and performance periods can be used. Period aging enables short running work to run at a high priority and long running work drops to a lower priority after using a designated number of service units. For example, assume that the following periods have been assigned the indicated service units:

- Period 1: 100000 service units
- Period 2: 1000000 service units
- Period 3: to end of transaction

Once a task uses 100000 service units, its priority will be dropped until it uses 1000000 services units after which its priority will be dropped again and remain there until the end of the transaction. Do be cautious of continuously active threads, they can go to a higher period and remain there even though there is a good deal of think time on behalf of the user.

Managing WLM Address Spaces

WLM panels are used to associate the application environment name specified in the WLM ENVIRONMENT parameter of the CREATE PROCEDURE statement. OS/390 WLM commands are used to start, stop, and display information on the WLM application environment when using goal mode. OS/390 commands are used to manage the address spaces when compatibility mode is used. DB2 commands are used to start, stop, and display information on procedures within the environment.

It is advisable is avoid having WLM create too many procedure address spaces by minimizing the number of WLM environments and OS/390 service classes. WLM creates an address space for each combination of WLM environment name and service class when a procedure is executed unless a particular environment or service class is not used for a long period of time. For example, if there are seven environment names and each one has four possible service classes, and all of the combinations are used, it is possible to have 28 procedure address spaces.

Interaction of Address Spaces

There are a number of steps required to execute a procedure as summarized in Figure SP.14 Each of these steps is described assuming a DB2-established procedure address space.

Figure SP.14. Interaction of address spaces

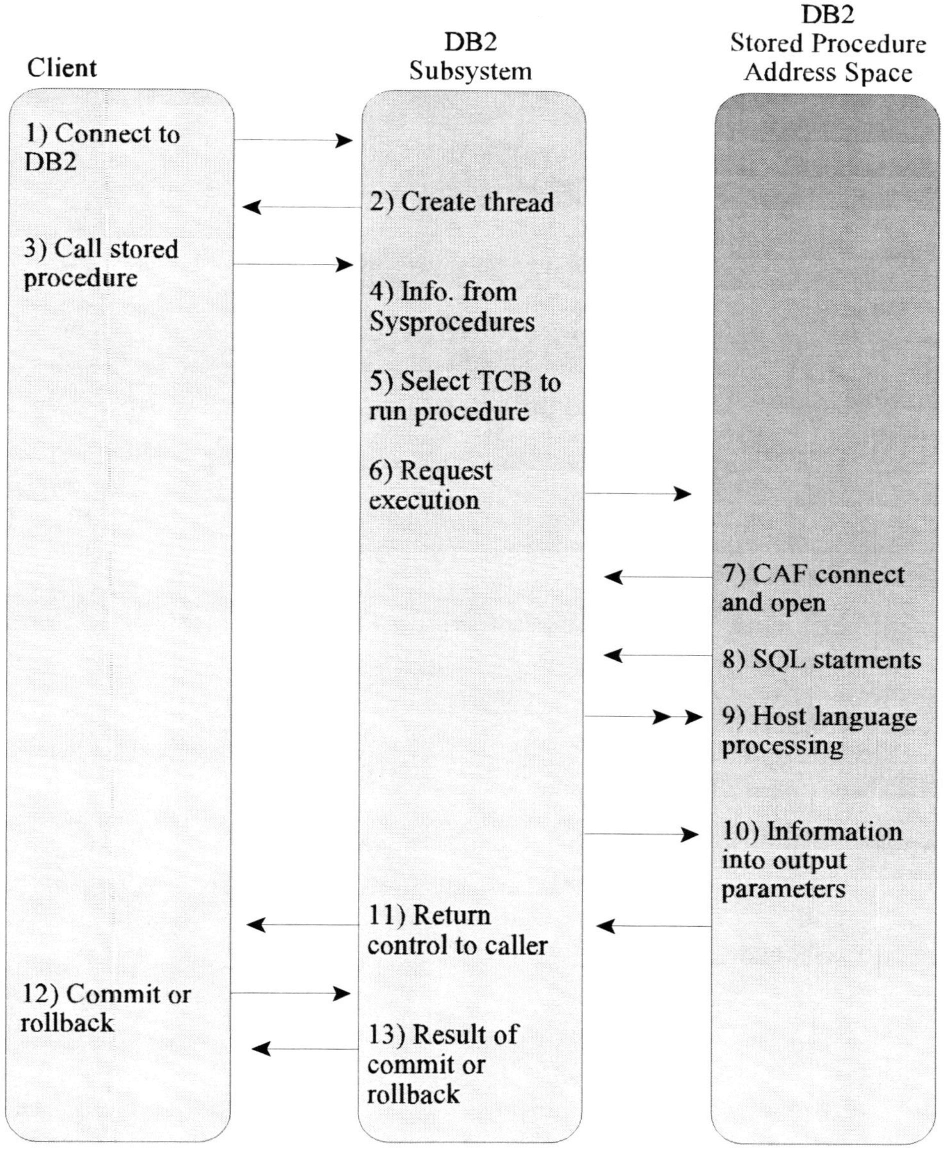

1) A connection between the caller at the client site and the DB2 subsystem is established.

2) A thread is created for the execution of the procedure.

3) A request to run the procedure is made to DB2 based on the SQL CALL issued by the client.

4) DB2 gets information about the procedure from the SYSROUTINES and SYSPARMS catalog tables as placed there by the developer. The information is cached to avoid further access to the table. DB2 verifies that the client is authorized to execute the package associated with the procedure.

5) An OS/390 TCB is selected under which to run the procedure.

6) DB2 requests execution of the procedure.

7) The procedure attach code issues a CAF CONNECT to the DB2 subsystem and opens (allocates) the package.

8) The SQL statements in the procedure are executed in DB2 alternating with host language code in step 9).

9) The host language code in the procedure receives results from DB2 and executes alternating with SQL statement execution in step 8).

10) The SQL CALL parameters are filled and the results returned to the client program.

11) Control is returned from the procedure to DB2 and the client program. All cursors opened by procedure are closed. (Cursors can be left open for fetching by the client when using WITH RETURN and WLM procedure address spaces.) Working storage used by the procedure is reclaimed.

12) The client program issues a commit or rollback which applies to SQL issued in the procedure and any SQL issued directly by the client program as a UR.

13) The result of the commit or rollback is returned to client program. This last message can be eliminated when using WLM address spaces and COMMIT ON RETURN of yes in the CREATE PROCEDURE statement.

If the procedure abends, a -935 SQLCODE is returned to the client and the client's UR is rolled back.

Data is returned to the client program using block fetch. Block fetch means that up to 32 KB of data is accumulated, formatted, and transmitted to the client. In order to use block fetch, the cursor must be read-only or ambiguous with CURRENTDATA of NO specified with a bind. The effect of OPTIMIZE FOR *n* ROWS is discussed in Chapter PD.

Timeout of a Client

A distributed user (thread) which is inactive, holding a lock, and has not committed can be timed out by specifying a timeout period in seconds on the installation panel DSNTIPR (no timeout is the default). If the specified time limit is exceeded, a rollback occurs and all resources are released. This does not apply to an inactive thread that is not holding a lock and indoubt threads. If a requester thread is terminated, DB2 effectively issues a -CANCEL DDF THREAD command. This avoids using resources to derive results that cannot be transmitted to the requester.

SP.12 COMMANDS FOR CONTROLLING PROCEDURES

DB2 START, STOP, and DISPLAY commands are used to manage procedures. These commands are also used to manage the DB2-established procedure address space. OS/390 WLM commands are used to manage WLM procedure address spaces with goal mode. OS/390 commands are used with compatibility mode. In this section we will describe the DB2 commands used to manage procedures in any address space and in the DB2-established procedure address space.

START Command

A -START command can be used to start a procedure like:

```
-START PROCEDURE (INORUP, SPJ*)
```

Specific procedures can be listed, or leading characters of procedures (SPJ*, for example) can be used, or '*.*' can be used to indicate that all procedures are to be started. Optionally, you can specify the schema or qualifier (GKWADM.INORUP, for example)

It is not necessary to start a procedure. A procedure is started automatically when it is called regardless of whether it is a newly defined procedure or one that has existed for some time.

The -START command causes DB2 to read SYSROUTINES and SYSPARMS (SYSPROCEDURES in V5) , and cache information for the identified procedures and mark the procedures as available to be called. It also causes any queued requests waiting for the procedures to execute. The START command is useful for refreshing a cached procedure after it has been modified. You may also want to start frequently executed procedures after starting DB2 to avoid the overhead of caching the information from the catalog tables when the procedures are first called. Another reason for using the -START command is to activate a stopped procedure.

The START command does not refresh LE when using WLM-established address spaces. The use of the following command refreshes the LE environment and load module. This applies to UDF as well.

```
MVS VARY WLM,APPLENV=applenv,REFRESH
```

Additional commands for managing WLM-established address spaces are described in the *Administration Guide* manual.

STOP Command

Procedures can be stopped using a format similar to the -START command -- specific procedures can be named or "*" can be used. Any currently running, queued, and scheduled procedures will complete execution. Here is an example of stopping the INORUP procedure.

```
-STOP PROCEDURE(INORUP) ACTION(QUEUE)
```

The ACTION(QUEUE) parameter means that all requests to execute the procedure will be queued for 180 seconds by default. If this does not give adequate time to make required changes, the timeout value can be made more generous -- up to 1800 seconds or no limit can be specified on the installation panel DSNTIPX or DSNZPARM STORMXAB. The -START command can be used to start the procedure at any time.

If it is necessary to stop the procedure without queuing requests, the ACTION(REJECT) parameter can be used to reject all requests for the procedure.

It may be necessary to stop a procedure that is not running correctly, to add or replace a procedure load module, or to allow for compression of the load library.

If a procedure exceeds the abend count specified on the installation panel DSNTIPX, calls to the procedure will be rejected. The abend count is 0 by default with a maximum of 225. The first abend of a procedure results in additional calls being rejected until the procedure is explicitly started. This may be appropriate in a production environment but is rather severe in a test environment. Some one will receive a good many calls to start a procedure that has abended during initial testing. Do consider increasing the count, particularly in a test environment.

Permanently Stopping a Procedure: The -STOP command does not permanently stop a procedure. If DB2 is stopped and started, a procedure that has been stopped can be executed. Permanently stopping a procedure can be accomplished by dropping the procedure, altering the EXTERNAL NAME (name of load module), or renaming or deleting the load module from load library.

DISPLAY Command

Information about procedures can be determined by using the -DISPLAY command like:

```
-DISPLAY PROCEDURE (*)
```

One can name specific procedures or use "*" as with the -START and -STOP command.

Figure SP.15 is an example of the results of the -DISPLAY commands.

Figure SP.15. Example Result of -DISPLAY PROCEDURE (*)

```
DSNX940I csect - DISPLAY PROCEDURE REPORT FOLLOWS -
PROCEDURE  MODULE    STATUS   ACTIVE   MAXACT  QUEUED  MAXQUE TIMEOUT
SPJSP01    SPJMOD01  STARTED       0        1       0       1       0
SPJSP02    SPJMOD02  STOPQUE       0        2       5       5       3
SPJSP03    SPJMOD03  STARTED       2        2       0       6       0
SPJSP04    SPJMOD04  STOPREJ       0        1       0       1       0
PROCEDURES A THROUGH Z99999999999999999 HAVE BEEN STOPPED WITH
  ACTION(QUEUE)
DISPLAY PROCEDURE REPORT COMPLETE

Brief description of each column in the report:

  PROCEDURE = Name of procedure
  MODULE = Name of load module
  STATUS = Started, stopped and queued, stopped and rejected
  ACTIVE = Number of threads currently running the load module
  MAXACT = Maximum number of threads that have run the load
           module concurrently since DB2 was started
  QUEUED = Number of threads that are waiting for the
           procedure to be scheduled
  MAXQUE = Maximum number of threads that have waited
           concurrently for the procedure to be scheduled
           since DB2 was started
  TIMEOUT= Number of times an SQL CALL statement timed out
           while waiting for a request for the procedure
           to be scheduled
```

The -DISPLAY THREAD command also provides information on procedures. SW means that the thread is waiting for a procedure to be scheduled. SP means that the thread is executing within a procedure.

SP.13 SUMMARY

A primary advantage of a procedure is to reduce the number of messages transmitted in a client/server environment. Another significant advantage of procedures is the ability of manage client processes centrally and minimize maintenance at client sites.

Procedures are straightforward to develop because the same host languages can be used as in developing any host program with embedded SQL statements. Cursors can be defined and opened in a procedure, and fetched from the calling program in any order after a locator host variable is declared, associated, and allocated for each cursor. The calling program controls the UR. A COMMIT or ROLLBACK statement applies to all SQL in the calling program and a number of called procedures at many locations within a UR.

The SPB is a good choice for those not versed in host languages and for quickly developing a procedure and getting it in production.

Multiple address spaces can be managed by WLM or a DB2-established address space can be used.

START, STOP, and DISPLAY commands provide for managing procedures. Commands used for managing the procedure address spaces depends on the environment.

EXERCISES

1. What are two primary advantages of procedures?

2. What are the differences in developing a procedure and preparing it compared to a subroutine or module?

3. What are the differences in calling a procedure compared to calling a subroutine or module?

4. Can a COMMIT or ROLLBACK statement be successfully executed in a procedure? Why?

5. What is a primary prerequisite to ensure that all changes to DB2 tables, DL/1 databases, recoverable VSAM files, and MQSeries messages are made or no changes are made when a COMMIT statement is executed?

6. Are there any restrictions on selecting and changing rows in a global temporary table compared to a base table?

7. Why should null indicator variables be used in the parameter list of an SQL CALL statement?

8. How does one specify that a procedure is to be executed in a WLM procedure address space?

9. ASUTIME in SYSROUTINES provides for limiting the number of service units used for what type of processing in a procedure?

10. If a procedure abends, how is the client program notified?

11. The START, STOP, and DISPLAY DB2 commands are used to manage which resources?

ANSWERS

1. The two primary advantages of procedures are to reduce network traffic and provide for managing client processes centrally.

2. There are very few differences in developing a procedure and preparing it compared to a subroutine or module. The differences are that a cursor should not be closed before the procedure ends when using WITH RETURN, it is necessary to describe the procedure to DB2 using the CREATE PROCEDURE statement, and it is necessary to bind the SQL into a package (not a plan).

3. There are basically no differences between calling a procedure compared to calling a subroutine or module with the exceptions that it is necessary to use an EXEC SQL CALL rather than a CALL statement and the procedure name is a three part name (location, server name, and procedure name).

4. COMMIT and ROLLBACK statements cannot be successfully executed in a procedure. This is to ensure that the caller has control over the UR. When the caller issues a COMMIT or ROLLBACK, the work is done in all called procedures at possibly multiple sites or none of them.

5. A primary prerequisite to ensure that all changes to DB2 tables, DL/1 databases, recoverable VSAM files, and MQSeries messages are made or no changes are made is the use of WLM procedure address spaces.

6. There are no restrictions on selecting rows in a global temporary table compared to a base table. Rows can be inserted into a temporary table. Specific rows identified in a WHERE clause cannot be deleted from a temporary table although all rows can be deleted without a WHERE clause. Rows cannot be updated in a temporary table although a temporary table can be referenced in the WHERE clause of an UPDATE statement on a base table.

7. Message traffic can be reduced by specifying a null indicator variable when values are frequently not specified for a parameter in the SQL CALL statement. If the null indicator variable is a negative value, DB2 does not transmit the content of the parameter.

8. The fact that a procedure is to be executed in a WLM procedure address space is specified by naming the application environment using the WLM ENVIRONMENT parameter of the CREATE PROCEDURE statement.

9. ASUTIME in SYSROUTINES provides for limiting the total number of service units used for host language code, static SQL, and dynamic SQL.

10. If a procedure abends, the client program is notified with a negative SQLCODE (-935).

11. The START, STOP, and DISPLAY DB2 commands are used to manage procedures in any address space.

FIGURES

User Defined Functions

UD.1 INTRODUCTION

User-defined functions (UDF) provide for developing frequently required functions that can be invoked for any SQL data manipulation statement. There are three types of user-defined functions (UDF) in V6.

1) **Sourced user-defined functions** are created based on existing functions. Sourced UDF are used primarily for management of distinct types (also known as user-defined data types and strong typing) as discussed in Chapters CT and PD)

2) **External scalar user-defined scalar functions** are implemented using a host language to perform the defined function. They are used to develop functions similar to built-in scalar functions like SUBSTR, CONCAT, STRIP, etc. Only one value is returned.

3) **External table functions** are similar to external UDF except that the table functions can return multiple columns (a table) one row at a time to the invoking SQL statement.

How to create and use the functions are described in this chapter.

UD.2 SOURCED USER-DEFINED FUNCTIONS

The purpose of sourced UDF is to provide for arithmetic operations on distinct types without having to use cast functions to designate a column, literal, or host variable as a particular distinct type. We will see how to create and use sourced UDF in this section.

An attempt to increase employee salaries in work department D11 by 20 percent will fail without the use of a sourced UDF or cast function. It is not possible to do an arithmetic operation on a column defined with a distinct type of US_DOLLAR and a literal or host variable.

```
UPDATE EMP
  SET   SALARY    = SALARY * 1.20
  WHERE WORKDEPT = 'D11';
```

A sourced function can be defined using existing built-in or external UDFs (except an external table function). They can be used to define infix operators (||, /, *, +, -) for distinct types. This avoids having to cast distinct types to their source to do arithmetic operations as described in Chapter CT. In addition, sourced functions are useful for supporting the use of built-in column and scalar functions for distinct types. Following is an example of creating a sourced function named "*" to allow multiplication of columns defined with a distinct type of US_DOLLAR. The input to the function are two values defined with the distinct type of US_DOLLAR and the results is in US_DOLLAR. The source of the function is SYSIBM."*" which indicates the usual multiplication operation used for built-in data types.

```
CREATE   FUNCTION "*"(US_DOLLAR,US_DOLLAR)
RETURNS  US_DOLLAR
SOURCE   SYSIBM."*"(DECIMAL(9,2),DECIMAL(9,2));
```

After successfully creating the sourced function, you can now successfully execute:

```
UPDATE EMP
  SET   SALARY    = SALARY * US_DOLLAR(1.20)
  WHERE WORKDEPT = 'D11';
```

Notice that the literal of 1.20 or a host variable must be cast to the distinct type of US_DOLLAR.

If you prefer not to create a sourced UDF, the SALARY can be increased by 20 percent by casting SALARY to decimal which matches the 1.20 literal (or host variable) built-in data type.

```
UPDATE EMP
  SET   SALARY    = DECIMAL(SALARY) * 1.20
  WHERE WORKDEPT = 'D11';
```

The SOURCE clause in the CREATE FUNCTION statement provides for specifying which built-in function the new function should use. Sourced functions can have the same name as the function upon which it is sourced as in the previous and next example. The function signature is used to determined which function to use as described in more detail later. Part of the signature consists of the number of input parameters for the function and their source must be compatible. If the data type and length differ, the lower level value must be promotable to the higher level value. For example, SMALLINT is promotable to INTEGER but DECIMAL(9,2) is not promotable to SMALLINT. The returned value must have a data type and length greater than or equal the input parameters. The SOURCE parameter does not apply to UDF scalar functions discussed in Section UD.4.

It is necessary to cast a distinct type (Euro) to a built-in data type (decimal) to use the TRUNCATE function as in the following example. The example assumes that a fraction of a Euro is not paid for commissions.

```
SELECT TRUNCATE(DECIMAL(COMM),0)
FROM   EMP
WHERE  EMPNO = '00200';
```

Use of Built-in Functions with Distinct Types

If you want to use of a built-in function on a column declared with a distinct type without receiving a -440 SQLCODE (no function by the name AVG having compatible arguments was found in the current path), it is necessary to create a sourced function for use on a column defined with a sourced data type. For example, if you want to compute the average salary of employees where the SALARY column is defined with a distinct type of US_DOLLAR, it is necessary to create a sourced function like:

```
CREATE   FUNCTION AVG(US_DOLLAR)
RETURNS  US_DOLLAR
SOURCE   SYSIBM.AVG(DECIMAL(9,2));
```

Now you can successfully compute the average SALARY with a distinct type of US_DOLLAR like:

```
SELECT AVG(SALARY)
FROM   EMP;
```

An alternative is to cast SALARY declared as US_DOLLAR to DECIMAL before using a function expecting a built-in data type like:

```
SELECT SUM(DECIMAL(SALARY))
FROM   EMP;
```

Distinct Types in the Catalog Tables

You can describe distinct types in the SYSDATATYPES catalog table with the COMMENT ON statement like:

```
COMMENT ON DISTINCT TYPE US_DOLLAR IS
 'SALARY IN US DOLLARS';
```

You can determine distinct types created by GKWADM like:

```
SELECT SCHEMA, OWNER, NAME, CREATEDBY,
  SOURCESCHEMA, SOURCETYPE, METATYPE,
  DATATYPEID, SOURCETYPEID, LENGTH,
  SCALE, SUBTYPE, CREATEDTS,
  ENCODING_SCHEME, IBMREQD, REMARKS
FROM   SYSIBM.SYSDATATYPES
WHERE  OWNER = 'GKWADM';
```

Here are the results.

SCHEMA	OWNER	NAME	CREATEDBY	SOURCESCHEMA	SOURCETYPE
GKWADM	GKWADM	US_DOLLAR	GKWADM	SYSIBM	DECIMAL
GKWADM	GKWADM	EURO	GKWADM	SYSIBM	DECIMAL

METATYPE	DATATYPEID	SOURCETYPEID	LENGTH	SCALE	SUBTYPE
T	-2147483647	484	9	2	
T	-2147483646	484	9	2	

CREATEDTS	ENCODING_SCHEME	IBMREQD	REMARKS
1999-09-01-20.43.03.299938		N	SALARY IN US DOLLARS
1999-09-01-20.43.44.092621		N	SALARY IN EURO

UD.3 COMPARISON OF SOURCED AND EXTERNAL FUNCTIONS

Column and scalar functions are supplied with DB2. You can create sourced functions similar to column functions. Column functions accept as input one or more values in a column, for example

AVG, SUM, MIN, MAX, COUNT. If no values qualify, a null is returned. External functions must be created like scalar functions (not column functions). Scalar functions accept as input a single value for each argument, for example SUBSTR, CONCAT, STRIP, etc. (over 100). Both column and scalar functions return a single value.

UDF can be used anywhere that built-in functions can be used in SELECT, INSERT, UPDATE, and DELETE statements. Do be cautious of using a UDF in a WHERE clause. This is because different results can be obtained if the optimizer chooses to use parallelism, for example. The DETERMINISTIC parameter discussed in Section UD.6 can be used to ensure that each invocation of a UDF returns the same results (disallows parallelism).

Invocation of an external scalar or column function can include:

- Host variable, constant, special register, qualified or unqualified column name
- Operators (+, -, *, /, ||, CONCAT)
- Scalar function
- CASE expression
- CAST specification with or without a parameter marker

UDF can be invoked from an SQL statement embedded in a stand-alone program, a stored procedure (discussed in Chapter SP), a trigger body (discussed in Chapter TR), another user-defined function, and interactively.

UD.4 EXTERNAL SCALAR USER-DEFINED FUNCTIONS

External UDF scalar functions are like scalar functions provided by DB2 in that the UDF name is followed by one or more arguments (also called operands) within parenthesis. Each argument can be specified as an expression. The result is a single value.

External functions are written in a host language (COBOL, PL/1, C, or Assembler) unlike sourced UDFs which are developed based on existing functions. Most operations performed in an application program can be performed in an external function including the use of embedded static and dynamic SQL. An exception is that a COMMIT and ROLLBACK cannot be successfully executed in the function. However, SAVEPOINT statements can be used as discussed in Chapter SP. An external function can be used to perform external actions. The function can issue I/O to files, send email messages, and more.

UDF programs go through program preparation like any application program. They do require the use of a package if the UDF contains SQL. UDF must run in a WLM (Work Load Manager) established address space (not DB2-established procedure address space).

Defining External UDF

The CREATE FUNCTION statement is used to establish a UDF. Here is an example of a function to convert US dollars to Euro based on an EXCHANGE_RATE table. Basically the function converts from one distinct type (US_DOLLAR) to another distinct type (EURO).

```
CREATE FUNCTION US_TO_EURO(AMOUNT US_DOLLAR)
RETURNS EURO
EXTERNAL NAME 'USTOEURO'
LANGUAGE COBOL
WLM ENVIRONMENT WLMENVCU
PARAMETER STYLE DB2SQL;
```

The function can be invoked by its name of US_TO_EURO. It receives one value in US dollars. The parameter name of AMOUNT is optional. The data type of input and output parameters of UDF are required. US_DOLLAR is the input data type and EURO is the output data type in the example.

The EXTERNAL NAME of USTOEURO is the name of the load module of the host program written in COBOL as indicated by the LANGUAGE parameters. The USTOEURO program must be developed and prepared like any application program. The additional parameters in the example as well as more parameters that can be specific are covered in Section UD.6.

The external function reads an exchange rate table and does the required calculations, for example:

```
EURO       = US_DOLLAR * RATE where RATE = 0.970204 in table
97.0204    = 100       * 0.970204
```

This means that 97.0204 Euro are received for 100.00 US dollars.

Using UDF with Distinct Types

Only values declared as US_DOLLAR can be input to the US_TO_EURO function. A literal or host variable must be cast to US_DOLLAR before invoking the UDF. Here is an example to determine employees whose COMM in Euro is greater than their SALARY in US dollars or US$20,000.00.

```
SELECT EMPNO, LASTNAME
FROM   EMP
WHERE  COMM > US_TO_EURO(SALARY)
OR     COMM > US_TO_EURO(US_DOLLAR(20000.00));
```

COMM in Euro is compared to SALARY after salary is converted to Euro by the US_TO_EURO UDF. The 20,000.00 literal needs to be designated as US dollars.

UNION and UNION ALL requires that unioned columns have the same distinct type assuming distinct type columns are selected. UDF can be used to UNION US_DOLLAR with EURO. This requires the conversion of US dollars to EURO or vice versa. The resulting unioned columns must have the same distinct type.

UDF to Calculate the Total Amount Paid for a Loan

This UDF function to demonstrate additional features and uses of external scalar function is also useful in personal life. Most of us have a mortgage on our home, car, and other items. We will develop a function to determine the total amount paid for buying a home where the total retail price is financed as a loan. Assume that the facts of the loan are:

- The loan is $100,000.
- The interest is 0.08.
- The payment period is 30 years

The formula for calculating the total amount paid for the loan is:

```
TOTAL_AMOUNT = LOAN    *INTEREST *YEARS / (1-(1 + INTEREST / 12)**(-12 * YEARS))
264,155.25 = 100,000 *0.08      * 30    / (1-(1 + 0.08      / 12)**(-12 * 30))
```

Here is the CREATE FUNCTION statement for a UDF to calculate total amount paid.

```
CREATE FUNCTION TOTAL_AMOUNT(LOAN DECIMAL(9,2),
  INTEREST DECIMAL(9,3), YEARS SMALLINT)
RETURNS DECIMAL(9,2)
EXTERNAL NAME 'TOTALAMT'
SPECIFIC TOTALAMT
LANGUAGE COBOL
WLM ENVIRONMENT WLMENVCU
PARAMETER STYLE DB2SQL;
```

UDF requires that a COBOL (LANGUAGE) program with a load module of TOTALAMT (EXTERNAL NAME) be developed and prepared to perform the calculations. The LANGUAGE parameter can be COBOL, PLI, C, or ASSEMBLE. The SPECIFIC parameter provides for assigning a name that can be used in managing functions as discussed in Section UD.6. The example uses a specific name which is the same as the load module name. This is not a requirement. It simply reduces the total number of names to deal with.

Alternatives for Invoking a UDF from a Host Program

UDF can be invoked using the SET, VALUES, and SQL statements from a host program. The SET and VALUES statements cannot be used interactively because a host variable is required to receive the results.

The SET statement can be used to assign the results of the UDF to a host variable. Either host variables or literals can be used as arguments to the function as in the following two examples.

```
EXEC SQL SET :TARESULT = TOTAL_AMOUNT(:LOAN,:INTEREST,
  :YEARS) END-EXEC.

EXEC SQL SET :TARESULT = TOTAL_AMOUNT(100000.00, 0.08, 30)
  END-EXEC.
```

The VALUES statement is functionally the same as the SET statement. It differs in syntax. Notice in the following example that the UDF is invoked within parenthesis following the keyword VALUES. The INTO clause is used to specify the host variable to receive the results. Like the SET statement the arguments of the UDF can be host variables or literals.

```
EXEC SQL VALUES(TOTAL_AMOUNT(:LOAN, :INTEREST, :YEARS))
         INTO   :TARESULT END-EXEC.

EXEC SQL VALUES(TOTAL_AMOUNT(100000.00, 0.08, 30))
```

```
                INTO   :TARESULT END-EXEC.
```

Of course, the UDF can be invoked from a SELECT, INSERT, UPDATE, and DELETE statement embedded in a host program as has been seen earlier in this chapter. However, this is the only way to invoke a UDF interactively. If the goal is to determine the total amount paid for a loan interactively, you can select from a one row table like:

```
SELECT TOTAL_AMOUNT(100000.00, 0.08, 30)
FROM   SYSIBM.SYSDUMMY1;
```

Abend of an Invoked UDF

If an invoked UDF abends, a -430 SQLCODE is issued. The UR (Unit of Recovery) that contains the invoking SQL statement is placed in a must-rollback state.

Explanation of CREATE FUNCTION Statement

The CREATE FUNCTION statement registers a UDF in the catalog table SYSROUTINES. Cast functions and stored procedures are also described in SYSROUTINES. The name of UDF can be <= 18 bytes (TOTAL_AMOUNT in the previous example) plus 8 or fewer bytes for a schema or qualifier name as the qualifier. SYSIBM is the schema name of DB2 provided functions. Creation and usage of schemas are discussed in Chapter CO.

Signature of a function uniquely identifies the function. It is used by DB2 to locate the correct function to execute when a UDF is invoked. It consists of the schema or qualifier name, function name, number of parameters, and the data type of the first 30 or fewer parameters. The signature must uniquely identify the UDF at the current server. The data type length, precision, scale, subtype, or encoding scheme attributes are not used to uniquely identify a UDF. For example, CHAR(10) and CHAR(20) are considered the same as are DECIMAL(8,2), DECIMAL(4,3), and NUMERIC(9,4). Details on locating the correct function is in the *SQL Reference* manual.

If the qualifier is not explicitly specified when creating a UDF, the schema or qualifier name and ownership are assigned as with the creation of triggers as discussed in Chapter TR. The qualifier cannot begin with SYS except it can begin with SYSADM. A UDF can be invoked with or without its schema or qualifier name. This is because the signature is used to determine which function to use.

The CREATE FUNCTION statement can be embedded in an application program or issued interactively. It can be dynamically prepared only from a package or plan bound with DYNAMICRULES(RUN).

Data Types of Input and Output Parameters

The data type of one or more arguments passed to a UDF follow the UDF name in parenthesis. Optionally, each argument can be given a name. The arguments can be a distinct type as in the US_TO_EURO example or built-in data type as in the TOTAL_AMOUNT example. However, they are passed as a built-in data types to be manipulated by the host program that constitutes the UDF.

Date/time data type parameters are passed as character data types in ISO format as described in Chapter CT.

Do specify the length for data type types that require a length, otherwise defaults are used:

- ♦ CHAR(1) is used if CHAR is specified.
- ♦ GRAPHIC(1) is used if GRAPHIC is specified.
- ♦ DECIMAL(5,0) is used if DECIMAL is specified.
- ♦ FLOAT DOUBLE has a length of 8 bytes.

It is necessary to use VARCHAR or VARGRAPHIC with an explicit length rather than LONG VARCHAR or LONG VARGRAPHIC.

The CCSID of EBCDIC is the default. You can specify the CCSID of ASCII but do keep in mind that an SQL statement must reference all EBCDIC or ASCII data.

UDF Privileges

Creation of a UDF can be done by a person with SYSADM or SYSCTRL authority or CREATEIN for the schema. The AUTHID that matches the schema name implicitly has the CREATEIN privilege. It is necessary to have privileges on the objects manipulated by SQL in a UDF as with any host program.

In order for others to use UDF, privileges are granted similar to the grant of privileges on the usage of a package except that the FUNCTION parameter is required. Here is an example to allow the public to use the US_TO_EURO function.

```
GRANT EXECUTE ON FUNCTION US_TO_EURO TO PUBLIC;
```

Optionally, you can specify specific name:

```
GRANT EXECUTE ON SPECIFIC FUNCTION USTOEURO TO PUBLIC;
```

Another option is to specify the data type of input parameters as well as the name of the input parameter like:

```
GRANT EXECUTE ON FUNCTION US_TO_EURO(AMOUNT US_DOLLAR)
  TO PUBLIC;
```

If there is more than one function named TOTAL_AMOUNT in a schema, it is necessary to specify the specific name or input parameters in the GRANT statement. Otherwise, -476 SQLCODE (reference to function GKWADM.TOTAL_AMOUNT was named without a signature, but the function is not unique within its schema) is issued when attempting to execute the GRANT statement. This applies to all references to a UDF except invocation of a function.

It is also necessary to grant execute privileges on the package that is created through program preparation as discussed in Section UD.7 like:

```
GRANT EXECUTE ON PACKAGE USTOEURO TO FLEUR; -- or PUBLIC
```

If the invoking package or plan contains static SQL, the AUTHID of invoking package owner is used to determine if the target package can be executed. If embedded dynamic SQL is used as the invoker and the package is bound with DYNAMICRULES(INVOKEBIND), the AUTHID that executes the statement must have execute privileges on the target package. Additional DYNAMICRULES parameters are available to control privileges.

Privileges in the catalog tables can be determined like:

```
SELECT GRANTOR, NAME, DATEGRANTED
FROM   SYSIBM.SYSRESAUTH
WHERE  OBTYPE  = 'D'
AND    GRANTEE = 'PUBLIC';
```

The results will include privileges on UDF, distinct types, cast functions, and stored procedures granted to the public.

The SYSPACKAUTH has information on AUTHIDs that have privileges to execute UDF and stored procedure packages as for all packages.

SYSROUTINES has detailed information including information on the parameter values specified when cast functions, user-defined functions, and stored procedures are created. The following statement gives you summary information on all existing UDF and cast function. If you need information on stored procedures as well, replace WHERE ROUTINETYPE='F' with WHERE ROUTINETYPE IN ('F', 'P'). You will want to add or replace some of the columns selected.

```
SELECT SCHEME, NAME, FUNCTION_TYPE, PARM_COUNT
FROM   SYSIBM.SYSROUTINES
WHERE  ROUTINETYPE='F';
```

UD.5 TABLE USER-DEFINED FUNCTIONS

A table function returns a table, one row at a time, based on one or more arguments it receives. Each input argument supplies one value (not a table). They are useful for applying SQL to non-DB2 data. The table function host program can read and process data from any source (file or WWW (World Wide Web), for example). Returned rows are processed like rows from a base table named in the FROM clause of the invoking SQL statement. A table function can only be referenced in the FROM clause. The UDF host program receives arguments and return results through an internal DB2 buffer. It must be an external UDF (not sourced or built-in functions).

Parameters for creating UDF external and table functions are the same as described in Section UD.6 except RETURNS TABLE and CARDINALITY are valid only for user-defined table functions. MODIFIES SQL DATA, ALLOW PARALLEL, and CAST FROM are valid only for external scalar UDF.

Creation and Usage of UDF Table Function

Order processing tables like those in Chapter TR are used to provide more realistic examples of table function processing. Assume that a function is required to return a row from a VSAM file for each item purchased by a given customer.

```
CREATE  FUNCTION CUST_ITEMS(CUSTNO INTEGER)
RETURNS TABLE (ITEMNO     INTEGER,
               TOTAL_COST DECIMAL(9,2),
               ORDER_DATE DATE,
               SHIP_DATE  DATE)
EXTERNAL NAME 'CUSTITEM'
CARDINALITY 20
LANGUAGE COBOL
WLM ENVIRONMENT WLMENVCU
PARAMETER STYLE DB2SQL;
```

A COBOL program needs to be developed with a load module name of CUSTITEM (EXTERNAL NAME) to read an ORDER file and returns a row for each item purchased by the given customer to the invoking SQL statement. The RETURNS TABLE clause defines the name (optional) and data type (required) of columns to be returned from the table function. Notice that four values are returned for each row (ITEMNO, TOTAL_COST, ORDER_DATE, and SHIP_DATE. In contrast, an external scalar UDF can return only one value. A returned column can be a result of calculated values. TOTAL_COST is calculated as UNIT_COST * QTY in the UDF host program (CUSTITEM), for example.

The CARDINALITY parameter has a value of 20. This informs the optimizer that 20 rows are expected to be returned from the UDF table function. The value can be 0 to 2,147,483,647. The cardinality is useful to the optimizer in determining the inner and outer table of a join and which join type should be used, for example. If CARDINALITY is specified without a value, the optimizer estimates the number of rows based on default statistics. If CARDINALITY is not specified, an infinite cardinality is assumed and an end-of-table condition is never returned.

Statistics Used by the Optimizer for Table Functions

RUNSTATS does not update the statistics in SYSROUTINES. The optimizer uses the statistics for a table function if you update them, otherwise, defaults are used as summarized in Figure UD.1.

Figure UD.1. Statistics used by the optimizer for table functions

Column	Default if -1 in col.	Description
IOS_PER_INVOC	0	Estimated number of IOs per invocation.
INSTS_PER_INVOC	4000	Estimated number of instructions per invocation.
INITIAL_IOS	0	Estimated number of IOs performed the first and last time the function is invoked.

Column	Default if -1 in col.	Description
INITIAL_INSTS	40000	Estimated number of instructions executed the first and last time the function is invoked.
CARDINALITY	10000	Predicted cardinality of a table function. Can be specified on CREATE FUNCTION statement.

You can update the floating point statistics used by the optimizer to determine the best access path when using table functions like:

```
UPDATE SYSIBM.SYSROUTINES
SET IOS_PER_INVOC    = 0.0,
    INSTS_PER_INVOC = 4.5E3,
    INITIAL_IOS     = 2.0
    INITIAL_INSTS   = 1.0E4,
    CARDINALITY     = 5E3
WHERE SCHEMA         = 'SYSADM'
AND   SPECIFICNAME   = 'FUNCTION1'
AND   ROUTINETYPE    = 'F';
```

Invoking a Table Function

Lets analyze an example of invoking a table function using the CUST_ITEM function just created to gain an understanding of how to execute a table function. The following statement reports on ITEMNO, TOTAL_COST, ORDER_DATE, and SHIP_DATE for customer 400 who ordered ITEMNO 782 with a TOTAL_COST > 1000.00 during 1999.

```
SELECT ITEMNO, TOTAL_COST, ORDER_DATE, SHIP_DATE
FROM   TABLE(CUST_ITEMS(400)) AS C
WHERE  ITEMNO      = 782
AND    TOTAL_COST > 1000.00
AND    YEAR(ORDER_DATE) = 1999;
```

Notice that the invocation of the table function appears in the FROM clause. The results are treated as a temporary table. Most SELECT clauses can be used when selecting from a table function.

Assume that is it also necessary to include the UNIT_PRICE of the item in the report. This requires a join with the INVENTORY table like:

```
SELECT ITEMNO, UNIT_PRICE, TOTAL_COST, ORDER_DATE, SHIP_DATE
FROM   TABLE(CUST_ITEMS(400)) AS C, INVENTORY AS I
WHERE  C.ITEMNO    = I.ITEMNO
AND    C.ITEMNO    = 782
AND    TOTAL_COST > 1000.00
AND    YEAR(ORDER_DATE) = 1999;
```

Using a Column as Input to a Table Function

A column value from a base table can be used as an argument of a table function. The name of the base table must appear before the table function in the FROM clause. The following statement applies CUST_ITEMS table function to the CUSTNO for Blake as retrieved from the CUSTOMER table.

```
SELECT ITEMNO, TOTAL_COST, ORDER_DATE, SHIP_DATE
FROM   CUSTOMER AS CB, TABLE(CUST_ITEMS(CB.CUSTNO)) AS C
WHERE  CB.ITEMNO    = C.ITEMNO
AND    CB.CNAME     = 'Blake'
AND    C.ITEMNO     = 782
AND    TOTAL_COST   > 1000.00
AND    YEAR(ORDER_DATE) = 1999;
```

The reference to the base table CUSTOMER AS CB can be replaced with another table function. The CUST_ITEMS table function can then reference a column from the first table function. This allows for joining two or more table function results.

Inserting rows into a base table from the results of a table function: You can populate a base table by using an INSERT statement with a subselect that retrieves rows by invoking a table expression in the FROM clause.

UD.6 CREATE PARAMETERS IN DETAIL

We have created several functions in the previous sections of this chapter and discussed some of the parameters that can be used when creating a function, particularly naming the function and the data type and length of the parameters. In this section we will discuss the remaining parameters preceded by an asterisk that have not been discussed in the previous SP Chapter in detail with reference to the following statement.

```
CREATE FUNCTION TOTAL_AMOUNT(LOAN DECIMAL(9,2),
  INTEREST DECIMAL(9,3), YEARS SMALLINT)
*RETURNS DECIMAL(9,2)
*CAST FROM FLOAT
EXTERNAL  NAME 'TOTALAMT'
LANGUAGE  COBOL
PARAMETER STYLE DB2SQL
WLM ENVIRONMENT WLMENVCU
*SPECIFIC TOTALAMT
PROGRAM TYPE SUB
STAY RESIDENT NO
CALLED ON NULL INPUT
READS SQL DATA
*NO EXTERNAL ACTION
*NO FINAL CALL
NO DBINFO
*ALLOW PARALLEL
DETERMINISTIC
*NO SCRATCHPAD
FENCED
ASUTIME LIMIT 80000
```

```
NO COLLID
SECURITY DB2
RUN OPTIONS
  'HEAP(,,ANY),BELOW(4K,,),ALL31(ON),STACK(,,ANY,)';
```

RETURNS DECIMAL(9,2) means that the UDF program does the required calculation and returns a decimal number.

CAST FROM FLOAT causes DB2 to convert the built-in data type of decimal to a floating point number and return it to the invoker. This data type conversion is not necessary. Indeed, declaration of input parameters as they are used in the UDF adds clarity. The data type conversion is not done with distinct data types.

SPECIFIC parameter is optional (TOTALAMT in example). It provides for a unique name (18 bytes or less) for the function which is implicitly or explicitly qualified with the schema name. If the SPECIFIC name is not specified, the default is name of function if it is unique. If the default name is not unique, DB2 generates a specific name in the form of:

SQLxxxxxxxxxxxx where x's represent 12 characters that make the name unique

The name is stored in the SPECIFICNAME column of the SYSROUTINES catalog table. The specific name can be used in ALTER FUNCTION, COMMENT ON, DROP, GRANT, and REVOKE statements as well as and in -START FUNCTION SPECIFIC, -STOP FUNCTION SPECIFIC, and -DISPLAY FUNCTION SPECIFIC commands to be discussed.

The function name (not the SPECIFIC name) must be used to invoke a function.

EXTERNAL ACTION (default) means that an action that changes the state of an object that DB2 does not manage can be taken. You can do I/O to a file or send a message, for example. If Resource Recovery Services (RRS) is used, changes made outside of DB2 can be committed or rolled back along with the DB2 operations. It does cause materialization of views referenced in SELECT, UPDATE, DELETE or INSERT statements that invoke the function. The function does not move one task control block (TCB) to another between FETCH operations. It is not possible for another function or stored procedure to use the TCB until the cursor is closed when using CURSOR WITH HOLD. Do use DISALLOW PARALLEL if parallelism can give incorrect result. This is the default when using EXTERNAL ACTION. If a function sends a note for each initial call to it, one note is sent for each parallel task instead of once for an invocation of the function if parallelism is used. EXTERNAL ACTION is a good choice if the function performs some external action that should apply to only one partition.

NO EXTERNAL ACTION means that no action that changes the state of an object not managed by DB2 can be taken.

NO FINAL CALL (default) means that a final call is not made to the function.

FINAL CALL means that a final call is made to the function when a COMMIT or ROLLBACK occurs in the invoking program (with or without CURSOR WITH HOLD). Do consider the use of DISALLOW PARALLEL which is the default when this parameter is used. This avoids sending an email message for each parallel task rather than one message for the invoking statement, for example. Parallelism is not appropriate for final call processing in most cases.

NO DBINFO (default) means that no additional information is passed to the UDF when it is invoked.

DBINFO means that additional arguments can be passed when the UDF is invoked, for example the run-time AUTHID, schema name, name of the table or column that the UDF might be inserting into or updating, and the database server ID that invoked the UDF. The *Application Programming and SQL Guide* manual contains additional details.

ALLOW PARALLEL means that a parallel path is allowed (does not encourage or discourage the choice of parallelism) for the SQL statement that invokes the UDF. This is a good choice if all invocations of the function are completely independent from one another.

DISALLOW PARALLEL means that a parallel path is not allowed for the SQL statement that invokes the UDF. This is a good choice if each invocation of the function updates the scratchpad to provide values that are of interest to the next invocation, such as incrementing a counter, for example.

The default is ALLOW PARALLEL in most cases. If one or more of the following parameters are specified when creating a UDF, the default is DISALLOW PARALLEL. It is always best to explicitly specify the parameter value that you require.

SCRATCHPAD 100 (default) provides an area for the function to save information from one invocation to the next. It is useful for saving information between invocations of reentrant UDF as well as for saving the results of each subselect in a UDF. The scratchpad area can be between 1 and 32,767. It is initialized to X'00's by DB2 when the function is invoked by an SQL statement. An exception is that the scratchpad is not reset when a correlated subselect begins to execute. DB2 does not change scratchpad areas after initialization. Each invocation of a function in an SQL statement has a scratchpad, for example two scratchpad areas are allocated for:

```
SELECT ORDERNO, UNIT_PRICE
FROM   ORDER
WHERE  UNIT_PRICE > US_TO_EURO(US_DOLLAR(:LIMIT))
OR     UNIT_PRICE > US_TO_EURO(US_DOLLAR(1000));
```

Scratchpads are allocated for each parallel task. If results should be accumulated for a statement rather for each parallel task, do use DISALLOW PARALLEL which is the default when a scratchpad is used. It avoids counting the number of invocations of the function for each parallel task when the intent is to count the number of times the function is invoked in total, for example. If a scratchpad is used only so that some expensive initialization processing is performed a minimal number of times, ALLOW PARALLEL is a good choice.

Do use FINAL CALL to ensure that DB2 invokes the function one more time so that the function can free the scatchpad areas.

If a scratchpad is used, like with the use of EXTERNAL ACTION, DB2 does not move the function from one task control block (TCB) to another between FETCH operations nor does it allow another function or stored procedure to use the TCB until the cursor is closed when using CURSOR WITH HOLD.

NO SCRATCHPAD means that a scratchpad is not allocated and passed to the function.

IBM strongly recommends the use a scratchpad and the use of reentrant code.

ALTER and DROP of UDF

Most UDF parameters can be changed with the ALTER FUNCTION statement. You can use the specific name to identify the function to be altered. For example, it has been decided to change the WLM environment to WLMENV1:

```
ALTER SPECIFIC FUNCTION TOTALAMT
  WLM ENVIRONMENT WLMENV1;
```

Optionally, you can alter a UDF by specifying its name provided that it uniquely identifies the function like:

```
ALTER FUNCTION TOTAL_AMOUNT
  WLM ENVIRONMENT WLMENV1;
```

If it necessary to uniquely identify a function, use the parameters specified when creating the function to identify the signature of the function like:

```
ALTER FUNCTION GKWADM.TOTAL_AMOUNT
  (LOAN DECIMAL(9,2), INTEREST DECIMAL(9,3), YEARS SMALLINT)
  WLM ENVIRONMENT WLMENV1;
```

Dropping a UDF: Identifying a UDF to drop is similar to altering a UDF. You can drop a function using its specific name. This avoids having to name additional parameters.

```
DROP SPECIFIC FUNCTION TOTALAMT RESTRICT;
```

You can also drop a UDF by specifying its name if it uniquely identifies the function like:

```
DROP FUNCTION TOTAL_AMOUNT RESTRICT;
```

The function name can be used along with the parameters specified when creating the function to identify the signature of the function when necessary.

```
DROP FUNCTION TOTAL_AMOUNT (LOAN DECIMAL(9,2),
  INTEREST DECIMAL(9,3), YEARS SMALLINT) RESTRICT;
```

The RESTRICT parameter is required. It is not possible to drop a UDF referenced in trigger definition. An error is issued.

UDF Commands

The -START FUNCTION SPECIFIC, -STOP FUNCTION SPECIFIC, and -DISPLAY FUNCTION SPECIFIC commands are similar in usage as the corresponding procedure commands described in Chapter SP. They apply to external UDF (not sourced or built-in functions). If a new UDF is not started, DB2 automatically activates it when the first SQL statement invokes the UDF. Following is an example of stopping the TOTAL_AMOUNT UDF using the specific name of TOTALAMT. The command will cause DB2 to refuse to execute any SQL statements that invoke the UDF. DB2 will go ahead and execute any UDF that have already been queued or scheduled.

```
-STOP FUNCTION SPECIFIC TOTALAMT
```

If the specific name is not known, it can be determined from the catalog tables like:

```
SELECT SPECIFICNAME, PARM_COUNT
FROM   SYSIBM.SYSROUTINES
WHERE  NAME   = 'function_name'
AND    SCHEMA = 'schema_name';
```

The 'function_name' is TOTAL_AMOUNT in our example and the 'schema_name' is GKWADM (schema name or qualifier of the UDF).

Optionally, you can specify the schema.specific-function name or schema.partial-name* rather than the specific name, or *.* applies to all UDF. Details on the usage of the commands can be found in the *Command Reference* manual.

UR.7 USER-DEFINED FUNCTION PROGRAM PREPARATION

External scalar and table UDF are prepared for execution much like any application program and stored procedure including a precompile, compile, linkedit into a load library, and bind. There are few things to keep in mind.

Do specify ATTACH(RRSAF) to the precompiler. RRSAF means to use the Recoverable Resource Services Attachment Facility of OS/390.

Do specify LE (Language Environment) run-time library and any language specific libraries to the link edit step. This establishes a common run-time environment for different programming languages. It provides storage management and condition handling to host programs. Details are in the *OS/390 Language Environment for OS/390 and VM Programming Reference* manual.

The load module name must be the same as specified in the EXTERNAL NAME clause of the CREATE FUNCTION statement, for example:

```
EXTERNAL NAME 'USTOEURO'
```

If the host program contains SQL, a package is required for each UDF. A plan is not used for UDFs.

There is sample program preparation JCL in SDSNSAMP. The members DSNHASM, DSNHC, DSNHCPP, DSNHICOB, and DSNHPLI contain sample JCL for assembler, C, C ++ , COBOL, and PL/I host programs.

Reentrant UDF and stored procedures have advantages: The operating system need not load UDF each time it is called. Multiple tasks in an address space can share a single copy of a UDF. This decreases the amount of virtual storage needed for code in an address space. Do use the RENT linkage editor option.

Use of DSN_FUNCTION_TABLE

If an external UDF contains SQL and a DSN_FUNCTION_TABLE exists, explain of yes with a bind or rebind results in inserting a row into the following table for each function invoked by an SQL statement.

```
CREATE TABLE DSN_FUNCTION_TABLE
  (QUERYNO          INTEGER        NOT NULL WITH DEFAULT,
   QBLOCKNO         INTEGER        NOT NULL WITH DEFAULT,
   APPLNAME         CHAR(8)        NOT NULL WITH DEFAULT,
   PROGNAME         CHAR(8)        NOT NULL WITH DEFAULT,
   COLLID           CHAR(18)       NOT NULL WITH DEFAULT,
   GROUP_MEMBER     CHAR(8)        NOT NULL WITH DEFAULT,
   EXPLAIN_TIME     TIMESTAMP      NOT NULL WITH DEFAULT,
   SCHEMA_NAME      CHAR(8)        NOT NULL WITH DEFAULT,
   FUNCTION_NAME    CHAR(18)       NOT NULL WITH DEFAULT,
   SPEC_FUNC_NAME   CHAR(18)       NOT NULL WITH DEFAULT,
   FUNCTION_TYPE    CHAR(2)        NOT NULL WITH DEFAULT,
   VIEW_CREATOR     CHAR(8)        NOT NULL WITH DEFAULT,
   VIEW_NAME        CHAR(18)       NOT NULL WITH DEFAULT,
   PATH             VARCHAR(254)   NOT NULL WITH DEFAULT,
   FUNCTION_TEXT    VARCHAR(254)   NOT NULL WITH DEFAULT);
```

The QUERYNO, QBLOCKNO, APPLNAME, PROGNAME, COLLID, and GROUP_MEMBER columns have the same meanings as in the PLAN_TABLE as discussed in Chapter EX. An explanation of remaining columns in DSN_FUNCTION_TABLE are summarized in Figure UD.2 as taken from the *Application Programming and SQL Guide* manual excluding the asterisk.

Figure UD.2. DSN_FUNCTION_TABLE columns

Column	Description
EXPLAIN_TIME	Timestamp when the EXPLAIN statement was executed.
SCHEMA_NAME	Schema name of the function that is invoked in the explained statement.
FUNCTION_NAME	Name of the function that is invoked in the explained statement.
SPEC_FUNC_NAME	Specific name of the function that is invoked in the explained statement.
FUNCTION_TYPE	The type of function that is invoked in the explained statement: SU - Scalar function TU - Table function
VIEW_CREATOR	The creator of the view, if the function that is specified in the FUNCTION_NAME column is referenced in a view definition. Otherwise, this field is blank.

Column	Description
VIEW_NAME	The name of the view, if the function that is specified in the FUNCTION_NAME column is referenced in a view definition. Otherwise, this field is blank.
PATH*	The value of the SQL path when DB2 resolved the function reference.
FUNCTION_TEXT	The text of the function reference (the function name and parameters). If the function reference exceeds 100 bytes, this column contains the first 100 bytes. For a function specified in infix notation, FUNCTION_TEXT contains only the function name. For example, suppose a user-defined function named / is in the function reference A/B. Then FUNCTION_TEXT contains only /, not A/B.

*PATH bind/rebind parameter is used to determines the SQL path that DB2 uses to resolve unqualified user-defined distinct types, functions, and stored procedure names in SQL CALL statements. Can be the schema name or USER. The default is "SYSIBM", "SYSFUN", "SYSPROC", or plan qualifier.

UD.8 DB2 SUPPLIED UDF

DB2 supplies over 100 UDFs in addition to the built-in functions discussed in Chapter SL. The DB2 supplied functions are written in C. The source code for the functions can be found in SDSNSAMP. They have a schema name of SYSIBM.

Examples of DB2 Supplied UDF

We will look closely at a few of the particularly useful functions and summarize all of the functions including the built in functions covered in detail in Chapter SL.

DAYOFWEEK: A rather complex calculation was required to determine the day of week prior to V6 as described in Chapter BP for those of you who have not yet migrated to V6. The DAYOFWEEK function like more most functions accept as arguments a column, host variables, special register, and literal (must be in a valid date format as described in Chapter CT) as shown in the following example.

```
SELECT ORDERNO, CUSTNO, ITEMNO,
  ORDER_DATE,       DAYOFWEEK(ORDER_DATE),
  'Host variable', DAYOFWEEK(:SHIP_DATE),
  CURRENT DATE,     DAYOFWEEK(CURRENT DATE),
  'Literal',        DAYOFWEEK('2000-12-25')
FROM   ORDER
WHERE  ORDERNO = 4873
```

```
AND     CUSTNO   = 7392
AND     ITEMNO   = 9844;
```

The DAYOFWEEK function returns an integer in the range of 1 to 7, where

1 represents Sunday
2 represents Monday
3 represents Tuesday
4 represents Wednesday
5 represents Thursday
6 represents Friday
7 represents Saturday

UDF arguments can be a column, host variable, special register, or a literal (must be in a valid date format for this function).

POSSTR UDF can be used to determine the position in a string of another string. A good use of this function is to determine the number of bytes before trailing blanks when inserting or updating a VARCHAR column. The following statement will return a value of 10 in the host variable CHARLENTH. There are 10 bytes in 'ERIC CLARK ' before trailing blanks.

```
EXEC SQL SET :CHARLENGTH =
  POSSTR('ERIC CLARK          ', '  ') - 1) END-EXEC.
```

The value can be moved to the length field of a VARCHAR column. Otherwise, trailing blanks are stored in column. Do be cautious that two blanks are not embedded in the string before trailing blanks. If the string contains 'EricbbClark' where 'bb' represents to blanks, only Eric will be stored in the column and Clark will be lost. Alternatives are discussed in Chapter PD.

The SET and VALUES statements are alternatives in a host program to avoid selecting from a one row table.

ROUND UDF can be used to round a number specified as the first argument as indicated by the second argument of SMALLINT or INTEGER. The value of 0.5 is rounded to the next higher number and -0.5 is rounded to the next lower number. The second parameter specifies the position to which the rounding is to occur. It is necessary to select from a one row table interactively. You can select from a one row table to retrieve a one row result or use the SET and VALUE ... INTO statements in host programs as discussed in Section UD.4.

```
SELECT ROUND( 12345.6789, 2),        Results
       ROUND( 12345.6789, 1),         12345.6800
       ROUND( 12345.6789, 0),         12345.7000
       ROUND( 12345.6789,-1),         12346.0000
       ROUND( 12345.6789,-2),         12350.0000
       ROUND(-12345.6789, 2),         12300.0000
       ROUND(-12345.6789, 1),        -12345.6800
       ROUND(-12345.6789, 0),        -12345.7000
       ROUND(-12345.6789,-1),        -12346.0000
       ROUND(-12345.6789,-2),        -12350.0000
       ROUND(-12345.6789, 8)         -12300.0000
FROM   SYSIBM.SYSDUMMY1;             -12345.6789
```

The result of the ROUND function has the same data type and length attributes as the first argument plus one for DECIMAL, if the precision is less than 31. For example the argument of DECIMAL(9,2) results in DECIMAL(10,2) and the argument of DECIMAL(31,2) results in DECIMAL(31,2). If the first or second argument is null, the result is the null.

Brief Description of DB2 UDF

Figure UD.3 summarizes character functions, Figure UD.4 summarizes date/time functions, Figure UD.5 summarizes data type conversion functions, Figure UD.6 summarizes statistical functions, Figure UD.7 summarizes mathematical functions, Figure UD.8 summarizes trigonometric functions, Figure UD.9 summarizes null management functions, Figure UD.10 summarizes LOB functions, Figure UD.11 summarizes double type character set functions, and Figure UD.12 describes the RAISE_ERROR function. These figures include the functions available prior to V6.

Figure UD.3. Character functions

Function	Description
CONCAT	Returns the concatenation of two strings
INSERT	Returns a string that is composed of an argument inserted into another argument at the same position where some number of bytes have been deleted
LCASE or LOWER	Returns a string with the characters converted to lowercase
LEFT	Returns a string that consists of the specified number of left most bytes of a string
LENGTH	Returns the length of its argument
LOCATE	Returns the position at which the first occurrence of an argument starts within another argument
LTRIM	Returns the characters of a string with the leading blanks removed
POSSTR	Returns the position of the first occurrence of an argument within another argument

Function	Description
REPEAT	Returns a character string composed of an argument repeated a specified number of times
REPLACE	Returns a string in which all occurrences of an argument within a second argument are replaced with a third argument
RIGHT	Returns a string that consists of the specified number of right most bytes of a string
RTRIM	Returns the characters of an argument with the trailing blanks removed.
SPACE	Returns a string that consists of the number of blanks the argument specifies
STRIP	Returns the characters of a string with the blanks (or specified character) at the beginning, end, or both beginning and end of the string removed
SUBSTR	Returns a substring of a string
TRANS-LATE	Returns a string with one or more characters translated
TRUNCATE or TRUNC	Returns a number truncated to the specified number of spaces to the right or left of the decimal point
UCASE or UPPER	Returns a string with the characters converted to uppercase
VARCHAR	Returns the varying-length character string representation of its argument

Figure UD.4. Date/time functions

Function	Description
DATE	Returns a date derived from its argument
DAY	Returns the day part of its argument
DAYOF-MONTH	Similar to DAY
DAYOF-WEEK	Returns an integer in the range of 1 to 7, where 1 represents Sunday
DAYOF-YEAR	Returns an integer in the range of 1 to 366, where 1 represents the first day of the year
DAYS	Returns an integer representation of a date
HOUR	Returns the hour part of its argument
JULIAN_DAY	Returns an integer that represents the number of days from January 1, 4712 B.C.

Function	Description
DATE	Returns a date derived from its argument
DAY	Returns the day part of its argument
SECOND	Returns the seconds part of its argument.
MICRO-SECOND	Returns the microsecond part of its argument
MIDNIGHT_SECONDS	Returns an integer in the range of 0 to 86400 that represents the number of seconds between midnight and the argument
MINUTE	Returns the minute part of its argument
MONTH	Returns the month part of its argument
QUARTER	Returns an integer in the range of 1 to 4 that represents the quarter of the year for the date specified in the argument
WEEK	Returns an integer that represents the week of the year
YEAR	Returns the year part of its argument

Figure UD.5. Data type conversion functions

Function	Description
CHAR	Returns a fixed-length character string representation of its argument (date/time, character, integer, decimal, floating point, or ROWID)
DECIMAL or DEC	Returns a decimal representation of its character or numeric argument
DIGITS	Returns a character string representation of a number
DOUBLE or DOUBLE-PRE-CISION	Returns a double precision floating-point representation of its argument
HEX	Returns a hexadecimal representation of its argument
RAND	Returns a double precision floating-point random number
INTEGER or INT	Returns an integer representation of its character or numeric argument
SMALLINT	Returns a small integer representation of its character or numeric argument

Function	Description
REAL	Returns a single precision floating-point representation of its argument
ROWID	Returns a row ID representation of its argument
TIME	Returns a time derived from its argument
TIME-STAMP	Returns a timestamp derived from its arguments

Figure UD.6. Statistical functions

Function	Description
AVG	Returns the average of a set of numbers
COUNT	Returns the number of rows or values in a set of rows or values (returns an integer)
COUNT_BIG	Same as COUNT, except the result can be greater than the maximum value of an integer (returns a decimal number with precision 31 and scale 0)
MAX	Returns the maximum value in a set of values
MIN	Returns the minimum value in a set of values
ROUND	Returns a number rounded to the specified number of places to the right or left of the decimal place
SQRT	Returns the square root of its argument
STDDEV	Returns the standard deviation of a set of numbers
SUM	Returns the sum of a set of numbers
VARIANCE or VAR	Returns the variance of a set of numbers

Figure UD.7. Mathematical functions

Function	Description
ABS or ABSVAL	Returns the absolute value of its argument
CEIL or CEILING	Returns the smallest integer greater than or equal to the argument
EXP	Returns the exponential function of an argument FLOAT Same as DOUBLE
FLOOR	Returns the largest integer that is less than or equal to the argument
MOD	Returns the remainder of one argument divided by the second argument

Function	Description
POWER	Returns the value of one argument raised to the power of a second argument

Figure UD.8. Trigonometric functions

Function	Description
ACOS	Returns the arccosine of an argument as an angle, expressed in radians
ASIN	Returns the arcsine of an argument as an angle, expressed in radians
ATAN	Returns the arctangent of an argument as an angle, expressed in radians
ATANH	Returns the hyperbolic arctangent of an argument as an angle, expressed in radians
ATAN2	Returns the arctangent of x and y coordinates as an angle, expressed in radians
COS	Returns the cosine of an argument that is expressed as an angle in radians
COSH	Returns the hyperbolic cosine of an argument that is expressed as an angle in radians
DEGREES	Returns the number of degrees for an argument that is expressed in radians
LOG	Returns the natural logarithm of an argument
LN	Same as LOG
LOG10	Returns the base 10 logarithm of an argument
RADIANS	Returns the number of radians for an argument that is expressed in degrees
SIGN	Returns the sign of an argument
SIN	Returns the sine of an argument that is expressed as an angle in radians
SINH	Returns the hyperbolic sine of an argument that is expressed as an angle in radians
TAN	Returns the tangent of an argument that is expressed as an angle in radians
TANH	Returns the hyperbolic tangent of an argument that is expressed as an angle in radians

Figure UD.9. Null management functions

Function	Description
COALESCE & VALUE	Returns the first argument in a set of arguments that is not null
IFNULL	Returns the first argument in a set of two arguments that is not null
NULLIF	Returns NULL if the arguments are equal; else the first argument

Figure UD.10. LOB functions

Function	Description
BLOB	Returns a BLOB representation of its argument
CLOB	Returns a CLOB representation of its argument

Figure UD.11. Double type character set functions

Function	Description
DBCLOB	Returns a DBCLOB representation of its argument
GRAPHIC	Returns a GRAPHIC representation of its argument
VAR-GRAPHIC	Returns a graphic string representation of its argument

Figure UD.12. RAISE_ERROR function

Function	Description
RAISE_ ERROR	Raises an error in the SQLCA with the specified SQLSTATE and error description

RAISE_ERROR function causes the statement that uses the function to return an error with the specified SQLSTATE and characters string. No further processing is done on the statement and the work done thus far is rolled back with a -438 SQLCODE returned.

Consider a statement to return the method of shipment depending on the weight of an item. If the weight does not fall within the three stated conditions, the user and program needs to be informed with a specified SQLSTATE and diagnostic string shown in parenthesis following the function name of RAISE_ERROR.

```
SELECT ORDERNO, CUSTNO, ITEMNO,
  CASE WHEN WEIGHT < 10.00 THEN 'Use local mail service'
       WHEN WEIGHT < 20.00 THEN 'Use Federal Express'
       WHEN WEIGHT < 30.00 THEN 'Use UPS'
    ELSE RAISE_ERROR('70001',              -- SQLSTATE
      'Consider another form of shipment')-- Diagnostic string
  END
FROM ORDER
```

```
      WHERE COUNTRY = 'USA   ';
```

If the WEIGHT is 30.00 or more, then the following error is received.

```
DSNT408I SQLCODE = -438, ERROR:  APPLICATION RAISED ERROR WITH DIAGNOSTIC TEXT:
Consider another form of shipment
DSNT418I SQLSTATE   = 70001 SQLSTATE RETURN CODE
DSNT415I SQLERRP    = DSNXRTYP SQL PROCEDURE DETECTING ERROR
DSNT416I SQLERRD    = 1  0  0  -1  0  0 SQL DIAGNOSTIC INFORMATION
DSNT416I SQLERRD    = X'00000001'  X'00000000'  X'00000000'  X'FFFFFFFF'
         X'00000000'  X'00000000' SQL DIAGNOSTIC INFORMATION
---------+---------+---------+---------+---------+---------+---------+-------+
DSNE618I ROLLBACK PERFORMED, SQLCODE IS 0
DSNE616I STATEMENT EXECUTION WAS SUCCESSFUL, SQLCODE IS 0
```

SQLSTATE and Diagnostic String: The SQLSTATE is a 5 character string consisting of letters and digits, and the diagnostic-string can be <= 70 bytes of EBCDIC CHAR or VARCHAR data. The values can be found in the SQLSTATE and SQLERRMC fields of the SQLCA as discussed in Chapter PD. You can avoid conflicts with the SQL92 SQLSTATE values by using a first character of the letters between I and Z or the digits 7, 8, or 9.

Comparison of RAISE_ERROR and SIGNAL SQLSTATE: The RAISE_ERROR can be used in any SQL statement and the statement can be used in a trigger. The SIGNAL SQLSTATE can only be used in a trigger as discussed in Chapter TR.

Performance Comparison of DB2 UDF, Host Code, Sub and Main External UDF

Tests were run comparing LCASE (convert to lower case) using DB2 UDF, host language code used to read a value and convert it to lower case characters, an external UDF written as a subroutine and the same external UDF written as a main program. All tests were done using C programs and the UDFs are written in C. One column in each of 510,000 rows are converted to lower case while processing the rows sequentially. Details of tests can be found in *DB2 UDB Server for OS/390 Version 6 Technical Update*, SG24-6108 manual

It can be seen in Figure UD.13 that DB2 UDF has performance advantages. A primary reason for this is that DB2 UDB execute in a DB2 address spaces. The use of host language code costs a little more than DB2 UDF for converting values to upper case. A primary reason for external UDF costing more than DB2 UDF is that they are fenced and executes under LE in a WLM address space. The use of sourced UDF do not have this overhead and compare favorably with CAST functions. The use of external UDF as a subroutine has somewhat lower costs than when defined as a main program. The use of subroutine and main program UDF would not show such a dramatic increase in CPU and elapsed time if more work were done in the function. A good deal of the cost is in setting up the environment.

Figure UD.13. Comparison of DB2 UDF, Host Code, Sub and Main External UDF

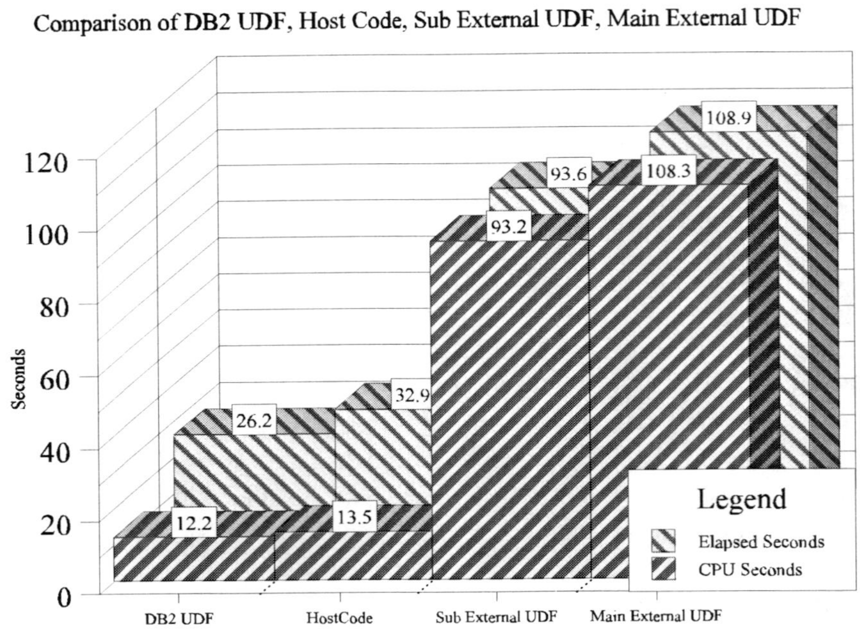

Performance of external UDF can be improved using a number of techniques. The use of an existing WLM address space avoids creating a WLM address space for each invocation of external UDF. However, it can be a challenge if you need to isolate different workloads and applications. The UDF load module should be reentrant. This can be done by specifying STAY RESIDENT YES (default is NO) when the UDF is created and using the RENT linkage editor option. The data type, length, and nullability of parameters between the invoker and UDF should match. Do minimize the number of parameters defined in an UDF. Costs increase with the number of parameters defined. The use a subroutine (rather than a main program) for external UDF improves performance. Do use EXPLAIN for all SQL in external UDF to ensure a good access path as discussed in Chapter EX.

Sample UDF

In addition to DB2 supplied UDF, sample UDFs can be found in SDSNSAMP as summarized in Figure UD.14. The sample UDF must be taken through program preparation with the use of DSNELI attachment facility. This is not necessary for the DB2 supplied UDF. Member DSNTEJ2U contains JCL for program preparation. The sample UDF can be invoked from SPUFI and DSNTEP2 as well as host programs.

Figure UD.14. Sample UDF

Function	SDSNSAMP Member	Description
ALTDATE1	DSN8DUAD	Converts the current date to <=34 user-specified formats
ALTDATE2	DSN8DUCD	Converts a date from one format to another

Function	SDSNSAMP Member	Description
ALTTIME3	DSN8DUAT	Converts the current time to a user-specified format
ALTTIME4	DSN8DUCT	Converts a time from one format to another
DAYNAME	DSN8EUDN++	Returns the day of the week for a user-specified date
MONTHNAME	DSN8EUMN++	Returns the month for a user-specified date
CURRENCY	DSN8DUCY	Formats a floating-point number as a currency value
TABLE_ NAME	DSN8DUTI	Returns the unqualified table name for a table, view, or alias
TABLE_ QUALIF	DSN8DUTI	Returns the qualifier for a table, view, or alias
TABLE_ LOCATION	DSN8DUTI	Returns the location for a table, view, or alias
WEATHER	DSN8DUWF	Returns a table of weather information from a EBCDIC data set

++UDF written in C++ (all other functions written in C)

Invocation of a UDF or Stored Procedure from a Trigger

UDF can be used with triggers and stored procedures. You may need to send an email message to the customer's email address thanking them for their order and to provide confirmation of the order after inserting into the ORDER TABLE. Here is a trigger created with the name of THANKU which can be used to call a stored procedure or invoke a UDF.

```
CREATE TRIGGER THANKU
  AFTER INSERT ON ORDER
  FOR EACH STATEMENT
  MODE DB2SQL
  CALL EMAIL(CUSTINF); - or EMAIL(CUSTINF) for UDF
```

An EMAIL stored procedure must be developed to send a thank you email message to the email address referenced in the CUSTINF input parameter. Optionally, you can use a UDF rather than a stored procedure as indicated in the note preceded by '--'.

UD.9 COMPARISON OF UDF AND STORED PROCEDURES

UDF and stored procedures have similarities and are managed alike in many ways by DB2. However, there are major differences between these objects. We will summarize the similarities and differences to aid in making your decision as to which object should be used under which condition and when to meet various requirements of your applications. This section has been written at the request of a reader who asked for clarification on the use of UDF and stored procedures. Details on the following similarities and difference are found throughout this chapter and Chapter SP.

Similarities

External UDF and stored procedures can be developed using host language programs (UDF cannot be written in REXX and Java as can procedures.) They both go through program preparation and result in the use of a package (if UDF contains SQL). Both external UDFs and procedures can contain SQL data manipulation statements (UDF cannot contain data definition statements). They can use SAVEPOINTs (COMMIT and ROLLBACK cannot be successfully executed). They both can issue I/O to files.

The host program that constitutes a procedures or UDF can invoke other procedures and UDFs. UDFs and procedures can be invoked from a trigger although the syntax differs.

Information about UDFs and procedures are automatically defined in SYSROUTINES when they are created (V6). Both can execute in WLM (Work Load Manager) established (UDF cannot execute in the DB2-established address space). OS/390 WLM commands are used to manage WLM address spaces with goal mode. OS/390 commands are used with compatibility mode. Both have advantages if they are reentrant. The operating system need not load the program each time it is invoked.

The START command does not refresh LE when using WLM-established address spaces. The use of the following command refreshes the LE environment and load module for procedures and UDF.

```
MVS VARY WLM,APPLENV=applenv,REFRESH
```

Additional commands for managing WLM-established address spaces are described in the *Administration Guide* manual.

Differences

Invocation of a UDF returns a single value except for table functions. Multiple input parameters can be defined with the CREATE FUNCTION statement. Procedures can return many values including a result set to the caller. Multiple input and output parameters are defined using the CREATE PROCEDURE statement. Procedures are invoked with an SQL CALL statement embedded in a host program. UDF can be invoked within SQL data manipulation statements interactive as well as with the SET and VALUES statements within a host program. The abend of UDFs and procedures are managed differently. The DSN_FUNCTION_TABLE table can be populated for UDF (not appropriate for use with procedures) when EXPLAIN is used. UDF are useful in managing distinct types. This can be done with procedures, however, it is more convenient with UDF. Utilities can be executed from a procedure (not UDF). The Stored Procedure Builder (SPB) can be used to build, modify, run, and manage procedures (not UDF). DECLARE handlers are supported in SQL procedures (not UDF).

The commands -START PROCEDURE, -STOP PROCEDURE, and -DISPLAY PROCEDURE are used to manage procedures. -START FUNCTION SPECIFIC, -STOP FUNCTION SPECIFIC, and -DISPLAY FUNCTION SPECIFIC commands are used to manage functions. The functionality of these commands have many common attributes.

Some similarities and differences are not clear cut. Some parameters used to defined procedures and UDF are the same, other are not as described in this chapter and Chapter SP. Privileges to create and use UDF and procedures have some similarities and differences. Details of the ALTER and DROP statements have some similarities and differences as well.

In general, procedures can be used to manage more complex tasks than UDFs.

UD.10 SUMMARY

Sourced functions are implemented by invoking another function (either built-in, external, or sourced) that is already registered with an application server. They are particularly useful in working with distinct types.

External scalar and table functions are written in a programming language. Multiple arguments can be passed to external functions. Scalar function return a single value. Table functions returns a table consisting of multiple columns, one row at a time.

External functions are written in a host language with or without SQL. They are prepared like a stand-alone program. It is necessary to issue a CREATE statement for an external function along with various attributes for registration with an application server.

You can invoke a sourced, external scalar, and table UDF in an SQL statement embedded in a stand-alone program, a stored procedure, a trigger body, another UDF, and interactively. The SET and VALUES ... INTO statements can be used in host programs.

UDF provide for application developers, IBM, and third party vendors to create functions to perform specific operations.

EXERCISES

1. Do sourced, external scalar, and table functions require a host program be developed and implemented?

2. Create a distinct type of fahrenheit and one for centigrade. Use the built-in data type of integer.

3. Will the following statement execute successfully? Why?

- Assume that the WEATHER table has a TEMP_F column defined with the distinct type of fahrenheit and a TEMP_C column with a distinct type of centigrade.

```
SELECT TEMP_F, TEMP_C
FROM   WEATHER
WHERE  TEMP_F > TEMP_C
```

```
AND    DATE_W = '2000-01-17';
```

4. Will the following statement execute successfully?

```
SELECT TEMP_F, TEMP_C
FROM   WEATHER
WHERE  INTEGER(TEMP_F) > 70
AND    DATE_W = '2000-01-17';
```

5. Will the following statement execute successfully? Why?

```
SELECT CAST(TEMP_F AS CENTIGRADE) + TEMP_C
FROM   WEATHER
WHERE  CAST(TEMP_F AS CENTIGRADE) > TEMP_C
AND    DATE_W = '2000-01-17';
```

6. Write a sourced function that allows the following statement to execute successfully.

```
UPDATE WEATHER
  SET    TEMP_F = TEMP_F + FAHRENHEIT(5)
  WHERE DATE_W = '2000-01-17';
```

7. Develop a sourced function that allows for the successful execution of:

```
SELECT MIN(TEMP_F)
FROM   WEATHER
WHERE  DATE_W BETWEEN '2000-01-01'AND '2000-01-31';
```

8. Develop a CREATE FUNCTION statement for a UDF that converts fahrenheit to centigrade with a name of F_TO_C. The input parameter is an INTEGER and the value to be returned is an INTEGER. The name of the load module is FTOC. ALTER statements are to refer to the function with the specific name of FTOC. The program that does the calculation is developed using the C language. The function should return a null only if the input arguments is null.

9. Develop a CREATE FUNCTION statement that has three floating point input variables and outputs a DECIMAL(8,4) value. Place the function in the ORDER schema. The function is to be invoked with the name CALCORD, referenced in ALTER statements as CALCORD, and have a load module name of CALCORD. The program is written in COBOL. It uses a scratchpad area once for initialization and to save some values.

10. It has been decided that the CALCORD UDF should be developed as a re-entrant program because it will be executed frequently and the program does not need a scratchpad area. Modify the following statement so that the UDF can be used according to the new requirements

```
CREATE FUNCTION ORDER.CALCORD(FLOAT, FLOAT, FLOAT)
RETURNS DECIMAL(8,4) CAST FROM FLOAT
EXTERNAL NAME 'CALCORD'
SPECIFIC CALCORD
LANGUAGE COBOL
WLM ENVIRONMENT WLMENVCU
DETERMINISTIC
NO SQL
```

```
FENCED
PARAMETER STYLE DB2SQL
NO EXTERNAL ACTION
STAY RESIDENT YES;
```

11. What are three alternatives for invoking external scalar functions. Which alternative is required to use a function interactively?

12. What privileges are required to use an external function?

13. What information is in the DSN_FUNCTION_TABLE.PATH column?

ANSWERS

1. External scalar and table functions require a host program be developed and implemented. Sourced functions are not implemented through a host program.

2. Here are the CREATE statements for two distinct type, one for fahrenheit and one for centigrade using the built-in data type of integer.

```
CREATE DISTINCT TYPE FAHRENHEIT AS INTEGER WITH COMPARISONS;

CREATE DISTINCT TYPE CENTIGRADE AS INTEGER WITH COMPARISONS;
```

3. The following statement will not execute successfully because a comparison cannot be made between a column defined with a distinct type of FAHRENHEIT and a column TEMP_C column defined with a distinct type of CENTIGRADE. An SQLCODE of -401 is returned.

```
SELECT TEMP_F, TEMP_C
FROM   WEATHER
WHERE  TEMP_F > TEMP_C
AND    DATE_W = '2000-01-17';
```

4. The following statement will execute successfully and the correct results received assuming that the value 70 is in fahrenheit (not centigrade). The statement results in a -401 SQLCODE without the use of the INTEGER cast function. The developer is taking an overt action to by using the INTEGER function to make the comparisons. The same principle applies if a host variable is used in place of 70. Host variables are always defined with built in data types. Host languages do not support the definition of a field as a distinct types.

```
SELECT TEMP_F, TEMP_C
FROM   WEATHER
WHERE  INTEGER(TEMP_F) > 70
AND    DATE_W = '2000-01-17';
```

5. The following statement will not execute successfully (-461 SQLCODE). It is not possible to cast a distinct type TEMP_F (distinct type of FAHRENHEIT) to a different distinct type (CENTIGRADE). One of the primary goals of distinct types is to avoid arithmetic operations and comparison of unlike distinct types. A UDF needs to be developed in a host language with the correct formula to convert fahrenheit to centigrade.

```
SELECT CAST(TEMP_F AS CENTIGRADE) + TEMP_C
FROM   WEATHER
WHERE  CAST(TEMP_F AS CENTIGRADE) > TEMP_C
AND    DATE_W = '2000-01-17';
```

6. Following is a sourced function that allows the UPDATE statement to execute successfully.

```
CREATE  FUNCTION "+"(FAHRENHEIT, FAHRENHEIT)
RETURNS FAHRENHEIT
SOURCE  SYSIBM."+"(INTEGER, INTEGER);

UPDATE WEATHER
  SET   TEMP_F = TEMP_F + FAHRENHEIT(5)
  WHERE DATE_W = '2000-01-17';
```

7. The following sourced function allows for the determining the minimum temperature in fahrenheit in January of the year 2000.

```
CREATE  FUNCTION MIN(FAHRENHEIT)
RETURNS FAHRENHEIT
SOURCE  SYSIBM.MIN(INTEGER);

SELECT MIN(TEMP_F)
FROM   WEATHER
WHERE  DATE_W BETWEEN '2000-01-01'AND '2000-01-31';
```

8. Following is a CREATE FUNCTION statement for a UDF that converts fahrenheit to centigrade with a name of F_TO_C. The input parameter is an INTEGER and the value to be returned is an INTEGER. The name of the load module is FTOC. ALTER statements are to refer to the function as FTOC. The program that does the calculation is developed using the C language. The function should return a null only if the input arguments is null.

```
CREATE FUNCTION F_TO_C (INTEGER)
RETURNS INTEGER
EXTERNAL NAME 'FTOC'
SPECIFIC FTOC
LANGUAGE C
DETERMINISTIC
NO SQL
FENCED
PARAMETER STYLE DB2SQL
RETURNS NULL ON NULL INPUT
NO EXTERNAL ACTION;
```

9. Following is a CREATE FUNCTION statement that has three floating point input variables and outputs a DECIMAL(8,4) value. Place the function in the ORDER schema. The function is to be invoked with the name CALCORD, referenced in ALTER statements as CALCORD, and have a load module name of CALCORD. The program is written in COBOL. It uses a scratchpad area once for initialization and to save some values.

```
CREATE FUNCTION ORDER.CALCORD(FLOAT, FLOAT, FLOAT)
RETURNS DECIMAL(8,4) CAST FROM FLOAT
```

```
EXTERNAL NAME 'CALCORD'
SPECIFIC CALCORD
LANGUAGE COBOL
DETERMINISTIC
NO SQL
FENCED
PARAMETER STYLE DB2SQL
NO EXTERNAL ACTION
SCRATCHPAD
NO FINAL CALL;
```

10. The STAY RESIDENT YES parameter has been added, and SCRATCHPAD and NO FINAL CALL parameters have been removed to make the UDF a reentrant program and eliminate the need for a scratchpad area resulting in the statement:

```
CREATE FUNCTION ORDER.CALCORD(FLOAT, FLOAT, FLOAT)
RETURNS DECIMAL(8,4) CAST FROM FLOAT
EXTERNAL NAME 'CALCORD'
SPECIFIC CALCORD
LANGUAGE COBOL
DETERMINISTIC
NO SQL
FENCED
PARAMETER STYLE DB2SQL
NO EXTERNAL ACTION
STAY RESIDENT YES;
```

11. The alternatives for invoking external scalar functions are use of the SET or VALUES ... INTO statement. It is necessary to select from a one row table to invoke a function interactively.

12. It is necessary to grant execute privilege on the function and package generated for the function.

13. The DSN_FUNCTION_TABLE.PATH column contains information on the path to locate the UDF to be executed (not the access path).

FIGURES

Program Preparation and Execution

PE.1 INTRODUCTION

Program preparation consists of a precompile, compile, linkedit, and a bind process. The precompiler extracts SQL statements from the host language code, substituting call statements. When the program runs, these call statements pass control through a host language interface to DB2's Database Services Address Space (DBAS), which does the processing called for by the SQL statements. The precompiler leaves copies of the SQL statements as comments in the modified host language program source code to maintain understandability. The modified source code is readied for execution through compilation and link editing which allows the programmer to include code from other libraries in the application program.

The precompiler places a copy of the SQL statements in a database request module (DBRM) library member. Each individual program, module, or subroutine that is precompiled separately has one DBRM member covering all of its SQL statements. Bind operates on the DBRM member to create an application plan or package. It first parses the SQL statements, a process akin to parsing a sentence for grammar. The parsing confirms that all of the necessary elements of a statement are present and syntactically correct. Bind also checks that the individual binding the plan or package is authorized to perform the statement's database activities. During bind, the optimizer interrogates the catalog tables describing the database, chooses the access path, and generates the machine code calls needed to execute the statements. DB2 stores information about the plan or package in the catalog tables and the plan or package in a directory table. SQL statements are written to the catalog tables SYSSTMT for a plan and to SYSPACKSTMT for a package. The compiled and link-edited host program and application plan work together when the program runs.

Program preparation can be accomplished through the use of DB2 interactive (DB2I) panels. There are panels for each stage of the process as described in the *Application Programming and SQL Guide* manual. Most companies use these panels to generate the JCL for the program preparation process and modify it for their specific requirements. Developers typically use this JCL for their program preparation.

PE.2 THE STEPS IN PROGRAM PREPARATION

Optional and required steps in program preparation and execution are diagramed in Figure PE.1.

Figure PE.1. Program preparation and execution

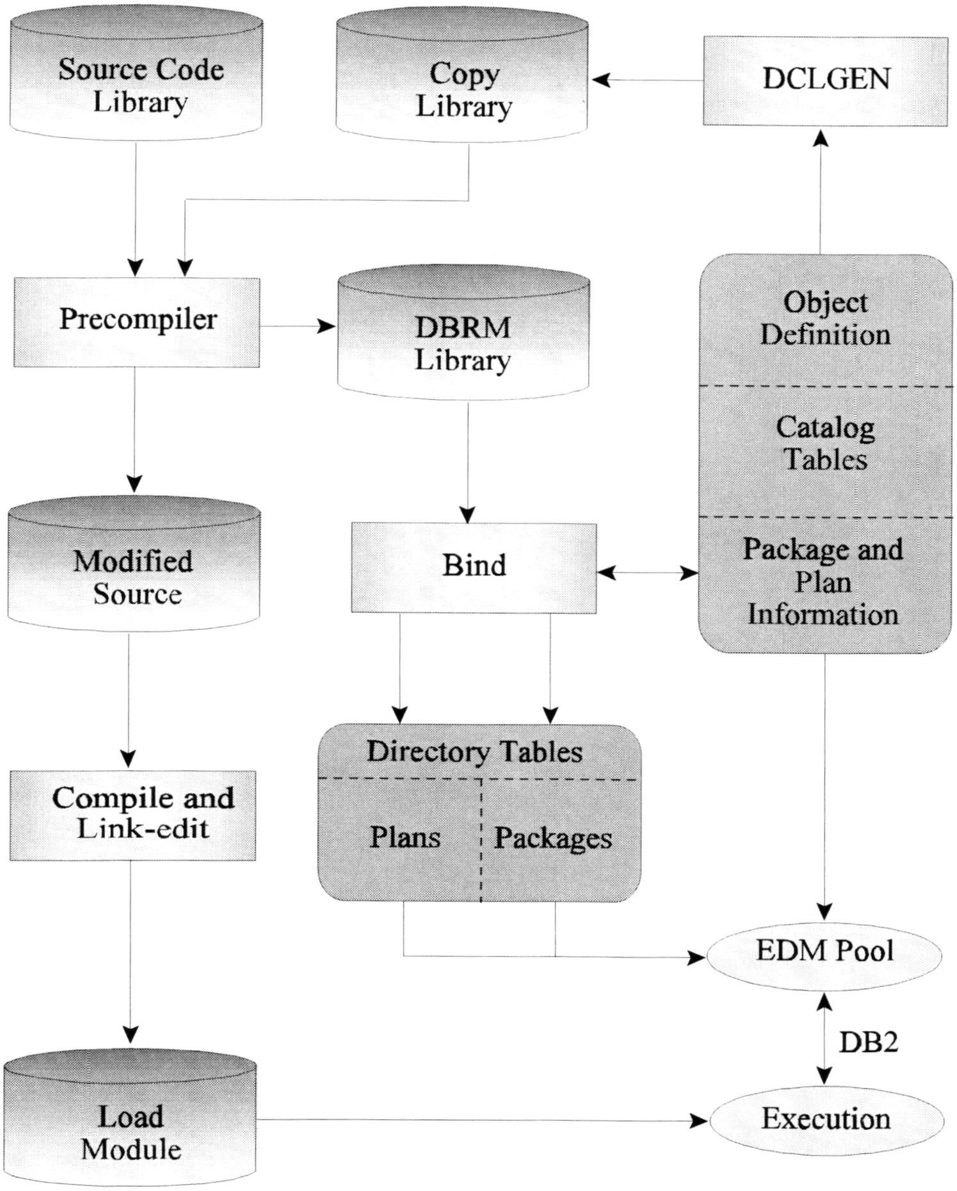

Generation of Data Structures and Declare Table

Prior to program preparation, DCLGEN can be executed to generate data structures and declare table statements that are included in each host program developed to manipulate tables. DCLGEN reads a description of a designated table or view from the catalog tables and generates a data structure with the same data type and length of columns in the table for supported languages. These data structures are used to receive column values selected from tables. The declare table statement is used by the precompiler to syntax check SQL statements referring to the tables. If the statement is not present, the precompiler issues a warning, with a return code of 4, for any table or view references that do not have DECLARE TABLE statements. Here is an example of a data structure and declare table statement generated for the S table:

```
01  DCLS.
```

```
    10  SN     PIC X(5).
    10  SNAME  PIC X(20).
    10  STATUS PIC S9(4) USAGE COMP.
    10  CITY   PIC X(15).

EXEC SQL
DECLARE AUTHID.S TABLE
(SN     CHAR(5)   NOT NULL,
 SNAME  CHAR(20)  NOT NULL WITH DEFAULT,
 STATUS SMALLINT  NOT NULL WITH DEFAULT,
 CITY   CHAR(15)  NOT NULL WITH DEFAULT)
END-EXEC.
```

Figure PE.2 is a sample of JCL for generating a data structure for the S table to be included in a COBOL program.

Figure PE.2. Generate a data structure for the S table

```
//SUPDATE  JOB ... USER=AUTHID
//*
//STEP1    EXEC PGM=IKJEFT01,DYNAMNBR=30
//STEPLIB  DD   DSN=DSN610.SDSNLOAD,DISP=SHR
//SYSPRINT DD   SYSOUT=A
//SYSTSPRT DD   SYSOUT=A
//SYSUDUMP DD   SYSOUT=A
//SYSOUT   DD   SYSOUT=A
//REPORT   DD   SYSOUT=A
//PARMIN   DD   DSN=PARMIN.FILE
//*
//SYSTSIN  DD   *
DSN SYSTEM(DSN)
DCLGEN TABLE(S)                                   -
       OWNER(AUTHID)                              -
       AT(STOCKHOLM)                              -
       LIBRARY('PROJECT.AUTHID.DCLGEN(STABLE)')   -
       ACTION(ADD)                                -
       LANGUAGE(COB2)
END
/*
```

Defaults are used for additional parameters not shown in the sample JCL. The parameters that can be specified for DCLGEN are summarized in Figure PE.3.

Figure PE.3. Explanation of DCLGEN parameters

DCLGEN Parameter	Description
TABLE(S)	S is the table name.
OWNER(AUTHID)	AUTHID is the table owner. Default is AUTHID of person who executes DCLGEN.
AT(STOCKHOLM)	STOCKHOLM is the location of the table. Default is the local location.
LIBRARY('PROJECT. AUTHID.DCLGEN (STABLE)')	Library and member name to receive generated structure. Can be changed using an editor.
ACTION(REPLACE)	Replaces existing member or adds a member if one does not exist. ACTION(ADD) adds a member only if one does not exist (default*).
LANGUAGE(COBOL)**	Language of the program that will include the generated structure. Default can be specified on installation panel.
NAME(ST)	ST is used as the prefix of sequence numbers assigned for each column in the table. If NAME is not specified, the column name is used as the field name (default*).
STRUCTURE (TAB-NAME)	Default structure name is the table name with a prefix of DCL for COBOL, PL/1, and C by default.
APOST	Apostrophe (') is the delimiter used by the host language and quote (") is the delimiter used for SQL statements (default*). QUOTE has the opposite meaning.
LABEL NO	LABEL YES causes labels to be used as comments. LABEL NO is the default.
DBCSSYMBOL(G)	Graphic data is denoted using G. DBCSSYMBOL(N) means that graphic data is denoted using N.
DBCSDELIM(YES)	DBCS table and column names are delimited (default). NO means they are not delimited.
COLSUFFIX(NO)	The NAME value is not used as a column suffix (default). YES means that the NAME value is used as the column suffix. For example, if NAME of 'S-' is specified, and a column has a name of SN, the generated name is S-SN.
INDVAR(NO)	Indicator variables are not generated (default). INDVAR(YES) means an indicator array is generated with a name of the table preceded by I. For example: 01 IS PIC S9(4) USAGE COMP OCCURS 4 TIMES. If DBCS is used the prefix is "<I>".

*Default can be specified on installation panels.

** The supported langages are:

Value	Description
COBOL	OS/VS COBOL (default)
IBMCOB	IBM COBOL
COB2	Other COBOL languages
PLI	PL/1
C	C/370
CPP	C++

DCLGEN writes the statements for a table or view to a member of a library designated to receive the statements. Developers use an INCLUDE statement to name the member of the DCLGEN library in the host program. Assuming that the statements are written to 'PROJECT.AUTHID.DCLGEN(**STABLE**)', the INCLUDE statement looks like:

```
EXEC SQL INCLUDE STABLE END-EXEC.
```

The precompiler includes the DCLGEN library member in the host program. The DCLGEN process is not required by DB2 but is highly advisable. It encourages use of host language variables that match the data types and lengths of columns in DB2 tables and the use of uniform naming conventions. Mismatched data types and lengths disallow the use of matching index scans and results in stage 2 processing as discussed in Chapter PP.

PE.3 PRECOMPILE PROCESS

The precompiler reads the host language source code with embedded SQL and includes the data structures and declare table statements generated by DCLGEN. The precompiler does an initial syntax check of the SQL based on the declare table statements, INSERT statements call statements, and data structures used in the call statements, and makes SQL into comments. This modified code is written to a file with the default name of USERID.TEMP.COBOL. It is input to the compile and linkedit process. The result is a load module that will be executed in conjunction with the application plan and packages. Figure PE.4 shows the JCL for this processing.

Figure PE.4. JCL for program preparation

```
//PROGPRE JOB ...
//********DB2 Precompile the COBOL program*******************
//PC       EXEC PGM=DSNHPC,
//    PARM='HOST(COB2),XREF,SOURCE,FLAG(I),APOST,VERSION(AUTO)'
//STEPLIB  DD   DISP=SHR,DSN=DSN610.SDSNEXIT
//         DD   DISP=SHR,DSN=DSN610.SDSNLOAD
//DBRMLIB  DD   DISP=OLD,DSN=PROJECT.AUTHID.DBRM(SUPDATE)
//SYSCIN   DD   DSN=&&DSNHOUT,DISP=(MOD,PASS),UNIT=SYSDA,
//              SPACE=(800,(500,500))
//SYSLIB   DD   DISP=SHR,DSN=PROJECT.AUTHID.DCLGEN
//SYSPRINT DD   SYSOUT=*
//SYSTERM  DD   SYSOUT=*
//SYSUDUMP DD   SYSOUT=*
//SYSUT1   DD   SPACE=(800,(500,500),,,ROUND),UNIT=SYSDA
//SYSUT2   DD   SPACE=(800,(500,500),,,ROUND),UNIT=SYSDA
//SYSIN    DD   DISP=SHR,DSN=PROJECT.AUTHID.COBOL(SUPDATE)
//*******Bind the SQL****************************************
//BIND    EXEC PGM=IKJEFT01, COND=((4,LT,PC))
//STEPLIB  DD   DISP=SHR,DSN=DSN610.SDSNEXIT
//         DD   DISP=SHR,DSN=DSN610.SDSNLOAD
//DBRMLIB  DD   DISP=OLD,DSN=PROJECT.AUTHID.DBRM(SUPDATE)
//SYSPRINT DD   SYSOUT=*
//SYSTSPRT DD   SYSOUT=*
//SYSUDUMP DD   SYSOUT=*
//SYSTSIN  DD *
 DSN SYSTEM(DSN)
 BIND PLAN(SUPDATE)  MEMBER(SUPDATE) ACTION(REP) -
   RETAIN ISOLATION(CS)
 END
//*******CICS procedure to translate, compile, & link-edit****
//CICS    EXEC DFHEITVL
//*******DB2 precompiler output is input to the CICS command**
//*******language translator
//TRN.SYSIN    DD  DSN=&&DSNHOUT,DISP=(OLD,DELETE)
//****Application load library to contain load module. Library
//****must be included in the DFHRPL DD statement of the CICS
//****execution JCL.*****************************************
//LKED.SYSLMOD DD  DSN=USER.RUNLIB.LOAD
//****DB2 load library that contains DSNCLI******************
//LKED.DB2LOAD DD  DISP=SHR,DSN=DSN610.SDSNLOAD
//LKED.SYSIN   DD  *
//**Include host language interface module for the CICS attach
  INCLUDE DB2LOAD(DSNCLI)
  NAME SUPDATE(R)
//*
```

Do pay close attention to the items in bold. The PROJECT.AUTHID.DCLGEN library contains data structures and DECLARE statements generated by DCLGEN in the example. PROJECT.AUTHID.COBOL(SUPDATE) contains source code with SQL statements. PROJECT.AUTHID.DBRM(SUPDATE) contains a copy of SQL from source code with a consistency token (pseudo timestamp) and version ID as written by the precompiler. It is the DBRM (Database Request Module) member that is input to bind process.

Consistency Token: The precompiler generates a consistency token which is the value in the OS/390 store clock shifted four bits. The consistency token and version ID are written to the DBRM member along with the SQL. This consistency token is a field in a data structure used as a parameter of the call statements added to the modified source code in USERID.TEMP.COBOL. It will ultimately be included in the load module. Figure PE.5 shows a fragment of code generated by the precompiler and placed in USERID.TEMP.COBOL. SQL-TIMESTAMP-1 and SQL-TIMESTAMP-2 in bold constitutes the consistency token.

Figure PE.5. Code fragment generated by the precompiler

```
 01   SQL-PLIST39.
        05   SQL-PLIST-CON    PIC S9(9) COMP-4 VALUE +2621440.
        05   SQL-CALLTYPE     PIC S9(4) COMP-4 VALUE +30.
        05   SQL-PROG-NAME    PIC X(8)         VALUE "SUPDATE".
        05   SQL-TIMESTAMP-1  PIC S9(9) COMP-4 VALUE +238837294.
        05   SQL-TIMESTAMP-2  PIC S9(9) COMP-4 VALUE +66273344.
        05   SQL-SECTION      PIC S9(4) COMP-4 VALUE +8.
        05   SQL-CODEPTR      PIC S9(9) COMP-4.
        05   SQL-VPARMPTR     PIC S9(9) COMP-4 VALUE +0.
        05   SQL-APARMPTR     PIC S9(9) COMP-4 VALUE +0.
        05   SQL-STMT-NUM     PIC S9(4) COMP-4 VALUE +362.
        05   SQL-STMT-TYPE    PIC S9(4) COMP-4 VALUE +232.

   01   SQL-VERS.
        05   SQL-VARS-PREF    PIC X(04) VALUE 'VER.'.
        05   SQL-VERS-DATA    PIC X(64)
                              VALUE '1992-01-01-09.15.30.123456'.

*****EXEC SQL
*****  INSERT INTO SPJTEST.S VALUES ("S4","Adams",30,"Athens")
*****END-EXEC.
          PERFORM SQL-INITIAL UNTIL SQL-INIT-DONE
          CALL "DSNHLI" USING SQL-PLIST39.
```

The consistency token is carried forward in the plan or package and the load module. It is checked at execution time to insure that the SQL and host language code came from the same source program. When the load module is executed, if DB2 cannot locate a plan or package with a matching consistency token, one of several SQLCODEs will be issued.

- -818 SQLCODE if cannot locate a plan to match the consistency token in the load module. (A -818 is also issued after a bind when using CICS if the CICS NEWCOPY command is not executed.)

- -805 SQLCODE if cannot locate the package named in the load module.

- -812 SQLCODE if current packageset special register is blank and the last or only entry in the package list has '*' as the collection ID. (The current packageset special register is discussed in Section PE.4.)

In most cases these conditions require complete program preparation process, including a precompile, bind, compile and linkedit, to avoid the error message when the program is next executed.

Notice the last line in Figure PE.5, 'CALL "DSNHLI" USING SQL-PLIST39'. DSNHLI is an alias for a language interface module, depending on the attach being used. The language interface modules for TSO, IMS, CAF, and CICS are modules DSNELI, DFSLI000, DSNALI, and DSNCLI, respectively. The "INCLUDE DB2LOAD(DSNCLI)" statement in Figure PE.4 JCL includes the CICS language interface module.

Additional Files Produced by the Precompiler

The precompiler writes messages about any errors that it detected to the file USERID.TEMP.PCLIST (default name). The line numbers for errors refer to the statements in this file (not the original source code input to the precompiler). When EXPLAIN is executed to describe the access path chosen by the optimizer, the line numbers are used as the query number in the PLAN_TABLE so that the rows in the PLAN_TABLE can be associated with specific SQL statements in USERID.TEMP.PCLIST as discussed in Chapter EX.

If CICS command translation is chosen, the precompiled code is written to USERID.TEMP.CICSIN by default. USERID.TEMP.CXLIST contains CICS command translation. The compiler output is written to USERID.TEMP.LIST by default.

Execution of batch programs is discussed in Chapter BP.

PE.4 BINDING SQL INTO PACKAGES AND PLANS

The SQL placed in a DBRM by the precompiler must be bound into a package or plan before it is executed. Packages, like plans, contain optimized code structures for SQL statements but for only the code structures for a single program, module, or subroutine are contained in a single member of the DBRM library. A plan is required when using packages, but it can contain only package identifiers. We will begin by looking at the benefits of packages and their naming convention. Then we will establish a collection and bind packages into it.

The Benefit of Packages

If an application plan is used without packages, all DBRM members for a transaction must be bound into a plan and specified to the CICS or IMS transaction manager. This makes the development and maintenance of each program, module, and subroutine that constitutes the transaction difficult to manage. When a program requires revision, a new program is added, or an existing program eliminated, all DBRMs used in the transaction must be identified and bound into a plan. While the bind takes place, the transaction cannot be used. If there is a failure as a result of the change, there are no facilities to fall back to the previous working version. Frequently common subroutines or modules are used by several programs. It is resource intensive to bind the same subroutine's DBRM into each of many plans that use it. There are performance benefits to having frequently executed programs in a single transaction since it facilitates thread reuse as discussed in Chapter CO. Packages also avoid the redundancy that results from IMS requiring that the transaction code, plan name, and program name be the same. In addition, it requires considerable I/O and CPU time to bind a large number of DBRM members together each time a change is made to only one program, subroutine or module. The likelihood of catalog contention is increased. The proper use of packages can avoid these problems and the resources required to bind many DBRM modules into a plan for use by a transaction or batch program.

One Versus Multiple Plans

There are disadvantages of one or very few plans. The primary disadvantage is that it makes it very difficult to monitor and tune programs. Many statistics are collected per plan rather than per package. An exception is to trace records by package for each execution of a transaction using CICS with TOKENI or TOKENE. Another disadvantage is that one or a very few plans requires more space in the EDM pool when using RELEASE(DEALLOCATE).

An approach to having multiple plans: You may want to consider one plan per functional group of packages (payroll, personnel, inventory, accounting, for example). This reduces space requirements in the EDM pool and provides for a finer granularity of the collection of statistics for analysis.

Package Naming Convention

Management of packages depends on their naming convention. Packages have a four part name like:

```
Location.Collection.Package_ID.Version
```

Location is the local DB2 subsystem where the package is bound by default. The location is blank in this case. Specification of location is required only if the SQL to be bound is on another DBMS which can be at a remote location. The remote location name must be placed in the catalog table SYSLOCATIONS at the local site. When binding at a remote location, the DBRM must be present there and the resulting package will be at the remote location.

Collection is a user defined name which is the anchor point for packages and has no physical existence in its own right. A collection is a grouping of packages used to associate packages with a plan. The collection is specified when a plan is established and for each package that is bound into the grouping of packages associated with a plan. Administration can be at the collection level including the granting of privileges.

Package-ID is the DBRM member name. There must be a one-to-one correspondence between a package and a DBRM member.

Version provides for having multiple versions of a package. If a package is bound multiple times with different version identifiers, each version must be in a different DBRM library. Multiple versions can be in the same collection. The version is specified to the precompiler. VERSION(AUTO) is specified on the fourth line of the sample JCL in Figure PE.4. This means that a character timestamp is used as the version (1998-04-01-09.15.30.141719, for example). Another option is to specify a string of up to 64 bytes as the version. If version is not specified, the default is blank. This results in a bind replacing the existing version of a package.

The precompiler records the version in the modified source and DBRM member. The version is *not* used to synchronize the package and load module at execution time. The consistency token assigned internally by DB2 at precompile time is used for synchronization. The version is for use by developers. There is no further use of the version by DB2.

Managing a Proliferation of Packages

The use of a timestamp or up to 64 byte string can result in a proliferation of package versions. The following SELECT statement generates DROP statements that can be executed using SPUFI to remove all but the most recent version of a package.

```
SELECT 'DROP PACKAGE(' CONCAT STRIP(COLLID)
        CONCAT '.' CONCAT NAME
        CONCAT '.(' CONCAT
        VERSION CONCAT '))'
FROM    SYSIBM.SYSPACKAGE P1
WHERE   TIMESTAMP <
  (SELECT MAX(TIMESTAMP)
   FROM    SYSIBM.SYSPACKAGE P2
   WHERE   P1.COLLID = P2.COLLID
   AND     P1.NAME   = P2.NAME);
```

The SELECT statement can be modified to generate FREE commands if you prefer the use of commands.

The use of collections is an alternative to using versions. For example, separate collections for unit test, system test, quality assurance, and production can be used.

Establishing a Collection

A collection should be created before binding packages. This is not a requirement, but it is a good approach. Here is an example of establishing a collection for the TRN1 plan.

```
BIND PLAN    (TRN1)         -
     PKLIST (SPJTEST.*)  -
     OWNER   (FLEUR)
```

Notice that the plan has a one part name as specified following BIND PLAN. The PKLIST (package list) is used to specify the collection name. In the example, SPJTEST is the collection name. The "*" following the collection name indicates that many packages can be bound to the collection.

A good approach, although not required, is to grant execute privileges on the collection to the plan owner like:

```
GRANT EXECUTE ON PACKAGE SPJTEST.* TO FLEUR
```

The GRANT *before* binding the DBRMs avoids authorization checking at execution time. Developers need BINDADD or BIND and CREATE IN collection privileges or PACKADM privileges to bind packages in the collection.

Many packages can be bound to the TRN1 plan by referencing the SPJTEST collection. The following example binds the SQL in the DBRM member PROGA in the PROJECT.AUTHID.DBRM library. There are a number of additional bind parameters that can be specified as discussed in Section PE.5.

```
BIND PACKAGE (SPJTEST)              -
     LIBRARY (PROJECT.AUTHID.DBRM)-
```

```
        MEMBER  (PROGA) ...
```

New packages can be added to the SPJTEST collection for programs that are added to a transaction as shown in the above example. Old programs can be modified without a bind of the plan, only the DBRM for the modified program needs to be bound into a package with a command like the one used to bind a new package.

An alternative to binding a package into a collection is to explicitly name one or more packages in the PKLIST qualified with the collection name like:

```
BIND PLAN -
     PKLIST (SPJTEST.SUPDATE, SPJTEST.SREPORT)
```

Disadvantage of explicitly named packages in PKLIST: If an explicitly named package in PKLIST is dropped or freed, the plan is invalidated. This is a result of the fact that an explicitly named package causes a plan dependency row to be inserted into SYSPLANDEP. In contrast, dependency rows are inserted into the catalog tables for each collection when SPJTEST.* (collection ID with an asterisk in place of the package ID) is specified. In addition, explicitly named packages in the PKLIST result in a sequential search of the named packages in the plan header. (The plan header is discussed in Chapter CO). The search algorithm used to locate a package bound into a collection is covered later in this section after further discussion of collections.

It is best to establish a collection with the BIND PLAN command before binding packages and to grant execute privileges to the plan owner. Packages are then bound with reference to the established collection.

Use of (*) in a Package List

An asterisk can be used in place of a package name, collection name, or location name. We will look at the consequences of using the asterisk when specifying a package list.

PKLIST(SPJTEST.*): If an asterisk is used in place of one or more package name, it means that many packages can be bound by referencing the SPJTEST collection. The plan owner must have authority to execute all of the SQL in all packages bound to the collection.

PKLIST(*.PROGA): If an asterisk is used in place of the collection name, the collection must be determined from the CURRENT PACKAGESET special register at execution time. The developer can set the special register by specifying the following statement after moving the collection name to the host variable :COL-ID.

```
SET CURRENT PACKAGESET = :COL-ID
```

If the CURRENT PACKAGESET special register is blank because it has not been set, a -812 SQLCODE is received when an attempt is make to execute the package. In addition, the use of an asterisk in place of the collection name causes authorization to be checked at execution time. This processing detracts from performance.

The value in the CURRENT PACKAGESET special register remains in effect until the end of a thread (end of task) or until it is reset with a SET command when using the TSO Terminal Monitor

Program (TMP), the Call Attachment Facility (CAF), or the Recoverable Resource Manager Services Attachment Facility (RRSAF). The register is not reset with a commit. When using CICS or IMS transactions, the value is lost when the thread is lost. If a thread is unprotected, the thread is lost at the commit point. This is because another thread can be used for the next SQL statement executed. The use of CURSOR WITH HOLD causes the thread to be held across commits. Therefore, the current packageset value is held.

PKLIST(*.SPJTEST.PROGA): If an asterisk is used in place of location name, the location must be determined at execution time. Authorization is always checked at execution time when the package is at a remote location. The location is determined from the CURRENT SERVER special register. The developer can set the special register by specifying the following statement after moving the location name to the host variable :CS.

```
SET :CS = CURRENT SERVER
```

The CONNECT TO statement also sets the CURRENT SERVER special register.

```
CONNECT TO :CURRENT-SERVER
```

If the register is blank, the local DB2 subsystem is assumed.

The duration of the value in the CURRENT SERVER special register is the same as for the CURRENT PACKAGESET special register as discussed in the previous subsection.

A Plan Can Have Multiple Collections

Collections can be added to an existing plan or a plan can be established with multiple collections. In the following example the NEWCOL collection is added to the TRN1 plan:

```
BIND PLAN    (TRN1) -
     PKLIST (NEWCOL.*)
```

Here is an example of a STRN plan established with four collections.

```
BIND PLAN    (STRN) -
     PKLIST (COL1.*, COL2.*, COL3.*, COL4.*) ...
```

There are performance advantages to placing frequently executed packages in one of the collections at the beginning of the list or to use only a few collections. Let's consider the work that must be done when a package is bound into the fourth collection like:

```
BIND PACKAGE    (COL4)                  -
  LIBRARY       (PROJECT.AUTHID.DBRM)  -
  MEMBER        (PUPDATE) ...
```

DB2 must build a package name consisting of the location.collection.DBRM-name.contoken and section number to locate the correct package in the directory table SCTR to execute. (The directory is discussed in Chapter CO). The DBRM name, consistency token, and section number are passed to DB2 from the host program as placed there by the precompiler. The collection and location can be determined from the special registers CURRENT PACKAGESET and CURRENT SERVER if they are set as discussed in the previous subsection. Developers are not required to set the CURRENT PACKAGESET and are unlikely to do so in most cases. Certainly, developers would not have set the CURRENT PACKAGESET in programs that were developed before packages were available in DB2 and later converted to use packages.

If the CURRENT PACKAGESET is not set to the collection name used when the package was bound, DB2 must try and locate the required package in each collection specified in the PKLIST. It does this with a matching index scan into the directory table SPTR for each of the four collections specified in the STRN plan PKLIST. This adds four matching index scans to the example transaction before it starts executing, assuming that the required SQL is not already in the Environmental Descriptor Manager (EDM) pool. CPU time and I/O are required to build each search argument and do the matching index scan for each collection until the package is located or an error message issued. If it is a frequently executed package and is not in one of the first few collections named in the PKLIST, the developer should set the CURRENT PACKAGESET to the collection that contains the required package. Also, message traffic is increased in a client/server environment in that a message is transmitted to the server for each search.

If a package from the same DBRM appears in multiple collections -- like COL1.PUPDATE.constoken and COL4.PUPDATE.constoken -- the first package found during the search is used. This may not be the required package. Again, SET CURRENT PACKAGESET can be used in the host program to designated the collection to use. It is best, however, to avoid having multiple packages from the same DBRM in a multiple collection plan in most cases.

PE.5 BIND PARAMETERS

There are many parameter values to choose from when doing a bind. Most of the parameters apply to both packages and plans; exceptions are noted. The advantages and disadvantages of the bind parameters will be considered so that you can make the best selections for your packages and plans.

Parameters that Apply to Packages and Plans

The BIND PACKAGE command in Figure PE.6 is an example of the command required to bind a package. The parameter values specified are good choices in many cases. Most parameters can be changed with the REBIND command discussed in Section PE.7. Parameter that cannot be changed are noted in the following descriptions of the parameters that can be specified with the BIND command.

Figure PE.6. BIND package command

```
BIND PACKAGE    (SPJTEST)                 - [Collection]
     LIBRARY    (PROJECT.AUTHID.DBRM)- [Required]
     MEMBER     (SUPDATE)                 - [DBRM member]
     OWNER      (POWNER)                  - [Primary ID]
     QUALIFIER (POTST)                    - [Owner value]
     CURRENTDATA   (NO)                   - [YES]
     NOREOPT       (VARS)                 - [Default]
     OPTHINT       ( )                    - [Default]
```

```
KEEPDYNAMIC  (YES)                    - [NO]
NODEFER      (PREPARE)                - [Default]
DYNAMICRULES (YES)                    - [NO]
VALIDATE   (BIND)                     - [RUN]
DEGREE     (1)                        - [Default]
IMMEDWRITE(NO)                        - [Default]
ISOLATION  (CS)                       - [Plan value]
RELEASE    (DEALLOCATE)               - [Plan value]
EXPLAIN    (YES)                      - [NO]
LANGUAGE   (COBOL)                    - [Default]
DBPROTOCOL(DRDA)                      - [Default]
PATH       (qualifier)                - [Default]
FLAG       (I)                        - [Default]
ENABLE     (*)                        - [Default]
ACTION     (REPLACE)                  - [Default]
SQLERROR   (NOPACKAGE)                  [Default]
```

Collection: The collection name is in parentheses following the key word PACKAGE, SPJTEST in the example, specifies that the package is to become part of the SPJTEST collection.

LIBRARY and MEMBER: The SQL for the bind is to come from the SUPDATE member in the DBRM library PROJECT.AUTHID.DBRM.

OWNER: The owner of the package is POWNER in Figure PE.6. POWNER must have privileges to perform operations on objects referenced by SQL statements in the DBRM to be bound. The owner can bind, rebind, free, or execute the package. If no value is entered, the default is the primary AUTHID of the binder. Ownership can be shared by making the owning AUTHID a secondary AUTHID to which several AUTHIDs are connected. The AUTHID should be associated with a function, not an individual, to avoid complexities when the individual transfers to another project or leaves the company. The owner's AUTHID is recorded in the CREATOR column and the primary AUTHID is recorded in the BOUNDBY column in the SYSPACKAGE catalog table or SYSPLAN catalog table, depending on whether a package or plan is bound. Ownership of a plan can be changed with a bind or rebind. The old owner retains bind and execute privileges with the grant option on the rebound plan. If privileges are revoked from the owner, the package or plan is marked invalid and must be rebound by an AUTHID with the required privileges when using validate of bind. The OWNER parameter value is used as the leading qualifier of all unqualified table references in the application plan unless the QUALIFIER parameter gives another value.

QUALIFIER: The QUALIFIER parameter value is used as the qualifier of all referenced tables and views that do not have an explicit qualifier coded. For example, if the FROM clause of an SQL statement is FROM SPJ, the POTST.SPJ table is processed when QUALIFIER(POTST) is used on the bind command. Unlike the owner value, privileges need not be granted to a qualifier value. If the qualifier is not specified, the owner parameter value is used to qualify all unqualified tables and views. It is advisable to use a qualifier rather than the owner value to qualify tables and views to avoid mixing naming conventions with security issues.

CURRENTDATA: CURRENTDATA of NO allows DB2 to assume read-only data for ambiguous cursors. This allows DB2 to use lock avoidance, blocking data for transmission, and parallel processing for SELECT statements that are ambiguous. CURRENTDATA of NO does have performance advantages, reduces lock contention, and allows for blocking of data before transmission. However, do study the integrity implications of CURRENTDATA of NO in Chapter

CC before overriding the default of CURRENTDATA of YES. The REBIND command cannot be used to change the CURRENTDATA value at a remote site. To change the value, it is necessary to issue the BIND command.

NOREOPT: NOREOPT(VARS) means that SQL statements are optimized once when doing a BIND or REBIND which is the default. REOPT(VARS) causes SQL statements to be optimized each time the plan or package is executed in addition to the original bind. This applies to SQL with host variables, dynamic SQL with parameter markers, and special registers. Reoptimization does not occur for an SQL statement that contains only literals in predicates.

Most bind processing occurs at run time when using REOPT(VARS) except that it is not necessary to parse the statement, authorization checking is not required, there is no dependency checking, and no view and table expression decomposition. Reoptimization of SQL at run time allows the optimizer to choose the best access path based on values entered by the user for predicates. All SQL statements in a package or plan are reoptimized at run time. This suggests that statements that require reoptimization be placed in a separate package.

There are a number of cases where the best access path depends on the values requested by the user. These cases as well as cases where reoptimization is of no value are discussed in Section OP.7.

OPTHINT: The OPTHINT (optimization hint) parameter can be used to request a specified access path in the plan table. If a parameter value less than or equal to 8 bytes other than blanks is specified, the optimizer can use the access path identified by a matching value in the column OPTHINT column of the in the PLAN_TABLE. Details on the use of optimization hints are covered in Chapter EX.

KEEPDYNAMIC: This parameter applies only when using dynamic SQL and has the default of KEEPDYNAMIC of NO. KEEPDYNAMIC of YES means that the prepared dynamic statements are retained past a commit point. CACHE DYNAMIC SQL of YES is required on DSNTIP4 installation panel (not the default) in addition to KEEPDYNAMIC of YES to minimize implicit prepares of dynamic SQL. It is also necessary to use NOREOPT(VARS), which is the default. Caching of dynamic SQL applies to executing local dynamic SQL and remote dynamic SQL using Distributed Relational Data Access (DRDA), not the private protocol. The use of caching dynamic SQL is discussed in Chapter PD.

NODEFER and DEFER: This parameter is particularly important when using dynamic SQL in a client/server environment. The default NODEFER(PREPARE) indicates that the prepare of SQL statements is to takes place immediately. DEFER(PREPARE) indicates that the prepare will be deferred until the first EXECUTE, OPEN or DESCRIBE is issued and the first INSERT, UPDATE, or DELETE is executed using the private protocol. Deferring the prepare is a good choice in a client/server environment since it avoids transmitting each prepare, describe, open and data manipulation (DML) statement separately. Do check the SQLCODE after an EXECUTE or DESCRIBE for any error condition that could have occurred with the prepare when using DEFER(PREPARE). This is because the prepare is done along with the EXECUTE or DESCRIBE. If NODEFER and DEFER are not specified for a local bind of a package, the plan value is used. For a remote bind, NODEFER(PREPARE) is used at the remote site. REOPT(VARS) implies DEFER(PREPARE) if neither option is specified and if an option is specified, it must be DEFER(PREPARE).

DYNAMICRULES: This parameter applies only when using dynamic SQL. DYNAMICRULES(BIND) has the advantage in that it is not necessary to grant privileges on tables to users. Users will be able to execute any SQL statements on any table referenced in the program that the binder has authority on. Unqualified object names are qualified with the value specified using the QUALIFER parameter. There are some restrictions. The program cannot use SET CURRENT SQLID and cannot use dynamic GRANT, REVOKE, ALTER, CREATE, or DROP statements. The default of DYNAMICRULES(RUN) requires that users be granted select and update privileges as required on the tables directly. This allows users to manipulate the tables directly using an interactive tool such as QMF rather than allowing them to manipulate the tables only through specific programs. Unqualified object names are qualified by the value in the special register CURRENT SQLID.

Following DYNAMICRULES parameter values can be used with packages (not plans). They are designed for use with stored procedures and user-defined functions.

- DYNAMICRULES(DEFINERUN) causes the rules of DYNAMICRULES(RUN) to apply when binding stored procedures and user-defined functions.
- DYNAMICRULES(DEFINEBIND) causes the rules of DYNAMICRULES(BIND) to apply when binding stored procedures and user-defined functions.
- DYNAMICRULES(INVOKERRUN) causes the rules of DYNAMICRULES(RUN) to apply when stored procedures and user-defined functions are invoked.
- DYNAMICRULES(INVOKEBIND) causes the rules of DYNAMICRULES(BIND) to apply when stored procedures and user-defined functions are invoked.

DEGREE: DEGREE(1) informs the optimizer not to consider a parallel path and is the default. DEGREE(ANY) allows the optimizer to consider a parallel path with any degree that is appropriate. The DEGREE parameter applies to static SQL. SET CURRENT DEGREE to ANY is required for dynamic SQL if you want the optimizer to consider parallelism as part of the access path. This sets the CURRENT DEGREE special register.

IMMEDWRITE: The IMMEDWRITE parameter applies only to a sysplex data sharing environment. The goal of IMMEDWRITE(NO) (default) is to accumulate updated pages in the buffer pool to minimize I/O. Less than or equal to 32 pages are written using deferred write after sorting the RIDs in sequence as the page appear on DASD. Details on the processing is in Chapter CO. This processing is always used in a non-sysplex data sharing environment.

IMMEDWRITE(PH1) means that updated pages that are group buffer pool dependent are written at or before phase one of a commit. If the transaction subsequently rolls back, pages are updated again during the rollback process and pages are written again at the end of abort.

IMMEDWRITE(YES) means that updated pages that are group buffer pool dependent are immediately written as soon as the buffer update completes. This is useful if PROGA can spawn PROGB on another member and PROGB must see the updates made by PROGA. However, writing the pages immediately can adversely effect performance.

VALIDATE: VALIDATE(BIND) requires that all objects referenced in an SQL statement exist and the owner of the package or plan must have privileges on the referenced objects for the bind to be successful. The executor need only have execute privilege. VALIDATE of BIND minimizes resource usage at execution time and catalog contention by avoiding checking the existence of objects and privileges at run time. When binding a package (not a plan) with SQLERROR(CONTINUE) as discussed in the next section, the bind succeeds but the SQL statements that have errors are not executable. The default of VALIDATE(RUN) does not require that referenced objects exist and appropriate privileges are held at bind time. Rather the object existence and privileges are checked at execution time which results in incremental binds until the objects and privileges exist. This has a negative impact on performance until all objects and privileges exist. Once all objects and privileges exist, incremental binds are no longer attempted and it is as if VALIDATE(BIND) had been specified.

ISOLATION, ACQUIRE, and RELEASE: The significance of the bind time parameters--ISOLATION, ACQUIRE, and RELEASE--that effect concurrency are discussed in Chapter CC. The isolation level of CS is frequently used rather than the default of RR to maximize update concurrency. The ACQUIRE parameter does not apply to packages since ACQUIRE(USE) is always used for packages. The RELEASE parameter can be specified with the value of COMMIT or DEALLOCATE for packages and plans.

If the ISOLATION and RELEASE parameters are not specified when binding a package, the plan parameter values are used. These two parameters are exceptions. Most package bind parameters use their own defaults and are not affected by the plan bind parameters. If you need to change the package's ISOLATION and RELEASE parameters from that inherited from the plan, it is necessary to bind (not rebind) the package with the required values.

EXPLAIN: EXPLAIN(YES) causes rows to be inserted into the PLAN_TABLE describing the access path chosen by the optimizer as discussed in Chapter EX. The default of NO should be overridden with a YES so that the developer can verify that the access path selected by the optimizer for a package or plan is likely to provide the required performance.

LANGUAGE parameter is useful in the conversion of private protocol programs to DRDA access. It provides for remotely binding COBOL program that use hyphens in cursor names, SCURSOR-1, for example. The valid values are COBOL, COBOL2 and IBMCOBOL.

DBPROTOCOL provides for specifying whether DRDA or private protocol is used in a client/server environment. DBPROTOCOL(DRDA) means that DRDA protocol is used (default unless changed on DSNTIP5 installation panel or DSNZPARM DSN6SYSP DBPROTCL). DBPROTOCOL(PRIVATE) means that the private protocol is used. This option is not advisable. There are no further enhancement planned for the private protocol. Indeed, the private protocol is likely to be removed from DB2 in the future.

FLAG parameter value indicates the level of messages to be displayed during the bind. The default of (I) results in displaying all informational, warning, error, and completion messages; (W) displays only warning, error, and completion messages; (E) displays only error and completion messages and; (C) displays only completion messages.

ENABLE/DISABLE: The ENABLE and DISABLE parameters provide for restricting execution to only specific connection types. Either of these parameters can be specified but not both. Execution of a local package or plan can be enabled or disabled for use with CICS, IMSBMP, IMSMPP, IMS, Batch, DB2CALL, DL1BATCH,or RRSAF, and can be further restricted by connection such as CICS application ID, IMSBMP IMS ID, and IMSMPP IMS ID. The bind parameter ENABLE

(CICS) CICS (TST4) allows only CICS and only one region, TST4, to execute the package or plan. The DISABLE parameter can be used to allow all connection types except the one specified. For example, all connection types except CICS PRD1 are allowed with the parameter DISABLE(CICS) CICS(PRD1). The ENABLE and DISABLE parameters are useful for designating a test or production region. This can avoid a test plan being accidentally executed in a production region.

The number of connection types named should be minimized. A long list detracts from performance since the list must be searched at execution time. Do use ENABLE or DISABLE based on which results in a shorter list of connection types. ENABLE(*) enables all environments and is the default.

If ENABLE or DISABLE is used at the plan level, the restriction applies to all packages executed from the plan. ENABLE and DISABLE can be used at the package level and not the plan level, in which case the values specified apply to the package regardless of which plan it is executed from.

ENABLE and DISABLE cannot be used to control the execution of packages at a remote site. The REMOTE parameter along with the location name as recorded in SYSLOCATIONS for the DB2 for OS/390 subsystem and logical unit (LU) name as defined to VTAM for other members of the DB2 family can be used to control the execution of remote packages.

ACTION parameter indicates whether the package or plan is new or a replacement. ACTION(ADD) results in an error if the object already exists. The default of ACTION(REPLACE) adds the object or replaces it if it already exists. BIND with REPLACE is required whenever the host program has been changed and precompiled, even if the SQL statements and the referenced tables have not been changed. Although the package or plan will be the same if the SQL and tables have not changed, DB2 requires that the consistency token in the load module and package or plan match, necessitating creation of a replacement package or plan when the revised program is precompiled. If the consistency tokens do not match, a negative SQLCODE is received at execution time as discussed in Section PE.3.

Parameters that Apply to Packages Only

Most bind parameters apply to both packages and plans as shown in the Figure PE.7 intersection diagram. The only parameters that do not apply to plans are REPLVER on ACTION, COPY, COPYVER, OPTIONS, and SQLERROR. If parameters are not explicitly specified when a package is bound, package default values are used in most cases--not the values specified when the plan is bound.

Figure PE.7. Parameters that apply to packages and plans

Packages and Plans	Packages only
COLLECTION	REPLVER on ACTION
LIBRARY	COPY, COPYVER
MEMBER	OPTIONS
OWNER	SQLERROR
QUALIFIER	
CURRENTDATA	
NOREOPT(VARS)	
OPTHINT	
KEEPDYNAMIC	
NODEFER	
DYNAMICRULES	
DEGREE	
IMMEDWRITE	
VALIDATE	
FLAG	**Plans only**
ISOLATION	
RELEASE	PKLIST
EXPLAIN	ACQUIRE
ACTION	RETAIN on ACTION
ENABLE/DISABLE	CURRENTSERVER
LANGUAGE	DISCONNECT
DBPROTOCOL	CACHESIZE
PATHDEFAULT/PATH	SQLRULES

PE.6 PARAMETERS THAT APPLY TO PACKAGES ONLY AND PLANS ONLY

In this section we will analyze parameters that apply only to packages and those that apply only to plans.

REPLVER: The REPLVER parameter can be specified along with ACTION(REPLACE) for packages. REPLVER(SAME) causes the existing package version ID to be replaced and is the default. The version ID comes from the DBRM member or COPYVER when the COPY option is used. REPLVER('1992-01-01-09.15.30.123456') causes a package with a version ID of '1992-01-01-09.15.30.123456' to be replaced. The REPLVER parameter is useful when migrating from test to production.

Copying a Package and Replacing a Version ID

The SQL statements for a package that has been tested can be copied and bound in the production environment. The source and destination collection cannot be the same when a package is copied within a DB2 subsystem. The following command takes the SQL from the catalog table SYSPACKSTMT for the PROGA package, version '1992-01-01-09.15.30.123456' as indicated with the COPYVER parameter, in the SPJTEST collection, binds the SQL, and places the new package in the SPJPROD collection.

```
BIND PACKAGE    (SPJPROD)                        -
     COPY       (SPJTEST.PROGA)                  -
     COPYVER    ('1992-01-01-09.15.30.123456')   -
     OWNER      (POWNER)                         -
     QUALIFIER  (POPROD)                         -
     ENABLE     (*)
```

This command conceptually copies SPJTEST.PROGA.'1992-01-01-09.15.30.123456' to SPJPROD.PROGA.'1992-01-01-09.15.30.123456' with a bind of the SQL from SYSPACKSTMT for SPJTEST.PROGA.'1992-01-01-09.15.30.123456'.

Most of the original bind parameters apply to the new package except for the OWNER, QUALIFIER, and ENABLE/DISABLE parameters. Do be cautious of the fact that the default values for these parameters are used if they are not specified.

A package can be bound over an existing package with the REPLVER parameter. This can be useful when migrating application systems from a test to a production environment. The following BIND command replaces the PROGA package in the SPJPROD collection after binding the SQL from SYSPACKSTMT to create the package in the SPJPROD collection with a version of '1992-01-01-09.15.30.123456'.

```
BIND PACKAGE    (SPJPROD)                      -
     COPY       (SPJTEST.PROGA)                -
     OWNER      (POWNER)                       -
     QUALIFIER  (POPROD)                       -
     ENABLE     (CICS) CICS (TST4)             -
     ACTION     (REPLACE)                      -
       REPLVER    ('1992-01-01-09.15.30.123456')
```

OPTIONS: The OPTIONS parameter specified on the BIND PACKAGE ... COPY command is used for the copied and bound package. Parameter options *not* specified depend on the OPTIONS parameter and whether the copy is local or to a downlevel server. A downlevel server is any server other than DB2 for OS/390. OPTIONS(COMPOSITE) means that options *not* specified are taken from SYSPACKAGE which has current bind options. OPTIONS(COMMAND) for a local new copy means that the BIND PACKAGE default options are used for the new copy when not specified. OPTIONS(COMMAND) for a downlevel new copy means that the server defined BIND PACKAGE default options are used for the new copy. OPTIONS(COMMAND) is required for a downlevel copy.

SQLERROR: The SQLERROR parameter provides for binding SQL statements that reference objects that do not exist at the bind site or the binder does not currently hold authority on the referenced objects. The example BIND command in Figure PE.6 uses the default of NOPACKAGE which means that a package will not be created if either of the condition is not met. The CONTINUE value results in a package being created but statements that caused the error are not executable. SQLERROR(CONTINUE) is required if the DBRM contains SQL for DB2 and non-DB2 DBMSs. An attempt to execute unresolved statements results in a negative SQLCODE at execution time. The SQLERROR parameter applies to packages only (not plans). It cannot be changed with a rebind.

Parameters that Apply to Plans Only

There are a number of parameters that apply only to plans--PKLIST, ACQUIRE, RETAIN on ACTION, CACHESIZE, NODEFER, CURRENTSERVER, DISCONNECT, and SQLRULES. Figure PE.8 shows a command to bind a plan without the use of packages. Notice that PKLIST is not specified in the BIND command. We have analyzed the parameters that apply to packages and plans, and only packages. We will now consider the parameters that apply only to plans. These parameters can be specified when using packages with plans.

Figure PE.8. Bind of a plan without the use of packages

```
BIND PLAN       (SUPDATE)                 - [Required]
     LIBRARY    (PROJECT.AUTHID.DBRM)- [Required]
     MEMBER     (SUPDATE)                 - [DBRM member]
     OWNER      (POTSTOWN)                - [Primary ID]
     QUALIFIER (POUNTST)                  - [Owner value]
     CURRENTDATA     (NO)                 - [YES]
     NOREOPT         (VARS)               - [Default]
     OPTHINT         ( )                  - [Default]
     KEEPDYNAMIC     (YES)                - [NO]
     DYNAMICRULES    (YES)                - [NO]
     VALIDATE        (BIND)               - [RUN]
     DEGREE          (1)                  - [Default]
     IMMEDWRITE      (NO)                 - [Default]
     ISOLATION       (CS)                 - [RR]
     ACQUIRE         (ALLOCATE)           - [USE]
     RELEASE         (DEALLOCATE)         - [COMMIT]
     EXPLAIN         (YES)                - [NO]
     FLAG            (I)                  - [Default]
     ENABLE          (*)                  - [All enabled]
     ACTION          (REPLACE) RETAIN - [No retain]
     CACHESIZE       (1024)               - [Default]
     CURRENTSERVER (DUBLIN)               - [Local]
     DBPROTOCOL      (DRDA)               - [Default]
     PATH            (qualifier)          - [Default]
     LANGUAGE        (COBOL)              - [Default]
     DISCONNECT      (EXPLICIT)           - [EXPLICIT]
```

```
SQLRULES        (DB2)                 [Default]
```

ACTION(REPLACE) RETAIN: The RETAIN parameter can be specified along with ACTION(REPLACE) when binding a plan. It is not the default. If the RETAIN parameter is used, execute and bind authorities continue to be in effect. If RETAIN is *not* specified with ACTION(REPLACE), which is the default, everyone but the plan owner loses EXECUTE privilege (but not BIND privilege). It is necessary to regrant EXECUTE privileges to the required AUTHIDs. If the plan owner changes, the new owner grants the BIND privilege to the previous owner without issuing a GRANT statement. In addition to being a security issue, when not using RETAIN, exclusive locks are taken on the SYSPLANAUTH table and its index to delete rows from the table. Other DBRMs cannot be bound or executed during this processing unless privileges are granted to the public. It is best to override the default and use the RETAIN parameter. It does not apply to packages because the equivalent of RETAIN is always used with packages. RETAIN is one of the few parameters that is specific to BIND and cannot be changed with REBIND.

CACHESIZE: The CACHESIZE indicates the size of the authorization cache which can be a value from 256 to 4096 bytes or zero. (The cache size specified is rounded up to the nearest multiple of 256 bytes.) The authorization cache will contain the most recent AUTHIDs which have executed the plan. It is used with the plan in the EDM pool to minimize I/O to the catalog tables to check if the appropriate authorities are held at execution time. The base portion is 32 bytes and each cached AUTHID requires 8 bytes. The default authorization cache size of 1,024 bytes holds the last 124 AUTHIDs which executed the plan. If more than 124 AUTHIDs frequently execute the plan, the CACHESIZE can be increased to 4096 bytes or set to 0.

A CACHESIZE of 0 saves space in the EDM pool and is a good choice when execution authority is granted to the public with the use of transaction level security. The grant of execution authority to the public causes a bit to be turned on for a plan after the first execution to avoid further authorization checks as long as the plan remains in the EDM pool. If this procedure is used, the default CACHESIZE of 1024 can be changed to 0 on the installation panel DSNTIPP to avoid the default being taken accidentally.

Package caching is at the subsystem level. There is one cache for all packages. The use of the cache can be specified in DSNZPARM or PACKAGE AUTH CACHE of DSNTIPP panel. The default global cache size for all packages is 32 KB which allows for about 400 AUTHIDs. It is necessary to GRANT EXECUTE ON collid.* TO AUTHIDs for use of the package cache. There is a plan cache for each plan by default.

PATHDEFAULT and PATH: These parameters are used to identify the correct user-defined distinct types, functions, and stored procedure to execute if the object is not explicitly qualified when invoked. The qualifiers of SYSIBM, SYSFUN, and SYSPROC are searched first regardless of the PATHDEFAULT (rebind parameters) and PATH (bind parameter) values. PATHDEFAULT means that the value specified for the QUALIFIER parameter is searched next. This is the default if PATH is not specified on BIND command. PATH (SCHEMA1, SCHEMA2, SCHEMA3, etc., USER) means that each schema name is used as the qualifier in the order specified to locate the object. The schema names must be specified in all upper case letters. USER (if specified) means that the primary AUTHID of the person executing the program containing the object is used as the qualifier if object is not found in previously listed schemas. This value requires granting privileges to users. The maximum length of the values specified for the PATH parameter is 254 or less. You can specify PATHDEFAULT or PATH (not both) on REBIND command.

CURRENTSERVER(DUBLIN): This parameter causes a connection to the named location before running the plan, Dublin in the example. The CURRENT SERVER special register is set to the location. The location must be placed in the catalog table SYSLOCATIONS. CURRENTSERVER can be used to avoid modifying an existing program to be executed at a remote site. However, it causes an implicit type 1 connection to be used. This means the use of the private protocol which will probably be replaced with DRDA in the future. Any explicitly executed CONNECT statement uses a type 1 connection. CURRENTSERVER does not apply to DRDA which uses a type 2 connection.

DBPROTOCOL(DRDA): This parameter provides for specifying whether DRDA or private protocol is used in a client/server environment. DBPROTOCOL(DRDA) means that the DRDA protocol is used (default unless changed on DSNTIP5 installation panel or DSNZPARM DSN6SYSP DBPROTCL). DBPROTOCOL(PRIVATE) means that the private protocol is used. This option is not advisable because no further enhancement are planned and the private protocol is likely to be removed from DB2 in the future.

DISCONNECT: A program can be connected to multiple sites at any one time. However, only one connection is active at any one time. It is advisable to physically destroy connections that are not to be used again in the program. The RELEASE statement should be used to indicate that the connection will not be used again so that it can be destroyed at the next commit. The DISCONNECT parameter provides for specifying which connection are to be destroyed at the next commit. DISCONNECT(EXPLICIT) means that all released connections will be destroyed at the next commit and is the default. This is a good choice if additional work needs to be done at a location after a commit is issued for some locations. The RELEASE statement should be used for locations that will not be visited again after a commit to reduce the resources required to hold connections. The RELEASE statement itself does not destroy the connect, rather it sets a condition so that the connection will be destroyed when a commit is issued for a plan bound with DISCONNECT(EXPLICIT). DISCONNECT (AUTOMATIC) means that all connections will be destroyed at the next commit even if they have not been released. This is a good choice if all the required work is completed at all locations before a commit is issued. DISCONNECT(CONDITIONAL) means that all connections will be destroyed except those with an open cursor defined using the CURSOR WITH HOLD clause.

Enforcement of SQL Standards

There are three ways that you can choose to have SQL syntax and processing conform to the DB2 or SQL standard:

- Bind plan options
- Precompile options
- SET statement in a program

SQLRULES: SQLRULES(STD) causes the bind to conform to the American National Standards Institute (ANSI) standard for SQL processing. SQLRULES(NO) does not require conformance to the standard and is the default. Optionally, the processing of SQL can be made to conform to the SQL standard or DB2 by specifying the precompiler parameter STDSQL with a value of NO or DB2.

Precompiler Option: You can have the precompiler check that the syntax conforms to the SQL standard or DB2 by specifying a value of STD or IBM for the SQLFLAG parameter. The default for the SQLFLAG parameter is IBM for the enforcement of IBMDB2 syntax.

SET CURRENT RULES: The CURRENT RULES special register is set based on STDSQL and SQLRULES parameter values. DB2 is the default. The bind parameter value overrides the precompiler parameter value. Optionally, you can set the special register to STD or DB2 like:

```
SET CURRENT RULES = 'STD'
```

The SET statement is useful prior to executing SQL with SPUFI. Rather than specifying the literal 'STD' as in the example, you can specify a host variable that contains a valid value. The current value of the special register can be determined like:

```
SET :CRULES = CURRENT RULES
```

SQLCODE and SQLSTATE Compliance with the SQL Standard: If STDSQL of YES is specified to the precompiler, SQLCODE and SQLSTATE must be stand-alone variables (not part of the SQLCA data structure) and defined like:

```
EXEC SQL BEGIN DECLARE SECTION END-EXEC.
01  SQLCODE  PIC S9(9) COMP.
01  SQLSTATE PIC X(5).
EXEC SQL END DECLARE SECTION END-EXEC.
```

Notice that "EXEC SQL BEGIN DECLARE SECTION END-EXEC." and "EXEC SQL END DECLARE SECTION END-EXEC." blanket the declaration of host variables based on the standard.

The SQLCA data structure must not be coded in the program according to the standard. The INCLUDE statement discussed in Chapter PD is acceptable:

```
EXEC SQL INCLUDE SQLCA END-EXEC.
```

You probably already follow this procedure. The SQLCA has SQLCADE rather than SQLCODE because the SQLCODE must be a standalone host variable based on the standard. Similarly, SQLCA has SQLSTAT rather than SQLSTATE because SQLSTATE must be a standalone host variable. The precompiler includes moves to avoid you having to rewrite existing host programs:

```
Move SQLCADE in SQLCA to SQLCODE
Move SQLSTAT in SQLCA to SQLSTATE
```

PE.7 REBINDING PLANS AND PACKAGES

The REBIND command is quite distinct from the BIND command. The REBIND command is useful to have the optimizer evaluate and perhaps choose another access path and to change most of the bind parameters. REBIND gets the SQL to be bound from the catalog tables (SYSSTMT or SYSPACKSTMT). BIND gets its SQL from the DBRM library and must be used after a host program has been precompiled.

DB2 automatically rebinds a plan or package if changes have invalidated it--if an index, table, or view has been dropped or a privilege revoked. There are times when developers may want to rebind plans and packages, such as when an added index may improve performance, a table's statistics have changed significantly so that the optimizer might choose a different access path, a new release of DB2 has been installed with enhancement that can improve performance, or the plan or package has been marked as invalid. If a rebind fails, DB2 marks the plan or package as inoperative to avoid many repeated rebinds. It is necessary to perform a bind replace once a plan or package has become inoperative.

Identify Invalid and Inoperative Packages and Plans

A SELECT from the catalog tables can be used to identify the packages and plans that have been invalidated (VALID = 'N') and an automatic rebind will be attempted. An automatic rebind uses the last owner AUTHID (SYSPACKAGE or SYSPLAN.CREATOR) of the person who performed the bind. OPERATIVE = 'N' indicates that an unsuccessful rebind (automatic or initiated) has occurred and an explicit bind is required. Packages and plans that are invalid or inoperative can be identified like:

```
SELECT COLLID, NAME, VERSION, CREATOR,
       BOUNDBY, VALID, OPERATIVE, BINDTIME
FROM   SYSIBM.SYSPACKAGE
WHERE  VALID     = 'N'
OR     OPERATIVE = 'N';

SELECT NAME, CREATOR, BOUNDBY, VALID,
       OPERATIVE, BINDDATE
FROM   SYSIBM.SYSPLAN
WHERE  VALID     = 'N'
OR     OPERATIVE = 'N';
```

The REBIND Command: The syntax of the REBIND command is similar to the BIND command. Most parameters can be changed when the REBIND command is executed. The exceptions that cannot be changed with a rebind are: SQLERROR, COPY, COPYVER, and ACTION REPLVER. If bind parameters are not specified, the parameters specified when the package or plan was last bound are used in most cases. The global operator "*" means that all packages or plans that your AUTHID is authorized to bind are to be rebound. Extreme caution should be exercised when using the global operator "*". If someone with the highest authorization, SYSADM, uses all packages and plans on the DB2 subsystem will be rebound ,which is probably not the intent. You can rebind more packages and plans than intended with most privileges. In particular, you will rebind all packages and plans where privileges have been granted to the public with a command like:

```
REBIND PACKAGE(*)
```

Optionally, an asterisk can be used in each position of the package name to rebind all of the package you are authorized to bind.

```
REBIND PACKAGE(*.*.(*))
```

You can rebind all plans you are authorized to bind like:

```
REBIND PLAN(*)
```

Each package or plan rebind is committed before processing the next one. A package being bound cannot be executed. However, a plan that references the package can be executed as can other packages referenced in the plan. Exclusive locks are taken on the package or plan table and on indexes in the directory where the package or package is placed when bound. These exclusive locks can interfere with the bind and execution of other packages and plans. The use of packages decreases the likelihood of lock contention since packages are typically small and require less time to bind .. Another parameter to use cautiously is REBIND PLAN(STRN) NOPKLIST. This command causes all collections and packages to be dropped from the STRN plan.

It is best to name one or more packages and plans that are to be rebound. A specific package (PROGA) and version ('1991-04-01-09.15.30.141719') of a package in the SPJPROD collection can be rebound with:

```
REBIND PACKAGE -
  (SPJPROD.PROGA.('1991-04-01-09.15.30.141719'))
```

Here is an example of rebinding one plan and three plans:

```
REBIND PLAN (TRN1)

REBIND PLAN (TRN1, TRN2, TRN3)
```

Generating REBIND Commands

REBIND commands can be generated using SELECT statements from the catalog tables. This provides for reviewing the packages and plans to be rebound before the commands are executed. In addition, if there is a failure during a rebind of many packages and plans, you will know which objects bound successfully and which objects still need to be rebound after the failure. The REBIND commands can be generated with the following statements.

```
SELECT 'REBIND PLAN('CONCAT STRIP(NAME) CONCAT ')'
FROM   SYSIBM.SYSPLAN
WHERE  BOUNDTS >= TIMESTAMP('1989-12-31-24.00.00.000000')
AND    BOUNDTS <= TIMESTAMP('1997-12-31-24.00.00.000000');
```

You can include all versions of all packages like:

```
SELECT 'REBIND PACKAGE(' CONCAT STRIP(COLLID)
       CONCAT '.' CONCAT STRIP(NAME) CONCAT '.(*))'
FROM   SYSIBM.SYSPACKAGE
WHERE  TIMESTAMP >= TIMESTAMP('1989-12-31-24.00.00.000000')
AND    TIMESTAMP <= TIMESTAMP('1997-12-31-24.00.00.000000');
```

You also have the flexibility of rebinding only packages and plans that meet specified conditions. Packages and plans that are bound with other than cursor stability can be identified by adding the condition ISOLATION ¬= 'S' to the WHERE clause; those that do not allow for lock avoidance can be identified with CURRENTDATA ¬= 'B'; and those that were bound without consideration for the use of parallelism can be identified with DEGREE = '1'.

PE.8 FREEING PLANS AND PACKAGES

The FREE command and DROP statement can be used to delete packages that are no longer needed. FREE is a DSN command to delete plans as well as local and remote packages. DROP is an SQL statement to delete local packages (not plans). It is executable from a program, SPUFI, QMF, etc. A plan or package cannot be deleted while it is executing.

A specific version of a package can be freed or dropped by specifying the fully qualified name. The leading qualifier of location can be included in a client/server environment. Here are examples of deleting a package with FREE and DROP:

```
FREE PACKAGE -
    (SPJTEST.PROGA.'1992-01-01-09.15.30.123456')

DROP PACKAGE SPJTEST.PROGA VERSION -
    '1992-01-01-09.15.30.123456';
```

Here is an example of deleting a plan with the FREE command.

```
FREE PLAN (TRN1)
```

When all versions of a specific package are outdated and should be deleted, this FREE command is useful with the asterisk in the version position of the package:

```
FREE PACKAGE(SPJTEST.PROGA.(*))
```

Multiple packages and plans can be deleted with an asterisk, similar to the way multiple packages and plans can be rebound. Like with REBIND, you should be extremely cautious about acting on more packages and plans than you intend. This FREE command deletes all packages in a collection at the local site:

```
FREE PACKAGE(SPJTEST.*)
```

The following FREE commands delete all packages and plans you are authorized to bind:

```
FREE PACKAGE(*) -- or
FREE PACKAGE(*.*.(*))

FREE PLAN(*)
```

Again, great caution should be exercised when using an asterisk, particularly when deleting packages and plans. If someone with SYSADM privileges invokes FREE PLAN(*) and FREE PACKAGE(*), all plans and packages for all application systems, and all plans and packages used by DB2 itself, such as the DCLGEN, SPUFI plans, and QMF, are deleted. This accident has been known to happen when well-meaning developers clean up unused plans, costing considerable extra work to restore the unintentionally deleted plans.

PE.9 INFORMATION ON PLANS AND PACKAGES IN THE CATALOG

DB2 records a good deal of information in the catalog tables about plans and packages when they are bound as summarized in Figure PE.9.

Figure PE.9. Catalog tables updated with bind

- **SYSPLANDEP and SYSPACKDEP** have one row for each index, table, view, alias, synonym, and tablespace used by the plan or package.
- **SYSSTMT and SYSPACKSTMT** have one or more rows with the text of each SQL statement.
- **SYSPLAN and SYSPACKAGE** have one row for creator, boundby, bind time and date, plan size, valid, operative, validate, isolation, etc.
- **SYSPLANAUTH and SYSPACKAUTH** have one row for each owner with plan or package authority.
- **SYSPLSYSTEM and SYSPKSYSTEM** have one row for each type of system enabled or disabled.
- **SYSPACKLIST** has one row for each collection_ID.package in the package list.
- **SYSDBRM** has one row for each DBRM creator, host language, PDS containing DBRM, etc, for plans and packages.

Plans and packages themselves are placed in separate tables in the directory as discussed briefly in this chapter and in detail in Chapter CO.

Impact Analysis

Information in the catalog tables is particularly useful for impact analysis. If a column is added or deleted from a table or the data type of a column is changed, it is necessary to determine programs that are affected. This can be done by selecting from SYSPLANDEP and SYSPACKDEP to identify all plans and packages that reference the table. A plan or package that references a table may not reference the column that has been changed. A finer level of identification can be made by selecting from SYSSTMT and SYSPACKSTMT ,which contain the text of SQL statements. A LIKE predicate can be used to find all references to a column that has been changed.

Following are two SELECT statements that identify plans and packages that use the named table and creator. Of course, the 'table name' represents the table name of interest, the 'creator' represents the AUTHID that created the plan or package, and the 'column name' represents the column name. The search can be narrowed to plans and packages that use a specified column by executing the statements again and changing the S1.TEXT LIKE '%table name%' predicate to S1.TEXT LIKE '%column name%'.

```
SELECT DISTINCT S2.PLNAME, S2.NAME,
                S2.STMTNO, S2.SEQNO,
                S2.TEXT, BNAME
FROM    SYSIBM.SYSSTMT S1,
        SYSIBM.SYSSTMT S2,
        SYSIBM.SYSPLANDEP
WHERE   BNAME          = 'table name'
AND     BCREATOR       = 'creator'
AND     BTYPE          = 'T'
AND     S1.PLNAME      = DNAME
```

```
AND     S1.PLNAME    = S2.PLNAME
AND     S1.NAME      = S2.NAME
AND     S1.PLCREATOR = S2.PLCREATOR
AND     S1.STMTNO    = S2.STMTNO
AND     S1.TEXT LIKE '%table name%'
AND     S1.TEXT NOT LIKE '%FETCH%'
AND      (S1.TEXT LIKE '%DECLARE%CURSOR%'
OR        S1.TEXT LIKE '%SELECT%'
OR        S1.TEXT LIKE '%INSERT%'
OR        S1.TEXT LIKE '%UPDATE%'
OR        S1.TEXT LIKE '%LOCK%')
ORDER BY S2.PLNAME,S2.NAME,
  S2.STMTNO,S2.SEQNO;

SELECT DISTINCT S2.COLLID, S2.NAME,
                S2.VERSION, S2.STMTNO,
                S2.SEQNO, S2.TEXT, BNAME
FROM    SYSIBM.SYSPACKSTMT S1,
        SYSIBM.SYSPACKSTMT S2,
        SYSIBM.SYSPACKDEP
WHERE   BNAME           = 'table name'
AND     BCREATOR        = 'creator'
AND     BTYPE           = 'T'
AND     S1.NAME         = DNAME
AND     S1.NAME         = S2.NAME
AND     S1.NAME         = S2.NAME
AND     S1.STMTNO       = S2.STMTNO
AND     S1.STMT LIKE '%table name%'
AND     S1.STMT NOT LIKE '%FETCH%'
AND      (S1.STMT LIKE '%DECLARE%CURSOR%'
OR        S1.STMT LIKE '%SELECT%'
OR        S1.STMT LIKE '%INSERT%'
OR        S1.STMT LIKE '%UPDATE%'
OR        S1.STMT LIKE '%LOCK%')
ORDER BY S2.COLLID,S2.NAME,
  S2.VERSION,S2.STMTNO,S2.SEQNO;
```

There are some limitations to the SELECT statements. They do not identify references to views, aliases, and synonyms. Nor do they identify tables where the FROM clause extends beyond the 254 bytes of the SQL statement stored in the TEXT/STMT columns.

The execution of the SELECT statements can take some time since they require a tablespace scan of all static SQL statements in all applications systems using DB2. However, it will take considerably less time than several programmers manually locating and searching through a large number of program listings.

PE.10 MANAGING SETS OF TABLES WITH PACKAGES

It may be necessary to manage a set of tables for each corporate division or branch office, or for some other functional grouping of the data. All of the tables have the same structure, that is the same columns with the same data types and lengths, but each division needs to maintain its data in a separate set of tables. This approach is sometimes referred to as mirror tables. (The use of views that identify groups of data in one large table is not always an acceptable alternative.) However, information systems professionals do not want to incur the cost of maintaining separate sets of programs. If a change needs to be made to one program, it would have to be made to all of the identical programs for each of perhaps five or more divisions. One set of programs using a number of sets of tables can be managed through the use of packages.

Each set of tables can be created with a qualifier indicating the division that uses the tables, for example DIV1, DIV2, DIV3, DIV4, and DIV5. The BIND PACKAGE and BIND PLAN commands provide for specifying the qualifier to be used for each table and view referenced in an SQL statement as discussed in Section PE.5. A single set of programs can be developed and prepared as usual resulting in a single set of DBRM members. The difference lies in the use of a collection and qualifier for each set of programs. Here is an example of binding a plan with five collections for each of five divisions:

```
BIND PLAN   (ALLDIV)                            -
     PKLIST (DIV1COL.*, DIV2COL.*,              -
     DIV3COL.*, DIV4COL.*, DIV5COL.*)
```

Each DBRM member is bound into each of the five collections. Here is an example of binding the SQL in one DBRM member into two of the collections established:

```
BIND PACKAGE    (DIV1COL)                  -
     LIBRARY    (PROJECT.AUTHID.DBRM)      -
     MEMBER     (PROGA)                    -
     OWNER      (FLEUR)                    -
     QUALIFIER  (DIV1) ...

BIND PACKAGE    (DIV2COL)                  -
     LIBRARY    (PROJECT.AUTHID.DBRM)      -
     MEMBER     (PROGA)                    -
     OWNER      (ERIC)                     -
     QUALIFIER  (DIV2) ...
```

The host program must determine which of the packages to be used based on who is executing the transaction and plan since all of the packages have the same consistency token as taken from the set of DBRMs. The program can be designed to determine at execution time who is executing the program using the LTERM, USERID, or some other means and move the appropriate collection name into :CUR-DIV followed by the execution of:

```
SET CURRENT PACKAGESET = :CUR-DIV
```

This results in accessing the set of tables for the specified division. If the set is not issued, the first package in the list with the same consistency token is used. The package will not reference the correct set of tables in most cases.

Current and Historical Data: Alternatives for managing current and historical data are as discussed in Chapter CD. Another alterative is to use two sets of mirror tables and to maintain current data in one set of tables and historical data in another set of tables. For example, current data tables can have a qualifier of CURRENT and historical tables can have a qualifier of HISTORY with corresponding CURRENT and HISTORY collections.

PE.11 EXECUTING PROGRAMS AND THE DSN PROCESSOR

The DSN command processor uses the TSO attach. It is used to execute programs and can be used to perform program preparation functions. Most TSO commands can also be used from within the DSN command processor. The DSN command processor can be used interactively under TSO, from a CLIST, or JCL.

Following is a CLIST to execute the SUPDATE program with the load module in the PROJECT.AUTHID.LOAD library. The parameter SYSTEM(DSN) uses the default name of DB2 which is DSN and should be changed to the name given to DB2 by the person who installed it. Frequently the name of DB2T is given to the test DB2 subsystem.

```
PROC 0
CONTROL MSG,MAIN,NOPROMPT,LIST
ALLOC F(SYSOUT) DA(*)
ALLOC F(REPORT) DA(*)
ALLOC F(PARMIN) DA('PARMIN.FILE')

DSN SYSTEM(DSN)
RUN PROGRAM(SUPDATE) PLAN(SUPDATE) -
    LIBRARY('PROJECT.AUTHID.LOAD')
END
```

The TSO TMP, CAF, or RRSAF can be used to execute batch programs. Section BP.10 has sample JCL to execute a batch program using the TMP and discusses the pros and cons of using CAF.

The execution of plans and packages in the EDM pool and thread creation, use, and termination are covered in Chapter CO.

PE.12 SUMMARY

This chapter has described how to prepare and execute programs including DCLGEN, precompile, bind, compile, linkedit, and execution. Do use the JCL customized by your company for this processing. If none is available, consider the use of the DB2I program preparation panels to generate the JCL and customize it for your purposes. If a program is precompiled, BIND with the REPLACE parameter must be used to create a new package or plan even if nothing has changed in the program before executing the program.

EXERCISES

1. Why is it important to have DCLGEN generate data structures and the DECLARE TABLE statements for tables manipulated in a program?

2. Is there a performance penalty for having many packages in a collection, say 10,000 ,as an example? Why?

3. Is there a performance penalty for having many collections associated with a plan, say 20, as an example? Why? How can you avoid this performance penalty?

4. Assume that a program has the following SQL statement.

```
SELECT SN, SNAME, STATUS, CITY
FROM   S
WHERE  CITY = 'Mexico City';
```

The developer who binds the associated DBRM into a package has an AUTHID of Fleur. How can you direct DB2 to use the table SPJTEST.S through the use of the BIND PACKAGE command?

5. If you use the COPY parameter to copy a package from a test DB2 subsystem to a production DB2 subsystem, will it have the same access path in production as it did in test? Why?

6. The use of an asterisk when rebinding and freeing plans and packages can save the time and effort in developing many commands or listing the names of many plans and packages. What is a major disadvantage of using this technique?

7. Revisions are made to a program after going through the complete program preparation process. The revised program is precompiled, compiled, link edited, and a rebind done to produce a new application plan. The program will not execute. What is a possible problem?

8. A new program was developed, prepared, and the package bound. The program will not execute. What is a possible problem?

9. What is the source of SQL when doing a bind of a package? What is the source of SQL when doing a rebind of a package?

10. Write a DSN command to run program SNCHANGE from library SUPPLY.DJK.LOAD. The application plan carries the program name. The facility has named its DB2 subsystem DB2.

11. If you do not have JCL to do program preparation, what are two alternatives for getting the JCL?

ANSWERS

1. Generation of data structures by DCLGEN insures that the data type and length of host variables used in SQL statements matches the data type and length of columns in a table. DECLARE TABLE statements allow the precompiler to check the syntax of SQL statements in a program and report any errors. This minimizes the possibility of errors when the SQL is bound.

2. There is no performance penalty for having many packages in a collection. This is because a matching index scan is used to locate the required package.

3. There is a performance penalty for having many collections associated with a plan If there are 20 packages in a collection 20 matching index scans may be required to locate a package before it is executed if it is in the last collection. The performance penalty can be avoided by setting the current package set to the collection that references the package before an SQL statement in the package is executed.

4. You direct DB2 to use the table SPJTEST.S by specifying QUALIFIER(SPJTEST) on the BIND PACKAGE command.

5. The COPY parameter can be used to copy a package to another DB2 subsystem. However, the SQL will be bound on the new DB2 subsystem which will probably have different catalog statistic and different subsystem parameters. If there are differences between the two subsystems, there can be differences between the access paths chosen by the subsystems.
6. All plans and packages are rebound or freed that you are authorized to bind including those granted to the public. You may well rebind or free many more plans and packages than you intended and it will be very resource intensive and frustrating to put things back the way they were. This is particularly true if you have SYSADM privileges.

7. If a program has been precompiled, its application plan must be bound with BIND REPLACE. A rebind of a plan results in an SQLCODE of -818 at execution time.

8. A plan must be bound in addition to binding the package.

9. The source of SQL when doing a bind is a member of a DBRM library. The SQL statements are placed in a DBRM member by the precompiler. The source of SQL when doing a rebind of a package is SYSPACKSTMT. The SQL is placed in the catalog table when the BIND command is executed.

10. Here is a DSN command to run the program SNCHANGE from library SUPPLY.DJK.LOAD:

```
DSN SYSTEM(DB2)
    RUN PROGRAM(SNCHANGE) PLAN(SNCHANGE) -
        LIBRARY('SUPPLY.DKJ.LOAD')
END
```

11. If you do not have JCL to do program preparation, two alternatives for getting the JCL are:

1) Ask an associate for a copy of the JCL that is used at your company for program preparation.

2) Use the DB2 I panels to generate the JCL and customize it to fit your requirements if established JCL is not available.

FIGURES

Join Performance

JP.1 INTRODUCTION

Joins are used to combine information from two or more tables by comparing all the values that meet the search criteria in the designated column or columns of one table with all the values in corresponding columns of the other table or tables. When the values meet the comparison criteria, the rows containing them are joined and used for the select. (This kind of join is called an *inner join*. *Outer joins*, discussed in Section JP.8, do not require a match in both columns to be joined.)

A Typical Join Example

A simple example illustrates the join concept. To find all suppliers of part P4, their names, cities, and amounts they supply, data must be drawn from tables S and SPJ.

- The first step is to find the P4 suppliers, identified by supplier number, in the SPJ table. Those rows, shaded in Figure JP.1, also provide the quantities supplied.
- The next step is to find the suppliers' names and cities by matching the SN values associated with P4 in the SPJ table with the SN values in the S table—that is, by comparing the values for equality.
- When a match is found, the selected columns from the S and SPJ table make up the result of the join.

Figure JP.1. A typical join

SPJ Table

SN	PN	JN	QTY
S1	P1	J1	200
S1	P1	J4	700
S2	P3	J1	400
S2	P3	J2	200
S2	P3	J3	200
S2	P3	J4	500
S2	P3	J5	600
S2	P3	J6	400
S2	P3	J7	800
S2	P5	J2	100
S3	P3	J1	200
S3	P4	J2	500
S4	P6	J3	300
S4	P6	J7	300
S5	P2	J2	200
S5	P2	J4	100
S5	P5	J5	500
S5	P5	J7	100
S5	P6	J2	200
S5	P1	J4	100
S5	P3	J4	200
S5	P4	J4	800
S5	P5	J4	400
S5	P6	J4	500

S Table

SN	SNAME	STATUS	CITY
S1	Smith	20	London
S2	Jones	10	Paris
S3	**Blake**	**30**	**Paris**
S4	Clark	20	London
S5	**Adams**	**30**	**Athens**

The FROM clause of the SELECT statement for the join must include the tables that participate. The WHERE clause identifies the columns to be compared for the join and the type of comparison. Although most joins involve a match of values called an equi-join *or* natural join any of the comparison operators may be used. The statement needed for this join example is:

```
SELECT SNAME, CITY, QTY
FROM   S, SPJ
```

```
WHERE   S.SN = SPJ.SN
AND     PN   = 'P4';
```

Returns:

SNAME	CITY	QTY
Blake	Paris	500
Adams	Athens	800

The "S.SN = SPJ.SN" portion of the statement is the join predicate. A predicate used to narrow the search is the local predicate, "PN = 'P4'" in the example.

Although not a requirement, it is recommended that the columns on which the tables are joined have the same name, data type, and length. When they have the same name, the column names must be qualified by the table name. Column SN appears in both the S and SPJ table and therefore must be qualified with the table name, as S.SN and SPJ.SN in the example. Optionally, columns can be qualified with a correlation name as discussed in Chapter SL.

General Join Guidelines

The simplest and most important guideline is to narrow the search to only the rows required by specifying as many predicates as possible to minimize the number of rows to be joined. The number of rows joined usually effects performance more than the number of tables joined. As the number of rows to be joined goes up multiplicatively, the join costs go up exponentially.

Proper index design and usage are critical to the performance of joins for anything other than the smallest of tables. DB2 uses indexes efficiently for joins. However, the indexed columns to be joined must match in data type and length. Otherwise, a matching index scan cannot be used in the join processing. Most joins are over the primary and foreign key columns, which should have matching data types. When they do not match it is usually a result of a keying error when the tables were created, or lack of communication between people who created the tables. The primary key might be defined as DECIMAL(8,2) and the foreign key as DECIMAL(8,3). The data types are similar and even require the same amount of storage on DASD, but indexes on these columns cannot be used to perform a join. The requirement for matching data types and lengths is discussed in Chapter PP.

Exception: An equi-join can be done on CHAR and VARCHAR columns of unequal length (V5 APAR PQ22046). This applies to nested loop and merge joins (not hybrid joins). (These join types are discussed in detail in the next section.) In the following example, assume that the length of the column is represented by the last one or two digits of the column name.

```
SELECT CHAR2, CHAR4, CHAR10, VARCHAR25
FROM   TA, TB
WHERE  TA.CHAR2      = TB.CHAR4
AND    TA.VARCHAR25 = TB.CHAR10
```

A matching index scan can be used on all column in the statement.

Join Methods

DB2 can implement joins using a merge join, nested loop join, or hybrid join. When DB2 processes a join, it decides which table should be processed first. This table is designated the outer table of the join. The second table used in the join is the inner table. The outer table is usually the table with the smallest number of qualifying rows. This choice requires less processing on the larger inner table.

JP.2 THE MERGE JOIN METHOD

The merge join method requires that the rows in the tables to be joined are in sequence. DB2 either sorts the rows or retrieves them in sequence using a high cluster ratio index (a large percent of rows are in the sequence of the indexed column on the data pages). If a sort is required, all predicates are applied before the sort so that a minimal number of rows are sorted. A row is read from the outer table and the inner table is read to find all matches, a second row is read from the outer table and the inner table is read from its last position to find all matches. The comparisons continue similar to standard match-merge processing.

Consider the following join to determine the supplier names of parts and the quantity of parts used on jobs where SN is between S1 and S5.

```
SELECT S.SN, SNAME, PN, JN, QTY
FROM   S, SPJ
WHERE  S.SN = SPJ.SN
AND    S.SN BETWEEN 'S1' AND 'S5'
ORDER BY S.SN;
```

S.SN is the primary key of the S table and has a unique index. SPJ.SN is the foreign key of the SPJ table. This is a one-to-many join. For each unique SN in the S table there are many corresponding SNs in the SPJ table. The optimizer will probably recognize this by analyzing the statistics in the catalog tables. This suggests that the S table contains the smaller number of qualifying rows and is made the outer table. The ORDER BY S.SN clause encourages the optimizer to choose the S table as the outer table if the index on S.SN has a high cluster ratio index. This is because the index can be used to avoid a sort for the ORDER BY and for the merge join. In general, ORDER BY on columns of a table encourages the table to be outer table for a merge and nested loop join.

When Merge Join is Favored

It is best not to try to influence the optimizer's choice of access paths. However, there are times when it may be necessary. The merge join can be encouraged by using an ORDER BY on a join column with a high cluster ratio index. Here is a summary of the factors that encourage a merge join:

- There is a high cluster ratio index on the inner or outer table. This indicates that a large percent of the rows are in the required sequence on the data pages and can be used to avoid sorts.
- Few columns are selected. This means the result rows to be sorted are shorter and the sort costs are reduced. The reduced cost increases the likelihood of a merge join. Large sorts discourage the use of the merge join method.

- There are a large number of qualifying rows to be joined (particularly many-to-many joins).
- There is a small buffer pool.
- There is no usable index on the join tables.

If the columns to be joined do not have matching nullability in addition to data type and length, a merge join involving composite indexes will have less than optimal performance if a sort is required. The sort will be on only the first column in the composite index, and the non-leading columns are evaluated at stage 2 which increases the path length. (Stage 2 predicates are discussed in Chapter PP.) The primary key should be declared as NOT NULL. If there is a conditional dependency or a self-referencing table, the foreign key may need to be declared as allowing for null. If this is the case and a sort is required, a merge join does not give its best performance.

Derived Predicates with a Merge Join

If a sort is required on the outer table, the optimizer can derive predicates that were not coded on the SQL statement. The purpose of these derived predicates is to minimize the number of rows to be processed. Consider determining the parts that were ordered on 1990-09-05:and their suppliers.

```
SELECT O.SN, O.PN, DATE_ORDERED, QTY
FROM   ORDERS O, SPJ
WHERE  DATE_ORDERED = '1990-09-05'
AND    SPJ.SN = O.SN
AND    SPJ.PN = O.PN
AND    SPJ.SN BETWEEN 'S2' AND 'S3' -- Derived predicate
AND    SPJ.PN BETWEEN 'P3' AND 'P4';-- Derived predicate
```

While processing the ORDERS table, the outer table in Figure JP.2, DB2 can determine that only S2, S3, P3, and P4 are required from the SPJ table. Two additional BETWEEN predicates are conceptually added and evaluated at execution time to narrow the number of rows to be joined in the inner table (the SPJ table).

Figure JP.2. Derived predicates with a merge join

Orders

SN	PN	DATE_ORDERED	...
S1	P1	1991-01-31	
S2	P3	1990-09-05	
S3	P3	1990-09-05	
S3	P4	1990-09-05	
S4	P1	1991-02-14	
S5	P5	1991-05-10	
S5	P6	1993-03-12	
Etc			

SPJ

SN	PN	JN	QTY
S1	P1	J1	200
S1	P1	J4	700
S2	P3	J1	400
S2	P2	J2	200
S2	P5	J3	200
S2	P4	J4	500
S2	P3	J5	600
S2	P6	J6	400
S2	P3	J7	800
S2	P6	J2	100
S3	P2	J1	200
S3	P4	J2	500
S4	P6	J3	300
S4	P6	J7	300
S5	P2	J2	200
S5	P2	J4	100
S5	P5	J5	500
S5	P5	J7	100
S5	P6	J2	200
S5	P1	J4	100
S5	P3	J4	200
S5	P4	J4	800
S5	P5	J4	400

JP.3 NESTED LOOP JOIN METHOD

Unlike the merge scan join, the nested loop join method does not require that the rows to be joined be sorted. Also, preprocessing of the data is never required, making it a good technique for joining a small number of rows, in particular for cursor repositioning as described in Chapter PD. With the nested loop join, DB2 reads the first value from the outer table and then, if there is no index on the inner table join column, it scans the inner table looking for matches. Then it reads the second value from the outer table, scans all of the inner table rows, and so on.

The repeated scan of the entire inner table can use considerable I/O operations and CPU time. If there is no index on the inner join column, it is very unlikely that a nested loop join will be performed. If there is an index on the inner table, it is very likely that a matching index scan of the inner table will be done for each qualifying row in the outer table. Costs are reduced further by using the index lookaside technique discussed in Chapter IU and sequential detection discussed in Chapter PP.

A high cluster ratio on the outer table join columns increases index lookaside efficiency with dynamic prefetch on the inner table. If the outer table join column index has a low cluster ratio or there is no usable index, the optimizer may choose to narrow the search according to the local predicates and sort the outer table qualifying rows to gain benefits for inner table processing.

Here is an example of a SELECT statement where the optimizer chose a nested loop join for determining the jobs using parts from suppliers in London.

```
SELECT SPJ.SN, SNAME, PN, JN, QTY
FROM   SPJ, S
WHERE  SPJ.SN = S.SN
AND    CITY = 'London';
```

An index on CITY can be used to narrow the search to suppliers in London. There are two suppliers in London as indicated by the shading in Figure JP.3. The leaf page contains the value of 'London' followed by two RIDs. The first RID is used to access the data page with the first supplier in London, S1. DB2 is using a derived predicate of SPJ.SN = 'S1'. It can use a matching index scan on the SPJ.SN index (or a composite index on SN, PN, and JN) to locate S1. On a SPJ.SN leaf page, it finds two RIDs referencing the two rows in the SPJ table for S1. DB2 can use the first RID to locate the page to retrieve the columns requested in the SELECT statement. A minimal amount of processing is required to return the first row to the program. This is a primary advantage of the nested loop join. Only two matching index scans into the S and SPJ table are required before returning the result row to the program. The first row returned to the program is shown as the first row in the table "Results of Join" in the lower left corner of Figure JP.3.

Figure JP.3. Nested loop join

S (Supplier Table)

SN	SNAME	STATUS	CITY
S1	Smith	20	London
S2	Jones	10	Paris
S3	Blake	30	Paris
S4	Clark	20	London
S5	Adams	30	Athens

SPJ

SN	PN	JN	QTY
S1	P1	J1	200
S1	P1	J4	700
S2	P3	J1	400
S2	P3	J2	200
S2	P3	J3	200
S2	P3	J4	500
S2	P3	J5	600
S2	P3	J6	400
S2	P3	J7	800
S2	P5	J2	100
S3	P3	J1	200
S3	P4	J2	500
S4	P6	J3	300
S4	P6	J7	300
S5	P2	J2	200
S5	P2	J4	100
S5	P5	J5	500
S5	P5	J7	100
S5	P6	J2	200
S5	P1	J4	100
S5	P3	J4	200
S5	P4	J4	800
S5	P5	J4	400
S5	P6	J4	500

Results of Join

SN	SNAME	PN	JN	QTY
S1	Smith	P1	J1	200
S1	Smith	P1	J4	700
S4	Clark	P6	J3	300
S4	Clark	P6	J7	300

The nested loop join processing continues by using the second RID following S1 in the SPJ.SN leaf page to access the data page and to return the second row to the program. DB2 can use the second RID following London to determine that S4 is a required supplier. DB2 can then use a second matching index scan on the SPJ.SN index to locate the RIDs following S4 and then subsequently access the data pages to retrieve the columns required.

The nested loop join is favored in the following circumstances:

- The number of rows to be joined is relatively small.

- OPTIMIZE FOR *n* ROWS is used where *n* is a small number. This encourages use of the nested loop join without having to perform a sort. This is useful in the situation where a SELECT statement qualifies a large number of rows but only a few of those rows are fetched to fill a screen. The optimizer recognizes that a large number of rows will qualify based on the specified predicates and statistics in the catalog tables. The optimizer has no way of knowing that the host program will fetch only a few of the many qualifying rows. The access path for processing a large number of rows will be less than optimal if only a few rows are fetched. It is necessary to inform the optimizer that only a few rows will be fetched even though many rows will qualify. To do this, use the clause OPTIMIZE FOR *n* ROWS on the SELECT statement, as described in Chapter PD.

- If there is an index on the inner table, it is likely that DB2 can use a matching index scan of the inner table for each qualifying row in the outer table.

Influencing which Table Is Processed First: There are times when you may want to influence which table should be the outer table. You can do this by adding a predicate that does not disqualify any rows to the desired outer table. For example, if you want SPJ to be the outer table, you can add the predicate "SPJ.QTY = SPJ.QTY". The optimizer allows itself to be fooled into thinking that the predicate narrows the search and few rows will qualify in the SPJ table. We are taking advantage of the fact that the optimizer usually makes the table with the smallest number of qualifying rows the outer table. If you already have a local predicate like SPJ.QTY = 400 on the column, the SPJ.QTY = SPJ.QTY predicate is ignored. The SPJ.QTY = SPJ.QTY predicate disallows the use of index-only processing.

Be very careful about influencing the optimizer. Even if you get the best access path today, it may not be the best access path in the future. Any changes to the characteristics of the data, the table or index design, or to DB2 itself might cause an undesirable access path because of the original influencing techniques that were used to get a particular access path.

Using the Host Language to Code a Nested Loop Join

Some developers code joins in the application. They may feel more comfortable with the record at a time processing that they have used with non-relational applications or be concerned about the performance of a join. Sometimes people say that they never code joins because they believe that joins will result in poor performance. Although they don't code the join in a SELECT statement, they are coding a join in their programs if they process two or more related tables. Figure JP.4 is the pseudo-code to perform a nested loop join in a host program.

Figure JP.4. Using host language code for a nested loop join

```
DECLARE SC FOR
     SELECT SN, SNAME, STATUS, CITY
     FROM   S

     DECLARE SPJC FOR
     SELECT SN, PN, JN, QTY
     FROM   SPJ
     WHERE  SN = :SN;

PROCESS-OUTER-TABLE
     OPEN SC
     FETCH SC INTO :SN, :SNAME, :STATUS, :CITY
     IF SQLCODE = 100
          GO TO CONTINUE-PROCESSING
     IF SQLCODE = 0
          OPEN SPJC
```

```
PROCESS-INNER-TABLE
     FETCH SPJC INTO :SPJ-SN, :SPJ-PN,
                     :SPJ-JN, :SPJ-QTY
          IF SQLCODE = 100
               CLOSE SPJC
               GO TO PROCESS-OUTER-TABLE
          IF SQLCODE = 0
               PERFORM PROCESS-RESULTS
               GO TO PROCESS-INNER-TABLE

CONTINUE-PROCESSING
```

Clearly, the join can be written much more easily in a SELECT statement like:

```
SELECT S.SN, SNAME, PN, QTY
FROM   S, SPJ
WHERE  SPJ.SN = S.SN;
```

DB2 joins perform better than application joins in the great majority of cases. This is because the join is done at a lower level within DB2 than is possible for a host program. The lower level of processing reduces the number of instructions that must be executed. For example, in one case where performance was measured for a join of 70,000 rows, the application join took 6:26 minutes elapsed time and 2:35 CPU minutes compared with DB2 join times of 4:09 minutes elapsed time and 1:44 CPU minutes. The application join would require even more time and resources in a client/server environment where a client program fetched the rows from the server and then joined them.

JP.4 THE HYBRID JOIN

The hybrid join, as its name indicates, is a mix between a merge and nested loop join. The process is as follows:

1. The outer table rows are either retrieved in sequence using an index with a high cluster ratio (>= 80 percent) or the qualifying values are retrieved and sorted. (This is like merge join.)

2. For each *unique* value in the outer table, find the RIDs for the inner table using a matching index scan. (Similar to nested loop join except that only unique values in the outer table must be evaluated against the inner table with the hybrid join.)

3. Build partial rows of qualifying RIDs from the inner table along with the qualifying columns from the outer table using the work tablespaces in the work database DSNDB07.

4. Sort the partial rows in RID sequence and conceptually eliminate duplicate RIDs on the first 3 bytes that point to a data page of the inner table. This is a type N hybrid join. The work file and sort is not required if the inner table join column has a cluster ratio of >= 80 percent. Also list prefetch can start before all partial rows are built. This is a type C hybrid join.

5. Process the inner table with list prefetch. (List prefetch is discussed in Chapter PP.)

Let's use the following SELECT statement in conjunction with Figure JP.5 to illustrate a hybrid join. Assume that there is a low cardinality index on SPJ.SN:

```
SELECT SPJ.SN, SNAME, PN, JN, QTY
FROM   SPJ, S
WHERE  SPJ.SN = S.SN
AND    SPJ.SN >= 'S1';
```

Figure JP.5. Hybrid join processing

SPJ

SN	PN	JN	QTY
S1	P1	J1	200
S1	P1	J4	700
S2	P3	J1	400
S2	P3	J2	200
S2	P3	J3	200
S2	P3	J4	500
S2	P3	J5	600
S2	P3	J6	400
S2	P3	J7	800
S2	P5	J2	100
S3	P3	J1	200
S3	P4	J2	500
S4	P6	J3	300
S4	P6	J7	300
S5	P2	J2	200
S5	P2	J4	100
S5	P5	J5	500
S5	P5	J7	100
S5	P6	J2	200
S5	P1	J4	100
S5	P3	J4	200
S5	P4	J4	800
S5	P5	J4	400
S5	P6	J4	500

SN	SNAME	STATUS	CITY	S RIDs	Partial
S1	Smith	20	London	1001	rows and
S2	Jones	10	Paris	2001	columns
S3	Blake	30	Paris	~~2002~~	from
S4	Clark	20	London	3001	outer
S5	Adams	30	Athens	4001	table

Partial result of join

SN	SNAME	PN	JN	QTY
S1	Smith	P1	J1	200
S1	Smith	P1	J4	700
S2	Jones	P3	J1	400
S2	Jones	P3	J2	200
Etc				

1. DB2 identifies the first S1 in the SPJ table using a matching index scan or a tablespace scan.

2. It uses a matching index scan into the S table to get the RID for S1.

3. It builds a partial row consisting of the RID referencing the S table and the required columns from the SPJ table. The hybrid join requires that an index be used on the inner table (SPJ table).

4. It is not necessary to do a second matching index scan into SPJ for the second S1 in the S table as would be required if a nested loop join were used. DB2 effectively remembers that it has already found S1in the S table. However, it does have to build a second partial row with the requested columns from the SPJ table.

5. It moves on to the S2 in the SPJ table, does a matching index scan into the S table to get the RID referencing S2 in the S table, and builds a partial row.

It does not have to do seven additional matching index scans for the seven additional S2s in the SPJ. This is a major advantage of the hybrid join compared to a nested loop join that would have done seven additional matching index scans or the merge join which would have done seven comparisons between the two tables. (Of course, seven is not a significant number. Your tables are likely to have very large numbers of duplicate values in one of the tables.)

When the Hybrid Join Is Favored

The hybrid join method is favored if the following conditions are true:

- The outer table has duplicate qualifying values. This means that DB2 can access the inner table only one time instead of the eight times that might be necessary for the eight occurrences of SPJ.SN='S2'. This is a fairly common occurrence in which one primary key is joined with many matching foreign key values.

- The inner table join column has a low cluster ratio index and a fairly small number of RIDs need to be sorted. This is because DB2 uses list prefetch to sequentially access the data rather than random access of data pages with potentially excessive seek time to locate the required inner table columns.

Disadvantages of Hybrid Join

There are some cases where a hybrid join can have disadvantages. If there are local predicates on the inner table, they are not applied until after the join processing when the required columns are gotten from the inner table data pages. This means that more rows can be joined than necessary. The rows that do not qualify according to the local predicates are discarded after the hybrid join processing. If there is a local predicate on CITY where only the suppliers in Athens are required, DB2 does the join processing for the London and Paris suppliers only to find that they are not required. Of course, the optimizer uses statistics in the catalog table to try and identify cases like this so it can avoid using the hybrid join.

There is an exception that improves performance where local predicates can be applied before join processing. DB2 can use multiple columns of a composite index to narrow the search and do the hybrid join processing.

The hybrid join must build partial rows for all of the qualifying rows in the outer table and perhaps sort the RIDs and manage the partial rows before it returns the first row to the program when using a type-N hybrid join. This is a major disadvantage if a large number of rows qualify and only a few are fetched to fill a screen, for example. OPTIMIZE FOR *n* ROWS, where *n* is small, can be used to discourage a hybrid join.

There is an exception where all qualifying rows need not be joined before the first row is returned to the program. If a RID pool threshold is reached, joined rows are returned to the program for the first batch of processed partial rows for type-N and type-C hybrid join.

JP.5 JOIN METHODS AND THE NUMBER OF ROWS TO BE JOINED

The choice of join methods depends on the number of rows to be joined. The merge join is good for joining a large number of qualifying rows. The initial cost of the merge join can be high if one or more qualifying rows in a table must be sorted. Notice in Figure JP.6 that the merge join has a potentially high cost due to a sort, but the costs go up slowly as more rows are joined. The elapsed time for the sort can be reduced dramatically if query parallelism is used, as discussed in Chapter PL. If an index with a high cluster ratio is used to avoid a sort of rows from one or more tables to be joined, the initial cost is reduced dramatically. If none of the qualifying rows need to be sorted, the merge join is competitive with the nested loop join.

Figure JP.6. Choice of join methods

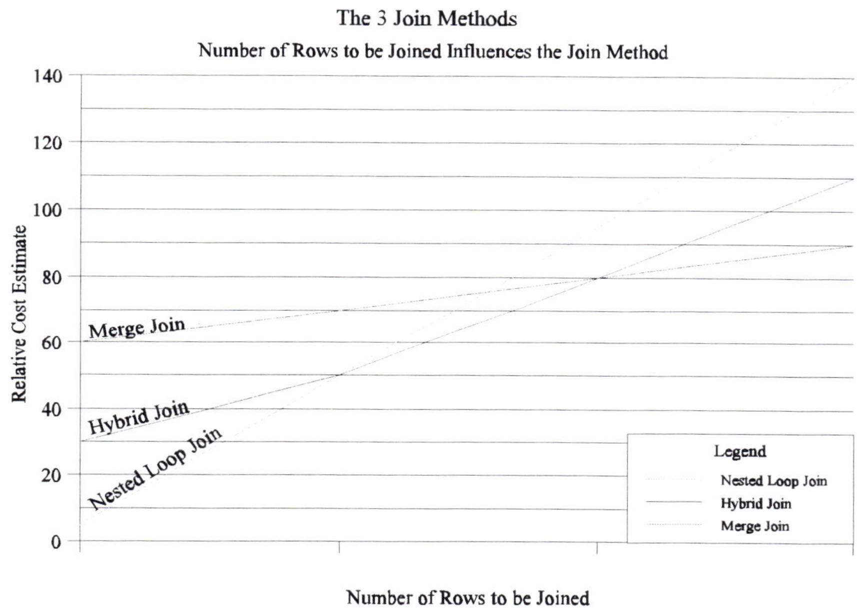

Best for a Small Number of Rows: The nested loop join is good for joining a small number of qualifying rows, which makes it a good choice for online transactions where only a few rows will be displayed to the user. Notice in the figure that the initial cost for the nested loop join is low. However, the cost increases rapidly as the number of rows to be joined increases. Figure BP.3 compares the I/O time of a matching index scan with a tablespace scan. The line for the matching index scan is rather like the line in Figure JP.6 for a nested loop join. This is because the nested loop join almost always uses a matching index scan on the inner table and can use a matching index scan on the outer table as well.

Best for a Larger Number of Rows: Batch processing benefits from match-merge processing and the merge join uses match-merge processing. This suggests that a merge join is a good choice for batch processing, provided CURSOR WITH HOLD is used to avoid a possible merge join sort each time a commit is issued and the cursor is re-opened. (CURSOR WITH HOLD is discussed in Chapter PD.)

Moderate Number of Rows: The hybrid join is good for joining a medium number of qualifying rows. It does have the initial costs of building and perhaps sorting the partial rows. The costs increase more rapidly than the merge join but less rapidly than the nested loop join when joining a large number of rows. Indeed, Figure JP.6 shows that the hybrid join has a rather narrow range where it performs better than the merge and nested loop joins.

Recommendation: It is very important for the optimizer to have a good estimate of the number of rows to be joined. If you have a local predicate on a column without an index, it is necessary to have the SYSCOLUMNS.COLCARDF updated with the number of distinct values in the column. COLCARDF can be used by the optimizer to compute a good estimate of the number of rows that will qualify. This also applies to predicates on the non-leading columns of a composite index where the leading column has not been specified with an equal predicate. The TABLE/COLUMN parameters must be specified when executing RUNSTATS to collect COLCARDF which is not the default. If you find that the optimizer did not choose the best access path for a join, do check that COLCARDF has been updated for columns that are used in local predicates.

JP.6 USE OF MULTIPLE INDEXES WITH A JOIN

Multiple index processing can be used on the inner table using all three join methods. An example shows how this works:

```
SELECT S.SN, SNAME, PN, JN, QTY
FROM   SPJ, S
WHERE  SPJ.SN  = S.SN
AND    JN      = 'J5'
AND    SNAME   = 'Adams';
```

A row with JN = 'J5' can be located in the SPJ table (outer table of nested loop join) where it is determined that S2 supplies the part. DB2 can use an index on SN in the S table (inner table of nested loop join) to locate the RID for S2, RID 2000 for example. An index on SNAME can be used to locate the qualifying RID for Adams, RID 5000 for example. RID 2000 and 5000 are not the same; therefore there is no need to access a data page. The next supplier is obtained from the outer table followed by a matching index scan or index lookaside to locate the RID for S5 which is 5000; in our example. The RID of 5000 obtained for Adams is also 5000, therefore the data pages should be processed to obtain the required columns.

This is very efficient processing and can result in significant savings. An oil company found that a join of rows in a 935,000-row table and a 34,000-row table required 2 hours and 40 minutes. They added an index to allow for multiple-index processing, and the time went to less than one minute. Figure JP.7 contains the results of their experience:

Figure JP.7. Experience with and without multiple index usages

Processing	No Multiple Indexes	Multiple Indexes
Total CPU	2:40:23.05	0:00:59.32
DB2 CPU	2:40:22.38	0:00:52.41
Lock Requests	1,269,424	92,352
Getpage Count	17,282,432	93,982
Sync. Reads	3,108	3,314
Prefetch Reads	542,936	5,630
Immed. Writes	0	0

Joining Multiple Tables Using Multiple Join Methods

The maximum number of tables that can be joined in a SELECT block (SELECT ... FROM ... WHERE, for example) is 15 except for star joins which allow for 225 table join (V6 APAR PQ31326). APAR PQ21815 allowing for 225 table join is removed due to excessive space required in RDS OP pool (861 MB for 23 table join in 1 case). If >15 table join is required, the systems administrator can change DSNZPARM and SPRMMXT SETC '15' to a value <= 225 and run first 2 steps of DSNTIJUZ job. Do be cautious of developing too complex of a statement. It can take a good deal of time to develop, test, and maintain a very complex statement. In addition, the statement can be very resource intensive in terms of I/O, CPU, and elapsed time.

The three join methods can be used in any combination. It is not necessary to complete a two-way inner join before processing a third table. Rather a row from each multiple tables can be joined and returned to the program one at a time. A three-way join illustrates the processing that can be done using the SPJ table, which is an intersection table that shows the relationship between the S and P tables. This is a type of join that is frequently required. In this case it is necessary to determine the supplier name for S3 and the part name of parts supplied by S3.

```
SELECT S.SN, SNAME, P.PN, PNAME
FROM   SPJ, S, P
WHERE  SPJ.SN = 'S3'
AND    SPJ.SN = S.SN
AND    SPJ.PN = P.PN;
```

- A matching index scan on S.SN can be used to locate S3 and used as the outer table of a nested loop join. Although a predicate of S.SN = 'S3' was not specified in the statement, the optimizer was able to deduce it based on the equi-join predicate of SPJ.SN = S.SN. If the S3s in the SPJ table are required, then the S3s in the S table are required.

- A matching index scan with index only processing on the SN, PN, and JN composite index of the SPJ table is used to locate S3. P3 and P4 can be obtained from the leaf page where S3 is located.

- A matching index scan on P.PN can be used to locate P3 and P4 one at a time as the inner table of a hybrid join.

This join strategy performs well provided not too many PNs qualify. It is necessary to build a partial row for each of the qualifying PNs. If many PNs qualify and only a few rows are fetched to fill a screen, consider adding the OPTIMIZE FOR *n* ROWS clause to inform the optimizer that only a few rows will be fetched.

JP.7 PREDICATE TRANSITIVE CLOSURE WITH JOINS

If a predicate is specified on one table of a join, the optimizer, in most cases, adds the predicate to the other table during access path selection. (Applies to outer joins with V5 APAR PQ18710 and after a rebind.) It does this in case it is best to narrow the search using the other table first rather than the table on which the predicate is coded. The outer table of the join is likely to be the table where the predicate is applied. To do this, at least one equal predicate is required. No more than nine tables are consider for predicate transitive closure. The example fulfills the criteria with the equal on the join predicate.

```
SELECT S.SN, SNAME, PN, JN, QTY
FROM   SPJ, S
WHERE  SPJ.SN = S.SN
AND    SPJ.PN > 'S4'
AND    S.SN   > 'S4'; <-- added by optimizer
```

Any predicate that the optimizer adds for access path selection is not evaluated at execution time if it is not used as part of the access path. In contrast, any predicates you code are evaluated at execution time and can add some CPU cost to the query. Generally, it is advisable to let the optimizer add the predicate rather than coding it in the statement. There are two types of predicate where it is advisable to code the predicate on both tables to be joined--IN (list of values) and LIKE predicates. The optimizer does not automatically add these two types of predicate on the second table to be joined. If there is mismatched nullability between the join predicates, added predicate is evaluated at stage 2 and cannot use a matching index scan.

JP.8 OUTER JOINS

In most cases, joins are performed by setting two columns equal to each other. If a value appears in one table but not the other table to be joined, the row with the value in the one table will not appear in the result when there is not a match in the other table. This is the correct result for an inner join. However, there are times when the row without a matching value in the other table is required. For example, assume that there is a requirement to identify all departments and employees in the DEPT and EMP tables shown in Figure JP.8.

Figure JP.8. Sample DEPT and EMP tables

DEPT

DEPTNO	DEPTNAME
D1	PROGDEV
D2	DBADM
D3	DATADM
D4	AI

EMP

EMPNO	LASTNAME	WORKDEPT
E1	Thomas	D1
E2	Clark	D2
E3	Johnson	(null)
E4	Blake	D1
E5	Adams	D2
E6	Jones	D1
E7	Smith	D3
E8	Giles	D3

The first thought might be to do an inner join on the DEPT and EMP like:

```
SELECT DEPTNO, DEPTNAME, EMPNO, LASTNAME
FROM   DEPT, EMP
WHERE  DEPT.DEPTNO = EMP.WORKDEPT;
```

The results of the inner join is in Figure JP.9.

Figure JP.9. Inner join on DEPT.DEPTNO and EMP.WORKDEPT results

DEPTNO	DEPTNAME	EMPNO	LASTNAME	WORKDEPT
~~D4~~	~~AI~~	~~(null)~~	~~(null)~~	~~(null)~~
D1	PROGDEV	E1	Thomas	D1
D1	PROGDEV	E4	Blake	D1
D1	PROGDEV	E6	Jones	D1
D2	DBADM	E2	Clark	D2
D2	DBADM	E5	Adams	D2
D3	DATADM	E7	Smith	D3
D3	DATADM	E8	Giles	D3
~~(null)~~	~~(null)~~	~~E3~~	~~Johnson~~	~~(null)~~

*(null) means that there is no match where DEPTNO = WORKDEPT

The inner join results do not show department D4 in the DEPT table because D4 does not appear in the column EMP.WORKDEPT in Figure JP.8 and is crossed out in Figure JP.9. In addition, employee E3 in the EMP table does not appear in the inner join result because WORKDEPT for E3 is null. Even if there was a null in the parent DEPT table, a null does not equal any value--including another null--and does not participate in a join.

Optionally, the syntax of an inner join can be specified like:

```
SELECT DEPTNO, DEPTNAME, EMPNO, LASTNAME
FROM   DEPT INNER JOIN EMP
ON     DEPT.DEPTNO = EMP.WORKDEPT;
```

The two tables to be joined are separated by INNER JOIN rather than a comma, and ON can be used rather than WHERE.

Coding Outer Joins

An outer join is required to identify all departments and all employees in a company including those departments that have no employees and employees who are not assigned to a department. Here are two ways to do this.

Alternative 1: SELECT with UNION ALL: One technique is to write a SELECT statement for the inner join and then UNION ALL it with a NOT EXISTS subselect to identify departments which do not have employees. Follow that with a UNION ALL and a NOT EXISTS subselect to identify employees who are not assigned to a department like:

```
                    |SELECT DEPTNO,DEPTNAME,EMPNO,LASTNAME,WORKDEPT
Inner join          |FROM   DEPT, EMP
                    |WHERE  DEPT.DEPTNO = EMP.WORKDEPT
                     UNION ALL
                    |SELECT D.DEPTNO,DEPTNAME,'null','null',WORKDEPT
                    |FROM   DEPT D
Departments         |WHERE  NOT EXISTS
  which have        |  (SELECT 1
  no employees      |   FROM   EMP E
                    |   WHERE  D.DEPTNO = E.WORKDEPT)
                     UNION ALL
                    |SELECT 'null','null',E.EMPNO,LASTNAME,WORKDEPT
                    |FROM   EMP E
Employees not       |WHERE  NOT EXISTS
  assigned to a     |  (SELECT 1
  department        |   FROM   DEPT D
                    |   WHERE  D.DEPTNO = E.WORKDEPT);
```

Alternative 2: FULL OUTER JOIN: The NOT EXISTS formulation is a rather lengthy statement to write, not to mention providing plenty of opportunities for errors. It is preferable to write:

```
SELECT DEPTNO, DEPTNAME, EMPNO, LASTNAME, WORKDEPT
FROM   DEPT FULL OUTER JOIN EMP
ON     DEPT.DEPTNO = EMP.WORKDEPT;
```

An ON rather than WHERE is required for outer joins. This indicates that rows without a match in both tables participate in the join. D4 in the DEPT.DEPTNO column is identified even though there is no match in the EMP.WORKDEPT column. E3 is identified even though there is a null in the EMP.WORKDEPT column.

Performance Consideration: A merge join is used for the FULL OUTER JOIN. This is a good choice if all qualifying rows are fetched. In the example, all rows in the two tables qualify. If only a few rows are fetched and many rows qualify, the merge join gives good performance if indexes can be used on both tables to avoid a sort of all rows in both tables.

It may be worth your while to write the more lengthy NOT EXISTS subselect formulation if only a few rows are fetched from an answer set in which a large number of rows qualify and must be sorted. The NOT EXISTS formulation can use a matching index scan on EMP.WORKDEPT in the third query block and on DEPT.DEPTNO in the fifth query block, assuming there are indexes on these columns.

Left Outer Join

Assume it is necessary to identify rows in one table that do not have a match in the other table but not the opposite. For example, if it is necessary to determine all departments regardless of whether they have employees assigned, but it is not necessary to determine all employees regardless of whether they are currently assigned to a department, use a LEFT OUTER JOIN. All rows from the left table (DEPT) are identified with a LEFT OUTER JOIN.

```
SELECT DEPTNO, DEPTNAME, EMPNO, LASTNAME, WORKDEPT
FROM   DEPT LEFT OUTER JOIN EMP
ON     DEPT.DEPTNO = EMP.WORKDEPT;
```

Notice that D4 in the DEPT (left table) is shown in the results of the LEFT OUTER JOIN in Figure JP.10. E3 in the EMP table that is not currently assigned to a department is not included in the result. The syntax of a LEFT OUTER JOIN clause can be written as LEFT OUTER or LEFT. Local predicates can be in ON or WHERE clause. This does not apply to a FULL OUTER join.

Figure JP.10. Results of a left outer join

DEPTNO	DEPTNAME	EMPNO	LASTNAME	WORKDEPT
D4	AI	(null)	(null)	(null)
D1	PROGDEV	E1	Thomas	D1
D1	PROGDEV	E4	Blake	D1
D1	PROGDEV	E6	Jones	D1
D2	DBADM	E2	Clark	D2
D2	DBADM	E5	Adams	D2
D3	DATADM	E7	Smith	D3
D3	DATADM	E8	Giles	D3
~~(null)~~	~~(null)~~	~~E3~~	~~Johnson~~	~~(null)~~

The optimizer may choose a nested loop or merge join for a left or right outer join.

Right Outer Join

The right outer join identifies all rows from the right table (EMP). This allows for determining all employees regardless of whether they are currently assigned to a department.

```
SELECT DEPTNO, DEPTNAME, EMPNO, LASTNAME, WORKDEPT
FROM   DEPT RIGHT OUTER JOIN EMP
ON     DEPT.DEPTNO = EMP.WORKDEPT;
```

E3 is identified because it is in the right table. Figure JP.11 shows that D4 is not identified. D4 is not in the right table.

Figure JP.11. Results of a right outer join

DEPTNO	DEPTNAME	EMPNO	LASTNAME	WORKDEPT
~~D4~~	~~AI~~	~~(null)~~	~~(null)~~	~~(null)~~
D1	PROGDEV	E1	Thomas	D1
D1	PROGDEV	E4	Blake	D1
D1	PROGDEV	E6	Jones	D1
D2	DBADM	E2	Clark	D2
D2	DBADM	E5	Adams	D2
D3	DATADM	E7	Smith	D3
D3	DATADM	E8	Giles	D3
(null)	(null)	E3	Johnson	(null)

Joins in the PLAN_TABLE

The JOIN_TYPE column in the PLAN_TABLE shows the type of join with a code:

- F = Full outer join
- L = Left outer join
- S = Star join as discussed in appendix
- blank = Inner join or no join

A right outer join is not shown with a R in the JOIN_TYPE column. This is because a right outer join is converted to a left outer join before access path selection. For example, the right outer join of:

```
SELECT DEPTNO, DEPTNAME, EMPNO, LASTNAME, WORKDEPT
FROM   DEPT RIGHT OUTER JOIN EMP
ON     DEPT.DEPTNO = EMP.WORKDEPT;
```

is converted to:

```
SELECT DEPTNO, DEPTNAME, EMPNO, LASTNAME, WORKDEPT
FROM   EMP  LEFT OUTER JOIN DEPT
ON     DEPT.DEPTNO = EMP.WORKDEPT;
```

The results are the same. If this can lead to confusion in interpreting the result in the PLAN_TABLE, consider using a guideline that one should write a LEFT OUTER JOIN and avoid writing a RIGHT OUTER JOIN. The PLAN_TABLE is discussed in Chapter EX.

Indeed, the left outer join is a good choice in most cases. The full outer join should not be necessary if RI (Referential Integrity) is enforced. There should never be a dependent row without a parent row.

If more than two tables are to be joined with an outer join, one or more temporary work areas for intermediate results is likely. If a temporary work area is needed (usually a full outer join involving three or more tables), the column PLAN_TABLE.TNAME will show a value of DSNWFQB(nn) (DSN Work File Query Block number) as the name of the temporary work area. If the AS clause is used to name a temporary result, the name specified in the AS clause will be shown in the column PLAN_TABLE.TNAME. The AS clause is discussed in Chapter ST

Forcing the First Table Processed in a Join

The first table specified with a left outer join is the first table processed (the outer table). This rule can be used to force the outer table of an inner join by using a left outer join provided there are no local predicates on second named table resulting in transformation to an inner join as discussed in the next subsection. An alternative to avoid the transformation is to a predicate like (DEPT.DEPTNO > ' ' OR 0 = 1) as shown in context in the following SQL statement assuming that (DEPT.DEPTNO > ' ' qualifiers all rows. For example, if you know that the DEPT table is the best table to be processed first in the join processing but the optimizer does not choose it as the first table processed, an inner join of the DEPT and EMP table can be written as:

```
SELECT DEPTNO, DEPTNAME, EMPNO, LASTNAME, WORKDEPT
FROM   DEPT LEFT OUTER JOIN EMP
ON     DEPT.DEPTNO = EMP.WORKDEPT
WHERE (DEPT.DEPTNO > ' ' OR 0 = 1)
AND    EMP.WORKDEPT IS NOT NULL;
```

The EMP.WORKDEPT IS NOT NULL predicate is necessary on the second table join column to achieve an inner join. This is not a good choice if many rows have null in EMP.WORKDEPT because many rows are joined and then discarded when the local predicate is applied as discussed in the next subsection.

Care should be exercised when using local predicates with outer joins as discussed in the next section.

The order of specifying tables for an inner join does not affect the access path chosen by the optimizer.

Local Predicates with Outer Joins

An example will be used to show how local predicates affect the results of outer joins. Here is a FULL OUTER JOIN similar to the statement used to introduce outer joins except that it has two local predicates on DEPTNAME and LASTNAME. These local predicates qualify all rows in the sample tables. That is all DEPTNAMEs and LASTNAMEs are greater than or equal to blank.

```
SELECT DEPTNO, DEPTNAME, EMPNO, LASTNAME, WORKDEPT
FROM   DEPT FULL OUTER JOIN EMP
ON     DEPT.DEPTNO     = EMP.WORKDEPT
WHERE  DEPT.DEPTNAME >= ' '
AND    EMP.LASTNAME  >= ' ';
```

The results of the statement are the same as an inner join as shown in Figure JP.12. Recall from Chapter CT and SL that null is =, >, < no value. Rows with a null EMP.WORKDEPT and DEPT.DEPTNO are excluded when tested for the local predicates. There are no employees in D4 which results in a null EMP.EMPNO, EMP.LASTNAME, and EMP.WORKDEPT that is crossed out in the figure. Similarly, the DEPT.DEPTNO, DEPT.DEPTNAME, and EMP.WORKDEPT are null because E3 is not currently assigned to a department.

Figure JP.12. Result of a full outer join with local predicates

DEPTNO	DEPTNAME	EMPNO	LASTNAME	WORKDEPT
~~D4~~	~~AI~~	~~(null)~~	~~(null)~~	~~(null)~~
D1	PROGDEV	E1	Thomas	D1
D1	PROGDEV	E4	Blake	D1
D1	PROGDEV	E6	Jones	D1
D2	DBADM	E2	Clark	D2
D2	DBADM	E5	Adams	D2
D3	DATADM	E7	Smith	D3
D3	DATADM	E8	Giles	D3
~~(null)~~	~~(null)~~	~~E3~~	~~Johnson~~	~~(null)~~

If the rows with null are required, it is necessary to add a condition to test for nulls for each of the two tables with local predicates. If the DEPT.DEPTNAME is greater than or equal to blank or DEPT.DEPTNO is null, the row should be included in the result. Similarly, if the EMP.LASTNAME is greater than or equal to blank or EMP.WORKDEPT is null, the row should be included in the result. Here is a statement that includes the result rows with null DEPT.DEPTNAME and EMP.WORKDEPT.

```
SELECT DEPTNO, DEPTNAME, EMPNO, LASTNAME, WORKDEPT
FROM   DEPT FULL OUTER JOIN EMP
ON     DEPT.DEPTNO     = EMP.WORKDEPT
WHERE (DEPT.DEPTNAME >= ' '
   OR  DEPT.DEPTNO IS NULL)
AND   (EMP.LASTNAME >= ' '
   OR  EMP.WORKDEPT IS NULL);
```

An alternative is to code the predicates on DEPT.DEPTNAME and EMP.WORKDEPT within nested table expressions as discussed in Chapter ST.

The principle applies to a full, left and right outer join. The local predicates can be on any column in the table.

Application of Local Predicates Before Outer Joins Processing

Outer joins are considered in transitive closure analysis (V5 APAR PQ18710). Like inner joins, it is not necessary to code local predicates on both tables to be joined with and without table expressions. Local predicates in the WHERE clause are applied after outer join processing prior to the APAR. (Recall from earlier in this chapter that local predicates are applied before inner join processing in the vast majority of cases.) Outer join statements are processed in the following order:

- Predicates on the first named table in the LEFT OUTER JOIN clause (V5 APAR PQ18710)
  - Opposite is true for a right outer join
  - Applies to FULL OUTER JOIN after transformation to a LEFT OUTER JOIN
- Predicates on second named table in the LEFT OUTER JOIN clause
  - Opposite is true for a right outer join
- FROM and ON clause for outer join (outer join processing)
- GROUP BY, HAVING, and SELECT clause

Local predicates can be applied to tables before outer join processing in many cases as shown in Figure JP.13.

Figure JP.13. Application of local predicates before outer join processing

Outer Join Type	Local Predicate on:	Predicate Applied Before Join Processing
Left	1st named table	Yes
Left	2nd named table	Yes after transformed to inner join
Full	1st or 2nd table	Yes after transformed to left outer join

WHERE clause restrictions for transformations: Transformation for application of local predicates before outer join processing does not apply if a CASE expression or user-defined function is used. It does not apply when using an IN (list) and LIKE predicate as with inner joins prior to the APAR. The predicate must be a Boolean term predicate. The predicate becomes false if one table supplies a null value for all of its columns. It is necessary to do a rebind to take advantage of the outer join enhancement after applying the APAR.

When Predicates are Applied with Outer Joins: Predicates in an outer join statement are referred to as table access predicates, during join predicates, after join step predicates, or totally after join predicates. Here is a brief explanation of each predicate type.

- Predicates applied before join predicates (also known as after table access predicates).
- During join predicates are local predicates in the ON clause.
- After join step predicates applied on pair of outer join tables followed by an outer join on another table.
- Totally after join predicates are applied after three of more tables participate in an outer join and predicates references two or more tables already joined, for example.

Examples of Applying Local Predicates Before Outer Join Processing

How DB2 can apply local predicates before outer join processing depends on whether the local predicate is on the first or second named table in the LEFT OUTER JOIN clause as indicated in Figure JP.13 after application of V5 APAR PQ18710.

First Named Table in the LEFT OUTER JOIN Clause: Local predicates can be applied on the first named table in the LEFT OUTER JOIN clause. An example of determining employees with an education level > 16 regardless of whether they are assigned to a department is used to demonstrate the advantages of applying local predicates before left outer join processing.

```
SELECT DEPTNO, DEPTNAME, EMPNO, LASTNAME, WORKDEPT, EDLEVEL
FROM   EMP LEFT OUTER JOIN DEPT
ON     EMP.WORKDEPT = DEPT.DEPTNO
WHERE  EMP.EDLEVEL > 16;
```

The EMP.EDLEVEL > 16 predicate is applied before the left outer join processing as indicated by the crossed out rows in Figure JP.14. The crossed out rows do not participate in the outer join processing. This improves performance significantly because the number of rows that need to be joined are reduced.

Figure JP.14. Results of a left outer join with a local predicate

DEPTNO	DEPTNAME	EMPNO	LASTNAME	WORKDEPT	EDLEVEL
D1	PROGDEV	E1	Thomas	D1	18
~~D1~~	~~PROGDEV~~	~~E4~~	~~Blake~~	~~D1~~	~~16~~
~~D1~~	~~PROGDEV~~	~~E6~~	~~Jones~~	~~D1~~	~~16~~
D2	DBADM	E2	Clark	D2	18
~~D2~~	~~DBADM~~	~~E5~~	~~Adams~~	~~D2~~	~~16~~
~~D3~~	~~DATADM~~	~~E7~~	~~Smith~~	~~D3~~	~~16~~
~~D3~~	~~DATADM~~	~~E8~~	~~Giles~~	~~D3~~	~~14~~
(null)	(null)	E3	Johnson	(null)	20

The opposite is true for a right outer join. Recall that a right outer join is transformed to a left outer join before access path selection by the optimizer.

Second Named Table in the LEFT OUTER JOIN Clause: If there is a local predicate on the second named table in the LEFT OUTER JOIN clause, the optimizer can transform the statement to an inner join to allow application of local predicates and the use of any of the three join methods. Here is an example to select departments that have employees with an education level > 16. The LEFT OUTER JOIN

```
SELECT DEPTNO, DEPTNAME, EMPNO,
       LASTNAME, WORKDEPT, EDLEVEL
FROM   DEPT LEFT OUTER JOIN EMP
ON     EMP.WORKDEPT = DEPT.DEPTNO
WHERE  EMP.EDLEVEL > 16;
```

gives the same results as the following inner join.

```
SELECT DEPTNO, DEPTNAME, EMPNO,
       LASTNAME, WORKDEPT, EDLEVEL
FROM   DEPT INNER JOIN EMP
ON     EMP.WORKDEPT = DEPT.DEPTNO
WHERE  EMP.EDLEVEL > 16;
```

The results of the LEFT OUTER JOIN and INNER JOIN are shown in Figure JP.15

Figure JP.15. Results of a left outer join and inner join

DEPTNO	DEPTNAME	EMPNO	LASTNAME	WORKDEPT	EDLEVEL
D1	PROGDEV	E1	Thomas	D1	18
~~D1~~	~~PROGDEV~~	~~E4~~	~~Blake~~	~~D1~~	~~16~~
~~D1~~	~~PROGDEV~~	~~E6~~	~~Jones~~	~~D1~~	~~16~~
D2	DBADM	E2	Clark	D2	18
~~D2~~	~~DBADM~~	~~E5~~	~~Adams~~	~~D2~~	~~16~~
~~D3~~	~~DATADM~~	~~E7~~	~~Smith~~	~~D3~~	~~16~~
~~D3~~	~~DATADM~~	~~E8~~	~~Giles~~	~~D3~~	~~14~~
~~(null)~~	~~(null)~~	~~E3~~	~~Johnson~~	~~(null)~~	~~20~~

E3 is eliminated from the inner join because null is generated for the column WORKDEPT in the join predicate. Null is not equal to any value in the DEPTNO column. Indeed, null compares to no value.

Transformation of a Full Outer Join to a Left Outer Join

If there is a local predicate on the first named table in the FULL OUTER JOIN clause, the statement can be transformed to a left out join to allow application of local predicates and the use of a nested loop or merge join. Here is a simple example to demonstrate why this is possible. Assume that all rows in the DEPT table qualify according to the DEPT.DEPTNAME >= ' ' predicate.

```
SELECT DEPTNO, DEPTNAME, EMPNO, LASTNAME, WORKDEPT
```

```
FROM    DEPT FULL OUTER JOIN EMP
ON      DEPT.DEPTNO    =   EMP.WORKDEPT
WHERE   DEPT.DEPTNAME >= ' ';
```

The result of a full outer join includes E3 Johnson. However, Johnson is not assigned to a department as indicated by the null in the DEPTNO and DEPTNAME columns after the full outer join shown in Figure JP.16. The application of the DEPT.DEPTNAME >= ' ' predicate eliminates the row. Recall from Chapter CT that null compares to no value. Therefore, the row is not returned as part of the result and is crossed out in the figure.

Figure JP.16. Results of a full outer join with a local predicate

DEPTNO	DEPTNAME	EMPNO	LASTNAME	WORKDEPT
D4	AI	(null)	(null)	(null)
D1	PROGDEV	E1	Thomas	D1
D1	PROGDEV	E4	Blake	D1
D1	PROGDEV	E6	Jones	D1
D2	DBADM	E2	Clark	D2
D2	DBADM	E5	Adams	D2
D3	DATADM	E7	Smith	D3
D3	DATADM	E8	Giles	D3
~~(null)~~	~~(null)~~	~~E3~~	~~Johnson~~	~~(null)~~

The same results are achieved with a left outer join like:

```
SELECT DEPTNO, DEPTNAME, EMPNO, LASTNAME, WORKDEPT
FROM   DEPT LEFT OUTER JOIN EMP
ON     DEPT.DEPTNO = EMP.WORKDEPT
WHERE  DEPT.DEPTNAME >= ' ';
```

The optimizer is able to transform the full outer join with a local predicate on the first named table to a left outer join and achieve the same results. This allows DB2 to narrow the search according to the local predicate and use a nested loop join or a merge join. (Recall that only a merge join is used for a full outer join.)

Local Predicates on the Second Named Table of a Full Outer Join

If there is a local predicate on the second named table in the FULL OUTER JOIN clause, the statement can be transformed to a right then left outer join to allow application of the local predicate. Consider an example to demonstrate why this is possible. In the following FULL OUTER JOIN, all rows qualify according to EMP.LASTNAME >= ' ' unless compared to null.

```
SELECT DEPTNO, DEPTNAME, EMPNO, LASTNAME, WORKDEPT
FROM   DEPT FULL OUTER JOIN EMP
```

```
ON      DEPT.DEPTNO   = EMP.WORKDEPT
WHERE   EMP.LASTNAME >= ' ';
```

The statement can be transformed to a RIGHT OUTER JOIN like:

```
SELECT DEPTNO, DEPTNAME, EMPNO, LASTNAME, WORKDEPT
FROM   DEPT RIGHT OUTER JOIN EMP
ON     DEPT.DEPTNO   = EMP.WORKDEPT
WHERE  EMP.LASTNAME >= ' ';
```

A RIGHT OUTER JOIN is transformed to a LEFT OUTER JOIN with the tables in the FROM clause reversed like:

```
SELECT DEPTNO, DEPTNAME, EMPNO, LASTNAME, WORKDEPT
FROM   EMP  LEFT OUTER JOIN DEPT
ON     DEPT.DEPTNO = EMP.WORKDEPT
WHERE  EMP.LASTNAME   >= ' ';
```

The results of the three formulations are the same as shown in Figure JP.17. The last LEFT OUTER JOIN formulation allows for application of the local predicate on the first named table as discussed earlier in this section.

Figure JP.17. Results of a full outer join with a local predicate on the second named table

DEPTNO	DEPTNAME	EMPNO	LASTNAME	WORKDEPT
D4	AI	(null)	(null)	(null)
D1	PROGDEV	E1	Thomas	D1
D1	PROGDEV	E4	Blake	D1
D1	PROGDEV	E6	Jones	D1
D2	DBADM	E2	Clark	D2
D2	DBADM	E5	Adams	D2
D3	DATADM	E7	Smith	D3
D3	DATADM	E8	Giles	D3
(null)	(null)	E3	Johnson	(null)

JP.9 ACCIDENTS THAT DO HAPPEN

The purpose of this section is to alert you to some accidents that have happened to many people, maybe even you. These accidents can occur when someone is rushed or tired, can mean bad performance and can give joins an undeservedly bad reputation. An awareness of these common accidents can help prevent them in the future.

Forgetting to Include a Join Predicate

Perhaps the distressing accident is a join statement for which the user has forgotten to include a predicate. The result is called a *Cartesian product*, after Descartes, the seventeenth-century mathematician and philosopher who originally defined the product of two vectors in coordinate geometry. In relational terms, a Cartesian product includes a row in the result table for every combination of rows in the participating tables. In other words, the number of rows in a Cartesian product equals the number of rows in one table multiplied by the number of rows in the second table. If S has 1,000 rows and SPJ has 10,000, the statement

```
SELECT S.SN, PN, JN
FROM   S, SPJ;
```

returns a Cartesian product with 10 million rows. It is unlikely that any application would have use for such a result. A more likely explanation is that the programmer or user forgot to key in the WHERE clause.

Forgetting to Specify a Join Condition

A partial Cartesian product can be less obvious and can occur when a join condition is forgotten. This is especially easy to do when the SQL statements are complicated. Consider the following select on the catalog tables that estimates the average number of values that appear on a page. Which join condition is missing, thus requiring a partial Cartesian product to be performed?

```
SELECT I.CREATOR, I.TBNAME, I.NAME,
       I.FIRSTKEYCARDF, I.FULLKEYCARDF,
       C.NAME, C.COLCARDF,
       T.CARDF, T.NPAGES,
       T.CARDF/T.NPAGES/I.FIRSTKEYCARDF,
       T.CARDF/T.NPAGES/I.FULLKEYCARDF
FROM   SYSIBM.SYSINDEXES I,
       SYSIBM.SYSTABLES  T,
       SYSIBM.SYSCOLUMNS C,
       SYSIBM.SYSKEYS    K
WHERE  I.FIRSTKEYCARDF > 0
AND    I.FULLKEYCARDF  > 0
AND    T.CARDF         > 0
AND    T.NPAGES        > 0
AND    I.CREATOR     = 'PAT'
AND    K.IXCREATOR = I.CREATOR
AND    C.TBCREATOR = I.CREATOR
AND    T.CREATOR   = I.CREATOR
AND    T.NAME      = C.TBNAME
AND    T.NAME      = I.TBNAME
AND    C.NAME      = K.COLNAME;
```

The missing join condition is I.NAME = K.IXNAME, which results in a partial Cartesian product.

An even more subtle oversight involves a composite index. If the first column in a composite index on K.IXCREATOR and K.IXNAME is forgotten, a matching index scan cannot be used, significantly degrading the join's performance.

Forgetting to Include a Local Predicate

A seemingly simple SELECT statement required 1.5 hours to run and gave many duplicate rows. The problem is shown using the SPJ and S tables using the following SELECT statement to determine information on suppliers who supply parts for J4 or are located in London.

```
SELECT S.SN, STATUS, CITY
FROM   SPJ, S
WHERE (SPJ.SN = S.SN
AND    SPJ.JN = 'J4')
OR     S.CITY = 'London'
ORDER BY S.SN, STATUS, CITY;
```

It is necessary to form a partial Cartesian product of SPJ and S for suppliers in London because there is no join predicate for the ORed predicate (OR S.CITY = 'London'). The results based on the rows in the sample database (Figure CT.6) are shown in Figure JP.18a and JP18b.

Figure JP.18. Cartesian results

SN	STATUS	CITY
S1	20	London
S1	20	London
S1	20	London
S1	20	London
S1	20	London
S1	20	London
S1	20	London
S1	20	London
S1	20	London
S1	20	London
S1	20	London
S1	20	London
S1	20	London
S1	20	London
S1	20	London
S1	20	London
S1	20	London
S1	20	London
S1	20	London
S1	20	London
S1	20	London
S1	20	London
S1	20	London
S1	20	London
S2	10	Paris
S4	20	London
S4	20	London

Results - continued

SN	STATUS	CITY
S4	20	London
S4	20	London
S4	20	London
S4	20	London
S4	20	London
S4	20	London
S4	20	London
S4	20	London
S4	20	London
S4	20	London
S4	20	London
S4	20	London
S4	20	London
S4	20	London
S4	20	London
S4	20	London
S4	20	London
S4	20	London
S4	20	London
S4	20	London
S4	20	London
S4	20	London
S5	30	Athens
S5	30	Athens
S5	30	Athens
S5	30	Athens
S5	30	Athens
S5	30	Athens

The statement can be reformulated to avoid a partial Cartesian product like:

```
SELECT S.SN, STATUS, CITY
FROM   SPJ, S
WHERE (SPJ.SN = S.SN
AND    SPJ.JN = 'J4')
UNION
SELECT S.SN, STATUS, CITY
FROM   S
WHERE  CITY = 'London'
ORDER BY 1, 2, 3;
```

DISTINCT is not used because UNION eliminates duplicates. This avoids a second sort.

The correct results as shown in Figure JP.19. required only a few seconds.

Figure JP.19. Results and no Cartesian product

SN	STATUS	CITY
S1	20	London
S2	10	Paris
S4	20	London
S5	30	Athens

Failing to Limit the Number of Rows Selected

Even the simplest omission can be costly. It most frequently occurs with developers new to the set processing capability of SQL. Accustomed to one-record-at-a-time processing, they feel comfortable joining two entire tables and using the host program to test for the desired values. For example, when looking for suppliers of part P5 and the jobs on which it is used, they might join the entire S and SPJ tables with this statement:

```
SELECT S.SN, PN, JN
FROM   S, SPJ
WHERE  S.SN = SPJ.SN;
```

Then they use a cursor to fetch the returned rows and test for those containing P5. This join is much more expensive than a join of only the P5 rows from one table with the other, which can be accomplished with this statement:

```
SELECT S.SN, PN, JN
FROM   S, SPJ
WHERE  S.SN = SPJ.SN
AND    PN   = 'P5';
```

JP.10 STAR JOIN

A star schema is sometimes used in decision support applications. It consists of a fact table and multiple dimension tables as shown in Figure JP.20. The schema has three dimension tables containing information on products, time, and location in the example. The sales fact table must have an ID column for each dimension. In our example, the column names are S.PRODUCT, S.LOCATION, and S.TIME. The product dimension table can have information on product item, class, inventory, etc. The location dimension table can have information on city, state, country, etc. The time dimension table can have information on the month, quarter, year, etc.

Figure JP.20. Star schema

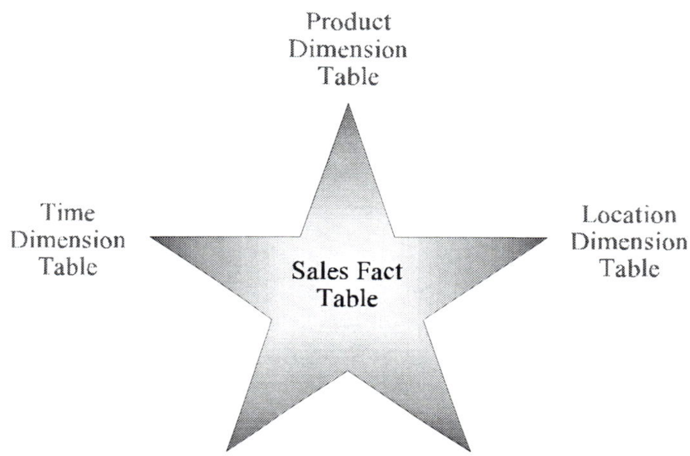

A star join of the fact and dimension tables can be written as:

```
SELECT *
FROM   SALES S, PRODUCT P, LOCATION L, TIME T,
WHERE  S.PRODUCT  = P.ID
AND    S.LOCATION = L.ID
AND    S.TIME     = T.ID
AND    P.CLASS    = 'Coats'
AND    L.CITY     = 'Omaha'
AND    T.YEAR     = 2000;
```

A distinguishing characteristic of a star join is that there are no join predicates between the dimension tables. Star join processing (V6 APAR PQ28813 and PQ36206) can be identified in a plan table as discussed in Chapter EX. Following are partial results from a plan table. Notice that the JT = JOIN_TYPE = S for a star join with the index indicated.

```
CREATE INDEX SPLTX ON SALES (PRODUCT, LOCATION, TIME) CLUSTER;
```

```
QN_B  MT  TNAME     PRE  AT  MC  XNAME  JT UJOG  UJOC
---------+---------+---------+---------+---------+--
1  1   0  Product   S    I   0   PRODX  S  NYNN  NNNN
1  1   1  Location  S    R   0          S  NYNN  NNNN
1  1   1  Time      S    R   0          S  NYNN  NNNN
1  1   1  Sales     S    I   3   SPLTX  S  NNNN  NNNN
```

It is important to create a composite index on fact table columns that correspond to each dimension table ID. Star join processing is performed in the order of columns in the composite index. The star join processing is done at stage 1 with the composite indexed created as specified.

Star join processing uses a work file for each column of the sales fact composite index created in DSNDB07 tablespaces which is used to store qualifying column values from corresponding dimension tables. A matching index scan is done into sales table using values in work file. A technique of next key feed back provides for the highest column combination in the index to be used to avoid unnecessary matching index scans into the sales table. This avoids generating duplicate rows and eliminating duplicates to return to the user and improves performance dramatically. In one test case star join processing required 5.10 and 4.34 seconds of CPU and elapsed time compared to 3007.82 and 126.41 seconds of CPU and elapsed time without star join processing.
Details on processing can be found in *DB2 UDB Server for OS/390 Version 6 Technical Update*, SG24-6108 manual.

There are a number of requirements for star join processing including:

- All join predicates are equi-joins between the fact table and its dimensions with Boolean term predicates or within tables of the same dimension.
- Fact table must have >= 25 times (default) the number of rows as the largest dimension table. The default can be changed using hidden DSNZPARM DSN6SPRC parameter SPRMSJR.
- Select references >= 2 dimensions.
- Cannot cross dimensions with correlated subselects.
- A single fact table column cannot be joined to columns of different dimension tables. Fact table column F1 cannot be joined to column D1 of dimension table T1 and also joined to column D2 of dimension table T2, , for example.
- Matching data types and length on equi-joins columns.
- Star join is not used for outer joins. An outer join can be transformed to an inner join with usage of star join processing.

The systems administrator can disallow and influence DB2s usage of a star join using hidden DSNZPARM DSN6SPRC parameter SPMSJR with the values shown in Figure JP.21.

Figure JP.21. Encourage or discourage a star join

Value	Description
0	Enable star join (default).
-1	Disable star join.
1	Fact table will be the largest table in star join. No Fact/Dimension ratio checking. More star join processing is exploited if ratio is 1.
>1	Value used as the star join fact table and the largest dimension root table ratio. The higher the ratio, the less chance the star join will be invoked.

Order of columns in composite index: A composite index on the fact table columns that correspond to each dimension table ID should be created. The order of column in the index are important to achieve good performance. Star join processing is performed in the order of columns in the composite index. We will describe a technique that can be used to determine that order. Assume that the cardinality of fact table columns are:

```
S.TIME     = 2,000
S.PRODUCT  =   433
S.LOCATION =   100
```

The cardinality of dimension tables are:

```
T.ID = 2,000
P.ID =   500
L.ID =   100
```

The cardinality of column pairs in fact table are:

```
S.TIME    and S.PRODUCT  = 625,000
S.TIME    and S.LOCATION = 196,000
S.PRODUCT and S.LOCATION =     994
```

The density of all pairs of columns in fact table can be calculated as follows. The density is a measure of the correlation of the columns.

```
Density (S.TIME and S.PRODUCT)   = 625,000 / (2,000 * 500)=0.625
Density (S.TIME and S.LOCATION)  = 196,000 / (2,000 * 100)=0.98
Density (S.PRODUCT and S.LOCATION) =   994 / (  500 * 100)=0.01988
```

By reviewing the prior results we can see that the pair of columns with the lowest density is S.PRODUCT and S.LOCATION with a value of 0.01988. The column not in the pair should be used a the third column of the composite index (S.TIME).

Repeat the process to determine:

```
Density of S.PRODUCT  = 433 / 500 = 0.866
Density of S.LOCATION = 100 / 100 = 1.0
```

The S.PRODUCT column has the lowest density of 0.866 and therefore should be made the first column of the composite index. The remaining column S.LOCATION should be made the second column of the index. The index can be created like:

```
CREATE INDEX SPLTX ON SALES (PRODUCT, LOCATION, TIME) CLUSTER;
```

The usage of the data overrides the order suggested by the formula. For example, if the PRODUCT table does not participate in most joins requested by the user, it should not be the first column in the index. If the user frequently narrows the search on LOCATION, consideration should be made to making this the first column in the index. An alternative is to have an index on LOCATION in the dimension table to allow DB2 to narrow the search to specific locations requested by the user. The dimension tables should be indexed for anticipated user requests using the guidelines in Chapter ID. The dimension table indexes are not used in star join processing

JP.11 SUMMARY

All three join methods can use multiple index processing and list prefetch to qualify rows for the inner table and all return the rows to the program as they are joined without having to complete the join of all rows. However, the merge and hybrid join methods may require a sort of the qualifying rows before the join can begin. It is only the nested loop join that never requires preprocessing of the data before beginning the join and returning rows to the program, thus its advantage for quickly returning a few rows to a program even though a large number of rows might qualify but will not be fetched.

Here is a summary of guidelines that can help improve join performance.

- Join only the required rows. Specify as many predicates as possible to limit the number of rows from each table. In most cases, the number of rows to be joined impacts performance much more than the number of tables.
- Ensure that the join columns have matching data types and lengths. If they do not, an index cannot be used. If a particular join runs unexpectedly slowly, this error might be the cause, because DB2 will not use an index that you know is there. Although SQL functions are available for converting data types and lengths to gain compatibility between columns to be joined, using those functions also disallows use of the index.
- In general, let DB2 perform the join in a single SELECT statement rather than writing application program code to join rows returned from separate SELECT statements.
- An index with a high cluster ratio improves the efficiency of the join.
- Avoid accidents when coding predicates and join conditions. Avoid partial and full Cartesian products.

EXERCISES

1. A join is taking an excessive amount of time. What are some factors that should be considered to reduce the processing time?

2. Assume indexes on the join columns but no index on the CITY column. What is a possible reason that the optimizer chose a less than optimal join method for the following SELECT statement?

```
SELECT SPJ.SN, SNAME, PN, JN, QTY
FROM   SPJ, S
WHERE  SPJ.SN = S.SN
AND    CITY = 'Athens';
```

3. Why does a nested loop join perform better than a merge or hybrid join for a small number of rows to be joined? Why is it a good join method for online transactions that need to process and display a few rows?

4. How can the use of a nested loop join be encouraged?

5. How can you encourage the use of a particular table, the TA table, as the outer table of a join?

6. How can you discourage the use of the TA table as the inner table of a join?

7. When is a merge join favored over the nested loop and hybrid join? How can you encourage a merge join?

8. What are the characteristics of tables that benefit from a hybrid join?

9. Is the foreign key table likely to be the outer table of a hybrid join? Is the primary key table likely to be the inner table of a hybrid join?

10. What are two disadvantages of the hybrid join?

11. How can the use of a hybrid join be discouraged?

12. If a supplier is not actively supplying parts for a job, consideration will be given to discontinuing the supplier. Develop a SELECT statement to determine the SN and SNAME of suppliers who have not supplied any parts to jobs in the SPJ table.

13. Will the following two SELECT statements correctly identify the SN and SNAME of suppliers who have not supplied any parts to jobs in the SPJ table? What is the disadvantage of each of the statements?

```
SELECT S.SN, SNAME
FROM   S FULL OUTER JOIN SPJ
ON     S.SN = SPJ.SN;

SELECT S.SN, SNAME
FROM   SPJ RIGHT OUTER JOIN S
ON     S.SN = SPJ.SN;
```

14. Assume that S.SN and SPJ.SN allow for nulls. (S.SN should be declared as NOT NULL because it is the primary key. SPJ.SN should be declared as NOT NULL because it is part of the primary key.) Will the following full outer join and inner join return the same results? Why?

```
SELECT S.SN, SNAME, PN, JN
FROM   S FULL OUTER JOIN SPJ
ON     S.SN   = SPJ.SN
WHERE  S.SN   > 'S4'
AND    SPJ.SN > 'S4';

SELECT S.SN, SNAME, PN, JN
FROM   S, SPJ
WHERE  S.SN   = SPJ.SN
AND    S.SN   > 'S4'
AND    SPJ.SN > 'S4';
```

15. a) Will the local predicate (EMP.EDLEVEL > 16) in the following example be used to narrow the search and reduce the number of rows to be processed in the join? b) Why?

```
SELECT DEPTNO, DEPTNAME, EMPNO, LASTNAME, WORKDEPT, EDLEVEL
FROM   EMP RIGHT OUTER JOIN DEPT
ON     DEPT.DEPTNO = EMP.WORKDEPT
WHERE  EMP.EDLEVEL > 16;
```

ANSWERS

1. Join performance can be improved with indexes on the join columns. It is best if those indexes have a high cluster ratio. The data type and length of the columns to be joined must be the same to use an index. For the best performance, the nullability of join columns with a composite index must match for a merge join that requires a sort. Narrow the search in the SELECT statement to avoid joining all rows if all rows are not required. Consult with the systems administrator on the size and usage of buffer pool BP0. A large buffer pool can significantly improve join performance. (The importance of sizing the buffer pool for the workload is discussed in Chapter CD.)

2. A possible reason that the optimizer chose a less than optimal join method is that the table/column parameter was not used when RUNSTATS was executed to update SYSCOLUMNS.COLCARDF. The optimizer does not have any statistics to estimate the number of qualifying rows according to the local predicate on CITY.

3. A nested loop join usually performs best for joining a few rows to be displayed to the user because a minimal amount of work must be done before the first and subsequent rows can be returned to the program. It is necessary only to locate a qualifying row in the outer table, do a matching index scan on the inner table, and return the result row for each of a few rows fetched by a program.

4. Use OPTIMIZE FOR *n* ROWS where *n* is a small number to encourage use of a nested loop join.

5. Use predicates to narrow the search on TA. The table with the smallest number of qualifying rows, as estimated by the optimizer, is usually chosen as the outer table. If it is necessary, set a column in TA equal to itself (C1 = C1, for example), assuming there is no other predicate in the WHERE clause defined on the C1 column.

6. Code a predicate on the join column of TA, and add OR 0 = 1 in parentheses: (C1 = 10 OR 0 = 1). This disallows the use of an index on TA.C1. It is very unlikely that TA can be used as the inner table of a nested loop or hybrid join if an index cannot be used.

7. A merge join has performance advantages over the nested loop and hybrid joins when a large number of rows qualify to be joined. This is particularly true when there is a high cluster ratio index on one or both columns to be joined. An index with a high cluster ratio on one or both columns to be joined encourages a merge join. Use range predicates so that it appears that many rows will qualify. Use an ORDER BY on a join column with a high cluster ratio index. The optimizer is likely to use an index with a high cluster ratio to avoid a sort for the ORDER BY and to avoid a sort for the merge join.

8. The hybrid join is likely if it is estimated that a medium number of rows will qualify for the join, and one of the tables has a low cardinality.

9. If the foreign key column has a low cardinality, it is likely to encourage a hybrid join and be made the outer table. A primary key column frequently has the clustering index with a high cluster ratio and thus is likely to be made the inner table of a type C hybrid join where a sort of the partial rows is not required and all partial rows need not be built before list prefetch can begin returning rows to the program.

10. a) DB2 builds partial rows consisting of the RIDs from the inner table and selected columns from the outer table. The partial rows are sorted if there is a low cluster ratio index on the inner table join column. This initial work is done before the first row is returned to the program resulting in an unacceptable delay for online transactions if a large number of rows qualify and are not fetched.

b) Local predicates on the inner table are applied after the join, thus more rows may be joined than necessary before the local predicates are applied.

11. The use of OPTIMIZE FOR *n* ROWS where *n* is small discourages the use of a hybrid join.

12. SELECT statement to determine the SN and SNAME of suppliers who have not supplied any parts to jobs in the SPJ table:

```
SELECT S.SN, SNAME
FROM   S LEFT OUTER JOIN SPJ
ON     S.SN = SPJ.SN;
```

A left outer join is required to satisfy the requirement. An inner join identifies only the suppliers who have supplied parts on currently active jobs.

13. Both of the SELECT statements give the required results. The full outer join is not necessary. It limits DB2 to using the merge join method, which may or may not be the best access path. In addition, if there are suppliers in the SPJ table without a matching supplier in the parent S table, a full outer join returns more rows than needed to satisfy the business requirement.

The optimizer can choose to use the nested loop join or merge join for a left or right outer join based on the statistics in the catalog tables. The right outer join is shown as a left outer join in the PLAN_TABLE, because the optimizer reformulates the FROM clause as a left outer join like: S LEFT OUTER JOIN SPJ.

14. The full outer join and the inner join will return the same result. Null does not compare to any value including itself. Therefore, if there is a null in the S.SN. or SPJ.SN columns, the corresponding rows will be excluded before it gets to the outer join processing by the local predicates on the columns.

15. a) The local predicate (EMP.EDLEVEL > 16) in the following example will not be used to narrow the search and reduce the number of rows to be processed in the join.

```
SELECT DEPTNO, DEPTNAME, EMPNO, LASTNAME, WORKDEPT, EDLEVEL
FROM   EMP RIGHT OUTER JOIN DEPT
ON     DEPT.DEPTNO = EMP.WORKDEPT
WHERE  EMP.EDLEVEL > 16;
```

b) The reason is that the optimizer transforms the right outer join to a left outer join and reverses the named tables like:

```
SELECT DEPTNO, DEPTNAME, EMPNO, LASTNAME, WORKDEPT, EDLEVEL
FROM   DEPT LEFT OUTER JOIN EMP
ON     DEPT.DEPTNO = EMP.WORKDEPT
WHERE  EMP.EDLEVEL > 16;
```

The local predicate is on the second named table to be joined. Local predicates are applied before a left outer join only if the local predicate is on the first named table.

FIGURES

Subselects and Table Expressions

ST.1 INTRODUCTION

Subselects are SELECTS that work in conjunction with other SELECTS, providing values that determine part of the search criteria. In *non-correlated* subselects, in contrast with *correlated* subselects, DB2 usually first performs the subselect, or inner select, presented within parentheses below the primary, or outer, select. The value or values returned for the subselect provide values for the search criteria for the primary select.

In correlated subselects, the subselect's search criteria depend on values from the table identified in the outer select. SQL evaluates the outer select first and passes a value to the subselect, which returns values one at a time to be used in completion of the outer select.

Nested table expressions are subselects in a FROM clause that are surrounded by parentheses. In many ways, they are similar to views, but they do not have to be created as a separate entity outside of the immediate SELECT statement. They can also be useful when using outer joins, which are described in Chapter JP.

The purpose of this chapter is to impart an understanding of how to use subselects and nested table expressions, but also to give information about how they work and what the performance implications of using them are. With knowledge of the processing used, and the examples we present for alternative ways to code statements, you will have the tools you need to develop good performing SQL and rewrite poor-performing statements.

ST.2 SUBSELECTS

This section contains information about non-correlated subselects, nested subselects, and correlated subselects.

Non-Correlated Subselects

To understand a non-correlated subselect, consider a search for parts that exceed the average weight of all the parts kept in London. A subselect can determine the average weight and pass that value to a primary select that locates the heavier parts:

```
SELECT PNAME, WEIGHT
FROM   P
WHERE  WEIGHT >
  (SELECT AVG(WEIGHT)
   FROM   P
   WHERE  CITY 'London');
```

PNAME	WEIGHT
Screw	17
Bolt	17
Cog	19

Subselects can also pass multiple values to the primary select, most frequently done by using the IN operator in the primary select to address a set of values returned by the subselect. To determine the part number and name of parts supplied by supplier S2, for example, a subselect can locate S2's part numbers in the SPJ table and pass that set to a select that finds those parts' names in the P table. The statement to do this is:

```
SELECT PN, PNAME
FROM   P
WHERE  PN IN
  (SELECT PN
   FROM   SPJ
   WHERE  SN = 'S2');
```

PN	PNAME
P3	Screw
P5	Cam

The primary select can also use three other operators—ALL, ANY, and SOME—to address sets of values returned by the subselect. Used in the select's WHERE clause, ALL, ANY, or SOME instructs the select to find rows based on their comparison to the values in the returned set. For ANY and SOME, which are equivalent, each satisfies the comparison against at least one value in the set. For ALL, each returned row satisfies the comparison against all values in the set. For example, the following statement determines all parts that weigh more than each and every part stored in Paris:

```
SELECT PNAME, WEIGHT, CITY
FROM   P
WHERE  WEIGHT > ALL
  (SELECT WEIGHT
   FROM   P
   WHERE  CITY = 'Paris');
```

Programming Recommendation: The words ANY and ALL are somewhat ambiguous and do not naturally carry to some users the operators' precise meanings. Moreover, SQL's handling of unknown values with respect to these operators can be misleading. Because searches provided by the ANY, ALL, and SOME operators can be performed with equivalent statements using more straightforward terminology, it may be wise to avoid these operators entirely rather than having to deal with their somewhat confusing distinctions. For example, selecting parts that weigh more than each and every part stored in Paris is the same as selecting parts that weigh more than the heaviest part stored in Paris. The MAX operator can identify those rows. Indeed, DB2 evaluates the > ANY subselect like the more straightforward formulation:

```
SELECT PNAME, WEIGHT, CITY
FROM   P
WHERE  WEIGHT >
  (SELECT MAX(WEIGHT)
   FROM   P
   WHERE  CITY = 'Paris');
```

Similarly, the MIN operator can perform the function of ANY or SOME. To say that a given value is greater than any or some of the values in a set is the same as saying that it is greater than the least value in the set. The different formulation returns the same results.

The Trouble with Nulls: When using ALL and MAX interchangeably, be careful if there is a possibility that no rows will qualify for the subselect--the results can be quite different. If there are no parts in Paris, ALL weights are greater than the empty set. However, no weights are greater than a null when using MAX. If there are parts in Paris, MAX returns the same results as does ALL. MIN and ANY or SOME return the same results regardless of whether rows qualify in the subselect--no weights are greater than the empty set, and no weights are greater than a null MIN.

Nulls are also troublesome if they appear in rows in a table processed in a subselect. Assume for a moment that the PN column contains a null in the SPJ table and that there is a P99 in the P table but not in the SPJ table. It is necessary to determine information on parts in P that are not used on jobs in SPJ with:

```
SELECT PN, PNAME, COLOR, WEIGHT, CITY
FROM   P
WHERE  PN NOT IN
   (SELECT PN
    FROM   SPJ);
```

The P99 in the P table is not identified. The rationale is that the unknown value in the SPJ table might be P99. Either of the following rewrites of the request identifies the P99 that is not currently being used on any job:

```
SELECT PN, PNAME, COLOR, WEIGHT, CITY
FROM   P
WHERE  PN NOT IN
   (SELECT PN
    FROM   SPJ
    WHERE  SPJ.PN IS NOT NULL);
```

The subselect excludes any nulls with the predicate WHERE SPJ.PN IS NOT NULL.

```
SELECT PN, PNAME, COLOR, WEIGHT, CITY
FROM   P AS P1
WHERE  PN NOT IN
   (SELECT PN
    FROM   SPJ
    WHERE  SPJ.PN = P1.PN);
```

The subselect is comparing part numbers between the SPJ and P tables. As stated earlier, null compares to no value, therefore any nulls are ignored.

These are just a few of the potential problems when dealing with nulls and the reason that most developers declare most columns as NOT NULL WITH DEFAULT, or they specify a default value like: DEFAULT 'London'. Recall from the previous examples that even then a subselect can return null, and aggregates can return null in inner or outer SELECTS if no rows qualify as a result of the WHERE clause.

Nesting Subselects

A subselect can pass an intermediate answer set to a subselect that uses it in defining the search criteria that allow it to pass an intermediate answer to another subselect, and so on for as many subselects as a search may need. The only limit is that any single SQL statement may not exceed 32 kilobytes and cannot reference more than 15 tables. In most cases, SQL executes the innermost subselect first and works its way up. For example, a search to locate the part number and name for parts supplied by supplier Jones would be similar to the search presented above in which we found the part numbers and names for parts supplied by S2. In this case, however, an additional subselect is needed to find Jones's supplier number. The necessary statement is:

```
SELECT PN, PNAME
FROM   P
WHERE  PN IN
   (SELECT PN
    FROM   SPJ
    WHERE  SN =
      (SELECT SN
       FROM   S
       WHERE  SNAME = 'Jones'));
```

PN	PNAME
P3	Screw
P5	Cam

Correlated Subselects

In a correlated subselect, the outer select identifies a table from which SQL draws values for use in the subselect. The outer select passes one row at a time from the identified table to the subselect, which uses the column specified in the subselect to perform the subselect. A correlated subselect uses a correlation name following the table or view name separated by AS or a space.
For example, P1 is the correlation name in FROM P AS P1 and FROM P P1.For example, to determine the names of parts used on job J1, the search can check each part listed in the P table against all the parts listed in the SPJ table. When the part number (PN) from P matches the PN from SPJ, and the job number equals J1, the select returns that part's name. This statement satisfies the search:

```
SELECT PNAME
FROM   P AS P1
WHERE  'J1' IN
   (SELECT JN
    FROM   SPJ
    WHERE  SPJ.PN = P1.PN);
```

To perform this search, SQL first passes the first part number from the P table to the subselect. The subselect uses the part number, P1, from that row in its search. This search finds P1 used in two jobs—J1 and J4—which make up the set returned to the outer select for evaluation with the IN operator. Because J1 is the first value returned, the outer select returns PNAME from the P1 row in the P table—NUT. SQL continues the process by passing to the subselect each subsequent part number from the P table in turn. Try continuing the search using the remaining values from the P table.

ST.3 SUBSELECTS THAT RETURN FEW OR MANY VALUES

Subselect of a SELECT, UPDATE, and DELETE statement can qualify a few or many rows when using IN, =ANY, =SOME, =ALL (with or without NOT and WHERE CURRENT OF). Consider the processing required to identify those parts that are being used in a quantity of 200 on jobs.

```
SELECT PN, PNAME, WEIGHT, CITY
```

```
FROM    P
WHERE   PN IN
  (SELECT PN
   FROM    SPJ
   WHERE   QTY = 200);
```

Whether the subselect returns a few or many values significantly effects the how the statement is processed and its performance. In any case, a matching index scan can be used to satisfy predicates in the subselect (WHERE QTY = 200 in the example). The goal is to minimize the number of values that must be processed in the subselect.

Subselects That Return Few Values

If few rows qualify in the subselect and many rows must be processed for the outer select, the qualifying values from the subselect are sorted, duplicates eliminated, and written to a work file (V5 APAR PQ23243). If P7, P7, P7, P5, P3, P8, P8, P9, P9, P1, P1, P1, P3, P3, P4, P8, P9, P2, P2, P5, P6, P1 qualify with a QTY = 200 in the subselect , the statement is executed like:

```
SELECT PN, PNAME, WEIGHT, CITY
FROM    P
WHERE   PN IN ('P1','P2',P3','P4','P5','P6','P7','P8','P9');
```

This allows for 9 matching index scans on a P.PN clustering index. The processing can be identified in the PLAN_TABLE. The column ACCESSTYPE = 'N' and MATCHCOL > 0. OPTIMIZE FOR 1 ROW encourages the transformation to IN (list) processing. The same principle applies to multi-level subselects.

Beware of many qualifying rows in the subselect in some cases based on the value requested by the user (QTY = 10 can cause many PNs to qualify, for example). An alternative is the use of reoptimization as discussed in Chapter OP Section 6. Another cause of concern is the possibility of the characteristics of the data changing such that many rows qualify in the subselect after the access path is chosen. This can be dealt with, once discovered, by doing a rebind. The optimizer will then recognize that many rows qualify in the subselect and not choose to use IN (list) processing.

Restrictions: This processing applies to non-correlated subselects (not correlated subselects). The column preceding the subselect must match the data type and length of the selected column in the subselect. The column preceding subselect cannot be part of an expression (PN + 4, for example).

Subselects That Return Many Values

Most subselects can be rewritten as a join. (The opposite is not true.) Usually the join is the more efficient of the two methods if the subselect qualifies many values for the following reasons:

- A join's WHERE clause can reduce the number of rows to be processed. The inner select of a subselect frequently qualifies a number of rows which are written to a temporary work area before processing of the outer select can begin. In contrast, a join can process one row from each of the tables to be joined and return them immediately to the program without processing perhaps a large number of rows from the inner select in an intermediate work area.

♦ DB2 does not use a matching index scan on the column preceding a non-correlated subselect prior to V5 APAR PQ23243. However, it can use a matching index scan on the column with an equivalent join.

Examples will clarify these points.

Subselect Compared with a Join

Lets reconsider the subselect at the beginning of this section with the assumption that many rows qualify in the subselect.

```
SELECT PN, PNAME, COLOR, WEIGHT, CITY
FROM   P
WHERE  PN IN
   (SELECT PN
    FROM   SPJ
    WHERE  QTY = 200);
```

A tablespace scan is required on the P table, comparing each PN with those identified in the inner select if many rows are estimated to qualify in the subselect. The number of comparisons is reduced by sorting the inner select result, eliminating duplicates, and building an in-memory sparse index in a temporary work area.

The purpose of the in-memory sparse index is to improve the performance of searching the work area containing the results of subselect for every qualifying row in the outer select. DB2 can create an in-memory sparse index that points to subsections of the qualifying result set from the subselect. It can then do a binary search on the values in each subsection for each qualifying row in the outer select. Figure ST.1 gives a conceptual picture of how this works. The rows that are crossed out are eliminated from the temporary work area before the in-memory sparse index is built.

Figure ST.1. In-memory sparse index

PN in-memory sparse index	Binary Search of Values
P1000	P1000, P1001, P1002, P1003, P1004, P1005, ...
P2000	P2000, P2001, P2002, P2003, P2004, P2005, ...
P3000	P3000, P3001, P3002, P3003, P3004, P3005, ...
~~P3000~~	~~P3000, P3001, P3002, P3003, P3004, P3005,~~ ...
~~P3000~~	~~P3000, P3001, P3002, P3003, P3004, P3005,~~ ...
~~P3000~~	~~P3000, P3001, P3002, P3003, P3004, P3005,~~ ...
~~P3000~~	~~P3000, P3001, P3002, P3003, P3004, P3005,~~ ...
P6000	P6000, P6001, P6002, P6003, P6004, P6005, ...

Getting back to our example, DB2 can locate P1004 from the outer SELECT, use the in-memory sparse index to find the subsection that contains the P1000s, and do a binary search of the parts to locate P1004. When P2002 is encountered during a tablespace of the outer table, the in-memory sparse index is used to locate the P2000's subsection and a binary search performed to locate the P2002 efficiently. This processing continues for each row in the outer table. In none of the evaluations does it use an index on PN in the P table prior to a V5 APAR PQ23243.

Transformation of NOT IN to NOT EXISTS: If the optimizer estimates that many rows qualify in the inner table and there is a usable index for locating rows in the subselect, it can transform a NOT IN non-correlated subselect to a NOT EXISTS subselect (V5 APAR PQ24284) for improved performance. This avoids the cost of in-memory sparse index processing. Rather, a matching index scan can be used to determine if the value exists in the inner table with the NOT EXISTS formulation. If the value does not exist in the inner table, a qualifying row from the outer table can be returned to the program immediately without first processing a work file. This is particularly important if many rows qualify in the subselect and few rows are fetched. For example, if one million rows qualify in the subselect, about 1,000 rows may need to be scanned with an in-memory sparse index for each qualifying row in the outer table.

Writing the query as a join: In contrast, an alternative join is likely to use indexes on both tables to locate matching values for the statement:

```
SELECT P.PN, PNAME, COLOR, WEIGHT, CITY
FROM   P, SPJ
WHERE  P.PN  = SPJ.PN
AND    QTY   = 200;
```

the join's results does not match those of the subselect exactly, however, because the subselect does not return duplicate rows, while the join does. The subselect returns:

PN	PNAME	COLOR	WEIGHT	CITY
P1	Nut	Red	12	London
P2	Bolt	Green	17	Paris
P3	Screw	Blue	17	Rome
P6	Cog	Red	19	London

and the join returns:

PN	PNAME	COLOR	WEIGHT	CITY
P1	Nut	Red	12	London
P2	Bolt	Green	17	Paris
P3	Screw	Blue	17	Rome
P3	Screw	Blue	17	Rome
P3	Screw	Blue	17	Rome

P3	Screw	Blue	17	Rome
P3	Screw	Blue	17	Rome
P6	Cog	Red	19	London

Duplicates can be eliminated from the join results using the DISTINCT operator:

```
SELECT DISTINCT P.PN,PNAME,COLOR,WEIGHT,CITY
FROM   P, SPJ
WHERE  P.PN = SPJ.PN
AND    QTY  = 200;
```

The DISTINCT operator here does require a sort to eliminate the duplicate rows from the join result. And it may be a more costly sort than the one needed to satisfy the inner select in the subselect formulation. That is because the rows returned by the join are longer than those returned by the subselect. In this particular example, the subselect may provide better performance since the rows to be sorted are shorter. However, if the data is such that there are no duplicates, you can remove the DISTINCT and the join performs best.

The earlier IN subselect has performance advantages if few rows qualify in inner select and an index is used on the column preceding subselect to do few matching index scans into the outer table.

Automatic Transformation of Subselects into Joins

The optimizer can transform a non-correlated or correlated subselect using the IN, =ALL, =ANY, or =SOME operator into an equivalent join and take advantage of any indexes the join would. So that the optimizer can be certain that the subselect and join are equivalent--that they will return identical results in all cases--there are restrictions on when it will make these transformations:

- The column in the inner select must have a unique index to ensure that no duplicates are returned as a result of the transformation.
- The subselect must access only one table
- Potential join columns must have the same data type and length
- The subselect cannot contain a GROUP BY or HAVING clause or use a column function
- The operator on the inner select cannot be negated (such as NOT IN).

After the transformation, a nested loop join is used in most cases, although a hybrid or merge join is possible. If the unique index is dropped, the plan or package is marked invalid. The next time the plan or package is executed, it is rebound without the transformation to a join.

Example: If there is a unique index on the SN column in the S table, this subselect:

```
SELECT SN, PN, JN, QTY
FROM   SPJ
WHERE  SN IN
  (SELECT SN
```

```
    FROM    S
    WHERE   CITY = 'London');
```

can be transformed into a join, like the following:

```
SELECT S.SN, PN, JN, QTY
FROM   SPJ, S
WHERE  CITY = 'London'
AND    SPJ.SN = S.SN;
```

Transformation can occur with composite indexes as well. If there is a composite index on CITY and SN in that order, the transformation can occur, provided the leading column in the composite index is specified with an equal predicate as is the case in the above example.

Recommendation: If a subselect is automatically transformed into a join, the access path can differ from that chosen when the join is explicitly coded. In most cases, it is best to code the join, and it also much clearer to the next person looking at the code to determine what is happening.

Conditions That Favor IN Versus EXISTS Subselect

An IN subselect using an in-memory sparse index compared to a join or EXISTS subselect has advantages in some cases:

- Many rows qualify in outer select and
- Most rows are fetched or must be processed for a COUNT, for example, and
- Inner table is small, and
- Low cluster ratio index used for matching index scans into the inner table when IN subselect is not used

The reason that the IN subselect has a performance advantage is that many matching index scans into widely dispersed rows are not required as is the case with a join or EXISTS formulation. This avoids the excessive seek time required for many matching index scans used by an EXISTS subselect and a nested loop join.

Michael Hannan in Melbourne, Australia, discovered this where 968,961 matching index scans were required for a join and EXISTS formulation. The IN subselect resulted in a non-matching index scan, sort, and build of an in-memory sparse index on 3,000 values qualifying in the subselect. The CPU and elapsed seconds for the three formulations are shown in Figure ST.2.

Figure ST.2. Comparison of IN subselect, join, and EXISTS subselect

Description	CPU Seconds	Elapsed Seconds
IN subselect	31.07	87
Nested loop join	124.96	348
EXISTS subselect	124.99	239.64

There is another case where an IN subselect has performance advantages. If few rows qualify in the inner select and an index is used on the column preceding subselect, the IN subselect formulation has performance advantages.

What about Updates?

One might ask if a subselect like that shown here can be rewritten as a join so that an index can be used on SPJ.SN:

```
UPDATE SPJ SET QTY = 0
WHERE  SN IN
   (SELECT SN
    FROM   S
    WHERE  STATUS = 10);
```

Unfortunately, the answer is no. DB2 does not update a join condition. That is, the update statement's predicate identifying the rows to be modified cannot call for a join.

An alternative for such updates that makes better use of indexes is to separate the update into component parts--in this case, a cursor select and an update. For example, you can use the following pseudo-code, which uses an index on SN in the SPJ table for setting QTY=0 for suppliers with a STATUS of 10.

```
DECLARE SCURSOR CURSOR FOR
   SELECT SN
   FROM   S
   WHERE  STATUS = 10
   OPEN SCURSOR
FETCH-NEXT-SN
   FETCH SCURSOR INTO :SN
   IF SQLCODE = 100
     GO TO COMPLETED-UPDATE
   UPDATE SPJ
   SET QTY = 0
   WHERE SPJ.SN = :SN
   GO TO FETCH-NEXT-SN
COMPLETED-UPDATE
```

If few rows qualify in the subselect, the IN subselect can be replaced with IN list of value processing.

ST.4 CORRELATED SUBSELECTS

In the subselects analyzed thus far, the inner select was evaluated first and written to a temporary work area. Indeed, the optimizer usually chooses the best access path for the inner and outer select independently. For correlated subselects, the access paths cannot be determined independently, but even then an in-memory table is used to store intermediate results in some cases. Another important point about correlated subselects is that any predicate that contain a correlated subselect is evaluated later, at stage 2. For more information about the implications of this, see Chapter PP.

Consider a search for the names of suppliers of part P5 which are used on jobs as indicated in the SPJ table. This same analysis holds true if the literal 'P5' is replaced with a host variable.

```
SELECT SNAME
FROM   S AS SX
WHERE  'P5' IN
  (SELECT PN
   FROM   SPJ
   WHERE  SPJ.SN = SX.SN);
```

The subselect cannot automatically be transformed into a join because there is not a unique index on SPJ.PN. It is necessary to search the SPJ.SN column in the inner select for each unique S.SN in the outer select. The outer SELECT returns the supplier name any time the returned set includes P5. The processing goes as follows:

- Take the first supplier from the S table, say S1; find all matches in the SPJ table as indicated by the predicate SPJ.SN = SX.SN and identify the parts supplied by S1--in this case P1 and P2, which are written to a temporary work area.
- Then return to the outer select and determine if P5 is in the work area. None qualify.
- Take the next supplier, S2, from the S table and locate it in the SPJ table to identify the two P3s and P5, supplied by S2.
- Again the processing returns to the outer select to determine if P5 is in the work area, which it is in this case.

In summary, each supplier in the outer select must be located in the inner SPJ table, written to a work area, with a return to the outer select to determine if the supplier supplies P5. The entire SPJ table must be read once for each unique SN in the S table. Clearly this processing is resource-intensive.

Write the Query as a Join: An alternative formulation that returns the same results is to use a join:

```
SELECT SNAME
FROM   S, SPJ
WHERE  S.SN = SPJ.SN
AND    PN   = 'P5';
```

The four P5 rows are identified in the SPJ table one at time and joined with the S table on SN. The procedure requires, at most, reads of only four rows in the S table.

Programming Recommendation: A good way to identify correlated subselects is to ask whether the inner select can be evaluated independently of the outer select. If the answer is no, it is a correlated subselect; be careful when using such subselects. If the answer is yes, the inner and outer SELECTS can be optimized independently, decreasing complexity and improving performance in many cases. Be cautious when coding correlated subselects, and use joins where possible.

Who Are the Top 10

A frequent requirement is to determine the 10 highest values. Who are the top 10 customers who made the largest purchase or who are the top 10 paid employees, for example. A correlated subselect can be used to satisfy the requirement.

```
SELECT EMPNO, SALARY
FROM   EMP AS EMP1
WHERE  10 >
  (SELECT COUNT(*)
   FROM   EMP AS EMP2
   WHERE  EMP1.SALARY < EMP2.SALARY)
ORDER BY SALARY DESC;
```

Of course, the literal of 10 in the statement can be replaced by another literal value or a host variable. However, more than the specified number of rows will qualify if there are duplicates within the top 10 occurring values in the example. The statement is resource intensive primarily because it is a correlated subselect. The sort of about 10 rows to satisfy the ORDER BY increases the costs very little. An alternative is to declare a cursor, open the cursor, and fetch the required number of employees with the highest salary. This will perform well if there is a good cluster ratio descending index to avoid sorting all rows in the EMP table. If a cursor cannot be used because the information needs to be retrieved using an interactive tool (QMF, for example), multiple one-fetch index accesses is an efficient method for satisfying the requirement.

```
SELECT EMPNO, SALARY
FROM   EMP
WHERE  SALARY >
  (SELECT MAX(SALARY) FROM EMP WHERE SALARY <
  (SELECT MAX(SALARY) FROM EMP WHERE SALARY <
  (SELECT MAX(SALARY) FROM EMP WHERE SALARY <
  (SELECT MAX(SALARY) FROM EMP WHERE SALARY <
  (SELECT MAX(SALARY) FROM EMP WHERE SALARY <
  (SELECT MAX(SALARY) FROM EMP WHERE SALARY <
  (SELECT MAX(SALARY) FROM EMP WHERE SALARY <
  (SELECT MAX(SALARY) FROM EMP WHERE SALARY <
  (SELECT MAX(SALARY) FROM EMP )))))))))
ORDER BY SALARY DESC;
```

If you have an ascending index on the column (SALARY in the example), the statement can be reformulated to allow for 1-fetch index access like:

```
SELECT EMPNO, SALARY
FROM   EMP
WHERE  SALARY <=
  (SELECT MIN(SALARY) FROM EMP WHERE SALARY >
  (SELECT MIN(SALARY) FROM EMP WHERE SALARY >
  (SELECT MIN(SALARY) FROM EMP WHERE SALARY >
  (SELECT MIN(SALARY) FROM EMP WHERE SALARY >
  (SELECT MIN(SALARY) FROM EMP WHERE SALARY >
  (SELECT MIN(SALARY) FROM EMP WHERE SALARY >
  (SELECT MIN(SALARY) FROM EMP WHERE SALARY >
  (SELECT MIN(SALARY) FROM EMP WHERE SALARY >
  (SELECT MIN(SALARY) FROM EMP )))))))))
ORDER BY SALARY DESC;
```

Caution: If there is a possibility of mismatched nullability or that no rows qualify in a subselect, do consider using COALESCE or VALUE as discussed in Section ST.6.

The maximum number of subselect in a statement is 14.

Comparison of Costs Using DB2 Estimator: DB2 Estimator is useful in comparing the costs of different formulations of challenging SQL statements. It is particularly useful when test tables are small in comparison to production tables and to test the value of having an index without the cost of building the index. The three formulations of determining the highest values in a column were estimated using a one million row table (Figure ST.3)

Figure ST.3. Comparison of formulation for top 10

Description	CPU Hr:Min:Sec	I/O Hr:Min:Sec	Elapsed Hr:Min:Sec
Correlated subselect and sort 10 rows	00:54:34.65	15:51:09.12	16:45:30.87
Fetch first 10 rows after tablespace scan and sort	00:05:52.05	00:01:04.30	00:06:52:93
MAX(SALARY) subselects with tablespace scans	00:05:13.90	00:00:34.15	00:05:13.90
MAX(SALARY) subselects with index on SALARY	00:00:10.29	00:00:00.70	00:00:10.33

The resources required for the correlated subselect is estimated to be very high. Sorting the values and fetching the first 10 rows is dramatically lower in cost. The MAX(SALARY) formulation is a bit lower in costs without a descending index to allow for one-fetch index accesses. If a descending index is available, the costs are reduced significantly.

Suresh Sane of Employers Reinsurance Corp. had a requirement to determine the top 10 sales amounts. He did a comparison of the correlated subselect, and the alternative to do a tablespace scan, sort and fetch the 10 highest values formulations. His results in Figure ST.4 are consistent with the CPU and elapsed time estimated by DB2 Estimator in that the correlated subselect is much more costly than a tablespace scan with a sort.

Figure ST.4. Comparison of correlated subselect and tablespace scan with sort

Description	CPU Hr:Min:Sec	I/O Hr:Min:Sec	Elapsed Hr:Min:Sec
Correlated subselect and sort 10 rows	00:01:30.91	Not reported	00:01:39.67
Fetch first 10 rows after tablespace scan and sort	00:00:00.31	Not reported	00:00:01:00

Use of In-Memory Tables

Another type of resource-intensive correlated subselect is demonstrated with an example to locate employees who have a salary less than the average salary in each department.

```
SELECT EMPNO, WORKDEPT, SALARY
FROM   EMP AS EMP1
WHERE  SALARY <
  (SELECT AVG(SALARY)
   FROM   EMP AS EMP2
   WHERE  EMP2.WORKDEPT = EMP1.WORKDEPT);
```

Conceptually the AVG aggregate is computed for each value passed from the outer select. Because the inner select always returns a single value to the outer select as a result of using a column function, DB2 can use an in-memory table to keep the result. The following analysis of the processing refers to the data in Figure ST.5.

Figure ST.5. In-memory table minimizes processing of inner select

EMP Table

EMPNO	WORKDEPT	SALARY
E1	D1	40000
E4	D1	50000
E6	D1	30000
E2	D2	40000
E5	D2	40000
E7	D3	20000
E8	D3	30000
E9	D5	45000
E3	(null)	70000

4 KB In-Memory Table

WORKDEPT	AVG for Each DEPT
D1	40000
D2	40000
D3	25000
D5	45000
(null)	70000

1. The first average SALARY is computed for the first occurrence of a WORKDEPT of D1 with an average of 40,000, and the pair of values are stored in a 4 KB in-memory table. Then all rows with SALARY values less than that average are selected through the use of a tablespace scan on the outer table. E6 in D1 has a salary less than the average of 40,000 for their department.

2. For the next outer select value to be evaluated, DB2 checks the in-memory table to see whether the evaluation has already been done. This saving of each unique WORKDEPT and its average avoids repeated searches of the inner table. The average is computed once for D1 rather than three times for the three employees in the department. This assumes that the

values fit in the 4 KB in-memory table. If all of the values do not fit, the space is reused after relocating the required values.

3. DB2 continues on, calculating the average SALARY for each WORKDEPT and saving the results in the in-memory table. A tablespace scan of the outer table is done to compare each SALARY with the average placed in the in-memory table. The next qualifying row is E7 in D3 with a salary of 20,000 which is less than the average for the department at 25,000.

With this method, the inner select can be evaluated once for each unique WORKDEPT in the outer table with a matching index scan while performing a tablespace scan of the outer table.

An in-memory table can be used for subselects preceded by simple operators (>, <, =, etc.) and EXISTS subselect (with or without negation). An in-memory table cannot be used if there are more than 16 columns or more than 256 bytes in the correlated columns. Also, if there is a unique index on the correlated columns in the outer select, an in-memory table is not needed because the index guarantees that there can be no duplicates.

Alternative to Correlated Subselect

Joining a table to itself with GROUP BY ... HAVING is an alternative to a correlated subselect with a column function.

```
SELECT EMP1.EMPNO, EMP1.WORKDEPT, EMP1.SALARY
FROM   EMP AS EMP1, EMP AS EMP2
WHERE  EMP1.WORKDEPT = EMP2.WORKDEPT
GROUP BY EMP1.EMPNO,EMP1.WORKDEPT,EMP1.SALARY
HAVING EMP1.SALARY < AVG(EMP2.SALARY);
```

The result of the join does not return duplicates as does the correlated subselect shown in Figure ST.6 with the duplicates crossed out. This is probably the desired result. The formulation does require a sort for the GROUP BY.

Figure ST.6. Result of GROUP BY and HAVING formulation

EMPNO	WORKDEPT	SALARY
E1	D1	20000
E2	D3	20000
~~E2~~	~~D3~~	~~20000~~
E2	D5	10000
E3	D3	20000
E3	D4	50000
E4	D6	30000
~~E4~~	~~D6~~	~~30000~~
E5	D2	10000

EMPNO	WORKDEPT	SALARY
E5	D5	10000
E5	D6	20000
E5	D1	10000
E5	D3	20000

ST.5 COMPARING EXISTS WITH JOINS AND IN

EXISTS and NOT EXISTS subselects are frequently correlated subselects like this one which determines suppliers who currently supply parts to active jobs:

```
SELECT SN, SNAME, STATUS, CITY
FROM   S AS S1
WHERE EXISTS
    (SELECT 1 -- can also use SPJ.SN or *
     FROM   SPJ
     WHERE  SPJ.SN = S1.SN);
```

EXISTS and NOT EXISTS tests the predicate, and a true or false is returned to the outer select. No column value is returned. Because of this, the subselect can use SELECT * or SELECT 1 instead of the SELECT SPJ.SN shown in the example. All three formulations give the same results, the same access path, and similar performance as indicated below.

EXISTS Subselect	Elapsed Seconds	CPU Seconds
SELECT SPJ.SN	3.93	0
SELECT 1	3.79	0.1929
SELECT *	3.87	0.1928

Comparing EXISTS to Nested Loop Join

In this example, we need to find information on parts used on job J2 where the supplier is located in Paris.

```
SELECT SN, PN, JN, QTY
FROM   SPJ AS SPJ1
WHERE  JN = 'J2'
AND    EXISTS
   (SELECT 1
    FROM   S
    WHERE  S.SN = SPJ1.SN
    AND    CITY = 'Paris');
```

It is likely that a tablespace scan will be performed on the outer table, SPJ, to locate a J2 and the first supplier of parts for that job, S2 as indicated by the shading in Figure ST.7.

1. An in-memory table for SPJ.SNs is searched for S2. If it is not present, S2 is saved in the in-memory table along with a true or false indicating whether the supplier is located in Paris.

2. S2 can be located in the S table with a matching index scan. The data page can be read to determine if S2 is in Paris. An index on S.CITY cannot be used.

3. Subsequent S2s from the SPJ table are found in the in-memory table in many cases (hence it is crossed out in the figure). If it is in the in-memory table, DB2 can avoid a matching index scan on S.SN for each S2 in SPJ.SN.

4. If S2 is not found because the in-memory space has been reused, the S2 value is saved again.

5. The processing is repeated for each unique outer table value (SPJ.SN) that supplies parts for J2.

Figure ST.7. Processing of an EXISTS subselect

SPJ

SN	PN	JN	QTY
S1	P1	J1	200
S1	P1	J4	700
S2	P3	J1	400
S2	P3	J2	200
S2	P3	J3	200
S2	P3	J4	500
S2	P3	J5	600
S2	P3	J6	400
S2	P3	J7	800
~~S2~~	P5	J2	100
S3	P3	J1	200
S3	P4	J2	500
S4	P6	J3	300
S4	P6	J7	300
S5	P2	J2	200
S5	P2	J4	100
S5	P5	J5	500
S5	P5	J7	100
~~S5~~	P6	J2	200
S5	P1	J4	100
S5	P3	J4	200
S5	P4	J4	800

S (Supplier Table)

SN	NAME	STATUS	CITY
S1	Smith	20	London
S2	Jones	10	Paris
S3	Blake	30	Paris
S4	Clark	20	London
S5	Adams	30	~~Athens~~

Result

SN	SNAME	PN	JN	QTY
S2	Jones	P3	J2	200
S2	Jones	P5	J2	100
S3	Blake	P4	J2	500

Alternative Using a Join: The same information as above (parts that are used on J2 with the supplier of the parts located in Paris) can be determined with a join:

```
SELECT SN, PN, JN, QTY
FROM   S, SPJ
WHERE  S.SN = SPJ.SN
AND    CITY = 'Paris'
AND    JN   = 'J2';
```

A comparison of the EXISTS processing with a nested loop join reveals some similarities and some differences, depending on whether indexes are available and whether the optimizer chooses to use those indexes. Nested loop joins are described in JP, but a summary of the process for this particular example is given here:

1. Assuming that the S table is chosen as the outer table of a nested loop join, a supplier in Paris can be located, S2 with a matching index scan or a tablespace scan as shown in the shading of Figure ST.8.

2. The inner table can be processed using a matching index scan on a composite index on columns SN, PN, and JN to locate S2.

3. If J2 is in the leaf page, the required columns on the SELECT clause are retrieved from the data page.

4. If J2 is not in the leaf page, the next supplier in Paris is located, S3, and steps 1 through 3 are repeated until there are no more suppliers in Paris.

The join has advantages over the EXISTS subselect if there is a usable index on S.CITY to narrow the search to suppliers in Paris and an index on SN, PN, and JN to narrow the search to suppliers which supply parts used by J2. However, the EXISTS subselect has advantages if there is no usable index on SPJ, because only unique SPJ.SNs need to be processed, using the in-memory table in most cases. If there is a composite index on S.CITY and S.SN, a matching index scan can be used on Paris and each SN in the inner SPJ table.

Figure ST.8. Nested loop join processing

S (Supplier Table)

SN	SNAME	STATUS	CITY
S1	Smith	20	London
S2	Jones	10	Paris
S3	Blake	30	Paris
S4	Clark	20	London
S5	Adams	30	Athens

SPJ

SN	PN	JN	QTY
S1	P1	J1	200
S1	P1	J4	700
S2	P3	J1	400
S2	P3	J2	200
S2	P3	J3	200
S2	P3	J4	500
S2	P3	J5	600
S2	P3	J6	400
S2	P3	J7	800
S2	P5	J2	100
S3	P3	J1	200
S3	P4	J2	500
S4	P6	J3	300
S4	P6	J7	300
S5	P2	J2	200
S5	P2	J4	100
S5	P5	J5	500
S5	P5	J7	100
S5	P6	J2	200
S5	P1	J4	100
S5	P3	J4	200
S5	P4	J4	800
S5	P5	J4	400
S5	P6	J4	500

Result of join

SN	SNAME	PN	JN	QTY
S2	Jones	P3	J2	200
S2	Jones	P5	J2	100
S3	Blake	P4	J2	500

Comparing IN and EXISTS Subselects

Subselect using IN: An IN subselect can be used to determine information on parts currently used on jobs with the assumption that many SPJ.PNs qualify:

```
SELECT PN, PNAME, WEIGHT, CITY
FROM   P
WHERE  PN IN
  (SELECT PN
   FROM   SPJ);
```

The statement cannot be converted to a join because there is no unique index on SPJ.PN. However, there is a composite index on SN, PN, and JN, which probably has fewer leaf pages than there are data pages in the table. There is a good chance that the optimizer will choose to perform a non-matching index scan on SPJ.PN index with sequential prefetch, then sort and eliminate duplicates, place the SPJ.PNs in a temporary work area, and build an in-memory sparse index. The in-memory sparse index is used to efficiently locate each P.PN in the temporary work area while doing a tablespace scan on the outer table (if many SPJ rows are estimated to qualify, therefore an index on P.PN is unlikely to be used). For each P.PN, the in-memory sparse index is used to locate a subsection of values in the temporary work area. Once the subsection is located, a binary search is done to determine if the row in the P table should be returned to the program.

Subselect using EXISTS: Information on parts currently used on jobs can also be determined with an EXISTS subselect:

```
SELECT PN, PNAME, WEIGHT, CITY
FROM   P AS P1
WHERE  EXISTS
  (SELECT 1
   FROM   SPJ
   WHERE  SPJ.PN = P1.PN);
```

Because there is no predicate to narrow the search on the table, a tablespace scan is needed on the outer P table, as is the case for the IN subselect. For each PN in the P table, a matching index scan on a nonunique PN index is used to locate the part number in the SPJ table. Index lookaside and dynamic prefetch can be used on the inner table. The processing is similar to a nested loop join--there is no initial inner table processing, which means minimal delay in returning the first row.

Analysis: If there is a usable index on SPJ.PN, or if that inner table is large, EXISTS performs better than the IN formulation because DB2 can avoid processing all SPJ.PNs in a work area. It is not necessary for the user to wait while all SPJ.PNs are processed before the first row can be seen. Less processing is required if all qualifying rows are not fetched.

In one case in which the inner table was large and had a usable index, it took 6.5 hours for an IN subselect to process 10 percent of the data compared to three minutes for an EXISTS subselect to process 100 percent of the data.

If there is no usable index on SPJ.PN, the IN subselect has advantages, as is the case in the example. PN is not the leading column of the composite index. The number of SPJ.PNs is sorted, reduced, and an in-memory sparse index is built to be used during a tablespace scan of P. If there are few rows that qualify in the subselect, it can be converted to an IN (list) formulation which allows for a matching index scan for each value in the list.

A comparison of NOT IN and NOT EXISTS is similar to that of IN and EXISTS. In one case in which the inner table was small and had no usable index, using NOT EXISTS took 60 minutes whereas a NOT IN formulation took only one minute.

It depends: We have seen that a comparison of (NOT) IN and (NOT) EXISTS depends on many factors.

ST.6 SUBSELECTS RETURNING A SINGLE VALUE

A subselect returning a single value usually performs well. Use of an index is not barred when comparing an outer select value to an inner select that returns only one value, those which have a simple operator like =, < or > preceding the inner select. If the subselect returns more than one value, an SQLCODE of -811 is received. The following SELECT statement determines information on suppliers that are located in the same city as P3:

```
SELECT SN, SNAME, STATUS, CITY
FROM   S
WHERE  S.CITY =
  (SELECT P.CITY
   FROM   P
   WHERE  PN = 'P3');
```

The inner SELECT can be evaluated using an index on P.PN to locate the city where P3 is housed, Rome. An index on S.CITY in the outer SELECT table can be used to locate information about the supplier who is located in Rome provided that the S.CITY and P.CITY columns have matching nullability and data types. At execution time, that statement is evaluated as if it were coded as:

```
SELECT SN, SNAME, STATUS, CITY
FROM   S
WHERE  S.CITY = 'Rome';
```

Subselects That Can be Reduced to a Single Value: A subselect using ANY, SOME, or ALL with a range predicate does not at first appear to qualify only one value in the inner select. Consider determining parts that are too heavy to be shipped on just any available truck due to the weight capacity of the various trucks:

```
SELECT PN, PNAME, WEIGHT, CITY
FROM   P
WHERE  WEIGHT > ANY
  (SELECT TRUCK_LIMIT
   FROM   TRUCK_CAPACITIES
   WHERE  CITY = 'Brussels');
```

The inner SELECT can be reduced to a single value from the leaf pages while performing a non-matching index scan. In the outer SELECT, DB2 can evaluate that single TRUCK_LIMIT value, say 9,000, against part weights with a matching index scan. At execution time, the statement is evaluated as if it were coded as:

```
SELECT PN, PNAME, WEIGHT, CITY
FROM   P
WHERE  WEIGHT > 9000;
```

This subselect returns the same results and seems more intuitive but is evaluated differently. Assume that WEIGHT does not allow for nulls:

```
SELECT PN, PNAME, WEIGHT, CITY
FROM   P
WHERE  WEIGHT >
```

```
  (SELECT COALESCE (MIN(TRUCK_LIMIT),0)
   FROM   TRUCK_CAPACITIES
   WHERE  CITY = 'Brussels');
```

A one-fetch index access can be used to determine the minimum weight of 9,000, assuming an ascending index on the TRUCK_LIMIT column. The > ANY subselect requires a scan of the leaf pages. COALESCE is required to substitute a value for the minimum if no rows qualify in the subselect. For example, if there are no trucks in Brussels, a tablespace scan is done on the P table. This is because a nullable value and a column that does not allow for nulls cannot be evaluated at stage 1. (Stage 1 and stage 2 processing is described in PP.)

The execution time evaluation will be as if the statement were coded as:

```
SELECT PN, PNAME, WEIGHT, CITY
FROM   P
WHERE  WEIGHT > 9000;
```

There is a good chance that a tablespace scan will be used on the P table to identify the parts that cannot be shipped on just any available truck. If there is a small number of TRUCK_LIMIT leaf pages, or only a few data pages in the table compared to the number of data pages in the P table, or if there is no ascending index on TRUCK_LIMIT, the >ANY subselect formulation performs best. However, if the relative size of the tables were reversed, and if there is an ascending index on a large inner table, the use of the MIN aggregate is best. A one-fetch index access on the large table to determine the minimum value and a tablespace scan on a small outer table would give the best performance.

The comparison is similar for a >ALL subselect and a MAX aggregate on columns with a descending index. Recall from Section ST.2 that >ALL and MAX do not return the same results if no rows qualify in the inner select. If there were no trucks in Brussels, all values are greater than the empty set, but no values are greater than a null from MAX. Again, it is advisable to use the COALESCE or VALUE function to what is done with the MIN column function above.

Recommendation: Sometimes it is necessary to know the size of tables as well as to understanding how the SQL statements are processed in order to identify why a particular a statement does not perform satisfactorily and to be able to formulate a statement that will perform as required.

ST.7 USING THE COALESCE FUNCTION

COALESCE is a function that allows you to substitute any numeric or character value for a null, based on the column data type. For example, assume a decision has been made to allow for nulls in a column containing insurance premiums to be deducted from employees salary. Some employees may have insurance deducted from their salary while other employees do not because their spouses have insurance deducted from their salary. Consider the computation of the net salary as the GROSS_SALARY - (TAXES + **INSURANCE** + SAVINGS) in the statement:

```
SELECT EMPNO, LASTNAME, GROSS_SALARY,
  GROSS_SALARY - (TAXES + INSURANCE + SAVINGS)
FROM   EMP;
```

Because any addition, subtraction and multiplication involving a null value is null, the result of the computation is null. So, if an employee has no insurance deducted from his or her salary, the result for gross salary is null (unknown). Although, it is logical that the result is null, an employee who receives a check with a null amount would not appreciate the logic of the matter. Use the scalar function of COALESCE or VALUE (COALESCE conforms to the SQL standard) to substitute any value for a null. The value of 0 is added to TAXES in the following example:

```
SELECT EMPNO, LASTNAME, GROSS_SALARY,
  GROSS_SALARY - (TAXES + COALESCE(INSURANCE,0) + (SAVINGS)
FROM   EMP;
```

Use COALESCE or VALUE to take the first non-null from two or more columns. The following table lists some possible values for the C1 column in table TA, C4 column in table TB, and C7 column in table TB. The result of COALESCE (TA.C1, TB.C4, TB.C7) is shown in the fourth column of the table in Figure ST.9.

Figure ST.9. Result of COALESCE on three columns

TA.C1	TB.C4	TB.C7	Result of VALUE (TA.C1,TB.C4,TB.C7)
(null)	400	(null)	400
100	300	(null)	100
(null)	(null)	700	700

The ability to take the first non-null value using COALESCE and VALUE is useful with a full inner join and an outer join but cannot be used with a left or right outer join.

Full Outer Join and COALESCE

Notice that the last row in the following EMP table has an employee E9 in WORKDEPT D5. There is no corresponding D5 in the DEPT.DEPTNO column. (This situation will not occur if referential integrity is enforced. It is not possible to iNSERT a row in a dependent table (EMP) if there is not a matching primary key in the parent table (DEPT) when referential integrity is enforced.)

DEPTNO	DEPTNAME
D1	PROGDEV
D2	DBADM
D3	DATADM
D4	AI

EMPNO	LASTNAME	WORKDEPT
E1	Thomas	D1
E2	Clark	D2
E3	Johnson	(null)
E4	Blake	D1
E5	Adams	D2
E6	Jones	D1
E7	Smith	D3

E8	Giles	D3
E9	Hollis	D5

Suppose it is necessary to write a report showing D5, even though that department is not in the DEPT table. Use a full outer join and COALESCE to do this. COALESCE is required for D5 to appear in the report. COALESCE takes the first non-null value, which is D5, in the second column of COALESCE(DEPTNO, WORKDEPT) in the statement:

```
SELECT COALESCE(DEPTNO, WORKDEPT) AS DEPTID,
         DEPTNAME, EMPNO, LASTNAME
FROM   DEPT FULL OUTER JOIN EMP
ON     DEPT.DEPTNO = EMP.WORKDEPT;
```

If the COALESCE function is not used, a null appears in the report under the column DEPTID because there is no matching D5 in the DEPT table. With or without COALESCE, E9 and Hollis appear in the report. The clause AS DEPTID, results in having DEPTID as the column heading in the report:

DEPTID	DEPTNAME	EMPNO	LASTNAME
D4	AI	(null)	(null)
D5	(null)	E9	Hollis
D1	PROGDEV	E1	Thomas
D1	PROGDEV	E4	Blake
D1	PROGDEV	E6	Jones
D2	DBADM	E2	Clark
D2	DBADM	E5	Adams
D3	DATADM	E7	Smith
D3	DATADM	E8	Giles
(null)	(null)	E3	Johnson

ST.8 USING 'AS' TO NAME A RESULT

The AS clause is useful for assigning a column heading for a report and for naming a calculated expression or literal for later reference. It can also be used with an alias or synonym. If you use DESCRIBE for an embedded dynamic SQL statement, the AS name is placed in the SQLDA along with other information about values to be returned from the statement execution.

Naming a Calculated Expression: Here is the SELECT statement to calculate the net salary once again, but this time we assume that INSURANCE does not allow nulls:

```
SELECT EMPNO, LASTNAME, GROSS_SALARY,
  GROSS_SALARY - (TAXES + INSURANCE + SAVINGS)
```

```
    AS NET_SALARY
FROM   EMP
ORDER BY NET_SALARY;
```

The AS clause is used to name the calculated expression, and that name appears as the heading of the column in the report produced using SPUFI and QMF. Also notice that the AS name is used in the clause "ORDER BY NET_SALARY". Without the AS clause it would be necessary to specify "ORDER BY 4" where 4 indicates the fourth expression in the SELECT clause. "ORDER BY NET_SALARY" adds clarity to the statement.

The AS clause is useful for a UNION with an ORDER BY . The following statement also shows an example of naming a literal. The literal 'PROGDEV' and 'DBADM' will have a column heading of DEPTID in a report.

```
SELECT EMPNO, LASTNAME, GROSS_SALARY,
  GROSS_SALARY - (TAXES + INSURANCE + SAVINGS)
    AS NET_SALARY, 'PROGDEV' AS DEPTID
FROM   EMP
WHERE  WORKDEPT = 'PROGDEV'
UNION ALL
SELECT EMPNO, LASTNAME, GROSS_SALARY,
  GROSS_SALARY - (TAXES + INSURANCE + SAVINGS)
    AS NET_SALARY, 'DBADM' AS DEPTID
FROM   EMP
WHERE  WORKDEPT = 'DBADM'
ORDER BY NET_SALARY;
```

ST.9 NESTED TABLE EXPRESSIONS

In this section, we look at nested table expressions, which can be thought of as in-line views. A table expression is a subselect that is the operand of the FROM clause. We'll first look at a simple table expression, to get an understanding of the syntax, and then we'll describe how to use table expressions with outer joins. As you'll see later in this section, table expressions can be used for doing a three-way outer join.

The table expressions in the first few examples are not actually necessary to achieve the required results, but they illustrate the mechanics of table expressions. In the first example, a table expression is used to determine information on employees with an education level >= 20. The SELECT in parentheses following the FROM clause is the table expression:

```
SELECT HIEMP.EMPNO, HIEMP.LASTNAME
FROM (SELECT EMPNO, LASTNAME
      FROM   EMP
      WHERE  EDLEVEL >= 20)
AS HIEMP;
```

It is necessary to assign a correlation name to a table expression with the AS clause. HIEMP is used to name the table expression in the above statement. HIEMP can optionally be used to qualify the EMPNO and LASTNAME in the outer SELECT clause. HIEMP is used to qualify the EMPNO column and is crossed out for the LASTNAME column to show that the use of the AS name is optional. If an AS name is not used within the table expression to name columns, the column names in the outer select need not be qualified with the table expression AS name.

If an AS name is used to name a column in the table expression, the AS name must be used in outer select (not LASTNAME) like:

```
SELECT EMPNO, SURNAME
FROM (SELECT EMPNO, LASTNAME AS SURNAME
      FROM   EMP
      WHERE  EDLEVEL >= 20)
AS HIEMP;
```

If table expression columns are referenced in outer SELECTS, it is necessary to select the columns in the table expression.

Table Expression Like an Inline View

You can think of a table expression as an inline view. Indeed, the optimizer merges the SELECT that defines the table expression with the first SELECT like it merges the SELECT that defines a view with the SELECT from a view. There are exceptions having to do with some outer joins and materialization.

You can get the same results as the first table expression by defining a view and selecting from it like:

```
CREATE VIEW HIEMP AS
SELECT EMPNO, LASTNAME
FROM   EMP
WHERE  EDLEVEL >= 20;

SELECT EMPNO, LASTNAME
FROM   HIEMP;
```

The optimizer transforms the table expression and the select from the view to:

```
SELECT EMPNO, LASTNAME
FROM   EMP
WHERE  EDLEVEL >= 20;
```

GROUP BY with a View and a Table Expression

It is not possible to GROUP BY the result of a date or time function. The following syntax is in error:

Invalid syntax:

```
SELECT YEAR(HIREDATE) AS HIREYEAR, AVG(SALARY)
FROM   EMP
WHERE  EDLEVEL >=20
GROUP BY HIREYEAR;
```

However, a view can be used to extract the year. A select from the view can then group by the year like:

```
CREATE VIEW YEAR_HIEMP (HIREYEAR, SALARY) AS
SELECT YEAR(HIREDATE), SALARY
FROM   EMP
WHERE  EDLEVEL >= 20;

SELECT HIREYEAR, AVG(SALARY)
FROM   YEAR_HIEMP
GROUP BY HIREYEAR;
```

A table expression and AS name are used below to avoid creating a view so that a GROUP BY can be done on the result of a date or time function. Another advantage of a table expression over a view is that a host variable can be specified, :NYEARS is an example.

```
SELECT HIREYEAR, AVG(SALARY)
FROM (SELECT YEAR(HIREDATE) AS HIREYEAR, SALARY
      FROM   EMP
      WHERE  EDLEVEL >= :NYEARS) AS HIEMP
GROUP BY HIREYEAR;
```

It is not necessary to materialize the view and table expression. The table expression SELECT YEAR(HIREDATE) is a subset of a table expression column. We will see that this condition does not require materialization in Figure ST.10.

String scalar functions can be grouped similar to date or time functions, like this:

```
SELECT J3, AVG(SALARY)
FROM (SELECT SUBSTR(JOB,1,3) AS J3, SALARY
      FROM   EMP
      WHERE  EDLEVEL >= 20) AS HIEMP
GROUP BY J3;
```

ne can also GROUP BY the results of an arithmetic function. In the following example the GROUP BY is on the calculated GROSS_SALARY.

```
SELECT WORKDEPT, GROSS_SALARY
FROM (SELECT WORKDEPT, SALARY + BONUS + COMM
                       AS GROSS_SALARY
      FROM   EMP
      WHERE  EDLEVEL >= 20) AS HIEMP
GROUP BY WORKDEPT, GROSS_SALARY;
```

View and Table Expression Materialization

View and table expression materialization means that intermediate results from the select that constitutes the view or table expression are written to a temporary work area in DSNDB07. Simple Boolean term predicates using =, <, <=, >, >=, ¬=, ¬>, ¬<, BETWEEN, LIKE, C1 IS NULL (with and without NOT) are applied to minimize the number of rows that must be written to the work area.

The use of GROUP BY, DISTINCT, and column functions can result in materialization. Whether materialization is required depends on the function performed in the view and table expression as well as the function performed by the SELECT from the view and table expression. The columns of Figure ST.10 are the functions in the CREATE VIEW or table expression. When those functions are combined with certain operations used in the select from the view or table expression, materialization is necessary.

Figure ST.10. Conditions that require materialization

	CREATE VIEW or table expression uses...(2):			
SELECT from view or table expression uses...(1):	GROUP BY	DISTINCT	Column Function	Column Function DISTINCT
Joins (3)	X	X	X	X
GROUP BY	X	X	X	X
DISTINCT	-	X	-	X
Column Function	X	X	X	X
Column Function DISTINCT	X	X	X	X
SELECT subset of view or table expression column	-	X	-	-

Table from *IBM DB2 UDB for OS/390 Administration Guide*, SC26-9003, manual (V6). Applies to V5 with APAR PQ18710.

X = Materialization is required

(1) Applies to INSERT, UPDATE, and DELETE statements. If a view is referenced, it must be updatable.
(2) If SELECT clause of a table expression contains a host variable, materialization is required.
(3) Materialization is required for outer joins only when:
  a) SELECT clause does not contain a column.
  b) SELECT clause of a full outer join does not contain a standalone column (no arithmetic expression, for example).
  c) If there is a WHERE clause, it must contain a column.

Table Expressions and Column Functions

Table expressions can be used to apply a column function to a computed column function. Look at a simple example of determining the average salary of employees by department like:

```
SELECT WORKDEPT, AVG(SALARY)
FROM   EMP
GROUP BY WORKDEPT;
```

Assume that there is a requirement to determine the average of averages for each department. The following statement will result in a syntax error:

Invalid syntax:

```
SELECT WORKDEPT, AVG (AVG(SALARY))
FROM   EMP
GROUP BY WORKDEPT;
```

A table expression or view materialization can be used to determine the average of the averages:

```
SELECT AVG(AVG_SAL) AS AVGAVG
FROM (SELECT WORKDEPT, AVG(SALARY) AS AVG_SAL
      FROM   EMP
      GROUP BY WORKDEPT) AS AVG_DEPT_SAL;
```

OR

```
CREATE VIEW AVG_DEPT_SAL (WORKDEPT, AVG_SAL) AS
SELECT WORKDEPT, AVG(SALARY)
FROM   EMP
GROUP BY WORKDEPT;

SELECT AVG(AVG_SAL)
FROM   AVG_DEPT_SAL;
```

Both the table expression and view result in materialization as shown in Figure ST.10. This can be resource-intensive if many intermediate rows must be written to a temporary work area.

Figure ST.11 shows examples of data and the two averages discussed. The last column is the average salary of all employees produced by:

```
SELECT AVG(SALARY)
FROM   EMP;
```

Figure ST.11. Result of averages

EMPNO	WORKDEPT	SALARY	AVG for Each DEPT	AVG of AVG for All DEPTs	AVG of All Employees
E1	D1	40000			
E4	D1	50000			
E6	D1	30000			
			40000		
E2	D2	40000			
E5	D2	40000			
			40000		

EMPNO	WORKDEPT	SALARY	AVG for Each DEPT	AVG of AVG for All DEPTs	AVG of All Employees
E7	D3	20000			
E8	D3	30000			
			25000		
E9	D5	45000			
			45000		
E3	(null)	70000			
			70000		
				44000	40,556

Two Levels of Aggregation

A common requirement is to determine a group that has an amount greater than any other group. For example, it may be necessary to determine a customer that purchases more than any of the other customers or the checking account with the highest balance over a three month period. In terms of the employee table, the following statement determines the work department that has the highest total pay for all employees in the department.

```
SELECT WORKDEPT, TOTAL_PAY
FROM (SELECT WORKDEPT, SUM(SALARY) + SUM(COMM)
                       AS TOTAL_PAY
      FROM EMP
      GROUP BY WORKDEPT) AS PAYROLL_BY_WORKDEPT1
WHERE TOTAL_PAY =
   (SELECT MAX(TOTAL_PAY)
    FROM (SELECT WORKDEPT, SUM(SALARY) + SUM(COMM)
                           AS TOTAL_PAY
          FROM EMP
          GROUP BY WORKDEPT) AS PAYROLL_BY_WORKDEPT2);
```

This statement demonstrates the high level of functionality provided through the use of table expressions. If the tables are large, however, it is necessary to be cautious regarding performance. The last query block named as PAYROLL_BY_WORKDEPT2 requires a tablespace scan of the EMP table. Each WORKDEPT and total pay for all employees in the department is materialized into a work area. The work area is scanned to determine the WORKDEPT with the maximum total pay (MAX(TOTAL_PAY)). A second tablespace scan of the EMP table is performed for the first and second query block to compare the TOTAL_PAY for each WORKDEPT with the maximum that has been determined. Each of the two GROUP BYs require a sort.

Table Expressions and Performance

Table expressions have performance advantages in some cases. We will first look at a case where materialization is required and has performance advantages. The requirement is to count the number of employees in each department and report on the DEPTNO, DEPTNAME, and MGRNO.

```
SELECT DEPTNO, DEPTNAME, MGRNO, COUNT(*)
FROM   DEPT, EMP
WHERE  DEPT.DEPTNO = EMP.WORKDEPT
GROUP BY DEPTNO, DEPTNAME, MGRNO;
```

All of the rows in the DEPT and EMP department must be joined and sorted on three columns to satisfy the GROUP BY. We would like to minimize the number of rows that must be joined as well as the number of rows and columns that must be sorted for the GROUP BY. The cost of sorts increases when the number of rows and columns that must be sorted depending on the size of the sort pool as discussed in Chapter PP. The join and sort costs can be reduced by writing the statement as a table expression.

```
SELECT DEPTNO, DEPTNAME, MGRNO, EMPCOUNT
FROM   DEPT, (SELECT WORKDEPT AS DEPTGROUP,
                     COUNT(*) AS EMPCOUNT
              FROM   EMP
              GROUP BY WORKDEPT) AS TEMP
WHERE DEPTNO = DEPTGROUP;
```

A sort can be done for the GROUP BY in the table expression on only the WORKDEPT. The count of the number of employees in each department can be done and written to a work area along with each WORKDEPT. Each unique WORKDEPT can be joined with the DEPTNO in the DEPT table. This is in contrast to joining the WORKDEPT for every employee with the DEPTNO, sorting on three columns, and doing the count. You do need to be cautious regarding the number rows that must be sorted and written to a temporary work area if an index cannot be used to avoid the sort for the GROUP BY. If an index can be used to avoid the sort, only the fetched rows need to be materialized in most cases. A plan report showing the access path for the join and table expression is in Chapter EX.

Apply Local Predicates with a Table Expression Before Outer Join

Recall from Chapter JP that local predicates are applied after outer join processing until V5 APAR PQ18710 is applied. If you do not have this APAR applied or want to use a table expression to apply local predicates before outer join processing to reduce the number of rows that must be joined, the use of a table expression is a good choice if materialization is not required. We will consider an example to show how a table expression can be used to cause local predicates to be applied before outer join processing. Here is a statement to determine all departments regardless of whether they have employees assigned to them and report on only departments with employees that have an EDLEVEL > 16.

```
SELECT DEPTNO, DEPTNAME, EMPNO, LASTNAME, WORKDEPT, EDLEVEL
FROM   DEPT LEFT OUTER JOIN EMP
ON     DEPT.DEPTNO = EMP.WORKDEPT
WHERE  EMP.EDLEVEL > 16;
```

If the local predicate EMP.EDLEVEL > 16 is not applied until after the join processing, all rows in Figure ST.12 are joined including those crossed out before application of V5 APAR PQ18710. The crossed out rows are not part of the results returned from the statement in any case.

Figure ST.12. Result of a left outer join with a local predicate

DEPTNO	DEPTNAME	EMPNO	LASTNAME	WORKDEPT	EDLEVEL
D1	PROGDEV	E1	Thomas	D1	18
~~D1~~	~~PROGDEV~~	~~E4~~	~~Blake~~	~~D1~~	~~16~~
~~D1~~	~~PROGDEV~~	~~E6~~	~~Jones~~	~~D1~~	~~16~~
D2	DBADM	E2	Clark	D2	18
~~D2~~	~~DBADM~~	~~E5~~	~~Adams~~	~~D2~~	~~16~~
~~D3~~	~~DATADM~~	~~E7~~	~~Smith~~	~~D3~~	~~16~~
~~D3~~	~~DATADM~~	~~E8~~	~~Giles~~	~~D3~~	~~14~~

A table expression without materialization can be used to apply the local predicate on EDLEVEL before the left outer join processing like:

```
SELECT DEPTNO, DEPTNAME, EMPNO, LASTNAME, WORKDEPT, EDLEVEL
FROM (SELECT DEPTNO, DEPTNAME
      FROM   DEPT) AS TDEPT
LEFT OUTER JOIN
     (SELECT EMPNO, LASTNAME, WORKDEPT, EDLEVEL
      FROM   EMP
      WHERE  EDLEVEL > 16) AS TEMP
ON TEMP.WORKDEPT = TDEPT.DEPTNO
WHERE WORKDEPT IS NOT NULL;
```

The WORKDEPT IS NOT NULL predicate is required to eliminate the departments with no employees who have EDLEVEL > 16 which are the crossed out rows in Figure ST.13.

Figure ST.13. Processing of ON Clause and Local Predicates

DEPTNO	DEPTNAME	EMPNO	LASTNAME	WORKDEPT	EDLEVEL
D1	PROGDEV	E1	Thomas	D1	18
D2	DBADM	E2	Clark	D2	18
~~D3~~	~~DATADM~~	~~(null)~~	~~(null)~~	~~(null)~~	~~(null)~~
~~D4~~	~~AI~~	~~(null)~~	~~(null)~~	~~(null)~~	(null)

The table expression formulation is not required to avoid joining rows before applying the local predicate when V5 APAR PQ18710 is applied. However, if materialization is not required as in this example, there is no need to change existing outer joins with table expressions.

An ON clause cannot contain an expression, for example:

```
ON ORDER_DATE + 60 DAYS = RECEIVED_DATE
```

The expression can be placed in a table expression and combined with an outer join.

Including Nulls in Outer Joins with Local Predicates

Recall from Chapter JP that the predicate EMP.LASTNAME >= ' ' includes all employees except those with a null last name. A full outer join causes a null last name to be generated for D4 because there are no employees in the department. Similarly, the predicate DEPT.DEPTNAME includes all departments except those with a null department name. A full outer join causes a null department name to be generated for E3 because the employee is not assigned to a department. If rows with null are required when using a local predicate, consider adding OR conditions to include nulls in the full outer join.

```
SELECT DEPTNO, DEPTNAME, EMPNO,
       LASTNAME, WORKDEPT
FROM   DEPT FULL OUTER JOIN EMP
ON     DEPT.DEPTNO    =
       EMP.WORKDEPT
WHERE (EMP.LASTNAME >= ' '
   OR  EMP.WORKDEPT IS NULL)
AND   (DEPT.DEPTNAME >= ' '
   OR  DEPT.DEPTNO IS NULL);
```

An alternative formulation is the use of the COALESCE scalar function to substitute blank if a null results and qualify the row with a WHERE clause to include blank values.

```
SELECT DEPTNO, DEPTNAME, EMPNO,
       LASTNAME, WORKDEPT
FROM   DEPT FULL OUTER JOIN EMP
ON     DEPT.DEPTNO    =
       EMP.WORKDEPT
WHERE  COALESCE(EMP.LASTNAME,   ' ') >= ' '
OR     COALESCE(DEPT.DEPTNAME,  ' ') >= ' ';
```

Another alternative formulation that adds clarity to the processing required is to use table expressions to apply the local predicates before the outer join processing like:

```
SELECT DEPTNO, DEPTNAME, EMPNO,
       LASTNAME, WORKDEPT
FROM  (SELECT DEPTNO, DEPTNAME
        FROM   DEPT
        WHERE  DEPT.DEPTNAME >= ' ') AS TDEPT
FULL OUTER JOIN
       (SELECT EMPNO, LASTNAME, WORKDEPT, EDLEVEL
        FROM   EMP
        WHERE  EMP.LASTNAME >= ' ') AS TEMP
ON TEMP.WORKDEPT = TDEPT.DEPTNO;
```

Figure ST.14 shows the results of the full outer join with tests for null, use of COALESCE, and table expressions to include null in the results.

Figure ST.14. Results of a full outer join and table expressions to manage nulls

DEPTNO	DEPTNAME	EMPNO	LASTNAME	WORKDEPT
D4	AI	(null)	(null)	(null)
D1	PROGDEV	E1	Thomas	D1
D1	PROGDEV	E4	Blake	D1
D1	PROGDEV	E6	Jones	D1
D2	DBADM	E2	Clark	D2
D2	DBADM	E5	Adams	D2
D3	DATADM	E7	Smith	D3
D3	DATADM	E8	Giles	D3
(null)	(null)	E3	Johnson	(null)

If materialization is not required as in this case, it is not necessary to change existing table expressions used to apply local predicates before outer join processing after applying the V5 APAR.

Multi-Way Outer Join in Steps

Left outer joins of three or more tables need not be performed two tables at a time with the results written to a work file followed by joining the next table prior to V5 APAR PQ18710 as indicated in Figure ST.15.

Figure ST.15. Steps of a multi-way outer join

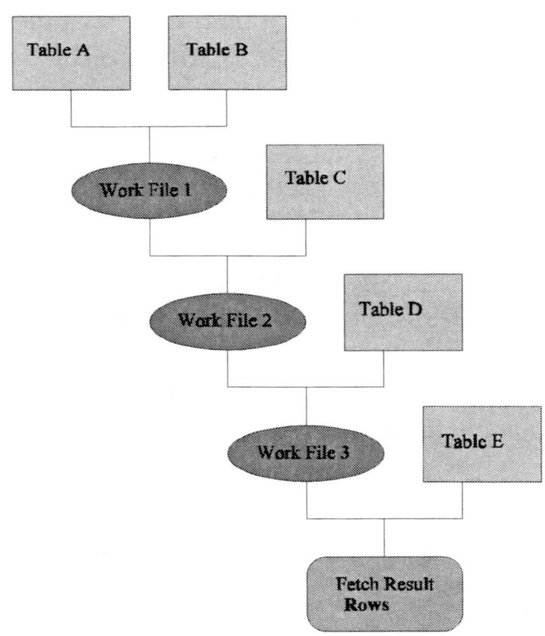

Full outer joins can requires work files. If this is the case, join on the smaller tables followed by right outer join with the large table. If TA is large and the other tables are small, consider doing a doing a full outer join on small tables followed by right outer join with the large table like:

```
SELECT C1, C2, C3
FROM   TB FULL OUTER JOIN TC
ON     TB.C1 = TC.C1
         FULL OUTER JOIN TD
           ON TB.C1 = TD.C1
                RIGHT OUTER
JOIN TA
                 ON TB.C1 =
TA.C1;
```

ST.10 SUMMARY

Non-correlated subselects performance depends on whether a few or many rows qualify in the inner select. An inner select that returns few rows can result in a few matching index scans. An inner select that returns many rows can be resource intensive because many result rows need to be sorted, duplicates eliminated, written to a work area, build of in-memory sparse index, and cannot use an index on column preceding the subselect. How much of a problem this is depends on how many rows qualify for the inner select. Try coding the query as a join, because joins often perform better than subselects.

Use correlated subselects with care, for they are often resource-intensive. The exceptions are EXISTS and NOT EXISTS, which frequently perform well if an index is used for processing the subselect. If no index is available for processing the subselect, or if the subselect qualifies very few rows, a subselect using IN and NOT IN can perform better.

Subselect that return a single value often perform well provided that there is matched nullability between the column compared to the column returned in the subselect. COALESCE needs to be used to substitute a value if no values qualify in the subselect to avoid null being returned to the outer select which can cause mismatched nullability and unexpected results in some cases.

Table expressions can be thought of as an inline view. They add a good deal of functionality to SQL. We have seen cases where table expressions have performance advantages and where they detract from performance depending on the processing required.

EXERCISES

1. Describe how the following statement is processed by DB2. The statement determines the suppliers who supply P5. Assume an index on S.SN, a composite index on SN, PN, and JN in the SPJ table and many rows qualify in the subselect.

```
SELECT SN, SNAME, STATUS, CITY
FROM   S
WHERE  SN IN
 (SELECT SN
  FROM   SPJ
  WHERE  PN='P5');
```

2. Under what conditions will the IN subselect perform well?

3. Reformulate the IN subselect in exercise 1 for improved performance. Describe how it can be processed, and list its advantages over the subselect formulation.

4. How can a correlated subselect be identified?

5. Why do correlated subselects perform poorly in many cases? How does DB2 enhance the performance of a correlated subselect?

6. What type of correlated subselects perform well in most cases? Why?

7. Describe how the following statement is processed by DB2. The statement determines information on parts supplied by Blake and the jobs that use the parts. Assume a unique index on the composite columns SN, PN, and JN in the SPJ table and an index on S.SNAME.

```
SELECT SN, PN, JN
FROM   SPJ
WHERE  SN =
  (SELECT SN
   FROM   S
   WHERE  SNAME = 'Blake');
```

8. The following SELECT statement determines the employees who have a salary greater than or equal to the highest salary in the AI (artificial intelligence) department. There is an index on SALARY and the column is declared as not allowing for nulls. The optimizer does not use a matching index scan. Reformulate the statement so that the optimizer can use the index on SALARY. Why is your new formulation necessary?

```
SELECT EMPNO, LASTNAME, SALARY
FROM   EMP
WHERE  SALARY >=
  (SELECT MAX(SALARY)
   FROM   EMP
   WHERE  WORKDEPT = 'AI');
```

9. Does the following table expression have performance advantages over the select from the view?

```
SELECT HIEMP.EMPNO, LASTNAME, HIDEPT
FROM (SELECT EMPNO, LASTNAME, WORKDEPT AS HIDEPT
      FROM   EMP
      WHERE  EDLEVEL >= 20) AS HIEMP
LEFT OUTER JOIN DEPT
ON HIDEPT = DEPTNO;

CREATE VIEW HIEMP AS
SELECT EMPNO, LASTNAME, WORKDEPT
FROM   EMP
WHERE  EDLEVEL >= 20;

SELECT EMPNO, LASTNAME, WORKDEPT
FROM   HIEMP LEFT OUTER JOIN DEPT
ON     WORKDEPT = DEPTNO;
```

10. The following select from the defined view requires view materialization. If the statement is reformulated to a table expression, will the materialization be eliminated?

```
CREATE VIEW AVGSAL (WORKDEPT, AVG_SAL) AS
SELECT WORKDEPT, AVG(SALARY)
FROM   EMP
GROUP BY WORKDEPT;

SELECT WORKDEPT, EMP.EMPNO, SALARY
FROM   EMP, AVGSAL
WHERE  EMP.SALARY > AVGSAL.AVG_SAL;
```

11. Will a temporary work area always be used when doing an outer join of more than two tables?

ANSWERS

1. A non-matching index scan can be done on the SN, PN, and JN composite index to identify the SNs who supply P5. The SNs are sorted and duplicates eliminated to minimize the number of SNs that must be scanned and reduce the size of the temporary work area. An in-memory sparse index is created on the subselect results. A tablespace scan is performed on the S table. For each S.SN, the in-memory sparse index is used to locate a subsection. A binary search is done on values in subsection for each qualifying row in the outer select. Qualifying rows are returned to the user.

2. The statement will perform well if there is a small number of leaf pages for the composite index on SN, PN, and JN, and a small number of SPJ.SN are identified to be sorted with elimination of duplicates, and the build of an in-memory sparse index. Also, if few rows qualify in the inner select and an index is used on the column preceding subselect, the IN subselect has advantages.

3. The optimizer will not reformulate the IN subselect into a join because there is not a unique index on SPJ.SN. You can reformulate the statement as a join like:

```
SELECT DISTINCT S.SN, SNAME, STATUS, CITY
FROM   S, SPJ
WHERE  S.SN = SPJ.SN
AND    PN   = 'P5';
```

A nested loop join can be performed with the composite index leaf pages on SN, PN, and JN scanned as the outer table until a P5 is found. Each supplier of P5 parts can be found in the composite index and used in a matching index scan on the S.SN as the inner table of the nested loop join. The first joined result row is returned to the user. The join formulation has the advantage in that a temporary work file need not be built, sorted, duplicates removed, and a sparse index built before the first row can be returned to the user. In addition, a matching index scan can be done on S.SN rather than a tablespace scan. However, the join formulation requires a sort for DISTINCT to eliminate duplicate rows. If few rows qualify in inner select and an index is used on the column preceding subselect to do few matching index scans into the outer table, the IN subselect formulation has advantages.

4. If a correlation name is used in the subselect predicate to refer back to the table in the outer select, it is a correlated subselect. The correlation name follows the table name in the FROM clause without a comma separating them. "D" is the correlation name in FROM DEPT D. You can also specify the correlation name by separating the table name from the correlation name with the AS clause like: FROM DEPT AS D. Another way to identify a correlated subselect is to cover the outer select and determine if the inner select can be evaluated independently of the outer select. If the inner select cannot be evaluated independently of the outer select, it is a correlated subselect.

5. The reason that correlated subselects can perform poorly is that correlated subselects require that the subselect be evaluated for each qualifying value in the outer select. DB2 optimizes this processing by not reevaluating duplicate values for the outer select. It does this by saving qualifying outer table values in a 4 KB in-memory table. When the value recurs, the in-memory table is checked to determine if the value has already been evaluated. If the value is in the in-memory table, that duplicate value is not evaluated in the inner table.

6. The EXISTS and NOT EXISTS subselects perform well in most cases because of the use of the in-memory table and the fact that a matching index scan can be performed on the inner table pseudo join predicate.

7. A matching index scan can be done on the SNAME index with access to the data page to determine that Blake's supplier number is S3. The statement can then be executed as if it had been written as:

```
SELECT SN, PN, JN
FROM   SPJ
WHERE  SN = 'S3';
```

A matching index scan can be done using the composite index on SN, PN, and JN with index only processing to retrieve the required information.

8. The following formulation of the statement allows the optimizer to use a matching index scan on SALARY.

```
SELECT EMPNO, LASTNAME, SALARY
FROM   EMP
WHERE  SALARY >=
   (SELECT COALESCE (MAX(SALARY), 0)
    FROM   EMP
    WHERE  WORKDEPT = 'AI');
```

The use of the COALESCE or VALUE clause is necessary because SALARY is declared as not allowing nulls and the subselect result will be null if there are no employees in the AI (artificial intelligence) department. Matched nullability is necessary to use an index. The subselect will not return null with the COALESCE clause. Therefore, there is matched nullability between the result of the subselect and the SALARY column.

9. It is very likely that the optimizer will choose the same access path for the table expression and the select from the view. Therefore, the performance will be the same.

10. Reformulation of the select from a view to a table expression will not eliminate the materialization. SELECTS from a view and table expressions are managed similarly by the optimizer.

11. A temporary work area will always be used when doing an outer join of more than two tables.

FIGURES

Parallel Processing

PL.1 INTRODUCTION

One of the major challenges in program design is to improve the response time for end users. Many chapters in this book can help you attain that goal, by giving you ideas about how to take the best advantage of DB2's processing to achieve the best performance. For very complex I/O-intensive or processor-intensive queries, such as those used by companies doing complicated data analysis to discover buying trends, the best way to reduce total elapsed time is to do as much of the processing as possible in parallel.

Parallelism is a good choice for the statements in which a large number of data or index pages are scanned, for column functions computed on a large number of rows, when few rows are returned from a complex operation, and for sorts and joins. Data warehousing and decision support systems benefit significantly from parallelism. The goal of parallelism to is reduce elapsed time without increasing processor time by more than 15 percent.

PL.2 MODES OF PARALLELISM

Depending on the type of statement being processed and the system resources available for doing the work, the optimizer can choose *I/O parallelism*, which creates multiple I/O streams for a single task, *CP parallelism*, which creates multiple tasks, each of which can have a single I/O stream, or *sysplex parallelism*, which uses multiple DB2 subsystems to execute an SQL statement.

CPU, CPC, and CP Acronyms: CPU (Central Processor Unit) has been a widely used acronym for the past 30 years. It originally meant one processor as indicated the "unit" portion of the acronym. Multiple processors have been included within a computer purchased from IBM and other companies for over a decade. The acronym "CPU" continued to be used to refer to these computers. With respect to parallelism, it is necessary to be more precise in the use of terms. Central processor complex (CPC) means a computer with more than one tightly-coupled processor. Central processor (CP) means one processor within a complex with multiple processors.

I/O Parallelism: I/O instructions are executed from one CP serially in a round robin fashion. Data is located on DASD devices in parallel (assuming data is spread across multiple DASD devices) and transferred over channels in parallel into a virtual pool. This mode of parallelism is good for I/O intensive SQL.

CP Parallelism: I/O instructions are executed from more than one CP in parallel. Data is located and transferred over channels as with I/O parallelism. This mode of parallelism is good for I/O intensive SQL with more than one CP.

Sysplex Parallelism: More than one DB2 subsystem on more than one CPC with sysplex data sharing can be used to process data for one SQL statement. I/O and CP parallelism can be used by each DB2 subsystem. Each subsystem processes the data that it reads. This mode of parallelism is good for CP intensive operations including SQL that require sorts, joins, and decompression of data.

Sysplex and CP parallelism requires OS/390 with preemptable service request blocks (SRBs) on a CPC. SRBs are discussed in Section PL.7.

PL.3 WHEN PARALLELISM CAN BE USED

Parallelism can be used on partitioned tablespaces and indexes. It can be used on work files output by an enterprise system architecture (ESA) sort which uses a hardware assist to maximize performance. The input to the sort can be from a partitioned or nonpartitioned tablespace. CP and sysplex parallelism can be used on one data set (one partition), nonpartitioned tables, nonpartitioned indexes (NPIs), and pieces of NPI for CP intensive operations. Parallelism applies to SELECT statements that are read-only or ambiguous with CURRENTDATA of NO as discussed in Chapter CC. It will probably apply to UPDATE and DELETE statements in a future release. Whether parallelism will be beneficial for INSERT statements remains to be seen. Insertions are basically a serial process in most cases.

Degree Parameter

DEGREE(ANY) must be specified with a bind or rebind of static SQL statements to allow the optimizer to consider parallelism. DEGREE(1) is the default. The default can be changed by the systems administrator using the DSNTIPK installation panel or the parameter CDSSRDEF in the DSN6SPRM macro of DSNZPARM. It is expected that the maximum degree of parallelism can be specified in the future. Parallelism can be used with host variables.

Dynamic SQL requires that the statement SET CURRENT DEGREE = 'ANY' be executed to allow parallelism for dynamic SELECT statements if the installation default of DEGREE(1) is used.

Data Set Placement on DASD

It is important to place partitions, pieces of NPI, and work tablespaces on separate packs. Otherwise, elapsed time of parallel processing can be greater than sequential processing due to excessive seek time. Seek time is depicted in Figure PL.1 showing the DASD arm movement from one partition to another on a single pack. I/O requests are queued. That is a second I/O request to a volume must wait for the first request to complete. The optimizer assumes that the underlying data sets for partitions, pieces of NPIs, and work tablespaces are on separate packs. The number of data sets per DASD controller and the number of channels per controller can also effect performance.

Figure PL.1. Excessive seek time with two partitions on a DASD pack

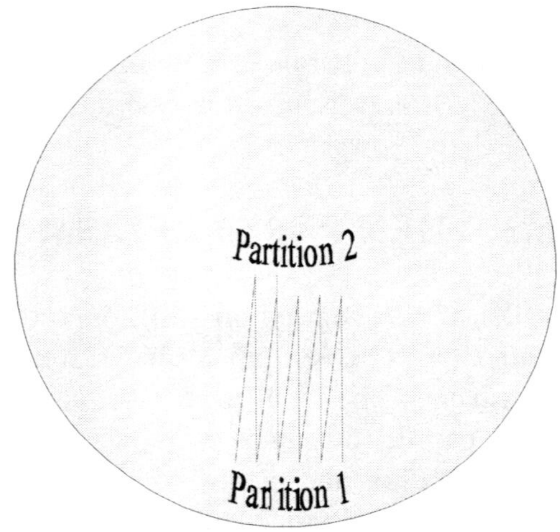

Recommendation: Place data sets to be processed in parallel on separate DASD packs. Consider one control unit per four to five data sets with two to three channels per controller. If you are using SMS to manage tablespaces and index, consider the guidelines in Chapter CD on data set placement.

Types of Processing that Can and Cannot Use Parallelism

Most commonly used SELECT statements can use parallelism. Sequential prefetch used for a tablespace scan and non-matching index scan of partitioned tablespaces and indexes are good candidates for parallelism. The mode of parallelism for use on indexes depends on the type of index. All modes of parallelism can be used on indexes. List prefetch can use I/O and CP parallelism. Sysplex parallelism cannot be used for list prefetch because the RID pool is not a shared resource in sysplex data sharing as discussed in Chapter PP.

The inner and outer SELECTS of a non-correlated subselect can use all three modes of parallelism but only the outer select of a correlated subselect can use the three modes of parallelism. The subselect of an INSERT statement can use parallelism. Subselects across UNION and UNION ALL can use parallelism. That is each SELECT can be processed independently in parallel.

Most types of joins can use all three types of parallelism including nested loop, merge, and hybrid type C join. A hybrid type N join does not use parallelism. This type of join would require a shared RID pool for sysplex parallelism. A merge join on more than one column does not use parallelism. Parallelism can be used with outer joins (V6). There are a number of cases where parallelism is currently not used but will probably be used in the future. Materialization of views and nested table expressions are also types of processing that cannot use parallelism at present but probably will in the future.

The type of processing and mode of parallelism that can be used are summarized in Figure PL.2.

Figure PL.2. Types of processing that can and cannot use parallelism

Processing	Mode of Par. I	C	X
Tablespace scan	Y	Y	Y
Non-matching and matching index scan	Y	Y	Y
Sequential prefetch	Y	Y	Y
List prefetch (no shared RID pool)	Y	Y	-
ESA Sort with hardware assist	-	Y	Y
Subselect using in-memory sparse index can use I/O parallelism only prior to V5	Y	-	-
Inner and outer select of non-correlated subselect can be run in parallel including use of in-memory sparse index with V5	Y	Y	Y
Outer select of correlated subselect with V5	Y	Y	Y
Subselect of INSERT with V5	Y	Y	Y
Subselects across UNION and UNION ALL. Each SELECT can be processed independently in parallel	Y	Y	Y
Nested loop, merge, hybrid type C join with a single join predicate, and star join (not sysplex parallelism)	Y	Y	Y
Outer joins with V6	Y	Y	Y
Hybrid type N join (no shared RID pool)	-	-	-
Merge join on > 1 column	-	-	-
Matching index scan for IN (list)(can be used on inner table of a join (V6))	-	-	-
Materialized views at view reference time	-	-	-
Materialized nested table expressions	-	-	-
SELECT from a global temporary table	-	-	-
Subselect of UPDATE and DELETE	-	-	-
Direct row access using a row ID column	-	-	-
Select defined with CURSOR WITH HOLD	Y	Y	-
RR Isolation level	Y	Y	-

I indicates I/O parallelism
C indicates CP parallelism
X indicates sysplex parallelism
Y indicates that the mode of parallelism can be used for the type of processing.

"-" indicates that the mode of parallelism cannot be used for the type of processing.

PL.4 DEGREE OF PARALLELISM

The degree of parallelism is the number of parallel operations that can be used for a specific activity. Figure PL.3 shows that four parallel operations are being used to bring data from the partitions of the SPJ table into the buffer pool.

Figure PL.3. Degree of parallelism

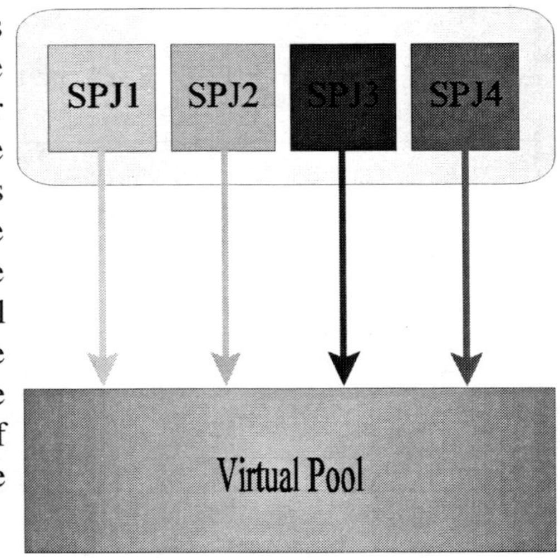

In this case, the degree of parallelism is the same as the number of physical partitions in the tablespace, but this is not always the case. In many cases, *logical partitions* are used. Logical partitions are based on page ranges of one or more physical partitions and a key range of more than one partition of a partitioning index. If some physical partitions are considerably smaller than other partitions, they can be combined into a logical partition. Looking back at Figure PL.3, for example, SPJ3 and SPJ4 might be small physical partitions and be treated as one logical partition. The degree of parallelism then would be three. The maximum degree possible is 254, the same as the maximum number of partitions in a tablespace. The maximum number of usable CPs for one SQL statement is 320.

Parallelism in the PLAN_TABLE

The PLAN_TABLE provides information on the access path chosen by the optimizer when EXPLAIN is used as discussed in Chapter EX. In this chapter we will consider information in the PLAN_TABLE relevant to parallelism. Figure PL.4 is a fragment of the PLAN_TABLE showing the TNAME (table name), METHOD of 0 indicates the first table accessed, ACCESS_DEGREE indicates the degree of parallelism, and ACCESS_PGROUP_ID is the step in the execution of the SQL statement where the degree of parallel is used.

Figure PL.4. Degree and parallel group in the PLAN_TABLE

TNAME	METHOD	ACCESS_ DEGREE	ACCESS_ PGROUP_ID
SPJ	0	4	1

The ACCESS_DEGREE of 4 describes the degree of parallelism shown in Figure PL.3. If the degree is blank, parallel processing was not chosen. If the degree is 0, the content of host variables for static SQL will be used to determine the degree of parallelism at run time or parallelism will not be used.

The additional columns in the PLAN_TABLE describing parallelism will be discussed later in this chapter as the operations performed in parallel are discussed.

Bind, Run, and Actual Degree

The parallel degree chosen at bind time is an optimal degree, based on the access path chosen by the optimizer and the amount of processor resource available. Even if the optimizer *plans* to use parallelism, it is possible that the degree of parallelism will have to be reduced at run time or that the SQL will have to run sequentially instead of in parallel. Even during execution, the *actual* degree used might be reduced because of virtual pool shortages that occur before or after parallel processing begins.

The planned bind degree of parallelism is chosen by the optimizer and shown in the PLAN_TABLE. This degree can be reduced before execution and during execution depending on the availability of prerequisites and resource availability. The bind degree will not be adjusted if there are fewer processors online at run time compared to bind time provided there is more than one processor online for sysplex and CP parallelism. For example, if four processors are online at bind time but only two processors are available at run time, the degree of parallelism is not adjusted downward. This can cause an increase in I/O wait time because there are not enough processors to handle the I/O workload.

The planned run degree is determined at run time based on content of host variables, ambiguous cursors, and availability of prerequisites. If the prerequisites are not available at run time, sequential prefetch will be used with no parallelism. The planned run degree prerequisites are:

- OS/390 for CP and sysplex parallelism
- One or more processors for CP and sysplex parallelism, and processor speed
- Availability of coordinator and assistants for sysplex parallelism as discussed in Section PL.7
- ESA Sort if a sort is required (not checked at bind time)

The actual degree can be less than the bind and run degrees based on buffer pool space to process the data, indexes, and work files. If there is insufficient buffer pool space before the start of parallelism, the degree is reduced or parallelism is not used. If there is insufficient buffer pool space after start of parallelism, the prefetch quantity is dynamically halved and quartered (from 32 to 16 to pages for example). This avoids flooding the buffer pool.

The performance trace records show the bind, run, and actual degrees as discussed in Section PL.7.

Parallel Groups

A *parallel group* is a discrete unit of processing for a particular statement. Each parallel group is assigned a parallel group ID. For example, a simple SELECT using a tablespace scan probably has just one parallel group, the one used to access the table as shown in Figs. PL.4 and PL.5. A series of nested loop joins for three tables might also all belong to the same parallel group, because the access is happening concurrently.

If operations have different parallel degrees, they are part of different parallel groups. A merge scan join of two tables might have one table accessed with a parallel degree of 2 and a second table might be accessed with a parallel degree of 8. These two operations are part of two separate parallel groups and are identified in the PLAN_TABLE with two different parallel group IDs. Each parallel group is executed serially. All tables within a join group have the same low and high keys for a physical or logical partition.

An SQL statement can have different parallel modes for each of several different parallel groups. However, there will not be multiple parallel modes within a parallel group.

Parallel groups are analogous to a job step except they can be executed in parallel with sysplex parallelism.

PL.5 THE OPTIMIZER AND PARALLELISM

The optimizer first chooses a good sequential access path. If it estimates that the elapsed time can be reduced by using a parallel path, and if a DEGREE of ANY is specified at bind time, the optimizer is likely to choose parallel processing. Both the sequential and parallel path are placed in plan or package if parallelism is chosen. This provides for fallback at execution time depending on factors to be discussed in this section.

Sysplex and CP parallelism are considered before I/O parallelism because the I/O can be issued in parallel using multiple parallel tasks. However, if the requirements for CP parallelism are not met, then only I/O parallelism is considered. I/O parallelism only is considered at bind if OS/390 is not available, and more than one processor is not available. CP and I/O (not sysplex) parallelism are considered when using CURSOR WITH HOLD and the isolation levels of cursor stability or uncommited read.

The optimizer takes the following factors into account when determining if parallelism should be used and how it should be used.

- Statistics collected by RUNSTATS as discussed in Chapter RR
- Estimated I/O cost of the largest partition
- Estimated processor cost considering the MIPS rating of the CPs and number of CPs and CPCs online
- Availability of coordinators and assistants for sysplex parallelism
- Virtual pool thresholds
- Number of physical partitions
- Number of pages in largest partition

Largest Partition Limits the Degree of Parallelism

The maximum degree of parallelism for a tablespace scan is the total number of pages in the tablespace divided by the number of pages in the largest partition. The total number of pages in the tablespace is in the NPAGES column of the SYSTABLES catalog table. The number of pages for each partition is in the NPAGES column of the SYSTABSTATS table. If a tablespace has 120,000 pages, and if the largest partition has 30,000 pages, the parallel degree can be no larger than 4 (120,000 / 30,000). Choosing a higher degree does not reduce elapsed time.

As an example, suppose there are 10 physical partitions with 120,000 pages total. Partition 1 is significantly larger than the rest in that it has 30,000 pages. The rest of the partitions have about

10,000 pages each. The highest degree of parallelism that can be achieved in this case is 4, divided as follows:

Logical partition 1 = 30,000 pages in partition 1
Logical partition 2 = 30,000 pages in partitions 2, 3, 4
Logical partition 3 = 30,000 pages in partitions 5, 6, 7
Logical partition 4 = 30,000 pages in partitions 8, 9, 10

However, if each physical partition has about 12,000 pages, it is more likely that a degree of parallelism of 10 can be achieved. Indeed, it may be possible to achieve a higher degree of parallelism for CP intensive SQL than there are physical partitions.

Examples of Estimating the Degree of Parallelism

The optimizer uses a number of rules and formula in determining the degree of parallelism. It is thought that one of the rules used by the optimizer is that it will not choose a parallel path if more than 15 percent increase in processor time is estimated. Here is a conceptual formula for estimating the maximum degree of parallelism for a single tablespace scan:

- Degree = `MAX (TIO, TCP) / MAX (TCP / N, MPIO)`

The acronyms used in the formula are:

```
♦  TIO  = Estimated total I/O time in minutes
♦  TCP  = Estimated total CP time in minutes
♦  N    = Total number of available processors,
          1 used if I/O parallelism
♦  MPIO = Estimated I/O time in minutes for the largest partition
```

Figure PL.5 contains examples of using a conceptual formulation for estimating the degree of parallelism for I/O bound, CP bound, and a mixture of I/O and CP bound processing. The mode column in the figure uses the same acronym as used in the PARALLELISM_MODE column of the PLAN_TABLE with the same meaning of:

```
♦  I for I/O parallelism
♦  C for CP parallelism
♦  X for sysplex parallelism
```

Figure PL.5. Conceptually estimating the degree of parallelism

SQL Type	Mode	TIO	TCP	N	MPIO	Degree
I/O bound	I	50	5	1	10	5
I/O bound	C	50	5	10	10	5
I/O bound	X	50	5	50	10	5

SQL Type	Mode	TIO	TCP	N	MPIO	Degree
CP bound	I	2	50	1	0.5	1
CP bound	C	2	50	10	0.5	10
CP bound	X	2	50	50	0.5	50
Mixed	I	50	5	1	0.2	10
Mixed	C	50	5	10	0.2	100
Mixed	X	50	5	50	0.2	250

Test Results

Figure PL.6 shows the IBM test results comparing the use of I/O, CP, and Sysplex parallelism in the following environment. Details of the laboratory results can be found in the *Version 5 Performance Topics*, SG24-2213, manual.

- I/O parallelism used one CP.
- CP parallelism used 10 CPs.
- Sysplex parallelism used 10 CPs on 2 CPCs.

The tests were run on a two member data sharing group using 9672-RX2 processors and a 9674-C02 coupling facility with 30 GB of data in 30 partitions.

The goal of parallelism to reduce elapsed time was accomplished with 7 to 29 X reductions in elapsed time at a cost of 5 to 14 percent increase in CPC time.

Figure PL.6. IBM test comparisons of parallelism

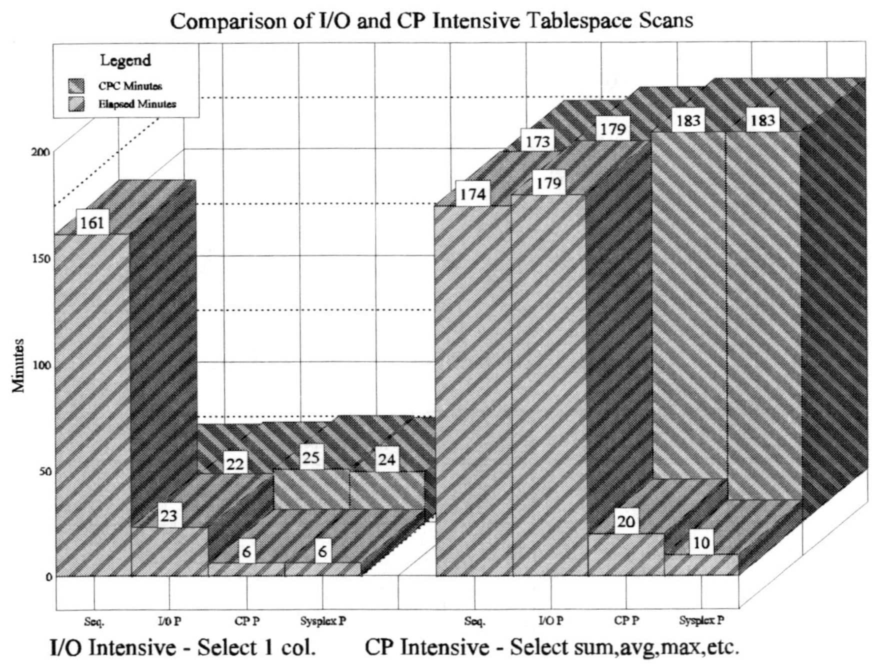

Increase Parallelism with Program Design

You can increase the benefits of parallelism through program design. The technique described is not necessary to achieve parallelism but can be used to achieve an additional level of parallelism. When a cursor is opened, it causes parallelism to begin. This allows for executing other SQL statements and host language code which will occur concurrently with the work in progress for the opened cursor. Figure PL.7 shows an example of this using pseudo code.

Figure PL.7. Pseudo code for increasing parallelism with program design

```
     EXEC SQL DECLARE PCURSOR CURSOR FOR
              SELECT COUNT(*)
              FROM   P
              WHERE  CITY = :CITY
     END-EXEC.

     EXEC SQL DECLARE SCURSOR CURSOR FOR
              SELECT SN, SNAME, STATUS, CITY
              FROM   S
              WHERE  STATUS > :STATUS
              ORDER BY SNAME
     END-EXEC.

OPEN-CURSORS. -- Causes parallel processing to begin

     EXEC SQL OPEN PCURSOR END-EXEC.
     EXEC SQL OPEN SCURSOR END-EXEC.

-- SELECTS using parallelism can be executed
-- concurrently

-- SELECT, INSERT, UPDATE, and DELETE from other tables
-- Execute host language statements
-- Work is being done to satisfy SCURSOR and PCURSOR

     EXEC SQL FETCH PCURSOR
              INTO :COUNT-FOR-CITY
     END-EXEC.

-- Execute more SQL and host language statements to
-- allow for more time to sort rows

     EXEC SQL FETCH SCURSOR
              INTO :SN, :SNAME, :STATUS, :CITY
     END-EXEC.
```

The example assumes that the P and S tables are partitioned and parallelism is used in a tablespace scan to satisfy both SELECT statements shown in the figure. (The CITY and STATUS columns in the WHERE clauses do not have indexes.) Parallelism is used to sort by SNAME to satisfy the ORDER BY in the second SELECT statement. The access path chosen by the optimizer can be determined by using EXPLAIN and analyzing the PLAN_TABLE. The planned bind, run, and actual degree of parallelism can be determined using a performance monitor or the program DB2QPMON. (DB2QPMON is provided by IBM at no charge.)

Limited Partition Scan

For partitioned tablespaces, the optimizer can limit the number of partitions that have to be scanned. This applies to scanning only some of the data partitions, index partitions, or data and index partitions. The purpose is to not scan partitions that the optimizer can determine ahead of time do not contain qualifying values. To determine this, the WHERE clause of the SELECT statement must have predicates on the leading column of the partitioning index. The predicates cannot contain host variables for static SQL, unless reoptimization is used as discussed in Section OP.7. If the number of partitions scanned can be reduced, the cost of reoptimization is almost certainly a good choice.

The LIMITKEY column in the catalog table SYSINDEXPART is compared to the user requested value to determine the data partitions that need to be scanned. It contains the upper range value for the partition as specified when the partitioning index is created. A limited partitioning scan does not require that the partitioning index be scanned. The PLAN_TABLE shows a limited partition scan with 'Y' in the PAGE_RANGE. It shows a 'R' in the METHOD column for a scan of one or more data or index partitions and an 'I' for a NPI logical partition scan.

For example, assume that a tablespace has 12 partitions, one for each month of the year, partitioned by the DATE_REC column. In the following statement, only data partition 9 must be scanned.

```
SELECT PN, PNAME, WEIGHT, CITY, DATE_REC
FROM   P
WHERE  DATE_REC = '1993-09-16';
```

Range predicates can also be used to limit the number of partitions that must be scanned. Suppose you have the following statement:

```
SELECT PN, PNAME, WEIGHT, CITY, DATE_REC
FROM   P
WHERE  DATE_REC >= '1993-09-16';
```

Conceptually, the optimizer can treat the statement as if it were written like this:

```
SELECT PN, PNAME, WEIGHT, CITY, DATE_REC
FROM   P
WHERE  DATE_REC BETWEEN '1993-09-16' AND '1993-09-30'
OR     DATE_REC BETWEEN '1993-10-01' AND '1993-10-31'
OR     DATE_REC BETWEEN '1993-11-01' AND '1993-11-30'
OR     DATE_REC BETWEEN '1993-12-01' AND '1993-12-31';
```

Only data partitions 9 through 12 must be scanned. The partitions scanned need not be contiguous. For example, parts 2, 4, 6 can be scanned. Only partitions being scanned are locked. This selective partition locking reduces the costs of a commit when using RELEASE of COMMIT as discussed in Chapter TS.

Restrictions: A data partition scan does not apply to host variables with static SQL. If parallelism is used, a limited partition scan applies only to single table access.

PL.6 SORTS AND JOINS USING PARALLELISM

Sorts and joins of a large number of rows can be resource intensive both in I/O time and CP time. I/O, CP, and sysplex parallelism are all useful in reducing the elapsed time. Sysplex parallelism is particularly useful for these operations because a good deal of the elapsed time is due to CP time in addition to I/O time in many cases. A number of examples of sorts and joins will be given along with how to understand the use of parallelism through analysis of the explain results in the plan table.

ESA Sort Parallelism

If the ESA sort is available, qualifying rows are passed to the sort as they are read. With CP and sysplex parallelism multiple processors can sort multiple portions of the data and write each portion to a work file. The merged rows from the work files are passed directly to the host program without the program having to wait for the merge process to complete. No parallelism and I/O parallelism differs from CP and sysplex parallelism in that the sort is done serially with one processor. In addition, it is necessary to merge the sorted work files into another work files in DSNDB07. I/O parallelism can be used to read work files for the merge process.

Figure PL.8 shows how a sort can be performed with three tasks using CP and sysplex parallelism. Each task can scan a logical partition, sort it, and place the sorted rows in work files. The work files need not be merged into another work file as is the case with I/O parallelism. Rather, the sorted rows are passed directly to the host program as they are merged.

Figure PL.8. Sort with CP and sysplex parallelism

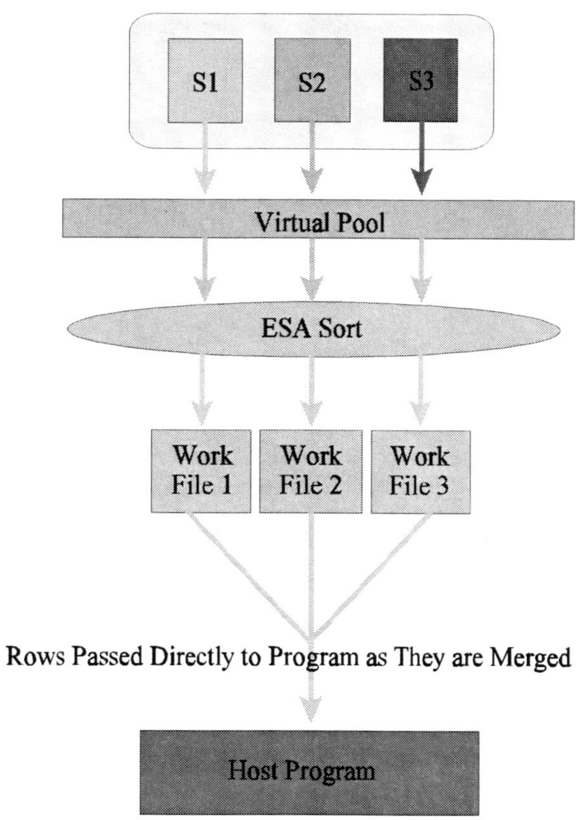

Join of Partitioned Tablespaces

We will analyze the parallel processing of a nested loop join with one sort to gain an understanding of the processing required and how to interpret it as described in a plan table. The first row of a partial PLAN_TABLE in Figure PL.9 shows that the S table is accessed first (MT=0), using a tablespace scan (AT=R) with sequential prefetch (PR=S). The first step of the parallel process (ACCESS_PGROUP_ID=1)) results in reading two S partitions in parallel (ACCESS_DEGREE=2) and two sorts are done in parallel in the first step (SORTN_PGROUP=1). The upper two-thirds of the diagram in Figure PL.10 shows the process.

Figure PL.9. Join of partitioned tablespaces - PLAN_TABLE

TNAME	MT	AT	PR	ACCESS_ DEGREE	ACCESS_ PGROUP _ID	SORTC_ PGROUP	SORTN_ PGROUP	JOIN_ DEGREE	JOIN_ PGROUP _ID
S	0	R	S	2	1		1		
SPJ	1	R	S	3	2			3	2

Figure PL.10. Join of partitioned tablespaces - diagram

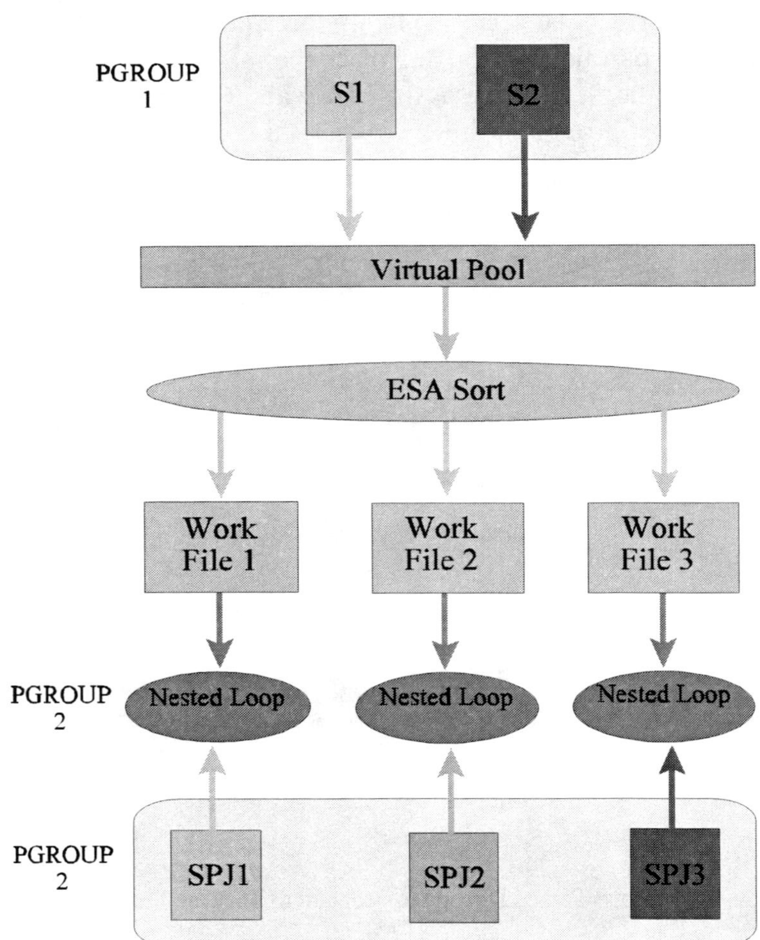

The second row of the plan table shows that the SPJ table is accessed second in a nested loop join (MT=1) using a tablespace scan (AT=R) with sequential prefetch (PR=S). The second step of the parallel process (ACCESS_PGROUP_ID=2)) results in reading three SPJ partitions in parallel (ACCESS_DEGREE=3). The join is done as part of the second step (JOIN_PGROUP=2) with a degree of 3 (JOIN_DEGREE=3). The lower one-third of the diagram in Figure PL.10 shows the process.

Nonpartitioned Tablespaces in Joins

Parallelism is considered for a nonpartitioned tablespace, particularly if a sort is required. All three of the join methods benefit from having the outer table in sequence as discussed in Chapter JP. Figure PL.11 shows a hybrid join of a nonpartitioned tablespace and a partitioned tablespace. Both sides of a join have the same degree of parallelism. The degree used to process the outer table of a join drives the degree of parallelism. The inner table has the same degree of parallelism as the outer table.

Figure PL.11. Join of nonpartitioned tablespace with a partitioned one

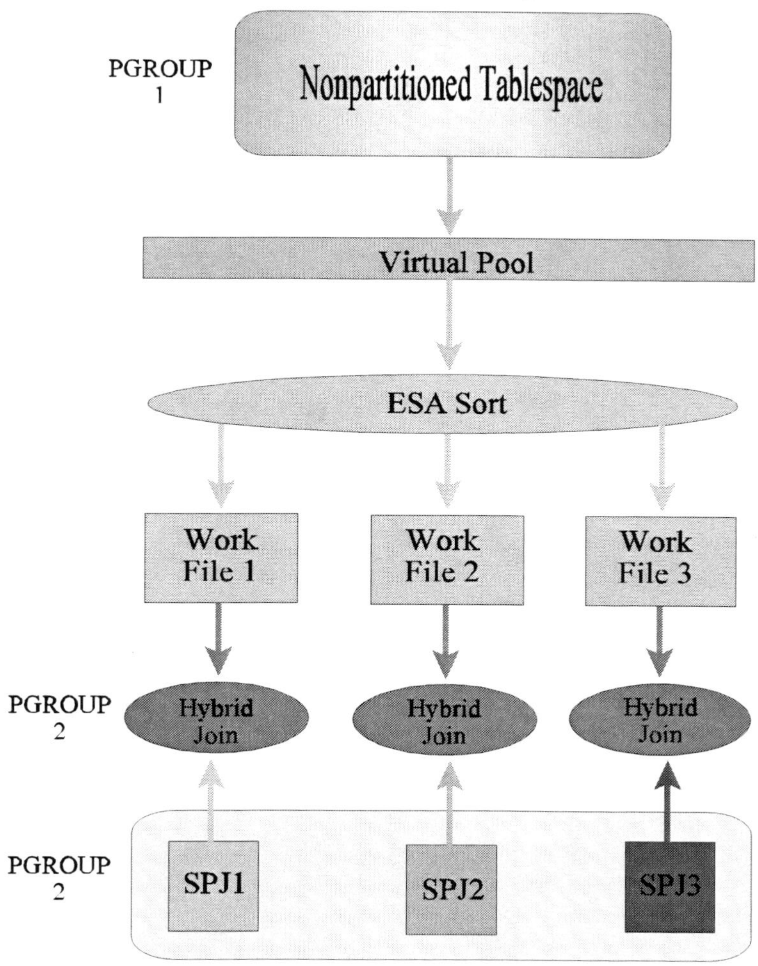

Parallel Sorts and a Merge Join

Two or more sorts for joining two or more tables can be done in parallel by two or more CPs concurrently (except not with I/O parallelism). The qualifying rows can be from partitioned or nonpartitioned tables. The partial PLAN_TABLE in Figure PL.12 is used to analyze and gain an understanding of the processing.

Figure PL.12. Merge join in parallel - PLAN_TABLE

TNAME	MT	AT	PR	ACCESS_ DEGREE	ACCESS_ PGROUP ID	SORTC_ PGROUP	SORTN_ PGROUP	JOIN_ DEGREE	JOIN_ PGROUP ID
S	0	R	S	3	1		1		
SPJ	2	R	S	4	2	1	2	2	3

The three parallel groups are processed as:

- The first step (ACCESS_PGROUP_ID=1) is to read the S table with a degree of 3. The qualifying rows from the S table are passed to an ESA sort as they are read (SORTN_PGROUP=1). Notice that the access and sort parallel groups are both 1 meaning that the work can be done concurrently.

- The second step (ACCESS_PGROUP_ID=2) is to read the SPJ table with a degree of 4. The qualifying rows from the S table are passed to an ESA sort as they are read (SORTN_PGROUP=2). Notice that the access and sort parallel groups are both 2 meaning that the work can be done concurrently.

- The third step (JOIN_PGROUP_ID=3) is to merge the pair of two work files from the S and SPJ tables.

The number of work files or partitions to be joined must match on both sides of the join in most cases as in this example shown in Figure PL.13. This example also shows how the output of a sort can be to a different number of work files than the number of partitions read.

Figure PL.13. Merge join in parallel - diagram

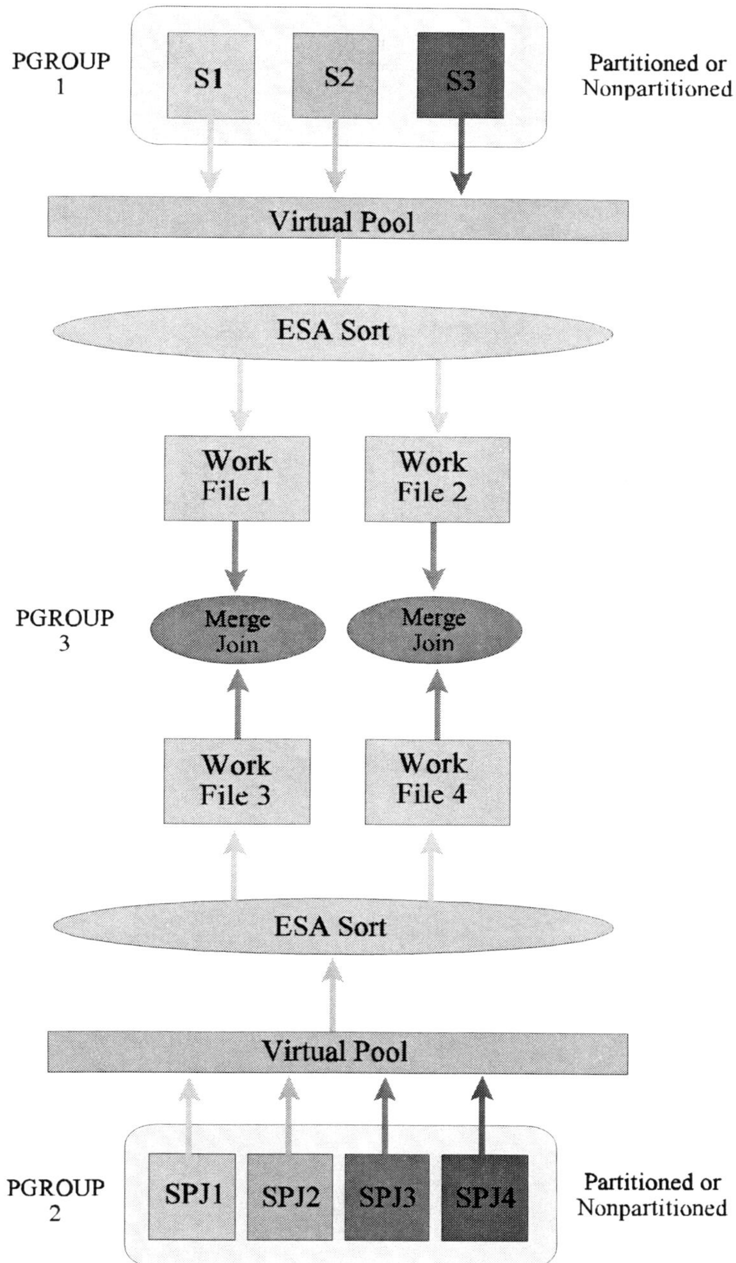

Nested Loop Join with No Sorts

Join parallelism can be achieved in cases where no sorts are required. The plan table in Figure PL.14 shows the same parallel group of 1 for reading the S and SPJ tables, and for performing the join.

Figure PL.14. Nested loop join with no sorts - PLAN_TABLE

TNAME	METHOD	ACCESS_ DEGREE	ACCESS_ PGROUP_ID	JOIN_ DEGREE	JOIN_ PGROUP_ID
S	0	4	1		
SPJ	1	4	1	4	1

All processing is done in parallel in one step; no serial processing is required. The accesses to the tables are done in parallel as are the joins. Figure PL.15 shows a diagram of the process based on the results in the PLAN_TABLE (Figure PL.14)

Figure PL.15. Nested loop join with no sorts - diagram

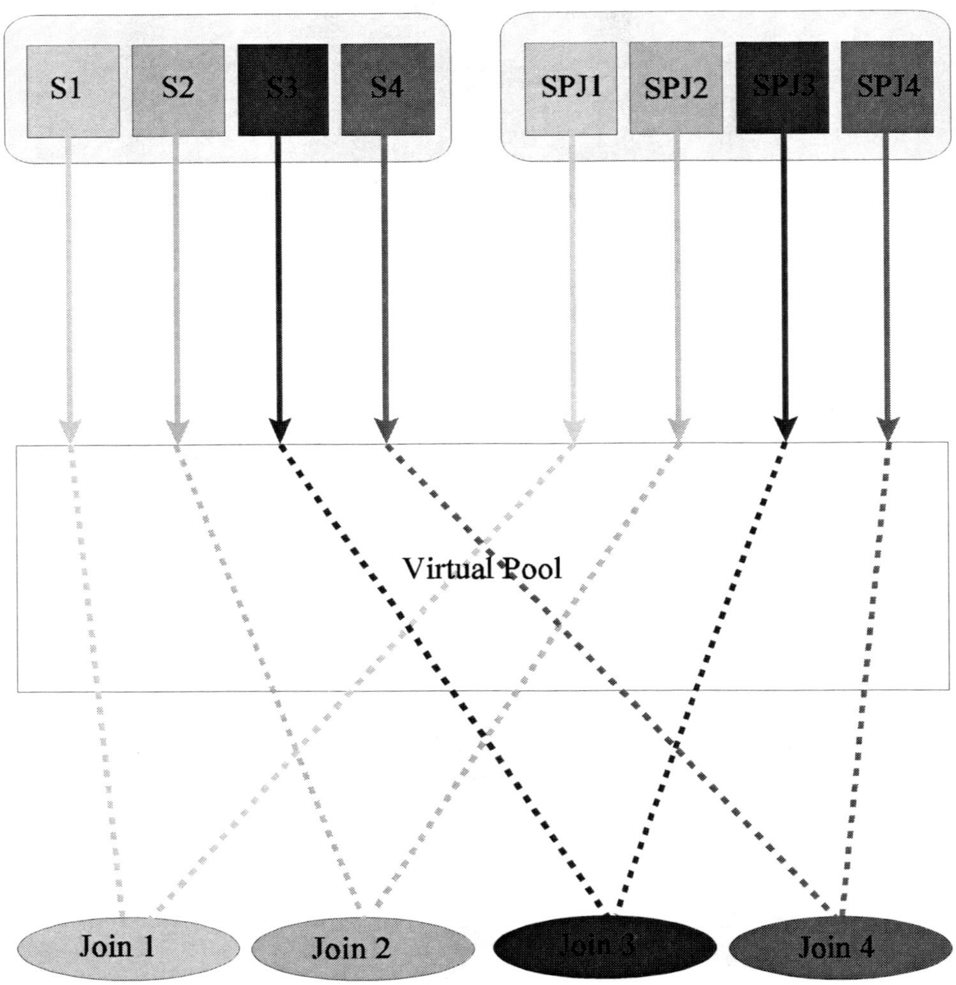

PL.7 IMPLEMENTING AND TUNING PARALLELISM

This section describes some of the system-level processing that is used to implement parallelism in DB2. It is probably of most interest to those who are responsible for understanding, implementing, and tuning parallel performance at the DB2 subsystem level. Developers who are not getting the parallelism expected will also be interested in this section.

Coordinator and Assisting DB2 Subsystems

A DB2 subsystem can be a coordinator and assistant when using sysplex parallelism. A coordinating DB2 accepts SQL for execution, decomposes the statement, and sends different parts of the statement to assisting DB2s for execution. The coordinator may execute part of the statement. Assisting DB2 subsystems will accept sysplex parallelism work from a coordinator. Each participating DB2 subsystem creates and uses its parallel tasks.

The results processed by the assistants are returned to the coordinating DB2 and host program via fiber-optic channels or work files (usually if a sort is required). The fiber-optic channels have a capacity of one million bytes per second. They are cross-system coupling facility links.

The DSNTIPK installation panel is used to designate whether a subsystem is a coordinator and/or assistant. (The default is no for both parameters.)

Controls on the Use of Parallelism

The designation of coordinators and assistants, virtual pool thresholds, performance periods, and the resource limit facility provide controls on the use of parallelism. Exercising these controls is advisable if processors are already running at more than 95 percent capacity. Parallelism does require more processing capacity to achieve a reduction in elapsed time.

Coordinator and assist parameters specified at installation provide controls over if and how each DB2 subsystem can be used for sysplex parallelism. The availability of coordinators and assistants is checked at bind and run time.

Virtual pool thresholds determine how much of a pool can be used for parallel processing as discussed in Chapter CD. There are two thresholds that are particularly important for parallelism, the VPPSEQT and VPXPSEQT thresholds. VPPSEQT limits the number of pages in a virtual pool that can be used for all modes of parallelism. If the threshold is set to 0 for a virtual pool, all modes of parallelism will be disabled for tablespaces assigned to the associated buffer pool. VPXPSEQT limits the number of pages in a virtual pool that can be used by the assisting DB2 for tablespaces assigned to the associated buffer pool using sysplex parallelism. If the threshold is set to 0, sysplex parallelism will be disabled for tablespaces assigned to the associated buffer pool.

Performance periods can be used to down grade the priority of a task at defined intervals of CP usage as defined in service classes to OS/390. Separate service classes can be defined for coordinators and assistants. Period aging is discussed in Chapter SP.

CURRENT DEGREE special register can be set to 1 (default) to disallow parallelism on installation panel DSNTIPB option 18 or DSNZPARM DSN6SPRM CDSSRDEF.

MAX DEGREE of parallelism can be set on DSNTIP4 installation panel or DSNZPARM DSN6SPRM SPRMMDEG (V6 APAR PQ 28414).

MAX DEGREE of parallelism can be set on DSNTIP4 installation panel or DSNZPARM DSN6SPRM SPRMMDEG (V6 APAR PQ 28414).

Can limit the degree of parallelism for a parallel group using the PARAMDEG parameter on DSNTIP4 installation panel (V6 APAR PQ 28414). The value can be between 0 and 254 where 0 means no limit.

The resource limit facility (RLF) can be used to disallow one or more modes of parallelism for dynamic SQL. This gives you the flexibility to disable parallelism for specific plans and authorization IDs. It also allows you to change the resource limit specifications for different times of day. It is possible to disable parallel processing during prime time, for example, when processor usage is at its highest and enable it during non-prime-time. The RLF is discussed in Chapter PP.

-CANCEL THREAD can be used to cancel a parent or child task. If a child task is canceled, the parent task and all child tasks will be canceled. The command -DISPLAY THREAD (*) will show 'PT' in the status column for threads using parallelism.

Tasks

When parallel processing is used, an *originating task*, sometimes called a *parent task* is created. This originating task is a task control block (TCB). That originating task creates a *parallel task*, sometimes called a *child task*, for each logical partition. If using I/O parallelism, each parallel I/O stream is assigned an SRB. SRBs are used for CP and sysplex parallelism, as well, but these are special types of SRBs called *preemptable* SRBs.

An SRB that is preemptable is able to be swapped out by OS/390 if it is running too long. This is in contrast with non-preemptable SRBs, which must run to completion, although they can be interrupted. The preemptable SRBs run under the priority of the allied address space, such as CICS or batch. Non-preemptable SRBs, on the other hand, run at the priority of the database services address space for DB2, usually quite high. One should be cautious about running parallelism within a high priority CICS or IMS dependent region. The processor time taken by parallel processing can detract from the performance of online transactions. These transactions typically do not use parallelism to process the few rows required for display to users.

OS/390 system resource manager (SRM) can be used to assign TCB execution priorities. A preemptable SRB inherits the priority of its parent TCB. Similarly, assistants inherit the priority of the coordinator.

OS/390 determines which processor a given SRB uses and handles the scheduling of SRBs. This scheduling is not controlled by the TCB. DB2 handles synchronization by suspending and resuming tasks. If a parallel task is too far ahead, it is suspended.

Pipes and Subpipes

A pipe is a DB2 construct that consists of data structures and logic to manage the transfer of data from the parallel tasks to the originating task.

A subpipe is a portion of the pipe that occurs under the control of each parallel task. Each logical partition is processed with a subpipe. The pipe is used to merge the results from the subpipes. This is done by moving pointers, not rows or pages. The pipe is terminated after the longest-running subpipe completes processing its logical partition.

There is processor time required to set up the pipes and subpipes and to do context switching. This time can result in a total increase in processor time of up to 15 percent of that expected with serial processing. This is consistent with the test results presented in Figure PL.6. The increase in processor time is usually justified by the dramatic decrease in elapsed time.

Statistics Collected on Parallelism

There are many useful statistics collected by statistics, accounting, and performance traces including the instrumentation facility component identifiers (IFCID) of 0002, 0003, 0015, 0017, 0018, 0022, 0096, 0108, 0201, 0221, 0222, 0231, and 0237. These trace records can be used to see how effective parallelism is and if the degree is being degraded because of a lack of buffer pool space. The statistics (IFCID 0002) and accounting traces (IFCID 0003) have information on:

- Maximum degree of parallelism
- Total number of parallel groups
- Number of times the parallel degree was reduced
- Number of times the prefetch quantity was reduced
- The SRB processor time for the parallel tasks

If you need to determine the cause of a specific response time problem for which the statistics and accounting trace do not provide enough information, you can do more detailed monitoring using IFCID 0221 in performance class 8. This provides information about the following:

- Package and statement identifiers
- Parallel group number (corresponds to the PLAN_TABLE report)
- Planned, run, and actual degree of parallelism
- Low and high keys of logical partitions

IFCID 0222 in the same trace class provides the identifiers found in IFCID 0221 and includes information about pipe creation and termination times, giving the elapsed time for the parallel group and the number of rows processed per pipe. Subpipe creation and termination times give the elapsed time for each I/O stream and the number of rows processed per I/O stream.

Figure PL.16 is an example of some of the information that is available from IFCID 0221 for an SQL statement that uses a tablespace scan on the first table accessed.

Figure PL.16. HPage ranges from IFCID 0221

Logical Partition	Low Page Range	High Page Range	Status
1	x'000001'	x'100640'	normal
2	x'100641'	x'200E9E'	normal
3	x'200E9F'	x'3014A0'	normal
4	x'3014A1'	x'40193A'	normal
5	x'40193B'	x'600000'	normal

Notice that logical partition 5 has more pages than the other partitions. Let's see what effect that has on the elapsed time for the pipe, as shown in Figure PL.17 for IFCID 0222.

Figure PL.17. Pipe and subpipe elapsed time from IFCID 0222

Pipe and Subpipes	Creation Time	Termination Time	Rows Processed by Pipe/Subpipe	Duration in Seconds
Pipe	18:39:42.40	18:40:20.81	97722	38.41
Subpipe 1	18:39:42.41	18:40:14.37	33188	31.96
Subpipe 2	18:39:42.41	18:40:14.32	22023	31.91
Subpipe 3	18:39:42.41	18:40:14.38	29279	31.97
Subpipe 4	18:39:42.41	18:40:14.34	13232	31.93
Subpipe 5	18:39:42.41	18:40:20.81	0	38.40

Subpipe 5, processing the fifth logical partition, takes about 6 seconds longer than the rest of the subpipes, even though no rows qualify. If the subpipe duration is exceptionally long compared to other subpipes, consider reducing the total elapsed time by redistributing rows across the partitions.

Let's look at another example in which a matching index scan is used, followed by index screening on the first table accessed. Figure PL.18 shows the key ranges of the index scanned and the status of each logical partition.

Figure PL.18. Key ranges from IFCID 0221

Logical Partition	Low Key Range	High Key Range	Status
1	x'0000..00'	x'21EBN'	normal
2	x'21EBN'	x'BOOT5'	normal
3	x'BOOT5'	x'FFFF..FF'	empty

Logical partition 3 contains no rows to be processed; therefore a third work file is not required and no subpipe is created as shown in Figure PL.19.

Figure PL.19. Pipe and subpipe elapsed time from IFCID 0222

Pipes and Subpipes	Creation Time	Termination Time	Rows Processed by Pipe/Subpipe	Duration in Seconds
Pipe	18:43:46.94	18:44:09.05	465	22.11
Subpipe 1	18:43:46.94	18:43:59.76	160	12.84
Subpipe 2	18:43:49.77	18:44:09.05	305	19.20

You will want to consider the resources used by all DB2 subsystems when sysplex parallelism is used. Each DB2 subsystem writes its own trace records. Performance monitors (DB2PM, for example) collect and report on records for all DB2 subsystems when using sysplex parallelism. The sum of all CP times in a CPC executing in parallel can be more than total elapsed time for CP intensive operations in particular.

Can summarize accounting statistics: Optionally, you can minimize the number of accounting statistics records that are written by setting PTASKROL to yes in DSNZPARM (default is no). If this is done, the coordinating member produces one accounting record for sequential processing and one accounting record for all parallel processing done on that member. An assisting member produces one accounting record for each parallel group. One accounting record is produced for multiple parallel groups when they complete, for example.

This option significantly reduces the number of account statistics records that are written. For example, assume that parallel group 1 has a degree of 20 and parallel group 2 has a degree of 10. If PTASKROL = N0, 32 (2 + 20 + 10) accounting records are written. If PTASKROL = YES, 3 (2 + 1) accounting records are written.

PL.8 SUMMARY

Parallel processing of read-only SELECT statements can significantly reduce elapsed time. Test results indicate a reduction of 50 percent in elapsed time with a range of 10 to 85 percent with an increase in processor time of less than 15 percent.

Parallelism is performed on separate data sets, either from a partitioned tablespace or index, pieces of a NPI, or work files output from an ESA sort. If DEGREE ANY is specified at bind time, the optimizer determines a planned degree of parallelism, which can be different than the run time or actual degree used. The planned degree of parallelism is determined after the best sequential access path is chosen. The optimizer uses formula and rules to determine whether parallelism should be used.

The run time degree and actual degree can be different than the planned bind degree. To avoid having the optimizer's decision overridden at run time, make sure that the prerequisites are available and there is enough buffer pool storage available for parallel processing.

EXERCISES

1. What is the goal of parallel processing?

2. If CP or sysplex parallelism is used, will I/O be executed in parallel?

3. Under what conditions is I/O parallelism considered without CP or sysplex parallelism?

4. Why is it important to place each partition of the data and partitioning index, and pieces of NPIs separate DASD packs?

5. Will the degree of parallelism indicated in the PLAN_TABLE always be used at run time? Why?

6. How can you determine the run and actual degree of parallelism?

7. If there are six processors available at bind time but only three at run time, how will this effect parallelism?

8. Why is it important that all partitions have approximately the same number of pages?

9. Can parallelism and/or a limited partition scan be used for static SQL with host variables?

10. Does a partition scan require a scan of the partitioning index?

11. Is it necessary to write a host program in any special way in order to use parallelism?

ANSWERS

1. The goal of parallel processing is to reduce the elapsed time of an SQL statement without increasing the processing time by more than 15 percent.

2. If CP or sysplex parallelism is used, I/O is executed in parallel.

3. I/O parallelism is considered without CP or sysplex parallelism if OS/390 and more than one processor are not available at bind time. It is considered when CURSOR WITH HOLD.

4. It is important to place each partition of the data and partitioning index, and piece of NPI on a separate DASD pack to avoid excessive seek time. If the data sets are not separated, a parallel path can require more elapsed time than a sequential path.

5. The degree of parallelism indicated in the PLAN_TABLE will not always be used at run time. If the prerequisites are not available, the planned run degree can differ from the bind degree. If there is insufficient space in the buffer pool, the actual degree can be less than the bind degree, parallelism will not be used, or the prefetch quantity can be reduced during execution.

6. The run and actual degree of parallelism can be determined using a performance monitor or DB2QPMON.

7. If there are six processors available at bind time but only three at run time, the degree of parallelism is not effected. However, I/O wait time will be higher than if six processors were available at run time.

8. It is important that all partitions have approximately the same number of pages because the partition with the largest number of pages determines the maximum degree of parallelism.

9. Parallelism can be used with host variables for static SQL. A limited partition scan cannot be used with host variables for static SQL unless reoptimization is used as will be discussed.

10. A partition scan does not require a scan of the partitioning index. The optimizer determines the data partitions that need to be scanned based on the SYSINDEXPART.LIMITKEY.

11. It is not necessary to write a host program in any special way in order to use parallelism. You can execute other SQL and host language code after opening a cursor that uses parallelism to achieve an additional level of parallelism.

FIGURES

Programming for Performance

PP.1 INTRODUCTION

There are several steps to consider in coding efficient SQL statements.

The First Step: The first step, and the goal, is to simply code SQL to achieve the required result. Let the optimizer determine the required processing to achieve the result. This gives good performance in the majority of the cases and has a number of advantages:

- It results in a high level of data independence and minimizes the need to change application programs when the structure of the data changes, new columns are added or deleted, a column is increased in length, a new index is added, new access strategies are introduced into DB2, and enhancements to the optimizer are made.
- It reduces the amount and complexity of host-language code that must be developed, tested, and maintained.
- It also enhances performance by reducing the path length. The more work that can be pushed down to DB2's level, the fewer instructions that must be executed in the host program.

The Second Step: If the first step does not produce acceptable performance, the second step is to rewrite the SQL so that a better access path can be chosen by the optimizer. A number of hints, tips, guidelines, and alternatives will be included in this chapter and throughout the book that should help you with this task.

The Third Step: If the required performance is still not achieved, the third step and last resort is to break the SQL into parts and introduce procedural code. This technique was used in the Section ST.3 to avoid an update with a subselect.

It was also used in Chapter PD for organization chart processing and as an alternative for cursor repositioning. However, it does lose the advantages of the first step and should be avoided in a distributed environment because that means more data must be transmitted over the wire.

Predicates are processed in two stages, *stage 1* and *stage 2*. Stage 1 predicate evaluation is done by data manager (DM) on data in the virtual pool. DM does tablespace scans and interfaces with the index manager for all matching and non-matching index scans. It narrows the search on just rows and columns that qualify based on stage 1 predicates and passes one column at a time to the next stage of processing. Stage 2 processing is done by the Relational Data System (RDS). RDS does data type conversions, arithmetic operations and scalar functions on columns passed from DM. RDS narrows the search on stage 2 predicates. It does sorts, joins, all correlated subselect processing, and non-correlated subselect processing where more than one row qualifies in the subselect. RDS uses the application program interface (API) to pass qualifying columns, one at a time, to the application program.

Passing rows and columns from DM to RDS and on to the application program requires CPU cycles. The more rows and columns that DM must pass to RDS to complete a search, the higher the processing cost is. An important performance goal is to write SQL statements so that DM can perform as much of the search as possible, minimizing the number of columns and rows that must be passed to RDS.

A predicate that is evaluated by RDS cannot use an index to narrow the search. Only DM interfaces with the index manager. This means that a predicate must be stage 1 in order to use a matching index scan. A non-matching index scan can be done for a stage 2 predicate. However, each value must be passed to RDS for evaluation against the predicate.

This chapter describes when sorts are required and how indexes can be used to avoid sorts. It describes various techniques you can use to take advantage of single and multiple indexes. The chapter also describes how to ensure that dynamic SQL does not adversely affect the online transaction processing that is going on. There are various ways of doing this, but we concentrate on DB2's Resource Limit Facility as a means of controlling processor resources.

PP.2 STAGE 1 PREDICATES

This section explains stage 1 predicates and how to encourage the use of matching index scans. Literals are used in most examples to ease the explanation and understanding of the material. If the use of a host variable rather than a literal effects the processing, the difference will be discussed.

Figures PP.1 and PP.2 contain summaries of stage 1 and 2 predicates. A table detailing these predicates and whether they are indexable can be found in the *Administration Guide* manual.

Figure PP.1. Summary of stage 1 predicates

Stage 1 predicates are of the form: WHERE C1 **OP** :HV. C1 represents a column name and :HV represents a host variable. The operator (OP) can be:

- A simple operator (=, >, >=, <, <=, ¬=, ¬>,¬<)
- IN (list of values), BETWEEN, or LIKE
- A test for null; that is, C1 IS NULL

Data type and length of C1 and :HV must match.

Predicates may be joined by Boolean operators (AND, OR).

Negated predicates are evaluated at stage 1 but do not use a matching index scan.

The column functions AVG, SUM, and COUNT can be computed from the leaf or data pages at stage 1.

MIN and MAX can be satisfied at stage 1 with a single fetch.

Column preceding a non-correlated subselect that returns a single value using >ALL, >ANY, and >SOME can be evaluated at stage 1.

Figure PP.2. Summary of stage 2 predicates

Summary of Stage 2 Predicates

A predicate comparing different data types: WHERE C1 > 1.1 if C1 is an integer, for example.
A predicate with an arithmetic or scalar function on a column: WHERE C1 * 4 > :HV.
IN (list) where list contains an expression
A subselect predicate using IN, =ALL, =ANY, =SOME. (These types of predicates are discussed in Chapter ST). Inner select predicates can be stage 1. If subselect can be executed as IN (list), evaluation is at stage 1.
A correlated subselect. (Correlated subselects are discussed in Chapter ST.)
A subselect predicate using EXISTS or NOT EXISTS. A matching index scan can be used on inner table "join" predicate or local predicate but not both.
A predicate that compares the same or different columns within the same or different tables, for example WHERE C1 BETWEEN C2 AND C3.

Make Sure Data Type and Length Match

When comparing the value of a column to a literal or host variable, the data types and lengths must match to be stage 1 and for a matching index scan to be considered by the optimizer. For example, if a column is declared as DECIMAL(8,2) and a host variable is declared equivalent to DECIMAL(8,3) in a predicate, a matching index scan is not used and the processing is done at stage 2. This is an easy mistake to make, but one that can have a significant negative affect on performance.

Precision Mismatch: If the data type of a literal or host variable has a greater precision than the column, a matching index scan is not used, and the data must be passed to stage 2 for data type conversion and to be evaluated. This is what happens in the following example, where QTY is defined as an integer data type.

```
SELECT SN, PN
FROM   SPJ
WHERE  QTY > 100.5
AND    PN  = 'P5';
```

Some predicates in a WHERE clause can be evaluated at stage 1 and others at stage 2. The predicate on PN is a stage 1 predicate and a matching index scan can be used to narrow the search according to the predicate. DM narrows the search and passes only rows and columns for P5s to RDS using a matching or non-matching index scan, or a tablespace scan. RDS applies the stage 2 predicate on QTY and passes the qualifying rows and columns to the host program.

Alternative: If the statement is written as follows, a matching index scan can be used on the QTY column as well as on the PN column and only qualifying rows are passed to stage 2:

```
SELECT SN, PN
FROM   SPJ
WHERE  QTY > 101
```

```
AND     PN   = 'P5';
```

Length Mismatch: If a literal or host variable is *longer* than a column in a predicate, a matching index scan is not used, and the data must be evaluated at stage 2. If the variable is *shorter*, it is padded with blanks before the search at stage 1. Rather than trying to remember the distinction, it is always best to use matching data types and lengths between a column and a host variable or literal.

Sometimes, it is not easy to detect a simple keying error that can negatively affect the access path. For example, in the following statement, it is not instantly obvious why the matching index scan is not used:

```
SELECT SN, SNAME
FROM   S
WHERE  SN = 'S1 ';
```

SN is defined as CHAR(2), but the literal has an extra blank, making it three characters long. All the rows must be passed to stage 2 to be evaluated. One can easily "remember" a column as being CHAR(3) and declare a working storage variable as 3 bytes in length. This can have drastic effects on performance even when the same access path is chosen by the optimizer. In one case, a table with 3 million rows in which only 1000 rows qualified, the elapsed time was 45 minutes because the host variable was defined with a length longer than the column. By correcting this error, the elapsed time went down to 10 minutes. The time was reduced because 3 million rows did not have to be passed from stage 1 to stage 2 for evaluation by RDS. Only the 1000 qualified rows were passed to RDS. It was not a matter of different access paths for the two timings. There was no index on the column so that the optimizer chose a tablespace scan in both cases. Double checking the column definition is well worth the effort.

Recommendation: DCLGEN can be used to generate data structures to be included in a host-language program as discussed in Chapter PE. Whenever possible, use DCLGEN, because data structures generated by DCLGEN always match the corresponding columns. Take special care when defining additional host variables in working storage to ensure that data types and lengths match the columns with which they are being compared.

Column Functions

The column functions--MIN, MAX, SUM, AVG, COUNT--can be evaluated at stage 1 or stage 2. The criteria for stage 1 evaluation are:

- GROUP BY, if used, does not require a sort.
- DISTINCT is not used.
- There are no arithmetic functions such as (SUM(C1) + SUM(C2) or (SUM(C1) + 100).
- If there is a join, the column function must be on the last table joined.
- There are no stage 2 predicates on the column.

If the function does not meet the above criteria, it is evaluated at stage 2. If a sort is required, the column function is evaluated during the final phase of the sort at stage 2. The PLAN_TABLE column COLUMN_FN_EVAL indicates when the evaluation takes place:

R = Evaluation as data is read from data or index pages (stage 1)

S = Evaluation during sort (stage 2)
(blank) = After data retrieval and after any sorts (stage 2)

Chapter EX has detailed information on the PLAN_TABLE.

Predicates Using Negation

In most cases, a stage 1 predicates can use a matching index scan. An exception is for predicates that use negation. For example, neither of the following statements uses a matching index scan:

```
SELECT SN, SNAME
FROM   S
WHERE  NOT STATUS = 20;

SELECT SN, SNAME
FROM   S
WHERE  STATUS ¬= 20;
```

NOT EQUAL: A negated predicate does not narrow the search sufficiently to make a matching index scan a good choice in most cases. If you do not want the suppliers with a status of 20, you want all of the other suppliers. The optimizer chooses a tablespace scan, which is the most efficient method for returning a majority of rows. Some people avoid using negated predicates, and they have the program discard the rows that are not needed. This is not the best use of resources. A negated predicate is applied at stage 1 and thus minimizes the number of columns and rows passed to RDS and to the host program.

Suppose that we need to find all suppliers in Dallas whose status is not equal to 20, as follows:

```
SELECT SN, SNAME
FROM   S
WHERE  STATUS ¬= 20
AND    CITY    = 'Dallas';
```

A matching index scan can be used to narrow the search on CITY, and the negated predicate on STATUS is applied at stage 1. If the negated predicate is not coded in the SELECT statement, many more columns and rows must be passed to RDS and to the host program only to be discarded. The example above where there was a reduction of 45 to 10 minutes applies here.

Recommendation for NOT EQUAL: It is best to use negation of predicates to narrow the search in SQL rather than retrieving unnecessary rows only to discard them in the host program.

NOT BETWEEN, LIKE, IN: A matching index scan is not used for NOT LIKE, NOT IN, and NOT BETWEEN, as shown in the following statement where we want to find all parts that are supplied outside the normal quantity range of 100 through 800:

```
SELECT SN, PN, JN, QTY
FROM   SPJ
WHERE  QTY NOT BETWEEN 100 AND 800;
```

Alternative 1: The NOT BETWEEN does not include the 100 and 800 as endpoints as does a positive BETWEEN. It is possible to rewrite the statement to allow use of a matching index scan and to include the 100 and 800 endpoints. Because we know that no duplicates are logically possible (no row can have a QTY both greater than 800 and less than 100), you can use UNION ALL. UNION ALL does not require a sort, UNION alone does.

```
SELECT SN, PN, JN, QTY
FROM   SPJ
WHERE  QTY < 100
UNION ALL
SELECT SN, PN, JN, QTY
FROM   SPJ
WHERE  QTY > 800;
```

With this rewrite, a matching index scan can be used above and below the UNION ALL.

Alternative 2: You may have a case where duplicate rows will qualify and UNION would have to be used. To avoid a sort of rows to eliminate duplicates, an alternative formulation can be used. In the following example, assume that QTY is declared in the host program as a positive small integer. Define endpoints and have those endpoints appear as host variables in the SQL statement as shown here:

In the host program:

```
ENDP   = 100 - 1
BEGINP = 800 + 1
```

The SQL statement:

```
SELECT SN, PN, JN, QTY
FROM   SPJ
WHERE  QTY BETWEEN  0       AND :ENDP
OR     QTY BETWEEN :BEGINP AND 32767;
```

A matching index scan can be used on QTY twice with multiple-index processing with the positive BETWEENs.

Alternative 3: The same information can be obtained with this formulation:

```
SELECT SN, PN, JN, QTY
FROM   SPJ
WHERE  QTY < 100   -- Assume host variable
OR     QTY > 800;  -- Assume host variable
```

If host variables are used rather than the literals of 100 and 800, a matching index scan may not be chosen by the optimizer as will be seen shortly in the Section PP.3.

Recommendation: To use a matching index scan, use a positive formulation of the predicates. As we see in the next example, sometimes the optimizer can reformulate a negative predicate to a positive predicate.

NOT > and NOT <: When negating greater-than or less-than predicates, the optimizer can reverse the condition so that a matching index scan can be used. Suppose you wrote the statement this way:

```
SELECT SN, SNAME
FROM   S
WHERE  NOT STATUS > 20;
```

The optimizer reformulates the statements as follows, to allow a matching index scan to be used:

```
SELECT SN, SNAME
FROM   S
WHERE  STATUS <= 20;
```

Range Searches with Host Variables

The optimizer uses default *filter factors* when determining the access path for range predicates. A filter factor (FF) is an estimate the optimizer uses to estimate how many rows will qualify for the predicate. Default FFs are used for range predicates, because the search values are not known until execution time when they are provided by the user and can vary from one execution of the program to another. The default FF is lower for BETWEEN than for other range predicates. The FF formula for range predicates include the values requested as described in Chapter OP.

Range Searches Using BETWEEN

SQL provides two ways to request a search for values that fall within a range: by using the symbolic operators >= and <= or by using the BETWEEN operator. These predicates are functionally equivalent but may perform differently. For example, compare the following two statements:

```
SELECT SN, PN, JN, QTY
FROM   SPJ
WHERE  PN >= 'P2';

SELECT SN, PN, JN, QTY
FROM   SPJ
WHERE  PN BETWEEN 'P2' AND X'FFFF';
```

Both versions of the statement are stage 1. The optimizer can choose to use an index on PN for the search in either case, but it is more likely to use an index for the statement using BETWEEN, particularly when using host variables. This is because the optimizer uses default FFs unless reoptimization is specified when binding a plan or package as described in Section OP.6.

The optimizer automatically transforms >= AND <= predicates to a BETWEEN predicate. For example, the WHERE clause

```
WHERE  PN >= 'P2'
AND    PN <= 'P9'
```

is transformed to

```
WHERE PN BETWEEN 'P2' AND 'P9'
```

by the optimizer.

Estimating the FF for Range Predicates

Example calculations will be used to demonstrate the difference between greater than and less than predicates compared to BETWEEN predicates using alternatives 2 and 3 for the NOT BETWEEN predicate. Here is the alternative 2 formulation:

```
SELECT SN, PN, JN, QTY
FROM   SPJ
WHERE  QTY BETWEEN  0       AND :ENDP
OR     QTY BETWEEN :BEGINP AND 32767;
```

The default FF for a BETWEEN predicate using host variables is 3 percent when using host variables assuming a column cardinality between 100 and 1000. The FFs for the two BETWEEN predicates (P1 and P2) are combined according to the OR Boolean factor with the formula:

```
FF   = FF(P1) + FF(P2) - FF(P1) * FF(P2)
```

A substitution of the 3 percent default FF in the formula results in an estimate that 6 percent of the rows will qualify as shown in the calculation:

```
0.06 = 0.03   + 0.03   - 0.0009
```

A matching index scan with multiple index processing on a single QTY index can be used for the ORed BETWEEN predicates. Multiple index processing is introduced in Chapter IU and discussed in detail in Section PP.8.

The third alternative for the negated predicate is:

```
SELECT SN, PN, JN, QTY
FROM   SPJ
WHERE  QTY < 100   -- Assume host variable
OR     QTY > 800;  -- Assume host variable
```

The default FF for greater than and less than predicates is 10 percent assuming a column cardinality between 100 and 1000. A substitution of the 10 percent default FF in the formula results in an estimate that 19 percent of the rows will qualify as shown in the calculation:

```
0.19 = 0.10   + 0.10   - 0.01
```

The optimizer is more likely to choose a matching index scan for the BETWEEN predicates with an estimate that 6 percent of the rows will qualify compared to the greater than and less than predicates where the estimated number of qualifying rows is 19 percent.

Rather than having to be concerned with how to formulate an SQL statement, you can let the optimizer know the values requested by the user at execution time by using reoptimization as discussed in Section OP.6. Indeed, many of the reformulations suggested in this chapter are not necessary when using reoptimization.

Transforming Range Predicates

The optimizer can sometimes transform predicates that you write to an equivalent predicate that makes better use of composite indexes. For example, suppose the following statement has a composite index on SN, PN, and JN:

```
SELECT SN, PN, JN, QTY
FROM   SPJ
WHERE  SN = 'S5'
AND   (PN BETWEEN 'P1' AND 'P3'
OR     PN BETWEEN 'P6' AND 'P7');
```

It appears that a matching index scan can only be used on SN, followed by a scan of the leaf pages to find the required PNs. However, the optimizer transforms that statement as follows:

```
SELECT SN, PN, JN, QTY
FROM   SPJ
WHERE (SN = 'S5' AND PN BETWEEN 'P1' AND 'P3')
OR    (SN = 'S5' AND PN BETWEEN 'P6' AND 'P7');
```

This transformation allows for two matching index scans on two columns (SN and PN) and multiple-index processing for the OR condition. The same principle applies to < and > predicate formulations.

Transforming Predicates Using OR

The optimizer can transform predicates that use the OR operator on a single column of a composite index to an IN (list). Once again, assume a composite index on SN, PN, and JN:

```
SELECT SN, PN, JN, QTY
FROM   SPJ
WHERE  SN = 'S4'
AND   (PN = 'P1' OR PN = 'P2' OR
       PN = 'P3' OR PN = 'P4')
AND    JN > 'J1';
```

The statement appears to allow a matching index scan only on the SN column, with a scan of the leaf pages to find the PN values and the JNs greater than J1.

The optimizer transforms the statement into:

```
SELECT SN, PN, JN, QTY
FROM   SPJ
WHERE  SN = 'S4'
AND    PN = IN ('P1','P2','P3','P4')
AND    JN > 'J1';
```

This allows for four matching index scans followed by index screening for JN > 'J1' on:

```
S4, P1, J1
S4, P2, J1
S4, P3, J1
S4, P4, J1
```

All three columns of the composite index are now being used and can thus use matching index scans on each of the three separate columns (SN, PN, JN).

Expressions in IN (list)

Expression like special-registers, labeled durations, case expressions, cast specifications, arithmetic expressions, scalar functions, constants, host variables, and non-table user-defined functions can be included in an IN (list) (V6). However, use of these expression in an IN (list) predicate does result in a stage 2 predicate and cannot use a matching index scan.

Here is an example of using DB2 supplied user-defined functions in the SELECT and WHERE clause. It is the expressions in the WHERE clause (not the SELECT clause) that causes stage 2 processing. This is true of all stage 1 and 2 processing.

```
EXEC SQL
SELECT PN, ROUND(19.99,0), CEILING(19.01), FLOOR(19.99)
INTO   :PN,:XROUND,       :XCEILING,      :XFLOOR
--Results   20.00          20.00           19.00
FROM   P
WHERE  WEIGHT IN (ROUND(19.99,0), CEILING(19.99),
       FLOOR(19.99), :QTY / 2)
AND    PN = 'P4'
END-EXEC.
```

The above example provides an opportunity to describe the meaning of the user-defined functions used in the SELECT statement. ROUND gives the expected results, rounding 19.99 gives 20.00. CEILING always rounds up even if there is a small value to the right of the decimal point. FLOOR always truncates any digits to the right of the decimal point. User-defined functions are discussed in detail in Chapter UD.

Comparisons Using LIKE

The index structure does not allow for a matching index scan to search for a character string if the leading character is not specified in the LIKE clause as shown in the examples below. However, a non-matching index scan can be used.

```
SELECT PN, PNAME
FROM   P
WHERE  PNAME LIKE '_CH%';

SELECT PN, PNAME
FROM P
```

```
WHERE   PNAME LIKE '%CH%';
```

It is as if someone asked you to find a name in a telephone book without giving you the first few characters. The only way that you can find a name that has CH in the second and third position is to scan the entire telephone book. You cannot use the first few characters in the upper right corner of a page in the telephone book to narrow the search. The index manager is faced with a similar problem because it must compare the specified value to the upper range values in the root and nonleaf page to traverse the index and find the value in a leaf page.

If the leading characters are specified, such as WHERE PNAME LIKE 'CH%', the index manager can use a matching index scan on PNAME. If the clause reads WHERE PNAME LIKE 'CH%J%', it can use a matching scan to locate strings beginning with CH and scan the remaining leaf pages and search for the names that also include a J. It can use a non-matching index scan to satisfy a string search on an indexed CHAR column beginning with '%' or '_' and scan all of the leaf pages.

VARCHAR exception: If a VARCHAR column is used in a LIKE comparison, the optimizer recognizes that index screening cannot occur (V5 APAR PQ22381). This is because strings are padded with blanks in the index. A tablespace scan is likely with or without the value beginning with "%" or "_".

Host Variables with LIKE: What if a host variable is used as the object of the LIKE, as shown in the following:

```
SELECT PN, PNAME
FROM   P
WHERE  PNAME LIKE :PNAME;
```

With host variables, the optimizer assumes at BIND time that a matching index scan will be used, and this is what it shows in the PLAN_TABLE output from EXPLAIN. It checks the value at execution time, and if the value begins with '%' or '_', it can do a non-matching index scan of the leaf pages if the cluster ratio is high (80 percent or better, for example). If the cluster ratio is low, it does a tablespace scan. DB2 can make this decision at execution time, without accessing the catalog tables, and a bind is not necessary. Thus, performance is not hurt by making the matching versus non-matching index scan decision at execution time.

Be Careful about Mismatching Lengths: What if you find that a SELECT statement returns the required results when you test it interactively using literals but that a different result is returned when the statement is embedded in a host program? This could be a problem with the length of the value placed in the host variable. If the host variable is declared as character data of length five to match the column length for example, the index manager is searching for a string of 'CH%bb' (lower case b represents a blank space). A fixed-length host variable must be padded with '%' or '_' to its full length like 'CH%%%' or 'CH%__' in order to find parts beginning with CH.

If PNAME is declared as variable length--49-levels in COBOL or VAR in PL/1--the padding is not required, provided the length of the search string (three in this example) is moved into the first 49-level length field.

PP.3 STAGE 2 PREDICATES

Stage 2 predicates cannot use matching index scans. A non-matching index scan can be used, but all values in the leaf pages must be passed to stage 2 for evaluation. This section describes the implications of stage 2 predicates, and how you can usually rewrite those predicates to perform more efficiently.

Predicates with an Arithmetic Expression

When using an arithmetic expression on a column in a predicate, a matching index scan is not used, and the arithmetic is performed at stage 2. In the following statement, *all* rows and selected columns must be passed to stage 2 for the multiplication and to narrow the search to rows for the predicate on QTY.

```
SELECT SN, PN, QTY
FROM   SPJ
WHERE  QTY * 4 > :QTY;
```

An arithmetic expression on a host variable must be evaluated at stage 2 and a matching index scan cannot be used on the column in the WHERE clause prior to V5. This restriction applies in V5 only if the product or quotient is an integer and the column is a declared FLOAT or DECIMAL. The following predicate can be applied at stage 1 and a matching index scan can be used assuming that the column is declared as an integer.

In the host program:

```
QTY = 200
```

The SQL statement:

```
SELECT SN, SNAME
FROM   S
WHERE  QTY > :QTY / 2;
```

Recommendation: It is necessary to rewrite the statement and have the division done in the host program prior to V5, as follows:

In the host program:

```
QTY = QTY / 2
```

The SQL statement:

```
SELECT SN, SNAME
FROM   S
WHERE  QTY > :QTY;
```

With this formulation, a matching index scan can be used, and only qualifying rows are passed to stage 2 before and after V5.

A Grandfather Clause: We have seen that predicates with arithmetic expressions on non-columns are evaluated at stage 1 and can use a matching index scan in V5. This obviously has advantages except in cases where developers used arithmetic expressions to avoid index usage in the past. Developers used arithmetic expressions to cause a predicate to be evaluated at stage 2 to avoid the use of a matching index scan before the availability of the construct "(C1 = :HV OR 0 = 1)" (discussed in Chapters PD and BP). They added or subtracted a 0 from a host variable, or multiplied or divided a host variable by 1, or concatenated a column with null. This technique continues to have the same effect in V5 and is evaluated at stage 1. The DB2 developers have made the techniques an exception to avoid having to modify programs written before V5. A matching index scan is not used on any of the columns in the WHERE clause:

```
WHERE C1  =  :HV  +  0
AND   C2  =  :HV  -  0
AND   C3  =  :HV  *  1
AND   C4  =  :HV  /  1
AND   C5  CONCAT''
```

The use of C1 = :HV + 0 requires less CPU time to disallow the use of an index for numeric data and C1 CONCAT" for character data compared to (C1 = :HV OR 0 = 1) which is evaluated at stage 2. The above predicates are not evaluated at run time. The CPU time savings that results from not having to evaluate a predicate can be important when processing a large number of rows. However, the OR 0 = 1 is more obvious and maintainable.

Scalar Functions

Scalar functions like arithmetic expressions on columns are evaluated at stage 2, and a matching index scan cannot be used. Scalar and arithmetic functions on non-columns are evaluated at stage 1 and a matching index scan can be used in V5 provided that the result of the function has the same data type and length of the column. Figure PP.3 lists the scalar functions. The same principle applies to user-defined functions discussed in Chapter UD.

Figure PP.3. Scalar functions

Date/Time Functions	String Functions
MONTH	VALUE/COALESCE
DAY	NULLIF (V5)
YEAR	STRIP (V5)
HOUR	SUBSTR
MINUTE	CONCAT
SECOND	LENGTH
MICROSECOND	DECIMAL
DAYS	FLOAT
DATE	INTEGER
TIME	HEX

TIMESTAMP	DIGITS
CHAR	VARGRAPHIC

In the following statement, for example, the use of the DECIMAL function on the column QTY causes the predicate to be evaluated at stage 2 and a matching index scan cannot be used:

```
SELECT SN, PN, JN, QTY
FROM   SPJ
WHERE  DECIMAL(QTY) > :CALC-QTY;
```

A scalar function used on a non-column can be evaluated at stage 1 and a matching index scan can be used in V5 unlike prior releases of DB2. For example, the DECIMAL function on the :CALC-QTY host variable allows for the stage 1 evaluation and a matching index scan can be used on the QTY column. (Assume that DECIMAL_QTY is another column in SPJ.)

```
SELECT SN, PN, JN, QTY
FROM   SPJ
WHERE  DECIMAL_QTY > DECIMAL(:CALC-QTY, 7,2);
```

Use of the DECIMAL scalar function on a host variable is particularly useful in the C host language because the decimal data type is not supported.

Date/time functions are scalar functions. Therefore, they are evaluated at stage 1 and are indexable when used on non-columns in V5. The two predicates in the following statement are evaluated at stage 1 and a matching index scan can be used on one or both of the columns in the WHERE clause.

```
SELECT PN, DATE_RECEIVED
FROM   SHIPMENTS
WHERE  DATE_RECEIVED < CURRENT DATE - 15 DAYS
AND    MONTH_REQUIRED = MONTH(:DATE-REQUIRED);
```

Arithmetic and Scalar Functions in SELECT Clause

Arithmetic and scalar functions can be performed in the SELECT clause without affecting the access path. It is only when these functions are performed in the WHERE clause that performance can be adversely affected.

Comparison of More than One Column in a Table

Let's assume that there is a requirement to determine parts received on '1997-07-01' and the date is between the ORDER_DATE and RECEIVED_DATE. One possible formulation is:

```
SELECT PN, ORDER_DATE, RECEIVED_DATE
FROM   ORDERS
WHERE '1997-07-01'
       BETWEEN ORDER_DATE AND RECEIVED_DATE;
```

However, the above formulation has a test of more than one column in a single condition. This causes the condition to be tested at stage 2 and a matching index scan cannot be used.

An alternative formulation is to test each of the columns in the table in separate conditions.

```
SELECT PN, ORDER_DATE, RECEIVED_DATE
FROM   ORDERS
WHERE  ORDER_DATE      <= '1997-07-01'
AND    RECEIVED_DATE   >= '1997-07-01';
```

Now the conditions can be tested at stage 1 and can use a matching index scan on one or both of the conditions

Comparing Two Columns in a Table

A comparison of two columns in the same table does not use a matching index scan and is evaluated at stage 2. For example, the following statement finds employees from the EMP table whose commission is greater than their salary:

```
SELECT EMPNO, LASTNAME, COMMISSION, SALARY
FROM   EMP
WHERE  COMMISSION > SALARY;
```

The above statement uses a tablespace scan to retrieve qualifying rows, and the comparison is done at stage 2. Some companies have a policy that a matching index scan must be used for all SQL statements that are used in an online transaction. To accommodate this requirement, the statement can be rewritten to use a matching index scan. To do so requires a join of the table to itself. A correlation name is required for each instance of the table. E1 and E2 are the correlation names in the statement:

```
SELECT E1.EMPNO, E1.LASTNAME, E1.COMMISSION, E1.SALARY
FROM   EMP AS E1, EMP AS E2
WHERE  E1.COMMISSION > E2.SALARY
AND    E1.EMPNO = E2.EMPNO;
```

DB2 can do a tablespace scan on the outer table and a matching index scan on an EMPNO and SALARY composite index on the inner table in a nested loop join.

Matching Index Scan Not Always Best: This is one of those cases where the matching index scan is not always the best idea. In one case, the processing of 70,000 rows used 2:02 elapsed time and 1:16 CPU minutes for a tablespace scan compared with 2:56 minutes elapsed time and 1:63 minutes of CPU time for a nested loop join with a matching index scan. The original policy requiring a matching index scan for all SELECT statements was intended to result in the best performance in all cases. Consider making exceptions to policies for those special cases that can result in better performance.

BETWEEN with Columns from the Same Table: BETWEEN used with columns from the same table must be evaluated at stage 2 and does not use a matching index scan. The following statement illustrates this:

```
SELECT C1, C2, C3
```

```
FROM   TA
WHERE  C1 BETWEEN C2 AND C3;
```

CASE Expressions

Avoiding Multiple Tablespace Scans: A CASE expression is a good alternative to multiple SQL statements or a statement with UNION ALL that requires multiple tablespace scans. Here is a statement that requires three tablespace scans to identify the male and female employees in WORKDEPT D4, assuming that there is not a suitable index to narrow the search.

```
SELECT EMPNO, LASTNAME, 'Male' AS GENDER
FROM   EMP
WHERE  WORKDEPT = 'D4'
AND    SEX      = 'M'
UNION ALL
SELECT EMPNO, LASTNAME, 'Female' AS GENDER
FROM   EMP
WHERE  WORKDEPT = 'D4'
AND    SEX      = 'F'
UNION ALL
SELECT EMPNO, LASTNAME, 'Unknown' AS GENDER
FROM   EMP
WHERE  WORKDEPT = 'D4'
AND    SEX NOT IN ('M', 'F');
```

CASE expression is a good alternative to UNION ALL if each SELECT clause has the same or compatible columns, the FROM clauses have the same table name when using UNION ALL, and WHERE clause conditions can be placed in WHEN clause. The above UNION ALL statement is reformualted into the following CASE expression that requires one tablespace scan rather than three.

```
SELECT EMPNO, LASTNAME,
CASE SEX
     WHEN 'M' THEN 'Male'
     WHEN 'F' THEN 'Female'
     ELSE 'UNKNOWN'
END AS GENDER
FROM   EMP
WHERE  WORKDEPT = 'D4';
```

The data types of columns and values within a WHEN or THEN clause must be compatible. That is the column and all values (literals or host variables) must be numeric or character values and should have the same length.

The CASE expression also allows for translating a code to a value ('M' is translated to 'Male' in the example) and specifying a column heading (GENDER) for reporting purposes. This is particularly useful when using an interactive tool. If a host program is used, the developer can test for specific codes and translate them to the required value for a report using the statement:

```
SELECT EMPNO, LASTNAME, SEX
FROM   EMP
WHERE  WORKDEPT = 'D4'
```

```
AND    SEX IN ('M', 'F', ' ');
```

If all employees in WORKDEPT D4 are required rather than only those that satisfy a predicate on the SEX column, the following simple SELECT statement will do the job:

```
SELECT EMPNO, LASTNAME, SEX
FROM   EMP
WHERE  WORKDEPT = 'D4';
```

As always the best formulation depends on your specific requirements.

The CASE expression also allows for translating a code to a value ('M' is translated to 'Male' in the example) and specifying a column heading (GENDER) for reporting purposes. This is particularly useful when using an interactive tool. If a host program is used, the developer can test for specific codes and translate them to the required value for a report using the statement:

Flexibility of CASE Expression: Special registers, arithmetic expression, and date durations can be used in a CASE expression. For example, consider reporting on the vacation time due employees. The number of vacation weeks depends on time with the company as follows.

Years of Seniority	Weeks
< 1 year	1
Between 1 and 10 years	2
Between 10 and 20 years	3
> 20 years	4

A CASE expression that will report on the vacation weeks allowed for each employee is:

```
SELECT EMPNO, LASTNAME,
CASE
  WHEN YEAR(CURRENT DATE - HIREDATE) < 1
      THEN '1 week'
  WHEN YEAR(CURRENT DATE - HIREDATE)
    BETWEEN 1 AND 10
      THEN '2 weeks'
  WHEN YEAR(CURRENT DATE - HIREDATE)
    BETWEEN 11 AND 20
      THEN '3 weeks'
  WHEN YEAR(CURRENT DATE - HIREDATE) > 20
      THEN '4 weeks'
  ELSE 'UNKNOWN'
END AS VACATION
FROM   EMP;
```

Notice that if a WHEN clause has a comparison other than equal and an arithmetic expression, the column name must be in the WHEN clause.

Arithmetic expressions, special registers, column functions, and scalar functions can be used in the WHEN and THEN clauses. AND, OR, and NOT can be used to specify conditions in the WHEN clause. If the WHEN clause has a comparison other than = and an arithmetic expression, the column name must be in the WHEN clause. Here is an example using some of these functions to determine the number of employees in WORKDEPT D1 and D2 that have a bonus plus commission greater than their salary:

```
SELECT SUM(CASE WHEN WORKDEPT = 'D1'
                AND  BONUS + COMM > SALARY
                     THEN 1 ELSE 0
           END) AS N_EMP_D1,
       SUM(CASE WHEN WORKDEPT = 'D2'
                AND  BONUS + COMM > SALARY
                     THEN 1 ELSE 0
           END) AS N_EMP_D2,
FROM   EMP
WHERE  WORKDEPT IN ('D1', 'D2');
```

The SELECT statement with a CASE expression requires only one tablespace scan assuming that an index is not available to satisfy the WORKDEPT IN ('D1', 'D2') predicate. Without the use of the CASE expressions, two SELECT statements with two tablespace scans would be required, one for D1 and one for D2.

Coding conditions in the WHEN and WHERE clauses: The test of WORKDEPT 'D1' is in the WHEN and WHERE clauses in the previous SELECT statement. The predicate in the WHERE clause provides for the optimizer choosing a matching index scan on WORKDEPT (assuming an index on the column). It is necessary to do a tablespace scan without the WHERE clause. A WHEN condition is evaluated at stage 2 and cannot use a matching index scan.

CASE expression in WHERE clause: CASE expression can be used in a WHERE clause. However, it detracts from performance because it is evaluated at stage 2. As with all stage 2 predicates, they are better than not coding the predicates at all. This is particularly true if the search is also narrowed with stage 1 indexable predicates. Always avoid returning rows to a host program only to be discarded with no action taken on the row fetched.

PP.4 ORDER OF PREDICATE EVALUATION

To offer the best performance, DB2 performs its evaluations of a row in a certain priority order. These priorities are based on both the type of criteria to be checked and the order in which they are expressed. Although setting this priority order improves performance overall, it also means that the order in which predicates are listed can make a difference in performance.

In most cases, this difference is slight. This is because *predicate order plays no part in the optimizer's choice of access path.* The optimizer always evaluates the use of indexes first before doing further evaluation of the predicates. At execution time, indexes are used to narrow the search before applying predicates on columns where indexes are not used.

What Part Does Predicate Order Play? Predicate order can influence the testing of rows already retrieved through an index or tablespace scan.

In general, after indexes are used to narrow the search, DB2 evaluates first those operations that disqualify the most rows so that it disqualifies them as early as possible, stage 1 before stage 2. The fewer rows that pass the earlier tests, the less processing is required for later tests. With a uniform distribution of values, it is usually the case that fewer values satisfy an equality rather than a range. Consequently, if a WHERE clause calls for both a range and equality search, it usually makes sense to perform the equality test first. If a request has two equality searches, with a uniform distribution, it does not matter which is performed first. They are likely to eliminate about the same number of rows. Therefore, the equal predicates are evaluated at execution time in the order in which they were coded.

Summary of Predicate Evaluation: Figure PP.4 summarizes the order that predicates are evaluated, assuming that no matching index is available. If one were, it would be evaluated first.

Figure PP.4. Order of Predicate Evaluation

First, DB2 evaluates stage 1 predicates in the following order:

1) Equal predicates such as C1 = :HV, IN (:HV), and C1 IS NULL.

2) Range predicates such as C1 *op* :HV (where *op* is BETWEEN, >, <, and so on).

Next, DB2 evaluates stage 2 predicates, in the same order as that listed above for stage 1 predicates.

Within each of these groups, DB2 evaluates predicates in the order in which they are coded in the statement. Parentheses also affect the order of evaluations. DB2 evaluates predicates expressed within parentheses before those presented outside them.

What does this order of evaluations mean for performance? Simply, processing can be minimized if the more restrictive predicates are performed before the less restrictive predicates. Consider the following statement, for example:

```
SELECT SN, SNAME, STATUS, CITY
FROM   S
WHERE  STATUS > 20 <-- Evaluated last
AND    CITY    = 'San Jose'
AND    SNAME   = 'Akira';
```

If there are no indexes on table S, DB2 performs the search with a tablespace scan. Because the two equal predicates are in the same priority group for order of evaluations, DB2 checks them in the order listed. When it evaluates each row, it first checks the CITY value. If CITY does not equal 'San Jose', DB2 need not check the SNAME value. But suppose Akira appears only a few times in a 500,000 row table, while 'San Jose' appears in 100,000 rows. All of those 100,000 rows pass the first test (CITY = 'San Jose'). But while DB2 goes on to perform the second test for Akira immediately after testing the row for 'San Jose', only a few of them pass this second test. If you know that the table includes only a relatively few 'Akira' rows, you could code the SNAME= 'Akira' predicate first so that only a few rows would pass the first test. That rewrite can avoid almost 100,000 comparisons. However, the CPU time necessary to perform a comparison is so small that it might not be worth the effort for each developer to memorize and use the rule each time they write an SQL statement.

The range predicate is evaluated last, regardless of the whether it is coded before or between the equal predicates.

Order of Join Processing: The table name coded to the left of the operator LEFT OUTER JOIN is the outer table (first table processed) of the join. The complement is true for RIGHT OUTER JOIN as discussed in Chapter JP. The order of coding table names and join predicates does not effect the access path chosen by the optimizer for inner joins. The optimizer determines the outer table based on its estimate of the table with the smallest number of qualifying rows.

Order of Subselect Processing: First, non-correlated subselects are processed reading from the bottom of the statement to the top. Second, correlated subselects are processed. Third, subselects joined by AND or OR are processed in the order in which they are coded. This suggests that the most restrictive subselects be written first. However, if the subselects vary significantly in path length, write the least resource intensive subselect first.

PP.5 OPTIMIZE FOR *N* ROWS

In many cases, a SELECT statement qualifies a large number of rows, but only a few are fetched, perhaps only enough to fill a screen to be displayed to a user. Based on the specified predicates, the optimizer chooses a good access path to process a *large* number of rows, perhaps using multiple indexes and list prefetch, a merge join, a hybrid join, or a tablespace scan with sequential prefetch. However, these technique can be less than optimal for processing only the first few rows that qualify.

What Access Path is Better? In this case, using a single index is better than using several indexes and list prefetch. List prefetch causes all of the qualifying RIDs to be retrieved from the index leaf pages and sorted before the first row is returned to the program. (Multiple index processing and list prefetch are introduced in Chapter IU and described in the following Section PP.7.) A nested loop join is better than a merge join, which requires a sort of the data. The nested loop join is also better than a hybrid join, which requires a sort of partial rows (RID and columns from the outer table).

Tell the Optimizer: Use the clause OPTIMIZE FOR *n* ROWS to inform the optimizer that only a few rows will be fetched even though many may qualify. OPTIMIZE FOR 1 ROW invokes the optimizer's rule not to use multiple indexes, list prefetch, and sequential prefetch.

DB2 returns all rows that qualify as they are fetched, even if they exceed the number of rows specified in the clause. Do not specify 15 rows in a program you know will fetch 10,000; a good access path for 15 rows is probably not a good access path for 10,000 rows. Using OPTIMIZE FOR *n* ROWS where *n* is small encourages the use of matching index scans and discourages the use of sequential prefetch, list prefetch for single and multiple index usage, join methods that require sorts, and parallel processing.

The optimizer uses the number of rows specified in some of the formula for estimating the cost of various access paths as discussed in Chapter OP. The chapter also discusses the hazards of trying to fool the optimizer. The OPTIMIZE FOR *n* ROWS clause significantly influences the access path chosen by the optimizer and thus the performance of a SELECT statement.

Restrictions: OPTIMIZE FOR *n* ROWS has no impact on operations which require a sort, like GROUP BY, DISTINCT and UNION. For ORDER BY, however, it does make it more likely that an index will be used, even one with a low cluster ratio, to avoid the sort. The clause has no effect on subselect processing where the inner select qualifies many rows since they must all be processed before the outer select can be processed. The clause cannot be used for the inner table of a subselect, it cannot be used in a CREATE VIEW statement and a table expression, and it cannot be used with INSERT, UPDATE, and DELETE statements.

PP.6 SORTING ROWS

The ORDER BY, GROUP BY, DISTINCT, and UNION operators can require that rows be sorted. ORDER BY presents rows in order, and GROUP BY sorts rows to put them in groups. For DISTINCT and UNION, ordered rows provide the most efficient means to eliminate duplicate values. UNION ALL, which does not eliminate duplicates, does not require a sort. Joins can also use sorts: the inner and outer table of a merge join, the outer table of a hybrid join, and sometimes the outer table of a nested loop join.

Using Indexes to Avoid Sorts

If the column to be sorted has an index with a good cluster ratio, the optimizer is likely to use the index to locate the rows in sequence and thus avoid a sort. DB2 scans the leaf pages where the values are maintained in sequence and follows the RID (record ID) to the rows to retrieve them in sequence. If the cluster ratio is 80 percent or better, sequential prefetch can be used on the leaf and data pages.

The index must be an ascending index to avoid an ascending sort. The index must be a descending index to avoid a descending sort.

Using Composite Indexes: Frequently, DB2 can avoid sorting rows for the GROUP BY, ORDER BY, and DISTINCT operators when the statements using those operators refer to columns that are part of composite indexes. DB2 can only avoid a sort, however, if all columns in the clause are in the composite index, and are used in the same order.

As an example, the optimizer can use a composite index SN, PN, and JN to avoid a sort in the statement:

```
SELECT SN, PN, JN, QTY
FROM   SPJ
WHERE  SN   = 'S4'
ORDER BY SN, PN, JN;
```

Here is a case where DB2 is not able to use the composite index to avoid a sort:

```
SELECT SN, PN, JN, QTY
FROM   SPJ
WHERE  PN   = 'P4'
ORDER BY JN, PN, SN, QTY;
```

It cannot avoid the sort because the columns in the ORDER BY clause are not sequenced as in the composite index, and QTY is not in the index.

The leading columns of a composite index must be in the WHERE clause with equal predicates if the ORDER BY does not reference the leading columns. Here is a case where a sort can be avoided on the JN column because the leading columns (SN and PN) are specified with equal predicates.

```
SELECT SN, PN, JN, QTY
FROM   SPJ
WHERE  SN  = 'S4'
AND    PN  = 'P6'
ORDER BY JN;
```

Here is a similar SELECT statement that will require a sort on JN because there is a range predicate on one of the leading columns of the composite index (PN >= 'P6'). If the composite index were used to avoid a sort, it is possible not to retrieve all J4s in sequence if it appears for P6, P7, P8, etc., for example.

```
SELECT SN, PN, JN, QTY
FROM   SPJ
WHERE  SN  = 'S4'
AND    PN >= 'P6'
ORDER BY JN;
```

DISTINCT and GROUP BY

A unique index can be used to avoid a sort for the DISTINCT operator, but it is doubtful that someone would intentionally code such a request since all values are distinct by definition with a unique index on the column. An index cannot be used to avoid a sort for DISTINCT on a nonunique index.

```
SELECT DISTINCT CITY  <--nonunique index
FROM S;
```

An alternative formulation is the use of GROUP BY that returns the same results and uses an index to avoid a sort:

```
SELECT CITY
FROM S
GROUP BY CITY;
```

For clarity of function, the DISTINCT can remain in the statement as long as the GROUP BY is included like:

```
SELECT DISTINCT CITY
FROM S
GROUP BY CITY;
```

Analysis: If an index cannot be used to avoid a sort, and if the values to be sorted have few distinct values, GROUP BY performs better because duplicate values are eliminated as the data is processed and placed in the sort tree. In contrast, DISTINCT sorts all the values and then eliminates the duplicates. This can be quite costly if there are many duplicates.

GROUP BY and DISTINCT Used Together: When DB2 uses a composite index to satisfy a GROUP BY, it can also avoid a sort of the grouped rows when it is retrieving distinct values from the groups. However, the column order of the GROUP BY and DISTINCT must match the index column order. Assume there is a composite index on PN and WEIGHT, in that order, in the P table. DB2 can use the index to group the rows by part number in:

```
SELECT PN, AVG(DISTINCT WEIGHT)
FROM   P
GROUP BY PN;
```

DB2 does not have to sort the rows to group the values nor to find the distinct weights. If a sort is required, perhaps because of a low cluster ratio, an aggregate like AVG is computed during the final phase of the sort to avoid passing the data again.

GROUP BY and ORDER BY: We have seen that GROUP BY can require a sort or an index can be used to avoid the sort. If you require that the rows be returned in sequence, do not count on GROUP BY always returning the rows in sequence. To be certain that the rows will be returned in sequence, use an ORDER BY clause. This turns responsibility over to DB2 to insure that the rows are always returned in the sequence specified by the ORDER BY clause. DB2 is likely to do one sort or use an index to satisfy sequencing for both the GROUP BY and ORDER BY where both clauses name the same columns in the same sequence and the columns are in the SELECT clause.

```
SELECT SN, PN, AVG(QTY)
FROM   SPJ
GROUP BY SN, PN
ORDER BY SN, PN;
```

When DB2 groups rows, it can sometimes avoid a sort to order the results. The columns used in the GROUP BY clause need not be part of the composite index, nor must they be expressed in the clause in any particular order. Again assume the composite index on SN, PN, and JN. Because the sample database does not offer a meaningful example, the following example illustrates the concept but probably would not be used in the real world:

```
SELECT SN, PN, JN, QTY
FROM   SPJ
GROUP  BY SN, PN, QTY   <-- PN placed first
ORDER  BY PN;
```

DB2 temporarily reorders the GROUP BY list to PN, SN, QTY, so it can avoid the second sort for the ORDER BY. The GROUP BY does require a sort because QTY is not in the index. The ORDER BY operation, because of the reordering, does not require an additional sort.

Requirements: Generally, for DB2 to be able to avoid a sort in this kind of situation, the following conditions must be met:

- The ORDER BY list is from the same table as the GROUP BY list
- The ORDER BY list's leading columns are the same as the leading columns of the GROUP BY list and DISTINCT columns
- GROUP BY columns must be in the SELECT clause

Recommendation: It is advisable although not required for columns in an ORDER BY clause to be in the SELECT clause (V5 APAR PQ23778). If the columns are not in the SELECT clause, GROUP BY, MIN, MAX, SUM, DISTINCT, UNION, UNION ALL cannot be in the SELECT clause.

Encouraging the Use of an Index to Avoid a Sort

It is possible to encourage the use of an index to avoid a sort. To do this, use the OPTIMIZE FOR 1 ROW clause as shown in the statement below:

```
SELECT SN, PN, JN, QTY
FROM   SPJ
WHERE  SN > 'S4'
ORDER BY SN
OPTIMIZE FOR 1 ROW;
```

Do not use the OPTIMIZE clause in every instance. It is not a good idea to encourage an index when the index has a low cluster ratio and many rows have to be retrieved in order. This is because the seek time on DASD can be excessive. Sequential and list prefetch are not used with OPTIMIZE FOR 1 ROW.

It can be best to retrieve and sort the qualifying rows rather than use an index to avoid a sort as discovered by an insurance company using an IBM 6-WAY 9021-720 computer. The CPU and elapsed minutes for fetching one million rows in sequence are summarized in Figure PP.5. It required almost four times the elapsed minutes to retrieve the rows in sequence using an index with a low cluster ratio of 33 percent primarily due to the excessive seek time on DASD to locate the widely scattered rows. Clearly in this case it is best to sort the rows rather than retrieving them in sequence.

Figure PP.5. Comparison of retrieving rows in sequence and sorting them

Description	Partial Access Path	CPU Minutes	Elapsed Minutes
SELECT SCHD_NEXT_DATE, POLICYNO FROM TSCHED ORDER BY SCHD_NEXT_DATE OPTIMIZE FOR 1 ROW;	Used index with a cluster ratio of 33 %	10:27	1:00:15
SELECT SCHD_NEXT_DATE, POLICYNO FROM TSCHED ORDER BY SCHD_NEXT_DATE;	Used tablespace scan and sorted rows	7:32	16:30

Avoiding a Sort for UNION

An index cannot be used to avoid a sort for UNION. All rows above and below the UNION operator must be retrieved, sorted, and duplicates eliminated.

```
SELECT S.CITY, 'Supplier'
FROM   S
UNION
SELECT P.CITY, 'Part'
FROM   P;
```

UNION **ALL** does not require a sort, because duplicates are not eliminated. In addition, all rows above and below the UNION ALL do not have to be processed before rows are returned to the program. For example, if enough rows are fetched to fill a screen from the S table, the P table need not be accessed. This can have performance advantages.

```
SELECT S.CITY, 'Supplier'
FROM   S
UNION ALL
SELECT P.CITY, 'Part'
FROM   P;
```

Analysis: UNION ALL is a good alternative to UNION when logically there can be no duplicates, or if duplicates are acceptable for the type of processing required.

Keep Rows to be Sorted Short

The length of the rows to be sorted affects the speed with which the sort can be accomplished. If an SQL statement requiring a sort takes too long, reduce the size of the returned rows by eliminating from the SELECT any columns that are not essential. If the sort time is still unacceptable, the system administrator should be consulted on the size of the sort pool and number and size of work tablespaces available to DB2.

Recommendation: Do work with the system administrator in sizing the sort pool and work file tablespaces for your workload as discussed in Chapter CO.

PP.7 AVOID SELECT *

It is best to select only the columns required and avoid the use of SELECT * which causes all columns to be returned to the host program. SELECT * is a temptation to code because it avoids having to name each of the columns required. However, this convenience can be costly in terms of CPU time, elapsed time, and maintenance of host programs. The impact of the first two reasons in Figure PP.6 was demonstrated to an insurance company using an IBM 6-way 9021-720 computer.

Figure PP.6. Reasons Not to Use SELECT *

- An unnecessary number of columns must be passed from DM to RDS and then on to the host program.

- It is less likely that a sort can be done in a sort pool in central storage and increases the number of work files that must be written to DASD and then merged before returning the rows to the host program.
- Transmitting an excessive number of bytes in a distributed environment can be very expensive.
- It increases the likelihood that a *compiled assignment procedure* is greater than 4 KB at bind time and thus not stored in the plan or package. A compiled assignment procedure is used rather than an interpretative process to move columns to host variable output area. If more than 100 rows are fetched, the procedure is compiled each time the SQL is executed rather than only at bind time, which increases the CPU time.
- Lack of data independence. The table could have columns added or taken away, returning different results or causing the program to abend.

Figure PP.7 summarizes the results of selecting all rows in a 90,000 row table and all columns in a table compared to selecting 20 columns with and without a sort. Notice that selecting 20 columns dramatically reduced CPU and elapsed time with and without a sort. These test results from an insurance company and the test results used throughout the book are to give you an idea of the order of magnitude of the guidelines presented.

Figure PP.7. Comparison of selecting all versus 20 columns with and without a sort

Description	CPU Minutes	Elapsed Minutes
SELECT * FROM TAGENT	11:16	14:21
SELECT 20 columns FROM TAGENT	1:36	3:00
SELECT * FROM TAGENT ORDER BY 5 columns	11:46	21:41
SELECT 20 columns FROM TAGENT ORDER BY 5 columns	1:55	7:53

PP.8 MULTIPLE AND SINGLE INDEX USAGE WITH LIST PREFETCH

Multiple index usage is designed to narrow the search using multiple indexes, reduce the number of I/Os to the data pages, access the data pages in sequence as they appear on DASD with list prefetch, and additional benefit as will be seen in this section. We will use some examples to show the benefits of multiple index processing and list prefetch starting with:

```
SELECT SN, PN, JN, QTY
FROM   SPJ
WHERE  SN = 'S1'
OR    (SN = 'S5'
AND    PN = 'P5');
```

Separate indexes on SN and PN can be used to narrow the search before accessing the data pages. The processing of multiple indexes is done in steps as outlined below. The shaded areas in Figure PP.8 show the indexes and RIDs used to process this example.

Figure PP.8. Using multiple indexes to access data

1) RIDs for S5 to list A

2) RIDs for P5 to list B

3) Intersection of list A & B to list C

4) RIDs for S1 to list D

5) Union of list C & D to list E

SN	PN	JN	QTY	RID
S1	P1	J1	200	1021
S1	P1	J4	700	~~1022~~
S2	P3	J1	400	1031
S2	P3	J2	200	1041
S2	P3	J3	200	1051
S2	P3	J4	500	1061
S2	P3	J5	600	1071
S2	P3	J6	400	1081
S2	P3	J7	800	1091
S2	P5	J2	100	1101
S3	P3	J1	200	1111
S3	P4	J2	500	1121
S4	P6	J3	300	1131
S4	P6	J7	300	1141
S5	P2	J2	200	1151
S5	P2	J4	100	1161
S5	P5	J5	500	1171
S5	P5	J7	100	1181
S5	P6	J2	200	1191
S5	P1	J4	100	1201
S5	P3	J4	200	1211
S5	P4	J4	800	1221
S5	P5	J4	400	1231
S5	P6	J4	500	1241

1. The RIDs for S5 are retrieved from the SN index and placed in a work area in the RID pool, call it list A.

2. The RIDs for P5 are retrieved from the PN index and placed in list B.

3. The RIDs for S5 and P5 are intersected. (This is also called ANDing of the RIDs.) That is the RIDs are sorted and duplicates are removed. The RIDs must be in both lists to qualify for ANDed predicates. The resulting RIDs 1171, 1181, and 1231 are placed in list C. Notice in Figure PP.8 that RIDs 1101, 1151, 1161, 1191, 1201, 1211, 1221, and 1241 references rows with S5 or P5 but not both. These RIDs can be discarded, and there is no need to do I/O to the data pages that those RIDs reference.

4. The RIDs for S1 are retrieved from the SN index and placed in list D.

5. Lists C and D are unioned, sorted, and duplicates are removed. The result is placed in list E. Notice in Figure PP.8 that RID 1022 is crossed out. This is because duplicates are eliminated on the first three bytes of the RID to avoid multiple I/Os to the same page to retrieve multiple

rows on a single page. The processing used to retrieve data pages in sequence from the RIDs in list E is called *list prefetch*.

List prefetch processes 32 or fewer pages with a single I/O, using skip-sequential processing. That is, if pages 5, 10, 15, 20, and 25 are required, the pages in between need not be read. If pages 10 and 20 are already in the buffer pool, buffer manager issues one I/O for pages 5, 15, and 25. Because the RIDs are sorted, the pages are retrieved in the sequence as they appear on DASD, thus reducing I/O seek time. DB2 processes the data pages only once regardless of how many rows qualify on a page and whether a clustering or non-clustering index is used.

Use of List Prefetch and Sequencing of Data

ORDER BY discourages the use of list prefetch, particularly if there is a good cluster ratio (such as greater than 80 percent) on the column to be sorted. This is because a sort of the RIDs would almost certainly result in the rows on the data pages being out of sequence, and a second sort would be required for the qualifying rows. Even if the cluster ratio is 100 percent at bind time, it cannot be assumed that all rows will be in sequence on the sequenced pages at execution time. There is a good chance that some inserted rows will not be placed in sequence on the clustering index due to a lack of free space after RUNSTATS has been executed and before a SELECT statement is executed.

Multiple index processing probably will not be used for the following statement because of the ORDER BY clause assuming that there is a good cluster ratio on PN.

```
SELECT PN, PNAME, COLOR, WEIGHT, CITY
FROM   P
WHERE  PN BETWEEN 'P2' AND 'P5'
AND    WEIGHT > 700
ORDER BY PN;
```

Multiple index processing can be used with range predicates as well as equal predicates, although in this example it probably will not be used because of the ORDER BY clause. A better strategy that was chosen by the optimizer for the SELECT statement is to use the index on PN with a good cluster ratio, retrieve the rows that satisfy the BETWEEN predicate in sequence using the index, apply the predicate on WEIGHT, and return the qualifying rows to the host program.

Interdependent Indexes

If two predicates qualify mostly the same rows and a large number of rows qualify, it is best *not* to use multiple index processing to avoid retrieving many of the same RIDs from the multiple indexes, sorting them, and eliminating duplicates. Many of the same RIDs will be retrieved from multiple indexes if the values in two or more indexes are interdependent. Here is an obvious example of interdependent indexes. At most companies most employees are over 18 years of age and have been with the company for more than one year. There is usually a correlation between the age of a person and the number of years of service at a company. This statement identifies employees who are over 18 years of age and have been with the company more than one year:

```
SELECT EMPNO, LASTNAME
FROM   EMP
```

```
WHERE   AGE         > 18
AND     SENIORITY > 1;
```

The RIDs for employees over 18 years of age are placed in list A, and the RIDs for employees who have been with the company for over one year are placed in list B. Many of the RIDs in list A and B are the same. It is a waste of resources to get basically the same RIDs from two indexes only to eliminate close to half of them when the RIDs are intersected.

It is best not to have indexes on columns that qualify mostly the same rows because one index narrows the search sufficiently and two indexes need not be maintained. However, both indexes might be required because of frequent searches on age or seniority with infrequent searches on both indexes.

Discouraging the Use of the Index: One way to avoid using one of the indexes is to code only the most restrictive predicate so that multiple index processing will not be used. However, this requires that unwanted rows be retrieved by the host program only to be eliminated with a test in the program. A technique used in early releases of DB2 is to add a zero to a numeric value or make the length of the host variable longer than the column length. This results in a stage 2 predicate that is not indexable as discussed above in Section PP.3. However, the techniques are very subtle and likely to result in a person revising the program correcting the "error" and cause a less than optimal access path to be chosen.

There is a better alternative that reduces CPU time usage and is clear to everyone once the rule is learned. That is to take advantage of the fact that ORed predicates on a column cannot use single index processing. You can add the predicate OR 0 = 1 within the parentheses like: (AGE > 18 OR 0 = 1). The ORed predicate can be on any non-equal values (OR 5 = 6, for example). However, it is best to simply use OR 0 = 1 so that everyone recognizes its meaning to disallow the use of an index on the column in parentheses.

These techniques, however, mean that any time the distribution of the data changes, or the optimizer is changed, a different access path might be appropriate. Recall from Section PP.5 that the clause OPTIMIZE FOR *n* ROWS where *n* is small (such as 15) makes it unlikely that multiple indexes will be used, and OPTIMIZE FOR 1 ROW invokes the optimizer's rule not to use multiple index processing for a single table SELECT statement.

Threshold for ANDing of Predicates

There is no architectural limit to the number of predicates that can be ANDed. There are times, however, when ANDing of additional indexes offers no benefits and can cost more. DB2 uses a threshold to avoid incurring additional costs when little or no benefit can be achieved. ANDing of predicates stops when 32 or fewer RIDs qualify from multiple indexes. The search has already been narrowed to a small number of pages, and DB2 can use a single I/O to retrieve 32 pages using list prefetch. Additional predicates are applied directly to the row. For example, if less than 32 RIDs qualify using the SN and PN indexes, the JN RIDs are not retrieved from the JN index and ANDed with the following SELECT. The JN predicate is applied directly on the row. This is a refinement of the access path chosen by the optimizer at execution time.

Here is an example of a statement where the optimizer chooses multiple index processing on three indexes on the columns SN, PN, and JN.

```
SELECT SN, PN, JN, QTY
FROM   SPJ
WHERE  SN = 'S5'
AND    PN = 'P5'
AND    JN = 'J4';
```

If the RID pool is too small to process the JN RIDs from a third or fourth index, for example, RIDs from the first two indexes can still be used for list prefetch. However, performance can be adversely affected when this happens.

If you find that the performance of an SQL statement varies with the workload, a shortage of space in the RID pool may be a factor. For example, if you find that the SQL performs well most of the time but when there is a heavy load on the system at say 10:00 A.M. when RIDs are being placed in the RID pool for many SQL statements, there may not be space to process the RIDs from all of the indexes. Consider checking with the system administrator to determine if this could a factor. There are many factors that affect performance during peak periods (the CPU may be used to near 100 percent of its capacity, for example). A shortage of space in the RID pool is only one of many possibilities that are worth investigating with the person responsible for tuning the DB2 subsystem.

Use of Multiple Indexes with OR

It is not logically possible to use only one of two separate indexes on SN and PN. If only the index on SN were used to locate the S2 rows, then the P4 rows would be missed as indicated by shading in Figure PP.9 for the statement:

```
SELECT SN, PN, JN, QTY
FROM   SPJ
WHERE  SN = 'S2'
OR     PN = 'P4';
```

Figure PP.9. Rows can be missed if one index were used

SN	PN	JN	QTY
S1	P1	J1	200
S1	P1	J4	700
S2	P3	J1	400
S2	P3	J2	200
S2	P3	J3	200
S2	P3	J4	500
S2	P3	J5	600
S2	P3	J6	400
S2	P3	J7	800
S2	P5	J2	100
S3	P3	J1	200
S3	P4	J2	500
S4	P6	J3	300
S4	P6	J7	300

S5	P2	J2	200
S5	P4	J4	100

Separate indexes on SN and PN can be used to narrow the search before access to the data pages for OR conditions on different columns. The process used for an OR condition is similar conceptually to that used for AND conditions. The RIDs for S2 are retrieved from the SN index, and those for P4 are retrieved from the PN index and placed in the RID pool. The RIDs are sorted and duplicates are removed. This is referred to as *OR*ing of the predicates or taking a union of the RIDs. List prefetch is used to retrieve the data pages in sequence as they appear on DASD using skip sequential processing.

Recall from Chapter IU that ORed predicates on different columns in a composite index cannot use a matching index scan because rows can be missed or all leaf pages must be scanned using a non-matching index scan.

Multiple index processing does not apply to ORed predicates on different columns of a composite index. It is necessary to do a non-matching index scan or a tablespace scan in this case. ORed predicates in general are complex to deal with.

ORed predicates on the same column with < and > predicates usually mean an index is not used, particularly when host variables are used and the column has a low cardinality. This has to do with the relationship of range predicates with host variables and how the computed filter factors are combined with ORed predicates as discussed in the above Section PP.2 as the third alternative for the negated predicate. Here is a statement that probably will not result in a matching index scan:

```
SELECT SN, SNAME
FROM   S
WHERE  SN <= 'S2'
OR     SN >= 'S4';
```

If you are sure that only a small percent of rows will qualify, use BETWEEN when using host variables to encourage the use of indexes like:

```
SELECT SN, SNAME
FROM   S
WHERE  SN BETWEEN X'0000'  AND 'S2'
OR     SN BETWEEN 'S4'     AND X'FFFF';
```

A matching index scan can be used to identify SNs greater than or equal to the lowest possible value of hexadecimal X'0000', to identify the qualifying RIDS, and to scan forward in the leaf pages until S2 is found. A second matching index scan can be used to find S4 and all those greater than S4. The RIDs are sorted, duplicates eliminated, and list prefetch is used to locate the rows on the data pages. Notice from this example that multiple index processing can be performed on a single index.

Threshold for ORing of Predicates

DB2 does not continue to use multiple index processing for ORed predicates if more than 25 percent of the RIDs qualify using some combination of indexes. If more than 25 percent of the RIDs qualify, DB2 stops ORing the RIDs, discards the RIDs, and uses a tablespace scan with sequential prefetch, which is a better way to process a large percent of rows. DASD seek time is shorter for sequential prefetch than list prefetch because fetched pages are contiguous with sequential prefetch. A good rule of thumb is that sequential prefetch requires about 1.7 milliseconds (ms) and list prefetch requires about 3 ms of I/O time. Any pages that are already in the buffer pool are not read again with both sequential and list prefetch.

The problem is that 25 percent of the RIDs must be retrieved before determining that a tablespace scan is best. At bind time, the optimizer estimates the percent of RIDs that will be processed and does not choose multiple index processing if it estimates that more than 25 percent of the RIDs will qualify. However, the actual number of qualifying RIDs to be processed depends on the values requested by the user at execution time and varies from one execution to another. The values requested by the user are not known by the optimizer when host variables are used with static SQL unless reoptimization is requested. In addition, predicates on interdependent indexes and an index on a column with a skewed distribution of values increases the likelihood that the 25 percent threshold will be reached.

Performance trace class 8 IFCID 0125 can be used to identify program and statement number that caused threshold to be reached as described in SDSNSAMP(DSNWMSGS) .

Recommendation: To avoid the 25 percent threshold being exceeded at execution time, use the OPTIMIZE FOR 1 ROW as discussed in Section PP.5, use "0 = 1" in parentheses to disallow the use of an index on the column, or use reoptimization. If there is a reason to believe that a large percent of the rows will qualify for most user requests, it is best to do a tablespace scan immediately rather than accumulate 25 percent of the RIDs, discard them, and then do a tablespace scan.

Considerations for Using Multiple Indexes

and OR predicates in combination can use ANDing and ORing of RID lists. There is no architectural limit on the number of indexes that are ANDed and ORed, although it is possible to run out of work space. RIDs from the first two indexes are combined into a temporary list, let's call that list A. RIDs from the third index are combined with temporary list A into temporary list B. RIDs from the fourth index are combined with temporary list B into temporary list C, and so forth with a current maximum set at 200 indexes.

Multiple indexes can be used with almost any cluster ratio, but it is more likely with a low cluster ratio. List prefetch is always used with multiple index processing and a hybrid join, and can sometimes be used with a single index as well.

List Prefetch with a Single Index

Multiple indexes are useful for narrowing a search so that fewer data pages must be processed. List prefetch can also be used with single index processing if two or more pages are to be processed and if sequential prefetch is not appropriate. It is better to issue one list prefetch I/O for two pages rather than to issue two I/Os. List prefetch has a number of benefits for multiple and single index processing: A page does not have to be read more than once to process multiple rows on the page, only pages with qualifying rows are read, and pages are read sequentially as they appear on DASD, which reduces seek time.

Without list prefetch, a page might have to be read more than once when it has multiple qualifying rows. This occurs when a column has a low cardinality or a skewed distribution of values. An example of a low cardinality index on a city column is used in Chapter IU. The cardinality is 20, meaning that a search for any one value, say Dallas, qualifies about 5 percent of the rows and that each page has on average two and a half rows located in Dallas. (The 5 percent is calculated as 1 divided by 20 because 1 value is required out of 20.) Clearly, it is desirable to avoid having to read each page two and a half times; list prefetch eliminates duplicate RIDs and accomplishes this goal. A similar situation occurs with a skewed distribution of values. Assume 80 percent of the parts are in the headquarters city and the remaining 20 percent are in branch warehouses. That means there is a good chance that each data page has even more than two and a half parts when a search is done on the headquarters city. Indeed, depending on the cardinality and other statistics, the optimizer many choose a tablespace scan with sequential prefetch.

A range search can benefit from list prefetch. If all the parts between P2 and P20 are required, there is a good chance that several qualifying parts are on a single page. If the index on PN has a high cluster ratio, the benefits of list prefetch are not as great since the cost of sorting the RIDs and eliminating duplicates is necessary. A high cluster ratio means that most of the values are clustered or grouped together on contiguous pages already and sequential prefetch can be used rather than list prefetch.

Difference between Sequential and List Prefetch: Sequential prefetch differs from list prefetch in that it does not require prior access to an index; it can be used on index and data pages (list prefetch is used only on data pages); and it reads the next 32 pages even if there are no qualifying rows on some of the pages.

List prefetch is more likely to be used if there is a low cluster ratio of less than 80 percent, for example. These factors are considered by the optimizer for both single and multiple index processing using list prefetch.

Use of a Composite Index with Index Screening

In Chapters IU, we described composite indexes and how they can be used for matching index scans when the user specifies the leading columns of the composite index in the WHERE clause. Assume there is a composite index on SN, PN, and JN for the following statement:

```
SELECT SN, PN, JN
FROM   SPJ
WHERE  SN = 'S1'
AND    JN > 'J5';
```

SN is the leading column of the index, and, with the equal predicate on that column, a matching index scan can be used to locate S1 in the leaf pages and then scan forward to apply the JN predicate on the leaf pages. (A matching index scan cannot be used on PN and JN because PN is not specified in the predicate.) The JN > 'J5' predicate can be applied to the leaf pages using index screening with or without list prefetch and multiple index usage (V5 APAR PQ15670). The goal is to reduce number of data pages that must be processed by applying predicates on index pages. Do be cautious of many qualifying RIDs that must be placed in the RID pool and only a few rows need to be fetched to fill a screen

Size of the RID pool

The RID pool is an area of central storage used to store and sort RID lists. No DASD work files are used to sort RIDs. The maximum RID pool size is the minimum of the value specified as RID POOL SIZE on install panel DSNTIPC (or DSNZPARM DSN6SPRM MAXRBLK). The default is 4,000 KB. It is advisable for the systems administrator to explicitly set the RID pool size to avoid having the size vary whenever someone changes the size of the buffer pools.

The size of the RID pool is considered by the optimizer at bind time when determining if list prefetch is a good choice. The optimizer will not choose list prefetch as part of the access path if more than 25 percent of the pages are estimated to contain qualifying rows, more than 50 percent of the RID pool is required for one statement, or more than 16 million RIDs qualify for one statement.

The optimizer estimate of the number of RIDs that will qualify can be inaccurate when host variables are used. For example, a user may request all suppliers with a status less than 30 in a host variable and few to medium number of rows qualify in which case list prefetch is a good choice. Another user may request all suppliers with a status >= 99 in a host variable and many rows qualify in which case list prefetch is a poor choice. If you are faced with a similar situations, consider reoptimization as discussed in Chapter OP.7.

- Interdependent columns with separate indexes

- Consider reoptimization (V5)

Each SQL statement is allowed a minimum of one RID block of 4,096 RIDs (4,096 RIDs * 4 byte RID = 16 KB). Even if there is a shortage of space in the RID pool, an SQL statement can process 4,096 RIDs before DB2 changes to a tablespace scan. This reduces the likelihood that transactions will vary in response time when RID pool space becomes scarce during peak periods of activity. The additional space is allocated in the general working storage of the database services address space up to the equivalent RID pool size. If the number of RIDs is less than 4,096 for an SQL statement, online transactions benefit from list prefetch in most cases.

Disabling List Prefetch: If the RID pool size is set to 0, list prefetch is disabled as is multiple index access and hybrid join. Be careful about disabling list prefetch, especially after plans and packages have already been bound. If the plan or package was bound and list prefetch was chosen by the optimizer, it reverts to a tablespace scan at execution time if there is no RID pool storage.

Monitoring RID Pool Processing: It is best to monitor the use of list prefetch rather than disabling it. List prefetch is usually a very good technique for processing the data. Indeed, if the RID list is beyond a 150 page boundary, other I/O requests are serviced to avoid one SQL statement causing delays for other statements.

DB2 collects statistics on the use of the RID pool in accounting trace records. A performance monitor (DB2PM for example) can be used to report on these statistics. The DB2PM "Instrumentation Accounting Data" panel shows a count of the number of times that the RID pool was used successfully, list prefetch was not used as requested by the optimizer because insufficient space was available for RID processing, and the number of times RID processing was terminated because a threshold limit was exceeded. The DB2PM "Statistic Trace - Long" panel shows the number of times the 2 GB limit was exceeded as "Failed-No storage". It shows a count of the number of times that more than 25 percent of table RIDs qualify, more than 50 percent of the RID pool is required for one statement, and when space for 4,096 RIDs (default) cannot be allocated as "Failed-RDS limit exceeded". The "Failed-DM limit exceeded" shows the number of times that one SQL statement required more than 16 million RIDs. The "Process limit exceeded" shows the number of times that no more space is available for processing the RIDs.

The SQL statements that caused one or more of the conditions should be identified. Consider using OPTIMIZE FOR 1 ROW, add "OR 0 = 1" in parentheses along with the predicate to disallow the use of an index, or use reoptimization. If there is insufficient space in the RID pool, do consider increasing its size.

PP.9 CAPPING THE COSTS

The Resource Limit Facility (RLF) in DB2 provides a flexible way to put a cap on the cost of any dynamic data manipulation statement executed by any AUTHID from any program and from any location. The limit applies to each statement execution. It does not include I/O costs, cost of parallel processing, triggers, user-defined functions, and large objects. You can use reactive and predictive governing. Limits can be set for QMF users in addition to or instead of RLF limits. The QMF governor provides for a great deal of flexibility in that assembler program logic is used. You can limit the number of rows selected, usage of specific tables, QMF commands, and more.

Reactive governing stops a currently executing statement when the designated processing limit is exceeded. A -905 SQLCODE is issued meaning that the limit has been exceeded. Execution stops and the unit of recovery is rolled back. The disadvantage of this type of governing is that the resources are used before the execution is stopped, usually without any results being returned. If you decide to use the reactive governor, do be cautious of setting too low of a limit. A rollback requires more processing than the original work that is rolled back, don't set limits that users frequently exceed; it may turn out to be more expensive than setting the higher limits they need. Even if only SELECT statements are used, set the limit high enough to satisfy most requests, or else the user might try the statement repeatedly, perhaps modifying it to try and stay within limits, thereby wasting more CPU time than if the user had been given a higher limit originally.

Predictive governing is used to inform users that designated processing limits for cost category 'A' from the DSN_STATEMNT_TABLE discussed in Chapter EX might be exceeded (V6). It has the advantages in that resources are not used to execute the SQL if the specified limit might be exceeded. A -495 SQLCODE is issued if the statement might exceed the specified limit and the statement is not executed at all. Optionally, you can set a warning limit. If this limit is exceeded, a warning of +495 SQLCODE is issued.

Predictive governing is used to inform users that designated processing limits for cost category 'A' from the DSN_STATEMNT_TABLE discussed in Chapter EX might be exceeded (V6). It has the advantages in that resources are not used to execute the SQL if the specified limit might be exceeded. A -495 SQLCODE is issued if the statement might exceed the specified limit and the statement is not executed at all. Optionally, you can set a warning limit. If this limit is exceeded, a warning of +495 SQLCODE is issued.

The RLF limits are not expressed directly in CPU seconds but rather in service units, called ASU time, which is derived by multiplying the CPU second limit by the service units per second for a given processor. This is done to avoid having to change the limits when a processor model is changed. Basically, more work can be done per CPU second on a faster CPU. The OS/390 system programmer can provide the service units per second for a processor model from the *OS/390 Initialization and Tuning Guide for the OS/390* manual in the section on the System Resource Manager. If the service units per seconds for your processor model is 800 and you want a CPU limit of 10 seconds, the ASU time is 8000, for example.

You will find the DSN_STATEMNT_TABLE discussed in Chapter EX useful in determining the ASU to use in the RLF table. The column PROCSU contains the optimizer's estimate of the processor time required and is useful in estimating the service unit limit that you want to specify in the RLF table. The COST_CATEGORY is useful in determining the cost category that is used in predictive governing described in the next section.

Resource Limit Specification Tables

The system administrator sets up the limits with RLF tables. More than one RLF table can be used to control a system, but only one is active at any one time. For example, one table may set the limits from 9 A.M. to 5 P.M.; another may enforce different limits from 5 P.M. to midnight; and a third still different limits from midnight to 9 A.M. Each table must be named DSNRLST*xx*, where *xx* is any two alphanumeric characters. The *xx* is used by the operator to designate the table to be used when starting the resource limit facility with the command: -START RLIMIT ID=xx. Here is an example of creating a DSNRLSTxx table.

```
CREATE TABLE AUTHID.DSNRLSTxx
  (AUTHID    CHAR(8)  NOT NULL WITH DEFAULT,
   PLANNAME  CHAR(8)  NOT NULL WITH DEFAULT,
   ASUTIME   INTEGER,
   LUNAME    CHAR(8)   NOT NULL WITH DEFAULT,
   RLFFUNC   CHAR(1)   NOT NULL WITH DEFAULT,
   RLFBIND   CHAR(1)   NOT NULL WITH DEFAULT,
   RLFCOLLN  CHAR(18)  NOT NULL WITH DEFAULT,
   RLFPKG    CHAR(8)   NOT NULL WITH DEFAULT),
   RLFASUERR        INTEGER,
   RLFASUWARN       INTEGER,
   RLF_CATEGORY_B CHAR(1)  NOT NULL WITH DEFAULT)
    IN DSNRLST.DSNRLSxx;
```

The first three columns are required. The remaining columns are used as needed. All or none of the columns used to control binds (RLFFUNC, RLFBIND, RLFCOLLN, RLFPKG) are required. All or none of the columns to control predictive governing are required (RLFASUERR , RLFASUWARN, RLF_CATEGORY_B). Figure PP.10 contains a description of each column in the DSNRLSTxx table.

Figure PP.10. Explanation of DSNRLSTxx columns

Column	Explanation
AUTHID	Primary AUTHID for which the limit applies.
PLAN-NAME	Plan for which the limit applies. Must be blank if limit applies to a package.
ASU-TIME	Service unit limit for reactive governing.
LUNAME	Location to which the limit applies.
RLF-FUNC	Type of function govern by row. ' ' = governs by plan name. '1' = governs bind operations. '2' = reactive governor by package or collection name. '3' = disables query I/O parallelism. '4' = disables query CP parallelism. '5' = disables sysplex query parallelism. '6' = predictive governor by plan name. '7' = predictive governor by package or collection. All other values are ignored.
RLF-BIND	'N' = bind operations are not allowed. Any other value allows bind operations. Column used only if RLFFUNC = '1'.
RLF-COLLN	Collection name that rows applies to if SQL executed from a package otherwise row is ignored. ' ' = applies to all collections at the specified LUNAME. If RLFFUNC = ' ', '1,' or '6', then RLFCOLLN must be ' '.
RLF-PKG	Package that rows applies to if SQL executed from a package otherwise row is ignored. ' ' = all packages specified in LUNAME. If RLFFUNC = ' ', '1', or '6', then RLFPKG must be ' '.
RLF-ASU-ERR	Row used for predictive governing (RLFFUNC= '6' or '7'). Used only for statements that are in cost category A. If service units specified in this column are exceeded, -495 SQLCODE is returned and statement is not executed. Null = No error threshold. 0 (zero) or a negative value = -495 SQLCODE.
RLF-ASU-WARN	Used for predictive governing (RLFFUNC= '6' or '7'). Used only for statements that are in cost category A. If service units specified in this column are exceeded, +495 SQLCODE is returned as a warning. Null = No error threshold. 0 (zero) or a negative value = +495 SQLCODE. RLFASUWARN should be < RLFASUERR, otherwise error is always issued with no warning.
RLF_CATE-GORY_B	Used for predictive governing (RLFFUNC='6' or '7'). Action to take if cost category = B: ' ' = Prepare and execute the SQL statement (default). 'Y' = Prepare and execute the SQL statement. 'N' = Do not prepare or execute the SQL statement. Return SQLCODE -495 to the application. 'W' = +459 SQLCODE, complete the prepare. Program logic determine whether to execute the SQL.

Figure PP.11 is used to clarify how the DSNRLSTxx table columns are used to control resource usage. The figure is followed by description of each entry.

Figure PP.11. Sample resource limit specification table

AUTH-ID*	PLAN-NAME	ASU-TIME	LUNAME	RLF-FUNC	RLF-COLLN	RLF-PKG	RLF-ASU-ERR	RLF-ASU-WARN	RLF_CATE-GORY_B
FLEUR	QMF310	40000							
FLEUR		20000	Perth						
	QMF310	10000	Oslo	2					
		2000							
ERIC		null	Sydney						
BILL		0	Dallas						
			Public	6			9000	7000	Y
			Public	7	SCOLL		8000	6000	N
			Public	7		SREP	7000	5000	W

*AUTHID is the primary AUTHID

In the example, the table sets limits as follows:

- Fleur cannot use over 40,000 ASU while executing any one SQL DML using QMF at the local site (LUNAME is blank). The blank in the RLFFUNC column means that the first row if for the reactive governor is by plan.
- Fleur cannot use over 20,000 ASU while executing any one SQL DML while using other plans or packages (SPUFI for example) coming from Perth.
- Any other AUTHID can use 10,000 ASU using QMF coming from Oslo. The value of 2 in the RLFFUNC means that the reactive governor is used by collection or package.
- Any AUTHID using any plan from any location can use 2,000 ASU.
- Null ASUTIME results in no limit for Eric coming from Sydney.
- Zero ASUTIME indicates that the use of dynamic SQL is not permitted by Bill coming from Dallas.

The following 3 examples apply if the cost category is 'A' (described for DSN_STATEMNT_TABLE in Chapter EX).

- Any AUTHID can use 9,000 ASU for each SQL statement executed from any plan (optionally, you can name a specified plan in this and other rows) from any location. If the estimate is exceeded, the statement is not executed, rather a -495 SQLCODE is returned. If 7000 ASU (from the warning column) is exceeded, a +495 SQLCODE is issued. The RLFFUNC column value of 6 means that this row applies to the predictive governor by plan name.
- Any AUTHID can use 8,000 ASU for each SQL statement executed from the SCOLL collection from any location. If the estimate is exceeded, statement is not executed and a -495 SQLCODE is returned. If 6000 ASU (from the warning column) is exceeded, +495

SQLCODE is issued. The RLFFUNC column value of 7 means that this row applies to the predictive governor.

- Any AUTHID can use 7,000 ASU for each SQL statement executed from the SREP package from any location. If the estimate is exceeded, the statement is not executed, rather a -495 SQLCODE is returned. If 5000 ASU (from the warning column) is exceeded, +495 SQLCODE is returned. The RLFFUNC column value of 7 means that this row applies to the predictive governor.
- If cost category is 'B' (described for DSN_STATEMNT_TABLE in Chapter EX), predictive governing is used, and the action to be taken depends on the value in the RLF_CATEGORY_B column:
  - 'Y' means to prepare and execute the statement.
  - 'N' means not to do a prepare and execute the statement and results in a -495 SQLCODE.
  - 'W' means to prepare the statement and program logic determines whether to execute the statement and result in a +495 SQLCODE.

Controlling Binds with RLF

Four of the columns in the DSNRLSTxx table are used to control whether bind operations are allowed by collection and package as described in Figure PP.10. They are:

- RLFFUNC - Function controlled
- RLFBIND - Binds are or are not allowed
- RLFCOLLN - Name of collection
- RLFPKG - Name of package

The RLFCOLLN column contains the name of a collection that the row applies to if RLFFUNC = 2. The column RLFPKG contains the name of a package that the row applies to if RLFFUNC = 2. If the column value for RLFPKG is blank, the row applies to all packages in a named collection or all plans if RLFFUNC = ' '. An entry in the LUNAME column is required when controlling binds.

Controlling Program Resource Usage

Developers have a number of ways to limit the cost of executing SQL and host language code. Program resource usage (and thus static SQL) can be controlled by OS/390 WLM (Work Load Manager) as described in the *OS/390 MVS Initialization and Tuning Guide* manual. The TIME parameter on job and step statement limits resource usage for batch jobs. The TSO time parameter in the logon procedure can be set by the OS/390 systems programmer as described in the *OS/390 TSO/E Programming Guide and OS/390 TSO/E Customization* manuals. CICS controls are described in the *CICS/ESA Performance Guide* manual. IMS controls are described in the *IMS/ESA Operator's Reference* manual.

You have the option of limiting the sum of CPU time used for static SQL, dynamic SQL, and host language code when using local and remote stored procedures as described in Chapter SP.

PP.10 SUMMARY

In a perfect world, it would only be necessary to write an SQL statement that achieves the results you want, no matter how it got there. And, DB2's optimizer does give you that capability most of the time. However, if a statement does not meet reasonable performance expectations, you can often rewrite the statement to take better advantage of DB2's way of processing predicates. SQL guidelines alone are not sufficient, an understanding of SQL processing is required to maximize performance for challenging SQL statements.

There are many guidelines throughout the book and in this chapter for writing SQL statements to achieve good performance. Based on your study and experience with DB2, do consider providing examples of customized model SQL statements using your application tables for developers new to DB2. Examples of statements that perform well and some that perform poorly will give your new developers a head start in developing high performing SQL statements.

EXERCISES

1. Give two reasons why it is important to use stage 1 predicates.

2. If a non-matching index scan is chosen to evaluate a predicate by the optimizer, is the evaluation of the predicate done at stage 1 by DM in all cases? Does the same principle apply to a tablespace scan?

3. Assume an index on QTY in the P table. Why is the index not being used in a matching index scan for the following statement?

```
SELECT PN, QTY / 100
FROM   P
WHERE  QTY + 10 > :QTY;
```

4. Assume that there is no index on the PN column, and the column is declared as CHAR(2). Why is the elapsed time to locate 100 rows with a p5 out of a million row table longer than expected?

```
SELECT SN, PN, JN, QTY
FROM   SPJ
WHERE  PN > 'P5 ';
```

5. Is the predicate in the following statement evaluated at stage 1? Why?

```
SELECT JNAME, CITY CONCAT ',' CONCAT STATE
FROM   J
WHERE  SUBSTR(JNAME,1,2) = 'SW';
```

6. Are any of the predicates in the following statement evaluated at stage 2? How many rows are passed to RDS, assuming that 10 rows have a JNAME with "PRO" in the second, third, and fourth position of the name, and five of the rows have a city of Dallas?

```
SELECT JNAME, CITY
FROM   J
WHERE  JNAME LIKE '_PRO%'
AND    CITY  ¬= 'Dallas';
```

7. Assume a separate index on each of the columns in the following WHERE clause. Which of the predicates can and cannot use a matching index scan?

```
SELECT SN, SNAME, STATUS, CITY
FROM   S
WHERE  SN      = 'S4  '
AND    SNAME   = 'Blake'
AND    CITY    = SUBSTR(:CITY,1,5)
AND   (STATUS  = :STATUS + 10
OR     STATUS  = 30.2);
```

8. Which of the following SELECT statements can use a matching index scan on a composite index composed of the columns SN, PN, and JN? The two statements do not yield the same result.

```
SELECT SN, PN, JN, QTY
FROM   SPJ
WHERE  SN = 'S3'
OR     PN = 'P3'
OR     JN = 'J3';
```

```
SELECT SN, PN, JN, QTY
FROM   SPJ
WHERE  SN = 'S3'
AND   (PN = 'P2' OR PN = 'P5')
AND    JN = 'J4';
```

9. a) Is it possible to use an index scan on one of three indexes on each of the columns SN, PN, or JN to satisfy the following statement? Why?

b) How can the three indexes be used to satisfy the following statement?

```
SELECT SN, PN, JN, QTY
FROM   SPJ
WHERE  SN = 'S5'
OR     PN = 'P5'
OR     JN = 'J5';
```

10. Can an index on DATE_RECEIVED be used to narrow the search for either of the predicates in the following statement? Why?

```
SELECT PN, CITY, DATE_RECEIVED
FROM   P
WHERE  DATE_RECEIVED > DATE(:DATE-REQUIRED) + 10 DAYS
AND    DATE_RECEIVED < CURRENT DATE;
```

11. Can an index on DATE_RECEIVED be used to narrow the search? Why?

```
SELECT PN, CITY, DATE_RECEIVED
FROM   P
WHERE  DATE_RECEIVED + 10 DAYS < DATE(:DATE-REQUIRED);
```

12. Assume an index on QTY. Is the summation on QTY done at stage 1 in the following statement?

```
SELECT SUM(QTY)
FROM   SPJ;
```

13. Assume a separate index on SN, PN, JN, and QTY. How is the following count of all the rows processed?

```
SELECT COUNT(*)
FROM   SPJ;
```

14. How is LIKE use of an index similar to the use of a composite index when the leading columns are not specified in the WHERE clause?

15. Here is a two-part question that draws on information in this chapter as well as Chapter JP.

a) Does the access path chosen by the optimizer differ for the following two formulations of the same request? The statements are to report on all suppliers in Lisbon who have a status of 20 and currently supply parts in a quantity of over 100 to 'J3'.

b) In what order are the predicates applied to the rows?

```
SELECT S.SN, SNAME, STATUS, CITY, PN, JN, QTY
FROM   S, SPJ
WHERE  S.SN   = SPJ.SN
AND    CITY   = 'Lisbon'
AND    STATUS = 20
AND    JN     = 'J3'
AND    QTY    > 100;

SELECT PN, JN, QTY, S.SN, SNAME, STATUS, CITY
FROM   SPJ, S
WHERE  QTY    > 100
AND    STATUS = 20
AND    S.SN   = SPJ.SN
AND    CITY   = 'Lisbon'
AND    JN     = 'J3';
```

16. Can an index with a good cluster ratio be used to avoid a sort for a UNION operator? Why?

17. Assume a composite index scan on SN, PN, and JN with a good cluster ratio. Can the index be used to avoid a sort for the ORDER BY clause? Why?

```
SELECT SN, PN, JN, QTY
FROM   SPJ
WHERE  PN  = 'P4'
AND    QTY = 200
ORDER BY SN, PN, JN, QTY;
```

18. What are two alternatives that can be used to allow for the use of an index to avoid a sort for the following statement assuming a composite index on SN, PN, and JN with a good cluster ratio? Give your reasons. Hint: One alternative has to do with the SELECT statement and the other alternative has to do with the index definition.

```
SELECT SN, PN, JN, QTY
FROM   SPJ
WHERE  PN  = 'P4'
AND    QTY = 200
ORDER BY SN, PN, JN, QTY;
```

19. A composite index on SN, PN, and JN on the SPJ table with a good cluster ratio is not used to avoid a sort for the following statement. How can you change the statement so that the index can be used to avoid a sort?

```
SELECT S.SN, PN, JN, QTY, CITY
FROM   S, SPJ
WHERE  S.SN = SPJ.SN
AND    PN   = 'P4'
AND    QTY  = 200
ORDER BY S.SN, SPJ.PN, SPJ.JN;
```

20. Assume a unique index on SN with a good cluster ratio. A sort is required for the following statement. Why? How can the statement be changed so that the index can be used to avoid the sort?

```
SELECT SN, SNAME
FROM   S
ORDER BY SN, SNAME;
```

21. What are three major advantages of list prefetch using multiple index and single index processing?

22. What does skip sequential processing mean regarding list prefetch?

23. How does list prefetch differ from sequential prefetch?

24. If the required pages are found in the buffer pool, are they read from DASD with list prefetch or sequential prefetch?

25. Why is the rule-of-thumb I/O time estimate per page higher for list prefetch (3 ms) than for sequential prefetch (1.7 ms)?

26. List prefetch is always used for what two types of processing?

27. Under what conditions is the optimizer likely to use list prefetch when using single index access? Why?

28. If an index can be used to avoid a sort, is it likely that the optimizer will choose to use list prefetch? Why?

29. What is a major advantage of multiple index usage for ANDed predicates?

30. Does the use of multiple indexes for ORed predicates reduce the total number of data pages that must be processed like it does for ANDed predicates?

31. How is multiple index processing for ORed predicates similar to that for ANDed predicates?

32. How is multiple index processing for ORed predicates different from that for ANDed predicates? What is a performance benefit of using multiple indexes for ORed predicates?

33. What is a major disadvantage of list prefetch and multiple index usage?

34. What type of processing frequently results in many qualifying RIDs but only a few rows being fetched?

35. When you identify a case where list prefetch and multiple index processing detract from performance, what can you do to influence the optimizer not to use this type of processing?

36. The optimizer has chosen to use multiple index processing on the STATUS and CITY indexes for the following statement. You believe that many RIDs will qualify and be processed in the RID pool but that only 15 rows will be fetched to fill a screen for an online transaction. Modify the statement to influence the optimizer not to use multiple index processing.

```
SELECT SN, SNAME, STATUS, CITY
FROM   S
WHERE  SN    > :SN
AND    STATUS BETWEEN :LOW AND :HIGH
AND    CITY = :CITY;
```

37. The optimizer has chosen to use the index on SN as part of the access path for the following statement. It is felt that the index on CITY should be used since there are very few suppliers in Canberra, not the index on SN. Modify the following statement so that is it very likely that only the CITY index will be used in the access path.

```
SELECT SN, SNAME, STATUS, CITY
FROM   S
WHERE  SN    > :SN
AND    STATUS BETWEEN :LOW AND :HIGH
AND    CITY = :CITY
OPTIMIZE FOR 15 ROWS;
```

38. What are the disadvantages of using the techniques discussed in the previous exercise?

39. What happens when more than 25 percent of the RIDs qualify when processing ORed predicates? Why?

40. The optimizer does not use list prefetch when it estimates that more than 25 percent of the RIDs will qualify. What is the most common cause for the optimizer's estimate being incorrect?

41. Under what condition is list prefetch not used even though the optimizer requested it?

42. How does DB2 minimize the possibility that a tablespace scan will be used for an SQL statement even when there is a shortage of space in the RID pool, particularly for online transactions that process a small number of rows?

43. Develop a SELECT statement with a case expression to count the number of employees hired during 1980 to 1989, 1990 to 1999, and 2000 to 2009. Develop a SELECT statement using UNION

ALL and without a case expression to determine the same information. Which of the two formulations perform best and why?

44. What is the distinction between reactive and predictive governing?

ANSWERS

1. 1) A matching index scan can be used for stage 1 predicates. 2) Significant reductions in CPU and elapsed time can be achieved by having DM evaluate predicates and narrow the search at stage 1 so that fewer columns and rows are passed to RDS for processing.

2. DM evaluates a predicate during a non-matching index scan only if it is a stage 1 predicate. If it is a stage 2 predicate, the values in all leaf pages are passed to RDS, one at a time, for stage 2 processing. The same principle applies to a tablespace scan.

3. A matching index scan cannot be used on a predicate that has an arithmetic expression on a column, because the expression is evaluated at stage 2. The expression "QTY / 100" in the SELECT clause does not influence the choice of whether an index is used to narrow the search.

4. The predicate PN > 'P5 ' is evaluated at stage 2 because 'P5 ' is 3 bytes in length and the column is 2 bytes in length. The same principle applies when using a host variable declared as equivalent to CHAR(3). There is a mismatch in the length of the character data type. A million SN, PN, JN, and QTY values must be passed to RDS one column at a time. 999,900 rows will be discarded by RDS before returning the 100 qualifying rows with the four selected columns to the host program.

5. The SUBSTR(JNAME,1,2) is not evaluated at stage 1 because SUBSTR is a scalar function used with a column. Scalar functions used with columns are evaluated at stage 2. The CONCAT scalar function in the SELECT clause has no effect. Every JNAME, CITY, and STATE in the table is passed to RDS during a tablespace scan. RDS does the SUBSTR processing and discards rows that do not qualify.

6. Both of the predicates on JNAME and CITY are evaluated at stage 1. Five rows are passed to RDS and then to the host program. Five of the 10 rows that have "PRO" in the JNAME column are discarded by DM because the jobs are not in Dallas.

7. A matching index scan cannot be used for the predicate SN = 'S4 ' because SN is declared as CHAR(2), and the literal is longer. A matching index scan can be used for the SNAME = 'Blake' predicate. This is true even if SNAME is declared as CHAR(10). 'Blake' is padded with 5 blanks to match the length of the column. A matching index scan can be used for the predicate SUBSTR(:CITY,1,5) because scalar functions used on non-columns are evaluated at stage 1. A matching index scan can be used for the predicate STATUS = :STATUS + 10 because the arithmetic expression is on a non-column. A matching index scan cannot be used for the predicate STATUS = 30.2 because the column is declared as INTEGER or SMALLINT and the literal is DECIMAL or FLOAT.

8. The first SELECT cannot use a matching index scan on a composite index. This is because once a position is found on a leaf page, a scan can continue forward but rows can be missed on pages before the scan began. It would not be efficient to start in, say, the middle of the leaf pages and scan forward, then reposition at the beginning of the leaf and scan forward. Too much DASD seek time

would be required. A non-matching index scan of all leaf pages from the beginning of the index is a better access path and might be chosen by the optimizer.

The second SELECT statement can be transformed by the optimizer into:

```
SELECT SN, PN, JN, QTY
FROM   SPJ
WHERE  SN = 'S3'
AND    PN IN ('P2', 'P5')
AND    JN = 'J4';
```

The reformulated statement can use two matching index scans to locate S3, P2, J4 and S3, P5, J4.

9. a) It is not possible to use an index scan on any one of the three indexes to satisfy the statement because the S5s can be identified by the SN index but the P5s and J5s would be missed.

b) All three of the indexes must be used to satisfy the ORed predicates in multiple index processing or none of the indexes can be used.

10. An index on DATE_RECEIVED can be used to narrow the search for the predicate DATE_RECEIVED < CURRENT DATE because it is evaluated at stage 1. An index can be used to narrow the search for the predicate DATE_RECEIVED > DATE(:DATE-REQUIRED) + 10 DAYS because scalar and arithmetic functions can be done on non-column data at stage 1.

11. An index on DATE_RECEIVED cannot be used to narrow the search because of the arithmetic operation on the column.

12. DM can calculate the summation of all of the QTYs in SPJ using a non-matching index scan at stage 1.

13. The optimizer chooses the index with the smallest number of leaf pages. DM counts all of the RIDs in the index chosen by the optimizer to determine the number of rows in the table, and passes the one value to RDS.

14. A matching index cannot be used if the leading characters in the index are not specified. There are no values to compare to the upper range values in the root and nonleaf pages.

15. a) The different formulations of the same request have exactly the same access path. The order in which the predicates are coded has no effect on the access path chosen by the optimizer.

b) The order in which the predicates are coded has an effect on the order in which they are tested, in some cases. For example, a possible access path is to access the S table first as the outer table of a nested loop join using an index on the CITY column to narrow the search to a supplier in Lisbon, and test the row for a status of 20. If the row qualifies, use the SN from the data page and do a matching index scan on the SPJ.SN index. After the row is retrieved, the predicates JN = 'J3' and QTY > 100 in the order indicated are applied to the row for both formulations of the request. This is because equal predicates usually narrow the search more than range predicates and are tested before range predicates regardless of the order in which they are coded. In addition, predicates are tested before join processing in most cases. (There are two exceptions. 1) Predicates on the inner table of a hybrid join are applied after the join. 2) Local predicates on the columns to be joined are applied after an outer join.)

If indexes are not used or there are several predicates of the same type on a table, the order in which the predicates are coded can affect the order in which they are tested at execution time and therefore the amount of CPU time used. Approximately 400 nanoseconds are required to do a comparison depending on the computer model. If one million rows are processed in a batch job and a comparison can be saved for most of the million rows by coding the most restrictive predicate first, about 0.4 seconds ($400 * (1 / 10^9) * 1,000,000$) can be saved. The savings of 0.4 seconds in a batch job does not seem to be worth the time required to be concerned with the order in which the predicates are coded.

If a tablespace scan is done on the two tables, the S table is likely to be the outer table because it is the smaller of the two tables. In the first formulation, the CITY = 'Lisbon' predicate is tested, followed by STATUS = 20, because equal predicates are tested first in the order in which they are coded before range predicates. In the second formulation, STATUS = 20 is tested first because it is the first equal predicate. It is likely that the result rows from the S table are sorted as the outer table of a merge join. Also, a derived predicate can be added at execution time during the sort of the outer table to narrow the search to, say, SN BETWEEN 'S30' AND 'S70' during a tablespace scan of the inner SPJ table. A nested loop join is very unlikely, and the hybrid join is impossible without an index on the inner table. During a tablespace scan on SPJ, the predicate JN = 'J3' is tested before the predicate QTY > 100 for both formulations, even though they are coded in the opposite order in the second formulation. This is because equal predicates are tested before range predicates.

16. An index cannot be used to avoid a sort for a UNION operator. This is because all of the qualifying rows above the UNION and then all of the rows below the UNION must be retrieved and sorted to eliminate duplicates.

17. The composite index on SN, PN, and JN cannot be used to avoid a sort to satisfy the ORDER BY clause. This is because the QTY column in the ORDER BY clause in not in the composite index. All columns in the ORDER BY clause must be in the composite index.

18. One alternative is to remove QTY from the ORDER BY clause. It is not needed because the WHERE clause has an equal predicate on QTY. The other alternative is to add QTY to the composite index. This is a good choice if an equal predicate on QTY is not in the WHERE clause, the specified sequence is needed frequently, many rows qualify, and there are no dependent tables with a foreign key on SN, PN, and JN referencing the SPJ table. The SN, PN, and JN columns are the primary key and would have to be carried in any dependent tables to have DB2 enforce referential integrity. In addition, a column should not be added to a unique index such that the index is no longer unique.

19. Change the column S.SN in the ORDER BY clause to SPJ.SN. All columns in the ORDER BY must be from the same index.

20. A sort is required for the statement because SNAME is not part of the index. SNAME can be removed from the ORDER BY to avoid the sort. The rows are returned in the correct sequence because of the unique index on SN. There is only one SNAME for each SN.

21. 1) A major advantage of list prefetch using multiple index and single index processing is that the RIDs are sorted and duplicates are eliminated. The duplicates are eliminated on the first three bytes of the RID which is the page identifier. This means that DM can get a page once and process all of

the rows on the page rather than getting the page for each qualifying row. 2) List prefetch means that up to 32 pages are read with a single I/O. 3) Pages are read sequentially as they appear on DASD.

22. Skip sequential processing regarding list prefetch means that only the pages identified by RIDs are read in sequence as they appear on DASD--the pages in between are skipped. For example, if RIDs 2, 4, and 6 are identified as containing qualifying rows, only those pages are read, not pages identified by RIDs 1, 3, and 5.

23. List prefetch differs from sequential prefetch in that list prefetch requires prior access to one or more indexes to obtain the RIDs. List prefetch I/Os are issued on only data pages, not index pages. Only pages with qualifying rows according to the predicate on the indexed column are read with list prefetch. In contrast, sequential prefetch reads the next 32 pages regardless of whether every page contains a qualifying row. Sequential prefetch can be used on the index and data pages. It does not require prior access to the index pages.

24. No, if the required pages are found in the buffer pool, they are not read from DASD with list prefetch or sequential prefetch.

25. The rule-of-thumb I/O time estimate is higher for list prefetch than sequential prefetch because only pages with qualifying rows are read from DASD, and it is unlikely that those pages are next to each other on DASD. Sequential prefetch reads the next set of pages, regardless of whether rows qualify, so they are next to each other on DASD. An exception is when some of the page are found in the buffer pool before the sequential prefetch I/O is issued.

26. List prefetch is always used for multiple index processing and a hybrid join.

27. If the optimizer estimates that two or more pages contain qualifying rows, an index has been chosen as part of the access path, and sequential prefetch is not a good choice, it is likely to use list prefetch. It is better to issue one list prefetch I/O than two I/Os.

28. If an index can be used to avoid a sort to retrieve rows in sequence, is it *not* likely that the optimizer will choose to use list prefetch. This is because list prefetch requires a sort of the RIDs and sequenced rows requires a sort of the rows. It is usually best to use an index with a good cluster ratio to avoid a sort of the rows. It is not logically possible to sort the RIDs from one or more indexes and to also use an index to avoid a sort of the rows.

29. A major advantage of multiple index usage for ANDed predicates is that the search can be narrowed from the index pages, thereby minimizing the number of data pages that must be read and processed. The RIDs that qualify according to each of the ANDed predicates are gotten from the multiple indexes and placed in the RID pool. An intersection is taken of the RIDs. This means that the RIDs are sorted, duplicates are eliminated, and only the RIDs of pages that contain rows satisfying all of the ANDed predicates are identified. The manipulation of the RIDs significantly reduces the number of I/Os to the data pages.

30. The use of multiple indexes for ORed predicates does not reduce the total number of data pages that must be processed. ORed predicates means that all rows that qualify for either of the ORed predicates are required.

31. Multiple index processing for ORed predicates is similar to that for ANDed predicates in that the RIDs from multiple indexes are placed in the RID pool, sorted, and duplicates are removed.

32. Multiple index processing for ORed predicates is different from that for ANDed predicates in that the RIDs are unioned rather than intersected. The major benefit of unioning the RIDs is that duplicate RIDs are eliminated. This means that DM gets the page once to process all of the qualifying rows on the page instead of having to get the page once for each qualifying row on the page.

33. The major disadvantage of list prefetch and multiple index usage is that all of the qualifying RIDs must be obtained from the leaf pages, placed in the RID pool, sorted, and a list prefetch I/O issued before the first qualifying row is returned to the user.

34. Cursor repositioning, scrolling, the use of range predicates, and equal predicates on a column with a low cardinality or a skewed distribution of values can result in many qualifying RIDs. Only a few of the qualifying rows are fetched to fill a screen for an online transaction. If a large number of RIDs qualify but only a few rows are fetched, the processing of many RIDs can be costly and is wasted if only a few of the qualifying rows are fetched.

35. You can influence the optimizer not to use list prefetch and multiple index processing by using the clause OPTIMIZE FOR *n* ROWS where *n* is small. This discourages the optimizer from using list prefetch and multiple index processing. OPTIMIZE FOR 1 ROW invokes the optimizer's rule not to use list prefetch and multiple index processing for an SQL statement that references a single table.

36. Inform the optimizer that you plan to fetch only 15 rows using the OPTIMIZE FOR 15 ROWS clause to avoid the use of multiple index processing. If this is not effective, use OPTIMIZE FOR 1 ROW to invoke the optimizer's rule not to use list prefetch and multiple index processing for single table processing.

```
SELECT SN, SNAME, STATUS, CITY
FROM   S
WHERE  SN    > :SN
AND    STATUS BETWEEN :LOW AND :HIGH
AND    CITY = :CITY
OPTIMIZE FOR 15 ROWS;
```

37. Use OR 0 = 1 in parentheses for each predicate where you do not want to have the index used as in the following example. If the index on CITY is not chosen as the part of the access path, use the clause OPTIMIZE FOR 1 ROW.

```
SELECT SN, SNAME, STATUS, CITY
FROM   S
WHERE (SN    > :SN OR 0 = 1)
AND   (STATUS BETWEEN :LOW AND :HIGH OR 0 = 1)
AND    CITY = :CITY
OPTIMIZE FOR 1 ROW;
```

38. Use of an index on CITY may appear to be the best access path but in fact is not. Use of the index on CITY may not be best in the future when the distribution of values change, another index is added, the processing done by DB2 is changed, or the optimizer is changed. Forcing an access path severely detracts from data independence.

39. The RIDs are placed in the RID pool until the 25 percent threshold is reached. When the threshold is reached, the RIDs are discarded and a tablespace scan is used. A tablespace is best if

more than 25 percent of the pages must be processed. The OPTIMIZE FOR clause is useful to discourage or disallow list prefetch when this threshold is likely to be reached.

40. When host variables are used, the optimizer does not have the value that will be requested by the user at execution time and the value can vary from one execution to another. For example, one user may request all of the rows in Tallahassee and a small to medium number of rows qualify. Another user may request all of the rows in the headquarters city of Dallas and over 25 percent of the rows qualify.

41. If there is a shortage of space for the RIDs, list prefetch is not used even though the optimizer requested it.

42. Even if the RID pool is full the space will be allocated in database services working storage. This minimizes the possibility that an online transaction will go to a tablespace scan at peak periods when the RID pool is full.

43. Here are two SELECT statements, one with a case expression and one with UNION ALL to count the number of employees hired during 1980 to 1989, 1990 to 1999, and 2000 to 2009. The SELECT statement has performance advantages because only one tablespace scan is required compared to three tablespace scans for the SELECT with UNION ALL if all of the qualifying rows are fetched.

```
SELECT SUM(CASE WHEN YEAR(HIREDATE)
           BETWEEN  1980  AND  1989
           THEN 1 ELSE 0
           END) AS HIRED_1980S,
       SUM(CASE WHEN YEAR(HIREDATE)
           BETWEEN  1990  AND  1999
           THEN 1 ELSE 0
           END) AS HIRED_1990S,
       SUM(CASE WHEN YEAR(HIREDATE)
           BETWEEN  2000  AND  2010
           THEN 1 ELSE 0
           END) AS HIRED_2000S
FROM   EMP;

SELECT COUNT(*) AS HIRED_1990S
FROM   EMP
WHERE  YEAR(HIREDATE) BETWEEN  1980  AND  1989
UNION ALL
SELECT COUNT(*) AS HIRED_1990S
FROM   EMP
WHERE  YEAR(HIREDATE) BETWEEN  1990  AND  1999
UNION ALL
SELECT COUNT(*) AS HIRED_2000S
FROM   EMP
WHERE  YEAR(HIREDATE) BETWEEN  2000  AND  2010;
```

44. There is a significant distinction between reactive and predictive governing. Reactive governing means that resources are used to execute a dynamic SQL statement until the a specified limit has been exceeded. If the limit is exceeded, -905 SQLCODE is issued and no results are received. Predictive governing means that if a the value in the RLFASUERR column is exceeded, -495 is issued and the

statement is not executed. If the value in the RLFASUWARN column is exceeded, a warning of +495 is issued.

FIGURES

The Optimizer

OP.1 INTRODUCTION

The optimizer's primary function is to determine efficient database search strategies for satisfying SQL statements. It is DB2's central component--in effect, its intelligence. The optimizer can be thought of as an expert system that incorporates the knowledge of programmers, and database administrators, and the expertise of many researchers into the science of database access. Catalog tables store information about a database--the sizes of tables, the availability of indexes, and more. The optimizer processes an SQL statement in terms of that information to determine the possible access paths to the needed data. It then applies formula and rules for determining relative costs of the various search options. The access path with the lowest estimated costs is chosen by the optimizer.

As an example, an SQL statement to select information about suppliers in the S table (Figure CT.6) that supply J7 with fewer than 200 of any part reads like this:

```
SELECT SN, SNAME, STATUS, CITY, JN, QTY
FROM   S, SPJ
WHERE  S.SN = SPJ.SN
AND    JN   = 'J7'
AND    QTY  < 200;
```

Several search strategies can fulfill that request. One strategy that is likely to be inefficient is to create the Cartesian product of the S and SPJ tables, creating a new virtual table with a row for every combination of rows from S and SPJ. Then the system could search for rows including both J7 and quantities of fewer than 200. If the S table has 1,000 rows and SPJ has 10,000, a Cartesian product will have 10 million rows, making this type of search costly indeed--consequently DB2's optimizer does not use this type of search when a large number of rows will result.

Another viable approach is to perform a tablespace scan on SPJ, searching for rows with J7 and quantities fewer than 200, and to join those rows with the S table on SN. If there is an index on job number, using it will provide a second, more efficient option. To choose the more efficient of the two viable searches, the optimizer needs to know the sizes of the tables and whether there is a useful index.

The DB2 optimizer gets that information from the catalog tables. The optimizer takes that information and uses formula and rules to determine an efficient access path.

Contrast with Non-Relational DBMSs: The optimizer's ability to find the most efficient path to the data needed to satisfy a request frees users and programmers from having to know the database structure. In marked contrast, users and programmers accessing databases within hierarchical or network database management systems must be familiar with the relationships between records.

Figure OP.1 shows a small portion of a network database. Pointers, instances of special data types within records, which are indicated by arrows in the figure, connect related records. To request information from the Employee ID/Project ID records, the user must know that there are pointers to them from Employee and Project records. And the user must include that information in the request. This is called navigating through the database. When changes are made to the database's design, users and programmers must learn about them and will probably have to modify programs to navigate through the new routes.

Figure OP.1. Network database

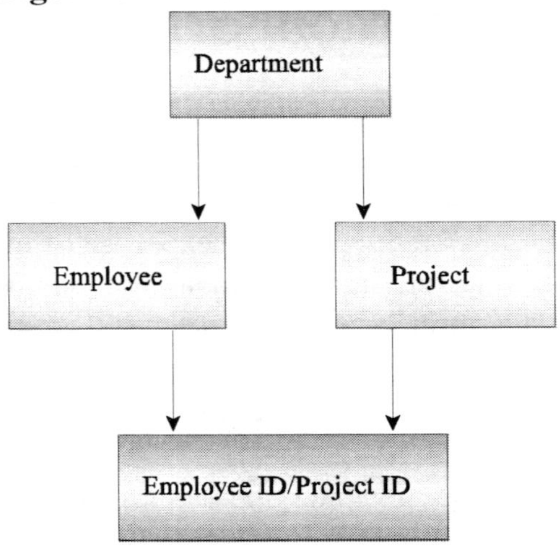

DB2's optimizer, on the other hand, can detect changes to the database's physical design in catalog table descriptions and itself find a new access path for any SQL statement that requests information from the changed database. Indeed, the optimizer should do better than a programmer in efficiently accessing a database because it can store and apply more information about the database than most people are able to remember--and it can keep up to date with changes much more quickly and accurately than even the most studious programmers.

Data Independence

The separation of the request for data from the need to specify its structure is called *data independence*. It has great practical value. Programmers and users can work more effectively when they don't have to worry about navigating through the data. Database administrators can change a database design without causing programmers to have to rewrite applications that access the database. And since design changes can be made easily, the database administrator can improve performance for applications by restructuring tables, adding or deleting indexes, and so on. DB2 developers are able to introduce new access techniques without requiring existing programs or queries to be changed.

Because the optimizer provides for data independence in a relational database management system and because independence is of such great value, relational products are likely to compete to a large extent on the basis of their optimizers' capabilities. Ideally, an optimizer chooses the best access path no matter how a user chooses to formulate a request. DB2's optimizer has not been perfected to the point where this is true in every case, but no other product's optimizer has reached that goal either. (A way to determine whether a database management system has a good optimizer is to find out whether it collects statistics for the optimizer's use. Then a simple test of the optimizer is to order the predicates of a data request in several ways and observe response times for each formulation. If the optimizer is effective, response times should not vary in most cases.) Researchers in a number of companies and universities are working on improving optimizers, and gains have and will continue to come steadily.

IBM guards information about how DB2's optimizer works quite closely. It is known, however, that DB2 grew out of earlier research, the System R project, about which much has been published. In this chapter, we assume that many of the principles upon which System R operated have been retained in DB2. Information on the System R project, IBM's few statements about DB2's optimizer, and information gleaned from EXPLAIN provide the basis for this chapter. Frank J. Ingrassia, considered by many to be the top DB2 optimizer expert outside of IBM, also contributed to this chapter.

Four Phases of Statement Processing

The optimizer contributes to statement processing in four steps:

1. *Parsing* checks that the statement is formulated correctly and breaks it down into the components upon which the optimizer bases its search strategy. DB2 checks to see that the statement's content is correct by verifying in the catalog tables that the referenced tables and columns exist.

Parsing analyzes an SQL statement much as a grammarian would analyze a natural-language sentence. The parsing process checks that the statement is syntactically and semantically correct and identifies the basic components that give the statement its meaning. The syntax check ensures that the statement exhibits the proper grammatical form for SQL. As a sentence must have a noun, verb, and period at the end, for example, an SQL statement must include certain keywords, commas between column names, and so on. The optimizer enforces these grammatical rules in the syntax check. In the semantic check, it sees that the statement's content is correct by verifying in the catalog tables that the referenced tables and columns exist.

The parsing process constructs a *parse tree* to identify the statement components that can be acted upon. An SQL statement parse tree is analogous to a parse tree a student might construct for a sentence. The tree branches down from the desired "RESULT" to the steps that must be performed to achieve it (Figure OP.2). In effect, a separate search must be performed for each nested subselect and each part of a union operation. In most cases, when a statement includes subselects, unions and in some cases outer joins, the optimizer constructs a separate section, called a *query block*, for each one.

Figure OP.2. Parse tree

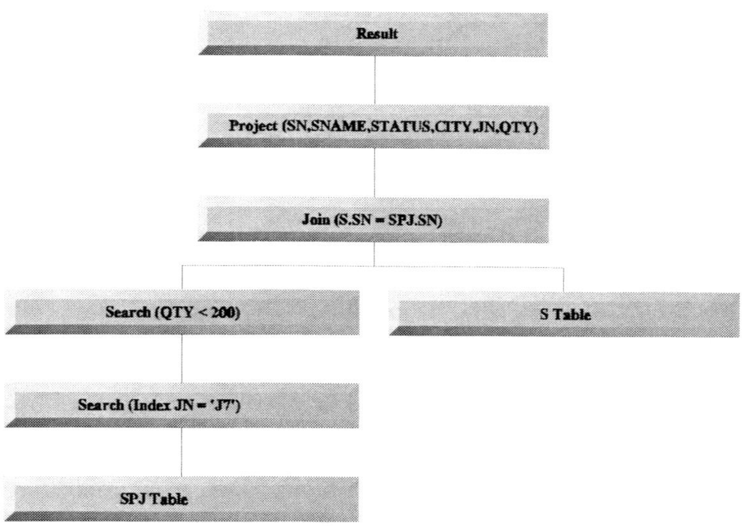

Optimization checks authorization, verifies information about the tables and columns from the catalog, verifies data type compatibility, and gets information about indexes and statistics about the data from the catalog tables. This catalog information is used for the task of selecting the best access path.

If the statement is referencing a view, views are replaced with the base table references. If the view references more than one table, additional tables are added to the FROM list. Predicates specified in the view definition are ANDed to the parse tree. If the view has subselects, additional blocks are added to the parse tree. The optimizer processes table expressions much like views.

The steps in *access path selection* include calculating filter factors, estimating I/O and CPU cost, determining the order in which predicates should be applied, estimate costs of materializing a table expression, view, and work files where required, and choosing the access path with the lowest timeron (cost estimate). All of these factors and more are discussed in this chapter.

Structure generation produces machine code calls needed to execute the access path: After calculating the estimated costs of the access path possibilities, the optimizer selects the low-cost estimate and builds from the access path tree the application plan or package for the search in Access Specification Language (ASL). It then generates from the ASL the machine-language calls needed to execute the plan or package. The generation process uses code structures--prewritten code for possible processes--and adds structures particular to the statement. Commonly used structures are stored in the relational database system (RDS) and data manager (DM) components in the database services address space, and are called from the plan or package.

The generated plan or package for static SQL is stored in the directory for retrieval at execution time. Plans are stored in the SCTR table in the SCT02 tablespace. Packages are stored in the table SPTR in the SPT01 tablespace. Plans and packages involving parallel access store both the parallel plan and the best sequential plan for possible fallback at execution time. Information about the plan or package is stored in the catalog tables as discussed in Chapter PE.

***Execution* of static SQL** requires checking if the user has authority to execute the plan or package. DB2 also checks to be sure the application plan or package is still valid, that is, that all necessary objects are still available. If the privilege to manipulate the objects in the plan or package has been revoked from the plan or package's owner or a dependent object has been dropped, DB2 attempts an automatic rebind. Reading the plan or package from the directory and its execution in the environmental descriptor management (EDM) pool are discussed in Chapter PE.

Cost Value: The Timeron

The cost of a search is a function of the number of I/O operations required to move pages from disk to main storage and the amount of processing that must be done to search those pages and manipulate the located rows. DB2 uses a number of formulas to determine the access path it will use. The following formula calculates a search cost estimate, called a *timeron:*

Cost = (I/O * W1) + (processor cost * W2)

The timeron is a unitless number that indicates only the search's relative cost. It can be found in the SQLCA in field SQERRD(4) as discussed in Chapter PD. QMF users see the timeron divided by 1024 of the chosen path prior to executing a search. The value of the QMF relative cost estimate is described in Chapter EX. (The divisor of 1024 is determined from the QMF governor exit DSQUEGV1).

W1 and W2 are weighting factors designed to give more or less importance to the I/O or processing costs. Those weighting factors are secret to IBM. Frank Ingrassia's research indicates that the timeron is presently weighted as follows:

Cost = (I/O * N) + (CPU / N * SU per second)

Service units (SU) per second is based on the speed of the processor used to bind plans and packages. The value is determined from the OS/390 relative performance power system resource manager (SRM). It is thought that N currently has a value of 10. Effectively, this means that 10 times the I/O, plus the raw CPU path length (instruction count) divided by 10 times the SU per second is used.

The use of the relative performance power of the processor used to bind plans and packages means that if SQL is bound on one CPU model and executed on another CPU model, the access path chosen may not be optimal for the execution CPU model. If a different CPU model is used in production and test, different access paths can result in the two environments. The DSNZPARM SPRMCPU variable in DSN6SPRC MACRO in DSN6SPRM CSECT can be modified to represent the microseconds of task or service request block (SRB) execution time per SU for the target CPU. The *MVS/ESA SPL Initialization and Tuning*, GC28-1828, manual contains a CPU/SU chart for various CPU models.

There are a number of factors considered by the optimizer that can vary between test and production DB2 subsystems including buffer pool and the RID pool sizes. Application data in test and production are frequently different, resulting in different statistics being seen by the optimizer as discussed in Section OP.9.

OP.2 STATISTICS

At the heart of the optimizer's work is its analysis of the catalog table statistics describing the target tables and the index availability. The optimizer gains efficiencies from these analyses in a number of ways. It uses the statistics in formula to estimate the number of qualifying rows, the number of I/O, and the CPU time. It also uses rules to refine the estimates. For one simple example, a predicate is not satisfied if either of the criteria combined with an AND operator is not satisfied. For the clause WHERE C1 = 10 AND C2 = 'ABC', it is more efficient to first search the column that narrows the search the most because it may not be necessary to perform the second search at all. If 10 is not found in C1, there is no need to look for 'ABC' in C2. The optimizer uses the catalog to check for any indexes on C1 and C2 and checks to see which index is likely to narrow the search the most, or whether multiple indexes should be used.

The statistics in the catalog describe a number of facts about each table being accessed: the number of rows, the number of pages that contain rows, the number of distinct values in columns, the highest and second highest values in columns, the lowest and second lowest values in columns, information on the distribution of data, the cluster ratio of each index and more. The statistics collected by the RUNSTATS utility and used by the optimizer are in Chapter RR, Section 4.

The optimizer uses distribution statistics collected by RUNSTATS for nonunique indexes and the first column of composite indexes. The statistics are used for local predicates with literals (not for join predicates with no local predicates on the join columns) and dynamic SQL. They are not used for static SQL with host variables because the value requested by the user at execution time is not known at bind time and can vary from one execution to another unless the bind option REOPT(VARS) is employed, causing a re-evaluation of the populated host variable at run time. Chapter PP discusses methods for managing a skewed distribution of values.

The distribution statistics are described in rows with a TYPE of 'F' in the SYSCOLDIST and SYSCOLDISTSTATS tables. There is a row for each of the frequently occurring values with a default of 10 rows for a table. COLVALUE contains the frequently occurring value in a single column index or the first column of a composite index by default. The number of frequently occurring values and the number of columns in a composite index can be specified to RUNSTATS as described in Chapter RR. Similar statistics are collected by partition for partitioned tablespaces and placed in SYSCOLDISTSTATS. Values not placed in COLVALUE are assumed to be uniformly distributed among the remaining percentage of rows.

Rows with a TYPE of 'C' describe the correlation statistic of composite indexes if requested with the RUNSTATS parameter KEYCARD. CARDF contains the number of distinct values for a column group. That is, if a composite index has five columns, there are three rows each with a CARDF containing the cardinality of columns:

```
1 and 2
1, 2, and 3
1, 2, 3, and 4
```

FULLKEYCARDF has the cardinality of columns 1, 2, 3, 4, and 5 (all columns in the composite index). These cardinalities can be used by the optimizer for equal predicates and IN (list) predicates on each of the column groups. The optimizer can also use the CARDF statistics that you iNSERT on non-leading columns (columns 2 and 3 for example). INSERT, UPDATE, and DELETE statements can be used on CARDF rows.

KEYCARD is not needed if the composite index has two or fewer columns because FULLKEYCARDF contains the cardinality of a two column composite index. A matching index scan can be used on all columns.

The Importance of Accurate Statistics: It is impossible to overestimate the importance of executing RUNSTATS after data is loaded and before SQL statements are bound. One company found statements requiring more than 20 minutes in CPU time before RUNSTATS had been executed on the tablespaces took only seconds after RUNSTATS was executed. If RUNSTATS has not been executed, the optimizer uses default values in the calculations as summarized in Chapter RR and assumes a uniform distribution of data for dynamic SQL and static SQL with literals as it does for static SQL with host variables. Similar default statistics are used for partitioned tablespaces. Obviously, the default statistics are not representative of the great majority of your tables.

OP.3 ESTIMATING I/O COSTS

The optimizer estimates the number of I/O operations required for many of the possible access paths by using statistics describing the table to be searched in a formula specific to the type of predicate coded in the SQL statement.

Filter Factors

An important element in estimating the number of I/O is the *filter factor* (FF), an estimate of the percentage of rows that will qualify as results. The higher the FF, indicating that a higher percentage of rows will be returned, the less likely the optimizer is to use an index. Much of the table will have to be read in any case. The smaller the FF, indicating that a relatively few rows must be found, the greater the likelihood that the optimizer considers an index efficient. The concept of the FF is similar to the notion of probability.

To determine the number of I/O needed, the FF is multiplied by the number of rows or pages in the table and adjusted using the cluster ratio of the index in most cases. Figure OP.3 lists some of the FF formulas used by the optimizer. If the predicate calls for a search based on an equality and there is an index on the column being searched--WHERE PN = 'P4', for example--the FF equals 1 divided by the cardinality of the column, stored as FIRSTKEYCARDF in the catalog table SYSIBM.SYSINDEXES. The term COLCARDF is used when describing the optimizer and its formula. In fact, COLCARDF, FIRSTKEYCARDF, or FULLKEYCARDF is used in the formula depending on whether there is an index on the column, the type of index and the specific predicate.

Figure OP.3. Basic filter factor formula

Predicate	Filter Factor Formula
WHERE C1 = :HV	1 / COLCARDF
WHERE C1 IS NULL	1 / COLCARDF
WHERE C1 IN (:HV,,:HV,...)	Number of values in list / COLCARDF
WHERE C1 >= Value	(HIGH2KEY - Value) / (HIGH2KEY - LOW2KEY)
WHERE C1 > Value	same as above
WHERE C1 <= Value	(Value - LOW2KEY) / (HIGH2KEY - LOW2KEY)
WHERE C1 < Value	same as above
WHERE C1 BETWEEN V1 AND V2	(High V - Low V) / (HIGH2KEY - LOW2KEY)

```
:HV   = host variable or literal value
Value = V = literal value
```

COLCARDF is used in the basic FF formula. However, FIRSTKEYCARDF, FULLKEYCARDF, CARDF or COLCARDF is used by optimizer if matching against an indexed column and depending on the number of columns matched, type of index, and predicates.

If RUNSTATS has not been executed, the following values are used:

- 25 = COLCARDF = FIRSTKEYCARDF = FULLKEYCARDF
- 0.04 = 1 / 25 FF for an equal predicate
- 0.33 = for range predicates (>, >=, <, <=) other than BETWEEN and LIKE
- 0.10 = BETWEEN and LIKE predicates

Default Filter Factors: If RUNSTATS has not been executed, the optimizer uses a default FF of 1/25 for equal predicates. For range searches with host variables--those using the BETWEEN operator, for example--the default FFs are summarized in Figure OP.4. DB2 adjusts the FF formula as the COLCARDF increases using a step function so that the FF decreases incrementally for larger table sizes. Because in general the lower the FF, the greater the likelihood the optimizer will choose an index, decreasing the default value as the cardinality and table size increases improves the chances of the optimizer's choosing to use an index over a tablespace scan for larger tables.

Figure OP.4. Default filter factors for BETWEEN, LIKE, and range predicates

COLCARDF	BETWEEN, LIKE	>,>=,<,<=
>=100,000,000	3/100,000	1/10,000
>= 10,000,000	1/ 10,000	1/ 3,000
>= 1,000,000	3/ 10,000	1/ 1,000
>= 100,000	1/ 1,000	1/ 300
>= 10,000	3/ 1,000	1/ 100
>= 1,000	1/ 100	1/ 30
>= 100	3/ 100	1/ 10
< 100	1/ 10	1/ 3
-1	1/ 10	1/ 3

Factoring in the Cluster Ratio

After the FFs have been determined using the formula like those in Figure OP.3 or the defaults for predicates in Figure OP.4, they are multiplied by the number of rows or the number of pages in the table based on the cluster ratio in most cases. Here is an example: for a predicate WHERE CITY = 'Dallas' assuming an index on CITY with a cardinality of 20 and 10,000 rows on 200 pages. The FF is 1/COLCARDF (1/20); that is, 5 percent of the rows are estimated to qualify.

Cluster ratio of 0: If the cluster ratio is zero (or less than 5 percent) a good estimate of the number of I/Os is the FF multiplied by the number of rows in the table. For the example above, the estimated number of I/Os is 500. However, because list prefetch will most likely be used with a low cardinality of 20, the number of pages read will most likely be reduced to the 200 pages occupied by the table. The optimizer assumes that each row will be found on a separate page for indexes with a low cluster ratio. Therefore, the I/O can be estimated at one data page per row required in the answer set. Prefetch can be used in the example in all cases and is not factored into the calculations for ease of explanation. Sequential prefetch will be used on data retrieved via indexes that have a cluster ratio of 80 percent or more, while list prefetch may be employed on data pages via index access with a cluster ratio less than 80 percent.

Cluster ratio of 100: If the cluster ratio is 100 percent, then all of the rows for Dallas are clustered together on the data pages. This means that the FF can be multiple times the number of pages in the table--0.05 * 200--giving an estimate of 10 I/Os.

Cluster ratio of 80: The cluster ratio is somewhere between 0 and 100 percent in most cases. Let's assume that the cluster ratio is 80 percent. This means that 80 percent of the rows are clustered together on the data pages and 20 percent are not. This can be factored into the formula by multiplying 80 percent by the 10 I/Os that will be required if the cluster ratio is 100 percent and adding 20 percent multiplied by the 200 I/O that will be required if there is no clustering. This gives a more accurate estimate of 48 I/Os (0.80 * 10 + 0.20 * 200).

If the COLCARDF is 3 or less, it is unlikely that an index will be used to narrow the search.

Frank Ingrassia has done a great deal of research on how the optimizer estimates I/O for a matching index scan and tablespace scan.

Matching index scans: Ingrassia's optimizer research offers the following formulas for matching index scan I/O:

```
Clustered indexes = NLEVD + (NLEAF * FF) + (NPAGES * FF) / 5
* CF

Random indexes* = NLEVD + (NLEAF * FF) + (CARD * FF) / 5 * CF

where NLEVD = MAX(NLEVELS - 2, 0)
and   CF    = cluster ratio factor or a penalty applied to
unclustered data. For example, 80 percent cluster ratio would
have a CF of 1.2 where 20 percent of the data is unclustered.

*This suggests the assumption on random indexes that each row
is found on another page.
```

Tablespace scans: Ingrassia states that the optimizers estimated I/O count for tablespace scans varies by tablespace type (segmented versus nonsegmented) and whether the access is sequential or parallel. In recent releases, a divisor of 5 has been employed to normalize the I/O page count from various sequential and list prefetches, as well as synchronous read I/O. This means that the optimizer's relative cost estimate (timeron) does not necessarily reflect the real world I/O counts anticipated, for nonsegmented tablespace scans, and partitioned tablespace scans not accessed in parallel:

```
I/O = NACTIVE / 5
```

for segmented tablespaces and parallel partitioned access:

```
I/O = NPAGES / 5
```

As an example, suppose a 4 partition tablespace is scanned with an access degree of 2, and the catalog tables have NACTIVE of 25,900, NPAGES of 25,000, and each partition's NPAGES of 6,250. The parallel tablespace scan of 2 partitions would be estimated by the optimizer as:

```
I/O = 12,500 / 5 = 2500
```

Use of Frequency Statistics

If the user requests one of the frequently occurring values in a column and the value is known during access path selection, a very good estimate of the percentage of rows required can be determined from SYSCOLDIST or SYSCOLDISTSTATS as identified by RUNSTATS. For example, assume that RUNSTATS has identified the 10 most frequently occurring cities and their frequency of occurrence shown as a non-uniform distribution of data.

Figure OP.5 is a graphic to demonstrate the difference between a non-uniform and uniform distribution of data. The dark shaded area represented a non-uniform or skewed distribution of data. The light shaded area represents a uniform or flat distribution of data.

Figure OP.5. Non-uniform and uniform distribution of data

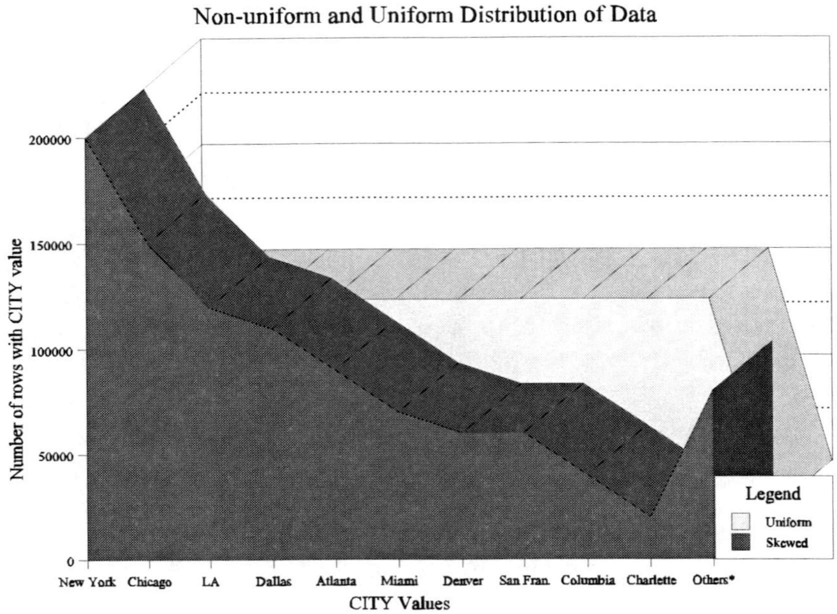

A predicate of CITY IN ('Columbia', 'Charlotte') means that the user requires all rows that have a city of Columbia or Charlotte. SYSCOLDIST indicates that 4 percent of the rows are for Columbia and 2 percent of the rows are for Charlotte. A good estimate for the percentage of rows required is 6 percent (4 + 2 percent). There were 6 percent of the rows in Columbia and Charlotte when RUNSTATS was executed.

The percentage of rows accounted for in SYSCOLDIST is used in estimating the percentage of rows that will qualify for values not in SYSCOLDIST. Assume that the cardinality of the index on CITY is 19 and there are 10,000 rows in the table. The total percentage of rows accounted for in SYSCOLDIST is the sum of the percentages which is 92 for the 10 cities. That leaves 8 percent of the suppliers in 9 (19 - 10) cities with about 89 (0.08 * 10,000) / 9) suppliers in each city. Assuming a uniform distribution of the 89 suppliers on the data pages, 3 (89/32) is a good estimate for the number of I/Os to the data pages using prefetch for a city that is not one of the 10 most frequently occurring cities. The use of sequential prefetch and list prefetch are discussed in Chapters BP and PP.

Column Correlation in a Composite Index

The optimizer is aware that columns in a composite index are correlated if the parameter KEYCARD is specified to RUNSTATS. Otherwise, the optimizer assumes that the distribution of values in columns of a composite index are statistically independent--that the distribution of values in one column is unrelated to the distribution of values in another column. That is, the columns are not correlated. Very often this is not the case. For example, the values in columns for city, state, and zip code are correlated as are the values for store ID, department ID, and location.

If given a value in a column (CITY, for example), the value in another column (STATE) is known, the columns are interdependent or perfectly correlated. If given a city of Chicago, you know that the state is Illinois, the columns are correlated (Figure OP.6). If Chicago can be any state in the STATE column, the columns are independent or there is no correlation.

Figure OP.6. Correlated and uncorrelated columns

a) Correlated
3 Distinct pairs

CITY	STATE
Chicago	IL
Dallas	TX
San Jose	CA

b) Uncorrelated
9 Distinct pairs

CITY	STATE
Chicago	IL
Chicago	TX
Chicago	CA
Dallas	IL
Dallas	TX
Dallas	CA
San Jose	IL
San Jose	TX
San Jose	CA

Actually, a two column composite index poses no problem to the optimizer because FULLKEYCARDF contains the number of distinct values in the two columns. However, if there are more than two columns in a composite index and they are correlated (city, state, and zip code, for example), more information is needed. This additional information is provided in CARDF of SYSCOLDIST and SYSCOLDISTSTATS with a TYPE of 'C'.

FF for Correlated and Non-Correlated Columns

Let's consider the different FF calculations with and without column correlation statistics for locating all of the suppliers in Dallas, TX. Assume that there is a composite index on city, state, and zip code. The user provides a value for city and state, but not zip code like:

```
SELECT SN, SNAME, CITY, STATE
FROM   S
WHERE  CITY  = 'Dallas'
AND    STATE = 'TX';
```

If city and state are perfectly correlated, we see that there are 3 distinct pairs of cities and states, therefore, CARDF is 3 and the FF is 0.33 (1 / 3 distinct city and state pairs). However, if city and state are not correlated the FF is 0.11 calculated as:

```
City  FF = 0.33 = 1/3 (1 / COLCARDF)
State FF = 0.33 = 1/3 (1 / COLCARDF)
```

The FFs are combined according to the ANDed predicates:

```
FF = 0.11 = 0.33 * 0.33
```

If the columns are correlated as in this case, the FF of 0.11 is too low. The index on city and state can be chosen when it should not be chosen. A tablespace scan or an index on another column can be a better access path. In addition, a less than optimal join method can be chosen or the chosen outer table can be less than optimal.

How to Determine if Columns are Correlated

Whether columns are correlated can be determined by looking at the number of distinct values in the columns that makeup the composite index. The cardinality of each column in a composite index is in the column COLCARDF of SYSCOLUMNS if requested of RUNSTATS using the TABLE and optionally the COLUMN parameters as discussed in Chapter RR. Otherwise, the cardinality of each column can be determined by counting the number of distinct values in a column. For example, the cardinality of the CITY and STATE columns can be determine like:

```
SELECT COUNT (DISTINCT CITY)
FROM   S;

SELECT COUNT (DISTINCT STATE)
FROM   S;
```

Once you have the cardinality of each column in the composite index, multiply the cardinalities. There are 3 distinct cities and 3 distinct states. The product of the cardinalities is 9.

We must also determine the number of distinct pairs of values in the CITY and STATE columns. This can be done with the statement:

```
SELECT COUNT (*) AS N_DISTINCT_PAIRS
FROM  (SELECT DISTINCT CITY, STATE
       FROM   S) AS DISTINCT_PAIRS;
```

If the number of distinct pairs is approximately equal to the product of the number of distinct values in each column, the columns are uncorrelated or independent of each other. For example, if the number of distinct pairs is 9 and the product of the cardinalities is 9, the columns are not correlated. It is not necessary to collect correlation statistics.

If the number of distinct pairs is less than the product of the cardinalities, the columns have some correlation. As the number of distinct pairs decreases compared to the product of the cardinalities of each individual column, the higher the correlation of the columns and the more likely that a less than optimal access path will be chosen. In this case, it is highly advisable to collect correlation statistics by specifying the parameter KEYCARD to RUNSTATS.

If the user asks for the state where Chicago is located, one row provides the answer if columns are perfectly correlated. If the user asks the same question and the columns are not correlated, 3 rows must be retrieved to provide the answer. Obviously, whether 1 or 3 rows qualify does not significantly affect performance. However, your tables are likely to be much larger than the example with a larger number of qualifying rows.

If there are three or more correlated columns in a composite index and the columns are correlated, the optimizer will be able to determine a good access path more accurately if you have RUNSTATS collect the needed statistics by specifying the parameter KEYCARD. An alternative is to use (... OR 0=1) to disallow the use of an undesirable index.

Other Factors Influencing the I/O Estimate

OPTIMIZE FOR *n* ROWS: If the OPTIMIZE FOR *n* ROWS clause is used, the result of the formulas is compared to the value specified for *n*. If *n* is less than the estimated number of rows, the optimizer determines the best access path for *n* rows in most cases. Calculating the number of pages that will contain that number of rows is straightforward (floor (page size / row length) * *n*). However, it is still necessary to factor in the cluster ratio, possible use of multiple indexes, whether list prefetch with a single index should be used, etc.

Multiple-Index Access: The optimizer factors in the use of multiple indexes for AND and OR conditions, the cost of sorting the record identifiers (RIDs), and performing an intersection or union of the RIDs followed by list prefetch in its formula to determine a good access path. The optimizer considers using list prefetch with a single index to avoid reading a page multiple times because of a low index cardinality or a skewed distribution of values in a column with a low cluster ratio index.

Non-Matching Index Scan: The number of leaf pages to be read in a non-matching index scan can be determined from SYSINDEXES.NLEAF. The partition statistics are used for partitioned indexes and tablespaces.

Tablespace Scan: The optimizer estimates the number of pages to be scanned based on the catalog values, SYSTABLES.NPAGES for segmented tablespaces, and SYSTABLESPACE.NACTIVEF for nonsegmented tablespaces. For segmented tablespaces, the space map pages are used to pull off just those data pages that contain rows of the table being scanned. This avoids scanning pages without rows for the table--such as pages with only deleted rows, free pages, or pages with rows from other tables in the case of nonsegmented tablespaces.

Partition Scan: The number of data pages to be read in a partition can be determined from SYSTABSTATS.NPAGES.

Page Size: 4, 8, 16, and 32 KB page sizes are considered by the optimizer in determining the access path.

Combining Filter Factors According to Boolean Operators

The calculated FFs are combined according to the Boolean operators in the WHERE clause. Consider a WHERE clause with two predicates and the FFs noted after each predicate:

```
WHERE C1 = 10   -- FF = 0.05
AND   C2 = 90   -- FF = 0.20
```

It is estimated that 5 percent of the rows will have a value of 10 in C1 and 20 percent of the rows will have a value of 90 in C2. The WHERE clause requires that a row have both a value of 10 and 90 in columns C1 and C2. It is less likely that a row will meet both conditions than either one of the conditions taken individually. This is taken into account by multiplying the two FFs for each of the predicates. Figure OP.7 shows the formula as FF(P1) * FF(P2) for a WHERE clause with two predicates (P1 and P2).

Figure OP.7. Formula to combine filter factors according to Boolean factors

WHERE Clause	Formula
WHERE P1 AND P2	FF(P1) * FF(P2)
WHERE P1 OR P2	FF(P1) + FF(P2) - (FF(P1) * FF(P2))
WHERE NOT P1	1 - FF(P1)
WHERE C1 IN Subselect	Expected cardinality of subselect result divided by product of cardinalities of all relations in the subselect from list

P1 = Predicate expression
P2 = Predicate expression

It is unlikely that the optimizer will choose to use a matching index scan for satisfying ORed range predicates on the same column unless multiple index ORing is selected as discussed in Chapter PP. An example of estimating the number of I/O will show why this is true. We will assume that the SN column has a cardinality of less than 100 for the following statement using host variables.

```
SELECT  SN, SNAME
FROM    S
WHERE   SN <= :SN1
OR      SN >= :SN2;
```

Notice in Figure OP.4 that the default FF for greater than and less than predicates when using host variables is 33 percent (1/3). The use of the formula for ORed predicates in Figure OP.7 results in an estimate that 55 percent (0.33 + 0.33 - 0.33 * 0.33) of the rows will qualify. A tablespace scan is best for processing 55 percent of the rows. The ORed predicate formula tends to cause the estimated number of rows that qualify to increase, thus increasing the likelihood of using a tablespace scan or a non-matching index scan. If the cardinality of an index on SN is high, a lower percentage of rows will be estimated based on the table of default FFs in Figure OP.4. For example, if the SN index cardinality is one million, the default FF is 0.1 percent (1/1000). Based on the ORed predicate formula, 0.2 percent of the rows are estimated to qualify, which makes the use of a matching index scan likely.

I/O Time Estimate

The elapsed time and response time are usually determined by the I/O time. The CPU time and I/O time overlap for most SELECT statements and the elapsed time is usually the greater of the two times. The optimizer can estimate the I/O time based on its decision as to how to read a page and the number of milliseconds required to read a page based on the DASD device. Figure OP.8 shows rough estimates of the number of milliseconds (ms) to read a page based on the type of read and the DASD device used.

Figure OP.8. Rule-of-thumb estimates for I/O time

Type of I/O and DASD Device	Time (ms)
Random page read	
3380	20.0
3390	16.0
List prefetch per page	
3380	4.0
3390	3
Sequential prefetch per page	
3380	2.2
3390	2
Random page write	
(Sorts RIDs before write)	
3380	4.0
3390	3.0
Work file prefetch read	
3380	4.0
3390	3.0
Work file write	
3380	2.2
3390	1.7

A matching index scan incurs random reads of index and data pages assuming that the pages required are not in the buffer pool. Indeed, the optimizer assumes that the required pages will not be found in the buffer pool with the exception of the root page of an index. The list prefetch I/O time estimate is for reading a data page after access to the leaf pages and RID processing as discussed in Chapter PP. The sequential prefetch I/O time estimate is used for tablespace and non-matching index scans as discussed in Chapter BP. Estimating I/O and processor time is discussed in Chapter PL.

Notice that the list prefetch I/O time is almost double that of the sequential prefetch I/O time. This is because it is likely that the pages read with list prefetch will not be contiguous as are the pages read with sequential prefetch. However, the pages read with list prefetch contain qualifying rows according to the index used to obtain the RIDs. Pages read with sequential prefetch may or may not have qualifying rows.

The random page write I/O time estimate is the same as list prefetch because the RIDs are sorted before the pages are written to reduce seek time, which is similar to reading pages with list prefetch. The work file prefetch read I/O time estimate is the same as list prefetch. Perhaps this is to allow for additional seek time when work files to be merged are on the same DASD device. The work file write I/O time estimate is the same as sequential prefetch.

List prefetch reads and random (asynchronous) writes are limited to a 150 page range to avoid long I/O chains that span more than 10 cylinders for a single I/O request.

Examples of Estimating I/O Time

A few examples of estimating I/O time will be given, assuming the use of 3390 DASD.

A matching index scan with access to a data page can be done in 48 ms (16 ms * (1 nonleaf page + 1 leaf page + 1 data page) assuming a three level index structure with the root page in the buffer pool.

A non-matching index scan without data reference of 4,000 leaf pages can be done in 6,800 ms (1.7 ms * 4,000 leaf pages) using sequential prefetch.

A tablespace scan of 30,000 data pages can be done in 51,000 ms (1.7 ms * 30,000 data pages) using sequential prefetch.

List prefetch of 1,500 data pages can be done in 4,500 ms (3.00 ms * 1,500) after access to the index pages and processing the RIDs.

OP.4 PROCESSING COSTS

The CPU costs are based on the number of I/O, getpages, predicates applied, number of columns selected, your choice of locking parameters, sort costs, compression costs, and more. This section will give cost estimates normalized to an IBM 3090-180J computer with one processor which is rated at 22.2 million instructions per second (MIPS). If you are using a 511 based computer, the estimates should be divided results 1.25. If you are using a 711 based computer, the estimates should be divided results 3.00.

There are a number of reasons that the optimizer attempts to minimize I/O. We have seen that I/O time frequently determines the elapsed time and the response time. It also has a significant effect on CPU time, about 0.33 ms per I/O plus the CPU time for DM to issue a getpage of 0.11 ms.

Data Manager and Relational Data System Cost Estimates

DM CPU Cost Component: CPU time is required to evaluate predicates by DM, about 0.0033 ms per predicate (not including a matching index scan). The optimizer factors in the CPU time for rows scanned by DM using a matching index scan at 0.0061 ms plus the time to apply predicates per row. Qualifying columns must be passed one at a time from DM to RDS at a cost of 0.0044 ms per column.

RDS CPU Cost Component: RDS then processes the rows at a cost of 0.06 ms plus 0.0015 ms times the number of columns per row. This cost is reduced by using stage 1 predicates as discussed in Chapter PP. The cost of passing the rows to the application program is about 0.12 ms plus 0.0015 ms times the number of columns per row. Notice that the number of columns selected by the application program is a multiplier in several components of the formula. This emphasizes the importance of the guidelines in Chapter PP that only the required columns should be select and that SELECT * should be avoided. Figure OP.9 summarizes the CPU cost factors.

Figure OP.9. DM and RDS CPU cost factors

- Number of physical I/Os initiated by buffer manager at 0.33 ms per I/O.
- Getpages issued by DM at 0.11 ms per getpage.
- Predicates applied by DM (not including matching index scan) at 0.0033 ms per predicate.
- Rows scanned by DM using a matching index scan at 0.0061 ms + time to apply predicates per row.
- Columns passed from DM to RDS at 0.0044 ms per column.
- Rows processed by RDS from a matching index scan at 0.06 + (0.0015 * N of columns) ms per row.
- Rows fetched by program at 0.12 + (0.0015 * N of columns) ms per row.

Combining the DM and RDS Cost Components: The cost factors are combined depending on the specific SQL statement. For example, consider a singleton SELECT with a matching index scan like:

```
SELECT SN, SNAME, STATUS, CITY
FROM   S
WHERE  SN = 'S4';
```

Figure OP.10 summarizes the cost components and the formula used to estimate the CPU time for a singleton SELECT statement.

Figure OP.10. DM and RDS cost components for a singleton select

Description	Formula
Page overhead	0.11 * NP
CPU time for I/O	+ 0.33 * NIO
Fixed overhead	+ 0.14
Data Manager component	+ (NDMS * (0.0061+x+(0.0033 * NSAN)))
RDS component	+ (NQ * (0.06+(0.0015 * NC)))
API fetch component	+ (1 * (0.12+(0.0015 * NC)))

```
NDMS is the number of rows scanned by Data Manager
 NSAN is the number of search arguments evaluated
 NQ is the number of qualifying rows
 NC is the number of columns fetched
```

Additional Cost Estimates

CPU Cost Estimate for a Sort: If an index cannot be used to avoid a sort as discussed in Chapter PP, the optimizer estimates the sort costs as 2 ms for initialization and terminate of the sort plus 0.04 ms times the number of rows plus 0.22 ms times the number of sort pages. If rows to be sorted cannot fit in the sort pool, logical work files must be written to the work tablespaces in the work database DSNDB07. The work files must be merged at a cost of about 0.01 ms times the number of rows plus 0.22 ms times the number of sort pages for each merge pass, depending on the size of the sort pool.

CPU Cost Estimate for Locking: CPU time is estimated for row or page locking and the choice of isolation level is factored into the costs. For example, row locking increases the CPU time. The uncommited read isolation level eliminates the need for locks and decreases the CPU costs.

Character Conversion: If character conversion is required, CPU must be estimated for this as well.

Data Compression CPU Cost Estimate

If the DB2 data compression is used on a tablespace, the costs of compression and decompression must be estimated by the optimizer.

DB2 Data Compression: DB2 applies the ESA compression algorithm to an entire row irrespective of the beginning and end of columns as discussed in Chapter CD. Therefore, the CPU cost for compression and decompression is estimated per byte. Compression can be done with software alone or with a hardware assist if the computer has the required hardware. There is a significant savings in the CPU costs when using hardware compression as shown in the Figure OP.11 The figure shows the average per-byte CPU time in milliseconds with a 50 percent compression ratio. The CPU cost estimates are normalized to a 3090-180J processor model.

Figure OP.11. CPU cost estimate per byte for DB2 data compression

Type	Compress 1 Row	Decompress 1 Row	Compress Multiple Rows	Decompress Multiple Rows
Hardware	0.00072	0.00017	0.00036	0.00008
Software	0.00278	0.00050	0.00139	0.00025

The costs for decompression are considerably lower than those for compression. This is because the algorithm has been refined to minimize the costs of decompression which occurs more frequently than compression. Most application systems select rows more frequently than they iNSERT, update, and delete rows. Indeed the general 80/20 guidelines applies here. Typically, rows are selected 80 percent of the time and changed 20 percent of the time. Also notice that the CPU time is less to compress and decompress when multiple rows are compressed compared to a single row. This suggests that there is an initialization cost to compression and decompression.

The optimizer factors in the row length and the percentage of rows compressed in its estimate of CPU time. The PCTROWCOMP column of the SYSTABLES and SYSTABSTATS catalog tables contains the information about the percentage of rows compressed in the table or partition. PCTROWCOMP is particularly important for decompression of rows.

A high value for PCTROWCOMP means a higher CPU cost per row estimate when reading data. This tends to encourage a matching index scan over a tablespace scan. The cost estimate for index only processing is not affected by compression because ESA compression is not used on the index pages. If the PCTROWCOMP is low, or if there is no compression, the CPU cost per row is lower, thus a tablespace scan and non-matching index scan with reference to the data pages is more likely.

EDITPROC Compression: The optimizer uses a fixed CPU costs when EDITPROC compression is used. There are a number of software products available that can be used for EDITPROC compression. The optimizer has no way of knowing the details of the compression algorithm used. Therefore, it factors in a fixed CPU cost which is typically lower then reality and may not result in an optimal access path.

Capacity Planning

Capacity planning requires an estimate of the CPU time and the I/O operations required. Before these estimates can be made it is necessary to have a great deal of information on how the data will be processed and the actual SQL that will be used. Much also depends on the processor model and DASD device used, the workload on the system, the size of the buffer pools, and the size of the tables. We have touched on a few formula that are used in capacity planning. More detailed information is available from the *Capacity Planning for DB2 Applications* (GG24-3512) and *DB2 V2.3 Nondistributed Performance Topics* (GG24-3823) manuals.

Figure OP.12 contains a gross estimate of number of instructions required to execute an SQL statement. Of course, the actual number of instructions depends on the chosen access path, index usage, number of columns selected, number of predicates, and more.

Figure OP.12. Number of instructions to execute SQL statements

Statement Type	Estimate of Number of Instructions
Simple fetch	3,500 to 9,000
Singleton select	12,000 to 40,000
Update/delete/iNSERT	40,000 to 90,000

The CPU estimate can be based on the MIPS (Million Instructions Per Second) rating of your computer.

Several software products are available for estimating the I/O and CPU costs. For instance, IMSI offers the Query Costing Facility (QCF ®) which can provide instantaneous read-world costs for any DB2 OS/390 query. QCF operates under TSO and batch, as a QMF governor intercept and as a stored procedure, allowing costing prior to execution from virtually any where in the DB2 environment. IBM provides DB2 Estimator with an order of DB2 that operates on a work station. The software products avoid the time required to do the calculations or to develop a program to perform the calculations. But in any case a great deal of information about the application system processing is required and the estimates are only as good as the estimate of the processing anticipated.

OP.5 TRANSFORMATION OF SQL

The optimizer transforms some SQL statements, recasting them to gain efficiencies. Suppose you write a WHERE clause like this:

```
WHERE SPJ.PN  =  P.PN
AND   P.PN    =  'P3'
```

If P3 is required from the P table, then P3 must also be required from the SPJ table based on the join predicate, SPJ.PN = P.PN. The optimizer adds the predicate AND SPJ.PN = 'P3' so that it can determine if narrowing the search on SPJ before the join will result in a more efficient access path. This is referred to as predicate transitive closure as discussed in Chapter JP. It applies for up to and including a 9-way inner join (not outer joins). If the additional predicate does not provide a good access path, it is not included in the plan or package, thus avoiding any added CPU time at execution time. If you, on the other hand, had coded the additional predicate, it will be evaluated at execution time.

The many cases where the optimizer can transform SQL to achieve improved performance are discussed in the chapters on the relevant topic, including Chapters JP, ST, PP, and EX. The transformations will occur only if the same results will be achieved and under the conditions discussed previously in the chapters. A number of the cases are summarized in Figure OP.13.

Figure OP.13. Cases where SQL can be transformed to achieve a better access path

- Local predicates (except IN (list) and LIKE) specified on one join table are added for the other join table such as:

```
WHERE TA.C1   = TB.C10
AND   TA.C1   > 10
AND   TB.C10  > 10 -- Added automatically by optimizer
```

- All join combinations are evaluated even though only some are coded such as:

```
WHERE TA.C1    = TB.C10
AND   TB.C10   = TC.C100
AND   TC.C100  = TA.C1 -- Added automatically by optimizer
```

- Outer joins can be transformed to allow for application of local predicates before join processing as discussed in Chapter JP

- Predicates can be derived on the inner table of a merge join to narrow the search if a sort is required on the outer table.

- IN, =ALL, =ANY, and =SOME subselect can be transformed to a join <u>or</u>
    - Use of in-memory sparse index and binary search on inner select results <u>or</u>
    - If few rows qualify in subselect, can transform subselect to an IN (list).

- Subselect preceded with a simple operator is evaluated as a simple predicate.

- Subselect preceded with a range predicate on ANY, SOME, ALL can be reduced to a single value and evaluated as a simple predicate.

- If the optimizer estimates that many rows qualify in the inner table, it can transform NOT IN non-correlated subselect to NOT EXISTS.

- Simple ORed predicates are converted to IN (list) when evaluating the use of a single index:

```
WHERE TA.C1  = 10
```

```
OR     TA.C1 = 30
```

Transformed to:

```
WHERE TA.C1 IN (10, 30)
```

- WHERE C1 IN ('S4') is treated as WHERE C1 = 'S4'

- >= AND <= predicates converted to BETWEEN

```
WHERE   C1 >= 10
AND     C1 <= 30
```

Transformed to:

```
WHERE C1 BETWEEN 10 AND 30
```

- NOT condition can be transformed to a positive expression.

- Columns can be re-ordered to avoid a sort.

- Transformation of ANDed and ORed predicates to allow for a matching index scan on an additional column of a composite index and multiple index processing on a composite index.

After the optimizer transforms the coded SQL, it then creates a tree of alternate access paths using these more efficient formulations. With the tree complete, the optimizer has the statement's information in the form it needs to develop an access path to satisfy the statement's request.

OP.6 CHOOSING THE ACCESS PATH

The optimizer processes all SQL data manipulation statements similarly with the exception of the INSERT statement. An INSERT always uses the clustering index to determine where a row is to be inserted. If a clustering index is not explicitly defined, DB2 uses the first index on the chain of indexes in the Database Descriptor (DBD). If no index exists, the iNSERT is positioned at the current cursor location or the point of the last iNSERT. UPDATE statements do require the application of a few additional rules compared to SELECT and DELETE statements to avoid missing rows or a looping condition as discussed in Chapter IU.

Before building a tree for each alternative access path, the optimizer eliminates obviously expensive paths, such as most of those that require formation of Cartesian products. The optimizer then estimates the costs of various access paths. The number of possible paths can be large.

Consider a statement requiring a join of three tables, each with four access paths that might satisfy the request (a path using any of three indexes or a tablespace scan). The four access paths could be used in 64 different ways (4 * 4 * 4). The joins might be performed in any one of six orders--Table A with Table B and the results with Table C, Table A with Table C and the results with Table B, and so on (3 * 2 * 1). Then three types of joins--nested loop, merge, or hybrid join--must be considered for each of the two join pairs (3 * 2). In this case, there are 3,456 possible paths--(4 * 4 * 4) * (3 * 2 * 1) * (3 ** 2). Efficient optimization depends on the ability to recognize and eliminate early those access paths certain to be poor performers. The DB2 optimizer will discard quickly a good many of these 3,456 possibilities and analyze closely only some of them.

Unique Indexes are Favored

If a particularly good access path is discovered, the optimizer discontinues the evaluation of alternative paths. For example, predicates on columns with a unique composite index on SN, PN, and JN is the best access path for:

```
SELECT SN, PN, JN, QTY
FROM   SPJ
WHERE  SN  = 'S4'
AND    PN  = 'P6'
AND    JN  = 'J3'
AND    QTY = 300;
```

An index on QTY is not considered. A single matching index scan can be done on the unique index. It is considered the best matching index scan. If the index cardinality is equal to the table cardinality, it was a unique index at the time that RUNSTATS was executed and it is favored by the optimizer as a unique index.

There is an exception. If there is a nonunique index that provides for index only processing, it can be chosen by the optimizer to avoid access to the data pages. For example, if there is a nonunique index on SN, PN, JN, and QTY, it likely to be chosen over the unique index on SN, PN, and JN to avoid access to the data pages to retrieve the QTY values.

Boolean Term Predicates

An objective of the optimizer is to determine which predicate should be evaluated first at execution time. If a predicate disqualifies a row, additional predicates need not be evaluated. A Boolean term predicate (simple or compound) is one where if the predicate is evaluated false, the entire WHERE clause is false. An example illustrates the point:

```
SELECT C1, C2, C3, C4, C5
FROM   TA
WHERE  C1 = 10
AND   (C2 = 20
OR     C3 = 30);
```

The column C1 must have a value of 10 to qualify a row. If 10 is not in C1, the row does not qualify, and there is no need to test additional conditions and use additional CPU time. If single index processing is chosen, an index on C1 is used first. It is considered a Boolean term predicate and a best matching predicate. Boolean terms are used for single index matching scans as well as for view and table expression materialization.

Constraint Checking

In determining access paths, the optimizer does not consider any processing that may be necessary for table check constraints and referential integrity constraint checking as discussed in Chapter CT. No code is added to a plan or package for constraint checking. DM gets information about the constraints from the DBD and checks the constraints directly without having to pass data to RDS and on the host program.

Referential integrity checking is done with index only processing (assuming indexes have been created). This and the fact that the path length is shorter means that DB2-enforced referential integrity usually outperforms application-enforced integrity.

Techniques Used at Execution Time

There are a number of techniques used by DB2 at execution time without having to be considered by the optimizer. These techniques are discussed in the chapters on the relevant topic including Chapters IU, BP, and ST. The techniques are summarized in Figure OP.14.

Figure OP.14. Techniques Used at Execution Time

- ♦ Index lookaside is used to minimize the number of matching index scans.
- ♦ Sequential detection is used to activate and deactivate dynamic prefetch if sequential or list prefetch is not chosen by the optimizer.
- ♦ An in-memory table can be used to remember values from the outer select that have already been evaluated against the inner select for correlated subselects with simple operators, EXISTS, and NOT EXISTS subselects.
- ♦ An in-memory sparse index is built for the result of subselects that can return many rows (subselects preceded by IN, =ANY, =SOME, =ALL). It is used to minimize the scan processing of the subselect results.
- ♦ The degree of parallelism is adjusted based on the content of host variables at execution time.

Optimizer Decisions can be Overridden

Thresholds are applied at bind time to determine if a particular access path will result in good performance depending on the resources made available to DB2. If the resources are already used at execution time, further thresholds are applied to avoid using an access path that requires resources that are already in use. Figure OP.15 summarizes the thresholds used at execution to override the optimizer's decision because there are insufficient resources available.

Figure OP.15. Thresholds applied at execution time

- ♦ If the virtual pool VPSEQT threshold for which a tablespace or index is assigned is set to 0, all types of prefetch are disallowed at execution time.
- ♦ If less than 10 percent of the buffer pool pages are stealable, sequential prefetch is not used as requested by the optimizer.
- ♦ If insufficient space is available in the buffer pool (most of the buffers allowed for parallelism are in use), parallel processing is not used, the degree of parallelism can be reduced, or the prefetch quantity is reduced.
- ♦ If OS/390 and more than one processor are not available, CPU and sysplex parallelism will not be used. I/O parallelism can be used.

- If less than 32 RIDs qualify using some but not all ANDed predicates, additional indexes specified for usage by the optimizer are not used.
- If more than 25 percent of the RIDs qualify using ORed predicates, the RIDs are discarded and a tablespace scan using sequential prefetch rather than the list prefetch requested by the optimizer is used.
- A matching index scan for a LIKE predicate will be changed to a non-matching index scan or a tablespace scan if the content of the host variable begins with "%" or "_". The cluster ratio of the index determines which fall back is chosen as discussed in Chapter PP.

The systems administrator needs to monitor the use of the buffer pools and RID pool closely. If there is insufficient space in the pools at execution time, even though the optimizer requested sequential or list prefetch, it will not be used or the processing will be degraded.

OP.7 RUN TIME ACCESS PATH SELECTION

The optimizer does not know the value that will be requested by the user when host variables are used in predicates. Indeed, the value requested changes from one execution to another based on the values requested by each of many users who execute a program. Reoptimization at run time allows the optimizer to choose the best access path based on values entered by the user for predicates. This applies to static SQL with host variables, dynamic SQL with parameter markers, and special registers. Reoptimization does not occur for an SQL statement that contains only literals in predicates.

Reoptimization can be requested when you do a bind or rebind with the parameter REOPT(VARS) as discussed in Chapter PE. This section analyzes the cases where reoptimization should and should not be considered. Although reoptimization is not a good choice for most SQL statements, it should be considered when the costs are less than the costs of executing an SQL statement with a poor access path.

Range Predicates

The FF calculation for range predicates is straightforward based on the formula in Figure OP.7. Assume that the HIGH2KEY value is 1000, the LOW2KEY value is 10, and that the user requests rows with a weight >= 900. It is estimated that 10 percent of the rows will qualify based on the calculation:

```
FF = (HIGH2KEY - Value) / (HIGH2KEY - LOW2KEY)
   = (1000     - 900  ) / (1000     - 10     )
   = 0.10
```

It is likely that the optimizer will use a matching index scan with a FF of 0.10. But what if the next user to execute the program needs to see all of the parts that weight >= 20. A tablespace scan is best with a FF of 0.99 ((1000 - 20) / (1000 - 10)). In most cases, the developer will use a host variable rather than a literal of 900 or 20 as used in the examples. When host variable are used in predicates, the optimizer uses a default FF based on the COLCARDF of the table as shown in Figure OP.4. There is no one best access path. Indeed, users will almost certainly request many different values, depending on their requirements when executing the transaction.

The same principle applies to range predicates with character data. Of course, arithmetic operations cannot be done on character data. Therefore, it is necessary to substitute numeric values for character values requested by the user. Base 37 calculations are done to derive the numeric value. The 37 is based on 1 blank, plus 26 letters in the alphabet, plus 10 digits. For example, if the user requests all PNAMEs >= 'XZZ', the value of 35,251 can be assigned by noting that the first letter 'X' is the 25th letter multiplied by 37^2, plus 27 * 37^1 (or 37) for the second letter 'Z', plus 27 for the third letter 'Z'.

A numeric value is assigned to the second lowest (LOW2KEY) value of ' A' (blank, blank, A) calculated as:

$$1{,}408 = 1 * 37^2 + 1 * 37^1 + 2$$

Similar calculations are done for the HIGH2KEY value calculated as:

$$36{,}620 = 26 * 37^2 + 27 * 37^1 + 27$$

The calculated numeric values are substituted in the same formula used for > and >= predicates with numeric values like:

```
FF = (HIGH2KEY  - Value)   / (HIGH2KEY  - LOW2KEY)
FF = (36,620    - 35,251) / (36,620    - 1,408)
   = 0.0388788
```

Reoptimization allows the optimizer to see the value requested by the user at run time and determine the best access path based on that value.

LIKE Predicate: The optimizer can estimate a FF for a LIKE predicate if the search string begins with '%' when the requested string is known during access path selection. The estimate is based on the number of bytes in the string and column. In addition, the distribution statistics in the catalog tables SYSCOLDIST and SYSCOLDISTSTATS are used by the optimizer under these conditions as will be discussed. A matching index scan is not possible when the string begins the '%' as discussed in Chapter PP. These techniques are useful in determining whether a non-matching index scan or tablespace scan should be done, perhaps even more important which join method should be used and which table should be the outer and inner table of the join. IBM test results of a 5-way join indicate significant improvements in performance with the elapsed time going from 518 to 109 minutes and the CPU time going from 604 to 402 minutes when the value is known by the optimizer for access path selection.

Alternatives for Managing a Skewed Distribution

It is best not to index a column with skewed distribution of values as discussed in Chapter ID. Nevertheless, there are cases where an index is required to retrieve infrequently occurring values. One way to handle this problem is to test various values requested by the user. Based on your knowledge of the data, catalog statistics, and formulas in this chapter, you can use host language logic to execute the appropriate access path depending on the value that users request.

A mini case study of an application design for dealing with a skewed distribution of values is used to show how a program can be designed to choose the required access path based on the value requested by the user. The technique is useful if the access path chosen by the optimizer is good for most user requests and poor for a small percentage of the requests.

An accounting application was designed such that accounts progress through a series of stages. For example, when an account application is first submitted, the account is assigned a status of 1, during credit check the account has a status of 2, when credit for the account is approved it receives a status of 3, when the first purchase is made it receives a status of 4, when payment is due it receives a status of 5, etc. as shown in Figure OP.16. Once the account has been paid it is considered a historical row and receives a status of 99. The account information is retained for a 2 year period so that after a fairly short period of time, 80 percent or more of the rows will have a status of 99. Obviously, a tablespace scan is the best access path for locating 80 percent or more of the rows. However, the users need to locate a few percentage of the rows with various statuses that occur in a small percentage of the rows. For example, the user may need to review 2 percent of the accounts with a status of 6 which are accounts where payment is past due. Indeed, a matching index scan is needed for all statuses except for the accounts with a status of 99.

Figure OP.16. Account status and frequency of occurrence

Status COLVALUE	% * 100 Occurrence FREQUENCYF	Description
1	3	Account application is first submitted
2	3	Credit is being checked
3	2	Credit is approved
4	5	First purchase is made
5	2	Payment is due
6	1	Payment is past due
7	4	Payment is received
8	1	Over payment
9	1	Unknown
99	80	Historical row

We will consider several alternatives for dealing with this skewed distribution of values.

Alternative 1: Using Host-Language Test

The application designers decided to check the status requested by the user in the COBOL programs. If the request is for active accounts only, those without a status of 99, the program encourages the use of an index on status by using the OPTIMIZE FOR 1 ROW clause, as shown here:

```
IF STATUS ¬= 99   <-- host-language test

  SELECT ACCOUNT_ID, ACCOUNT_NAME
```

```
FROM    ACCOUNTS
WHERE   STATUS = :STATUS
OPTIMIZE FOR 1 ROW;
```

For an inactive account, for which 80 percent of the rows qualify, a tablespace scan is a better method. Using the OR operator in the predicate disallows use of the index, as shown here:

```
IF STATUS = 99  <-- host-language test

  SELECT ACCOUNT_ID, ACCOUNT_NAME
  FROM   ACCOUNTS
  WHERE (STATUS = :STATUS OR 0 = 1);
```

This procedure was effective for the particular application system because the meaning of the statuses was constant with the possibility of adding additional statuses but there would always be a high percentage of historical rows with a status of 99.

The design is not advisable for an application system where the distribution of values can change in the future. For example, the design was considered by an insurance company in Vancouver. Vancouver is the largest city in western Canada and the insurance company has most of its policies in Vancouver. There are a few policies in the smaller cities in western Canada. Users would like to be able to see the few policies without a tablespace scan of a multiple million row policy table. However, the design used for the accounting application is not advisable because the insurance company may decide to open an office in Toronto. If more polices are sold in Toronto than Vancouver, it will be necessary to revise all the programs that depend on most policies being in Vancouver.

Alternative 2: Distribution Statistics in the Catalog

It is not be necessary to resort to the method described above, which will require changes to programs if the characteristics of the data change in the future. The application can select from SYSCOLDIST using host variables to determine if the value chosen by the user is present, and, if so, the frequency of its occurrence. The application can use this knowledge to execute the SELECT statement with the appropriate access path, as described above.

An even better alternative is to place the distribution statistics in an application table after executing RUNSTATS. This means the application does not have to go directly against the catalog. Here is how you can iNSERT those distribution statistics into a table called APPL_COLDIST:

```
INSERT INTO APPL_COLDIST
       (COLVALUE, FREQUENCYF)
  SELECT COLVALUE, FREQUENCYF
  FROM   SYSIBM.SYSCOLDIST
  WHERE  TBCREATOR = 'POSYSTEM'
  AND    TBNAME    = 'S'
  AND    NAME      = 'STATUS';
```

Pseudo-code for how the application can use the distribution statistics to choose the appropriate SELECT statement for suppliers who have a status of '04' follows. Host language logic is used to determine whether to execute a SELECT statement which cannot use an index or one that can use an index. In this example, we use literals for ease of understanding. In the program, you can replace all literals with host variables.

```
      SELECT FREQUENCYF
      FROM   APPL_COLDIST
      WHERE  COLVALUE = '04';

IF   SQLCODE = 0    <-- One of the top 10 occurring values
AND FREQUENCYF >10 <-- Value occurs in >10 percent of rows

      SELECT SN, SNAME, STATUS, CITY
      FROM   S
      WHERE (STATUS = 99 OR 0 = 1);
      GO TO CONTINUE-PROCESSING

IF   SQLCODE = 100 <-- Not one of the top 10 values

      SELECT SN, SNAME, STATUS, CITY
      FROM   S
      WHERE  STATUS = '04'
      OPTIMIZE FOR 1 ROW;
```

Alternative 3: Using Embedded Dynamic SQL

When a host variable is specified in a predicate, the optimizer does not use the information on the distribution of values because it does not know what value will be requested each time a user executes the transaction. Consequently, embedded dynamic SQL with literals requested by the user for which the indexes are used appropriately may be more efficient than static SQL for which they are not.

In one case, for example, it was found that retrieval of 77 percent of 510,000 rows required 100 seconds elapsed time and 19 seconds of CPU when the optimizer assumed a uniform distribution of all values and used an index inappropriately. When the optimizer considered the distribution of values with dynamic SQL, the test required only 14 seconds elapsed time and 7 seconds of CPU time. The cost of embedded dynamic SQL is not likely to offset such savings. That cost, however, will be incurred each time the SQL is executed regardless of the frequency of the value sought.

Alternative 4: Using Reoptimization

Reoptimization, like embedded dynamic SQL with literals, allows the optimizer to choose an access path based on the value requested by the user. It does not require that the developer build dynamic SQL statements with literals, prepare, and execute them. Rather static SQL is written with host variables and the bind parameter REOPT(VARS) is used. Reoptimization also has advantages over alternatives 1 and 2. It is not necessary to develop the program to test the value requested by the user, write multiple SQL statements influencing the optimizer to give the needed access paths, and execute the appropriate SQL statement based on logic in the program.

There is a disadvantage of reoptimization in this mini case study. If users request infrequently occurring statuses 90 percent of the time and use a matching index scan, it is a waste of resources to reoptimize the SQL 100 percent of the time to get a tablespace scan 10 percent of the time, for example. Most application systems are not this straightforward. There are usually more factors to be considered. Lets introduce one more factor to the example. Most companies have more customers in one city than another as indicated in Figure OP.17.

Figure OP.17. City value and frequency of occurrence

FREQUENCYF	COLVALUE
20	New York
15	Chicago
12	Los Angeles
11	Dallas
9	Atlanta
8	Other*
7	Miami
6	Denver
6	San Francisco
4	Columbia
2	Charlotte

We will assume that the company does business in 20 cities and there are 10 statuses. The following SQL statement is executed to satisfy user requests to see the accounts in a given city with a given status.

```
SELECT ACCOUNT_ID, ACCOUNT_NAME
FROM   ACCOUNTS
WHERE  CITY   = :CITY
AND    STATUS = :STATUS;
```

If a uniform distribution of values is assumed, a small percentage of rows is estimated to qualify. The FF for the equal predicate on CITY is 1 / 20 (1 / cardinality of CITY from Figure OP.9) or 0.05. The FF for the predicate on STATUS is 1/ 10 or 0.10. The FFs for CITY and STATUS are multiplied based on the formula for ANDed predicates in Figure OP.7 to give a FF of 0.005 (0.05 * 0.10). A matching index scan is likely with low FFs.

If the user requests the accounts in New York (FREQUENCYF of 20) with a status of 4 (FREQUENCYF of 5) and these values are known to the optimizer, the FF is 0.16 (0.20 * 0.80) and a tablespace scan is a good choice. If the user requests the accounts in Charlotte (FREQUENCYF of 2) with a status of 4 (FREQUENCYF of 5) and these values are known to the optimizer, the FF is 0.001 (0.02 * 0.05). A matching index scan is a good choice on CITY based on the FF of 0.02 which is lower than the FF 0.05 on STATUS.

We are getting into too many options to be considered in developing program logic to determine the access path using the techniques discussed as alternatives 1 and 2 above. Users can request any combination of city and status values at different times. If reoptimization is used, the optimizer is able to choose the best access path among the many that it will evaluate based on the values requested by the users.

Additional Uses of Reoptimization

We have reviewed a number of cases where reoptimization can be useful. There are some additional situations where reoptimization can be considered.

The formula used to combine FFs for ORed predicates on the same column results in a larger FF than either of the ORed predicates taken individually, making the use of a matching index scan less likely. (An example of this using range predicates is in Chapter PP.) If the user requested values are known during access path selection, the calculated FFs can be lower than the default FFs which increases the likelihood that a matching index scan will be used.

Joins with local predicates on the join columns using host variables benefit from reoptimization. If the values required are known, the optimizer has more information in order to choose the best join method and which table should be the outer and inner table of the join.

If equal predicates are not specified for all columns of a composite index, reoptimization has advantages, particularly if the cardinalities of the non-leading columns of the composite index are collected by RUNSTATS (not the default).

In order to take advantage of a limited partition scan, the required value in the partitioning index must be known at run time. A limited partition scan allows for scanning some but not all data partitions or index and data partitions. This avoids scanning all partitions of a large partitioned tablespace.

The optimizer may not choose a matching index scan when it should with a special register in the WHERE clause. This is because the value in the special register is not known until run time similar to when using host variables. It is unlikely that the optimizer will choose a matching index scan for the following predicate with a special register and range predicate.

```
WHERE REQ_DATE > CURRENT DATE - 1 MONTH
```

If the user requested values are known, the optimizer is likely to recognize when more than 25 percent of the RIDs will qualify or that more than 50 percent of the RID pool is required for an SQL statement and choose a tablespace scan rather than multiple index processing. If the thresholds are reached at run time, the RIDs identified from processing the index pages are discarded and a tablespace scan is used. Obviously, it is best for the optimizer not to choose multiple index processing when these thresholds are reached at bind time.

Statistics vary a great deal between rebinds for some tables and indexes. For example, data entry tables that begin with no rows on a daily or weekly basis and grow to be sizable over the time period. It is necessary to execute RUNSTATS for reoptimization to see the changing statistics.

The use of reoptimization can be used to avoid a suboptimal access path generated on one processor model with the statements executed on another processor model in a sysplex data sharing environment.

You will find that it is not necessary to influence the optimizer with OPTIMIZE FOR *n* ROWS and (C1 = :HV OR 0 = 1) to achieve the required access path in most cases. It is best not to influence the optimizer. Even if the best access path is achieved today, it may not be the best access path in the future with changes to the characteristics of the data, values requested by users, database design, and the DB2 subsystem.

An Analysis of Costs Using DB2 Estimator

The resources required for access path selection at run time can be estimated using DB2 Estimator. The estimates summarized in Figure OP.18 are for using a 9672 RX3 Central Processor Unit (CPC) with a 50 MIPS rating and 3390-2 DASD. DB2 Estimator provides the options of estimating costs using static and dynamic SQL. The costs of executing three SQL statements were estimated using the dynamic SQL option shown with the column heading of "Run Time Path" and a value of "Yes" in the column. The estimate using the static SQL option has a "No" in the column. This results in a bit of an over estimate of what would be expected when using reoptimization. (DB2 Estimator has an option for dynamic SQL but not reoptimization.) Reoptimization of static SQL does not require parsing of the statement, authorization checking is not required, there is no dependency checking, and there is no view and table expression decomposition. The "CPU Min:Sec" column gives an estimate of the CPU time in minutes and seconds. Two companies that I have worked for recently charge their users at $0.50 per second of CPU time. If this charge is close to what is charged at your company, the "CPU $ Costs" column is useful in giving you a rough idea of the costs in dollars.

Figure OP.18. Estimating resources with DB2 Estimator

Description	Run Time Path*	CPU $ Costs**	CPU Min:Sec.	I/O Seconds	Elapsed Min:Sec.
Simple select with	Yes	0.151	0.302	3.152	3.455
2 local predicates	No	0.140	0.279	3.090	3.370
Difference		0.012	0.023	0.062	0.085
4-way join with	Yes	0.764	1.527	0.353	1.790
9 local predicates	No	0.711	1.422	0.106	1.439
Difference		0.053	0.105	0.247	0.351
1 join, 2 union	Yes	368.558	12:17.116	2.050	12:17.259
alls, 2 not exists 3 local predicates	No	368.533	12:17.066	1.926	12:17.086
Difference		0.025	0.050	0.124	0.173

The "Difference" row is the estimate with access path selection at run time minus the estimate with the access path not to be chosen at run time. The simple select with 2 local predicates requires about 8 percent more CPU time when the access path is chosen at run time. Another way of evaluating the costs is to multiply the difference in CPU time by the amount charged per CPU second at your company. If your company charges 50 cents a CPU second, the additional cost for access path selection at run time is a little over 1 cent. About 7 percent more CPU time is estimated for the 4-way join with nine local predicates. In this case the additional costs for access path selection at run time is a little over 5 cents. The percent CPU time increase for choosing the access path at run time does not increase with the costs of executing a statement. Indeed, in the last case, for a complex SQL statement that had a join, two union alls, two not exists subselects, and three local predicates, the difference is a very small percentage of the CPU time for executing the statement. The estimates depend heavily on the number of rows estimated to qualify and are fetched by the program. We will include these factors in another example in a moment.

DB2 Estimator was told that the buffer hit ratio is 90 percent for all cases reported. When a 20 percent buffer hit ratio was used, the estimated costs were significantly higher. However, the difference between choosing and not choosing the access path at run time did not vary between using a 90 percent and 20 percent hit ratio. This suggests that DB2 Estimator does not assume that the catalog pages needed for access path selection at run time are in the buffer pool. We will address the impact of keeping the catalog pages in the buffer pool in a moment.

The *DB2 for OS/390 Version 5 Performance Topics,* (SG24-2213), manual has test results that will prove useful in your analysis to determine if reoptimization is appropriate for your environment.

An analysis of the costs and savings of reoptimization depends on the number of times an SQL statement will be executed with a good access path and a poor access path. We will consider a method for the analysis using a SELECT statement to determine information on jobs in a user requested city for a period of time using the statement:

```
SELECT JN, JNAME, CITY, BEGIN_DATE
FROM   J
WHERE  CITY = :CITY
AND    BEGIN_DATE > :REQUESTED-DATE;
```

This is the simple SELECT with two local predicates used as the first example in Figure OP.18. It is assumed that the user requests jobs over a long period of time (jobs that began during the last year, for example) about 20 percent of the time, in which case the use of the CITYX index is best. Use of the DATEX index is not a good choice because a large percent of the rows qualify. However, the user requests jobs over a short period of time (jobs that began during the last week, for example) about 80 percent of the time, in which case the DATEX index is best because only a low percentage of the rows qualify according to the predicate on date.

The optimizer is likely to choose the CITYX because of the equal predicate on city even though the column has a low cardinality of 20 and a cluster ratio of 30 percent. It is unlikely to choose the DATEX index despite the cluster ratio of 85 percent because of the range predicate on date with the use of a host variable. Indeed, DB2 Estimator chose the CITYX index. You might calculate the FF for the two predicates to determine if DB2 Estimator made a good choice.

The estimate that 1,500 rows qualify according to the CITY predicate have to be tested to locate 12 rows that satisfy the DATE predicate was provided to DB2 Estimator. The 1,500 row estimate is based on having to test 1 percent of 150,000 rows for each city. The 150,000 row estimate is based on the optimizer formula for equal predicates 1 / COLCARDF of 20 times 3,000,000 rows in the table.

DB2 Estimator allows for forcing the access path to use the DATEX index. In this case, it was estimated that 1,000 rows are tested to determine if the row qualifies according to the CITY predicate to locate the 12 rows to be displayed to the user.

If the CITYX index is always used with static SQL and no access path selection at run time, it will cost about $13,950 to execute the statement 100,000 times per day (Figure OP.19). However, if the access path is chosen at run time and the CITYX index is used for 20,000 executions and the DATEX index is used for 80,000 executions, the total cost is $5,900. Clearly, choosing the access path at run time reduces the costs dramatically. The costs of choosing the access path at run time is included in the cost estimates by DB2 Estimator.

Figure OP.19. Cost Estimates

Description	Index Used	Run Time Path*	CPU $ Costs **	CPU Seconds ***	Number of Executions Per Day
Simple select with 2 local predicates	CITYX	Yes	3,020	0.302	20,000
	CITYX	No	2,790	0.279	20,000
	DATEX	Yes	2,880	0.072	80,000
	DATEX	No	1,920	0.048	80,000
Total for 100,000	CITYX or DATEX	Yes	5,900	N/A	100,000
CITYX always used	CITYX	No	13,950	0.279	100,000
DATEX always used	DATEX	No	2,400	0.048	100,000

If users usually request a narrow date range and city has a low cardinality and the DATEX index is always used, the costs are reduced further to $2,400. In this particular case, it might be best to influence the optimizer to choose the DATEX index and not have the access path chosen at run time. This can be done by adding OR 0 = 1 in parentheses with the CITY predicate.

The goal of this analysis is to demonstrate one approach to determine if the access path should be chosen at run time. Do consider using DB2 Estimator to test the many assumptions and conditions that are appropriate for your challenging SQL statements where it might be appropriate to have the access path chosen at run time. You can then test the more reasonable alternatives with representative test data and values that the users require.

The Costs of Reoptimization

If the use of reoptimization reduces run time costs significantly, the costs of choosing an access path at run time can be acceptable. DB2 Estimator results in Figure OP.19 provide a rough idea of the CPU time required for binding SQL statements that vary in complexity. The additional CPU time required to choose an access path at run time may or may not be acceptable, depending on the application requirements. You probably have some programs where the additional CPU time is acceptable. However, if subsecond response time is required with a high transaction rate, the additional CPU time required may not be acceptable.

A good deal of the CPU time required for the bind is used to issue I/O to the catalog tables. Indeed, 30-40 I/Os and share locks are typically taken on the catalog tables during the bind. Obviously, this depends on the complexity of the SQL statement. Share locks on the catalog and DBD are taken for binds. This means that lock contention will be low in a production environment in most cases.

The costs of binding SQL statements can be reduced dramatically if the required catalog pages are in BP0. The goal is to use 30-40 getpages without 30-40 I/O by sizing BP0 to contain catalog pages frequently used for binds. This can be accomplished by sizing BP0 to basically page fix the catalog and directory tables and indexes required for reoptimization. It will also minimize the possibility of an I/O bottleneck on the tables and indexes. Application tablespaces and indexes can be assigned to other buffer pools to avoid overwriting catalog and directory pages used for reoptimization.

You will want to analyze the costs and savings of using reoptimization to determine if it should be used and if configuring BP0 for the processing is worthwhile.

Reoptimization and the PLAN_TABLE

The column WHEN_OPTIMIZE in the PLAN_TABLE will prove useful in your analysis of whether SQL statements should be reoptimized at bind time. Rows are inserted into the PLAN_TABLE during reoptimization if explain is requested. (Reoptimization occurs if there is no PLAN_TABLE.) The column WHEN_OPTIMIZE indicates when the access path was chosen. If the column is blank, the access path described was chosen at bind time with the use of NOREOPT(VARS) and no reoptimization takes place. If the column contains 'B', the access path is determined at run time with REOPT(VARS) for static SQL and dynamic SQL when DESCRIBE or PREPARE INTO is executed before OPEN or EXECUTE. Static SQL will be reoptimized at run time and dynamic SQL at OPEN or EXECUTE time. If the column contains 'R', the access path was determined at run time with real values for variables. The 'B' and 'R' access paths can be compared to analyze different access paths chosen at bind and run time for a statement. You may want to consider counting the number of different access paths chosen and the number of times a particular access path is used. This will be useful in analyzing the costs of reoptimization and execution of SQL. If the reoptimization costs are high compared to the savings, consider the alternatives that have been discussed in this chapter and Chapter PP.

Reoptimization in IFCID Records

Access path information like in the PLAN_TABLE plus the timeron is written to the instrumentation facility component ID (IFCID) 0022 (with EXPLAIN of YES and NO) for the PREPARE of dynamic SQL statements, reoptimized statements, and when binding static SQL with VALIDATE(RUN) and the required objects or privileges do not exist. The IFCID records can be related to rows in the plan table using the plan and package name, timestamp, and statement number. The variable value used for access path selection can be found in IFCID 0247 and the SQL statement text in IFCID 0063. The costs of collecting these records can be minimized by starting the performance trace for only the specific IFCIDs and specific plans like:

```
-START TRACE (PERFM)
 PLAN(name)
 DEST(SMF)
 CLASS(30)
 IFCID(0022,0247,0063)
```

Using Reoptimization on Some But Not all SQL in a Package or Plan

Optimization hints, as discussed in Chapter EX, can be used to reoptimize some but not all SQL in a package or plan. This avoids having to split out SQL into a different package or plan. The method involves binding with REOPT(VARS) and OPTHINT (HINTA). Replace the hint name HINTA with your value. Update the PLAN_TABLE for each SQL statement not to be reoptimized like:

```
UPDATE PLAN_TABLE
   SET OPTHINT       = 'HINTA',
       WHEN_OPTIMIZE = 'B' --results in no reoptimization
WHERE QUERYNO    = 400
AND   APPLNAME   = ' '
AND   PROGNAME   = 'PROGA'
AND   VERSION    = ' '
AND   COLLID     = 'SPJCOLL';
```

The setting of WHEN_OPTIMIZE to 'B' informs the optimizer not to use reoptimization. The value of 'R' means to reoptimize with or without providing hints. It is necessary to execute a similar UPDATE statement for each statement (QUERYNO) not to be reoptimized in the package or plan bound with REOPT(VARS) and OPTHINT (HINTA). You can use a different hint name for each statement.

Reoptimization in the Catalog Tables

Plans and packages bound with REOPT(VARS) and for which the access path will be chosen at run time can be determined from the catalog tables using the following SELECT statements.

```
SELECT PLNAME, SEQNO, TEXT
  CASE WHEN STMTNOI <> 0
    THEN STMTNOI
    ELSE STMTNO
  END AS STMTNUM,
FROM SYSIBM.SYSSTMT
WHERE STATUS IN ('B','F','G','J')
ORDER BY PLNAME, STMTNUM, SEQNO;

SELECT COLLID, NAME, VERSION, SEQNO, STMT
  CASE WHEN STMTNOI <> 0
    THEN STMTNOI
    ELSE STMTNO
  END AS STMTNUM,
FROM SYSIBM.SYSPACKSTMT
WHERE STATUS IN ('B','F','G','J')
ORDER BY COLLID, NAME, VERSION, STMTNUM, SEQNO;
```

If the STATUS column has a 'B', the plan or package uses static SQL and distributed processing with the private protocols. All SQL statements will be bound at the server using the values requested by the user each time the plan or package is run. The value 'F' means that the plan or package was bound with VALIDATE(RUN) and will be bound at run time under the conditions described for the value 'B' except the SQL statements are not executed in a distributed environment. 'G' means that the plan or package was bound with REOPT(VARS) and will be bound at run time. 'J' means that the plan or package contains dynamic SQL, was bound with REOPT(VARS), and will be bound at run time.

You can determine if REOPT(VARS) was used with a bind or rebind by selecting from SYSPLAN and SYSPACKAGE. The column REOPTVAR contains 'Y' if the statements in the plan or package are reoptimized at run time.

Challenges in Estimating Costs and Savings

There are certainly challenges in estimating reoptimization costs and savings. There are a number of questions that should be addressed to estimate the costs and savings. A first step might be to explain the access path for SQL interactively using different literal values expected to be requested by users and determine if you are getting significantly different access paths for different values. Do estimate the costs and savings based on test results for your SQL in your environment including the I/O, CPU, and response time. Estimate the percentage of executions that will have a good access path for the value requested by the user and compare that to the percentage of executions that will have a better access path when using reoptimization. If an SQL statement processes > 1 row, do consider the costs of reoptimization per row processed although reoptimization occurs at OPEN time. This is particularly important if many rows must be processed at OPEN time and few rows are fetched. Reoptimization has minimal impact for batch programs. The resources required is a very small percentage of total resources required for a batch program in most cases.

Do estimate the costs and savings based on test results for your SQL in your environment including the I/O, CPU, and response time.

Reoptimization Has No Advantages in Some Cases

Reoptimization has no advantage in some cases. An equal predicate used on an indexed column or equal predicates used on all columns of a composite index where the index is unique or there is a uniform distribution of values in the indexed columns do not benefit from reoptimization. If there are no stage 1 indexable predicates, host variables, special registers, and parameter markers, there are no advantages to reoptimization. Predicates used on columns that do not participate in any index do not benefit except for local predicates used on a non-indexed column where a join is required. In this case, reoptimization has an advantage in determining the join method and which tables should be the inner and outer tables of the join.

INSERT statements do not benefit from reoptimization because the optimizer does not choose an access path for the insertion of rows. The clustering index or first index on the chain of indexes in DBD is always used by DM to determine where a row should be inserted.

Reoptimization Compared to Dynamic SQL

There are a number of pros and cons in deciding whether to use reoptimization or dynamic SQL as discussed in Chapter PD. Indeed, reoptimization is required when using dynamic SQL with parameter markers. Reoptimization requires a bit fewer resources than dynamic SQL with literals.

Embedded dynamic SQL is complex to develop, test, and maintain. REOPT(VARS) is simply a bind parameter and can be used when binding existing SQL without modifying the program.

Dynamic SQL is at the statement level and can be used for specific SQL statements. In contrast, reoptimization is at the package or plan level. In order to use reoptimization for some but not all SQL statements in a program, it is necessary to isolate statements to be reoptimized into a separate package or use optimization hints as discussed later in this section and Chapter EX.

Reoptimization is a good choice if the user requested value significantly affects the access path in a number of cases, particularly for long running statements where the cost of reoptimization is a small percentage of the total costs.

Dynamic SQL using the cache as discussed in Chapter PD is a good choice for short running statements where the bind costs are high compared to the cost of running the SQL. Reoptimization cannot be used when using the dynamic SQL cache.

The purpose of the cache is to avoid bind processing including access path selection. In contrast, the purpose of reoptimization is to determine a good access path for given values requested by users.

OP.8 FOOLING THE OPTIMIZER

There are times when you know more about the characteristics of the data than is available to the optimizer. You can influence or force a specified access path if you think it might mean better performance over the access path chosen by the optimizer. This is possible by updating the statistics used by the optimizer. The primary benefits of updating the statistics, however, are to allow for simulating large production tables in a test environment with small test tables and for capacity planning. Most statistics used by the optimizer can be manually updated.

Correcting for Outliers

When a column includes a few extremely high and low values, the optimizer may inaccurately estimate the proportion of rows included in a range--and make the improper choice about whether to use an index to find values in that range. For example, the optimizer uses a formula like the following to determine the FF for a statement requiring a greater-than search of a column's upper range:

```
FF = (HIGH2KEY - V1) / (HIGH2KEY - LOW2KEY)
```

HIGH2KEY is the second highest value in the column; LOW2KEY, the second lowest. DB2's developers used the column's second highest and second lowest values in the formula rather than highest and lowest values to eliminate extreme values that are not representative of the distribution of values and nulls. Sometimes that correction is not enough to give a true picture of the column.

Consider a WEIGHT column in the P table in which almost all parts weigh between 100 and 1,000 pounds. RUNSTATS has found, however, a HIGH2KEY of 8,000 and a LOW2KEY of 10.

Assume there are frequent searches of the P table for parts weighing more than 900 pounds. The optimizer can calculate the FF for that search as follows:

```
FF = (8,000 - 900) / (8,000 - 10) = 0.89
```

This indicates that 89 percent of the rows will satisfy the search and the optimizer will probably not choose to use an index to find them. However, we know that the extreme values found by RUNSTATS for HIGH2KEY AND LOW2KEY provide a distorted view of the column. By updating those values to 1,000 and 100 respectively, we can change the optimizer's calculation for the range search:

```
FF = (1,000 - 900) / (1,000 - 10) = 0.11
```

With this FF, indicating only 11 percent of the rows will be returned, the optimizer will likely choose to use a clustering index or perhaps a non-clustering index using list prefetch to avoid processing pages more than once. One major problem with this technique is that it will be effective only for predicates using literals and dynamic SQL. Recall that default FFs are used for range predicates when host variables are used.

Forcing an Access Path

It is necessary to have a great deal of information in order to force an access path. An indepth understanding of how the optimizer chooses an access path is required which is a non-trivial task as has been seen in this chapter. What values should be used to cause the desired access path? How will the data be processed by a large number of programs in the application system and by casual users for ad hoc processing? If catalog statistics are updated directly with an UPDATE statement, RUNSTATS cannot be executed since it replaces the updated values or the values will have to be updated after each execution of RUNSTATS.

Consider the following statement and statistics. Which index should the optimizer choose to use?

```
SELECT SN, PN, QTY
FROM   SPJ
WHERE  JN = 'J1'
AND    QTY < 20000;
```

Relevant statistics:

```
SPJ has 10,000 rows on 100 pages

JN has an index with 50 unique values

QTY has a clustering index with 6,000 unique values

QTY has a LOW2KEY of 10,000 and a HIGH2KEY of 40,000
```

Some people might think that using the index on JN will provide the best access path since an equal predicate is specified. They might be tempted to force the use of the index by setting the index cardinality approximately equal to the cardinality of the table:

```
UPDATE SYSIBM.SYSINDEXES
SET FIRSTKEYCARDF = 10000
WHERE NAME    = 'JNINDEX'
AND   TBNAME  = 'S'
AND   CREATOR = 'POSYSTEM';
```

But before using the update, let us look closer at the statistics, FF calculations, and estimate I/O to the data pages:

1. The JN FF estimates that 2 percent (1/50 = 0.02) of the rows will qualify, requiring 100 I/O plus a sort of the RIDs for list prefetch or 200 I/O (0.02 * 10,000 rows) if list prefetch is not used. The estimates are not divided by 32 since sequential or list prefetch can be used in all three cases considered.

2. 100 I/O will be required for a tablespace scan since there are 100 pages.

3. The QTY FF will estimate that 34 percent (ceiling (20,000 - 10,000) / (40,000 - 10,000) = 0.333) of the pages with rows in sequence on QTY with a clustered index will require 34 I/O (0.34 * 100 pages) and no RID sort is required.

The calculations indicate that the QTY index will require significantly fewer I/O than using the JN index. The point is that what appears initially to be a good access path may not be or even if it does result in a better access path for a specific statement, it may cause a poor access path for other SQL statements in many application programs.

The Perils of Tampering with Statistics

Before attempting to fool the optimizer, consider these important issues:

The danger of suboptimization: By inducing the optimizer to choose a better path for one statement, you may force it to choose a poor path for other statements. One way of avoiding that problem is to modify the statistics, bind the application plan or package to achieve the desired path, and reset the statistics to their original values. Such an approach is hazardous, because any automatic rebind uses the current statistics.

The situation changes: Another danger is that the situation that prompted the modification in catalog statistics may change over time. Changes to the data's characteristics from updates and insertions can turn what was once a good access path into a poor performer. And changes in the way an organization uses a table can also make a good access path decision look bad. Choices that seemed proper when a table was used solely for online transactions and batch processing may not appear so when the organization gives users direct access to the tables for ad hoc queries. In addition, application developers may add or drop indexes and the DB2 developers are likely to continue to enhance the optimizer which cannot be taken advantage of when "fooling" the optimizer.

An administrative nightmare: Modifying statistics requires much administrative overhead. Your organization needs to set up controls for the execution of RUNSTATS to avoid undoing the alterations. Careful documentation is required to explain why values were chosen. Bound plans need to be reviewed periodically to determine that the rationale for the statistics used when they were bound continues to hold. Finally, all decisions to fool the optimizer need to be reexamined with each new release of DB2 containing changes in the optimizer's algorithms, formula, and rules.

Recommendation: The optimizer will almost always choose a good access paths and, although it may sometimes be tempting to "fool" the optimizer by changing the statistics, doing so is rarely worth the cost. When it is necessary, a better approach is to use the OPTIMIZE FOR 1 ROW clause to encourage the use of an index or "OR 0 = 1" in parenthesis with a predicate to discourage the use of an index as discussed in Chapters PD and BP. However, even these approaches have many of the hazards discussed.

OP.9 SIMULATING PRODUCTION DATA IN A TEST ENVIRONMENT

Production tables can be quite large. It may be too costly in DASD space to maintain a full copy of the production data in test for development and maintenance of an application system. A few alternatives will be considered to reduce the DASD space costs in a test environment.

Estimating Statistics: An alternative to loading full production data during testing is to update the statistics to be like what is expected in the production data. The challenge is determining the statistics that should be used for the updates. One approach is to estimate the statistics based on a knowledge of the data. Interviews of the users for whom the application system is being developed can provide some information. They will have a good idea of the number of rows in the tables, and the number of pages can be calculated without much difficulty. But the cardinality of the columns, particularly those that are indexed, is very important but not so easily estimated. In addition, the distribution of values in terms of the second highest and lowest values, the 10 most frequently occurring values and their percent occurrence are difficult to estimate.

Using a Sample of the Data: An alternative that can provide more representative test data is to take a sample of the data that will be used in the production environment for a new application system under development. It is very likely that the data already exists on DASD or tape as used by previous application systems. Most likely it will be necessary to extract the data anyway when the system is migrated to production. If you write the extract programs early, you can take a sample of the data to be used during testing of the new DB2 programs. A 10 percent sample is a good target.

The optimizer will in most cases choose the same access path for a 100,000 row table as it will for a similar 1 million row table if the indexed columns in each have about the same distribution of values. The index cluster ratios should contain typical values. A cluster ratio of 100 percent will probably not exist most of the time when tables are being updated and reorganized periodically. Load the test table with data that closely matches the COLCARDF, FIRSTKEYCARDF, and FULLKEYCARDF of the data in the production table. If the index cardinality cannot be reproduced exactly (if a large production table has an index with a large number of distinct values), the cardinality of the test table indexes should be proportionate to the table size. For example, if a 1 million row production table has 10,000 distinct values in a column, a 100,000 row test table should have 1,000 distinct values, maintaining the 10 to 1 ratio.

Try to have the test table's distribution of values match that of the production table's. That is, if each SN value occurs 10 times for every PN value in the production table, the test data should show the same relationship. If a skewed distribution of values will exist in a column in the production data, then the skewed distribution should be proportionate in the test data. Finally, each column's distribution of values as reflected by the top 10 occurring values and the second highest and second lowest values in the test table should correspond to the production table.

One way to develop a test table with the same statistical characteristics as the production table is to select rows from the production table at random. Numbers between zero and one from a random number generator can be multiplied times the number of rows in the table to extract rows to be included in the test table's sample. For example, in a 1 million row table, if the random number generates 0.835722, the production table's 835,722nd row should be included in the test table

(0.835722 * 1,000,000). A simple pseudo-random number formula to generate numbers between zero and one is to take the remainder of a value divided by a prime number. If it is difficult, time-consuming, or resource intensive to process the data using the random number, you might simply use every tenth row from the production table.

The access paths chosen by the optimizer for the test tables will be very similar with a 10 percent sample of large tables. Use EXPLAIN to determine the access path. This can give a good indication of the performance of the SQL when using the large production tables. The elapsed time used by a test program, particularly when using a tablespace scan, will not be the same. However, the cost of a tablespace and non-matching index scan go up linearly as the size of the table increases. If a scan of 100,000 rows requires one minute, a scan of 1 million rows will require about 10 minutes.

Use Existing Production Statistics: Testing is much simpler if the production tables already exist. Then the catalog statistics for the production data can be used to update the catalog for the test tables. This means that large tables for testing or maintenance do not have to be maintained for additional programs being developed, tuned, or modified to accommodate new business requirements. Even though the test table may be very small, the optimizer will choose the same access path for it as for the larger production table if their statistics match in most cases. Sample program DB2PLI8 can be used to generate UPDATE statements for changing the statistics in test catalog tables to be like the production catalog tables.

When updating catalog statistics do consider updating the STATSTIME column in the catalog tables used by the optimizer to a value that will not occur (9999-12-31 or 0001-01-01, for example) to indicate that the statistics have been updated manually rather than by RUNSTATS.

Extract a sample of production data for testing: Even with production statistics in the test catalog tables, you will also need representative data for testing programs. If there is a time or timestamp column in the table, the following statement extracts a 10 percent sample of the production data and placed it in the corresponding test table.

```
INSERT INTO SPJTEST
  SELECT *
  FROM   SPJPROD
  WHERE  SECOND(TIMECOL) < 6;
```

If you would like to use a larger percent of the production data in test, the value of 12, 18, or 30 can be used in place of the value of 6 in the preceding statement to iNSERT between 20 to 50 percent of the data into a test table based on:

```
 6 for 10 percent ( 6 / 60 seconds)
12 for 20 percent (12 / 60 seconds)
18 for 30 percent (18 / 60 seconds)
30 for 50 percent (30 / 60 seconds)
```

If the tables do not have a column with seconds, you can use a column with a pseudo random number between 0 and 99. For example, assume that positions 3 and 4 of QTY contain a pseudo random number. The following statement iNSERT statements about 10 percent of the production data into the test table.

```
INSERT INTO SPJTEST
  SELECT *
```

```
FROM    SPJPROD
WHERE   SUBSTR(DIGITS(QTY),3,2) < '10';
```

Recommendation: It is very important to have representative test data in application tables and statistics in the catalog tables. If test data is not representative of production data, test performance will not be representative of production performance.

OP.10 SUMMARY

The original architecture of the optimizer as developed in System R is sound and is being enhanced with each version and release of DB2. DB2 has a cost based optimizer. That is, it considers both I/O and CPU cost when determining the best access path. There are many factors that influence those costs, including the distribution of data, whether the data is compressed, the size of the buffer pools, the size of the RID pool, the size of the sort pool, and many others.

Many factors are considered in the formula and a number of rules are applied. The cluster ratio is considered for all matching index scans. Sequential prefetch is considered for tablespace and non-matching index scans and list prefetch is considered with single and multiple index usage. The optimizer can reformulate SQL statements in a number of cases for improved performance. Thresholds are applied at bind and execution times to provide good performance across many SQL statements that will be executing with different workloads.

The optimizer does not have sufficient information at bind time for static SQL with host variables for range predicates, a skewed distribution of values, and limited partition scan. Several alternatives and their pros and cons have been discussed including reoptimization and program logic to influence or choose an access path. Reoptimization of static SQL with host variables at run time is a good choice when the value requested by the user at run time will result in an access path that reduces costs more than the cost of the reoptimization.

It is advisable to reserve modifying statistics used by the optimizer for modeling a production system on a test system and for capacity planning. Chapter EX provides information on how to determine the access path chosen by the optimizer using EXPLAIN.

EXERCISES

1. Why is it important to execute RUNSTATS after data have been loaded and before binding SQL?

2. How does the optimizer estimate access costs if the catalog tables do not contain statistics on a table being accessed?

3. Why is the a) formulation more likely to use a matching index scan than the b) formulation? Will the a) and c) formulations give the same access path? Why?

a)
```
SELECT PN, PNAME, WEIGHT, CITY
  FROM    P
  WHERE   PN BETWEEN :HOST-VAR AND :HIGH-VALUES
```

b)
```
SELECT PN, PNAME, WEIGHT, CITY
```

```
    FROM    P
    WHERE   PN >= :HV
```

```
c) SELECT PN, PNAME, WEIGHT, CITY
    FROM    P
    WHERE   PN >= :HOST-VAR
    AND     PN <= :HIGH-VALUES
```

4. Assume 10,000 rows on 500 pages and an indexed column with a cardinality of 200.

a) Estimate the number of I/O to the data pages for an equal predicate with a 100 percent cluster ratio.
b) Estimate the number of I/O to the data pages for an equal predicate with a 5 percent cluster ratio.
c) Estimate the number of I/O to the data pages for an equal predicate with a 60 percent cluster ratio.

5. Assume that a select from SYSIBM.SYSCOLDIST reveals the following distribution of suppliers in 10 cities.

COLVALUE	FREQUENCY
Dallas	55
Chicago	12
Miami	8
New York	7
St. Paul	5
Omaha	4
San Diego	3
Atlanta	1
Bolivar	1
Denver	1

What is the I/O estimate to the data pages for the suppliers in Dallas and Chicago using an index with a cluster ratio of 70 percent? Assume 10,000 rows on 500 pages.

6. Estimate the I/O time to process 235 data pages using list prefetch and sequential prefetch assuming the use of 3390 DASD. Assume 10,000 rows on 500 pages.

7. Estimate the CPU time to read 235 pages at random and using prefetch. Assume that the required pages are not in the buffer pool.

8. Assume that the TA table contains 10,000 rows and that the C1 column is declared as an integer. Each distinct value in C1 represents about 20 percent of the total. Assume that the C2 value exceeds the C2 plus C3 values about 30 percent of the time. This exercise assumes that you understand stage 1 and stage 2 processing (discussed in Chapter PP). Estimate the number of rows that will be processed by DM, RDS, and passed to the application program for the following statement.

```
SELECT C1, C2, C3, C4, C5, C6, C7, C8, C9, C10
FROM   TA
WHERE  C1 = 7689
AND    C2 > C2 + C3
```

9. Using the assumptions in the previous exercise with the added assumption that C1 is declared as DECIMAL(8,2), how many rows will be passed from DM to RDS? What is an estimate of the CPU time to pass the additional rows from DM to RDS?

10. Will the access path chosen by the optimizer be used at execution time in all cases?

11. In general, when should reoptimization at run time be considered?

ANSWERS

1. RUNSTATS collects statistics describing the table, tablespace, partition, indexes, and columns that the optimizer uses to determine a good access path.

2. In the absence of statistics, the optimizer uses default values to estimate costs.

3. The a) formulation is more likely to use a matching index scan than the b) formulation because the default FFs are used to estimate the I/O required for range predicates when host variables are used. This is because the content of the host variable is not known until the user keys the value when the transaction is executed and the value can vary from one execution to another. The default FF is 33 percent for a >= or <= predicate and 10 percent for a BETWEEN predicate if the column cardinality is < 100.

The a) and c) formulations will give the same access path because the optimizer transforms the c) formulation into the a) formulation before access path selection.

4. a) The I/O estimate to the data pages for the clustering index is 3 (1/200 * 500 pages). (The ceiling is taken for the calculations. A fraction of an I/O cannot be done.) List prefetch can be used if the I/O estimate is two or more, reducing the I/O to one.
b) The I/O estimate to the data pages for the non-clustering index is 50 (1/200 * 10,000 rows). Sequential prefetch can be used, reducing the I/O to two.
c) The I/O estimate to the data pages using an index with a cluster ratio of 60 percent is 22 (0.60 * 3 from a) + 0.40 * 50 from b)).

5. The I/O estimate to the data pages can be estimated as:

- The FF for WHERE CITY = 'Dallas' AND CITY = 'Chicago' is 0.07 (0.55 * 0.12).
- If the cluster ratio is 100 percent, the I/O estimate is 35 (0.07 * 500).
- If the cluster ratio is 0 percent, the I/O estimate is 700 (0.07 * 10,000).
- With a cluster ratio of 70 percent, the I/O estimate is 235 (0.70 * 35 + 0.30 * 700).

6. The 235 data pages to be read using list prefetch and sequential prefetch can be divided by 32 giving 8 I/O (235/32). The list prefetch I/O time estimate is 24 ms (3 ms * 8). The sequential prefetch I/O time estimate is 13.6 ms (1.7 ms * 8).

7. The CPU time estimate to read 235 pages at random is 103.4 ms (235 * 0.11 ms per getpage + 235 * 0.33 ms per physical I/O). The CPU time estimate to read 235 pages with prefetch is 3.52 ms (8 * 0.11 ms per getpage + 8 * 0.33 ms per physical I/O).

8. The C1 predicate is stage 1 which results in DM scanning 10,000 rows and passing 2,000 rows to RDS. RDS scans the 2,000 rows and applies the stage 2 predicate on C2 after performing the addition of C2 and C3. The qualifying 600 rows are returned to the user.

9. C1 = 7689 must be evaluated by RDS if C1 is declared as DECIMAL(8,2). This means that all 10,000 rows (rather than 2,000 rows) must be passed to RDS one column at a time. The additional 8,000 rows with 10 columns will increase the CPU time by about 352 ms (8,000 * 10 * 0.0044 ms).

10. The access path chosen by the optimizer will not be used at execution time if insufficient resources are available in the buffer pool or RID pool, for example, or if an execution time threshold is exceeded.

11. Reoptimization at run time is a good choice when the value requested by the user at run time will result in an access path that reduces costs more than the cost of the reoptimization.

FIGURES

Explaining the Access Path Chosen by the Optimizer

EX.1 INTRODUCTION

Determining the access path chosen by the optimizer early in the interactive testing of SQL statements before embedding the statements in a host program can save a good deal of time and frustration. If the statements are not performing as required, a good deal of effort can be wasted rewriting and retesting SQL and a large amount of host language code. There is considerable resistence to rewriting host language code that is operating correctly because the SQL must be rewritten to achieve the required performance. It is recommended that the SQL statements be written and tested for the correct results and good performance before writing the host program. The use of EXPLAIN to determine the access path chosen by the optimizer during this early testing has significant benefits. You can also use EXPLAIN when testing programs with static SQL, to verify the access path chosen when migrating to a production environment, and finally to monitor changes to access paths in a production environment.

EXPLAIN also provides for early verification of the table and index design. Perhaps the tables need to be normalized or denormalized. Perhaps additional indexes are needed or some that were thought to be needed are not being used by the optimizer and can be dropped.

The SQL generated by CASE tools and 4th generation languages can be checked for potential performance problems and poor programming practices can be identified before they are proliferated throughout the application system.

EX.2 METHODS FOR GETTING INFORMATION ON PERFORMANCE

EXPLAIN can be used interactively, at bind, or at rebind time. Any SQL data manipulation (DML) statement can be explained. However, the use of the clustering index to determine where to insert a row is not shown as discussed in other chapters and an example given toward the end of this chapter. EXPLAIN is one of the best methods for getting information about how SQL statements will perform. Similar information as generated by EXPLAIN is also available using the performance trace class 3 IFCID 0022. This provides for analysis of the access paths chosen for dynamic SQL.

Some early indication of the expected performance of different formulations of SQL statements can be gleaned from the QMF relative cost estimate. This value is useful only when comparing different formulations of an SQL statement that produce the same result. If one formulation has a significantly lower relative cost estimate than another formulation, there is a good chance that the statement with the lower value will have performance advantages. The relative cost estimate should be used cautiously. It is the timeron divided by 1024 as calculated by the optimizer including many factors considered in the access path selection as discussed in Chapter OP.

The statistics collected by DB2 and reported by performance monitor products are an excellent source of information on the CPU, I/O, getpages, elapsed time, and synchronous (random) and asynchronous (prefetch) I/O. These statistics are available from instrumentation facility component ID (IFCID) 0003 and the text of SQL statements can be found in IFCID 0063 and 0124. If there is excessive wait time for I/O and CPU, do investigate to determine if resources are being used to capacity. You may have tuned the SQL for the best possible performance but resources are being over utilized. Another possibility, particularly when DB2 has been installed at a company for a short period of time, is that DB2 needs higher priority for improved performance. Perhaps other older systems have been given higher priority than DB2.

The performance trace provides for a detailed analysis of the work done by DB2. However, it does require high I/O and CPU costs during the trace and the trace is time consuming to read and interpret. If you believe that the performance trace is necessary to resolve the problem, do limit the trace as much as possible by specifying only the required AUTHID, PLAN, CLASS, and IFCID parameters as discussed in Chapter CO.

The catalog tables SYSPLANDEP and SYSPACKDEP have information on the indexes used by plan and package. This information is of limited value because it does not show index usage by SQL statement. However, it does have some value in being able to identify indexes that are frequently and infrequently used by plans and packages. If an index is frequently used, it should be kept well organized. If an index is infrequently used, do an analysis to determine if its usage justifies the cost of maintaining it.

EX.3 PREPARING TO USE EXPLAIN

Before using EXPLAIN, it is necessary to have a AUTHID.PLAN_TABLE to receive rows describing the access path chosen by the optimizer. The table qualifier AUTHID must be the qualifier matching the user's primary AUTHID or the ID specified as the owner of the plan or package when it is bound. The CREATE PLAN_TABLE statement in Figure EX.1 can be keyed and executed or copied from the sample library prefix.SDSNSAMP DSNTESC).

Figure EX.1. Create plan table statement

```
CREATE TABLE PLAN_TABLE
 (QUERYNO            INTEGER        NOT NULL,
  QBLOCKNO           SMALLINT       NOT NULL,
  APPLNAME           CHAR(8)        NOT NULL,
  PROGNAME           CHAR(8)        NOT NULL,
  PLANNO             SMALLINT       NOT NULL,
  METHOD             SMALLINT       NOT NULL,
  CREATOR            CHAR(8)        NOT NULL,
  TNAME              CHAR(18)       NOT NULL,
  TABNO              SMALLINT       NOT NULL,
  ACCESSTYPE         CHAR(2)        NOT NULL,
  MATCHCOLS          SMALLINT       NOT NULL,
  ACCESSCREATOR      CHAR(8)        NOT NULL,
  ACCESSNAME         CHAR(18)       NOT NULL,
  INDEXONLY          CHAR(1)        NOT NULL,
  SORTN_UNIQ         CHAR(1)        NOT NULL,
  SORTN_JOIN         CHAR(1)        NOT NULL,
```

```
SORTN_ORDERBY      CHAR(1)        NOT NULL,
SORTN_GROUPBY      CHAR(1)        NOT NULL,
SORTC_UNIQ         CHAR(1)        NOT NULL,
SORTC_JOIN         CHAR(1)        NOT NULL,
SORTC_ORDERBY      CHAR(1)        NOT NULL,
SORTC_GROUPBY      CHAR(1)        NOT NULL,
TSLOCKMODE         CHAR(3)        NOT NULL,
TIMESTAMP          CHAR(16)       NOT NULL,
REMARKS            VARCHAR(254)   NOT NULL,
PREFETCH           CHAR(1)        NOT NULL,
COLUMN_FN_EVAL     CHAR(1)        NOT NULL,
MIXOPSEQ           SMALLINT       NOT NULL,
VERSION            VARCHAR(64)    NOT NULL,
COLLID             CHAR(18)       NOT NULL,
ACCESS_DEGREE      SMALLINT,
ACCESS_PGROUP_ID   SMALLINT,
JOIN_DEGREE        SMALLINT,
JOIN_PGROUP_ID     SMALLINT,
SORTC_PGROUP_ID    SMALLINT,
SORTN_PGROUP_ID    SMALLINT,
PARALLELISM_MODE   CHAR(1),
MERGE_JOIN_COLS    SMALLINT,
CORRELATION_NAME   CHAR(18),
PAGE_RANGE         CHAR(1)        NOT NULL WITH DEFAULT,
JOIN_TYPE          CHAR(1)        NOT NULL WITH DEFAULT,
GROUP_MEMBER       CHAR(8)        NOT NULL WITH DEFAULT,
IBM_SERVICE_DATA   VARCHAR(254)   NOT NULL WITH DEFAULT,
WHEN_OPTIMIZE      CHAR(1)        NOT NULL WITH DEFAULT,  -- V5
QBLOCK_TYPE        CHAR(6)        NOT NULL WITH DEFAULT,  -- V5
BIND_TIME          TIMESTAMP      NOT NULL WITH DEFAULT,  -- V5
OPTHINT            CHAR(8)        NOT NULL WITH DEFAULT,  -- V6
HINT_USED          CHAR(8)        NOT NULL WITH DEFAULT,  -- V6
PRIMARY_ACCESSTYPE CHAR(1)        NOT NULL WITH DEFAULT)  -- V6
  IN DAGKWDB.DAGKWTSP;
```

Optionally, the DSN_STATEMNT_TABLE (V6) can be created as indicated in Figure EX.2. It is populated along with the PLAN_TABLE if it has been created.

Figure EX.2. Create statement table statement

```
CREATE TABLE DSN_STATEMNT_TABLE
 (QUERYNO         INTEGER       NOT NULL,
  APPLNAME        CHAR(8)       NOT NULL,
  PROGNAME        CHAR(8)       NOT NULL,
  COLLID          CHAR(18)      NOT NULL,
  GROUP_MEMBER    CHAR(8)       NOT NULL,
  EXPLAIN_TIME    TIMESTAMP     NOT NULL,
  STMT_TYPE       CHAR(6)       NOT NULL,
  COST_CATEGORY   CHAR(1)       NOT NULL,
  PROCMS          INTEGER       NOT NULL,
  PROCSU          INTEGER       NOT NULL,
  REASON          VARCHAR(254)  NOT NULL)
    IN DAGKWDB.DAGKWTSP;
```

A good alternative to creating the rather length tables is to ask a friend to grant you select privileges on their PLAN_TABLE and DSN_STATEMNT_TABLE, and execute a CREATE ... LIKE statements using your database and tablespace in the IN clause.

```
CREATE TABLE PLAN_TABLE LIKE FRIEND.PLAN_TABLE
  IN DAGKWDB.DAGKWTSP;

CREATE TABLE DSN_STATEMNT_TABLE LIKE
  FRIEND.DSN_STATEMNT_TABLE
  IN DAGKWDB.DAGKWTSP;
```

Do be cautious of sharing plan and statement tables among several developers in a test environment. It is a nuisance at best to identify rows that describe your SQL statements without having to be concerned with the rows in the tables that describe the statements of others. Having your own tables also gives you the flexibility of easily deleting rows of previously explained statements so that you can concentrate on the explanation of the most recent formulation of your statements without concern for outdated explanations. The DASD space cost of each developer having their own tables is very low; typically the minimum space allocation of one track is sufficient. This is because developers usually want to delete rows that are no longer needed to avoid confusion in interpreting the results.

The use of EXPLAIN causes rows to be inserted into the PLAN_TABLE describing the steps to be executed for interactive SQL and for each SQL statement in a plan or package. The rows provide information on how the data is processed at execution time. Information provided includes the use of indexes and how they are used, the method used to perform joins, the use of sequential and list prefetch, any sorts that are required, and the type of table or tablespace lock that will be used. These processes used at execution time are described throughout the book, in particular Chapters IU, BP, JP, ST, and PP. This chapter re-enforces a good deal of the material covered throughout the book on available access paths and performance through the analysis of the reports from the plan and statement tables.

If the DSN_STATEMNT_TABLE has been created, rows are also inserted into the table with an estimate of the processor time in milliseconds and in service units as will be discussed.

It is necessary to select from the PLAN_TABLE and DSN_STATEMNT_TABLE to view of the results placed in the tables by the optimizer. A report from these tables is very wide and does not fit on the screen or a hard copy report without wrapping of the report lines. Views can be created to narrow the column names and retrieve only the columns required as shown in Figure EX.3. The first view definition identifies the columns most frequently reviewed to determine if the appropriate access path has been chosen for the required processing and provides an estimate of the processor time expected at run time. This view is used for most examples in this chapter. The processor time estimate is reported in seconds based on the PROCMS/1000.0 calculation in the PLAN_CP view. The second view provides additional columns from the plan table and does not include any columns from the statement table. The third view definition identifies columns with information on parallelism, limited partition scan, correlation names, and additional useful information for your analysis. If you change the SPUFI maximum numeric and character field to 10 and 4 on the default panel, most of the column will fit on the screen when selecting from the views. You can customize the view definitions to meet your particular preferences and requirements. For example, you can identify rows that describe SQL statements in a specific program by adding a predicate:

```
WHERE P.APPLNAME   = 'PROGA'
```

where PROGA represents the program of interest.

Figure EX.3. View definitions of the plan and statement table

```
CREATE VIEW PLAN_CP
 (QN_B, MT, TNAME, PRE, AT, MC_O, XNAME,
  UJOG, UJOC, CP_S, CC, REASON, XCP) AS
SELECT STRIP(DIGITS(P.QUERYNO),LEADING,'0') CONCAT '  '
  CONCAT STRIP(DIGITS(QBLOCKNO), LEADING,'0') AS QN_B,
         STRIP(DIGITS(METHOD),   LEADING,'0') AS MT,
  TNAME, PREFETCH, ACCESSTYPE,
  SUBSTR(DIGITS(MATCHCOLS),5,1) CONCAT '  ' CONCAT
  INDEXONLY, ACCESSNAME,
  SORTN_UNIQ CONCAT SORTN_JOIN CONCAT SORTN_ORDERBY CONCAT
    SORTN_GROUPBY AS UJOG,
  SORTC_UNIQ CONCAT SORTC_JOIN CONCAT SORTC_ORDERBY CONCAT
    SORTC_GROUPBY AS UJOC,
  ROUND(DECIMAL(PROCMS/1000.0,9,2),2), COST_CATEGORY, REASON
FROM PLAN_TABLE P, DSN_STATEMNT_TABLE S
WHERE P.APPLNAME  = S.APPLNAME
AND   P.PROGNAME  = S.PROGNAME
AND   P.COLLID    = S.COLLID
AND   P.BIND_TIME = S.EXPLAIN_TIME;

CREATE VIEW PLAN_VIEW
 (QN,QB,PN,MT,TNAME,PRE,AT,MC,XNAME,
  XO,MX,CF,UN,JN,ON,GN,UC,JC,OC,GC,TB) AS
SELECT QUERYNO, QBLOCKNO, PLANNO, METHOD, TNAME,
  PREFETCH, ACCESSTYPE, MATCHCOLS, ACCESSNAME,
  INDEXONLY, MIXOPSEQ, COLUMN_FN_EVAL,
  SORTN_UNIQ, SORTN_JOIN, SORTN_ORDERBY,
  SORTN_GROUPBY, SORTC_UNIQ, SORTC_JOIN,
  SORTC_ORDERBY, SORTC_GROUPBY, TSLOCKMODE
FROM PLAN_TABLE;

CREATE VIEW PLAN_VIEW2
 (QN,QB,PN,AD,AP,JD,JP,SC,SN,PM,JC,CN,PR,
  JT,GM,IBM,WO,QT,BT) AS
SELECT QUERYNO, QBLOCKNO, PLANNO,
  ACCESS_DEGREE, ACCESS_PGROUP_ID,
  JOIN_DEGREE, JOIN_PGROUP_ID,
  SORTC_PGROUP_ID, SORTN_PGROUP_ID,
  PARALLELISM_MODE,MERGE_JOIN_COLS,
  CORRELATION_NAME, PAGE_RANGE,JOIN_TYPE,
  GROUP_MEMBER,IBM_SERVICE_DATA,
   WHEN_OPTIMIZE, QBLOCK_TYPE, BIND_TIME
FROM PLAN_TABLE;
```

You will want to associate the rows in the plan table with those in the statement table. This can be accomplished with the first view definition in Figure EX.3.

Figures EX.4. a, EX.4.b. EX.4.c, EX.4.d, EX.4.e, and EX.4.f summarizes the view column names, table column, and a brief explanation of the codes used by the optimizer to represent the access path chosen and give a processor time estimate.

Figure EX.4. a. Summary of access path codes

Report	Column	Explanation
QN	QUERYNO	Set QUERYNO = N on EXPLAIN, SET statement, or assigned by DB2
_B	QBLOCKNO	A number indicating a subselect, outer join or union block
-	APPLNAME	Name of application or blank for dynamic SQL
-	PROGNAME	Name of DBRM or blank for dynamic SQL
PN	PLANNO	Number of step within the QBLOCKNO being processed. Each new table accessed has a new step.
MT	METHOD	0, first table accessed, continuation, or not used 1, nested loop join (inner table) 2, merge join (inner table) 3, additional sorts needed 4, hybrid join (inner table)
-	CREATOR	Creator of the table accessed
TNAM	TNAME	Name of the table, materialized view, table expression, or temporary table for a full outer join.
-	TABNO	Distinguishes different references to a table. Indicates 1st, 2nd, 3rd, etc. table processed in a join.

Figure EX.4.b. Summary of access path codes

Report	Column	Explanation
PRE	PREFETCH	S,sequential prefetch
		L,list prefetch
		,(blank), no prefetch or unknown
AT	ACCESSTYPE	I, index scan
		I1, one-fetch index access
		R, tablespace scan
		N, IN (list) of values, index access
		M, multi index scans, followed by MX, MI, or MU
		MX, one of many index scans
		MI, intersection of multiple indexes
		MU, union of multiple indexes
		, (blank) not applicable to the current row or where current of cursor (update, delete)
MC	MATCHCOLS	Number of matched columns
-	ACCESS CREATOR	Creator of the index
XNAM	ACCESSNAME	Name of index if AT = I, I1, N, MX
O	INDEXONLY	Y, If no data access

Report	Column	Explanation
-	MIXOPSEQ	Step sequence for access type MX/MI/MU

Figure EX.4.c. Summary of access path codes

Report	Column	Explanation
-	COLUMN_FN EVAL	R, evaluation as is data read from data or index pages (stage 1) S, evaluation during sort (stage 2 , (blank)after data retrieval and after any sorts (stage 2)
U	SORTN_UNIQ	Y, sort on new table to remove duplicate rows*
J	SORTN_JOIN	Y, sort on new table for method 2 or 4
O	SORTN ORDERBY	Y, sort on new table for ORDER BY*
G	SORTN GROUPBY	Y, sort on new table for GROUP BY*
U	SORTC_UNIQ	Y, sort on composite to remove duplicate rows
J	SORTC_JOIN	Y, sort on composite for method 2 or 4
O	SORTC ORDERBY	Y, sort on composite for ORDER BY
C	SORTC GROUPBY	Y, sort on composite for GROUP BY

* UN, ON, GN not used in DB2 for OS/390

Figure EX.4.d. Summary of access path codes

Report	Column	Explanation
TB	TSLOCKMODE	Table lock mode if segmented tablespace. Tablespace lock mode if nonsegmented tablespace or LOCKSIZE is tablespace. IS, Intent Share IX, Intent Exclusive S, Share U, Update X, Exclusive SIX, Share with Intent Exclusive ,(blank) if the column is blank, no locks on the data are taken. N, UR isolation. Locks are not acquired on the tablespace, with the exception of mass delete and drop of table.*

*Following locks are like N except isolation level could not be determined at bind time. If the isolation level at execution time is UR, then no lock will be acquired (except as noted above). The condition noted will determine the lock mode at execution time:

NS, If the isolation level is CS, RR, or RS,

```
  then an S tablespace lock is acquired.
NIS,If the isolation level is CS, RR, or RS,
  then an IS tablespace lock is acquired.
SS,If the isolation level is CS or RS,
  then an IS tablespace lock is acquired.
If the isolation level is RR,
  then an S tablespace lock is acquired.
SS, If the isolation level is UR, CS, or RS,
  then an IS tablespace lock is acquired.
If the isolation level is RR,
  then an S tablespace lock is acquired.
```

Figure EX.4.e. Summary of access path codes

Report	Column	Explanation
-	TIMESTAMP	YYYYMMDDHHMMSSmmmmmm when EXPLAIN was processed
-	REMARKS	Can be used by developers
-	VERSION	Package version identifier
-	COLLID	Package collection identifier
-	ACCESS DEGREE	Degree of parallelism for accessing the new table
-	ACCESS PGROUP_ID	Parallel group identifier for accessing the new table
-	JOIN_DEGREE	Degree of parallelism for joining composite table with new table
-	JOIN_PGROUP ID	Parallel group ID for joining composite table with new table
-	SORTC_ PGROUP_ID	Sort outer or composite table in parallel*
-	SORTN_ PGROUP_ID	Sort inner or new table in parallel*
-	PARALLELISM _MODE	C = CPU Parallelism (includes parallel I/O) I = I/O Parallelism X = Sysplex query parallelism
-	MERGE_JOIN_ COLS	Number of columns used in merge join

* All members of a PGROUP_ID have the same degrees of parallelism. Thus, finding a previous ACCESS_DEGREE or JOIN_DEGREE with the *same* PGROUP_ID will yield the degrees of the sort.

Figure EX.4.f. Summary of access path codes

Report	Column	Explanation
-	CORRELATION_NAME	Name of table or view for the statement as specified in AS clause
-	PAGE_RANGE	Scan of >=1 partition planned (not all partitions)
-	JOIN_TYPE	F = Full outer L = Left or right outer S = Star join
-	GROUP_MEMBER	Data sharing group member that executed EXPLAIN
-	IBM_SERVICE_DATA	Internal use only
-	WHEN_OPTIMIZE	blank - Access path determined at bind time
		'B'-Access path determined at bind time and reoptimize at run time
		'R'-Access path determined at run time with values for variables
-	QBLOCK_TYPE	For each query block, the type of SQL operation performed. For the outermost query, it identifies the statement type. Values can be SELECT, INSERT, UPDATE, DELETE, SELUPD (SELECT with FOR UPDATE OF), DELCUR (DELETE WHERE CURRENT OF CURSOR), UPDCUR (UPDATE WHERE CURRENT OF CURSOR), CORSUB (correlated subquery), NCOSUB (non-correlated sub.)
-	BIND_TIME	Timestamp of bind for static SQL. 4 bytes are appended to the timestamp for dynamic SQL.
-	OPTHINT	A string that you use to identify this row as an optimization hint for DB2. DB2 uses this row as input when choosing an access path.
-	HINT_USED	If DB2 used one of your optimization hints, it puts the identifier for that hint (the value in OPTHINT) in this column.
-	PRIMARY_ACCESSTYPE	Indicates whether direct row access will be attempted first: 'D'-DB2 will try to use direct row access. If DB2 cannot use direct row access at runtime, it uses the access path described in the ACCESSTYPE column of PLAN_TABLE. blank-DB2 will not try to use direct row access.

Figure EX.5 contains a brief explanation of the columns in the DSN_STATEMNT_TABLE. The primary purpose of this table is to provide an estimate of the processor time in milliseconds and in service units for each SQL statement explained. The PROCMS column contains a value less than or equal to 2,147,483,647 which represents the estimated number of milliseconds. (The maximum value allows for about 24.8 days of processor time.) If the estimated value exceeds this maximum, the maximum value is reported. The PROCSU column is similar to the PROCMS column except that the cost estimate is in service units rather than milliseconds of processor time. Chapter PP discusses the use of service units in the resource limit facility table to control the amount of processor time that a dynamic SQL statement is allowed to use. Service units are specified to avoid having to change the limits when a company changes processors which have different speeds.

Figure EX.5. Statement table explanation

Report	Column	Explanation
QN	QUERYNO	Set QUERYNO = N on EXPLAIN, SET statement, or assigned by DB2
-	APPLNAME	Name of application or blank for dynamic SQL
-	PROGNAME	Name of DBRM or blank for dynamic SQL
-	COLLID	Package collection identifier or blank
-	GROUP_ MEMBER	Data sharing group member that executed EXPLAIN or blank
-	EXPLAIN_ TIME	Time of statement processing. Same as PLAN_TABLE.BIND_TIME.
-	STMT_TYPE	SELECT, INSERT, UPDATE, DELETE, SELUPD, DELCUR, UPDCUR
CC	COST_ CATEGORY	'A' - DB2 made cost estimate without using default values. Everything not in 'B' goes in 'A'. 'B' - Default values were used as indicated in REASON column
MS	PROCMS	Estimated processor time in <= 2,147,483,647 milliseconds (24.8 days). Maximum value is reported if exceeded.
-	PROCSU	Estimated service unit time <= 2,147,483,647. Maximum value is reported if exceeded.
-	REASON	Reason that cost estimate is placed in category B, for example: HOST VARIABLE - Statement uses host variables, parameter markers, or special registers. TABLE CARDINALITY - Cardinality statistics are missing for >=1 table named in the statement. UDF - Statement uses user-defined functions. TRIGGERS - Triggers are defined on the target table of an INSERT, UPDATE, or DELETE statement. REFERENTIAL CONSTRAINTS - Referential constraints of the type CASCADE or SET NULL exist on the target table of a DELETE statement.

Many factors can effect the accuracy of the estimates. The estimates are placed in one of two categories as shown in the COST_CATEGORY column. A cost category of A indicates a higher degree of accuracy than a cost category of B. The cost category of A means that the optimizer made the estimate without having to rely on default values as discussed in Chapter OP. Less confidence should be placed on an estimate with in a B cost category because the optimize does not have sufficient information available to calculate a good estimate and had to use default values.

The REASON column in Figure EX.5 contains reasons that a B cost estimate is not as accurate as an A cost estimate. Recall from Chapters PD and OP that there can be more than one best access path when host variables, parameter markers, and special registers are used in SQL statements. This is because the user can request different values at different times when the SQL is executed. The optimizer must use default values to estimate the costs of executing the statement. The optimizer must also use default values if the cardinality statistics have not been updated in the catalog tables as discussed in Chapters RR and OP. If the SQL statement references a user defined functions (UDF), triggers, or referential constraints involving cascade or set null, the optimizer does not have a cost estimate of doing the additional work.

EX.4 HOW TO USE EXPLAIN WITH A SIMPLE SELECT

EXPLAIN can be invoked when doing a bind or rebind of static SQL and when using dynamic SQL. The EXPLAIN(YES) parameter is used on the BIND and REBIND commands to get an explanation of static SQL embedded in a host program. EXPLAIN(NO) is the default. Here is an example of a partial BIND command with the EXPLAIN(YES) parameter.

```
BIND PLAN (SUPDATE)                -
LIBRARY   (PROJECT.AUTHID.DBRM)-
MEMBER    (SUPDATE)                -
EXPLAIN   (YES) ...
```

You may want to determine if you would get a different access path with new statistics, a new program temporary fix (PTF), or a new release of DB2 but do not want to replace the plan in the directory for execution unless it is the same or better access path. This can be done by doing a BIND without specifying the plan name in parentheses. The same goal can be accomplished with a package by specifying a collection other than the one from which you execute the package. In the following REBIND command, a new package for each member in the TESTEX collection is replaced in the collection. We are assuming that another collection is used for execution. An alternative is to do the explain using a test plan for the packages.

```
REBIND PACKAGE(TESTEX) MEMBER(*) EXPLAIN(YES)
```

The EXPLAIN clause is used to get an explanation of dynamic SQL embedded in a host program or executed interactively like:

```
EXPLAIN PLAN SET QUERYNO = 1 FOR
SELECT SN, SNAME
FROM   S
WHERE  CITY = 'Dallas';
```

QUERYNO = 1 on the EXPLAIN line identifies the rows in the plan table that apply to the SQL statement. There are frequently many rows in the plan table and the QUERYNO provides for identifying the rows that apply to a specific SQL statement in a program or assigned with the EXPLAIN clause. The QUERYNO and SQL statement can be found in the file USERID.TEMP.PCLIST containing the modified source code and the DBRM library member created by the precompiler. The catalog tables SYSSTMT and SYSPACKSTMT contain the QUERYNO and text for static SQL. This information can be gotten with the following SELECT statements. However, the statements are not in blocked format as they were keyed in a program.

```
SELECT NAME, PLNAME, PLCREATOR,
  SEQNO, STMTNO, SECTNO, TEXT
FROM   SYSIBM.SYSSTMT
WHERE  NAME = 'P1';

SELECT COLLID, NAME, VERSION,
  SEQNO, STMTNO, SECTNO, STMT
FROM   SYSIBM.SYSPACKSTMT
WHERE  NAME    = 'PK1'
AND    COLLID  = 'UNITEST'
AND    VERSION = 'V1';
```

Execution of EXPLAIN does not execute the SQL statement. It simply INSERT statements rows in the plan and statement tables. It is necessary to select from one of the views in Figure EX.3 or the base tables to see the results. In the following example of selecting from the PLAN_CP view, the rows are sorted for ease of interpreting the report:

```
SELECT *
FROM   PLAN_CP
ORDER BY QN_B;
```

The report from the view in Figure EX.6 reveals that a matching index scan on the PCIT index (AT=I, MC=1, XNAM=PCIT) is used to locate the suppliers in Dallas. The initial thought might be that 3 I/O are required to traverse a 3 level index on the CITY column plus 1 I/O to a data page (XO=N) to retrieve the columns requested. But notice that list prefetch (PRE=L) is being used. This suggests that the optimizer has estimated that more than one data page is expected to contain the required rows. The PCIT index probably has a low cardinality. This can be verified by selecting FIRSTKEYCARDF from SYSIBM.SYSINDEXES. Indeed, the cardinality is 20, which means that 5 percent (1/20 is the filter factor) of the index leaf and data pages are expected to be processed.

Figure EX.6. A simple plan and statement report

```
QN_B  MT     TNAM  PRE  AT  MC_O  XNAM  UJOG  UJOC       CP_S  CC  REAS
---------+---------+---------+---------+---------+---------+---------
1  1         P     L    I   1  N  PCIT  NNNN  NNNN       3.31  A
```

Initially, it is surprising that the processor time is 3.31 seconds with a matching index scan. Lets analyze the processing to determine why the processor time is high. If the P table has 1 million rows on 30,000 data pages, about 1,500 data pages (0.05 * 30,000) need to be read in addition to the index pages. List prefetch is be used to read 32 pages with 1 I/O (assuming a buffer pool size of 1000 pages or larger). This reduces the I/O to 47 (1500 / 32). Actually the number of I/O is probably less than 47 since the RIDs (Record IDs) are sorted and duplicate page identifiers eliminated before the I/O requests are issued. There is a good chance that many of the data pages identified by the RIDs contain several parts in Dallas with such a low cardinality of 20. The RID sort is not shown in the report. It is assumed that the analyst knows that RIDs are almost always sorted before list prefetch. An exception has to do with a hybrid join as discussed in Chapter JP.

If the indexed column is 10 bytes in length, there will be about 3,000 leaf pages, and about 150 (0.05 * 3,000) leaf pages will need to be read before reading the data pages. The report does not indicate that sequential prefetch on the leaf pages is part of the plan. However, it is likely that sequential or dynamic prefetch will be used on the leaf pages, reducing the number of I/O to 5 (150 / 32). (List prefetch applies only to data pages, not to index pages. It is merely coincidental that the code PRE=L appears adjacent to the code AT=I indicating index usage.)

Figure EX.7 summarizes the statistics used by the optimizer for most tables and indexes analyzed in this chapter. The total number of pages for the three tables is 405,000 from SYSTABLESPACE.NACTIVEF

Figure EX.7. Indexes and statistics available to the optimizer in examples

```
→    CREATE UNIQUE INDEX SX   ON S   (SN)           CLUSTER;
→    CREATE UNIQUE INDEX JX   ON J   (JN)           CLUSTER;
→    CREATE UNIQUE INDEX PX   ON P   (PN)           CLUSTER;
→    CREATE UNIQUE INDEX SPJX ON SPJ (SN, PN, JN) CLUSTER;
→    CREATE INDEX PCIT ON P (CITY);
→    CREATE INDEX SCIT ON S (CITY);
→    CREATE INDEX STX  ON S (STATUS);
```

SYSTABLES

NAME	CARDF	NPAGES
S	500000	15000
P	1000000	30000
J	2000000	60000
SPJ	10000000	300000

SYSINDEXES

NAME	CLUSTER RATIOF	FIRSTKEY CARDF	FULLKEY CARDF	NLEAF	NLEV-ELS
SX	0.99	500000	500000	10	3
SCIT	0.20	20	20	3000	3
STX	0.60	10	10	2000	3
PX	0.99	1000000	1000000	4000	3
PCIT	0.20	20	20	3000	3
JX	0.99	2000000	2000000	8000	3
JCIT	0.20	20	20	3000	3
SPJX	0.99	10000000	10000000	40000	3

SYSCOLUMNS

TBNAME	Column	COLCARDF	HIGH2KEY	LOW2KEY
S	SN	500000	ZZZZXX	AAAABB
S	SNAME	400000	Smith	AAAAAAAA
S	STATUS	10	..	..
S	CITY	20	Paris	AAAAAAAA
P	PN	1000000	ZZZZXX	AAAABB
P	PNAME	900000	Screw	Bolt
P	COLOR	100	Red	Blue
P	WEIGHT	1000	..	..
P	CITY	20	Rome	London
J	JN	2000000	ZZZZXX	AAAABB
J	JNAME	1500000	Terminal	Collator
J	CITY	20	Rome	AAAAAAAA
SPJ	SN	100000	ZZZZXX	AAAABB
SPJ	PN	200000	P6	P1
SPJ	JN	300000	J7	J2
SPJ	QTY	10000	....	...

EX.5 ANALYSIS OF EXPLANATIONS IN THE PLAN TABLE

It takes some time and practice to interpret and understand the access paths as summarized in the plan and statement tables. We will analyze the explanation of a number of SQL statements to get you started in this direction. Information that can be gleaned from reading between the lines of the reports are also discussed. The analysis in this chapter will enhance your knowledge and provide a good foundation for writing good performing SQL in the future. Your analysis and tuning of SQL statements that you have written will further enhance your ability to write good performing statements.

Information in the reports is very useful but care must be exercised in interpreting the codes describing the access paths chosen. For example, a predicate WHERE SNAME LIKE :SNAME usually shows the use of a matching index scan. However, at execution time a non-matching index scan or tablespace scan with sequential prefetch is used if the host variable has a value beginning with "%" or "_".

A number of SELECT statements will be analyzed to demonstrate how to interpret the results of EXPLAIN. The optimizer evaluates access paths using the same rules and formula for SELECT, UPDATE, and DELETE statements. There is no access path evaluation for INSERT statements.

Data manager always uses the clustering index to insert the row in sequence on the column with the clustering index if one exists.

It is advisable to use a parameter marker ("?") in place of a literal when testing SQL statements interactively that will be embedded in a host program using host variables. This is because coded literals are used in formula to estimate the number of I/O and CPU time, and the access path chosen differs in many cases when host variables are used. The value of a host language variable changes from one execution of the program to another and during the execution of the program depending on the information requested by the user. Therefore, the optimizer uses default filter factors (estimates of the percentage of rows that will qualify) for range predicates (such as >, <, BETWEEN and LIKE) and does not use distribution statistics when host variables are used except for LIKE predicates.

You can get different access paths selected than the ones described in this chapter for the same SQL statements. This is because the access path chosen varies with the version/release of DB2, current PTFs installed, buffer pool sizes and thresholds, RID pool size, and the computer model being used to do the explains.

Processor Time Estimates with Different BETWEEN Values

The purpose of analyzing the following statement is to point out how the values in a BETWEEN predicate can effect the processor time estimate as well as the use of sorts and prefetch. Three explains were done to generate three explanations. The QUERYNO used for each explain is shown preceded by two hyphens in the WHERE clause.

```
EXPLAIN PLAN SET QUERYNO =  (--noted) FOR
SELECT SN, PN, JN, QTY
FROM   SPJ
WHERE     QTY BETWEEN 1000 AND 3000 --QUERYNO = 1
--WHERE   QTY BETWEEN  100 AND  300 --QUERYNO = 2
--WHERE   QTY BETWEEN    ? AND    ? --QUERYNO = 3
ORDER BY QTY;
```

Figure EX.8 shows the results of explaining the previous statement by selecting from the PLAN_CP view. This provides for analyzing the processor time estimate. The estimate (in column CP_S) applies to the entire SQL statement (not each row in the explanation). Notice that the optimizer has given the highest processor time estimate (CP_S) for the QTY BETWEEN 1000 AND 3000 predicate used as QUERYNO = 1. It has estimated that more rows qualify with the wider range of values than the narrower range of values used for the QTY BETWEEN 100 AND 300 predicate (QUERYNO = 2) result in a processor time estimate of only about one-third that of the wider range of values (QUERYNO = 1). Both of these cost estimates have a cost category (CC) of 'A' because literals are used in the predicates. However, the use of the parameter marker '?' to represent a host variable results in CC = 'B' and a much lower processor time estimate. The Optimizer estimated fewer rows need to be retrieved and sorted based on default FF (filter factor). The default FF of 3/1,000 for a BETWEEN predicates based on a column cardinality of 10,000 is given in Chapter OP.

Figure EX.8. Estimate of processor time report

QN	B	MT	TNAM	PRE	AT	MC_O	XNAM	UJOG	UJOC	CP_S	CC	REAS
1	1		SPJ	S	R	N		NNNN	NNNN	1425.95	A	
1	1	3				N		NNNN	NNYN	1425.95	A	
2	1		SPJ	S	R	N		NNNN	NNNN	505.74	A	
2	1	3				N		NNNN	NNYN	505.74	A	
3	1		SPJ	S	R	N		NNNN	NNNN	49.31	B	HOST
3	1	3				N		NNNN	NNYN	49.31	B	HOST

A tablespace scan (AT = R) with sequential prefetch (PRE = S) on SPJ and a sort is required for the ORDER BY for all three formulations. There is no index on the QTY column to narrow the search and possible avoid a sort.

Multiple Index Usage Explanation

The following three SELECT statements identify suppliers who are in a city and have a SN between values specified by the user. The three access paths for the three formulations will be analyzed to gain an understanding of how to interpret the results in the report and which access path is likely to give the best performance under what conditions.

```
EXPLAIN PLAN SET QUERYNO = 1 FOR
SELECT SN, SNAME, CITY, STATUS
FROM   S
WHERE  CITY = ?
OR     SN BETWEEN ? AND ?;

EXPLAIN PLAN SET QUERYNO = 2 FOR
SELECT SN, SNAME, CITY, STATUS
FROM   S
WHERE  CITY = ?
OR     SN BETWEEN ? AND ?
OPTIMIZE FOR 1 ROW;

EXPLAIN PLAN SET QUERYNO = 3 FOR
SELECT SN, SNAME, CITY, STATUS
FROM   S
WHERE  CITY = ?
UNION ALL
SELECT SN, SNAME, CITY, STATUS
FROM   S
WHERE  SN BETWEEN ? AND ?;
```

Use of multiple indexes (QUERYNO=1): The first four rows in the Figure EX.9 report describes the access path for using multiple index processing. The rows are frequently not executed in the order in which they are listed. One reason is that the SELECT from PLAN_CP view that produced the report used an ORDER BY on the QUERYNO to arrange the rows for ease of analysis. The order of the rows does not reflect the order of execution even if an ORDER BY is not used to produce the report. The first row indicates that multiple index processing is used with list prefetch (PRE=L, AT=M). Obviously, list prefetch cannot be used until the RIDs are identified from the leaf pages and processed as discussed in Chapters CO, IU, and PP.

Figure EX.9. Multiple index usage report

QN	B	MT	TNAM	PRE	AT	MC	_O	XNAM	UJOG	UJOC	CP_S	CC	REAS
1	1		S	L	M	0	N		NNNN	NNNN	3.46	B	HOST
1	1		S		MX	1	Y	SX	NNNN	NNNN	3.46	B	HOST
1	1		S	S	MX	1	Y	SCIT	NNNN	NNNN	3.46	B	HOST
1	1		S		MU	0	N		NNNN	NNNN	3.46	B	HOST
2	1		S		R	0	N		NNNN	NNNN	4.61	B	HOST
3	1		S	L	I	1	N	SCIT	NNNN	NNNN	3.50	B	HOST
3	2		S	S	I	1	N	SX	NNNN	NNNN	3.50	B	HOST

The second and third rows indicate that a matching index scan will be done using the SX and SCIT indexes with index only processing (AT=MX, MC=1, XNAM=SCIT and XNAM=SX, XO=Y). There is a good chance that a number of leaf pages will be processed, assuming that both of the indexed columns have a low cardinality. Each index is processed serially. One might speculate that this is a good opportunity for parallel processing in the future. One processor of a central computer complex (CPC) might process the SCIT index and sort the RIDs while at the same time a second processor can be processing and sorting the RIDs from the SX index. A third processor can merge the sorted RIDs, eliminate duplicates, and issue the prefetch I/O.

The last row of QUERYNO 1 shows that a union of the RIDs is done for the ORed condition (AT=MU). It is implied that a union of the RIDs and an intersection of the RIDs for ANDed conditions requires a sort to eliminate duplicates, although a sort is not shown in the report. The sort results in the RIDs being in sequence as they appear on DASD, making the list prefetch processing efficient by reducing DASD seek time. If some of the required pages are already in the buffer pool, they will not be read again. For example, if pages 5, 10, 15, 20, 25 are in the buffer pool and pages 5, **7**, 10, 15, 20, **23, 27** are required, only pages **7, 23, 27** will be read from DASD using skip sequential processing.

OPTIMIZE FOR 1 ROW (QUERYNO=2) is used to discourage the use of list prefetch. If list prefetch is not used, multiple index processing cannot be used. The first thought is that one of the indexes can be used to narrow the search. However, this is not possible because if the index on CITY is used, rows within the range of SN designated in the BETWEEN predicate can be missed. Conversely, if the index on SN is used, suppliers in a specified city can be missed. Chapter PP discusses this situation in more detail. The tablespace scan does increase the processor time estimate as would be expected with sizable tables.

The UNION ALL formulation allows for use of the index on SN followed by the use of the index on CITY to locate the required rows. This is the best formulation if only a few non-duplicate rows are fetched and many rows qualify. The few required rows are located one at a time and returned to the user as they are fetched. However, if the same row is for a supplier in a city and SNs within the specified range of values, duplicate rows are returned to the user. If duplicate rows can qualify and are not acceptable to the user, UNION rather than UNION ALL can be used. However, UNION requires that all qualifying rows above and below the UNION are retrieved, sorted, and duplicates eliminated. This is not a good access path if many rows qualify and few rows are fetched.

Comparison of three access paths: The first formulation (QUERYNO=1) will perform well if there are not a large number of qualifying RIDs for a given city and there is not a large number of values that qualify within the specified range of SNs. If there are a large number of qualifying RIDs because of a low cardinality or skewed distribution of values in one or both of the indexed columns and only a few rows are fetched, this is not a good access path because it is necessary to locate and process all of the qualifying RIDs before the first few rows can be returned to the user. The second formulation is a good alternative if it is likely that enough qualifying rows can be located after issuing only a few sequential prefetch I/O or many rows qualify and must be processed by a batch program. If a large number of rows qualify, only a few will be fetched, no duplicate rows will qualify or duplicate rows are acceptable, the third formulation (QUERYNO=3) is best. This is because an index on CITY can be used to locate the rows in a given city one at a time as they are fetched followed by the use of the index on SN to locate one row at a time to satisfy the BETWEEN predicate on SN. Indeed, if there are enough suppliers in a given city to display to the user, the index on SN need not be used at all.

EX.6 JOIN EXPLANATIONS

We will review the explanation of several joins to gain an understanding of how to interpret the explain report and gain insight into the performance of the join methods described in Chapter JP.

Hybrid and Nested Loop Join with Literals and Host Variables

Hybrid and nested loop joins are analyzed using the following statements:

```
EXPLAIN PLAN SET QUERYNO = 1 FOR
SELECT S.SN, SNAME, PN, QTY
FROM   SPJ, S
WHERE  SPJ.SN = S.SN
AND    SPJ.SN > 'S2'
AND    S.SN   > 'S2';--Added by optimizer

EXPLAIN PLAN SET QUERYNO = 2 FOR
SELECT S.SN, SNAME, PN, QTY
FROM   SPJ, S
WHERE  SPJ.SN = S.SN
AND    SPJ.SN > 'S2'
AND    S.SN   > 'S2' --Added by optimizer
OPTIMIZE FOR 12 ROWS;

EXPLAIN PLAN SET QUERYNO = 3 FOR
SELECT S.SN, SNAME, PN, QTY
FROM   SPJ, S
WHERE  SPJ.SN = S.SN
AND    SPJ.SN > ?
AND    S.SN   > ?;  --Added by optimizer
```

The optimizer uses transitive closure (discussed in Chapter JP) and adds the predicate S.SN > ? based on the local predicate SPJ.SN > ? and the join predicate SPJ.SN = S.SN in all three statements. This is a deduction based on the matching index scans on the S.SN index shown in Figure EX.10. The optimizer recognizes the unique index on S.SN. It uses the S table with 500,000 rows as the outer table of the join and the SPJ table with 10,000,000 rows as the inner table. It has estimated that the local predicates on the two tables qualifies fewer rows in the S table than the SPJ table.

Figure EX.10. Hybrid and nested loop join report

QN	B	MT	TNAM	PRE	AT	MC	O	XNAM	UJOG	UJOC	CP_S	CC	REAS
1	1		S	S	I	1	N	SX	NNNN	NNNN	34.07	A	
1	1	4	SPJ	L	I	1	N	SPJX	NNNN	NNNN	34.07	A	
2	1		S	S	I	1	N	SX	NNNN	NNNN	37.10	A	
2	1	1	SPJ		I	1	N	SPJX	NNNN	NNNN	37.10	A	
3	1		S	S	I	1	N	SX	NNNN	NNNN	.02	B	HOST
3	1	1	SPJ		I	1	N	SPJX	NNNN	NNNN	.02	B	HOST

The hybrid join (QUERYNO = 1, MT = 4) has a bit lower processor time estimate than the nested loop join (QUERYNO = 2, MT = 1) due largely to no sorts required for the hybrid join. Sorts are avoided through the use of high cluster ratios indexes on the inner and outer tables.

The optimize for a small number of rows influenced the optimizer to choose a nested loop join (QUERYNO = 2, MT = 1) over a hybrid join to show the difference in processing. The nested loop join is the better access path if only a few rows are fetched despite increasing the processor time by about 3 seconds. This is because the processor time is based on fetching all qualifying rows.

Both the hybrid and nested loop join have a high estimated cost based on many rows estimated to qualify with the SN > 'S2' predicate.

The parameter marker '?' is used to represent a host variable (QUERYNO = 3). The processor time is significantly less based on the default FF on the S.SN column with a high cardinality which is equal to the cardinality of the table (unique index).

Nested Loop and Merge Join with Host Variables

Determine the SN, SNAME, PN, JN, and QTY for SNs within a range of values requested by the user and sequence the data.

```
EXPLAIN PLAN SET QUERYNO = 1 FOR
SELECT SPJ.SN, SNAME, JN, PN, QTY
FROM   SPJ, S
WHERE  SPJ.SN = S.SN
AND    S.SN   BETWEEN ?  AND ?
ORDER BY SPJ.SN, SPJ.PN, SPJ.JN;

EXPLAIN PLAN SET QUERYNO = 2 FOR
SELECT SPJ.SN, SNAME, JN, PN, QTY
FROM   SPJ, S
WHERE  SPJ.SN = S.SN
AND    S.SN   BETWEEN ?  AND ?
ORDER BY SPJ.SN, SPJ.PN, SPJ.JN
OPTIMIZE FOR 1 ROW;
```

Concern for a merge join motivated OPTIMIZE FOR 1 ROW even though indexes are used to avoid sorts for QUERYNO = 1 in Figure EX.11. This clause encourages a nested loop join as shown in for QUERYNO = 2. However, the nested loop join has a higher processor time estimate. The actual costs depends on the actual number of rows fetched. Therefore, if few rows are fetched, the actual processor times can be less than using the merge join.

Figure EX.11. Nested loop and merge join with host variables

```
QN_B  MT     TNAM  PRE  AT  MC_O  XNAM  UJOG  UJOC        CP_S  CC  REAS
---------+---------+---------+---------+---------+-------+---------+-
1 1          SPJ   S    I   1  N  SPJX  NNNN  NNNN        1.49  B   HOST
1 1   2      S     S    I   1  N  SX    NNNN  NNNN        1.49  B   HOST
2 1          SPJ   S    I   1  N  SPJX  NNNN  NNNN        1.83  B   HOST
2 1   1      S          I   1  N  SX    NNNN  NNNN        1.83  B   HOST
```

Explaining a Three-way Join

Assume that a three-way join is required as indicated in the following statement. The second formulation uses the OPTIMIZE FOR 12 rows clause to encourage a nested loop join.

```
EXPLAIN PLAN SET QUERYNO = 1 FOR
SELECT S.SN, P.PN, QTY, S.CITY
FROM   S, P, SPJ
WHERE  S.SN   = SPJ.SN
AND    P.CITY = S.CITY
AND    S.SN   = ?
ORDER BY SPJ.SN, SPJ.PN, SPJ.JN;

EXPLAIN PLAN SET QUERYNO = 2 FOR
SELECT S.SN, P.PN, QTY, S.CITY
FROM   S, P, SPJ
WHERE  S.SN   = SPJ.SN
AND    P.CITY = S.CITY
AND    S.SN   = ?
ORDER BY SPJ.SN, SPJ.PN, SPJ.JN
OPTIMIZE FOR 12 ROWS;
```

Two sorts are required for the merge join despite the clustering index on SN, PN, JN in the SPJ table as shown in Figure EX.12. The two smaller tables (S and P) are joined first with a nested loop join and list prefetch is used on the P table. The results of the join of the qualifying S and P rows are written to a work file. The work file is sorted as well as SPJ columns to allow for a merge join. List prefetch used on the SPJ table requires RID precessing before the join. List prefetch also makes it necessary to sort the qualifying rows for the ORDER BY clause.

Figure EX.12. Three-way join report

QN_B		MT	TNAM	PRE	AT	MC_O		XNAM	UJOG	UJOC	CP_S	CC	REAS
1	1		S		I	1	N	SX	NNNN	NNNN	791.19	A	
1	1	1	P	L	I	1	N	PCIT	NNNN	NNNN	791.19	A	
1	1	2	SPJ	L	I	1	N	SPJX	NYNN	NYNN	791.19	A	
1	1	3				0	N		NNNN	NNYN	791.19	A	
2	1		SPJ		I	1	N	SPJX	NNNN	NNNN	1149.68	A	
2	1	1	S		I	1	N	SX	NNNN	NNNN	1149.68	A	
2	1	1	P		I	1	N	PCIT	NNNN	NNNN	1149.68	A	

The two nested loop joins do not require a sort for the joins nor ORDER BY (QUERYNO = 2). However, there is a higher processor time estimate. This may be a result of an estimate that many rows must be processed in the 10,000,000 row SPJ table in the first step. The matching index scan is a result of transitive closure. SPJ.SN = ? is added by the optimizer based on the coded predicate of S.SN = ? and the join predicate S.SN = SPJ.SN. The processor time estimate includes fetching all qualifying rows despite the OPTIMIZE FOR 12 ROWS clause. If you do plan to fetch only 12 rows, the two nested loop joins have performance advantages. Considerably less work as described for the first formulation needs to be done before the first 12 rows are fetched.

EX.7 Subselect Explanations

Non-correlated subselects are processed bottom up. That is the bottom select is processed prior to the select above it. Additional factors are included in subselect processing as discussed in Chapter ST. We will analyze several explain reports to understand how subselects are processed.

IN Subselect with Transformation to a Join

The following statement to determine information on parts and their supplier that are being used on jobs will be used to show several points.

```
             EXPLAIN PLAN SET QUERYNO = 1 FOR
QBLOCKNO=1   SELECT SN, PN, JN, QTY
             FROM   SPJ
             WHERE  PN IN
QBLOCKNO=2    (SELECT PN
               FROM   P);

             EXPLAIN PLAN SET QUERYNO = 2 FOR
QBLOCKNO=1   SELECT SN, PN, JN, QTY
             FROM   SPJ
             WHERE  PN IN
QBLOCKNO=2    (SELECT PN
               FROM   P);
```

QUERYNO = 1 was explained with an index on P.PN that has a cluster ratio of 20 percent and is not declared as unique with the results shown in Figure EX.13. QUERYNO = 2 was explained with a unique index on P.PN that has a cluster ratio of 99 percent as all examples in this chapter unless noted otherwise.

Figure EX.13. Subselect with and without transformation to a join

```
QN_B   MT      TNAM   PRE   AT   MC_O   XNAM   UJOG UJOC          CP_S CC REAS
----------+----------+----------+----------+----------+---------+----------+
1  1           SPJ    S     R         N        NNNN  NNNN  2147483.64   A
1  2  3                               N        NNNN  YNYN  2147483.64   A
1  2           P      S     R         N        NNNN  NNNN  2147483.64   A
2  1           SPJ    S     R         N        NNNN  NNNN     4187.42   A
2  1  1        P            I    1    Y  PX    NNNN  NNNN     4187.42   A
```

Query blocks: An SQL statement can consist of several query blocks. A good rule of thumb for identifying query blocks in a statement is to notice each occurrence of the keywords SELECT, INSERT, UPDATE, and DELETE. The optimizer sequence numbers the query blocks in the order in which they are written in the statement. One or more rows are inserted into the PLAN_TABLE for each query block along with the sequence number assigned by the optimizer. The query blocks are noted in the previous SELECT statements (QBLOCKNO=1 and QBLOCKNO=2). Query blocks are frequently not executed in the order of the assigned sequence numbers.

Sequence of execution: An IN subselect is an example of a case where the second query block is executed before the first query block. It is also a good example of how it is necessary to read between the lines of the report based on how SQL statements are processed. Recall from Chapter ST that non-correlated subselects are processed bottom up. In the example, the bottom select (QBLOCKNO=2) is processed before the top select (QBLOCKNO=1). This is logical if you think of the question being asked. It is necessary to first get the PNs from the P table before determining the JNs from the SPJ table that use the parts along with the SNs that supplied the parts used on the job.

Notice that a tablespace scan with sequential prefetch is used to retrieve all PNs from the P table (QN_B = 1 2, AT = R, PRE = S). The PNs are written to a work area, and sorted, duplicates eliminated, and an in-memory sparse index is built as described in Chapter ST. Although two sorts are shown in the report, only one sort is done for two reasons. The two reasons are to eliminate duplicates (U = Y) and to sequence the PNs from the P table (O = Y). A tablespace scan is done on the SPJ table using sequential prefetch (QN_B = 1 1, PRE=S, AT=R). For each PN in the SPJ table, the sparse in-memory index is used to determine if the PN is in the work area created from the P table. If the SPJ.PN is in the work area, the SN, PN, and JN are returned from the SPJ table.

The PN in the P table should have a unique index because it is the primary key. QUERYNO=2 was explained with a unique index on P.PN and a cluster ratio of 99 percent. The optimizer recognizes the unique index on the column selected in the bottom select. This means that the same results will be returned if the subselect is transformed into a join. The use of a nested loop join with the P table as the inner table of the join allows for a matching index scan on the PN index and index only processing (MT=1, AT=I, MC_O = 1 Y). Typically the subselect is transformed into a nested loop join with the second selected table as the inner table of the join.

The primary requirement for transformation of a subselect to a join is that there is a unique index on the column selected in the bottom select. A few additional requirements are described in Chapter ST. Transformation into a join does not occur for a NOT IN subselect.

Comparison: The use of the join with the unique index avoids having to retrieve all P.PNs, write them to a work area, sort them, eliminate duplicates, and build a sparse in-memory index. If many rows qualify and only a few rows are fetched, the join access path has significant performance advantages in avoiding a good deal of processing before the first few rows can be returned to the program. This is reflected in the processor time estimate being dramatically lower for the join compared to the subselect processing. Indeed, the subselect processing shows the maximum possible time estimate.

Comparison of NOT IN and NOT EXISTS Subselects

NOT IN like IN subselects are non-correlated subselects. NOT EXISTS and EXISTS are correlated subselects. Several factors affecting the performance of these types of subselects are discussed in Chapter ST. Here we will analyze a NOT IN and NOT EXISTS subselect. The following two statements select the SNs from SPJ where there is not a matching supplier in the parent S table. If any rows qualify, there is a violation of referential integrity (Chapter RI).

```
EXPLAIN PLAN SET QUERYNO = 1 FOR
SELECT SN, PN, JN, QTY
FROM   SPJ
WHERE  SPJ.SN NOT IN
  (SELECT S.SN
   FROM   S);

EXPLAIN PLAN SET QUERYNO = 2 FOR
SELECT SN, PN, JN, QTY
FROM   SPJ SPJX
WHERE  NOT EXISTS
  (SELECT 1
   FROM   S
   WHERE  S.SN = SPJX.SN);
```

We pointed out that a NOT IN formulation can be automatically transformed into NOT EXISTS if few rows are expected to qualify in the outer select which means few matching index scans into the inner table are required. The previous QUERYNO = 1 is not automatically transformed to a NOT EXISTS formulation based on the SPJ.SN cardinality of 100,000 in the 10,000,000 row SPJ table because 100,000 matching index scans into the S table would be required based on the statistics in Figure EX.7.

We see from the explain report in Figure EX.14 that the NOT IN formulation is estimated to require a very large amount of processor time. Indeed, the maximum possible time is reported. This largely due to the tablespace scan of 10,000,000 row SPJ table (QN_B = 1 1), a non-matching index scan of the index on S.SN with index only processing (QN_B = 1 2), and a sort of 500,000 S.SN values (there is no local predicate to narrow the search) (MT = 3).

Figure EX.14. Comparison of NOT IN and NOT EXISTS subselects

QN_B		MT	TNAM	PRE	AT	MC_O		XNAM	UJOG	UJOC	CP_S	CC	REAS
1	1		SPJ	S	R	0	N		NNNN	NNNN	2147483.64	A	
1	2	3				0	N		NNNN	YNYN	2147483.64	A	
1	2		S	S	I	0	Y	SX	NNNN	NNNN	2147483.64	A	
2	1		SPJ	S	R	0	N		NNNN	NNNN	3807.17	A	
2	2		S		I	1	Y	SX	NNNN	NNNN	3807.17	A	

We can rewrite this statement using a NOT EXISTS formulation (QUERYNO =2). Each SPJ.SN is estimated to appear 100 times in SPJ (10,000,000 table cardinality / 100,000 column cardinality). Each SPJ.SN can be evaluated against the S table only once in most cases because the first occurrence of a SPJ.SN can be placed in an in-memory table for the correlated subselect. This avoids evaluation of each 100 occurrences of a single SPJ.SN value in most cases.

NOT EXISTS formulations frequently perform better than NOT IN. However, if you find that an EXISTS or NOT EXISTS formulation performs poorly, do review the cases where IN and NOT IN have performance advantages in Chapter ST.

IN Subselect Transformed to IN (list)

QUERYNO = 1 and 2 determines information on parts being used on jobs in a specified quantity. The only difference between the two statements is that the first statement uses a literal in the subselect predicate (QTY = 100) and the second statement uses a parameter marker (QTY = ?) to represent a host variable which will be used when the statement is embedded in a host program.

```
EXPLAIN PLAN SET QUERYNO = 1 FOR
SELECT PN, PNAME, WEIGHT, CITY
FROM   P
WHERE  PN IN
   (SELECT PN
    FROM   SPJ
    WHERE  QTY = 100);

EXPLAIN PLAN SET QUERYNO = 2 FOR
SELECT PN, PNAME, WEIGHT, CITY
FROM   P
WHERE  PN IN
   (SELECT PN
    FROM   SPJ
    WHERE  QTY = ?);
```

Notice that the processor time estimate is the same with an equal predicate on a literal and a parameter marker to represent a host variable in Figure EX.15. Both statements have a cost category of A. This is because the formula for calculating the FF is the same, both are calculated as 1 divided by the cardinality of the QTY column.

Figure EX.15. IN subselect transformed to an IN (list)

QN_B	MT	TNAM	PRE	AT	MC_O	XNAM	UJOG	UJOC	CP_S	CC	REAS
1 1		P		N	1 N	PX	NNNN	NNNN	13601.51	A	
1 2	3				N		NNNN	YNYN	13601.51	A	
1 2		SPJ	S	R	N		NNNN	NNNN	13601.51	A	
2 1		P		N	1 N	PX	NNNN	NNNN	13601.51	A	
2 2	3				N		NNNN	YNYN	13601.51	A	
2 2		SPJ	S	R	N		NNNN	NNNN	13601.51	A	

The AT = N for QN_B = 1 1 and QN_B = 2 1 means that the IN subselect is transformed to IN (list) processing. A matching index scan can be done on P.PN for each qualifying row in the SPJ table.

The YNYN (QN_B = 1 2, MT = 3 and QN_B = 2 2, MT = 3) means that one sort of the subselect results is done for two reasons (unique values and sequential order) for QUERYNO = 1 and 2.

EX.8. ADDITIONAL EXPLANATIONS

Table/Tablespace Lock Explanation

It can be surprising to discover that no program can update any rows or pages in the SPJ table while the following statement is being executed despite the fact that it is a SELECT statement and a row or page lock size was requested along with LOCKMAX of 0 when the tablespace containing the SPJ table was created.

```
EXEC SQL DECLARE CSPJ CURSOR FOR
SELECT SN, PN, QTY
FROM   SPJ
WHERE  PN IN (?, ?, ?)
AND    QTY > ?
END-EXEC.
```

The problem can be identified by reviewing the table/tablespace lock in the plan table. Notice that the column TB in Figure EX.16 contains S indicating that a share lock is taken at the table/tablespace level at run time. We know based on Chapter CC that an X lock on a row or page cannot be taken when an S lock is held at the table/tablespace level. The lock is taken at the table level for segmented tablespaces and at the tablespace level for nonsegmented tablespaces.

Figure EX.16. Table/tablespace lock that does not allow updates

QN_B	MT	TNAM	PRE	AT	MC_O	XNAM	UJOG	UJOC	CP_S	CC	REAS	TB
1 1		SPJ	S	I	0 N	SPJX	NNNN	NNNN	46.33	B	HOST	S

If a plan or package is accidentally bound with the default isolation level of RR and the optimizer chooses a tablespace or non-matching index scan, it wants to avoids taking a lock on each and every row or page during the table/tablespace scan and thus uses a table/tablespace lock. A bind time warning with a +806 SQLCODE and message DSX103I is issued if a table or tablespace lock will be taken at run time under these conditions. However, this warning is not always noticed or understood.

Recommendation: Do review your plan tables for inappropriate S, X, and SIX locks to avoid having an SQL statement unnecessarily lock out all other processing.

An alternative to identifying this potential problem and other related problems is to investigate all plans and packages bound with the RR isolation level to be sure that this isolation level is necessary by selecting from the SYSPLAN and SYSPACKAGE catalog tables.

Once the problem has been identified, it is straightforward to fix. All that is necessary is to bind the SQL with an isolation level other than RR and verify that you now have an IS or IX lock at the table/tablespace level (TB=IS) in the plan table as shown in Figure EX.17.

Figure EX.17. Table/tablespace lock that does allow updates

```
QN_B   MT      TNAM   PRE   AT   MC_O   XNAM   UJOG   UJOC   CP_S   CC REAS    TB
---------+---------+---------+---------+---------+---------+-------+--
1  1           SPJ     S     I    0  N  SPJX   NNNN   NNNN   46.33   B HOST    IS
```

An IS and IX lock on a table or tablespace allows exclusive page or row locks for updates by other SQL statements provided that the page or row is not locked.

Update Explanation

The optimizer basically uses the same formula and rules for determining an access path for UPDATE statements as it does for SELECT statements with some additional rules applied to UPDATE statements.

```
EXPLAIN PLAN SET QUERYNO = 1 FOR
UPDATE S
SET    SN = ?
WHERE  SN = ?;

EXPLAIN PLAN SET QUERYNO = 2 FOR
UPDATE S
SET    SN = ?
WHERE  SN > ?;
```

The first access path for QUERYNO = 1 in Figure EX. 18 is the same for the UPDATE statement and a comparable SELECT statement. The MC_O = 1 Y indicating a matching index scan with index only processing is surprising for an UPDATE statement. Access to data pages is required for an update despite the index only of 'Y'. This is documented in the manuals.

Figure EX.18. UPDATE statement access paths

QN_B	MT	TNAM	PRE	AT	MC_O		XNAM	UJOG	UJOC	CP_S	CC	REAS
1	1	S		I	1	Y	SX	NNNN	NNNN	.00	A	
2	1	S	L	I	1	N	SX	NNNN	NNNN	.13	B	HOST

The optimizer has chosen a matching index scan followed by list prefetch (PRE = L) for QUERYNO = 2. The use of list prefetch avoids the halloween problem and allows for a matching index scan for an UPDATE statement with a range predicate. This is because it is necessary to check values after processing RIDs for most list prefetch processing to ensure that the values have not changed during RID processing. The parameter marker (host variable) results in a cost category of "B" with use of default FF because of the range predicate.

PROCMS = 1 ms without division by 1000 .00 (QUERYNO = 1, CP_S = .00) for reporting purposes.

Delete with ORed Predicates Explanation

No special rules are required for choosing an access path for DELETE statements compared to SELECT statements. We will consider the explanation of four DELETE statements for completeness and to review how composite indexes can be used as discussed in Chapters IU and PP.

```
EXPLAIN PLAN SET QUERYNO = 1 FOR
DELETE FROM SPJ
WHERE  SN < 'S1'
OR     PN > 'P1'
OR     JN > 'J1';

EXPLAIN PLAN SET QUERYNO = 2 FOR
DELETE FROM SPJ
WHERE  SN = 'S1'
OR     PN > 'P1'
OR     JN > 'J1';

EXPLAIN PLAN SET QUERYNO = 3 FOR
DELETE FROM SPJ
WHERE  SN = 'S1'
OR     PN = 'P1'
OR     JN = 'J1';

EXPLAIN PLAN SET QUERYNO = 4 FOR
DELETE FROM SPJ
WHERE  PN = 'P1'
OR     JN = 'J1';
```

Figure EX.19 shows a tablespace scan with sequential prefetch (QUERYNO = 1, PRE = S, AT = R) because of the ORed conditions as would be the case if the same WHERE clause were used in a SELECT statement. This is because rows can be missed if a matching index scan is used as discussed in Chapter PP.

Figure EX.19. DELETE statement access paths

QN	B	MT	TNAM	PRE	AT	MC_O		XNAM	UJOG	UJOC	CP_S	CC REAS
1	1		SPJ	S	R	0	N		NNNN	NNNN	3478.41	A
2	1		SPJ	S	R	0	N		NNNN	NNNN	3478.41	A
3	1		SPJ	S	I	0	Y	SPJX	NNNN	NNNN	290.47	A
4	1		SPJ	S	I	0	Y	SPJX	NNNN	NNNN	39.34	A

Even if an equal predicate is specified on the first column of the composite index, a tablespace scan is still necessary because of the ORed predicates on columns of the composite index (QUERYNO = 2, AT = R). This holds true for a comparable SELECT statement.

If equal predicates are specified on all columns of the composite index, the optimizer chooses to use a non-matching index scan with sequential prefetch on all of the leaf pages and index only processing (QUERYNO = 3, PRE = S, AT = I, MC_O = 0 Y) as it can do for a comparable SELECT statement. Rows will not be missed nor will a looping condition occur when scanning all of the leaf pages. Even though index only processing is indicated, DB2 does access the data pages to mark the qualifying rows as being deleted. The estimated processor cost is significantly lower using the non-matching index scan compared to the tablespace scan in QUERYNO = 1 and 2 because there are fewer index pages to identify the rows to be deleted compared to the total number of data pages.

We know from Chapter IU that a matching index scan cannot be used if the leading column of a composite index is not specified in the WHERE clause. However, a non-matching index scan can be used. Notice that the access path for QUERYNO = 3 and 4 are the same even though the leading column of the composite index is not specified in the WHERE clause. QUERYNO = 4 has a lower processor cost compared to QUERYNO = 3 despite the same access path. This is surprising since it seems that fewer rows would be expected to be deleted with 3 equal predicates in QUERYNO = 3 compared to 2 equal predicates in QUERYNO = 4. Either I or the optimize are not perfect.

EX.9 COMPARING CURRENT AND PREVIOUS ACCESS PATHS

Do EXPLAIN all plans and packages when they are bound for production use using representative production data. This provides for verifying that you do have a good access path for production. It also provides for comparisons of changes to access paths as will be discussed.

The use of the EXPLAIN(YES) on the BIND and REBIND commands leaves explain on until EXPLAIN(NO) is specified. Automatic rebinds and explicit rebinds result in rows being inserted into the plan table for monitoring if you specify YES for the EXPLAIN PROCESSING field on the installation panel DSNTIPO. Of course, it is necessary to have an existing plan table with the appropriate AUTHID as discussed in Section EX.3. If a PLAN_TABLE does not exist, automatic rebinds are successful.

Do retain the PLAN_TABLE and DSN_STATEMNT_TABLE. This allows for tracking changes in access paths due to changes in the statistics used by the optimizer as the data changes and RUNSTATS is executed, the restructuring of tables, addition and deletion of indexes, changes with new DB2 releases, and new PTFs.

Determine the Most Recent Access Path

You will want to determines the most recent access paths from among a number of access paths chosen for programs when you are accumulating different access paths that are chosen under various conditions over various time periods. This applies to a test environment where you have tried various formulation of SQL statements and want to locate the access path for the most recent formulation. It is particularly useful when it is difficult to delete rows from a PLAN_TABLE shared by a number of developers for fear of deleting rows that others may need for further analysis. In a production environment you will want to identify the access path that is currently being used at run time. Here is a statement developed by Michael Hannan that identifies the most recent access paths from among a number of access paths chosen for programs.

```
SELECT A.*
FROM PLAN_TABLE A
  INNER JOIN
   (SELECT DISTINCT NAME, COLLID, VERSION, BINDTIME
    FROM SYSIBM.SYSPACKAGE A
    WHERE LOCATION = ' '
    AND   BINDTIME >= '2000-01-15-00.00.00.000000'
    AND   COLLID IN ('SPJCOLL','EMPCOLL')
    AND   NOT EXISTS
       (SELECT 1 FROM SYSIBM.SYSPACKAGE
        WHERE LOCATION = ' '
        AND   NAME = A.NAME
        AND   COLLID IN ('SPJCOLL','EMPCOLL')
        AND   PCTIMESTAMP >= A.PCTIMESTAMP
        AND  (PCTIMESTAMP >  A.PCTIMESTAMP
        OR    BINDTIME    >  A.BINDTIME))) AS P
  ON A.COLLID    = P.COLLID
AND A.PROGNAME   = P.NAME
AND A.VERSION    = P.VERSION
AND A.BIND_TIME  = P.BINDTIME
ORDER BY A.PROGNAME, A.TIMESTAMP, A.QBLOCKNO, A.PLANNO,
A.MIXOPSEQ;
```

Compare Most Recent Access Path with Previous Access Paths

You can report on current access paths that differ from the access paths chosen previously by the optimizer using the statement:

```
SELECT X.QUERYNO,X.QBLOCKNO,X.APPLNAME,X.PROGNAME,
  X.PLANNO,X.METHOD,X.CREATOR,X.TNAME,X.TABNO,
  X.ACCESSTYPE,X.MATCHCOLS,X.ACCESSCREATOR,
  X.ACCESSNAME,X.INDEXONLY,X.SORTN_UNIQ,
  X.SORTN_JOIN,X.SORTN_ORDERBY,
  X.SORTC_GROUPBY,X.SORTC_UNIQ,X.SORTC JOIN,
  X.SORTC_ORDERBY,X.SORTC_GROUPBY,X.TSLOCKMODE,
  X.TIMESTAMP,X.PREFETCH,X.COLUMN_FN_EVAL,
  X.MIXOPSEQ,Y.QUERYNO,Y.BLOCKNO,Y.APPLNAME,
  Y.PROGNAME,Y.PLANNO,
  Y.METHOD,Y.CREATOR,Y.TNAME,Y.TABNO,Y.ACCESSTYPE,
  Y.MATCHCOLS,Y.ACCESSCREATOR,Y.ACCESSNAME,
```

```
    Y.INDEXONLY,Y.SORTN_UNIQ,Y.SORTN_JOIN,
    Y.SORTN_ORDERBY,Y.SORTC_GROUPBY,Y.SORTC_UNIQ,
    Y.SORTC_JOIN,Y.SORTC_ORDERBY,Y.SORTC_GROUPBY,
    Y.TSLOCKMODE,Y.TIMESTAMP,Y.PREFETCH,
    Y.COLUMN_FN_EVAL,Y.MIXOPSEQ
  FROM  PLAN_TABLE X,PLAN_TABLE Y
  WHERE X.PROGNAME = Y.PROGNAME
  AND   X.QUERYNO  = Y.QUERYNO
  AND   X.QBLOCKNO = Y.QBLOCKNO
  AND   X.TABNO    = Y.TABNO
  AND   X.TIMESTAMP=
   (SELECT MAX(C.TIMESTAMP)
    FROM  PLAN_TABLE C
    WHERE X.PROGNAME  = C.PROGNAME
    AND   X.QUERYNO   = C.QUERYNO
    AND   X.TABNO     = C.TABNO
    AND   X.QBLOCKNO  = C.QBLOCKNO)
  AND       Y.TIMESTAMP      < X.TIMESTAMP
  AND NOT Y.METHOD           = X.METHOD
  AND NOT Y.ACCESSTYPE       = X.ACCESSTYPE
  AND NOT Y.MATCHCOLS        = X.MATCHOLS
  AND NOT Y.ACCESSNAME       = X.ACCESSNAME
  AND NOT Y.INDEXONLY        = X.INDEXONLY
  AND NOT Y.PREFETCH         = X.PREFETCH
  AND NOT Y.SORTN_UNIQ       = X.SORTN_UNIQ
  AND NOT Y.SORTN_JOIN       = X.SORTN_JOIN
  AND NOT Y.SORTN_ORDERBY    = X.SORTN_ORDERBY
  AND NOT Y.SORTN_GROUPBY    = X.SORTN_GROUPBY
  AND NOT Y.SORTC_UNIQ       = X.SORTC_UNIQ
  AND NOT Y.SORTC_JOIN       = X.SORTC_JOIN
  AND NOT Y.SORTC_ORDERBY    = X.SORTC_ORDERBY
  AND NOT Y.SORTC_GROUPBY    = X.SORTC_GROUPBY
  AND NOT Y.TSLOCKMODE       = X.TSLOCKMODE
  AND NOT Y.COLUMN_FN_EVAL = X.COLUMN_FN_EVAL
  AND NOT Y.MIXOPSEQ         = X.MIXOPSEQ
  ORDER BY X.PROGNAME,X.QUERYNO,X.QBLOCKNO,
           X.PLANNO,X.MIXOPSEQ;
```

If you are interested in comparing additional columns in the plan table, particular those added with a new release, it is necessary to add predicates on the new columns.

EX.10 OPTIMIZATION HINTS IN V6

Optimizer hints are useful if it is neccessary to fallback to a previous access path after installing a new PTF, APAR, release, or version of DB2 followed by a rebind that results in an undesirable access path. Hints can be used to influence an access path. Do be cautious with this usage. Even if it is the best access path today, it may not be the best access path in the future with changes to the DB2 subsystem, database design, index design, and characteristics of the data.

Prerequisites: It is necessary to specify YES in the OPTIMIZATION HINTS field of the DSNTIP4 installation panel (default is NO). You must bind or rebind a plan or a package with the OPTHINT('hintnam') parameter. The 'hintnam' can be 8 bytes or less in length. It is used by the optimizer to locate the rows in the PLAN_TABLE that contains the hint. A hint name that contains blanks means typical optimization without hints. This is the default when binding plans and packages.

It is advisable, although not required, to have a composite ascending index on the QUERYNO, APPLNAME, PROGNAME, VERSION, COLLID, and OPTHINT columns in the PLAN_TABLE assuming that it is sizable. (The member DSNTESC in SDSNSAMP has a create index statement for this purpose.) Otherwise, the optimizer must do a tablespace scan to locate a hint.

Procedure for Creating a Hint

SQL should be explained as programs are migrated to production with retention of the PLAN_TABLE as discussed in Section 7. You need to identify the statement number of an access path that you want to use as a hint. The statement number can be found in the QUERYNO column of the PLAN_TABLE. It is necessary to tag the access path that you want to use with a hint name. For example, assume that you want to use the access path identified by QUERYNO 400 when you next do a bind or rebind. The hint name of OLDPATH (any value of 8 characters or less) is used to tag the rows like:

```
UPDATE PLAN_TABLE
SET OPTHINT = 'OLDPATH'
  WHERE QUERYNO  = 400
  AND   APPLNAME = ' '
  AND   PROGNAME = 'PROGA'
  AND   VERSION  = ' '
  AND   COLLID   = 'SPJCOLL';
```

The hint name of OLDPATH can be specified with the OPTHINT parameter using the REBIND statement like:

```
REBIND PACKAGE (SPJCOLL.PROGA.(''))
  OPTHINT (OLDPATH)
  EXPLAIN (YES)
```

If the hint is used by the optimizer, the column HINT_USED in the PLAN_TABLE contains OPTHINT. Otherwise, the column contains blank. A +394 SQLCODE is issued at bind time if the hint is used. If a hint is found but cannot be used, +395 SQLCODE is issued at bind time.

Set the QUERYNO if the query number can change: The procedure described thus far works if the QUERYNO does not changed for the statement. However, the QUERYNO can change if the program has changed such that the SQL statement is assigned a different QUERYNO (a statement is added, deleted, or moved, for example). If the QUERYNO can change and you plan to use an optimization hint, use the QUERYNO clause like:

```
SELECT SN, SNAME
FROM   S
WHERE  CITY = 'Dallas'
QUERYNO = 900400;
```

Now QUERYNO 900400 appears in the PLAN_TABLE along with the access path for the statement when an explain is requested. Do consider a numbering convention to indicate rows where hints have been used. Hints begin with 9 in the 6th position counting from the right in the example. The statement number in SYSSTMT and SYSPACKSTMT is not affected by the QUERYNO clause. The clause can be used with static and dynamic SQL. Once the QUERYNO has been set, update the PLAN_TABLE and bind/rebind the plan or package as discussed earlier in this section.

Here is a useful SELECT statement to group together access paths chosen by the optimizer and hints used for the SQL.

```
SELECT *
FROM   PLAN_TABLE
ORDER BY BIND_TIME, QUERYNO, QBLOCKNO, PLANNO;
```

Hints for dynamic SQL: The QUERYNO clause is particularly useful where the same statement in a program prepares dynamic SQL. This is because the same statement number is used for all SQL statements processed by the program. The sample program DSNTEP2 is an example of where all SQL processed by the program is assigned the same QUERYNO. You can compensate for this by setting the current optimization hint special register to the hint name by executing a SET statement similar to the following before the interactive or embedded dynamic SQL statement is executed.

```
SET CURRENT OPTIMIZATION HINT = :OLDPATH - Can be a literal
```

The CURRENT OPTIMIZATION HINT special register can be set equal to the content of a host variable as in the example or a literal. The hint in the PLAN_TABLE with OPTHINT = 'OLDPATH' is used assuming that the content of the host variable is 'OLDPATH'. If the CURRENT OPTIMIZATION HINT special register is not set, the value specified for OPTHINT at bind time is used. If the value is blank, hints are not used. If the CURRENT OPTIMIZATION HINT special register contains non-blanks and OPTIMIZATION HINTS field of the DSNTIP4 installation panel is NO, a warning is issued indicating that the hint is not used.

If WHEN_OPTIMIZE = 'R', reoptimization (discussed in Chapter OP) occurs with or without providing hints.

Columns Considered by the Optimizer with Hints

Only the columns described in Figure EX.20 are considered by the optimizer when using hints.

Figure EX.20. Columns considered by optimizer with hints

Columns	Description
CREATOR, TNAME	Must identify an existing table or view.
TABNO	Used only if CREATOR, TNAME and CORRELATION_NAME do not uniquely identify the row.
METHOD	Must be 0, 1, 2, 3, or 4 (not S for star join).

Columns	Description
ACCESSTYPE	Must be 'R', 'I', 'I1', 'N', or 'M'. Optimizer will determine how to use the index when 'I', 'I1', or 'N' (all indicate matching index scan) is specified.
ACCESSCREATOR, ACCESSNAME	Ignored if ACCESSTYPE is 'R' or 'M'. If the ACCESSTYPE is 'I', 'I1', or 'N', ACCESSNAME must identify an index on the table
SORTN_JOIN, SORTC_JOIN	Must be 'Y', 'N' or blank. Ignored if a sort is required for join processing.
PREFETCH	Must be 'S', 'L' or blank.
WHEN_OPTIMIZE	Must be blank, 'B' or 'R'. If blank or 'B', reoptimization does not occur. If 'R', reoptimization does occur provided there is a valid hint.
PAGE_RANGE	Must be 'Y', 'N' or blank. If 'Y' is specified, limited partition scan is used only if optimizer can determine the partition to scan.
PARALLELISM_MODE	Must be either 'I', 'C', 'X' or null. If null is specified, optimizer determines the mode of parallelism if used.
ACCESS_DEGREE, ACCESS_PGROUP_ID	Ignored if parallelism is not used. Specified degree can be adjusted by the optimizer.
JOIN_DEGREE, JOIN_PGROUP_ID	Ignored if parallelism is not used. Specified degree can be adjusted by the optimizer.
CORRELATION_NAME	Used if specified as an additional qualifier to TNAME if necessary to resolve ambiguities when the same table is referenced multiple times.

Forcing an access path with hints: You can force an access path using a similar method as using an old access path. The following index is created and the SELECT statement is explained to determine the 10 highest paid employees with one SQL statement as discussed in Chapter ST. This formulation developed by Michael Hannan in Melbourne, Australia, provides for a one-fetch index access with an ascending index in contrast to the Chapter ST example which requires a descending index for the one-fetch index access using MAX.

```
→    CREATE INDEX SALX ON EMP (SALARY);

     SELECT EMPNO, SALARY
     FROM   EMP
```

```
WHERE  SALARY <=
  (SELECT MIN(SALARY) FROM EMP WHERE SALARY >
  (SELECT MIN(SALARY) FROM EMP WHERE SALARY >
  (SELECT MIN(SALARY) FROM EMP WHERE SALARY >
  (SELECT MIN(SALARY) FROM EMP WHERE SALARY >
  (SELECT MIN(SALARY) FROM EMP WHERE SALARY >
  (SELECT MIN(SALARY) FROM EMP WHERE SALARY >
  (SELECT MIN(SALARY) FROM EMP WHERE SALARY >
  (SELECT MIN(SALARY) FROM EMP WHERE SALARY >
  (SELECT MIN(SALARY) FROM EMP )))))))))
ORDER BY SALARY DESC;
```

Figure EX.21 shows the access path chosen by the optimizer with an ascending non-clustering index on SALARY.

Figure EX.21. Top 10 access path

QN	B	MT	TNAM	PRE	AT	MC	O	XNAM	UJOG	UJOC	CP_S	CC	REAS
1	1		EMP	S	R	0	N	SALX	NNNN	NNNN	2.78	A	
1	1	3				0	N		NNNN	NNYN	2.78	A	
1	1		EMP		I1	0	Y	SALX	NNNN	NNNN	2.78	A	
1	2		EMP		I1	1	Y	SALX	NNNN	NNNN	2.78	A	
1	3		EMP		I1	1	Y	SALX	NNNN	NNNN	2.78	A	
1	4		EMP		I1	1	Y	SALX	NNNN	NNNN	2.78	A	
1	5		EMP		I1	1	Y	SALX	NNNN	NNNN	2.78	A	
1	6		EMP		I1	1	Y	SALX	NNNN	NNNN	2.78	A	
1	7		EMP		I1	1	Y	SALX	NNNN	NNNN	2.78	A	
1	8		EMP		I1	1	Y	SALX	NNNN	NNNN	2.78	A	
1	9		EMP		I1	1	Y	SALX	NNNN	NNNN	2.78	A	

The PRE = R, AT = R, and XNAM = ' ' can be updated to be PRE = L, AT = I, and XNAM = 'SALX ' as shown in Figure EX.22.

Figure EX.22. Modified access path for top 10 values

QN_B		MT	TNAM	PRE	AT	MC_O		XNAM	UJOG	UJOC	CP_S	CC REAS
1	1		EMP	L	I	0	N	SALX	NNNN	NNNN	2.78	A
1	1	3				0	N		NNNN	NNNN	2.78	A
1	1		EMP		I1	0	Y	SALX	NNNN	NNNN	2.78	A
1	2		EMP		I1	1	Y	SALX	NNNN	NNNN	2.78	A
1	3		EMP		I1	1	Y	SALX	NNNN	NNNN	2.78	A
1	4		EMP		I1	1	Y	SALX	NNNN	NNNN	2.78	A
1	5		EMP		I1	1	Y	SALX	NNNN	NNNN	2.78	A
1	6		EMP		I1	1	Y	SALX	NNNN	NNNN	2.78	A
1	7		EMP		I1	1	Y	SALX	NNNN	NNNN	2.78	A
1	8		EMP		I1	1	Y	SALX	NNNN	NNNN	2.78	A
1	9		EMP		I1	1	Y	SALX	NNNN	NNNN	2.78	A

The update of PRE = S and AT = R to PRE = L, AT = I, and XNAM = SALX is legitimate. Indeed, this is the chosen access path when the index on SALARY has a high cluster ratio. However, it is not the best access path for the existing index with a low cluster ratio in most cases. This is because seek time to the data pages to get the EMPNO can be high with a low cluster ratio.

The update of O = Y for the composite table can be updated to O = N. It is not legitimate. It is not possible to avoid the descending sort for the top 10 occurring values that have been gotten from the one-fetch index accesses in QBLOCKNO 2 through 10.

Asking for An Impossible Access Path

You can insert rows in the PLAN_TABLE describing the desired access path. Column values in the PLAN_TABLE must conform to allowable values described in Figure EX.5. Do be cautious about asking for a worse access path or an impossible access path. Following are a few impossible access paths that can be requested through hints but will not be used. If a hint cannot be used, the optimizer chooses an access path as if no hint was given.

- Use an index that does not exist.
- Use a matching index scan where the leading column of a composite index is not specified in the WHERE clause.
- Change PRE = 'S' to 'L' without index access to get the RIDs to use in list prefetch.
- Change MT = 2 (merge join) to 4 (hybrid join) without index access to the inner table.
- Many more impossible access paths ...

The optimizer ignores hints if they result in unnecessary processing compared to its choice of access path. For example, the optimizer will use its access path rather than a hint that requires additional sorts, multiple index usage, view and table expression materialization, and etc.

EX.11 REVIEW STATISTICS USED BY THE OPTIMIZER

Knowledge of the statistics used by the optimizer in determining the access paths aids a great deal in your evaluation of whether the chosen access paths are best for the processing you require. A good method for getting the statistics is to specify the REPORT parameter when RUNSTATS is executed.

This causes the utility to write a report of the statistics that it collects. An alternative is to select the statistics from the catalog tables like:

Index and clustering information:

```
SELECT NAME, UNIQUERULE, CLUSTERRATIOF,
  CLUSTERED, CLUSTERING
  FIRSTKEYCARDF, FULLKEYCARDF,
  NLEAF, NLEVELS, PGSIZE, STATSTIME
FROM   SYSIBM.SYSINDEXES
WHERE  DBNAME = 'DASPJDB';

SELECT NAME, UNIQUERULE, CLUSTERRATIOF,
  FIRSTKEYCARDF, FULLKEYCARDF,
  NLEAF, NLEVELS, STATSTIME
FROM   SYSIBM.SYSINDEXSTATS
WHERE  DBNAME = 'DASPJDB';
```

Size of table information:

```
SELECT NAME, CREATOR, CARDF, NPAGES,
  EDPROC, PCTROWCOMP, PCTPAGES, STATSTIME
FROM   SYSIBM.SYSTABLES
WHERE  DBNAME = 'DASPJDB'
AND    TYPE   = 'T';

SELECT NAME, OWNER, CARDF, NPAGES,
  PCTROWCOMP, TSNAME, STATSTIME
FROM   SYSIBM.SYSTABSTATS
WHERE  DBNAME = 'DASPJDB';

SELECT NAME, DBNAME, NACTIVE, LOCKRULE,
  CLOSERULE
FROM   SYSIBM.SYSTABLESPACE
WHERE  DBNAME = 'DASPJDB';
```

Cardinality and highest and lowest values:

```
SELECT NAME, TBNAME, COLCARDF,
       HIGH2KEY, LOW2KEY,
       HEX(HIGH2KEY), HEX(LOW2KEY),
       STATSTIME
FROM   SYSIBM.SYSCOLUMNS
WHERE  TBNAME  IN ('S','P','J','SPJ')
AND    COLCARDF >= 0;

SELECT NAME, TBNAME, COLCARDF,
       HIGH2KEY, LOW2KEY,
       HEX(HIGH2KEY), HEX(LOW2KEY),
       HIGHKEY, LOWKEY, HEX(HIGHKEY),
       HEX(LOWKEY),STATSTIME
FROM   SYSIBM.SYSCOLSTATS
WHERE  TBNAME  IN ('S','P','J','SPJ')
AND    COLCARDF >= 0;
```

Distribution information:

```
SELECT TBNAME, NAME, FREQUENCYF,
       COLVALUE, HEX(COLVALUE), CARDF,
       COLGROUPCOLNO,
       HEX(COLGROUPCOLNO),
       NUMCOLUMNS, TYPE, STATSTIME
FROM   SYSIBM.SYSCOLDIST
WHERE  TBCREATOR = 'AUTHID'
AND    TBNAME     IN('S','P','J','SPJ')
UNION
SELECT TBNAME, NAME, FREQUENCYF,
       COLVALUE, HEX(COLVALUE), CARDF,
       COLGROUPCOLNO,
       HEX(COLGROUPCOLNO),
       NUMCOLUMNS, TYPE, STATSTIME
FROM   SYSIBM.SYSCOLDISTSTATS
WHERE  TBCREATOR = 'AUTHID'
AND    TBNAME     IN('S','P','J', 'SPJ')
ORDER BY NUMCOLUMNS, NAME,
       COLGROUPCOLNO, TYPE,
       FREQUENCYF DESC;
```

The table layout of the tables used in the SQL statements you are analyzing is also very useful:

```
SELECT NAME, COLTYPE, LENGTH, SCALE,
  NULLS, FOREIGNKEY, COLNO
FROM   SYSIBM.SYSCOLUMNS
WHERE  TBCREATOR = 'AUTHID'
AND    TBNAME     IN('S','P','J','SPJ')
ORDER BY COLNO;
```

EX.12 MIRRORING PRODUCTION STATISTICS IN TEST

Access path selection can vary a great deal between small test tables and large production tables, buffer pool sizes and thresholds, the RID pool size, the computer model and number of processors being used to do the explains. If you have small test tables and large production tables, do update the test catalog table statistics used by the optimizer to be like production statistics.

UPDATE statements to be executed on the test catalog tables can be generated from the production catalog tables. Following are the statements that will generate the UPDATE statements. After you have generated the UPDATE statements, execute them on the test catalog tables.

```
SELECT DISTINCT
  'UPDATE SYSIBM.SYSTABLESPACE SET NACTIVE='
  CONCAT DIGITS(DECIMAL(NACTIVEF,31,0))
  CONCAT ' WHERE NAME='''CONCAT TS.NAME
  CONCAT ''' AND CREATOR ='''CONCAT TS.CREATOR
  CONCAT''';'
FROM SYSIBM.SYSTABLESPACE TS, SYSIBM.SYSTABLES TBL
```

```
WHERE TS.NAME = TSNAME
AND   TBL.NAME IN ('S', 'P', 'J', 'SPJ')
AND   TBL.CREATOR IN ('AUTHID1', 'AUTHID2');

SELECT 'UPDATE SYSIBM.SYSTABLES SET CARDF='
  CONCAT  DIGITS(DECIMAL(CARDF,31,0))
  CONCAT',NPAGES='CONCAT DIGITS(NPAGES)
  CONCAT ' WHERE NAME='''CONCAT NAME
  CONCAT ''' AND CREATOR ='''CONCAT CREATOR CONCAT''';'
FROM SYSIBM.SYSTABLES
WHERE NAME     IN ('S', 'P', 'J', 'SPJ')
AND   CREATOR IN ('AUTHID1', 'AUTHID2');
AND   CARDF >= 0;
SELECT 'UPDATE SYSIBM.SYSINDEXES SET FIRSTKEYCARDF='
  CONCAT DIGITS(DECIMAL(FIRSTKEYCARDF,31,0))
  CONCAT ',FULLKEYCARDF='
  CONCAT DIGITS(DECIMAL(FULLKEYCARDF,31,0))
  CONCAT ',NLEAF=' CONCAT DIGITS(NLEAF)
  CONCAT ',NLEVELS=' CONCAT DIGITS(NLEVELS)
  CONCAT ',CLUSTERRATIOF=.'
  CONCAT   DIGITS(DECIMAL(CLUSTERRATIOF,31,0))
  CONCAT ' WHERE NAME=''' CONCAT NAME
  CONCAT ''' AND CREATOR =''' CONCAT CREATOR CONCAT ''';'
FROM SYSIBM.SYSINDEXES
WHERE TBNAME  IN ('S', 'P', 'J', 'SPJ')
AND   CREATOR IN ('AUTHID1', 'AUTHID2');
AND   FULLKEYCARDF >= 0;

SELECT 'UPDATE SYSIBM.SYSCOLUMNS SET COLCARDF='
  CONCAT DIGITS(DECIMAL(COLCARDF,31,0))
  CONCAT',HIGH2KEY='''CONCAT HIGH2KEY
  CONCAT''',LOW2KEY='''CONCAT LOW2KEY
  CONCAT''' WHERE TBNAME='''CONCAT TBNAME
  CONCAT''' AND COLNO=' CONCAT DIGITS(COLNO)
  CONCAT  ' AND TBCREATOR ='''CONCAT TBCREATOR
  CONCAT''';'
FROM SYSIBM.SYSCOLUMNS
WHERE TBNAME    IN ('S', 'P', 'J', 'SPJ')
AND   TBCREATOR IN ('AUTHID1', 'AUTHID2');
AND   COLCARDF >= 0;
```

EX.13 VISUAL EXPLAIN

Visual explain is a no additional cost option of DB2 that runs on a PC or workstation. It can get SQL statements, the PLAN_TABLE, and catalog statistics from the DB2 subsystem on a mainframe using DB2 universal database (UDB) on a PC or workstation through Distributed Relational Data Access (DRDA).

The use of visual explain has several prerequisites including:

- Windows 2000, NT, 98, 95, Unix, AIX, Linux, HP-UX, Solaris, UNMA-Q, OS/2, OS/400, or other platforms in the future

- DB2 UDB or DB2/2 on a PC or workstation
- DB2 Connect or Distributed Database Connection Services (DDCS)
- Stored procedures enabled on the DB2 subsystem for DSNZPARM support

Visual explain has options to explain by plan, package, or DBRM. You can have SQL statements listed and choose the statements of interest. The dynamic explain option provides for the cut and paste of a statement from another window into visual explain or you can key in a statement directly.

An access path diagram is used to show the access path chosen by the optimizer on the mainframe. Various shapes are used to describe the access path from the PLAN_TABLE in the diagram. Figure EX.23 is an example of a diagram showing the access path for a 3-way join. The polygon at top of the diagram shows the type of statement – SELECT, UPDATE, DELETE, or INSERT. Polygons are also used to represent operations, including joins and sorts, for example. Triangles represent index usage. Rectangles represent tables.

Figure EX.23. Access path diagram of a 3-way join

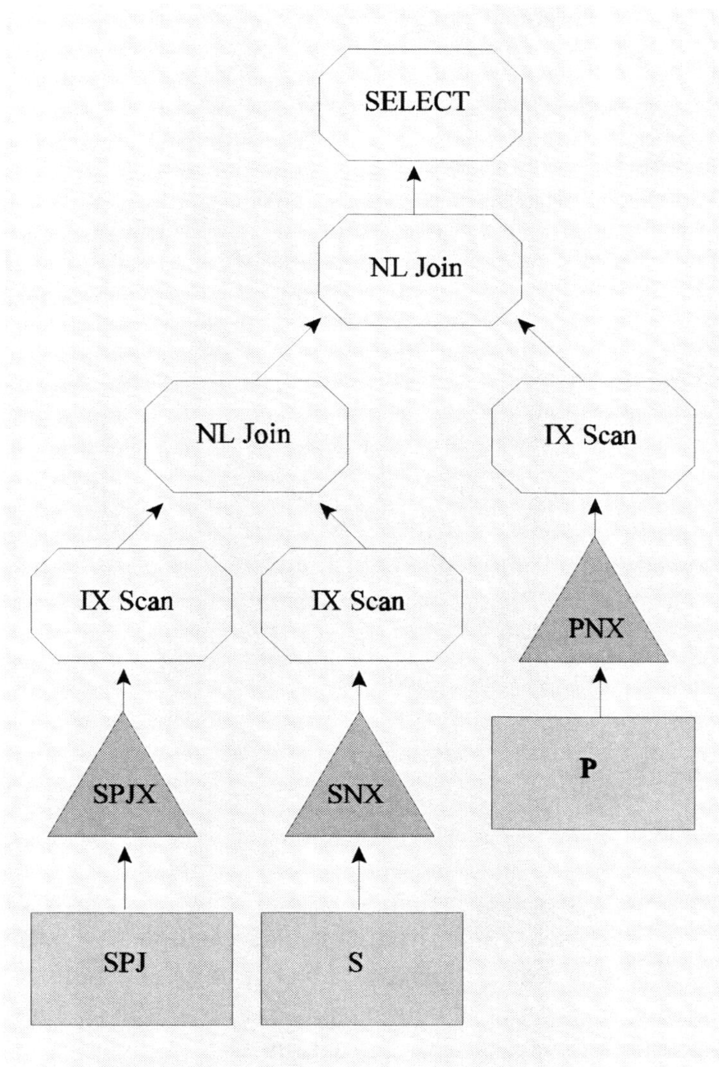

The diagram should be read from the bottom up and left to right to determine the approximate processing sequence. For example, the SPJ and S tables are accessed using an index scan (IX) on the

SPJX and SX indexes for a nested loop (NL). The P table is accessed using an index scan on the PX index and brought in as the third table of the 3-way join using a nested loop join.

There are many options available when using visual explain. Textual description of codes in the plan table can be given. There is an option that provides a textual description of the operation, for example:

> "With a nested loop join, DB2 scans the inner table once (usually with an index scan) for each row of the outer table. A nested loop join does not require a join predicate but you will get better performance by using a join predicate."

The suggestions option provides a textual description of how to get a better access path. An example of a suggestion to achieve a better access path is to create an index.

You have options to view the catalog statistics by column, index, and, tablespace.

There is an option to select only SQL statements that perform one or more operations. You can filter by selecting a combination of criteria including:

- Sorts
- Tablespace scan
- Sequential and list prefetch
- Matching and non-matching index scan
- Non-index only
- Multiple index
- IN-list
- 1-fetch index access
- Nested loop, merge, and hybrid join
- I/O, CP, and sysplex parallelism

There is a subsystem parameter browser option for finding a specific DSNZPARM parameter. For example, you can determine the current value for CTHREAD which is the maximum number of allied threads that can be allocated concurrently. There are options to give a description of a parameter, install panel name, field number, macro, etc. Visual explain determines this information by calling a stored procedure on the DB2 subsystem which issues an IFI call to get trace record 0106 containing current DSNZPARM values. This option requires that the user have authority to call the stored procedure.

EX.14 SUMMARY

The analysis of explain reports is a non-trivial pursuit and requires a great deal of understanding of how SQL statements are processed. Visual explain and a number of products from software companies on the market describe the codes produced by EXPLAIN in phrases and sentences. Some products include recommendations on what actions to take to improve performance and display the statistics used by the optimizer in access path evaluation. Caution must be exercised in using the recommendations. They are very general and may no longer be valid after a new release or PTF and before the product has been updated and installed at your site. There is no substitute for a good understanding of SQL processing to deal with statements that do not perform as required.

It is advisable to know the statistics used by the optimizer to understand why certain access paths are chosen and what actions to take. The statistics should be saved along with a copy of the report on all plans and packages when they are migrated to a production environment. The specification of EXPLAIN(YES) on the bind or rebind command results in rows being inserted into the plan table whenever an automatic rebind occurs or the user initiates a bind without specifying EXPLAIN(NO). It is advisable to leave explain on in a production environment. The cost is low, only a few rows are inserted into the plan table for each SQL statement at bind time, and it may prove very useful in identifying and correcting a statement in a plan or package that was performing well but is currently using excessive I/O and CPU time. It may be that indexes have been added or dropped, tables have been restructured, statistics have changed dramatically, a reorganization is required, or a new release or PTF has been installed. Optimization hints can be used to fallback to a previous access path in the plan table.

It depends! We have considered many factors that it depends on.

EXERCISES

1. Following is an index definition, an INSERT statement, and the results of explain. How does DB2 determine where to insert the row?

```
CREATE UNIQUE INDEX SX ON S (SN) CLUSTER;

     EXPLAIN PLAN SET QUERYNO = 1 FOR
     INSERT INTO S (SN, SNAME, STATUS, CITY)
     VALUES ('S99','GONZALES',90,'MEXICO CITY');
```

```
QN_B  MT    TNAM  PRE  AT  MC_O  XNAM  UJOG  UJOC       CP_S  CC REAS
---------+---------+---------+---------+---------+---------+--------
1  1        S              0  N          NNNN  NNNN       .00   A
```

2. Why might you want to use the UNION ALL formulation compared to the multiple index processing shown in Figure EX.9 even though its estimated cost is a bit higher than the multiple index usage?

3. Will the following SELECT statement provide good response time for cursor repositioning for an online transaction based on the access path chosen in the plan report?

```
EXPLAIN PLAN SET QUERYNO = 1 FOR
SELECT SN, PN, JN, QTY
FROM   SPJ
WHERE  SN >= 'S2' AND
 ((SN  =  'S2' AND
   PN  =  'P3' AND
   JN  >  'J3') OR
  (SN  =  'S2' AND
   PN  >  'P3') OR
  (SN  >  'S2'))
ORDER BY SN, PN, JN
OPTIMIZE FOR 12 ROWS;
```

```
QN_B   MT      TNAM   PRE   AT   MC_O   XNAM   UJOG UJOC         CP_S   CC REAS
---------+---------+---------+---------+---------+---------+---------+--
1  1           SPJ           I    1  N  SPJX   NNNN  NNNN        620.59  A
```

4. Describe how the qualifying rows will be located based on the statement:

```
SELECT SN, PN, JN, QTY
FROM   SPJ
WHERE  SN = 'S4'
AND   (PN = 'P1' OR PN = 'P2' OR
       PN = 'P3' OR PN = 'P4')
AND    JN > 'J1';
```

```
QN_B   MT      TNAM   PRE   AT   MC_O   XNAM   UJOG UJOC         CP_S   CC REAS
---------+---------+---------+---------+---------+---------+---------+--
1  1           SPJ           N    3  N  SPJX   NNNN  NNNN          .00   A
```

5. Do you expect a different access path or processor time estimate if the following statement used host variables rather than literals? (The processor time estimate is 1 milliseconds before division by 1000 to report in seconds.) What is an exception?

```
EXPLAIN PLAN SET QUERYNO = 1 FOR
SELECT SN, PN, JN, QTY
FROM   SPJ
WHERE  SN = 'S4'
AND    PN = 'P1';
```

```
QN_B   MT      TNAM   PRE   AT   MC_O   XNAM   UJOG  UJOC        CP_S   CC   REAS
---------+---------+---------+---------+---------+---------+---------+--
1  1           SPJ           I    2  N  SPJX   NNNN  NNNN          .00  A
```

6. Why does QUERYNO = 1 use matching index scans (AT=N) to locate the rows to be updated and QUERYNO = 2 uses a tablespace scan?

```
EXPLAIN PLAN SET QUERYNO = 1 FOR
UPDATE SPJ
SET QTY =
  CASE
    WHEN SN = 'S1'
      THEN QTY * 1.1
    WHEN SN = 'S2'
      THEN QTY * 1.2
  ELSE QTY
  END
WHERE  SN IN ('S1', 'S1');

EXPLAIN PLAN SET QUERYNO = 2 FOR
UPDATE SPJ
SET QTY =
  CASE
    WHEN SN = 'S1'
       THEN QTY * 1.1
    WHEN SN = 'S2'
```

```
        THEN QTY * 1.2
    ELSE QTY
    END;
```

QN	B	MT	TNAM	PRE	AT	MC	O	XNAM	UJOG	UJOC	CP_S	CC	REAS
1	1		SPJ	S	N	1	N	SPJX	NNNN	NNNN	113.36	A	
2	1		SPJ	S	R	0	N		NNNN	NNNN	668.07	A	

7. Why does the optimizer choose to use a matching index scan on S.SN when there is no local predicate coded on the column?

```
EXPLAIN PLAN SET QUERYNO = 1 FOR
SELECT S.SN, SNAME, PN, QTY
FROM   SPJ, S
WHERE  SPJ.SN = S.SN
AND    SPJ.SN = 'S2';
```

QN	B	MT	TNAM	PRE	AT	MC	O	XNAM	UJOG	UJOC	CP_S	CC	REAS
1	1		S		I	1	N	SX	NNNN	NNNN	305.61	A	
1	1	1	SPJ	S	I	1	N	SPJX	NNNN	NNNN	305.61	A	

8. a) Does the following two SELECT statements always return the same results? b) How is the access path chosen by the optimizer similar for the two statements.

```
EXPLAIN PLAN SET QUERYNO = 1 FOR
SELECT S.SN, SNAME, STATUS, CITY
FROM   S, SPJ
WHERE  S.SN = SPJ.SN
AND    CITY = ?;

EXPLAIN PLAN SET QUERYNO = 2 FOR
SELECT SX.SN, SNAME, STATUS, CITY
FROM   S SX
WHERE  CITY = ?
AND    EXISTS
  (SELECT 1
   FROM   SPJ
   WHERE  SX.SN = SPJ.SN);
```

QN	B	MT	TNAM	PRE	AT	MC	O	XNAM	UJOG	UJOC	CP_S	CC	REAS
1	1		S	L	I	1	N	SCIT	NNNN	NNNN	53.30	A	
1	1	1	SPJ		I	1	Y	SPJX	NNNN	NNNN	53.30	A	
2	1		S	L	I	1	N	SCIT	NNNN	NNNN	19.67	A	
2	2		SPJ		I	1	Y	SPJX	NNNN	NNNN	19.67	A	

9. Describe the processing that will be done at execution time based on the following information.

```
EXPLAIN PLAN SET QUERYNO = 1 FOR
SELECT SN, PN, QTY
FROM   SPJ AS SPJX
```

```
 WHERE  QTY <
  (SELECT AVG(QTY)
   FROM   SPJ
   WHERE  SPJ.SN = SPJX.SN);
```

QN_B	MT	TNAM	PRE	AT	MC_O	XNAM	UJOG	UJOC	CP_S	CC REAS
1	1	SPJ	S	R	0	N		NNNN	NNNN	18623.60	A
1	2	SPJ	L	I	1	N	SPJX	NNNN	NNNN	18623.60	A

10. The following FULL OUTER JOIN and EXISTS statements give the same results. Indeed, the exists formulation was the most common way to achieve full outer join results prior to the introduction of the FULL OUTER JOIN into DB2. Look first at the access path chosen by the optimizer and decide which of the three formulations are likely to perform best. Then look at the processor time estimates in seconds and give your option based on both factors.

```
EXPLAIN PLAN SET QUERYNO = 1 FOR
SELECT SPJ.SN, SPJ.PN, SPJ.JN
FROM   SPJ FULL OUTER JOIN S
ON     SPJ.SN = S.SN
   FULL OUTER JOIN P
    ON SPJ.PN = P.PN
   FULL OUTER JOIN J
    ON SPJ.JN = J.JN;

SELECT SPJ.SN, SPJ.PN, SPJ.JN
FROM   SPJ, S, P, J
WHERE  SPJ.SN = S.SN
AND    SPJ.PN = P.PN
AND    SPJ.JN = J.JN
UNION ALL
SELECT SPJX.SN, SPJX.PN, SPJX.JN
FROM   SPJ AS SPJX
WHERE  NOT EXISTS
  (SELECT 1
   FROM   S
   WHERE  SN = SPJX.SN)
UNION ALL
SELECT SPJX.SN, SPJX.PN, SPJX.JN
FROM   SPJ AS SPJX
WHERE  NOT EXISTS
  (SELECT 1
   FROM   P
   WHERE  PN = SPJX.PN)
UNION ALL
SELECT SPJX.SN, SPJX.PN, SPJX.JN
FROM   SPJ AS SPJX
WHERE  NOT EXISTS
  (SELECT 1
   FROM   J
   WHERE  JN = SPJX.JN);
```

QN_B		MT	TNAM	PRE	AT	MC_O		XNAM	UJOG	UJOC	CP_S	CC	REAS
1	1		DSNW	S	R	0	N		NNNN	NNNN	1801.48	B	TABL
1	1	2	J	S	I	0	Y	JX	NNNN	NYNN	1801.48	B	TABL
1	2		DSNW	S	R	0	N		NNNN	NNNN	1801.48	B	TABL
1	2	2	P	S	I	0	Y	PX	NNNN	NYNN	1801.48	B	TABL
1	3		SPJ	S	I	0	Y	SPJX	NNNN	NNNN	1801.48	B	TABL
1	3	2	S	S	I	0	Y	SX	NNNN	NNNN	1801.48	B	TABL
2	1		S	S	I	0	Y	SX	NNNN	NNNN	15334.40	A	
2	1	1	SPJ		I	1	Y	SPJX	NNNN	NNNN	15334.40	A	
2	1	2	J	S	I	0	Y	JX	NNNN	NYNN	15334.40	A	
2	1	2	P	S	I	0	Y	PX	NNNN	NYNN	15334.40	A	
2	2		SPJ	S	I	0	Y	SPJX	NNNN	NNNN	15334.40	A	
2	3		S		I	1	Y	SX	NNNN	NNNN	15334.40	A	
2	4		SPJ	S	I	0	Y	SPJX	NNNN	NNNN	15334.40	A	
2	5		P		I	1	Y	PX	NNNN	NNNN	15334.40	A	
2	6		SPJ	S	I	0	Y	SPJX	NNNN	NNNN	15334.40	A	
2	7		J		I	1	Y	JX	NNNN	NNNN	15334.40	A	

11. The following SELECT statement to determine suppliers who have and have not provided parts for active jobs has three query blocks, unlike the previous SELECT statements which have one query block each SELECT keyword. A good rule of thumb to determine the number of query blocks that a statement has is to count the number of occurrences of the key words SELECT, UPDATE, and DELETE in a statement. It is not an absolute rule, as is the case for all rules of thumb. The following statement has 4 occurrences of the key word SELECT but only 3 query blocks are shown in the plan report.

```
            EXPLAIN PLAN SET QUERYNO = 1 FOR
QBLOCKNO=1  SELECT SN,'PARTS IN SPJ     ',QTY
            FROM   SPJ
            WHERE  SN IN
              (SELECT SN
               FROM   S)
            UNION
QBLOCKNO=3  SELECT SN,'PARTS NOT IN SPJ',-1
            FROM   S
            WHERE  SN NOT IN
QBLOCKNO=4   (SELECT SN
              FROM   SPJ);
```

QN_B		MT	TNAM	PRE	AT	MC_O		XNAM	UJOG	UJOC	CP_S	CC	REAS
1	1		S	S	I	0	Y	SX	NNNN	NNNN	2147483.64	A	
1	1	1	SPJ		I	1	N	SPJX	NNNN	NNNN	2147483.64	A	
1	1	3				0	N		NNNN	YNNN	2147483.64	A	
1	3		S	S	I	0	Y	SX	NNNN	NNNN	2147483.64	A	
1	4	3				0	N		NNNN	YNYN	2147483.64	A	
1	4		SPJ	S	I	0	Y	SPJX	NNNN	NNNN	2147483.64	A	

a) Why does the third row in the report indicate that an additional sort is required to obtain unique values?

b) Is the sort performed in the middle to the processing as suggested in the explain report?

c) How can the sort be avoided?

d) Is the third query block (QB_B = 1 3) showing a non-matching index scan of all the leaf pages for the SX index with sequential prefetch on the leaf pages and index only processing (PRE = S, AT = I, MC_O = 0 Y) processed next?

e) What is the next query block processed after the join?

f) What is the last step processed before the sort for the UNION?

ANSWERS

1. DB2 attempts to insert the row in sequence according to the SN index. If there is sufficient free space on the target page, the row S99 is inserted on the page that contains S98 and S100, for example, according to the clustering index on the SN column. This is not reflected in the plan table because the optimizer does not choose an access path for an INSERT statement. Data manager determines the clustering index (or the index with the lowest object ID if a clustering index was not explicitly defined) from the DBD and INSERT statements the row accordingly. If there is no index on the table, the row is inserted at the end of the table. The PROCMS is 1 millisecond before division by 1000 to report the CP_S in seconds.

2. The UNION ALL formulation might have advantages in some cases even though its estimated cost is a bit higher than multiple index usage. If the user requests a large range of values for the WHERE SN BETWEEN ? AND ? predicate but only a small number of rows are displayed on the screen, it is not necessary to scan many leaf pages to get the qualifying RIDs, place them in the RID pool, sort them (not required with a high cluster ratio index), and issue list prefetch with the UNION ALL formulation. The rows are retrieved as they are fetched with the matching index scan used for the UNION ALL formulation without prior RID processing. In addition, the UNION ALL formulation avoids hitting some of the negative list prefetch thresholds discussed in Chapter PP.

3. The unique clustering index on SN, PN, and JN is very good. However, the matching index scan is on only 1 of the 3 columns because of the OR predicates on different columns. If suppliers supply many parts, it will be necessary to scan many leaf pages to reposition the cursor. Indeed, the 620.59 processor second estimate is probably due to the low value specified in the SN >= 'S2' predicate even though the cardinality of the column is good at 100,000 in the 10 million row table. The response time will vary depending on the value used for repositioning and the cardinality of the column. These factors determine the number of leaf pages that must be scanned.

4. The optimizer has transformed the ORed predicates to an IN (list) formulation based on the AT value of N for:

```
SELECT SN, PN, JN, QTY
FROM   SPJ
WHERE  SN = 'S4'
AND    PN IN ('P1', 'P2', 'P3', 'P4')
AND    JN > 'J1';
```

Four matching index scans will be done starting with S4, P1, and J1 followed by index screening. The second matching index scan will be on S4, P2, and J1, the third on S4, P3, and J1, and the fourth on S4, P4, and J1. Each matching index scan will be followed by index screening because of the > predicate on JN.

5. Whether host variables or literals are used, the access path and processor time estimate will not differ in most cases because equal predicates are used. An exception is if the literal is in SYSCOLDIST as being a frequently occurring value, a tablespace scan, non-matching index scan, or matching index scan can be chosen as the access path as discussed in Chapter OP.

6. QUERYNO = 1 uses matching index scans (AT=N) to locate the rows to be updated because SN is in the WHERE clause. QUERYNO = 2 uses a tablespace scan because CASE expressions are evaluated at stage 2 and there is no WHERE clause to provide for stage 1 processing and matching index scans.

7. The optimizer added the predicate S.SN = 'S2' based on the coded predicate SPJ.SN = 'S2' and the join predicate SPJ.SN = S.SN (transitive closure). It discovered a unique index on S.SN. Only one row will qualify with a unique index and an equal predicate. This is an example of a best matching index scan. The S2 row is made the outer table of the nested loop join. Clearly, it contains the smallest possible number of qualifying row and is accessed first. It also reduces the access to the SPJ inner table to one matching index scan. The optimizer has estimated that there are several S2s in the SPJ table since it chose to use sequential prefetch.

8. a) The join and EXISTS formulations return the same results. b) The access path chosen by the optimizer is very similar. Both of the formulations result in the S table as the first table to be processed with the use of list prefetch and both use a matching index scan on the second SPJ table processed with index only processing. The only difference in the access path is that a nested loop join (MT=1) is shown for the join formulation.

9. This is a correlated subselect with use of an in-memory table. It is necessary to deduce the use of the in-memory table based on the fact that the inner select can be reduced to a single value (AVG(QTY)). A tablespace scan is performed on the SPJ table as the outer table with sequential prefetch. For each unique SN, a matching index scan is done on the SN, PN, JN composite index. The AVG(QTY) is computed for all matching SPJ.SN = SPJX.SN and recorded in a 4 KB in-memory table. The quantity in the outer SELECT statement is compared to the computed value and if it is less than the average, the SN, PN and QTY columns are returned to the user. Notice the high processor cost estimate of 18,623.60 seconds. Correlated subselects are frequently resource intensive.

10. This exercise is a review of material discussed in Chapters JP and ST. The full outer join of more than two tables can require intermediate work files as indicated by the two 'DSNW' in the TNAM column. (Left and right outer joins do not require an intermediate work files.) A merge join is always used for full outer joins (QUERYNO = 1, MT = 2). (Left and right outer joins can use a nested loop or merge join.) It is necessary to sort the two work files before doing the merge join processing. In contrast, the EXISTS formulation does not require intermediate work files. This suggests that the EXISTS formulation would require less processor time. However, significantly more processing time is estimated for the EXISTS formulation (15,334.40 seconds) compared to the full outer joins (1801.48) if you fetch all of the qualifying rows. If you fetch only a few rows, the EXISTS formulation gives the best performance because work files of all of the qualifying rows need not be built, sorted, and scanned.

11. The rule of thumb failed in this example because the optimizer discovered a unique index on S.SN and transformed the first subselect to a nested loop join with a matching index scan and index only processing on the inner table in parentheses (QBLOCKNO=1 noted by the SELECT statement, QN_B = 1 1, MT=1, AT=I, MC_O = 0 Y, and XNAM=SX in the explain report).

a) It is necessary to deduce that the sort shown as the third row in the explain report is for the UNION.

b) The sort for the UNION is performed at the end of the processing, not in the middle to the processing as suggested in the explain report. This is deduced by the fact that all rows before and after the UNION must be processed before the sort is performed to eliminate duplicate rows.

c) The UNION sort can be avoided by changing the statement from the use of a UNION to a UNION ALL. Logically there can be no duplicates. A supplier cannot both supply and not supply parts to active jobs.

d) The third query block (QB_B = 1 3) showing a non-matching index scan of all the leaf pages for the SX index with sequential prefetch on the leaf pages and index only processing (PRE = S, AT = I, MC_O = 0 Y) is not processed next. The sequence of query blocks as well as the sequence of rows in the report do not reflect the sequence of operations at run time. An SQL statement is frequently not processed in the sequence that it is coded. The optimizer usually processes a statement in a sequence to minimize the number of intermediate rows that must be carried forward for further processing.

e) The next query block processed after the join is QN_B = 1 4 with MT = 3 to satisfy the very last subselect (QBLOCKNO = 3) with the results written to a work area for in-memory sparse index processing as discussed in section ST as indicated by YNYN for the composite sort. Also in this case, logically it is necessary to process the last inner select on the SPJ table shown as QBLOCKNO=3 before QBLOCKNO=2 on the S table. All the SPJ.SNs are retrieved from the SPJX index with sequential prefetch of all the leaf pages during a non-matching index scan and index only processing (QBLOCKNO=3, PN=1, PRE=S, XNAM=SPJX, MC=0, XO=0). The values are then sorted to get them in sequence (OC=Y) and to eliminate duplicates (UC=Y). There is one sort for two reasons. The sequenced and reduced intermediate answer set is placed in a temporary work area, and a sparse in-memory index is built as discussed in Chapter ST.

f) The last step processed before the sort for the UNION is the non-matching index scan on the S.SN index (SX). For each S.SN a search is performed of the work file using the in-memory sparse index. QBLOCKNO = 2 and 3 are not transformed into a join because of the NOT IN operator and there is not a unique index on SN in the SPJ table.

FIGURES

Load and Check Data Utilities

LC.1 INTRODUCTION

The LOAD utility offers a great deal of flexibility in loading data into a table as read from a sequential file. It provides for selectively loading some fields from records in the input file and ignoring others. You can specify conditions on the LOAD control statement such that only the records meeting the conditions are loaded into a table. Records that do not meet the conditions or contain errors are written to a discard data set by default. Multiple tables in a tablespace can be loaded from a single input file and you can specify which fields are to go into which columns of the various tables. One or all of the partitions of a partitioned tablespace can be loaded. LOAD can convert a variety of data types and lengths of fields to match the data types and lengths of the table columns. It is necessary only to describe the field and the LOAD utility converts the data to the type and length of the column as described in the catalog table. LOAD can be used replace existing data or add additional data to a table. LOAD validates the data before it is loaded to ensure that there are no referential integrity (RI) and table check constraint violations by default.

The CHECK DATA utility can be used to check that there are no violations of RI and table check constraints. This is particularly useful when constraints are added to a populated table with the ALTER statement. It can also be used to check data for violations after loading data and overriding the default of checking the data during the load process. Optionally, CHECK DATA can delete rows that violate constraints and write a copy of the rows to an exception table for later investigation.

LC.2 DESCRIBE INPUT FIELD POSITION AND DATA TYPE

The LOAD control statement is used to describe input field positions and data types. The following statement instructs the LOAD utility to read a sequential file from SYSREC and load the data into the AUTHID.S table. The INDDN SYSREC parameters are the default and are optional on the statement. An example of the JCL needed to allocate the required files and execute the LOAD utility is described in Section LC.13.

```
LOAD DATA INDDN SYSREC
INTO TABLE AUTHID.S
 (SN     POSITION  (1)     CHAR(2),
  SNAME  POSITION  (5:19)  CHAR,
  STATUS POSITION  (*)     INTEGER,
  CITY   POSITION  (*+2)   CHAR)
```

The position of a field in the file can be described in a variety of ways using the POSITION parameter following the column name and data type and length of the field.. You will probably want to choose a technique that is convenient for you from among the examples given.

The starting and ending positions of a field can be described in a number of ways. For example, the SN column begins in position 1 and is character data with a length of two bytes as indicated by

CHAR(2). The data type and length of a field are described much like describing a column when creating a table as discussed in Chapter CT. The length of the field need not be specified. For example, SNAME is described in the example as beginning in position 5 and ending in position 19, and is character data. LOAD calculates the length as 15 (19 - 5 + 1). The field that contains data for the STATUS column follows the SNAME with no bytes in between as indicated by the "(*)" and appears as an integer data type of four bytes on the file. The field that contains the data for the CITY column follows the STATUS field with two bytes in between as indicated by the "(*+2)" description following the POSITION parameter. The length of CITY is not given in the statement; therefore, LOAD checks the catalog tables to determine the number of bytes specified for CITY when the table was created and assumes that number of bytes on the sequential file.

If a table has a column defined as an identity column with the GENERATED ALWAYS clause as discussed in Chapters CT and BP, the column should not be named in the list of column descriptions. LOAD generates sequential values for the column. If the identity column is defined with GENERATED BY DEFAULT, LOAD will generate the sequential values if DEFAULT is specified. An alternative is to name the column in the list of column descriptions and load values into the identify column. This is useful for data propagation.

Records can be written to the sequential file with fields in the same sequence as columns in the table with no bytes between the fields using exactly the same data type and length as the rows to be loaded into the table. If the sequential file format matches the table, fields on the sequential file need not be described. This avoids errors when coding the LOAD statement and the utility gives better performance when it does not have to do data type conversions. Optionally, the sample program DSNTIUAL can be used to generate a LOAD statement once the table has been created. This program is discussed in Chapter RR.

Converting from External to Internal Integer Format

LOAD supports data type conversion between numeric data types and between character data types. In general, it does not support conversion from character to numeric data types and from numeric to character data types. An exception is that LOAD converts an external integer data type to a internal integer format.

The QTY field may have been written to a sequential file using a COBOL program that declared the field as PIC X(3), for example. This means that the value of 783 is represented with the hexadecimal format of X'F7F8F3'. It is necessary to describe the field accurately to the LOAD utility as INTEGER EXTERNAL(3). LOAD reads the field as described and converts it to an internal integer format based on the statement:

```
LOAD DATA
INTO TABLE AUTHID.SPJ
 (SN  POSITION (1)   CHAR(2),
  PN  POSITION (3)   CHAR(2),
  JN  POSITION (5)   CHAR(2),
  QTY POSITION (7)   INTEGER EXTERNAL(3))
```

Loading Packed Decimal Values

There are three types of packed decimal formats: external, packed, and zoned. If a field contains an external value of -100, for example, it must be described as DECIMAL EXTERNAL with a length and scale. The declaration of DECIMAL EXTERNAL(4,0) results in a value of -100 when selected from the table after it is loaded. The placement of the decimal point is described in parentheses. The first digit is the length or total number of bytes occupied by the field. A comma separates the length from the scale which is the number of digits to the right of the decimal point. The declaration of DECIMAL EXTERNAL(4,3) results in a value of -.100 when selected. DECIMAL EXTERNAL provides for loading a number with an implicit decimal point in an input field.

If the field is written as packed decimal, each digit is represented by four bits with the last four bits being the sign bits. The sign of a positive number is represented by A, C, E, or F. The sign of a negative number is represented by B or D. For example, the value X'000C' represent a positive zero in packed decimal format and must be described as DECIMAL PACKED.

If the field is written as zoned decimal, each digit is represented in the right four bits and the left four bits of a byte are the zone. The left four bits of the rightmost byte represents the sign. Like with packed decimal, A, C, E, or F can represent a positive number and B or D can represent a negative number. The value X'F0D1' represents a zoned decimal value of -1.

The following statement describes the input record as beginning with a two byte character value (the length is determined from the catalog tables) to be loaded into the PN column, followed immediately by a zoned decimal field to be loaded into the COST column, followed by a packed decimal field to be loaded into the QTY_DISCOUNT field, and finally an external decimal field to be loaded into the DISCOUNT field.

```
LOAD DATA
INTO TABLE AUTHID.P_COST
 (PN            POSITION(*) CHAR,
  COST          POSITION(*) DECIMAL ZONED,
  QTY_DISCOUNT POSITION(*) DECIMAL PACKED,
  DISCOUNT      POSITION(*) DECIMAL EXTERNAL)
```

The CREATE TABLE statement, formats of fields in the sequential file, and LOAD statement are all considered when loading a table. Assume that a table is created as follows.

```
CREATE TABLE COSTS
  (COST     DECIMAL (8,2)
   DISCOUNT DECIMAL (8,2));
```

The sequential file has the following values for COST and DISCOUNT.

```
 COST         DISCOUNT
(ZONED)      (EXTERNAL)
00000503        503
0000050L       -503
0000050L      -.503
```

The following LOAD statement is used to populate the COSTS table.

```
LOAD DATA
 INTO TABLE AUTHID.COSTS
```

```
(COST     POSITION (1:8) DECIMAL ZONED,
 DISCOUNT POSITION (9:16)DECIMAL EXTERNAL(8,1))
```

The result of SELECT * FROM COSTS; is:

```
COST   DISCOUNT
 5.03     50.30
-5.03    -50.30
-5.03      -.50
```

Notice that the DECIMAL(8,2) declaration for COST on the CREATE table statement as recorded in the catalog tables determines the number of digits to the right of the decimal point because the length and scale are not specified on the LOAD statement. The EXTERNAL(8,1) declaration for DISCOUNT on the LOAD statement (not the DECIMAL(8,2) on the CREATE TABLE statement) is used to determine the placement of the decimal point unless there is an explicit decimal point in the field. If there is an explicit decimal point in the field, it is used to determine the placement of the decimal point.

Loading Variable Length Data

Care needs to be exercised when loading variable length data where the column is declared as VARCHAR as will be demonstrated with an example. Assume that BUYER_NAME is defined as VARCHAR(20) in the CREATE TABLE statement and the input file contains C'FLEUR' starting in position 5. The LOAD statement must describe the field as it exists in the file as follows:

```
LOAD DATA
INTO TABLE AUTHID.S_BUYER
 (BUYER_NAME   POSITION(5)  CHAR(20),
  S_NAME       POSITION(30) VARCHAR(20),
  ASSIGN_DATE  POSITION(60) DATE EXTERNAL(10),
  ASSIGN_TIME  POSITION(*)  TIME EXTERNAL(8))
```

FLEUR is loaded into the column followed by 15 blanks with the correct description of BUYER_NAME as it appears on the file as CHAR(20). However, the requirement is to load the data without trailing blanks. To accomplish this, it is necessary to have a two byte SMALLINT (PIC S9(4) in COBOL) with the number of significant characters in the name immediately preceding the field. The field is then described as VARCHAR(20).

If S_NAME is defined as VARCHAR(20) in table and the input file contains X'0005' followed immediately by C'KATHY' starting in position 30 and the LOAD statement describes the field as VARCHAR(20), KATHY will be loaded with no trailing blanks. This is the required result.

Loading Date and Time Data

If a column is declared as DATE, TIME, or TIMESTAMP on the CREATE TABLE statement, the fields on the sequential files must be in character format with punctuation. For example, if the default international standards organization (ISO) format is used, 1994-05-23 is a valid date, 20.10.30 is a valid time, and 1994-05-23-20.10.30.123456 is a valid timestamp. The fields must be declared as

DATE EXTERNAL, TIME EXTERNAL, or TIMESTAMP EXTERNAL with the appropriate number of digits for LOAD as shown in the previous LOAD statement. If the input file to LOAD is a result of using REORG UNLOAD EXTERNAL (described in Chapter RR), the same procedure is used. However, if you are loading data as output by REORG UNLOAD, do not specify DATE EXTERNAL. This is because this option of the REORG utility outputs date/time in an internal format acceptable to the LOAD utility.

If NOT NULL WITH DEFAULT is specified and the date/time is not in the input file, the date/time at the start of load is used for all rows loaded without a date/time in the record. This may or may not be the desired result. If it is not the desired result, the input file must have a valid date/time to be loaded.

We have reviewed a few of many data type and length conversions that can be done by LOAD. The *Utility Guide and Reference* manual has a table of all data type conversions that can be done by LOAD.

Loading ASCII Data

An American Standard Code for Information Interchange (ASCII) input file can be loaded into an ASCII table by specifying the parameter ASCII on the LOAD statement like:

```
LOAD DATA ASCII
INTO TABLE AUTHID.SPJ
 (SN   POSITION (1)    CHAR(2),
  PN   POSITION (3)    CHAR(2),
  JN   POSITION (5)    CHAR(2),
  QTY POSITION (7)    INTEGER EXTERNAL(3))
```

The example assumes that the input file contains the installation specified default Coded Character Set Identifier (CCSID). If this is not true, it is necessary to specify the CCSID.

Loading Data that Spans Records

If the columns of a row appear in fields on multiple records, the CONTINUEIF parameter is used. The CONTINUEIF(80:80) = 'C' parameter in the following example causes the physical record following the record with a 'C' in position 80 to be treated as a continuation of the first physical record. The two physical records are treated as one long logical record.

```
LOAD DATA
  CONTINUEIF(80:80)  = 'C'
  INTO TABLE AUTHID.P
   (PN      POSITION    (1:2)   CHAR,
    PNAME  POSITION    (5:24)  CHAR,
    COLOR  POSITION   (30:35)  INTEGER,
    WEIGHT POSITION   (90:93)  INTEGER
           DEFAULTIF  (90:93)  = -1,
    CITY   POSITION  (100:114)  CHAR
           NULLIF    (100:102)  = '***')
```

Dealing with Nulls when Loading Data

Loading data depends on how nulls are declared for a column when the table is created.

If the column is declared NOT NULL (without default), data must be loaded into the column. If there are no values for the column in the input file, an alternative is to describe a field in the record that contains zero or blank for loading into the column.

If the column is declared NOT NULL WITH DEFAULT, a field need not be designated as containing a value for the column. If no field description is specified for a column declared as NOT NULL WITH DEFAULT, zero is loaded into a numeric column, blank is loaded into a character column, and the date/time of the start of the utility is loaded into date/time columns. If in the past a value has been specified to indicate that the true value is unknown, the DEFAULTIF parameter can be used to substitute the default value for the data type in the column. In the previous LOAD statement the parameter DEFAULTIF (90:93) = -1 means to load zero in WEIGHT if positions 90-93 contain -1 in binary.

If the column is declared DEFAULT 9999 and no field is described for the column, the value of 9999 is loaded in the column for each row loaded. If in the past, 0 has been used to indicate that a valid value is unknown and the field contains 0, the parameter DEFAULTIF(90:93) = 0 loads 9999 in the column.

If the column allows nulls and no field is described for the column, no value is loaded into the column. Rather, a one byte column prefix is loaded with X'FF' indicating that there is no value for the column as discussed in Chapter CT. If in the past, '***' has been used to indicate that a value is unknown and the field contains '***', the NULLIF(100:102) = '***' parameter describing the CITY column in the previous LOAD statement causes X'FF' to be loaded in the one byte column prefix indicating that the value is not known.

Loading a Fixed Repeating Group

There are times when it is necessary to load a varying number of columns depending on the month when the data is being loaded. For example, assume that a sequential file has a field in positions 18-19 which gives the number of expenditure buckets to be loaded into 12 columns in the table. If the field in positions 18-19 contains 01, only the first value for January is present on the record in positions 20 through 29. If the field contains 02, then the first two values for January and February are present on the record in positions 20 through 29 and positions 30 through 39. If the field contains 03, the first three values for January, February, and March are present on the record as indicated in the LOAD statement:

```
LOAD DATA
INTO TABLE AUTHID.EXPENDITURES
   WHEN (18:19)= '01'(EXPENSE1 POSITION (20:29))
   WHEN (18:19)= '02'(EXPENSE1 POSITION (20:29),
                      EXPENSE2 POSITION (30:39))
   WHEN (18:19)= '03'(EXPENSE1 POSITION (20:29),
                      EXPENSE2 POSITION (30:39),
                      EXPENSE3 POSITION (40:49))
```

There can be a description for each record , which can contain from 1 to 12 expense fields. If a varying number of columns are to be loaded throughout the year, the expense columns cannot be declared NOT NULL.

LC.3 SORTKEYS PARAMETER

The SORTKEYS parameter causes LOAD, REORG, and REBUILD INDEX to pass indexed values to an external sort (DFSORT, for example) directly without having to write the values to a file before the sort begins. The sort is done in memory as data is written to the table (REBUILD INDEX does not write data to the table). SORTWKnn data sets are used to contain portions of the sorted values, which are called runs. The runs are merged and passed to the build index phase. If there is more than one index, all indexed values are sorted together and built serially with or without the SORTKEYS parameter in V5. This increases the elapsed time to complete the load and build of a number of indexes. The values for each index are sorted separately and built in parallel with the SORTKEYS parameter in V6. The indexed values are not written to the SYSUT1 and SORTDATA data sets when the SORTKEYS parameter is used. However, these data sets do need to be allocated for processing errors during the reload, validate, and enforce phases of the utility.

The number of indexed values to be sorted should be given, along with the SORTKEYS parameter as shown in the following statement. The example LOAD statement assumes that the fields in the sequential file match the columns in the table to be loaded because the fields are not described.

```
LOAD DATA
INTO TABLE AUTHID.SPJ
SORTKEYS 300000
RESUME NO REPLACE
STATISTICS
 INDEX(ALL)
COPYDDN (SYSCOPY)
DISCARDS 1000
```

The 300,000 estimate is calculated as the number or rows times the number of indexes plus the number of FK if not indexed when using ENFORCE YES. We are assuming 100,000 rows and 3 indexes in the example. If the estimate is too high or too low, the sort can abend. If the default of SORTKEYS 0 is used, more I/O is required in most cases.

Parallel build of indexes (V6): A separate task is used for each parallel index sort and build which can overlap with the reload phase. The parallel build of indexes can take advantage of multiprocessing and multiple processors. If sufficient virtual storage resources are available, sort and build index phases assign subtasks for each index to be built. If this is not possible, each of several available subtasks can build indexes serially. That is the subtasks build several indexes in parallel and then the subtasks build several more indexes in parallel. If there are more indexes than sort tasks, assignment of indexes to available sort tasks is done in a round robin fashion. If DB2 is used to enforce RI, foreign keys are sorted first. Multiple parts of the partitioning index can be built in parallel. Nonpartitioning index (NPI) can use multiple sort subtasks to sort the indexed values in parallel. The sorted results are merged and the index built serially.

Data sets for parallel build of indexes: Utilities can dynamically allocate the required data sets to maximize parallel build of the indexes. It is necessay to specify SORTDEVT in addition to the

SORTKEYS parameter. The SORTWKnn must not be specified in the utility JCL. Rather, SWnnWKmm data sets are needed for sort runs of each index built in parallel. Optionally, you can allocate SWnnWKmm and UTPRINnn to determine the number of indexes built in parallel. Each sort subtask must have its own group of sort work data sets and know where to print messages (each NPI requires its own message output), for example:

- SW01WK01 for 1st subtask to use as its 1st work data set to build the 1st index.
- SW01WK02 for 1st subtask to use as its 2nd work data set to build the 1st index, etc. if more sort work data sets are wanted.
- UTPRIN01 for 1st index build messages or allocate UTPRINT DD statement to SYSOUT or a data set.
- SW02WK01 for 2nd subtask to use as its 1st work data set to build the 2nd index.
- SW02WK02 for 2nd subtask to use as its 2nd work data set to build the 2nd index, etc. if more sort work data sets are wanted.
- UTPRIN02 for 2nd index build messages or allocate UTPRINT DD statement to SYSOUT or a data set.
- Etc. for each index to be built in parallel.

The space required for the work data sets can be estimated using the formula:

2 * (longest indexed column to be built by a subtask + 20 bytes)
* number of indexes to be sorted by the subtask * number of rows

There are several advantages of allocating data sets compared to having them dynamically allocated. You have the opportunity to control the size and placement of data sets, minimize device contention, limit the number of utility subtasks used to build indexes, and optimally utilize DASD free space.

IBM tested the LOAD utility with serial build of indexes with and without the SORTKEYS parameter. The elapsed and CPU times are shown in Figure LC.1. The timings were done for loading a 5 million row table in 10 partitions, 118 byte row with 26 columns, and there were two indexes on the table. The tests were done using V5 of the DB2 subsystem, a 10-way RX3 9672 V0C, and RAMAC DASD. The details of the test can be found in the *DB2 for OS/390 Version 5 Performance Topics* manual, SG24-2213. There is a good savings in elapsed time using SORTKEYS and a bit less CPU time as can be seen in the figure.

Figure LC.1. LOAD without and with SORTKEYS

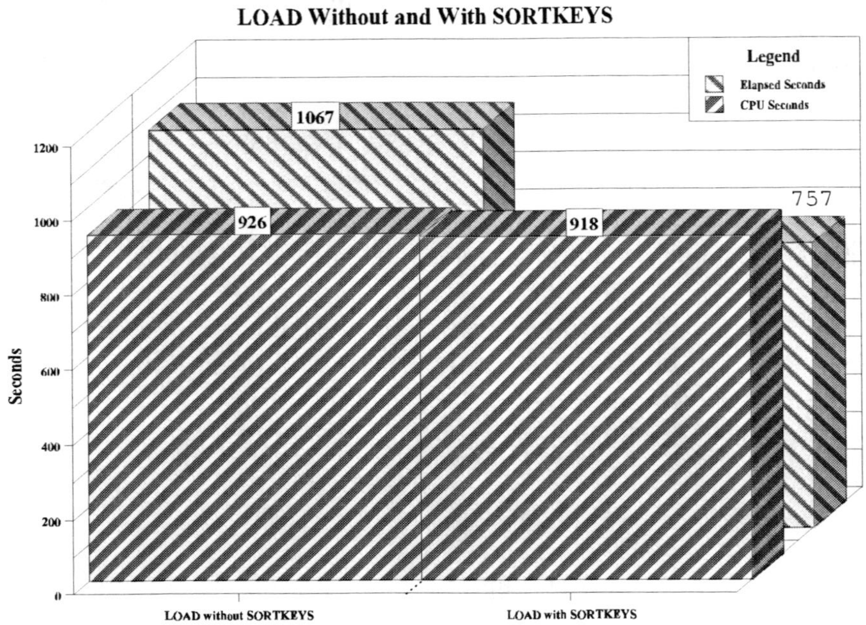

Indexed values are always sorted with SORTKEYS unless there is only one clustering index and the records have been sorted in sequence according to the clustering index columns.

Recommendations: The sequential file should always be sorted in sequence according to the clustering index columns before loading the data. Otherwise, the rows are not in clustering sequence until after a reorganization. LOAD never sorts the records and rows.

The SORTKEYS parameter is a good choice for improved performance and parallel build of indexes if there is more than one index on the table. However, there is a trade-off regarding restartability of the utility. It is only restartable from the beginning of the RELOAD phase, regardless of how restart is requested when SORTKEYS is specified.

LC.4 RESUME AND REPLACE PARAMETERS

The LOAD utility can be used to load a table that has never had rows in it, to replace rows in a table, or to add rows to a table.

RESUME NO REPLACE causes the LOAD utility to write into an empty data set. This is the default. If data is present in the table, the utility does not place any rows in the table.

REPLACE causes the LOAD utility to write over existing data. You can replace data in individual partitions. If the partitioned tablespace has a NPI, the RIDs pointing to the replaced rows must be deleted, the new indexed values sorted, and the new RIDs pointing to the new rows inserted into the NPI. This increases the costs of replacing data in a partitioned tablespace. Be cautious of the placement of the PART parameter when loading one or a few partitions to avoid replacing the entire tablespace. The PART parameter needs to follow the INTO TABLE clause like:

```
INTO TABLE AUTHID.SPJ PART 1 REPLACE
```

Beware of replacing a single table in a multi-table tablespace. All tables are lost when replacing a single table.

RESUME YES causes the LOAD utility to add new rows at the end of the tablespace. This is a good choice for adding rows to a table compared to using SQL INSERT statements. In general the LOAD utility has performance advantages when loading a table for the first time, replacing rows, and adding rows to a table as discussed in Chapter BP. However, deleted row space is not used unless all secondary extents are filled.

LC.5 INLINE STATISTICS (V6) AND COPY WITH LOAD

LOAD can optionally collect statistics and make an image copy during the load processing. The STATISTICS parameter causes statistics to be collected by LOAD (not with RESUME YES), REORG, and REBUILD INDEX similar to RUNSTATS as discussed in Chapter RR with default parameters (no explicitly specified parameters). Tablespace statistics are collected during the reload phase. Index statistics are collected during index build phase if index parameters are specified. You can specify specific parameters like with RUNSTATS including TABLE, COLUMN, SAMPLE, INDEX, REPORT, UPDATE, KEYCARD, FREQVAL, NUMCOLS, and COUNT. Do specify STATISTICS and optionally additional parameter to LOAD. This avoids passing the loaded data again to collect tablespace statistics. Figure LC.2 shows a comparison of the elapsed and CPU time using LOAD followed by RUNSTATS (914 and 554 seconds) and using LOAD with the collection of inline statistics (603 and 560 seconds). Notice that there is a significant reduction in elapsed time with a small increase in CPU time when loading a 5 million row table in 10 partitions, 118 byte row with 26 columns, and 2 indexes using V6. Details of tests are in *DB2 UDB for OS/390 Version 6 Performance Topics*, SG24-5351, manual. The test results show a significant advantage of using inline statistics.

Figure LC.2. Comparison of LOAD followed by RUNSTATS with inline statistics

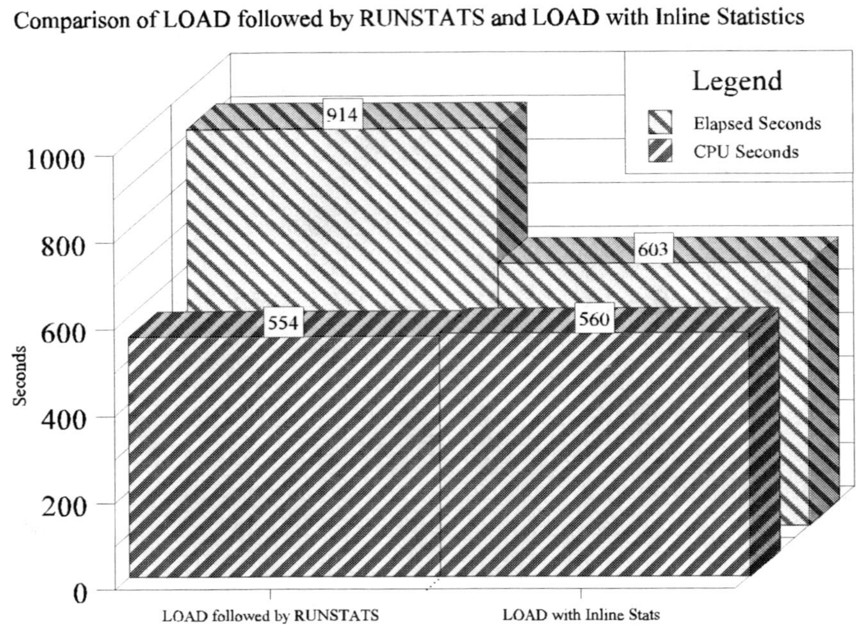

An image copy of the tablespace (not indexes) can be made during the load process. An inline copy is not the default. It is necessary to specify the COPYDDN parameter and optionally the RECOVERYDDN parameter. Up to four copies (two local copies and two remote copies) can be made asynchronously as the data is loaded. This avoids having to pass the data a second time to make a copy after the load. The COPYDDN parameter is used in the previous LOAD statement example. The COPYDDN and RECOVERYDDN parameters are discussed in detail in Chapter CR.

Inline copies can be made when replacing an entire tablespace or partition using the parameter RESUME NO REPLACE. LOAD issues an error message if the COPYDDN parameter is coded on the LOAD statement along with RESUME YES or RESUME NO without REPLACE. The copy pending state is not turned on with a successful inline copy regardless of whether LOG of YES or NO is used.

An inline copy produced by the LOAD utility is logically equivalent to a full image copy made with SHRLEVEL REFERENCE. Data and space map pages may be out of sequence and some may be repeated. The last duplicates are used to ensure data integrity. If the data is compressed, the second set of dictionary pages are used when building a new dictionary.

An inline copy should not be used with the RECOVER TOCOPY utility. The use of a point-in-time recovery to an image copy places the indexes on the tables in the tablespace and the dependent tables in recovery pending. This is necessary because there can exist uncorrected unique index violations and constraint violations in the inline copy. REBUILD INDEX and CHECK DATA should be run to remove the recovery pending state.

Comparison of Costs

None of the test results in this book apply directly to your environment. You have a different computer, DASD, workload, virtual pool size and usage, different table sizes, and many other differences from the test environments used. However, the test results do give you a rough order of magnitude idea as to whether a particular alternative presented in this book might be useful in your environment.

The test results in Figure LC.3 compare the elapsed and CPU times of loading data followed by an image copy, with an inline copy, and not including a copy. The tests were done by IBM on the same data and environment as the tests comparing the LOAD utility with and without the SORTKEYS parameter in Section LC.3. The results suggest that a load with an inline copy costs less than loading a table followed by a full image copy. Notice in the figure that the load followed by an image copy has a higher elapsed time than loading the data with and without an inline copy. The one second difference in CPU time is not significant. A little more CPU time and elapsed time are required for the load with an inline copy compared to the load with no inline copy and no image copy taken. The additional time to take an inline copy is certainly advisable to avoid a long recovery in case of a failure after the load.

Figure LC.3. LOAD followed by copy, with an inline copy, and not including a copy

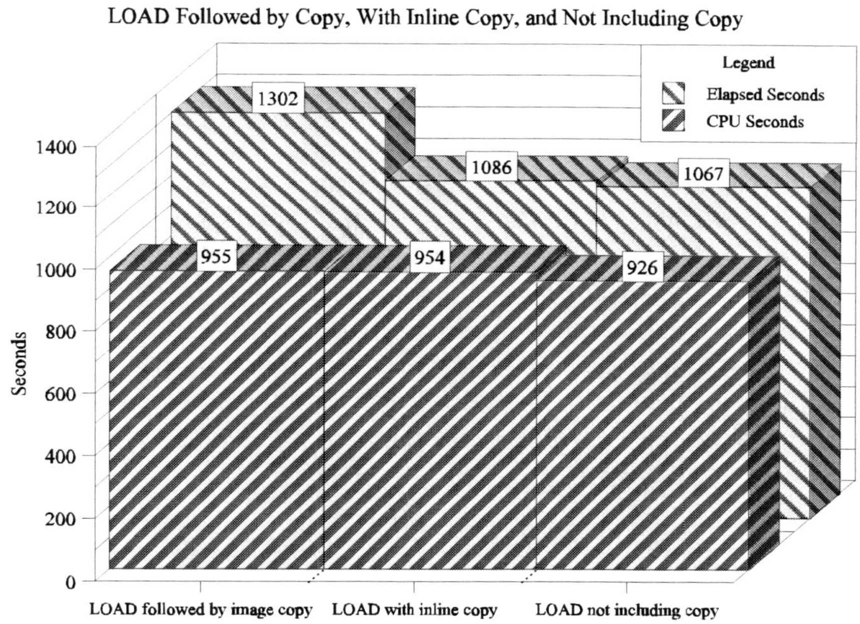

LC.6 LOAD WITH LOG OF NO

We have seen that an inline copy cannot be made when adding rows to a table using the RESUME YES parameter. In this case it is advisable to use the LOG NO parameter followed by a full image copy to improve performance as shown in the following LOAD statement. This reduces the number of bytes that must be logged. The time and resources required to follow the load with an image copy are almost always less than the cost of logging the data as it is loaded, assuming that a medium to large number of rows are added to the table.

```
LOAD DATA
INTO TABLE AUTHID.SPJ
RESUME YES
LOG NO
```

The relative amount of log data for a load of 100,000 rows (115 byte row length) is 108,000 bytes with log of no and 2,130,000 bytes with log of yes. Obviously, log of no saves a good deal of logging. There is some logging when loading a partition of a partitioned tablespace that has one or more NPI. Logging is done for the NPIs even when log of no is specified. The copy pending restriction is set on for a tablespace or partition when a table is loaded with log of no. This means that updates cannot be executed and the tablespace cannot be recovered. The restriction can be removed by following the load with a full image copy using the SHRLEVEL REFERENCE parameter, a reorganization with log of yes, execution of the REPAIR utility with the NOCOPYPEND parameter, or starting the database and tablespace with ACCESS(FORCE).

The copy pending restriction need *not* be removed for read-only access. A read-only table can always be reloaded in case of a failure, assuming that the sequential file used for the LOAD is retained in good condition.

Recommendation: Use load with log of no and follow it immediately with a full image copy using SHRLEVEL REFERENCE when adding rows to a table. Use load with log of no with an inline copy when replacing data.

LC.7 DISCARDING ERROR RECORDS

Records that cannot be loaded are written to a discard data set. It is recommended that you use the default to discard records that cannot be loaded. However, the parameter DISCARDS should be coded along with a maximum number of error records that should be discarded. Otherwise, the default is DISCARDS 0. The zero means that all records that cannot be loaded are written to the discard data set. A reasonable limit should be specified with the DISCARDS parameter to avoid writing all input records to the discard data set because of a keying error on the LOAD statement or using the wrong file as input by accident. The DISCARDS 1000 parameter is used in the LOAD statement as an example in Section LC.3. Discarding all records can take several times longer than loading the data.

Recommendation: Exercise caution when writing the sequential file to be used as input to the LOAD utility. Errors in the file detract significantly from the performance of a load because records must be written to the discard data set, messages are written to SYSERR, and a cross reference map of RIDs and records numbers is written to SYSMAP.

Conditions that Cause Discards

A number of conditions can cause records to be discarded. Perhaps the most common reason for not being able to load records into a table is simply a keying error on the LOAD statement. The second most common reason for discarding records is that the data types and lengths of the fields on the sequential file are not described correctly on the LOAD statement or it is not possible to convert a field to the column data type and length.

There are a number of other conditions that cause records to be written to the discard data set. If the WHEN clause condition is not met by the record, it is discarded. If the goal is to load a particular partition but there are records for another partition in the input file, they are discarded. If NOSUBS parameter is used and conversion of one CCSID to another or to/from ASCII/EBCDIC would result in a substitution byte, the record is discarded if there is a discard data set, otherwise, LOAD abends. Records which violate RI and check table constraints are discarded if the default of ENFORCE CONSTRAINTS is used. Duplicate values in columns with a unique index cause records to be discarded. When RESUME NO REPLACE is used, all duplicates are discarded. One of the duplicates is not written to the table because all of the columns may not be duplicates. When RESUME YES is used, the duplicate to be loaded into the table is not included in the table. It is written to the discard data set.

A report of records not loaded along with the discard data set is written with descriptive error messages including the sequence number of the input record and the RID in the table depending on the options chosen. Based on this information, you can correct records in the discard data set and execute LOAD RESUME YES with the discard data set as input to the load.

LC.8 REUSE AND PREFORMATTING DATA SETS

The REUSE parameter can be used to cause a logical reset of data sets with several utilities including LOAD REPLACE (V5 APAR PQ19077).

```
LOAD DATA
INTO TABLE AUTHID.SPJ
REPLACE
REUSE
PREFORMAT
ENFORCE CONSTRAINTS
COPYDDN (SYSCOPY)
DISCARDS 1000
```

REUSE avoids delete and redefine of DB2 managed data sets for utilities that rewrite tablespaces and indexes including LOAD REPLACE, REORG TABLESPACE with SHRLEVEL NONE, REORG INDEX, RECOVER TABLESPACE, REBUILD INDEX, and RECOVER INDEX. The purpose is to keep data sets in the same location on DASD. This eases maintenance of data set placement on DASD and improves performance over deleting and redefining the data sets. REUSE applies to partitions of a partitioned tablespace and the partitioning index. The savings of 0.6 seconds (0.3 to delete plus 0.3 seconds to define) per data set can be significant, particularly with a large number of data sets (data partitions, partitioning index, and nonpartitioned indexes, for example).

Caution: The REUSE parameter should not be used if the DASD space of the current location of data set has been damaged.

The PREFORMAT parameter causes the LOAD and REORG utilities to write X'00' on the tablespace and index pages for the full primary quantity and the last secondary quantity required. The high used RBA equals the high allocated RBA after using PREFORMAT. Pages are preformatted after loading rows and building indexes. This will increases the time for executing the utilities but avoids the time to preformat pages during inserts with some inserts requiring more time than others. Do estimate the space required carefully to avoid wasting space on DASD.

If you require preformatted space, the PREFORMAT parameter must be specified in addition to the REUSE parameter.

LC.9 ENFORCEMENT OF CONSTRAINTS

The LOAD utility enforces RI and table check constraints by default. Optionally, you can specify the ENFORCE CONSTRAINTS parameter. If you do not want to enforce the constraints, it is necessary to override the default by specifying the ENFORCE NO parameter. The use of ENFORCE NO always causes check pending to be set on because the LOAD utility does not check for any constraint violations and some may exist. It is necessary to turn checking pending off in order to select and update rows. A good method for turning check pending off is to use the CHECK DATA utility as discussed in Section LC.14. Load with ENFORCE CONSTRAINTS is more efficient than ENFORCE NO followed by CHECK DATA.

When loading tables that are part of a RI set, it is advisable to load the parent tables first to maximize performance and minimize complexities when loading the dependent tables. There will be no violations of RI constraints when loading a parent table because parent rows may or may not have dependents. You will want to resolve any duplicates on the primary key (PK) before loading the dependent tables. This avoids discarding dependent rows that are dependents of parent rows that were discarded because of duplicate PK values. In addition, you can read the parent table while loading the dependent tables.

After you have loaded one of each duplicate PK row, you are ready to load the dependent tables. All orphans (dependent rows without matching parent rows) are discarded. These rows are identified as having a primary error. Dependents of rows not loaded within the same load job are not loaded. These rows are identified as having a secondary error. The tablespace and indexes are immediately usable after a load when enforcing the constraints. You will want to review the discarded rows, correct them, and use LOAD RESUME YES with the discard data set as input to the load.

If the parent and dependent tables are in same tablespace, it is necessary to load the dependent tables using the RESUME YES parameter.

LC.10 KEEPDICTIONARY AND PART PARAMETERS

The LOAD utility builds a compression dictionary by default when replacing data if the tablespace was created with the COMPRESS YES parameter as discussed in Chapter CD. In most cases the characteristics of the data do not change with respect to compression and it is not necessary to build the compression dictionary when LOAD is used to replace existing rows in a table. If this is the case with your data, you will want to use the parameter KEEPDICTIONARY to avoid the costs of building a new dictionary as shown in the following LOAD statement.

```
LOAD DATA
INTO TABLE AUTHID.SPJ
PART 4
REPLACE
KEEPDICTIONARY
COPYDDN (SYSCOPY)
```

The PART parameter can be used to load only specific partitions in a partitioned tablespace as indicated by the partition number specified, part 4 in the above LOAD statement. The PART, KEEPDICTIONARY, REPLACE, RESUME, and COPYDDN parameters must be positioned after the INTO TABLE clause when loading a partition.

LC.11 PARTITION INDEPENDENCE

Partition independence means that most utilities can be executed on one partition while other partitions are available for processing by SQL or other utilities. The primary goal is to improve the availability of data. The execution of a utility on one partition usually requires considerably less time than executing the utility on the entire tablespace. For example, you can load one partition while reorganizing another partition and recovering another failed partition while allowing normal SQL access to all partitions not currently being processed by the utilities. Even the START, STOP, and DISPLAY commands can operate at the partition level.

Processing multiple partitions in parallel reduces the elapsed time that data is unavailable compared to processing the entire tablespace. However, the total elapsed and CPU times for processing each partition individually is higher in most cases than for processing the entire tablespace. This is particularly true when there is one or more NPI. But even without NPI some increase in resource consumption can be expected due to contention for the CPU, I/O, locks, and latches.

Claims and Drains on Objects

Claims and drains on objects and restrictive states are used to provide partition independence. Most utilities do *not* take transaction locks and latches as do SQL statements to serialize processing. Utilities do lock some catalog tables. For example, locks are taken to check authorization to execute a utility and several utilities record information in SYSCOPY.

Claims (not drain locks) are taken by SQL statements, DB2 commands, DB2 restart on objects placed INDOUBT, and some utilities, including RUNSTATS and COPY with SHRLEVEL CHANGE. A claim is taken on an object to avoid a utility taking a drain lock and executing. A claim is a counter of all users that are accessing an object. There are three classes of claims for physical and logical objects as summarized below. A physical object is a partition of a partitioned tablespace, a partition of a partitioning index, an entire segmented tablespace, a simple tablespace, and the entire index on a table in a nonpartitioned tablespace. A logical partition is the RIDs in a NPI that reference a partition.

1) Write claim
2) CS (Cursor Stability) read claim including a count of users using UR (Uncommitted Read) and RS (Read Stability)
3) RR (Repeatable Read) read claim

One or more claims can be active for a user at any one time. A commit decrements the counter of claims on an object, except when using CURSOR WITH HOLD, LOCK TABLE, or the RUNSTATS or COPY utility with SHRLEVEL CHANGE.

Programs can disallow a utility from executing by using CURSOR WITH HOLD or LOCK TABLE. This is advisable if you establish quiesce points periodically while a program is executing. You would not want to establish an RBA (Relative Byte Address) with the QUIESCE utility during the execution of a batch program for example. This is because if you recover to the established RBA, you will not know exactly which insert, update, and delete statements were and were not successfully executed in the batch program before the QUIESCE utility executed. Therefore, you will not know which changes remain in effect after a partial recovery to the established RBA.

Draining an Object

In order for a utility to execute, it must drain one or more claim classes depending on the utility phase that needs to be executed. Claim counters are decremented by one when a user does a commit. A utility submitted for execution must wait for all claims in the required claim classes to be released. No new claims within a class are allowed. Basically, the utility does quiesce processing for up to and including 6 to 18 minutes depending on the number of active physical claim classes. The maximum wait time is 2 times the number of claim classes that must be drained times the resource timeout (60 second default) times the utility timeout (6 minutes by default).

A utility or command can take complete or partial control of an object. Complete control is obtained by draining all claim classes and taking a drain lock. A share or exclusive drain lock is taken by the Internal Resource Lock Manager (IRLM). Partial control is obtained by draining writers only and taking a claim. Claim and drain processing are managed by data manager and buffer manager. After a utility does a commit and releases its drain lock, SQL can take a claim.

Execution of SQL and LOAD Utility

Let's consider how SQL and the LOAD utility can execute concurrently on different partitions. If a unit of recovery (UR) is *not* active on, say, partition 2, LOAD can load partition 2. Indeed the load can begin before or after the SQL claims are taken on partition 1. Figure LC.4 shows that a user has an intent exclusive (IX) lock, and a write claim on partition 1, and is updating data in the partition. These factors allow the LOAD utility to execute on partition 2.

Figure LC.4. SQL executed on partition 1 and load on partition 2 concurrently

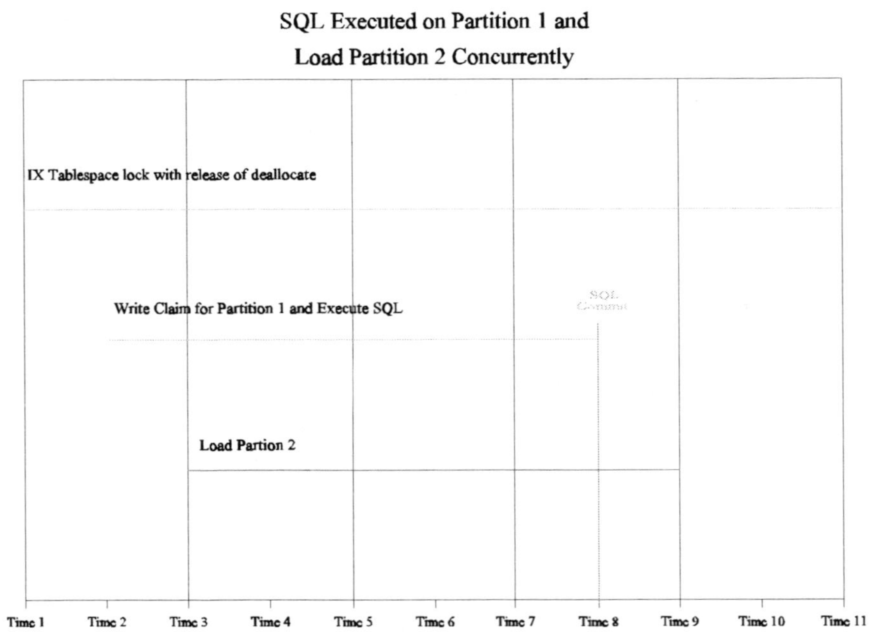

Utility Test Results

In most cases LOAD inserts all values and RIDs on the appropriate index pages as rows are loaded. However, it is necessary to process one entry for each row at a time for a logical partition of a NPI. This detracts from performance.

Test results give a rough idea of the difference between loading one partition at a time compared to loading the entire tablespace. The tests were done using a 5 million rows table on 147,000 pages in 10 partitions. The table had 2 indexes and 26 columns (21 character or internal integer and five internal decimal columns) using V4 on a 3090-180J computer and 3390 DASD. If you are using a 511 based computer, divide the results by 1.25. If you are using a 711 based computer, divide the results by 3.00 to adjust the IBM test results for your computer model. Figure LC.5 shows the test results.

Figure LC.5. Comparison of loading by partition and loading the entire tablespace

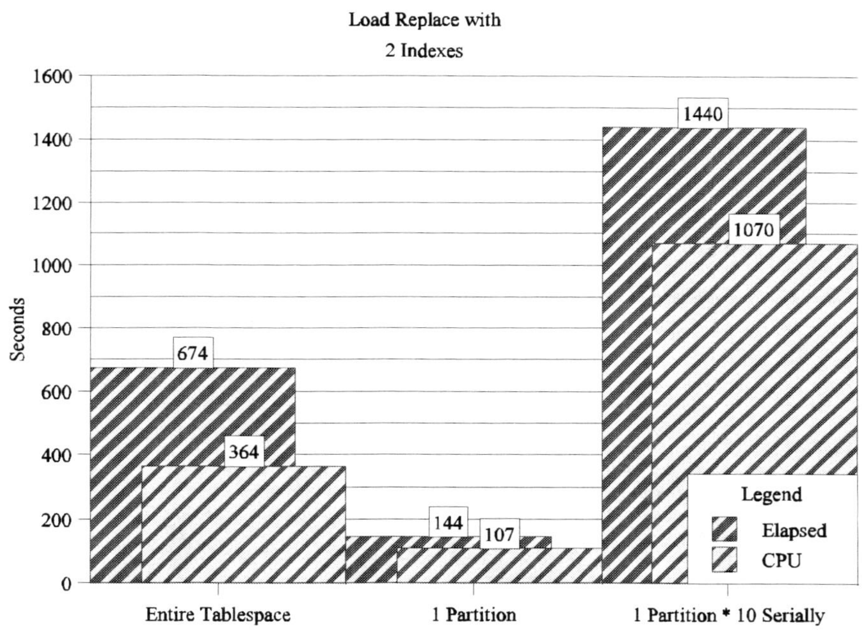

We see from the test results that the goal of partition independence is accomplished. All partitions except the one partition being loaded are available during the load. The one partition was unavailable for only 144 elapsed seconds with 107 CPU seconds compared to the entire tablespace being unavailable for 674 elapsed seconds with 364 seconds of CPU time while the entire tablespace is being loaded. However, if a batch window is available, CPU and elapsed times can be saved by loading the entire tablespace at one time. Notice that the total costs of loading the 10 partitions one at a time is 1440 elapsed and 1070 CPU seconds are considerable more than loading the entire tablespace at 674 elapsed and 364 CPU seconds. However, the entire tablespace is unavailable for 1440 elapsed seconds. You need to evaluate the trade-off between improved availability of the data and the costs of executing the utilities.

LOAD Drains and Restrictive States

Each utility requires different drains and restrictive states at different times of its processing. The *Utility Guide and Reference* manual has a summary of this processing for each utility. Figure LC.6 is a summary from the manual for the LOAD utility and Figure LC.7 has an explanation of the codes describing the drains and restrictive states, and the access allowed during the processing.

Figure LC.6. Summary of load drain processing and restrictive states

Target	LOAD	LOAD PART
Tablespace, index, or physical partition of a tablespace or index	DA/UTUT	DA/UTUT
Nonpartitioned index	DA/UTUT	DR
Logical partition of an index		DA/UTUT
Primary index (with ENFORCE option only)	DW/UTRO	DW/UTRO
RI dependents	CHKP(NO)*	CHKP(NO)*

*CHKP(NO) - Concurrently running applications will not see CHECK PENDING after commit

Figure LC.7. Summary of codes used in describing drain processing and restrictive states

Code	Description	Access Allowed
DA	Drain all claim classes	No concurrent SQL access
DR	Drain repeatable read class	No concurrent access for SQL repeatable readers
DW	Drain the write claim class	Concurrent access for SQL readers
UTUT*	Utility restrictive state	None - Utility has exclusive control
UTRO*	Utility restrictive state	Read only access allowed
UTRW*	Utility restrictive state	Read/write access allowed
Blank	Object is not affected	All

*SYSUTILX has information on restrictive states, UTSERIAL lock, serialization, utility restart, and checkpoint status

Operations During Utility Execution

If SQL needs to be executed on an object, avoid submitting a utility that acts on the *same* object before the SQL is to execute. Application programs need to check for a -904 SQLCODE (resource unavailable) due to losing claims after a commit, getting another claim when crossing partition boundaries within a UR, and restrictive states left by an abended utility. Careful planning is required to keep SQL on available partitions while utilities are executing on other partitions.

No SQL DDL (Data Definition Language) is allowed on an object when a utility has a restrictive state. However, DB2 commands and utility commands are allowed.

Displaying Information on Claims and Locks

You can get information on claimers using the DISPLAY DATABASE command and specify the database and optionally all or some of the tablespaces and index spaces. The following command produces information on all claimers on all tablespaces and indexes in the DASPJDB database.

```
-DISPLAY DATABASE(DASPJDB) SPACENAM(*) CLAIMERS
```

Figure LC.8 is an example of displaying information on all claimers on all objects in the DASPJTSP database. Notice that part 3 (PART column) of the DASPJTSP tablespace (TYPE = TS) and part 3 of the DASPJIX1 index space (TYPE = IX) have a CS claim that is held by CONNID BATCH for commit duration.

Figure LC.8. Results of displaying information on claimers

```
DSNT360I ( *********************************************************
DSNT361I ( * DISPLAY DATABASE SUMMARY
           *   GLOBAL CLAIMERS
DSNT360I ( *********************************************************
DSNT362I (   DATABASE = DASPJDB   STATUS = RW
             DBD LENGTH = 4028
DSNT397I (
NAME     TYPE PART STATUS          CONNID   CORRID     CLAIMINFO

DASPJTSP TS    01  RW,COPY,UTRO
DASPJTSP TS    02  RW,COPY,UTRO
DASPJTSP TS    03  RW,COPY,UTRO    BATCH    S2410406   (CS,C)
DASPJIX1 IX    01  RW,UTRO
DASPJIX1 IX    02  RW,UTRO
DASPJIX1 IX    03  RW              BATCH    S2410406   (CS,C)
DASPJIX2 IX        RW
DASPJIX2 IX   L01  RW
******* DISPLAY OF DATABASE DASPJDB ENDED      *********************
```

The codes used to describe claims are summarized in Figure LC.9.

Figure LC.9. Codes used in describing claims

1st Code	Claim Class Descriptor
CS	CS claim class
RR	RR claim class
WR	Write claim class
2nd Code	Claim Duration Descriptor
A	Claim is held until deallocation
C	Claim is held until the next commit point
H	Claim is held across commit

Information on locks can also be gotten using the DISPLAY DATABASE command. The keyword LOCKS is used rather than the keyword CLAIMERS.

```
-DISPLAY DATABASE(DASPJDB) SPACENAM(*) LOCKS
```

Figure LC.10 is an example of the results of displaying information on all locks on all objects in the DASPJTSP database. Notice from the LOCKINFO column with the values (H(IS,P,C) that part 1 of the DASPJTSP tablespace has an intent to share (IS) lock on the partition (P), and is held for commit duration by CONNID BATCH.

Figure LC.10. Results of displaying information on locks

```
DSNT360I  ( ********************************************************
DSNT361I  ( * DISPLAY DATABASE SUMMARY
            *   GLOBAL LOCKS
DSNT360I  ( ********************************************************
DSNT362I  (   DATABASE = DASPJDB   STATUS = RW
              DBD LENGTH = 4028
DSNT397I  (
NAME      TYPE PART STATUS          CONNID    CORRID      LOCKINFO

DASPJTSP  TS    01  RW,COPY,UTRO    UTILITY   S2410405
DASPJTSP  TS    01  RW,COPY,UTRO    BATCH     S2410406    (H(IS,P,C)
DASPJTSP  TS    01  RW,COPY,UTRO    UTILITY   S2410404    (H(IX,W,A)
DASPJTSP  TS    02  RW,COPY,UTRO    UTILITY   S2410405    (H(IX,W,A)
DASPJTSP  TS    02  RW,COPY,UTRO    BATCH     S2410406    (H(IS,P,C)
DASPJTSP  TS    02  RW,COPY,UTRO    UTILITY   S2410404
DASPJTSP  TS    03  RW,COPY,UTRO    UTILITY   S2410405
DASPJTSP  TS    03  RW,COPY,UTRO    BATCH     S2410406    (H(IS,P,C)
DASPJTSP  TS    03  RW,COPY         UTILITY   S2410404
DASPJIX1  IX    01  RW,UTRO         UTILITY   S2410405
DASPJIX1  IX    01  RW,UTRO         BATCH     S2410406
DASPJIX1  IX    01  RW,UTRO         UTILITY   S2410404    (H(IX,W,A)
DASPJIX1  IX    02  RW              UTILITY   S2410405    (H(IX,W,A)
DASPJIX1  IX    02  RW              BATCH     S2410406
DASPJIX1  IX    02  RW              UTILITY   S2410404
DASPJIX1  IX    03  RW              UTILITY   S2410405
DASPJIX1  IX    03  RW              BATCH     S2410406
DASPJIX1  IX    03  RW              UTILITY   S2410404
DASPJIX2  IX        RW
******* DISPLAY OF DATABASE DASPJDB ENDED      *********************
```

The codes used to describe locks are summarized in Figure LC.11.

Figure LC.11. Codes used in describing locks

1st Code	Lock Qualifier
H	Lock is held by the agent
W	Agent is waiting for the lock
R	Retained lock in a sysplex data sharing environment
2nd Code	Type of Lock
IS	Tablespace lock with read intentions (shared)
IX	Tablespace or lock with update intentions (exclusive)
SIX	Tablespace lock that does not lock a page while reading, but locks the page with an X lock while updating
S	Share lock
X	Exclusive lock
3rd Code	Unit of Locking
S	Tablespace lock
P	Partition lock
T	Table lock
C	Cursor-stability read drain lock
R	Repeatable-read drain lock
W	Write drain lock
PP	Page set or partition physical lock
4th Code	Lock Duration If Lock Qualifier is H
A	Freed at deallocation
C	Freed at commit
H	Freed when all cursors are closed
M	Freed by the system
P	Freed when the plan is complete

LC.12 LOAD PHASES

Each utility has a number of phases for accomplishing the required work. The first phase of most utilities is initialization and setup which is referred to as the UTILINIT phase. The last phase is for cleanup and is referred to as the UTILTERM phase. The additional phases for processing a load are summarized in Figure LC.12.

Figure LC.12. Phases of the LOAD utility

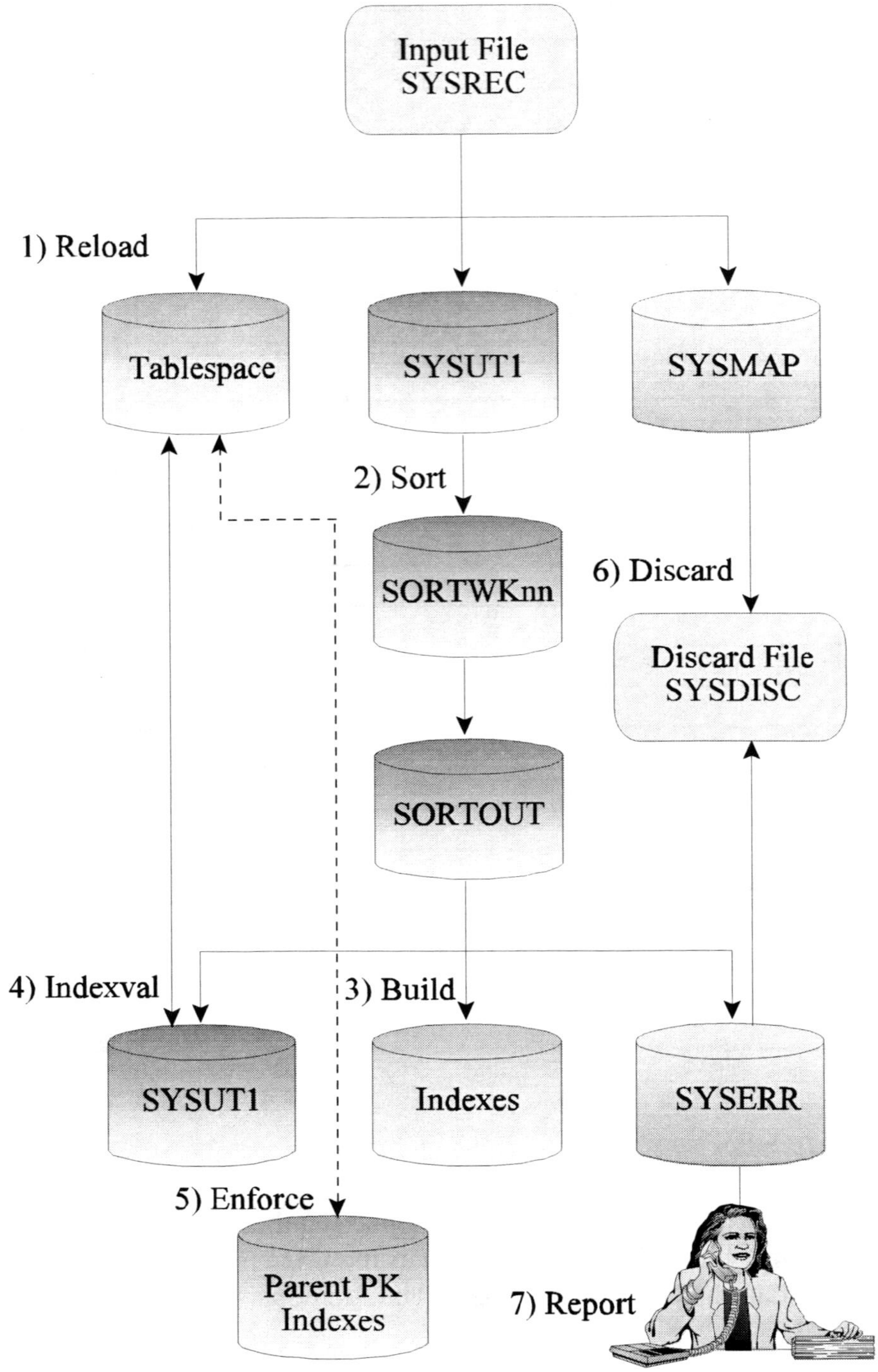

Each phase is described briefly with reference to the sequence numbers in the graphic.

1) RELOAD phase reads the sequential input file and writes rows to the table. If error records are detected, information about the errors are written to SYSERR. If ESA compression is used on the tablespace, the compression dictionary is built. The indexed values and non-indexed foreign key (FK) values are written to SYSUT1, and a cross reference of the RID and record number is written to SYSMAP if ENFORCE CONSTRAINTS is used.

2) SORT phase sorts SYSUT1 by index, key, and RID into SORTWKnn and merges the intermediate sorted work files into SORTOUT. Any non-indexed FK values are written at the end of SORTOUT.

3) BUILD phase builds indexes from the sorted and merged indexed values in SORTOUT. Information about unique index violations are written to SYSERR or SYSUT1 depending on the options specified.

4) INDEXVAL phase deletes duplicate rows and indexed values using information from SYSERR and SYSUT1 if there is a unique index.

5) ENFORCE phase is executed if the table being loaded is a dependent table, a FK has been defined to DB2, and the default of ENFORCE CONSTRAINTS is used. This phase checks that FK values exist as a PK in the dependent table using the PK index. Violating FK rows are deleted and messages written using the SYSERR, SYSUT1, and SORTOUT data sets. The deletion of a FK row may cause a cascade on a PK in the row to dependent tables if they are loaded within the scope of a single load. Not all processing is shown in the graphic.

6) DISCARD phase processes error records. It sorts SYSERR, SYSMAP and SORTOUT, and does a merge depending on parameters specified when the objects were created and the parameters on the LOAD statement. Identified input error records are copied from SYSREC to SYSDISC. Not all processing is shown in the graphic.

7) REPORT phase sorts records by primary errors, secondary errors, and input sequence number. A report of the results is printed. Not all processing is not shown in the graphic.

LC.13 EXECUTING THE UTILITIES

JCL to execute the utilities can be generated using DB2I or the DSNU CLIST. Typically, someone at your company used one of these methods to generate the JCL and customized it for your environment. We will briefly look at the alternatives for generating the JCL if you cannot locate it at your company.

If you select the UTILITIES option from the main DB2I panel, you will see a panel like the one shown in Figure LC.13.

Figure LC.13. DB2 utilities panel

```
DSNEUP01                          DB2 UTILITIES
===>

Select from the following:

 1 FUNCTION ===> EDITJCL    (SUBMIT job, EDITJCL, DISPLAY, TERMINATE)
 2 JOB ID   ===> LOADSPJ    (A unique job identifier string)
 3 UTILITY  ===> LOAD       (CHECK DATA, CHECK INDEX, CHECK LOB,
                             COPY, DIAGNOSE, LOAD, MERGE, MODIFY,
                             QUIESCE, REBUILD, RECOVER, REORG INDEX,
                             REORG LOB, REORG TABLESPACE, REPORT,
                             REPAIR, RUNSTATS, STOSPACE.)

 4 CONTROL CARDS DATA SET     ===> 'PROJ.AUTHID.CNTL(LOADSTMT)'

To RESTART a utility, specify starting point, otherwise enter NO.

 5 RESTART  ===> NO  (NO, At CURRENT position, or beginning of PHASE)

* The data set names panel will be displayed when required by a
utility.


PRESS:  ENTER to process     END to exit    HELP for more information
```

The items that you need to specify are shown in bold. You will probably want to edit the JCL before submitting it once it is generated as indicated in option 1. Do specify a JOB ID for option 2 and make a note of it so that you can display information about the utility as it executes, or terminate it if it abends. DB2 tracks the progress of the utility in the SYSUTILX directory table. If the utility abends and you do want to restart it, do terminate it with the -TERM UTILITY(LOADSPJ) command from the DB2I commands panel. An alternative is to key TERMINATE on line 1 of the DB2 UTILITIES panel. Do not submit the utility again until after you make corrections and terminate it even after it abends. DB2 retains information about abended utilities in SYSUTILX in case you need to restart them. If you do not want to restart the utility, terminate; otherwise it will not execute. Some people rename the utility and resubmit it. This results in execution of the utility but it causes an accumulation of abended utilities in SYSUTILX. Someone will periodically terminate all of the abended utilities if a large number accumulate in SYSUTILX and you do not want a utility to be terminated if you want to restart it. The bottom line is that it is best to terminate a utility if it has abended and you do not want to restart it.

Key the name of the utility that you want to execute using option 3 of the DB2 UTILITIES panel. You specify the data set that contains the utility control statement in option 4. You will want NO for restart in option 5 if it is the first execution of the named utility.

After you have completed the first utility panel, a second panel is displayed when you are requesting the generation of JCL for the LOAD, REORG, and COPY utilities as shown in Figure LC.14. You need to key the name of the data set that contains the data that is to be loaded into a table as option 1 and the name of a data set to contain discards as option 2 when using the LOAD utility.

Figure LC.14. Data set names panel

```
DSNEUP02                                    DATA SET NAMES
===>

  Enter data set name for LOAD or REORG TABLESPACE:
1 RECDSN    ==> 'PROJ.AUTHID.SPJDATA'

  Enter data set name for LOAD:
2 DISCDSN   ==> 'PROJ.AUTHID.DISCARD'

  Enter output data sets for local/current site for COPY or MERGECOPY
3 COPYDSN   ==>
4 COPYDSN2  ==>

  Enter output data sets for recovery site for COPY:
5 RCPYDSN1  ==>
6 RCPYDSN2  ==>

PRESS:  ENTER to process     END to exit     HELP for more information
```

The generated JCL is placed in a data set with the name USERID.DSNname.CNTL where USERID is your TSO user ID, "name" following DSN is an abbreviation of the utility name, and CNTL is a constant. Before considering how you might want to customize the generated JCL for your particular requirements, we will look briefly at generating the JCL using the DSNU CLIST.

Generate JCL Using DSNU CLIST

The DSNU CLIST can be executed from TSO or parameters can be passed to the TSO terminal monitor program (TMP). Figure LC.15 is an example of using the TSO TMP by executing PGM=IKJEFT1B to generate JCL.

Figure LC.15. Example of generating JCL using DSNU CLIST

```
//LOADJOB   JOB ... USER=AUTHID
//*
//TERM      EXEC PGM=IKJEFT1B,DYNAMNBR=30
//*
//SYSPRINT DD  SYSOUT=A
//SYSTSPRT DD  SYSOUT=A
//SYSUDUMP DD  SYSOUT=A
//SYSOUT   DD  SYSOUT=A
//*
//SYSTSIN  DD  *
%DSNU                   -
  UTILITY (LOAD)        -
  SYSTEM  (DB2T)        -
  INDSN   ('PROJ.AUTHID.CNTL(LOADSTMT)') -
  EDIT    (YES)         -
  SUBMIT  (YES)         -
  UID     (LOADSPJ)     -
  RESTART (NO)
/*
```

Figure LC.16 is an example of the JCL that can be generated using DB2I or the DSNU CLIST.

Figure LC.16. Sample JCL to execute LOAD

```
//LOADSTEP EXEC PGM=DSNUTILB,REGION=1024K,
//              PARM='V61A,DSNTEX'
//STEPLIB  DD DSN=PREFIX.SDSNLOAD,DISP=SHR
//*
//**************************************************************
//*  DATA SETS USED BY THE UTILITY                             *
//**************************************************************
//SORTOUT  DD  UNIT=SYSDA,SPACE=(4000,(20,20),,,ROUND)
//SORTWK01 DD  UNIT=SYSDA,SPACE=(4000,(20,20),,,ROUND)
//SYSDISC  DD  UNIT=SYSDA,SPACE=(4000,(20,20),,,ROUND)
//SYSERR   DD  UNIT=SYSDA,SPACE=(4000,(20,20),,,ROUND)
//SYSMAP   DD  UNIT=SYSDA,SPACE=(4000,(20,20),,,ROUND)
//SYSREC   DD  DSN=PROJ.AUTHID.SPJDATA
//             DISP=SHR
//SYSUT1   DD  UNIT=SYSDA,SPACE=(4000,(20,20),,,ROUND)
//SYSCOPY  DD  DSN=INLINE.COPY.SPJ1,SPACE=(CYL,(42,5))
//             DISP=(NEW,CATLG,CATLG),UNIT=SYSDA,
//SYSPRINT DD  SYSOUT=*
//UTPRINT  DD  SYSOUT=*
//SYSIN    DD  *
   LOAD DATA
   INTO TABLE AUTHID.SPJ
   SORTKEYS 300000
   RESUME NO REPLACE       -- Replace existing rows
   COPYDDN (SYSCOPY)       -- Make an inline copy
   DISCARDS 1000
//*
```

Customize Generated JCL

You can customize the JCL generated by DB2I, the DSNU CLIST, or JCL that you have gotten from a friend. The generated JCL is for small to medium sized tables. If you are loading a large table, for example, you will want to maximize the performance of sorting the indexed values. The same guidelines apply to other utilities that sort the indexed values and data rows.

Sorts in Hiperspace: Sort performance can be improved by the use of a hipersort if expanded storage is available. DFSORT uses HIPRMAX=OPTIMAL by default which results in the maximum amount of space being used for the best performance. If you are executing multiple utilities that sort in parallel, be careful not to let the first submitted utility take a large percentage of the space such that subsequently submitted utilities do not have enough space. Consider dividing the available hiperspace by the number of utilities and include the estimate in the utility job before the sort. For example, assume that you have 200 MB of hiperspace available and need to execute 5 utilities that do a sort in parallel, specify the space for each utility sort as 40 MB (200 MB / 5 parallel sorts) like:

```
//DFSPARM DD *
  OPTION HIPRMAX = 40
/*
```

Use a large sort size above the 16 MB line if available (more than 20 MB, for example).

Sort Work Data Sets: Several work data sets are used to sort and build indexes. The default DD names are:

- SYSUT1 contains the values for all indexes that are extracted while reading the sequential file and writing rows to the table. The RIDs of where the rows are written to the table are included along with the indexed values.
- SORTWK01, SORTWK02, etc., contain sorted runs which are merged into SORTOUT.
- SORTOUT contains sorted and merged runs.

The SYSUT1 and SORTOUT data set sizes should be calculated based on the longest indexed column plus 12 bytes times the number of indexes to be sorted times the number of rows in the table. Multiply this value by 2.15 to estimate the space required for the work data sets (SORTWKnn). It is not necessary to allocate space to sort the values for the clustering index if you have sorted the input file in clustering sequence. Sort of the input file is highly advisable as discussed in Section LC.3.

The blocking factor is calculated by the utilities unless specified on the DD statement (27,998 bytes are used for 3390 DASD). If you do specify the blocking factor, do use large blocking factors for the output data sets, for example, 28 KB which is a half track on 3390 DASD and 22 KB which is half a track on 3380 DASD. Do use cylinder allocation for improved performance.

Do make every effort to place the sort work data sets on separate DASD, channels, and control units from the sort input and output files to spread out the I/O activity and minimize I/O contention. If there are a few volumes available, one or two large sort work data sets have advantages over several smaller work data sets on the same volume. In general, apply guidelines used for large sorts irrespective of DB2 for utilities that use a sort including the LOAD, REORG, RECOVER INDEX prior to V6, and REBUILD INDEX in V6.

DFSORT can be used to dynamically allocate work data sets. This can be done by removing SORTWKnn DD statements and adding:

```
//DFSPARM DD *
  DYNALLOC=(,n)
/*
```

The maximum number of work data sets to be allocated is specified with *n* and cannot exceed 100.

Utility Buffers: You can specify the number of central storage buffers used by the utilities to process input and output files. The default utility buffers is 20 which requires about a 5000K region size including 560 KB for 3390 DASD. If you are processing large tables, consider more buffers (maximum of 99) and a larger region size. The region size can be specified on the job statement and the BUFNO can be specified on the DD statement like:

```
//LOADSPJ  JOB  MSGLEVEL=(1,1),CLASS=A,REGION=5000K,
//            USER=SPJTEST,PASSWORD=SPJPASS
//SYSUT1     DD DSN=WORKDAT1,UNIT=SYSDA,
//               SPACE=(4000,(20,20),,,ROUND),
//               DCB=(BUFNO=20),DISP=(MOD,DELETE,CATLG)
```

Disposition of Data Sets for Restart: Consider changing the SORTOUT work data set disposition from DISP=(MOD,**DELETE**,CATLG) to DISP=(MOD,**CATLG**,CATLG). This provides for minimizing restart processing after an abend with a return code of 8.

Utility Statement Comments: Comments can be specified on the utility control statements as long as they are preceded by two hyphens (--).

Executing Utilities from a Stored Procedure

Utilities can be executed by calling the DSNUTILS stored procedure from an application program as discussed in Chapter SP. The Control Center can be used to generate and submit utilities using DSNUTILS. However, it cannot submit utility jobs on a scheduled basis.

Restarting Utilities

A utility that abends can be restarted in most cases depending on the specific utility and parameters specified. Most utilities can be restarted at the current position after successful completion of a phase. The exceptions are the CHECK, QUIESCE, and REPORT utilities. It will be seen that these utilities require few resources and can simply be resubmitted after an abend and termination of the utility.

RESTART(CURRENT) indicates the utility is to be restarted after the last successful commit point. Most utilities take an internal commit after processing about 1000 pages. This option has performance advantages over RESTART(PHASE) because less processing is required.

RESTART(PHASE) restarts after the last successfully completed phase. This phase can be determined with the -DISPLAY UTILITY(*) command which displays information on all active utilities and utilities that have abended but have not been restarted or terminated. Rather than using "(*)" in the command, you can name one or more utilities that are of interest to you. Also the report written by each utility to SYSPRINT has the successfully completed phases. RESTART(PHASE) must be used for the REBUILD INDEX, REORG UNLOAD of compressed data, and REORG PAUSEd jobs.

The RESTART(CURRENT) or RESTART(PHASE) parameter can be specified on the EXEC DSNUPROC statement or you can specify CURRENT or PHASE on line 8 of the utilities panel.

A resubmitted utility should be the same as the original. This is because restart processing tracks the relative position of the utility statement in the input stream.

LC.14 CHECK DATA FOR INTEGRITY VIOLATIONS

Check pending is set on if there is a *potential* violation of a constraint. It applies to dependent tablespaces of a RI structure and table check constraints. The CHECK DATA utility uses index only access when an index is available and no sort is required. However, if there is no index available on a FK or the index contains additional columns that are not part of the FK, the FK values are extracted and sorted before checking the constraints.

Operations Permitted and Not Permitted

Once check pending is set on, for an object no data manipulation statements (SELECT, INSERT, UPDATE, and DELETE statements) can be successfully executed on the object. Rather a resource unavailable message is received (-904 SQLCODE). This message is also received if there is an attempt to update a PK when the FK table has the check pending set on because it is necessary to access the FK table to determine if there are any FKs with the old PK value. The COPY and REORG utilities give a -904 SQLCODE if there is an attempt to execute the utilities. The only utilities that can be successfully executed are CHECKDATA, RECOVER, REPAIR, LOAD REPLACE, and RUNSTATS. The only SQL statements that can be executed are the DROP and ALTER statements.

Operations that Cause Check Pending

A number of operations can cause check pending to be set on. If the ALTER statement is used to add a FK or check table constraint to a populated table, check pending is set on because there may exist violations of the constraints in the table. Similarly if there is a load of a dependent table with ENFORCE NO or a load replace of a parent table in its own tablespace, the dependent tablespaces have a status of check pending (but not descendants of the parent). If some but not all tablespaces in a referential structure are recovered, check pending is set on for the dependents. If the CHECK DATA utility is executed with DELETE NO and violations are detected, check pending is set on.

How to Reset Check Pending

The best way to turn check pending off is to execute the CHECK DATA utility. You can have the utility delete the rows that violate RI and table check constraints, and have the deleted rows written to an exception table with the parameter of DELETE YES which is not the default. If you take the default or specify DELETE NO and there are violations, a report is generated describing the constraint violations but the check pending state remains on because the violating rows are still in the table. The check pending state is turned off if no violations exist.

Other methods for setting check pending off is to recover tablespaces to a quiesce point, drop the tables in the tablespace that caused the violation or execute the REPAIR utility with the NOCHECKPEND parameter as discussed in Chapter CR. The check pending state can be ignored by starting the database and optionally naming one or more tablespaces like:

```
-START DATABASE DASPJDB ACCESS (FORCE)
```

This last method is the least desirable alternative because *all* restrictions and problems are ignored.

CHECK DATA Statement

Related tablespaces need to be named in the CHECK DATA statement when checking for RI constraint violations. These related tablespaces can be identified using the REPORT utility discussed in Chapter CR. Here is a statement to check that every FK in the dependent tablespace SPJTSP has a parent row in the STSP, PTSP, and JTSP tablespaces.

```
CHECK DATA TABLESPACE DASPJDB.STSP
           TABLESPACE DASPJDB.PTSP
           TABLESPACE DASPJDB.JTSP
           TABLESPACE DASPJDB.SPJTSP
SCOPE PENDING
FOR EXCEPTION
  IN AUTHID.SPJ USE AUTHID.SPJEX
EXCEPTIONS 100
DELETE YES
LOG NO
```

The parameters used for controlling the CHECK DATA utility are described.

SCOPE PENDING means that only rows added by the LOAD utility should be checked. This is the default for the SCOPE parameter.

SCOPE ALL means that all rows should be checked.

FOR EXCEPTION means that a copy of the invalid rows are to be written to an exception table.

DELETE YES means that violating rows are to be deleted and a copy of the deleted rows written to an exception table. An exception table is required for each dependent table and its descendants. In addition, a report is written identifying the deleted rows. Checking pending is turned off when the utility completes successfully.

DELETE NO means that only the report describing the constraint violations is written. The report includes error messages identifying the table, constraint name, and RID of the invalid rows. The violating rows are not deleted and check pending remains on if there are any rows that violate the constraints. If there are no rows that violate the constraints, check pending is turned off.

LOG NO is a good choice to reduce logging (is not the default) (V6).

Creating Exception Tables for DELETE YES

An exception table must be created for each table to be checked when DELETE YES is specified. The table must contain the same columns with the same data type and length as those of the table being checked plus a column for the RIDs. The RID column must be declared CHAR(4) or CHAR(5) if the tablespace is greater than 64 GB (discussed in Chapter TS). Optionally, a timestamp column can be included in the table. This allows you to determine when the exception rows were written to the table. The CHECK DATA utility inserts rows into the exception table that are deleted each time it is executed, thus rows from different executions of the utility can be in the exception table with different timestamps. You can also specify additional columns for your own purposes provided that the columns are not declared NOT NULL. Here is a convenient method for creating the SPJEX exception table to receive deleted rows from the SPJ table and add the RID and TIMESTAMP columns to the table with ALTER statements.

```
CREATE TABLE SPJEX LIKE SPJ;

ALTER  TABLE SPJEX ADD RID CHAR(4);
```

```
ALTER  TABLE SPJEX ADD TIMESTAMP TIMESTAMP;
```

After you have investigated and corrected rows in the exception table, the following statement can be used to add the rows to the original table if there are only a few rows.

```
INSERT INTO SPJ
  SELECT SN, PN, JN, QTY
  FROM   SPJEX;
```

If there are more than a few thousand rows in the exception table, performance can be improved by unloading the table into a sequential file, sorting it in clustering sequence, and using the LOAD utility with the RESUME YES parameter to add the rows to the original table.

Check Pending in the DBET and Catalog Tables

The scope of check pending can apply to the entire tablespace, a partition of a partitioned tablespace, a table in a segmented tablespace, rows beyond a specific RID, or some combination. The status and scope are tracked in the database exception table (DBET) which is an internal table kept in main memory. The DISPLAY DATABASE command is used to determine information from the DBET. You can also determine information about the scope of the check pending condition by selecting from the catalog tables like:

```
SELECT NAME, CHECKFLAG,
       HEX(CHECKRID),'TABLE'
FROM   SYSIBM.SYSTABLES
WHERE  CHECKFLAG = 'C'
UNION
SELECT TSNAME, CHECKFLAG,
       HEX(CHECKRID), 'TABLESPACE'
FROM   SYSIBM.SYSTABLEPART
WHERE  CHECKFLAG = 'C'
ORDER BY 1, 4;
```

If the CHECKFLAG column contain 'C', the table is in check pending. If the CHECKRID and CHECKFLAG columns contain blank, the table is not in check pending. If the CHECKRID column contains X'00000000', rows in the table can violate a constraint. The use of the parameter SCOPE ALL is appropriate. If there is a value other than zero, the CHECKRID column contains the first row of the table that may violate a constraint and SCOPE PENDING is appropriate.

Recommendation: You can always use the SCOPE PENDING parameter. If the CHECKRID column contains X'00000000', CHECK DATA checks all of the rows.

LC.15 CHECKING INDEXES

The CHECK INDEX utility checks that each RID points to a row with a value matching the indexed value. If the index is declared as unique, the utility checks that the values in the index are unique. You can name specific indexes to be checked like:

```
CHECK INDEX (AUTHID.SNX, AUTHID.SPJX)
```

or check all indexes on all tables in the tablespace SPJTSP like:

```
CHECK INDEX ALL TABLESPACE SPJTSP
```

The PART parameter can be used to check a physical or logical index partition. Duplicate values in separate logical parts are not detected.

CHECK INDEX should be executed on the PK and FK indexes before CHECK DATA if there is reason to believe there can be inconsistencies. This is because index only processing is used by CHECK DATA.

Space for the work files can be calculated like estimating space to build indexes.

LC.16 SUMMARY

The LOAD utility offers a good deal of flexibility in loading a table for the first time, replacing data in a table, and adding rows to a table. The utility has dramatic performance improvements compared to SQL INSERT statements but does not allow for access to the data during most of the load processing.

Do build the sequential file used as input to load carefully. Few or no errors in the data improves performance dramatically and avoids check pending complexities.

Do create indexes and sort the data in clustering sequence before loading it. Otherwise, there will be a low cluster ratio until the data is reorganized. Inline copy has performance advantages and avoids passing the data again after it is loaded. If inline copy is not used, do load with log of no and follow the load with a full image copy.

Utilities and SQL can be executed concurrently on multiple partitions. SQL claim counters disallow utilities from taking control until commits result in counters of 0 and drain processing allow utilities to take control and execute.

Do use exception tables when checking data and override the default by specifying DELETE YES so that the table is immediately usable after successful completion of the CHECK DATA utility.

Do check indexes if there is reason to believe that there is an inconsistency between the indexes and data. This is particularly important before executing CHECK DATA because it uses index only processing.

Do terminate or restart a utility that has abended.

EXERCISES

1. Under what conditions is it necessary to describe the fields in a sequential file that are to be loaded into a table?

2. a) What is an advantage to specifying SORTKEYS?

b) Under what condition should SORTKEYS not be specified?

3. Which of the following options is required to make an inline copy while loading the data?

```
RESUME NO REPLACE
RESUME YES
REPLACE
```

4. If RESUME NO REPLACE is not the required option when loading data, what should be specified for the LOG parameter for improved performance and what additional utility should be executed?

5. Should the default of DISCARDS 0 be used when loading data? What is a good alternative and why?

6. Should statistics and an inline copy be made while loading data RESUME NO REPLACE?

7. a) Why should the JCL generated by DB2I for LOAD and REORG be customized?

b) What should you concentrate on in particular?

8. Should an abended utility be terminated if restart is not required? Why?

9. Give a brief overview of claim and drain processing.

10. What is the basic purpose of the CHECK DATA utility?

11. What is the purpose of the FOR EXCEPTION and DELETE YES parameters of CHECK DATA?

12. What is the basic purpose of the CHECK INDEX utility?

13. If the DISCARD parameter is not specified and a column is described as numeric when in fact it is character on the input file, what will happen and how will performance be affected?

14. Assume that the EMP_NAME is declared as VARCHAR(20) and HIREDATE is declared as a DATE data type. The input file has an employee name of Blake and a date of 19941130. Will the following LOAD statement load the data properly?

```
LOAD DATA
INTO TABLE AUTHID.EMP
 (EMP_NAME      POSITION(*)   CHAR(20),
  HIREDATE      POSITION(*)   DATE)
```

ANSWERS

1. If the fields in a sequential file to be loaded into a table do not match the columns of the table exactly in terms of their relative position, data type and length, the fields must be described on the LOAD statement.

2. a) The advantage of specifying SORTKEYS is that indexed values are passed directly to an external sort and on to the build index phase. (SORTWKnn is used for the sort.)

b) SORTKEYS should not be specified if there is only one index which is the clustering index and the data has been sorted in clustering sequence. This avoids a sort of the indexed values that are already in sequence.

3. RESUME NO REPLACE is required to make an inline copy while loading the data.

4. If RESUME NO REPLACE is not the required option when loading data, LOG NO should be specified to improve performance and an image copy should be taken after executing LOAD with LOG NO to remove the copy pending status, assuming that the table is not read only.

5. DISCARDS 0 should not be specified when loading data. A good alternative is to specify a reasonable number of records that will be discarded (DISCARDS 1000, for example). This avoids discarding all records if there is a keying error on the LOAD statement, for example. Discarding all records requires significantly more resources than loading the records.

6. It is advisable to collect statistics and make an inline copy be while loading data with RESUME NO REPLACE in most cases to avoid passing the data to collect statistics and passing it again to make an image copy. Performance is improved in most cases.

7. a) The generated JCL assumes small to medium tables. Performance can be improved by customizing the JCL.

b) Particular attention should be paid to allocating sufficient memory and DASD for the sorts.

8. An abended utility should be terminated if restart is not required. This allows for correcting the problem and resubmitting the utility with the same name. Otherwise, submission of the corrected utility with the same name as the abended utility will not execute. Also, it avoids accumulating a record of a large number of abended utilities in the SYSUTILX directory table.

9. A claim counter is incremented by one for an object referenced by an SQL statement. Most utilities must drain the claim counters before they can execute. The utility does quiesce processing of a target object until the required claim counters are zero. The utility executes once the required claim counters are zero. The goal of partition independence is to allow SQL access to all partitions not currently being processed by a utility. Claim and drain processing is used on partitioned and nonpartitioned tablespaces and indexes.

10. The basic purpose of the CHECK DATA utility is to identify any FKs that do not have matching PKs and to identify any rows that violate table check constraints.

11. The FOR EXCEPTION parameter provides for specifying the table where rows that violate a constraint are to be inserted after they are deleted assuming that DELETE YES is specified to CHECK DATA.

12. The basic purpose of the CHECK INDEX utility is to verify that each RID points to a row that contains the indexed value.

13. If the DISCARD parameter is not specified and the data cannot be loaded, all records on the input file go through discard processing. Load takes several times longer to discard the data than to load it.

14. EMP_NAME is loaded as Blake followed by 15 blanks because there is no length field preceding the name. HIREDATE must be on the input file in a supported date format (1994-11-30 if the ISO format is used, for example) and the LOAD statement must declare the date as DATE EXTERNAL(10).

FIGURES

Runstats and Reorganization

RR.1 INTRODUCTION

The RUNSTATS utility collects statistics used by the optimizer to choose a good access path and statistics that are useful in space management and determining the frequency of reorganizations. There are a number of optional statistics that can be collected for use by the optimizer. The importance of these statistics and the cost of collecting them will be discussed in this chapter.

It is important to reorganize tablespaces and indexes periodically to maintain good performance of transactions and batch programs. The challenge is in determining how often objects need to be reorganized and which parameters are best for your data as will be discussed in this chapter.

RR.2 WHY AND WHEN TO EXECUTE RUNSTATS

It is crucial that the RUNSTATS utility be executed after loading data and before binding plans and packages. It is necessary to provide the optimizer with accurate statistics describing the tablespaces and indexes so that it can choose an efficient access path for processing the data. The statistics collected by RUNSTATS are very useful in determining when the tablespaces and indexes should be reorganized, if more or less space is required, and to provide current documentation.

An example serves to demonstrate the importance of RUNSTATS. It was extremely puzzling as to why the following select used over 20 minutes of CPU time and over 75 minutes of elapsed time before it was canceled out of frustration. The tables were not large. The customer table (CUSTTAB) had 1,100 rows with a unique index on the primary key CUST_NO and the account table (ACCT_TAB) had 42,000 rows with a unique index on the foreign key CUST_NO.

```
SELECT CT.CUST_NO, CUST_NAME
FROM   CUSTTAB CT
WHERE  NOT EXISTS
   (SELECT AT.CUST_NO
    FROM   ACCT_TAB AT
    WHERE  CT.CUST_NO = AT.CUST_NO);
```

After considerable analysis, it was discovered that RUNSTATS had not been executed. Indeed, developers at the company never executed RUNSTATS since they had a bill-back system and were under pressure to keep costs down. They felt that the optimizer usually chose the best access path without RUNSTATS so it seemed an unnecessary cost.

It was decided to execute RUNSTATS and try the select once more. The costs went down dramatically to 1.29 seconds of CPU time and 9.14 seconds of elapsed time. The optimizer was now aware of the characteristics of the data and indexes and chose to use an index rather than repeatedly scanning the ACCT_TAB for the correlated subselect.

This is an extreme case. Usually performance will not be improved this dramatically by simply executing RUNSTATS. However, it does demonstrate the importance of RUNSTATS. If RUNSTATS has not been executed, the optimizer sees only a -1 where there should be statistics describing the data and has no other choice than to use the default statistics summarized in Figure RR.1 which rarely are representative of the actual data. It is critical to execute RUNSTATS at these times:

- After a table and indexes have been created and the data loaded
- After a tablespace or index has been reorganized *and* statistics have changed significantly
- After heavy insert, update, and delete activity
- Before binding and rebinding plans and packages
- Before monitoring the catalog tables

Recommendation: Collect statistics during LOAD (Chapter LC) and REBUILD INDEX (Chapter CR) processing as well as during a reorganization as discussed in Section RR.18 in most cases (V6). Most RUNSTATS parameters discussed in the first half of this chapter can be specified to these utilities.

These guidelines are straightforward. The real challenge is determining the schedule of the RUNSTATS utility and rebinds in a production environment.

Figure RR.1. Default statistics used by the optimizer if RUNSTATS has not been executed

SYSIBM.SYSTABLES

CARDF	10,000 rows
NPAGES	501 = CEILING(1 + CARDF / 20)
PCTROWCOMP	0
EDPROC	blank = EDITPROC not used

SYSIBM.SYSINDEXES

CLUSTER-RATIOF	0 (95 % IF CLUSTERED = Y)
CLUSTERED	Y if CLUSTER used when index was created
FIRSTKEY-CARDF	25
FULLKEY-CARDF	25
NLEAF	33 = CARDF / 300
NLEVELS	2

SYSIBM.SYSCOLUMNS

COLCARDF	25
FOREIGNKEY	B for SBCS (Single Byte Character Set)

SYSIBM.SYSTABLESPACE

NACTIVE	501 = CEILING(1 + CARDF / 20)

- Uniform distribution of data is assumed.

RR.3 SCHEDULING RUNSTATS, REORG, AND REBIND

A good procedure for determining the scheduling of RUNSTATS is also useful in determining the scheduling of reorganizations. The procedure can be generalized to scheduling rebinds of your plans and packages.

Scheduling RUNSTATS: Create a table. We will call it the STAT_HISTORY table in the example, into which statistics collected by RUNSTATS are inserted after each execution of the utility over a period of time. (The statistics updated by RUNSTATS are summarized in Section RR.4.) Next, estimate the frequency of executing RUNSTATS based on a knowledge of the update activity expected on the tables, perhaps daily, weekly, monthly, etc. After RUNSTATS is executed, insert into the STAT_HISTORY table, selecting from the catalog tables updated, and accumulate a history of the statistics over a period of time and update cycles. Then use SQL to analyze the statistics accumulated. If the statistics are spiking, that is some statistics are going up and others are going down, a good schedule has been chosen or perhaps RUNSTATS should be executed more frequently than originally estimated. If the statistics are all going up, are all going down, or remaining constant, it probably is not necessary to execute RUNSTATS as frequently as originally estimated.

Scheduling reorganizations: The analysis of the STAT_HISTORY table provides good information on the scheduling of reorganizations as well. Indeed, it may be that the scheduling of reorganizations is more important than the scheduling of RUNSTATS. Frequently, the statistics do not spike, and it is important to reorganize the tablespace to regain storage efficiencies so that the original access path chosen by the optimizer remains efficient. If reorganizations are not executed as needed, what was a good access path can rapidly become a poor access path.

Scheduling rebinds: The periodic execution of RUNSTATS after the first execution does not affect the access path and performance of static plans and packages bound with the default of NOREOPT(VARS) even if statistics are spiking unless the plans are rebound and a more efficient path is found. The optimizer does use the current statistics each time dynamic SQL statements are executed and each time static plans and packages are executed if they are bound with REOPT(VARS) as discussed in Chapters OP and PE.

The next question is how often should static plans and packages bound with NOREOPT(VARS) be rebound. The plans and packages do not need to be rebound after reorganizations, assuming that the statistics remain proportional. A general rule of thumb is to rebind plans and packages in conjunction with reorganizations and collecting if statistics have changed more than 20 percent and the changes are disproportionate. The statistics to pay close attention to are the number of leaf and data pages, whether the number of levels in the index has increased, the table, partition, index, and column cardinalities, the cluster ratio, frequently occurring values and their percent occurrence, and the range of the second highest and lowest values.

The scheduling of rebinds can be done using a similar technique for scheduling reorganizations with the collection of statistics. Accumulate a history of the paths chosen by the optimizer by rebinding plans and packages periodically after collecting statistics and with EXPLAIN(YES). Use SQL to analyze the paths chosen as recorded in the PLAN_TABLE by DB2. If the paths chosen are improving because statistics are changing disproportionately, then rebinds should be scheduled after reorganizations with collection of statistics.

Recommendation: It is important to collect statistics initially before binding plans as discussed. There is no need to accumulate costs over the life of a production system for periodic execution of RUNSTATS and rebinds if they are not needed. Indeed, most applications system do not require frequent execution of RUNSTATS and rebinds. If there is reason to believe that periodic execution of RUNSTATS and rebinds would improve performance, it is worth taking a day or two of time to accumulate a history and do an analysis of the history for scheduling purposes on an application system that will be in production for 5, 10, 15 years or more.

An alternative is to develop or purchase software to submit utilities as required based on statistics in the catalog tables. (REORG has threshold for this purpose as discussed in Section RR.9.) Do be cautious of automatically submitting utilities taking more time than batch window allows.

RR.4 CATALOG TABLES UPDATED BY RUNSTATS

In this section we will summarize the statistics collected by RUNSTATS and used to update the catalog tables. We will distinguish the statistics used by the optimizer and those used to determine reorganization requirements and information for space management. This applies to statistics collected by specifying the STATISTICS parameter to the LOAD and REBUILD INDEX, and REORG utilities. These utilities effectively execute RUNSTATS during their processing. Therefore, references to executing RUNSTATS apply to the utilities that support the STATISTICS parameter.

Statistics Used by the Optimizer

Figure RR.2 summarizes the statistics updated by RUNSTATS and used by the optimizer. How RUNSTATS calculates each statistic is described briefly along with a description of the column updated. The timestamp of when RUNSTATS was executed is in the STATSTIME column of these catalog tables. Most of the statistics can be updated with SQL statements. Those that cannot are indicated by an asterisk (*).

Figure RR.2. Statistics used by the optimizer

SYSIBM.SYSTABLES

CARDF	Number of rows in the table from tablespace scan
NPAGES	Number of pages that contain rows of the table from tablespace scan
PCTROWCOMP	Percentage of rows compressed in table from tablespace scan * 100
EDPROC	blank means that EDITPROC not used

SYSIBM.SYSCOLUMNS

COLCARDF	Estimated number of distinct values in column from tablespace scan or scan of leaf pages if the column is indexed
HIGH2KEY	First 8 bytes of second highest value in the column collected like COLCARDF
LOW2KEY	First 8 bytes of second lowest value in the column collected like COLCARDF

SYSIBM.SYSINDEXES

CLUSTER-RATIO	Percentage of rows in clustering sequence from leaf pages * 100. Counted if RID >= RID from previous RID pair and function applied
CLUSTERED	Y if >=95 % of rows in sequence from CLUSTERRATIOF
FIRSTKEY-CARDF	Number of distinct values of the first key column from leaf pages
FULLKEY-CARDF	Number of distinct values of the full key from leaf pages
NLEAF	Number of active leaf pages in the index from leaf pages
NLEVELS	Number of levels in the index tree from traversing index

SYSIBM.SYSTABLESPACE

NACTIVE	Number of active pages in the tablespace from HURBA (High Used RBA) in VSAM/ICF catalog.

It is best not to update the statistics recorded by RUNSTATS with SQL statements to influence the optimizer as discussed in Chapter OP. However, updating the test catalog tables based on the production catalog tables is advisable if full production data cannot be loaded into test tables. This allows the optimizer to choose access paths similar to what it will do in the production DB2 subsystem. The SQL statements to generate the UPDATE statements are in Chapter EX.

Partition Statistics

Partition statistics are collected like nonpartitioned statistics as summarized in Figure RR.3. At present a few of the partition statistics are used by the optimizer, including the CARDF and NPAGES in SYSTABSTATS and LIMITKEY in SYSINDEXPART are used when the optimizer considers parallel processing. The other statistics in the figure may be used in the future. The *Administration Guide* manual summarizes the statistics that are and are not used by the optimizer in the current release of DB2.

Figure RR.3. Partition statistics updated by RUNSTATS

SYSIBM.SYSTABSTATS

CARDF~	Number of rows in partition
NPAGES~	Number of pages that contain rows in the partition
PCTROW-COMP	Percentage of rows compressed in the partition * 100
NACTIVE	Number of active pages in the partition

SYSIBM.SYSCOLSTATS

COLCARDF~	Estimated number of distinct column values in partition
HIGHKEY*~	First 8 bytes of highest value in the column
HIGH2KEY	First 8 bytes of second highest value in the column
LOWKEY*~	First 8 bytes of lowest value in the column
LOW2KEY	First 8 bytes of second lowest value in the column

SYSIBM.SYSINDEXSTATS

CLUSTER-RATIO	Percentage of rows that are in clustering sequence
CLUSTERED	Y if >=95 % of rows in sequence from CLUSTERRATIOF
FIRSTKEY-CARDF	Number of distinct values of the first key column
FULLKEY-CARDF	Number of distinct values of the full key
NLEAF	Number of active leaf pages
NLEVELS	Number of levels in index
KEYCOUNT	Number of index keys/entries in index
IOFACTOR	Not used
PREFETCH-FACTOR	Not used

SYSIBM.SYSINDEXPART

LIMITKEY~*	The upper range value specified when the partitioning index is created.

~Statistics used by the optimizer if parallelism is considered.
*Statistics that cannot be updated with the UPDATE statement.

Frequency and Correlation Statistics

Frequency statistics are used by the optimizer when the user requested value is known for access path selection. The value requested by the user is known when predicates are coded with literals, dynamic SQL is used with literals (not parameter markers), and reoptimization of static SQL is used. The INDEX parameter must be specified on the RUNSTATS statement for the statistics to be collected.

Ten rows (default) containing the ten most frequently occurring values are inserted into SYSCOLDIST for nonpartitioned tablespaces and SYSCOLDISTSTATS for partitioned tablespaces as shown in Figure RR.4. These rows have a value of 'F' in the TYPE column. The column COLVALUE contains one of the most frequently occurring values and the FREQUENCYF column contains the percentage of rows that contain the value times 100 for a single column index. The first column of a composite index is described in COLVALUE and FREQUENCYF by default. You can request more than the default of 10 most frequently occurring values on more than the first column of a composite index as discussed in Section RR.7. A uniform distribution is assumed for the remaining percentage of rows.

Figure RR.4. Frequency and correlation statistics

SYSIBM.SYSCOLDIST and SYSIBM.SYSCOLDISTSTATS

COLVALUE	One of up to *n* values of the first and additional (optional) key columns that occur most frequently
FREQUENCYF	Percentage of rows that contain the value specified in COLVALUE * 100 from leaf pages
TYPE	'F' for frequency statistics 'C' for correlation statistics
CARDF	Number of distinct values for a column group
COLGROUP-COLNO	Each SMALLINT array element contains the sequence number of the column in the row for which statistics are collected
NUMCOLUMNS	Number of columns associated with the statistics

Correlation statistics provide the number of distinct values for a column group in a composite index as discussed in Section RR.7. The rows describing column correlation statistics have a value of 'C' in the TYPE column.

You can use the INSERT statement to insert frequency and correlation statistics. The UPDATE and DELETE statements can also be used on the rows in SYSCOLDIST and SYSCOLDISTSTATS.

However, when RUNSTATS is executed on a tablespace, all rows all deleted. If you need to maintain these statistics without using RUNSTATS, the SQL statements must be executed after every execution of RUNSTATS.

Statistics for Reorganization and Space Management

RUNSTATS updates statistics that are not used by the optimizer. These statistics are useful for determining if a reorganization is needed and for space management. Section RR.9 and RR.10 gives SELECT statements from the catalog tables summarized in Figure RR.5 along with guidelines on when to reorganize the tablespace and indexes as well as when more or less space is required. Most catalog table columns updated by RUNSTATS contain -1 until the utility is executed.

Figure RR.5. Statistics for reorganization and space management

SYSIBM.SYSTABLEPART

CARDF	Number of rows in the table space or partition from tablespace scan
SPACE (V6)	KB of space as determined by RUNSTATS or STOSPACE
NEARINDREF	Number of rows moved to a nearby page (within 2 segments or 16 pages for a nonsegmented tablespace) due to row length increase from tablespace scan
FARINDREF	Number of rows moved to a faraway page due to row length increase from tablespace scan
PERCACTIVE	Percentage of space occupied by active rows containing actual data from active tables (not space from deleted rows). Calculated as active row space bytes / SYSTABLEPART active page bytes.
PERCDROP	Percentage of space occupied by rows from dropped tables. Dropped simple tablespace bytes / SYSTABLEPART active page bytes.
PAGESAVE	Percentage of pages saved in the tablespace or partition as a result of using ESA compression * 100

SYSIBM.SYSINDEXPART

CARDF	Number of rows referenced by the index or index partition from leaf pages
SPACE (V6)	KB of space as determined by RUNSTATS or STOSPACE
NEAROFFPOS	Number of times the next row was not in sequence of index but was in a near page from leaf pages. Counter incremented by 1 if RID >1 and < cutoff pages away from last RID sequence or in a previous page from the RID.

FAROFFPOS	Number of times the next row was not in sequence of index but was in a faraway page from leaf pages. Counter incremented by 1 if RID > cutoff pages away from last RID sequence.
LEAFDIST	100 times the average number of pages between successive leaf pages during scan of leaf pages

PCTPAGES in SYSTABLES and SYSTABSTATS is the percentage of total pages that contains rows. The percentage is calculated as NPAGES divided by NACTIVE for nonsegmented tablespace and NPAGES divided by the number of segments * SEGSIZE for segmented tablespaces.

RR.5 RUNSTATS STATEMENT AND PARAMETERS

We will review the many parameters that can be specified in the RUNSTATS statement. These parameters are used to control the operation of the utility.

Index Statistics

The name of the database and tablespace for which statistics are to be collected is named in the RUNSTATS statement. In the following example, statistics are collected on the DASPJTSP tablespace in the DASPJDB database.

```
RUNSTATS TABLESPACE DASPJDB.DASPJTSP
INDEX(ALL)
SHRLEVEL CHANGE
REPORT YES
UPDATE ALL
```

You will almost always want to collect statistics on all indexes on all tables in the named tablespace as indicated by the INDEX(ALL) parameter. These statistics are very valuable to the optimizer in determining a good access path and to you in determining reorganization requirements and for space management. Indeed, there are times when collecting statistics on only the indexes after the first execution of RUNSTATS with representative data can be sufficient if it is necessary to reduce the costs of RUNSTATS which are dominated by CPU usage. RUNSTATS collects the index statistics based on an index scan. A tablespace scan and the CPU time required to calculate the statistics on tablespaces and tables can be avoided if you believe that the statistic have not changed significantly since the last collection of these statistics.

You can name specific indexes for which statistics are to be collected. For example, we need to collect statistics on the AUTHID.SPJX and AUTHID.QTYX indexes but there is no need to collect the table and tablespace statistics. Use the statement:

```
RUNSTATS INDEX (AUTHID.SPJX, AUTHID.QTYX)
```

SHRLEVEL of CHANGE and REFERENCE

SHRLEVEL (share level) of CHANGE and REFERENCE control whether SQL statements can select and update data while RUNSTATS is executing.

SHRLEVEL CHANGE allows others to update data while the utility is executing. RUNSTATS uses the uncommited read (UR) isolation level (discussed in Chapter CC) and takes a read claim (claims are discussed in Chapter LC). This means that RUNSTATS basically ignores any locks held by other programs. Indeed, it collects statistics on a page even if there is currently a share, update, or exclusive lock held by another program on the page. This does *not* adversely affect statistics in most cases because typically only a few pages are locked at any one time. RUNSTATS does wait for a mass delete lock to be released when all rows are being deleted from a table using the mass delete algorithm discussed in Chapter BP.

SHRLEVEL REFERENCE allows others to select data while RUNSTATS is executing. Others cannot insert, update, and delete rows. SHRLEVEL REFERENCE is the default. The utility holds a share lock taken at table/tablespace level during execution.

Recommendation: SHRLEVEL CHANGE is a good choice. It does not use significantly more resources than SHRLEVEL REFERENCE.

REPORT Parameter

REPORT YES causes statistics to be written to SYSPRINT in addition to updating the catalog tables. It is advisable to override the default of REPORT NO to have a report of the statistics updated by RUNSTATS.

UPDATE Parameter

There are several parameters that can be used to control which statistics should be updated.

UPDATE ALL is the default and causes the update of non-optional statistics summarized in Figures RR.2, RR.3, and the frequency statistics (not the correlation statistics) in Figure RR.4 as those used by the optimizer and the statistics summarized in Figure RR.5 as those used to determine reorganization requirements and for space management.

UPDATE SPACE causes the update of statistics summarized in Figure RR.5 as those that can be used to determine reorganization needs and space management. This parameter does not cause the statistics used by the optimizer to be updated and therefore avoids the possibility of losing current access paths with explicit or automatic rebinds.

UPDATE ACCESSPATH causes the update of non-optional statistics summarized in Figs. RR.2, RR.3, and the frequency statistics (not the correlation statistics) in Figure RR.4 as those used by the optimizer to determine a good access path. There is a savings of CPU time when not updating the statistics used to determine reorganization requirements and for space management. There is not a significant reduction in costs when using the UPDATE ACCESSPATH parameter in most cases.

UPDATE NONE can be useful when used with REPORT YES. This combination causes RUNSTATS to collect the statistics, report on them, but not update the catalog tables. You have the opportunity to review the statistics and decide if it is likely that the new statistics would result in a different access path when plans and package are explicitly bound or an automatic rebind occurs. In order to update the statistics in the catalog tables RUNSTATS must be executed without the UPDATE NONE parameter.

Update Statistics on a Partition

Statistics can be updated on a specific tablespace or index partition. The PART parameter is used to specify the partition. Statistics are collected on part 2 of the tablespace and SPJX index with the statement:

```
RUNSTATS TABLESPACE DASPJDB.DASPJTSP
PART 2
INDEX (SPJX PART 2)
```

Updating statistics on specific partitions is a good choice where specific partitions are updated frequently and other are updated infrequently. Certainly, updating statistics on one or a few partitions is less costly that updating statistics on the entire partitioned tablespace and indexes.

It is advisable to execute RUNSTATS on the entire partitioned tablespace before executing the utility on individual partitions. If this is not done, the tablespace statistics are not updated until statistics have been gathered on each and every partition when using the PART parameter.

You can name a specific index and its partition like:

```
RUNSTATS INDEX (AUTHID.SPJX PART 3)
```

RUNSTATS can be executed on the catalog tables and indexes. These statistics are useful for SELECT statements but are not used for internal manipulation of the catalog tables when objects are created, altered, and dropped, plans and packages are bound and freed, privileges are granted and revoked, and other operations performed on the catalog tables within DB2.

RR.6 COLLECTING STATISTICS ON NON-INDEXED COLUMNS

There are several statistics used by the optimizer that are not updated unless specific parameters are specified. The cardinality of non-indexed columns, and the second highest and second lowest values in the column are optional statistics that can be collected by RUNSTATS and used by the optimizer. If you request that these statistics be collected, they will be placed in the COLCARDF, HIGH2KEY, and LOW2KEY columns of the SYSCOLUMNS catalog tables. The statistics are used in two general cases and more are expected in the future.

First, the cardinality of non-indexed columns is useful in estimating the number of qualifying rows according to local predicates when doing a join. If there is no index on the columns tested in the local predicates, the optimizer does not have a good estimate of the number of qualifying rows without the cardinality of the columns. If the optimizer has these statistics, it can better estimate the number of qualifying rows in the tables to be joined, determine which tables should be the inner and outer tables of the join, and which join method should be used. Second, the cardinality of non-leading columns of a composite index are very useful in determining if and how a composite index should be used to narrow the search when equal predicates are not specified on all columns of the composite index.

You can request that the COLCARDF, HIGH2KEY, and LOW2KEY statistics be collected on all columns of a table by specifying the TABLE parameter and optionally naming a specific table in a tablespace. If you want to collect the statistics on only some columns in a table, a maximum of 10 specific columns can be named with the COLUMN parameter. The following statement causes RUNSTATS to collect the statistics on all columns of the S table and on only the PN and JN columns of the SPJ table. It is not necessary to collect statistics on the leading column of the composite index on SN, PN, JN because the cardinality of SN is in FIRSTKEYCARDF in SYSINDEXES and COLCARDF in SYSCOLUMNS.

```
RUNSTATS TABLESPACE DASPJDB.DASPJTSP
TABLE (S)   COLUMN (ALL)
TABLE (SPJ) COLUMN (PN,JN)
SAMPLE 25
INDEX (ALL)
SHRLEVEL CHANGE
UPDATE ALL
REPORT YES
```

The collection of non-indexed column statistics increases the CPU time required by RUNSTATS to calculate the statistics based on a simulation method. The costs can be reduced by naming only columns that are used in the WHERE clauses with the COLUMN parameter and the non-leading columns of composite indexes where it is not possible to specify equal predicates on all of the columns. It is obviously difficult to identify such columns. An alternative is to have RUNSTATS estimate the cardinality of non-indexed columns using the simulation method based on a sample of data in the columns.

Sampling to Reduce CPU Costs

You can specify the percentage of rows that are to be used as a sample to estimate the cardinality of non-indexed columns. This is done by specifying the parameter SAMPLE along with the percentage times 100. If you specify the SAMPLE parameter without giving a value, the default is 25. That is, 25 percent of the data will be sampled to estimate the cardinality of non-indexed columns. This is somewhat like using every 4th row.

An idea of the cost savings using sampling can be gotten using DB2 Estimator. Figure RR.6 is the V5 results for RUNSTATS of a 1 million row table, 100 byte row length, and 3 indexes.

Figure RR.6. RUNSTATS costs with and without non-indexed column cardinalities

Utility	CPU Min:Sec	I/O Min:Sec	Elapsed Min:Sec
RUNSTATS TABLESPACE T100 INDEX(ALL) SHRLEVEL REFERENCE REPORT NO UPDATE ALL	1:23.005	1.02.723	1:37.096
RUNSTATS TABLESPACE T100 INDEX(ALL) TABLE **COLUMN(ALL) SAMPLE 25** SHRLEVEL REFERENCE REPORT NO UPDATE ALL	1:47.134	1:02.723	1:47.134

The CPU costs are increased by about 24 seconds when collecting cardinality statistics on non-indexed columns with a sampling of 25 percent of the data. It is likely that the reduced costs of executing SQL with improved access paths frequently will offset the additional costs of having RUNSTATS collect statistics on non-indexed columns infrequently. CPU costs tend to increase with large tables, many columns in the table, long columns, low cardinality columns, VARCHAR columns, and a high sampling percentage.

If the additional RUNSTATS CPU costs are still too high, even with sampling, consider collecting non-indexed column cardinalities on only columns used in predicates and the non-leading column of composite indexes where not all columns of a composite index are specified in the WHERE clause.

RR.7 COLLECTION OF FREQUENCY AND CORRELATION STATISTICS

We have seen in Section RR.4 that frequency and correlation statistics can be collected by RUNSTATS. We will look at these statistics in more detail.

Collection of Additional Frequency Statistics

The 10 most frequently occurring values in a column are identified and written to the COLVALUE column in SYSCOLDIST and SYSCOLDISTSTATS for partitioned tablespaces if there is a non-uniform distribution of values by default. The FREQUENCYF column contains the percentage of rows times 100 that have a value in COLVALUE. This applies only to the first column of a composite index by default. You can collect frequency statistics on any number of the most frequently occurring values and more than the first column of a composite index. The FREQVAL parameter provides for specifying the number of the most frequently occurring values with the COUNT parameter and the number of columns in a composite index with the NUMCOLS parameter. The following statement instructs RUNSTATS to collect the percent occurrence of the 15 most frequently occurring values in the first column of the composite index AUTHID.SPJX, the 25 most frequently occurring values in the first two columns of the index, and the 35 most frequently occurring values in the first three columns of the index.

```
RUNSTATS INDEX (AUTHID.SPJX)
  FREQVAL NUMCOLS 1 COUNT 15
  FREQVAL NUMCOLS 2 COUNT 25
  FREQVAL NUMCOLS 3 COUNT 35
```

Do be cautious about specifying only FREQVAL NUMCOLS 3 COUNT 35, for example. The frequency statistics can be used only if a matching index scan can be used on all 3 columns of the composite index.

Recommendation: Do consider requesting frequency statistics for indexed columns that have a skewed distribution of values. The FREQUENCYF column provides the optimizer with the exact percentage of rows that will qualify for an equal predicate immediately after RUNSTATS has been executed. This information continues to be useful between executions of RUNSTATS because the frequency statistics do not vary significantly in most cases.

Collection of Correlation Statistics

The collection of correlation statistics is important if you have composite indexes where the columns within the index are correlated and it is not possible to specify equal predicates on all columns of the composite index in the WHERE clause of SQL statements. Chapter OP describes the meaning of correlation statistics and how the optimizer can use the statistics for improved access path selection.

The use of the KEYCARD parameter in the following RUNSTATS statement causes rows describing the correlation of columns within a composite index to be written to SYSCOLDIST and SYSCOLDISTSTATS for partitioned tablespaces. There is one row for each column group with a 'C' in the TYPE column rather than the 'F' used for distribution statistics.

```
RUNSTATS TABLESPACE DASPJDB.DASPJTSP
INDEX (ALL) -- Can name an index & partition
KEYCARD
```

An example will show the meaning of a column group. Assume that a composite index consists of four columns, CARDF in a row describing the correlation statistics has the cardinality of the column group consisting of the first and second column of the composite index. Another row is inserted with the cardinality of the column group consisting of the first, second, and third column of the composite index. A row is not inserted for the first, second, third, and fourth column because FULLKEYCARDF in SYSINDEXES contains the cardinality of all columns in a composite index. A row is not inserted for the first column of the composite index because FIRSTKEYCARDF in SYSINDEXES and COLCARDF in SYSCOLUMNS contain the cardinality.

You can insert rows in SYSCOLDIST and SYSCOLDISTSTATS describing the cardinalities of column groupings not including the leading columns of a composite index, for example, the cardinality of the second and third columns. The optimizer can use these statistics in determining the access path. However, keep in mind that all rows describing the correlation and frequency statistics for a tablespace are deleted when RUNSTATS is next executed. In order for any rows that you insert, update, or delete to remain in effect, it is necessary to execute the SQL statements after each RUNSTATS.

There is no reason to specify the KEYCARD parameter if an index has only one or two columns. Of course, there is no column group with a one column index and the cardinality of the column group of two columns in a composite index is in FIRSTKEYCARDF of SYSINDEXES.

Report on Correlation and Frequency Statistics

You can report on a summary of the correlation and distribution statistics. Here is a statement that will report on all indexes on the SPJ table.

```
SELECT NAME, TYPE, INTEGER(CARDF),
CASE
  WHEN NUMCOLUMNS = 2 THEN
       HEX(SUBSTR(COLGROUPCOLNO, 1, 4))
  WHEN NUMCOLUMNS = 3 THEN
       HEX(SUBSTR(COLGROUPCOLNO, 1, 6))
  ELSE NULL
```

```
END AS COLGRPCOLNO,
CASE
  WHEN FREQUENCYF <> -1 THEN
       INTEGER(FLOAT(FREQUENCYF) * 100)
  ELSE -1
END AS FQY, COLVALUE
FROM   SYSIBM.SYSCOLDIST
WHERE TBNAME   = 'SPJ'
AND   TBOWNER = 'AUTHID'
ORDER BY NAME, TYPE, COLGRPCOLNO,
      FQY DESC, COLVALUE;
```

The COLGROUPCOLNO column contains an array of SMALLINT columns. Each array element contains the sequence number of the column in the row for which statistics are collected. The NUMCOLUMNS contains the number of columns for which the statistics are collected. A WHEN condition is needed for each column in the composite index with the most columns minus 1. For example, the composite index on the SN, PN, and JN needs the first two WHEN clauses. The WHEN NUMCOLMNS = 2 THEN HEX(SUBSTR(COLGROUPCOLNO, 1, 4) clause includes the cardinality of the first two columns. The WHEN NUMCOLMNS = 3 THEN HEX(SUBSTR (COLGROUPCOLNO, 1, 6) includes the cardinality of the first three columns.

RR.8 CATALOG TABLES UPDATED BY STOSPACE

The STOSPACE utility updates the SPACE column in SYSTABLESPACE for each tablespace, SYSTABLEPART for each data partition, SYSINDEXES for each index, SYSINDEXPART for each index partition, and SYSSTOGROUP for each storage group. The high allocated relative byte address (RBA) of VSAM linear data set is used for the SPACE column. This applies to objects created using storage groups (not user defined data sets). It also does not apply to objects on DASD managed by SMS. Here is an example of instructing the STOSPACE utility to place the number of kilobytes of space in the SPACE column of the catalog tables for the DASPJSTO and DAZIPSTO storage groups.

```
STOSPACE STOGROUP (DASPJSTO, DAZIPSTO)
```

We will be looking at a number of SELECT statements from the catalog tables in the Section RR.10 on space management. Some of these statements use the SPACE column in the calculations. If STOSPACE has not been executed, the SPACE column and calculations based on the column will not be accurate.

RR.9 WHEN TO REORGANIZE USING THE CATALOG & REORG THRESHOLDS (V6)

There are a number of factors that suggest when a tablespace and indexes should be reorganized as summarized in Figure RR.7. Most of these conditions can be checked using SELECT statements from the catalog tables and three of the conditions (V6) can be checked by the REORG utility based on specified thresholds. We will look at each of the conditions, the SELECT statements that are useful in determining when the REORG utility should be executed, and the thresholds that can be specified to determine if the utility should to a reorganization when submitted.

Figure RR.7. Conditions that suggest a reorganization

- After rows have lost more than 20 percent of their clustering
  - OFFPOSLIMIT threshold, 10 percent default
- After a number of rows have overflowed to near or far pages
  - INDREFLIMIT, 10 percent default
- After filling free space
- After index page splitting
  - LEAFDISTLIMIT threshold, 200 default
- After losing compression savings
- After heavy insert, update, and delete activity
- After dropping a table in a nonsegmented tablespace to reclaim space

Here is an example of using the OFFPOSLIMIT and INDEFLIMIT parameters with default values on the REORG TABLESPACE statement.

```
REORG TABLESPACE DASPJDB.DASPJTSP
OFFPOSLIMIT 10
INDREFLIMIT 10
```

The REORG TABLESPACE utility also reorganizes all indexes on all tables in the tablespace. If you need to reorganize only a specific index as discussed in Section RR.22, here is a statement to show the use of the LEAFDISTLIMIT parameter .

```
REORG INDEX AUTHID.SPJX
LEAFDISTLIMIT 200
```

There are many more parameters discussed in the remainder of this chapter that you will want to include in the REORG TABLESPACE and REORG INDEX statements.

The REPORTONLY parameter can be specified along with OFFPOSLIMIT, INDEFLIMIT, and LEAFDISTLIMIT (V6) to determine if a reorganization is recommended based on these thresholds. The reorganization is not performed regardless of the result. If the return code is 1, no limit is met and no REORG is performed or recommended. This means that no limit is met. If the return code is 2, REORG is performed (not performed if REPORTONLY is specified) or recommended. The catalog statistics should be current for the thresholds to be useful.

Recommendation: Increase percent free if REORG needs to be executed more frequently than desired and there is random insert, update, and delete activity. Do use the ALTER statement before a reorganization to increase the free space.

Determine Data that is Losing Clustering

If less than 80 percent of the rows in a table are in sequence according to the clustering index, it is advisable to reorganize the tablespace. The CLUSTERRATIOF in SYSINDEXES contains the percentage of rows that are in sequence according to the values in the column declared as the clustering index by specifying the CLUSTER parameter when the index was created. CLUSTERRATIOF rather than CLUSTERRATIO is used by the optimizer once it is populated in V6. It is a floating point number rather than the previous integer that was used prior to V6. A value of 'Y' in the CLUSTERING column indicates that the row describes the clustering index. If the index has been designated the clustering index, the data is assumed to be in sequence according to the index if RUNSTATS has not been updated. The CLUSTERED column contains 'Y' if 95 percent or more of the rows are in sequence. The optimizer no longer uses this column in access path selection.

The following SELECT statements reports on the cluster ratio of all indexes in the DASPJDB database. You can add the predicates CLUSTERING = 'Y' and CLUSTERRATIOF < 80 to identify only the clustering indexes with a cluster ratio of less than 80 percent.

```
SELECT CREATOR, NAME, TBNAME,
       CLUSTERRATIOF,
       CLUSTERING, CLUSTERED
FROM   SYSIBM.SYSINDEXES
WHERE  DBNAME = 'DASPJDB';

SELECT OWNER, NAME, PARTITION,
       CLUSTERRATIOF
FROM   SYSIBM.SYSINDEXSTATS
WHERE  DBNAME = 'DASPJDB';
```

In general, if the cluster ratio of the clustering index falls below 80 percent, a good access path chosen by the optimizer based on a high cluster ratio deteriorates as the cluster ratio decreases. The value of locating and processing rows using an index with a high cluster ratio has been discussed extensively throughout the book. The 80 percent figure is a guideline, not a hard and fast figure. The optimizer does not use the 80 percent cluster ratio as a cut off point in most cases. An exception is that if the cluster ratio is 80 percent or higher, sequential prefetch can be used on the data pages to locate rows identified using a non-matching index scan.

The OFFPOSLIMIT REORG threshold provides for reorganizing the tablespace if a good deal of clustering has been lost. If REORG finds that (NEAROFFPOSF + FAROFFPOSF) * 100 / CARDF in SYSINDEXPART > OFFPOSLIMIT (10 percent default) assuming that the limit parameter is specified, a reorganization of the tablespace or named partitions are performed along with the indexes on the objects. This applies only to explicitly defined clustering indexes.

NEAROFFPOSF is the number of times it is necessary to access a different, "near-off" page when processing rows in sequence according to the index. A segmented tablespace row is near-off position if the difference between the two page IDs on the leaf page is greater than or equal to two and less than the SEGSIZE times two (16 rather than SEGSIZE times two is used for nonsegmented tablespaces).

FAROFFPOSF is the number of times it is necessary to access a different, "far-off" page when processing rows in sequence according to the index. A segmented tablespace row is far-off position if the two page IDs differ by SEGSIZE times two or more (16 rather than SEGSIZE times two is used for nonsegmented tablespaces). This makes it likely that an I/O is required to locate the required row.

Variable Length Rows That Have Been Relocated

If a variable length row is expanded in length and there is no free space on the page, the row is moved to a near or far page with a pointer left behind in the row's original position, pointing to the new location of the row as discussed in Chapter CD. If the percentage of rows relocated is sizable, more than 5 percent for example, consider reorganizing the tablespace. This avoids two rather than one I/O to a data page to locate a row as a result of a matching index scan. It avoids interrupting prefetch processing to do a synchronous I/O to locate the moved row when doing a tablespace scan. It minimizes seek time on DASD to locate the moved row. This is particularly important if the row is moved to a far off position.

The following SELECT statement calculates the percentage of moved rows. You can add additional predicates to analyze only tablespaces created by a particular AUTHID or use a LIKE predicate to search for only tablespaces for a specific application system. If all tablespaces in an application system begin with SPJ, the LIKE 'SPJ%" predicate can be used to locate only the tablespaces for the particular application that have more than 5 percent of the rows moved to a near or far position.

```
SELECT TSNAME,NEARINDREF,FARINDREF,CARDF,
       (NEARINDREF+FARINDREF)*100/CARDF,
       PCTFREE, FREEPAGE
FROM   SYSIBM.SYSTABLEPART
WHERE  CARDF > 0
AND   ((NEARINDREF+FARINDREF)*100/CARDF)>0;
```

If rows are frequently relocated, consider increasing the percent free with the ALTER statement if you have random insert, update, and delete activity. If the tablespace is nonsegmented, consider converting to a segmented tablespace. As discussed in Chapter TS, free space can be located more efficiently in segmented tablespaces.

Recommendation: Consider reorganizing a tablespace if 5 percent or more of the rows have been moved to a near or far position.

Determine the Availability of Free Space

If a good deal of the free space specified when the tablespace was created or last altered has been filled, it is advisable to reorganize the tablespace to regain the specified free space assuming that insert, update, and delete activity is at random. The following statement reports on all tablespaces in the DASPJDB database along with the percentage of space that is active (PERCACTIVE).

```
SELECT TSNAME, DBNAME, PERCACTIVE
FROM   SYSIBM.SYSTABLEPART
WHERE  DBNAME = 'DASPJDB';
```

If the PERCACTIVE is greater than 95 percent, some of 5 percent free space (default) has been used. You can add a predicate to report on only tablespaces that have a PERCACTIVE greater than 100 minus the percent free specified when the free space was specified.

Recommendation: Reorganize a tablespace when a good deal of the free space has been filled and you are doing random inserts, updates, and deletes. This allows for more efficient inserts and updates of variable length rows.

Reuse of Space from a Dropped Table

It is necessary to reorganize a simple tablespace in order for the space from a dropped table to be reusable. The following statement identifies all tablespaces with a PERCDROP greater than zero.

```
SELECT TSNAME, DBNAME, PERCDROP
FROM   SYSIBM.SYSTABLEPART
WHERE  PERCDROP > 0;
```

Recommendation: If tablespaces are frequently identified as having unusable space as a result of dropped tables, consider converting the simple tablespace to a segmented tablespace. The space from a dropped table in a segmented tablespace is immediately reusable and PERCDROP always equals zero.

Deleted row space is immediately reusable for all types of tablespaces. Scattered free space is gathered when updates require space on the page. However, the costs of gathering the free space is avoided by reorganizing the tablespace periodically.

Reorganization of the Catalog and Directory

All catalog tablespaces and the directory plan, package, DBD, and SYSLGRNX tablespaces can be reorganized. These objects need to be reorganized less frequently than application tablespaces in the great majority of the cases. They may need to be reorganized to reallocate space to gain more or less space, reclaim fragmented space not being reused, allocate free space for additional inserts, and move objects to another DASD device. Reorganization can also improve performance of SQL against the catalog tables but does not improve performance of DB2 processing of the catalog in most cases. This is because DB2 uses links for internal processing of the catalog tables.

There are some special considerations regarding the reorganization of the catalog and directory that are covered in detail in the *Utility Guide and Reference* manual.

REORG INDEX on catalog and directory indexes is not supported. However, RECOVER INDEX PRIOR to V6 and REBUILD INDEX in V6 can be used to rebuild the indexes.

RR.10 SPACE MANAGEMENT

The goal is to have a primary space allocation (PRIQTY) of sufficient size to contain a tablespace or index, and to allow for inserting additional rows without having to use secondary space allocation (SECQTY) too often as discussed in Chapter CD. A number of SELECT statements against the catalog tables are useful in space management.

Allocated Space and Actual Space Used

The following statement provides a report so that you can compare the space allocated with the space used for all tablespaces in the DB2 subsystem. Again, predicates can be added to restrict the report to just specific databases or creators, or a LIKE predicate can be used to identify tablespaces that follow a naming convention for a particular application system.

```
SELECT NAME, SPACE, NACTIVE,
       NACTIVE*PGSIZE*100/SPACE AS SPACE_USED,
       SPACE - (NACTIVE * PGSIZE) AS SPACE_NOT_USED
FROM   SYSIBM.SYSTABLESPACE
WHERE  SPACE > 0;
```

The NACTIVE column contains the number of active pages up to the high preformatted page in the tablespace. The SPACE column contains the number of KB allocated to a tablespace. This column needs to be updated by the STOSPACE utility before executing a statement that references SPACE to receive accurate results as discussed in Section RR.10.

If less than 80 to 90 percent of space is used as calculated with NACTIVE * PGSIZE * 100, perhaps you expect to insert 10 to 20 percent more rows before the next reorganization, too much space has been allocated for the data, or you need to reclaim space occupied by a dropped table.

The amount of space that is not actively being used is calculated as SPACE - (NACTIVE * PGSIZE).

Primary and Secondary Space

Tablespaces and indexes that are using multiple extents can be identified by calculating the space allocated as a percentage of the primary allocation. If the percentage is high, multiple extents are being used. The maximum number of extents that can be taken by DB2 on multiple volumes is 119 (4 of the 123 VSAM extents are reserved by DB2) prior to V6. The maximum number of extents on multiple volumes is 251 with 4 of the 255 VSAM extents reserved by DB2 in V6.

The following SELECT statement gives a report of the space allocated to the primary and secondary allocations for tablespaces located in storage groups beginning with SPJST.

```
SELECT TSNAME, PQTY, SQTY, TP.SPACE,
       TP.SPACE*100/(PQTY*4)
FROM   SYSIBM.SYSTABLEPART TP,
       SYSIBM.SYSTABLESPACE
WHERE  TSNAME     = NAME
AND    PARTITIONS = 0
AND    STORNAME LIKE 'SPJST%';
```

This SELECT statement gives a report similar to the previous one for indexes on tables in the DASPJDB database.

```
SELECT NAME, PQTY, SQTY, IP.SPACE,
       IP.SPACE*100/(PQTY*4)
FROM   SYSIBM.SYSINDEXES,
       SYSIBM.SYSINDEXPART IP
WHERE  NAME      = IXNAME
AND    PARTITION = 0
AND    DBNAME    = 'DASPJDB';
```

Tablespace PRIQTY Compared to Pages Used by a Table

If you prefer to look at absolute values rather than at percentages, the following statement proves useful for tablespaces with one table in them.

```
SELECT T.TSNAME, TP.PQTY, T.NAME,
       T.NPAGES, T.CARDF
FROM   SYSIBM.SYSTABLEPART TP,
       SYSIBM.SYSTABLES    T
WHERE  TP.TSNAME = T.TSNAME
AND    T.CREATOR = &TABLECREATOR
AND    T.TYPE    = 'T';
```

The PQTY column contains the primary space allocation in units of 4 KB pages. The NPAGES column contains the number of pages in the tablespace which contain rows of the table. This does not include pages formatted without active rows or empty pages due to rows being deleted. If there is more than one table in the tablespace, comparing NPAGES and PQTY is not valid. This is because NPAGES is the number of pages used by a table and PQTY is the pages allocated to a tablespace.

Recommendation: Do adjust the PRIQTY space to match the used space plus expected growth. The ALTER statement can be used to adjust the PRIQTY and SECQTY quantities prior to a reorganization. The REORG utility leaves the new space allocation.

Determine Tablespaces and Indexes in Secondary Extents

The number of tablespace extents can be determined in a specified database that exceed a specified number of extents using a SELECT statement like the one that follows. Change the 'DASPJDB' database name to your database name and the 0 in the WHERE #EXTENTS > 0 clause to a value of interest to you.

```
SELECT * FROM
  (SELECT TS.DBNAME AS DB, TS.NAME AS TS,
     TP.PARTITION   AS PART, TP.SPACE,
     TP.PQTY, TP.SQTY,
     CASE TS.PGSIZE
       WHEN 4 THEN
          (TP.SPACE-
           CASE
             WHEN TP.PQTY<3 THEN 12
             ELSE TP.PQTY*4
           END)
           / (CASE
                WHEN TP.SQTY=0 THEN 1
                WHEN TP.SQTY<3 THEN 12
                ELSE TP.SQTY*4
              END) +1
       WHEN 8 THEN
          (TP.SPACE-
           CASE
             WHEN TP.PQTY<6 THEN 24
             ELSE TP.PQTY*4
```

```
            END)
            / (CASE
                WHEN TP.SQTY=0 THEN 1
                WHEN TP.SQTY<6 THEN 24
                ELSE TP.SQTY*4
              END) +1
      WHEN 16 THEN
          (TP.SPACE-
            CASE
              WHEN TP.PQTY<12 THEN 48
              ELSE TP.PQTY*4
            END)
            / (CASE
                WHEN TP.SQTY=0 THEN 1
                WHEN TP.SQTY<12 THEN 48
                ELSE TP.SQTY*4
              END) +1
      WHEN 32 THEN
          (TP.SPACE-
            CASE
              WHEN TP.PQTY<24 THEN 96
              ELSE TP.PQTY*4
            END)
            / (CASE
                WHEN TP.SQTY=0 THEN 1
                WHEN TP.SQTY<24 THEN 96
                ELSE TP.SQTY*4
              END) +1
    END AS #EXTENTS
  FROM SYSIBM.SYSTABLESPACE TS,
       SYSIBM.SYSTABLEPART  TP
  WHERE TS.NAME = TP.TSNAME AND
        TS.DBNAME = TP.DBNAME AND
        TS.DBNAME = 'DASPJDB' AND
        TP.SPACE  > 0)
  AS DUMMY
WHERE  #EXTENTS > 0
ORDER BY DB, TS, PART;
```

The number of extents used by indexes can be determined in a specified database that exceed a specified number of extents using a SELECT statement like the one that follows. Change the 'DASPJDB' database name to your database name and the 0 in the WHERE #EXTENTS > 0 clause to a value of interest to you.

```
SELECT * FROM
  (SELECT
    TS.DBNAME     AS DB,
    IX.NAME       AS IX,
    IP.PARTITION AS PART,
    IX.BPOOL, IP.VCATNAME, IP.SPACE, IX.PGSIZE,
    IP.STORNAME, IP.PQTY, IP.SQTY,
    CASE IX.PGSIZE
      WHEN 4096 THEN
        (IP.SPACE-
```

```
                CASE
                  WHEN IP.PQTY<3 THEN 48
                  ELSE IP.PQTY*4
                END)
                / (CASE
                     WHEN IP.SQTY=0 THEN 1
                     WHEN IP.SQTY<3 THEN 48
                     ELSE IP.SQTY*4
                   END) +1
         END AS #EXTENTS
       FROM   SYSIBM.SYSTABLESPACE TS, SYSIBM.SYSTABLES    TB,
              SYSIBM.SYSINDEXES    IX, SYSIBM.SYSINDEXPART IP
       WHERE IX.NAME    = IP.IXNAME AND
              TB.NAME   = IX.TBNAME AND
              TS.NAME   = TB.TSNAME AND
              TS.DBNAME = 'DASPJDB' AND
              IP.SPACE  >0)
       AS DUMMY
     WHERE  #EXTENTS > 0
     ORDER BY DB, IX, PART;
```

Alternatives to Determine Secondary Extents

The LISTCAT access method services (AMS) command can be used to determine secondary extents from the ICF catalog. The ISPF option 3.4 can be used as well, for example:

```
Dsname Level . . . DSNP.DSNDBD.DSNDB07.* with option 2
```

gives the space allocated for work tablespaces. The use of SORT XT lists the data sets in multiple extents first. The method can be used on any tablespaces and indexes and are particularly useful for partitioned tablespaces and indexes.

Expanding and Contracting Space Allocation USING VCAT

The DB2 ALTER statement cannot be used for changing the PRIQTY and SECQTY when USING VCAT. An alternative is to use the REORG utility to unload the data with the UNLOAD PAUSE parameter:

```
REORG TABLESPACE DASPJDB.DASPJTSP
UNLOAD PAUSE
SORTDATA
```

During the pause, delete and redefine or alter the VSAM data sets. You then restart the REORG utility by specifying the RESTART(PHASE) parameter on the EXEC DSNUPROC statement or enter PHASE on line 8 of the utilities panel. It is not necessary to drop tablespace and its dependencies.

Unloading data to be loaded into the same or another table is discussed in Section RR.19.

RR.11 THE REORGANIZATION UTILITY

Sections RR.9 and RR.10 of this chapter have provided guidelines on when to reorganize a tablespace and indexes to regain processing efficiencies and manage space. In this section, we will discuss how to use the REORG utility and the many parameters that significantly affect the availability of the data during the reorganization and performance of the utility.

REORG SHRLEVEL Parameters

The SHRLEVEL parameter determines the accessibility of the data during reorganization and the destination of the reloaded data.

SHRLEVEL NONE means that the data can only be read during the unload of the data and no SELECT, INSERT, UPDATE, and DELETE statements are allowed while the data is being reloaded. The REUSE parameter can be used to reload data into original data sets with the benefits discussed in Section LC.8. The data is reloaded into the original data sets. This is the default if the SHRLEVEL parameter is not specified and is always used for reorganizing the catalog and directory tables regardless of the value specified.

SHRLEVEL REFERENCE means that the data can only be read during most of the reorganization processing. The data is reloaded into the shadow data sets. (Shadow data set are discussed later in this section.)

SHRLEVEL CHANGE means that SELECT, INSERT, UPDATE, and DELETE statements can be executed on the original data during most of reorganization processing. The reorganized data is reloaded into shadow data sets. This is referred to as online reorganization.

Logging is not done during reload when using SHRLEVEL of REFERENCE and CHANGE. This is because an image copy is made during the reorganization. LOG of YES or NO can be specified when using SHRLEVEL NONE. If SHRLEVEL NONE is used, LOG NO is a good choice followed by a full image copy to reduce costs and provide for recovery using the copy made after the reorganization. If a full image copy is not made after the reorganization when using LOG NO, the tablespace and indexes are placed in recovery pending as discussed in Chapter CR.

Reorganization with SHRLEVEL CHANGE Overview

Online reorganization provides for read and write processing of the data in the original tablespace during most of reorganization process. It also applies at the partition level for partitioned tablespaces. An exception is that you cannot issue DDL (Data Definition Language) statements. We will begin this section with an overview of the basic processing of an online reorganization and discuss the details throughout the section.

The data and indexes are reorganized into a shadow copy of the objects as indicated in Figure RR.8. An image copy is made asynchronously while doing the reorganization into the shadow copy (not after the reorganization). Log records describing all insert, update, and delete activity during the reorganization are written to the active and archive log in the same manner as is done when a reorganization is not being done. The log records written during the reorganization are used later to update the reorganized shadow copy. Finally there is a switch processing where the shadow becomes the active tablespace and the original tablespace is deleted in most cases.

Figure RR.8. Online reorganization processing

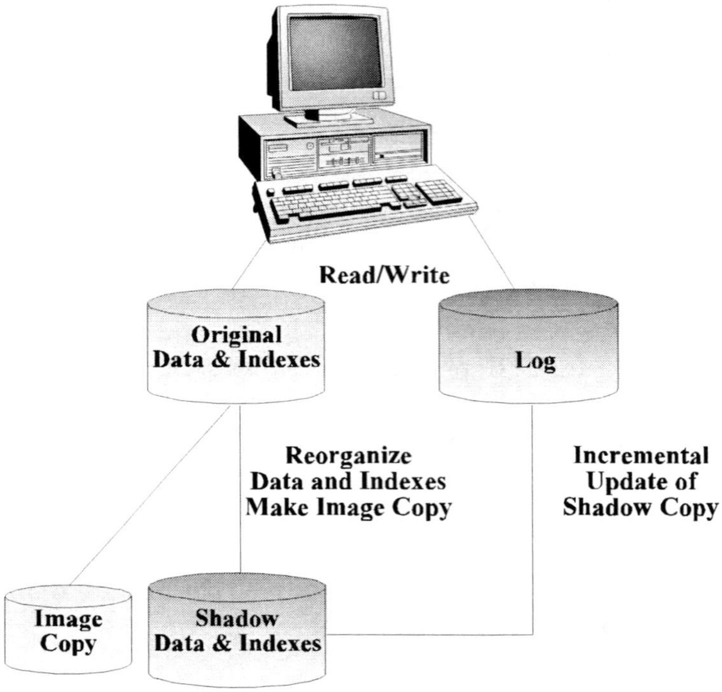

Here is an example of a REORG statement to do an online reorganization using the SHRLEVEL CHANGE parameter.

```
REORG TABLESPACE DASPJDB.DASPJTSP
  SHRLEVEL CHANGE
  MAPPINGTABLE MAPSPJ
  MAXRO  300
  DELAY 1200
  LONGLOG CONTINUE
  TIMEOUT TERM
  DRAIN WRITERS
  DEADLINE NONE
```

This statement causes REORG to reorganize the data and indexes. If you like, only the indexes can be reorganized with all three SHRLEVEL parameters.

Space for Online REORG

Additional DASD space is required for the shadow copy of the tablespace and indexes being reorganized. If a partition of a partitioned tablespace is reorganized, then only space for the shadow tablespace partition, partitioning index, and the logical part of nonpartitioned indexes (NPI) is required. Space is also required for the image copy made during the reorganization. To offset this additional space requirement, there is a space savings in that few work files are required.

It is necessary to have enough space for the REORG utility to create the data sets in the storage group containing the original data sets for the tablespace and indexes. You may want to use the ALTER statement to add one or more volumes to the storage group for the shadow copies and remove the volumes containing the original data after the reorganization. (Tablespaces and indexes on the removed volume are placed on another volume in the storage group when they are reorganized, load replace, or recovered as discussed in Chapter CD.) This procedure increases the likelihood the shadow copies will be allocated by the REORG utility on separate volumes from the original data which minimizes seek time and maximizes performance. Another consideration is to place the mapping take on a newly added volume and remove the volume after the reorganization.

If user defined data sets (USING VCAT) are used, then you must create the required shadow data sets and optionally delete the original data sets after the reorganization is complete. A strict naming convention must be followed as detailed in Chapter CD Section 2 and the *DB2 Utility Guide and Reference* manual.

Mapping Table

It is necessary to create a mapping table and a composite index on all columns in the table when using SHRLEVEL CHANGE. The purpose of the table is to map the location of rows in the original table to the new location of the rows in the shadow table. It is used to locate rows in the shadow to apply log records generated when the original data is updated during the reorganization. Sample statements to create the mapping table and index are in prefix.SDSNSAMP(DSNTEJ1). Here is an example of creating a mapping table and index for reorganizing the SPJ table.

```
CREATE TABLE MAPSPJ
 (TYPE         CHAR(1) NOT NULL,
  SOURCE_RID   CHAR(5) NOT NULL,
  TARGET_XRID  CHAR(9) NOT NULL WITH DEFAULT,
  LRSN         CHAR(6) NOT NULL)
IN DASPJDB.MAPTSP;

CREATE UNIQUE INDEX MAPSPJX
  ON MAPSPJ (SOURCE_RID ASC, TYPE, TARGET_XRID, LRSN)
  USING STOGROUP DASPJSTG
    PRIQTY 7200
    SECQTY  720
    ERASE NO;
```

You will need to calculate the space required for the shadow based on the number of rows in the original tablespace plus 10 percent for growth during the reorganization. The mapping table can be in the same or a different tablespace from the one containing the data to be reorganized. It must be in a segmented tablespace. A separate mapping table is required for each concurrently executing REORG TABLESPACE. A mapping table is not needed when using REORG INDEX.

How the Mapping Table Is Built and Used

The mapping table is built during the unload phase of the original table and during the reload phase of the shadow. It is cleared at the end of the reorganization. The build of the mapping table is not logged.

After the data has been reorganized into the shadow, the log records of all inserts, updates, and deletes of the original tablespace are read and applied to the shadow. A batch of log records are read for an iteration of the log apply, an internal sort of source RIDs is done, the log RIDs from the source data are translated to the target RIDs using the mapping table, an internal sort of target RIDs is done, and the batch of log records are applied to the shadow. This work is done with index only processing. The overall processing allows for efficiently locating rows in the shadow and processing a shadow page once for multiple log records. A 10 MB buffer in the REORG utility address space is used for the processing.

RR.12 INCREMENTAL UPDATE OF THE SHADOW COPY

Figure RR.9 is an example of how the log records written to the log as a result of insert, update, and delete activity to the original tablespace are applied to the shadow when using SHRLEVEL CHANGE (does not apply to SHRLEVEL REFERENCE).

Figure RR.9. Incremental update of the shadow

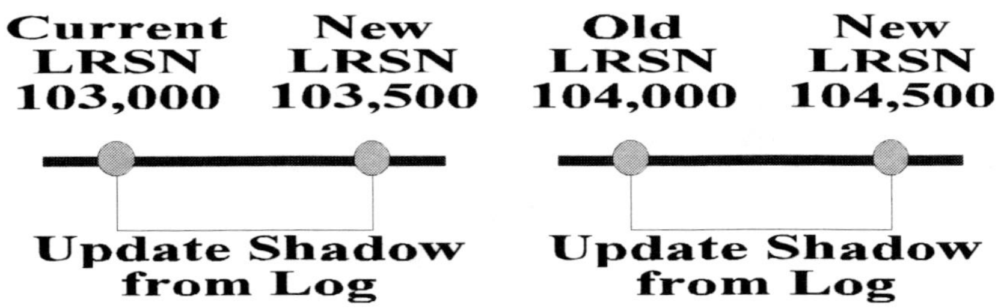

The log record sequence number (LRSN) is a timestamp of when the log record was written truncated to 6 bytes. The LRSN is written along with each log record. In Figure RR.9 we assume that the current LRSN is 103,000, when the reorganization began. The first batch of log records to be applied to the shadow have LRSNs between of 103,000 and 103,500. These log records are applied to the shadow as the first incremental log apply. The next log record that applies to the reorganized tablespace has a LRSN of 104,000 and the REORG utility decides to end the batch of log records to be applied to the shadow with LRSN of 104,500, for example. These log records are applied to the shadow as the second incremental log apply. The third incremental log apply is the next range of LRSNs that identify log records that describe inserts, updates, and deletes on the original tablespace. These log records are applied to the shadow. The process continues until all inserts, updates, and deletes written to the original tablespace are applied to the shadow.

The LRSN range depends on the REORG maximum read-only (MAXRO) parameter. The MAXRO is the maximum number of seconds that the original data can be in read-only (RO) mode during the last iteration. (This maximum can be exceeded depending on factors to be discussed.) REORG updates the shadow from the log when it estimates that the work can be done within the specified

MAXRO time, which is 300 seconds by default. Data manager (DM) tracks the number of updates within the range of the old and new LRSN.

Last Iteration of the Log Apply

Writers are drained during the last iteration of updates to the shadow. New writers are queued during the drain process and update of the shadow. Utilities wait 6-18 minutes by default to complete a drain, depending on how many of the 3 claim classes are active. It is advisable to have the active log large enough to contain logs records written during the reorganization. This will avoid delays of going to archive logs.

Pages updated on the shadow are appended to the image copy taken during the reorganization processing, resulting in a single data set. This is an incremental copy taken during the last iteration and appended to the original copy. The complete copy can be used as input to the RECOVER TOCOPY utilities discussed in Chapter CR.

Completing the Process

If DB2 estimates that all remaining log records can be applied to the shadow within the MAXRO time, this signifies the last iteration of the log records. Switch processing occurs after the last iteration. No access is allowed during switch processing. This is accomplished by draining all readers and writers from the original data.

The shadow tablespace and indexes are renamed to the original names of the objects (not including the logical part of NPIs). Processing is switched over to the renamed objects. Updated pages are appended to the copy, which provides for a point-in-time of recovery. The original data sets are deleted when using storage groups. You are responsible for deleting data sets when using user defined data sets.

The time required for switch processing depends on the number of readers and writers that must be drained, their commit frequency, and the number of data sets to be renamed.

FASTSWITCH parameter alternative (V7): The use of this parameter causes the REORG utility to update the catalog to reference the newly reorganized data sets. The data sets themselves are not renamed. Rather the reorganization utility alternates the I0001 and J0001 node of the data set name in the catalog tables. (Data set naming conventions are discussed in Chapter CD Section 1.) This reduces the time for switch processing which is particular significant for a large number of objects including partitioned tablespaces and index.

Switch processing applies to SHRLEVEL of CHANGE and REFERENCE.

Do avoid heavy update activity during the instant between processing the last increment of updates and the drain of all claim classes. For example, avoid submitting a batch update program during the last phase or allowing the last phase to be executing at 9:00 A.M. with a rush of online updates coming in. Once the switch processing begins, REORG continues processing without looking at the parameters to be discussed. This can result in data being unavailable longer than MAXRO seconds.

The DISPLAY UTILITY command can be executed to provides information on the processing as will be discussed.

Do be cautious of a failed member in a sysplex environment having restart pending on the target page set. The drain processing will fail. The -DB1G DISPLAY GROUP command provides information on the member and -DB1G DISPLAY DATABASE with the LOCKS parameter shows held locks.

Reorganization of a partition with NPI: If you are reorganizing a partition with NPIs, it is necessary to update the original NPI RIDs during the BUILD2 phase to reference rows in the shadow based on a mini index of the logical part that has been built. No access is allowed using the logical part of the NPI during this lengthy process. You can access data using the partitioning index, limited partition scan, and tablespace scan. Contention can result when updating NPIs from multiple concurrent reorganizations of multiple parts. This applies to SHRLEVEL CHANGE and REFERENCE.

RR.13 PARAMETERS FOR CONTROLLING ITERATIVE LOG APPLY

There are a number of parameters for controlling iterative log apply for a reorganization with SHRLEVEL CHANGE (not NONE and REFERENCE). The DEADLINE parameter can be used with SHRLEVEL REFERENCE.

DEADLINE Parameter

The DEADLINE parameter provides for specifying a labeled duration (V5 APAR) or an absolute time when REORG is terminated if it has not begun the switch processing to the shadow. The time must be a time beyond when REORG started processing. DEADLINE NONE can be specified which means that there is no deadline. This is the default. The REORG utility is terminated if the utility estimates that processing cannot be completed by the deadline. REORG issues a -DISPLAY UTILITY command before it terminates to provide information on its progress before the termination. After the termination, the original data continues to be used without any effect of a reorganization.

Recommendation: Specification of a labeled duration using the CURRENT DATE or CURRENT TIMESTAMP special registers is a good choice compared to specifying an absolute time when REORG is terminated. It allows for setting the time such that the utility statement need not be changed each time the utility is executed. For example, if you require that the reorganization always complete within 1 day, 2 hours, and 30 minutes, the parameter can be specified like:

```
DEADLINE CURRENT DATE + 1 DAY + 2 HOURS + 30 MINUTES
```

MAXRO Parameter

The MAXRO parameter provides for specifying the maximum allowable seconds (300 by default) that RO access to the page set is allowed. An option is to specify MAXRO DEFER which means the switch processing is deferred indefinitely or until an action is taken to cause the switch, -ALTER

UTILITY for example. This allows you to choose when to do the switch. Indeed, the shadow can be used as a hot standby.

The MAXRO seconds that you specify determines the number of updates that can be done before applying them to the shadow and the size of the LRSN range as discussed in the previous section. A small value reduces the time data cannot be updated but increases reorganization time. A very large value makes it likely that REORG will complete during the next iteration.

Recommendation: Consider using DB2 Estimator to estimate the time to do a reorganization and use this estimate as a guideline for specifying the MAXRO value. DB2 Estimator V5 estimated 305 seconds to reorganize one million rows with five indexes and SHRLEVEL NONE in one case.

DELAY, LONGLOG, DRAIN, and TIMEOUT Parameters

If the number of log records that the next iteration will process is not sufficiently lower than the number of log records processed in the previous iteration, the shadow copy cannot be updated as fast as the original tablespace. The message DSNU377I is written to the operator (WTO) console regarding the condition. Processing continues for the number of seconds specified with the DELAY parameter.

The DELAY parameter provides for specifying the number of seconds (1200 default) to wait before taking the action specified using the LONGLOG parameter after message DSNU377I is written to console.

The LONGLOG parameter is used to specify the action to take if REORG is not catching up on log processing. The action can be CONTINUE, DRAIN, or TERM. CONTINUE means that the reorganization continues and is the default. DRAIN means that the write class will be drained, all remaining log records will be applied, and switch processing is done after the DELAY time. TERM means that REORG will be terminated after the DELAY time. The LONGLOG parameter is ignored when the next iteration is estimated to be less than or equal to MAXRO, the -ALTER UTILITY or -TERM UTILITY is executed, or REORG terminates for any reason.

LONGLOG CONTINUE is a good choice when using the MAXRO DEFER parameter. It avoid DRAIN and DELAY parameter processing.

The DRAIN parameter controls when writers and readers are drained (V5 APAR PQ20032). The use of the WRITERS (default) with the DRAIN parameter causes a drain of writers during the log phase when MAXRO is reached and a drain all during the switch phase. This provides for early and frequent drains of writers. It minimizes drain processing during the switch phase. The use of ALL with the DRAIN parameter causes all writers and readers to be drained during the switch phase. This is useful in minimizing -911 SQLCODEs with high update activity during the log phase. Writers are not drained when MAXRO is reached (does drain all during the switch phase). DRAIN applies to SHRLEVEL CHANGE of REORG (not SHRLEVEL NONE and REFERENCE).

The TIMEOUT parameter is used to specify the action to take if while draining objects during the log or switch phase and a timeout occurs (V5 APAR PQ18941). TERM causes the utility to be terminated (implicit -TERM UTILITY) with a return code of 8, issues the DSNU590I and DSNU170I messages, and leaves the objects in RW mode. This is a good choice. ABEND causes the utility to abend and leaves objects in UTRO or UTUT mode which is the default. The object is left in UTRO if the abend occurs during last log iteration phase or UTUT if during the switch phase.

A timeout can occur if a cursor defined WITH HOLD is open on an object in the tablespace during the last log iterations or switch phase.

Getting Information on Reorganization

The -DISPLAY UTILITY command provides useful information to determine what to do if REORG is not catching up. Figure RR.10 shows an example of displaying the progress of an online reorganization of the SPJ tablespace.

Figure RR.10. Results of -DISPLAY UTILITY(REORGSPJ)

```
DSNU105  . DSNUGDIS  - USERID = SYSADM 973
                MEMBER =
                UTILID = REORGSPJ
                PROCESSING UTILITY STATEMENT 1
                UTILITY = REORG
                PHASE = LOG   COUNT = n
                STATUS = ACTIVE
DSNU347I  . DSNUGDIS  - 974
                DEADLINE = 1996-04-02-08.30.00.000000
DSNU384I  . DSNUGDIS  - 975
                MAXRO = 300 SECONDS
                LONGLOG = CONTINUE
                DELAY = 1200 SECONDS
DSNU383I  . DSNUGDIS  - CURRENT ITERATION NUMBER = 4 976
WRITE ACCESS ALLOWED IN THIS ITERATION = YES
ITERATION BEFORE PREVIOUS ITERATION:
   ELAPSED TIME = hh:mm:ss
   NUMBER OF LOG RECORDS PROCESSED = nnnnnn
PREVIOUS ITERATION:
   ELAPSED TIME = hh:mm:ss
   NUMBER OF LOG RECORDS PROCESSED = nnnnnn
CURRENT ITERATION:
   ELAPSED TIME = hh:mm:ss
   ACTUAL ELAPSED TIME SO FAR = hh:mm:ss
   ACTUAL NUMBER OF LOG RECORDS BEING PROCESSED = nnnnnn
CURRENT ESTIMATE FOR NEXT ITERATION:
   ELAPSED TIME = hh:mm:ss
   NUMBER OF LOG RECORDS TO BE PROCESSED = nnnnnn
DSN90221  . DSNUGCCC '-DIS UTI' NORMAL COMPLETION
```

The display utility report shows the current values for the parameters that control an online reorganization. Notice in the middle of the report, we see the current values for DEADLINE, MAXRO, LONGLOG, and DELAY. The elapsed time and number of log records processed for several iterations and an estimate for the next iteration will prove useful to you in determining whether the reorganization should be allowed to continue, all remaining log records should be applied, or the utility should be terminated. Indeed, it is this information that is used by the REORG utility to determine if the DSNU3771 message should be written to the console.

What to Do If REORG Is Not Catching Up

A number of actions can be taken after the DSNU3771 message is written to the console and before the DELAY time expires. The -ALTER UTILITY command can be issued to change the MAXRO, LONGLOG, DELAY, and DEADLINE parameters. If some of the parameters are not specified, the defaults are used for the unspecified parameters. Parameter changes take effect after the currently effective DELAY time. Here is an example of altering all of the parameters.

```
-ALTER UTILITY (REORGSPJ) REORG
   MAXRO 600
   LONGLOG DRAIN
   DELAY 2400
   DEADLINE 1997-06-30-08.00.00.000000
```

A very large value for MAXRO causes the next iteration to be the last assuming that the value is large enough for all of the log records to be applied within the specified time. LONGLOG DRAIN forces final processing, you can continue the iterative log apply, or you can terminate the utility and revert to the original data that has not been reorganized. You can increase the DELAY time to allow for more time to do an analysis and make a decision as to the disposition of the reorganization.

There are additional alternatives for dealing with a situation where the log apply is not catching up. The -START DATABASE (DASPJDB) SPACENAM (PTSP) ACCESS (RO) command followed by executing the QUIESCE utility to drain the write claim class disallows additional updates so that the log apply can catch up. After REORG has had some time to catch up, you can start the database with ACCESS(RW) to allow others to continue their update processing of the original data. Scheduling priorities of the reorganization and application programs can be adjusted to increase the chances of REORG being able to catch up on the log processing. The amount of buffer space allocated to REORG can be increased and the amount allocated to applications can be decreased. You also have the option of issuing the -TERM UTILITY (REORGSPJ) command to terminate the utility. However, keep in mind that REORG with SHRLEVEL CHANGE is not restartable in most cases.

Restartability of REORG

The restartability of the reorganization depends on whether REORG INDEX or REORG TABLESPACE is executed, the SHRLEVEL parameter specified, and the availability of required data sets. Data set availability depends on several parameters discussed in Section RR.15. Figure RR.11 summarizes these factors by phase of the REORG utility and whether the utility is restartable during each phase.

Figure RR.11. Restartability of REORG by phase

PHASE	REORG INDEX	SHRLEVEL NONE	SHRLEVEL REFERENCE	SHRLEVEL CHANGE	Data Sets Required
UNLOAD	Current Phase	Current Phase	Current Phase	None	SYSREC
RELOAD		Current Phase	Current Phase	None	SYSREC SYSUT1
SORT	Current Phase	Current Phase	Current Phase	None	SYSUT1
BUILD	Current Phase	Current Phase	Current Phase	None	SORTOUT
LOG				None	
SWITCH			Current Phase	Current Phase	Originals and shadows
BUILD2			Current Phase	Current Phase	Shadows for NPI

RR.14 DIFFERENT SHRLEVELs AND UPDATE ACTIVITY TEST RESULTS

IBM did a number of tests comparing reorganization with difference SHRLEVELS, and simulating batch and online update activity during online reorganizations. These results are reported in the *DB2 for OS/390 Version 5 Performance Topics* manual, SG24-2213. We will review a few of the test results as input to your decision as to which SHRLEVEL should be used and the effect of reorganizations on the programs doing the updates. As always your results will vary depending on your data and environment.

The tests were done on a 5 million row table in 10 partitions, the table had a row length was 118 bytes with 26 columns, and there were 2 indexes on the table. Version 5 of the DB2 subsystem running on a 10-way RX3 9672 V0C and 3390 DASD were used in the tests.

Comparison of Different SHRLEVELs and Cluster Ratios

Figure RR.12 summarizes the test differences using SHRLEVEL of NONE, REFERENCE, and CHANGE when reorganizing the tablespace with a 100 and 83 percent cluster ratio. Notice that there were some increases in elapsed and CPU times when using SHRLEVEL of CHANGE with a 100 percent cluster ratio. The increase was much more significant when reorganizing the tablespace with a cluster ratio of 83 percent. As would be expected, the reorganization costs increase with the increased availability of data and a decrease in cluster ratio.

Figure RR.12. REORG tablespace with 3 SHRLEVELS and 2 cluster ratios

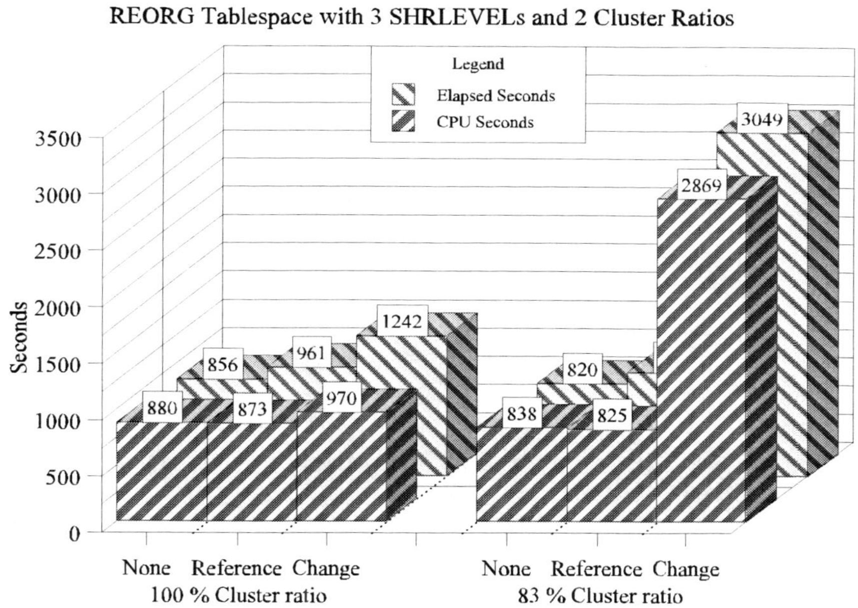

Online Reorganization with Concurrent Batch Updates

It is expected that updates executed during an online reorganization will delay the process. The question is to what degree. A batch job that updates a table with a cluster ratio of 83 percent was submitted after the REORG utility unloaded the data. The program updated the data sequentially and did not update the indexed columns.

Figure RR.13 shows an almost linear increase in elapsed and CPU times as the number of rows updated by the batch program increased from no updates to updating 5 million rows in increments of 1 million updates. Indeed, about 300 CPU and 400 elapsed seconds were required for each 1 million rows updated. This increase is due to the interactive log apply of the online reorganization.

Figure RR.13. REORG tablespace with concurrent updates

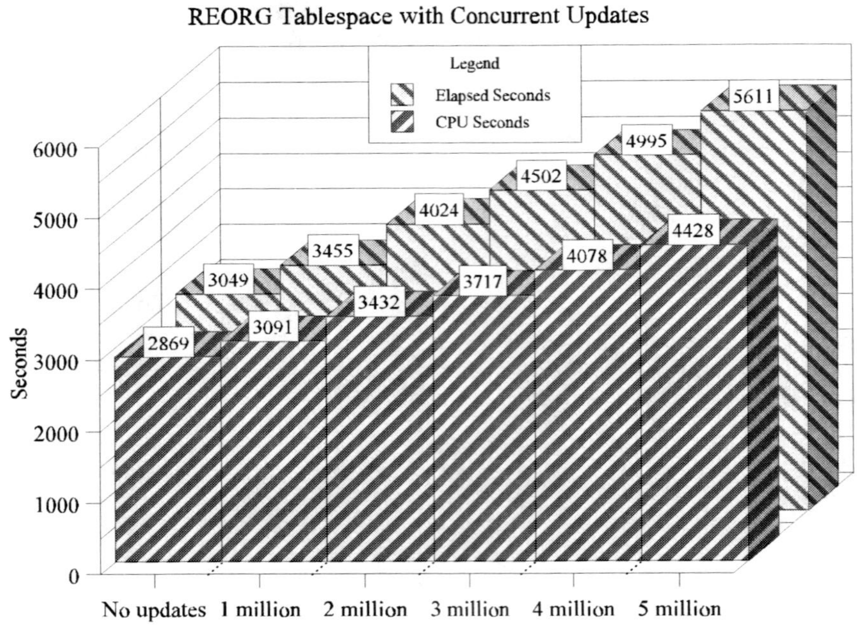

Online Reorganization with Concurrent Online Inserts

Online activity during online reorganizations was simulated by submitting 25 programs each of which inserted 10,000 rows into an eleventh partition that already had 2.5 million rows with a cluster ratio of 83 percent. The first test was to establish a base line by doing an online reorganization with no concurrent updates. The second test was to submit the 25 insert programs after the REORG utility had unloaded the data, and the third test was to have the 25 insert programs inserting rows during the time that REORG was unloading the data. It can be seen from the three tests results summarized in Figure RR.14. that the reorganization elapsed and CPU times increased substantially with the 25 programs inserting rows after the utility had unloaded the data. There was a little higher increase when the 25 insert programs were executing during the unload of the data (right most pair of bars) due in part to the I/O contention of REORG unloading the data while the application programs were inserting rows. Some of the increase in elapsed and CPU times can be attributed to the REORG utility having to reorganize and copy (inline copy) 250,000 more rows than in the base line test with no insert activity during the reorganization. Also the 2 indexes had to be updated to reference the 250,000 rows inserted by the application programs.

Figure RR.14. Reorganization with and without concurrent updates

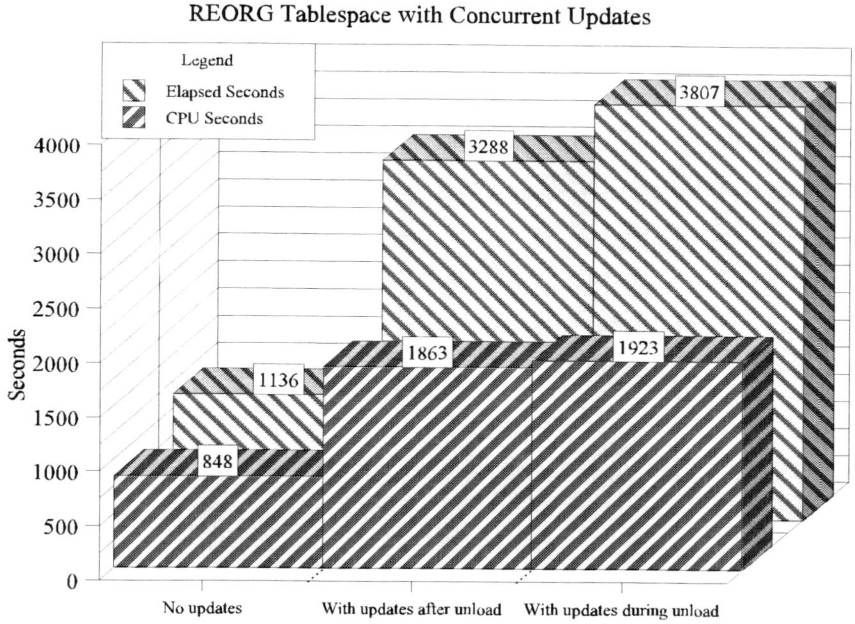

Recommendation: Do execute the REORG utility during low insert, update, and delete activity to achieve lower elapsed and CPU time (left most pair of bars in Figure RR.14.

Effect on Online Insert Activity

Tests were done to measure the effect of online reorganization on the 25 online insert programs executing concurrently with the reorganization. The elapsed and CPU times were measured for each of the 25 programs. Figure RR.15 shows the times of the first, middle, and last of the 25 programs which are representative of all 25 programs. The measurements were done for each of the 25 program with no concurrent reorganization, after REORG unloaded the data, and during the reorganization. There was some increase in elapsed time and even less of an increase in CPU time for the insert programs.

Figure RR.15. Online transactions executing with no reorganization, after unload, and during unload

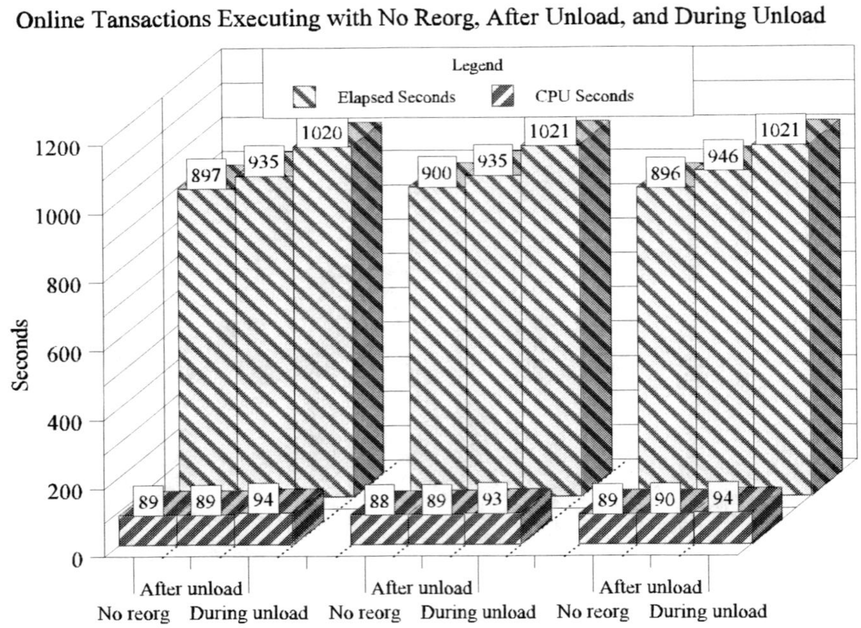

RR.15 PHASES OF REORG, SORTKEYS, AND NOSYSREC PARAMETERS

REORG with SHRLEVEL NONE and without SORTKEYS unloads data into the SYSREC data set as shown in Figure RR.16. Rows are written to the tablespace and indexed values are written to SYSUT1 during the reload phase. Indexed values not in sequence are sorted using SORTWKnn files and output to SORTOUT. Indexes are built from sorted indexed values in SORTOUT.

Figure RR.16. REORG phases with SHRLEVEL NONE and without SORTKEYS

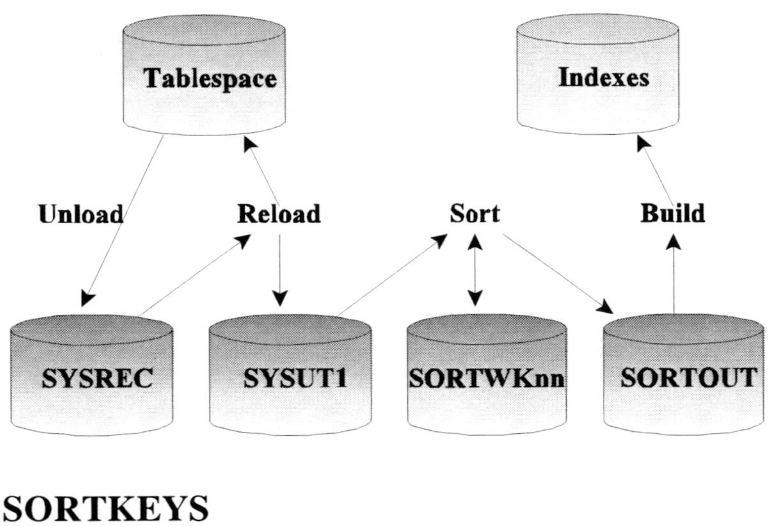

REORG with SORTKEYS

The use of SORTKEYS causes indexed values to be passed to an external sort (DFSORT by default) as the rows are reloaded into the tablespace (Figure RR.17). The sort begins in memory while the rows are being reloaded without first writing the indexed value to a sort data set (SYSUT1) as is done without the use of SORTKEYS. Runs (batches of sorted rows) from the sort are written to SORTWKnn data sets. The sort is executed as a subtask in parallel with the reload and build phases.

Sorted index values are passed to the build index phase. The indexes are built serially in V5. (Multiple indexes are built in parallel when using SORTKEYS in V6 as described in Chapter LC Section 3.) SYSUT1 and SORTOUT are not used when SORTKEYS is specified. This reduces the total elapsed time particularly when there are several indexes. This saves DASD space and reduces CPU and elapsed time. However, restart is from the RELOAD phase regardless of how restart is requested.

Figure RR.17. REORG phases with SHRLEVEL NONE and with SORTKEYS

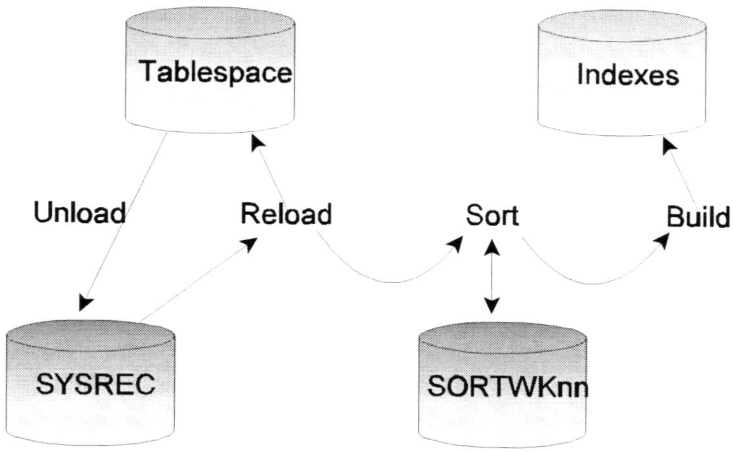

Here is an example of a REORG statement with the SORTKEYS and REUSE (discussed in Section LC.8) parameters:

```
REORG TABLESPACE DASPJDB.DASPJTSP
REUSE
SORTKEYS
```

Omitting the Output Data Set Using NOSYSREC

Use of the parameter NOSYSREC means that unloaded data is passed directly to the reload phase without writing to the unload data set (SYSREC). It is necessary to explicitly define a clustering index on each table in the tablespace. If there is no explicitly defined clustering index, rows are written to SYSREC and the data set is sorted even if NOSYSREC is specified.

REORG with SHRLEVEL REFERENCE and NOSYSREC improves performance. However, it is not possible to restart using data unloaded into SYSREC because NOSYSREC means that the rows are not written to SYSREC if there is an explicitly defined clustering index.

REORG with SHRLEVEL NONE and NOSYSREC also improves performance. However, it is not possible to restart because data is written back to the original tablespace. If you choose to use SHRLEVEL NONE and NOSYSREC, do make an image copy before the reorganization to allow for recover to the copy.

REORG with SHRLEVEL CHANGE operates as if using NOSYSREC, SORTKEYS, and SORTDATA parameters.

Comparison With and Without SORTKEYS and NOSYSREC

IBM test results of reorganizing a 5 million row table in 10 partitions with 118 byte rows and 26 columns, and 2 indexes using V5 on a 10-way RX3 9672 V0C and RAMAC DASD suggests that elapsed and CPU times are reduced the most with the use of SORTKEYS and NOSYSREC as summarized in Figure RR.18. There is also a good reduction in elapsed and CPU times when using SORTKEYS without NOSYSREC compared to when not using SORTKEYS and NOSYSREC.

Figure RR.18. REORG with and without SORTKEYS and NOSYSREC

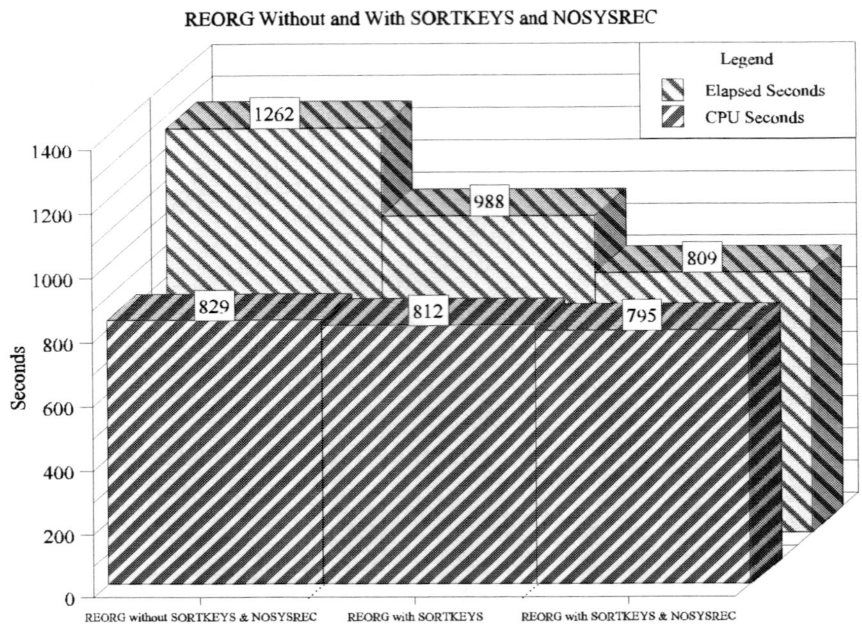

RR.16 HOW REORG UNLOADS AND RELOADS DATA AND SORTS

How REORG unloads and reloads data depends on whether the tablespace is segmented or nonsegmented and whether or not SORTDATA is used.

Segmented Tablespace without SORTDATA

When you reorganize a segmented tablespace and do not specify the SORTDATA parameter, each table is unloaded individually in sequence using the clustering index leaf pages. That is, the clustering index leaf pages are read with the indexed values in sequence and the RIDs following theindexed values are used to locate the rows on the data pages in sequence. Each table is reloaded in clustering sequence. Each table's segments are in contiguous space.

If there is no explicitly defined clustering index, rows are unloaded in the physical order of segment blocks with the space map pages used to locate segments. The data is not loaded in clustering sequence. All segments of a table are contiguous after the reload.

Nonsegmented Tablespace without SORTDATA

If there is one table in the tablespace, rows are unloaded in sequence using the clustering index leaf pages. If there is more than one table in a nonsegmented tablespace, the data is not reclustered. This is because data is unloaded with a tablespace scan and the rows are not sorted.

Indexes are rebuilt from the indexed values extracted during the reload of the data. Values are not sorted if they are already in sequence, that is, if the values were extracted from sequenced rows.

SORTDATA Parameter and Processing

The SORTDATA parameter has significant performance advantages. It results in a tablespace scan to unload the data and passes the data directly to an external sort via a sort exit. This avoids scanning the leaf pages and pulling the rows off in sequence. This reduces seek time and avoids processing a data page multiple times to pull rows off in sequence. In addition, clustering is restored for multiple tables in all types of tablespaces if a clustering index is declared.

Test results gave 20 percent less elapsed time with a 95 percent cluster ratio and 74 percent less elapsed time with an 80 percent cluster ratio. About the only indicated disadvantage of using SORTDATA was when the cluster ratio was 100 percent, 4 percent more elapsed time was required in the test. Of course, it is very doubtful that the tablespace needs to be reorganized with a very high cluster ratio.

Here is an example of a REORG statement using the SORTDATA parameter.

```
REORG TABLESPACE DASPJDB.DASPJTSP
SHRLEVEL NONE
LOG NO -- Do follow reorg with an image copy
SORTDATA
SORTDEVT SYSDA
SORTNUM 6
```

The SORTDATA parameter is ignored if there is no explicitly defined clustering index.

Sort Work Space for REORG

SORTDEVT or DD statements for sort work space are required. The sort work data sets are used to sort data and indexes if SORTDATA is specified. If SORTDATA is not specified, the data sets are used to sort indexed values before the build of the indexes. SORTNUM is the number of sort work data sets required. If this parameter is not specified, DFSORT uses its defaults.

If SORTDATA is specified, DB2 estimates the number of rows to be sorted. The estimate is doubled if compression is used on the tablespace. The estimate is passed to DFSORT using the FILSZ parameter. If VARCHAR is used, the estimate can be low. You can estimate the space and allocate it with SORTWKnn DD statements or the following JCL statements can be used to specify the file size in hexadecimal.

```
//DFSPART DD *
  OPTION FILSZ=E005000
/*
```

Do estimate the sort space for indexes using formula and volume separation as discussed for the LOAD utility and build of indexes. If insufficient sort space is provided, REORG abends.

Estimate Space for SYSREC

You need to estimate the space for SYSREC assuming that you plan to unload the data into SYSREC. This estimate depends on whether rows are fixed or variable length. If the rows are fixed length, the estimate can be calculated as the number of rows times (6 + the record length). If the rows are variable in length, the estimate can be calculated as the number of rows times (6 + the maximum record length) or the number of rows times (6 + the average record length).

Sort of Indexed Values and RIDs by REORG

REORG of a unique index never sorts indexed values. Values are extracted in sequence and only one RID follows a value. Further, if values are extracted in sequence, REORG tablespace, REORG index, LOAD, and RECOVER do not sort indexed values.

Exception: Reorganization of a non-unique index (not tablespace) always sorts the indexed values and RIDs. The utility developers assume that no one would reorganize a perfectly organized index (all values are in sequence and all RIDs following a value are in sequence). This saves the CPU time to check if the values are in sequence.

RR.17 REORG WITH INLINE COPY

An inline image copy of a tablespace (not indexes) can be made during a reorganization. The copy is made asynchronously as the reorganization is performed. This avoids passing the data again after the reorganization to make a full image copy. The use of inline image copy avoids the copy pending state being set on with LOG of YES or NO. There are likely to be some duplicate pages at the end of the copy, assuming that others are updating the data while the copy is being made. The last page is the most current. The inline image copy is logically equivalent to a full image copy made with SHRLEVEL REFERENCE as discussed in Chapter CR. The COPYDDN and optionally the RECOVERYDDN statement must be specified to make up to two local and two remote copies of the tablespace as discussed in Chapter CR. Here is an example of a REORG statement that will make one local and one remote copy.

```
REORG TABLESPACE DASPJDB.DASPJTSP
COPYDDN      (DDNSPJ)
RECOVERYDDN (DDNSPJR) -- optional
```

Figure RR.19 summarizes some tests run by IBM doing a reorganization of a 5 million row table in 10 partitions, 118 byte row with 26 columns, and 2 indexes using V5 on a 10-way RX3 9672 V0C and RAMAC DASD.

Figure RR.19. Comparison of REORG followed by a copy, with an inline copy and not including a copy

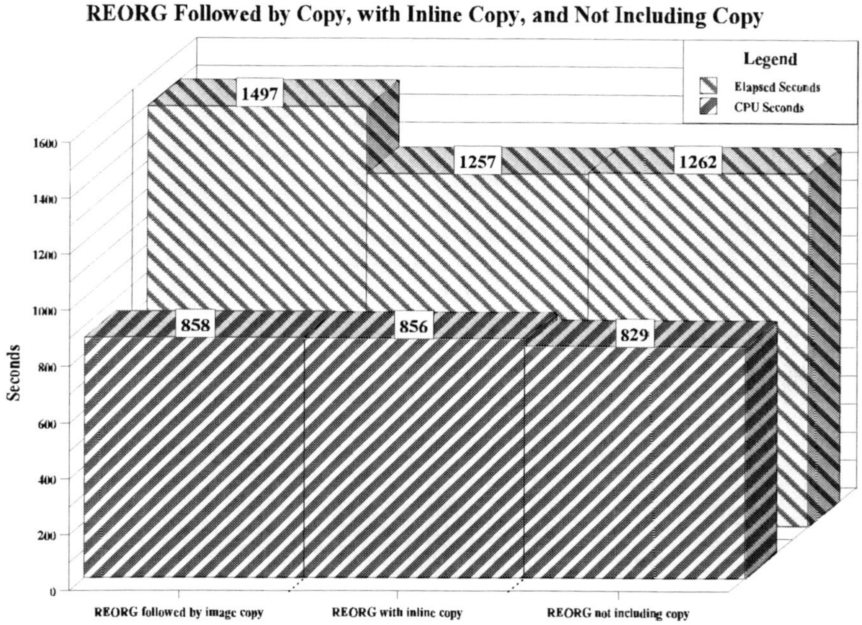

Notice from the test results that the REORG followed by an image copy required the most elapsed time while the REORG with an inline copy and with no copy required about the same amount of elapsed time. There was not a dramatic difference in CPU time in all three cases.

RR.18 REORG WITH INLINE STATISTICS (V6)

The statistics collected by RUNSTATS can be collected inline while doing a reorganization. The STATISTICS parameter must be coded on the utility statement (not the default). Optionally, you can specify the same parameters that are used to collect a variety of statistics with RUNSTATS. These parameters can be used along with the STATISTICS parameter to collect additional statistics over and above the default statistics.

Following is an example REORG statement that collects all statistics that can be collected by RUNSTATS. The STATISTICS and related parameters can also be specified on the LOAD and REBUILD INDEX utilities. In all cases, if a utility is restarted, the statistics are not recorded in the catalog tables. It is necessary to submit RUNSTATS to collect and record the statistics.

```
REORG TABLESPACE DASPJDB.DASPJTSP
  STATISTICS
    TABLE (SPJ) COLUMN (ALL)
      SAMPLE 25
    UPDATE ALL
    INDEX (ALL)
    KEYCARD
      FREQVAL NUMCOLS 1 COUNT 15
      FREQVAL NUMCOLS 2 COUNT 25
      FREQVAL NUMCOLS 3 COUNT 35
    REPORT YES
```

If only the STATISTICS parameter is specified without the requesting specific additional statistics over and above the default statistics, it is as if the following statement is coded. The optional parameters are made into comments by specifying '--' in front of the parameters. These statistics are not collected by default.

```
REORG TABLESPACE DASPJDB.DASPJTSP
  STATISTICS
  --TABLE (SPJ) COLUMN (ALL)
  --   SAMPLE 25
    UPDATE ALL
    INDEX (ALL)
  --KEYCARD
  --   FREQVAL NUMCOLS 1 COUNT 15
  --   FREQVAL NUMCOLS 2 COUNT 25
  --   FREQVAL NUMCOLS 3 COUNT 35
  --REPORT YES
```

Recommendation: The guidelines for the frequency of collecting inline statistics with REORG and REBUILD INDEX are similar to those suggested for the frequency of executing RUNSTATS discussed in Section RR.3. Do specify the parameters of all optional statistics that you require. Otherwise, fewer statistics are collected than what might be expected. Also you will not receive a hardcopy of the statistics collected and recorded in the catalog tables without the REPORT YES parameter.

RR.19 REORG WITH KEEPDICTIONARY AND PART

The use of the KEEPDICTIONARY parameter has performance advantages when reorganizing data compressed with ESA compression. This is because it is not necessary to recompress data when the data is reloaded and the dictionary is not rebuilt. Data is decompressed when the data is unloaded so that indexed values can be extracted. Overriding the default of rebuilding and recompressing the data with the KEEPDICTIONARY parameter is a good choice if the characteristics of the data have not changed with respect to compression. It often results in significantly reduced CPU costs. However, a compression report is not generated to determine if the dictionary should be rebuilt and the data recompressed.

It is necessary to monitor SYSTABLEPART.PAGESAVE after executing RUNSTATS to determine if the dictionary needs to be rebuilt. If PAGESAVE decreases with update activity, the dictionary should be rebuilt and the data recompressed which is the default when the KEEPDICTIONARY parameter is not specified.

Here is an example of reorganizing the DASPJTSP in the DASPJDB using the existing dictionary.

```
REORG TABLESPACE DASPJDB.DASPJTSP
KEEPDICTIONARY
PART 4
```

Optionally you can specify a partition or range of partitions with or without compression. In the above example, the PART 4 parameter instructs the REORG utility to reorganize only the fourth data and index partition. If there are NPIs, the RIDs in logical part 4 are updated in place which increases the costs of the reorganization.

RR.20 Unloading Data Using REORG

REORG can be used to unload rows for refreshing test data after updates, transporting data from one DB2 subsystem to another, to load data into a restructured table, and more.

The UNLOAD CONTINUE parameter means that the reorganization utility should continue its processing after unloading the data and the unloaded data is not retained beyond the reorganization. This is the default. Here is an example of specifying the parameter:

```
REORG TABLESPACE DASPJDB.DASPJTSP
UNLOAD ONLY
SORTDATA
```

The UNLOAD ONLY parameter can be used to cause the unload data to be saved in a file. However, the unloaded data can be loaded only into the same object from which it is unloaded. The data is saved in an internal format which makes it difficult to develop a program to read the file. Indeed, LOAD must be informed that its input file contains data in an internal format by specifying the parameter FORMAT UNLOAD to accept the unloaded data

The UNLOAD EXTERNAL parameter causes the data to be unloaded in an external format that can be loaded into any table and read easily by a program (V5 APAR PQ19897) . Following is an example REORG statement to unload rows from a named table only if the rows meet certain conditions as specified in the WHEN clause.

```
REORG TABLESPACE DASPJDB.DASPJTSP
UNLOAD EXTERNAL
FROM TABLE AUTHID.SPJ
WHEN (JN = 'J5' OR JN = 'J7')
SHRLEVEL NONE
```

The unloaded records are decompressed if compression is used on the tablespace. SMALLINT, INTEGER, FLOAT, and DECIMAL are converted from DB2 internal format to OS/390 format. VARCHAR data is padded to its full length when written to the file by default. The NOPAD parameter can be used to avoid the padding. However, if a host program is to read the unloaded data, it must be prepared to deal with a varying length field. If the data is stored in EBCDIC format, it is written to the file in the same format. If the data is stored in ASCII format it is written to the file in the same format. EDITPROC and FIELDPROC processing is performed (VALIDPROC is ignored).

The WHEN clause can be used to specify simple conditions under which the rows are to be unloaded. The conditions that can be specified are similar to those specified in a WHERE clause including the operators:

=, <, <=, >, >=, ¬=, ¬>, ¬<, IS NULL, IS NOT NULL, LIKE and NOT LIKE

LIKE and NOT LIKE cannot be used on columns defined with a FIELDPROC.

The conditions can be combined with AND and OR to unload only rows that meet several conditions.

Safety net: If there is no WHEN clause, all records are unloaded when using the UNLOAD EXTERNAL parameter. In addition, only rows from the named table are discarded in a multiple table tablespace.

A LOAD utility statement is generated for loading the data into any table. The statement is written to the DDNAME specified using the REORG PUNCHDDN parameter (SYSPUNCH is the default). EBCDIC, ASCII, SBCS, DBCS, mixed CCSIDs, etc. parameters are generated for the LOAD statement as required. A WHEN clause is included to allow for loading multiple tables in a tablespace. Do customize the generated statements based on your requirements and the guidelines discussed in Chapter LC.

The SHRLEVEL NONE (not CHANGE or REFERENCE) parameter must be specified when using UNLOAD EXTERNAL. Therefore, it is not possible to select and update rows during REORG unload external.

Caution: If there is more than one table in the named tablespace, all rows in the tables not named in the FROM clause are unloaded. This is because there is no WHEN clause on the other tables.

Unloading Rows Using DSNTIAUL

DSNTIAUL is a frequently used sample assembler batch program to unload data before the UNLOAD EXTERNAL functionality was added to DB2 in 1998. REORG has performance advantages over the sample program as indicated by IBM test result of 78 CPU and 97 elapsed seconds for DSNTIAUL to unload 1 million rows with 10 columns each defined as DECIMAL with significantly less resources for REORG UNLOAD at 11 CPU and 22 elapsed seconds for REORG UNLOAD. Details of tests are in *DB2 UDB for OS/390 Version 6 Performance Topics*, SG24-5351 manual.

DSNTIAUL does have advantages in that data can be unloaded based on the WHERE clause of a SELECT statement, join of multiple tables, subselects, calculations in expression, based on a view definition, and using an access path chosen by the optimizer (use of an index, for example). (REORG does not use an index to unload the data.) The program is in prefix.SDSNSAMP library along with sample JCL in the DSNTEJ2A member. Figure RR.20 contains an example of JCL to execute DSNTIAUL.

Figure RR.20. Sample JCL to execute DSNTIAUL

```
//EXTRACT  JOB ... USER=AUTHID
//*
//STEP1     EXEC PGM=IKJEFT1B,DYNAMNBR=30
//STEPLIB  DD   DSN=DSN610.SDSNLOAD,DISP=SHR
//SYSPRINT DD   SYSOUT=A
//SYSTSPRT DD   SYSOUT=A
//SYSUDUMP DD   SYSOUT=A
//SYSOUT   DD   SYSOUT=A
//REPORT   DD   SYSOUT=A
//PARMIN   DD   DSN=PARMIN.FILE
//*
//SYSTSIN  DD   *
DSN SYSTEM(DB2T)
RUN PROGRAM(DSNTIAUL) PLAN(DSNTIB61) -
    LIBRARY('DSN610.RUNLIB.LOAD') PARM('SQL')
END
/*
//SYSIN    DD *
  SELECT SN, SNAME, CITY
  FROM   S
  WHERE  CITY = 'Copenhagen';
//*
```

The data to be unloaded can be described using a SELECT statement. Do use PARM('SQL') to allow for specifying a SELECT statement as you would when using SPUFI or QMF. If the blocking factor is not specified on the DD statement, DSNTIAUL computes the block size.

DSNTIAUL generates LOAD statements but does not include many of the parameters that can be included by REORG ... UNLOAD EXTERNAL.

RR.21 Deleting Rows During a Reorganization

The reorganization utility can be used to efficiently delete rows that meet specified conditions during the reorganization process (V5 APAR PQ19897). This is done by specifying the DISCARD parameter, the table from which to delete the rows, and conditions under which to delete the rows like:

```
REORG TABLESPACE DASPJDB.DASPJTSP
DISCARD
FROM TABLE AUTHID.SPJ
WHEN (JN = 'J5' AND QTY > 600)
```

Optionally, the discarded rows can be written in the external format to a file for archival purposes. The records are written to the DDNAME specified using the REORG DISCARDDN parameter (SYSDISC is the default). If no discard data set is specified in the JCL, discarded records are not written to a data set records will not be written to a data set. If records are discarded from a referential integrity (RI) structure, check pending is turned on if there can be a violation of RI as a result of deleting a row. The NOPAD parameter can be used as with UNLOAD EXTERNAL to avoid padding VARCHAR columns to their full length.

The WHEN clause is much like the WHEN clause used with the EXTERNAL LOAD parameter discussed in Section RR.19. Simple conditions (=, <, <=, >, >=, ¬=, ¬>, ¬<, IS NULL, IS NOT NULL, LIKE and NOT LIKE) combined with and OR conditions can be specified. WHEN clause constants must be specified in hexadecimal for tables defined as ASCII. If the WHEN condition is found to be true for a row, it is discarded. If there is no WHEN clause, no records are discarded when using the DISCARD parameter. This is a good feature that avoids accidentally discarding all rows in a table.

A LOAD control statement is generated similar to when using the EXTERNAL LOAD parameter. The statement can be used to load the discarded rows into any table from the discard data set. You will find this useful when populating an archival table.

SHRLEVEL NONE or REFERENCE (not CHANGE) must be specified to use discard processing. This means that other programs can read but not update data while deleting rows with the REORG utility. REORG DISCARD can be used with UNLOAD CONTINUE AND UNLOAD PAUSE (not UNLOAD ONLY and UNLOAD EXTERNAL).

Recommendation: REORG ... DISCARD has significant performance advantages over DELETEing rows followed by a reorganization. It avoids having to delete reference to the discarded rows from one or more indexes. There is little or no increase in the cost of a reorganization when using the DISCARD parameter, particularly if the discarded rows are not written to a discard data set. Indeed, the costs of the reorganization can be reduced because fewer rows must be reorganized and referenced in one or more indexes that are rebuilt with a reorganization of a tablespace.

RR.22 Use of REORG to Rebalance Altered Partitions (V6)

After ALTER INDEX has been used to modify the limit key for partitions, the tablespace is placed in reorg pending (REORP) status. No DML statements are allowed on tablespace until the status is removed. It is necessary to reorganize the altered partitions to remove REORG pending. Here is a statement to reorganize parts 4 through 6 assuming that the limit key has been altered for one or more of the partitions.

```
REORG TABLESPACE DAZIPDB.ZIPTSP PART 4:6
SHRLEVEL NONE - - required if REORG pending is on
SORTDATA
NOSYSREC
SORTKEYS
COPYDDN SYSCOPY
STATISTICS TABLE INDEX(ALL)
```

SHRLEVEL NONE is required if REORG pending is on. An image copy of reorganized partitions that were in REORG pending is required before any type of recovery is allowed. The COPYDDN SYSCOPY parameter is a good choice to ensure recoverability after rebalancing partitions.

If the limit key is reduced on the last partition of a tablespace where DSSIZE or LARGE has been specified, DISCARDDN and PUNCHDDN must be specified. DISCARDDN must be specified to receive rows that cannot be loaded with the new limit key if any. PUNCHDDN must be specified to receive the generated LOAD statement that can be used to reload discarded rows if required. If these data sets are not specified, message DSNU035I with return code of 8 is issued without a reorganization.

If the KEEPDICTIONARY parameter is specified, it is honored only for partitions that are not in REORG pending.

RR.22 REORG INDEX

All indexes on a nonpartitioned tablespace are rebuilt when a tablespace is reorganized. Optionally, you can specify that only named indexes or partitions are to be reorganized. The following statement cause partition 4 of the AUTHID.SPJX index to be reorganized. It uses the REUSE parameter discussed in Section LC.8.

```
REORG INDEX AUTHID.SPJX PART 4
REUSE
```

The reorganization of only the indexes frequently has greater impact on performance than reorganizing a tablespace and its indexes in a number of cases. If you have mostly transaction processing and you are processing only a few rows with matching scans and most of your heavy insert activity is at the end of a table, consider reorganizing the indexes frequently and reorganizing the tablespace less frequently. If the tablespace is compressed, you have another advantage of reorganizing only the indexes. This is because the rows need not be decompressed and recompressed irrespective of the KEEPDICTIONARY parameter. Rather only the uncompressed leaf pages are scanned and the indexes rebuilt.

Reorganizing the indexes on the catalog tables and directory improves performance primarily when selecting from the catalog tables. In most cases, DB2 does not use the catalog table indexes for internal processing. It is particularly important to keep the indexes on the directory tables that contains plans and packages well organized so that they can be located efficiently when executed.

The reorganization of an entire NPI is described in the Chapter LC Section 3.

Indicators to Determine REORG INDEX Requirements

There are two primary factors in addition to the factors that suggest a reorganization of the tablespace as discussed in Section RR.9 that suggest indexes need to be reorganized. Both of these factors, leaf page distance and an increase in the number of levels in the index, are a result of page splitting as discussed in Chapter ID.

LEAFDIST: The leaf distance is calculated by RUNSTATS based on the number of gaps between what should be contiguous leaf pages divided by the number of contiguous pages and recorded in the SYSINDEXES.LEAFDIST. Gaps can be free pages, nonleaf pages, deleted pages, and split pages, for example.

Figure RR.21 is an example of 15 leaf pages with 4 gaps. Four pages are interspersed between what should be 15 contiguous active leaf pages (SYSINDEXES.NLEAF contains the number of leaf pages). The LEAFDIST is calculated as the number of gaps divided by the number of leaf pages times 100. In the example, the LEAFDIST is 27 ((4 / 15) * 100).

Figure RR.21. Example of gaps within leaf pages

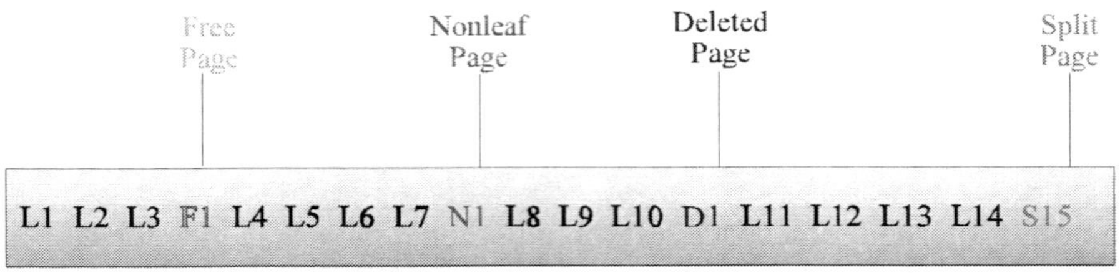

If the LEAFDIST is greater than 200, consider reorganizing the index. The following SELECT statement can be used to identify all indexes with a LEAFDIST greater than 200.

```
SELECT IXCREATOR, IXNAME, LEAFDIST
FROM   SYSIBM.SYSINDEXPART
WHERE  LEAFDIST > 200;
```

The LEAFDISTLIMIT threshold parameter (V6) can be specified to REORG such that if the LEAFDIST exceeds the limit an index or partitioning index, the index is reorganized. The index is reorganized if the LEAFDIST is greater than 200 by default or the number specified with the parameter.

The LEAFDIST can be greater than zero after building an index with the REORG, LOAD, or RECOVER INDEX prior to V6 and REBUILD INDEX in V6. This is because free pages and nonleaf pages are included in the computation.

Recommendation: Do maintain a low LEAFDIST by reorganizing the indexes or the tablespace which causes the indexes to be reorganized as well. This improves performance for non-matching index scan, sequential and dynamic prefetch on the leaf pages, and index lookaside.

NLEVELS: The number of levels in an index is the number of getpages required to do a matching index scan and perhaps the number of I/O depending on the availability of pages in the buffer pool. RUNSTATS places the number of levels in an index in SYSINDEXES.NLEVELS. If NLEVELS is greater than the NLEVELS for an index right after it has been built, it is likely a great deal of page splitting has occurred as a result of insert and update activity. The index needs to be reorganized. If it is not feasible to compare NLEVELS before and after insert and update activity, the following statements are useful in determining indexes and index partitions that exceed 3 levels. It may be that some of the identified indexes are large and are at the minimum number of levels.

```
SELECT NAME, INDEXSPACE, NLEVELS
FROM   SYSIBM.SYSINDEXES
WHERE  NLEVELS > 3;

SELECT NAME, NLEVELS, PARTITION
FROM   SYSIBM.SYSINDEXSTATS
WHERE  NLEVELS > 3;
```

Another indication that an index needs to be reorganized is when the current number of leaf pages (SYSINDEXES.NLEAF) is greater than the number of leaf pages when the index was last built. If the difference is high, REORG INDEX is advisable.

If the LEAFDIST, NLEVELS, and NLEAF frequently increase, consider increasing the free space for the index if you have random insert, update, and delete activity. It may be necessary to reorganize the indexes more frequently than the tablespace, depending on the factors that suggest the need to reorganize the tablespace as discussed in Sections RR.9 and RR.10.

Comparison of Building Indexes with REORG and REBUILD

REORG INDEX has performance advantages over REBUILD INDEX (discussed in Chapter CR) if the elapsed time is acceptable and if the sum of leaf pages for the indexes to be reorganized are less than the number of data pages.

DB2 Estimator V5 was used to compare REORG and REBUILD INDEX on a million row table, 100 byte row length, and 3 indexes using a 9672 RX3 with 10 CPUs and 3390-1 DASD. The estimates in Figure RR.22 are in minutes:seconds.

Figure RR.22. Comparison of REORG INDEX and REBUILD INDEX

Utility	CPU	I/O	Elapsed
REORG INDEX T100.C1X UNLOAD CONTINUE SORTDATA	0:30.000	Not Applicable	0:33.333
REBUILD INDEX* (T100.C1X)	1:01.130	Not Applicable	1:19.828

*REBUILD INDEX and RECOVER INDEX are synonyms in V5

Notice that REORG INDEX is estimated to require about half as much CPU time as REBUILD INDEX, and the savings in elapsed time is even greater when using REORG INDEX. This is because REORG INDEX scans only the leaf pages and the rebuild processing is more efficient than REBUILD INDEX. REBUILD INDEX does a tablespace scan and extracts values for all indexes.

The elapsed time for building several indexes can be excessive because each index is built serially prior to V6. If you need to reduce the elapsed time, consider submitting a separate REBUILD INDEX job for each index. This allows multiple indexes to be built in parallel. It does requires a tablespace scan for each index which increases the CPU and elapsed times for each index rebuilt individually. However, the overall elapsed time for rebuilding several indexes is reduced.

RR.23 SUMMARY

Do execute RUNSTATS after loading data and before binding plans and packages. Consider collecting optional statistics to achieve better access paths and reduce the costs of executing SQL. However, it does increase the costs of executing RUNSTATS. The additional costs of collecting the additional statistics are frequently less than the costs of repeatedly executing SQL statements with a less than optimal access path. The use of SHRLEVEL CHANGE avoids taking locks and allows for SQL updates during the collection of statistics. Do analyze statistics before finalizing the schedule for production RUNSTATS, REORG, and REBIND.

Do reorganize a tablespace when data has lost a good deal of clustering, rows have overflowed to near or far pages, after heavy update activity, and after altering the primary and secondary quantities.

Do consider using SORTKEYS, inline copy, or LOG NO followed by an image copy. Use the appropriate SHRLEVEL parameter depending on availability and performance requirements. You may find that you can reorganize tablespaces less frequently and reorganize indexes more frequently to reduce costs and improve performance.

EXERCISES

1. Should RUNSTATS be executed after each reorganization in a production environment?

2. What is the advantage of using SHRLEVEL CHANGE rather than SHRLEVEL REFERENCE when executing RUNSTATS?

3. Is it necessary to specify a parameter to RUNSTATS in order to get a report of the statistics collected?

4. a) What statistics are collected when the TABLE parameter is specified with RUNSTATS?

b) What are the benefits of collecting these statistics?

5. a) What is the disadvantage of specifying the RUNSTATS TABLE parameter?

b) What are two approaches that can be used to reduce the impact of the disadvantage?

6. Is it necessary to collect the cardinalities of non-leading columns of a composite index if equal predicates are specified on all leading columns (no intermediate column is skipped) and the KEYCARD parameter is specified? Why?

7. Under what conditions should the KEYCARD be specified to RUNSTATS?

8. If the NUMCOLS and COUNT parameters are not specified to RUNSTATS, how are frequency statistics collected?

9. When should the REORG TABLESPACE utility be executed on a tablespace?

10. When should the REORG INDEX rather than the REORG TABLESPACE utility be executed on indexes?

11. What parameters are specified to cause a reorganization of a tablespace only if 20 percent or more of the rows have lost clustering and 10 percent or more of the rows have overflowed to near or far pages?

12. What parameter is specified to cause a reorganization of an index if many leaf pages have been split?

13. What parameter should be specified on the REORG TABLESPACE and/or REORG INDEX statements to cause the rows and/or index to be written back to the same data sets?

14. What parameter is specified to indicate that an online reorganization with read/write access by SQL statements during most of the reorganization process is required?

15. Which SHRLEVEL parameter values causes a shadow copy of the data and indexes to be made by REORG TABLESPACE?

16. Is logging done during reload when using SHRLEVEL of REFERENCE and CHANGE? Why?

17. Is it advisable to specify LOG NO when using REORG with SHRLEVEL NONE? Why?

18. A mapping table must be created when using which SHRLEVEL parameter value?

19. If the number of log records that the next log apply iteration will process is not sufficiently lower than the number of log records processed in the previous iteration, what action is taken by online REORG?

20. There are a number of actions that can be taken before the DELAY time has expired. One possibility is to alter the LONGLOG parameter value to CONTINUE, DRAIN, or TERM. What action will REORG take based on each of the values?

21. Online REORG is restartable during which two phases?

22. Is it advisable to specify SORTDATA, SORTKEYS, and NOSYSREC with REORG ... SHRLEVEL CHANGE?

23. a) What is the advantage of using SORTKEYS with SHRLEVEL NONE when doing a reorganization?

b) What is the disadvantage of using SORTKEYS with SHRLEVEL NONE when doing a reorganization?

24. Should the SORTDATA parameter be used with SHRLEVEL NONE and REFERENCE when reorganizing a tablespace? Why?

25. Is it advisable to specify the COPYDDN parameter when using SHRLEVEL NONE, REFERENCE, or CHANGE with a reorganization?

26. a) Should KEEPDICTIONARY be specified when doing a reorganization if ESA compression is used? Why?

b) What is a disadvantage to using KEEPDICTIONARY? How can the disadvantage be managed?

ANSWERS

1. RUNSTATS need not be executed after each reorganization in a production environment. In most cases, the statistics do not change in such a way as to affect the access path chosen by the optimizer. If the statistics do change significantly, it is necessary to rebind plans and packages to allow the optimizer to choose a different access path based on the new statistics, assuming the use of static SQL.

Executing RUNSTATS immediately after each REORG is not useful in determining if a reorganization should be done since the data is well organized after a REORG. There is some value in executing RUNSTATS after a REORG for space management. LISTCAT is a less costly alternative.

2. SHRLEVEL CHANGE allows for concurrent execution of update programs. The fact that RUNSTATS collects statistics on uncommited data is not a problem in most cases. SHRLEVEL REFERENCE allows for SELECTS but INSERT, UPDATE, and DELETE statements cannot be executed during the execution of RUNSTATS.

3. Yes, it is necessary to specify REPORT YES to RUNSTATS in order to get a report of the statistics collected. REPORT NO is the default.

4. a) The TABLE parameter causes RUNSTATS to estimate the cardinality of non-indexed columns and of the non-leading columns of a composite index.

b) The cardinality of non-indexed columns and of the non-leading columns of a composite index provides the optimizer with more information to choose the best access path. These statistics are particularly important for determining the join method and which tables should be the inner and outer tables of a join when there are local predicates on non-indexed columns. The cardinalities of non-leading columns of a composite index are used to determine if and how a composite index should be used when the user does not specify information so that equal predicates can be specified on all columns of a composite index.

5. a) The disadvantage of specifying the RUNSTATS TABLE parameter is that the CPU costs are increased.

b) The increase in CPU costs can be reduced by specifying the SAMPLE parameter so that only a sample of the data will be used in estimating the cardinalities rather than using all rows in the table. The second approach that will reduce the costs of collecting the cardinalities is to name the columns used in predicates and the non-leading columns of a composite index if equal predicates cannot be specified on all columns of the composite index.

6. It is not necessary to collect the cardinalities of non-leading columns of a composite index if equal predicates are specified on all leading columns (no intermediate column is skipped) and the KEYCARD parameter is specified. This is because the column group cardinalities collected as a result of KEYCARD can be used when equal predicates are specified on the leading columns of a composite index.

7. If there are more than two columns in a composite index and the columns are correlated or equal predicates cannot be specified on the "middle" columns of a composite index, it is advisable to specify the KEYCARD parameter to RUNSTATS to provide the optimizer with the needed statistics to choose a good access path.

8. If the NUMCOLS parameter is not specified to RUNSTATS, only the first column of a composite index is used to determine the frequency of occurrence of a value in the column. If the COUNT parameter is not specified to RUNSTATS, the 10 most frequently occurring values are identified and inserted into the catalog tables along with their frequency of occurrence.

9. REORG TABLESPACE is advisable after rows have lost more than 20 percent of their clustering, after a number of rows have overflowed to near or far pages, after filling free space, after index page splitting, after losing some compression savings, after heavy insert, update, and delete activity, after dropping a table in a nonsegmented tablespace to reclaim space, and to take advantage of a new space allocation.

10. REORG INDEX rather than the REORG TABLESPACE may be sufficient if you have mostly transaction processing retrieving only a few rows with matching index scans or mostly heavy insert activity at the end of a table. If the primary reason for a reorganization is page splitting as indicated by increased LEAFDIST and NLEVELS, REORG INDEX is a good choice. Also if compression is used, decompressing the data is not required with REORG INDEX.

11.The OFFPOSLIMIT 20 and INDREFLIMIT 10 parameters cause a submitted REORG TABLESPACE utility to execute only if 20 percent or more of the rows have lost clustering and 10 percent or more of the rows have overflowed to near or far pages.

12. The LEAFDISTLIMIT parameter is specified to cause a reorganization of an index if many leaf pages have been split.

13.The REUSE parameter should be specified on the REORG TABLESPACE and/or REORG INDEX statements to cause the rows and/or index to be written back to the same data sets.

14. An online reorganization with read/write access by SQL statements during most of the reorganization process is requested by specifying the parameter SHRLEVEL CHANGE.

15. The parameters SHRLEVEL REFERENCE and SHRLEVEL CHANGE cause REORG TABLESPACE to reorganize the data and indexes into shadow copies.

16. Logging is not done during reload when using SHRLEVEL of REFERENCE and CHANGE. This is because an image copy is made during the reorganization.

17. It is advisable to specify LOG NO when using REORG with SHRLEVEL NONE. This will reduce the costs of a reorganization. REORG with LOG NO should be followed by an image copy to turn off the copy pending status and allow for updating the data. Logging is done for NPI when reorganizing a partition with LOG of NO or YES.

18. A mapping table must be created when using SHRLEVEL CHANGE.

19. A message (DSNU3771) is written to the console regarding the fact that the shadow copy cannot be updated as fast as the original tablespace. The reorganization process continues for the number of seconds specified in the DELAY parameter.

20. If LONGLOG CONTINUE is specified, the reorganization will continue. If LONGLOG DRAIN is specified, REORG will drain the write class, apply all remaining log records, and do the switch processing after the DELAY time. If LONGLOG TERM is specified, the reorganization will be terminated and the original data will continue to be used.

21. Online REORG can be restarted during the switch phase and during the build phase of NPIs.

22. It is not necessary to specify SORTDATA, SORTKEYS, and NOSYSREC with REORG ... SHRLEVEL CHANGE. These parameters are effectively used with SHRLEVEL CHANGE.

23. a) The advantage of using SORTKEYS with SHRLEVEL NONE when doing a reorganization is that indexed values extracted during reload phase are passed directly to sort and the sort is done in memory. (SORTWKnn is used for the sort.) The sorted values are passed to the build index phase.

b) The disadvantage of using SORTKEYS with SHRLEVEL NONE when doing a reorganization is that restart is from the RELOAD phase regardless of how restart is requested.

24. SORTDATA used with SHRLEVEL NONE and REFERENCE has significant performance advantages in most cases assuming that the cluster ratio is not 100 percent. The rows are unloaded during a tablespace scan and passed directly to an external sort. This avoids scanning the leaf pages and pulling the rows off in sequence, avoids excessive seek time, and avoids processing a data page multiple times to pull rows off in sequence.

25. Is it advisable to specify the COPYDDN parameter when using SHRLEVEL NONE with a reorganization to avoid having to pass the data a second time after the reorganization to make an image copy. COPYDDN is not necessary when using SHRLEVEL of REFERENCE or CHANGE because an inline image copy is always made with these parameters.

26. a) KEEPDICTIONARY is a good choice if the characteristics of the data have not changed with respect to data compression when doing a reorganization. It reduces CPU costs significantly.

b) The disadvantage of KEEPDICTIONARY is that a compression report is not generated so that it is difficult to know when the dictionary should be rebuilt to gain greater efficiencies in compression. The column SYSTABLEPART.PAGESAVE contains the percentage of pages (times 100) in the tablespace or partition as a result of using ESA compression after RUNSTATS has been executed. This percentage can be monitored. If it decreases with update activity, consider rebuilding the dictionary.

FIGURES

Copy, Quiesce, Report, Rebuild, & Recover

CR.1 INTRODUCTION

It is critical to have a good backup and recovery strategy in case of a failure due to hardware, software, or human error. DB2 is actually capable of logonly recovery since the tablespace was first created, assuming that all of the archive logs are available. This is obviously impractical for tablespaces created years in the past or even months in the past, assuming a reasonable amount of update activity.

The goal is to make image copies periodically to minimize the amount of time required for a recovery. Indeed, a good strategy is to estimate the time to recover depending on whether an image copy is made on a daily, week, or monthly basis. If the time to recover is unacceptable to the business, copies need to be made more frequently.

Overview of the Backup and Recovery Process

We will start with an overview of the backup and recovery process and then look at each of the utilities that can be used in the processing throughout the chapter.

All inserts, updates, and deletes issued on a table are written to dual active log data sets as well as to the table and indexes. Each log record has a relative byte address (RBA) assigned to it. This is analogous to a sequence number of the log record written to the log. When the active log data sets becomes full, they are written to archive log data sets. The range of RBAs for each log data set is written to the boot strap data set (BSDS). The BSDS contains an inventory of active and archive log data sets with start and end RBA for each log data set. It is used to locate the required log data sets with updates made after a copy. These updates are applied to the copy that the RECOVER utility writes to the tablespace being recovered as shown in Figure CR.1. All processing in the figure will be described in this chapter.

Figure CR.1. Backup and Recovery Process

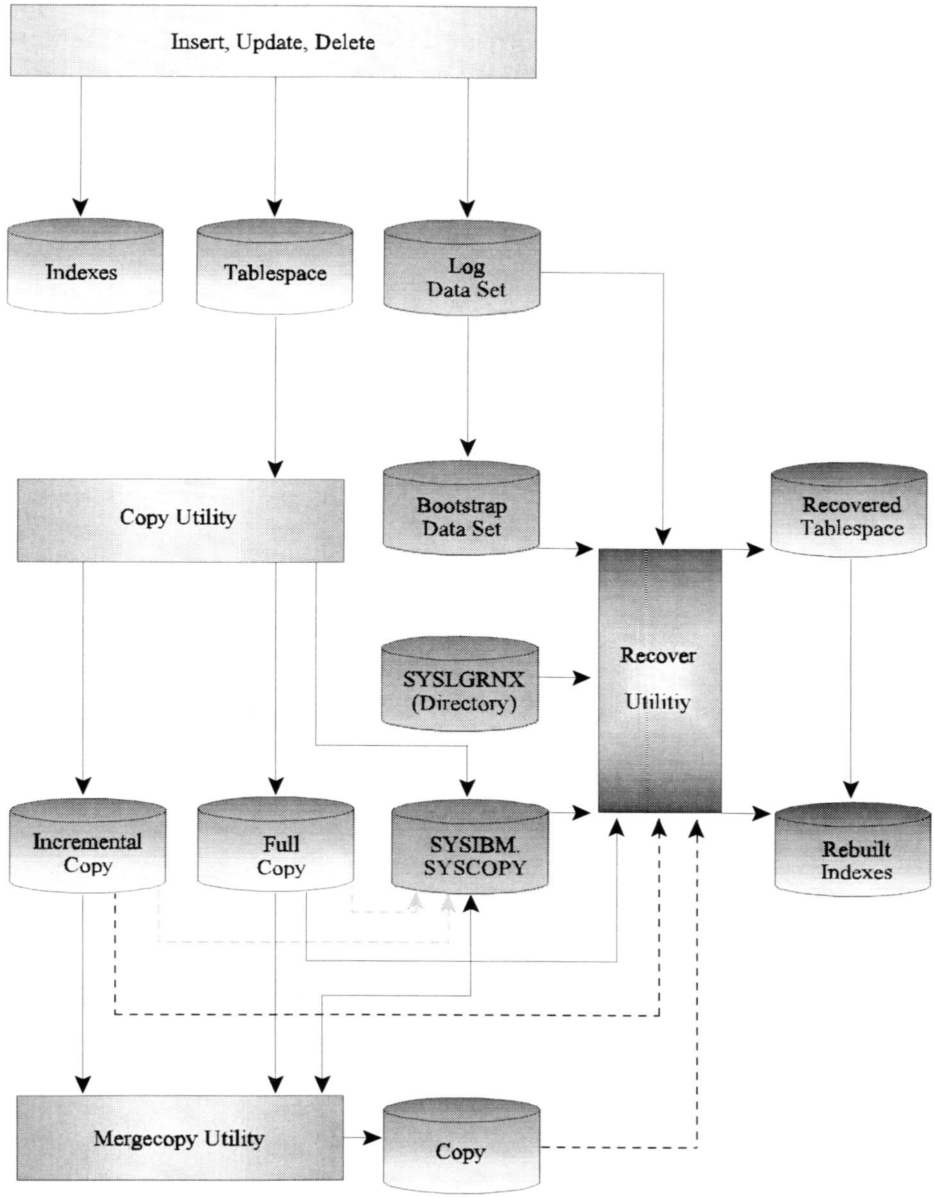

Recording and Locating Log Records

When the COPY utility is executed, the RBA at the time of the copy is written along with a copy of the tablespace and optionally the indexes (V6) on the tables in one or more tablespaces to an image copy data set for each object named in the COPY statement. An RBA is written to SYSLGRNX when the tablespace or partition is first updated after the copy, when it is switched to read-only status, and the data set is closed. SYSLGRNX in the directory database (DSNDB01) defines the range of records in the log to be processed for a recovery.

The RECOVER utility reads the RBA in the image copy and locates the RBA in SYSLGRNX that is greater than or equal to the RBA in copy. The log is read from the RBA written with the first update after a copy is made until the RBA written when the data set is switched to read-only status or the data set is closed. The log records between the ranges for the named objects can be skipped. They apply to other objects not named in the COPY statement.

Figure CR.2 shows how the RBAs are tracked and used to apply log records to a copy placed on a tablespace by the RECOVER utility. The example assumes that the start of the log has an RBA of 1 which is written to the BSDS, an image copy of a tablespace is taken with the RBA of 5 written to the image copy and the catalog table SYSCOPY. The first update to the tablespace is assigned an RBA of 9 and written to SYSLGRNX. The tablespace is closed or switched to read-only processing with an RBA of 13 which is also written to SYSLGRNX. The log records of 9 through 13 are applied to the restored copy made with an RBA of 5. Log records less than 9 need not be scanned because they do not apply to the tablespace being recovered. Log records with an RBA of 14 through 16 are for other tablespaces and can be skipped during the recovery of the target tablespace. Updates to the target tablespace continue with an RBA of 17 and the RBA is written to SYSLGRNX to establish the beginning of a second range of RBAs for log records to be applied to the copy by the RECOVER utility. We assume that the active log is filled with an RBA of 21 which is written to the BSDS to delineate the end of a specified log data set. Log records with an RBA beginning with 17 and continuing on to the second log data set are applied to the copy.

Figure CR.2. Recording and Locating Log Records

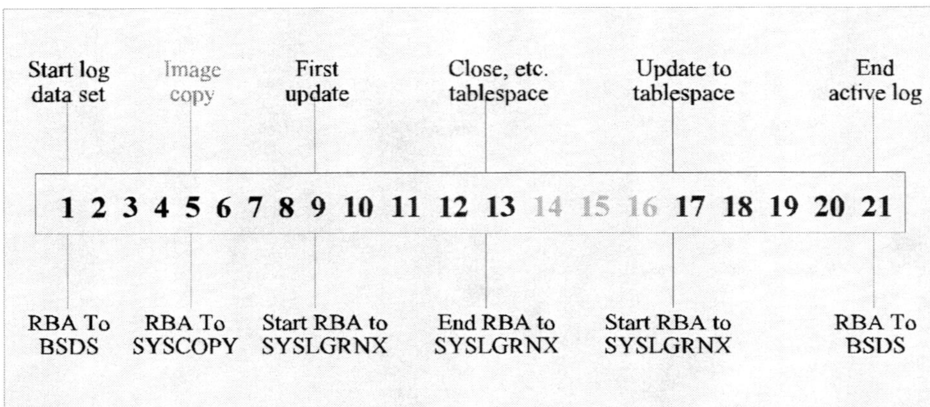

Scan of Active and Archive Logs

If there is frequent update activity and the data set is not switched to read-only processing or closed, the end RBA is not written to SYSLGRNX. All active and archive logs must be read since the first update after the copy was made for a recovery. There is no opportunity to skip portions of the logs, which increases the time to recover. Do make frequent image copies to reduce the number of logs that must be scanned and the recovery time.

Recovery time is improved significantly if the archive log is on DASD. As mentioned, DB2 does dual logging. If you believe that the cost of keeping both copies of the log on DASD is too high, one of the archive logs can be written to tape and one archive log can be written to DASD. One or both of the logs on DASD can be migrated to tape periodically with SMS. (DSNTIPA installation panel allows for the selection of DASD or tape.)

Recommendation: Do consider sizing the active log for a 24 hour period if sufficient DASD space is available and take an image copy every 24 hours. This minimizes the possibility of requiring an archive log and delaying the recovery process.

CR.2 FULL AND INCREMENTAL COPIES

You have a choice of making a full image copy or a copy of only the pages changed since the last copy of a tablespace. A full image copy (not an incremental copy) is always made if a copy of an index is requested. A full image copy is the default or you can specify FULL YES after naming the database and tablespace (DASPJDB and DASPJTSP) in the COPY statement as shown in the example.

```
COPY TABLESPACE DASPJDB.DASPJTSP
FULL YES
```

If you prefer to make a copy of only those data pages that have changed since the last full or incremental image copy, the FULL NO parameter must be specified. There is a bit map at the bottom of each space map page as discussed in Chapter TS. A bit on the space map page corresponds to each page within the range of pages covered by the space map (about 5000 pages, depending on the segment size). Bits are turned on in the space map pages when pages are updated after making a copy. For example, if page 10 has been updated after it has been copied, the tenth bit is turned on. These bits are used by the COPY utility to determine which pages need to be copied when making an incremental copy. The COPY utility turns off the bits when a copy is made.

It is necessary to make a full image copy before making an incremental copy for recovery to currency. A full image copy is required after a REORG or LOAD REPLACE without an inline copy and after making a concurrent copy. If an incremental copy is requested and there is not a valid non-concurrent full copy, COPY takes a full image copy based on an analysis of SYSCOPY rows and issues the DSNU402 message when an incremental copy is requested. Do be cautious with this polite feature of the COPY utility. There may not be sufficient time to make a full copy within the time allocated for an incremental copy which can delay the availability of the tablespace depending on the SHRLEVEL parameter to be discussed. There may be insufficient space on a volume for a full copy when an incremental copy is requested. Also, you can use a naming convention to distinguish between a full and incremental copy. If you do, the full copy will be named as if it were an incremental copy.

Guidelines for Making an Incremental or Full Copy

Your choice of making an incremental or full copy depends on the percentage of pages that have been updated and need to be copied, and whether the updated pages are contiguous. An incremental copy is a good choice if less than 50 percent of the pages are updated and are contiguous, less than 5 percent of the pages are updated and are randomly distributed in the tablespace, or less than 10 percent of the pages are updated and the distance of the updated pages are unknown. These percent guidelines can be adjusted upward to allow for the management of incremental copies and the merging of incremental copies prior to a recovery.

Figures CR.3 and CR.4 summarize test results of the elapsed and CPU times required to make an incremental and full copy with SHRLEVEL of CHANGE and REFERENCE. (These parameter are discussed in Section CR.3.) For now, notice that there is not a significant performance difference for a copy made with SHRLEVEL of CHANGE and REFERENCE. The primary point of the figures is to show that test results indicate that an incremental copy requires less elapsed and CPU times than a full copy up to about 90 to 95 percent changed pages. This suggests that an incremental copy is almost always more economical than a full copy. The use of TRACKMOD NO to reduce contention increases resources required by incremental copy as discussed in Chapter TS. In addition, we must consider the management of incremental copies before deciding on reasonable guidelines.

Figure CR.3. Comparison of the elapsed seconds for a full and incremental copy

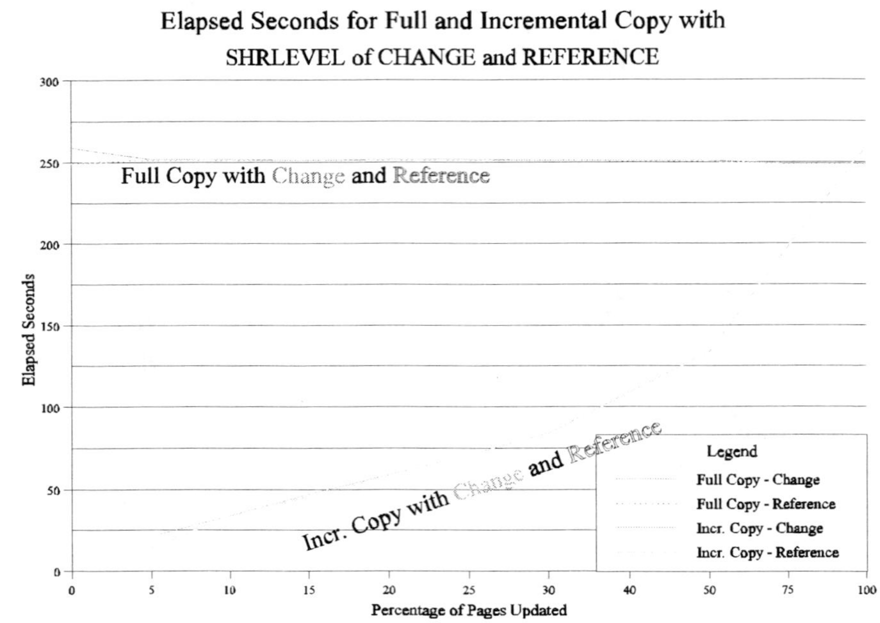

Figure CR.4. Comparison of the CPU seconds for a full and incremental copy

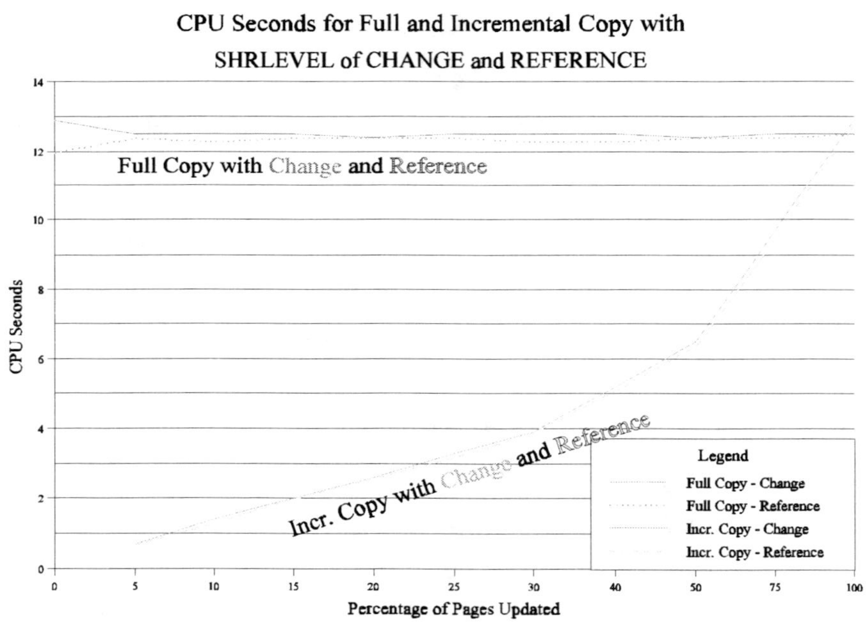

CR.3 MERGING INCREMENTAL COPIES

Incremental copies must be merged before a recovery. You can merge them periodically to avoid the delay of the RECOVERY utility having to merge them before it can begin a recovery. Here is a statement to instruct the MERGECOPY utility to merge all existing incremental copies made on tablespace DASPJTSP in database DASPJDB.

```
MERGECOPY TABLESPACE DASPJDB.DASPJTSP
NEWCOPY YES
```

The MERGECOPY utility calls for the required copies for the merge based on information in SYSCOPY.

NEWCOPY YES causes all incremental copies to be merged with the full image copy to create a new copy.

NEWCOPY NO causes all incremental copies to be merged. The RECOVER utility uses the last full copy and the merged incremental copies for the recovery. NEWCOPY NO is not a valid option at a recovery site.

Too Many Incremental Copies

The MERGECOPY utility merges the number of copies that can be mounted on available tape units. If there are more copies than tape units, an intermediate work file is built to be merged with additional copies. If a DD statement has not been specified for the work file, message DSNU454I gives the number of copies merged. MERGECOPY can be executed again to merge the remaining incremental copies. If MERGECOPY has not been used to merge the incremental copies, the RECOVER copy must merge the copies before writing the copy to the tablespace

If the RECOVER utility must merge the incremental copies, only the oldest copies that can be mounted on the available tape units are merged. If there are not enough tape units for the number of incremental copies, the remaining incremental copies are not used in the recovery. Rather it is necessary to go further back in the log to locate log records of updates made after the incremental copies that could be merged with available tape units.

Recommendation: Make no more incremental copies than available tape units to merge them. Consider making periodic incremental copies (Monday through Thursday, for example) and a full image copy occasionally (weekly, for example) rather than doing a merge of the incremental copies.

CHANGELIMIT Copy Parameter

Your choice of making no copy, an incremental copy, or a full copy can be specified in terms of the percentage of changed pages as indicated using the CHANGELIMIT parameter. This parameter applies to tablespaces (not indexes). Here is an example of using the parameter specifying the default values.

```
COPY TABLESPACE DASPJDB.DASPJTSP
CHANGELIMIT (1, 10)
```

If the percent of changed pages is less than or equal 1 percent, an image copy is not taken. If the percent of changed pages is greater than 1 and less than 10 percent, an incremental copy is taken. If the percent of changed pages is greater than or equal to 10 percent, a full image copy is taken.

One value can be specified, CHANGELIMIT 20 for example. This means that if the percent of changed pages is greater than 0 and less than 20, an incremental copy is made. If the percent of changed pages is greater than or equal to 20 percent, a full copy is taken.

Return codes indicates the type of copy if any and whether a damaged space map page was encountered as summarized in Figure CR.5.

Figure CR.5. Return codes indicating the type of copy if any

Return Codes	Description
1	If successful and no CHANGELIMIT value is met, no image copy is recommended or taken.*
2	If successful and the percent of changed pages is within the range specified for an incremental image copy, then an incremental copy is recommended or taken.*
3	If successful and the percent of changed pages is greater than or equal to the high CHANGELIMIT value. A full image copy is recommended or taken.*
8	Broken space map page, report given along with broken page number.

*REPORTONLY parameter determines if copy is recommended or taken.

REPORTONLY Copy Parameter

The COPY utility can be instructed to produce a report without taking an image copy using the REPORTONLY parameter.

```
COPY TABLESPACE DASPJDB.DASPJTSP
REPORTONLY
```

A report is always produced when a copy is made regardless of whether the REPORTONLY parameter is specified. Figure CR.6 is an example of a report showing the total number of pages, the number of empty and changed pages, and the percent of changed pages.

Figure CR.6. Image copy report

```
DSNU000I DSNUGUTC - OUTPUT START FOR UTILITY, UTILID = RPRTO
DSNU050I DSNUGUTC - COPY TABLESPACE DASPJDB.DASPJTSP
                    CHANGELIMIT(10,40) REPORTONLY
DSNU440I DSNUBCHG - IMAGE COPY INFORMATION

                                 4KB     EMPTY   CHANGED   PERCENT OF
 DBNAME    TSNAME   DSNUM  PAGES    PAGES    PAGES   CHANGED PAGES   ICTYPE
--------  --------  -----  -------  -------  -------  -------------   ------
DASPJDB   DASPJTSP   ALL    64000     5000    25000           39.0       I

DSNU443I DSNUBCHG - INCREMENTAL CHANGE LIMIT MET
DSNU010I DSNUGBAC - UTILITY EXECUTION COMPLETE, HIGHEST RETURN CODE=2
```

Managing Empty GDG Copies

If you are using generation data groups (GDG) for your copies, you probably do not want to make a copy with no pages, record it in SYSCOPY, and have RECOVER call for the empty copy during a recovery. This can be accomplished by executing the COPY utility with the REPORTONLY parameter in a step preceding a step that makes a copy if certain criteria are met. Figure CR.7 is an example of doing this.

Figure CR.7. JCL to avoid making an empty GDG copy

```
//COPYREPT EXEC PGM=DSNUTILB,PARTM='DSN,COPYR'
//SYSCOPY   DD DUMMY
//SYSIN     DD *
  COPY TABLESPACE DASPJDB.DASPJTSP CHANGELIMIT 20 REPORTONLY
/*
//          IF (COPYREPT.RC.3) THEN MADE A FULL COPY
/*
//COPYFULL EXEC PGM=DSNUTILB,PARM='DSN,COPYF'
//SYSCOPY   DD DSN=FCOPY.DASPJTSP,SPACE=(CYL,(15,1)),DISP=(,CATLOG)
//SYSIN     DD *
  COPY TABLESPACE DASPJDB.DASPJTSP FULL YES
/*
//          ENDIF
/*
```

Notice that the first step executes the COPY utility with the REPORTONLY parameter and the full image copy requested in the second step is executed only if the return code from the first step is equal to 3. If both the CHANGELIMIT and REPORTONLY parameters are specified, do specify DUMMY for SYSCOPY to avoid allocating and opening a data set with no rows.

Share Level Parameters

The share level (SHRLEVEL) parameter instructs the image copy utility to allow others to only read the data or to read and change the data while the image copy is being made. It applies to both tablespaces and indexes.

SHRLEVEL REFERENCE means that others can read the data but not update it while the copy if being made. With this parameter, the COPY utility establishes a point of consistency by draining all writers before starting to make the copy. The log RBA is written to SYSCOPY at end of copy. This means that fewer log records need to be processed during a recovery made with SHRLEVEL REFERENCE. The log records written for other tablespaces while making a copy need not be scanned.

SHRLEVEL REFERENCE results in all objects having the same RBA or LRSN (if sysplex data sharing is used) written to SYSCOPY.START_RBA. This allows for a recovery of all objects to TOCOPY, TOLOGPOINT, or TORBA which is particularly important to keep related tablespaces synchronized as discussed in Section CR.8.

SHRLEVEL CHANGE means that others can read and update the tablespace while the copy is being made. The COPY utility uses the uncommited read (UR) isolation level and takes a read claim. Both pages with committed data and pages with uncommited data are copied. This means that a page that has an exclusive (X) lock and is currently being updated by an SQL statement is included in the copy. For this reason, a point-in-time recover using the TOCOPY parameter should not be done because the copy can contain uncommited updates. The log RBA is written to SYSCOPY.START_RBA at the beginning of the copy which can require a longer recovery time because more log records must be scanned. However, different objects are likely to have different values which does not provide for synchronizing related tablespaces.

The COPY utility updates SYSCOPY and SYSUTILX with information on the copy that has been made and holds a lock during the process. Lock contention can be minimized by deleting rows from SYSCOPY and SYSUTILX describing copies made before the oldest retained archive logs using the MODIFY utility as will be discussed.

Local and Recovery Site Copies

Up to and including four image copies can be created by the COPY utility with a single tablespace scan. If separate I/O channels can be used, multiple copies adds little to the costs of making a copy. One or two local copies can be requested with the COPYDDN parameter. Figure CR.8 contains a sample COPY statement embedded in JCL to execute the utility. The COPYDDN(L1DDNAME, L2DDNAME) parameter indicates that two local copies are to be written to the data sets identified by the L1DDNAME and L2DDNAME DD statements. The RECOVERYDDN(R1DDNAME, R2DDNAME) parameter indicates that two remote copies are to be written to the data sets identified by the R1DDNAME and R2DDNAME DD statements. The recovery site copies can be merged at the remote or local site.

Figure CR.8. COPY Statement and JCL

```
//COPYSPJ EXEC DSNUPROC,SYSTEM=DB2T,UID='CSPJ',UTPROC=''
//L1DDNAME DD DSN=LOCALC1,UNIT=SYSDA,VOL=SER=SERID1,
//             SPACE=(TRK,(15,1)),DISP=(NEW,CATLG,CATLG)
//L2DDNAME DD DSN=LOCALC2,UNIT=SYSDA,VOL=SER=SERID1,
//             SPACE=(TRK,(15,1)),DISP=(NEW,CATLG,CATLG)
//R1DDNAME DD DSN=REMOTC1,UNIT=SYSDA,VOL=SER=SERID1,
//             SPACE=(TRK,(15,1)),DISP=(NEW,CATLG,CATLG)
//R2DDNAME DD DSN=REMOTC2,UNIT=SYSDA,VOL=SER=SERID1,
//             SPACE=(TRK,(15,1)),DISP=(NEW,CATLG,CATLG)
//DSNUPROC.SYSIN    DD   *
  COPY TABLESPACE DASPJDB.DASPJTSP
       CHANGELIMIT (1, 10)
       SHRLEVEL CHANGE
       COPYDDN     (L1DDNAME, L2DDNAME)
       RECOVERYDDN (R1DDNAME, R2DDNAME)
       DSNUM ALL
/*
```

The remote copies are intended for disaster recovery at a remote site but can be used for local recovery if the local copies are damaged or lost. The DB2 subsystem site is designated as local or remote in SITETYPE of DSNZPARM, and SYSCOPY.ICBACKUP contains 'LB' for local copies and 'RB' for remote copies. Remote site recovery assumes copies of catalog tables, directory, logs, etc. at the remote site. Disaster recovery is beyond the scope of this book. The Administration Guide and DB2 UDB Server for OS/390 Version 6 Technical Update, SG24-6108 manuals are good sources of information.

The COPY utility is rather friendly in that if local and recovery site copies have been made in the past and only local or recovery copies are made, a full recovery may not be possible at one of the sites and a warning is issued:

```
DSNU406I FULL IMAGE COPY SHOULD BE TAKEN FOR
BOTH LOCAL SITE AND RECOVERY SITE
```

The DSNUM ALL parameter in Figure CR.8 is the default and means that all data sets for the tablespace are copied. A numeric value can be specified to indicate that a specific partition or data set within a multi data set tablespace is to be copied. If DSNUM *n* is specified with the COPY utility, the DSNUM must also be specified when executing the MERGECOPY and RECOVER utilities.

Copy of Multiple Indexes and Tablespaces (V6)

Multiple indexes and tablespaces can be copied in parallel in a single COPY utility execution. Indexes must be created or altered to COPY YES (COPY NO is the default) to enable the copy and recovery of indexes from the log. Here is an example of changing the SNX index to COPY YES.

```
ALTER INDEX SNX
  COPY YES;
```

Indexes defined with COPY YES are marked in the catalog table SYSINDEXES with a 'Y' in the COPY column. SYSCOPY is updated for the copies as with copies of tablespaces. Similarly, SYSLGRNX is maintained for copies of indexes as well as tablespaces. REPORT, MODIFY, REPAIR, and downlevel detection support indexes defined with COPY YES similar to tablespaces.

Following is an example of a COPY statement that copies four tablespaces and each of the indexes on tables in the tablespaces. The statement identifies the indexes by their name. Optionally, you can use the INDEXSPACE name rather than the INDEX name as in the example.

```
COPY
  TABLESPACE DASPJDB.DASPJTSP
  CHANGELIMIT (1, 10)
    INDEX AUTHID.SNPNJNX
    INDEX AUTHID.PNX
    INDEX AUTHID.JNX
  TABLESPACE DASPJDB.DASTSP
  CHANGELIMIT (1, 10)
    INDEX AUTHID.SNX
  TABLESPACE DASPJDB.DAPTSP
  CHANGELIMIT (1, 10)
    INDEX AUTHID.PNX
  TABLESPACE DASPJDB.DAJTSP
  CHANGELIMIT (1, 10)
    INDEX AUTHID.JNX
PARALLEL(4)
SHRLEVEL REFERENCE
```

You can recover indexes using TOLOGPOINT, TORBA, TOCOPY, ERROR RANGE, PAGE, and LOGONLY. PIT (Point-in-Time) recover of indexes places them in check pending. REBUILD index is an alternative to avoid check pending

CHANGELIMIT does not apply to indexes. It applies to the percentage of data pages that have been changed. If the percentage indicates that a copy should be made, copies of the tablespace are made. Each named tablespace has a REPORT phase.

The PARALLEL parameter provides for specifying the maximum number of objects in the list that can be processed in parallel. If PARALLEL or PARALLEL (0) is specified, COPY determines the optimal number of objects to process in parallel. Once a parallel task completes, the task starts working on the next copy.

When copy parallelism is not used: Copy parallelism does not apply to copying objects to tape. If an object is copied to tape, parallelism is discontinued until the copy to tape completes at present. Copy and recovery parallelism does not apply when using CONCURRENT. CONCURRENT is discussed in Section CR.5. If PARALLEL is not specified, each object in the list is copied serially in the order listed.

CHECKPAGE parameter can be added to copy statement for a more thorough check of data and index pages during the image copy (V6 APAR PQ25084). This parameter checks for damaged data pages by invoking the data manager routine DSNICPGD and checks for damaged index pages by invoking the index manager routine DSNKCHKP. Copy pending is turned on if damaged pages are detected. The REPAIR utility can be used to correct errors or you can recover to a previous copy. There is a low increase in CPU time for coping 147,090 data and 32,440 index pages:

- 3.88 CPU and 293 elapsed seconds with CHECKPAGE
- 3.45 CPU and 296 elapsed seconds without CHECKPAGE

COPY Pending Advisory Status

The COPY pending status (ICOPY) for indexes is an advisory status that can be set on by the REORG INDEX, REORG TABLESPACE with LOG YES or NO, LOAD TABLE with LOG YES or NO, and the REBUILD INDEX utilities for an index that has been defined as COPY YES. The status allows read and write processing. You can determine if the status is active using the -DISPLAY DATABASE command with the ADVISORY parameter.

If the COPY pending status is on for an index, REBUILD INDEX rather than RECOVER INDEX is required. The status can be turned off by running making an image COPY of the indexes so that indexes can be recovered rather than having to rebuild them.

If an index defined with COPY YES might be inconsistent with the data, CHKP (check pending) is turned on for the index. In this case, no DML (Data Manipulation Language) statements are allowed until the status is removed. The status is not recorded in the catalog tables. It can be determined suing the -DISPLAY DATABASE command with the RESTRICT parameter.

Ensure That a Recent Copy Has Been Made

It is advisable to periodically ensure that a recent copy has been made. This can be done by selecting from the catalog tables. The following SQL statement identifies tablespaces in a given database that do not have an image copy recorded in SYSCOPY. You will want to replace 'dbname' with your database name.

```
SELECT DBNAME, NAME, CREATOR
FROM   SYSIBM.SYSTABLESPACE
WHERE  DBNAME = 'dbname'
AND    NAME NOT IN
  (SELECT TSNAME
   FROM   SYSIBM.SYSCOPY
   WHERE  DBNAME = 'dbname')
ORDER BY DBNAME, NAME;
```

This SQL statement reports on most current image copies on all tablespaces in the dbname database:

```
SELECT DBNAME, TSNAME, MAX(TIMESTAMP)
FROM   SYSIBM.SYSCOPY
WHERE  DBNAME = 'dbname'
GROUP BY DBNAME, TSNAME;
```

If you are interested in only full image copies, add the predicate:

```
AND ICTYPE = 'F'
```

CR.4 CONCURRENT COPY

The DUMP option of SMS is used to make a concurrent copy. It requires SMS and 3990-3 or -6 DASD with extended platform.

Concurrent copy first makes a logical copy. This consists of setting on a bit for each track to be copied in the DASD controller. No updates are allowed during the logical copy. Typically a logical copy requires a few seconds or less depending on the number of tracks to be copied. In one case the logical copy required 30 seconds for full pack copy. A message is issued when the logical copy is complete. The next step is to make the physical copy.

The physical copy turns off the bits as each track is copied. Updates can be written on a track after that track is copied. Pages updated on a track before the track is copied and the bit is turned off are written to a DASD cache sidefile. If there is insufficient space in the DASD cache, the cache sidefile is written to OS/390 processor storage sidefiles to free space in the DASD cache. Sidefile pages are merged and written to DASD after the physical copy is complete.

Pages required for selects and updates are located and processed in the sidefiles. As with any copy process, it is best to make copies during low update activity to avoid delaying the copy process.

Comparison of Image and Concurrent Copy

There are pros and cons of using the image copy utility and of using concurrent copy. Image copy provides for taking an incremental copy and the use of CHANGELIMIT to specify the percentage of changed pages that indicate no copy, an incremental copy, or a full copy. Concurrent copy does not take an incremental copy. Therefore, the limit used to indicate that an incremental copy should be taken is ignored.

Concurrent copy allows for copying multiple tablespaces with one execution of the utility. A filter list can be specified such that all objects beginning with SPJ indicating a particularly application are copied with a point of consistency at the end of the logical copy. Both DB2 and non-DB2 data sets can be copied in one job step. Concurrent copy can be used to copy volumes of DASD to ease disaster recovery. It can be instructed to compress the data before it is written to the copy. These features are not available with the image copy utility.

The DSN1COPY, DSN1PRNT, and DSN1COMP services aids can be used to read an image copy but they cannot read a concurrent copy. DB2 security is used for an image copy. In contract, you must have privileges on the underlying data sets to use concurrent copy. There is not a significant difference in performance of making tablespace copies with image copy and concurrent copy. Figure CR.9 summarizes the comparison of image and concurrent copy plus a few additional items.

Figure CR.9. Comparison of image and concurrent copy

Item	Image Copy	Concurrent Copy
CHANGELIMIT	Yes	Full copy taken if limit is met
SHRLEVEL REFERENCE	No updates allows	Updates allowed after quiesce & logical copy
SHRLEVEL CHANGE	Yes	Yes, except for 32 KB pages
Recovery of indexes	Yes	No
Parallel copy and recovery	Yes	No, data unavailable during logical copy and all of recovery
Incremental copy	Yes	No
List >1 tablespace	Yes (V6)	Yes, except SYSUTILX, SYSLGRNX, SYSCOPY
Filter list	No	Can take advantage of a naming convention to copy all tablespaces in a database
Multiple copies on a tape	Complex to manage with labels and ddname refer backs	1 dump data set can contain multiple data sets
Volume copies	No	Yes, useful for disaster recovery. Data unavailable for minutes during logical copy of volumes.
DB2 and non-DB2 data sets	No	Can be copied in 1 job step

Item	Image Copy	Concurrent Copy
Execution of multiple copy jobs	<= 64 copy jobs can be supported on a 3990 with <= 16 on a volume	>= 4 copy jobs (each job can be for >1 tablespace) can result in excessive queuing and extended elapsed time. <= 2 is best or reduce the OPTIMIZE value to reduce demand on DASD subsystem.
Compression	No	Yes, CPU increased
DSN1COPY,DSN1PRNT, and DSN1COMP	Can read copy	Cannot read copy
Security	DB2 security	Privileges required on underlying data set or volume

Concurrent Copy JCL

Figure CR.10 is an example of JCL to make a concurrent copy. Notice that more than one tablespace can be specified with CONCURRENT copy. This is in contrast to being able to specify only one tablespace when making an image copy. If there is an abend during a concurrent copy, all successfully copied tablespaces before an abend are useable. A row is inserted into SYSCOPY after each tablespace is copied with an ICTYPE = 'F' and STYPE = 'C'.

Figure CR.10. Concurrent Copy JCL

```
//COPYSPJ EXEC DSNUPROC,SYSTEM=DB2T,UID='COPYSPJ',UTPROC=''
//SYSCOPYS DD DSN=CSPJ.MEMBER1.COPYSPJ.SYSCOPYS,
//            DISP=(MOD,KEEP,CATLG),UNIT=SYSDA,
//            SPACE=(4000,(20,20),,,ROUND)
//SYSCOPYP DD DSN=CSPJ.MEMBER1.COPYSPJ.SYSCOPYP,
//            DISP=(MOD,KEEP,CATLG),UNIT=SYSDA,
//            SPACE=(4000,(20,20),,,ROUND)
//SYSCOPYJ DD DSN=CSPJ.MEMBER1.COPYSPJ.SYSCOPYJ,
//            DISP=(MOD,KEEP,CATLG),UNIT=SYSDA,
//            SPACE=(4000,(20,20),,,ROUND)
//DSNUPROC.SYSIN    DD  *
    COPY TABLESPACE DASPJDB.DASTSP
         COPYDDN(SYSCOPYS)
         TABLESPACE DASPJDB.DAPTSP
         COPYDDN(SYSCOPYP)
         TABLESPACE DASPJDB.DAJTSP
         COPYDDN(SYSCOPYJ)
         CONCURRENT SHRLEVEL CHANGE
/*
```

The execution of the RECOVER utility will see the STYPE = 'C' and invoke DFDSS RESTORE for the recovery. All recovery functions are the same as recovery from an image copy with the exception that one cannot use page and error range recovery. The RECOVER utility uses the log to compensate for committed updates in the virtual pool but not written to DASD for recovery to currency as with an image copy.

CR.5 RECOVERING TABLESPACES AND INDEXES

There are a variety of ways to recover tablespaces and indexes. Indexes can be recovered in V6. Prior to this version, indexes must be rebuilt if recovery of the tablespace can result in the indexes being inconsistent with the data which is true in most commonly used recovery scenarios. We will begin this section with a recovery to currency of all tables in four named tablespaces and seven named indexes in the DASPJDB database with the following statement in mind. If there are a number of data sets, the savings from the use of REUSE parameter can be significant (saves 0.6 seconds saved per data set as discussed in Chapter LC).

```
RECOVER
  TABLESPACE DASPJDB.DASPJTSP
    INDEX AUTHID.SNPNJNX

    INDEX AUTHID.PNX
    INDEX AUTHID.JNX
  TABLESPACE DASPJDB.DASTSP
    INDEX AUTHID.SNX
  TABLESPACE DASPJDB.DAPTSP
    INDEX AUTHID.PNX
  TABLESPACE DASPJDB.DAJTSP
    INDEX AUTHID.JNX
PARALLEL(4)
```

The PARALLEL parameter (V6) of RECOVER means that multiple objects can be recovered in parallel. The image copies are written to the named objects during the RESTORE phase. The log records are applied to the restored copies of the tablespaces and indexes with a single pass of the log. If PARALLEL or PARALLEL (0) is specified, the RECOVER utility determines the optimal number of objects to process in parallel. The example RECOVER statement requests that four task be used for parallel recovery.

There must exist a full image copy of the indexes defined with COPY YES for a recovery of the indexes. It is necessary to have the copies on DASD for a parallel recovery. If a copy is on tape, parallelism is discontinued until tape processing completes and then parallel recovery resumes. Parallel recovery cannot be done on a logical part of a nonpartitioning indexes (NPI) and a single data set of a NPI.

The REUSE parameter can be used to reload data into the original data sets with the benefits discussed in the LC Chapter. The parameter also applies to recovering and rebuilding indexes. However, do not use the parameter if there has been a media failure involving the data set to be recovered or rebuilt.

Comparison of single and parallel COPY and RECOVER test results show significant reductions in elapsed time with little or not increase in CPU time as indicated in Figure CR.11 and Figure CR.12. The tests were done on a 5 million row table in 10 partitions, 118 byte row with 26 columns. Details of tests are in DB2 UDB for OS/390 Version 6 Performance Topics (SG24-5351).

Figure CR.11. Comparison of COPY all data serially and 10 parallel tasks

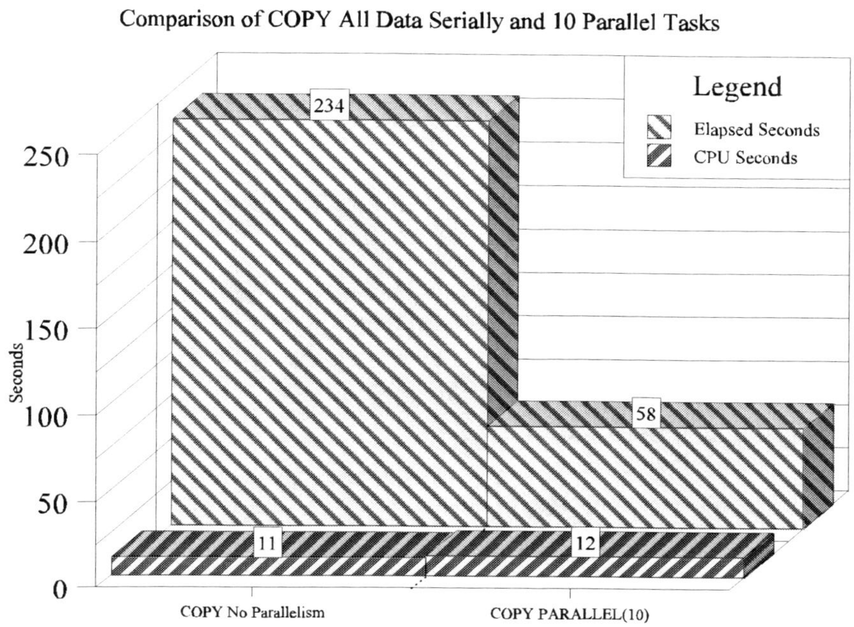

Figure CR.12. Comparison of RECOVER of all data serially and 10 parallel tasks

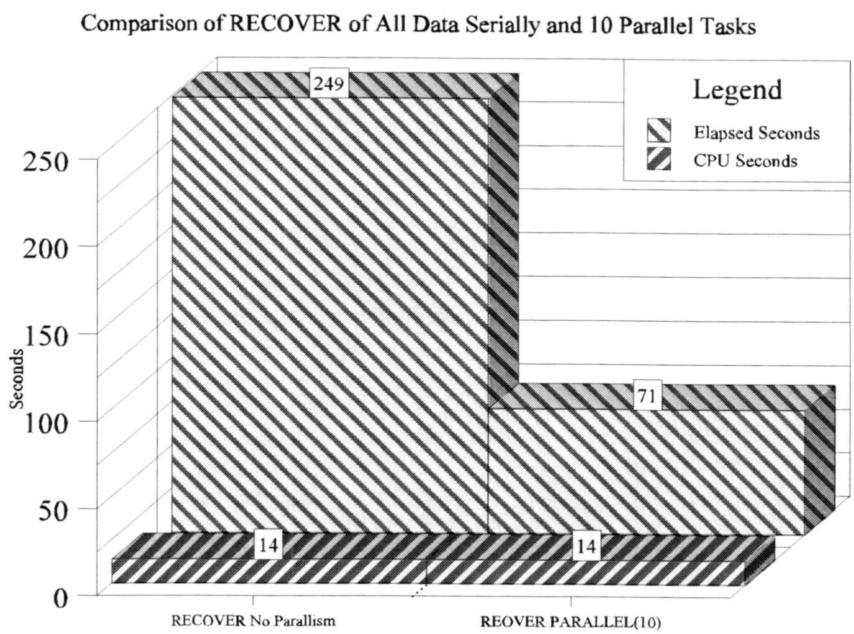

One might expect a 10 time reduction in elapsed time with 10 parallel tasks. This was not experienced primarily due to I/O contention. However, the decrease in elapsed time suggests that parallel copies and recoveries are a good choice when resources are available.

Fast Log Apply

Fast log apply applies multiple log records to a page or series of pages (V6). It applies to the RECOVER utility, forward phase of DB2 restart, START DATABASE for LPL and GRECP recovery.

The process consists of sorting the log records for a page set by DBID, OBID, PART, PAGE, and LRSN or RBA with a single pass of the log for objects named in RECOVER statement and groups by DBID, PSID, PART in the buffer. There is sort task for each recovery process in most cases. One log apply task is dispatched for each group within a page set. There is a maximum of 98 tasks that can be run in parallel. If 99th recovery is required, it must wait for a task to complete. List prefetch used to apply multiple log record to pages in sequence. This avoids accessing a page for each log record that applies to the page.

The use of fast log apply is not the default. It must be enabled by specifying a non-zero value for the buffer with DSNZPARM DSN6SYSP macro LOGAPSTG parameter or LOG APPLY STORAGE field on the DSNTIPL installation panel. The space requested is divided among recovery jobs (minimum of 64 KB for each job). If space is unavailable for one or subsequent recovery jobs, non-fast log apply is used for additional jobs and an error message is issued. DB2 restart uses 10 MB or amount specified up to 100 MB even if fast log apply is not enabled. This speeds recovery a great deal and the space is available during a DB2 restart.

Significant saving can result from the use of fast log apply. For example, the log apply phase went from 955 to 101 elapsed and 12 to 1.8 CPU seconds to recover 44,000 rows at random in a 5 million row table. The time went from 1,086 to 693 elapsed and 317 to 160 CPU seconds when the rows were in sequence. The details of these tests and more can be found in the *DB2 UDB for OS/390 Version 6 Performance Topics* (SG24-5351) manual.

We will review the work performed by the RECOVER utility to accomplish a recovery which will complete the explanation of the recovery portion of Figure CR.1.

Locate Image Copy for Recovery

The RECOVER utilities locates the most recent usable image copies for the current site in the catalog table SYSCOPY, calls for the copies, and writes them to DASD. If the most recent image copy is not available (one to four local and remote site copies), the RECOVER utility uses the previous image copy which requires that it go further back in the log to locate log records describing inserts, updates, and deletes done after the image copy was made. These log records are applied to the copies written to DASD with a single pass of the log.

If the local copies have been damaged or lost and the recovery site copies can be obtained, the RECOVERYSITE parameter causes the recovery site copy to be used at the local site. Conversely, if the recovery site copies have been damaged or lost, the local copy can to use at the recovery site provided that the LOCALSITE parameter is specified.

The DSNUM parameter must be specified to recover a partition or data set of a multi data set tablespace if the parameter was used to make the copy.

Recommendation: Do make copies frequently enough to avoid the use of archive logs particularly if they are on tape. Otherwise, the recovery process will take longer than necessary. Also, do follow the recovery with a full image copy to avoid a lengthy recovery in the future.

ERROR RANGE Parameter

If only specific tracks and cylinders are damaged on DASD, it is probably unnecessary to recover the entire tablespace and rebuild all of the indexes. The messages DSNU086I indicates an I/O error. The I/O error range is maintained internally by DB2 and you can determine the range with the DISPLAY DATABASE command. If the error range is a small percent of the total space, use of the ERROR RANGE parameter is advisable. This improves performance because only the damaged pages are recovered.

Do use the ICKDSF service utility to deal with the error before a recovery. Then submit a RECOVER statement with the ERROR RANGE parameter.

```
RECOVER TABLESPACE DASPJDB.DASPJTSP
ERROR RANGE
```

Logical Page List

Logical page list (LPL) is a list or range of page IDs with committed updates that could not be written to DASD because of a failure. For example, there may have been a transient disk read or write problem that can be fixed without redefining new tracks or volumes. An SQL statement that attempts to process a page on the LPL receive a -904 SQLCODE (resource unavailable).

If the cause of the error is unknown, the page IDs are first recorded in the LPL. If recovery is not successful, the page IDs are recorded in the error page range and the pages are considered physically damaged.

The LPL parameter can be added to the DISPLAY DATABASE command to determine the pages on the list. Here is an example to determine the LPL pages in the SPJTEST database. The command is to be executed on the -DB2A member of a data sharing group.

```
-DB2A DISPLAY DATABASE(SPJTEST) LPL
```

In the example output in Figure CR.13 from the DISPLAY command, we see that pages 10, 80 through 90, and 700 are on the LPL list.

Figure CR.13. Pages on the LPL list

```
DSNT362I DATABASE = SPJTEST   STATUS = RW DBD LENGTH = 200
SPACE    TYPE PART STATUS                LPL PAGES
------   ---- ---- ---------------       ------------------
SPJ      TS        RW,LPL                10,80-90,700
-                            MEMBER NAME DB2A
DSNT390  DISPLAY OF DATABASE SPJTEST ENDS
```

Recovery can be done with the RECOVER utility or simply execute the START DATABASE command with an ACCESS parameter of read/write (RW) or read-only (RO) on the affected database and tablespace like:

```
-DB2A START DATABASE(DASPJDB) SPACENAM (DASPJTSP) ACCESS(RW)
```

CR.6 RECOVER AND REBUILD INDEXES

REBUILD INDEX is an alias for RECOVER INDEX in V4 with PTF UQ11204 and in V5 with UQ11205 installed. If an index is to be rebuilt from indexed values extracted with a tablespace scan in V6 as in previous versions of DB2, specify REBUILD INDEX. If an index is to be recovered from an image copy of the index and log in V6, specify RECOVER INDEX. Optionally, the SORTKEYS parameter of REBUILD INDEX can be used to sort and rebuild multiple indexes on a table in parallel as described in Chapter LC Section 3 in V6.

Recommendation: Do use RECOVER INDEX and REBUILD INDEX in V4 and V5 the way that you want the indexes processed in V6. Do review your RECOVER INDEX jobs developed before V6 and change them to REBUILD INDEX where you want to rebuild an index rather than recover the index using a copy and the log in V6. If RECOVER INDEX is executed in V6 without the index being defined with COPY YES and an existing image copy of the index, the utility will fail.

Indexes must be recovered or rebuilt when recovering tablespaces unless only the tablespace is damaged and the table and indexes agree. If you believe that they agree, the CHECK INDEX utility can be used to verify agreement as discussed in Chapter LC. The following statement causes the DASPJDB.DASPJTSP tablespace to be recovered to currency and all of the indexes on all of the tables in the tablespace to be recovered by writing the image copy of the index to a data set and applying log records (V6). In contrast, REBUILD INDEX does a tablespace scan, extracts the indexed values, sorts them in most cases, and builds the index. (This is the processing done by RECOVER INDEX prior to V6.)

```
RECOVER INDEX (ALL)
TABLESPACE DASPJDB.DASPJTSP
```

One or more indexes can be specified to the RECOVER INDEX and REBUILD INDEX utilities. The following statement causes the AUTHID.ISN and AUTHID.IPN indexes to be rebuilt prior to V6. If you want to rebuild the indexes in V6, specify REBUILD INDEX in V4, V5, and V6.

```
RECOVER INDEX (AUTHID.ISN, AUTHID.IPN)
```

Both of the preceding statements cause a tablespace scan to extract the indexed values, sort of the indexed values, and build of the indexes serially prior to V6. The build of several indexes serially can delay the recovery time and when the data can be made available to the users.

REBUILD INDEX in V6: REBUILD INDEX does a tablespace scan, extracts the indexed values, sorts them, and optionally rebuilds the indexes in parallel. Figure CR.14 is an example of JCL to rebuild all indexesf on all tables in the tablespace DASPJTSP, and database DASPJDB. Optionally, you can name one or more indexes and one or more partitions for which indexes are to be rebuilt. The indexes are rebuilt in parallel as discussed in Chapter LC Section 3. The STATISTICS parameter with or without INDEX(ALL) causes statistics to be collected and recorded in the catalog tables similar to RUNSTATS without having RUNSTATS process the indexes after they are built (V6). This has performance advantages if the index statistics in the catalog tables are no longer representative of the rebuilt indexes. Additional parameters and details are discussed in Chapter RR.

Figure CR.14. Example of rebuilding all indexes on all tables in a tablespace

```
//REBLDX JOB   ...
//STEP1   EXEC DSNUPROC,UID='AUTHID.REBLDX',
//        UTPROC='', SYSTEM='DSNT'
//SYSIN   DD *
  REBUILD INDEX (ALL) TABLESPACE DASPJDB.DASPJTSP
    SORTKEYS
    SORTDEVT SYSWK
    SORTNUM 4
    STATISTICS
/*
```

Comparison of RECOVER and REBUILD Indexes: DB2 Estimator V6 is used to estimate the elapsed and CPU time to RECOVER and REBUILD three indexes on a million row table with a 100 byte row length using 9672 RX5 with 10 CPUs and 3390-3 DASD.

The REBUILD statement used is:

REBUILD INDEX(ALL) TABLE T100

The RECOVER statement used is:

RECOVER INDEX(ALL) TABLESPACE TSP100

Figure CR.15 shows a comparison of the using the utilities. Clearly RECOVER requires dramatically less elapsed and CPU time than REBUILD. The RECOVER utility estimate is based on 10 percent of the pages being changed.

Figure CR.15. Comparison of RECOVER and REBUILD indexes

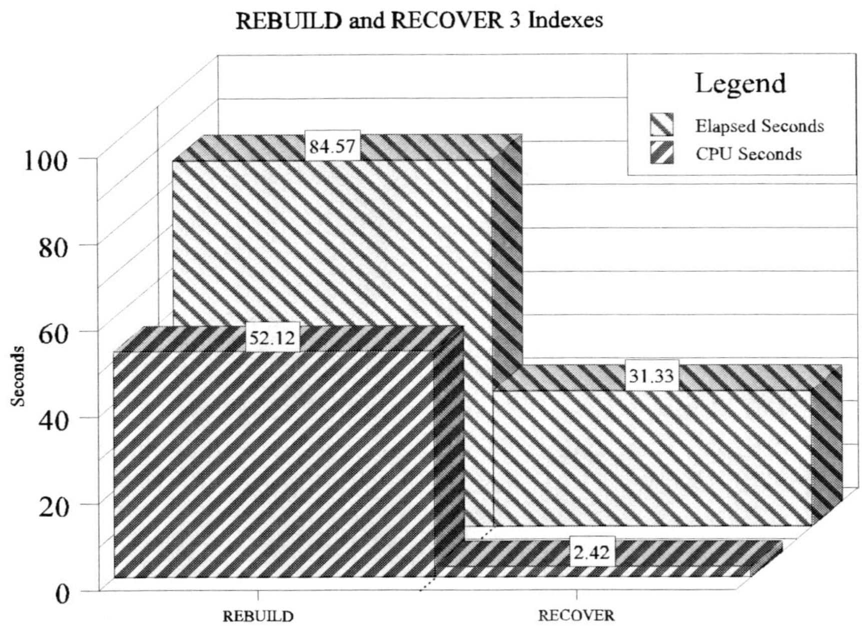

Recommendation: Do consider using DB2 Estimator to estimate differences for your data using your computer and DASD, and an estimate of the percentage of pages changed. This will give you good information on which utility is best for your tables in your environment.

Recovery of an Index Part

The PART parameter can be used to specify a specific physical or logical partition of a partitioned index or logical part of a nonpartitioned index on a partitioned tablespace. Recovery of a NPI logical part checks to determine if the RID has changed. If it has not changed, the RID is not deleted and a new RID inserted. This significantly improves performance.

Restart of REBUILD INDEX

There is a good deal of flexibility in restarting a REBUILD INDEX job as summarized in Figure CR.16.

Figure CR.16. Restartability of REBUILD INDEX

Phase	Description	Restart if Failure Occurs During Phase
UTILINIT	Initialization and setup	No
UNLOAD	Unload indexed values and write to SYSUT1	At beginning of phase
SORT*	Sort unloaded indexed values and write to SYSUT1 again	At beginning of phase
BUILD	Build indexes	At the last index built

Phase	Description	Restart if Failure Occurs During Phase
UTILTERM	Cleanup	No

Notice that if there is a failure during the build of multiple indexes serially, the restart is after the last successfully built index. If a failure occurs during a short period after the SORT phase, restart at the beginning the UNLOAD phase is required. This avoids an additional SORTOUT data set.

REBUILD INDEX With and Without SYSUT1

The elapsed time of REBUILD INDEX can be reduced significantly and there is some savings in CPU time by not specifying WORKDDN(SYSUT1) which is the default. This means that the indexed values extracted during a tablespace scan are not written to SYSUT1. Rather the indexed values are passed directly to the external sort and the external sort passes the sorted values directly to the build index phase. I/O to SYSUT1 is avoided. However, REBUILD INDEX is not restartable.

IBM tested the effect of omitting WORKDDN on a recovery of a 5 million row table in 10 partitions, 118 byte row length with 26 columns, and 2 indexes using DB2 V5 on a 10-way RX3 9672 V0C with RAMAC DASD. Figure CR.17 summarizes the tests results. Notice that recovery of 2 indexes was reduced from 796 elapsed and 593 CPU seconds to 579 elapsed and 527 CPU seconds by omitting WORKDDN and not using SYSUT1.

Figure CR.17. REBUILD INDEX ALL with and without SYSUT1

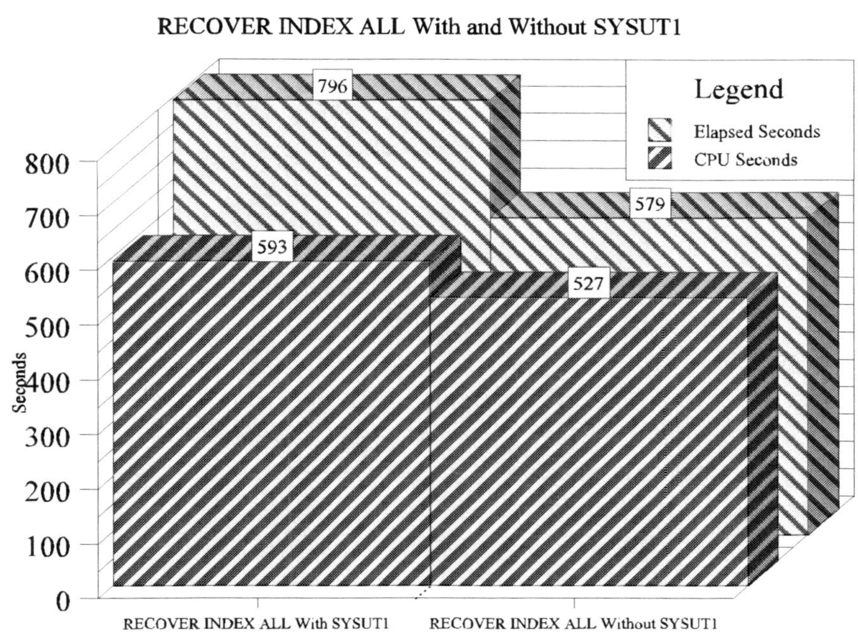

If the REBUILD INDEX fails and must be resubmitted, the total elapsed time is likely to be longer than if the utility could have been restarted. If it is unlikely that the REBUILD INDEX job will fail, omitting WORKDDN is a good choice to reduce the elapsed and CPU times for the recovery.

CR.7 POINT-IN-TIME RECOVERY

Point-in-Time (PIT) recovery can be to an image copy or a point of consistency. The point of consistency can be established by the QUIESCE utility discussed in Section CR.8 by recording the RBA or log record sequence number (LRSN) in a sysplex data sharing environment in the START_RBA column of SYSCOPY. The older term RBA is often used rather than LRSN and is used in this chapter. Keep in mind that it is actually the LRSN in a sysplex data sharing environment. The RECOVER utility parameter TOLOGPOINT should be used rather than TORBA. It has the same effect in a data sharing and non-data sharing environment. It is required in a data sharing environment and should be used in a non-data sharing environment if there is any possibility of using data sharing in the future. This avoids having to change TORBA to TOLOGPOINT if it is decided to use data sharing.

The goal of recovery to an RBA is to eliminate updates made after the PIT recovery. For example, assume that updates U20 through U30 are in the log for a tablespace as shown in Figure CR.18.

Figure CR.18. Point-in-time recovery

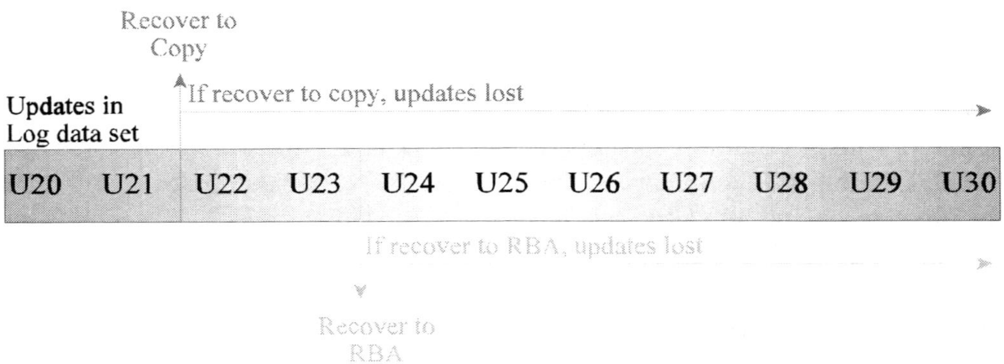

Assume that an image copy is made after U21 and there is a requirement to recover to that copy using the RECOVERY utility parameter TOCOPY. Update U22 and all subsequent updates are no longer on the tablespace after the recovery. This is because the RECOVER utility writes the image copy to the tablespace and does not apply the log records.

Another requirement might be to recover to an established RBA for update U24. All updates made after and including the RBA are no longer on the tablespace after a TOLOGPOINT or TORBA recovery. This is because the RECOVER utility writes the image copy to the tablespace and applies the log records up to and including the RBA for U24.

An image copy is not required after a PIT recovery although it is advisable to avoid having to go too far back in the log for future recoveries. The records between the RBA for U24 and the start RBA in SYSCOPY (U31 in the example) are not included in subsequent recoveries.

The QUIESCE and REPORT utilities are useful for PIT recoveries. We will look first at the QUIESCE utility.

CR.8 PURPOSE AND USE OF QUIESCE

A primary purposes of the QUIESCE utility is to establish a point of consistency (RBA or LRSN) for a referential integrity (RI) structure, any group of tablespaces and indexes, one or more tablespaces and optionally indexes. A full or PIT recovery of a RI structure must be to a quiesce point for all related tablespaces. Otherwise, the check pending status is turned on by recover. QUIESCE is not necessary if the RI structure is in a single tablespace. QUIESCE is often used to establish a point of consistency for a single unrelated tablespace to provide an RBA for a PIT recovery. Also, the PART parameter can be used to establish an RBA for a partition.

QUIESCE forces updated pages in virtual pool to DASD if the WRITE YES parameter is specified. The pages remain in the virtual pool and can be read or updated without physical I/O to DASD. QUIESCE has advantages over using the STOP DATABASE command and stopping the DB2 subsystem to force updated pages to DASD. If the database or tablespace is stopped, pages in the virtual pool must be reread from DASD incurring additional unwanted and unneeded I/O. In addition the underlying data sets are closed and must be reopened when next accessed. The stop of one or more tablespaces in a database disallows access to the data during the stop processing and while the tablespaces are stopped. Certainly, one would not want to have to stop the DB2 subsystem to force updated pages to DASD.

Executing QUIESCE

It is necessary to identify and name all tablespaces that are to have the same RBA or LRSN established. This is required to avoid a check pending status for an RI structure (V5). We will look at how to use the REPORT utility to do this in the next section. Here is an example of quiescing four related tablespaces as identified using the REPORT utility.

```
QUIESCE TABLESPACE DASPJDB.DASTSP
        TABLESPACE DASPJDB.DAPTSP
        TABLESPACE DASPJDB.DAJTSP
        TABLESPACE DASPJDB.DASPJTSP
WRITE YES
```

One tablespace can be named with the parameter TABLESPACESET (V6). QUIESCE processes all RI related tablespaces.

The WRITE YES parameter causes all outstanding updates in the virtual pool to be written to DASD, updates the STOPRBA in SYSLGRNX if it is 0, and writes the LOGRBA to header page of the tablespace.

The WRITE NO parameter does not externalize updates from the buffer. It updates the RBA while exclusive locks are being held for an update by an application program. A PIT recovery to the established RBA does not include updates that have not been committed.

Both WRITE of YES and write of NO cause the RBA and timestamp for each tablespace to be written to SYSCOPY which establishes a point of consistency.

QUIESCE updates SYSCOPY with its established RBA. This can result in a deadlock when multiple QUIESCE jobs execute concurrently. Contention involving the DSNUCX01 and DSNUCH01 indexes can occur.

CR.9 PURPOSE AND USE OF REPORT

There are three primary purposes of the REPORT utility. First, it is useful in identifying all tables and tablespaces in a RI structure to quiesce as a tablespace set (not required in V6), given a specific tablespace. Also, it provides good documentation of an RI structure. Second, it can report on indexes on tables in the specified tablespaces (V6). The identified indexes can be named in the RECOVER or REBUILD statements. Third, REPORT can be used to determine information on what is needed for a tablespace recovery. It reports on image copies and quiesce points from SYSCOPY, the start and stop RBA from SYSLGRNX, and information on active and archive log data sets from the BSDS.

Reporting on RI Structures

All of the tables and tablespaces that have a RI relationship can be determined by naming a specified tablespace like:

```
REPORT TABLESPACESET
TABLESPACE DASPJDB.DASPJTSP
```

Figure CR.19 is an example of a report showing the tables and tablespaces related to the DASPJTSP tablespace in the DASPJDB database.

Figure CR.19. Related tables and tablespaces

TABLESPACE	TABLE	DEPENDENT TABLE
DASPJDB.DASPJTSP	**AUTHID.S**	AUTHID.SPJ
		AUTHID.S_BUYER
	AUTHID.P	AUTHID.SPJ
	AUTHID.J	AUTHID.SPJ
		AUTHID.J_ASSIGN
	AUTHID.SPJ	
DASPJDB.DALOCTSP	AUTHID.VALID_CITY	**AUTHID.S**
		AUTHID.P
		AUTHID.J
	AUTHID.VALID_STATUS	**AUTHID.S**
DASPJDB.DAEMPTSP	**AUTHID.EMP**	AUTHID.S_BUYER
		AUTHID.J_ASSIGN
		AUTHID.DEPT
	AUTHID.J_ASSIGN	
	AUTHID.S_BUYER	
DASPJDB.DADEPTSP	**AUTHID.DEPT**	**AUTHID.EMP**
		AUTHID.J_ASSIGN
		AUTHID.DEPT

Notice that the AUTHID.S is one of four tables in the DASPJDB.DASPJTSP tablespace. It is a parent table as indicated by the second column heading. It is a dependent of the AUTHID.VALID_ CITY and AUTHID.VALID_STATUS tables in the DASPJDB.DALOCTSP tablespace as indicated by the third column heading. The AUTHID.EMP table is a parent table in the

DASPJDB.DAEMPTSP tablespace and also a dependent of the AUTHID.DEPT table in the DASPJDB.DADEPTSP. Further, the AUTHID.DEPT table is a parent table in the DASPJDB.DADEPTSP tablespace and the AUTHID.EMP in the same tablespace is a dependent table. This indicates that the DEPT and EMP tables are in a cyclic relationship as discussed in Chapter CT. Notice that the DEPT table is both a parent and dependent table in the DASPJDB.DADEPTSP tablespace. This indicates that the DEPT table is a self-referencing table as discussed in Chapter CT.

Reporting on Indexes (V6)

It is necessary to specify the index or indexspace name in order to recover or rebuild an index. The following statement reports on all indexes on all tables in the named tablespace. Multiple tablespaces can be named.

```
REPORT RECOVERY INDEX ALL
TABLESPACE DASPJDB.DASPJTSP
```

The INDEX ALL parameter is a good choice to determine all indexes on the tables in one or more tablespaces. INDEX NONE is the default.

Optionally, a report on named indexes or indexspaces can be requested using the INDEX AUTHID.SPJX or INDEXSPACE DASPJDB.INDSPACE parameter.

Reporting on Information Used for Recovery

The REPORT utility can be used to determine the resources required for a recovery of a name tablespace like:

```
REPORT RECOVERY
TABLESPACE DASPJDB.DASPJTSP
ARCHLOG 1
```

It reports on images copies and the start RBA from SYSCOPY, range of log records that need to be scanned from SYSLGRNX, and the range of log records found on log data sets from the BSDS.

The ARCHLOG parameter can be used to specify that information is required on 1 archive log or the value 2 or ALL indicates that information is required on both archive logs (V6). The default is 1.

Figure CR.20 is an example of information from SYSCOPY on the timestamp of when the START_RBA was written and TYPE indicates what caused the START RBA to be written to SYSCOPY. The meaning of the TYPE column will be discussed in the next section. The data set name (DSNAME) of image copies is also provided. The RECOVER utility uses this information to determine which copy to use, which log ranges to scan based on information from SYSLGRNX, and which log data sets contains the log records from the BSDS.

Figure CR.20. Information from SYSCOPY

TIMESTAMP	TYPE	DS NUM	FILE SEQ	START RBA	SHR LVL	DEV TYPE	REQD	DSNAME
1988-06-08-11.10.00.278362	*Q*	0000	0000	000008CF501A			Y	
1988-06-08-11.10.06.548910	*X*	0000	0000	000008CF98EE			N	
1988-06-14-14.16.25.843679	*Q*	0000	0000	000008E05F8A			Y	
1988-06-14-14.17.18.039184	F	0000	0000	000008E0BD09	R	SYSDA	N	C8145GD...
1988-06-14-04.16.15.387643	*Q*	0000	0000	000008F10D98			Y	
1988-06-14-10.09.20.843913	*Q*	0000	0000	000008F2CFE9			Y	
1988-06-14-10.11.01.560183	F	0000	0000	000008F411F3	R	SYSDA	N	C8145GD...
1988-06-14-09.11.08.495230	*Q*	0000	0000	000008F58320			Y	
1988-06-14-09.12.15.334827	**F**	**0000**	**0000**	**000008F5C300**	**R**	**SYSDA**	**N**	**C8145GD...**

REPORT provides information from directory table SYSLGRNX, an example of which is in Figure CR.21. It summarizes the START and STOP RBA in the log that need to be scanned for a log apply to the copy laid down by the RECOVER utility. If the image copy RBA is less than the SYSLGRNX RBA, this indicates to start applying updates to the copy from the SYSLGRNX RBA in the log data set.

For example, if the last image copy in the previous Figure CR.20 is used by the RECOVER utility, the log records between last start and stop RBA in Figure CR.21 must be scanned by the RECOVER utility to locate log records that must be applied to the copy laid down on the tablespace.

Figure CR.21. Information from SYSLGRNX

DSNU583I - DSNUPPLR - REPORT RECOVERY TABLESPACE DASPJDB.DASPJTSP SYSLGRNX ROWS

UCDATE	UCTIME	START RBA	STOP RBA	PARTITION
060888	10200532	0000088F5573	0000088F6994	0000
060888	10211502	000008C6E2BD	000008C6F9E1	0000
060888	22190320	000008CDD8D8	000008CDEED0	0000
060888	22211177	000008CF9C6D	000008CFB2B7	0000
061488	08373692	000008E0A5E3	000008E0BC84	0000
061488	19230279	000008F3F918	000008F30F6D	0000
061488	**19253341**	**000008F5AE3C**	**000008F5C4EE**	**0000**

The REPORT utility provides the start and end RBA for each log data set as shown in Figure CR.22. This information is used by the RECOVER utility to determine which log data sets contain updates made after an image copy and are required for the recovery.

Figure CR.22. Log record ranges in the log data sets

DSNU583I - DSNUPPLR - REPORT RECOVERY TABLESPACE DASPJDB.DASPJTSP BSDS VOLUMES

START TIME	END TIME	START RBA	END RBA	UNIT	VOLSER
19882882420449	19883882620449	000008C5AE5D	000008C6AE2E	3380	WAV01
19883882420538	19883882620538	000008E5AE2B	000008E6AE40	3380	WAV02
19883882437183	**19883882437183**	**000008F5AE4C**	**000008F6AE4B**	**3380**	**WAV03**

ICTYPES in SYSCOPY

You can select directly from SYSCOPY to determine information on copies and RBAs rather than using the REPORT utility. The following SELECT statement gives the same information from SYSCOPY as does the REPORT utility.

```
SELECT DBNAME, TSNAME, DSNUM, ICTYPE, ICDATE, HEX(START_RBA)
FROM   SYSIBM.SYSCOPY
WHERE  DBNAME = 'DASPJDB'
AND    TSNAME = 'DASTSP'
ORDER BY DSNUM, ICDATE;
```

The ICTYPE column is the same as the TYPE column in the REPORT output from Figure CR.22. Figure CR.23 summarizes the meaning of the ICTYPE and TYPE columns.

Figure CR.23. Description of ICTYPEs from SYSCOPY

ICTYPE	Description	START_RBA
F	COPY FULL YES	RBA of first update after the copy STYPE can have the values of: blank = DB2 image copy C = SMS concurrent copy R = LOAD REPLACE(YES), inline copy S = LOAD REPLACE(NO), inline copy W = REORG LOG(NO), inline copy X = REORG LOG(YES), inline copy
I	COPY FULL NO	RBA of first update after the copy
P	RECOVER TOCOPY, RECOVER TORBA, or RECOVER TOLOGPOINT	RBA after the log-apply phase of the PIT recovery. Used to avoid having to take a full image copy after a recovery to an RBA or image copy.
Q	QUIESCE	RBA after a successful quiesce. COPY ... CONCURRENT SHRLEVEL REFERENCE inserts a Q record at beginning of the job and updates row to a F at the end of the job and STYPE = C.
T	COPY terminated or stop database	End of log when utility terminated or stop database. Used to change a requested incremental copy to a full copy automatically.
R	LOAD REPLACE LOG(YES)	End of log before the start of LOAD
S	LOAD REPLACE LOG(NO)	End of log before the start of LOAD
W	REORG LOG(NO)	End of log before reload phase
X	REORG LOG(YES)	End of log before reload phase
Y	LOAD LOG(NO)	End of log before reload phase
Z	LOAD LOG(YES)	End of log before reload phase

CR.10 POINT-IN-TIME RECOVERY PROCEDURES

We have seen how information for a PIT recovery can be determined using the REPORT utility or you can select directly from SYSCOPY to determine the RBA to use with the TOLOGPOINT or TORBA parameter and the copy to use with the TOCOPY parameter.

Recover To an RBA

Lets assume that it is necessary to recover to the X'000008A50B9C' RBA based on information from executing the REPORT utility or from selecting from SYSCOPY. The RBA identified is specified in the TOLOGPOINT or TORBA parameter like:

```
RECOVER TABLESPACE DASPJDB.DASPJTSP
TOLOGPOINT X'000008A50B9C'
```

The RECOVER utility determines the most recent available image copy from SYSCOPY, writes it to the tablespace and applies the log records to the copy up to the specified RBA. All updates made after and including the RBA are lost as planned.

```
RECOVER TABLESPACE DASPJDB.DASPJTSP
TOLOGPOINT X'4A970C310154'
```

Indexes must be recovered with a PIT recovery. The existing indexes include updates effectively discarded from the tablespace with the PIT recovery. Here is an example of requesting the rebuild of all indexes on all tables in the DASPJDB.DASPJTSP.

```
REBUILD INDEX (ALL)
TABLESPACE DASPJDB.DASPJTSP
```

The most recent RBA written to SYSCOPY by the QUIESCE utility for a specified database and tablespace can be determined like:

```
SELECT HEX(START_RBA)
FROM   SYSIBM.SYSCOPY
WHERE  DBNAME = 'dbname'
AND    TSNAME = 'tsname'
AND    ICTYPE = 'Q'
AND    TIMESTAMP =
   (SELECT MAX(TIMESTAMP)
    FROM   SYSIBM.SYSCOPY
    WHERE  DBNAME = 'dbname'
    AND    TSNAME = 'tsname'
    AND    ICTYPE = 'Q');
```

Logonly Recovery

If an image copy is not available, a logonly recovery is attempted by scanning the log since the tablespace was first created. This can obviously be very resource intensive and it is unlikely that archive logs have been retained if the tablespace was created months or years ago. Also a logonly recover will not be successful if any non-recoverable event occurred, for example a load or reorganization with log of no. However, if LOAD fails during the RELOAD phase, it is possible to recover to the RBA written to SYSCOPY at the beginning of phase with log of no or at the end of the phase with log of yes. It is also possible to recover to a previous copy.

A logonly recover can be explicitly requested as discussed in Section CR.14.

Related Dependent Tablespaces

Any related dependent tablespaces not in the named tablespaces for a PIT recovery are placed in the check pending status. An exception is if the named RBA was established on all related tablespaces with the QUIESCE utility. This is because there can be inconsistencies between the parent and dependent tables after a PIT recovery. Figure CR.24 shows how inconsistencies can occur if a PIT recovery is not done to a quiesce point.

Figure CR.24. Problems of not doing a PIT recovery to a quiesce point

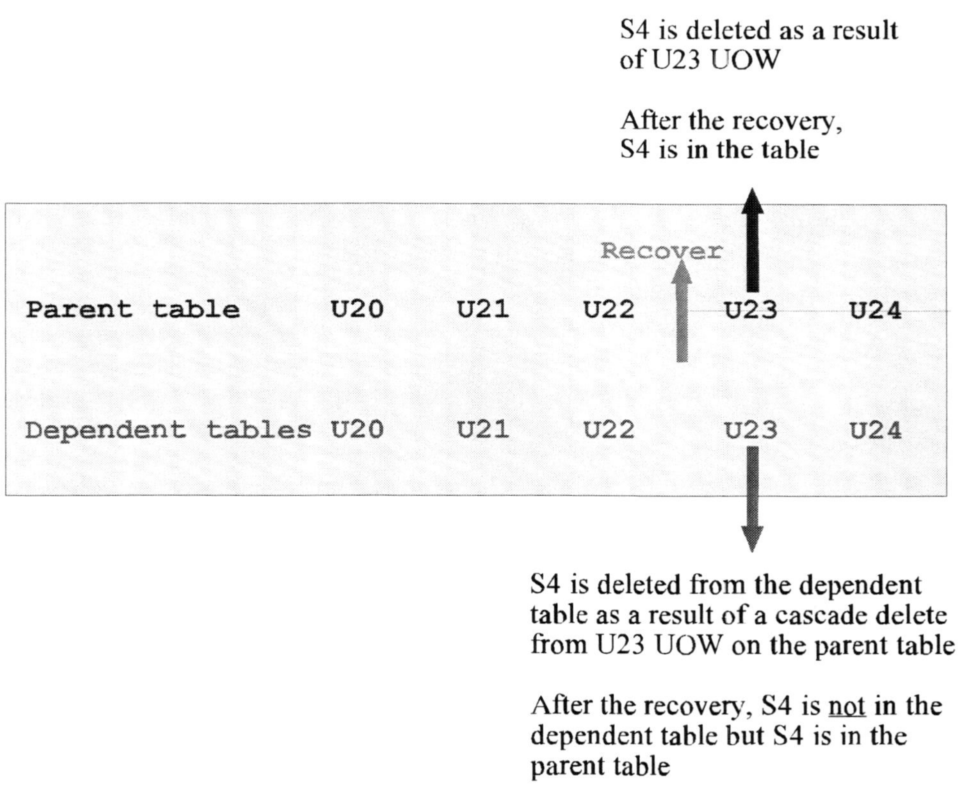

Lets assume that a TOLOGPOINT recovery is done such that the U23 and U24 work are removed from the parent S table. There is no recovery of the dependent table. Further assume that U23 is a delete of S4 from the S table with a cascade to the dependent table where it is also deleted. After the TOLOGPOINT recovery, S4 is in the S table again but is not in the dependent table. The effect of U23 is removed from the parent table but not the dependent table. This is an example of why check pending is set on.

Prepare for Recovering Related Tablespaces

It is advisable to prepare for recovering related tablespaces. This can be done by quiescing the related tablespaces before making image copies to ensures that all pending states are off and that all updates in the virtual pool are written to the tablespaces and indexes if WRITE YES is used. Make image copies of the related tablespaces. Do another quiesce of the related tablespaces after the image copies to provide for a TOLOGPOINT recovery. A recovery using TOCOPY will set check pending on because each of multiple copies probably completed at different times and can contain different update activity.

There are performance advantages to recovering TOLOGPOINT compared to a recovery to currency. This is because the log need not be scanned beyond the specified RBA.

Recovering a RI Structure to an RBA

After the QUIESCE utility has been used to establish an RBA for all tablespaces that are part of a DB2 defined RI structure or group of tablespaces that need to be kept synchronized, the tablespaces must be named in the RECOVER statement along with the established RBA value like:

```
RECOVER TABLESPACE DASPJDB.DASPJTSP
        TABLESPACE DASPJDB.DALOCTSP
        TABLESPACE DASPJDB.DAEMPTSP
        TABLESPACE DASPJDB.DADEPTSP
TOLOGPOINT X'000008A50B9C'
```

The recovery of the multiple tablespaces uses a single scan of the log. The utility is restartable in case of failure. Indeed, do restart the RECOVER utility rather than terminating it and resubmitting the utility. Termination of the utility places all of the named tablespaces in a RECOVERY PENDING state.

All indexes on all tables in all tablespaces recovered using TOLOGPOINT, TORBA and TOCOPY must be rebuilt prior to V6 like:

```
REBUILD INDEX (ALL)
        TABLESPACE DASPJDB.DASPJTSP
        TABLESPACE DASPJDB.DALOCTSP
        TABLESPACE DASPJDB.DAEMPTSP
        TABLESPACE DASPJDB.DADEPTSP
```

All indexes on all tables in the named tablespaces can be named in the RECOVER statement in V6 as discussed in Section CR.5.

Recover TOCOPY

Recovery can be to a specific image copy. All updates made after the image copy are lost. Here is an example of recovering the DASPJDB.DASPJTSP table to a named image copy.

```
RECOVER TABLESPACE DASPJDB.DASPJTSP
TOCOPY C8145GD.DASPJTSP.TIC.G0007V00
```

The copy named in the TOCOPY parameter can be a full or incremental copy. If the copy is not available, it is necessary to use the previously made copy and go further back in log for the log apply.

The named copy should be an image copy made with SHRLEVEL REFERENCE (not concurrent copy). Otherwise, data pages could have been changed during the copy after the space map page was copied resulting in an inconsistent copy. If an attempt is made to recovery to other than an image copy made with SHRLEVEL REFERENCE a warning is issued that the DB2 object has been recovered to an indeterminate point.

If a TOCOPY or TOLOGPOINT recovery is done of some but not all data sets in a multi data set nonpartitioned tablespace, a warning is issued prior to the recovery that the data set to be recovered might have been compressed with a different dictionary.

As mentioned early, it is necessary to recover or rebuild all indexes on all tables in all tablespaces that have been recovered with TOCOPY, TOLOGPOINT, and TORBA.

CR.11 LOGONLY RECOVERY

An offline copy is a copy made independently of DB2, not using the image copy utility. It can be made with the service aid DSN1COPY or a utility from a third party company. A record of an offline copy is not written to SYSCOPY.

It is your responsibility to track offline copies and write them to a tablespace to be recovered usually using the same tools used to make the copy. The LOGONLY parameter specified on the RECOVER statement indicates that the restore phase of the utility is to be skipped and that the log records must be applied to the copy that you placed on the tablespace. LOGONLY recovery applies to only a single tablespace. The recover can be to currency or TOLOGPOINT.

Do be careful and place the correct copy on the tablespace. LOGONLY assumes that offline copy cleared errors and resets error range flags. The RECOVER utility does validates the DBID, PSID, and etc. from the catalog tables. If the IDs do not match the IDs on the copy, the DSNU548 message is issued with a return code of 8.

RB-RBA Used in LOGONLY Recovery

LOGONLY recovery uses the recovery based RBA (RB-RBA) to determine where to start in the log to locate updates and apply them to the copy that you have placed on the tablespace.

The (RB-RBA) is written to tablespace header page (field HPGRBRBA) and SYSLGRNX to close the log range when the tablespace is switched to read-only status, the data set is closed, QUIESCE is executed with WRITE YES, the tablespace is stopped, and when the DB2 subsystem is stopped.

If any non-recoverable event (LOAD or REORG with LOG NO and no inline copy, for example) has occurred, message DSNU546 and return code of 8 is issued and the job is terminated. This is based on an analysis by the RECOVER utility as to whether SYSCOPY records have a START_RBA between RB-RBA and the current RBA.

After you have written the offline copy to the tablespace and submitted the RECOVER utility with the LOGONLY parameter, the utility reads the header page to determine the RB-RBA and uses this value to start reading the log and applying the log records to the copy as shown in Figure CR.25.

Figure CR.25. RB-RBA used in LOGONLY recovery

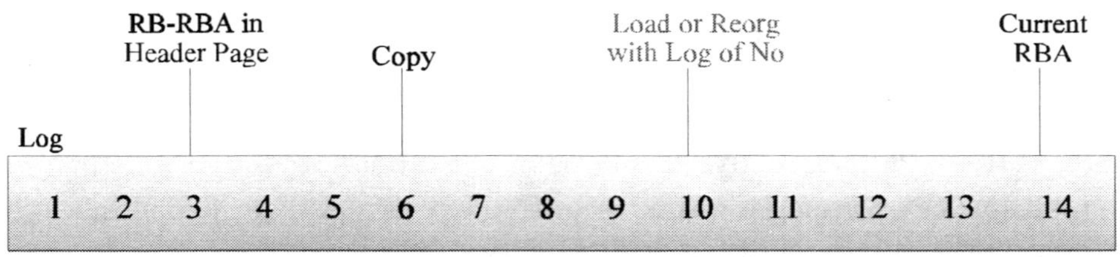

Procedures for LOGONLY Recover

If LOGONLY recover TOLOGPOINT is required, a procedure is needed to avoid capturing an update after the RB-RBA is captured in the copy. The goal is to lose updates made after TOLOGPOINT. Here is a procedure to create a copy that can be used safely in a TOLOGPOINT recovery

- -START DATABASE with ACCESS(RO) on all objects to be copied
- QUIESCE with WRITE YES
- Make Offline copies
- -START DATABASE with ACCESS(RW)

A procedure is needed for the LOGONLY recovery TOLOGPOINT to insure that no transaction can access data until recovery is complete like:

- -STOP DATABASE on all objects to be recovered
- -START DATABASE with ACCESS(UT)
- Write offline copy to tablespace
- RECOVER ... LOGONLY
- -START DATABASE with ACCESS(RW)

Level ID

A level ID is used to determine if the wrong copy has been placed on the tablespace. If the wrong copy has been placed on the tablespace, it is considered a down level error. The level ID is on the header page of each page set or partition and is written to SYSLGRNX at the same time as the end RBA is updated. If level IDs do not agree when SQL or a utility first attempts access of an unopened data set, it is considered a down-level data set. The following error message is issued along with the expected level ID, the current level ID, and the data set name.

```
DSNB232I UNEXPECTED DATA SET
  LEVEL ID ENCOUNTERED
```

You can determine the level ID in the header using DSN1PRNT with the options PRINT(1) and FORMAT to print the header page.

If you are confident that a down-level error will not occur or that you can manage the situation, you can disable level ID verification in DSNZPARM.

Recovering from a Down-Level Error

It is necessary to replace the data set with one at the proper level using DSN1COPY, SMS, or another copy utility. Then use the RECOVER utility to recover to the current time or prior point-in-time.

There are times when you need to explicitly reset the level ID. For example, you need to reset the level ID when using a production copy of a tablespace to populate or refresh a test copy of the tablespace. This can be done using DSN1COPY with the RESET option. An alternative is to use the REPAIR utility with the LEVELID option to reset the level ID.

CR.12 RECOVERY PENDING STATE

The recovery pending state can apply to a tablespace and an index space. A recovery TOCOPY, TOLOGPOINT, and TORBA can cause recover pending to be set on. Only the indexes are in recover pending if recovery is successful. Check pending is set on for dependent tablespaces when a single tablespace is recovered in a RI structure. Abend of RECOVER, LOAD, and REORG without a successful restart sets recovery pending on.

Operations Allowed While Recovery Pending is On

Once recovery pending is set on, no SQL DML (Data Manipulation Language) statements are allowed on the tablespace. You can execute RECOVER, LOAD REPLACE, or REPAIR to set recovery pending off. Less attractive alternatives are to use the REPAIR utility to set the recovery pending state off or start the database, tablespace, and index space with access of force. If you must ignore the problem, REPAIR is the better choice.

Managing Pending States

The recovery pending state can be forced off using the REPAIR utility like the check pending and copy pending states as mentioned in Chapter LC. Indeed, the utility can be used to force off one or more the pending states. Here is an example of turning off all of the pending states.

```
REPAIR SET TABLESPACE DASPJDB.DASPJTSP
NOCHECKPEND
NOCOPYPEND
NORCVRPEND
```

The disadvantage of using REPAIR is that the underlying problem is ignored. Only the flag indicating the pending state is set.

There are a variety of operations that can be performed using the REPAIR utility as described in the *DB2 Utility Guide and Reference* manual including the ability to dump, delete, and modify rows. Here is an example of deleting a FK row that has no parent row by specifying its RID.

```
REPAIR
LOCATE TABLESPACE DASPJDB.STSP
RID (X'0000070C') DELETE
```

The START DATABASE command with the ACCESS(FORCE) parameter can be used to ignore all pending states like:

```
-START DATABASE(DASPJDB) SPACENAM
 (DASPJTSP) ACCESS(FORCE)
```

However, all problems are ignored including pending deferred restarts, write error ranges, read-only access, and all pending states. The REORG pending state set on by altering the limit key of partitions is not set off.

Recommendation: It is best to resolve a problem rather than ignore it with REPAIR and start database with access of force.

CR.13 ARCHIVE LOG MANAGEMENT

Tape processing of the archive logs can be managed with the COUNT and TIME parameters in DSNZPARM. Also the parameters can be changed until the next stop and start of the DB2 subsystem with the SET ARCHIVE READ command.

The COUNT parameter allows for specifying the maximum number of tape units dedicated to reading archive logs.

The TIME parameter allows for specifying the number of minutes and seconds an allocated archive read tape unit can remain unused before it is deallocated.

SET ARCHIVE READ Command

The COUNT and TIME values specified in DSNZPARM can be modified until the next stop/start of DB2 with the SET ARCHIVE READ command. Here is an example of allocating 4 tape units (COUNT(4)) for 5 minutes and 30 seconds (TIME(5,30).

```
-SET ARCHIVE READ COUNT(4) TIME(5,30)
```

An alternative is to specify the maximum number of tape units with no time limit like:

```
-SET ARCHIVE READ COUNT(99) TIME(NOLIMIT)
```

The parameter values can be reset to the values specified in DSNZPARM like:

```
-SET ARCHIVE DEFAULT
```

DISPLAY ARCHIVE Command

The currently set count and time can be determined using the DISPLAY ARCHIVE command like:

```
-DISPLAY ARCHIVE
```

An example of a report produced by the command is in Figure CR.26.

Figure CR.26. Example output of the -DISPLAY ARCHIVE command

```
 DSNJ322I DISPLAY ARCHIVE REPORT FOLLOWS -
           COUNT          TIME
        (TAPE UNITS)   (MIN,SEC)

 DSNZPARM      1             0
 CURRENT       4             5
==========================================================
 ADDR     STATUS CORR_ID VOLUME      DATASET
 290      BUSY   RECJOB1 TAPE1       DSNCAT.ARCHCOPY1.A0000040
 293      PREM   RECJOB1 SCRO1       DSNCAT.ARCHCOPY1.A0000041
 294      AVAIL  ******* TAPE2       DSNCAT.ARCHCOPY1.A0000042
END OF DISPLAY ARCHIVE REPORT.
DSN9022I ( DSNJC001 '(DIS ARC' NORMAL COMPLETION
```

The DISPLAY ARCHIVE report indicates that one tape unit with no time limit is dedicated to reading the archive log. The SET ARCHIVE READ command has been used to change the count of tapes to 4 with a time limit of 5 minutes. These values will remain in effect until the SET ARCHIVE DEFAULT command is issued or the DB2 subsystem is stopped and restarted.

You can monitor the count and time values through the use of the performance and accounting traces. The performance class 5, IFCIDs 0228 and 0229, gives the time a tape unit is allocated and not busy. The accounting class 3, IFCIDs 0117 and 0118, gives the elapsed time waiting for the archive read.

CR.14 RESTORING A DROPPED TABLE/TABLESPACE

It is difficult to restore a table or tablespace that is accidentally dropped. This is because the DROP causes DB2 to remove all references to the object from the catalog tables. It is advisable to use the WITH RESTRICT ON DROP when creating a table or add the restriction with the ALTER statement as discussed in Chapter CT.

If a dropped table or tablespace needs to be restored it is necessary to create the objects as new objects. You need to determine object IDs of the new objects. The tablespace DBID and PSID are in SYSTABLESPACE, the table OBID is in SYSTABLES, and the index DBID and ISOBID are in SYSINDEXES. You must also determine the old identifiers. This can be done using DSN1COPY with the SYSXLAT parameter to translate old identifiers in an old image copy to the new identifiers and reset the log RBAs to zero. Do stop the tablespace before using DSN1COPY. If the old identifiers are unknown, translate the identifiers on the old image copy to 9999. DSN1COPY responds with an error message and the identifier on the image copy. The process needs to be repeated for each unknown identifier. If you are restoring a dropped tablespace or multiple tables in a tablespace, the identifiers can be obtained from header page with DSN1PRNT. The offsets of the object IDs can be found in the *Diagnosis Guide and Reference* manual. The next step is to use DSN1COPY to copy the old image copy to the newly created objects. And finally, take a full image copy for future recoveries.

CR.15 MODIFY UTILITY

The MODIFY RECOVERY utility deletes rows from SYSCOPY and SYSLGRNX. Rows should be deleted that describe copies made before the oldest retained archive logs to reduce lock contention and save DASD space. The image copy data sets are not deleted by the MODIFY RECOVERY utility.

The rows can be deleted based on a date using the DATE parameter or number of days using the AGE parameter. Here is an example of deleting all rows written before June 1, 1997:

```
MODIFY RECOVERY TABLESPACE DASPJDB.DASPJTSP
                DELETE DATE (19970601)
```

Here is an example of deleting all rows older than 90 days:

```
MODIFY RECOVERY TABLESPACE DASPJDB.DASPJTSP
                DELETE AGE (90)
```

Rows can be deleted from SYSCOPY and SYSLGRNX with any and all dates and ages using DATE(*) and AGE(*). You probably do not want to use the "*" in the great majority of cases. Do be cautious about deleting too many rows and compromising future recoverability with any date and age value specified.

CR.16 STAND-ALONE UTILITIES

Stand-alone utilities (also known as service aids) operate outside the control of DB2. Indeed, DB2 need not be operational in most cases. These utilities will be reviewed briefly.

DSNJU003 can change the BSDS including adding and deleting active and archive log data sets, checkpoint records, passwords, conditional restart control record, etc.

DSNJU004 can print most of the information that can be changed with DSNJU003. You probably want to use this utility to review parameter values before they are changed and to provide documentation.

DSN1LOGP can produce a summary or detailed report of the recovery log somewhat like the REPORT utility with the RECOVERY parameter. Information is provided on the resources required to do a recovery.

DSNJLOGF can preformat newly defined active log data sets. This avoids DB2 having to format the log when log records are written, thus improving logging performance.

DSN1CHKR verifies the integrity of catalog tables and the directory by checking for broken hashes and links. This utility is useful if you suspect errors in the catalog or directory tables.

DSN1PRNT Prints the contents of tablespaces, indexes, image copies, and sequential data sets created by DSN1COPY.

DSN1SDMP can be used to force dumps when selected DB2 events occur or after a utility abend. It write DB2 trace records to a user defined OS/390 data set.

DSN1COMP estimates ESA data compression savings and is covered in detail in Chapter CD.

DSN1COPY is perhaps the most popularly used service aid. It can be used to copy tablespace and index spaces to and from sequential files or to and from DB2 VSAM data sets. It can be used to perform object ID translations and reset the log RBA to 0 as recorded in each data and index page as discussed in Section CR.16 regarding recovering a dropped table or tablespace. The COPY utility cannot be used since rows describing image copy are deleted when objects are dropped. DSN1COPY also has the option to print hexadecimal dumps of data and index pages.

DSN1COPY is often used to copy image copies from one DB2 subsystem to another. For example, from production to test or from production to a data warehouse environment. You can copy both the tablespace and all indexes on tables in the tablespace to a sequential file and then to the target objects. This avoids having to rebuild the indexes. Additional steps are required if the table has an identity column as described in the DB2 UDB Server for OS/390 Version 6 Technical Update, SG24-6108 manual.

Performance of DSN1COPY can improved significantly by using cylinder allocation. In one case performance was improved by a factor of 10 (from 11.4 minutes to 1 minute elapsed time by increasing blocking factor like:

```
//SYSUTn    DD   ICFNAME.DSNDBD.DASPJDB.PTSP.I0001.A001,DISP=OLD,
                 AMP=('BUFND=181') -- for 3390 cylinder allocation
```

CR.17 SUMMARY

Do consider taking an incremental copy periodically (Monday thru Thursday, for example) and a full copy less frequently (weekly, for example). Of course, the scheduling depends on the update frequency and allowable time for recovery. The CHANGELIMIT parameter is useful to determine if a copy should be made and whether it should be an incremental or full copy based on the percentage of changed pages that you specify. Do consider using inline copy with REORG and LOAD RESUME NO REPLACE to avoid logging and having to pass the tablespace again to make a copy. Parallel recovery reduces elapsed time for both tablespaces and indexes.

Do establish procedures to avoid pending states. Use QUIESCE after copying related tablespaces to avoid pending states with a partial recovery. Keep in mind that a PIT recovery turns on check pending if all related tablespaces are not recovered together. The use of QUIESCE with WRITE NO minimizes timeouts. The REPORT utility is useful for PIT recoveries and documentation. Offline copies are supported with logonly recovery but must be managed outside of DB2. SMS concurrent copy is supported by DB2 with and without the use of logonly recovery.

EXERCISES

1. Why is it important to make a copy of the data periodically?

2. Test results indicate that an incremental copy requires less CPU and I/O time than a full image copy when < 90 percent of the pages have changed since the last copy. What additional factors need to be considered when deciding whether to do full or incremental copies?

3. a) What is a good guidelines for the number of incremental copies to make before a MERGECOPY is executed?

b) What is an alternative to a MERGECOPY?

4. What action will the COPY utility take based on the parameter CHANGELIMIT (1, 50)?

5. There is not a dramatic difference in CPU and I/O times between making a copy with SHRLEVEL of CHANGE and REFERENCE. What is an advantage having to do with availability and a disadvantage having to do with performance of using SHRLEVEL CHANGE?

6. Should a TOCOPY recovery be done using an image copy made with SHRLEVEL CHANGE? Why?

7. What are some of the advantages of using concurrent copy over an image copy?

8. a) If a few tracks or cylinders of a tablespace are damaged, is it necessary to recover the indexes?

b) What parameter can be used to recover only the damaged pages?

9. How can the elapsed time for the following recovery be reduced in V5, assuming that the named tablespaces are related through RI? What is a good alternative in V6?

```
RECOVER TABLESPACE DASPJDB.DASPJTSP
        TABLESPACE DASPJDB.DALOCTSP
        TABLESPACE DASPJDB.DAEMPTSP
        TABLESPACE DASPJDB.DADEPTSP

RECOVER INDEX (ALL)
        TABLESPACE DASPJDB.DASPJTSP
        TABLESPACE DASPJDB.DALOCTSP
        TABLESPACE DASPJDB.DAEMPTSP
        TABLESPACE DASPJDB.DADEPTSP
```

10. a) What are the advantages of a separate recovery job for each tablespace to be recovered and in some cases separate recovery jobs for each index?

b) What are the disadvantage of a recovery job for each tablespace to be recovered in V5? What is the effect on REBUILD INDEX in V5?

11. REORG INDEX has performance advantages over REBUILD INDEX in some cases. Can REORG INDEX be used after recovering the tablespace rather than REBUILD INDEX, assuming that the indexes have been damaged?

12. QUIESCE with WRITE of YES or NO establishes an RBA for a PIT recovery. How does WRITE NO differ from WRITE YES?

13.What is the purpose of LOGONLY recovery?

14. a) What DML statements are allowed when each of the following pending states are set on?

- COPY PENDING
- CHECK PENDING
- RECOVERY PENDING

b) In general, what utilities can be executing when the pending states are set on?

15.The 3 pending states can be set off with:

- REPAIR ... NOCOPYPEND
- REPAIR ... NOCHECKPEND
- REPAIR ... NORCVRPEND

- -START DATABASE(DASPJDB) SPACENAM (DASPJTSP) ACCESS(FORCE)

What are the disadvantages of using these approaches?

ANSWERS

1. It is important to make a copy of the data periodically to minimize the time to recover when a failure occurs.

2. Incremental copies must be merged with MERGECOPY or RECOVER merges the copies before a recovery. The cost of managing and merging incremental copies should be considered in making a decision as to whether to make incremental copies or a full image copy.

3. a) One should not make more incremental copies than the number of tape units available for the merge process.

b) A full copy is a good alternative to a MERGECOPY.

4. COPY takes one of the following actions based on CHANGELIMIT (1, 50):

- If the percent of changed pages is <= 1 percent, no copy will be made.
- If the percent of changed pages are between 1 and 50 percent, an incremental copy will be made.
- If the percent of changed pages is > 50 percent, a full image copy will be made.

5. The advantage of using SHRLEVEL CHANGE is that users can update the data during the copy process. A disadvantage having to do with performance is that the recovery can take longer using a copy made with SHRLEVEL CHANGE compared to REFERENCE because the RBA is written to

SYSCOPY at the beginning of the copy job and can require a longer recovery time. The impact of this depends on the time required to make the copy and the number of updates made during the copy.

6. An image copy made with SHRLEVEL CHANGE should not be used in a TOCOPY recovery. The copy may contain uncommited data because the image copy utility copies a page even though an application program is in the process of updating the page and holding an exclusive lock on the page. A warning is issued that the recover has been made to an indeterminate point when using a copy made with SHRLEVEL CHANGE.

7. Some of the advantages of using concurrent copy over an image copy are:

- Can copy multiple tablespaces
- Can copy DB2 and non-DB2 objects to synchronize them
- Can use a filter list to copy a number of tablespaces based on a naming convention
- Can do volume copies for disaster recovery

8. a) If the tracks or cylinders of a tablespace are damaged, is it not necessary to recover the indexes.

b) The ERROR RANGE parameter can be specified on the RECOVER utility statement to recover only the damaged pages. If a small percentage of the data has been damaged based on information provided by DISPLAY DATABASE, the ERROR RANGE parameter reduces recovery time. The ICKDSF service utility should be used to deal with the damaged tracks and cylinders before a recovery.

9. The indexes on the recovered tablespaces can be recovered in parallel to reduce the elapsed time by submitting a separate rebuild index job for each index in V5. The procedure is not needed in V6 when naming the indexes and using the PARALLEL parameter on the RECOVER statement.

10. a) Multiple tablespaces can be recovered in parallel with reduced elapsed time for recovery. (There is more competition for BP0 and I/O as well as more CPU time and DASD space for sorts.) It avoids all tablespaces on the RECOVER statement being unavailable until all have been recovered. In addition, if a small percentage of the data pages have been updated and needs to be recovered, recover can skip areas of the log not for the tablespace being recovered.

b) A disadvantage of a recovery job for each tablespace is contention for the log. Perhaps more important is the fact that if all related tablespaces are not named in the RECOVER statement, check pending is set on for the dependent tables. Separate REBUILD INDEX jobs allows for parallel recovery and reduced elapsed time without concern for check pending being set on in V5.

11. No, REORG INDEX cannot be used in a recovery situation if the indexes have been damaged. The utility rebuilds the index based on the values and RIDs in the leaf pages which have been damaged.

12. WRITE NO does not externalize updates from buffer to the tablespace. It does write an RBA for PIT recovery even if exclusive locks are being held for an update by an application program. If there is a recovery to the established RBA, it will not include updates that have not been committed.

13. The purpose of LOGONLY recovery is to allow for recovery with a non-image copy. The LOGONLY parameter tells the RECOVER utility not to place a copy on the tablespace. RECOVER assumes that the correct copy has already been placed in the tablespace and does the log apply.

14. a) COPY PENDING allows SELECT statements only. CHECK PENDING and RECOVERY PENDING allow no DML.

b) COPY PENDING allows all utilities. CHECK PENDING allows COPY, REORG, LOAD REPLACE, CHECK, and REPAIR. RECOVERY PENDING allows RECOVER, LOAD REPLACE, and REPAIR.

15. REPAIR and START DATABASE simply sets the indicator off but does not correct the problem. START DATABASE effectively removes all pending states and restrictions without correcting any problems.

FIGURES

INDEX